STAY TUNED

A HISTORY OF
AMERICAN BROADCASTING

STAY TUNED

A HISTORY OF AMERICAN BROADCASTING

THIRD EDITION

CHRISTOPHER H. STERLING
The George Washington University

JOHN MICHAEL KITTROSS
K\E\G Associates

LEA **Lawrence Erlbaum Associates, Publishers**
2002 Mahwah, New Jersey   London

Acquisitions Editor:	Linda Bathgate
Textbook Marketing Manager:	Marisol Kozlovski
Editorial Assistant:	Karin Wittig
Cover Design:	Jennifer Sterling/Spot Color Incorporated
Textbook Production Manager:	Paul Smolenski
Full-Service Compositor:	TechBooks
Text and Cover Printer:	Hamilton Printing Company

This book was typeset in 10.5/13 pt. Melior, Melior Bold, Melior Italic
and Melior Bold Italic.
The heads were typeset in ACaslon Bold, ACaslon Bold Italic,
and Melior Bold.

Library of Congress Cataloging-in-Publication Data

Sterling, Christopher H., 1943–
    Stay tuned: a history of American broadcasting / Christopher H.
Sterling, John Michael Kittross.—3rd ed.
        p. cm.—(LEA's communication series)
    Includes bibliographical references and index.
    ISBN 0-8058-2624-6 (alk. paper)
    1. Broadcasting—United States—History. I. Kittross, John M., 1929–
II. Title. III. Series.
    HE8689.8.S73   2001
    384.54'0973—dc21   2001040808

To our parents—
who were there and thus listened
to many things we missed

CONTENTS
(CHRONOLOGICAL)

ALTERNATE
CONTENTS (TOPICAL)

The Broadcast Audience

Regulatory Trends

Broadcasting and Society (and Foreign Broadcasting)

LIST OF BOXED FEATURES, ILLUSTRATIONS, AND TABLES

PREFACE
TO THE THIRD EDITION
(2002)

Broadcasting—if, indeed, the term "broadcasting" is still a valid label for the subject matter of this book—isn't what it used to be. In some respects, it is better, in some worse than it was in decades past—but it certainly is different and more complex.

Nearly a quarter of a century ago, when the first edition of *Stay Tuned* was published, the broadcasting industry was relatively simple and placid. The second edition, published a dozen years later, reflected the technological, organizational, economic, and legal developments that then had started to change the industry.

Today, it is almost an entirely new ball game. Keeping up is a major task. To understand the game's unwritten rules, it is more important than ever to understand how the broadcasting industry has evolved to what it is today. That is the purpose of this new edition of *Stay Tuned*.

Accordingly, we have reviewed every single word of the second edition, removed ambiguities and a gratifyingly-small number of reported errors, added in new and sometimes unpublished scholarship in broadcasting history—such as research by Louise Benjamin, Donna Halper, Don Godfrey, Harold Cones, Paul Beck, Gordon Greb, and Mike Adams and many other known and unknown contributors to the body of knowledge found in this volume—and eliminated discussion of a few "dead ends" that earlier we didn't know were dead ends.

To bring this account of broadcasting history up to 2001, we've written a new chapter 11 to describe what in our judgment are significant historical developments from 1988 until the present and completely rewritten chapter 12 ("Lessons From the Past for the Future") in light of new lessons.

To make this edition even more useful, we've expanded the Bibliography (Appendix D) substantially, supplied "Selected Further Reading" for each chapter in an alphabetical format (within topics) in order to avoid the risk of influencing readers with our own biases, and expanded both the

Chronology of Appendix A and the Glossary of Appendix B. The historical tables in Appendix C have been thoroughly updated and reorganized and several new ones have been added on topics from public television programming to the relationship of television to presidential elections.

We've also moved most of the data from the "Key Indicators" tables for every five years found in the second edition to Appendix C—partly because what once were "key" no longer may be so, and partly because of the increasing unavailability of current data. Nothing significant from earlier editions has been omitted.

We've seen many developments since the second edition. Digitized technologies, the convergence of broadcasting and computers, viable new broadcast networks, an ever-growing tendency toward concentration of ownership of networks and stations, commodification of everything from industries to programs and audiences, the possibly temporary triumph of the ideology of deregulation, programming more highly specialized than had been imagined a few years earlier and lowest-common-denominator "reality" (such as *Survivor*) and quiz programs, DTV and DVD and a myriad of additional technological acronyms, streaming, changes in the copyright law, and literally dozens of other developments all are to be found in the pages of this edition of *Stay Tuned*.

These developments all have at least one thing in common: None of them appeared full-blown, out of nowhere. They all evolved from earlier developments, inventions, trends, and principles—and this is where we hope *Stay Tuned* will be most valuable. The reader can both understand what is behind what she or he sees or hears today and develop a sense of historical evolution that will make it possible to be better prepared for what will show up tomorrow.

We are trying to concentrate on trends and principles, even though they are reflected in myriad developments and events. We do try to point out that "what everyone thinks happened" isn't always what actually occurred. For example, was the first U.S. broadcasting station KQW, KDKA, WWJ, or 1XE or one of several other claimants? Did Marconi deserve his reputation for having invented radio, or should the praise go to Tesla? Why has Armstrong been largely forgotten—but de Forest remembered? We try to provide data that may help you decide these questions, but we are not egotistical enough to act as "the" judge. Although both of us are trivia buffs, we also are well aware that trivia of person, time, place, and gadget is much less important than are trends.

In preparing this edition, we owe special thanks to our long-suffering families, perceptive readers such as Lou Benjamin and Don Godfrey, and the helpful staff, particularly Linda Bathgate, at Lawrence Erlbaum Associates, our new publishers. The many production problems inherent in a book of this length and scope were handled with aplomb by Susan Detwiler, of TechBooks; Ruth Mandel was of great help in locating photographs; and Jennifer Sterling (who was less than a year old when this project was conceived) and her colleagues at Spot Color Inc. were responsible for the design of this edition's cover.

The professional interests of both authors have changed—Kittross is deeply into media ethics, and Sterling into telecommunications policy—and our book jacket photographs from earlier editions no longer look like us. While Sterling is still at George Washington University, Kittross now is managing director of K\E\G Associates, an academic consulting firm, and editor of *Media Ethics* magazine.

Although the authors are as excited about the history of broadcasting as they ever were, a look around our homes—filled with computers, new television sets with bells and whistles, VCRs, CD players, radios, and other paraphernalia, but no longer containing children (all of ours now have their own homes, computers, television sets, etc.) or parents—tells us that the rate of change has, if anything, speeded up. If one claims to be knowledgeable about broadcasting, there is a lot, past and present, that one needs to know.

While predicting the future is even more problematic than interpreting the past, it is an impossible task unless one understands *both* the present and how it evolved from the past. For example, will today's new technologies and programming, providing hundreds rather than only scores of content choices every minute, ultimately be beneficial or harmful to society? Will the raging growth of deregulation-spawned concentration of control of broadcast outlets remove the last vestiges of "localism"? Will our growing dependence on space communication satellites render us more vulnerable to accidental sundering of our communications connections? What will be the effect of replacing the "public interest, convenience, and necessity" licensing standard with auctions and lotteries? Stay tuned!

In 1958, acclaimed newsman Edward R. Murrow said to his colleagues, "This instrument [of television] can teach, it can illuminate; yes, and it can even inspire. But it can do so only to the extent that humans are determined to use it to those ends. Otherwise it is merely wires and lights in a box. There is a great and perhaps decisive battle to be fought against ignorance, intolerance, and indifference. This weapon of television could be useful."

In its own small way, we hope this third edition of *Stay Tuned* also will be useful to you as you fight the battle.

C.H.S. and J.M.K.

PREFACE
to the SECOND EDITION
(1990)

In the decade since publication of the first edition of *Stay Tuned*, the world has not stood still. Indeed, the jury is out as to whether this period has not seen more changes in broadcasting than any other decade since broadcasting became an industry in the 1920s.

It may be argued that the late 1970s were the period of highest complexity, even achievement, of the broadcasting industry, as described in chapters 3 through 9. It was a period of real scarcity of outlets, with limited opportunity for entry. But it also was the last period when the people running the industry had come up through the ranks and perhaps still believed in broadcasting as a public interest, convenience, and/or necessity.

Actually, 1978 marked the start of a new ball game. At that time, only three-quarters of today's full-power stations were on the air; cable served only half the number of homes it serves today—and pay-cable was only starting; home VCRs were virtually unknown; PBS rarely made the ratings books; nobody talked about LPTV or HDTV; the FCC was still a force to be reckoned with; "indecency" was left to the pulpit and the pamphlet; and nobody ever dreamed that all three networks, the most stable part of the industry, would be sold.

There are those who now say that the "gee-whiz" or "glamorous something special" hallmark of broadcasting has dissipated. They say that broadcasting is only one small but inseparable part of our current culture and economy. By 1980, it was clear that the new breed of MBAs were in control of broadcasting, as they were in many other industries, and were treating broadcasting as "just another business" that could be manipulated for improvement of the short-term "bottom line" according to the gospel of the graduate business schools. Additionally, the Reagan administration had the political clout to expand the "marketplace ideology" policies supporting arbitrary deregulation that had surfaced late in the Carter administration. These views are held by many outside of broadcasting and, due to the influence of the present crop of business managers who do not think of broadcasting as a calling, by many now in positions of leadership in radio and television. The authors of *Stay Tuned*, however, are not convinced that we should dismiss the special nature of broadcasting that easily. We believe that it *is* special, even if its shape has changed.

We have tried to cover the turbulent first decade of this new shape of the industry in an all-new chapter 10, while retaining those portions of earlier chapters that have withstood the test of time and the slings and arrows of our colleagues and students. Rewritten chapters 9 and 11 benefit from what we have learned since the first edition. Corrections and minor updatings have been made in chapters 1 through 8, and the greatly expanded glossary and bibliography include the results of current knowledge and scholarship. Tables in Appendix C have been updated, a difficult task since the FCC, in the name of "deregulation," no longer collects much of the data we had access to earlier.

To do all this required help. Frank Kahn voluntarily supplied a surgical overview of the first edition; George Shiers brought his technical knowledge to bear, as did Paul Beck; Amy Vossen gleefully unlimbered her blue pencil on the new sections; Donald G. Godfrey, Harry Sova, and Michael J. Stanton provided useful feedback as they reviewed chapters 10 and 11; the ever-patient Becky Hayden had every excuse to stop being patient; those who called upon us for information (and the settling of bets) found themselves pumped for information; those who complained about our subtitling the book "American," ignoring the other nations of this hemisphere, received apologies; and several classes of guinea pigs suffered good-humoredly.

As individuals, we have noted some changes that are not explicitly included in *Stay Tuned*. Our children are not children any more; there are new pets to feed; only one of the parents to whom we have dedicated this volume is still alive; we have both dabbled in academic administration; we have both moved to new locations (the George Washington University and Emerson College, respectively) and owe thanks to new presidents and chairpersons. We have both subscribed to cable and acquired VCRs. But the important things remain the same: the steadfast support of our wives, and our belief in—and excitement over—the importance of the history of broadcasting.

C.H.S. and J.M.K.

PREFACE
TO THE FIRST EDITION
(1978)

"... it might be advantageous to 'shout' the message, spreading it broadcast to receivers in all directions, and for which the wireless system is well adapted, seeing that it is so inexpensive and so easily and rapidly installed—such as for army manoeuvres, for reporting races and other sporting events, and, generally, for all important matters ..."—J. J. Fahie, *A History of Wireless Telegraphy* (1901), p. 259

"In 1928 we were watching it grow.
"And in 1950 the radio art will have influenced this whole people for more than thirty years, breaking down their distance barriers, making all the world their neighbor, carrying the electric word from coast to coast and nation to nation ... promoting understanding, sympathy, peace ...

"It will have played its part in the development of music ... in education, and in business, and in happiness ..."—Paul Schubert, *The Electric Word* (1928), p. 311

We think that the history of broadcasting is important.

The ambiguous mirrors of radio and television, reflecting the world about us and projecting our interests and concerns upon themselves, are a major part of all our lives. In fact, most of us spend more time listening to and watching radio and television in an average week than doing anything else except perhaps sleeping.

But we feel, in addition, that any institution—such as broadcasting—must recognize its roots and learn from its history in order to compete with other institutions and to grow in a constantly changing environment. Even though the past never exactly repeats itself, our knowledge of it will shape our future course.

Our goal is to tell how American broadcasting got where it is today and, by analyzing principles, events, and trends, suggest what directions it may take in the future. We emphasize trends rather than incidents and trivia, key individuals rather than random examples, and basic principles rather than isolated facts. Instead of just listing events, we try to explain them, interrelating developments in technology, organization and structure of the industry, economics, news and entertainment programming, audience research, and public policy and regulation.

We have arranged our material both chronologically and topically. The chapters are built around well-defined, consecutive periods of broadcasting's development. The topical arrangement of sections within chapters is consistent throughout the book except for the first two chapters. Tables of contents for both approaches are provided.

Within each chapter describing an era, we start with technology—the conditions, inventions, and innovations of that period relating to broadcasting. Man-made laws are more easily changed than are natural laws governing the electromagnetic spectrum. Allocations of spectrum space trigger political attention because broadcasting is important to the public. Allocations of time and money are important to other technologically based media and industries. Technological innovation involves economic antecedents and consequences, from the acquisition and control of patents, the unwillingness to discard investment in obsolescent studio equipment and receivers, to the entire range of relationships between government, industry, and the public, as the financial stakes grow over the years. These relationships are often far more important than the individual inventors, innovators, or electronic devices they develop.

Within each chapter beyond the earliest, we then discuss the basic unit of broadcasting—the individual station, originally thought of as the outlet for local expression and regulated by Congress accordingly.

Stations soon found it more profitable to establish affiliation with a national network, helping create the power of nationwide broadcasting organizations, to which we turn our attention in the third section of most chapters. We see the changing cast of haves and have-nots among stations and networks constantly jockeying for position and often creating or coloring important trends in the not-so-monolithic broadcasting industry.

In the fourth section of chapter 3 and later chapters, we examine the checkered development of educational, later public, broadcasting and the often precarious fortunes of noncommercial broadcasters, supported by donations, schools, government, and, more recently, corporate underwriting.

However, radio and television in the United States have become overwhelmingly commercial in respect to overall investment, audience interest, or nearly any other criterion. By the late 1920s advertising agencies had assumed a dominant position in network programming policy-making, a position they held for nearly three decades. Also discussed in the fifth section of most chapters are the changing roles of different media as new broadcast advertising competitors arrived on the scene.

Certainly listeners value broadcasting almost exclusively for its programming. In the sixth part of all but the first two chapters we review the development of program types, the apparent cycles of their invention-imitation-decline over the years, and the borrowing by one medium of another's content. We explore reasons for television's rapid development of program diversity compared with radio; we see why entertainment programming has been most popular while specific news broadcasts are often most memorable. Broadcast programming helps us maintain our surveillance of the world, to integrate what we see and hear, and transmits our culture—whether we like it or not—from person to person, country to country, and generation to generation. At the same time, its entertainment is a counterbalance to the stresses of our increasingly complex society.

One cannot discuss programming without looking at the audiences, of which we are all a part. The seventh part of chapters 3 through 10 [11 in the second edition] covers various aspects of the audience for radio and television—how it evolved, its reflection in the development and sale of receivers, ways of measuring its size, needs, and desires, and the effects that broadcasting is believed to have on people.

Because the radio spectrum is considered to be a national natural resource, it is administered by the federal government. We devote the eighth section to the roles of the legislative, judicial, and executive branches of government as well as to that creature with characteristics of all three, the Federal Communications Commission and its predecessors. Communications policy in this country is an intricate combination of politics, economics, technology, and sometimes logic, formed in a crucible of opposing public and private interests. Because the regulatory policies and judicial doctrines form slowly, many problems in broadcasting continue without apparent solution for years or even decades.

Finally, each chapter ends with a very brief account of the parallel events in broadcasting elsewhere in the world and notes some relationships of American radio and television to other social expressions of the period, such as wars, fads, the Depression, and Watergate.

Within this topical structure, we follow not only trends and continuing problems but the contributions of individual persons. Problems often return in other guises with other casts of characters. Personnel changes create policy changes in or among networks, stations, advertisers, the FCC, Congress, and citizen groups that can affect the entire institution of broadcasting. In reviewing the lives of radio and television's pioneers, we are reminded that broadcasting has been a part of American life for little more than a lifetime.

The authors of this book are, quite frankly, fascinated with the subject of broadcasting. We have tried to share our enthusiasm and show why broadcasting history is interesting as well as important. Our method lacks some of the trappings of serious historiography (footnotes) but does include a detailed glossary in unusual format, a lengthy bibliography of sources for further reading, supplementary tables, a chronology, and an index. In *Stay Tuned* we have tried to note the important events and themes in American broadcasting's story through careful selection of items to include in this single volume and subjects to analyze at length.

To find what we included, we suggest that you pay particular attention to the two tables of contents (chronological and topical), skim through the appendixes to get a sense of their contents, and then dig in where the book seems most relevant or interesting. No matter where you start or how you use the book, we hope you will obtain a better understanding of how broadcasting became the industry-art-babysitter-hero-villain-advertising medium-entertainer-news communicator and everything else it is today.

In the research, writing, and editing of this volume, we have had the help of many people. Among those who deserve our warmest thanks are (alphabetically): Joseph E. Baudino, of the Westinghouse Broadcasting Company and the Broadcast Pioneers, for his unparalleled knowledge of radio's early days; Joseph Berman, of Ohio University, for helpful criticism and encouragement; Gordon Greb, of San Jose State University, for his expert knowledge of early radio pioneer "Doc" Herrold; Kenneth Harwood, Dean of Temple University's School of Communications and Theater; the ever-patient Becky Hayden, of Wadsworth, who more than any other person is responsible for keeping us going for half a decade and hence for many of the strengths of this book; Temple colleague Sydney Head for his page-by-page criticism; Cathie Heinz and her staff at the Broadcast Pioneers Library in Washington; the *Journal of Broadcasting*'s many contributors during the long years when one or the other of us was editing it (1960–1976); collector of broadcast data *par excellence* Lawrence W. Lichty; consummate manuscript editor Jean Schuyler, who overcame the turgid prose of early drafts; Elliot Sivowitch of the Smithsonian's division of electricity and nuclear energy, who set us straight on many occasions; Robert R. Smith of Boston University, who offered valuable and constructive criticism at several stages of the book's gestation; Dallas W. Smythe of Simon Fraser University, who showed how to look behind the scenes; and Nathan B. Stubblefield, for obvious reasons.

We also owe gratitude to our many sources, among which are the books listed in the bibliography, many that are not so listed, several different libraries, countless secondhand bookshops, various Temple University departmental chairmen—one a former Iowa radio station manager and network operations supervisor, the second a former Philadelphia weekend television anchorman, and the third the son-in-law of radio's *The Whistler*—who ignored the mounting quantity of xerography requisitions, and many others.

As with most such volumes, our families gave far beyond the call of duty, without even the inner spur of scholarship or the outer spur of academic politics, and we hope that this recognition of the Sterling (Ellen, Jennifer, and Robin), and Kittross (Sally, David, Julie, and Serendipity) clans will be an aid to them during the transition of becoming reacquainted with husbands and fathers.

And, of course, for several years we have had each other to fight with, leading us to adopt the cheerful injunction in Backstrom and Hursh's *Survey Research* that "the authors will attribute any errors to each other."

C.H.S. and J.M.K.

ABOUT the AUTHORS

Christopher H. Sterling is a professor of Media and Public Affairs and of Telecommunications, and served as associate dean for graduate affairs in the arts and sciences at George Washington University, having joined that faculty in 1982. From 1980 to 1982, he served as a special assistant to FCC commissioner Anne Jones. Before that, he served for a decade on the faculty of Temple University's School of Communications and Theater. Sterling founded *Communication Booknotes Quarterly* in 1969 and still edits this review service, edited the *Journal of Broadcasting* for five years, and was chairman of the Broadcast Education Association from 1985 to 1987. Among his other books, he co-authored, with Sydney Head, four editions of *Broadcasting in America*, authored *Electronic Media: Trends in Broadcasting and Newer Technologies, 1920–1983,* co-authored *History of Telecommunications Technology: An Annotated Bibliography*, plus a number of other books on the telephone and telecommunications industry. He has lectured on American telecommunications policy in the United States, Europe, Asia, and Latin America. Among his avocations are collecting books about communications policy and history, passenger air and sea travel, codebreaking, Winston S. Churchill, and medieval castles. He and his wife have two grown daughters and live in the Virginia suburbs of Washington, D.C.

John Michael Kittross currently is Managing Director of K\E\G Associates, an academic consulting firm, and editor (since 1989) of *Media Ethics* magazine. After nine years on the faculty of the University of Southern California and more than 16 on the faculty of Temple University (where he was associate dean for graduate matters in the School of Communications and Theater), he moved to Emerson College in January 1985 as academic vice president, returned to teaching in the Fall of 1987, and "retired" in the mid-1990s. His interest in radio was kindled in high school, and his first full-time job in broadcasting was in the newsroom of WNYC at the side of his Antioch College classmate, Rod Serling. Other jobs in the media followed before Kittross earned his doctorate in communications at the University of Illinois. Among other scholarly publication efforts, he co-authored two editions of *Controversies in Media Ethics* (with A. David Gordon, John C. Merrill and Carol Reuss), wrote *Television Frequency Allocation*

Policy in the United States, was editor of the *Journal of Broadcasting* for more than 12 years, edited *Administration of American Telecommunications Policy, Documents in American Telecommunications Policy*, and *Free & Fair: Courtroom Access and the Fairness Doctrine* (with Kenneth Harwood), and compiled *A Bibliography of Theses and Dissertations in Broadcasting, 1920–1973*. He considers himself a jack of all trades and a gadfly, appreciates and uses gadgets, holds an amateur radio license, is thrilled by the experience of learning something new, enjoys academic, journalistic, and legal consulting on a variety of topics, walks a great deal in the U.S. and U.K., and is inordinately proud of his personal library. With their two grown children now located elsewhere, Kittross and his wife (and his books) live in the western suburbs of Boston.

STAY TUNED

A HISTORY OF
AMERICAN BROADCASTING

"My God, it talks!"——*attributed to the Emperor of Brazil, Dom Pedro, on first hearing the telephone at the 1876 Centennial Exhibition in Philadelphia*

CHAPTER 1

OPERATING-ROOM OF THE WESTERN UNION COMPANY, NEW YORK.

"What Hath God Wrought?"——*first non-test message over the initial (1844)*
American telegraph line

THE CONTEXT OF BROADCASTING

ONE WING OF TELEPHONE EXCHANGE, CORTLANDT STREET, NEW YORK CITY, WITH OPERATORS AT POSITIONS.

Chapter Outline

W hat was the world like before television? Or radio broadcasting? An elderly few can remember the world before radio, and many can remember television's advent. It wasn't all that long ago. Today, however, most Americans spend more time with radio and television than they do at any other activity, including working and sleeping, and most Americans get most of their news from television. Obviously, we are dealing here with a phenomenon that is not only relatively recent but extremely important, one whose cultural impact is almost inestimable. Why, then, do we know so little about its development?

Unfortunately, most early broadcasters and inventors were too busy creating an industry, and surviving in what they had created, to think of recording its development for those who followed. Now most of them are no longer with us. At the same time, pragmatic reasons for knowing about broadcasting's history are cropping up, and more people are becoming interested in it—and need to.

For example, regulation of space communications satellites follows principles established in international agreements in 1906, and even some from 1865. Early television programming of the 1940s and 1950s resembles the evolution of radio programming in the 1920s and 1930s. The beginnings of both cable television and pay-TV are discernible in a telephonic system in Budapest a century ago that distributed music and information for a fee. Videodisc recording is a descendant of Baird's television experimentation in England during the 1920s. In 1945, Arthur C. Clarke wrote a description of space communications satellites. Programming on the Internet has borrowed extensively from broadcasting practices.

In addition to basic principles, current problems have their roots in the past. For instance, placing the international distress ("SOS") frequency at 500 kHz in 1912—a location it didn't leave until the late 1990s—led some years later to placing standard (AM) broadcasting on a portion of the spectrum utterly unsuited to competitive local broadcasting. New Jersey's 1970s fight for a VHF television channel was really an attempt to overturn a 1945 political decision by the FCC that is a cornerstone of the United States television system. The still-mentioned Fairness Doctrine stems from specific statutory language in 1959, a 1949 FCC policy decision, a 1941 licensing case, the "public interest, convenience, and necessity" language in the Communications Act of 1934, and interstate commerce regulation right back to the Constitution in 1789. Indeed, there is hardly an argument on any aspect of modern broadcasting that does not leave one with a feeling of having heard all this before!

1.1 The Concept of Mass Communication

"*Mass communication*" is the effort to share information or entertainment with lots of different people through a technological intermediary. We can trace this concept all the way from primitive spoken language and cave drawing, and we can follow the development of modern mass communication from the introduction of print 500 years ago to the increasingly elaborate technologies of the motion picture, radio, and television.

When one imparts ideas and information "to whom it may concern" through some mechanical or electromechanical means, usually rapidly, over considerable distance, to a large and essentially undifferentiated audience, and when there are many copies of the message (duplicates of a newspaper or individual television sets tuned in)—then we have *mass* communication.

A *mass medium* is (a) the means—a printing press or broadcast transmitter—by which the communicator produces and distributes copies of the message to the mass audience or (b) the industry that operates that means. A *mass audience*, usually large but sometimes not, consists of people who typically are related only by their attention to the same message. The distance between the source and the audience can usually be measured in miles, but a newspaper restricted to a campus is still a mass medium. The audience may be highly specialized rather than undifferentiated—an abstruse scientific journal may reach only a few specialists in that field. Circulation can be small. Although Letters to the Editor and call-in programs on radio involve some person-to-person communication, they still reach a large audience. Unit cost to the consumer, typically low, may be high, as it was with early-day television. Messages usually are transmitted and received at or about the same time—but many books are timeless in appeal. And there are gray areas, such as truckers using CB radio and a chat room on the Internet.

1.2 Early Communication

Mass communication began when cave dwellers first shouted a warning to all the tribe within earshot or, closer to modern methods, used technology such as a horn, bells, a hollow-tree drum, a signal fire, a flag of cloth or wood, or a piece of reflecting metal to maintain surveillance of their surroundings and improve their chances of survival. Eventually, people used more complex ways to transmit their culture to the next generation. The prehistoric but realistic paintings of animals and animal hunts on cave walls probably served as hunting lessons for younger members of the tribe and possibly also as religious symbols intended to ensure good fortune on future hunts. In this way the tribe could refresh their memories and build on the lessons already learned without each generation having to start all over again. These two types of communication, transient and recorded, are to be found today.

Slowly, over thousands of years, pictures of people, places, animals, and things became conventionalized and stylized into symbols. Although most people still learned through oral tradition or storytelling, small ruling classes and religious elites developed a system of pictographs and hiero-glyphics—the printed, stamped, inscribed, painted, or carved "word." But written language was a code that only a tiny fraction of society could understand, with oral tradition serving the rest.

Communication typically depended on human senses and abilities. When *speed* was uppermost—a prearranged code of signal fires carried news of the fall of Troy across most of Greece in a single night—the *amount* of information transmitted had to be small. Sending a long or complicated message took longer—as with the Romans' semaphore and flashing light devices—and sometimes involved a human carrier using any available means of travel, whether it was a horseman using a Roman road or an Incan royal messenger using a high-speed foot trail in the Andes.

After the fall of Rome in the fourth century A.D., the Roman Catholic Church preserved much of the knowledge of the past in its monasteries. By painstakingly reproducing books by hand, the monks managed to preserve some of the culture of the past that was not being transmitted by word of mouth among the illiterate masses.

The first real change in mass communication came with the introduction of the printing press and movable type—separate wood block or tin letters that could be temporarily combined into desired words that would form a page from which to print many copies. The first use of movable type in the Western world is ascribed to Johannes Gutenberg of Mainz, Germany, who either developed his own press, type, and ink, or applied Far Eastern techniques in 1456. The new process soon spread across Europe and its colonies, although its use was sometimes held up by the Church, which objected strongly both to losing its monopoly of recorded communications and to the increase of secular publishing that the Renaissance had stimulated.

Although greatly faster than hand copying, printing was restricted to the relatively slow speeds of hand-operated presses until the 1800s, when steam-driven presses became practical and common. Low-cost printing made books available to many more people, was a stimulus to literacy, standardized the appearance of alphabets, and enhanced the idea of the utility of books, reducing their artistic and increasing their social importance.

1.3 The Rise of Mass Society

Significant changes were taking place in Western society in Gutenberg's day. A new middle class of traders and merchants, between the upper nobility and the peasant poor, kept themselves informed of foreign developments in technology, commerce, and politics. Reformation within the Catholic church and revolt from without brought new patterns of societal control to Europe. The spread of secular news and knowledge brought a loosening of religious control over everyday life. In addition, the long-lasting feudal system began to give way to parliamentary government as the population, spear-headed by the growing merchant middle class, began to question the spending practices of monarchs.

At the same time, a renaissance of learning and art was taking place. Starting in southern Europe, the fine arts flourished, science and technology advanced, knowledge was acquired from the East, and new ideas once again became acceptable. Versatile men appeared, like Leonardo da Vinci, who could work in medicine, science, military technology, art, and music. Sometimes noble families, who still held most of the money, and consequently power, acted as patrons of a *high culture* of artists, musicians, architects, and some scientists—all of whom produced their work for this small elite or for the Church.

In many civilizations, the common people who provided the economic base for high culture had their own thematically and technically simple *folk culture* from which the high culture often borrowed. Folk culture of the Middle Ages took the form of fairs, circuses, traveling minstrels, song and story sessions, and morality plays, providing some religious instruction and a great deal of diverting entertainment.

In the 1700s the Industrial Revolution spread from England to the continent. Machines, driven by water and steam instead of human and animal power, supplied an increasing amount of manufactured goods that the home couldn't produce, at prices that individual craftsmen couldn't match. By the 1800s, manpower needs of industry, expansion of international commerce, and the start of mechanized agriculture led people toward city living.

The growing cities furnished an industrial base, great amounts of information and people who wanted it, and a market for mass-produced entertainment and information. The density of population made distribution easy. The local tavern or coffee shop continued to serve as a center of communications as it had for hundreds of years, but information now came in posted broadside advertisements or printed newspapers in addition to the traditional word of mouth from travelers. This situation was analogous to the "first color TV set in town" being in the local bar.

Although literacy was increasing, thanks to public and private schooling in the 19th century, improvements in transportation and technology were more important to communication in the increasingly urbanized society. Steam power permitted the mechanization of printing presses, made transportation by water faster and more reliable, and allowed the railroad (supplemented by improved carriage and wagon roads) to knit all parts of a country together. Greater occupational specialization, particularly in cities, led to an increased use of money instead of barter and to an increased need for news and entertainment—mass communication.

Most important, in the 19th century the first electrical communication devices (the telegraph and then the telephone) decisively overcame the problem of speed without dependence on unaided senses or transportation. By the mid-1800s, both the socioeconomic systems of the more developed countries and their emerging technologies were ready for introduction of the components of the mass electronic media we know today: radio and television broadcasting.

1.4 Early Electrical Communication

For centuries the technological development of communication involved distance, speed, number of copies, and quantity of content. Each new technology was a balance of these demands. The Pony Express could deliver mail faster than any other method, but only a few pounds at a time. If many copies of a communication were required, or if each copy contained many pages, production might take much more time and space than for a more limited output.

While printing answered the fundamental question of quantity, it did so at the expense of speed—the time needed for gathering information, setting it in type, and printing, binding, and distributing newspapers, magazines, or books. Improving routes and methods of transportation shortened distances, but the speed with which news could travel still was limited by how fast man, animal, train, or ship could go.

Combining distance with speed became possible with the development of telegraph systems, such as the mechanical semaphore originated by the Romans and forgotten during the Middle Ages. Rediscovered, the semaphore systems of several European countries reached a high degree of efficiency in the late 1700s. They were fast and simple for *short* messages, but the equipment was expensive to build and operate, and many towers would be needed to relay signals over long distances. Their inefficiency for long messages and their high personnel costs limited use to the most urgent needs. Although lights could be used at night, the semaphore was essentially a daytime, good-weather system that, like all telegraphs, achieved point-to-point rather than broadcast communication.

1.4.1 The Electrical Telegraph

The semaphore was quickly rendered obsolete by the electrical telegraph. Electricity could travel through a wire at almost the speed of light, and it needn't worry about fog or bad weather. Wherever a wire could be strung, there the electrical telegraph could go; nor did operators have to be within sight of each other. All that was needed was a source of electricity, a switch or key to manipulate the current, a wire to conduct electricity, and a mechanism—the element inventors changed most frequently—to "read" the transmitted message visually or audibly.

In the United States, the first practical telegraph was invented by Samuel Finley Breese Morse, then well-known as an artist. In 1832 he learned from a fellow passenger on a ship returning from Europe about the electromagnet and work being done on electrical signaling for railways in England. Morse's first electrical telegraphy instrument, in 1835, used pulses of current to deflect an electromagnet, which moved a marker to produce a written code on a strip of paper. A year later he modified the device to emboss the paper with dots and dashes. These were elements in what is now called "Morse code," even though it probably was actually developed by Morse's financial partner Alfred Vail. This code was carefully constructed, in keeping with what we now call Information Theory, with the most common letter, *e*, coded in the easiest form, one dot. With such a code, the inventor needed only one wire circuit to send sequentially even the longest messages. Some earlier devices had needed a separate wire circuit for each letter of the alphabet!

In 1840, Morse secured a patent on the system. His ultimate source of funds, as with so many later inventions, was the United States government. In 1843 Congress appropriated $30,000, and Morse used it to construct a demonstration line to span the 40 miles between Washington and Baltimore. He had to solve many technological problems—particularly insulating the wires so that the electricity wouldn't leak into the ground—as is often the case when scaling up from a laboratory model. The official first message, "What hath God wrought," was sent May 24, 1844.

In 1847 Congress sold the demonstration line to Morse interests, and the United States opted out of governmental control of telecommunications for the time being. Morse soon found that it was extremely hard to defend his patent because the technology was so simple. As a result, more than 50 telegraph companies were operating by 1851, and many more followed. But the number of important companies shrank steadily after the creation of the Western Union Telegraph Company in 1856, as uneconomical duplications and poorly engineered lines led to mergers and absorptions. By the early 1900s only Western Union and Postal Telegraph remained strong—and, at the start of World War II, after Congress passed a special antitrust law exemption, Western Union took over Postal Telegraph.

The telegraph was so efficient that it quickly eliminated competing forms of communication, such as the Pony Express, which died less than two years after its founding when the first transcontinental telegraph line opened in 1861. While the telegraph had important military applications, major emphasis in the United States was on commercial development. In the late 1840s five New York newspapers organized the Associated Press to get pooled telegraphic reports of the Mexican War. In England, Julius Reuter, who began a "pigeon post" in the 1850s to provide market prices to businessmen, adopted telegraphy and expanded his reports into a general news service for newspapers.

In Europe, development of land telegraphy followed a different path. Governments retained controlling interest in telegraphy and subsequent means of telecommunication. They placed military and political uses first and often postponed commercial telegraphy.

The telegraph and the railroads intertwined to spearhead the economic development of the United States. The telegraph needed a right-of-way between centers of population while the railroads needed some means of dispatching trains; both needed agents or operators. Their problems were solved by combining the jobs of station agent and telegraph operator in one person who handled railroad service messages and public messages alike. This system almost doubled the freight-handling capacity of the railroad and substantially reduced the cost of telegraph operators. As the number of competing railroad companies declined, so did the number of telegraph lines running between the same pairs of cities.

1.4.2 Submarine Cables

Although the telegraph could deliver a message almost instantaneously, its capability stopped at the ocean's edge. The first underwater cable, laid in 1850 across the English Channel, lasted only a short time, since its wire bundles were highly susceptible to damage from fishermen, dragging anchors, and corrosion and short-circuiting by sea water. In 1858, after several short cables had been installed successfully, wealthy American businessman Cyrus W. Field organized the first of several transatlantic cable layings. The first between England and the United States lasted about six months and was unreliable. In 1866, Field and his associates laid a new cable from Ireland to Newfoundland that worked. Transmission speed was only six words a minute, but the success of this transatlantic cable inspired installation of cables between other continents, and spurred commercial and diplomatic communication. The reliability of and the new modulation techniques for underseas cable have continued to make it attractive, with— in 1999 alone—enough underwater cable laid to encircle the globe five times!

Although pairs of nations had previously reached bilateral agreements, by 1865 there was enough general need and basis for agreement on operational techniques and finances for an International Telegraph Convention to meet in Paris. The convention agreed on priority of messages (governmental, then telegraph administration, and then commercial or private), uniformity of rates (set by distance), methods for settling accounts between countries, and meetings scheduled to update regulations. This gathering was the genesis of the International Telegraph Union—now the International

Telecommunication Union (ITU), a world organization under the United Nations that allocates radio spectrum space and sets standards for international telegraph and telephone.

1.4.3 The Telephone

The early electrical telegraph had several drawbacks: It could transmit only a few words per minute, it required trained operators, it conveyed emotion or emphasis poorly, it required a new alphabet (Morse code), and it was one-way. If the human voice could be transmitted in a two-way system, all of these problems would be overcome.

On February 14, 1876, Alexander Graham Bell, a successful teacher of the deaf, filed for a patent on such a device. He demonstrated his invention at the Philadelphia Centennial Exhibition of 1876 and attracted considerable attention. The first telephone system, with 21 subscribers, was established two years later in New Haven, Connecticut. Although Bell benefited financially, his financial backer and father-in-law, Gardner Hubbard, and his excellent business manager, Theodore Vail, a distant cousin of Morse's backer, had control.

After an unsuccessful attempt to sell the invention for $100,000 to Western Union in 1877, Bell and his associates redoubled their efforts to fight patent infringements and conflicts, purchase improvements on the telephone, and put systems into the most populated parts of city after city. Competition came from numerous small companies, many with a cavalier attitude toward the patent system, and from Western Union. This immensely wealthy and powerful company, realizing its earlier mistake, had set out to establish a rival telephone company based on other patents.

However, when financial baron Jay Gould threatened to establish a rival telegraph company in association with Bell's company in an effort to depress Western Union's stock and then buy it cheaply, Western Union hurriedly made peace with the Bell interests in 1879, giving up all ideas about competing in the telephone field in exchange for the Bell interests staying out of the telegraph industry. By 1909 the Bell system was so successful that the American Telephone and Telegraph Company (as it had been named in 1885) was able to purchase Western Union—only to have to resell it in 1914 because of the antitrust laws.

In its first 10 years, AT&T made some of the corporate decisions that guided it until it was split into several parts in 1984. Since it could expect competition when Bell's basic patents expired in 1894, AT&T decided to initiate research to improve the telephone in small but patentable steps, to purchase inventions by independent inventors—such as Michael Pupin's loading coil, which made long-distance telephony practical—and to concentrate on a part of the industry that, at the time, only one company could feasibly operate—long distance communication. While an estimated

6,000 firms battled in the late 1890s for local telephone business, AT&T worked to create transcontinental telephone service, which they accomplished in 1915. (Until stopped by a threatened antitrust action just before World War I, AT&T also bought many local competitors.)

This philosophy is still evident. AT&T has made large concessions to the antitrust laws—relinquishing royalties in 1956 on all patents, including the transistor—in order to keep control of its manufacturing subsidiary, Western Electric. Even when the court-approved 1984 "divestiture" led to the end of the integrated "Bell System" consisting of research, manufacturing, and long-distance and local telephone service facilities owned by AT&T, the company tried to carve out a niche for itself (in information transmission, combining long-distance communication and computers), leaving the aging local systems to the seven spun-off regional Bell operating companies and telephones to be made and sold by anyone. By 2000, AT&T was the nation's largest multiple cable systems operator. Although what originally were the local Bell companies still serve less than 90% of the nation's land line telephones (and a much smaller proportion of cellular phones), keeping them reasonably safe from the antitrust laws, it is in the long-distance business that competition has recently been most fierce. Fighting hard are such giants as AT&T, MCI, and Sprint and a host of small companies that lease facilities in bulk, then resell them at a discount. Recently, the regional Bell companies have agitated for permission to get into the long-distance business, and prepared for additional local competition from resellers and from new antagonists such as cable television operators, and some have merged in order to enhance their strength.

AT&T also searched for a "natural monopoly" in broadcasting. During the 1920s, when it could not maintain a monopoly of commercial "radio telephony for hire" or "toll broadcasting," it sold its stations to competitors; in the 1950s when it no longer sold the lion's share of transmitters and speech-input equipment, AT&T dropped that business completely. Domestic communications satellites have taken over station interconnection for the broadcasting networks, forcing AT&T into the competitive mode it avoided for more than a century.

Although most European countries placed telephone and telegraph within a government department, usually the post office, in the United States private ownership of the telephone was challenged only once. This occurred during World War I, when the federal government took over telephone, telegraph, and railroad companies to assure the priority of military operations and war production during a time of communication and transportation shortages. Some earlier proposals for government ownership of electrical communication, notably by Postmaster General Burleson in 1914 and an earlier postmaster general in 1872, got nowhere. This wartime takeover did not hamper the operations of the Bell System, however, since all details and virtually all policy were left to Bell executives, who inaugurated (as federal policies) installation and other fees that state regulatory agencies previously had blocked. After the war, although the Navy still wished to control wireless, AT&T easily retrieved its facilities.

1.4.4 The Electrical Manufacturing Industry

The successful development of telegraph and telephone in the United States led to near-monopolies by Western Union (telegraph) and AT&T (telephone). At the same time, as electricity was used more after 1880, companies appeared that manufactured electric lights, electric motors, and the like. The most important electrical manufacturing firms were Westinghouse, started in 1886, which brought the alternating current power system to the United States, and General Electric (GE), formed in 1892 as an amalgamation of two older firms, including Thomas Edison's. After several years of competition and patent arguments, GE and Westinghouse agreed in 1896 that GE should receive two-thirds of the business growing from their shared patents. This early patent "pool" agreement was an important precedent for the radio manufacturing industry. Another important firm was Western Electric, which specialized in telephone communications equipment and was taken over by AT&T in 1881.

All these firms were interrelated, not necessarily through ownership but because the manufacturing companies provided equipment and services to communications organizations while the latter, fed by increasing public use of their facilities, provided a demand on the electrical manufacturing companies. Each was so wrapped up in its own business that research was limited to perfecting existing products and little time, personnel, or money was spent on new systems such as wireless—as discussed in chapter 2.

1.5 Broadcasting: A New Mass Communication Medium

Radio *broadcasting* was a new electrical communications concept. Telegraph, telephone, and early radio were only faster means of point-to-point or interpersonal communication. History tells us that nothing could beat the speed of the royal Incan messengers, until the horse was introduced to the Western Hemisphere. Similarly, the Pony Express lasted 16 months, until the transcontinental telegraph was completed. The limits of the telegraph—its low words-per-minute capacity and need for trained operators—were "impassable," until the innovation of the telephone permitted rapid two-way conversation by distant laymen. Radio removed our dependence on wires, and finally "broadcasting" presented a new concept, just as movable type had when it bypassed the barrier—slow production of copies—of hand-lettering, and made widespread literacy worthwhile. Americans living when radio was new felt that it was a miracle—a cheap and pervasive national mass medium.

Although radio seemed to spring up full-blown in America in the early 1920s, amateur operators had been transmitting and listening to speech and music since 1906. A man named Charles David Herrold may have first envisioned the concept, in 1909, and RCA's David Sarnoff claims to have proposed a "radio music box" a few years later (see pp. 46–47). After commercial broadcasting started in 1922 and networks were fully established in 1926, everyone agreed that radio was truly a mass medium: a few programming sources (networks) geared to reach as large an undifferentiated audience as possible, for the purpose of purveying goods and services through advertisements. Even when, in the late 1950s and in the 1960s, radio networks virtually disappeared, and radio became a local medium serving specialized groups while television took over the national business, radio remained a mass medium.

But just what is *broadcasting*? It clearly has a different method of delivery from the other media of mass communication—and often a different message to deliver. According to Section 3(0) of the Communications Act of 1934, broadcasting is "the dissemination of radio communications intended to be received by the public, directly or by means of intermediary relay stations." The three essential elements here are "radio communication" (meaning use of wireless electromagnetic radiation—see Appendix B); "intended for" (meaning that everyone "whom it may concern or interest" is welcome to listen in, distinguishing a broadcast from the private interchange of telephone, postal service, e-mail or even CB radio); and "the public" (including the merely curious). Although *broadcasting* is more fully discussed on pp. 63–69, we should establish here that broadcasting signifies transmission of music, speech, and/or pictures in forms that the general public can understand, on a regular and announced schedule, on a frequency band for which the general public has receivers, by a station licensed by the government for that purpose (if licensing was then required).

Broadcasting is an industry, an institution, and a process, and we intend to examine all three. The system of broadcasting in the United States is virtually unique in the world (not necessarily better; simply different), and this book explores how the system is unique, how it got that way, and why.

As recently as 35 years ago, for example, the number of radio stations supposedly was limited by "technology" (the more stations, the more interference), or, more likely, by economics (only networks could finance expensive programming, by spreading costs over many stations), and politics (rural areas need clear-channel stations, and rural areas elect more than their share of legislators). We ignored the technological barriers—who cares about long-distance interference if the audience lives within a score of miles of the transmitter? The economic "necessity" of networks disappeared with the development of less expensive but still effective local program formats. The political "imperatives" of radio allocation shifted significantly as a result of "one man, one vote" Supreme Court decisions.

Television might some day travel the same road—but it also might follow a different path. VCRs and cable are already parts of the industry and broadcasting from satellites that cover most of a continent is growing stronger. The barriers that still face television are the speed of light, the ranges over which our senses operate, and the number of hours in the day. Can these be any more impassable than the walls that used to hamper older forms of communication? For instance, although propagation speeds may be limited, research indicates that "compression" of the television picture and sound is possible without loss of comprehension; a form of "fast motion." All of the strictly-entertainment media might be replaced in an Orwellian future by direct electrical stimulation of the brain, rather than by the slower and more imperfect use of sensory inputs. Telepathy is now a science-fiction concept, as were television and the atomic bomb; but we all know how many hours of subjective time our minds can cover in a few seconds of dreaming. More likely is the possibility of completely random access to nearly unlimited amounts of television programming through the use of computer scheduling, multiplexed additional channels (wired or broadcast), multiple-pickup playback video disc recorders in the stations, and inexpensive home VCRs, DVD players, and computers.

The limits we live with are in our own minds. By learning how previous limits were breached, perhaps we can look more wisely at the problems of today, such as fairness, access, ever more channels, fewer ownership entities, limits on the number of on-air channels, deregulation, direct broadcast satellites, audience fragmentation, high-definition television, pay-TV, indecency and violence, automation, and advertising and programming standards. In order to affect the future wisely, we *must* become aware of past principles, trends, decisions, and events.

New ways of applying or modifying old solutions may change the ground rules of broadcasting as completely as the vacuum tube supplanted the old rotary-generator transmitters or the iconoscope removed the mechanical limitations of the television scanning disc. It may take time—3-D color TV was first shown in 1926—but technology, structure, function, and regulation will adapt when and if the will, desire, and imagination are ready for another chapter in the unfinished story of broadcasting.

Selected Further Reading

(Alphabetical within topics. For full citations, see Appendix D.)

Boorstin (1973) provides excellent background context for American social history. Beniger (1986) focuses on the impact of communication, as does Czitrom (1982). Good studies of the rise of popular culture are Csida (1978), the three-volume Inge (1979–81), Hogben (1949), Nye (1970), and Toll (1982). Useful general media history is found in Baughman (1992), Blanchard (1998), Fang (1997), and Hudson (1987).

For various print media, see Desmond's four-volume study of international media to 1945 (1978–84), Lee's classic 1937 study of newspapers, Peterson (1964) on magazines, and Tebbel (1975) for books and periodicals. The growth of news agencies is reviewed in Blondheim (1994), Gramling (1940), Morris (1957), Rosewater (1930), Schwarzlose (1989,1990), and Unesco (1953).

Contextual surveys of telecommunication technology and policy include Brock (1981), Collins (1977), Davis (1981–85), Dummer (1997), Harlow (1936), Herring & Gross (1936), Lacy (1996), Lebow (1995), McMahon (1984), and Winston (1998). For the telegraph, see Coe (1993), Fahie (1884), King (1962), Marland (1964), Standage (1998), Thompson (1947), and Wilson (1976). Standard biographies of Morse were written by Mabee (1943) and Prime (1875). Submarine cable history is described in Bright (1898), Carter (1968), Clarke (1975), Coates & Finn (1979), and Dibner (1964). Telephone history is described in Boettinger (1983), Brooks (1976), Bruce (1973), Coe (1995), Danielian (1939), FCC (1939), Henck & Strassburg (1988), Pool (1977), Rhodes (1929), Smith (1985), Temin & Galambos (1987), and Young (1991). Sterling & Shiers (2000) provides an annotated bibliography of all of these technologies, including radio and television.

"...Signor Marconi gave a practical demonstration which showed that even in its present state the instruments can be made useful in signaling between ships and shore, and there is a certainty of working under all conditions of weather which is not common to any other mode of communication at sea."———*Lt. G. W. Denfield, U.S. Navy, in report to Secretary of the Navy, 1899*

CHAPTER 2

Guglielmo Marconi with early equipment. *Marconi Company, Ltd.*

"...a company incorporated for $2,000,000, whose only assets were de Forest's patents chiefly directed to a strange device like an incandescent lamp which he called an Audion and which device had proven worthless."———*Government prosecutor in 1912 mail fraud stock case*

THE PREHISTORY OF BROADCASTING (TO 1919)

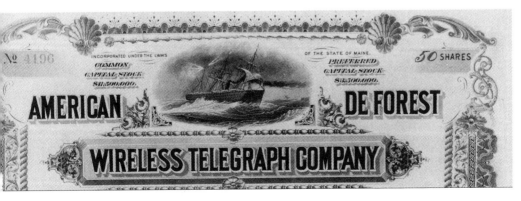

Chapter Outline

Broadcasting's earliest development was slow. It had many technological challenges and required the application of fundamental wireless discoveries. Although 30 years passed between the first theorizing about wireless in 1865 and Marconi's first practical system experiments, our concern is mostly with the subsequent rise of wireless communication from an isolated invention to a widespread, practical innovation. Even after it was in use, people in many nations saw it only as a point-to-point medium that could straddle natural barriers and operate more cheaply than the wire telegraph or telephone, a goal that has being met only in the last few years with the development of cellular and PCS (personal communication service) telephones. Few then thought that the absence of privacy protection from listeners-in would one day become one of radio's strongest advantages.

As radio's military and commercial values became obvious, major countries tried to develop their own systems so as not to have to depend on others in emergencies. This competition increased the importance of patents because by controlling essential patents one country, firm, or even person could dominate broadcasting's development for years. The different systems that succeeded have subtle and complicated distinctions, but in this chapter we concentrate more on the impact and application of wireless, or radio, than on its technical intricacies. More technical material is located in the glossary in Appendix B.

2.1 Fundamental Wireless Discoveries

As with many other 19th-century inventions, radio developed in widely separated places when the conditions were right. Typical of that period was the importance of the individual inventor or innovator who, unlike the 20th-century research team working in industrial laboratories, borrowed one element, added another, and was frequently ignorant of work done elsewhere. The invention or innovation (an invention introduced commercially as a new or improved product or process) was often the result of luck or curiosity rather than systematic scientific research applied to a specific problem.

In retrospect, wireless, or radio, is a logical extension of wired telegraphy and telephony. Wires were easily broken and hard to string between distant communities or over physical obstacles. With wireless techniques, communication could take place as rapidly as with wired devices but did

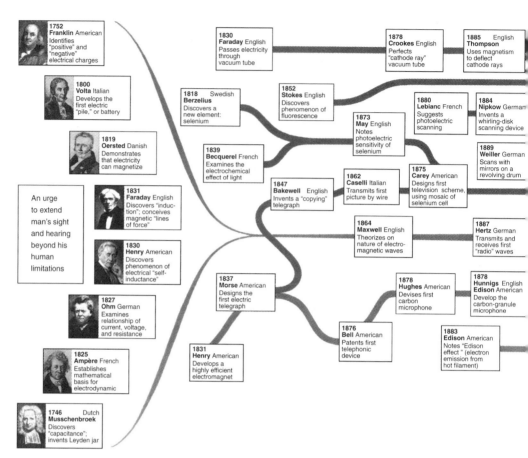

■ **Flow Chart on Invention of Radio and Television**   This chart traces the development of radio and television, showing how broadcasting was the result of experimentation and research by many scientists and inventors. It was drawn by Max Gschwind for *Fortune* magazine (December 1954) and is reproduced here by permission.

not require a physical connection. Distant locations could be contacted quickly, relaying might be unnecessary, and ships could keep in touch with land. The penalty for this was that a radio message would go out in all directions at once and could be picked up by anyone who cared to listen. A wired circuit, on the other hand, was relatively private.

2.1.1 Conduction and Induction

There are three important kinds of electrical transmission: conduction, induction, and radiation. *Conduction* means the sending of impulses through a medium capable of transmitting electricity—a wire, salt water, or the earth. *Induction* refers to the appearance of a current in one circuit when it is placed near another, already charged, circuit, without a physical connection. Induction can cause cross-talk on a telephone circuit, and

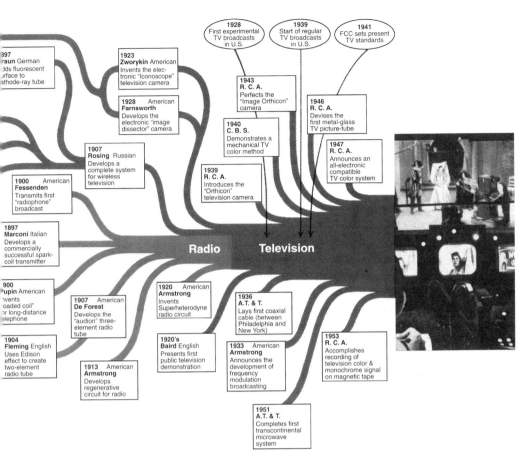

Photo credits: Volta, Oersted, Henry, Ampère (Culver Service); Faraday (Associated Press); Ohm (Brown Brothers); Musschenbroek (from *Grote Nederlanders* by Dr. G. C. Gerrits, E. J. Brill, Leiden, 1948); photo on right page (Andreas Feininger, *Life*).

induction coils permit the recording of telephone conversations without wire hookups. *Radiation* means the generation of electromagnetic waves, generally sent out from an antenna. The radio transmissions of today use this last method, which became practical just before 1900.

A Spaniard, Salvá, proposed using sea water as a conductor in 1795, 50 years before the first practical wired electrical telegraph system. In 1838 Carl August Steinheil, a Munich physics professor, proposed using railway rails as conductors and then experimented with the bare earth, sending messages for 50 feet. Morse, after constructing his wired system, suggested using water to extend land lines. Some of his assistants succeeded in receiving water-borne electrical signals over a distance of two miles.

Many other experimenters contributed to our knowledge of transmitting electricity. One of the most resourceful was Mahlon Loomis, a Washington, D.C., dentist who succeeded in 1866 in sending signals between mountains nearly 20 miles apart in Virginia. In 1872 Loomis received

■ **Two Early American Radio Inventors**   The Loomis patent of 1872, the first wireless patent granted in the United States.

UNITED STATES PATENT OFFICE.

MAHLON LOOMIS, OF WASHINGTON, DISTRICT OF COLUMBIA.

IMPROVEMENT IN TELEGRAPHING.

Specification forming part of Letters Patent No. **129,971**, dated July 30, 1872.

To all whom it may concern:

Be it known that I, MAHLON LOOMIS, dentist, of Washington, District of Columbia, have invented or discovered a new and Improved Mode of Telegraphing and of Generating Light, Heat, and Motive-Power; and I do hereby declare that the following is a full description thereof.

The nature of my invention or discovery consists, in general terms, of utilizing natural electricity and establishing an electrical current or circuit for telegraphic and other purposes without the aid of wires, artificial batteries, or cables to form such electrical circuit, and yet communicate from one continent of the globe to another.

To enable others skilled in electrical science to make use of my discovery, I will proceed to describe the arrangements and mode of operation.

As in dispensing with the double wire, (which was first used in telegraphing,) and making use of but one, substituting the earth instead of a wire to form one-half the circuit, so I now dispense with both wires, using the earth as one-half the circuit and the continuous electrical element far above the earth's surface for the other part of the circuit. I also dispense with all artificial batteries, but use the free electricity of the atmosphere, co-operating with that of the earth, to supply the electrical dynamic force or current for telegraphing and for other useful purposes, such as light, heat, and motive power.

As atmospheric electricity is found more and more abundant when moisture, clouds, heated currents of air, and other dissipating influences are left below and a greater altitude attained, my plan is to seek as high an elevation as practicable on the tops of high mountains, and thus penetrate or establish electrical connection with the atmospheric stratum or ocean overlying local disturbances. Upon these mountain-tops I erect suitable towers and apparatus to attract the electricity, or, in other words, to disturb the electrical equilibrium, and thus obtain a current of electricity, or shocks or pulsations, which traverse or disturb the positive electrical body of the atmosphere above and between two given points by communicating it to the negative electrical body in the earth below, to form the electrical circuit.

I deem it expedient to use an insulated wire or conductor as forming a part of the local apparatus and for conducting the electricity down to the foot of the mountain, or as far away as may be convenient for a telegraph-office, or to utilize it for other purposes.

I do not claim any new key-board nor any new alphabet or signals; I do not claim any new register or recording instrument; but

What I claim as my invention or discovery, and desire to secure by Letters Patent, is—

The utilization of natural electricity from elevated points by connecting the opposite polarity of the celestial and terrestrial bodies of electricity at different points by suitable conductors, and, for telegraphic purposes, relying upon the disturbance produced in the two electro-opposite bodies (of the earth and atmosphere) by an interruption of the continuity of one of the conductors from the electrical body being indicated upon its opposite or corresponding terminus, and thus producing a circuit or communication between the two without an artificial battery or the further use of wires or cables to connect the co-operating stations.

MAHLON LOOMIS.

Witnesses:
BOYD ELIOT,
C. C. WILSON.

the first American patent for wireless and the next year persuaded Congress to grant his company a federal charter. However, the financial panic of 1872 dried up potential sources of investment because the Chicago fire of 1871 had bankrupt some of his backers. Although no commercial system using the Loomis technique was successful, as late as 1924 the U.S. Signal Corps still recommended as a "field expedient" receiver his remarkably simple apparatus involving kite-flown aerials with a galvanometer in series with

A diagram from a 1908 patent of Nathan Stubblefield showing how his system would work near a waterway (other diagrams applied to railroads and roadways).

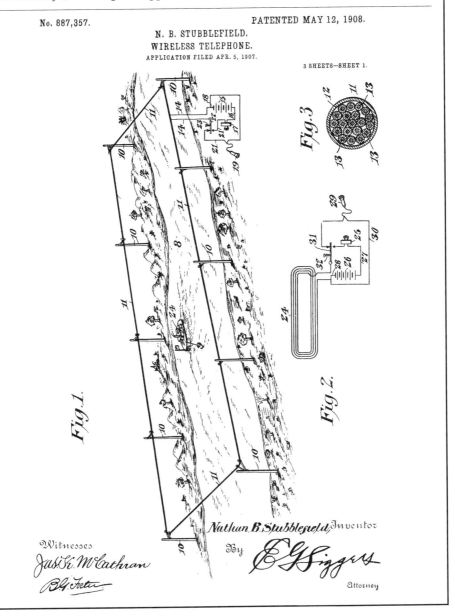

the aerial and ground. Another early experimenter, William Henry Ward of Auburn, New York, patented a "telegraphic tower"—looking remarkably like the early commercial space satellite communications receiving station at Andover, Maine—in 1872, which reportedly could send signals to many receiving antennas if all were "connected to the earth."

Most early experimenters believed in the concept of "ether" or "aether" as a medium (thought to be part of the atmosphere, hence "airwaves") that existed specifically to transmit electrical impulses. They thought that if they could successfully tap it and insert an impulse, the ether would carry the impulse for great distances. The idea of the ether, defined later and circularly as "that which carries radio waves," apparently served as a mental crutch, because it hung on in physics and radio engineering literature until the end of the 1930s.

In the early 1870s, Elihu Thompson and Thomas A. Edison individually began to detect sparks created by generators some distance from the measurement point. Edison in 1885 took out his only patent in wireless for an induction system that used antennas to get above the conducting earth. A year later, Professor Amos Dolbear of Tufts College in Massachusetts took out a patent for his "electrostatic telephone," a system of telephonic (voice) induction communication using a tin roof or a wire hanging from a kite to induce current into the "ether." Some energy may have been radiated from his antenna as well, but Dolbear had no good means of detecting the weaker radiated waves, even though they could reach a greater distance. A contemporary Harvard physicist, John Trowbridge, proposed inductive methods to reach ships at sea.

Another American inventor who attempted commercial application was Nathan B. Stubblefield of Kentucky. Having read about recent electrical radiation experiments in popular science magazines, he started experimentation in the late 1880s. In 1892 he demonstrated ground conduction voice signals over several hundred yards. Later, although possibly not recognizing that there were three distinct types of transmission, he switched to induction and communicated from the shore to ship stations on lakes or rivers. Stubblefield was particularly interested in relatively short distance communication with moving vehicles. Like Loomis, he got caught in a commercial scheme that, in this case, was in the stage of nationwide-publicity and funding before Stubblefield pulled out, claiming that his business partners were making crooked deals, cheating and using him as a scapegoat. Although he was a prolific inventor, even patenting the tin-cans-connected-by-string telephone, Stubblefield eventually died of starvation.

It is not surprising that commercial attempts at harnessing both induction and nonmetallic earth and water conduction failed. There were variations in conductivity, losses caused by the signal going in all directions at once, and limits to the amount of power that a sending coil of reasonable size could handle. Induction and non-metallic conduction could not hope to compete with the wire telegraph and telephone except possibly for short distances to and from moving vessels or vehicles. Researchers also had difficulty in demonstrating reliability of their signals, or even any results at all. Typically, they used galvanometers to register that a signal had been sent or received, but these meters could easily confuse interpreters, react to other electrical impulses, like lightning flashes, or fail to register adequately the minute amounts of current transmitted. Furthermore, a radiation component in many of the inductive experiments may have accounted for much of whatever success they had.

2.1.2 Radiation

The development of radiation for wireless communication rested on a firm theoretical framework. The major findings of Scottish mathematician and physicist James Clerk Maxwell, published in 1864, suggested that a signal could be sent out electromagnetically that would be completely detached from the point of origin. Using mathematical equations, he demonstrated that electricity, light, and heat are essentially the same and that all radiate at the same speed in free space.

German physicist Heinrich Hertz demonstrated the correctness of Clerk Maxwell's theories in a series of experiments in 1887 and 1888. The fundamental unit of frequency, the Hertz (Hz), is named for him. Hertz measured the speed of electromagnetic radiation (the speed of light), the length of various waves, and similar parameters but did not promote the use of wireless for communication. His crude but reasonably effective detector of radiated waves was a device that allowed an electric spark to jump a small gap between two charged steel balls when the receiving coil was placed facing a nearby transmitting spark coil. Hertz never achieved much range, and this detector was superseded by the much more efficient invention of French physicist Édouard Branly, in the early 1890s. His "*coherer*" consisted of a glass tube filled with metal filings that cohered or packed together and permitted an electrical current to pass whenever a wireless signal was being received. Although the coherer received very weak radiated currents, it had to be tapped mechanically after each pulse in order to restore the filings to their prereception looseness. In the late 1890s, English physicist and author Sir Oliver Lodge worked out the principle of resonance *tuning* that allowed both receiver and transmitter to operate on the same wavelength or frequency without dissipating the signal broadly over the spectrum.

In addition to Hertz, Branly, and Lodge, we find numerous persons whose work, while not universally recognized, either led or could have led to a practical wireless system. Among the most prominent was Alexander Popoff. This Russian professor at the University of Kronstadt developed a better coherer and vertical antenna around 1895 and noted the connection between Hertzian waves and static, but he wanted to develop a detection–prediction system for thunderstorms rather than a system of communication. (An analogous system for the purpose of detecting tornados by their *noise signature* on television channel 2 was tested in the United States in the early 1970s.) Popoff, whom Russia considers the inventor of radio, worked extensively in wireless and made equipment for the Russian Navy.

The most important electrical/wireless inventor of that time whose name is not a household word is Nikola Tesla. Tesla was known to the public chiefly for his showoff "taming" of lightning, but the electrical power transmission industry knew him chiefly for his development and championing of alternating current. Strangely, although Edison's direct current (DC) system lost the technical war to Tesla's alternating current

(AC) system, apparently Edison won the public relations war. Born in Croatia, Tesla spent much of his career working on AC equipment for Westinghouse—but he also worked on radio, commenting, when he heard of Marconi's 1901 sending of the letter "S" across the Atlantic, that "He is using 17 of my patents." These patents, starting with the first in 1893, fared well in the courts—one, filed in 1897 and granted in 1900, was held by the U.S. Supreme Court in 1943 to have anticipated Marconi's work—but Tesla never was deeply involved in innovating radio and never got full credit for his work.

2.1.2.1 *Marconi*

The most widely known inventor–innovator in the field of wireless, the man most historians credit with inventing radiotelegraphy, is the Italian Guglielmo Marconi. Marconi was interested in making radio work and only secondarily in *how* it worked. In 1894, at the age of 20, he read of Hertz's experiments and aimed to apply this knowledge to communication. Supported by a wealthy father, Marconi was able during the next year to improve the Hertz transmitter, to note that a signal sent from an elevated antenna would go farther, to use a ground connection as well as an antenna, to make the Branly-Lodge coherer more sensitive, and to add a telegraph key and batteries. By 1896 he could transmit and receive two miles or more on his father's estate near Bologna.

It was obvious to his family that the young man would shortly develop a commercially valuable, wireless telegraphy system. After the Italian government expressed no interest, the family decided to send him to England, which, as the most important naval and maritime power with its empire and control of most of the world's cables, was the country most concerned with development of long-range communication. At age 22, Marconi arrived in London. His Irish-born mother's contacts carried him to the head of the telegraph system of the British Post Office, William Preece, who had done some wireless experimentation himself. Preece took the young Italian under his wing and helped him to improve his system and show it to important persons in British finance and government.

Marconi's work progressed rapidly. Soon, his signals reached eight miles or more; in 1899 he spanned the English Channel, and two years later he transmitted the letter "S" in Morse code across the Atlantic to Newfoundland. However, wire telegraph interests in Newfoundland invoked their monopoly franchise and forced Marconi to dismantle his station. Then, incorporating Lodge's tuning principle into his apparatus, Marconi achieved a standard of reliability that overcame the skepticism his "miraculous" invention had provoked. Actually, Marconi may not have invented anything, as others had, but he assembled the fruits of many lines of development into a working apparatus.

◾ Marconi and the Transatlantic "S": 1901

Winds, as much as or more than distance, nearly undid Marconi's hopes of sending a wireless signal across the Atlantic Ocean late in 1901. First, a gale nearly wrecked the large Poldhu station in Cornwall, England. Then, just two months later, a similar storm demolished the new Marconi station on Cape Cod, threatening a long postponement of the tests. Then, with the Poldhu apparatus jury-rigged, Marconi and his assistants sailed for Newfoundland, which was somewhat closer, in the dead of winter. Marconi described what happened in a speech given a year later:

A 7340 Marconi's Wireless Telgraph Experimental Station, South Wellfleet, Mass.

The first experiments were carried out in Newfoundland last December, and every assistance and encouragement was given me by the Newfoundland Government. As it was impossible at that time of the year to set up a permanent installation with poles, I carried out experiments with receivers joined to a vertical wire about 400 ft. long, elevated by a kite. This gave a very great deal of trouble, as in consequence of the variations of the wind constant variations in the electrical capacity of the wire were caused. My assistants in Cornwall had received instructions to send a succession of "S's," followed by a short message at a certain pre-arranged speed, every ten minutes, alternating with five minutes' rest during certain hours every day. Owing to the constant variations in the capacity of the aerial wire it was soon found out that an ordinary syntonic receiver was not suitable, although a number of doubtful signals were at one time recorded. I, therefore, tried various microphonic self-restoring coherers placed in the secondary circuit of a transformer, the signals being read on a telephone. With several of these coherers, signals were distinctly and accurately received, and only at the pre-arranged times, in many cases a succession of "S's," being heard distinctly although, probably in consequence of the weakness of the signals and the unreliability of the detector, no actual message could be deciphered. The coherers which gave the signals were one containing loose carbon filings, another, designed by myself, containing a mixture of carbon dust and cobalt filings, and thirdly, the "Italian Navy Coherer," containing a globule of mercury between two plugs. . . .

The result of these tests was sufficient to convince myself and my assistants that, with permanent stations at both sides of the Atlantic, and by the employment of a little more power, messages could be sent across the ocean with the same facility as across much shorter distances.

Source: G. Marconi, "The Progress of Electric Space Telegraphy," delivered Friday, June 13, 1902, before the Royal Institution, London. Reprinted in Eric Eastwood (ed.) *Wireless Telegraphy* (New York: John Wiley, 1974), pages 72–88, at page 86. Courtesy of Applied Science Publishers Ltd., England.

Marconi managed to attract excellent business and technical managers and advisers, who put together the first wireless firm that could cultivate a profitable market. His company, formed in 1897, was first called the Wireless Telegraph and Signal Company but was changed in 1900 to Marconi's Wireless Telegraph Co., Ltd., or simply "British Marconi." Together with an American subsidiary formed two years later (and a Canadian subsidiary organized shortly after that), it quickly became dominant in both marine and transatlantic communication, remaining so until after World War I. Marconi, although something of a showman, winning the Nobel Prize for physics in 1909, was primarily interested in experimentation, and he let his well-qualified advisers and staff run the business. The companies concentrated on commercial applications of wireless telegraphy, as well as the British Empire's worldwide communications needs. Although the Marconi companies had some difficulty persuading land-line telegraph companies and government administrations to relay messages from wireless receiving stations to their final destinations, wireless marine business made money— at lower rates than the telegraph cable—as early as 1910.

2.1.2.2 *Fessenden and the First Broadcast*

The first major experimenter in the United States to work with wireless was Reginald A. Fessenden, a Canadian with far less business acumen than Marconi and a temper that repeatedly alienated his backers. He became a professor of electrical engineering at the University of Pittsburgh after having worked for Edison and with the U.S. Weather Bureau on a system of wireless transmission of forecasts. He wanted to develop a workable system of transoceanic wireless using continuous waves rather than Marconi's spark gap technique. Fessenden believed that this method would provide the power necessary for more effective Morse code transmissions and simultaneously create the quieter carrier wave required for voice transmission.

In 1900, Fessenden asked GE to make him a high-speed generator of alternating currents, or alternator, to use as a transmitter. The electrical manufacturing firms accepted special orders for machinery from communications inventors and organizations, and this was the first major request for wireless apparatus. The customer received the essential equipment, and the manufacturing company made a profit and kept the ideas.

It took three years for GE to design and deliver the first alternator to Fessenden. One of GE's engineers, E. F. W. Alexanderson, later perfected the alternator for GE, working along different lines from Fessenden. To fund his experimentation, Fessenden found financial backing for the National Electric Signaling Company in 1902. When the financial panic of 1907 wiped out an opportunity to sell the company to AT&T, Fessenden founded a company in which his original backers had no part. This led to lengthy law suits between backers and inventor and the eventual sale

■ **Site of the World's First Voice and Music Broadcast: 1906** This is a postcard view of Fessenden's Brant Rock station, showing the tall tubular tower with its adjustable antenna at the top, and the two summer cottages that were converted into living quarters and station headquarters. The tower was demolished in 1912 or 1913. This particular card was mailed in July of 1907, just six months after the Christmas Eve broadcast discussed in the text—and bears the handwritten comment on the back "Did you get my wireless?"

The Wireless Station-Brant Rock, Mass.

No. 1691 Moore & Gibson Co., New-York. Germany

of assets—primarily patents—to Westinghouse after World War I (see pp. 58–63). This firm failed chiefly because of the backers' lack of technical knowledge and understanding and the inventor's difficult personality.

Fessenden continued to contribute important technological developments for many years. He is most remembered for transmitting probably the first publicly announced broadcast of radio telephony, from his station at Brant Rock, Massachusetts, on Christmas Eve 1906. Following a private demonstration a month before, Fessenden alerted ships up and down the East Coast of the United States by wireless telegraphy and arranged for New York newspaper reporters to listen to the Christmas Eve broadcast, followed by one on New Year's Eve. If one considers the "general public" of the day as those few who owned and used receiving equipment, mainly ships at sea, and the newspapers are serving as representatives of the public, then the 1906 transmissions were the first broadcasts. They were scheduled, they were for the general public, and listening required no special knowledge of code since they consisted of voice and music. The publicity they received included apocryphal stories of shipboard radio operators hearing angels' voices. However, since Fessenden's purpose was to make money from his inventions of long- and medium-range radio apparatus, he meant these broadcasts as publicity and not as a program service to the public.

2.1.2.3 *De Forest*

Another important American inventor–innovator of radio was Lee de Forest. After earning a Ph.D. from Yale in 1899 with a dissertation on wireless telegraphy, de Forest worked briefly for Western Electric. In 1900 and 1901 he developed his own wireless telegraphy system as competition for Marconi, who was then getting established. De Forest's system was a technical failure but a publicity bonanza. He had arranged to send by wireless the results of a 1901 yacht race from a boat to one of the smaller press associations, but a Marconi set on another boat created such interference that neither signal could get through. The newspaper publicity about the attempt, however, reached stock promoter Abraham White, who decided to back de Forest.

The De Forest Wireless Telephone Company was established in 1902, with de Forest concentrating on research and White promoting heavy sales of stock. Customers included the Army, the Navy, and the United Fruit Company, which needed radio to communicate with its plantations in Central America, but sales were limited compared to stock sold and expectations engendered. As a result, in what was to become a common tale, the backers dissolved the company in 1907. Its assets were sold to the United Wireless Telegraph Company, in an effort to freeze out the inventor.

Fortunately de Forest retained the rights to his most important invention, the Audion or triode vacuum tube (see pp. 34–36), and immediately set up his own firm, the De Forest Radio Telephone Company. During the next few years, de Forest produced some spectacular publicity events: In 1907 he offered occasional telephonic, classical music broadcasts; in the summer of 1908, he broadcast a long phonograph record concert from the Eiffel Tower, with reception reported 500 miles away, although it was more reliable at 25 miles; in 1910 he broadcast Enrico Caruso in two operas from the Metropolitan Opera House in New York to perhaps 50 people. Financial problems, law suits, and criminal stock fraud charges forced de Forest to sell some of the Audion rights to a covert agent of AT&T at a low price. Even so, the De Forest company went bankrupt in 1911, the first of his several business catastrophes. Clearly, de Forest was a better inventor than he was businessman or scientist, and his reputation as the "father of radio" is based largely and deservedly on the Audion, which played a key role in electronics for several decades.

2.2 Improvements in Wireless

With basic wireless principles known, attention turned, over the next several years, to perfecting both transmission and reception of radio signals.

2.2.1 Transmission

Marconi's early experiments and initial commercial installations used the spark gap transmission pioneered by Heinrich Hertz in the 1880s. Although simple to construct, the spark gap transmitter required a large amount of power, radiated energy over a broad band, was bulky, and produced a thunderous and disagreeable crash. Furthermore, it was either "on" or "off," and it could not be modulated for speech and music.

An early improvement on the spark gap transmitter was the *arc*. Danish inventor Valdemar Poulsen patented an arc generator in 1902 that, by using a much narrower gap, could give a nearly continuous series of sparks, or arc. Because this system, called *CW* or *continuous wave*, was inherently more efficient for communication than was the spark gap, it could be used over longer distances. The Poulsen arc was normally a huge, expensive, water-cooled device, but it could be used in smaller shipboard installations. In 1909 Cyril F. Elwell purchased United States rights to it and set up the Federal Telegraph Company of California. In the years just before American entrance into World War I, the U.S. Navy's enthusiasm for this device resulted in contracts for several shore stations capable of long-distance communication with the fleet. The largest Poulsen arc station, started during the war but not finished until 1920, was at Bordeaux, France. This 1,000 kw station may have been the high point of trying to span the Atlantic with brute power. Federal's Poulsen patents also were important immediately after World War I (see p. 60), and the Poulsen arc remained in shipboard installations until the start of World War II.

■ **Typical Early Wireless Transmitter**   Taken from a typical book of the time intended for radio experimenters, this is both a drawing and an electrical schematic of a spark-gap transmitter (to the left)—the standard wireless transmitter from the time of Hertz in the 1880s through World War I. That it was used for wireless telegraphy (code) and not telephony (voice and music) is evident by the telegraph key. With a battery, the system was self-contained, not requiring plug-in sources of power. The receiving end might consist of a coherer (in the earliest days), and after 1900 a crystal detector as is shown in the box on page 90.

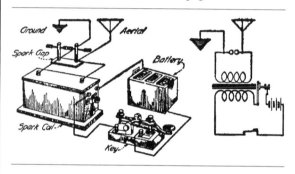

Source: Yates and Pacent (1922), page 61.

The next major system, also developed before World War I, was the alternator, a Fessenden idea built to his specifications by GE. The first was delivered in 1906 and soon others followed. By 1911, after Fessenden had ended his association with his financial backers, GE engineer E. F. W. Alexanderson rapidly perfected ideas of his own.

The Alexanderson alternator was a huge piece of machinery, very much like a power-plant generator but rotating much faster. Such high-speed rotation created complex mechanical problems, but by 1909 Alexanderson had developed a 100,000-cycle alternator that produced smooth, continuous waves. Although the first successful unit produced only 2,000 watts, higher power soon followed, and, by 1915, 50 kw units were being built. After long negotiations, GE and buyer British Marconi agreed that Marconi would have exclusive rights to use the alternator, and GE would have exclusive rights to make it. The first 50 kw unit was installed in 1917, and the following year a 200 kw unit, the most powerful and efficient transmitter in the world, was installed at New Brunswick, New Jersey. Using the government call letters NFF, the powerful unit announced President Wilson's Fourteen Points to the world in 1918. The agreement between Marconi and GE was set aside during the war but was to become instrumental in structuring American radio immediately afterward (see p. 57).

The next means of transmission, still in use today, involved vacuum tubes. Although experimentation began around 1912, high-powered

■ **The Alexanderson Alternator**   Alternator developer E. F. W. Alexanderson is seen watching one of the 50-kw alternators in action. These huge machines were the first reliable and effective means of long-distance and transatlantic communication by wireless.

Photo courtesy of General Electric.

vacuum-tube transmitters did not become common for more than a decade. Thomas Edison first noted that a heated filament gave off electrons—the blackening of a light bulb, or "Edison effect." In 1904 John Ambrose Fleming, working for British Marconi, discovered that, since electrons were negative, a positively charged plate could attract them. Therefore, electricity would flow whenever the plate was positively charged. When the plate was negatively charged, no current would flow. This made the tube a perfect one-way gate or *valve* that could be used to change alternating current, such as a radio wave, to pulsating direct current. This one-way flow, in a process known as *detection*, enabled one to hear an audible signal of dots and dashes or speech no matter how high above audible range the radio wave frequency was. Detection was essential to radio reception (see p. 37). De Forest inserted into the Fleming valve a third element, a grid carrying a slight charge that could be varied from neutral, which offered no hindrance to current, to slightly negative, which would block current. This invention made a vacuum tube function as an amplifier, since the larger current flowing from filament to plate would vary in step with a much smaller control current placing a charge on the grid. (This is analogous to the small current surviving to the end of a wire telegraph line being used to trigger a relay controlling a much greater current). De Forest first used his triode, or Audion, as an amplifier as well as a detector early in the century. AT&T engineers (see p. 32), improved the device, by using a high rather than partial vacuum, for instance, and put it to work as an amplifier on long-distance telephone lines, including the first transcontinental one in 1915.

Because of their lighter weight and low current demand, vacuum tubes were used during World War I for specialized receivers and transmitters—after the Navy had agreed to indemnify manufacturers for patent infringement suits. This was necessary since de Forest controlled the use of the third element (the grid) and Marconi owned the rights to the first two elements (the diode, or Fleming valve). As early as October 1915, speech and music traveled from the U.S. Navy station at Arlington, Virginia (NAA), to the Eiffel Tower in Paris—using several hundred triodes connected in parallel. Even though this experiment showed the advantages of the vacuum-tube transmitter, such as its freedom from problems of moving machinery and its small bulk and weight in relation to distance covered—even greater a relative saving than the transistor offered a third of a century later—the alternator still was used for code transmissions for many years. It was for the transmission of music and speech that the vacuum-tube transmitter became essential.

2.2.2 Reception

In 1900 the only device generally available for detecting radio waves was the Branly-Lodge coherer, as modified slightly by Marconi. It was very delicate, permitted only slow message speeds because of its need to be tapped regularly between incoming pulses, occasionally gave false indications, and was not readily adaptable to tuning. Marconi's 1902 magnetic detector was more sensitive, permitted reception over 500 miles by day and 1,500 by night, but was hard to construct. During the period from 1903 to 1908, Fessenden developed an electrolytic detector that was used extensively until about 1913. This silent and automatic device needed no "tapper" since it used liquid rather than particles.

A completely different approach led to the development of the crystal detector around 1906 by Greenleaf W. Pickard and H. H. C. Dunwoody. Pickard had found that a crystal of silicon would allow electricity to flow in one direction. Using a small metal point, called a *cat's whisker*, to find the most effective spot on the crystal, he constructed a detector of radio waves far less expensive than previous models and just as effective. Dunwoody discovered that carborundum, an extremely hard, electrical furnace by-product, also would work well. By allowing electricity to flow in one direction only, it converted the very rapidly alternating *radio-frequency* wave into a series of pulses whose variations in strength (amplitude) were in the audio-frequency range to which earphones and the human ear could respond. These detectors were the first *solid state* devices and, for several decades, the only ones. The crystal detector permitted hundreds of thousands of hobbyists and the general public to pick up radio signals—for the price of a pair of earphones and a few cents' worth of wire, crystal, and cat's whisker. The major drawbacks of the crystal set, which was in general use for decades and which hobbyists still use, were the difficulty of finding the right spot with the cat's whisker (solved by permanently affixing the whisker at the factory and sealing the crystal in a case) and the inability of such a simple receiver to amplify the weak incoming signals. But as late as World War II, all ships were required to have a crystal set for emergencies.

In its original form, the Fleming valve (see pp. 35–36), which permitted electricity to flow in only one direction, could function as a detector. Although the 3-element de Forest Audion, patented in 1906 and 1907, also could be used as a detector, it did not improve detection per se. Its greatest value was in amplifying weak incoming radio waves. A radio-frequency amplification stage or two before the detector and an audio-frequency amplification stage or two afterward would permit reliable reception of exceedingly weak radio signals. Eventually amplification led to the use of loudspeakers instead of earphones. Manufacturing tolerances were at first loose, permitting inconsistent results that kept de Forest tied up in lawsuits for many years. Although associated circuitry was not well understood at the time, the invention of the amplifying triode proved critical to the future development of radio.

At about the time de Forest sold telephonic rights to the Audion to AT&T, Edwin Howard Armstrong, best known later as the inventor of FM, was working on circuitry that would use the Audion as a transmitter, as well as an amplifier and detector in a radio receiver of unsurpassed sensitivity and selectivity. Within a few months of each other in 1914, de Forest and Armstrong individually applied for patents on what became known as the regenerative or *feedback* circuit. One of the longest and most bitter fights in radio history resulted from this conflict over patent priority, leading in 1928 and again in 1934 to the United States Supreme Court. Although the engineering community generally believed that Armstrong had a sounder grasp of the principles behind the circuit than de Forest had, the court held in favor of de Forest. Today, engineering texts and organizations generally give Armstrong credit for this crucial invention, but the law gave it to de Forest. The struggle embittered both men.

The regenerative and superregenerative receivers were very sensitive, but required extremely delicate tuning to keep them from oscillating. Oscillation interference would not only prevent signals from being heard, but would disrupt reception elsewhere in the vicinity. The solution lay in the heterodyne receiver, patented by Fessenden as early as 1905, and in the superheterodyne receiver, invented by Armstrong in 1918 and still in use today. These circuits were not practical until the development of the Audion.

Besides detecting and amplifying incoming signals, it was necessary at the turn of the century to find a means of *tuning* to a single station so that stations on nearby frequencies could operate without interference. Techniques were being explored: Sir Oliver Lodge had patented a system he called *syntonic tuning* as early as 1897, and, shortly afterward, both Marconi in England and John Stone Stone in America developed ways of selecting desired frequencies and rejecting unwanted ones through the principle of resonance. When a singer sings a note that hits the resonant frequency of a glass, acoustical energy is transferred so efficiently that it shatters the glass. In the same way, proper adjustment of the inductance or capacitance in a tuning circuit of a receiver—or transmitter, for that matter—can set up a condition whereby only the desired or resonant frequency is picked up. As usual, a patent fight ensued, but both patents, and the lives of the two inventors, expired before the case was settled.

2.3 Maritime Applications

Radio equipment for more than experimental purposes was first installed on oceangoing ships and in the shore stations that were built to communicate with them. Much as the telegraph had nearly doubled the railroad's freight-carrying capacity through more efficient scheduling and routing, so radio enabled ships to improve their cargo pickup schedules, to inform owners of their approach, and to learn of weather and other conditions en route. Over and above these commercial benefits, however, at least in the public mind, was the safety of lives and property at sea.

2.3.1 Wireless and Commercial Shipping (to 1914)

As early as 1899 ships in distress were calling for help by radio. Marconi's reputation in Great Britain grew after the crew of a coastal lightship was saved from a severe storm in this way. In 1909 when the liner *Republic* collided with the *Florida* in a fog off the East Coast of the United States, the radio operator on the sinking liner stayed at his post and issued a call for help that resulted in saving all those aboard, except one who died of a heart attack. In that same year, passengers and crew on 18 other ships with radio installations were saved, thanks to radio, but those on many more ships without radio were not.

Known to almost everyone today because of the popularity of the 1998 movie, one of the biggest peacetime maritime disasters was the sinking of the liner *Titanic* on her maiden voyage in April 1912. The ship collided with an iceberg and three hours later went to the bottom off the Newfoundland Banks together with 1,500 passengers and crew. Some 700 were saved by a ship that received *Titanic's* wireless call for help 58 miles away, but a much nearer ship did not assist because its only radio operator, after many hours on duty, was sound asleep when the messages came over the radio.

This disaster pointed up the necessity not only for radio installations but for enough qualified operators to man the apparatus on passenger and larger ocean-going cargo ships. While later research denies that it happened, David Sarnoff (years later president, then chairman of the board, of RCA) encouraged the story that, as a young Marconi operator assigned to the New York station atop the John Wanamaker department store, with the airwaves cleared by government order, he stayed at his post during the *Titanic* disaster, sending messages to coordinate rescue traffic and compile a list of survivors. Sarnoff soon was named commercial manager of American Marconi, perhaps because of his gift for self-promotion.

When Marconi first started installing wireless in ships, his was the best equipment available. Other apparatus could be used, but Marconi and his business associates found ways to keep Marconi apparatus most in demand. A 1901 agreement with the Lloyds of London insurance pool to equip Lloyds' signal stations served to gain acceptance and prestige for Marconi equipment early on; and Marconi allowed its shore stations to communicate only with ships that rented Marconi equipment and trained operators. As various nations began passing laws regulating radio to save lives at sea, and as ship-owners became more aware of its commercial benefits, more and more vessels acquired Marconi apparatus, complete with Marconi operators. To support their own manufacturers, nations other than England permitted or suggested other brands of wireless apparatus, but ships equipped with them could not, until after 1903 (see pp. 41–42), communicate with Marconi shore stations.

By the start of World War I, British Marconi stood preeminent in the field. It controlled wireless communications throughout the British Empire and had taken over the assets of de Forest's United Wireless, thus controlling—through its subsidiary, the American Marconi Company—90% of all American ship-to-shore commercial communication.

Some specialized radio operations did not need interconnection with Marconi installations. As early as 1904, the United Fruit Company used de Forest apparatus to make ships available for loading fruit as soon as it was ready to pick. In 1907, switching to Fessenden equipment, United Fruit constructed the first radio-transmitting facilities in most of the Central American republics. It established an operating subsidiary, Tropical Radio Telegraph Company, in 1913 and was among the leaders in upgrading transmitting and receiving equipment—sometimes because a hurricane had conveniently blown away older gear. By the early 1920s, United Fruit had invested nearly $4 million in establishing radio in the region, equipping its ships, and even acquiring patents on a crystal receiver.

For dispatching of ships, radio had no equal. For point-to-point messages, however, undersea cable offered strong competition. In 1907 British Marconi offered transatlantic wireless telegraphy at only 18 cents a word, as compared to the cable companies' 25-cent rate. The greater reliability of cable evened the odds and helped to prolong this commercial war for many years. Radio had more luck in the Pacific, where fewer cables meant less competition and less interference meant greater reliability.

2.3.2 Wireless and the U.S. Navy

The first important armed-forces tests of radio were conducted independently by the United States Navy and the British Royal Navy in 1899. The American tests were made of Marconi apparatus aboard the U.S. battleships *New York* and *Massachusetts.* Although radio signals bridged distances of up to 40 miles, it was clear that the lack of suitable tuning devices led to unacceptable interference. Furthermore, the just adopted Marconi policy of renting rather than selling equipment and services was politically unacceptable. Obviously, the Navy could not accept being dependent on a foreign power, no matter how friendly.

For the next few years, the Navy searched for a different, reliable radio system, while not using any wireless at sea. Neither the de Forest nor the Fessenden systems seemed to do the trick, nor did various European systems. In 1903 the Navy installed some German (Slaby-Arco) apparatus on ships of the North Atlantic Fleet, which gave them a clear advantage in war games over another part of the fleet without radio communications. At the same time, the Navy started to build powerful shore stations, and by 1904, 20 of these were in operation. One of these, in Arlington, Virginia, broadcast precise time signals, a useful aid to navigation.

As early as 1905, after further comparative tests, the Navy began a conscious swing to American-made equipment. In 1907 it gave de Forest a scant month to install radiotelephone transmitters on the ships of the Great White Fleet, being readied for an around-the-world "show the flag" mission. Partly because of hasty installation, these devices worked poorly, except for the one on the U.S.S. *Ohio*, which transmitted voice and music to the crew, to other ships in the fleet, and to listeners in ports of call. However, these unreliable radio telephones were removed when the fleet returned in 1909, and interest in naval wireless telephony languished for nearly a decade until the United States entered World War I in 1917.

During this period, the Navy concentrated on expanding shore stations and shipboard wireless telegraphy installations. In 1912 it began building a chain of stations to connect American bases in the Pacific, including Hawaii and the Philippines, at the same time that British Marconi was constructing the "Empire system" for use of the Royal Navy and to eliminate the British Empire's dependence on easily severed cables. After contracting with the Federal Telegraph Company for a Poulsen arc installation at the Arlington station in 1913, the U.S. Navy installed similar transmitters in the Pacific, including one of 500 kw in Manila. Coastal shore stations in the United States were located so that, if one station was out of operation, another could reach naval units at sea. Unfortunately, most of this equipment could function over a range of only a few hundred to 2,000 or so miles—a serious drawback if the Navy expected the fleet to be in action across the Atlantic or Pacific.

Another drawback to the Navy's use of radio was the resistance of personnel to innovation. Most shipboard installations were primitive, hand-built affairs. Few men were adequately trained to get the most from them, and fewer still cared to learn. Doubtful senior officers discouraged diversion of scarce Navy funds for wireless, and field commanders disliked being tied to headquarters by an electronic umbilical cord. The telegraph had already limited the freedom of army commanders to "fight their own war," but, until the advent of wireless, naval commanders retained independence due to the nature of their forces and battleground. Nevertheless, foresighted naval officers realized that wireless would be useful in wartime—if its problems could be overcome.

2.4 First Attempts at Regulation

Radio clearly was such a potential saver of lives and property in peril at sea that otherwise acceptable practices that interfered with its maritime operation had to be overcome. British Marconi's policy not to communicate with users of other companies' facilities, even sometimes in an emergency, was seen as a blatant attempt to establish a monopoly. Interference was increasing as more stations went on the air and receivers became more sensitive. It occurred not only between ship stations but between ships, land stations, and a growing number of amateur stations.

Other factors helped to sway public opinion in the direction of government control of radio. Business scandals involved de Forest in the U.S. and Marconi stock in the United Kingdom. The growing militant nationalism in most technologically developed countries worsened the confusion over rates, equipment standards, and interconnection procedures. How could radio achieve full stature when each nation rallied around its own radio equipment manufacturers, and based industry standards on political policy rather than on technology? Some international solution to these problems was indicated.

In 1903, the government of Imperial Germany called the first international convention on radio, in Berlin. This meeting stemmed partly from the refusal of the Marconi Company to relay signals from a yacht belonging to a German prince on a visit to North America. The eight nations attending—except for Italy and the United Kingdom, which not surprisingly supported the Marconi position—called for all wireless systems to communicate under all conditions with all other wireless systems. With the provision that each country would have to pass the enabling laws, the meeting adjourned with plans to reconvene the following year.

The subsequent meeting was postponed once because Great Britain and Italy still were not ready, and then again because of the Russo-Japanese War of 1905, and finally took place in Berlin in 1906. Delegates from 27 nations—including the U.S. with a naval officer delegation—worked out two protocols, one for ship-to-ship and the other for ship-to-shore communication, both calling for communication without regard for the type of equipment used. Also the international distress call was changed from CQD (roughly, "calling all stations, disaster") to an arbitrary three dots, three dashes, and three dots all run together—the famous SOS.

These agreements were to take effect on July 1, 1908, but there were many delays and complications. Countries with Marconi contracts asked for time to work them out. In the United States, Congress initially refused

---

■ **The Beginnings of Radio Regulation**   (Excerpts from three key acts).

An Act to Require Apparatus and Operators for Radio Communication on Certain Ocean Steamers, approved June 24, 1910   . . . it shall be unlawful for any ocean-going steamer of the United States or of any foreign country, carrying passengers and carrying fifty or more persons, including passengers and crew, to leave or attempt to leave any port of the United States unless such steamer shall be equipped with an efficient apparatus for radio-communication, in good working order, in charge of a person skilled in the use of such apparatus, which apparatus shall be capable of transmitting and receiving messages over a distance of at least one hundred miles . . .

That for the purpose of this act apparatus for radio communications shall not be deemed to be efficient unless the company Installing it shall contract in writing to exchange, and shall, in fact, exchange, as far as may be physically practicable, to be determined by the master of the vessel, messages with shore or ship stations using other systems of radio-communication.

An Act to Amend the Act of 1910, approved July 23, 1912   . . . an auxiliary power supply, independent of the vessel's main electric power plant, must be provided which will enable the sending set for at least four hours to send messages over a distance of at least one hundred miles day or night, and efficient communication between the operator in the radio room and the bridge shall be maintained at all times. The radio equipment must be in charge of two or more persons skilled in the use of such apparatus, one or the other of whom shall be on duty at all times while the vessel is being navigated . . .

An Act to Regulate Radio Communication, approved August 13, 1912   . . . That a person, company, or corporation within the jurisdiction of the United States shall not use or operate any apparatus for radio communication as a means of commercial intercourse among the several States . . . except under and in accordance with a license, revocable for cause, in that behalf granted by the Secretary of Commerce and Labor upon application therefore . . .

That every such license shall be in such form as the Secretary . . . shall determine and shall contain restrictions . . . on and subject to which the license is granted; . . . that every such license shall be issued only to citizens of the United States . . . shall specify the ownership and location of the station . . . and other particulars for its identification and to enable its range to be estimated; shall state the purpose of the station . . . shall state the wavelength or the wavelengths authorized for use by the station for the prevention of interference and the hours for which the station is licensed for work . . .

to ratify the agreements, accepting the testimony of American wireless manufacturing firms that they would stifle development of radio and place it under international rather than national control. It was not until the planners of a third conference, to be held in London in 1912, quietly withdrew their invitation to the United States that Congress passed the first radio law in this country, the Wireless Ship Act of 1910.

The absence of a specific law did not mean that Americans were not trying to settle the problem of interference between stations, which was caused largely by the uncoordinated use of radio by private commercial and experimental stations, the Army, the Navy, the Weather Bureau, and the Department of Agriculture. A board set up in 1904 by President Theodore Roosevelt to resolve these difficulties recommended Navy control of most radio, especially in wartime; legislation to prevent commercial interests from controlling radio; peacetime direction of radio by the Department of Commerce and Labor; and installation of government stations in all United States territories. Although none of these suggestions was formally adopted, one could trace them in American radio regulation for more than two decades.

The Wireless Ship Act of 1910, which Congress passed after several attempts, contained in one page nearly everything called for in the 1906 Berlin protocol: Ocean-going vessels with 50 or more passengers traveling between ports 200 or more miles apart had to carry radio apparatus capable of reaching 100 miles day or night and an operator to run it. Partly because of the lesson learned from the *Republic* disaster, and partly because the law created a market for more sales, the manufacturers accepted this act. It met the demands of the 1903 and 1906 conferences indirectly, calling for "an efficient apparatus for radio-communication" and then defining "efficient" by stating that "apparatus for radio-communication shall not be deemed to be efficient unless the company installing it shall contract in writing to exchange, and shall, in fact, exchange . . . messages with shore or ship stations using other systems of radio-communication." (By the late 1950s and early 1960s, this precedent was overlooked when television was faced with the problem of sets that couldn't pick up UHF channels.) Together with similar laws passed in other countries (one in the United Kingdom as early as 1904 called for trained radio operators), this Act solved the problem.

In 1912, 29 nations met in London and agreed to strengthen the 1906 protocol, particularly, as a result of the *Titanic* disaster that year, in recommending that two operators be available on most vessels. The United States amended the 1910 act to provide that any ship with 50 or more passengers, regardless of distance between customary ports and including the Great Lakes for the first time, had to have radio, an auxiliary power supply capable of operating it, two or more operators, and good communication between the radio operator and the bridge. A month later, in August, Congress passed the Radio Act of 1912, which took seven pages to spell out public policy (stations had to be licensed by the Secretary of Commerce and Labor, government stations had priority, etc.) and standards of operation (messages were to be secret, wavelengths and transmitter power were to be selected for minimal interference, etc.). This law governed the regulation of radio, including the as yet little-known concept of broadcasting, until 1927.

2.5 The First Broadcasters

In selecting the most important early broadcasters, one has to use a detailed definition of broadcasting (see p. 15). For example, although Stubblefield transmitted speech successfully (see p. 26), he hardly intended to reach the general public, a major criterion in our definition, and his transmissions apparently relied on induction, inherently short-range, rather than on radiation. In another example, Théodore and Francois Puskás linked telephone subscribers in Budapest to a central unit that provided a news and music service. However, this "Telephonic Newspaper," which ran from 1893 until at least the middle 1930s, used wire, not radio—in a process called *rediffusion*, still used in some countries. This might be thought of as the precursor of cable television, but it was not broadcasting by radio to the general public. Early in the century an ingenious operator at the Mare Island Navy base in California had produced musical tones by rapidly changing the speed of rotary generators of radio waves so that the musical pitch of the signal changed—similar to the musical games one can play today with "touch tone" telephone equipment.

However, there were numerous examples of true broadcasting before its commonly accepted U.S. inauguration on KDKA late in 1920 (see pp. 63–66). Fessenden's Christmas Eve 1906 broadcast was one. Fessenden had tried to ensure a maximum audience, and, although some ship operators and a smattering of reporters in New York had to act as surrogates for the general public, this transmission was intended for a general audience; it was telephony (speech and music); it required no special knowledge for decoding; and anyone with a receiver could pick it up.

But neither Fessenden nor de Forest, who made a number of broadcasts in 1907 and 1908, had incentive to establish a regular series of public broadcasts. Their stations were experimental and promotional, and the service they provided to listeners was incidental. Although better known and with more powerful equipment than most, they were amateur radio operators, or hams. By 1912 there were more than a thousand such hobbyists, most of them interested primarily in communicating with fellow amateurs, almost exclusively by Morse code. However, by 1915, having formed a national organization, the American Radio Relay League, and established a magazine, *QST*, they had become a potential political power, a source of trained operators for wartime, and an important group of listeners, as well as tinkerers whose curiosity and work led to many important advances of the technical radio art.

Perhaps the strongest claimant to being first to intentionally broadcast on a schedule to a general audience, with voice rather than code transmission, using electromagnetic waves, was Charles D. "Doc" Herrold, who operated a College of Engineering and Wireless in San Jose, California. He was not the first to broadcast speech and music, not even in California, but early in 1909, as an adjunct to his school, Herrold presented regularly scheduled news reports and musical programs. Starting with a spark gap transmitter, he soon developed an arc that transmitted better quality voice and music. At first he broadcast only on Wednesday nights for an hour or so but soon changed to every day. Herrold built some receivers and made them available for public use in hotel lobbies. In 1915, during the San Francisco Exposition, the station broadcast six to eight hours a day with de Forest apparatus receiving its transmissions at the fair site. De Forest later said that Herrold's station "can rightfully claim to be the oldest broadcasting station of the entire world. . . ." When the Radio Act of 1912 was passed, Herrold's station was licensed and operated until World War I, when all amateur stations were closed down. Herrold resurrected the station in December 1921 or January 1922, eventually using the call letters KQW and more conventional apparatus than the "Herrold System of Radio Telephony," which would not work on wavelengths the Secretary of Commerce then assigned for broadcasting. KQW, later sold and moved to San Francisco, still broadcasts as 50,000-watt KCBS, with a legitimate claim to be the descendant of the *first* broadcasting station in the United States—even though the delay in returning to the air after World War I had destroyed its claim as the *oldest* station now operating (see pp. 63–64).

Perhaps the most important part of the Herrold story is that he was interested in providing a program service to the general public almost from the start. He wasn't in the business of selling equipment, and his own apparatus wasn't of sufficiently high quality to allow him to establish and maintain a patent position that would bring him royalty income. But, in a number of ways, it can be argued that he had thought through the concept of what we now call "broadcasting," and never wavered from his opinion that it was important. In that sense, he was a true inventor.

However, Herrold was but one of a growing number of experimental broadcasters. From 1912 to 1914, Alfred Goldsmith operated station 2XN at City College of New York. 1XE, operated at Tufts College by Harold Power, founder of American Radio and Research Company (AMRAD), also broadcast music on a more-or-less regular basis from Medford, Massachusetts, as early as 1916. It later became WGI. In 1916, G. C. Conner and C. V. Logwood also broadcast music over 2ZK in New Rochelle, New York, for an hour most evenings. In East Pittsburgh, Pennsylvania, Westinghouse engineer Frank Conrad began that same year to send voice and music programs from his home to the Westinghouse plant five miles away. Soon he was scheduling music broadcasts for friends—a humble beginning for an enterprise we will discuss in the next chapter (see pp. 65–66). At the University of Wisconsin, Professor E. M. Terry set up 9XM (later WHA) for telegraphic

■ Herrold's KQW: The First Real Station?

WIRELESS TELEGRAPH TO BE DEMONSTRATED

PROF. HERROLD, FORMER SAN JOSEAN, HAS MADE MANY INTERESTING EXPERIMENTS

WILL PERFORM FEAT OF FIRING MINIATURE POWDER MINE BY WIRELESS

Public interest is focusing on a novel form of entertainment to be given in the Y.M.C.A. Hall, Friday evening July 16th. Chas. D. Herrold, a former San Josean will appear here for the first time in a lecture "The Story of Wireless." He has devoted a number of years to a careful experimental study of wireless telegraphy and telephony. For several months past he has had a system installed on board the sloop Dorothy on the San Joaquin River and a permanent station at Stockton. A portable outfit was also sent to Vernalis, Cal. and his assistant in charge kept in touch with him by ether waves. In the Friday evening entertainment he will show the public how it is possible to time two stations so that other stations cannot get the messages. He will perform the feat of firing a miniature powder mine by wireless and will have installed on the stage a complete wireless station. The equipment includes two large Rumkoeff Tesla [sic] coils capable of producing 400,000 volts of electricity. A feature of the entertainment will be a perfect imitation of lightning. A series of long, zig-zag discharges will be led over a plate 12 feet long under the enormous tension of nearly 500,000 volts.

"Doc" Herrold stands at the doorway of his second station, about 1913. The large circular cones on the table are part of Herrold's own system of wireless telephony, which he used until World War I.

Source: San Jose *Daily Mercury* news item Thursday morning, July 15, 1909. Courtesy of San Jose *Mercury*. Photo courtesy of KCBS Radio.

weather forecasts and market reports for mariners on the Great Lakes and farmers. Allowed to stay on the air during World War I, Terry also experimented with voice broadcasts, the genesis of WHA's claim to be the first station. Some experimenters of this period reached great distances with their low-power transmitters because there were few stations to offer interference.

Even as experimentation in broadcasting progressed, most radio people believed that the future of radio lay with *narrowcasting* or point-to-point communication, particularly between mobile stations or over difficult terrain. "Radio people" in this instance included the major electrical and wireless firms, who would have to support any new use of radio. There were exceptions of course. "Doc" Herrold understood the concept, and it can be argued that his wife, Sybil, was the first deejay; de Forest's love of opera and classical music led him to use music when testing his transmitters and subsequent telephoned requests for particular pieces made him realize

■ **Conrad's "Home" Station**   Equipment used by Dr. Frank Conrad, assistant chief engineer of Westinghouse, in the years before KDKA was established in 1920. Conrad transmitted radio telephone programs from his garage, using the call letters 8XK.

Photo courtesy of Westinghouse and Joseph E. Baudino.

that unknown others would like to hear music over the air. David Sarnoff, who had been promoted to commercial manager of American Marconi some years after his service at the Marconi station in New York during the Titanic disaster, claimed to have written a memo in 1915 or 1916 suggesting a "radio music box." Although this claim was generally accepted for decades, research by Louise Benjamin in 1993 and 2001 demonstrates that he really wrote the oft-quoted memo in 1920, when broadcasting was almost a reality, but that an earlier version apparently had been written to Marconi General Manager E. J. Nally in 1916.

However, by 1917 there were more than 8,500 licensed amateurs, some of whom transmitted voice and music, and most of whom listened. However, the complexity and unreliability of equipment, the necessity for earphones, and the limited programming tended to limit radio to the engineering-minded. Neither engineers nor businessmen had much interest in visionary schemes.

2.6 Radio at War

Armies had used the telegraph for 50 years, and World War I added all the newer devices that could be converted to warfare—the automobile, the airplane, the radio—and stimulated their development as well. Although the war halted most private experimentation and closed amateur stations, the

Army and Navy's need for reliable, efficient apparatus for communication hastened the introduction of wireless in all forms.

2.6.1 Radio in World War I

In the Gulf of Mexico, the U.S. Navy was able to intercept some ships during an incident prior to America's entry into World War I, thanks to radio. In Europe, Germany had had to turn to radio when Britain cut Germany's cable connections. Germany used radio sometimes for propaganda but usually for scheduling and dispatching commercial and naval vessels. Its "broadcast" nature, however, permitted the British to intercept German messages and decipher them with the aid of a captured code book. One message, sent by the German Foreign Ministry to their ambassador in Mexico City, proposed offering the Mexicans large chunks of United States territory if Mexico would join Germany in the event of war with the United States—the famous "Zimmermann Telegram." The British were delighted to inform the United States government, and the world, about the perfidy of the Germans and provided Washington with the key to the German code. What made this more infuriating to the Americans was that a German-owned but American Navy-operated station in New Jersey had relayed the original message, still in code, as a diplomatic courtesy.

The Navy was operating the German-owned transmitter because the government had taken over all high-power stations—even American Marconi's—as a national security measure. All amateur stations, including broadcast experimenters, were closed down in 1917. The Navy's own 35 coastal stations, its high-power chain across the Pacific, and radio telegraph apparatus on nearly all major vessels had cost about $20 million by April 6, 1917, when the United States entered the war. After that date, the Navy also acted as censor on all wireless and cable communication channels and the government took over the railroad and telephone industries, the latter assigned to the Post Office Department. The Navy communicated with the fleet in European waters from major shore stations including the American Marconi installation at New Brunswick, New Jersey. This station used a 200-kw Alexanderson alternator, which had replaced the 50-kw one and could be heard all over Europe.

With its great interest in rapid and efficient communication, the Navy was in an excellent position to use wireless. However, it suffered from two shortages: trained personnel and top-flight equipment. The first shortage was solved through recruiting amateur operators and establishing radio schools around the country, including one at Harvard University. By the Armistice, November 11, 1918, some 7,000 men had been trained and 3,400 were under instruction. This group, added to the thousands of hams who managed to keep up their interest in wireless during the war, strongly influenced postwar radio developments.

Technologically, radio advanced during the war. Lightweight vacuum-tube transmitters and receivers were developed. Even airplanes carried them, including one set designed by Major Edwin Armstrong. Low-power, tactical radio sets were not nearly so prevalent as they are today. In World War I, an Army division of 20,000 men rarely would have more than six radio sets—one for each of four regiments, one for the artillery, and one at headquarters. (By the early 1950s, one transmitter served every 6.3 men in an army division, and today most units have far more.) Although radio added greatly to the flexibility of ground communication during World War I, the demands of reliability, secrecy, and relatively immobile trench warfare made telephone and telegraph service more common than wireless.

2.6.2 The First Patents Pool

The Navy could requisition high-power (in those days, anything from 50 watts up) stations from private companies, train operators for them, and close down domestic stations to prevent the transmittal of espionage; but obtaining efficient and modern shipboard radio equipment was another story.

Vacuum-tube equipment was obviously the best, but nobody could legally make triode vacuum tubes so long as de Forest controlled the patent on the third electrode and Marconi controlled the Fleming patents on the first two electrodes. Furthermore, some of the Navy's earlier sources were busy making equipment for either the Germans or the Allies. Litigation on the de Forest and Fleming patents had continued for years, and court decisions in 1916 tied most companies into knots. Years before, Western Electric (AT&T) had purchased some rights to the triode from de Forest, but not enough. If tube equipment was to become available, the patent situation would have to be resolved.

The wartime solution was an emergency pool of patents set up under Navy protection. This offer of indemnification, in effect, said: "Use what you need to give us the best equipment, and if you are sued for patent infringement, we'll pay the bill." As the result, the Navy could get its equipment, mostly from civilian plants.

At the end of the war, all the temporarily shelved problems came back, together with some caused by the war itself. Should the Navy relinquish control over transoceanic wireless? What about the telephone industry, and the amateurs? How could the triode legally be manufactured and used? The patents pool had worked well; could it or should it continue? What about jobs for the returned radio operators? What about factories that had been turning out war-related radio apparatus? Should the government allow Marconi to expand its monopoly, particularly with respect to messages from America to Europe and the Pacific? Should Marconi alone have the Alexanderson alternator? The next chapter tells how these questions were answered.

■ **Use of Radio by the U.S. Army and Navy in 1917 and 1918**

The Army Signal Corps   Although a transatlantic radio station was built near Bordeaux, the War Department in Washington had no radio contact with its commanders in the field, and these commanders had no very dependable wireless systems among themselves. Radio carried little of the war's communications load. In the first place, the tactical situation again and again brought the Western Front into small areas and mired it there. For another reason, although nearly 10,000 radio sets, chiefly airborne radiotelegraph, were produced for the Signal Corps and Air Service, the conflict was over too soon for the combat signalman or aviator to use them much. Finally, radio was too new to have passed the awkward age. Spark-type equipment did have the advantage of not requiring a skilled man to tune it or mend it, but was so heavy it could scarcely be moved, was often unintelligible, and was frequently out of commission. Tube equipment generally replaced it. Radio's chief use was for intelligence work. At goniometric stations it took what were later called "fixes" upon enemy transmitters and identified their location by the intersection of the angles. It intercepted German ground telegraph, telephone, aircraft, and artillery signals. . . . The most interesting aspect of Signal Corps radio in World War I was the consolidation of the hitherto scattered efforts in scientific research . . . [but] for the most part, none of the laboratory improvements got into production before the Armistice. Had any been developed before the war, radio history would have been made, for the critical inadequacy of equipment necessitated remarkable advances in the field.

Source: Dulany Terrett, *The Signal Corps: The Emergency* (Washington: Government Printing Office, 1956), pages 18–19.

Naval Radio   In the operating field the Navy became the sole agency, with the exception of U.S. Army field communications, for providing U.S. radio communications, both military and commercial, from the date we entered the war until 1 March 1920. Much was done during the period to increase the reliability of long-range communications by encouraging the development of higher powered arcs and alternators and by the Navy's own design of heterodyne and neutrodyne receivers, multiple-stage amplifiers, and other ancillary apparatus. By the end of the war, sufficient progress had been made in the development of static-reducing balanced antenna systems, together with improvements to transmitters and receiving equipments, to insure reliable transatlantic radio communications.

Iconographic Collection, State Historical Society of Wisconsin. (WHi (×3) 32888)

Source: Captain L. S. Howeth, *History of Communications–Electronics in the United States Navy* (Washington: Government Printing Office, 1963), page 209.

2.7 The Stage Is Set

We can think of developments up to 1895 as background, for it was only with Marconi's active experimentation in that year that wireless began to move from theory to practice. The key people include Clerk-Maxwell, who first theorized about wireless communication; Hertz, who experimentally proved Clerk-Maxwell correct; Marconi, who took wireless from experiment to practical reality; Fleming, who developed the first vacuum tube with two elements; Fessenden, the first important American (actually, a Canadian working in the U.S.) experimenter and the first broadcaster; de Forest, who made amplification possible with his three-element vacuum tube; Alexanderson, who achieved the first reliable means of long-range wireless communication and unwittingly Americanized broadcast development; and Armstrong, who invented receiver circuits that greatly improved reception.

We can divide this time into the wireless experimental period (up to about 1900), practical maritime application (1900–1914), and radio in World War I (1914–1919). We see in these years first attempts at international and American regulation of wireless; intense nationalism in wireless development, with British interests dominating; and the first broadcasts and broadcasting stations both here and abroad. Of overriding importance was the control of key patents, determining which countries, business firms, and individuals would play leading roles. Originally, the most important concept, generally held, was that wireless was essentially a means of rapid, long-distance, point-to-point (or narrowcast) communications, for international and maritime message transmission. Only a handful of experimenters grasped its potential for *broad*casting to the public.

Selected Further Reading

(Alphabetical within topics. For full citations, see Appendix D.)

For early wired electrical communications and general bibliographies, see the books noted in chapter one. Standard early histories of wireless development are Fahie (1901), Fleming (1906), and Lodge (1900). More recent valuable studies include Aitken (1976, 1985), Coe (1996), Dalton (1975), Douglas (1987), Leinwoll (1979), Schubert (1928), Sivowitch (1970–1971), and Wedlake (1973). For the history of radio detection and vacuum tubes, see Phillips (1980), Stokes (1982), and Tyne (1977).

For more on the work of (and patent fights among) specific inventors, see Appleyard (1930), Blake (1928), Dunlap (1944), Hawks (1927), Howeth (1963), Lewis (1991), Maclaurin (1949), McNicol (1946), and Sturmey (1958). The many early U.S. wireless firms are sorted out in Mayes (1989). The role of amateur operators is described in Berg (1999), DeSoto (1936) and *Fifty Years of A.R.R.L.* (1965). Biographies of Marconi include those of Dunlap (1937), Jolly (1972), and his daughter, Marconi (1962). Baker (1972) reviews Marconi company history, Hancock (1950) relates Marconi's maritime role, and Jensen (1994) focuses on equipment development. DeForest's story is told in de Forest (1950) and Hijiya (1992). Other biographies include Cheney & Uth on Tesla (1999), Fessenden (1940), Lessing (1956) on Armstrong, and Bilby (1986) on Sarnoff. Sobel (1986) offers an informal history of RCA. Worldwide technical, application, and legal developments are reviewed in the annual *Year-Book of Wireless Telegraphy and Telephony* (1913–1925).

CHAPTER 3

Eunice Randall, announcer at 1XE/WGI, in 1921. *Donna Halper.*

THE BEGINNINGS OF BROADCASTING (1920–1926)

First factory-built consumer radio for home listening in the early 1920s. *Station KDKA, Westinghouse.*

Chapter Outline

World War I was over. America began to emerge from its isolation from the world, although the failure of the U.S. Senate to ratify the League of Nations Covenant showed we had a long way to go. Politically, the country drifted until the "normalcy" of the Harding administration starting in 1921. While many rural areas endured economic hardship, businesses in the cities faced the pent-up demand for all the goods and services unavailable since early 1917. Migration from countryside to city accelerated, while restrictive legislation slowed immigration from abroad. The new mobility of the automobile, adding congestion to the cities and creating the suburbs, expanded the immediate horizons of Americans. At the same time, the motion picture shattered barriers of time and distance and showed ordinary audiences a new, faster life outside their immediate surroundings. The changes in American attitudes that accompanied both these developments were ready targets for men and women who preferred a rigid, traditional, moral climate—such as the reformers who were flushed with Prohibition, their victory over Demon Rum.

The period became known as the Roaring Twenties. Radio would play a big part in communication of that frenzied lifestyle. The country's literary life was prolific, with young writers here and abroad turning out essays, novels, poetry, and plays that depicted the age. The first tabloid newspaper, the *New York Daily News*, appeared in 1919, followed by such untraditional magazines as *Reader's Digest* (1922), *Time* (1923), and *The New Yorker* (1925). Magazines generally used more photographs than print media previously had and covered a greater variety of events and developments—not just the effects of the car and motion pictures, not just political scandals, but sports events, sensational crimes and trials, the rise in aviation, trends in science, and the latest fads. Behind this surge of activity in the media was the expanding role of business and the prosperity that business brought to many Americans who suddenly had more leisure and money than ever before.

It was within this environment of national change that radio broadcasting began. Starting slowly, it quickly gathered pace to become one of the biggest and longest lasting fads. But before broadcasting could become an industry, several important economic, technological, and social developments had to occur both here and abroad. While foreign countries faced the same problems, the American solution was unique.

3.1 Important Precedents

Though often forgotten today, several developments in the 1918 to 1922 period helped to set American broadcasting's pattern, although they received little public attention at the time.

3.1.1 What Almost Happened: Government Control

The sometimes destructive competition between rival telegraph and telephone companies, the monopolistic trend in each field of communications due largely to the benefits of economies of scale, the Navy experiences during the war (see pp. 47–50), and the example of many European countries—all led to a strong push for a government-owned-and-operated wireless system. In Europe, almost all telegraph and telephone systems were part of the postal service. In the United States, at the end of World War I, the belief recurred that Congress had made a wrong turn in the 1840s when, after providing capital for Morse, it allowed the telegraph to revert to private hands (see pp. 9–11).

Before the United States entered the war, an effort to establish government control reached Congress. An interdepartmental radio committee proposed, on November 21, 1916, revision of the Radio Act of 1912 to allow, among other changes, government stations to compete with commercial interests for purchase of private stations. The Marconi interests fought virtually every section of this proposed legislation, but it was finally introduced into the House as the Alexander bill, named for the representative who introduced it. Secretary of the Navy Josephus Daniels strongly urged its adoption as did, to the surprise of other amateur organizations, Hiram Percy Maxim, head of the American Radio Relay League and a noted inventor. Spirited debate arose over the provisions for limiting foreign ownership of any operating commercial company, with the Marconi interests objecting particularly. Their concern raised suspicions that Marconi *was* bent on establishing postwar dominance in the field.

The U.S. entrance into the war, and the Navy's assumption of operational control of all stations on April 7, 1917, lifted the pressure on Congress. However, one month after the Armistice, Secretary Daniels, still strongly favoring government ownership, helped to revive hearings on the Alexander bill before the House Merchant Marine Committee. But the Navy had run into criticism for using wartime emergency powers to purchase the stations of the Federal Telegraph Company, some of the coastal Marconi stations, and installations in all seagoing vessels of American registry through the Shipping Board. This criticism and the Republican congressional sweep in the 1918 elections sounded the death knell of the Alexander bill. Until he left office in 1920, Secretary Daniels continued to press for commercial use of Navy-controlled stations or, failing that, at least making overseas radio communication from the United States a private monopoly in American hands, but the bill was tabled on January 16, 1919.

Furthermore, after the war, the Navy not only suffered from a lack of funds and of trained operators (after volunteers left), but faced a strong and growing clamor for return of government-operated stations to their owners. This outcry, joined by amateurs, as well as AT&T and Marconi, led President Wilson, on July 11, 1919, to order all seized stations returned to their owners as of March 1, 1920. The amateurs were allowed back on the air on October 1, 1919.

3.1.2 The Birth of RCA

The trigger that led to establishment of the Radio Corporation of America was the renewal of negotiations between British Marconi and GE over the Alexanderson alternator in March 1919, a bare 4 months after the end of World War I (p. 34). It was the second round in a series of discussions that had begun in 1915. Marconi now offered to buy 24 large alternators, 14 of which American Marconi would use, for $127,000 each—a vast sum for a time when a day's labor was worth only a dollar or two. This represented more than $3 million worth of business to GE, which, like other firms, was then painfully adjusting to the end of wartime government spending. At that time GE had no interest in the communications business itself. The following month Marconi offered to pay an additional million dollars to compensate GE for development costs *if* GE, which would retain manufacturing rights, granted Marconi the exclusive right to buy the Alexanderson alternator. Because this machine was the best and most reliable transatlantic radio communication device known at that time, acceptance of the offer would give Marconi a monopoly on American radio communications with Europe.

Most Americans, whether or not they favored government control, deplored the idea of allowing a foreign company to control American communications facilities (see p. 56). When Owen D. Young, then head of GE's legal department, approached Acting Secretary of the Navy Franklin D. Roosevelt for the Navy's view of the proposed Marconi contract, he found strong opposition.

Documentation of what happened next is sparse. Two American naval officers, Admiral William H. G. Bullard and Commander Stanley C. Hooper, known as the "father of naval radio," played a part in organizing governmental support for a "chosen instrument" in international radio; but their role apparently was insufficient to justify RCA's later claim that the firm was organized in response to a government request. The architect of the scheme that finally resolved the Marconi contract and many other postwar problems (see p. 49) was Owen D. Young, later to become chairman of the board of GE. A genius at negotiation, Young persuaded GE's directors to buy a controlling interest in American Marconi. British Marconi sold its holdings without much fuss, since it was clear that Congress would *not* accept foreign control of communications and since the Navy still held the American Marconi stations. GE then bought out the holdings of American stockholders of American Marconi. This first block in the Young edifice gave GE control of most United States-based ship-to-shore and international radio stations as well as rights under existing Marconi contracts with ship operators. Marconi, in return, could use the Alexanderson alternator for its own stations in the British Empire.

Since GE preferred the manufacturing business, it established the Radio Corporation of America in October 1919 to operate these stations. RCA's corporate charter required that at least 80% of its stock be in American hands, that all officers be American citizens, and that the government have a representative on the board of directors to "present and discuss informally" the government's views. Admiral Bullard, whom President Wilson appointed to the post, had little influence on corporate decisions, however. The unilateral placing of this provision in RCA's by-laws did not carry the same weight as it would have with a public corporation or quasi-official arm of the government organized or chartered by Congress. Young was named chairman of the board, and two former American Marconi officers, Edward J. Nally and David Sarnoff, became respectively president and commercial manager of the new firm. On the day of RCA's formation, GE and RCA signed a cross-licensing agreement calling for mutual use of each other's radio patents. A month later, GE transferred to RCA the tangible assets of what had been American Marconi, and the Navy promptly turned over the former American Marconi stations.

RCA's primary role was to be an instrument of American policy in the international communications field. Some of its other roles were not assumed for several years, and the most important of these was the resolution of a decade-old conflict over patent rights for technology that included the triode vacuum tube.

3.1.3 Patents Pooling: Westinghouse versus RCA

At the end of the war, it looked as though the design and manufacture of radio apparatus would be set back several years as the Navy program of indemnifying manufacturers against patent infringement suits came to an end and the advanced designs that had come from this period could no longer be used. Radio required the use of many patents, which were held by many individuals and companies. Amateur operators, however, could pirate these designs and techniques—with the exception of vacuum tubes and high-powered transmitters—and build their own equipment fairly easily. They could get the few items that were hard to produce at home from small manufacturers, many of whom were rather lax about paying royalties. The greatest hindrance to the manufacture of advanced radio receivers was the unavailability of the triode, de Forest's Audion. De Forest still controlled some rights to the third element, and he had sold some to Western Electric (AT&T) years before, but British Marconi still controlled the basic two-element tube, the diode or Fleming valve (see p. 37).

The pieces of this jigsaw puzzle fell into place when GE, RCA, and AT&T signed a further patents pooling agreement on July 1, 1920. Since AT&T, through its subsidiary Western Electric, had the right to use the third element of the triode, and since GE and RCA, through their purchase of Marconi assets, could use and license the patents for the diode, the cross-licensing agreement made the commercial sale of triodes legal for the first time.

What was Westinghouse doing all this time? GE's role was clear; it was the patron of RCA and the busy manufacturer of electrical and electronic apparatus. RCA not only operated overseas radio communications as the result of agreements with Marconi and various foreign post and telegraph administrations, but also managed a large and growing pool of important radio patents. AT&T retained the rights to use all patents necessary for the rental of radio and wire telephony service. Among other small companies, United Fruit had joined the patents pool, bringing in its crystal receiver and loop antenna patents in March 1921. But where was Westinghouse, one of the largest and most energetic electrical manufacturing firms in the world?

Although RCA–GE–AT&T had all the elements necessary to construct and operate a profitable communications system, their patent situation did not give them a monopoly. At the end of the war there was still room for a communications system that did not rely on the RCA–GE–AT&T patents pool. Westinghouse, as a major competitor of GE, decided to fill that hole. The company had done considerable radio research and manufacturing during the war, and it owned many important patents. Westinghouse wanted to get into the international communications market, which, together with maritime radio, was considered the future profit center of wireless. It acquired control of the International Radio Telegraph Company, which had Fessenden's heterodyne and continuous-wave transmitter patents (see p. 34), as well as some useful foreign contacts, in May 1920, a few months after RCA's establishment. That summer, Westinghouse President Samuel M. Kintner traveled to various countries in an attempt to line up traffic agreements. He met great difficulties because of RCA's iron-clad agreement with British Marconi, and received cooperation only from a war-cowed Germany. Not yet discouraged, Westinghouse purchased the Armstrong regenerative and superheterodyne receiver patents in October 1920 for $335,000 and arranged with the U.S. Navy for the non-exclusive use of a large block of important patents.

These patents included some German patents, which the Navy had acquired from the custody of the Alien Enemy Property Custodian, and the

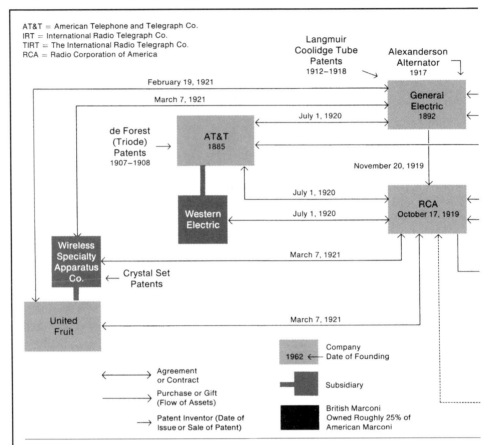

AT&T = American Telephone and Telegraph Co.
IRT = International Radio Telegraph Co.
TIRT = The International Radio Telegraph Co.
RCA = Radio Corporation of America

■ **The Origins of the Patents Pool: 1919 to 1922**   (See the text for discussion of participants' motivations.) In essence, GE bought American Marconi at the instigation of naval officers, in April 1919, in order to found RCA as a "chosen instrument" of American overseas communications. GE, RCA, and AT&T formed a patents pool, bringing in United Fruit and others not shown on the accompanying chart. Westinghouse attempted to compete head-to-head with RCA using purchased patents and others obtained nonexclusively from the Navy. The Navy had acquired some of these from the Alien Enemy Property Custodian during World War I, and some, the Poulsen arc patents, purchased along with several stations from Federal Telegraph of California. In returning the stations and the patents to Federal without payment shortly after Federal contracted to establish radio links between the United States and China, the Navy automatically restricted Westinghouse from using them. RCA agreed to "cooperate" with Federal, later establishing Federal Telegraph of Delaware as a subsidiary. Westinghouse, now without transmitter patents and prevented by RCA–British Marconi relationships from establishing competing traffic agreements with many countries, joined the patents pool in June 1921, in a relatively

very important patents for the Poulsen arc transmitter, which the Navy had bought from the Federal Telegraph Company in 1917, when it looked as though Federal was going to sell to Marconi. This sale had some questionable aspects, with at least one historian pointing out its "suspicious circumstances," the subsequent suicide of one of the chief actors and the resignations of several officials. The $1.6 million purchase of May 15, 1918,

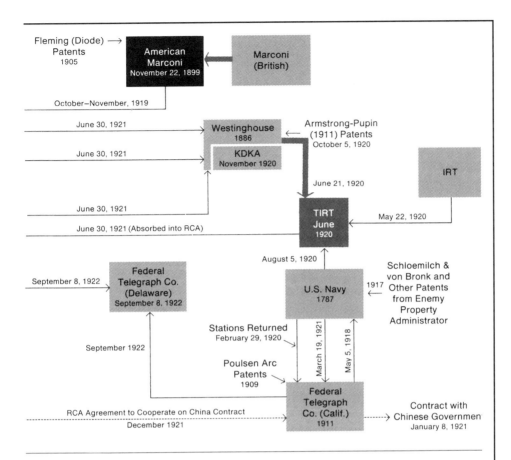

strong position thanks to its ownership of the Armstrong patents and its early commitment to domestic radio broadcasting.

The patents pool agreements established the following division of functions, among others, until the participating companies modified or abrogated the agreements in the mid-1920s:

- Each of the major participants (RCA, GE, AT&T, Westinghouse) could build equipment for its own use, including broadcasting transmitters.
- AT&T could sell broadcast transmitters to outsiders, and reserved the right to use radiotelephony for hire.
- GE and Westinghouse could manufacture radio receivers and supply them to RCA, which acted as sales agent (GE built approximately 60%, Westinghouse 40%).
- RCA would administer the patents pool, collecting royalties from outsiders.
- RCA would also operate all maritime and transoceanic radio communication for hire.

(It was not until several years later that RCA was allowed to manufacture receivers and engage in broadcasting and networking in its own name.)

gave the Navy not only the Poulsen and other patents but a chain of high-power stations on the Pacific Coast.

Therefore, by late 1920, Westinghouse was in an excellent position to challenge RCA and its associates. It had an operating company, the Armstrong and Pupin patents, the Fessenden patents, rights to use the Poulsen arc and many other devices, the glimmer of a profitable receiving-set manufacturing business in conjunction with broadcasting stations (more on this on p. 65), and the possibility of beating RCA to a lucrative communications circuit or two. Yet, within nine months, Westinghouse gave up its independent course and joined the patents pool. Why?

The story may never be clear, but it appears that Westinghouse was neatly mousetrapped by RCA. On January 8, 1921, the Federal Telegraph Company (which still existed as a corporation) entered into a contract with the Chinese government to build stations in China to communicate with a high-power California station. By some means, Federal persuaded the Navy to return the Poulsen patents on March 19, 1921—with no exchange of money—so that it could construct these stations. Apparently, the government considered $1.6 million a worthwhile price for three years' use of Federal's stations and patents, without concomitant infringement suits, and for the retained right to use the patents in question and any later ones developed by Federal. But once it had returned the patents to Federal, the Navy could no longer grant Westinghouse a license to use them. Perhaps by coincidence, only a few months later, in December 1921, David Sarnoff wrote the government that RCA was "ready to cooperate with and assist" Federal in its project. This move led to the establishment, in September 1922, of the Federal Telegraph Company of Delaware, which was organized so that RCA could take over the contract with China and, as a matter of fact, control the Federal Telegraph Company of California—and the Poulsen patents.

A major corporation such as Westinghouse does not survive by making mistakes or moving slowly. Then again, the entire gambit by Westinghouse may have been nothing more than a stratagem devised by its patent chief Otto Schairer, later to hold the same post at RCA, to ensure that Westinghouse would enter the patents pool on as favorable terms as the original members. Within six months after Federal's repossession of the Poulsen patents and long before RCA overtly took charge of Federal's activities, Westinghouse quietly joined RCA, AT&T, and GE in a patents pooling agreement. The International Radio Telegraph Company's business was absorbed into RCA on June 30, 1921, the same day that RCA concluded its cross-licensing agreement with Westinghouse.

Who won? The infant radio manufacturing industry did. The American people, tired of waiting for the squabbling over patent rights to subside, probably won as well. RCA finally fitted together the last sections of "Owen D. Young's famed jigsaw puzzle." GE could now manufacture, and RCA sell, radio receiving sets for the general public, using Westinghouse's Armstrong patents and demonstration of a market for them. AT&T could manufacture transmitters and use radio telephony in its domestic business. The Navy could breathe more easily and deal with one company instead of several. Westinghouse, in 1922 the second largest participant after GE, controlled 20.6% of RCA's common and preferred stock compared to 25.8% for GE, 4.1% for AT&T, 3.7% for United Fruit, and 45.8% for other owners including the general public and former American Marconi shareholders.

According to agreements with both GE and Westinghouse, RCA would be the sole selling agent for the manufacturing firms' radio receivers; with approximately 60% from GE and 40% from Westinghouse. Nearly 2,000 patents were pooled. Everyone was to have a piece of the action in the field of radio as it was then understood—the fields of international, maritime, and amateur radio. The signers did not realize that the development of radio *broadcasting* to the general public would make the patent agreements uncomfortably binding within only a few months.

3.2 The Pioneer Stations

In 2.5 we tentatively honored Fessenden for delivering the *first broadcast* in America and Herrold for maintaining the *first broadcasting station* with a regular schedule of programs. However, a controversy remains as to which is the *oldest* broadcasting station in the United States; depending on the definitions and the data accepted, there are several legitimate candidates. Our criteria for making this determination are that a broadcasting station must (a) utilize radio waves, (b) to send noncoded sounds by speech or music, (c) in a continuing or regularly scheduled program service, (d) intended to be received by the public, and (e) if after 1912, be licensed by the government. The *first* station is the one that had all these characteristics at the earliest date, although the *first broadcast* needn't meet the third criterion. The *oldest* radio station is the *one presently operating* that met all five criteria at the earliest date.

3.2.1 The Oldest Stations

Fessenden's 1906 transmissions fit our definition of the first true broadcasts but did not meet the third criterion. It was Herrold's continuous service of music and voice to the general public—at least to the extent of supplying receivers for boarding house or hotel lobbies—that earned the distinction of "first station." Determining the oldest station is more difficult.

A lack of data and a question of definition place Herrold's station KQW in San Jose, now KCBS in San Francisco, in an ambiguous position. Although "Doc" Herrold started in 1909 and was broadcasting one night a week regularly by 1912, his station had a substantial gap in service during *and after* World War I. Our criteria should tolerate a short-term suspension of service, technical failures, "acts of God," and other matters outside the station operator's control; and the wartime closing of amateur stations in 1917 could be considered in this light. However, despite the present operators' claim that the station returned to the air "very shortly" after the war (amateurs were on the air as early as October 1, 1919, and stations seized by the Navy were returned on March 1, 1920), their documentation is not adequate. Licenses for experimental stations 6XE and 6XF were issued to

Herrold in mid-1920, but there is no evidence, even though Gordon Greb and Mike Adams have done a staggering amount of research since the late 1950s, that Herrold *broadcast* anything over these stations, and, indeed, although KQW received a regular broadcast license on December 9, 1921, there is no record of the station having gone on the air until January 1922.

Professors Earle M. Terry and Edward Bennett, and others, were issued licenses for 9XM to operate at the University of Wisconsin at Madison before World War I. After 1915, this station (now WHA) was licensed to the university. Providing radio-*telegraphed* weather reports and communicating with the Navy's Great Lakes Training Station, 9XM was one of the few to stay on the air during much of the war. Although it may have transmitted by radiotelephone as early as February 1919 to Great Lakes, broadcast service apparently started between September 29, 1920, and January 19, 1921— almost certainly toward the end of this period—since Professor Terry wrote the Federal Radio Commission in 1928 that KDKA (see the following) antedated 9XM "by a few months."

There are numerous other claims to the title of "oldest station in the United States," each with its supporters. Some are little known: KQV, Pittsburgh, overshadowed by KDKA, has never pushed for recognition. WRUC, Union College, according to a 1970 article, signed on October 14, 1920; however, it no longer uses radiation to serve its campus-limited audience.

If it weren't for the fact that this book focuses on the United States, it could be argued that the oldest North American broadcasting station is the Canadian CFCF, which originated as Canadian Marconi station XWA. On May 20, 1920, well before KDKA went on the air, this Montreal station began broadcasting operations with a bang, which jumpstarted the purchase of receiving sets in Canada. The Royal Society of Canada, the Prime Minister, and other notables assembled in a well publicized meeting to listen to an address on wartime inventions and hear the songs of Dorothy Lutton. (Other stations, in other countries, make similar claims. For example, PCGG in the Netherlands claims to have started in November 1919.)

Some other U.S. claimants rely on variations in the definition of broadcasting: WEAF, New York, did not go on the air until 1922 but reputedly was the first broadcasting station to be established solely for the purpose of *commercial* broadcasting, or selling time (see p. 79). IXE (later WGI), Medford, Massachusetts, actually sold time earlier—apparently it charged a dollar a minute by April 1922, 4 months before WEAF—but also was used for experimentation for the AMRAD corporation and amateur transmissions. WBZ, Boston, which took to the air in September 1921, was erroneously listed as the first station to receive a "broadcasting" license from the Department of Commerce, evidently because its licensing coincided with the adoption of a new classification system.

While early stations backed by large corporations with big public relations departments (see KDKA and WWJ, following) tend to be better known, as are those associated with major early inventors such as Fessenden and de Forest, it is only when criteria for "first" and "oldest" are rigorously applied that we can award valid accolades. Some stations that might have been in the running for "oldest" if the question had been asked earlier—such as 1XE/WGI, whose little known history is parallel to and maybe ahead of 8XK/KDKA until it left the air in 1925—lose out because there is no supporting documentation or, as in the WGI example, they no longer exist and thus, while they might still be "first" (if they had started before Herrold's station) they logically cannot be "oldest" today. But some recent claimants have merely been asserting their claim as "oldest" in a brochure or on a web page without logic or data to back it up. Others, such as 1XE/WGI, whose previously unknown story was assiduously researched by Donna Halper in the 1990s, do not meet the necessary historical criteria.

KDKA, Pittsburgh, and WWJ, Detroit, both backed by large corporations, have jousted for years over the primacy title, and are the best known candidates. Since both stations apparently went on the air in 1920, they antedate most other claimants as continuing broadcasting services.

KDKA started as a 1916 amateur experimental station licensed to Dr. Frank Conrad, a Westinghouse engineer. When the war ended, Conrad was able to reopen his 8XK quickly—probably between June 15 and August 1, 1919—since during the war he had operated a station from his home in connection with designing equipment for the Navy. On October 17, 1919, Conrad delighted and amazed hams for miles around when he placed his microphone before a phonograph—an act that not only spared his voice but apparently initiated postwar broadcasting. Amateurs and veterans trained to build and operate radio receivers made so many requests for musical selections that Conrad decided to broadcast a program of records for two hours each Wednesday and Sunday evening instead of trying to comply with single requests. He sometimes added talks, sports scores, and live vocal and instrumental renditions by his young sons.

Late in the summer of 1920, growing interest in these broadcasts led the Joseph Horne Company, a Pittsburgh department store, to advertise amateur wireless sets for $10 and up on which to listen to Conrad's station. This ad struck the eye of H. P. Davis, Westinghouse vice president, who was eager to establish a postwar market for the company's radio manufacturing capability. At an executive meeting on September 30, 1920, Davis suggested that Westinghouse build a station and promote nightly broadcasts so that people would acquire the habit of listening. He observed that if there were sufficient interest to justify a department store in speculatively advertising radio sets for sale, there would probably be sufficient public interest to justify the expense of rendering a regular broadcasting service, looking both to the further sale of receivers and promotion of the Westinghouse Company name as return for the costs of broadcasting. An application was filed with the Department of Commerce on October 16, and a license for KDKA was issued 11 days later.

The first broadcast, on election night, November 2, 1920, came from a 100-watt transmitter in a tiny makeshift shack atop a Westinghouse manufacturing building at East Pittsburgh. Conrad was not there; he was at home, standing by with 8XK in case KDKA's new transmitter (licensed as 8ZZ for the first two days) failed to work properly. The election returns, courtesy of a telephone connection with the *Pittsburgh Post*, were broadcast to an estimated few thousand listeners, including some at a Pittsburgh country club, over Westinghouse-supplied loudspeakers. The broadcast started at 6 P.M. and continued until the following noon, even though Governor James M. Cox had earlier conceded the presidential election to Senator Warren G. Harding. The next evening KDKA broadcast only from 8:30 until 9:30. The transmitter soon was relocated and increased in power, but the studio remained on the roof for months in somewhat more spacious, airy, and sound-controlled quarters: a tent. When the tent blew down in a gale, it was re-erected inside, providing the necessary acoustic control.

In Detroit, amateur station 8MK went on the air on August 20, 1920, with voice and phonograph music, from a makeshift "radio phone room" on the second floor of the *Detroit News* building. The Radio News and Music Company, formed by associates of de Forest to sell his radio equipment, held the license. Although the *News*, a Scripps paper, apparently financed the broadcasts, it gave them no mention for days. On October 15, 1921, a broadcasting license with the call letters WBL, changed to WWJ on March 3, 1922, was issued to the *Detroit News.*

While it isn't easy to compare and adjudicate such conflicting claims, it can be done. As to *broadcasting* licenses, KDKA led WBL (WWJ) by nearly a year. Conrad's *amateur* station, 8XK, successor to the prewar station, went on the air more than a year before 8MK and was broadcasting music 10 months earlier. As to license-holding, in either case Westinghouse or one of its officers held a license before the *Detroit News* did. Only by maintaining that 8XK is *not* the precursor of KDKA, *and* that 8MK *is* the precursor of WWJ, can one uphold WWJ's claim—and both Conrad's status as a Westinghouse employee and the *Detroit News*'s delay in applying for a broadcasting license belie that position.

Radio broadcasting appeared to grow slowly for the first year or so after KDKA went on the air. By January 1, 1922, the Commerce Department had authorized only 30 broadcasting stations; and only 100,000 receivers were sold during 1922. However, the statistics are misleading. Hobbyists made many additional thousands of receivers, since a crystal set was inexpensive and could be put together easily, while thousands of war-trained radio experts produced advanced equipment. Some stations with amateur licenses broadcast regular programs of speech and music. By May 1, 1922, the *Radio Service Bulletin* of the Bureau of Navigation, Department of Commerce, listed 218 stations "broadcasting market or weather reports, and music, concerts, lectures, etc.," many of them on the air only a few hours a week.

■ **Early Radio Announcer**   One of the first full-time radio announcers was Harold W. Arlin of station KDKA, shown here as he broadcast in the early 1920s—complete with tuxedo, then almost mandatory for evening announcing duties. He did the first play-by-play sports and introduced many noted personalities in their radio debuts.

Photo courtesy of Group W and Broadcast Pioneers Library.

By March 1, 1923, there were 556, and in that year 550,000 radio receivers were produced commercially, with an average retail value of $55 each. The boom was on.

Westinghouse was the first company to move decisively into radio broadcasting, characterized until then by the haphazard operations and unreliable equipment of hobbyists and amateurs. In September 1921, when

KDKA was on its feet, Westinghouse opened WBZ, Springfield, Massachusetts, and WJZ, Newark, New Jersey, although they were licensed on different dates. In keeping with KDKA's makeshift quarters, WJZ started out in a curtained-off section of the ladies' lounge at the Westinghouse plant in Newark. This first station in the New York area later became the key station of the Blue Network. WBZ moved to Boston in later years and for some time operated station WBZA in Springfield *synchronized* on the same frequency. Westinghouse also established KYW in Chicago, which after several shifts now is located in Philadelphia, and stations in Hastings, Nebraska (a remote-controlled *repeater* station duplicating the KDKA signals), and Cleveland. Many Westinghouse officials enjoyed being associated with broadcasting, but the company backed these ventures chiefly to spark public interest in receiver sales. But by 1972, little less than 60 years after H. P. Davis had noticed that advertisement for radio receivers in a Pittsburgh newspaper, Westinghouse no longer made radio receivers domestically. On the other hand, in 1995 it spun off its broadcast operations, then known as "Group W," which bought the Columbia Broadcasting System, and today operates under the CBS name.

RCA delayed entering domestic radio broadcasting until it had set up the international communication links for which it had been established. The company's first broadcasting facility, WDY, went on the air on December 14, 1921, from the General Electric factory in Roselle Park, New Jersey. Its transmitter was one that RCA had installed, under the call letters WJY, for one night for a blow-by-blow account of the Dempsey–Carpentier heavyweight boxing championship match on July 2, 1921 (see p. 87). The estimated 200,000 listeners were lucky, for the transmitter burned out only a minute or so after the end of the fight. Even with 500 watts of power, a high output for the day, WDY was too far (approximately 16 miles) from New York City to attract live talent of any stature. Also, music from records played at home on an acoustic, spring-powered phonograph would have been probably cheaper and certainly more enjoyable than WDY's static-ridden transmission through earphones. WDY lasted only until February 24, 1922, when RCA agreed to share half the operating expense of Westinghouse's better-located and better-engineered WJZ.

General Electric entered the broadcasting business a bit behind its patents pool partners. Like Westinghouse, its original purpose was to encourage the sale of radio receivers. Its first station, WGY, operated from the GE plant at Schenectady, New York, with 1,500 watts of power when it went on the air on February 22, 1922. With favorable atmospheric conditions, the well-engineered station could reach the Pacific Coast and England. Such ranges were not uncommon, even with relatively low power, when there were few stations on the air to cause degradation of the signal; even WDY could be heard as far west as Omaha. GE also founded KOA in Denver and KGO in Oakland. For the next two-thirds of a century, GE was a major force in manufacturing, but was a limited factor in broadcasting until, in 1986 (see p. 512) GE bought RCA/NBC, which it had been so instrumental in establishing.

3.2.2 Boom (1922–1925)

By 1922 the country was afire with radio fever. More than 600 stations went on the air that year, but many went off again in a few months, weeks, or even days. Of the survivors we can identify many by their three-letter call signs (KYW, WHN), although some of the earliest had four letters (KDKA). Stations going on the air before 1908 could identify themselves in any way they choose, but when the U.S. started to enforce the Wireless Ship Act of 1910, the initial letters of call signs assigned by international agreement, the Berlin Convention of 1908, were used. W, K, N (which was used by the U.S. Navy), and later much of A were made available to the United States. In 1911, after the Radio Division of the Department of Commerce was established, W calls were assigned to ships plying the Atlantic and K calls to ships in the Pacific. After the Panama Canal opened in 1914, of course, this distinction became meaningless. However, by custom, and in 1923 by rule, when broadcasting started, W calls typically belonged to broadcasting stations east of the Mississippi and K west, although there are a handful of exceptions (see Appendix B). Radio and electrical manufacturers and dealers, ranging from giants like GE and Westinghouse to one-man repair shops in small towns, owned by far the largest number of stations.

Most station licensees spent little money on broadcasting and could expect little direct return. The manufacturing companies, and many dealers, provided the program service to encourage people to buy sets. Department stores owned a station as a publicity investment; although it wasn't advertising, the simple announcement of ownership or location was deemed worth the cost. Virtually all the stations that went on in 1921 and 1922 were operated as a side line. Licensees were seeking publicity, fun, or prestige in the community. Educational institutions used radio as an extension service or a physics department laboratory. Churches and other crusading organizations were early operators of radio to further their own ends. Newspapers built stations to keep up with new entertainment and news technology, for publicity, and as a symbol of their perceived public service role.

The names of the founders—and the engineers, programmers, and managers—of these early stations are largely forgotten. Even the names of such outstanding figures as John Shepard III, whose support of broadcasting in New England starting in 1922—including the first networking in 1923, organization of the Yankee Network, and a commitment to FM broadcasting in the late 1930s—led to national recognition as the first Vice President of the National Association of Broadcasters, are unknown to most broadcasters and researchers in the 1990s. Few stations today have any connection to

■ **Who Were the Early Broadcasters?**   As noted in this section, a radio station was seldom the primary interest of early broadcasters. It was nearly always an arm of some other business or activity, often promotional but mostly noncommercial. The best tabulation was done by the Department of Commerce as of February 1, 1923.

Type of Owner	Number of Stations	Percentage of Total
Radio and electrical manufacturers and dealers	222	39%
Educational institutions	72	13
Newspapers and other publications	69	12
Department stores	29	5
Automobile, battery, and cycle dealers	18	3
Music, musical instrument, and jewlery stores	13	2
Churches and YMCAs	12	2
Police and fire departments, and cities	7	1
Hardware stores	6	1
Railroad, power, and telephone companies	9	1
Other commercial businesses	19	3
Other and unknown	100	17
	576	100%

Source: U.S. Department of Commerce, *Radio Service Bulletin* (February 1, 1923), as reprinted in Banning (1946), pages 132–133, and adapted herein.

the past, although as late as the 1950s one might still find an engineer or bookkeeper who remembered when the station started in the 1920s. This collective forgetfulness should in no way diminish the importance of the work the pioneers accomplished. Every year, some researcher finds the roots of program formats of today, or important precedents in regulation and business strategy.

Some of these pioneers were women, perhaps a reflection of the low salaries paid to members of broadcast station staffs. Job descriptions were vague—one might book talent one day, engineer them the next, and sub-stute for them on the third. One such person was Eunice Randall, whose father disowned her because of her radio interests. A very early amateur operator, she joined the American Radio and Research Company (AMRAD) as a draftsman (her term), and by late 1919 she became "announcer ER," and assistant chief operator and the "story lady" for children shortly after, on AMRAD's 1XE/WGI. When AMRAD decided to reduce its investment in the station, Randall returned to the parent company as an engineer/draftsman.

Another female pioneer, Bertha Brainerd, started in radio in 1922 and became program director of WJZ, Newark/New York, before becoming commercial program director for NBC. Another woman who made her mark at both the local and national levels was Judith Waller, general manager of WMAQ (Chicago) from 1922 until 1931, when she became director of public affairs and education at NBC, a job that lasted until 1957. In those later days, popular children's television programs such as *Kukla, Fran & Ollie* were produced under her aegis. Waller also is remembered for an outstanding book (*Radio: the Fifth Estate*) and for having discovered the immensely popular *Amos 'n' Andy.*

While most stations were owned and operated by men, several women were pioneer station licensees. For example, Marie Zimmerman received the license for WIAE, Vinton, Iowa, on July 21, 1922, when she was 25 years old, and Aimee Semple MacPherson, the evangelist, controlled KSFG in Los Angeles.

Similarly, members of minority groups played a role in early broadcasting, usually as talent, but their names also are largely forgotten. One black disc jockey, Jack L. Cooper, may have been on WCAP (Washington, D.C.) as early as 1925, and had his own program by 1929. Black gospel singers and jazz musicians were popular as early as 1922. A Philadelphia station broadcast the NAACP's annual convention in 1924. After 1928, when broadcasting became profitable, it wasn't nearly as hospitable to women and blacks until the manpower shortage caused by World War II.

Early stations were primitive. Many operated from hotels, trading publicity for free room; but, because the hotel often was the tallest building in town, then it was thought to be an excellent location for antenna towers. Most studios had little equipment. A piano was a must, as was a microphone. Burlap served as sound control for years. Volume control and mixing were not yet available and phonograph records were played on a conventional acoustic phonograph with a microphone stationed before the open doors. At first, almost all transmitters were handmade, with indifferent results. Lack of volume controls and limiting devices made it possible for an opera singer to blow out a tube and throw the station off the air. Carbon telephone-type microphones tended to "freeze up" when very loud sibilant sounds were spoken into them.

Many transmitters of the early 1920s usually radiated less wattage than a studio light. Within a few years, most stations were rated from 100 to 500 watts, although about 15 were as high as 1,000 watts and five or six were "high power," running 5,000 watts. Such amounts of transmitter power were satisfactory when only a few hundred stations were on the air. A 100-watt station of the middle 1920s would send a reliable signal out 20 to 50 miles, a feat that today—with almost 5,000 transmitters on the standard (AM) broadcast band in the United States—would take many times as much radiated power. Because poor quality receivers had low sensitivity, broadcasters kept asking the Secretary of Commerce, the licensing authority, for *superpower* that would enable them to deliver a clearer signal to more people. Late in 1925, WGY experimentally broadcast with 50,000 watts. Of course, if *everyone* had higher power, interference would remain.

As broadcasting stations went on the air in large numbers, they also went off. For example, in just five months of mid-1923, 150 stations left the

■ **Early Radio Studios**   Early radio studios reflected their times: chintz-covered furniture, plants, the almost required piano, and draped walls to improve acoustics. The announcer and piano player appear in KDKA's inside studio at Christmas of 1922; the second draped studio is Westinghouse's WBZ in Springfield, Massachusetts, in 1922 (note the record player, used for music to fill between live presentations); and the third picture shows a large-station prestige studio from sometime in the 1926 to 1928 period. In all cases the studios are fairly large and have many chairs for performers to sit on while waiting to broadcast.

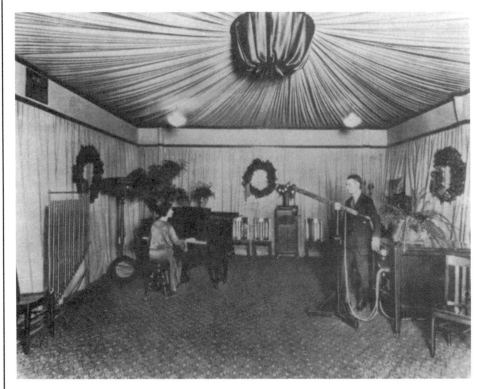

Courtesy of Group W and Broadcast Pioneers Library

Smithsonian Institution Photo No. 76-14663

Smithsonian Institution Photo No. 76-14657

air. Their failure was financial rather than technical. When a station had been on the air for some time, and its novelty had worn off, the licensee became more concerned about its cost. Although electrical current for low-power stations was not very expensive, transmission tubes and other parts were. The station needed consistent sources of programming, and record stores soon tired of lending or giving records in exchange for an occasional plug. Talent began demanding payment for their time or effort. It became clear that, if broadcasting were to become more than an adjunct to another enterprise, it had to have a direct source of income. In June 1922, RCA's David Sarnoff proposed a nonprofit broadcasting company supported by a 2% tax on receiver sales, but his idea went nowhere.

Nevertheless, people were starting to listen to radio for its content and not for its novelty. Although homemade receivers, typically crystal sets requiring minimal construction skill and no power, were still common, more and more persons purchased ready-made receivers. For example, in the summer of 1923, Gimbel Brothers department store in New York purchased from RCA 20,000 Westinghouse receiving sets with a retail value of at least $3 million. The total value of sets sold in 1923—excluding tubes, which were sold separately—was between $30 and $45 million, a figure that increased to approximately $100 million in 1924. The average retail value of sets climbed steadily from $50 in 1922 to over $135 in 1929. More than 4.1 million sets were manufactured commercially between 1922 and 1925 for America's 27 million homes.

By 1925 the growth of radio began to create problems. In major cities there were too many stations on a limited band for good reception (see p. 93); for instance, 23 in Los Angeles and 40 in Chicago. Receivers were unselective; transmitters tended to drift. With the limited spectrum space and equipment available, the typical large city could accommodate only seven stations without resorting to *share-time* operations. In Los Angeles and Chicago, share-time might allow a single station as little as one or two hours of air time daily, divided into widely separated parts of the day. With four or five stations using the same channel, no one of them could build an audience. Because many of their listeners were DX fans, who listened for distant stations, some cities designated "silent nights," when local stations signed off early to improve distance reception.

3.2.3 Conflict: Radio Group versus Telephone Group

Although interference between stations was the conflict most apparent to listeners, it was less important than the issue of financial support. Broadcasting was not considered when the original patents pool agreements were signed. Since no money was expected at first from broadcasting operations, Westinghouse, GE, and RCA all built stations without worrying about the agreements. After assuming control of WJZ in 1923, RCA opened another

New York station, WJY, and moved them both to Aeolian Hall—WJZ with a light, popular format and WJY with a "quality" program of talks, music, and education. By this time, RCA was spending approximately $100,000 a year to maintain its three stations, now including WRC in Washington, without any direct income from them. Westinghouse was not far behind in outlay.

It remained for AT&T to find a way to make radio broadcasting pay. In the original patent agreements, AT&T had reserved the right, the sole right, it claimed, to use radio telephony for hire. In July 1922 it built station WBAY in New York, only to discover that the location of a transmitter in a city of large steel-framed buildings decisively and negatively affects reception, and that this kind of engineering is an art, not a science. AT&T's second attempt was successful. WEAF, equipped with the best studio apparatus and an excellent transmitter, received much praise after it went on the air on August 16, 1922.

AT&T was now ready to move. Under the 1919 through 1921 patent agreements, what became known as the Telephone Group (essentially, AT&T and its manufacturing subsidiary Western Electric) held that it had the *exclusive* right to (a) manufacture and sell radio transmitters for broadcasting, (b) sell time for advertising, which they called *toll broadcasting* in a parallel to toll long-distance telephone calls, and (c) interconnect stations by wire for network or chain broadcasting. Each of these points was opposed by the Radio Group—GE, RCA, and Westinghouse.

Although AT&T's legal grounds with respect to the first point were excellent, the company actually lost in the court of public opinion. When station WHN (New York) settled out of court in the winter of 1924, agreeing to pay AT&T $4 per watt of power over the life of the patents, whether or not Western Electric had made the transmitter, it was merely acknowledging a hopeless legal position. But to the public, already disturbed at the growth and power of trusts and cartels, AT&T seemed to be jumping with hobnailed boots all over the little fellow.

The second point burst like a skyrocket over the radio scene when WEAF, shortly after going on the air, offered to sell time by the minute to whomever wished to use it (see p. 79).

The third point became increasingly important between 1923 and 1926 as the Telephone Group interconnected its affiliated stations with Bell System wires, engineered to carry music as well as voice, while the Radio Group had to make do with inferior Western Union telegraph circuits. Of course, AT&T received no revenue from the Radio Group when they used other circuits, but the poor voice quality over Western Union wires caused the Radio Group to lose much public favor. Throughout most of the history of American broadcasting, until space communications satellites became available for this purpose, AT&T's role in interconnecting stations has been an important one. When broadcasters objected to high AT&T video connection rates in the late 1940s and boycotted Bell System facilities, they found themselves turning again to Western Union lines for local loops if not for intercity circuits. One program was involved both times: the six-day bicycle races from Madison Square Garden in New York (see pp. 286–287).

Stations that took out transmitter licenses from AT&T were generally able to sell advertising time and afford interconnections by telephone lines. Few stations, however, were willing to pay a high price for what might be an unprofitable business. After WHN signed, many stations capitulated, but others went off the air or hoped that they were small enough for AT&T to overlook.

The Radio Group maintained (a) that only the firms in the patents pool (see pp. 51–58) had the right to make and sell radio receivers to the public, (b) that any station could at least recoup program costs from sponsors, and (c) that stations could be interconnected by any means available. RCA sued the A. H. Grebe radio company in support of the first point and won an important legal precedent: Manufacturers had to take out licenses from RCA in order to make many receiver parts. The royalties ran high—in 1927, for example, at 7 1/2% of the net selling price, including cabinets. RCA granted licenses solely to larger customers and even limited these purchases to relatively inefficient circuits—for which, of course, they had to buy RCA tubes. The royalty situation, as well as poor management, inadequate sales promotion, and rapid development of newer and better designs, drove many manufacturers out of business. Of the 748 radio manufacturing companies established between 1923 and 1926, only 72 lasted until 1927, and only 18 of these survived into 1934. As for the second and third points, there was a certain degree of fuzziness: Although some stations were able to sell advertising time for cash, most simply traded air time for products or services. As noted above, the Radio Group tried to meet the question of interconnection head-on.

Throughout the period from 1922 to 1924, unsuccessful attempts were made to reconcile the differences between the two groups. As the fight grew hotter, AT&T sold its RCA stock, although it remained a member of the patents pool. In 1923, Congress, concerned over RCA actions against Grebe and others, ordered the Federal Trade Commission to investigate RCA for violation of the antitrust laws. Clearly, RCA no longer had the image that it had in 1919. The FTC report of 1924, which examined manufacturing, international communications, and the role of radio, resulted in complaints against seven companies besides RCA. This proceeding dragged on for six more years (see p. 108).

In 1925 the Radio Group and the Telephone Group agreed to binding arbitration. After months of hearings, the arbitrator decided nearly all issues in favor of the Radio Group. As a result, the telephone company's lawyers announced that since the 1920 and 1921 agreements must have been illegal to have given RCA such a monopoly, AT&T would have to withdraw from them. With the prospect of putting the patent hassle back six years, both sides tried again to agree on what the words written in 1920 meant in the radically changed world of 1925.

Early in 1926 the stalemate was broken with an involved, three-part agreement that clearly settled the functions of the telephone and radio interests. First, the license or patents pool agreement was redefined in light of the realities of the broadcasting industry of 1926. Second, AT&T received a monopoly of providing wire interconnections between stations. Third, AT&T sold WEAF to RCA for $1 million and agreed not to re-enter broadcasting as a station owner for eight years, under penalty of having to refund part of the price.

Not only had AT&T wearied of the battle, but such a competitive business did not fit its longstanding corporate philosophy. This philosophy favored monopoly, such as it had in long-distance telephony, over head-to-head competition—which it really didn't have to face until the 1970s. AT&T also favored the cautious introduction of technological innovations (see pp. 12–13). In addition, many Bell executives were disturbed to see time, effort, and money going into entertainment and other broadcasting instead of into the firm's traditional point-to-point communications business.

3.3 The Start of Networking

The idea of connecting two or more stations for simultaneous broadcast of a program probably existed from the start of broadcasting. In this way a given message could reach a far larger audience, at reasonable cost, than from a single station. The earliest known efforts at relaying a program were *remote* reports from sports events sent over telephone lines. True chain or network broadcasting started on January 4, 1923, when telephone circuits connected WNAC in Boston and WEAF in New York for a five-minute saxophone solo originating at WEAF. Although generally satisfied with the experiment, AT&T engineers knew that substantial improvements in their lines would be necessary for the regular transmission of music.

In June 1923, WEAF (New York), WGY (Schenectady), KDKA (Pittsburgh), and KYW (then in Chicago) were connected for a special program on the anniversary of the electric light. A month later, the first "permanent"—more than one program—chain was established when WEAF piped programs to WMAF, a South Dartmouth, Massachusetts, station owned and supported as a public service by eccentric millionaire E. H. R. Green, who picked up the bill for three or four hours a day of New York programming.

The WEAF group made ambitious plans for nationwide broadcasting of President Warren G. Harding's speeches during the summer of 1923, but his illness and death abbreviated the effort. President Coolidge's first message to Congress, on December 4, was heard over a number of stations as far away as Missouri and Texas. Radio covered both political conventions of 1924, and AT&T was building a permanent hookup connecting Washington, New York, Providence, Buffalo, Pittsburgh, and Chicago. On October 24, 1924, President Coolidge spoke to the U.S. Chamber of

Commerce in Washington, and to the United States through 22 stations from coast to coast. When Coolidge was inaugurated the following March, 15 million people heard the ceremony over 24 stations. By this time, WEAF (AT&T) had an operating network of more than 20 stations; the WJZ (Radio Group) network, concentrated in the East, was much smaller. These networks were more engineering and programming devices than sales organizations.

Although telephone lines were the best medium for interconnecting stations, other techniques were tried. Westinghouse used shortwave transmissions in 1923 and 1924 to connect KDKA with satellite stations KFXX in Hastings, Nebraska, and KDPM in Cleveland. Amateur radio operators had opened up the shortwave spectrum, earlier thought useless, and had even sent a signal across the Atlantic in 1921. With higher shortwave power, KDKA relayed programs in the winter of 1923–1924 to a station in Manchester, England, for rebroadcast. This followed an ambitious experiment during the last week of November 1923, when stations in Great Britain picked up about fifteen American stations using their regular medium-wave transmitters.

Another interesting network experiment was a precursor of cable television. Early in 1923, a company in Dundee, Michigan, offered subscribers a wired radio system, providing programs from several stations for $1.50 a month. In Europe and the Soviet Union, earlier rediffusion systems such as the Puskás brothers' Telephonic Newspaper in Budapest (see p. 44) were a major technique for aural dissemination, but never caught on in America.

3.4 Early Educational Broadcasting

The prospect of educating larger numbers of people attracted universities and colleges to radio in 1921 and 1922. They first established stations as informal laboratories for engineering schools and physics departments or for publicity. Even before World War I, radio telegraph and some radio telephone experimentation had taken place at colleges and universities such as Arkansas, Cornell, Dartmouth, Iowa, Loyola, Nebraska, Ohio State, Penn State, Purdue, Tulane, Villanova, and Wisconsin. Afterward, many of these stations and many new ones went on the air: New York University, Nebraska, and Tufts were among the schools that offered extension courses by radio in the early 1920s. A few others tried to use radio for fund-raising without much success; land-grant colleges, in particular, offered adult education, primarily in home economics and agriculture. Of the more than 200 stations licensed to educational institutions in the early and middle 1920s, 72 were on the air in 1923 and 128 in 1925.

Noncollege broadcasters also scheduled educational programs in the form of "radio schools of the air," lectures, and even courses for credit. WJZ began such broadcasts in 1923. WEAF followed, and WLS in Chicago began its *Little Red Schoolhouse* series in 1924.

3.5 The Problem of Financial Support

The primary problem that broadcasters faced in the early 1920s was how to pay for programming. Stations struggled along as adjuncts to other enterprises or as hobbies. David Sarnoff suggested a 2% tax on receiver sales. In 1924, New York businessmen formed a committee to solicit funds from the radio audience for the hiring of high-class talent for WEAF. This effort failed partly because the fractionated radio audience distrusted such a benefit to the AT&T station. The idea of voluntary audience contributions to a common fund controlled by an elected or appointed board also failed. Another gimmick was for a station to establish an "invisible theater of the air," in which the audience could "buy seats." One New York station tried to gather $20,000 in this way but gave up and returned the contributions when it could collect only $1,000. This idea still survives: some stations sell printed program schedules to augment income, and many public television stations and noncommercial radio stations depend today largely on audience donations.

One approach that was not tried in this country became the standard practice abroad: levying an annual tax on radio receivers for the support of broadcasting. In this way, the audience supported the programming by buying and using sets, and the government, as collector and distributor of fees, had a say in the programming. In America a few municipalities and states have used general tax revenues to support broadcasting stations such as New York City's WNYC until 1995, but the national approach never took hold—perhaps for fear of governmental control of content, belief that free enterprise should determine radio operation, or dislike of taxation in general. (Current discussions over the financing of public television reflect these debates of the 1920s.)

The financial technique that eventually succeeded was direct advertising—the purchase of time from a station for the presentation of commercial messages. While there is evidence, in the form of a complaint to headquarters by a Federal Radio Inspector that WGI, and probably other stations, had accepted money some months earlier for promoting a retail establishment, the first *commercial*—so named from AT&T accounting practices—that is fully documented is one that lasted for 10 or 15 minutes on WEAF in the early evening of August 28, 1922. It was a pitch by the Queensboro Corporation for a cooperative (similar to a condominium) apartment house complex in Jackson Heights, a section of New York City recently opened up by a new rapid transit line. A salesman for the company, which owned most of Jackson Heights, referred briefly to author Nathaniel Hawthorne, namesake of the apartment house, and devoted the rest of the broadcast to a sales talk very much like today's offerings of land in Florida or Arizona. This short broadcast cost $100; it was repeated for five days, and then again a month later. Several thousand dollars in sales were reported.

Tidewater Oil and American Express also bought time in those first weeks, but after two months WEAF had sold only three hours and collected

$550. As with television two decades later, only a few far-sighted firms—including a department store, a political organization, and a motion picture producer—saw the great potential of radio as an advertising medium in those first four months when the station realized a net income of only about $5,000. By 1923 Gimbel's department store and other advertisers had begun sponsoring entertainment programs.

Some other stations, adopting this means of recouping expenses, ran afoul of AT&T's policy of exacting additional royalties for the use of radio telephony for hire. By the end of 1925, about half the stations on the air paid these royalties, which were part of the transmitter royalty payment and ranged from $500 to $3,000 in a lump sum.

Stations soon developed pricing policies geared to the market. Important stations in major markets, such as WEAF, could charge $500 for an hour of time. Boston stations might charge $250, Cincinnati and Detroit around $200, and Washington, D.C., $150. An advertiser might "buy" the 13-station WEAF chain for $2,600, a saving of $300 over the individual station rates.

The advertising heard in the early 1920s was what we would call *institutional*, with no mention of price or sometimes even place of sale, much like underwriting announcements on PBS. Announcers described their products glowingly but generally, often postponing mention of the sponsor's name until the end. Increasingly, the sponsor attached its name to the program, such as the *A & P* (food store) *Gypsies*, the *Cliquot Club* (soft drink) *Eskimos*, and the *Lucky Strike* (cigarette) *Hour*.

As soon as the Radio Group and the Telephone Group had signed the 1926 agreements, all stations could accept advertising. However, *direct advertising*, mentioning product, place, and price, was still frowned on (see quote at start of this chapter). The president of AT&T, trying to protect its "monopoly" of broadcast advertising, expressed doubt as to the feasibility of the listener's having to buy or lease receivers from the broadcasting company. Sarnoff was still calling for outright philanthropic endowment. A GE spokesman opined that broadcasting eventually would be supported by voluntary contributions or by licensing individual receivers, another scheme doubted by AT&T. It was not until 1928 that broadcast advertising clearly became the breadwinner for American radio broadcasting, even though many persons still objected to the mixing of programming and advertising.

3.6 Early Radio Programming

Early radio programs, resembling vaudeville in that there were several acts, usually musical, presented with awesome seriousness. Announcers wore tuxedos, at least at the larger stations, and studios were decorated with potted palms. The tuxedos and palms lasted for decades in Great Britain but were soon discarded in the United States for everyday use. The earliest

▪ **Types of Programs Broadcast in 1925**   This chart shows the kinds of programs broadcast in a period in February 1925 on three stations in New York, one in Chicago, and one in Kansas City. These powerful outlets in major cities were the stations most listened to at night but were not typical of local radio. Compare to table on page 133 for comparable data for 1932, and to table on page 300 for postwar radio in 1946.

Program Type and Subtypes		Percentage of Total
Music		**71.5%**
Dance	22.9%	
Vocal	8.1	
Combination	14.1	
Concert orchestras	4.3	
Soloists	7.6	
Phonograph records	—	
String ensembles	10.1	
Sacred	1.0	
Miscellaneous	3.4	
Drama		**.1**
Continued plays, reading, etc.	.1	
Sketches	—	
Onetime plays	—	
Other Entertainment		**6.8**
Women's	2.4	
Children's	3.7	
Feature	.7	
Star (other than music)	.0	
Information		**11.5**
Education	4.9	
News	.7	
Political	1.8	
Market reports	3.6	
Weather	.3	
Sports	.2	
Other		**10.1**
Foreign-originated	—	
Health exercises	1.8	
Church services	3.1	
Miscellaneous	5.2	
Total		**100.0%**

Source: William Albig, *Modern Public Opinion* (New York, McGraw-Hill, 1956), Table 20, page 447. By permission.

announcers were selected for their ability to speak with dignity, to sing or play an instrument in a pinch, and, until volume controls were developed, to push singers in and out from the carbon microphones. Instead of using names, announcers were known by certain initials: Thomas H. Cowan, apparently the first so identified in New York radio, was ACN (*A*nnouncer *C*owan, *N*ewark) when he started broadcasting over WJZ in October 1922.

An announcer for more than 30 years, Cowan became chief announcer of WNYC when it went on the air in 1924. Milton Cross, whose career spanned more than half a century (to his death in 1974), closely followed Cowan over WJZ, as AJN, using his middle initial since "C" was already taken. Cross became best known for his broadcasts from the Metropolitan Opera. Perhaps the most famous announcer of this period was Graham McNamee, who went to work for WEAF in 1923 and quickly created a following for his sports broadcasts.

Many stations tried to broadcast on a schedule, but luck played a large part in a given night's actual content. Major programs were announced and publicized, but poor weather or slow transportation often prevented a guest artist from appearing. When stations arranged to broadcast special talent or dance bands—usually from the studio but sometimes by remote telephone line from a hotel ballroom—they might run the program as long as the individual or group had something to offer. Although phonograph records sometimes were used, they were considered a low-class source of programming. There were few planned programs at first, only short segments like articles in a magazine. Often, the programs of several stations that shared time on a single channel sounded so much alike that none of the stations could build an individual audience. Stations with only a few hours' air time on occasional nights early in the 1920s realized the desirability of regular hours—even on a shared channel. The addition of daytime programming advanced station recognition in the larger markets. However, regardless of the quantity of a station's production, program elements were similar. By 1925, the percentages of time devoted to various types of programs on five stations in major cities was as shown in the boxed table on page 81.

3.6.1 Music

Because familiarity often makes it more enjoyable, music has been an entertainment staple for centuries; it is not "used up" in the same way as comedy or dramatic material. However, live music production is not cheap. Phonograph records were initially the answer, but their imperfect quality meant poor sound reproduction; in fact, in 1922 the Secretary of Commerce prohibited large stations from using records and giving the public nothing more than what it could enjoy without a radio (see p. 93). The networks refused as a matter of pride to air records, even battlefield recordings during World War II, until the late 1940s, and only in the early 1950s did records become the mainstay of radio programming (see pp. 298–299).

In the 1920s, many artists were glad to appear for publicity value alone. Dance bands provided "potted palm" music, named for the decor of the hotel ballrooms in which they played. One of the first to be broadcast by remote pickup was the Vincent Lopez group, which had a weekly 90-minute program on WJZ in 1921. For years the radio audience instantly recognized the salutation "Lopez speaking." The same year, a group known as "Coon Sanders' Nighthawks" became so popular over WDAF in Kansas City, especially with DX-ers all over the country, that the group moved to Chicago.

Local stations imitated the larger ones, frequently nurturing talent up to the big time. The WLS (Chicago) *Barn Dance* country and western music program began in 1924 and lasted for many years. Of the big bands that were becoming popular, many had begun as small groups and built their reputations over radio, such as Lawrence Welk's, which was first heard on the air in 1927 in Yankton, South Dakota, and which lasted for more than 30 years on television.

Classical music was also a staple on radio in the 1920s. In 1921, when Westinghouse put KYW on the air in Chicago, it programmed little more than the Chicago Opera, using a sophisticated 10–microphone system on the stage. In March 1922, WJZ brought orchestra and singers into the studio for a 75-minute presentation of Mozart's *The Impresario*. The New York Philharmonic began weekly broadcasts over WEAF that November. The prestige associated with classical music appealed to advertisers, with the National Carbon Company's *Eveready Hour* becoming the first sponsored network program in February 1924.

3.6.2 Variety and Vaudeville

Vaudeville—or traveling stage musical, comedy, and acrobatic acts— inspired several kinds of programs: professional acts, typically touring from theater to theater, local talent nights, and song-and-patter teams. The motion picture already had damaged the profitability of organized stage vaudeville circuits, and radio pushed it into its grave as talented performers gave up the nomadic life for broadcasting. Some of these gave more to radio than they got in return; some were one-man programming departments. Singer Wendell Woods Hall, a red-haired ukulele player with some stage and records following, worked a 3 P.M. to 3 A.M. shift on KYW for $25 a week in 1922, after several months' work for nothing but publicity. Although this program made him one of the first well-known radio performers, the station carried him on a *sustaining* (no advertising) basis. In 1924, Hall was married over the air (WEAF), one of the earliest radio news stunts. In New York, movie-theater owner Samuel S. Rothafel, known as "Roxy," joined the radio bandwagon as an impresario and master of ceremonies by putting his Capitol Theater show *Roxy's Gang* on WEAF almost intact in January 1923. The program, a happy mixture of music, comedy routines, and other things, lasted for 15 years. Al Jolson and Eddie Cantor were among the vaudeville and variety people who had switched to radio by the end of the 1920s, although "big name" comedy-variety network programming didn't start until 1933 (see p. 129). For those who were not headliners, performing on radio

■ **An Early Station Schedule: 1922**   This form letter was sent to letter writers who reported reception of the Westinghouse Chicago station KYW and requested a schedule. Between programmed reports, the station either played light studio music or simply went off the air.

Westinghouse Electric & Manufacturing Company

To....Chicago...........................   From..........Chicago.................

For Mr......W...C...Evans.,..Chief............. Department..Radio..Station.KYW
                              Operator

Subject: Date: April 21,1922.

The attached is a copy of our present schedule
for broadcasting, with the exception of the evening
performance, which has in no wise been changed,
namely:

        7:30 – – Bedtime story
        7:40 – – Special feature
        8:00 to 9:00 – – Musical Program.

If for any reason it is not possible to broadcast on
this schedule, please let me have a memorandum to
that effect for each case, with the exception of the
present 3:00 o'clock period, with which, as you
know, I am familiar.

For your information, it is also possible that the
7:30 to 9:00 period may be changed shortly, but
at present we will maintain that schedule.

G.H.Jaspert-MR

                              RADIO PUBLICITY DEPARTMENT.

became more attractive than making one-night stands and more secure because the vaudeville circuits were in trouble.

Although *talent night* could produce a sure-fire audience of the performers' friends and relatives, there was not enough talent in smaller towns, not enough local identification, not enough audience interest in this free entertainment to attract the kind of audience that the broadcaster desired.

Westinghouse Electric & Manufacturing Company

General Offices and Main Works
East Pittsburgh, Pa.

IN REPLY PLEASE ADDRESS THE COMPANY
AND REFER TO_____

M. G. SYMONDS
DISTRICT MANAGER
MALCOLM CARRINGTON.
ASST. DISTRICT MANAGER

III WEST WASHINGTON STREET, CHICAGO, ILL.

Your letter commenting on the reception of our broadcasting
of Chicago Board of Trade quotations, U. S. Bureau of Markets
reports, financial summary, and baseball news, is indeed
appreciated.

Our schedule is:

    9:25 A.M.   Opening Market Quotations,
                Chicago Board of Trade.

    10:00 A.M. Market Quotations, Chicago Board
                of Trade; Quotations every half
                hour thereafter until 1:00 P.M.

    1:20 P.M.   Closing Market Quotations,
                Chicago Board of Trade.

    2:15 P.M.   News and Market Reports

    3:00 P.M.   American and National League baseball
                team line-ups; progress of games every
                half hour thereafter until close of
                all games.

    4:15 P.M.   News, Markets, and Stock Reports

    6:30 P.M.   News, Final Market, Financial, and
                summaries of principal games played in
                American and National League.

    9:00 P.M.   Summaries of principal games played in
                American and National League.

It is our purpose to make this service as completely satisfactory to you as possible. We are pleased to have your
comments concerning the reception of our broadcasting.

Yours very truly,

G. H. Jaspert

G.H.Jaspert-MR   RADIO PUBLICITY DEPARTMENT.

Both local talent shows and vaudeville, but primarily vaudeville, produced the song-and-patter teams. These two-man (most women then on
radio were singers only) teams would travel from station to station, offering
songs and light chatter, often in dialect, for several weeks before moving on.
Some stayed with one station and became well known, like Billy Jones and
Ernie Hare, who began broadcasting on WEAF in mid-1923 and became

known over the first few years as the Happiness Boys (Happiness Candy), the Interwoven Pair (Interwoven socks), and the Tastee Loafers (a baking company). Called radio's first real comedy team, their combination of light comedy, music, and topical comment appealed to audiences.

3.6.3 Politics and News

Music and variety made up more than three-fourths of the average station's programming in the early and mid-1920s. They were relatively easy to provide, were flexible to program, and could be accomplished with available talent. However, even in the infancy of broadcasting, stations were experimenting with ways of providing information to their listeners.

From the 1920 election returns over KDKA—and, indeed, a 1916 election-night broadcast by Lee de Forest—to today's talk shows, broadcasting and politics have been linked. Radio's first major political project was the 1924 election. From President Coolidge's December 1923 speech to Congress, through the nominating conventions, and to the election returns, radio was an ever fascinating source of firsthand information for millions of Americans. Chains of stations carried major speeches and comment. Coolidge's renomination by the Republicans was cut and dried; the Democratic convention went through 103 ballots before deciding on compromise candidate John W. Davis. For years afterward, radio listeners remembered or were reminded by comedians of the sound of a leather-lunged Alabama delegate starting off each roll call with "Alabama casts 24 votes for Oscar W. Underwood," a favorite son candidate. After a few ballots, the convention began to echo the call, and radio made it a catch-line all over the country. The night before the election, the President addressed the nation over 26 stations hooked up coast-to-coast by AT&T, reaching an estimated 20 to 30 million people of a total population of roughly 110 million. Several big-city stations started what became the traditional practice of interrupting regular programming to carry returns and some crude analysis—a practice that seemed to be dying out in the 1990s as interest in politics dwindled and audiences complained about missing their entertainment programming—until the cliff–hanger presidential count in 2000 rekindled public interest. KDKA was on the air from 7 P.M. until 4 A.M. the next morning, and many other stations stayed on past midnight. Between reports, stations offered musical interludes. For the first time, the whole nation was able to hear election returns virtually as soon as they were known. Newspapers were annoyed to have been scooped by radio.

Other kinds of news programs were less common. There were no daily newscasts at first. Many people felt that radio should provide entertainment and occasional special presentations and that newspapers could carry the news. Newspaper-owned stations sometimes used news bulletins as teasers to stimulate newspaper sales, and other stations sometimes read news as a filler, without bothering to pay or, often, to identify the source. Lecturers or commentators often discussed current news events. Perhaps the best-known commentator was Hans ("H.V.") Kaltenborn, an assistant editor of the *Brooklyn Eagle*, which sponsored him for a weekly news commentary over WEAF starting in October 1923. His clipped pronunciation and incisive comment later distinguished him as network news reporter-commentator.

Many stations *did* carry special events, or "emergency" news where speed was important. Since all stations in the early 1920s were required to listen periodically to the maritime distress frequency of 500 kHz, reports of shipwrecks were prominent in news broadcasting, and the nearest powerful stations could, and indeed were required to, relay the SOS messages themselves.

Probably the best-known special news coverage of the mid-1920s was WGN's (Chicago) broadcasts from the 1925 Scopes "monkey" trial (teaching of Darwin's theory of evolution) in Dayton, Tennessee. The famous confrontations between Clarence Darrow for the defense and William Jennings Bryan for the prosecution were carried live to Chicago audiences, reputedly costing the station $1,000 a day in personnel, telephone line, and other items. There was little concern then over radio's presence in the courtroom; the microphone stood squarely in front of the bench, and all parties accepted the wider forum it provided. This was a far cry from the furor over coverage of the Hauptmann trial (Lindbergh kidnaping) a decade later (see p. 197).

3.6.4 Other Talk Programs

Many program types familiar today were first tried in the 1920s, including religion, education, and sports. Educational programming has been discussed (see p. 78). Religious programming started when the U.S. Army Signal Corps (apparently unconcerned about separation of church and state) broadcast a church service in Washington, D.C., in August 1919. KDKA was probably the first private station to broadcast religious services when, on January 2, 1921, it transmitted an Episcopalian service, with microphones for organ, choir, and clergyman and with two technicians (a Jew and a Catholic) dressed in choir robes, on standby in case anything went wrong. As the years went by, stations traditionally broadcast a religious service or talk each week, usually on Sunday.

Considering their later popularity, it is odd that sports programs were seldom scheduled in the early 1920s. In April 1921, KDKA gave a blow-by-blow account of a boxing match. In July RCA broadcast the Dempsey–Carpentier heavyweight fight (see p. 68), with Major J. Andrew White, an early radio promoter and founder of *Wireless Age*, managing the broadcast. Later that summer KDKA covered a tennis tournament and a baseball game. Although few teams liked the idea of letting radio siphon off their attendance, the World Series was carried as early as 1922 over WJZ and other stations of the Radio Group, using Western Union lines, and noncommercial events such as sailing regattas were commonly described over the air.

During the mid-1920s, radio aired almost any subject discussed in public from astrology to politics; it programmed academic and popular lectures, cooking lessons, exercise programs. Programs for farmers, first market and weather reports and then how-to talks, began to appear on Midwest stations in 1921 or 1922, particularly those operated by land-grant colleges with strong departments of agriculture. The battery-powered radio found a tremendous audience among rural Americans, nearly half the population (48.8% in 1920), who lived days away from the news at the end of poor roads and without telephones.

The *public service* program or announcement was an early feature. A marathon broadcast by WLS in March 1925, which raised $200,000 for tornado relief in Illinois, set a standard for other disasters: first news or warnings of a flood or storm and then appeals for help and funds for its victims.

3.6.5 Drama

When radio drama first was thought of, producers had the fortunately–erroneous impression that the action of a drama would have to take place in a tunnel or cave so that the audience could identify with something they couldn't see. Probably the first play broadcast on radio was "The Perfect Fool," which was having a successful run on Broadway with Ed Wynn in the lead. Wynn, starring also in the WJZ version on February 19, 1922, "froze" before the microphone and later complained that only with an audience to react against could he correctly time his delivery. When he became a regular radio performer, using the "perfect fool" character, Wynn insisted on a studio audience.

In the fall of 1922, GE's WGY offered the first dramatic series, the weekly *WGY Players*, and in 1925 established a contest for audience-submitted scripts. Other stations, particularly in major cities with access to acting troupes, began to offer plays adapted from the stage or films. Probably the first play designed for radio was called "When Love Wakens" (note the "W-L-W"), written and directed by Fred Smith, program director of WLW (Cincinnati) in April 1923. Although original drama was tried elsewhere, it often lacked the audience-pulling power of a proven story and required enormous talent to produce successfully.

3.7 Creation of the Radio Audience

The increase in radio listening was both spontaneous and created: Spontaneous in that experimenters and early listeners were motivated to build or buy receivers, and created in that many more Americans had to be persuaded that the sizable investment of time and money was worth-while—that radio was more than a fad.

3.7.1 Development of the Receiver

Until late 1920, just before KDKA's first broadcast, all receivers were home-made. Some, like the crystal set, were cheap and simple—all it took was some wire and an oatmeal box to wind it on, a purchased piece of galena or other crystal and cat's whisker to probe it with, and a pair of earphones. More complicated sets were more expensive—the price of tubes, like many weekly wages, started at $6—though not beyond the capabilities of experienced amateurs or the thousands of ex-servicemen trained in radio. Early sets varied in cost, looks, and effectiveness, until more advanced superregenerative or superheterodyne circuits became available and design more standard. Almost all had limited sensitivity (ability to pick up weak signals) and very limited selectivity (ability to tune sharply and pick up only one frequency at a time); and tube sets required not only tubes but several types of expensive batteries, including cumbersome and heavy automobile storage batteries. Receivers needed earphones for listening, making radio a solitary pastime, although more than one pair of phones could be hooked up at a time. Even when loud-speakers were developed, the additional amplification they demanded was so expensive, in both components and batteries, that they were not widely used. Early receivers were hard to tune, their many controls requiring an artist's touch, and their audio quality left much to be desired.

In Fall 1920, commercially manufactured radios became available, principally in large department stores. The Westinghouse "Aeriola Jr." was a crystal set that cost $25, and the "Aeriola Sr." was a tube set for $60. By 1922 there were hundreds of manufacturing companies varying considerably in size. Many smaller companies assembled parts supplied by other companies. RCA, as sales agent for sets made by Westinghouse and GE, was the foremost distributor, but Crosley, Grebe, and Atwater Kent also became familiar brands. Fortunately for the companies competing with RCA, the RCA–GE–Westinghouse agreements (see pp. 57–63) that required RCA to market GE and Westinghouse receivers worked against RCA because the long lead-time needed for this intercompany ordering made its "Radiola" sets obsolete by the time they hit the market. The public soon realized that inexpensive sets were no bargain due to their lack of quality and performance, and the average price per set climbed well above $100.

After 1923, advertising and merchandising of radio receivers stressed brand name and product dependability. A National Radio Chamber of Commerce, later the Radio Manufacturers Association and now the Electronic Industries Association, was established to improve quality standards, collect sales data, and speak for the industry in forums or before government and private bodies. After Westinghouse brought the Armstrong superheterodyne patent into the patents pool, RCA marketed the first superheterodyne receivers, which were expensive but sold well because they improved reception. Crosley, hoping to reverse the trend toward expensive sets, marketed the $10 Crosley "Pup" in 1924, a small metal box with a single tube on top that could receive stations from up to 15 miles away.

By 1924 radio manufacturers were going bankrupt at nearly the same rate they were being established. In 1925, in spite of fall "radio shows" in major cities when set makers released next year's models just like automobiles, more manufacturers went out of business than started. The survivors usually were the larger and stronger companies—including several thousand that made components, in addition to the manufacturers and assemblers of complete sets—but virtually every year saw fewer of them.

As an industry, radio receiver manufacture became big business as the 1920s wore on (see Appendix C, table 6A). Circuit designs were changed annually, with emphasis on easier operation by nontechnically minded listeners, especially women. The public bought sets enthusiastically—a half million in 1923, a million and a half in 1924, two million in 1925, one and three-quarters million in 1926. When Gimbel's department store had a sale

---

■ **The Early Radio Receiver: Homemade Variety**   This is from one of many published instructions for a do-it-yourself radio receiver that could be assembled at a fraction of the cost of a commercially manufactured set.

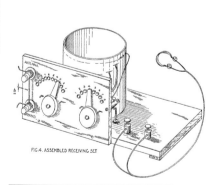

FIG 4. ASSEMBLED RECEIVING SET

8. APPROXIMATE COST OF PARTS

The following list shows the approximate cost of the parts used in the construction of the receiving station. The total cost will depend largely on the kind of apparatus purchased and on the number of parts constructed at home.

Antenna:
Wire, copper, bare or insulated, No. 14 or 16, 100 to 150 feet	$0.75
Rope, 1/4 or 3/8 inch, 2 cents per foot.	
2 insulators, porcelain	.20
1 pulley	.15
Lightning switch, 30-ampere battery switch	.30
1 porcelain tube	.10

Ground connections:
Wire (same kind as antenna wire).	
2 clamps	.30
1 iron pipe or rod	.25

Receiving set:
3 ounces No. 24 copper wire, double cotton covered	.75
1 round cardboard box	
2 switch knobs and blades complete	1.00
18 switch contacts and nuts	.75
3 binding posts, set screw type	.45
2 binding posts, any type	.30
1 crystal, tested	.25
3 wood screws, brass, 3/4 inch long	.03
2 wood screws for fastening panel to base	.02
Wood for panels (from packing box).	
2 pounds paraffin	.30
Lamp cord, 2 to 3 cents per foot.	
Test buzzer	.50
Dry battery	.30
Telephone receivers	4.00
Total	10.70

If the switches are constructed as directed and a single telephone receiver be used, the cost may be kept well below $10.

If a head set consisting of a pair of telephone receivers instead of a single telephone receiver is used, the cost of this item may be about $8 instead of $4. Still more efficient and expensive telephone receivers are available at prices ranging up to about $20.

WASHINGTON, March 27, 1922.

Source: U.S. Department of Commerce, Bureau of Standards. *Construction and Operation of a Simple Homemade Receiving Outfit.* Washington: Government Printing Office, 1922 (pp. 12 and 16).

in May 1925 of Freed-Eisemann Neutrodyne five-tube receivers—including one "Prest-O-Lite" A battery of 90 amperes, two 45-volt B batteries, one phone plug, a complete antenna outfit, vacuum tubes, and a choice of loudspeakers—it took 240 clerks to sell the 5,300 receivers, at $98.75, $15 down—even though this price represented as much as several months of a worker's wages. These 5,300 sets joined the 2.5 million already in use at the end of 1924.

In 1926 "battery-eliminator" or plug-in models reached the market to the delight of everyone except the battery manufacturers and households with no electricity, a rapidly shrinking proportion. A simple connection to house current eliminated 40 to 50 pounds of batteries and a maze of wiring. Common in the later 1920s were improvements in appearance—a mahogany box was more acceptable in the living room than a homemade *bread-board* receiver without a cabinet; in convenience—John V. L. Hogan's *uni-tuning* reduced controls to one tuning knob and a volume control; and in economy—the plug-in model was cheaper. As listeners updated their installations, older sets went to the attic to provide parts for future experimenters, or out to rural areas without electricity.

3.7.2 A National Craze

By the end of 1921 about one in every 500 American households had a radio receiver; by 1926 one radio receiver had been sold for every six households. Considering that some high-income households probably had purchased more than one receiver in this period and that home-built sets, not included in the statistics, counteracted this bias in the figures, it was estimated that one family in six had a radio. All over the country, newspapers, magazines, clubs, and classes fed the urge for more information about this marvel. Prearranged groups listened around sets in hotel lobbies or stores. Because of Prohibition, there were no legal saloons where people could enjoy radio on the house. (However, when television came in, the local tavern typically was the first to buy one.) Some radio retailers installed a mobile receiver in the back of a car to promote sales. Radio basically was an urban medium in its early years, although the number of farm sets increased rapidly when stations offered market and weather reports and when county extension agents explained radio's technicalities and cost and its potential benefits to the farmer.

During the early and middle 1920s audience research and listener feedback were slight. Broadcasters programmed to suit their own desires since they knew little about the audience's makeup, listening habits, or preferences, other than what they picked up in social and business conversations. The station could determine its area coverage from the postmarks on listener requests for DX cards, which it sent to verify long-range reception; and could get additional feedback through comment cards (supplied by radio shops to enable listeners to relate where they heard a certain broadcast, what they thought of it, and what receiving equipment was used); signal coverage maps

The Early Radio Receiver: Commercial Models

prepared by engineers; receiver sales records kept by retail outlets; and station mail counts of listener response, often to a *giveaway* offer. At best, these data enabled station owners to make an educated guess as to audience size and potential size. Most did not bother, at least not until advertising became their main support. Then, the audience became the station's most valuable asset, and knowledge of it made the difference between success and failure.

3.8 Further Attempts at Regulation

All these developments took place within the inadequate regulatory pattern of the Radio Act of 1912, which was passed long before broadcasting was conceived (see p. 43). It empowered the Secretary of Commerce to license all stations and operators for commercial or amateur radio transmissions; indeed, it gave him no discretion, but required him to license all applicants meeting the minimal standards, essentially United States citizenship, and assign call letters. On President Warren G. Harding's election in 1920, the Secretary of Commerce appointment went to Herbert Hoover, fresh from an active engineering and public service career, most recently providing food relief to war-torn Europe. Until 1921 the Bureau of Navigation of the Department of Commerce kept track of amateur and commercial (maritime) radio operations.

When broadcasting to the public started, the department allocated a single wavelength for it, although experimentation frequently took place elsewhere on the spectrum. This wavelength of 360 meters, or 833.3 kHz, was in the same range as the international distress and calling frequency of 600 meters (500 kHz), long familiar to experimenters and amateur hobbyists. (The 600-meter wavelength had been selected partly because it was the longest for which an antenna could be strung between the masts of a typical ship.) In December 1921, before the number of broadcasting stations began to climb sharply, a second wavelength of 485 meters (618.6 kHz) was added, primarily for crop reports and weather forecasts. To broadcast such "government services," stations would switch from 360 meters up to 485 meters, since the transmitters were tuned, like a radio receiver, rather than fixed by crystal control on a particular frequency as they are today.

During Spring 1922, there were so many stations on the air that the department *had* to provide a third wavelength of 400 meters (750 kHz) for Class B stations. These typically "better" stations were required to operate with at least 500 to 1,000 watts and could not use phonograph records. The new rule tended to create a privileged class on 400 meters, with most stations still crowded on the 360-meter wavelength. Although those who ran the powerful stations, and the typical listener, liked this move, it did not relieve the increased crowding on the airwaves. In a way, it was surprising that this system worked at all for its short life, until May 1923, since the Radio Act of 1912 gave the Secretary of Commerce very little power beyond that of persuasion.

3.8.1 Hoover and the National Radio Conferences

As the number of broadcasting stations grew from 30 to more than 500 in a single year, government, as well as commercial and amateur operators, faced new problems. Complaints of interference were filed, and pressure mounted for greater coordination. Secretary Hoover, in need of constructive advice, convened a conference of civilian and government experts, to discuss radio's problems and suggest legislative solutions. Fifteen official delegates, 10 representing governmental interests and 5 nongovernmental interests, particularly in science and engineering, gathered in Washington on February 27, 1922. (Members of the American Radio Relay League, meeting a little earlier in the same city, were very unhappy at the prospect of additional regulation!) Disagreement marked the conference when AT&T, GE, Westinghouse, and RCA favored keeping the Commerce Department in control of broadcasting rather than giving that role to the Army or the Navy, and the Navy and the Post Office had different ideas. The conference agreed, however, on some recommendations:

1. That the government regulate technical aspects of broadcasting by assigning stations to specific frequencies, with specific power and hours of operation.
2. That more channels be added to reduce interference.
3. That radio be considered a public utility, operating in the public interest.
4. That advertising be limited to naming the sponsor.
5. That four classes of station be recognized: government, private (educational), private (others), and toll (paid service).

These recommendations, as introduced into the House of Representatives by Congressman Wallace H. White, Jr., (R-Maine) called for administration by the Secretary of Commerce with no provision for court review, while his opponents called for an independent commission. The bill passed the House on the second try early in 1923 but died in the Senate Interstate Commerce Committee.

While waiting for congressional action, Hoover opened up the new Class B 400-meter frequency, as the number of stations increased from 60 to nearly 600. Three channels were clearly insufficient for satisfactory nationwide broadcast service, and Hoover called the second National Radio Committee conference. It convened on March 20, 1923, with 20 delegates. Its report reiterated the need for congressional action and called for various holding actions:

1. Establishment of three classes of stations.
2. Division of the country into five regions, with stations assigned accordingly to provide more equal service—an obvious political need.
3. Giving the Secretary of Commerce discretion to choose among applicants for the same facilities, instead of prolonging the voluntary allotment of segments of time on a single wavelength to several stations.
4. Discussion of station financing and copyright, suggested by the American Society of Composers, Authors, and Publishers (ASCAP), a music performing rights licensing organization.

As one result of the conference, Secretary Hoover announced a new system of frequency assignments on May 15, 1923. There would be, eventually, two classes of stations occupying the band from 550 kHz to 1,350 kHz (see the diagram below). Stations originally operating on 833.3 kHz were designated Class C until they could be reclassified into A or B. Class A stations, transmitting with less than 500 watts, were assigned to the top and

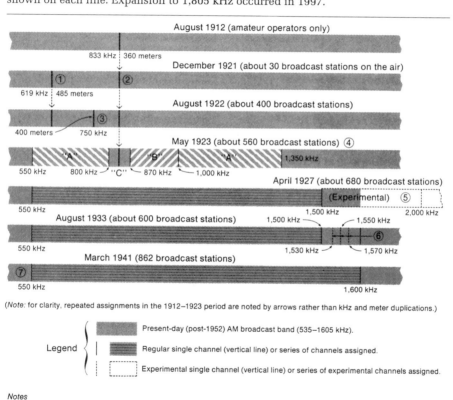

■ **Growth of the Standard (AM) Broadcast Band**   In the diagrams below, each bar represents the standard (AM) broadcast band (medium-wave) frequency allocation in the United States in the mid-1970s. Superimposed on those bars are earlier allocations for AM stations (see pp. 74 and 83). Small circled numbers refer to notes at end of diagrams. Actual allocations extend 5 kHz above and below the end numbers shown on each line. Expansion to 1,805 kHz occurred in 1997.

August 1912 (amateur operators only)

833 kHz | 360 meters

December 1921 (about 30 broadcast stations)

① ②

619 kHz | 485 meters

August 1922 (about 400 broadcast stations)

③

400 meters   750 kHz

May 1923 (about 560 broadcast stations) ④

"A"   "B"   "A"   1,350 kHz

550 kHz   800 kHz — "C" 870 kHz   1,000 kHz

April 1927 (about 680 broadcast stations)

(Experimental) ⑤

550 kHz   1,500 kHz   2,000 kHz

August 1933 (about 600 broadcast stations)   1,500 kHz   1,550 kHz

⑥

550 kHz   1,530 kHz   1,570 kHz

March 1941 (862 broadcast stations)

⑦

550 kHz   1,600 kHz

(*Note:* for clarity, repeated assignments in the 1912–1923 period are noted by arrows rather than kHz and meter duplications.)

Legend {
Present-day (post-1952) AM broadcast band (535–1605 kHz).

Regular single channel (vertical line) or series of channels assigned.

Experimental single channel (vertical line) or series of experimental channels assigned.
}

Notes
1. Used only for government reports (weather, crops, etc.).
2. Used for all other program types: entertainment, lectures, etc.
3. Called Class B with more stringent technical and some programming requirements. By October 1922, six months after this allocation, congestion was so great that time-sharing was necessary for stations on this wavelength in larger cities.
4. For this allocation, the following restrictions were in force: Class A—less than 500 watts, located on top and bottom of band; Class B—500 or more watts in middle of the band; Class C—temporary for stations on 360 meters (833 kHz) until they were reassigned to Class A or B. Because such stations, often the older ones, were seldom equipped to stay exactly on frequency, space was left on either side of the single channel; Class D—(not shown) for developmental work, with frequencies assigned to radio equipment manufacturers.
5. For experimental use only, including AM and visual (TV) experimentation. Most 1,500–2,000 kHz assignments were temporary.
6. Specific 20 kHz-wide channels (twice the normal AM channel width) were set aside on 1,530, 1,550 and 1,570 kHz for high-fidelity AM experimental broadcasting. Only a few stations were assigned here.
7. The 540 kHz channel was added to the U.S. AM band in December 1952.

bottom of this band: 550 to 800 kHz and 1,000 to 1,350 kHz. Class B stations, using 500 watts or more, were assigned to 870 to 1,000 kHz, leaving 833.3 kHz unmolested with "guard band" of nearly 35 kHz on either side. This vast increase in spectrum space made many receivers out of date but established AM radio broadcasting firmly in the heart of its current band and made adequate regulation possible.

But adequate regulation was not to come from the Department of Commerce, at least not under the 1912 Radio Act. In Summer 1923, the U.S. Court of Appeals for the District of Columbia ruled in *Hoover v. Intercity Radio* that the Secretary of Commerce could not regulate radio other than assigning wavelengths, and that his license-issuing function was purely clerical. A 1912 opinion of the attorney general had come to essentially the same conclusion, and a later opinion and the 1925 *Zenith-WJAZ* case (see pp. 97–98) concurred.

During 1923 and 1924, Congress still couldn't pass a new radio bill. Hoover called the Third National Radio Conference in October 1924 and told the 90-some delegates that the country needed a broadcasting system controlled largely by self-regulatory bodies rather than by the government. President Coolidge echoed some of Hoover's philosophy when he advised the conference that the government should not operate stations in competition with private broadcasters and that there should be no monopoly in broadcasting. David Sarnoff's announcement that RCA was planning a chain of superpower (50,000 watt) stations, starting with one in New York, led to objections from smaller broadcasters and study by a conference committee. The conference concluded that:

1. It strongly opposed monopolistic practices.
2. The power of the Department of Commerce should be extended in technical areas only.
3. National broadcasting through wired interconnection of stations, rather than shortwave, should be encouraged.
4. Experimentation with superpower should have strict supervision.
5. Power of existing stations should be increased, particularly where rural listeners would benefit.
6. The top of the broadcasting band should be extended to 1,500 kHz, and the regional zoning system should be revised to increase the number of channels by 30, to 96.
7. The classifying and labeling of stations should be changed.

The third conference made no call for congressional action; in fact, Hoover asked Congressman White not to introduce a bill until some of the problems raised at the conference could be corrected or put into more specific recommendations for legislative action.

A year later, the fourth and largest National Radio Conference was held in Washington on November 9, 1925. Its 400 delegates considered three topics: limiting the number of stations, granting licenses on the basis of "public interest" service to the listener, and appointing local committees, familiar with their own areas, to help the Secretary of Commerce select recipients of broadcast franchises. The conference strongly supported limiting the number of stations, even if it meant allowing the secretary to remove some of the 80 stations still on 833.3 kHz. The principle agreed to was that having a few stations broadcasting high quality programs was more desirable than having many stations offering mediocre programs, and that adding new channels would be irrelevant to this problem and unfair to other radio services. The conference found it difficult to define "public service" but supported the suggestion that a prospective licensee offer more than desire and money in order to procure a license. The idea of local committees was rejected. The conference decided that advertising was a proper means of support for broadcasting if it was indirect or institutional—apparently an acknowledgment that advertising was the best support option available. Matters discussed at earlier conferences were again raised. As to copyright, since the courts had made it plain that broadcasting constituted a public performance, it was decided that stations needed permission of the originator to rebroadcast programs. Public utility status as advocated by the first conference was rejected. Superpower experiments had proved that smaller stations need not be as worried about being "blanketed" by larger stations. Congressional action was again urged, specifically for administrative flexibility for the secretary, a commission or some other administering body, and renewable and revocable for cause five-year license terms. A baker's dozen of formal recommendations were introduced as H.R. 5589 by Congressman White in December 1925, and an amended version became the Radio Act of 1927 (see pp. 141–145).

3.8.2 Chaos

The already tenuous authority of the Secretary of Commerce disintegrated shortly after the Fourth National Radio Conference. Late in 1924 the Zenith Radio Corporation, a receiver manufacturer, applied for a permit, built a station, and in due course received a license for 930 kHz, which it had to share with several other stations. Zenith soon outgrew the two hours a week it had originally requested and asked for permission to broadcast longer hours on an unused wavelength at 910 kHz, which the United States had agreed to reserve for Canadian stations. Permission was refused. When Zenith defiantly "jumped" to 910 kHz, other stations announced similar intentions. The Commerce Department took Zenith to court, but an Illinois Federal District Court decided on April 26, 1926, that there was then "no express grant of power in the Act to the Secretary of Commerce to establish regulations." Although the Commerce Department

▪ **An FRC Commissioner Describes the Chaos of 1926 and 1927**   In a
June 1927 speech in Chicago, newly appointed FRC Commissioner Orestes H. Caldwell
looked back on the post-Zenith case confusion that precipitated the Radio Act of 1927.
(see pp. 141–145).

... many stations jumped without restraint to new wave lengths which suited them better,
regardless of the interference which they might thus be causing to other stations. Proper separation between established stations was destroyed by other stations coming in and camping in the
middle of any open spaces they could find, each interloper thus impairing reception of three
stations—his own and two others. Instead of the necessary 50-kilocycle separation between
stations in the same community, the condition soon developed where separations of 20 and
10 kilocycles, and even 8, 5, and 2 kilocycles, existed. Under such separations, of course, stations
were soon wildly blanketing each other while distracted listeners were assailed with scrambled
programs. ... Some of the older stations also jumped their power ... and heterodyne interference
between broadcasters on the same wave length became so bad at many points on the dial that
the listener might suppose instead of a receiving set he had a peanut roaster with assorted whistles. Indeed, every human ingenuity and selfish impulse seemed to have been exerted to complicate the tangle in the ether.

Source: Federal Radio Commission. *First Annual Report: 1927.* (Washington: Government Printing
Office, 1927) pp. 10–11.

tried to rush the pending bill, introduced by Senator Clarence C. Dill and
Representative White, through Congress, the Dill–White bill came too late
in the session. The attorney general, in a requested opinion issued on July
8, 1926, held that the secretary did not have adequate legal power to deal
with the situation. The department then had no choice but to continue processing applications and, in a period of seven months in 1926, more than
200 new stations went on the air, creating intolerable interference in major
urban areas.

3.8.3 Initial Self-Regulation

Secretary Hoover had preached that industry could avoid governmental
control through self-regulation. The cacophony on the air after mid-1926
was ample proof that broadcasters could not cooperate sufficiently to
function without outside regulatory force. Indeed, what self-regulation
there was resulted mostly from external threat rather than internal conviction. In the earliest years, self-regulation meant little other than "silent
nights." Time-sharing was mostly voluntary, but, except for the period after the Zenith decision, there was always the threat of government action.
In technical matters, broadcasting clearly needed a governmental traffic
cop; in programming, broadcasting managed alone, typically exercising
its freedom by censoring many dissenting points of view and presenting a
conservative, business-oriented middle-class viewpoint. The avoidance
of controversy became almost a fetish in later years.

Although a matter more of self-interest than self-regulation, the broadcasters' fight with ASCAP (American Society of Composers, Authors, and Publishers) in the early 1920s led the way toward organizing the broadcasting industry, a necessary step toward self-regulation. ASCAP—a performing rights, copyright-licensing agency founded in 1914—was concerned that record sales and, increasingly, broadcasting were the cause of declining revenues from sheet music sales. In 1922 and 1923, ASCAP demanded royalties from several selected stations for playing ASCAP-licensed music. Although AT&T's WEAF agreed to pay a few hundred dollars a year for a blanket license, possibly because of AT&T's own stance on patent rights, most stations balked because they had no income and relatively large expenses. Broadcasters contended not only that they ran a nonprofit business but that the publicity they gave to the music probably boosted record and sheet music sales. When ASCAP threatened to bring suit, as the Copyright Act of 1909 clearly allowed, a few stations capitulated but others dropped ASCAP-controlled popular music from their repertoires.

On April 25 and 26, 1923, a small group of broadcasters met in Chicago to establish a common front against ASCAP, leading to, in later years, its own music-licensing organization. This group, calling itself the National Association of Broadcasters, picked the head of Zenith, Commander Eugene F. McDonald, Jr., as its first president. Representatives from about 20 stations attending NAB's initial convention in New York that fall discussed politicians on the air, the need for technical cooperation and control, and possible revisions in the copyright law. The new group was small and largely ineffective at first—ASCAP got its royalties—but the groundwork had been laid for a powerful organization that would face ASCAP again with somewhat different results (see p. 214).

3.9 Radio's Early Impact

There were indicators of the roles of radio in this country and abroad beyond the impact on the American home of the 1920s that we have already noted (see pp. 91–93).

3.9.1 Domestic Effects

The radio craze or fad of 1921 and 1922 perhaps is best seen in the popular literature that grew up to feed and support, and be supported by, the national interest in wireless. Technical magazines about wireless had been around for some time, but they catered to the experimenter and not to the general public. Shortly after the first broadcasting stations went on the air, some general interest radio periodicals appeared. *Radio Broadcast*, which began in May 1922, concentrated on programming and industry economics, but in 1924 it began a column of radio criticism, particularly of musical programs. Then other popular radio periodicals, mixtures of fan and how-to-do-it technical magazines, lured an avid public. Almost all general magazines of information, opinion, and entertainment featured articles about broadcasting.

In its early years, newspapers devoted considerable attention to radio. In 1922 the *New York Times* started a regular radio section with the late Orrin E. Dunlap, Jr., now better known for his many books on radio and television, as columnist–critic; in 1924 the *Christian Science Monitor* started a radio section; in 1925 Ben Gross began his 45-year career with the *New York Daily News* and a writer signing himself "Pioneer" offered technical tips and brief reviews in the *New York Tribune*. Books appeared in increasing numbers, many on "how to build your own radio set," a few of the "gee whiz!" school covering all aspects of radio, and no less than four different series of boys' thrillers with the same series title of "The Radio Boys."

Broadcasting to the public had by no means killed the amateur radio service. Ham operators deserved credit for the development of efficient equipment and circuits and the opening up of higher frequencies of the electromagnetic spectrum.

Radio had a telling effect on other industries. Hardest hit was the phonograph record industry, which suddenly faced competition from "free" music sent over the air. As radio-transmitted sound improved and as the amount of broadcast music increased, demand for expensive but low-fidelity phonographs lessened and the companies that made them suffered. Radio also undermined vaudeville, although the traveling shows, some of which survived into the 1930s, were also a victim of the motion picture. Many of the acoustic and electronic principles that produced radio were applied to the sound motion picture, which made its appearance in the late 1920s. Without the Audion, sound motion pictures would have been impossible. The weekly bible of show business, *Variety*, started a special radio section in 1924 in testimony to the growing importance of the medium.

All in all, radio was a common household device by 1926. Although serious technical interference and economic problems existed, its potential for supplying entertainment to the American public was evident. Fortuitously but fortunately, the leisure time of most Americans was expanding just as radio was developing. Effects from the rapid spread of news and the loss or reduction of regional speech dialects and patterns were more subtle or more gradual.

3.9.2 Radio Abroad

Although much attention was diverted to broadcasting, a strong interest in the market for point-to-point international communications remained. With the end of the Navy's control of radio facilities in March 1920, commercial transatlantic wireless service returned, with RCA, the "chosen instrument" of American communications policy, profiting from traffic agreements with British Marconi and with other administrations.

Interestingly enough, the alternator that led to the birth of RCA was quickly superseded by high-power vacuum-tube transmitters. Discovery of the propagation characteristics of shortwaves suddenly made much-prized longwave frequencies less desirable. Shortwaves had been ignored commercially, with the belief that nothing below 200 meters (1,500 kHz) would work except for very short distances, but amateur operators had found ways to use them for long-range transmissions. Ham operators bridged the Atlantic with shortwave as early as December 1921 but did not know how to overcome a high level of interference. However, after the major manufacturing and operating companies, including Marconi, had been shown the possibilities of long-range skywave transmissions on shortwave frequencies, it did not take long. By the late 1920s, shortwave was used for long-distance telephone as well as the "Empire Chain" of stations connecting all the British Empire. The amateurs were "kicked upstairs" again, to yet higher frequencies, when their playground just below 200 meters was taken over by commercial and governmental radio services.

Radio broadcasting developed in many other countries at the same time it developed in the United States. Less developed nations did not establish indigenous radio broadcasting for some years, although some colonies had a radio system modeled on the mother country's. The first broadcasting station in Great Britain began in February 1920, near London. When a few other stations began experimental voice and music transmissions, interference and political and financial considerations caused the General Post Office, the licensing authority, to step in. This led to the establishment of the single British Broadcasting Company, owned and operated by a consortium of major manufacturing firms. It began operations in 1922, with eight stations, and received income in the form of royalties on receiver sales (discontinued in 1924) and yearly license fees for sets. In return for the risks taken by the manufacturers, the post office agreed to have imported receivers banned from the market. For a number of reasons the private company was politically disturbing. When the House of Commons called for an investigation in 1923, the Sykes Committee recommended governmental control, but it was not accomplished until 1927. Just as Sarnoff was to rise from obscurity to dominate the development of RCA, so did John C. W. Reith, the managing director of the privately owned British Broadcasting Company, advance to develop the publicly owned British Broadcasting Corporation. In his 15 years leading the BBC ending in mid-1938, he imposed his personal values on the system, which pays at least lip service to them today, more than 60 years later. For his service he was knighted and later made a peer.

Broadcasting also got underway in other parts of the world. In Europe, a Netherlands station claims a starting date of 1919 (see p. 64), Spain started by 1921, France and the Soviet Union in 1922, Germany in 1923, Italy in 1924. By 1926 there were 170 broadcasting stations in Europe, 5 in Africa, 40 in Latin America, 10 in Asia (mainly in Japan, which had begun the government-owned NHK in 1925) and 20 scattered about Oceania, chiefly in Australia, New Zealand, and the Philippines. Broadcasting in Canada began experimentally in 1919 over a Marconi-operated transmitter in Montreal that provided regular service started in May, 1920. There were 34 privately owned Canadian stations by 1922 or 1923, and roughly 75 by 1926. The first Mexican station was established in 1921, the second opened in 1923, and by 1926 there were about 10 privately owned stations and one government-owned educational operation, started in 1924. Few sets were manufactured domestically, and few sets were imported until Mexico issued its first radio law in 1926.

In 1926, an estimated 12 1/2 million homes had radio; half of them were in the United States, which also had half the broadcast transmitters then operating—and the real growth was just around the corner.

3.9.3 Period Overview

Surprisingly, only one important precedent emerged as radio spread over the country: Broadcasting in the United States essentially was to be privately owned and commercially supported. This was a time of both program and technical experimentation. The way was paved for permanent networks, educational broadcasting had its brief fling with AM stations, the radio receiver developed from an ugly battery-powered apparatus to a handsome piece of plug-in furniture, which became more sensitive, selective, and reliable each year. Regulation, however, was a patchwork based on the 1912 Radio Act, which was never intended to cover broadcasting, and the era ended with chaos and federal helplessness.

Radio's product was new and free—once you had a receiver—and that was enough to create a tremendous nationwide boom. A similar period of excitement would occur three decades later with the initial spread of television. Radio was both a hobby for searchers for distant stations and a pastime for listeners, and program types showed that duality. Led by a few big stations, radio quickly settled into a pattern of quarter-hour and half-hour programs offered at set times. It began as an evening medium and slowly spread into daytime hours as the audience increased and program material and advertising support became available for music, variety, and talk.

The early 1920s were a period of widespread experimentation where successful trials sometimes became precedents for newer stations. It was an exciting time for workers in broadcasting and often a frustrating one for an audience that could not hear clearly or hear all it wanted. By 1926 some wondered whether the industry's lack of financial and organizational stability was bringing the radio fad to an end.

Selected Further Reading

(Alphabetical within topics. For full citations, see Appendix D.)

Barnouw (1996) offers the best social history of this period, while Archer (1938, 1939), with an RCA bias, and *The Radio Industry* (1928) providing business-oriented histories. Halper (2001) reports on early women broadcasters. Banning (1946) relates the story of WEAF's pioneering, Hettinger (1933) covers early radio advertising, Jaker, Sulek, & Kanze (1998) relate the complex story of AM radio in New York City, and Schroeder (1998) does the same for Texas. For a thorough analysis of the "oldest station" controversy, see Baudino & Kittross (1977), and for the claim of CFCF, see Godfrey (1982).

For contemporary views of radio's rise, see Jome (1925), McNamee (1926), *Radio Broadcast* (1922–30), Rothafel & Yates (1925), and Yates & Pacent (1922). Regulatory developments are found in Benjamin (2001), Bensman (2000), Federal Trade Commission (1924), Kittross (1977), McChesney (1993), Rosen (1980), annual reports of the U.S. Department of Commerce (1923, 1924, 1926) and the U.S. Department of Commerce's Bureau of Navigation, later the Radio Bureau (1921–26, 1927–32).

For the early development of radio in Great Britain, see Briggs (1961) and Pawley (1972). For Canada, see Godfrey (1982), McNeil & Wolfe (1982), and Vipond (1992); for Japan, see the two histories issued by NHK (1967, 1977). Unesco (1947–51) provides a wealth of data for these and other nations.

CHAPTER 4

THE *Screen-Grid*

RADIOLA

gives you the Reserve Power you need for modern broadcasting

RCA Radiola advertisement, 1929.

THE COMING
OF COMMERCIALISM
(1926–1933)

TIONAL BROADCASTING COMPANY, INC.

| CARD NO. 11 | New York Cleveland | Boston Chicago | Schenectady Denver | Washington San Francisco | NOVEMBER 5, 1932 |

NBC NETWORKS
SHOWING WIRE CONNECTIONS

- - - - NBC RED NETWORK
·········· NBC BLUE NETWORK
—·—·— NBC INTERCHANGEABLE RED & BLUE NETWORK GROUPS
—×—×— NBC INTERCHANGEABLE RED, BLUE & PACIFIC COAST NETWORK GROUPS
+·+·+·+ NBC PACIFIC COAST NETWORKS
+ + + + NBC PACIFIC COAST SUPPLEMENTARY GROUP
↭↭↭ RADIO FACILITIES

...ional Broadcasting Company and Associated Stations are interconnected by special wire lines for the simultaneous transmission of a radio program throughout the United States.

NBC radio network rate card, 1932.

Chapter Outline

This was a frenzied time in America—perhaps best epitomized by one man and one trend. The man was Charles A. Lindbergh, whose May 1927 solo flight from New York to Paris made him the greatest hero of his time. This country and others pressed parades and awards on him for months, and his subsequent flying exploits and personal life were always front-page news, as were more tragic events (see pp. 136 and 197).

The trend was the rising stock market, which symbolized and encouraged the spirit of progress that pervaded the country. Nearly everyone, so it seemed, was "in the market," usually buying stock on margin. In 1928, when Herbert Hoover won the presidency, films were beginning to talk, Prohibition was a joke, automobiles were competing with railroads, and airmail pilots were attempting national airline service. Navy officer Richard E. Byrd explored the Arctic and then the Antarctic, and in 1929 and 1930 the nation could hear his broadcasts from "Little America" near the South Pole. Rumors were abroad of something called television—radio programs you could see as well as hear.

Then, in late 1929, the stock market crash brought this period of expansion and excitement to a sudden stop. In a few weeks, many investors were wiped out and, more important, the nation's spirit also sank into psychological depression. In late 1930, when millions were unemployed and breadlines formed in all major cities, the Hoover administration kept saying that the economy would soon turn for the better. But 1931 and election year 1932 were even worse. On a warm night in 1932, army troops with tear gas routed World War I veteran "Bonus marchers" from their tarpaper shacks in Washington, D.C. New York Governor Franklin D. Roosevelt won the November election and swept into the White House in March, brandishing a combination of skills—including his frequent use of radio—that would help move the country out of the Depression.

The present pattern of American broadcasting was set in the years between 1926 (the end of the so-called "roaring '20s") and 1933 (the depths of the Great Depression). Modernizing of federal regulation, the rise of national networks, acceptance and success of advertising, and a phenomenal increase in the radio audience all took place in that short period. Only the years just after World War II saw changes of similar magnitude, and these were superimposed on the existing pattern rather than basically altering it. The 1926–1933 developments were more than evolutionary; they were basic directional decisions. Made by a wide variety of people, they removed broadcasting from the role of experimental novelty and made it an industry. The rapid shift from boom to crash of the economy had important effects on radio's growth and role. Most of the changes in broadcasting that took place during this period were begun before 1930, and were merely consolidated after that year, paralleling the changes in the nation's social fabric.

A good example of this consolidation was the major change in character and function of the Radio Corporation of America, then the most important single voice in the radio manufacturing and broadcasting industries. In 1930 the radio-receiver manufacturing divisions of GE and Westinghouse were absorbed by RCA, and facilities and key personnel, like television experimenter Vladimir Zworykin (see p. 161) and patent chief Otto Schairer (see p. 59), transferred from Westinghouse to RCA. However, a few months later, the federal government began to pursue antitrust prosecution recommendations, some made as early as 1923 by the FTC (see p. 74). In May 1930, the Justice Department sought to undo RCA's newly unified ownership, contending that it was an unfair monopoly in restraint of trade in the field of radio apparatus. AT&T, by then divested of RCA stock, pulled out of the arrangements with little trouble (see pp. 116–117). Over the next two and one-half years, lawyers tried to figure out ways for GE and Westinghouse to ease out of RCA control and manufacturing agreements without harming any of the firms irreparably. Finally, in November 1932, they worked out a compromise acceptable to the Justice Department, and a consent decree was issued. GE and Westinghouse had a short transition period in which to divest themselves of RCA stock and get their representatives off the RCA board. Exclusive license agreements made from 1919 to 1921 (see pp. 58–63) became nonexclusive. GE and Westinghouse could not compete with RCA for two years, after which they could manufacture and sell their own radio receivers. RCA was to program radio stations owned by the two other firms for a decade, a boon to its subsidiary, NBC. RCA became a totally independent manufacturing, selling, international communications, and broadcasting concern, separate for the first time since its formation from GE (but see p. 512), Westinghouse (but see p. 617), AT&T, and other firms. As a convenience, it also continued to administer the patents pool, now nonexclusive. Although little noticed at the time, this agreement had major effects in the 1930s.

4.1 Technology: Better Sound and Early Television

By the late 1920s, technical changes in radio broadcasting were evolutionary rather than basic. They had to do mostly with improving the poor quality of transmitted sound and the elimination or lessening of over-the-air static. At the same time, reports began to reach the public of laboratory developments that were to eventuate in television. Breathless accounts of "television around the corner" began to show up regularly in the press.

4.1.1 Improvement of Sound

By the late 1920s, radio transmitters could send out a clean signal that would stay on its assigned frequency, and directional antennae that would limit interference with nearby stations were to be designed in later years. At the *studio*, however, the earlier standard of the telephone, capable of adequate voice but very poor music reproduction, was no longer acceptable.

In planning studios, new stations were beginning to rely on architects to improve sound quality instead of using cut-and-try burlap-covered walls. The carbon microphone, with its narrow frequency response and habit of freezing up for sibilant sounds, began to give way in the 1930s to the condenser, which had survived 10 years of testing, and the still–most–common dynamic microphones, both of which made radio talk and music sound more real because of their better frequency response.

Throughout the 1920s, radio stations generally presented music "live," or used regular, home-variety 78-rpm records, which had very poor frequency response and played for only three or four minutes a side. In 1929, WOR became one of the first stations to use electrical transcriptions: 33 1/3-rpm discs, which were as large as 16 inches in diameter and played for 15 minutes a side. (*Microgroove* LPs, which pretty much disappeared in the 1980s, had higher quality and played for a longer time at that speed.) These first transcriptions were substantially the same as those used for the earliest sound motion pictures, when silent films were synchronized to disc recordings in the projection booth. This new kind of recording made programming more flexible and improved sound, and more than 100 stations regularly began to use transcriptions, some received from program syndicators.

All attempts to broadcast better sound were limited by what the station could produce and transmit, the network carry on its lines, and the home set receive and reproduce. By 1933 the typical station transmitter could transmit an audio-frequency bandwidth of at least 3,750 cycles per second—the necessary radio-frequency bandwidth is exactly twice as much, or 7,500 Hz—and the best transmitters were capable of 5,000 Hz audio (10 kHz radio bandwidth). Low-frequency limits on transmission were in the 30 to 50 Hz range. Essentially the same bandwidth (30 to 5,000 Hz) is used today in standard (AM) broadcasting, although (a) a few stations take advantage of an FCC regulation that permits them to use a wider bandwidth if they do not adversely affect other stations and (b) at one time a number of "high-fidelity" stations in the 1,500 to 1,600 kHz band were allowed to transmit 10,000 Hz audio. Although all these standards seem inadequate, considering that the young human ear can hear up to 20,000 cycles or higher, 5,000 Hz sounds quite real compared to the 2,500 Hz bandwidth of a regular telephone instrument and circuit. Indeed, the main limitation on good network sound was the inability of AT&T lines to carry more than 4,000 Hz tones. The use of specially engineered lines overcame this difficulty but at considerable expense to the broadcaster. The home receiver typically lagged behind the studio and transmission facilities. Its audio had a tinny sound and rarely reproduced the higher and the lower portions of the audio spectrum. Unfortunately for the innovators of FM radio (see pp. 156–160) and true high-fidelity music reproduction systems, the public became very used to this "radio sound," which was, in all fairness, better than the hand-wound acoustic Victrola phonograph or the telephone.

4.1.2 Technological Prehistory of Television

Although television in the form of mechanical scanning systems (see Appendix B) was developed in the 1920s, it had a long history. One popular history of television (Hubbell) claims that the story goes back 4,000 years, but modern development started with the 1873 discovery by Joseph May and Willoughby Smith that the element selenium was capable of producing small amounts of electricity in direct response to the amount of light falling on it. Later inventors, such as George R. Carey in 1877, found that banks of selenium cells, placed in a mosaic analogous to the human eye and wired individually, could send the elements of a picture as electrical signals from each cell simultaneously to a bank of lamps that lit in response to the electricity. In 1880, Maurice Leblanc and others developed the principle of scanning, or viewing picture elements successively, rather than all at once as in a mosaic device, and transmitting them sequentially over a single circuit. This approach was analogous to the solution of the similar problem faced by the telegraph industry at its start (see pp. 9–10). A major refinement was the mechanical device—the mirror drum and, in 1883, Paul Nipkow's scanning disc—capable of scanning and transmitting even a moving picture. (See Appendix B under "Television's Early Technological Development").

4.1.3 Development of Mechanical Television

Of the many who worked on mechanical television in the 1920s, three made outstanding progress: Herbert E. Ives of Bell Telephone Laboratories, who worked with all the resources of a major corporation; John Logie Baird, a self-taught Scottish inventor whose system almost became the British standard; and Charles Francis Jenkins, an American whose "radio movies" ran neck and neck with Baird.

Ives was assigned, with substantial funds and staff, to keep AT&T "abreast of the general advances in the art of television." From research on wire-photo transmission in 1923 and 1924, his work culminated in 1927 with wire transmissions of still and moving pictures over hundreds of miles. In one example, Secretary of Commerce Herbert Hoover spoke over a circuit from Washington to New York and was viewed on a 2 × 2 1/2-foot neon-tube screen. In this April 7, 1927, demonstration, the picture was low definition—50 lines, compared to today's 525—but had synchronized sound. By the next year, outdoor scenes could be picked up and a three-channel color system was demonstrated. Bell Labs never promoted its system commercially, being content to keep "abreast of the art" with an eye eventually to interconnecting television stations. These experiments also generated Picturephone service, which AT&T has trotted out of the lab at intervals from 1927 to the present.

Baird (not to be confused with Hollis S. Baird, an American television experimenter) generally is credited with establishing television in Great Britain. In 1923, using a mechanical scanning system of his own design, he transmitted the first silhouette television picture by wire—almost simultaneously with Jenkins (see the box below). In 1925 both men transmitted

---

▥ Eyewitness Accounts of the First Television   The first public demonstration of television was conducted in January 1926 in London by John Logie Baird.

The proof of Baird's achievement came on Tuesday, January 26. During the evening some forty members of the Royal Institution and other guests gathered at 22 Frith Street to see what the inventor had to offer. Besides Baird and Hutchinson, the only other "official" host was W. C. Fox, a Press Association journalist and friend of Baird. Fox greeted the visitors, who were allowed to enter the cluttered rooms in small groups after they signed a register. He recalls the event:

> It was a cold January night and the members of the Royal Institution arrived in twos and threes. When they came out after the demonstration their remarks, such as I overheard, were much as one would expect. Some thought it was nothing worth consideration; others considered it the work of a young man who did not know what he was doing, while a few, a very few, thought there was something there capable of development. There was no realisation of the fact that they had been present at the birth of a new science.

Fox was at the head of the stairs on this occasion, but Baird had given him a personal demonstration a few days earlier:

> The received image was admittedly crude, but it was recognisable as—whatever it might be—a face, a vase of flowers, a book opened and shut, or some simple article of every day life. The image received was pinkish in colour and tended to swing up and down. It was not possible to see much of the apparatus as it was covered by screens of one sort and another—extraneous light was not wanted and would interfere with the image.

A short, factual account of the demonstration appeared in *The Times* two days later. The reporter described the transmitting machine and the results:

> . . . consisting of a large wooden revolving disk containing lenses, behind which was a revolving shutter and a light sensitive cell. The head of a ventriloquist's doll was manipulated as the image to be transmitted, though the human face was also reproduced. First on a receiver in the same room as the transmitter and then on a portable receiver in another room, the visitors were shown recognizable reception of the movements of the dummy and of a person speaking. The image as transmitted was faint and often blurred, but substantiated a claim that through the "Televisor," as Mr. Baird has named his apparatus, it is possible to transmit and reproduce instantly the details of movement, and such things as the play of expression on the face.

Source: Shiers, George. (Fall 1975). "Television 50 Years Ago," *Journal of Broadcasting*, 19, 393–394. By permission.

moving silhouettes, and in 1926 Baird succeeded in producing shades of gray. Turning next to live action scenes, in February 1928 he televised a woman's image from London to Hartsdale, New York, using the shortwave band to achieve that distance. Later that year he transmitted to the liner *Berengaria* a thousand miles at sea, and in 1932, foreshadowing today's large-scale closed-circuit transmissions of sports events, he transmitted the Derby horserace to a London movie theater where 4,000 persons watched the race. Alexanderson had conducted a similar demonstration in Schenectady in 1930 and later at a Brooklyn theater. Many individuals and small firms constructed Baird "Televisors," as the television receivers were called.

In 1935, when the Television Committee of the British government had to choose television standards for the United Kingdom, comparative tests were held of the Baird mechanical system, which included some components based on Philo Farnsworth's work in Philadelphia, and an electronic system controlled by the giant EMI (Electric and Musical Industries Ltd.) company based partly on Zworykin's work in the United States (see pp. 161–165). The committee decided in favor of the latter because they believed that Baird's system, although it tested well, was near the end of its potential development, while the electronic system could be improved considerably. Although greatly disappointed, Baird stayed in the field. In December 1941 he demonstrated improved color and stereoscopic three-dimensional television, areas he had worked in since 1928.

Jenkins, who invented a variety of devices based on drum and disc scanners, gave the first public U.S. demonstration of mechanical picture transmission in 1923 when he transmitted, by wireless, a photograph of President Harding from Washington to Philadelphia. From still silhouettes in 1923, Jenkins went to moving silhouettes, and then motion pictures, over Navy station NOF in Washington, in 1925. His equipment was not as well engineered as Ives', but he was a good publicist and aroused interest among amateurs and other experimenters. His system could transmit limited motion, achieving about 60 lines resolution at its best, compared to Ives' 48 lines and the 525 lines currently used in the United States. Claiming an amateur viewing audience of thousands, he organized the Jenkins Television Company in 1929 to manufacture both transmitting and receiving apparatus. The company announced commercial programs for 1930 and licensed other manufacturers to use its patents, but it could not make a profit selling expensive novelties during the Depression and quickly went into receivership. The De Forest Company purchased its assets, selling them in turn to RCA. Allen B. DuMont, chief engineer of the De Forest firm, became interested in television as a result, and later became a manufacturer of cathode-ray tubes and other television equipment and a television broadcasting entrepreneur (see p. 290).

The scanning disc in many different forms held sway for roughly 50 years of television experimentation. Although mechanical scanning could be improved, mechanical problems increased with every increase in picture definition. However, these investigations led to useful and practical

■ **Vaudeville Faces Television**   Famous producer Flo Ziegfeld (right) looks into a Charles Francis Jenkins mechanical television receiver in 1928. From his expression, it may be that he did not think television was the show business medium of the future.

Smithsonian Institution Photo No. 76-14655.

results. Arthur Korn's 1902 facsimile experiments led to developments in television. In the late 1940s, CBS used the spinning disc principle for a system of color television (see pp. 253 and 321) and that system was modified to send the first color transmissions from the moon to earth.

4.1.4 Television Goes Public

The television that promoters touted around 1930 was a collection of uncoordinated and incompatible systems. The Federal Radio Commission did little to establish television standards; perhaps it preferred to imitate the development of AM radio's equipment standards, which had evolved with a minimum of government supervision. To provide for orderly development of television, the Radio Manufacturers Association in 1931 set non-mandatory standards at 48 lines and 15 pictures per second, with a secondary standard of 60 lines for more advanced research efforts. These standards were set somewhat below the most advanced state of the art, presumably for the benefit of promoters, inventors, and manufacturers who were impatient to introduce television commercially. Pressure for high standards in the 1920s and early 1930s might have been heavier had it not been possible, with a little adjustment, to receive signals from a station using one mechanical scanning system on a receiver designed for a different system.

However, with the advent of rival electronic camera and complex synchronization systems in the mid-1930s (see p. 160) the lock-and-key aspect of
television standards became operative; no electronic commercial television
system would succeed until the government determined, or the whole industry adopted, common standards.

When early television experimenters were trying signal transmission by
radio, they had little trouble obtaining frequencies. Nearly the entire spectrum above the standard broadcast (AM) band, then ending at 1,500 kHz,
was available, although techniques for transmitting at these high frequencies generally were not then known. An associate of one experimenter complained that during the 1920s "there were no usable radio channels broad
enough to carry the television signal required for adequate detail in the received image." Accordingly, in 1928, the FRC made the first provisions for
television—*within* the standard broadcast band. Since these 10 kHz-wide
channels were of no practical use to television, the allocation was changed
to five 100 kHz-wide channels in the 2 to 3 MHz band. Despite the wider
channels, some promoters agitated in 1929 for the return of visual broadcasting to the AM band, where transmission characteristics and equipment
were familiar. This move was successfully opposed by radio broadcasters,
networks, and manufacturers. Although transmissions on the 2 MHz band
could travel thousands of miles, the FRC maintained at a 1930 television
conference (a) that the pressure of other services and the need for a wider
band-width for all-electronic scanning and higher definition would soon
force television from that band and (b) that, to expand successfully, television would have to enter the largely uncharted spectrum above 30 MHz.
This logical conclusion was taken seriously, and many experimenters and
manufacturers started to investigate the properties and the implications of
use of the VHF frequencies.

The willingness of speculators to back television in the late 1920s and
the 1929 pleading with the FRC for television space on AM channels were
not altruistic. Promoters saw television as the next great get-rich-quick opportunity. Pamphlets and magazines carried flamboyant articles urging the
general public to "get on the bandwagon" and exaggerated claims of television's spread. They implied that experimental television stations (18 of
them in cities such as Chicago, Boston, New York, and Detroit by 1931)
were broadcast stations serving the public and quoted often questionable
surveys indicating far more television receiving sets in homes than other
sources estimated. Jenkins alone claimed an audience of "some 25,000
lookers-in scattered throughout the States."

Programming was sketchy. A New York newspaper carried weekly program listings of four New York stations and one in Boston that largely presented test patterns and inexpensive or free motion picture short subjects for
irregular brief periods. But attempts at more imaginative programming
began early with a production of *The Queen's Messenger*, an old melodrama,
over the GE station in Schenectady, New York, on September 11, 1928.

Although television seemed to be imminent, opposition by larger radio broadcasters and manufacturers delayed its arrival and then the Depression dried up capital. The Depression also gave radio broadcasting a chance to expand its audience and profits, accumulating funds for later investment in television, and gave manufacturers time to learn more about electronic television.

4.2 Stations: Structure and Stagnation

The number of radio broadcasting stations on the air declined from a high of 681 in 1927 to a low of 599 in 1933. While the Depression was a major factor beginning in 1932–1933, as business generally slowed down and advertising-based radio followed, a glance at the numbers (see Appendix C, table 1) shows that the major decline took place in 1928 and 1929 *before* the Depression began. The number of educational stations also fell from the 1927 total of 100 as schools could no longer afford them.

This decline was due not so much to economic factors as to the establishment of the Federal Radio Commission (FRC) in 1927 (see pp. 141–143). The FRC's first accomplishment was to lessen interference, which had become acute after the 1926 *Zenith* decision (see pp. 97–98), by setting up a classification system that distinguished stations by type and service, reassigned many stations, and eliminated portable, low-power fringe operations. By late 1928 there was much less interference and the quality of the remaining stations was improved by requirements for 100% modulation, crystal frequency control, and the like. Nighttime interference (see Appendix B, under Allocation, Assignments, Licensing) was reduced largely by forcing stations to curtail operating hours and use lower power at night. These decisions now had the force of law, and the FRC could revoke a broadcasting license—a power that Secretary of Commerce Hoover lacked earlier in the decade. The elimination of channel jumping and unauthorized power changes soon brought stability. The Federal courts consistently upheld the FRC, establishing a firm legal base for its subsequent decisions.

Another development of this period was a steady increase in station transmitting power. Not only was higher power seen as a way of overcoming natural static, but also, as more stations came on the air, it became necessary just for a station to be heard. Where, in 1927, 28% of all stations used less than 100 watts, six years later only 3% were as low as 100 watts. Where in 1927 only three stations were using the 30,000-watt maximum, by 1933, 22 stations were using 50,000 watts, the limit for AM stations established in 1928 and still in effect today (see p. 171). Stations WGY in Schenectady (General Electric), WEAF, New York (RCA–NBC), and KDKA, Pittsburgh (Westinghouse), were among the first stations to transmit at the new power limit in 1928. In smaller communities, however, power ratings of 250 and 500 watts were the norm, with some using even less. Some man-made interference, often caused by oscillating receivers, and lots of natural static still plagued radio, but FRC regulatory actions had lessened it.

Both regulation and the trend toward more power and better equipment led to higher operating costs for nearly all stations. This increased economic burden, coming just before and during the Depression, brought about important changes in station ownership. The typical small operators of the 1920s, in some instances running 5- and 10-watt stations in their homes or garages for a couple of hours a week, could not meet the costs of improving equipment and paying for programming as well as other increasing demands on time, energy, and money. Many hobbyists and other shakily financed operators were forced off the air; many educational stations crumbled. In their places came the commercial broadcasting companies, groups of people in business solely to operate radio stations. Not gone, but declining numerically, were the laundries, hotels, department stores, and restaurants that had operated broadcasting stations as a sideline. Only in the smaller cities and towns did radio bring the carefree aspect of its first years into the 1930s. In bigger cities, business methods and operators were converting it into an advertising-based, money-making industry.

Newspaper ownership of radio stations grew from approximately 5% of all stations in the mid-1920s to 13% by 1933. Newspapers were both hedging their bets in news communications competition and seeking prestige by having a hand in the new enterprise. Typical were the *Milwaukee Journal*, which had reported on the growth of radio in the early 1920s, purchased station KWAF in 1927 for its frequency assignment, junked its equipment, and gone on the air with new equipment and higher power in mid-1927 as WTMJ (*The Milwaukee Journal*); and the *Chicago Tribune*, which in 1924 took over a station that had had three owners in two years and renamed it WGN (*World's Greatest Newspaper*).

4.3 The Rise of National Networks

The national chains developed in the late 1920s from temporary and experimental networks put together earlier in the decade (see p. 77). They were to affect radio development more than any organization other than the federal government.

4.3.1 Creation of NBC

The network of stations based on AT&T-owned WEAF in New York operated successfully while the Telephone Group and Radio Group were negotiating in 1925 and 1926 (see p. 74). In May 1926, AT&T made its broadcast properties a semi-independent subsidiary, both to pressure the Radio Group into granting more concessions to AT&T on matters other than broadcasting and to prepare for the expected purchase of their stations by

RCA. Announcement of initial agreement in July 1926 caused consternation among the closely knit staff at WEAF, and numerous problems developed in merging the operations and personnel of Radio Group station WJZ and Telephone Group station WEAF. The following month, RCA absorbed WCAP, Washington, which had been sharing time with RCA's WRC. On September 9, RCA formed a new corporation, the National Broadcasting Company (NBC), with ownership held by RCA (50%), GE (30%), and Westinghouse (20%), naming as president Merlin H. Aylesworth, former managing director of the National Electric Light Association—who did not even own a radio at the time. On November 1, NBC turned over a check for $1 million, which consummated the purchase of WEAF, took AT&T out of the broadcasting business, and firmly established NBC. Partly to broaden public interest plans for the network-to-be, and partly for public relations, NBC appointed an advisory council of 12 (later 19) distinguished Americans to advise it on programming. This committee, proving to be more valuable for its public relations and publicity contributions than for its real effect on network operations, was disbanded a decade later, without fanfare.

The network era was inaugurated the night of November 15, 1926, with a program presented live—as were all network programs until the late 1940s—before 1,000 guests in the Grand Ballroom of the Waldorf-Astoria Hotel in New York. Aylesworth was master of ceremonies for the four-hour program, which originated in the ballroom with singers, orchestras, comedy teams and from *remote* pickups in other cities—a singer in Chicago, Will Rogers from Kansas City. Newspapers reported that this extravaganza cost $50,000 to produce, half for talent and the rest mostly for technical arrangements, but Aylesworth later admitted that most of the talent appeared free in return for publicity. Twenty-one affiliates and four other stations carried the show, which was heard as far west as Kansas City. The stations, most of them independently owned but formerly affiliated with the old AT&T network, were connected by 3,600 miles of special telephone wire.

In the same period, NBC took over operation of RCA's WJZ in New York as the base for a second network, which would incorporate the old Radio Group network. In December the second network was announced, and, on January 1, 1927, it joined the WEAF-based network in a broadcast of Graham McNamee's play-by-play coverage of the Rose Bowl game between Stanford and Alabama. The WJZ-based network's first coast-to-coast hookup had only six affiliates. The WEAF-based chain became known as the Red network, and the WJZ-based chain as the Blue. How this came about is not clear, but some say that AT&T engineers kept the network routings straight on a map by coloring the circuits for one red and the other blue.

In April 1927 NBC started the Pacific Coast Network, stretching from Los Angeles to Seattle, based on stations KGO and KPO in San Francisco, and primarily organized for sales rather than for programming. It lasted only until late 1928, when NBC began full-time coast-to-coast programming on both Red and Blue.

■ **An Era Begins (1926)**

Announcing the

National Broadcasting Company, Inc.

National radio broadcasting with better programs permanently assured by this important action of the *Radio Corporation of America* in the interest of the listening public

THE RADIO CORPORATION OF AMERICA is the largest distributor of radio receiving sets in the world. It handles the entire output in this field of the Westinghouse and General Electric factories.

It does not say this boastfully. It does not say it with apology. It says it for the purpose of making clear the fact that it is more largely interested, more selfishly interested, if you please, in the best possible broadcasting in the United States than anyone else.

Radio for 26,000,000 Homes

The market for receiving sets in the future will be determined largely by the quantity and quality of the programs broadcast.

We say quantity because they must be diversified enough so that some of them will appeal to all possible listeners.

We say quality because each program must be the best of its kind. If that ideal were to be reached, no home in the United States could afford to be without a radio receiving set.

Today the best available statistics indicate that 5,000,000 homes are equipped, and 21,000,000 homes remain to be supplied.

Radio receiving sets of the best reproductive quality should be made available for all, and we hope to make them cheap enough so that all may buy.

The day has gone by when the radio receiving set is a plaything. It must now be an instrument of service.

WEAF Purchased for $1,000,000

The Radio Corporation of America, therefore, is interested, just as the public is, in having the most adequate programs broadcast. It is interested, as the public is, in having them comprehensive and free from discrimination.

Any use of radio transmission which causes the public to feel that the quality of the programs is not the highest, that the use of radio is not the broadest and best use in the public interest, that it is used for political advantage or selfish power, will be detrimental to the public interest in radio, and therefore to the Radio Corporation of America.

To insure, therefore, the development of this great service, the Radio Corporation of America has purchased for one million dollars station WEAF from the American Telephone and Telegraph Company, that company having decided to retire from the broadcasting business.

The Radio Corporation of America will assume active control of that station on November 15.

National Broadcasting Company Organized

The Radio Corporation of America has decided to incorporate that station, which has achieved such a deservedly high reputation for the quality and character of its programs, under the name of the National Broadcasting Company, Inc.

The Purpose of the New Company

The purpose of that company will be to provide the best program available for broadcasting in the United States.

The National Broadcasting Company will not only broadcast these programs through station WEAF, but it will make them available to other broadcasting stations throughout the country so far as it may be practicable to do so, and they may desire to take them.

It is hoped that arrangements may be made so that every event of national importance may be broadcast widely throughout the United States.

No Monopoly of the Air

The Radio Corporation of America is not in any sense seeking a monopoly of the air. That would be a liability rather than an asset. It is seeking, however, to provide machinery which will insure a national distribution of national programs, and a wider distribution of programs of the highest quality.

If others will engage in this business the Radio Corporation of America will welcome their action, whether it be cooperative or competitive.

If other radio manufacturing companies, competitors of the Radio Corporation of America, wish to use the facilities of the National Broadcasting Company for the purpose of making known to the public their receiving sets, they may do so on the same terms as accorded to other clients.

The necessity of providing adequate broad-

casting is apparent. The problem of finding the best means of doing it is yet experimental. The Radio Corporation of America is making this experiment in the interest of the art and the furtherance of the industry.

A Public Advisory Council

In order that the National Broadcasting Company may be advised as to the best type of program, that discrimination may be avoided, that the public may be assured that the broadcasting is being done in the fairest and best way, always allowing for human frailties and human performance, it has created an Advisory Council, composed of twelve members, to be chosen as representative of various shades of public opinion, which will from time to time give it the benefit of their judgment and suggestion. The members of this Council will be announced as soon as their acceptance shall have been obtained.

M. H. Aylesworth to be President

The President of the new National Broadcasting Company will be M. H. Aylesworth, for many years Managing Director of the National Electric Light Association. He will perform the executive and administrative duties of the corporation.

Mr. Aylesworth, while not hitherto identified with the radio industry or broadcasting, has had public experience as Chairman of the Colorado Public Utilities Commission, and, through his work with the association which represents the electrical industry, has a broad understanding of the technical problems which measure the pace of broadcasting.

One of his major responsibilities will be to see that the operations of the National Broadcasting Company reflect enlightened public opinion, which expresses itself so promptly the morning after any error of taste or judgment or departure from fair play.

We have no hesitation in recommending the National Broadcasting Company to the people of the United States.

It will need the help of all listeners. It will make mistakes. If the public will make known its views to the officials of the company from time to time, we are confident that the new broadcasting company will be an instrument of great public service.

RADIO CORPORATION OF AMERICA

OWEN D. YOUNG, *Chairman of the Board*

JAMES G. HARBORD, *President*

In October 1927 headquarters of NBC and operations for both WEAF-Red and WJZ-Blue were moved to new quarters at 711 Fifth Avenue. Eight studios, four of them two stories high, with elaborate sound-proofing, allowed simultaneous broadcasting, recording, and rehearsal. Since the studios were tightly sealed from one another and from their own control rooms, special air conditioning had to be installed.

In May 1930, with the short-lived unification of GE–Westinghouse–RCA interests, RCA took over full control of NBC operations. Two years later RCA gained complete ownership when NBC became one of the corporate entities that it retained after a 1932 antitrust consent decree separated the radio manufacturers. Within five years of its establishment, NBC was planning to move its operations into Radio City, a central building in the new Rockefeller Center complex in midtown New York City. Indeed, this expression of confidence, in the middle of the Depression, caused the name Radio City frequently to be applied to the entire center. People still remembered with nostalgia the dizzying heights to which RCA stock (called "Radio" on Wall Street) had climbed before the Depression—and to which it didn't rise again until well after World War II. The new headquarters in the 70-story RCA Building were occupied late in 1933, combining almost all New York operational facilities of NBC, except the transmitter of the New York station. Now that GE owns RCA, the building name has changed, but many New Yorkers still refer to the complex as "Radio City."

By 1933, NBC owned 10 stations outright, seven using 50,000 watts and all but one licensed for unlimited time operation. There were two stations each in the cities of New York (WEAF, later known as WRCA and now WNBC; and WJZ, later WABC), Chicago (WMAQ and WENR), San Francisco (KPO and KGO), and Washington (WRC and WMAL) plus one station each in Denver (KOA, later sold) and Cleveland (WTAM, later WKYC). In a city with two owned-and-operated (O & O) stations, one would be affiliated with the Red Network, the other with the Blue. Besides their O & O stations, the networks had affiliations with many independently owned stations, some of which contracted (affiliated) with one of the two networks and some of which joined either network for a particular broadcast depending on demand from the advertisers, the network, or the station. In 1927, 22 stations were affiliated with the Red Network, and 6 with the Blue, for a total of nearly 7% of all stations. By 1933, Red had 28, Blue had 24, and 36 were supplemental; these 88 stations constituted nearly 15% of all stations at that time. Although the two networks were of similar size, NBC-Red had the pick of stations and programs and far more advertising income (see Appendix C, table 2-C). Having two affiliates in each of most large cities also gave NBC an advantage over independent stations and competitive networks. By programming one affiliate against the other and by engaging in competitive price cutting that few independent stations could afford, NBC developed a strong lead in the industry—a role that became the focus of an important investigation a few years later (see pp. 172 and 210).

4.3.2 CBS Develops

The birth of NBC's major competitor, the Columbia Broadcasting System, Inc., was far more complicated and drawn out. It probably began at the fourth convention of the National Association of Broadcasters in September 1926 when promoter George A. Coats, speaking before 25 to 30 delegates, called for a broadcasting program bureau as a way of lessening the industry's reliance on ASCAP music (see p. 99). Within a month (which also saw the announcement of NBC) one of the audience, Arthur Judson, had organized the Judson Radio Program Corporation in New York. As business manager of the Philadelphia Orchestra, and with good contacts throughout the entertainment field, he hoped to sell cooperative booking of talent to the NBC networks. But NBC turned him down, and Judson considered establishing a rival radio network.

Late in January 1927, when both NBC networks were operating, Judson and three other stockholders, including Coats, formed the United Independent Broadcasters, Inc. Like NBC, the company's purpose was to purchase time on radio stations, sell this time to advertisers, and provide programming. Coats and another stockholder accomplished the first aim when they negotiated with Dr. Leon Levy, owner of WCAU in Philadelphia, a weekly price of $500 for 10 hours of station time. Soon, they had 12 prospective affiliates—with WOR, which covered the New York area from its Newark, New Jersey, location, as the key station—for a total commitment of $6,000 a week. The network had no income as yet, and no figures for the costs of AT&T-supplied wire connections and programming material. The shaky condition of this "paper network" led AT&T to deny line service to UIB for fear that it would be unable to pay its bills.

Now came a series of providential rescues. A rumor was flying in the phonograph industry that RCA was going to merge with the Victor Talking Machine Company, then in desperate straits because of obsolescent recording technology and radio competition. (The two firms did merge, in early 1929.) Hearing the rumor, Victor's chief competitor, the Columbia Phonograph Corporation, became interested in a possible merger with UIB. This situation was analogous to the financial "raid" on Western Union in the late 1870s (see p. 12). The scenario in 1927 was different. UIB, with 16 signed-up stations, now had commitments of $8,000 a week just for time. On April 5, 1927, the record company and UIB merged resources, while retaining separate corporate identities, and created the Columbia Phonograph Broadcasting System, Inc. The agreement gave the network $163,000 in cash to start operations. In return, the record firm gained some operational control over the radio network, stealing a march on its rival, and gained the station–network identification title that it hoped would sell Columbia phonographs and records.

During the summer, CPBS secured AT&T line service and finally, after nearly a year of gestation and several postponed opening dates, went on the air September 25, 1927, with a broadcast of *The King's Henchman from the Metropolitan Opera*, with composer–critic Deems Taylor as narrator. The network's problems were reflected in the debut program, which, besides its postponements, was afflicted halfway through by a violent thunderstorm, adding electrical static to financial concern. The Judson Radio Program Corporation, which had retained that part of the business, was supposed to provide programs, and UIB had to pay stations for time, whether or not there was a sponsor to cover costs. After losing $100,000 in the first month, the record company opted out of the merger, and again the fledgling network seemed to have reached the end of its string.

Arthur Judson went to WCAU owner Levy for help. Levy and his brother, in turn, while purchasing some shares, persuaded millionaire sportsman Jerome H. Louchheim to buy control of UIB, in spite of a negative reaction from Louchheim's lawyer. With the added funds, UIB was able to guarantee payments to the telephone company for several months. On November 19, Columbia Phonograph Broadcasting System became plain Columbia Broadcasting System, with UIB and CBS briefly existing side-by-side to operate the radio network. One of UIB's key officials, pioneer announcer J. Andrew White, even persuaded the affiliate stations to take a lower weekly guarantee for their 10 hours in order to give CBS a chance.

However, CBS losses continued as advertisers flocked to the increasingly successful NBC. Louchheim and the Levys advanced money as it was needed for operation, and more shares of stock were issued to them to cover their advances. After a couple of months, the new backers got cold feet and offered the controlling interest in CBS–UIB for sale.

A purchaser was already on the scene. In one of its first time sales, CBS had contracted with the Congress Cigar Company of Philadelphia, through the latter's young vice president, William S. Paley, son of the firm's owner, for a series of 26 programs to advertise La Palina cigars. The show started in 1928, and in short order there were highly satisfactory results. On September 28, 1928, Paley, with his own money and money from his family, bought a controlling interest in CBS for approximately $300,000. He planned to take a six-month leave of absence from the cigar company, get CBS–UIB in better shape, and then go back to selling cigars. He changed his mind in only three weeks—and ran CBS for nearly half a century, stepping down as chief executive only in the spring of 1977. Additional family investments, including $400,000 for flagship station WABC (now WCBS) in New York in December 1929, brought the total to $1.5 million, but Paley created a business worth hundreds of times what his family paid for it, largely through his ability as a negotiator, first with affiliates and then with the stars that made CBS programming famous (see pp. 172 and 297).

Paley's first change was to merge the two existing networks into one—Columbia Broadcasting System, Inc. He sold stock to get badly needed liquid reserves. Then, contracts with affiliated stations were changed in

March 1929 so that the network paid stations $50 for each hour actually used rather than $500 a week for 10 hours regardless of whether it was used, and the stations paid the network for sustaining (nonsponsored) programs, which they often sold to local sponsors. This way, it was felt, both stations and network would be lowering their financial sights until the operation was on its feet. Paley retained Judson and White as program advisers.

In September 1929, just a year after Paley had taken over, CBS moved into the top 10 floors of 485 Madison Avenue, where it remained until the mid-1960s. Another sure sign of success was the increased number of its affiliated stations from 17 (4% of all stations) in 1928 to 91 (nearly 16% of all stations) in 1933 (see Appendix C, table 2-A).

The CBS network, like both NBC networks, depended on its stable of owned-and-operated (O & O) stations for major and predictable income. By 1933 CBS owned seven stations, one each in New York (WABC, later named WCBS), Washington (WJSV, later sold), Cincinnati (WKRC, later sold), Chicago (WBBM), Charlotte, North Carolina (WBT, later sold), Minneapolis (WCCO, later sold), and St. Louis (KMOX). All these stations operated unlimited time and were broadcasting with 50,000 watts of power by the early 1930s.

4.4 The Decline of Educational AM Radio

Although more than 200 educational AM stations had been started in the early 1920s, almost all of them had left the air by the end of the decade. Their problems began in 1925, mainly because of financial pressures on the schools (increasing greatly during the Depression), school administrators' indecision and lack of purpose and interest, and share-time commercial broadcasters' efforts to gain air time and stifle competition for listeners. Under this load, educational stations dropped out at an increasing rate after 1926. Added factors were the cost of providing programming and making major technical improvements in order to meet the FRC requirements of 1927 and 1928 (see pp. 141–145). Some educational stations were sold to commercial interests that promised to air educational programs, a few converted to commercial operation, and most simply went off the air. Even with a handful of new stations early in the 1926–1933 period, the number of operating educational standard broadcast stations dropped steadily from 98 in 1927 (approximately 13% of all stations) to 43 in 1933 (about 7%).

The possible benefits from using radio as a teacher were not recognized at first. Schools' money went in other budgetary directions because of a shortage of trained and interested personnel and lack of support from administrators. Besides the high costs of upgrading facilities to meet FRC technical standards, the FRC's 1927 through 1929 reallocations and elimination of marginal stations (see p. 143) often gave channels to commercial operators at the expense of educational institutions. Commercial stations had more lobbying clout and, in many cases, appeared to be more stable. Commercial stations sometimes promised free time to educational institutions if the school's educational station would go off the air—and then forgot their promises once they were in control.

Concern for their dwindling numbers and interest in new ways of using radio effectively led radio educators to form national groups. In mid-1929, the Advisory Committee on Education by Radio started with backing from the Payne Fund, the Carnegie Endowment, and J.C. Penney, but it died before 1930 without having had much effect. In 1930, two rival organizations appeared that would represent educational radio for 10 years: the National Advisory Council on Radio in Education and the National Committee on Education by Radio. The *Council* worked with grants from the Rockefeller Foundation and Carnegie Endowment and called for time on commercial stations to meet educators' needs. The *Committee*, with support from the Payne Fund, asked that nonprofit educational operations fill 15% of all frequency assignments (more than twice the existing proportion), attacked "commercial monopolies," and disagreed with the "halfway" measures of the Council.

The controversy over educational radio's predicament led, in 1932, to a Senate-mandated survey of educational programs on both commercial and noncommercial stations. Having carefully timed their survey for National Education Week, when commercial stations typically scheduled educational programs, the FRC found that commercial stations were adequately filling educational needs. Congress was not yet convinced (see pp. 175–177), and in 1933 12 of the few remaining educational stations began to take advertising to meet costs and cover ASCAP music licensing fees.

Although educational stations' future looked bleak, radio still performed educational functions. Beginning in early 1929, the Payne Fund supported daily *Ohio School of the Air* broadcasts on commercial station WLW for in-school listening. The Ohio legislature appropriated money for some production—in the studios of WOSU, Ohio State University's station—of this series of instructional programs with related teacher guides and pupil materials. It later moved to WOSU. Another early primary/secondary educational series for classroom listening was the *Wisconsin School of the Air*, which began on university-owned WHA in Fall 1931. WHA started a *College of the Air* two years later. National commercial networks also regularly scheduled some educational programs.

During the years 1927 to 1933, many educators, acutely aware of their lost opportunities, searched for other broadcast outlets, debated the issue nationally, and scrambled for local funds and facilities. Despite problems of money and policy, educational radio's champions kept its foothold in American broadcasting.

4.5 Depression Radio Advertising

In the Depression, and partly because of it, advertising became the accepted means of support for stations and the expanding networks. Advertisers turned to radio even while retrenching in other media purchases, because radio's audience grew larger and more loyal even as it had less money for other leisure-time pursuits. Large stations and the networks began to make high profits, paving the way for new programs and more promotion.

4.5.1 Advertising Becomes King

Radio became an accepted medium of mass advertising in 1928 because:

- Coast-to-coast network coverage made programs available to 80% of the nation's homes, although only 30% of them possessed receivers.
- Far less mutual interference and reduced time-sharing made listening more enjoyable.
- Better and less expensive radio receivers led to larger audiences.
- The first scientific radio listener research was underway.
- Potential advertisers recognized radio's commercial role and value as a result of successful campaigns.
- Major national advertising agencies showed increasing interest in radio.
- The public accepted advertising on networks by 1927–1928.

NBC had nearly 40 sponsors that year, as CBS was struggling with 4, but the following year their combined total was 65. Many stations were still losing money, but the pattern was set and favorable.

The Depression pushed down many of the last barriers to *direct* advertising. Advertising had begun on radio as a genteel sales message broadcast in "business" (daytime) hours, with no hard sell or mention of price. Under the pressures of a Depression economy, stations began to accept more and longer ads—including some 15- and 30-minute "programs" of advertising content—harder selling ads, and even barter ads, whereby stations traded time for hard goods they could use. Advertising spread to all hours of the broadcast day, and evening *prime time* hours with the most listeners commanded the highest prices.

Broadcast advertising, network and local, became so complex that a number of middleman institutions evolved for the mutual benefit of sponsors and radio stations or networks. First were advertising agencies, which typically had considered radio a fad in the early 1920s. One 998-page book on advertising published in 1923 dismissed radio broadcasting in two sentences: "The development of radio broadcasting is presenting another possibility of mass communication which probably will be utilized for advertising purposes. It is too early to predict what its possibilities may be or how successfully it may be used." (Starch, 1923, p. 866) With national programs on major networks becoming more complicated to produce, and more expensive, the axiom of "he who pays the piper calls the tune" came into full operation. At first, agencies merely purchased air time for their sponsor clients, and stations or networks developed programs. Soon, however, some agencies attempted to create a profitable *package* of program and advertising pleasing to the sponsor by producing programs themselves. The networks concurred. Without having to worry about either production or pleasing the sponsor, they reaped their normal income by simply providing air time for the finished product. By the 1931–1932 season, the agencies had taken on program selection, casting, direction, and other production aspects on networks and a few larger stations, frequently renting studios from the former. In smaller markets and stations, apart from the influence of network programs supplied to affiliates, the agency's role was restricted pretty much to purchase of time and placing of sponsor ads.

Except for network advertising, purchasing time on stations across the nation was difficult and time consuming. Few local stations could afford to have full-time representatives in New York and other big cities where advertisers and advertising agencies were located. Hence, they took to hiring a firm to represent them and paid it a commission—nominally 15% of the involved time sales, after the 15% advertising agency commission had been deducted—on national advertiser time or spot sales. The first true station representative (rep) firm, Edward Petry & Co., was formed early in 1932 to help local stations sell time in the major cities. Before that, most rep firms were brokers for sponsors, and played off one station against another. (Advertising agencies also originally were brokers, which accounts for their income typically coming from commissions paid by the media rather than from fees paid by the sponsor.) The new type of rep firm would represent only one station in a market and "sell" it to a sponsor through the sponsor's ad agency. But station reps existed to serve their media clients, not the sponsor. This practice gave important individual stations more national and regional advertising business, since sponsors' agencies and stations' reps bought and sold station time with the idea of getting the widest coverage for a message—sometimes with programs, sometimes with spot advertising—without having to concern themselves with programs. The station rep business started slowly, but had an increasing financial impact later in the decade.

Broadcast advertising was becoming more sophisticated. By the early 1930s, an advertiser could prerecord messages on electrical transcriptions and mail them to many stations, often for simultaneous use. Even though the networks stuck to their ban on recordings in either program or advertising material, the volume of broadcast advertising increased. Advertising copy became more versatile as agency copywriters vied with one another

for the best approach for a given client. Sometimes agencies turned to research for ideas and answers, but other times the sponsor made decisions
by intuition.

According to McCann–Erickson data, radio advertising volume climbed
from less than 1% ($14 million) of advertising expenditures in 1928 to
nearly 5% ($62 million) in 1932 (see Appendix C, table 3-A). Even though
the deepening Depression caused an advertising decline of $5 million a
year later, this reduced the volume by only half a percentage point. Radio
had become an important element of the advertising "mix," and much of
this gain was at the expense of newspapers and magazines.

In 1932, an FRC study of advertising time found that, overall, 36% of air
time had commercial sponsorship—and 78% of that was local advertising—
leaving 64% unsponsored or *sustaining*; that is, the station or network
sustained the program's production and time costs. This pattern varied little by station size or power. Sustaining time was slightly more prevalent before 6 P.M., mainly because radio was only just beginning to offer regular
daytime programs.

4.5.2 Network-Station Economics

The following table indicates that network broadcast advertising expanded
sharply in the 1927–1930 period. By 1932, the Depression was causing
the networks to decline in most categories of advertising, or at best hold
their own. Since less commercial time was supporting a larger number of
sustaining hours, the amount of time sold was crucial to the entire
medium.

Network management originally thought, or at least said, that they
would not make money. NBC President Aylesworth expressed this belief to
a Senate committee in 1927, but one year later the network made a half-
million-dollar net profit. CBS had a rockier start, offering no effective competition to the two NBC chains, with their 75 stations, for nearly two years.
As shown in the table on the next page, however, all three chains, especially because of their O & O stations, soon began to make healthy profits.

In 1932 and 1933 CBS surpassed NBC, in number of stations and income, before they resumed a rough parity. RCA and NBC officials claimed
that this income discrepancy was due partly to NBC's providing public
service programs, which were typically sustaining, while CBS made money
on sponsored entertainment programming. This position was not supported by the facts; all three networks produced many public service programs. The networks' income decline after 1931 occurred when businesses
that were losing money in the Depression pared advertising expenditures
for economy's sake. Surprisingly enough, radio increased its income during
the first two years of the Depression. The fact that radio was "free" once
the set was bought created a large audience. This audience, supplied to

■ **The Economics of Network Advertising: The First Six Years** The following figures show the expansion of national advertising on CBS and the NBC-Red and -Blue networks combined.

Year	Money Expended for Time on All Networks		Commercial Time as Percentage Total Hours Broadcast		Net Pretax Income of All Networks	
	$	% Increase	%	% Increase	NBC Red and Blue	CBS
1927	$ 3,832,150	—	20.5	—	$(464,400)	$(220,100)
1928	10,252,497	167.5	27.7	35.1	427,200	(179,400)
1929	19,729,571	80.6	24.7	(10.8)	798,200	474,200
1930	26,819,156	43.2	29.2	18.2	2,167,500	985,400
1931	35,787,299	33.5	36.5	25.0	2,663,200	2,674,200
1932	39,106,776	9.3	25.5	(30.1)	1,163,300	1,888,100

Sources: First four columns from Herman S. Hettinger, *A Decade of Radio Advertising* (Chicago: University of Chicago Press, 1933), Tables 19, 20, and 23, pp. 113–118; last two columns from FCC, *Report on Chain Broadcasting* (Washington, D.C.: U.S.: Government Printing Office, 1941), pp. 17, 24. Data for 1927 in last two columns includes two months of 1926 for NBC but only eight months of 1927 for CBS. Figures in last two columns rounded to nearest 100. Data in parenthesis indicates loss.

advertisers at a small price per thousand, created such a tempting market that they stuck with radio while they could, particularly for high volume–low unit cost merchandise or services.

Local stations suffered more. Many faced business communities buttoning down for the Depression and showing little interest in a new advertising medium. Potential advertisers often waited to see results and gain experience from network advertising, agencies were just starting to get interested in radio, and reps were a new business. At the same time, though, an increasing flow of books, articles, and talks on how best to advertise on radio persuaded many advertisers to take the initial plunge during this period.

Gross receipts varied from a few hundred dollars per station to more than $1.5 million, for an industry total of $18.5 million. Networks earned another $37.5 million, giving radio broadcasting a total income of nearly $56 million in 1931. However, the industry spent more than it earned by several hundred thousand dollars. Of the 513 stations reporting to the FRC for 1931, 333 reported a profit ranging from $14 to $376,000 while the remaining 180 stations were in the red, with losses ranging from $22.50 to $178,000 for a firm operating two stations. Radio was making and spending a lot of money; networks and their O & O stations accounted for half and all other stations for the other half. Income had risen rapidly from less than $5 million in 1927 to nearly $56 million just four years later, thanks to the formation of three networks and acceptance of advertising by the business community and the listening audience. More than 6,000 persons worked in radio stations and networks in the 1930–1931 season.

4.6 Developing Program Diversity

In 1928, radio offered more features, less education, more plays, and fewer children's programs than in 1925 (see p. 81), but generally the time devoted to particular types of programs remained proportionately similar for years. A 1928 study of 100 stations in the western United States by Federal Radio Commissioner Harold Lafount showed that the average station was on the air 54 hours a week, with 1 hour of network programs, 25 hours of studio programs, 7 hours—only 13%—of "mechanical" (records and electrical transcriptions) programs, 4 hours of orchestras from remote locations, 8 hours of religion, 5 hours of education and lectures other than on farm subjects, 3 hours of farm reports, talks, and so forth, and 1 hour of weather and stock reports.

Although music remained the mainstay of both networks and independent stations, music programming on radio after 1927 was of two distinct types: network, usually more lavish and diversified, and local, mainly music and sometimes recorded. The majority of programs were sustaining throughout the 1927–1933 period. In 1926–1927, the first season of formally organized networks, more minutes of a sample January 1927 week were devoted to concert music (585) than to musical variety and light music (570). All other programming together—general variety, news and commentary, religious, homemaker and miscellaneous talk programs—occupied only 420 minutes a week. In other words, the two NBC networks (CBS was not yet on the air [see pp. 120–122]) programmed only 26 hours a week, or about 3 1/2 hours per day.

Like individual stations before them, networks programmed at first only in the evening hours. As the supply of sets, programming, the interest of advertisers, and the demands of affiliated stations increased, they added daytime hours, pretty much filling them by 1933. In the process, most major network program types made their appearance (see Appendix C, table 4-A).

4.6.1 Variety

Heavily sponsored from the start, radio variety programs grew in number and importance throughout the 1926–1933 period. The so-called *general variety* show, a sort of magazine of entertainment, was first programmed in the 1926–1927 season and reached daytime schedules as early as 1929–1930. "Radio's first really professional variety show," which started in October 1929, was the Fleischmann Yeast program, featuring the young crooner Rudy Vallee. Popular from the start, it remained with the same sponsor for a decade. Hillbilly and country-western variety also started early, with *Dutch Masters Minstrels* appearing in 1928–1929 and the even more famous *National Barn Dance* reaching a national audience late in 1933.

This type of programming, which had begun earlier on local stations in the South, soon became popular all over the country through network distribution. Combination orchestra and talk formats, or *semivariety*, appeared in the 1930–1931 season. Newspaper entertainment columnist Ed Sullivan, whose subsequent television variety program ran for more than two decades, made his first broadcast series appearance in the 1931–1932 season.

Also popular were *comedy variety* programs, usually comprised of a comedian or comedy team with a backup orchestra. On NBC's first season, Smith Brothers cough drops made use of their famous two faces trademark with a comedy team named "Trade and Mark," backed by an orchestra. Reflecting the social standards of that period, *Majestic Theater: Two Black Crows* featured black dialect (spoken by white actors) and was very popular in the 1928–1929 season and for several years thereafter. In 1931–1932, one of the early big stars, "Banjo Eyes" Eddie Cantor, began a comedy–variety series that drew large audiences for more than 10 years. The next season saw a parade to the network microphones of soon-to-be-famous radio comedians, many of whom were former vaudevillians. Al Jolson, famous as the singer in the early Hollywood talkie *The Jazz Singer*; George Burns and Gracie Allen, a husband and wife team; Ed Wynn, fresh from *The Perfect Fool* on Broadway; Jack Benny; Fred Allen, who was to maintain a fake feud with Benny for years; the Marx Brothers, best known for their movies; and Jack Pearl, who created on radio the German tall-tale teller, Baron Munchausen—all appeared in their own network shows for the first time that year. Most of these comedians lasted on radio for a decade or more, Burns and Allen and Benny each for more than 30 years on radio and then on television, with George Burns performing up to his death in 1996. Each added his or her own bit to radio's traditions; Wynn's program, for instance, introduced studio audiences to provide reaction to liven the program (see p. 88) and distract Wynn from the frightening microphone. Comedy shows all had orchestras and typically used "second bananas" (a burlesque term) or "sidekick" foils (or "straight men") but relied most heavily on comedy sketches and monologues.

Local stations also depended on variety programming, although it was usually sustaining. As vaudeville tours played to dwindling paying audiences and stalled all over the country, many troupes turned to local radio for short-term employment. Some performers left the traveling circuit altogether and began to work in radio, full time if possible, although pay often was only food and shelter. On many stations local talent was even cheaper, as anyone with any musical or comedy accomplishment was invited on the air just to fill time. One such early starter was (Arthur) "Red" Godfrey, known in Baltimore radio as the "warbling banjoist," who was later to find great success in radio and television. Formats generally were informal, although some stations tried to create low-cost versions of well-known network shows.

4.6.2 Music

Music programs occupied the most hours per week on both networks and local stations. As with variety programs, there were several types, but the typical program was built around an orchestra or a singer specializing in popular or light classical music. These programs usually had sponsors from the start and, as early as 1926–1927, many bore the sponsor's name in the title as in *Cliquot Club Eskimos* and *Michelin Tiremen*. Some performers sang under "house names," but the audience soon recognized such voices as that of the mysterious "Silver Masked Tenor," Joseph M. White, of the Goodrich Silvertown Orchestra, who never sang unmasked.

At first, orchestras alone were most popular, but after 1930 the network audience apparently began to prefer light musical variety programs. These were variety shows built around singers or orchestras rather than masters of ceremony or comedians. Most ran 15 or 30 minutes, and some were used as sustaining filler between sponsored shows. Falling in this category were the vaudeville-derived song and patter teams discussed on p. 83 and radio appearances of famous crooner Bing Crosby as early as 1931.

Sponsors sought and gained prestige through broadcast concert music. The Atwater Kent Sunday evening music hours began on the old AT&T network in 1925 and stayed with NBC for several years. The Boston Symphony Orchestra, Chicago Civic Opera, and National Symphony Orchestra joined another half-dozen concert orchestras in the first (1926–1927) network season. The New York Philharmonic, conducted by Arturo Toscanini, who later conducted NBC's own symphony orchestra, made its first radio broadcasts in fall 1927—a year that saw some 20 "concert music" programs. Until the late 1940s the networks always scheduled at least 20 such programs, usually sponsored by prestigious firms. (As television came in during the early 1950s, the number of concert music programs dropped slightly but rose again later, although mostly as sustaining programs, until network radio essentially ceased to exist.) One program that still goes on is the Saturday afternoon broadcast of the Metropolitan Opera, which started in the Fall of 1931. Announcer Milton Cross (see p. 80) gave the commentary on these broadcasts from their start until his death in 1974. Many other concert music programs had large audiences and long life: NBC's *Music Appreciation Hour*, with noted conductor Walter Damrosch as host, became an educational hit over the Blue network during Friday morning school hours after 1928; and the Mormon Tabernacle Choir broadcast live from Salt Lake City weekly for more than 50 years.

As local station schedules expanded to 12- and 18-hour broadcast days in larger cities, music became increasingly important. Music of all kinds comprised 50 to 60% of most schedules, with popular and semiclassical works predominating. The specific content varied tremendously, depending on local talent, audience composition, competition on the air, and

---

▨ **An Evening's Network Programming:
1930**   These are evening schedules for WEAF (NBC-Red's flagship station) and WABC (the key CBS station), both in New York. Blank time periods indicate that the previous program continues. Programs with an asterisk are sustaining (not sponsored). Naturally, programs would vary from night to night.

Tuesday, November 4, 1930

	WEAF	WABC
6:00	*Black and Gold Room Orchestra	*Harry Tucker and his Barclay Orchestra
6:30	*Who's Behind the Name?	*Crockett Mountaineers
6:45	*Black and Gold Room Orchestra	*Tony's Scrap Book
7:00	Air Scoops with Elinor Smith (Daggett & Ramsdell Co.)	*Columbia Educational Features
7:15	*Laws that Safeguard Society	Westchester County Salon Orchestra (Westchester Realty Board)
7:30	Soconyland Sketches (Standard Oil Co. of New York)	Wise Shoe Program (Wise Shoes, Inc.)
7:45		*The Early Book Worm— (Alexander Woolcott)
8:00	*Troika Bells	Blackstone Program (Waitt & Bond, Inc.)
8:15	*Snoop & Peep	
8:30	Florsheim Frolic (Florsheim Shoe Co.)	Kaltenborn Edits the News (S. W. Straus & Co.)
8:45		Premier Salad Dressers (Francis H. Leggett & Co.)
9:00	Eveready Program (National Carbon Co., Inc.)	Henry and George (Consolidated Cigar Co.)
9:30	Happy Wonder Bakers (Continental Baking Corp.)	Philco Symphony Concert (Philadelphia Storage Battery Co.)
10:00	Enna Jettick Songbird (Dunn & McCarthy Go.)	Graybar's Mr. and Mrs. (Graybar Electric Co.)
10:15	B. A. Rolfe and his Lucky Strike Dance Orchestra (American Tobacco Co.)	Paramount-Publix Radio Playhouse (Paramount-Publix Corp.)
11:00	*Mystery House	*Will Osborne and his Orchestra
11:15		*Columbia's Radio Column
11:30	*Vincent Lopez and his Hotel St. Regis Orchestra	*Mickey Alpert and his Orchestra from Boston
12:00	*Duke Ellington and his Cotton Club Orchestra	*Asbury Park Casino Orchestra
12:30	Jack Albin and his Hotel Pennsylvania Orchestra	*Nocturne—Ann Leaf at the Organ

Sustaining program

Source: "Radio Advertising," *Fortune* (December 1930), page 113. Courtesy of Fortune Magazine.

---

network affiliation, if any. Musical programs were nearly always live, with orchestras and soloists playing in studios or at remote pickup locations. The still strong antagonism toward records on the networks sometimes filtered down to local stations (see p. 92).

Although announcers of musical programs sometimes performed so well that they became radio personalities, some listeners found commercials and talk annoying. In 1928–1929 a Chicago firm attempted to overcome these drawbacks, which most listeners still preferred to the home phonograph, by providing a musical service over telephone lines for a fee—a throwback to the Puskás brothers' service in Budapest (see p. 44) and forerunner of cable.

4.6.3 Drama

Of all radio program types, drama had the slowest start; broadcasting theater to an unseeing audience was difficult for both actors and audience. The initial efforts were light "homey or love interest" half-hour shows, leading in a few years to the women's serial. The first of these, in late 1929, was the ethnic, immensely popular *Rise of the Goldbergs*, written by Gertrude Berg, who also starred as "Molly," as even her friends came to call her over the years. This program, built on an urban Jewish family, helped establish the idea of a continuing cast in a different situation each week. *Vic and Sade* was another superbly written popular program, lasting from 1932 to 1945. An increasing number of these light programs originated from Chicago. The first program from the West Coast was the supremely popular *One Man's Family*, written by Carlton Morse, which originated in San Francisco in April 1932. Serial drama established a daytime standard of several 15-minute programs—three at first, five later—per week in 1932–1933. By spring 1933, daytime *soap opera*—so called because of the soap company sponsorship common to the genre—included long-lived *The Romance of Helen Trent* and *Ma Perkins*. All these, written by a handful of writers, would have long runs, *Ma Perkins* until 1960, and were the prelude to a flood. The soap opera was a true serial, with stories slowly unfolding day after day, over years.

Comedy drama usually presented standard characters getting into and out of various situations week after week, each episode being complete in itself. The first and most famous, however, began as a two-character dialogue. Freeman F. Gosden and Charles J. Correll, who had started together in vaudeville, created a blackface routine in return for free meals from a small station in a Chicago hotel. The *Chicago Tribune's* station, WGN, then hired the pair for nearly 600 episodes of their *Sam 'n' Henry* act over the next two years. With success came an unsuccessful demand by the performers for more money, and Gosden and Correll moved to WMAQ. When WGN refused to release the program name to a competitor, the performers had to come up with a new one. Thus, *Amos 'n' Andy* came into being, with the two vaudevillians playing all the parts in an increasingly complicated series built around the Freshair Taxicab Company and the fraternal lodge Mystic Knights of the Sea. Although the program was carefully scripted, with even the pronunciation written in, it usually was aired without rehearsal in order to maintain spontaneity. Five-minute bits on 78-rpm records were both officially and unofficially syndicated to smaller stations. The whole show went to NBC-Blue in summer 1929 for a reputed $100,000 a year for the team. It was well worth it. *Amos 'n' Andy* quickly became a craze and then an institution. Almost everyone tuned in five, and later six, nights a week, and movie theaters were known to interrupt films for 15 minutes so that the audience could hear the evening's episode. While blacks would find the dialogue insulting today, a large number, as well as the country's white majority, enjoyed it in its time. Many suggest that this

■ **Types of Programs Broadcast in 1932**   Shown below are the program types broadcast by nine major-market radio stations (four in New York, four in Chicago, and one in Kansas City) in a 2-week period in February. When compared to 1925 data, there have been declines in music and "other" categories and an increase in drama and other entertainment (see table on page 81). Compare this also with Appendix C, table 4-A, to see what the networks were programming in 1932, and with p. 300 for 1946 station programming.

Program Type and Subtypes	Percentage of Time
Music	**64.1%**
Dance	23.5%
Vocal	13.0
Combination	3.6
Concert orchestras	8.4
Soloists	4.5
Phonograph records	3.2
String ensembles	3.3
Sacred	.6
Miscellaneous	4.0
Drama	**6.5**
Continued plays, reading, etc.	2.0
Sketches	3.3
Onetime plays	1.2
Other Entertainment	**13.3**
Women's	4.9
Children's	3.5
Feature	4.0
Star (other than music)	.9
Information	**12.1**
Education	7.2
News	1.2
Political	1.4
Market reports	.5
Weather	.1
Sports	1.7
Other	**4.0**
Foreign-originated	.5
Health exercises	.6
Church services	2.2
Miscellaneous	.7
Total	**100.0%**

Source: William Albig, *Modern Public Opinion* (New York: McGraw-Hill, 1956), Table 20, page 447. By permission.

■ **Amos 'n' Andy**   Though racist in today's view, this program helped propel network radio into faster and wider acceptance in the late 1920s and early 1930s, with the comic misadventures of two taxi drivers and their friends and relations. Freeman F. Gosden and Charles J. Correll, originators of *Amos 'n' Andy*, were white—but are shown here in blackface.

Photo courtesy of National Broadcasting Company, Inc.

program helped more than any other to sell radio to advertisers and the public alike. Other comedy programs came and went, but *Amos 'n' Andy* remained popular into the 1950s.

Thriller drama—action, western, crime, and suspense—began about the same time. The first was *Empire Builders*, a semi-informative show sponsored by a railroad and heard only in the Midwest in its first

(1928–1929) season. In 1930, the western came to radio with *Death Valley Days*, an anthology of tales introduced by a host, which retained its format in television a quarter-century later. In 1931, the crime program began with *Sherlock Holmes*, which remained on network radio for many years with different casts, straying far from the Arthur Conan Doyle original. The classic crime drama was *The Shadow*, whose chief character, Lamont Cranston, played at one time by Orson Welles, was a "wealthy young man-about-town" who had a "hypnotic power to cloud men's minds so they cannot see him." The invisible effect was created aurally and psychologically by putting Cranston's voice through a filter that made it sound like a telephone conversation. For two decades a bloodcurdling laugh and the slogan "Crime does not pay . . . the Shadow knows!" identified the Shadow. *Little Orphan Annie*, based on the comic strip, took to the air in fall 1931, the first of many children's adventure serial programs.

A very different kind of drama began in 1931 when the weekly newsmagazine *Time* created a radio program. Whether the *March of Time* should be classified as drama or news has been a source of argument. Each program contained the three or four most easily dramatized events of the week before, with actors selected to sound as much as possible like the personages they portrayed. In the late 1930s, pressure from the White House forced the removal of a sound-alike for President Roosevelt. The program's signature, announcer Westbrook Van Voorhis's impressive vocal "Time . . . marches on!" became a catch phrase.

Drama was rare on local stations because of the costs of good talent and production, but some stations tried amateur dramatic presentations and a few became known nationally. For example, WXYZ in Detroit rapidly built a following with *The Lone Ranger*, a western program mainly for children, which started in 1933. The program soon became a factor in the formation of the Mutual network (see p. 174). Stations also could produce a dramatic program series, and then offer to rent or sell recordings of it to other stations. This syndication process permitted stations in smaller and more remote towns to have professional drama without network dependency. The opposite also occurred, with local acts eventually receiving national exposure through syndication. For example, a comedy team known as "Smackouts" began with small bits on the air in Chicago, graduated to the network level *National Farm and Home Hour*, and later achieved national success with a network family show of their own as *Fibber McGee and Molly*.

4.6.4 News

Prior to 1930, the public could hear Frederick William Wile, David Lawrence, and H. V. Kaltenborn in separate once-a-week news commentaries and expect radio to inform it in times of high public interest or tension. This was demonstrated by the attention listeners gave to bulletins that were issued on Charles

Lindbergh's solo airplane flight across the Atlantic in 1927. But regular *hard news* broadcasting, as it is known today, did not exist until Lowell Thomas began a 15-minute newscast five times a week on NBC-Blue in Fall 1930, which was aired until early in 1976. Kaltenborn soon switched to three times a week, and in 1932 Boake Carter and Edwin C. Hill adopted similar 15-minute formats. The networks had no daytime newscasts during this period.

In its coverage of the Lindbergh baby kidnaping in 1932, radio showed a new responsibility. The networks scrapped evening schedules for several days—although NBC had waited a day, thinking the news too sensational for even brief bulletins. The positive audience reaction to such occasional reporting and the regular newscasts made network planners realize that news could be a powerful ingredient in programming. Coverage of the 1932 presidential campaign (see pp. 137–138) helped strengthen this feeling.

During this period, radio received its hard news mostly from the wire services, Associated Press, United Press, and International News Service, which were controlled by the newspaper industry. The nation's newspapers, already feeling the competition for advertising revenues, became alarmed over radio's small incursions into news reporting. When newspaper pressure made the wire services unavailable to radio, CBS began its own newsgathering, frequently ignoring the copyright law with a copy of a newspaper, scissors, and paste, in mid-1933. Rival NBC tried telephone inquiries, but both the Blue and the Red networks relied primarily on the wire services—when they could get them.

Late in 1933, tension between print and broadcasting came to a head, in a time called the "Newspaper–Radio War." Newspapers held the upper hand. Many papers stopped free listings of radio programs, demanding payment for such "advertisements." In a major agreement signed in December at New York's Biltmore Hotel between the newspaper industry and the networks, radio stations were restricted to:

1. Issuing only two 5-minute newscasts per day, at 9:30 A.M. and 9 P.M. or later, to protect both morning and afternoon papers.
2. Broadcasting interpretation and comment as opposed to hard news reporting.
3. Using news provided by the Press-Radio Bureau, a new service to which the wire services would funnel copy for rewriting in radio style.
4. Depending *only* on the new Press-Radio Bureau, stopping their own newsgathering activities.
5. Broadcasting only unsponsored news.

Radio had to accept the agreement, since it was a relatively new business supposedly dependent on the wire services controlled by newspapers for hard news and since newspaper ownership of many stations divided the radio industry.

The Press-Radio Bureau came into existence on March 1, 1934, and immediately ran into competition. As only the networks had signed the Biltmore Agreement for radio, many independent stations and affiliates decided to set up separate newsgathering operations not bound by the agreement. Of those, Transradio Press Service, headed by the former director of the CBS News Service, quickly became the largest. Local and regional services, such as the Yankee Network News Service, which augmented Transradio in New England, also provided news to other stations. Yankee started on March 1, 1934—the day that the Press-Radio Bureau commenced operations.

Within a year, with fewer than half of the radio stations subscribing to the Press-Radio Bureau and its restrictions, the newspaper industry realized it was losing. The directors of commercially based INS and UP—AP was a cooperative, owned by member papers—decided to sell news to radio stations without restriction, if the competition warranted. It did; thus, after about a year, the Biltmore Agreement was effectively dead. Few local stations broadcast hard news during the 1926–1933 period although some newspaper-owned outlets gave brief headlines. Radio was primarily for entertainment rather than for information, and except for local highlights, most stations let newspapers handle news.

4.6.5 Election Broadcasting

Radio's election coverage, which dated back at least to 1916, continued to expand. In the 1928 campaign between Republican Herbert Hoover and Democrat Alfred E. Smith, governor of New York, approximately $2 million was spent on radio for national and local candidates, with the Democrats outspending the GOP for national candidates by more than $200,000. The new practice of charging candidates for time (remember, few stations sold time for any purpose in 1924) accounted for much of the rising cost, and the increased use of radio time—especially the one-minute spot announcements pioneered by the Republicans—for the rest. Neither candidate was an ideal radio speaker, but Smith's constantly mispronounced "raddio" was probably most noticeable. On election eve both candidates made one-hour nationwide broadcasts, Hoover from his home in Palo Alto and Smith from New York City. Election night was a network affair, with both NBC and CBS interjecting news reports into special entertainment programming. Most national and local election reports were sustaining.

Four years later, in the midst of the Depression, the incumbent Hoover took on another New York governor, Franklin D. Roosevelt. Although the GOP used nearly twice as much time on national radio as in 1928, F.D.R. soundly beat Hoover. It is estimated that the two parties spent upwards of $5 million on the radio campaigns, with 25% going for national hookups. Election night broadcasts resembled those four years earlier, but they began earlier (6 P.M. instead of 8 P.M.) and included analysis as well as returns.

4.6.6 Other Talk Programs

Various kinds of talk shows filled many hours a week, especially during the day, as network schedules expanded. In these years, only special sports events were covered in play-by-play detail, and some local stations broadcast more than others. From the beginning of network programming, religious programs were prominent, especially multidenominational services and talks. Harry Emerson Fosdick began a long-running Protestant program, which became *National Vespers* on NBC-Blue in 1929. The *Catholic Hour* appeared a year later. Of a different order, though still professing to be a religious program, were the CBS commentaries of Catholic priest Charles E. Coughlin. Broadcasting from his Shrine of the Little Flower in Royal Oak near Detroit, Michigan, beginning late in 1930, the program grew out of a regional broadcast first aired in 1926. Discussing economics and politics as well as his religious views, the "radio priest" backed Roosevelt fervently until his policies had crystallized. Then Father Coughlin turned against F.D.R. and became a notorious "rabble rouser" (see p. 199).

Talk programs in daytime featured cooking, beauty hints, gossip, and other shows designed for the housewife. The long-running *National Farm and Home Hour*, produced with U.S. Department of Agriculture help, began in Fall 1928. *Cheerio*, an inspirational talk show, began a long career that season. Walter Winchell started his celebrated gossip show on NBC-Blue in 1932.

Both major networks offered educational programs. NBC introduced its *Music Appreciation Hour* (see p. 130) in 1928, and CBS followed in February 1930 with its *American School of the Air*, a sustaining program except for the first three months. Both of these programs were aimed at classroom listeners. In 1932 the *American School of the Air* reached some 20,000 schools with a number of different course offerings each week. The *National Farm and Home Hour* and the *March of Time* were typical of such programs.

Most local stations placed talk programs between musical presentations. Astrologers, children's storytellers, cooking teachers, gossipers, and advisers all found their way to the air. More than 1 1/2% of air time was devoted to health exercise programs until 1932. Some stations became famous for a particular talk program, such as the Kansas station that broadcast a "medical question box" (see p. 146), and some stations offered a particular type of program, such as local sports coverage in towns with college or professional teams, even though there was some fear of radio's effect on gate receipts.

4.7 Audience: Craze to Consequence

Radio's real impact in the 1926–1933 period occurred in the growing audience. By 1928–1929 the home radio tinkerer had given way numerically to the family that purchased a ready-made receiver, plugged it in, and listened. By 1933 about two-thirds of the nation's homes had radios (see Appendix C, table 6-A). Once a mystery and a novelty, radio listening had become the habit of millions.

4.7.1 The Changing Receiver Market

By 1928 there were about 60 U.S. makers of radio broadcast receivers, two of which had one-third of the market, and four of which had two-thirds. In addition to GE and Westinghouse, important independent producers included Atwater Kent, which turned from making automobile ignition systems to building radios in a huge factory in Philadelphia, and Grigsby-Grunow, which built a reputation on its console "Majestic" model, turning out 5,000 sets a day in its Chicago plant in 1929. Stromberg-Carlson turned from telephone equipment to fine, expensive receivers, and Crosley, owner of WLW, Cincinnati, began at the other extreme, making inexpensive receivers that most could afford.

In 1927–1928 the heavy, large, expensive-to-operate, and inconvenient battery-operated receiver became obsolete, as alternating-current (plug-in) sets became available except in places without power lines. By May 1928 it was estimated that 7 1/2 million of the nearly 12 million radio receivers in use were the "standard" type, with loudspeakers—the others being crystal sets or obsolete one-tube models. The radio audience was reportedly nearly 40 million out of a total population of 120 million. Receivers became furniture, the larger loudspeakers sounded better, and prices went up in a boom market, peaking in 1929 at an average of $136. The result was overproduction by perhaps a million units. Manufacturers, faced with unloading these sets in the Depression, dropped prices to below $90 in 1930 and to an average of $47 by 1932. Many makers and retailers went out of business, and others began to produce smaller and cheaper sets including table models.

Competition grew as the Philadelphia Storage Battery Company (Philco), bereft of most of its radio battery business by plug-in circuits, converted quickly to making radio sets and tubes. Tube production was very important, as tubes—costing at least a dollar or two apiece—were sold separately from receivers until the mid-1930s. RCA, because of its patent position, sold perhaps 60% of all radio tubes until 1931, when Philco stopped buying from RCA in a fight over specifications and price and started to make its own. In 1934 Philco had attracted 20% of the tube market compared to RCA's 40%. But Philco already outshone other radio manufacturers by producing fully one-third of *all* receivers manufactured in the country, having completely converted to the superheterodyne circuit in home and automobile radios. Though the new circuits were more expensive, volume production drove prices down and markets up. In 1933, when the Depression caused lower sales of expensive radios, many makers, notably Crosley and Emerson, made small tube radios to sell for less than $15—an unheard-of price for anything but a crystal set a year or so earlier. Quality suffered, but the audience grew nonetheless. To a great extent, radio circuits became standardized, and experimentation with new or expensive models decreased. Consoles still were made, but smaller table receivers predominated.

4.7.2 Development of Audience Research

Little was known about the radio audience except that it was growing. The 1930 U.S. Census collected information about radio ownership, showing that, while half the urban families in the country had receivers, only 21% of rural farm and 34% of rural nonfarm families had them. Receivers were concentrated in the Northeast, in midwestern cities, and in the Far West. Penetration of radio ranged from New Jersey's high of 63% to Mississippi's low of 5% of families. Of special interest was the increase in farm listeners, as the spread of electricity to rural areas made fast, direct communication possible for the first time—especially important in a crisis like the Depression.

The first system of program ratings appeared in 1929, when Archibald M. Crossley (no relation to Powel Crosley, Jr., the WLW owner and set maker) formed the Cooperative Analysis of Broadcasting (CAB). This national service, which benefited advertising agencies but was paid for largely by networks and stations, was the standard for five years. Crossley researchers would call a preselected sample of homes the morning following the program(s) to be rated and ask whoever answered "who had listened to what" the night before. The rating produced by this technique—a percentage of set-using families listening to one program or network—only applied to sponsored shows, as the service was established for the Association of National Advertisers. Noting that ratings were costing about 40 cents a call, CAB tried a postcard system (these were the days of the penny postcard) but got only a 3 to 5% response rate. Dividing each day into four parts, CAB found that most people listened to radio at night: fully half the sets were in use at 9 and 10 P.M., with perhaps a third at 7 P.M. and 11 P.M., thus, establishing the concept of *prime time.*

Local stations began to conduct audience research under pressure from advertisers who demanded such information before they would purchase time. Most stations were content to solicit reactions to programs and read incoming mail. Others, using FRC-required engineering surveys of their coverage area, simply thought of the population residing within the coverage area as their audience. Under sponsor pressure, they acknowledged that such figures did not reflect actual listenership and turned to active methods of discovering audience loyalty and interest. Stations variously made free premium offers to boost audiences and to gauge their size; analyzed set sales figures to establish the size and approximate location of the potential audience; and mailed questionnaires that sought data on audience size, preferences, and basic demographic characteristics. Although costly, a few larger stations used personal interviews to avoid a sampling bias of telephone interviews: only about half the American homes had telephones in the early 1930s. The stations that interviewed by telephone started using both recall and coincidental (calling when the program was on the air) methods around 1930.

Most broadcasters, however, had too few sponsors and too little money for this kind of effort. Thus, throughout the 1927–1933 period, little was known about radio listeners' reactions. While ratings were affecting network programs, local stations still made programming decisions and placed advertising without much knowledge of their audience.

4.8 Regulating Order out of Chaos

After the 1926 Zenith decision (see p. 97), Secretary of Commerce Hoover figuratively threw up his hands over the worsening interference situation. His call for industry self-regulation apparently fell on deaf ears. Congress made sporadic attempts to replace the obsolete 1912 Radio Act. In 1926 both houses of Congress finally passed radio bills, but major differences had to be resolved by a joint conference committee. The House bill called for the Secretary of Commerce to have strong licensing authority, with a new Federal Radio Commission (FRC) to serve as a board of appeal from the secretary's decisions. The Senate bill called for the FRC to have the licensing authority. Facing the delay of the joint conference committee, and the Christmas recess, Congress passed a stopgap bill giving all broadcast stations 90-day licenses, which could be renewed only if the station waived all rights to a specific frequency. But the new Christmas radios of 1926 still received a vast amount of unchecked interference from nearly 700 stations.

4.8.1 The Federal Radio Commission

The Radio Act of 1927 was passed on February 18 and sent to President Coolidge, who signed it into law on February 23. It created a Federal Radio Commission of five members, appointed to overlapping six-year terms and representing five geographical regions of the country. The FRC was to have licensing authority for only one year, in order to straighten out the interference and regulatory chaos, and then the Secretary of Commerce was to regain it as the FRC became an appellate body (but see pp. 143–145).

The House–Senate compromise is clearly reflected in this scheme. The FRC would have initial control over all interstate and foreign radio communications that originated in the United States. Specifically, it would have the power to:

1. Classify stations
2. Prescribe the nature of service to be provided
3. Assign frequencies
4. Determine power and location of transmitters
5. Regulate apparatus used
6. Make regulations to prevent interference
7. Set up zones of service (coverage areas)
8. Make special regulations concerning chain (network) broadcasting when necessary.

However, it would have no power to censor broadcasts. The act established a maximum period of three years for a license, renewable only to those stations adhering to FRC regulations and the law, and revokable for cause. The FRC was to keep radio service relatively equal throughout the country. Its decisions were not absolute but could be appealed to the U.S. Court of Appeals for the District of Columbia.

There were several key assumptions underlying the Radio Act of 1927. Equality of transmission facilities, reception, and service was a political goal. The public at large owned the radio spectrum, but individuals could be licensed to use frequencies. Because the number of channels that could be used without interference was limited, and because the number of applicants was larger than the number of channels, some criterion for choosing licensees had to be devised. Congress labeled this criterion the "public interest, convenience, and/or necessity" but did not define it in the 1927 act. Indeed, it remains undefined in statute to this day. It was the basis, however, on which discretionary control could be built, and it would be defined, however loosely, in the body of case law that was sure to develop. Essential to the operation of this principle was the concept that the broadcaster was ultimately responsible for his operation and that the government would step in only if the licensee did not adequately serve the listeners. This was a recognition that earlier self- and governmental-regulation had not worked and that broadcasting was a unique service requiring unique regulation. Although channels were scarce, radio as a form of expression was covered by the First Amendment and the Radio Act of 1927, thus precluding heavy-handed censorship.

Armed with these powers, the FRC began to function in March 1927. President Coolidge nominated five commissioners, but Congress approved only three before it adjourned. Two of these, including the chairman,

Admiral Bullard, died before the year was out, leaving the FRC with only one salaried appointee for much of its first year. In addition, since Congress had neglected specific funding for the FRC, the new agency camped out for many months in the Department of Commerce with a very small staff, much of it lent by the Commerce and Navy departments.

4.8.2 Clearing the Interference

Because the immediate job of reducing interference between stations was primarily technical, most of the original FRC members were radio experts. They included a naval officer (former RCA board member Admiral Bullard), an engineer and editor, a station manager, a radio inspector for the Department of Commerce, and a lawyer; and their earliest replacements were a former educational broadcaster and a set manufacturer. Their work was cut out for them because, in passing the Radio Act, Congress had stipulated that all licenses would expire two months after the act became law. Faced with an April 24 deadline, the FRC first extended amateur and ship licenses indefinitely in order to concentrate on broadcasting. It sent a questionnaire to all stations to determine who was broadcasting where, when, and with what power. It "summarily removed" some 40 stations operating on six frequencies reserved for Canada. It granted temporary extensions—initially for 60 days, later for 90—to most broadcasting stations, specifying power and times of operation on particular frequencies with minimum 50 kHz separations between stations in the same city. This action went a long way toward moving or eliminating the nearly 130 stations that had been off-frequency when the Act was passed (see p. 97).

It soon became clear that merely moving stations around was not going to reduce interference permanently. A classification system similar to that developed by Hoover in the mid-1920s would be necessary. The first step in this direction was a series of FRC general orders, which progressively widened the broadcast band to the entire spectrum between 550 kHz and 1,500 kHz (General Order No. 4); notified portable stations that they would be eliminated by fall but allowed temporary service with up to 100 watts on 1,470 kHz and 1,490 kHz (General Order No. 6); tightened allowable frequency deviations (General Order No. 7); and designated, in preparation for hearings, 600 to 1,000 kHz as a band to be kept free from heterodyne or other interference (General Order No. 19). Although these steps were constructive, the job was only partly done. The FRC, empowered to act in this way for only a year, had almost run out of time when Congress extended its licensing authority in March 1928 for another year.

Congress added a provision intended to promote equality of service throughout the country and stop the trend toward more stations in the larger eastern cities. Named the Davis Amendment after the Tennessee representative who introduced it, the new law required the licensing

---

■ **The FRC Establishes the Basic AM Allocation: 1928**

General Order No. 40, issued yesterday by the Federal Radio Commission, supplies the official basis for an adjustment in the assignment of the country's broadcasting facilities, under a plan which it is believed will provide an improved standard of radio reception generally. . . . The plan calls for full-time assignments for 100-watt stations equalling in number the total of all other classes of broadcasters put together. Of the 74 channels made available for high-grade reception, 34 will be assigned for regional service, permitting 125 full-time positions for this type of station, and 40 channels will be assigned to stations with minimum power of 5,000 watts and a maximum to be determined. . . . On these 40 channels only one station will be permitted to operate at any time during night hours, thus insuring clear reception of the station's program up to the extreme limit of its service range.[1]

A majority of the commission believes that this plan is the best which could be devised with due regard to existing conditions. It provides, or at least makes possible, excellent radio reception on 80 per cent of the channels. The few other channels will suffer from heterodyne interference except in a small area close to each station.[2]

The basic plan of allocation of regular broadcast facilities placed into effect by the Federal Radio Commission has been continued unchanged insofar as concerns the general plan of allocation of stations by frequencies, power, and hours of operation.[3]

Sources: [1] Statement to Accompany General Order No. 40, FRC, August 30, 1928 as reprinted in 1928 *Annual Report* of FRC, pages 49–50.

[2] FRC *Annual Report* (1928), page 17.

[3] FCC *Annual Report* (1935), page 23 (first report of the FCC).

---

authority—the FRC for another year, and then, presumably, the Secretary of Commerce—to work out means for assigning equal numbers of stations and equal amounts of power and air time to each of the country's five zones. In addition, all commissioners were to be legislated out of office by early 1929, thus in effect putting them on probation to clean up the remaining interference problems. Heedful of the Davis Amendment as well as their basic charge, the FRC, in May 1928, issued General Order No. 32, which was aimed at 164 stations believed to be causing the most interference. After a series of hearings requested by most of the affected stations, the commission removed 109 stations from the air, reducing the total number to around 590 by July 1. Portable stations were eliminated, since they caused interference and insurmountable regulatory problems under the Davis Amendment.

In July and August, the FRC issued the outline of its station classification plan, particularly General Order No. 40. The 96 available frequencies, each 10 kHz wide, were classified. There were to be 40 "cleared" channels, eight per zone, on which only one station would be placed anywhere in the country during evening hours, thus allowing better skywave reception in rural areas. These stations would operate with high power: 25,000 and later 50,000 watts. An additional 35 channels, seven per zone, would provide regional service with only two or three stations on each regional frequency using no more than 1,000 watts. The remaining 21 channels were either for low-power (100 to 5,000 watts) local stations, with many stations per frequency, or reserved by international agreement for Canada or Mexico. Claiming that this plan, which although modified still governs AM station assignment, would allow "excellent reception on 80 percent of the channels," the FRC reassigned existing stations in November 1928.

Once again, just as the FRC was beginning to have some major effect, its licensing authority was about to expire. Once again Congress extended it, this time to the end of 1929. A shift from technical to legal problems was apparent in congressional approval of an FRC general counsel and legal staff. By mid-1929, the FRC staff had more than tripled in one year to nearly 100 persons. Since it was also clear that some of the FRC's functions were less temporary than originally conceived, the FRC licensing authority was extended at the end of 1929 "until such time as is otherwise provided by law." To handle broadcasting's complexities, a body was needed to put congressional policy into regulation, administer those regulations, and adjudicate disagreements.

Even with license extensions, reduced interference and fewer stations, the FRC still had to equalize radio service in the country's five zones as called for by the Davis Amendment. When it tried quota systems, given states usually ended up with fractions of stations, an obvious impossibility. In 1930, it devised a system giving every broadcast station a number of points reflecting its power and time on the air; but even with some station changes, radio service remained "under quota" in the South and Far West and "over quota" in the Midwest and Northeast. It became obvious to many that the FRC was spending an inordinate amount of time trying to overcome financial, political, and technical problems in order to meet Congress's arbitrary and politically stimulated requirements. Except for the equalization issue, however, the FRC had effectively dealt with interference by the early 1930s and was ready to pursue legal and programming issues.

4.8.3 Improving Content

An early FRC programming concern had been the airing of phonograph records, which were considered to be inferior to live music and hence "deceptive" to the audience as well as generally available in stores and thus wasteful of air time, since people easily could buy and play them on phonographs. General Order No. 16 of August 1927 required clear identification of such "mechanical reproductions" with the exception of electrical transcriptions, which were of better sound quality and could not be purchased by the public.

Between 1927 and 1934, the federal courts—particularly the U.S. Court of Appeals for the District of Columbia—handled some 60 broadcast-related cases, 41 of which involved the FRC's basic role and the constitutionality of all or parts of the 1927 Radio Act. The courts generally were sympathetic to the FRC claim of special expertise and its position that the overriding criterion was to be the "public interest, convenience, or necessity," general and undefined as that standard was.

The appellate courts quickly supported congressional authority to regulate broadcasting, the right of the FRC to make regulations, the Commission's right to reject an application, power to prevent transfer of ownership, the public interest standard, and FRC discretionary powers. Numerous cases touched on programming—using a station for personal editorializing and defamatory attacks, overcommercialization, lack of programming balance—and some of the most interesting focused on programming and the public interest standard. Unless the FRC ignored evidence or procedural requirements, the courts usually upheld it, even if the case involved some aspect of programming.

Four early programming cases stand out. One was that of Dr. John R. Brinkley, who used his Milford, Kansas, station KFKB for a "medical question box" program in which he prescribed his own patent medicines—by number, to be dispensed by his own or friendly pharmacies—for unseen patients and promoted a questionable goat gland male sexual rejuvenation operation. The American Medical Association was particularly displeased, and the FRC eventually failed to renew Brinkley's license, with the reviewing court pointing out in 1931 that consideration of past behavior was not censorship. Brinkley moved to the border town of Del Rio, Texas, and continued broadcasting from Mexico, beyond the writ of the FRC. He was finally forced off the air in 1940 in a frequency reallocation. A similar case was that of Norman Baker, whose license in Muscatine, Iowa, was not renewed in 1931 because he used station KTNT to make "bitter attacks" on persons with whom he disagreed, as well as to exploit his medical theories and practices, and to promote his cancer hospital and merchandise. The Brinkley case figured as a precedent in the Baker decision. In a 1930 case, William B. Schaeffer was denied renewal for his Portland, Oregon, station KVEP because he allowed former political candidate Robert Duncan to attack his former opponent and backers over the air with "indecent and obscene" language. Schaeffer contended that, once having sold the time to Duncan, he was no longer responsible, but the Commission insisted that the licensee has to maintain control over material aired over the station. The Court of Appeals determined that this FRC dictum did not constitute censorship, and Schaeffer went off the air. Another case involving content was that of the Reverend Robert P. Schuler of the Trinity Methodist Church in Los Angeles, licensee of KGEF. Schuler had been convicted of attempting to use radio to "obstruct orderly administration of public justice" in "sensational rather than instructive" broadcasts, as he attacked religious organizations, public officials, the courts, institutions, and individuals in violent language. Citing the Brinkley case, the Court of Appeals upheld the FRC, and the Supreme Court refused to review.

The FRC established important technical, procedural, and legal precedents that still stand today. In 1932 it stopped issuing general orders and codified a set of rules and regulations, some of which provided precedent for its successor organization. In its seven years, the FRC cleared away the worst of the growth period's interference, established detailed regulations and standards, and made them stick in a series of court cases. Broadcasting gained the solid regulatory underpinning even broadcasters agreed was needed.

4.8.4 Development of Self-Regulation

The fledgling National Association of Broadcasters (see p. 99), which had fought for creation of the FRC because established stations had most to lose from unrestrained competition, worked with it throughout the FRC's seven years of life. Up to the late 1920s the NAB had primarily fought ASCAP demands (not very successfully), sought technical regulation, and acted as an information exchange and trade organization to promote radio. Now it added lobbying for commercial broadcasting's interests before Congress and the FCC, and pushing self-regulation of the industry to disarm rising governmental and public concern. The NAB feared that a Pandora's box had been opened now that the government had, and intended to use, the power to regulate *all* radio stations closely. On March 25, 1929, the NAB convention approved NAB's first Code of Ethics, a brief statement of general dos and don'ts relating to programming and advertising practices. The major aim of the code was to prevent the broadcast of fraudulent, deceptive, or indecent programs or advertising material that might offend any group of listeners. Distributed to NAB members only was a Code of Commercial Practice, which called for most advertising to be aired before 6 P.M. and for only "goodwill" or institutional advertising to be broadcast in prime time hours.

4.8.5 Music Licensing

As in the 1920s, however, NAB's major concern was ASCAP's demand for higher royalties; in early 1932 the increase asked for was an estimated 300%. Though it tried to establish a solid broadcaster front, NAB was undermined when ASCAP offered a lower rate to newspaper-owned stations— a successful attempt to divide and conquer as well as make the press grateful. After many newspaper-owned stations took this bait, other broadcasters had to sign and pay greatly increased rates for music. NAB again tried to set up a competitive music licensing agency, but its Radio Program Foundation soon died of broadcaster disinterest.

4.9 A Growing Social Impact

Radio was becoming a major institution. In 1933, high school and college students nationwide debated the question "Resolved: that the United States should adopt the essential features of the British system of radio operation and control," informing many people about the good points and the shortcomings of both systems. During the latter part of the 1926–1933 period, a large radio trade press developed. The most important advertising/business-oriented journal, *Broadcasting*, began as a twice-monthly periodical in 1931 and today is a weekly bible for much of the industry. *Variety* moved its radio section to second-place importance in space and location, right behind films, forcing vaudeville to third place. Fan magazines came and went, with one of the best, *Radio Broadcast*, dying during the Depression.

The potential of radio as material for a university course of study was realized in several schools during the late 1920s. Among the first was the University of Southern California in 1929. Most such early courses were in the English or speech departments and aimed particularly at basic training for on-the-air announcing. The earliest textbooks on radio also appeared in these years, including books on radio advertising for agencies and advertisers, announcing techniques, and even dramatic scripts.

4.9.1 Effects on Other Media

The Depression, together with radio's grip on people's leisure and money, nearly killed off phonographs and the recording industry. Many smaller companies disappeared because they couldn't afford to switch from mechanical to electronic recording methods to improve sound quality. The scarcity of capital caused many record firms to merge with stronger companies. Victor merged with RCA in 1929; Columbia Phonograph, weakened by losses during its fling at owning a broadcast network, became part of the American Record Corporation and later CBS, which had achieved strength and size since their previous association. Victor, building on work done for films and radio stations, introduced the 33 1/3-rpm disc in 1931, but the absence of high-quality records and a good inexpensive player kept this experiment from catching on. Radio stations used the slower-speed discs, which provided more content per side, but the public had to make do with 78-rpm records for another 17 years.

Broadcast music affected musicians too. Some, like orchestra leader Fred Waring, complained that playing songs on the radio hurt record sales; others that they weren't played or paid enough. In Chicago, the American Federation of Musicians struck to express its concern over radio's effects on musicians' employment (see p. 257).

The print media also felt radio's encroachment. During the "Press-Radio War" (see p. 136), most newspapers dropped free radio program listings and cut news about radio. Radio's share of advertising placed in the five major media increased from less than 2% in 1928 to more than 10% by 1933—and much of this was at the direct expense of newspapers. Magazines, too, felt the pinch, some of them losing ads to radio as early as 1928.

The motion picture industry was changing over from silent to sound movies. Warner's introduction of sound-on-disc pictures late in the 1920s had thrown Hollywood into chaos. Picture companies faced not only the immense costs of sound-conversion for the studios and thousands of theaters across the country but also the need for techniques for silencing noisy cameras and protecting fragile microphones and hiding them from view. Motion picture studios limited the appearance of their contract actors on radio for fear of both overexposure and competition. Like radio, the movie industry did well during the Depression, although it had to endure flurries of cost reductions, give-away free dishes, and often lower admission prices. To a great extent, film and radio complemented one another in the 1930s— fulfilling related but not duplicated interests and needs of their audiences.

4.9.2 Growth of Radio Abroad

The series of international radio conferences begun in 1903 (see p. 41) continued. The fourth meeting, postponed from 1917 due to wartime and postwar technical and political changes, was held in Washington in October 1927 with 300 or so delegates from nearly 80 countries. Its job was to minimize the interference caused by the rise in number and power of radio broadcasting and amateur stations. The conference (a) allocated for amateurs specific bands with minimal technical limitations, allowing for flexibility and change; (b) issued new general regulations covering radio in all countries and more detailed supplemental regulations that referred only to nations with government-run radio systems, thus excluding the United States with its commercial system; and (c) set up a technical committee to work on a frequency allocation table for the world. The fifth radio conference, held in Madrid in 1932, was the least important of the series since the 1927 regulations and the worldwide Depression had limited technical progress and financial investment. However, the conference decided to combine telegraph and radio regulations and to change the name of the International Telegraph Union to International Telecommunications Union.

To the north, Canada had some 75 stations by 1927 that provided service to every province although most of the stations, with half the total power, were concentrated in such major cities as Montreal and Toronto. Canada was principally concerned with two problems familiar to American broadcasting— the amount of advertising carried by stations and the lack of radio in rural areas—and two unique to that country—the cultural and social impact of increasing amounts of programming from another country, the United States, and a large French-speaking minority. In 1928 the Canadian government appointed a study commission (the "Aird Commission") to recommend a new system of broadcasting, which was to have far-reaching consequences. An operating body, the Canadian Radio Broadcasting Commission, was established in 1932 to set up a national system of broadcasting and to regulate radio.

To the south, a limited number of Mexican stations in the larger cities were using increasing amounts of power to reach rural listeners. Government agencies placed receivers in schools and workingmen's centers to receive the government-supported educational station. License periods up to 20 years, weak enforcement of its 1926 basic law, and unlimited transmitter

power all helped to make Mexico a haven for shady border station operations aimed at United States audiences but free from FRC control. By 1934,
12 such high-powered border stations, including John Brinkley's XER, were
operating or under construction.

Radio grew apace in Europe as well. In Great Britain, the British Broadcasting Company owned by manufacturing companies gave way to the
British Broadcasting Corporation on January 1, 1927. This government-
chartered monopoly, supported by post office-collected license fees on receivers, set an enduring standard for public service broadcasting. By 1932
United Kingdom radio operations were centralized in the handsome new
Broadcasting House in London, although lip service was paid to broadcasting in outlying regions such as Scotland and Wales. Germany and France
were advanced in radio, both technically and in station growth. International broadcasting became common in the early 1930s, with Radio
Moscow initiating one of the first shortwave broadcasting stations in 1929.
In late 1932, England began its BBC Empire Service to the Commonwealth,
and France broadcast extensively to its many colonies. The League of
Nations opened a shortwave station in 1932. In most European countries,
the government either directly operated or chartered and controlled broadcasting, and supported it by collecting annual taxes on receiving sets in the
same way the British government supported the BBC. Advertising rarely
was used for support. Colonies adopted the practices of their colonial masters, but broadcasting rarely affected the indigenous populations. Short-
and longwave frequencies augmented medium-wave ones in Europe
because the medium-wave broadcast band used in the United States could
not adequately contain and separate the many broadcasting stations and
languages of the many countries on the closely packed European continent.

4.9.3 Period Overview

The 1926 to 1933 period is one of the two most important in the history of
broadcasting; only 1946 to 1952 (Chapter 7) exceeds its importance in setting present-day patterns of radio and television, although television broadcasting was still in the laboratory in 1933. National radio networks and the
FRC were established, creating the structural and regulatory basis for broadcasting until the mid-1990s. Of nearly equal importance, the stabilizing effects of networks and the FRC led to increasing dominance by advertisers,
especially in network broadcasting.

Each of these factors helped bring permanence and standards to what
had been a day-to-day fad. Radio now could compete with other media for advertising dollars and audience. The FRC's clearing of technical interference
and the wider diversity of programs connected radio with its audience.
News and drama made their first appearances on network and major station
program schedules.

The importance of this period is underscored when we realize that the 1933 broadcast industry was very much like today's in structure, while the industry of 1926—only seven years earlier—was only roughly formed. In this short space of time, broadcasting had been molded to a pattern that would hold for decades to come and to which newer broadcast media, like FM, television, and even cable, would have to adapt.

Selected Further Reading

(Alphabetical within topics. For full citations, see Appendix D.)

Allen (1931, 1940) does the best job of relating the social history of the 1920s and 1930s, while Covert & Stevens (1984) discuss media between the World Wars. Barnouw (1966) is the best radio history of the period. Contemporary analyses of radio include Aly & Shively (1933), the first *Annals* collection (1929), Archer (1938, 1939), Buehler (1933), Codel (1930), Goldsmith & Lescarboura (1930), and the NAB (1933).

Mechanical television is described in Dinsdale (1932), Dunlap (1932), Felix (1931), and Sheldon & Grisewood (1929). The best histories of early television are Abramson (1987), Burns (1986, 1998), Pawley (1972) and Shiers (1997). Biographies of Baird include Moseley (1952) and McArthur & Waddell (1986). The rise of educational radio is reviewed in Frost (1937a), Lingel (1932), Perry (1929), Tyler (1933), and Wood & Wylie (1977). The development of radio advertising is discussed in Arnold (1933), Felix (1927), the FRC (1932), Hettinger (1933), Smulyan (1994), and Spalding (1963–1964). The rise of networks is traced in Bergreen (1980) and FCC (1941), while Paley (1979) and Smith (1990) detail William S. Paley's role.

The most useful directories of radio programs (for both this and subsequent chapters) include Buxton & Owen (1972), Dunning (1998), Sies (2000), Summers (1958) and Terrace (1998). Ely (1991) concentrates on *Amos 'n' Andy.* Recent assessments of radio's golden age development and impact are found in Barfield (1996), Douglas (1999), Godfrey & Leigh (1998), and Nachman (1998). Focused works on radio progrmming include Arnheim's (1936) unique volume on aesthetics, Cox (1999) on radio serials, Harmon (1967, 1970) on drama and comedy, Stedman (1977) on serials, and Wertheim (1979) on comedy. Picture histories (covering all of radio's development) focusing primarily on stars and programs include Rhoads (1996), Settel (1967), and Slide (1982). Guides to recorded programs include Pitts (1986) and Swartz & Reinehr (1993). Sterling (2002) is a general encyclopedia of radio.

Two examples of early audience research are Cantril & Allport (1935), and Lumley (1934). For the 1927 Act and operation under it see Davis (1927), FRC *Annual Reports* (1927–33), Kahn (1984), Kittross (1977), Rosen (1980), and Schmeckebier (1932). For broadcasting abroad, see Batson (1930), Briggs (1965) for the BBC, and Peers (1969) for Canada.

Anncr: "Ladies and gentlemen, I have a grave announcement to make. Incredible as it may seem, both the observations of science and the evidence of our eyes lead to the inescapable assumption that those strange beings who landed in the Jersey farmlands tonight are the vanguard of an invading army from the planet Mars."———*Orson Welles's "War of the Worlds" broadcast, October 30, 1938, on CBS*

CHAPTER 5

**MODEL RC-1
PHONOGRAPH RECORD
CABINET TO MATCH
PHONOGRAPH-RADIO**

An ideal stand for Phonograph-Radio, as it matches the 59F-1 exactly in size and finish. The two together make a harmonious, attractive furniture and musical unit. Or it can be used separately in another part of the room.

Mahogany finish. Size 26⅝ in. high, 15 in. wide and 10½ in. deep. 6 sloping record shelves. Space at bottom for record catalogs. HOLDS 100 RECORDS either 10 or 12-inch size.

Motorola
AMERICA'S FINEST AUTO RADIO

When you own a Motorola Car Radio you can enjoy the world's finest entertainment as you drive. Come in and see Motorola's many new and outstanding features: Electric Push-Button Tuning; Improved Acoustinator Personal Preference Selector; Automatic "Spot" Tuning. Motorola Exactly Matches Dash of Your Car —and at no extra cost.

Model "8-60" Push
6 Latest Style M
at Popular Pri

All Prices and Specifications Subject to Change Without

Made by Galvin Manufacturing Corporation, Ch

Printed in U.S.A.

> "The country has as many stations as it can support. Additional facilities will necessitate the commercialization of stations to the exclusion of public service."———*former FRC Commissioner H. A. Lafount, 1936*

RADIO'S GOLDEN AGE
(1934–1941)

Radio, the great storyteller, probably late 1930s or early 1940s. *National Archives.*

Chapter Outline

The blackened hulk of the cruise liner *Morro Castle* lying off the beach at Asbury Park, New Jersey, was a grisly remnant of the disaster in which 134 passengers and crew had burned to death or drowned in September 1934. On the beach a horde of salesmen hawking souvenir postcards and candy bars to tourists gave shape to former President Coolidge's stand that "the business of America is business." For most Americans, the *Morro Castle* was a distraction from worry over jobs and paychecks. Franklin Roosevelt's New Deal fight to bring the nation out of the Depression had just begun—and the still smoking ship was less depressing and more interesting than the bread lines of the unemployed.

Money was still tight and unemployment high, as radio came into its own. Once you had a set, radio was free, unlike newspapers, magazines, books, the movies, or the stage. While Americans turned to radio primarily for entertainment, they also absorbed news of conditions in other parts of the country, and the social upheaval in other parts of the world. They became both politically aware and dependent on radio for information.

Radio reported the sudden disasters—the *Morro Castle*, floods, the assassination of Louisiana populist Senator Huey P. Long in 1935—and slow political change—Hitler rearming Germany, war clouds gathering in the Far East, then in Spain, and finally throughout Europe as Germany lit the match of World War II. In 1936 King Edward VIII of England used radio to tell the world directly that he was giving up the throne for the "woman I love."

The "Fireside Chats" on radio of Franklin Roosevelt carried his plans for the country into the American home, aided by the REA (Rural Electrification Administration), which brought centrally generated electricity, and thus batteryless radio, to farm dwellers for the first time. He talked about the many federal agencies created to conquer the Depression. Citizens began to turn to Washington for leadership instead of to state capitals—and the federal government responded with new agencies and programs.

Radio reflected a country that was drinking legally again, with the lifting of Prohibition, and traveling farther; DC-3s were flying coast-to-coast overnight (with stops), transatlantic air service was promised, and Pennsylvania was building an unlimited-speed, multilane turnpike. Listeners in Maine knew that duststorms on the Great Plains were blowing away the rich Midwest topsoil, that floods on the Mississippi and Ohio were threatening river towns, and that "Oakies" dispossessed by the duststorms and economic conditions wandered across the country by car or freight train.

To most Americans, the 1930s brought new leisure. The five-day work week and the eight-hour day were becoming common. More people flocked to the movies every week. Walt Disney's first all-cartoon feature film *Snow White* appeared in 1937, and the highly creative *Fantasia* followed in 1940. The movie version of Margaret Mitchell's *Gone With the Wind* even permitted a spoken "damn"! Such big dance bands as Benny Goodman, Glenn Miller, and the Dorsey Brothers brought swing music to college proms and roadhouses alike, thanks to radio and juke boxes. People also read books. A generation of novelists came to maturity, including Sinclair Lewis, Edna Ferber, Ernest Hemingway, and John Steinbeck. The new picture magazines *Life* and *Look* quickly achieved high circulations.

Perhaps the most popular pastime was radio. This was truly radio's golden age, before World War II battlefield reports or television diverted listeners. Radio audiences grew steadily and broadcasting pioneers of the 1920s reaped a considerable profit. Although radio was still innovative and experimental, the medium was no longer novel—it was not only accepted but welcomed.

5.1 Innovations Around the Corner

Even during a period of relative stability in the broadcasting industry, seeds of change were germinating in laboratories across the country. Books and periodicals dwelled on technological improvements "just around the corner" that would change people's lives as AM radio had in the 1920s. These included static-free radio—FM; still pictures by wireless—facsimile; and perhaps most interesting to the public, moving pictures sent to the home by wireless—television (see p. 160). Their respective backers believed that FM radio, facsimile, or television was *the* future of broadcasting, while the AM radio broadcasters feared that these technologies would endanger their industry. This conflict was clear by the time this country entered World War II, when the battle in broadcasting had to defer to the battles against Germany and Japan.

5.1.1 Invention of FM Radio

Static always had interfered with radio reception, especially during summer thunderstorms and in the semitropical American South. Since the rasping "jamble" caused by lightning was amplitude modulated, a possible solution was to use frequency modulation for radio. Although the concept of FM dated back to the Poulsen Arc (see p. 33) in the early 1900s, experimentation had stopped in the early 1920s because most radio engineers thought that FM's drawbacks, such as distortion, outweighed its benefits and that the only solution was to overpower static by forcing a huge amount of transmitter power through as narrow a channel as possible. AM stations based their drive for additional power in the 1930s on the same idea (see p. 171).

An important radio engineer who disagreed with this conclusion was Edwin Armstrong, inventor of the feedback circuit (see p. 37) and other devices. Following his Signal Corps service in World War I, Armstrong began a search for a way to eliminate static, working at first with his former teacher, Professor Michael Pupin, at Columbia University and later alone. After devoting two years to frequency-modulated radio waves, Armstrong arrived in late 1930 at the key to successful FM broadcasting: the FM broadcast channel had to be many times *wider* than the standard AM channel of 10 kHz. Using a channel 200 kHz wide, with low power, Armstrong got excellent audio frequency response and virtually no static, even during electrical storms. (Actually, the swing of the modulated FM signal occupied only 75 kHz, but the additional bandwidth protected against interference from adjacent channels due to the instability of receiving equipment on the very high frequencies employed). Armstrong applied for the first four patents on his FM system in 1930 and received them just after Christmas in 1933.

With the basic FM patents secure, Armstrong gave his first demonstration to David Sarnoff of RCA. He and Sarnoff had known each other for nearly 20 years. RCA had used Armstrong's earlier inventions, to their mutual profit, and had an option to purchase new ones; Armstrong was the largest individual stockholder in RCA because of RCA's purchase of his feedback patents, and his wife had been Sarnoff's secretary. Sarnoff was impressed with FM but also was worried because Armstrong touted FM not as a means of solving the static interference problems but rather as a total replacement for AM. RCA, with its huge investment in AM broadcasting, would not readily undertake the heavy costs of developing a totally new system, especially one belonging to someone else.

Still, RCA scientists went to Columbia to observe FM and, on their advice, Sarnoff invited Armstrong to install equipment in RCA space atop the Empire State Building to test FM under broadcast conditions. RCA engineers, working with Armstrong for several months in 1934, made comparative broadcasts of music and other material using both AM and FM transmissions picked up by a receiving station 70 miles away. In November they transmitted at the same time on a single multiplexed FM carrier wave both the NBC-Red and -Blue programs of that day, a facsimile copy of part of the front page of the *New York Times*, and a telegraph message.

The parting of the ways came in Spring 1935. On April 26, Armstrong publicly announced FM and made plans for demonstrations for other engineers and the press. Just 10 days later, RCA announced its decision to spend $1 million developing television. RCA had decided to go with television, a totally new medium, rather than what it considered only an improvement

■ **The First Public Demonstration of FM: 1935**   Edwin Armstrong's biographer Lawrence Lessing provides a gripping account of the first public demonstration of what FM could do. Remember, thunderstorms and other interference could ruin AM station reception—and many then felt the only answer was greater power. Armstrong's audience was made up of fellow engineers, who listened to the inventor's highly technical paper with no hint of the demonstration to come. Meanwhile, 17 miles north of the Manhattan meeting site, Armstrong's friend, C. R. Runyon, was making last-minute adjustments to the world's first FM radio station—and in the process was burning out a generator halfway into Armstrong's talk. Armstrong continued the technical talk until he received word that Runyon was ready. An FM receiver—handmade, and one of the few then in existence—was set up near the lectern in the lecture hall.

For a moment the receiver groped . . . until the new station was tuned in with a dead unearthly silence, as the whole apparatus had been abruptly turned off. Suddenly out of the silence came Runyon's supernaturally clear voice: "This is amateur station W2AG in Yonkers, New York, operating on frequency modulation at two and a half meters." A hush fell over the large audience. Waves of two and a half meters ([approx.] 110 megacycles) were waves so short that up until then they had been regarded as too weak to carry a message across a street. Moreover, W2AG's announced transmitter power [100 watts] was barely enough to light one good-sized electric bulb. Yet these shortwaves and weak power were not only carrying a message over the seventeen miles from Yonkers, but carrying it by a method of modulation which the textbooks still held to be of no value. And doing it with a life-like clarity never heard on even the best clear-channel stations in the regular broadcast band. . . . A glass of water was poured before the microphone in Yonkers; it sounded like a glass of water being poured and not, as in the "sound effects" on ordinary radio, like a waterfall. A paper was crumpled and torn; it sounded like paper and not like a crackling forest fire. An oriental gong was softly struck and its overtones hung shimmering in the meeting halls' arrested air. . . . The absence of background noise and the lack of distortion in FM circuits made music stand out against the velvety silence with a presence that was something new in auditory experiences. The secret lay in the achievement of a signal-to-noise ratio of 100-to-1 or better, as against 30-to-1 on the best AM stations.

Source: Lawrence Lessing, *Man of High Fidelity: Edwin Howard Armstrong.* (Philadelphia Lippincott, 1956), pages 209–210. By permission.

on an existing system. The potential profits of television were clearly more attractive. Late in 1935 Armstrong was asked to remove his FM apparatus from the Empire State Building so that room could be made for expanded RCA television experimentation.

5.1.2 Early Innovation of FM

Edwin Armstrong believed that FM was bound to replace AM and that static-free and better quality sound would prevail. With the end of RCA cooperation, he moved to promote his system by using his own substantial fortune (from the sale of earlier inventions, mostly to RCA) and by persuading influential broadcasters to back him. In November 1935 Armstrong demonstrated FM to an engineering society meeting, publishing the key parts of that paper a few months later. Despite skepticism of Federal

Communications Commission engineers, Armstrong received permission to
build his own experimental FM station at Alpine, New Jersey, on the Hudson
River Palisades, near New York City. That fall the FCC held frequency allocation hearings and provided the experimental radio service with space for
13 of Armstrong's 200-kHz channels but in three widely separated places in
the spectrum. Only five channels were suitable for the existing transmitting
and receiving technology. (See allocation chart on p. 251).

However, Armstrong plowed ahead. Support for FM came from the
Yankee Network, a large New England AM network developed in the 1930s
by John Shepard III, with 10 stations in 1933 and twice as many a decade
later. In Spring 1937, Yankee applied for permission to build a 50-kw FM
station near Worcester, Massachusetts, to experiment with long-range and
relay broadcasting. Armstrong's own station, W2XMN in Alpine, began
low-power tests in April 1938. The first Yankee Network FM station started
in 1939, followed by a second a few months later. General Electric established stations in Albany and Schenectady, New York, to test FM reception
and made plans to manufacture receivers. Before the year was out, stations
were on the air from Washington, D.C., New York City, several places in
Connecticut, and Massachusetts. Three experimental stations, including
one owned by NBC (RCA liked to hedge its bets) and two in Wisconsin,
opened in early 1940, broadcasting engineering test programs, a lot of music, and no commercials. Several New England stations experimented with
relay broadcasting, whereby one station broadcast a program and others
picked it up with sensitive antennas and rebroadcast it. In this way, they
could avoid AT&T line connection expense and achieve better sound quality. Without static, and with an audio-frequency response up to 15 kHz,
such relaying was possible on FM but not on AM (though there was experimentation with wide-band high audio fidelity AM).

The success of these experiments led to demand for receivers, and firms
started making FM sets. Several stations attempted to promote interest
among listeners in the better sound of the new system, although FM table
model receivers cost at least $60. Supporters demonstrated FM reception to
engineering, political, and social groups, and early in 1940 formed an FM
trade association to persuade the FCC to allow commercial operation of FM
stations.

More than 20 experimental FM stations were on the air, with more
being built, when the FCC began eight days of hearings on FM's status in
mid-March 1940. A wide variety of views was heard, and to most observers'
surprise, RCA, then deep in television promotion, presented no objections to
FM. The commission announced its approval of commercial FM on May 20
to begin January 1, 1941, on 40 channels provided in a new and larger band
of 42 to 50 MHz with the lowest five channels reserved for educational stations. To accommodate FM, experimental television lost an existing channel and government services seven MHz of spectrum space, but they both
gained even more space in other parts of the spectrum. Engineering rules

released in June called for three classes of FM stations, defined by area served rather than power and frequency as with AM. The first construction permits for commercial FM stations were issued to 15 applicants in October, and in December the FCC issued an FM call-letter plan, which used numbers and letters in a code signifying station geographic and frequency locations.

A number of factors held up FM's initial growth. Construction permits were frozen during the FCC investigation of newspaper control of radio stations (see p. 211). While about 40 stations were on the air by 1941's end, only half were operating commercially. Of the rest, operating with experimental licenses, few had full power. Nearly all FM stations were affiliated with an AM station in the same city or town and thus lacked impetus for a rapid push to full-fledged commercial operation. Preparations for national defense put increasing demands on construction materials. By the time the United States entered the war in December 1941, FM was a commercial service, but just barely. Fewer than 400,000 receivers were in the hands of the public, and few of the 50 or so stations were in the West or South.

5.1.3 Facsimile

The notion of sending print and still pictures by wire or wireless was not new. The newspaper industry used a process called *wirephoto*, by which a photograph was scanned and sent by wire. By the late 1930s, interest developed in the idea of sending entire newspapers by radio rather than having them hand-delivered to the home. Receivers were designed and some stations experimented with *fax*, but facsimile never got off the ground as a broadcast medium. There were several reasons: the greater interest in the *moving* pictures of television, competition with new FM and older but still expanding AM radio services, high costs of facsimile paper, and inability of the system to transmit quickly. Facsimile seemed to have more applications for industry than for the home. Only in the late 1960s did industrial and public safety uses of fax systems become important, and the office and home "fax revolution" that started in the 1970s moved in a nonbroadcast direction.

5.1.4 Electronic Television

Although many early television experimenters used mechanical devices for both transmitting and receiving (see p. 110), later experimenters realized that the cathode-ray tube, which had been developed by Sir William Crookes and others in the 1870s, could better display the televised image. In 1897, Professor Karl Ferdinand Braun of the Physical Institute of Strassburg produced the cathode-ray oscilloscope, which used the tube for the visual observation of electrical signals. A decade later, Professor Boris Rosing of the St. Petersburg Technological Institute modified a Braun tube to display very faint images from a mechanical scanner that fed into a photoelectric cell connected to the Braun tube.

The outlines of a practical home television system were now clear. Lee de Forest's Audion (see pp. 35–36) would amplify the weak video current; the cathode-ray tube could be developed for reception; and methods of transmitting by wireless and synchronizing transmitting and receiving apparatus devised—but the basic idea was there. True, a television camera had to be designed that would break the picture down into very small elements and make sharp distinctions between light and shadow. Developing present technical standards took several decades.

The two paths of development of electronic scanning, which merged in the late 1930s, are associated with the names of Zworykin and Farnsworth. Vladimir K. Zworykin had been a student of Rosing's before World War I and had started extensive work on television as early as 1917 as an employee of the Russian Wireless Telegraph and Telephone Company. He came to the United States in 1919, with ideas for a television system in mind. Joining the Westinghouse research staff in 1920, he spent several frustrating years, including a year and a half at another company, due to Westinghouse's lack of interest in television. He eventually received approval to work on television, photoelectric cells, and sound motion picture reproduction. Although Westinghouse took out the first patent on Zworykin's camera tube in 1923, a practical demonstration of what he called the *iconoscope*—from the Greek words *eikon* (image) and *skopein* (to view)—could not be made until 1928. This device used a storage–discharge effect to achieve sensitivity to lower light levels, and magnetic deflection to aim a beam of electrons across a target that had been charged by light impinging on it. Unbeknownst to Zworykin, the British physicist A. A. Campbell Swinton had anticipated the iconoscope in 1908 independently of Rosing's need for an electronic scanner, but Campbell Swinton had never developed it. David Sarnoff, then vice president and general manager of RCA, became interested in Zworykin's invention and offered him support, which increased in 1930 when RCA took over research functions from GE and Westinghouse.

The other major inventor of electronic television was Philo T. Farnsworth, who worked under conditions very different from Zworykin's association with RCA's large industrial laboratory. As a boy in Rigby, Idaho, Farnsworth read popular electrical and radio magazines. In 1921, at age 15, he started studying the cathode-ray tube and photoelectricity. His high school notebooks later became crucially important in a major patent fight. While studying and building radios in Salt Lake City, he met San Francisco businessman George Everson, who arranged financial backing for the young inventor and later wrote a book about him. Like many other inventors, Farnsworth consistently had difficulty working within an organization and in pressing an idea through to commercial

■ **The Rise of Electronic Television: 1930s**   An experimental model television receiver (with a mirror to reflect the picture tube, which faces straight up) is tried out by RCA's Vladimir Zworykin—inventor of the iconoscope tube and one of the key figures in the development of electronic television.

Courtesy of Group W and Broadcast Pioneers Library.

success, although his scientific and engineering skills were exceptionally high. Working in his first San Francisco laboratory, by 1927 he had transmitted his first picture—a 60-line image of a dollar sign! By 1930 he had developed and patented an image dissector and a new television scanning and synchronizing system that he hoped to refine for commercial use. The Depression and increasing expenditures led him to accept financing from

Philco (the Philadelphia Storage Battery Company, soon to be an important radio manufacturer) and move to Philadelphia, where he worked from 1931 to 1933.

Starting on August 25, 1934, Farnsworth gave the first general public demonstration of electronic television, at the Franklin Institute in Philadelphia, using a 220-line system. Scheduled to run for 10 days but extended another week, the general public could see a new demonstration every 20 minutes until late into the night, and even see themselves on television as they entered the room. The opening session was attended by some 200 scientists, engineers, and others and received a great deal of attention in the newspapers. One headline had Farnsworth predicting television in the home in only 10 years as well as other wonders. It was predicted that sets could be sold for $250 (a sum now worth more than $3,000). The first demonstration's content wasn't merely dollar signs, talking heads, or tennis stars showing their techniques in a studio. A camera was taken outside to show some football players in action and even televised the moon!

However the Philco management, who wanted to get in on the ground floor of television independently of RCA, decided that they could not wait for Farnsworth, despite his ability, to develop a a commercial system of television. No longer supported by Philco, but continuing his work in Philadelphia with the support of his California backers, Farnsworth steadily improved his system.

By 1938 more than $1 million had been spent on Farnsworth's research, development, and legal fees—with only about 7% of that sum recovered from license fees and royalties. However, working with a series of excellent patent attorneys, the Farnsworth interests had 73 patents and 60 applications, approximately three-quarters of which represented the inventor's work on the image dissector, the image amplifier, and other devices. The strength of Farnsworth's patent position was proven by his winning in a number of important patent interference cases. In two of these, the Patent Office, concluding that the image dissector operated on different principles from the iconoscope, gave basic patents to both Farnsworth and Zworykin. In 1941 Farnsworth won a patent interference case against RCA that secured basic patents on synchronization and other important aspects of his television system. As a result, both RCA and AT&T decided to take out television licenses from Farnsworth in 1939. For the first time RCA had to pay royalties to another company; RCA patent manager Otto Schairer reportedly signing the royalty agreement with "tears in his eyes." Farnsworth's radio and television company went into manufacturing in 1939, but television wasn't yet ready to become a mass medium—and production of receivers was shut down by the government early in World War II. After 1940 Farnsworth, partly because of ill health that plagued him until his death in 1971, no longer acted as the company's research director.

Even more than Edwin Armstrong, Farnsworth typified the lone inventor in technological development. Uncomfortable when he had to work with the public or within a large group, he was obviously happier working in a small laboratory than as vice president of a manufacturing company. Television is an especially complex field, and the lone inventor or innovator was at a disadvantage compared to the research team whose work receives finance, publicity, continuity, and support from large corporations, government, or universities.

Picture definition was very limited at first, but both Farnsworth and Zworykin soon produced more detailed pictures with their delicate and expensive electronic gear than mechanical systems could produce (see pp. 110–113). As early as 1927 Farnsworth demonstrated an electronic system with a resolution around 100 lines at 30 pictures per second, compared with the 30- to 60-line definition of the best mechanical systems of that time. RCA transmitted 120-line pictures electronically in 1931 and 343-line pictures four years later. Although mechanical systems eventually exceeded 200 lines, they had clearly approached the limits of their technology, while electronic television promised much improvement.

Continuing experimentation led to an increasing demand for spectrum space. Stations at Purdue University in Indiana and GE in Schenectady, New York, were sending recognizable images thousands of miles on the shortwave 2-MHz band, but the experimenters needed more and much wider channels and hoped for commercial operation on higher bands. Under pressure from conflicting FM and television interests, the FCC held a series of allocations hearings and decided in 1937 (a) to accept applications for experimental television stations in the band from 20 to 300 MHz, already rapidly filling with other services, and (b) to allocate seven channels, each 6-MHz wide, in the band between 54 and 108 MHz, with an additional 12 channels in the 156- to 294-MHz band set aside for experimentation and expansion. Only the lower seven channels were put to use, however, as receivers of the period could not pick up the higher band transmissions, and transmitting devices at these frequencies were then not very efficient.

By the end of the 1936–1937 Informal Engineering Conference, the FCC concluded that "television is not yet ready for public service on a national scale," but that "the rate of [television] progress is rapid and the energies of the laboratories of the country are being concentrated on the technical development of television." Still, the FCC warned, "There does not appear to be any immediate outlook for the recognition of television service on a commercial basis," and it prohibited sponsorship of programs. It also required that licensees must conduct research and report on the result of that research to the FCC.

In 1938 RCA proceeded toward standardizing television for commercial use. It had spent millions of dollars on research and acquired competing and secondary patents. After negotiating an agreement on Farnsworth's patents in 1939 almost entirely on Farnsworth's terms, it was ready to innovate television on its own standards and terms. Despite the displeasure of other experimenters and manufacturers, RCA persuaded the Radio Manufacturers Association (RMA) to consider adopting its television standards. When an RMA committee found that the only other practical system, Farnsworth's, was being merged with RCA's in a patents pool, the RMA adopted the RCA system. But before RCA could begin regular programming and sell receivers to the public, the FCC had to accept the proposed standards and then approve commercial operation. Several months after the RMA presented the proposed new standards on September 10, 1938, the FCC appointed a committee of three commissioners to investigate the status of television preparatory to recommending a course of action. The RMA request had aroused considerable public interest about television's future. Newspaper columnist Walter Winchell predicted on September 18 that "the local stores will be selling television sets for as little as $3.95 by October 1." Things did not move quite that fast.

5.1.5 Television's False Dawn

The FCC television advisory committee moved cautiously. Its initial report of May 22, 1939, recommended that further delay in setting standards would best serve the public interest and straddled the fence by condemning premature standards while praising the proposed RMA–RCA standards as adequate.

In its second report, on November 15, 1939, the television advisory committee reversed itself and proposed standards of 441 lines, 30 pictures per second, which were, of course, supported by their author, RCA. Relying heavily on "the thoughts of the present leaders of the industry"— rather than on such nonmanufacturing outsiders as Armstrong and CBS—the committee concluded that more rapid progress could be expected by "allowing commercial operation to recoup some developmental expense."

Opposition to the RCA proposals crystallized at FCC hearings starting January 15, 1940. Many—including the DuMont and Zenith companies, the latter of which particularly disliked the weak synchronization technique, and Edwin Armstrong, who wanted additional frequencies for FM radio (see pp. 156–160)—objected to various technical standards and allocations. Some called for higher definition. In fact, virtually the entire manufacturing industry objected to being "frozen out" by the adoption of RCA's standards. RCA had the support of only its engineers and Farnsworth.

In the face of this controversy, the FCC reached a typical compromise: some television stations would be permitted "limited" commercial operation, to give program developers a chance to recoup some costs, starting September 1, 1940. At the same time, no standards of transmission would

■ **The First Television Sets Go on Sale: 1938–1939**   Television sets probably were first offered for public sale in the United States in April 1938 (England had beaten this date by nearly two years) at Piser's Furniture Store in the Bronx, New York. About 4,000 customers jammed the store for the first showing of a 3-inch ($125) and a 5-inch ($250) set offered by Communications System, Inc. The first table below shows what was available by Christmas 1938. Macy's department store had four different brands on sale in May 1939, and by July, as seen in the second table, 14 manufacturers were in production or planning for same. By December 1939, 8 set-makers had produced 5,000 television receivers—all before final FCC approval of standards. Prices ranged from $200 for 5-inch screens up to $600 for 9-inch sets. Most of these sets were used as demonstrators and very few were sold. *Note:* The dollar in those days was worth roughly 12 times what it will buy today.

TV Sets Available in December 1938

Company	Size of Screen (in inches)	Price Range (in dollars)
American Television Corp.	3, 5	$125–395
Andrea Radio Corp.	na	175–595
Dumont	14	395–445
General Electric	5, 9, 12	175–600
RCA	5, 9, 12	175–600

TV Sets Available in July 1939

Company	No. of Models	Size of Tube (in inches)	Retail Price (in dollars)
American Television Corp.	3	5	$185–395
Andrea Radio Corp.	2	5-12	190–350
Crosley	2-4	Announced for August	
Dumont	2	5	190–600
Farnsworth	2-4	Announced for the Fall	
General Electric	5	5-12	195–1,000
International Television	1-3	Announced for December	
Majestic	1	5	na
Majestic (kit)	1	5	125
Philco	6	5-9	200–425
Pilot	3	9-12	250–425
RCA	4	5-12	150–600
Stewart-Warner	1	9	600
Stromberg-Carlson	1	9	575
Westinghouse	3	5-12	200–600
Zenith	None for sale, but some for loan		

na = not available

Source: Alfred R. Oxenfeldt, *Marketing Practices in the TV Set Industry* (New York: Columbia University Press, 1964), pages 9–11. By permission.

be fixed, since "crystallization of standards at the current level of the art, by whatever means accomplished, would inevitably stifle research in basic phases of the art in which improvement appeared promising." This decision meant that, despite the dangers of equipment obsolescence, the public was to have the "opportunity" to buy various types of receivers to determine which system it preferred.

Throughout this period, the FCC was concerned with public investment in receivers. Even in its order of March 23, 1940, granting RCA limited commercial television, the FCC pointed out that "public participation in television experimentation at this time is desirable only if the public understands that it is experimenting in reception and not necessarily investing in receiving equipment with a guarantee of its continued usefulness." Despite this, RCA emphasized the sale of receivers to the public in its publicity for a broadcast on April 30, 1939, from the New York World's Fair.

Notwithstanding the FCC's admonition against encouraging "a large public investment in receivers which may become obsolete in a relatively short time," RCA took the approval for "limited commercial broadcasting" as a green light to manufacture and sell television receivers. It launched an intensive promotion and advertising campaign on March 20, 1940, that said, in essence, television is here, the commission has approved it, and a new commercial service to the American home will start—in the New York area, at least—on September 1, 1940. This publicity campaign was preceded by a bitter fight within the RMA when RCA's chief television engineer presented the company's position to an RMA committee as a *fait accompli*, and when President David Sarnoff threatened to pull RCA out of the RMA, refusing to discuss "any program the purpose of which is to delay the commercialization of television"—a far cry from its January FCC testimony. Philco withdrew from the RMA television standards committee, saying that the committee could serve no further purpose, since widespread sale of RCA equipment would make consideration of any other standard futile. All members of the committee except RCA and Farnsworth voted to consider new proposals, but none were forthcoming.

However, the FCC reacted strongly and issued a vigorous order only two days after the RCA publicity campaign started. Chairman James Lawrence Fly delivered his opinion of RCA, and a description of the issues, in a nationwide broadcast on April 2. The FCC order called for a new series of hearings, to start April 8, reopening the question of standards and a starting date for commercial broadcasting. The hearings lasted five days, with the same cast of characters. President Roosevelt announced on April 12 that the administration would exert every effort to prevent television from coming under monopolistic control. The FCC stated that it would have acted sooner if it had known about the RCA statement and hostilities at the RMA February meetings. (Ten years later General Sarnoff claimed that he had "personally" shown FCC Chairman Fly the objectionable RCA advertisement *before* it was published.)

Put on the defensive at the hearings, RCA stimulated a Senate investigation of the FCC's television policy in mid-April. This tactic failed to soften Chairman Fly's determination, and the FCC issued a scathing report on May 28 that condemned RCA, fostered research and development by other companies, limited station owning, and rescinded permission for commercial broadcasting until the entire industry could agree on standards. A brief fight centered on the right of the FCC to regulate the manufacture and sale of, and public "right" to buy, television receivers; but Fly was able to give as good as he got, and RCA clearly lost this fray, known as the "false dawn" of television.

Political and legal arguments did not stop engineering developments. In July the RMA established a National Television System Committee (NTSC), chaired by W. R. G. Baker of GE. By January 27, 1941, after 5,000 man-hours of work, the industry was able to present a united front to the commission, which the next day called for a public hearing. At these hearings, starting March 20, 1941, the FCC found that the NTSC standards had virtually unanimous industry approval, and that the 525-line, 30-picture standards were far superior to those of 1940. In addition, the new standards substituted FM for AM sound in television and greatly strengthened the synchronization system. In its report of May 3, 1941, the FCC accepted the NTSC recommendations and approved commercial television operation using the new standards starting July 1, 1941. These basic standards are still in use today.

The FCC's decisions did give television a green light, although they took away one of its 19 channels, deferred action on CBS's suggestion that color television be considered, created a very minor problem of receiver obsolescence—affecting only a few thousand sets, which the manufacturer could convert—and, in general, reflected the salutary effects of knocking together the heads of engineers and manufacturers to achieve cooperation.

5.2 Station Expansion

As the country slowly emerged from the Depression, radio broadcasting began to expand again. In the 1935–1941 period, more than 200 new AM stations took to the air, while few went off (see Appendix C, table 1-A). By the late 1930s, cumulative investment in tangible broadcast property, in addition to receivers, was in the order of $65 million. Many communities got their first radio station, while most large cities added one or more stations. This expansion, however, was not uniform throughout the country. In 1936, 43% of *all* stations were in markets of 100,000 people or more, as were 60% of the regional and 90% of the clear-channel operations. Smaller communities usually had to make do with low-power (100 to 250 watts) local stations, 75% of which were located in such communities; most places under 10,000 in population, and many under 50,000, had *no* local station. Thus radio was still a large-town or city service, and many listeners in rural areas had only secondary service (see p. 204).

The major reasons for this urban bias were economic and technical. In a country still in a depression with restricted advertising budgets, placing a station in a market too small to support it adequately was economically

■ **The First Television Rate Card: 1941**   Here is a partial reproduction of the first of a long series of television rate cards for NBC's New York outlet (now WNBC-TV), dated for the beginning of U.S. commercial television.

NBC *Television* RATES
Station WNBT

EFFECTIVE JULY 1, 1941

I TRANSMISSION RATE

GROSS

	60 Min.	30 Min.	15 Min.
6:00 PM to 11:00 PM Daily	$120.00	$60.00	$30.00
8:00 AM to 12 Noon Daily	60.00	30.00	15.00
12 Noon to 6:00 PM Daily, exclusive of Saturday and Sunday	60.00	30.00	15.00
12 Noon to 6:00 PM Saturday and Sunday	90.00	45.00	22.50
11:00 PM to Sign Off Daily	90.00	45.00	22.50

{ Rates for other units of time in exact proportion to corresponding one-hour rate. No periods less than 5 minutes sold except for Service Spots.

SERVICE SPOTS (News, Weather, Time, Etc.)

Evening (6:00 PM to Sign Off)—$8.00 for maximum of 1 minute.
Day (8:00 AM to 6:00 PM)   —$4.00 for maximum of 1 minute.

II PROGRAM FACILITIES RATE

TYPE OF FACILITIES (Based on time on the air to nearest 5 minutes.)

	60 Min.	30 Min.	15 Min.	10 Min.	5 Min.
Main Studio	$150.00	$90.00	$60.00	$53.00	$45.00
Small Studio	75.00	45.00	30.00	26.00	22.00
Film Studio	75.00	45.00	30.00	26.00	22.00
Field Pickups	75.00	(Minimum Charge—$75.00)			

{ Rates for units of time longer than one hour in exact proportion to corresponding one-hour rate.

Service Spots—Facilities and Handling—$5.00 per spot.
(Must originate in small or film studio.)

foolish. Many cities without radio stations were served by numerous outlets in nearby metropolitan areas. Advertisers and their agencies, to avoid splitting up one audience with many stations, usually favored the larger operations.

The technical problems were more involved. For one thing, radio station power continued to increase. Whereas only 37 stations broadcast with from 5 to 10 kw in 1935, 140 stations broadcast with such power in 1940. Stations with 50 kw of power had increased from 29 to 39, but the number of low-power (100 watts or less) stations had dropped from

179 to 98. Since new stations in these years typically were established in areas with limited radio service, they created few interference problems. But the Davis Amendment (see pp. 143–144) allowed the commission little flexibility in approving construction permit applications, as equality of facilities in the five zones had to be maintained. On June 5, 1936, the Davis Amendment was repealed, allowing more radio growth in highly populated areas by removing this artificial lid on expansion. A rush of applications followed for areas with the most population, again short-changing rural areas and suburbs. The clear-channel stations in large cities were expected to provide service to thousands of square miles of rural areas at night, when sky-wave propagation allows radio waves to travel longer distances.

5.2.1 Minimizing Interference

A number of ways to reduce interference was proposed. One, first tried by the FRC, was to reduce nighttime power and number of stations on the air. By the late 1930s, about 10% of radio stations were licensed to operate during daytime hours only and another 30% reduced power at night. A small proportion (4% in 1937) could broadcast only during specific, usually daytime, hours, and another 18% shared operations on the same frequency with another station in the same community. Another, more important means of limiting interference was the *directional antenna* (DA), which sent a station's signal out more strongly in one direction than another, protecting other stations in the suppressed directions from much man-made interference. This engineering technique was used by only 12 stations in 1934 but by more than 200—roughly one-quarter of all stations—by 1941. When adjacent or co-channel stations in different communities used it, they both normally could stay on the air serving their audiences, without overlapping. Sometimes the directional pattern—often a figure 8 or more complicated shape—required two to four expensive towers and great engineering skill.

Late in 1939 the Federal Communications Commission modified the 1928 FRC broadcast station classification system to allow four types of stations: Class I, high-power stations operating on the 25 clear channels; Class II, secondary stations operating on clear channels (but using less power at night, DAs or, most often, going off the air at night to protect a dominant clear station); Class III, regional stations; and Class IV, low-power local operations on the few channels set aside for them. The major change was the establishment of Class II.

There was, and is, a continuing debate on the role of clear-channel stations, typically 50-kw operations in major cities. Some observers consider them to be the first at the spigot, skimming off the best advertising dollars. Others, including rural spokesmen and their many defenders in government, saw them as the only effective means of reaching most of the country at night. More than one-third of the nation's voters got their only reliable night radio service in the 1930s from clear-channel stations. The conflict between this coverage and the equally important desire for more stations on the air, especially local stations in areas with no primary service, led to major debates in the late 1930s.

5.2.2 Superpower

The licensees of clear-channel stations fueled the debate by forming a pressure group that pushed the commission for more power. *Superpower* was not a new term, but whereas it once had meant 1,000 or 5,000 or even 20,000 watts, 50,000 watts was now the limit for AM stations. Clear-channel operators said that yet greater power would allow better service to a wider coverage area, which usually meant more nighttime coverage for the rural areas. Opponents of superpower saw this demand as another ploy to get more power and economic clout for stations already too powerful.

Superpower was put to the test in Cincinnati. In 1934 Powel Crosley, Jr.'s clear-channel station WLW was allowed to broadcast with 500,000 watts from 1 A.M. to 6 A.M. as an experiment. On April 17, 1934, Crosley secured a short-term license for 500,000 watts around the clock to experiment with audience and advertiser reaction to the increase, as well as to measure day and night interference. The power increase somewhat extended the station's already wide coverage, but its main effect was to improve the signal substantially in areas already reached. It also caused interference to CFRB in Toronto, and the Canadians complained. To protect CFRB, the FCC required WLW to install a directional antenna in February 1935, and the experiment continued. Listener surveys showed WLW as "first" in preference polls in 13 states, and "second" in six additional states—all of the Midwest and a chunk of the South and East. WLW acquired a national focus, dubbed itself the "Nation's Station," and soon subsisted completely on national and regional advertising. Local advertising disappeared partly because the station raised its rates by 20%—WLW explaining to the commission that additional use of electricity and some expensive rewiring had helped push operating costs up 68% ($25 more per operating hour). With the rate card increase, WLW's income was soon three times that of other 50-kw stations, although additional operating costs kept its net profit about the same. But more important, WLW did not want to relinquish the national prestige that the higher power rating had brought.

Others, however, distrusted one station's having such a wide audience. Some United States senators expressed concern that regional and local stations might find it harder to serve local interests. Fifteen other 50-kw clear-channel stations filed applications with the FCC to operate with the higher power. Networks fretted that wide-coverage competition might affect their business, and smaller stations in WLW's coverage area complained about the station's domination. A 1938 "Sense of the Senate" resolution (not an actual law) stated that 50 kw was plenty for any AM station within the American broadcasting structure—a limit still in effect. In March 1939 the FCC rescinded the 500-kw fulltime authorization for WLW, allowing only early morning experimentation once again. The station appealed, but the decision stuck. An attempt by some broadcasters to obtain 500-kw operation in 1940 because of the defense buildup also failed. WLW's early morning experiments continued until early 1942, when wartime restrictions ended them. The 500-kw transmitter eventually was broken up into smaller units and used for shortwave broadcasting.

In some ways, this superpower debate and experiment can be seen as the high-water mark of AM broadcasting facilities. Wartime shortages soon hobbled AM radio expansion; and, after the war, although there were many new stations, attention was diverted to FM and television development. Most clear channels were nibbled away over the next decades (see p. 414).

By 1941 radio broadcasting was a full-time business, and most station owners were full-time broadcasters. The commission increased the stability of the industry in 1939 when it extended the license period from six months (which it had been since 1928) to one year, although the Communications Act permitted and the FCC later adopted a three-year period which remained in effect until the 1990s. Of all stations on the air in 1939, networks owned 4% and newspapers 28%. Such figures conceal the true concentration of power, however. With respect to clear-channel and high-power regional stations, networks owned 25%, newspapers 27%, and radio/electrical manufacturers about 13%—roughly two-thirds of the total. Broadcasting was to a great extent individually and locally owned, but the big-audience and big-profit stations were concentrated in fewer hands.

Another sign of growth amid relatively stable conditions was the near doubling of broadcast employees—stations and networks, full- and part-time—from 14,000 in 1935 to 27,000 in 1941. The National Association of Broadcasters estimated in 1940 that approximately 350,000 persons were employed because of radio in advertising agencies, radio manufacturing companies, and as talent as well as in stations and networks.

5.3 Network Domination

With a few exceptions, success in radio station operation in the 1930s required having a network affiliation—preferably NBC-Red or CBS. By late 1938 the four national networks had affiliated all the 52 clear-channel stations but two (and they had ties with Mutual), half the regional stations, and even some low-power local stations. In all, almost half the unlimited-time stations were network affiliates. These stations took in the lion's share of broadcast revenues, because the big audiences that popular network programs drew attracted local advertisers.

By 1941 there were four national networks—NBC-Red, NBC-Blue, CBS, and Mutual—and some 20 regional networks. Of the latter, 14 operated in only one state, while six had wider coverage, including the Don Lee Network on the West Coast and the Yankee Network in New England. Many regional networks offered special programming to their affiliates, others merely facilitated program exchange, but all networks made time-buying easier for the advertising agencies by offering a block of stations and wide coverage with one order.

NBC was totally controlled by RCA—then a publicly held corporation, now owned by GE. In 1941, after government antitrust action a decade earlier, no one individual or firm held more than one-half of 1% of its stock. During the 1930s NBC operated two separate networks: the more important Red Network with larger stations as affiliates and far more advertising income and popular programs, and the Blue Network with its less powerful stations and more public service and sustaining programming. In 1935, 14% of stations were affiliated with one of the NBC networks, a figure that went up to 25% by 1941, not including 100 stations listed as optional (at the sponsor's request) affiliates for either network. NBC owned 10 stations and, from 1932 to 1940, was responsible for operating 5 others owned by Westinghouse—an agreement that ended when the FCC required licensees to program their own stations. Of the 10 owned-and-operated (O & O) outlets, all but 3 were unlimited-time 50-kw stations. In 1930 NBC opened a short-lived talent agency. In 1934 it began a transcription service, first for its affiliates and then for other stations, which provided a regularly supplemented and renewed library of prerecorded music on large discs.

In the late 1930s CBS was about one-third owned and controlled by its president, William S. Paley, and his family. It affiliated with some 15 or 16% of all the stations on the air and from 1936 to 1939 owned nine stations outright. In 1939 CBS sold its Cincinnati outlet and picked up a large minority interest in two other stations. All but one of its O & Os were unlimited-time 50-kw operations. Like NBC, CBS operated an "artist's bureau"—a talent agency, which actually did more business with NBC than with CBS—and, starting in 1940, a transcription service. That CBS was not in the phonograph record business until the end of 1938, when it bought the American Record Corporation—which then had Columbia Phonograph Company as a subsidiary—and changed its name to Columbia Record Corp., can partly explain the six-year lag behind NBC. CBS was devoted to broadcasting and other program-related services, while NBC was only a small part of a large electrical manufacturing and communications firm.

In summer 1934, four major eastern and midwestern stations decided to make themselves available to advertisers at a group rate by interconnecting themselves by wire lines. The four stations were WGN (Chicago), owned by the *Chicago Tribune*; WOR (Newark, New Jersey), owned by the Bamberger (Macy) department store; WLW (Cincinnati), owned by Powel Crosley, Jr., and just starting its 500-kw experiments; and WXYZ (Detroit), by George W. Trendle. The first three were 50-kw clear-channel stations trying to improve their economic condition outside the established networks, while WXYZ brought an especially popular new program, *The Lone Ranger*, to the new network. On September 29, 1934, the group changed its name from the Quality Network to the Mutual Broadcasting System, a name that stressed its unique organizational structure.

Unlike CBS and NBC, Mutual did not have a central ownership with O & O stations and contractual affiliates. From the beginning it was a cooperative venture, more or less equally operated by its four partners, although technically only WGN and WOR owned the firm's nominal amount of stock. For two years Mutual remained limited to its original four stations but was heard in most of the eastern United States. When WXYZ left Mutual for NBC in late 1935, its place was taken by CKLW in Windsor, Ontario, which served the same region. In 1936 the 13 affiliates of the New England-based Colonial Network and the 10 affiliates of the West Coast-based Don Lee Network affiliated as well with Mutual, making it a true national network. The addition of other independent stations and networks, including a 23-affiliate Texas network, brought Mutual from less than half of 1% of all stations in 1935 to more than 19% by 1940, and brought the first network service to many communities. However, many of its new stations were primarily affiliated with NBC or CBS and used Mutual programs only as fillers and were regional and local outlets with low power and relatively small audiences. Not surprisingly, therefore, this network lagged behind NBC and CBS in audience size and in advertising income. Because Mutual was a cooperative venture, most programs came from the founding or affiliate stations, although it did operate a small central news service in New York.

Perhaps the clearest indication of the importance of networks in the late 1930s was the increasing control that CBS and NBC exerted over their affiliates. Stations were bound to these networks for five-year periods, although the networks could end a contract after any single year. Mutual's one-year term for both sides was an exception. Affiliations were tightly exclusive: Networks would provide programs only to their affiliates, and affiliates could provide time to other national chains only on occasions when their primary network did not care. Stations gave option periods to the network for its national commercial programming. CBS had the right to take all day, NBC most of the day, but it gave 28-day notice, and Mutual averaged four hours a day. Finally, although stations legally could reject sustaining programs from the networks in order to air local shows, rejecting commercially sponsored programs could jeopardize their affiliation.

The one-sided nature of network contracts was a result of relative strength. Local stations did give networks and national advertisers access to audiences in their communities. But networks had the advertising money to produce programs that stations needed to attract audiences. No single station could afford to produce programs that would be as popular as those of the networks. Networks also supplied sustaining programs that the stations could use as free "fill." Hence, the affiliated stations, even with regional coverage, needed the networks more than vice versa, and other stations always were waiting for a chance to affiliate. Networks could demand and get major concessions, although powerful clear-channel stations could sometimes get better terms than smaller stations. In Mutual's cooperative arrangements, contracts tended at first to treat the two parties as equals. But when the proposed Transcontinental Network, which never materialized, threatened Mutual in 1938, MBS tightened its contracts in order to hold onto its affiliates. Clearly broadcasting in the 1930s was centrally controlled by the networks, and this concentration of programming authority brought government attention (see p. 210).

5.4 Educational Radio: Talk but Little Progress

The 38 AM educational stations on the air in 1936 had dropped to 35 by mid-1941 and today number no more than 25. About half the survivors in 1941 had been on the air more than 15 years, 12 were commercially supported, and 7 of these were affiliated with a network as well, airing educational programs only a few hours a day. One was operated by a high school, 2 by church-affiliated educational groups, nine by agriculture schools or state agricultural departments, and 11 by land-grant universities, mainly in the Midwest. Only 11 stations were licensed for unlimited broadcast time, about half of them in the 250 to 5,000 watt category.

Educational radio consisted of a few hardy survivors of the 200+ educational stations that had started in the 1920s. Although they provided in-school instructional and at-home educational and cultural programs to supplement educational offerings of the networks and a few commercial stations, their dwindling numbers made educational radio a shadow of what its adherents wanted.

Seemingly, more organizations were interested in educational radio than there were stations on the air during the late 1930s! Two of them (see p. 123), the National Advisory Council on Radio in Education and the National Committee on Education by Radio, continued their separate approaches to the problem. The council sponsored a series of useful publications and continued to push for cooperation with commercial broadcasters—although one of its experiments, using many commercial stations, was constantly rescheduled at less and less valuable air times. The committee worked for allocation of educational channels and sponsored annual conferences from 1931 until 1938, when its Rockefeller Foundation support ended. One of the committee's more lasting influences was to help local groups establish listening councils: groups of critical listeners who worked with local broadcasters to improve existing programs and plan new ones.

The Institute for Education by Radio was established at Ohio State University in 1930 and ran an annual conference on educational radio until 1960. The Federal Radio Education Committee, officially sponsored by the FCC, had 39 members under the chairmanship of the U.S. Commissioner of Education and existed to eliminate conflicts and promote cooperation between commercial and educational licensees. Like the other groups, it sponsored conferences and studies and promoted educational radio but did little of substance to expand the service.

The National Association of Educational Broadcasters (NAEB) evolved in 1934 from the Association of College and University Broadcasting Stations, which had been established in 1925 amid the rush to get education on the air. The NAEB, the only one of these educational radio groups to survive until the 1980s, operated throughout the 1934–1941 period with about 25 member stations and little money. Acting primarily as a program idea exchange, it also sponsored off-the-air rebroadcast experiments.

The notion of reserving spectrum space for the exclusive use of education arose during the 1930s. The National Committee on Education by Radio deserved much of the credit for lobbying through this proposal. Educators had lost interest when they realized that stations assigned to the part of the spectrum originally sought (1,500–1,600 kHz, just above the standard broadcast band of that time) typically would have less range than other stations, that they had to purchase expensive equipment, and that few receivers could receive signals on those frequencies. When the Senate was considering the 1934 Communications Act, Senators Wagner and Hatfield sponsored an amendment allocating 25% of broadcast facilities (essentially, spectrum space) to nonprofit organizations. However, dissension among educators and solid commercial broadcaster opposition led to this proposal's defeat. In response to a congressional order for investigation contained in the Communications Act, the commission recommended in 1935 against reservation of special frequencies and for educator cooperation with commercial stations and networks. Hearings brought forth testimony that networks and big stations were much more cooperative with educators than were small and independent stations.

Early in 1938, however, the FCC reversed itself and provided the first specific spectrum reservations for noncommercial broadcast use, selecting channels in the 41 to 42 MHz band, far above the standard broadcasting band. On January 26, it set aside 25 channels in this band for in-school broadcasting. The first station licensed was the Cleveland Board of Education's WBOE, in November 1938. In 1939 the educational broadcasting allocation was shifted to 42 to 43 MHz, and stations were required to change from AM to the newer FM mode. Since FM required a wider bandwidth, this allocation provided only five channels, on which seven stations were transmitting to radio-equipped classrooms by late 1941. When commercial FM went into operation, the educational allocation was for channels at the bottom of the band, which were fractionally easier for listeners to receive than higher ones.

Although the potential for educational radio was considered good, financial realities restricted most FM broadcasts to in-school use. The few surviving educational stations on the standard AM band supplied a little adult education programming in evening hours. Most important, the precedent of setting aside channels for education had been established.

5.5 The Advertising Agencies Take Over

Just as the radio business reflected the Depression (see the drop in overall advertising income for 1933 shown in Appendix C, table 3-A) so it reflected the country's recovery in the second half of the decade. Total revenues of $112 million in 1935 grew to more than twice that figure just six years later. In the same period, radio increased its portion of the advertising dollar from 7% to 11%—not a bad showing for a medium supported by advertising for little more than a decade. Much of this growth, of course, was due to the peculiar relationship between broadcasting and its audience. Once a person owned a radio receiver, he or she paid nothing for professional entertainment of high quality, but the advertiser paid dearly for the privilege of entertaining potential customers among the listeners. Every year set owners had more time for radio because of household labor-saving devices, shorter work weeks, and Depression-caused unemployment.

Another factor in radio's success was the growing role of middlemen. The station time broker, active in radio's early advertising years, was replaced in the late 1930s by the station representative (see p. 125) who promoted to advertising agencies a single station in a given market, thus avoiding the time broker's conflict of interest in dealing with several stations in the same market. The station rep received 10 to 15% of the station's advertising rate, after deducting the advertising agency commission of 15%. Rep firms grew from 28 in 1935 to about 40 five years later. The reps began to have a standardizing effect on their client stations, often suggesting which programming or advertising policies would appeal most to potential sponsors.

Representing the advertisers in all but the smallest markets were the advertising agencies, which as early as 1935 were placing three-quarters of the radio advertising orders. While many smaller agencies around the country were content to purchase time on existing programs through station reps in New York, in a few other big markets large agencies worked closely with their clients and the radio networks, or big stations, to develop compatible program and advertising packages. The agency created both the ads and the programs, contracted for talent and studio facilities— often from the networks—to produce programs, and then presented the finished program, with integrated commercials, to the network. In effect, the agencies bought time in large chunks from the networks and a few of the largest independent stations. Stations got the popular shows, networks provided facilities and collected the money—and Madison Avenue had all but total control over network prime time and daytime programming.

Another example of the trend toward centralized program control was the musical program package recorded by transcription companies and sold to individual local stations in ready-to-air form, often including advertising. Stations that had created their own programs in the 1920s now recognized the economy of centralized programming and the accessibility of the limited amount of popular talent through networks with which they were affiliated. In turn, the networks were glad to hand over their programming worries to the advertising agencies, which welcomed the opportunity to tie together program and commercial. Since the networks economically served the agencies, they felt free to let the agencies do the work and take the rap from the sponsors if anything went wrong.

Agency control of network programming continued until the advent of television in the late 1940s and early 1950s, with its enormous programming costs, discouraged agencies from making programming investments. At this stage, the television networks took over programming and, later, high prices virtually eliminated single sponsorship of programs with integrated commercials. In the 1970s, ironically, agitation grew for divorcing the networks from program production—a few people even suggesting that the agencies again take over that function.

By the mid-1930s, radio's advertising pattern for the next 15 years, and television's thereafter, was clearly established. The networks and their handful of O & O stations earned 60% of time sale revenues, leaving 700 other radio stations to share the remaining 40%. Since most network O & Os were 50,000-watt clear-channel stations in the country's biggest markets, they naturally attracted advertising. National and regional advertisers turned first to the networks and spent relatively little on local station sponsorship or spot advertising (see Appendix C, table 3-A). Most small and medium-size stations had to rely on local advertising revenues.

The networks differed greatly. NBC-Red and CBS had the most popular programs, the highest charges for time, and the largest incomes. NBC-Blue was a distant third. Although it had about as many affiliates as NBC-Red, its usually lower-powered stations could not get the same advertiser support as the Red network's clear-channel and powerful regional affiliates. Also, the Blue network presented many sustaining programs—not just because they could not attract sponsors but also to counterbalance, in a public relations sense, the culturally lower but popular sponsored shows on the Red network. The fourth national network, Mutual, had little national advertising impact, since most of its stations arranged their own time sales outside Mutual's limited program exchanges. Some regional networks made a profit but were handling only a fraction as much business as any one of the national networks.

By the mid-1930s, the advertising agencies could recommend two time periods during the day as most desirable for their clients. Many food and soap manufacturing companies purchased daily time on agency-packaged serial *soap opera* programs in the late morning and early afternoon. These programs (see p. 183), named after their typical sponsors, dominated daytime scheduling and acquired large and loyal housewife audiences. The other key time, *prime time*, generally was 7 P.M. to 11 P.M. on the East and West coasts and 6 P.M. to 10 P.M. in the Central and Mountain time zones. Prime time was most desirable because it had the most listeners.

Agencies and sponsors considered the best combination a high-power station operating on a channel toward the low-numbered end of the broadcast band in a large and prosperous market, and attracting a large audience, typically as a network affiliate. For example, in the late 1930s more than half of the total revenue went to stations in markets of more than 400,000 population, and one-quarter of the revenue went to the 50 or so 50-kw stations. In 1938 the average station in a market of over a million population had a net income of $60,000 before taxes, while a station in a market of fewer than a half-million population might earn $20,000. In the same year, according to FCC data, about one-third of all radio stations lost money.

A station's expenditures, like its revenues, varied with market size and station type. Powerful stations in large markets would spend about 19% of the average expense dollar on technical items, 43% on programming, and 38% for sales and administration. A small station in a small market would spend about the same proportion on technical items, about half as much on programming, and maybe twice as much on sales and administration. With less revenue and fewer national advertisers, local stations often offered simpler programming; recorded music cost much less than live orchestras and other talent.

A 1938 FCC survey of 633 stations showed that fully two-thirds of their programs carried advertising, compared to one-third at the start of the decade. About three-quarters of the musical programs were sponsored, about two-thirds of drama, talks and dialogues, and news were sponsored, and half of the variety programs were sponsored and half sustaining. Most other programs, like religion and special events, were sustaining.

While the radio industry's income varied with the country's economic condition, radio advertising was clearly accepted. Of the many trade publications and books on radio advertising in the late 1930s, nearly all were optimistic about radio's value.

5.6 The Golden Age of Programming

In the last half of the 1930s, most full time radio stations broadcast at least 12 hours a day, and many for 18 hours or more. Generally stations filled the expanded air time with variations of program types already developed. Three departures from this pattern were news and commentary, the daytime serial drama, and quiz and audience-participation programs.

A March 1938 survey of programming by the FCC showed that 53% was devoted to music, 11% to talks and dialogues, 9% to drama, 9% to variety, 9% to news (which would not have been measurable a few years earlier), 5% to religion and devotion, 2% to special events, and 2% to miscellaneous. While affiliates got from 50% to 70% of programming from their network, they also had more time devoted to local and live programming. Of all radio programming in the survey period, 64% was live—roughly half network and half local—while 21% was from electrical transcriptions and 12% was from phonograph records—a definite increase in nonlive programming on the typical station. (See box on the next page for one major station's 1937 schedule.)

5.6.1 Music and Variety

Music remained radio's staple. Several transcription companies, operated both by networks and some independents, offered local stations prerecorded music, sometimes assembled into programs. By early 1939 more than 575 stations subscribed to at least one transcription service, and nearly half of them used two or more. RCA's transcription operation probably accounted for 35% of the industry's business, although 25 or 30 companies had combined annual revenues of $5 million in the late 1930s.

A station usually signed a contract with a transcription firm to deliver several hundred recorded musical selections—usually on 16-inch discs, running at 33 1/3 rpm, with approximately 15 minutes per side—to start, and then perhaps 50 additional selections a month. The transcription firm usually dealt with only one station in a particular market to avoid program duplication, and payment by the station was either a percentage of its gross

▦ **A Radio Station's Programs: 1937**   This is a typical weekday schedule for WTMJ, the *Milwaukee Journal* AM station, as taken from a telephone audience report. The listing does not show programs on the air before 8 A.M. or after 10 P.M. as calls were not made earlier or later than that. Actually, WTMJ went on the air around 6 A.M. and did not go off until about midnight—hours since extended, as is the case with most large city radio stations. Programs followed by # originate at the network level—in this case, NBC-Red.

A.M.

8:00	Winter Wonderland	10:00	Household Hints
8:15	Your Home Town	10:15	Backstage Wife #
8:30	Party Line	10:30	How to Be Charming
8:45	Bandmaster	10:45	Hello Peggy
9:00	What's New in Milwaukee	11:00	Helen Gahagan
9:30	Morning Melodies	11:15	Blue Room
9:45	Today's Children	11:30	Behind the Mike
		11:45	Heinie [German band music]

P.M.

12:30	Rhythm Rascals	3:45	Road of Life #
12:45	Sidewalk Reporter	4:00	Friendship Circle
1:00	Livestock Reports, News	4:30	Kitty Keene #
1:15	Remote Control	4:45	News
2:00	Pepper Young's Family #	5:00	Jack Armstrong [children's action-adventure] #
2:15	Ma Perkins #	5:15	Heinie
2:30	Vic & Sade #	5:45	Sports Flash
2:45	The O'Neills #	6:00	Dairy Council
3:00	Around the Town	6:15	Uncle Ezra [country music] #
3:15	Guiding Light #	6:30	Easy Aces [comedy] #
3:30	Paul Skinner	6:45	Kilowatt Hour

(Here is the Monday schedule for the evening "prime time")

7:00	Burns & Allen [comedy] #
7:30	Firestone Program [music] #
8:00	Fibber McGee & Molly [comedy] #
8:30	Hour of Charm [female orchestra] #
9:00	Contented Hour [music] #
9:30	Glen Gray and his Casa Loma Orchestra #

Source: Milwaukee Journal radio station audience research report information for November 1937, based on 49,100 completed telephone calls comparing WTMJ with six other area stations. Material now on file with, and supplied through the courtesy of, the Mass Communication History Center of the State Historical Society of Wisconsin.

revenues or a flat sum. While such material averaged only 10 to 15% of time on network-affiliated stations, nonaffiliated stations used it much more, some for 80% of their schedules. Popular songs and instrumentals predominated, but all kinds of music were offered.

Although more music was aired locally, classical musical programs declined in importance on the networks after the early 1930s. A notable exception was the NBC Symphony Orchestra, one of the outstanding cultural creations of radio in America. The orchestra was founded when David Sarnoff helped persuade Arturo Toscanini, the just retired conductor of the

New York Philharmonic, to return from Italy to conduct 10 concerts, starting Christmas night 1937. NBC hired the best musicians to work in the new symphony orchestra. Three months later NBC announced that Toscanini would lead the orchestra for another three years; but, as it turned out, he continued for nearly 17 years until his final retirement, well into his 80s, in 1954. The broadcasts normally originated from specially built Studio 8H, then the world's largest, in the RCA Building in Rockefeller Center, and were broadcast on NBC-Blue on a sustaining basis, at the conductor's insistence. From 1948 the NBC Symphony was seen on television as well. After the NBC Symphony formally disbanded, the orchestra continued to play independently as the "Symphony of the Air."

Large dance bands were increasingly heard on both national and local programs. The 1930s were the "big band era," and many famous orchestras were heard first locally and then on the networks. Both industries benefited from such broadcasts, since the publicity of a major radio appearance attracted more people to the band's concerts. By 1937 the bands of Benny Goodman, Ozzie Nelson, Russ Morgan, Sammy Kaye, and Tommy Dorsey had played on network radio. *Your Hit Parade*, one of the top long-running radio programs, presented the most popular songs of the previous week, as determined by a national "survey" of record and sheet music sales, performed live by major singers and orchestras. The show began in Fall 1935 and was sponsored on radio until 1953, and from 1951 until 1959 on television, by the American Tobacco Company's Lucky Strike (and, toward the very end, Hit Parade) cigarettes.

Local stations presented a wide range of live music, some stations supporting a full orchestra, and an increasing amount of recorded music. The conflict between broadcasters and ASCAP (see p. 214) had a substantial effect on radio music in 1940 and 1941.

Compared to the highly professional variety programs, local or national *amateur hour* broadcasts presented unknowns who would sing, tap dance, or do imitations in the hope of making a career. Such programs were used as fillers for years. Although the quality was uneven, the audiences who had cheered hometown talent supported contestants from all over the country. The most famous amateur variety show, *Major Bowes and His Original Amateur Hour*, began on New York station WHN in 1934 and moved to NBC-Red in March 1935. Within a few months, it was the most popular program on radio—at one time reaching a near-unbelievable rating of 45 when 20 was more typical! It presented amateurs who went on to fame—including Frank Sinatra, who made his radio debut in this program's first year—and others who went down to defeat and anonymity. Bowes became known by his catch-phrases and for his abrupt, even brutal manner with a gong as an aural equivalent of the "hook" used to remove inept or stage-frightened performers. The program continued on radio until 1952 and went on television from 1949 to the late 1960s, with Ted Mack serving as MC after Bowes' death.

Many other national and local programs were built around a single performer, almost always a male singer or comic, usually backed by a musical group and supplemented by weekly guest performers. Most of these variety stars were products of vaudeville, burlesque, legitimate theater, or music halls. One was Bob Hope, who began his weekly show on CBS in 1935.

Such variety programming remained a network favorite, with little change, until inauguration of the draft just before World War II gave a military slant to programs of the early 1940s. The *Army Show* (later the *Army Hour*), *This Is Fort Dix*, the Navy Band hour, and *Wings over America* were typical. The formats resembled earlier radio variety shows, with bits of song, humor, and chatter, but the participants frequently were military personnel, and the programs often originated from military bases.

5.6.2 Drama

By far the most important network dramatic programming, in hours broadcast per week, was the woman's serial drama, or soap opera. Starting in 1935, the weekly hours of such fare increased sharply until, in 1940, the four networks combined devoted 75 hours a week to such programs, nine of every ten sponsored daytime network hours. These programs lasted 15 minutes, came on at the same time each weekday, and had soap and food manufacturers as sponsors. Typical of the longer running programs were *Back Stage Wife* ("what it means to be the wife of a famous Broadway star—dream sweetheart of a million other women"), which began in 1935; *The Guiding Light* (about a kindly cleric); *Lorenzo Jones* (inventor of useless gadgets); *Our Gal Sunday* ("Can this girl from a mining town in the West find happiness as the wife of a wealthy and titled Englishman?"); and *Road of Life* (doctors and nurses, although it began as the tale of an Irish-American mother's attempt to raise her children). In each case, domestic life was emphasized with its ups, and more usually, downs. Many of the actors and actresses played the same parts for decades. For a portion of each day, they performed a live, convincing, emotion-filled episode with little rehearsal, but their evenings were free for the stage or other professional activities. Behind many of the serials was the husband and wife team of Frank and Anne Hummert, who originally wrote all their own work but eventually employed dialogue writers to work within their character development and story lines. Elaine Carrington and Irna Phillips also wrote "soapers," sometimes several at the same time.

The typical serial format was wonderfully simple: a brief musical introduction played on the studio organ, a narrator opening the day's episode with a recap of what had happened before, two segments of action separated by a commercial break, and a closing word from the narrator suggesting the problems ahead. Dialogue and organ music were somber and simple; story progress was very slow, giving time for character development

▓ **Suggestions for Hopeful Radio Playwrights**　This copy, reproduced exactly as the Aubrey, Moore and Wallace agency of Chicago sent it out to those requesting it, shows some of the limitations and problems of writing for a prime time radio network drama program. Note some of the period taboos, such as women smoking. Similar, though usually much longer, guidelines exist for current television programs—but the price paid to authors has increased sharply from the $100 of 1938.

Suggestions for
Radio Playwrights
Campana's "First Nighter"(Friday NBC)
and "Grand Hotel" (Sunday NBC)

Regarding BOTH Programs

　　Both of these programs are very successful. They have
　　a large audience. During the years they have been on the
　　air we have received hundreds of thousands of letters all
　　of which have aided us in knowing what our audiences like.
　　Please keep this in mind as you read these suggestions.

　　Our radio listeners are primarily the family type of audience.
　　Consequently, we are interested in

　　　　　　　Comedy and Farce
　　　　　　　Melodrama
　　　　　　　Light and Heavy Romances
　　　　　　　Mystery
　　　　　　　Adventure

　　that will provide wholesome entertainment for all members
　　of an average family. This means there are certain re-
　　strictions. As a suggestion, we offer a few taboos:

　　　　　　　Sex
　　　　　　　Profanity
　　　　　　　Drunkenness or even drinking
　　　　　　　Smoking by Women
　　　　　　　Glorification,of crime of
　　　　　　　　criminals
　　　　　　　Anything that will offend
　　　　　　　　members of racial, political
　　　　　　　　or religious groups.

　　On the other hand, there is a wide range of possibilities
　　with real live characters, with plenty of action and dra-
　　matic conflict.

　　A few pointers:

　　　　1.　Plays which have a definite love interest or a
　　　　　　mystery with an original "twist" before the end-
　　　　　　ing are particularly desirable. While the con-
　　　　　　ventional happy ending is not essential, it is
　　　　　　generally conceded to be better box-office.

　　　　2.　"Plant" your characters -- i.e., tell us who they
　　　　　　are and where they are in the fewest possible words
　　　　　　as soon as possible after their entrance. Do not
　　　　　　use an announcer, narrator, or interpretor to de-
　　　　　　scribe scene or play. Characters must do all this
　　　　　　by their lines.

-2-

3. Do not shift scene unnecessarily. On the other hand, do not allow the whole play to become static.

4. If you have any good ideas on sound effects, write them in -- otherwise leave it alone. This part of the production is quite efficiently handled during rehearsals.

5. Radio drama is of necessity a natural and intimate form of entertainment, dialogue should not be stiff, or stagy. Make your characters real people.

6. Motivate all your characters and situations. Also remember that action is more entertaining than talk. Long conversations, unbroken by action, do not make good shows.

7. There is an efficient orchestra included in these programs, so that if you understand something about music and would like to use a little in your story, do so. The leading man, Don Ameche, has a pleasant and appealing singing voice and has successfully put over several roles in which he worked as a night club entertainer or a song writer, etc., etc.

8. When you have completed the first draft of your play -- read it over to yourself and then to someone of average intelligence and carefully note the reaction ... do they grasp the essentials of the plot?... does it sustain their undivided interest and attention? The most important requirement of a play is that it provide good entertainment. It must not be obvious, dull, trite, "draggy", etc.

9. Put plenty of color, action and motivation into your plot but keep the whole structure clear and well focused. Brevity is the soul of wit and simplicity is the essence of good showmanship.

10. Suspense is important in order to carry the audience over the intermissions and make them await eagerly the climax of the play.

-3-

<u>FIRST NIGHTER</u> (Three Acts)   This is the "opening night" in the
"Little Theatre Off Times Square"

Dramatic construction should be on an ascending line with
the "Big Scene", if possible, for the third act. As musical interludes occur between each act, in this series, it is
essential to build up the endings of Acts 1 and 2 in such a
manner as to leave a good carry-over. Usually suspense is
the best method.

Each act should average between five and six minutes actual
playing time, totaling 16 or 17½ minutes for three acts.
A manuscript of 2500 or 2600 words, averaging from 825 to
900 words per act makes the best play.

 <u>Players</u>

  Don Ameche -- leading man
  June Meredith -- leading lady
  Clifford Soubier -- an experienced heavy, villain
    or "character" actor. Very
    good in negro dialect also.

Other actors vary according to the requirements of the
script. It is desirable to have no more than four or
five characters in order to keep the plot clear and
understandable by the audience. Odd voices, taxi
drivers, doormen, etc. may be used at your discretion.

<u>GRAND HOTEL</u> (Two Acts.)

Often the scenes are associated with or start in "Grand Hotel"
anywhere.
A musical interlude occurs between the acts and it is essential that the ending of Act I be built up to leave a good
carry-over.
The acts should be evenly divided with roughly 21 or 22
minutes for the total length, figuring about 150 words to
the minute.

 <u>Players</u>

  Don Ameche -- leading man
  Anne Seymour -- leading lady
  Other actors vary according to the requirements of
  the script. It is desirable to have no more than
  four or five as more than that number may become
  confusing to the audience.

   - - x - -

<u>Note</u>: Authors are required to furnish <u>only</u> the <u>play</u>. Do not worry
about the "Shell" or "Framework" of the program.

For plays produced the author is remunerated on the day
following the broadcast. Price $100 each.

<u>Please type your name and address clearly on the manuscript.</u>
  Address scripts to
  L. T. Wallace, Vice President
  AUBREY, MOORE & WALLACE, INC.
  410 North Michigan Avenue
  Chicago, Illinois.

and allowing a listener to miss an episode or two painlessly. Audiences were loyal, and many programs lasted 15 or more seasons, until radio's programming character changed in the 1950s. Listeners to soap operas were among the first studied by social psychologists, and much criticism was levied at the genre in 1940 and 1941. These complaints dropped off as the number of serials decreased during the war years.

"Prestige" drama increased in the 1930s. These programs usually were "anthologies" offering different stories with new casts each week, sometimes adaptations from other media, but often original radio plays. Writers such as poet Archibald MacLeish, later Librarian of Congress, and new authors such as Norman Corwin and Arch Oboler gained recognition almost overnight. Prestige series included the *experimental Columbia Workshop* on CBS, started late in 1936, and the more conventional *Lux Radio Theater*, which presented such stars as Helen Hayes, Leslie Howard, and an unknown player named Orson Welles in hour-long versions of current films.

Welles at 23 was the guiding light behind a new CBS series in Fall 1938, the *Mercury Theater on the Air.* As writer, director, and star, he built up a company of actors whose names were famous for decades: Joseph Cotton, Agnes Moorehead, Everett Sloane, and Ray Collins. His Sunday evening, October 30, 1938, Halloween program probably ranks as the most famous single radio show ever presented. It was an adaptation by Welles and Howard Koch of H. G. Wells' science fiction story "War of the Worlds." The location was changed to northern New Jersey, the time was moved to the present and, even more important, the narrative was changed to reflect radio's format. Listeners to the program's beginning, or who listened carefully to the between-acts announcements, understood these circumstances. But those who tuned in late—and many had a habit of listening to the first few minutes of ventriloquist Edgar Bergen and his dummy Charlie McCarthy on NBC before tuning over to CBS for the play—were due for a surprise. The program in progress seemed to feature a band performing in a hotel. A few moments later, an announcer broke in with a "news bulletin" saying that a gas cloud had been observed on the planet Mars. Then back to the music; another interruption, asking observatories to keep watch; more music; an interview with a "noted astronomer" on the possibility of life on Mars (unlikely); more music—and, suddenly, a bulletin saying that a large meteorite had fallen in the vicinity of Grovers Mill, New Jersey. The pace built in a series of news bulletins and on-the-spot reports of the opening of the cylindrical "meteorite," the emergence of the Martians, the assembly of Martian war machines, the rout of U.S. military forces, and government reaction. Reports of casualties, traffic jams, transmissions from hapless military pilots, ominous breaking off of on-the-spot reports, the later report of the "death" of the field reporter, and use of familiar names and places—all gave it reality. As the Martian war machines headed toward New York to discharge their poison gas—to the sounds of fleeing ocean liners, the last gasps of a

▪ Orson Welles's Halloween Broadcast: 1938   Orson Welles acted/narrated the famous "War of the Worlds" broadcast on October 30, 1938—creating the kind of panic reported in the *New York Times* the following day.

Photo credit: Culver Pictures, Inc.

newsman atop the broadcasting studio, and the cracked voice of a solitary ham radio operator calling "Isn't anybody there? Isn't anybody?"—many listeners did not wait to hear the mid-program announcement that it was all a hoax. By 8:30, thousands of people were praying, preparing for the end, and fleeing the Martians.

These reactions were not silly, although it may look that way today. The pacing of the program undermined critical faculties. It convinced the listener that a reporter had traveled the miles from Grovers Mill "in ten minutes,"

NEW YORK, MONDAY, OCTOBER 31, 1938.

Radio Listeners in Panic, Taking War Drama as Fact

Many Flee Homes to Escape 'Gas Raid From Mars'—Phone Calls Swamp Police at Broadcast of Wells Fantasy

A wave of mass hysteria seized thousands of radio listeners throughout the nation between 8:15 and 9:30 o'clock last night when a broadcast of a dramatization of H. G. Wells's fantasy, "The War of the Worlds," led thousands to believe that an interplanetary conflict had started with invading Martians spreading wide death and destruction in New Jersey and New York.

The broadcast, which disrupted households, interrupted religious services, created traffic jams and clogged communications systems, was made by Orson Welles, who as the radio character, "The Shadow," used to give "the creeps" to countless child listeners. This time at least a score of adults required medical treatment for shock and hysteria.

In Newark, in a single block at Heddon Terrace and Hawthorne Avenue, more than twenty families rushed out of their houses with wet handkerchiefs and towels over their faces to flee from what they believed was to be a gas raid. Some began moving household furniture.

Throughout New York families left their homes, some to flee to near-by parks. Thousands of persons called the police, newspapers and radio stations here and in other cities of the United States and Canada seeking advice on protective measures against the raids.

The program was produced by Mr. Welles and the Mercury Theatre on the Air over station WABC and the Columbia Broadcasting System's coast-to-coast network, from 8 to 9 o'clock.

The radio play, as presented, was to simulate a regular radio program with a "break-in" for the material of the play. The radio listeners, apparently, missed or did not listen to the introduction, which was: "The Columbia Broadcasting System and its affiliated stations present Orson Welles and the Mercury Theatre on the Air in 'The War of the Worlds' by H. G. Wells."

They also failed to associate the program with the newspaper listing of the program, announced as "Today: 8:00-9:00—Play: H. G. Wells's 'War of the Worlds'—WABC." They ignored three additional announcements made during the broadcast emphasizing its fictional nature

Mr. Welles opened the program with a description of the series of

Continued on Page Four

when less than three minutes actually had elapsed. Already sure that mobs were fleeing, listeners who looked out their windows and saw lots of people going about normal pursuits assumed that everyone was trying to get away from the Martians, just as the radio said. If no one was in sight, they assumed that everyone else had fled and left them behind. Few heard the three announcements of the program's fictional nature or the last half-hour, which was mostly a monologue by Welles, as a scientist who believes that he is one of the few survivors and who observes the demise of the Martians

■ **Radio's Comedy Stars of the 1930s**   Two of radio's longest running comedians were Jack Benny (shown here, in the left photo, with his wife and comedy partner, Mary Livingstone) and Fred Allen (with his wife Portland Hoffa, in the right photo). The two—who actually admired each other—had a running on-air "feud," based on their very different approaches to radio comedy. Another ex-vaudevillian, George Burns, supplied straight lines to his zany and "confused" wife, Gracie Allen (see p. 721). With the exception of Fred Allen, who appeared infrequently on television, these stars made the transition from radio to television in the late 1940s and had broadcast careers of more than three decades.

Photos courtesy of National Broadcasting Company, Inc.

from the effects of earthly bacteria. If they had heard this obviously dramatic material, many persons might have caught on. In the East, especially near the "landing site," thousands of people—a small proportion of the population but a large number nevertheless—called police, fled their homes, or otherwise reacted as though the invasion was real.

This panic had a number of causes, notably the way the program's "Halloween prank" nature was glossed over in the introduction. Afterward researchers learned that many listeners did not try to double check the "news" on another station or telephone friends; and that others, who found normal programming elsewhere on the dial, decided that these stations had not yet received the word. The panic was also a reaction to the "Munich Crisis" just one month before, when Americans had been glued to their radios expecting the world to go to war (see p. 194).

Welles was only slightly abashed at the program's impact. The FCC made clear that it would not consider such "scare" programs and formats as broadcasting in the public interest. Although "War of the Worlds" was much later rebroadcast in the United States as a "period piece" without much effect, its original adaptation broadcast in other countries brought the same sort of panic. Decades later, several persons were killed in a riot in South

Oddly popular on radio, where the visual trick of ventriloquism could not be seen, were Edgar Bergen and his wooden dummy, Charlie McCarthy—though the wise-cracking dummy clearly walked away with the show. Famed comedy star W. C. Fields is about to perform a frontal lobotomy on McCarthy—the two traded barbs on the air for years.

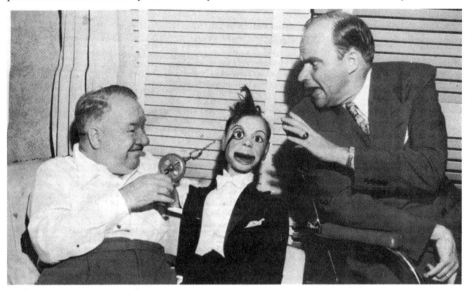

Photo credit: Culver Pictures, Inc.

America, when resentment over having been fooled boiled over. This drama showed better than any other program or episode the impact of radio on society—"if it was on the radio, then it must be true."

Thrillers and situation comedies filled more network time per week than any other form of drama. Adventure programs, starting in the early 1930s (see pp. 134–135), were heard both in the evenings, as crime-detective shows for adults, and in the late afternoons, as 15-minute action–adventure serials for children. These live, mostly network shows could be technically complicated, with large casts, sound effects, and split-second timing. Programs included the true story-recreating *Gangbusters* starting in 1935, whose loud opening of sirens, machine-gun fire, and marching feet gave rise to the phrase "coming on like Gangbusters"; *Mr. Keen, Tracer of Lost Persons*; and *I Love a Mystery*, which had one of radio's most loyal audiences. The last was written by Carlton E. Morse, writer of the enduringly popular *One Man's Family. Mr. District Attorney's* opening with the DA reciting his oath of office provided a generation with the concept of the law as protector as well as prosecutor.

Programs aimed at children included *Jack Armstrong—The All-American Boy; Tom Mix*, a cowboy-adventure program; *Captain Midnight* and *Hop*

Harrigan, both with pilot-heroes; *Terry and the Pirates*, based on the Milton Caniff comic strip; and a number of other serials that made the American "children's hour" far different from the period of silence that the British offered for several decades. Two of the most important children's adventure programs were not serials. *The Lone Ranger* and *The Green Hornet*, which began over Mutual in 1938, were both written and acted by a team at WXYZ, Detroit (see p. 132) that included Fran Stryker. Indeed, the publisher–hero Green Hornet was identified as the Lone Ranger's grandnephew! *The Green Hornet* used a hard-punching opening: "He hunts the biggest of all game! Public enemies who try to destroy our America. . . . With his faithful valet, Kato, Britt Reid, daring young publisher, matches wits with the underworld, risking his life that criminals and racketeers, within the law, may feel its weight by the sting of—the Green Hornet!" Until FBI Chief Hoover objected, the Green Hornet's targets were "public enemies that even the G-Men cannot catch." When the United States entered World War II, the faithful valet-chauffeur Kato's background was quickly changed from Japanese to Filipino.

Radio's half-hour situation comedies were a staple. *Li'l Abner* began over NBC in 1939, originating in Chicago as many programs then did; Fanny Brice, about whom the musical *Funny Girl* was written, created her immortal *Baby Snooks*, the child demon who created crisis after crisis for her father and her baby brother Robespierre; *Blondie*, a 1939 CBS entry based on the Chic Young comic strip, featured the tribulations of Dagwood and Blondie Bumstead—another example of broadcasting's penchant for weak father figures; and *Henry Aldrich*—the misadventures of a crack-voiced adolescent—after appearing for some years as a segment on other programs, aired on its own over NBC-Blue in 1939.

Except for daytime serials and thriller programs, most network drama—anthology or serial like *One Man's Family* and *Those We Love*—aired in the evening. Only the largest stations produced their own dramatic programs regularly, most being content with network offerings, although many stations supplied dramatic or sound effects for commercials and special programs.

To an audience reared largely on movies, amateur theatricals, and traveling companies, radio provided something new and fascinating. The resulting loyal audience was very attractive to advertisers. Since it could perceive radio only by ear, the audience had to use its imagination to fill in the setting and the action. This it did well with the help of numerous musical and sound-effect conventions. Everyone understood transitions of time and space; the absence of carpet in radioland homes told the listener when somebody was entering or leaving a room. A filter that removed some of the audio frequencies placed a voice on the telephone; a bit more filter and some reverberation or "echo" would transport a ghost to fantasyland. But without the audience's imagination, radio drama never would have succeeded.

5.6.3 News

By the late 1930s, news broadcasts and commentary programs had become common radio fare, as the Press–Radio war ended and tensions in Europe and the Far East mounted.

The Biltmore Agreement of late 1933, which was intended to end the Press–Radio war (see p. 136), proved short-lived. As soon as the networks stopped gathering and reporting news, local stations or groups of stations took over. Transradio Press Service, Inc., a news agency whose news could be sponsored, served more stations in early 1935 than did the Press-Radio wire authorized by the Biltmore Agreement. Both UP and INS copied this service in 1935, leaving only AP, controlled by the newspaper industry, as a holdout. To save wire line costs, Transradio, UP, and INS sent short dispatches that required rewriting at the station. In July 1936 UP started offering a special radio wire transmitting news summaries written and edited for radio delivery. By 1938 UP and INS had many more subscribers than Transradio, and many stations subscribed to more than one service. The Press-Radio wire, restrictive in news coverage and prohibiting sponsorship, withered and died in 1938 in the face of such competition, and the "war" ended with it. AP began to let newspaper-owned stations use its news on the air in 1939, opened up its news service, and permitted sponsorship on all stations a year later, and began a special radio wire in early 1941. The attempts of the press to limit radio news failed because most people saw them correctly as limiting news dissemination on a competing medium. As real war drew nearer, people wanted more news. Print media groups tried repeatedly in the late 1930s to regain control of radio news, but they had lost the issue already.

In the late 1930s, individual radio stations across the country began to offer news programs varying in length and depth. In the New York market, WOR aired its own newscasts early in the decade. Most stations had local news service, sometimes no more than headlines, often in cooperation with a local newspaper and supplemented by one or more of the wire service radio wires. The FCC's 1938 programming survey showed that one-tenth of broadcast programming was news; one-sixth was news and special events/public affairs; and more news and special events programs originated locally than were supplied by national networks. Compared to newspapers, radio carried more international and crime-related news but fewer social events and stock and commodity market reports. Radio's ability to report natural and man-made disasters faster doomed the newspaper "extra."

To the networks, the end of the Press–Radio war brought expansion of both domestic and foreign news reporting. NBC Director of News and Special Events A. A. Schechter earned a reputation for getting stories through skillful use of the long-distance telephone and producing color or human interest stories rather than *hard news.* There was coverage of sports events, talks from famous people beamed from abroad by short-wave and then rebroadcast, a singing mouse contest, launching of ocean liners; both networks were establishing the personnel and technical means for regular international reporting. CBS News Director Paul White directed César Saerchinger to cover the 1936 abdication of Great Britain's King Edward VIII and the 1937 coronation of King George VI. This latter broadcast may have been the first heard around the world, thanks to the British Broadcasting Corporation. In another memorable CBS broadcast, H. V. Kaltenborn reported on a 1936 skirmish in the Spanish Civil War while hiding in a haystack between the two armies; listeners in America could hear bullets hitting the hay above him while he spoke. In 1937 28-year-old Edward R. Murrow took Saerchinger's place as CBS European Director, arranging educational talks and other broadcasts from his base in London.

News reporting from abroad naturally picked up in quantity as diplomatic tensions increased. Radio reported the latest actions of dictators Hitler and Mussolini, and the often weak ripostes from Britain and France. Upon Germany's March 1938 annexation of Austria, CBS news chief White, at the urging of CBS owner William Paley, devised a new broadcasting technique. Reporters in four or five European nations would stand by microphones connected to shortwave transmitters and discuss events of the day from their various vantage points, frequently being able to hear and comment on their colleagues' reports, coordinated by transatlantic radio and telephone from New York. Because this was done live in the evening on the East Coast of the United States, the reporters had to broadcast in the wee hours of the morning. CBS presented sixteen such roundups in the six days of the Austrian crisis. The techniques developed and personnel trained became vitally important when Hitler threatened Czechoslovakia in September 1938. NBC provided more than 460 broadcasts in those 18 days of the Munich crisis, including Max Jordan's scoop—a broadcast of the complete text of the four-power agreement just minutes after it was signed. At CBS, H. V. Kaltenborn—who could readily translate into English several languages used during the crisis—won acclaim by doing 85 broadcasts over the 18 days. He virtually lived in Studio 9, having food brought in and sleeping on a cot. News Director White orchestrated the coverage, pulling in as needed wire reports, CBS reporters abroad, and commentary from New York or Washington. In those 18 days of speeches, threats, and communiqués, Americans grew used to news bulletins cutting into their entertainment programs at any hour. Kaltenborn later said that he felt the crisis passed (only for a year as it turned out) because radio had mobilized public opinion against war. However, the audience's new faith in radio reporting was tested a month later when the Welles broadcast (see pp. 187–190) scared millions.

The networks' news organizations were put to the test in the 1939–1941 period as war came to Europe and spread. By late 1939 CBS had 14 full-time employees in European capitals, headed by Murrow in London, Eric Sevareid in Paris, and William L. Shirer in Berlin. NBC had a similar staffing pattern. When war came, both networks were able to provide a running commentary: Murrow from London on the beginning of the war; NBC providing eye-witness live coverage of the bleak winter on the Russo-Finnish front; NBC's scoop live from Montevideo harbor in December when the Germans scuttled their pocket battleship *Graf Spee*; conflicting reports from all over as Hitler invaded the low countries, Scandinavia, and France in 1940; the combined broadcast by NBC's William Kerker and CBS's William L. Shirer in the forest of Compiègne in June 1940 when France surrendered to Hitler (most other correspondents were waiting for the news in Berlin); a *London after Dark* broadcast over CBS in August 1940 in the midst of a German air raid at the height of the Battle of Britain.

Wartime censorship restrictions forced many on-the-spot reports to be recorded originally, but most were live—a tribute to the newsmen's professionalism and the combatants' trust in their good faith. Edward R. Murrow led the way by proving to British censors, through trial broadcasts for several nights in a row, that he could broadcast without giving away military information. In his nightly "This...is London" reports to CBS, Murrow, from 1939 to 1941, probably gave Americans their best feel for the war in England. Night after night, he told how the war affected typical Londoners—in their homes, hiding from bombs in the London subway system, or working in factories turning out goods for the war.

Not only did radio report the news faster than competing media, it often reported directly from the scene, with the added color and interest of interviews and background sounds. Perhaps radio's outstanding performance in a domestic crisis was its cooperative coverage of the disastrous Ohio and Mississippi Valley floods of early 1937. Stations that were flooded out provided their personnel to stations still on the air. The latter scrapped program schedules and stayed on the air day and night directing flood victims to food and shelter. Some stations conducted fund-raising efforts to alleviate suffering; others provided a message service for official agencies that normally might have been illegal point-to-point use of a broadcasting station. Reporters fanned out over the entire area, serving local stations and networks alike. Radio's immediacy and portability were amply demonstrated.

In May 1937 Herb Morrison of Chicago station WLS, making a disc recording for archival purposes, watched the German airship *Hindenburg* come in for a routine landing at Lakehurst, New Jersey. As those on the ground watched in horror, the giant hydrogen-filled dirigible caught fire and, in less than a minute, burned to a mass of twisted girders on the ground, with the death of 30 passengers and crew. New York station WHN carried the news first, some eight minutes after the fire, and CBS and NBC followed within a half-hour. As the shock of this unexpected catastrophe overwhelmed Morrison, he sobbed, "This is one of the worst catastrophes in the world . . . oh, the humanity" but stayed at his post and recorded some 30 minutes of the aftermath—between stints of helping in the rescue work. The recording, rushed back to Chicago and aired on WLS the next morning, was so newsworthy that the three networks temporarily suspended their no-recordings rule to play portions.

To cover foreign and domestic events adequately, all networks and many larger stations began to hire newsmen–commentators to report and analyze the rapid and bewildering developments around the world. News commentary had been exempted from the short-lived Biltmore Agreement ban on sponsored news programs, and Lowell Thomas had broadcast on NBC-Blue since 1930 (continuing until June of 1976). Boake Carter and H. V. Kaltenborn were on CBS for several seasons. Other commentators broadcasting between 1935 and 1939 were Gabriel Heatter, famous for his coverage of the Lindbergh kidnaping trial (see next page); newspaper columnist Drew Pearson; Dorothy Thompson, the first important woman commentator; Raymond Gram Swing; conservative Fulton Lewis, Jr.; veteran broadcaster Norman Brokenshire; and respected newspaperman Elmer Davis.

The war increased news broadcasting in America. From some 850 hours of news and on-the-spot news specials broadcast by all networks in 1937, the yearly total went up to 1,250 hours in 1939 and nearly tripled 2 years later to 3,450 hours. Evening commercial network time devoted to commentators, news, and talks went from 6.7% in winter 1938–1939 to 12.3% in winter 1940–1941. CBS consistently provided the most news programming in the period 1937–1941, with NBC-Red and -Blue jockeying for second position and Mutual a distant third. Nearly all radio stations scheduled regular news programs by the 1940–1941 season, with a few providing summaries every hour.

5.6.4 Political Broadcasting

Radio as a political instrument in the United States came into its own with the presidency of Franklin D. Roosevelt starting in 1933. Adapting a practice from his New York governorship, F.D.R. began a series of "Fireside Chats" with the American public on the problems of Depression-hit America. There were 28 chats—8 in each of his first two terms, and 12 in the third, wartime term, nearly all of them half-hour programs broadcast in prime time—and they generally received ratings near the top. Roosevelt had a natural approach to radio, and his words came across more as a conversation between friends than as a political speech. In the third "chat," when he

---

▪ The Lindbergh Kidnaping Case: Trial by Circus?

Early in 1932, the 19-month-old son of aviation hero Charles Lindbergh was kidnaped from the Lindbergh estate near Hopewell, New Jersey. The crime attracted the attention of the country for over 10 weeks as the police and a weird variety of hangers-on attempted to recover the child by making payment to the kidnaper. They all failed, and the child's long-dead body was found on May 12. The kidnaper had not been found, and newspaper, newsreel, and radio reporters withdrew from covering the story.

Two-and-one-half years later, however, Bruno Richard Hauptmann was arrested in New York in the act of passing one of the ransom bills. That event, and the trial of Hauptmann for the kidnaping early in 1935 brought back the press in droves to focus the nation's concentration on the small town of Flemington, New Jersey, where the trial took place, much as the media swarmed around the O. J. Simpson home after his wife's murder. Hundreds of reporters and photographers squeezed into the courtroom and surrounding rooms in an attempt to bring every detail of the trial to the country's newspaper readers and radio listeners. Photographers—many of whom were freelance and aggressive— were all over and the scene was pandemonium. Near the front rail with the press was Gabriel Heatter, a reporter for the new Mutual radio network, given this special place because the judge's wife enjoyed his broadcasts! The trial lasted for six weeks and was front-page news for most of that time.

Late on the evening of February 13, 1935, the verdict came in and was soon flashed across the country—Hauptmann was guilty and sentenced to die. (An Associated Press employee using a secret radio transmitter in the courtroom to get a scoop on rivals got the verdict wrong, and about 10 minutes later AP had to send out a correction. The employee was fired.) Heatter's most famous moment came in early 1936 when Hauptmann finally went to the electric chair. Holding scripts to cover four eventualities—escape, suicide, reprieve, or delay—Heatter had to ad-lib for three-quarters of an hour when the execution was delayed—all this live on a coast-to-coast hookup.

The trial was important not only for its titillating effect on American lives in 1935 but for what came out of it—severe restrictions on reporting of courtroom events by radio and photographers (after 1952, such rules included television). Developed by the American Bar Association as a canon or rule of judicial procedure, Canon 35 limited radio access to the courtroom ostensibly to alleviate the circus-like atmosphere prevalent during the Hauptmann trial. Canon 35, now Canon 3A(7), is still hotly debated as a conflict of the First (free speech) and Sixth (fair trial) amendments to the Constitution. And it all dates back to that overcrowded courtroom!

The heavy media coverage of the Lindbergh trial is evident in the massed photographers facing the jury. United Press International Photo.

---

stopped for a moment and drank from a glass of water, it seemed perfectly natural and correct.

In the 1936 presidential election campaign, a desperate Republican party tried a number of innovative uses of radio. The GOP nominee, Kansas governor Alfred Landon, gave a lengthy radio interview just prior to his nomination. More than 200 stations carried the convention in

■ **Remote Broadcasts Become Truly Portable** This hand-held transmitter, touted by NBC in 1936 as the "smallest practical radio broadcasting station ever devised," was used in covering the national political conventions (including the Socialist) of that year. It liberated the reporter from wires connected to a companion staggering under the heavy weight of a "portable" backpack transmitter, and permitted the announcer to "wander freely about." Forty years later, however, all of the components (microphone, amplifiers, batteries, transmitter, antenna) in the 1936 device, and additional cueing circuits from the director back to the reporter, were contained in a lightweight telephone operator-type headset, with the transmitter itself a small box somewhat smaller than a cigarette pack sticking above the earphone with a tiny antenna waving jauntily above.

Photo courtesy of Broadcast Pioneers Library and National Broadcasting Company, Inc.

Cleveland, and the convention floor bristled with microphones. Once the campaign got underway, frequent spot radio commercials emphasized aspects of the GOP platform. In October, Senator Arthur Vandenberg presented a "debate" on CBS in which he asked questions of an absent President Roosevelt and then played carefully selected recordings of earlier

F.D.R. speeches and promises. The program violated CBS policy against recordings, and many of the network's affiliates either refused to carry it or cut out during the program when they realized its unfair approach. Finally, when the networks refused to sell the Republicans time after the convention, the GOP used Chicago station WGN to present an allegorical play depicting its campaign promises.

On the other hand, the Democrats used nothing special—only F.D.R. That consummate political speaker had huge audiences listening to his broadcast speeches. On election night, the networks initially interrupted regular programs with ballot bulletins from time to time, supplementing with commentary. CBS went full-time to election results at 10:30 P.M., while Mutual reported its first election that year.

There was increased use of radio in the second Roosevelt administration, not just by the President and his cabinet but also by federal agencies. The Office of Education, for example, produced 11 network educational programs; the Federal Theater Program—part of the Depression-spawned Works Progress Administration—produced more radio programming in its short life than any other agency; the departments of Agriculture and Interior supplied recorded programs to individual stations. Many local stations also benefited from the forecasting services of the U.S. Weather Bureau, and produced local programs featuring county agricultural agents.

The 1940 election campaign saw F.D.R. run again, this time against Republican Wendell Willkie, a little-known utilities executive before a whirlwind public relations campaign had propelled him into the limelight. Willkie pushed himself so hard that his voice weakened during the campaign—perhaps one of the reasons why Roosevelt consistently got higher ratings. Surveys conducted during this campaign suggested that most voters now considered radio more important than newspapers as a source of political news and tended to listen most to the candidate they favored; in other words, radio strengthened voters' predispositions. On election eve the Democrats mounted a special radio program of speeches, party propaganda, and entertainment by stage, screen, and radio stars. Full-time election coverage, as in 1936, came after the regular prime time entertainment, although bulletins were provided throughout the evening. Human interest pieces and voter interviews were more common than before.

Political broadcasting was not limited to the presidential campaign. Louisiana Senator Huey Long made anti-F.D.R. populist speeches until his 1935 assassination. Like Roosevelt, he had an informal approach, inviting listeners to call a friend or two and tell them Huey Long was on the air, and then delaying the meat of his address for the next several minutes. Catholic radio priest Coughlin (see p. 138), after promising to leave the air in 1936 if his third-party candidate got less than nine million votes (he got less than one million) came back to rail against the New Deal. He became increasingly rightist, criticizing Jews and defending many of the tenets of Nazism, until pressure from the Church hierarchy and other sources forced him off the air.

Common on local stations were talks and discussions of local and national topics of interest. Such programs were inexpensive and easy to produce, particularly in college towns where professors were willingly drafted into occasional radio commentary. One of the better-known national programs, *The University of Chicago Roundtable*, began in 1931, went network (NBC) in 1933, and lasted for nearly 25 years. The surprisingly popular format consisted of faculty members and, occasionally, distinguished guests discussing a current topic. This program often out-rated commercial programs and drew substantial mail from listeners seeking transcripts of programs. Another program of this type, NBC's *America's Town Meeting of the Air*, first aired in 1935 and involved members of the studio audience expressing their opinions on important issues.

5.6.5 Other Programs

Popular local station programs included man-on-the-street interviews and call-in interview programs, during which listeners could request a favorite musical selection or converse on an announced topic with a program host. People listened and participated because they enjoyed hearing themselves and other ordinary people on the radio. Common both to local and network schedules were Sunday morning religious services, typically a live remote broadcast from a community church.

Some children's programs had large audiences. Featuring storytelling and music interspersed with commercial announcements, they made ingenious use of radio's aural qualities and their ability to stimulate the imagination.

On the networks, quiz and human-interest programs grew on prime time from 2 to 10 hours a week from 1935 to 1941 but were less important during daytime hours. Some quiz programs used audience members as participants and others used professional panels, but each offered human interest, drama, and an opportunity for the listener to test himself and occasionally outguess the participant. In 1938 came *Kay Kyser's Kollege of Musical Knowledge*, a combination musical-variety and quiz format; the urbane *Information, Please!*, whose professional panel tried to answer questions sent in by the audience; *Dr. I.Q.*, whose host, broadcasting from theaters around the country, offered "ten silver dollars for that lady in the balcony if she can tell me. . . ." In *Truth or Consequences*, which aired in 1940, willing contestants from the audience who answered silly questions incorrectly had to perform silly stunts as a consequence.

5.7 Systematic Audience Research

In the late 1930s, the radio audience continued to grow, and radio was readily accepted all over the house (and increasingly in the car). That growth in size led to higher rates to advertisers, who demanded more refined research about the audience to justify increased expenditures. As the number of listeners increased, so did information about who listened and why.

5.7.1 The Radio Receiver

The years 1935–1941 saw the radio audience grow by seven million homes to a total of 28.5 million, or 81% of American homes as compared with 67% at the start of the period. At the same time, a previously insignificant element of the radio audience grew even more rapidly: by 1941, 7.5 million automobiles, more than 27%, were equipped with radio—as compared with 9% in 1935. By 1938 the United States housed half the world's radio receivers, and more homes had radios than telephones, vacuum cleaners, or electric irons. The number of sets had grown by more than 100% since 1930.

Philco (see p. 139) remained behind RCA as a seller of radios until 1940, when it sold an equal volume of sets. Heavy promotion, pioneering battery-operated portable (but heavy!) radios and automobile radios, and aiming a line of efficient battery radios at rural listeners—all helped make Philco the growing giant of the period. Next in importance was Zenith, whose dynamic president Commander Eugene F. McDonald preferred aggressive selling and concentration on the home radio market to diversification. Here, too, innovations brought success—large, round, and easily read dials on radios starting in 1935, a simple radio antenna to improve reception, and an inexpensive shortwave–AM portable radio. Another relatively new firm, Emerson Radio, was primarily responsible for introducing the small, inexpensive table radio in 1933, a type which had almost four-fifths of the home radio market by 1941. Prices kept getting lower until, by 1939 and 1940, Emerson was marketing small sets at under $10—a price that encouraged many families to have more than one set. Another aggressive firm, Motorola, moved into the automobile market and by 1941 was selling about one-third of all car radios, offering push-button sets tailored for specific car instrument panels. The hallmark of all these firms was aggressive salesmanship and price cutting rather than major technical development.

The one time leader in the radio receiver field, RCA, was losing out in other fields as well. While it remained the largest maker of radio tubes in 1941, Sylvania and Raytheon were moving in on this market; Magnavox and other firms were taking part of RCA's loudspeaker business. Mail order firms frequently cut prices and traded for profit rather than loyalty to a given manufacturer. Part of RCA's problem was the long antitrust litigation of the early 1930s, which resulted in GE and Westinghouse making and selling radio sets independently starting in 1935. Other firms once important in radio set manufacture, such as Grigsby-Grunow and Atwater Kent, disappeared during the Depression. Crosley declined sharply. Increasingly tight competition among the surviving firms led to narrow profit margins

The Radio Receiver Market in the Late 1930s   These two advertisements, from Motorola and RCA, show the variety of radio sets available in the prewar years.

and little research. Radio circuits became standardized; parts were frequently interchangeable, and manufacturing techniques were streamlined and simplified. Many firms sold similar small table models, chairside radios, large floor consoles (some with phonographs) and automobile radios. The major results: More reliable radios at low prices and a growing multiset radio audience.

One of the most aggressive radio manufacturing companies, Zenith Radio Corporation, under the direction of Eugene F. McDonald, Jr., focused in 1935 on the 11 million U.S. homes that weren't yet connected to electricity. Financing and then buying a company that manufactured wind-powered battery chargers, McDonald, a master salesman and developer of new products, made a success out of this "niche" product, selling many thousands for as little as $10—if a Zenith radio were bought at the same time. Some of these units reportedly were still in use 40 years later. McDonald also pioneered the "Radio Nurse" household audio monitoring system and the hearing aid. He had been involved in two of Donald MacMillan's Arctic expeditions, was a radio and television broadcaster, and is featured elsewhere in this volume for becoming the first president of the National Association of Broadcasters, for the WJAZ case that took away regulatory power from the Secretary of Commerce and led to the "chaos" of 1926 and the establishment of the FRC, and for promoting "Phonevision," a form of pay-per-view television in the early 1950s. (The name "Zenith" came from the call letters 9ZN, held by two men who had built the first set McDonald owned—and who held a license under the Armstrong patents, making them quite desirable to a young salesman on his way to becoming a manufacturer.) Commander McDonald may not have made "Radionics" a household word for radio-electronics, but it has been argued that his offer to use all five stations belonging to the NAB to advertise a fan magazine marked the start of network (as contrasted to single station) commercial advertising.

5.7.2 Audience Patterns

By 1938 more than 91% of urban homes, and nearly 70% of rural homes, had radio. Half the homes in the country had at least two radios, and there were few differences in regional distribution. Radio was nearly universal in higher income homes, but even 57% of lower income homes earning less than $1,000 a year had at least one set. Radio was played in the average household more than five hours a day.

Urban and rural audiences used radio differently. Although fewer rural homes had sets, those with receivers tended to listen a few minutes more each day than urban homes. However, because of the dawn-to-dusk working schedules of farmers, rural audiences listened less than urban audiences in the evening—a pattern reflected today in scheduling of network programs an hour earlier in the Central and Mountain time zones than on either Coast because of line costs for separate feeds and presumed earlier-to-bed habits in the Midwest. As might be expected, rural homes (76%) preferred clear-channel stations to regional (21%) or local (2%) stations, because they represented the only reliable service in many rural areas. The problems of radio coverage were well known to station owners and engineers and the FCC; large areas of the country got no decent service at night, and some lacked reception around the clock. In June 1938 the FCC reported that 8% of the population had no reception in daytime and more than 17% were without it at night. This neglected segment of more than 20 million people was concentrated in rural areas where 16% had no daytime radio and fully one-third had no reception at night. This was particularly troubling to a political body like the FCC, since a lot of voters were in rural areas. Examination of popularity of network evening programs in 1938 revealed other urban–rural differences. Urban listeners had less interest in news—it ranked fifth in urban areas but third in rural areas—perhaps because newspapers were more accessible in cities, and because rural families had a stronger need for weather and market information. Urban listeners had more interest in drama—it ranked third in urban areas but fifth in rural areas. All other program types were ranked the same: amateur (1), variety (2), serial drama (4), dance band music (6) and classical music (7).

Early research into listening habits found that, as income and education went up, the amount of radio listening (and later television watching) went down. Advertisers and networks applied the concept of *audience flow*, which describes a program's ability not only to attract an audience but to increase the audience for the shows before and after it. This led stations and networks to schedule *blocks* of compatible programs, such as one serial drama following another all afternoon, so as to build ever larger audiences throughout the evening.

5.7.3 Increased Research

In the late 1930s and early 1940s, there were two competing broadcast rating organizations. The Cooperative Analysis of Broadcasting (CAB; see p. 140), based in 33 cities, 14 on the East Coast, was run by advertisers and advertising agencies on a nonprofit basis for the benefit of radio time buyers. Using a modified recall telephone interview system, CAB called numbers at random from a sample four times a day and asked the respondents what they had heard on the radio during the previous two or three hours. Ratings, processed and published every other week, were based on a total of 3,000 calls a day nationwide. Any single program's rating was based on at least 1,500 calls over the two-week period.

In the Fall of 1934, Clark-Hooper, Inc., began to sell to advertisers audience research on magazines and radio. The radio portion split off in 1938, becoming C. E. Hooper, Inc., which provided monthly ratings of sponsored, not sustaining, programs on radio networks. Hooper pioneered national use of the coincidental telephone method, which avoided the limitations of the listener's memory by asking what he or she was listening to *at that moment*. However, the coincidental technique required nearly 10 times as many calls as the recall method in order to report data at 15-minute intervals. Both techniques suffered from problems of telephoning in sparsely settled areas (which required going through operators) and discounting the radio homes without telephones.

Radio rating service reports were prepared both for broadcast time buyers (advertisers and their agencies) and sellers (networks and stations).

Although they were expensive, particularly for the sellers, they soon gained a reputation for detail and accuracy. Both firms—Hooper and CAB, whose service was called the "Crossley rating" after Archibald M. Crossley, its founder—reported ratings or percentages of radio receivers tuned to a given station, network, or program in relation to total receivers whether in use or not. This raw quantitative data satisfied most advertisers until CAB started to supply qualitative information by breaking down program rating data by income groups and geographic areas—an innovation of great value to alert advertisers. To index listening behavior in a small sample of homes, marketing research company A.C. Nielsen was developing, but did not commercially introduce until 1942, an automatic "Audimeter" that recorded whether a set was on and to which channel it was tuned. More reliable and to some extent more valid for measuring *tuning* rather than *listening* behavior than the telephone techniques, this device was expensive and dependent on the audience member's returning the data, but eventually became important for television research (see pp. 247–248).

In addition to the ratings, which merely gave size-of-audience estimates, the first serious research analyses of radio's effect on its audience began to appear. In 1934 Frederick Lumley's *Measurement in Radio* supplied detailed information on the use of audience research. The size of his bibliography suggests that advertiser pressure had made management look seriously at the size and particulars of their prime and only "product"—their audience. In 1935 the first report of in-depth audience research, Hadley Cantril and Gordon W. Allport's *The Psychology of Radio*, examined the mental setting of radio—how listeners perceived music and speakers—and potential uses of this experimentally derived data. The first extensive study of a program, Cantril's 1940 *The Invasion from Mars: A Study in the Psychology of Panic*, which investigated listener reaction to Orson Welles's famous 1938 program (see pp. 187–191), still is considered basic to the study of group panic and the mass media.

Founded late in 1937 by a Rockefeller Foundation grant to Princeton University, the Office of Radio Research was established there with Paul F. Lazarsfeld as director. He was assisted by two young researchers, Frank Stanton, who had worked in audience studies at CBS since 1935, and Hadley Cantril. The organization's first major publication was H. M. Beville's *Social Stratification of the Radio Audience* (1939), which is the earliest detailed description of audience ratings and their fruits. Beville later became head of research for NBC, and Stanton started a three-decade tenure as president of CBS in 1946. In 1940 the Office of Radio Research moved to Columbia University in New York and issued its first commercial publication, Lazarsfeld's *Radio and the Printed Page*, a report on several studies comparing newspapers and radio. A year later it published the first of an intended annual series, Lazarsfeld and Stanton's *Radio Research 1941*, which contained reports on research into radio music, radio in rural life, foreign language broadcasting, and use of radio and the press by young people. Only two other volumes, 1942–1943 and 1948–1949, followed in this series. Lazarsfeld and Stanton also developed the *program analyzer*, still in use at CBS and elsewhere, to obtain minute-by-minute reactions of a test audience to new programs.

The output of the Columbia-based project, which lasted well past the war years, is perhaps the clearest indication of academic concern for and interest in radio's influence. Other colleges and universities mounted similar but smaller projects, focusing mostly on audience effects but also on programming control and regulation. By 1939 at least 28 doctoral dissertations and 159 masters theses that dealt with broadcasting had been completed.

5.8 Formative Years of the FCC

Major changes in federal regulatory structure and approach after 1933 were built on the precedents of the Federal Radio Commission. Several problems had hindered the governmental role in electrical communications: Regulation of closely related means of electrical communication was spread among various agencies, which frequently had little to do with one another. The Interstate Commerce Commission (ICC) controlled interstate telegraph and telephone traffic as little as possible; the FRC controlled most aspects of radio, including broadcasting; and the Department of Commerce had some regulatory voice in the wire and wireless common carrier industries. Congress had attempted over the years to amend the Radio Act of 1927 to make the FRC a permanent administrative agency, since it had not been able to become the part-time adjudicatory body envisioned by the 1927 act. Because President Hoover did not favor these bills, they were killed by pocket veto.

5.8.1 Creation of the FCC

Soon after becoming President, Franklin D. Roosevelt appointed an interdepartmental committee on communications to examine the roles of the nine governmental agencies involved with public, private, and governmental use of radio. In December 1933, this committee recommended creation of a Federal Communications Commission that would contain nearly all these functions, serving as an enlarged version of the FRC and regulating interstate telegraph and telephone as well. In February 1934, Congress moved to establish such a commission, the "services affected to be all of those which rely on wires, cables, or radio as a means of transmission." The President specifically called for broad and nonrestrictive legislation so that the new organization would have utmost flexibility. Representative, later Speaker, Sam Rayburn (D-Texas) introduced the House bill, which would replace the FRC with the FCC and modify the Radio Act of 1927 without abolishing it. Senator Clarence C. Dill (D-Washington) sponsored the Senate version. It would replace the 1927 act and combine the duties of the different agencies in the new FCC, with rigidly defined radio and telegraph divisions, but would add more power to the new agency. FRC members generally backed the proposed changes, while the broadcasting industry, with the National Association of Broadcasters acting as spokesman, opposed them because the NAB feared any stronger governmental role in radio broadcasting. Both houses passed their bills, and the President signed a Senate–House compromise bill to go into effect July 1, 1934.

The Communications Act of 1934 incorporated in its Title III most of the provisions of the Radio Act of 1927, retaining the three-year broadcast license term, although the FRC was then restricting licenses to six months and the Senate had toyed with a one-year period. Title I set up the new commission with seven commissioners (two more than the old FRC) appointed to staggered terms of seven years each, providing that no more than four members could have the same political affiliation. Charged with designating internal operations and divisions, the commissioners initially established broadcast, telegraph, and telephone divisions but abolished them late in 1937. From then on they acted as a committee of the whole, occasionally appointing ad hoc subgroups to prepare investigative reports into specific subjects. Commissioners were to be nominated, and the chairman appointed, by the U.S. President, with the advice and consent of the Senate, and could not have a financial interest in the industry. The commission was to report annually to Congress. Title II dealt with common carriers, generally reflecting existing ICC rules. Title IV was concerned with procedural and administrative matters, Title V with penal provisions and forfeitures, and Title VI with miscellaneous matters including the presidential emergency power to take over electrical and electronic communications in time of war or other emergency.

Most of the men—the first female commissioner, Frieda Hennock, didn't join the FCC until 1948—appointed to the FCC in the 1930s were lawyers with public utility experience or governmental service. Although one engineer usually served on the commission, technical expertise was thought less needed now that basic interference-reducing decisions had been made by the FRC and upheld by the courts.

5.8.2 Program Cleanup

The first FCC regulatory project was a concern of the old FRC—changing substandard program and advertising policies in broadcasting. Although the act forbade the FCC to censor, it could decide whether a station's policies and programs were in the public interest. This concern was apparent in a variety of hearings in the 1930s: on renewal of a 1935 Missouri station for carrying broadcasts by an astrologer (this was frowned on by the FCC not only because such individual messages were not broadcasting but because they took advantage of listeners' credulity); on a New York licensee for showing poor taste in accepting contraceptive advertising; on New Jersey and New York stations for broadcasting horse race information, using a code that only subscribers to a certain racing newspaper could decipher (held to be unfair, since the broadcast excluded some listeners); on a New York station for relinquishing responsibility as well as authority when it sold blocks of time for others to program; on several stations for promoting fraudulent products, especially patent medicines; and on several stations for airing misleading personal advice programs. Perhaps the most publicized case involved an episode of the popular Chase and Sanborn-sponsored *Edgar Bergen and Charlie McCarthy Show* in December 1937, in which guest star Mae West added some racy inflections to an "Adam and Eve" sketch. The FCC was inundated with complaints from offended listeners. Other than reprimanding NBC and its affiliates, the commission took no action.

In very few cases did stations actually lose licenses or fail to get a renewal or a construction permit. In fact, only two licenses were revoked and eight weren't renewed between 1934 and 1941. But FCC "raised eyebrow" displeasure was sufficient to change operating policy at an offending station. In a 1939 memo, the FCC listed 14 kinds of program material or practices deemed not to be in the public interest:

1. Defamation
2. Racial or religious intolerance
3. Fortune-telling or similar programs
4. Favorable reference to hard liquor
5. Obscenity
6. Programs depicting torture
7. Excessive suspense on children's programs
8. Excessive playing of recorded music to fill air time
9. Obvious solicitation of funds
10. Lengthy and frequent advertisements
11. Interruption of "artistic programs" by advertising
12. False or fraudulent or otherwise misleading advertising
13. Presentation of only one side of a controversial issue—an early statement of the Fairness Doctrine (see pp. 463–466)
14. Refusal to give equal treatment to both sides in a controversial discussion.

The commission, until the deregulation of the 1980s, held the first nine to be poor programming practice at all times, and some of the last five under some circumstances.

The Federal Trade Commission took over the major portion of advertising regulation, thanks to the Wheeler-Lea Act of early 1938. This act amended the FTC's original mandate to allow it to seek out and stop unfair and deceptive advertising in any medium, specifically for drugs, cosmetics, foods, means of product distribution, and marketing practices.

5.8.3 Investigations of Monopoly

The FCC also looked at monopoly practices in various industries. Under the strong guidance of Commissioner Paul Walker, it undertook a massive investigation of American Telephone and Telegraph's rate structure between 1936 and 1939, resulting in a limited rate reduction. Congress added pressure to this investigation and also, questioning FCC apparent unconcern about monopoly control of radio, considered several bills calling for FCC examination of the entire industry.

Under this pressure from its funding source, in March 1938 the FCC issued Order No. 37, an inquiry into "all phases of chain broadcasting and into the broadcasting industry generally" to see whether rules were needed to control network tendencies to monopolize. From November 1938 through May 1939, a subcommittee of four commissioners heard 73 days of testimony from 94 witnesses, resulting in thousands of pages of testimony and hundreds of exhibits on all aspects of network operation and its effect on the broadcasting industry. On June 12, 1940, the subcommittee issued a tentative, 1,300-page, mimeographed report of summarized testimony and recommended rule changes. Following hearings on these findings, the full commission, on May 2, 1941, released its *Report on Chain Broadcasting* containing specific regulations "designed to eliminate the abuses uncovered."

Of these regulations, the following were most important:

1. Network affiliation contracts would be limited to a single year for both parties—previously, stations had been bound to networks for five years, but the networks were bound for only one year.
2. Affiliations could no longer be exclusive—an affiliate could use programs from other networks or sources.
3. Networks could no longer demand options on large amounts of station time, because the FCC believed that stations—that is, licensees—should be in charge of and responsible for their own program content and arrangement.
4. An affiliate could reject any network program that in its view did not meet the public interest, convenience, or necessity, and could not sign away that right in its affiliation contract.
5. Networks would have no control over a station's rates for other than network programs.

6. "No license shall be issued to a standard broadcast [AM] station affiliated with a network organization which maintains more than one
   network" except where such networks operated at different times or
   covered substantially different territory.

These rules, and a seventh rule (not part of the chain broadcasting regulations) prohibiting duopoly, or the owning of two stations in the same
service area by one licensee, would drastically affect the industry.

Immediate network reaction was generally antagonistic. CBS and NBC
both published booklets claiming that the proposed rules could destroy the
American system of broadcasting. NBC stood to lose the most, as the sixth
rule would force it to drop either the Red or the Blue chain, and the seventh
would force it to sell one of the two stations it owned in New York, Chicago,
Washington, and San Francisco—one affiliated with the Red and the other
with the Blue network. Only Mutual applauded the new rules and had supported them in the hearings in the belief that they would make it more competitive with the other networks.

In October 1941, NBC and CBS brought suit in the Federal District Court
in New York to set aside the regulations; Mutual entered the case on the
other side. The FCC had twice postponed implementation of the new rules
and now postponed them again. As the country entered World War II, the
network rules were one of the hottest topics in the broadcasting industry.
The commission, many local broadcasters, and many critics of broadcasting
in Congress contended that by removing their dependence on network
fare, the new rules would enable stations to develop better programming.
(Two decades later, program syndicators also employed this reasoning in an
effort to get FCC backing for more local television programming in prime
time theretofore considered "network" time—see pp. 418–419.) The networks and their defenders claimed that the rules would weaken network
operating flexibility and lower program quality.

The commission also began to move on the issue of co-ownership of
newspapers and broadcast stations in the same market. In spite of congressional hearings and some FCC action by 1936, the proportion of newspaper-
owned stations increased through the decade, until by 1940 more than
30% were in this category, many located in the same market as their
owners. The FCC finally took action early in 1941, aware perhaps that
the Democratic administration would be concerned about Republican
newspapers' controlling of *all* news media and certainly that nearly
one-quarter of the FM construction permits had gone to newspaper-
connected applicants. FCC Chairman James Lawrence Fly announced in
March 1941 FCC Order No. 79, which called for "... an immediate investigation to determine what statement of policy or rules, if any, should be
issued concerning applications for high frequency [stations] with which
are associated persons also associated with the publication of one or more
newspapers...." While press ownership of AM stations also would be

■ **One Network Reacts to the Chain Broadcasting Report: 1941**   Seldom had the broadcast industry been as aroused as when the FCC issued its Chain Broadcasting Report and new rules in Spring 1941. Here are some of the reactions to the report, which, although it survived a Supreme Court test (see p. 259), did not have the dire effects the broadcasters anticipated.

Columbia Broadcasting System here states ... that, instead of benefiting the public, instead of promoting sound competition, instead of improving radio broadcasting, what the Commission proposes to do will have these effects: (1) It will threaten the very existence of present network broadcasting service, bring confusion to radio listeners, to radio stations, and to the users of radio [advertisers], and deprive business of an orderly and stable method of presenting sponsored programs to the public. (2) It will threaten the continuance to radio listeners of their favorite sustaining programs sent out by the networks, such as ... symphony broadcasts, educational and religious programs, world news service. We do not see how, under these "regulations," Columbia or anyone else can afford to, or has any real inducement to, produce and improve the character of its public service. (3) It will establish radio monopolies in many sections of the country. ... (4) In weakening the ability of the radio industry to give the kind of broadcasting service that people have come to demand, it may, in the end, encourage the government to take over broadcasting altogether. Meantime it opens the door to the complete domination of radio by whatever government happens to be in power. (5) It will cripple, if it does not paralyze, broadcasting as a national service at a time when radio should be encouraged to continue and enlarge its contribution to national unity and morale.

(NBC reacted as strongly. See Appendix C, tables 2-A and 3-A, to see how "badly" radio was "harmed," how the networks "all but disappeared," and how radio profits "plunged.")

Source: "What the New Radio Rules Mean" (New York: CBS, May 1941) p. 4.

examined, issuance of construction permits to newspaper-controlled FM stations was frozen for the duration of the hearings, which lasted from July through October 1941 and then recessed. There was dissension within the industry and even within the FCC over the hearings. Two commissioners thought that the FCC was overstepping its authority and the First Amendment by in any way considering the newspaper business. Station owners claimed that anyone or any group should be allowed to own radio stations, and that newspapers were no exception. Critics of co-ownership argued that to have both media under single control could limit expression of different viewpoints and might encourage combined advertising practices that would squelch the establishment of new stations or newspapers in such a market (see p. 259).

5.8.4 Self-Regulation

Industry self-control in the late 1930s essentially is the story of the reorganization of the National Association of Broadcasters, the revision of its radio code, and the long fight with ASCAP over music rights (see p. 214). While the period left broadcasters with a stronger trade organization and more unified clout, fundamental problems obviously remained unsolved.

Members of the NAB had begun to realize its limitations, as battles with unions, music copyright organizations, Congress, and private groups came and went with little broadcaster input or impact. Until 1938 the association, operating on $80,000 a year, with a salaried managing director and an unpaid broadcaster as ceremonial president, lacked personnel and funds to function effectively as a trade and lobby group. Representation of broadcaster interests had to come mostly from the networks and larger stations and reflected their views. Realizing the need to centralize, coordinate, and concert its efforts in the face of government investigations and other problems, the 1938 NAB convention voted to increase the budget threefold, to support a paid president and staff with dues proportional to a member station's earning, and to form operating subdivisions focusing on law, labor questions, management problems, engineering issues, and the role of education on the air. In this way, it was hoped that NAB—and therefore most broadcasters—would keep up to date on issues, and the broadcasting industry's position on issues, and communicate unified views to Congress and the FCC.

Under a National Recovery Administration (NRA) ruling in 1933, the broadcasting industry's 1929 code became law for all stations including earlier nonsubscribers. When the Supreme Court declared the NRA unconstitutional in 1935, the mandatory code went by the boards. Because of the antibroadcasting industry sentiment shown at the 1934 Communications Act hearings, the NAB hastily issued a 10-point, unenforceable ethical code in 1935. After the NAB reorganization of 1938 and during the FCC investigation of chain broadcasting, the NAB implemented in July 1939 a greatly expanded and revised radio code—a later edition of which was in use until 1982 (see p. 561). The new code allowed only 6 to 10 minutes of commercials per evening hour, with a bit more during the day. It permitted no separate scheduling of controversial issues; they were to be covered in news and special programs for the expression of opinions. It dealt with other issues in generalities and platitudes that had little effect on existing practices. Advertising agencies had helped to assure flexibility in the code, and a Code Compliance Committee supervised implementation. One effect was a reduction of Father Coughlin's access to the air after code-subscribing stations learned that they would have to provide opportunity for other points of view. Many stations also thought labor union news to be controversial. In practice, the requirements for controversial issues or fund-raising appeals served to limit access to radio drastically for all but commercial advertisers. Backers of the code claimed that selling time for controversial issues would overload the air with fractious arguments that would bore the listener seeking relaxation and entertainment. Critics of the code agreed that controversy might annoy some listeners and most certainly would not appeal to advertisers but argued that it was a necessary aspect of public interest broadcasting—another anticipation of the Fairness Doctrine. Despite these differences, broadcasters widely publicized the code as a symbol of their acceptance of responsibility to serve public needs.

5.8.5 The Music Licensing Battle

In the meantime, the original nemesis of NAB was flexing its muscles again. The American Society of Composers, Authors and Publishers (ASCAP), whose demands had led to formation of the NAB (see p. 99), had collected more than $800,000 (40% of its income) from radio music performance fees in 1930, $2.7 million in 1937 (60%), and $4.15 million (about two-thirds) in 1939. Many ASCAP members approved of such fees because they thought that radio was helping to kill the sheet-music and record businesses.

In 1937 ASCAP went too far—in the broadcasters' eyes—and imposed a rate increase of 70% or more. This demand caused broadcasters late in 1939 to create a fund to establish a temporary music licensing agency to compete with ASCAP: Broadcast Music, Incorporated (BMI). The $1.5 million fund was about half what stations had paid ASCAP in 1937, but BMI used it to advantage and set out to build an alternative library of music. When ASCAP increased its rates again in 1940, broadcasters decided to make BMI permanent and not to renew ASCAP contracts ending that year.

For 10 months beginning January 1, 1941, listeners heard BMI's few selections and a good deal of public domain music—music on which copyright had expired. Stephen Foster's "Jeannie with the Light Brown Hair" found sudden new popularity, and programs had new theme music. Although the networks and many stations stuck to their guns, some broadcasters chose to pay for ASCAP licenses rather than face checking each tune used or risk paying a statutory fine of $250 for each performance of music without a license. The battle became more confusing early in 1941 when the Justice Department filed antitrust suits against not only ASCAP but the networks as principal backers of BMI. Some musicians and publishers switched from ASCAP to BMI and vice versa, but ASCAP music still was not played over most stations. In May 1941 Mutual defected and signed with ASCAP, and in October the industry and ASCAP compromised on payments much closer to the old rates than to the new demands. The standoff had cost ASCAP some $4 million in revenue, the need to operate under a consent decree signed with the Justice Department, and the permanent addition of BMI as a competitor. But by late October and early November, ASCAP music again was playing on networks and local stations, under new contracts that would last until 1950.

5.9 Radio's Role Here and Abroad

As a medium of entertainment and news, radio really came into its own both here and abroad during the late 1930s. Radio was not only accepted and enjoyed—it had rapidly become an essential element of government and business as well.

5.9.1 Here . . .

By the time the United States entered World War II in December 1941, radio had become a part of American life. Three events showed radio's impact clearly: the 1938 Orson Welles "War of the Worlds" broadcast, which created panic because listeners had learned to believe what they heard on radio (see p. 189); the ASCAP hassle, which limited popular music in early 1941 at the height of the big band craze (see p. 214); and the FCC investigation of the networks (see p. 210), by which the 10-year-old networks were shown to have attained the importance of much older businesses.

Politically, radio brought the government home to the average American, who hung onto President Roosevelt's words during the first 100 days of the New Deal, in the heart of the Depression. More people heard more candidates and political opinions than had been heard throughout the country's history. Some commentators claimed that radio caused the 87% increase in number of votes cast in national presidential elections from 1920 to 1940, while the population grew only by 25%.

Furthermore, by its coverage of domestic and international news events, radio became the news medium to which people turned first, replacing the century-old dominance of the newspaper.

Radio's increasing importance to the listener can be indexed in other ways: newspapers' attempts to build or buy AM and FM stations as a hedge against the future; the use of motion picture stars and stories to promote films, as on *Lux Radio Theater*; the inclusion of radio-related questions on national polls and surveys, including the 1940 census; increased use of radio by public office seekers or, like Huey Long and Father Coughlin, opinion molders; ASCAP's reliance on revenue from radio; the increase in car radios; and refinement of radio audience research, primarily to serve hard-nosed advertisers.

Another indication of radio's impact was the sharp rise in criticism of its programs and organization. Books, pamphlets, and articles charged that big business interests had taken over radio, particularly the networks, to the detriment of the average listener. Special interest groups bemoaned the lack of religious programming, the paucity of educational programs, the increasing flood of advertisements. Many critics believed that radio's chief problems were no longer technical, as they had been through the mid-1930s, but social, and that programming aimed at the lowest common denominator would make radio a societal liability.

In the late 1930s, Americans were both struggling up from the Depression and preparing for a war that by 1941 seemed inevitable. Radio broadcasting prospered accordingly: its increasing popularity filled a major marketing function when other media were suffering from lower revenues; it provided news and other information to the public; and it filled pleasurably the leisure hours that the Depression and then the shorter work week provided. Radio also prepared itself for service in the war that was to come.

5.9.2 . . . and Abroad

Radio broadcasting also was developing in Canada, Mexico, and Cuba. As the stations in these neighboring nations multiplied, they used greater power, spent longer hours on the air, and consequently produced greater interference. Both Canada and Mexico complained that the United States was hogging most of North America's clear channels and was ignoring their needs. This dissension led to a meeting early in 1937 to plan a fair division of the broadcast spectrum among the four countries, and a November 1937 conference in Havana, where representatives of the United States, Canada, Mexico, Cuba, Haiti, and the Dominican Republic drew up a North American Regional Broadcasting Agreement (NARBA). After ratification by the various legislatures, NARBA went into effect in late March 1941. This agreement forced many stations to change frequency. In the United States, the FCC's moving 777 of the 862 stations on the air—only one to four channels for most of them—caused a minor technical expense rather than a major audience loss. About 100 Canadian stations were changed, and Mexico closed down many border stations that had long broadcast to the United States immune from FCC controls. In the end, Mexico and Canada gained better frequency allocations, and interference for all six countries was substantially reduced.

The story of radio abroad in the years 1934–1941 is essentially one of "haves" and "have-nots." While this country had fully half the world's radios, one for every 3.5 people, and Europe had one radio for every eight people, vast areas had little or no radio service or facilities. For example, rapidly industrializing Japan had but one receiver for every 28 people. Mexico, importing most sets from the United States, had only one radio for every 64 persons, concentrated in major cities.

Patterns of control and organization were evident overseas. In most European countries, government controlled radio, sometimes indirectly, usually with annual license fees on receivers for support. Under Hitler, radio became a part of the German Propaganda Ministry. In the United Kingdom, the British Broadcasting Corporation was a government-chartered monopoly, a kind of public utility, supported by license revenue. Director-general until 1938 was the strong-minded Sir John Reith, who during his 15-year tenure put a philosophical stamp of "public service" on both commercial and noncommercial British broadcasting that has lasted to this day. Since European colonies tended to copy the mother country's, the majority of African and Asian systems—where radio existed at all—had central government control of facilities, finances, and programming. Countries of the Western Hemisphere, except for Canada and some of the West Indies and Latin America, tended to follow the commercially based system of the United States.

The use of shortwave for international broadcasting increased sharply during the 1930s as world tension rose. In this hemisphere, both commercial—

primarily CBS and NBC—and governmental transmitters beamed broadcasts to Latin America by shortwave for rebroadcast over either medium- or short-wave domestic stations. By 1935 the Soviet Union, Germany, Italy, and Great Britain were sending regular shortwave broadcasts to North America and the rest of the world, in appropriate languages. Since many floor-model console radios and some table radios sold here were equipped for shortwave listening, Americans frequently listened to shortwave in a time of crisis in Europe. Although much European shortwave propaganda was intended for other European nations (Germany, in particular, used radio to soften up enemy resolve before starting a diplomatic or military move) even after World War II began, some was directed at other parts of the world.

5.9.3 Period Overview

In these years prior to our entry into World War II, there were few departures from the trends established in the 1926–1933 period. Major technological changes were brewing for FM in the Armstrong laboratory and for television in the RCA and Farnsworth laboratories. While these new media already were competing for spectrum space, attention, and backing, only in the last months before Pearl Harbor would the public become aware of them. Their real impact would come after the war. After the initial shocks of FRC regulation and the Depression, broadcasting stations increased in number and power, and brought many communities their first local service. Radio carried news of political and economic changes and also took people's minds off their troubles.

Radio's winners and losers were easily identified in this period. Networks and their supporting advertisers, influenced by the increasingly powerful advertising agencies, determined program content. What the networks presented, local stations carried, and copied in local programming. Commercial support, determined largely by audience ratings, was the substance of program and station survival. Many young entertainers began long careers on radio, and later on television. On the other hand, educational radio languished almost into nonexistence. Until Americans acknowledged the worldwide threat of events in Europe, news and public affairs were limited in both national and local programming. Once war came, however, such previously unknown reporters as Edward R. Murrow became household names through their coverage of radio's first war.

Other than program domination by networks and advertising agencies, the most important development of the late 1930s was the growth of federal regulation. The FCC completed the major technical receiver-interference reduction started by the FRC and turned to program content and media economics, areas that would demand increasing attention. Questionable program practices were brought to light and eliminated. Broadcast ownership and control, particularly as affected by the networks, was the subject of serious studies, numerous FCC hearings, and decisions. The general public neither knew nor cared about the behind-the-scenes battles—with the exception of the ASCAP–broadcasters fight that removed most popular music from the air for several months.

Radio as an increasing force in tying the nation together was illustrated in the first significant academic research into broadcasting. Radio's potential as both a positive and a negative propagandistic tool emerged in its early coverage of both the New Deal and the war in Europe. But the most important test for American radio was yet to come.

Selected Further Reading

(Alphabetical within topics. For full citations, see Appendix D.)

See most of the sources noted in the "Selected Further Reading" section of chapter four as well as the second and third *Annals* compilations (1935, 1941), Barnouw (1968), Lichty & Topping (1975), MacDonald (1979), and *The First 50 Years of Broadcasting* (1982). Contemporary views are recorded in Chase (1942), and Husing (1935). The rise of FM is best found in Lessing (1956), while television's development is in Abramson (1955 & 1987), Burns (1998), Eckhardt (1936), Fisher & Fisher (1996), Ritchie (1994), and Udelson (1982). Everson (1949), and Godfrey (2001) relate Farnsworth's life, while Abramson (1995) does the same for Zworykin. Contemporary descriptions of television include Fink (1943), Hubbell (1942), Lohr (1940), Porterfield & Reynolds (1940), and Waldrop & Borkin (1938). Eoyang (1936), and FCC (1938) offer assessments of the industry's economics. For insight into the growing role of advertising in radio, see Barnouw (1978), Dygert (1939) and Hettinger & Neff (1938). The struggle of educationl radio in the 1930s and early 1940s is found in Atkinson (1941, 1942a-d), Blakely (1979), Cooper (1942), and Frost (1937a-b).

Reference works describing radio programs are provided in the readings for chapter four. Music on radio is discussed by DeLong (1980), and Eberly (1982), while Poindexter (1978) focuses on the announcer. Norman Corwin's life (to date) is related in Bannerman (1986), Skutch (1998b) interviews him and four others, and collections of his scripts are listed in the bibliography (Corwin, 1942, 1944, 1945, 1947). The story of farm radio is told in Baker (1981). Radio news in this period is discussed in Bliss (1991), Brown (1998), Culbert (1976), Fang (1977), and Hosley (1984); contemporary views appear in Murrow (1941), Schechter & Anthony (1941), and Shirer (1941 and 1999). Carpenter (1998), Marcus (1973), and Warren (1996) all tell the story of Father Coughlin.

Radio audience research is reviewed in Beville (1988), Connah (1938), and Lazarsfeld (1940). The FCC (1941), Robinson (1943), and Sarnoff (1939), relate the network investigation story. Flannery (1995) offers brief biographies of FRC and FCC commissioners. Other studies of policy during this period include Dill (1938), Edelman (1950), FCC annual reports (1935 on), Foust (2000) on the clear channel controversy, Frost (1937b), Herring & Gross (1936), Paglin (1989), Rose (1940), and Socolow (1939).

The BBC's introduction of televisiion is told by Burns (1986), Norman (1984), Pawley (1972), and Swift (1950), while the growing social impact of radio in Britain is related by Briggs (1965), Maine (1939), and Scannell & Cardiff (1991). For studies of radio during World War II, see chapter six.

"Seems like free men have done it again!"————*ON A NOTE OF TRIUMPH,*
Norman Corwin, 1945

CHAPTER 6

Broadcasting Fights
Its First War

"... radio has nothing but a front page."———*Elmer Davis, 1942*

RADIO GOES TO WAR
(1941–1945)

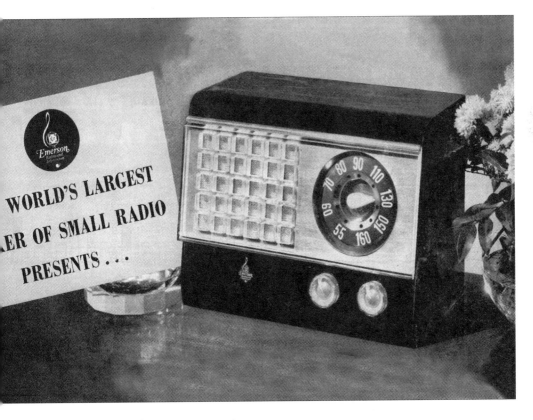

Chapter Outline

Tension between the United States and Japan had been building. While members of the America First Committee and others thundered against participating in a foreign war, the U.S. government was selling arms to the Allies in Europe, the Navy had orders to shoot back if fired on, and the tiny U.S. Army was priming itself with the draft and extensive maneuvers in Louisiana. Overseas, Hitler neared Moscow after his midsummer invasion of Russia; and General Douglas MacArthur, an American officer technically working for the government of the Philippines, said that he had what it took to resist a Japanese invasion of "up to five million men." At home, war-related industries were humming as the country geared for the war that seemed to be coming.

December 7, 1941, was a Sunday, and across the country people were wading through the newspaper, going for a day's outing or Christmas window shopping, or just relaxing. In Washington, Secretary of State Cordell Hull expected two Japanese emissaries in the latest of many attempts to reduce the tension.

Radio in those years devoted Sunday afternoon largely to public affairs and classical music. Audiences were not large, but they were loyal, and such programming was thought probably to please the FCC. At 2:30 P.M., eastern standard time, NBC-Red was about to broadcast a *University of Chicago Roundtable* program while NBC-Blue was in the middle of a Foreign Policy Association talk. A labor talk sponsored by the CIO had just finished on CBS, and the weekly New York Philharmonic broadcast would begin at 3 P.M. Listeners tuned in for the interim program were startled to hear newsman John Daly cut in at 2:31 with "The Japanese have attacked Pearl Harbor, Hawaii, by air, President Roosevelt has just announced. The attack was also made on naval and military activities on the principal island of Oahu." In his haste, Daly stumbled on the pronunciation of Oahu before repeating the incredible announcement. The other networks soon delivered similar bulletins, and Americans began to realize that war had come. For an hour or so, bulletins broke into regular programming, adding new details as military or Hawaiian authorities released them.

As afternoon wore on to evening on the East Coast, five time zones away, military censorship clamped down, leaving radio with limited information and unlimited demand for it. Hence, analysis and commentary—much of it badly informed—filled networks' programming that Sunday

---

▪ **How United Press Covered the Peart Harbor Story**

United Press Associations

INCORPORATED IN NEW YORK

GENERAL OFFICES
NEWS BUILDING NEW YORK CITY

FRANK H. BARTHOLOMEW
VICE PRESIDENT
814 MISSION STREET
SAN FRANCISCO, CAL.

December 11, 1941

United Press Pacific Division Clients:

So many of you wired or wrote your thanks for the beat we gave you last Sunday forenoon from Honolulu on the Japanese attack that we are using this blanket method of answering your inquiries as to how it was done.

Several days earlier, we had issued advance orders to the telephone company to put all leased wires into operation at a moment's notice. San Francisco bureau -- focal point of news from the Pacific -- was ready.

James A. Sullivan, San Francisco bureau manager, was on duty Sunday, Dec. 7.

At 11:24 a.m. the telephone rang. It was Mrs. Frank Tremaine, wife of our Hawaii manager in Honolulu.

"Fifty unidentified planes attacked Honolulu this morning," she began, relaying the information coming into our Honolulu bureau from Tremaine at Fort Shafter, from Night Manager William F. Tyree at another post, and from staff members on other assignments.

Ringing of the flash signal on our leased wire in San Francisco bureau, with the White House announcement of the attack, came at 11:26, while Mrs. Tremaine continued to dictate:

"Several of the planes were shot down. Their attack seemed to center on Pearl Harbor and Hickam Field. Some bombs fell in the city.

"Just a minute -- there's an explosion or something outside. I'll run to the window and see what it was....There's a lot of excitement outside. I'll call you back later."

(The excitement was when an incendiary bomb landed 25 feet from The Advertiser building, home of the United Press bureau.)

Sullivan, in San Francisco, telephoned the story to United Press in New York, from whence the first direct account of the attack was placed on United Press wires.

Advance arrangements perfected several days earlier went into operation. Leased wires were opened to clients. United Press men in San Francisco telephoned you by long-distance to go to your office and turn on your teletypes. Cable re-write men and operators bulletined onto the wires the steady flood of urgent cables pouring in from Honolulu.

Reprinted by permission of United Press International.

---

evening. Military personnel were ordered, by radio, to report for duty in uniform immediately—including headquarters officers and technical personnel who had not worn uniforms for years. Stations and networks tossed aside program schedules, canceling some shows and delaying others to make room for news bulletins. Even commercials gave way to news.

On the West Coast, people were worried about possible air raids or naval bombardment of major cities or southern California airfields. Some antiaircraft guns were fired at nonexistent enemy airplanes. The federal

United Press Pacific Division Clients -- Page 2

In Honolulu, United Press was well pre~red for the Japanese attack.

As Staffer Francis McCarthy said in the last story telephoned from Honolulu before all press communications were halted for nearly two days: "Now it is possible to reveal that the attack was not entirely unexpected."

McCarthy himself had arrived in Honolulu via Pan-American Clipper only four days before the attack, further augmenting the staff of the largest bureau operated in Hawaii by any news service.

Only United Press serves both morning and evening newspapers in Hawaii. Only United Press operates both day and night bureaus there.

United Press owns and operates the only news transmission system in Hawaii, including a full leased wire on the Island of Oahu and its own wireless-telegraphy plant for reception of news from the mainland. Other news services utilize the commercial routes and must yield priority to governmental traffic. With its own private system, handling press exclusively, United Press has no traffic-priority problem and has a clear channel at all times.

In Manila -- news center #2 in the War of the Pacific -- United Press similarly operates around the clock and owns and operates its own communications system for instantaneous and exclusive transmission of news.

Your news service has its own men at the places where news is going to originate in the next few days and weeks.

They include Harold Guard at Singapore; Francis M. Fisher at Chungking; Robert P. Martin at Shanghai; Jack Raleigh at Batavia; Darrell Berrigan at Bangkok; George Baxter at Hongkong.

History's biggest news story is breaking in territory strongly staffed by the largest world-wide press association.

Sincerely yours,

Frank A. Bartholomew

Manager, Pacific Division.

government took emergency measures. Because enemy ships or planes could use radio transmissions to "home in" on targets, and because spies might use amateur radio, the FCC ordered all amateurs to get off the air and dismantle their equipment. It also shut down many West Coast broadcast stations for periods up to a week until initial fears of attack had died down. While some stations were silent for a few days, others broadcast only important news. Silencing amateurs followed World War I precedent, while restricting regular radio broadcasting in Oregon, California, Washington, and the Territory of Hawaii was an isolated episode in this country's history, not just during World War II.

Personnel at all stations were confused as to what they should or should not transmit. The Naval Observatory stopped transmitting weather forecasts almost immediately, and station operators soon learned that, with a few exceptions, weather forecasts from other sources would be banned as well. The Army prohibited the broadcast of any information on troop movements outside the country. In New York, the networks began to limit visitors and station extra guards over control centers and transmitters—security precautions that quickly spread to stations in other regions.

On Monday, December 8, the wire services and networks kept stations supplied with bulletins on Japanese attacks throughout French Indochina and the Philippines. At 12:40 P.M., Speaker Sam Rayburn introduced President Roosevelt, who delivered his famous "Yesterday, December 7, 1941, a date which will live in infamy . . ." speech as millions of Americans listened on radio. That evening Roosevelt spoke to more than 62 million listeners, the largest audience for a single radio program up to that time.

American broadcasting rapidly switched to a wartime footing. The government established an Office of Censorship, which, within a month of the Pearl Harbor attack, published a voluntary code of censorship for broadcasting and other media. The chief censor was highly respected news commentator Elmer Davis. In January 1942 the FCC limited new station construction, and in April the War Production Board froze new receiver manufacture—both steps taken to preserve war-needed materials and labor supply. The government declared radio an essential industry to maintain its manpower strength, but the draft and enlistments shrank the work force anyway and equipment shortages hindered production and repairs. Broadcasting could not expand in number of stations or receivers, but programming services, news staffs, and time on the air increased sharply. Patriotic elements became more common in regular and special programs on networks and local stations. Songs like "Remember Pearl Harbor" and "Praise the Lord and Pass the Ammunition" had brief popularity, and tension-relaxing humor and entertainment went into high gear.

6.1 Innovations: Recording Methods

As during World War I, there were many technological advances in the uses of radio, from radar and proximity fuses to regular use of frequencies that hadn't been practical earlier. Yet, old technologies remained in use: Each merchant ship carried a crystal receiver for emergency use, and Morse code was the mode of choice for many kinds of tactical communication.

An important technical trend was toward miniaturization of components. By 1943 and 1944 military units carried two-way radio sets, the famous *walkie-talkies*, a new kind of radio transceiver (transmitter/receiver) construction that made equipment smaller, lighter, and more rugged. FM radio's great value in ground tactical communications was facilitated by FM inventor Armstrong's waiving his rights to royalties on FM military applications. Military research also produced knowledge about interference, propagation, and efficient use of very high and ultra high frequencies, crucial to the 1944 and 1945 FCC hearings on spectrum allocations for FM and television services (see pp. 249–256).

Worked on before the war, refined during wartime here and abroad, and destined to have great postwar applicability was the magnetic tape recorder. Until the mid-1930s, recordings of music or broadcast programs were made with a disc recorder for either the common 78-rpm speed (for music) or 33 1/3-rpm (broadcast transcriptions) or sometimes on 35 mm film. But the equipment was too bulky and heavy for stability, carrying, or easy operation. Besides, shellac, then the primary ingredient in records, was in short supply for civilian use. Original transcriptions were switched from metal to very fragile glass bases.

In the late 1930s, several technologies were under development as supplements or replacements for discs. In this country, magnetic wire and steel tape recorders received what little attention there was. By 1935 Bell Telephone Laboratories had an experimental system for which the high-grade steel tape cost $1.50 per foot. By 1938 the Brush Development Company had a steel tape dictating machine for sale. Overseas, the Germans used a steel tape magnetic recording machine to give time signals over various telephone systems, and the BBC used a similar machine for recording its half-hour Empire Service programs. The sound fidelity was not very high, but such recorders would be adapted to record conferences or radio programs during the war. Since their manufacture had low priority, however, they tended to be constructed by hand.

Another American firm, the Armour Research Foundation, developed a magnetic wire recorder when steel tape became scarce. This very thin— 1/100 inch or so—wire could hold up to an hour of material per reel, although its quality was even poorer than steel tape and it often broke. One could repair a break by melting both ends with a lighted cigarette or by tying a square knot, but the resulting bumps could damage the delicate recording and playback heads. In 1943 Armour and its licensee Webster-Chicago (Webcor) began to manufacture a limited number of "portable" (50 pounds or more!) wire recorders for the military.

Other techniques were explored. One used a base similar to motion picture film, on which grooves were magnetically etched. The Recordgraph, weighing 75 pounds, was so rugged it could be operated upside down. Although used by a few war correspondents—including George Hicks in his famous D-Day reports—portable film recorders could be used only for low-quality voice recordings. These could be stored for a long time and were very cheap, but the film wore out after it had been played 20 or 30 times.

The eventual winner was the paper or plastic base magnetic tape, which provided excellent sound quality with little or no surface noise. In 1941 the Germans programmed Radio Luxembourg, which they had captured in

1940, with prerecorded tapes operating at 30 inches per second (ips), four times the present broadcast standard. They provided such good sound that American forces moving across Europe in 1944 were surprised to capture radio stations operating with large reels of tape and not live performers. By 1945 some German Magnetophones, including portable ones, had been brought to the United States for evaluation. The implications for post-war broadcasting were not overlooked (see pp. 273–274).

6.2 Stations: Status Quo for the Duration

During the war, from 1942 through 1945, only 34 new AM and 28 FM stations took to the air; previously the number of stations had increased by 30 to 50 each year. This reduction was due not to economics but to government policy.

6.2.1 The AM Industry

On February 23, 1942, the FCC announced that, to save building materiel and electronic equipment for war needs, it would not issue permits for new station construction. In April, the War Production Board limited construction of any kind to applicants who had all the needed materials in hand, or to builders of noncommercial educational stations. The FCC also froze major alterations to existing stations "for the duration" and, to conserve electrical power, tubes, and components, reduced requirements for minimum number of hours of broadcast service, and required stations to lower their power output by a rarely noticeable 20%. It ordered a massive inventory of tubes and unused transmitters in the hands of licensees and distributed the information to military and commercial broadcasters so that available supplies could be fully used. As trained engineers became scarcer beginning in 1943, the FCC reduced requirements and restrictions so that other persons could read meters and do minor maintenance.

By early 1944, electronic production had improved enough for the FCC to authorize a limited number of new Class IV 250-watt local stations and allow facilities changes when matériel seemed to be available. Conditions tightened up again early in 1945, and new construction was limited to towns lacking primary service and to situations requiring minimal construction materials. Full wartime restrictions remained until August 1945 (see p. 276).

A strong indication of the FCC's faith in broadcasting's stability and ability to function in the public interest was the announcement on December 14, 1943, that for the first time it would license stations for the full statutory three years. Although both the 1927 and the 1934 acts had authorized three-year terms, for many years license renewal had been required every six months, then one year, and later two years. The full license period, of course, meant less paperwork for stations and commission, both of which were operating with severe manpower shortages.

6.2.2 FM Pioneering

When construction of new stations was frozen during the war, there were more than 900 AM stations. FM service, however, was just getting started. Many applications for construction permits were withdrawn because of lack of materials, and the FCC eased its rules to allow FM stations that provided some public service to operate with whatever equipment they could gather. Philadelphia stations kept FM going in the face of replacement equipment shortages by rotating time on the air so that no station was broadcasting more than two days a week. They pooled all spare parts, programming material, and personnel.

In August 1943, the FCC dropped the cumbersome system of FM call letters using letter and number combinations, and many FM stations owned by AMs in the same market now took their sister station's call letters with an -FM suffix.

6.2.3 Television During the War Years

When the FCC gave television a green light for commercial development in Spring 1941 (see pp. 165–168), it also deleted one of television's 19 channels and deferred action on CBS's suggestion to consider color television. This decision created a small problem of receiver obsolescence for a few thousand sets (see box, p. 251).

On July 1, 1941, both CBS and NBC New York stations converted from experimental to commercial status, becoming WCBW (CBS) and WNBT (NBC). By FCC regulation, both stations were on the air about 15 hours a week. Most programs—discussions, game shows, musical programs, and wrestling and boxing matches—were produced within the studio. Some sports events were covered live on a remote basis. Films, particularly free ones, were widely used; indeed, program schedules were divided into 20-minute multiples—just right for two reels of film (18 minutes in 35 mm) and some commercials. Newscasts resembled motion picture newsreels in content. The first television commercial reportedly was a picture of a Bulova watch showing the correct time, and Lever Brothers, Procter & Gamble, and Sun Oil also were early sponsors of television programs. According to the first television rate card, WNBT's, one hour of prime time in New York cost $120, compared to $10,700 in 1975 and the 1941 radio rate of $1,200. (See box on p. 169)

A handful of other stations converted to commercial operation in later 1941 and early 1942: WPTZ (the station Farnsworth had put on the air for Philco) in Philadelphia, what would become KTLA in Los Angeles, WRGB (named after GE engineer W. R. G. Baker) in Schenectady, what would become WBBM-TV in Chicago, and a Zenith-owned station (W9XZN) in the same city. But the audience grew very slowly, since very few sets—90 a month in New York early in 1942—were for sale, and their price was very high–several hundred dollars for a 5- or 8-inch picture when minimum wage was 25 cents an hour. By the time we entered World War II, between 10,000 and 20,000 sets were in use, half in New York and the rest in Philadelphia, Chicago, Schenectady, and Los Angeles.

In December 1941, WCBW produced a 90-minute documentary on the Pearl Harbor attack, only hours after it happened. It included the latest news bulletins and analysis backed up by maps, charts, and models of affected areas in Hawaii and the Philippines. Later both New York stations promoted War Bond drives and other patriotic material. WNBT carried a series of training programs for air raid wardens in New York, which many of them viewed on sets that individual owners loaned to firehouses and other posts.

The green light given to television in mid-1941 changed to red on May 12, 1942, when a War Production Board order, implemented by the FCC, forbade further building of stations so that materials could go to the war effort. Ten commercial stations, mostly converted from experimental ones, were then on the air, together with some remaining experimental transmitters. The commission allowed licensees who had construction permits and the necessary equipment to finish building in order to "keep alive this new art during the war." The FCC had previously dropped the minimum telecast hours from 15 to four per week in order to stretch matériel and manpower. Six stations throughout the country continued regular program service throughout the war. In New York, only the DuMont station, started in June 1942, maintained regular service. Both NBC and CBS cut down to skeleton organizations and dropped television broadcasting altogether until Summer 1944, after DuMont had begun a full commercial schedule.

Everyone was learning during the 1942–1945 wartime hiatus. The military learned how to use many of the higher-band television frequencies. Many of the few thousand people with sets learned how to keep them working; about three-quarters of prewar sets survived the war, although many were in poor condition. While viewers enjoyed increased entertainment programming on the few stations, it was still in the era of monochrome (shades of gray) makeup and extremely strong (and hot) lighting that caused perspiration to fall from actors and then literally to boil off tabletops. A young man hired off the street as a cable puller one day could become a cameraman the next and a director shortly thereafter; for a brief interval cameramen were considered artists rather than technicians, and ingenuity compensated for small budgets and limited manpower. Program innovations were legion. GE presented the first complete televised opera in 1943; three stations interconnected to show an original short film a year later; and a New York station, with a commercial sponsor, offered the first musical program specially written for television. The presidential election of 1944 was sketchily covered, with local coverage in the convention city of Chicago sent on film to New York, since there was no direct coaxial cable or microwave link between the East and the Midwest.

Television's first trade association, the Television Broadcasters Association, was formed early in 1944, and both NBC and CBS announced plans for postwar television networks. The new image orthicon camera tube could get excellent pictures with only a small fraction of the light needed by the older iconoscope. Experiments with lighting, makeup, UHF transmissions, and film projection were conducted. On V-E and V-J days in 1945, WNBT telecast 15 hours of special programming about the end of shooting in Europe and Asia that was carried live on stations in Schenectady and Philadelphia as well as New York. Baseball broadcasts on one New York station could cause workers at another station to desert their posts and flock around a receiver (behind closed doors). But, it must be remembered, few people saw any of this, and television marked time behind the scenes during the war, planning for the day when the light would turn green again.

6.3 The Split-up of NBC and Formation of ABC

With the limited growth in AM stations, the proportion of network radio affiliates rose from 60% of all stations in 1940 and 1941 to 95% in 1945. Never before or since would network programming so dominate radio. Almost all the approximately 950 stations on the air had affiliations with one network, and many with more than one, especially if they were the only station in a smaller community. An increasingly large proportion—more than 40% at war's end—was affiliated with Mutual, usually smaller and less important stations. The NBC-Red and -Blue networks combined affiliated with about 35% of all stations and CBS affiliated with another 16%.

The major development during the war years was the appearance of two new networks. The Keystone Broadcasting System, established in 1940, was a network in name only, as it existed to supply programs by transcription to secondary market affiliates—some 200 by the end of the war. It provided up to 28 hours a week in scripted and transcribed programs to stations that were apt also to be affiliated with Mutual or another major network.

An important aftermath of the FCC chain broadcasting rules and extended litigation over their implementation (see pp. 210–212) was RCA's splitting its Red and Blue NBC networks into separate but wholly owned divisions. Red was called "NBC" over the air, and Blue "the Blue Network." When the Supreme Court upheld the FCC in 1943, NBC had to divest itself of one networks (see p. 259). NBC sought a cash buyer for Blue, which had always had less important affiliated stations and had carried more sustaining programs than the powerful and popular Red network. At the end of July, just two months after the Supreme Court decision, RCA announced that the Blue network had been sold to WMCA (New York) owner Edward J. Noble, a candy manufacturer who had earned his fortune with Life Savers, for $8 million. The FCC approved the sale in mid-October, changing the ownership of New York flagship station WJZ and several others, and divorcing the Blue Network, Inc. from RCA. In 1945 the network became the American Broadcasting Company (ABC).

The war killed another attempt to establish a broadcast network. In 1940, just as the FCC announced commercial FM authorization effective for the coming year, some 15 FM station owners led by John Shepard III announced plans for an FM-only commercial network. They obtained a construction permit for a New York station, to be the "American Network" flagship, with the idea of relaying FM programs directly off the air, since FM was static-free, instead of leasing telephone circuits from AT&T as AM networks had to do. The first program was so relayed by seven northeastern stations in December 1941, but when the war froze FM station construction, the American Network was left with a bunch of paper affiliates unable to get on the air. This delay, plus pressure by the AM chains, led to the plan's demise and sale of its name to the Blue Network in mid-1944.

6.4 Education Struggles On

While educational broadcasting on AM remained limited through the war years, a new hope had appeared when the FCC reserved FM channels for potential educational broadcasting licensees (see p. 176). By the end of 1941, however, only two educational FM stations had gone on the air. Although the construction freeze of 1942 exempted educational stations, the scarcity of construction materials and broadcast equipment coupled with the slow decision-making processes of educational institutions limited educational FM growth during the war to 12 authorizations and 6 stations on the air when the war ended in mid-1945.

Still, educational institutions made known their plans to apply for construction permits at the end of the war. Some states, notably Wisconsin, envisioned statewide educational networks of FM stations to broadcast school, college, and adult education programming. Educators realized that, after more than a decade of talking about educational radio, they finally had means to accomplish it—after the war.

6.5 Advertising: 10-Cent Dollars

While it may not be politic to say so, World War II was one of the best things to happen to radio advertising. The impetus for AM radio's gravy years was the government imposition of a 90% excess-profits tax on American industry to discourage profiteering on war contracts. However, the tax law had a provision that made excess profits used in advertising taxable at only the normal rates, if at all. Advertisers soon realized they could buy a dollar's worth of advertising time or space for what was, in effect, 10 cents. As paper rationing during the period 1943–1945 and shortages of newsprint led to smaller newspaper editions and often less advertising space, many advertisers switched to radio, which faced no such problem. Radio's share of advertising dollars increased from 12% in 1941 to 18% of a much larger base in 1945. Radio broadcasting passed newspapers as a national advertising medium in 1943. By 1945 more than 37% of national (but not local or regional) advertising dollars went to radio, with magazines a close second and newspapers third (see Appendix C, table 3-A).

From 1940 to 1945, gross revenues for the networks and their owned-and-operated stations rose from $56.4 million to $100.9 million. Before-tax profits, however, remained proportionately static—25% to 23% of revenues over the years covered—partially due to greatly increased expenses in covering war news around the world. The overall network advertising pattern was concentrated. Three advertising agencies, J. Walter Thompson, Young & Rubicam—both of which are still important—and Dancer-Fitzgerald-Sample, purchased about 25% of the time on the Red, Blue, and CBS networks. In 1945 CBS had 13 sponsors each of which bought more than $1 million worth of time, and 3 that bought more than $4 million worth, General Foods, Lever Brothers, and Procter & Gamble—still among the largest advertisers in the 1990s. Just seven sponsors and six agencies accounted for half of CBS's billings. The NBC-Red network had 11 purchasers of more than $1 million in time, ABC had 9, and Mutual had 3. Twelve sponsors and 5 agencies accounted for 40% of ABC's 1945 billings, while 6 sponsors and 5 agencies accounted for one-third of Mutual's. This concentration was not a wartime creation, but the high rate of income and profit was, thanks to the 10-cent dollars and the wartime rationing of paper.

While the networks and their 30 or so stations skimmed off the cream of revenue, more than one-third throughout these war years, the remaining 800 or so stations prospered as well. Gross revenues of the non-network-owned operations more than doubled from 1940, when 734 stations collected $90.6 million, to 1945, when 873 stations earned $198.3 million; but their net before-tax profit increased even more, from 21 to 30.5% of revenues in the same years. Some stations either had no income or did not report it to the FCC, for Appendix C, table 1-A, shows about 30 to 50 more stations on the air each year than reported financial data. While one-third of all stations reported losses in 1939, less than 6% were in the red six years later—probably the lowest such figure in the history of radio. The entire radio industry, and especially the local stations, were profiting. While all radio stations increased their return on investment twofold, local stations enjoyed an 800% increase from 1939 to 1945.

Most radio advertising in these years was for insurance and for processed foods, drugs, toiletries, and tobacco—items that were often rationed but never unattainable during the war. Regional and national firms whose normal consumer manufacturing was halted for the duration turned to institutional advertising. For example, the major auto makers advertised mainly to keep the corporate name in the public's mind; the slogan "when better cars are built, Buick will build them" could be used even while the automobile firm was making tanks for the Army. Since companies seeking to enhance their corporate name rather than sell a specific product often chose to sponsor prestige drama or musical programs on the larger stations or the networks, such programming became more common. Advertising agencies remained in control of most radio advertising and much of the programming.

The few commercial FM stations carried little or no advertising, not because they did not want to or try to sell time but because their audiences were too small and their broadcasting hours too few to attract sponsors. FM survived the war either on the profits of co-owned AM stations or out of the pockets of their respective owners. Stations kept expenses down by duplicating network shows or by programming recorded music.

6.6 **Programming Patriotism**

Like virtually all other aspects of American life, American radio was affected by and reflected the war. There had been no overall radio industry planning for wartime operation, Thus, when war came, radio took a while to adjust. With the exception of news broadcasts, radio in the first weeks after Pearl Harbor sounded much like prewar broadcasting. An indication of what was to come aired on December 15, when Norman Corwin's *We Hold These Truths* reminded Americans that the Bill of Rights was worth fighting for. The program was a combination of documentary, inspiration, news, and patriotic fervor, but it elicited favorable comments.

Essentially, radio programs took three related approaches to the war. Getting most attention were special programs—appeals for scrap materials, the sale of War Bonds, and the like—built around major screen and radio stars. Probably the best-known was singer Kate Smith's 57 appearances during one day, February 1, 1944, in a War Bond appeal. She was later credited with having helped sell $112 million worth of War Bonds.

The second and most common approach was to insert war-related material into existing program series. Drama programs included references to rationing or to a son in the service; variety shows made increasing use of servicemen or took place at military camps, and musical programs featured war-related songs. Although "Coming in on a Wing and a Prayer" and "He Wears a Pair of Silver Wings" did well on *Your Hit Parade*, so did a woman's complaint, "They're Either Too Young or Too Old." As usual, most songs dealt with romance rather than warfare.

The third approach was to introduce a new program series devoted to the war or heavily reflecting its impact on the home front. An early example was *This Is War!*, a 13-week series of hour-long programs aired on 700 stations, counting those that aired it by transcription rather than live, on all four networks. The series was developed by and supported with funds of the government and the networks. Norman Corwin was the director and wrote half of the programs. The first went on the air on Valentine's Day 1942 while American eyes were focused on the worsening situation in the Philippines. Each succeeding Saturday evening for the next 12 weeks a different program attracted an estimated 20 million listeners while focusing on some aspect of the war—the White House role in this and past wars; the Navy; the Army; the Army Air Corps; our allies, now being referred to as the United Nations; the enemy and his propaganda. Famed writers Norman Corwin, Maxwell Anderson, Philip Wylie, and Stephen Vincent Benét and many Hollywood and radio stars contributed their efforts. According to the prospectus for the series, the producer's aim was to inspire, frighten, and inform all at the same time. Reaction to the series was generally positive, except for the complaint that the series aired simultaneously on all four networks and gave listeners no alternatives. This first all-network production also gave rise to a fear that government might dominate programming.

6.6.1 Office of War Information

Section 606 of the Communications Act of 1934 gives the President power to control operations of telecommunications facilities in time of war or other national emergency. Many broadcasters feared that the government would take over radio completely, as it had in World War I, thus silencing commercial broadcasting for the duration. As it happened, Section 606 was not invoked for broadcasting; but two government agencies were set up to handle issues of vital communication on the one hand and censorship on the other (see p. 258).

In June 1942, President Roosevelt established the Office of War Information (OWI) and named veteran and highly respected *New York Times* and CBS news commentator Elmer Davis to head it. OWI, combining the operations and functions of four older and overlapping agencies, was intended to meet three needs of audiences in the United States and abroad: the need for news; the need for information as to what the public should do and when and how to do it; and the need for truthful explanations of war issues, the enemy and our allies, and, especially, the role of work and war production at home as well as the sacrifices war forced on everyone. Roughly two-thirds of OWI's budget went for overseas operations (see p. 263), leaving only one-third for the domestic branch. A section of the latter, the Radio Bureau, headed by a radio industry executive, was created to deliver important war-related messages efficiently to radio listeners.

In its first weeks of frenzied activity, the Radio Bureau established a general policy: Government was to steer—with "suggestions" for voluntary compliance—rather than direct or command the flow of information. It devoted a great deal of effort to involving station managers and respecting their views. In line with this policy, the Radio Bureau decided to tailor war messages for specific publics and to favor inserting war messages into regular popular entertainment programs instead of creating special programs. It would emphasize quality rather than saturation, and it would help broadcasters modify existing programming rather than force major changes in content. In that way, popular radio programs would help maintain morale while delivering their large audiences to OWI for its war-related messages. OWl was behind several special program series, however. *This Is Our Enemy* appeared on the networks to inform listeners as to what the Axis powers stood for and had done. *You Can't Do Business With Hitler* ran by transcription on hundreds of stations, describing Nazi broken promises.

Perhaps OWI's key job was to *limit* the flood of material that hit broadcasters in early 1942 as the country switched to a war footing. The problem was epitomized by the station that received a 20-inch stack, 16 pounds, of messages, scripts, and transcriptions for free-time and urgent broadcast in a single month! OWI had the task of coordinating and clearing all government messages, including those of the military services, and establishing priorities as to their importance at any given time. By limiting and setting up specific ways of allocating them across the broadcast schedule, both advertisers and broadcasters could bear the costs of government messages as a contribution to the war effort. At the same time, these practices kept the public from being saturated with government information and exhortation on top of the war news and consequently ignoring the whole issue.

6.6.2 News

The major role of radio during the war was, of course, to report the war's progress. The amount of radio news, including specials and on-the-spot coverage, increased by more than 1,000 hours a year to 1943, when it began to taper off. A look at the last column in the table on the next page indicates that scheduled newscasts, at least, dropped off in the final year of the war. Although specific data are lacking, overall time devoted to news probably dropped off that year too, since the war ended in Europe in May and in the Pacific in August, and since audiences were tiring of constant war news by early 1945, when the final result of the fighting seemed clear. Within that trend, other changes were noticeable. Network news increased mainly in evening hours, and by 1944 news specials and newscasts made up 16 to 20% of network program schedules. In many cases, fewer commercials were given during newscasts, CBS considering jingles and other "undue gaiety" unfitting for serious wartime news.

At first, because of technological limitations and censorship, war reporting was an after-the-fact recitation of events. The networks still adhered to their ban against recordings except under most unusual conditions. But military censors distrusted live reports for the same reason that they eliminated or severely restricted weather reports: The danger that apparently

■ **The Growth of Network Wartime News: 1940 to 1945**   That the war stimulated an increase in the amount of radio network time devoted to news seems obvious—but here are figures that demonstrate how great that increase was. See text for other comment.

Year	NBC(Red)	CBS	Blue(ABC)	Mutual	Total	Scheduled Newscasts (quarter hours per week) All Four Networks Combined
	Total Yearly Hours of News*					
1940	636	769	681	310	2,396	70
1941	983	829	796	840	3,448	66
1942	1,280	1,385	836	1,131	4,632	108
1943	1,641	1,454	909	1,370	5,274	123
1944	1,726	1,497	1,062	1,237	5,522	145
1945	#	#	#	#	#	135

* = includes regularly scheduled newscasts, specials, on-the spot broadcasts
\# = indicates figures not available

Source: First five columns from *Broadcasting* (April 23, 1945), page 23; last column figured from data in H. Summers. *A Thirty Year History of Programs Carried on National Radio Networks in the United States: 1926–1956* (Columbus: Ohio State University, 1958; reprinted by Arno Press, 1971).

innocuous phrases or events—a station going off the air during an air raid, the absence of a reporter who might be expected to accompany an invasion force—would give information to the enemy.

But slowly censors were convinced that radio would not harm the war effort, as long as broadcasters took precautions against unauthorized persons using their facilities (see p. 258). Technicians were able to transmit usable shortwave signals to the United States. When reporters were allowed in the war zones or even neutral foreign capitals, they began filing live, on-the-scene stories such as Edward R. Murrow's 1940 and 1941 evening reports to CBS (see pp. 194–195).

Radio reporters with the invasion fleet off North Africa in November 1942 provided a blow-by-blow account of the troops landing against the Vichy (collaborationist) French. By 1944 reporters for the radio networks were covering commando raids against the coast of France, going on air raids with bomber fleets, reporting on England at war, and covering early U.S. island invasions in the South Pacific. Reporters unknown before the war became identified with the area from which they spoke. The American radio audience associated ex-newspaperman Eric Sevareid with the fall of France in 1940 and later, reporting his survival of a plane crash deep in the jungle, in the China-Burma-India theater. Howard K. Smith reported from Europe. Charles Collingwood reported the North African war and, later, D-Day and troop movements through France and into Germany. Webley Edwards and others reported Pacific naval battles and island-hopping invasions that first stopped and then turned the tide against the Japanese. Edwards reported live from a B-29 during an air raid against Japan. Earlier, one of Murrow's most memorable broadcasts came after he flew on an air-raid mission over Berlin, against the orders of his CBS superiors.

■ **A Great Reporter: World War II**   Edward R. Murrow's reports about World War II in Europe, particularly his "This . . . is London" signature on early CBS broadcasts from Britain, made the war—and our future allies—familiar to millions of Americans.

Photo credit: Culver Pictures, Inc.

Some famous reporters and commentators worked at home: H. V. Kaltenborn, an anchorman for NBC; Lowell Thomas, continuing his evening CBS newscasts begun in 1930; John Daly; Robert Trout; and others. Pioneer announcer Graham McNamee, only six months before his death, was on hand in New York when the giant French liner *Normandie*, being converted to a troopship, burned and capsized.

Of many notable broadcasts, D-Day—June 6, 1944, when the Allies invaded France—was particularly important. As George Hicks of CBS recorded troops going ashore from a Navy ship, listeners could hear aircraft and anti-aircraft guns in the background. The recording was sent to the United States by shortwave for later broadcast. Radio's role on D-Day was both tactical, calling on resistance groups to hamper the German army, and morale-boosting here and in Europe—although the BBC lost some of its tremendous credibility when it broadcast, under orders, some false reports to mislead the Germans.

Radio's first intensive reporting of a President's death in office came on April 12, 1945, when Franklin D. Roosevelt, just starting his fourth term, died of a stroke in Georgia. First reports from network reporters around 5:45 P.M. produced stunned confusion. The deaths of other public figures were reported erroneously. In the middle of a children's adventure program, one character departed from the script to say "Just a minute, kids—President Roosevelt just died"—followed by a few seconds that seemed like minutes until the news announcer confirmed the report. Within two hours of the first

---

■ The Show Must Go On Versus Circumstances Beyond Control

The tradition that the show must go on in spite of disasters received a severe test from World War II. Many individuals and stations managed to give recognition to the tradition, even when normal programming was impossible. Among them was the reporter speaking from Manila who was cut off in mid-sentence when a Japanese bombing attack knocked the station off the air shortly after Pearl Harbor. At the end of the war, he was freed from a Japanese prison camp, returned to the station and went on the air with "Hello, NBC—as I was saying before being so rudely interrupted ..." followed by his 4-year-old report! A similar story is told about BBC television, which was ordered to leave the air immediately after mobilization in 1939 so that its transmitters and towers could be used for the first crude radar aircraft warning system. Without even signing off, it "went to black" after a Walt Disney cartoon, "Mickey's Gala Premiere." When the service returned to the air approximately seven years later, the same cartoon was included in the Inaugural broadcast.

---

radio flash of the President's death, stations were reporting national and international reaction. Radio listeners heard four days of repeated news, reviews of the President's career, overviews of the war, predictions of the effect of F.D.R.'s death on the war effort, and somber music. The networks and many local stations deleted all commercials for the four days between his death and burial in Hyde Park, New York. Broadcasters themselves were strongly affected. When Arthur Godfrey reported the funeral procession moving down Washington's Pennsylvania Avenue over CBS, listeners heard him break into tears at the end as he quickly turned the program over to a studio announcer. Although the Republicans bitterly opposed Roosevelt at election time, most Americans considered him the architect of the victory that was only a few weeks off; and the suddenness and irony of his death, after more than a dozen years in office, disturbed them deeply.

After a false alarm, radio finally reported the end of the war in Europe in early May 1945. Microphones stuck out of studio windows over the next several hours brought the sounds of celebrating America to listeners beyond the celebration sites. Three months later, radio reported the awesome effects of the first (Hiroshima) atomic bomb. Shortly after the dropping of the second (Nagasaki) atomic bomb came the report of V-J (Victory over Japan) day, and in September came the broadcast of the surrender ceremonies on the battleship *Missouri* in Tokyo harbor.

For the true flavor of what radio sounded like during four years of war, one must listen to the many recordings that have survived. Reading about a broadcast, or even reading the script, cannot convey the excitement of that spoken report. Besides, the unscarred American listener could hear the first three short notes and one long note of Beethoven's Fifth Symphony, signifying the Morse code three dots and a dash of "V for Victory," with a different reaction from the impact underground guerrilla fighters felt when they heard those notes broadcast to Nazi-occupied Europe.

Radio and television news for decades reflected traditions that developed in the 1941 through 1945 period, when broadcast journalism came of age. Newscasters of World War II became the anchormen of the 1950s and 1960s, and their traditions survived into the 1980s.

▪ **Radio Brings the War to the Home Front**   In mid-April 1945, reporters followed the advancing allied armies into what was left of Nazi Germany. On April 15, 1945, CBS radio correspondent Edward R. Murrow broadcast his impressions of the liberation of a large concentration camp.

. . . Permit me to tell you what you would have seen, and heard, had you been with me on Thursday. It will not be pleasant listening. If you are at lunch, or if you have no appetite to hear what Germans have done, now is a good time to switch off the radio, for I propose to tell you of Buchenwald. It is on a small hill about four miles outside Weimar, and it was one of the largest concentration camps in Germany, and it was built to last. As we approached it, we saw about a hundred men in civilian clothes with rifles advancing in open order across the fields. There were a few shots; we stopped to inquire. We were told that some of the prisoners had a couple of SS men cornered in there. We drove on, reached the main gate. The prisoners crowded up behind the wire. We entered.

And now, let me tell this in the first person, for I was the least important person there, as you shall hear. There surged around me an evil-smelling horde. Men and boys reached out to touch me; they were in rags and the remnants of uniform. Death had already marked many of them, but they were smiling with their eyes. I looked out over that mass of men to the green fields beyond where well-fed Germans were ploughing.

A German, Fritz Kercheimer, came up and said, "May I show you round the camp? I've been here ten years." An Englishman stood to attention, saying, "May I introduce myself, delighted to see you, and can you tell me when some of our blokes will be along?" I told him soon and asked to see one of the barracks. It happened to be occupied by Czechoslovakians. When I entered, men crowded around, tried to lift me to their shoulders. They were too weak. Many of them could not get out of bed. I was told that this building had once stabled eighty horses. There were twelve hundred men in it, five to a bunk. The stink was beyond all description.

When I reached the center of the barracks, a man came up and said, "You remember me. I'm Peter Zenki, one-time mayor of Prague." I remembered him, but did not recognize him. He asked about Benes and Jan Masaryk. I asked how many men had died in that building during the last month. They called the doctor; we inspected his records. There were only names in the little black book, nothing more—nothing of who these men were, what they had done, or hoped. Behind the names of those who had died there was a cross. I counted them. They totalled 242. Two hundred and forty-two out of twelve hundred in one month.

As I walked down to the end of the barracks, there was applause from the men too weak to get out of bed. It sounded like the hand clapping of babies; they were so weak. The doctor's name was Paul Heller. He had been there since 1938.

From Murrow broadcast of April 15, 1945, from Buchenwald. Reprinted courtesy of the Estate of Edward R Murrow.

6.6.3 Political Broadcasting

In 1944, because of his carefully concealed deteriorating health and his understandable preoccupation with the war effort, Roosevelt carried his fourth presidential campaign almost exclusively on radio. Although the Republican nominee, the articulate and respected Governor Thomas E. Dewey of New York, was the most effective radio speaker to run against Roosevelt, the Republicans proposed a series of half-hour dramatizations of campaign issues rather than long, dry speeches. The networks refused to air them, however, fearing that listeners, used to drama as entertainment, would confuse entertainment with news. Dewey and his supporters had to resort to

As we walked out into the courtyard, a man fell dead. Two others—they must have been over sixty—were crawling toward the latrine. I saw it but will not describe it.

In another part of the camp they showed me the children, hundreds of them. Some were only six. One rolled up his sleeve, showed me his number. It was tattooed on his arm. B-6030, it was. The others showed me their numbers; they will carry them till they die.

An elderly man standing beside me said, "The children, enemies of the state." I could see their ribs through their thin shirts. The old man said, "I am Professor Charles Richer of the Sorbonne." The children clung to my hands and stared. We crossed to the courtyard. Men kept coming up to speak to me and to touch me, professors from Poland, doctors from Vienna, men from all Europe. Men from the countries that made America.

. . . Murder had been done at Buchenwald. God alone knows how many men and boys have died there during the last twelve years. Thursday I was told that there were more than twenty thousand in the camp. There had been as many as sixty thousand. Where are they now?

As I left that camp, a Frenchman who used to work for Havas in Paris came up to me and said, "You will write something about this, perhaps?" And he added, "To write about this you must have been here at least two years, and after that—you don't want to write any more."

I pray you to believe what I have said about Buchenwald. I have reported what I saw and heard, but only part of it. For most of it I have no words. Dead men are plentiful in war, but the living dead, more than twenty thousand of them in one camp. And the country round about was pleasing to the eye, and the Germans were well fed and well dressed. American trucks were rolling toward the rear filled with prisoners. Soon they would be eating American rations, as much for a meal as the men at Buchenwald received in four days.

If I've offended you by this rather mild account of Buchenwald, I'm not in the least sorry. I was there on Thursday, and many men in many tongues blessed the name of Roosevelt. For long years his name had meant the full measure of their hope. These men who had kept close company with death for many years did not know that Mr. Roosevelt would, within hours, join their comrades who had laid their lives on the scales of freedom.

conventional speeches, which they did in the heaviest use of radio in a campaign up to that time. On the Democratic side, a committee of Hollywood personalities made effective one-minute spot announcements to point out Republican problems and limitations. Afterwards, more than half of those asked in a national poll identified radio as their most accurate source of political information, while just over one-quarter chose newspapers and only 6% chose magazines. Political radio perhaps came of age on election night 1944 when, for the first time, all the networks dropped their regular programs in favor of continuous election returns and analysis. This was to become the standard format in later elections, until the 1990s. Reports were beamed overseas to the armed forces by OWI and Armed Forces Radio.

6.6.4 Music and Variety

Despite the increase in war-related news programming, music remained the staple of radio. The networks scheduled about one-third of their hours to popular music, with some classical music and opera on weekends. Popular music was still synonymous with the big bands of Glenn Miller, Benny Goodman, Harry James, and others. Of the new stars coming up, Frank Sinatra was most notable. The young singer created a sensation among the "bobby-soxers," and vast crowds of teenage girls crammed New York's Paramount Theater on Times Square to hear him and squeal their delight. Sinatra soon had his own radio show and also appeared on United Service Organization (USO) tours to entertain the armed forces. Many musical groups kept their home front programs and commitments while touring before military audiences, but some joined the armed forces and served in the "Special Services."

The prime listening periods for classical music were Saturday and Sunday. On Saturday afternoons Milton Cross narrated the broadcasts of the Metropolitan Opera from New York for the Blue Network; Arturo Toscanini conducted the NBC Symphony Orchestra, first for NBC-Blue on Tuesday and Saturday evenings on a sustaining basis and then as a sponsored program for NBC-Red on Sunday evenings. On Sunday afternoons CBS offered the New York Philharmonic, first sustaining and then sponsored. Besides airing most of the network musical programs, affiliates added some of their own. Many large stations employed an orchestra and popular music groups. At smaller stations and nonaffiliates, where music averaged about half their total schedule, recorded music became more common. During the protracted American Federation of Musicians (AFM) dispute (see p. 257), more live orchestras played than otherwise might have been the case.

Almost all programs had at least a thin veneer of wartime topicality. Musical programs often included war songs, but the variety programs featured soldiers as participants, originated in military camps and naval bases, and nearly always tried to build up patriotic fervor. Programs built around the military included NBC's *Army Hour*, beginning in April 1942, an Army-produced drama–news feature–music combination that gave the civilian an image of army life, and *Command Performance*, produced by the OWI Radio Branch starting in March 1942, a collection of music and variety acts requested by servicemen. It was broadcast on networks here and by Armed Forces Radio stations overseas.

Many stars got their radio start in the war years. Arthur Godfrey, after some years in Washington, went to the New York big time for CBS in 1941. Two years later Perry Como and Ed Sullivan began their own radio programs. Sullivan, a veteran Broadway newspaper columnist, was no smooth "personality" on the air, as audiences were to see for two decades on television, but he and his staff put together a well-balanced and audience-attracting program.

Some variety programs might have been classified also as situation comedies, especially those starring Jack Benny, ventriloquist Edgar Bergen and his dummy Charlie McCarthy (an unlikely but very popular gimmick on a sound medium) and Bob Hope. These were among the 10 most popular network shows during the war, perhaps because they helped audiences forget the world outside. Variety was somewhat harder for local stations to produce, but many middle- or large-size stations tried. Their shows usually reflected local culture and background—"country" dominated in the South and West, Scandinavian farm life in the upper Midwest—and centered on a local orchestra, vocalist, or station-created talent agent. Amateur hours still were popular, and stations near military installations were likely to inject more military flavor into their programs than stations further removed.

6.6.5 Drama

There were two trends in wartime network drama: daytime serial soap opera declined by one-third, and serious drama increased noticeably, fueled by the advertisers' 10-cent dollars (see pp. 232–233). Although soap operas had been at their peak in the 1940–1941 season with nearly 75 hours a week, in the early 1940s they gave way somewhat to quiz programs and other variety daytime programming. There were just too many *soaps*, and they were too similar, and at first they ignored wartime events except for an occasional "son lost in action" or suitor "gone off to a war industry job," when an actor left for war. New soapers went on the air, but more went off, while popular standards like *Helen Trent* and *Ma Perkins* plodded quietly on.

Wartime action–adventure programs also showed slight effects of war. The children's serial hero Jack Armstrong was on the Philippine island of Mindanao looking for uranium-235—3 1/2 years prior to announcement of the atomic bomb—when war came, and script writers moved fast to remove him from uncertainty and danger. Other thriller heroes went to war against the Axis, and stereotypical Japanese and German villains soon were common in *Suspense, Inner Sanctum*, and, starting in 1944, *The FBI in Peace and War* as well as in children's adventure serials. These action–adventure and crime detective programs were building to a postwar peak of popularity.

Favorite situation comedies that started in the 1941–1945 period included *The Great Gildersleeve*, which grew out of a character on *Fibber McGee and Molly*—a spin-off, the way many later radio and television programs originated, *The Life of Riley*, and *Ozzie and Harriet*. The last, a long-running radio and later television series, began in 1945 after Ozzie Nelson gave up his band and married his lead vocalist Harriet Hilliard.

The serious drama programs that advertiser 10-cent dollars made possible were both dramatic and documentary, the latter dealing almost always with military affairs. Some programs, like *First Line of Defense*, *Service to the Front*, and *Pacific Story*, the networks offered to stations on a sustaining basis, with production help from various government agencies. Of the dramatic type, U.S. Steel sponsored the *Theater Guild on the Air* and Revlon backed the *Gertrude Lawrence Theater*. Although such prestige shows had fairly low ratings, their appeal to audiences in the higher socioeconomic brackets assured the advertiser of keeping the company name before prospective postwar purchasers and decision makers.

6.6.6 Other Programs

The program darling of the late 1930s, the audience participation show, also grew in popularity during the war, because of its human interest—the entertainment value inherent in the way people behave in often-amusing situations. Art Linkletter's long-running *People Are Funny*, *Blind Date* (a program catering to soldiers and somewhat like television's *Dating Game*), a backwards quiz called *It Pays to Be Ignorant*, and a gambler-appealing *Double or Nothing* quiz show all began network runs. Some ran in prime time, and others began to encroach on daytime soap opera hours.

The 40 or so FM stations on the air during the war programmed orchestral music or duplicated co-owned AM station programming. FM operations generally broadcast from noon to 10 P.M. until equipment and personnel shortages led the FCC to allow a shorter schedule (see p. 229). AM-FM program duplication was very limited until the networks announced early in 1944 that an FM station could duplicate programs of its AM affiliate only if it carried *all* network programs, because the networks considered it unfair to network sponsors if only selected programs were carried. Although this cut down the amount of independent FM programming, networks, AM stations, and many FM proponents publicly argued further that only by carrying popular AM programs would FM attract and build a large audience. This argument was to be tested in the postwar years.

6.7 The Audience Tunes to Radio's War

World War II was broadcasting's first major war, and reporting the conflict made radio indispensable to the home front from 1941 to 1945. With a multicampaign war cutting across time zones, often half a world away, radio nearly always brought the first news of major events to increasing numbers of listening Americans. Newspapers provided depth and illustration, but radio nearly always delivered the scoops—frequently directly from the battlefield.

6.7.1 The Freeze on Receivers

The coming of war brought shortages and the meaning of "priorities" home to Americans. Within a month of Pearl Harbor, the Office of Price Administration (OPA) set price ceilings on radios and other consumer products, as a hint of stronger measures, such as rationing, yet to come. In the early months of 1942 governmental agencies examining Army and Navy needs for raw materials and production facilities discovered that nearly all consumer product production would have to be reduced drastically or stopped for the duration of the war. Advertisements began warning consumers of shortages ahead. Permits for new broadcast station construction were canceled in February (see p. 228), and in April the War Production Board ordered manufacturers to cease making civilian radio receivers immediately and turn full time to military communication needs. This ban originally affected only producers of AM sets but quickly affected the fledgling FM and television receiver industries.

The freeze did not completely halt expansion of the radio audience at early 1942 levels. As seen in Appendix C, table 6-A, 31 million homes and more than 9 million automobiles had radios. More homes had radios than electricity, bathtubs, telephones, or cars. Because households with more than one receiver loaned, gave, or sold extra sets to persons without, the radio audience actually expanded during the next two years even with no new receiver construction. While car radios declined by three million during the war—most of them were junked along with the car—the number of radio homes increased by nearly four million.

Still, the overall number of receivers in service declined as older sets wore out and were junked or gutted for spare parts. This increased after April 1943 when the War Production Board ruled that a replacement part could be obtained only in return for the old part, which was rebuilt and recycled when possible. Even more important, radio repair became virtually impossible in 1943–1945 as the best technical personnel were in the service or working in war plants. As a result, set manufacturers by 1943 or 1944 were predicting a massive postwar radio replacement market.

During the war there probably were 400,000 FM receivers in use plus 10,000 television sets. It was estimated in 1945 that, while possibly 4,400 television sets existed in New York, one-quarter of them did not work. Nearly all FM and television sets were located in New England, New York, Philadelphia, Chicago, and Los Angeles but there was little for them to tune to (see pp. 229–231). FM was able to provide minimal service in a few regions, but television practically closed up shop from 1942 until 1944—just as their growth began.

▪ The Attraction of the Daytime Serial

In size, the audience numbered approximately half of the women who were home during the daytime hours. In composition it included women of all cultural, economic and social levels. Among the faithful audience were many individuals whose relationship to the programs exceeded passive entertainment. For these listeners, the line between illusion and reality was too finely drawn to remain in view for an extended period of time. Whatever the level of rationalization employed, this segment of the audience did not regard the serial characters wholly as fiction. If one of the episodes involved the birth of a child the program could expect to receive not only notes of congratulations but baby gifts from all over the country. The same phenomenon occurred on the occasion of birthdays and anniversaries mentioned in any script. There were offers to loan money or to extend other assistance to destitute characters.

The primary reasons for listening, while often interrelated, can be distinguished as: (a) emotional escape from monotony, personal disappointment, and difficulty; (b) provision of moral values and guidance in family and interpersonal problems; (c) bolstering of the female ego; (d) companionship and, lastly, (e) entertainment.

The housewife increasingly has been free to indulge in whatever diversion, real or imaginary, might lighten the drudgery of her workload and brighten her glamourless life. The convenience and accessibility of radio served for many either to create heroic fantasies or to channel existing reveries at little or no cost in time or work accomplished. At the same time the listener was exposed to a generally consistent sequence of problem–solution case studies designed as entertainment but from which, if she so desired, the modern woman could derive sufficient strength and conviction to meet her share of personal grief. Whether or not the serials expected to function as educational or therapeutic instruments, the fact remains that nearly half of the listeners placed heavy emphasis on the guidance, inspiration and practical assistance thus afforded.

The listener's sense of security was enhanced by emphasis placed in the serials upon such matters of special interest as marriage ties, the problems encountered by career women (a role the listener had avoided), the importance attached to the role of the wife and homemaker and, in all things, the ultimate triumph of good over evil. It was not by chance that nearly all of the moral, emotional and spiritual strength was invested in the female characters.

At a more widely shared level of appreciation, the serials were enjoyed simply for the companionship provided by characters who became familiar to the listener over a period of months and years. The punctuality and dependability of the daily visits doubtlessly lent a sense of order to many a pointless day.

Source: Willey, G. A. (Spring 1961) "End of an Era: The Daytime Radio Serial." *Journal of Broadcasting* 5(97–115), at 109–110. By permission.

6.7.2 Wartime Radio Usage and Research

Apart from the predictable increase in listening to news and other war-related programs, audience listening patterns did not change much, even though many people's lives changed drastically during the war, with more than 16 million persons, including 200,000 women, in service during some part of it. Restrictions on travel and other activities caused a slight increase in radio listening that had practically disappeared by 1945. With the motion picture industry producing several hundred films a year, people exhibited no overwhelming need to turn more to radio for entertainment. There were nearly always more women tuned in than men, more lower than upper income listeners, everything else being equal, and more urban than rural listeners.

Initial research into specific types of programs and listeners disclosed, among other things, that different kinds of programs had varying amounts

▪ In their heyday, networks and advertisers sent out thousands of pictures to fans, showing the stars in costume—which, unfortunately, rarely matched listeners' imaginative expectations. This one, from the long-running soap opera *Ma Perkins*, stresses the tie of serial to listener with its printed salutation, "Your radio friend..."

Photo courtesy of the State Historical Society of Wisconsin. (WHi (×3) 32887)

of *holding power*—the ability of a program to keep its initial audience for the entire show. Women's serial drama managed an 85% holding rating (in other words, only 15% tuned out before the show ended) and wartime news reports 79%. Drama usually held three-quarters of its audience, and variety shows did nearly as well. Rated typically lower were the new audience participation and quiz shows, popular music, and, lowest of all with only 59%, concert music programs.

Audience research developments in 1941–1945 fell into three categories: audience ratings, in-depth program research, and propaganda analysis—the last done mainly by or for the military. In 1943 the Cooperative Analysis of Broadcasting (CAB; see p. 140) was dissolved, mainly in recognition of C. E. Hooper's "Hooperratings" as the final arbiter of network radio program success. Hooper continued using his coincidental telephone technique, even though some American homes had unlisted numbers and many had no telephone. He published the best description of his research technique in 1944 with Matthew Chappell in *Radio Audience Measurement.* However, other organizations had other techniques. In New York City, The Pulse used a roster-recall method, by which a selected audience member reviewed a list (roster) of programs for a prior period of time, usually a day, and indicated those he or she had listened to. This aided recall system could be done in person or by telephone. In the eastern states, A. C. Nielsen introduced its Nielsen Radio Index, using mechanical meters attached to radio sets, in Fall 1942 (see p. 206). The meter produced a small length of film every week or so that showed to what station that radio had been tuned at a given time. The meter required no human service or interaction other than mailing the film to Nielsen, in exchange for a few quarters that came out of a slot in the meter, and inserting the new film that arrived in the mail. It worked at all hours as no other audience research technique could. The Nielsen equipment was expensive to install, the sample could not easily be changed, and people with meters might exhibit different listening habits from people without them, but the technique had promise. By the end of the war, the Nielsen Radio Index had become the first serious competition to Hooper.

CBS backed a great deal of intensive research on programs and their audiences. Their electromechanical program-audience analyzer allowed intensive study of minute-by-minute reactions of 30 to 100 subjects to a specific program. Respondents sat in a room equipped with hand-held devices that allowed them to indicate their opinion of what they were hearing whenever a light signaled for a pro or con response. The hand devices were connected to a graphic recorder that told the researchers what moments in the program and its supporting commercials most appealed to or appalled the listeners. In this way, researchers learned what kinds of characters, language, situations, and events to put into programs and commercials to increase their appeal and audience holding power.

Researchers thoroughly examined the appeal and effects of serial soap operas, analyzing their educational aspects, the typical program formula's ability to attract and hold listeners, and characteristics of daily serial listeners. This was the first in-depth study of a segment of the radio audience since the "War of the Worlds" research of 1938–1940. It was learned that serial listeners felt tremendously loyal to the programs, their key characters, and often the sponsors' products (a fact of considerable interest to advertisers), and believed that they learned how to solve everyday problems from what they heard, and responded differently to different serials. Most serial listeners were from lower socioeconomic groups, and most listened to several serials each day. Ironically, this companionship role of soap operas was adequately understood only as the serial form began to slip in daytime radio schedules (see p. 243).

Finally, researchers looked into the presumed effect of propaganda on military and civilian subjects. The study of German radio programs and films, and some Allied efforts in the same media, gave clues as to how persuasion took place under various audience conditions. Findings bore fruit in Allied propaganda in both Europe and the Pacific—and domestic advertisers applied many of the basic results after the war.

6.8 Postwar Planning and Wartime Control

Four major regulatory developments occurred in the early 1940s: a lengthy allocation process; governmental wartime censorship; the FCC attempt to control ownership of broadcast networks and stations, with a resulting congressional investigation of the commission; and an incredible wrangle between radio broadcasters, the American Federation of Musicians, and the federal government. Oddly enough, censorship, which one might expect to be the most controversial and sticky, became an example of successful voluntary cooperation between government and broadcasters. Real sparks flew only over other developments.

6.8.1 Allocations Conflict: Television versus FM

As the war neared its end, in addition to hundreds of new AM station applications and requests for changes in existing stations, some 600 FM and 158 television applications to construct new facilities were piling up in the FCC's offices. Some applications were frivolous, some were "insurance policies" filed by older media concerned about television competition, many were withdrawn, but most reflected a belief that radio and television broadcasting were headed for a postwar bonanza—tapping of the pent-up consumer demand of the war years. For the next decade, the struggle between services over spectrum space and channel allotments to various communities was to absorb the attentions of broadcasters, regulators, manufacturers, and politicians. The decisions of the 1944–1953 period (see also pp. 321–331) shaped broadcasting, especially television, down to the present day.

During the 1930s, as new uses for radio developed, the usable, assigned part of the spectrum was continually moved upward. By the start of World War II, the practical limit for radio use was in the neighborhood of 100 MHz. Wartime research quickly opened the region above 100 MHz to tactical communication, radar, and many other uses. Early in World War II larger manufacturing concerns realized that overcoming technical drawbacks to use of the VHF and UHF portions of the spectrum would probably be easier than overcoming political and economic objections to their use for television broadcasting and other civilian services. Some frequency bands were better than others for certain applications; for example, frequencies above 30 MHz generally were restricted to little more than the "line of sight" distance from the antenna to the horizon—50 to 90 miles, depending on antenna height—with the lower frequencies being somewhat better. The enormous inertia of investment in equipment, particularly home receivers, designed to operate in a particular band was another limiting factor. Technical aspects of the propagational characteristics of a given band were uppermost in the minds of engineers, but economic "realities" were uppermost in the minds of those who hired the engineers.

The complexity of these economic realities must be understood to perceive why certain decisions were made. At least four separate but related factors led to the 1944–1945 allocations decision climax:

1. The wartime freeze, which led to a pent-up consumer demand for new goods and services and made feasible the planning of changes long in advance of production.
2. The new international responsibilities of the United States, requiring a tremendous amount of spectrum space for the armed forces, and leadership and cooperation with the ITU and other world agencies in reestablishing allocations guidelines after the war.
3. The fight between FM radio and television for essentially the same spectrum space, since the VHF band was believed best suited to both.
4. The feud between those industry forces that wanted immediate postwar television and those that argued for further changes and improvements in standards and allocations before the postwar boom began.

These economic and social problems complicated technical hearings already confused by military research findings on spectrum propagation characteristics. In addition, all parties recognized that the FRC and FCC allocation practice of the 1920s and 1930s merely to regularize existing uses and allow a service to spread out, as exemplified by AM radio (see pp. 93–97 and 143–145), was inefficient and impractical.

All this came to a head in several allocations hearings. The FCC had long been a member of the Interdepartmental Radio Advisory Committee (IRAC), the U.S. government body comprised of major federal government *users* of the radio spectrum—the military services, FBI, Forest Service, and so forth. The FCC represented both its own limited needs and the far larger and more important needs of civilians, including common carrier, safety and special services, amateur, and radio and television broadcasting. In June 1943 an IRAC committee began to plan for postwar use of the spectrum, for not only had military needs mushroomed, but a plan would be needed to replace the prewar worldwide Cairo agreement of 1938. IRAC submitted a tentative plan to the FCC in the latter's capacity as a member, for the FCC has no control over federal governmental usage. The FCC, seeing the military's proposals as a naked spectrum grab, balked at approving anything until a public hearing on the issues had been held, as required by the Communications Act of 1934, because many allocation changes affected nongovernmental users. Although the Department of State announced it would use the IRAC proposals in postwar international meetings, the FCC stood ground and effectively won after not participating in the State Department's government–industry meetings.

■ **The Changing Allocations for Television: 1937–1952**   Though this chart covers a greater period than the chapter, the major allocation decision was made in 1945 (the third bar of the chart). Note the changing interrelationship of TV channels and FM channels. See notes.

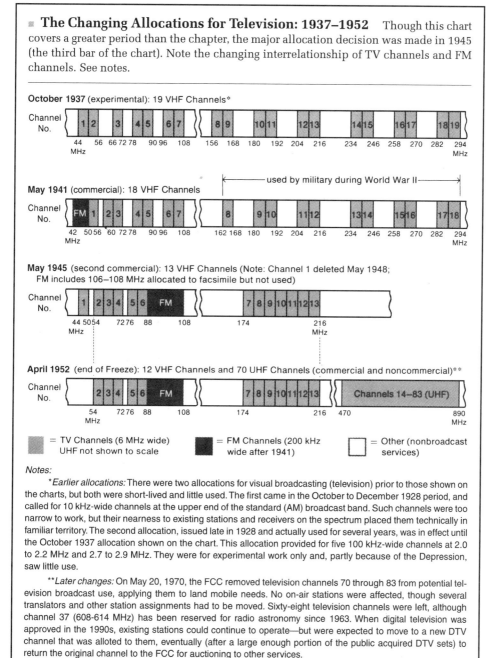

Notes:

   Earlier allocations: There were two allocations for visual broadcasting (television) prior to those shown on the charts, but both were short-lived and little used. The first came in the October to December 1928 period, and called for 10 kHz-wide channels at the upper end of the standard (AM) broadcast band. Such channels were too narrow to work, but their nearness to existing stations and receivers on the spectrum placed them technically in familiar territory. The second allocation, issued late in 1928 and actually used for several years, was in effect until the October 1937 allocation shown on the chart. This allocation provided for five 100 kHz-wide channels at 2.0 to 2.2 MHz and 2.7 to 2.9 MHz. They were for experimental work only and, partly because of the Depression, saw little use.

   **Later changes:* On May 20, 1970, the FCC removed television channels 70 through 83 from potential television broadcast use, applying them to land mobile needs. No on-air stations were affected, though several translators and other station assignments had to be moved. Sixty-eight television channels were left, although channel 37 (608-614 MHz) has been reserved for radio astronomy since 1963. When digital television was approved in the 1990s, existing stations could continue to operate—but were expected to move to a new DTV channel that was alloted to them, eventually (after a large enough portion of the public acquired DTV sets) to return the original channel to the FCC for auctioning to other services.

Source: FRC and FCC Annual Reports (1928–1946) and Background of Frequency Modulation, in Milton B. Sleeper (ed.) *FM Radio Handbook: 1946 Edition* Great Barrington, MA: FM Company. pp. 3–7.

Late in 1943, to make use of the rapidly increasing military spectrum and propagation research findings, the FCC called on the manufacturing industry to establish a Radio Technical Planning Board (RTPB) of industry and government engineers and other technical people, to evaluate wartime data in relation to prospective postwar changes in broadcasting and other allocations. Faced by the IRAC situation, the FCC urged the RTPB to present its case or cases at an extensive public hearing in Fall 1944. RTPB was divided into several panels, each of which would consider a major topic—FM, television, facsimile, allocations in general—and make recommendations at the hearings.

The hearings lasted from September 28 to November 2, 1944, the most extensive conducted by the FCC up to that time. More than 230 witnesses testified, 4,559 pages of testimony were gathered, and 543 exhibits were submitted for the record. The presentation of still-secret military data required that some sessions be held behind closed doors. One of the first issues considered was the fight between FM and television interests (see pp. 156–158).

In 1943, during Senate Commerce Committee hearings, Edwin Armstrong pleaded in favor of allocating additional frequencies for relaying FM broadcasts. By this time there were more applications than available FM channels in New York and New England, and it was apparent that this region at least would need additional channels.

By 1944, however, Armstrong was fighting to retain the channels FM already had. His fight for additional space succumbed to the pressures of the wartime spectrum propagation research and the 1944 allocations hearings. During those hearings, the 1945 decisions, and ensuing appeals and suits, FM and television struggled for the mutually exclusive right to occupy various parts of the VHF spectrum, especially the 42 to 50 MHz band then occupied by 55 pioneer FM stations. This fight, lasting from 1944 through 1947, grew more and more bitter as giant RCA used all its power to back television against FM and its solitary inventor. Since Armstrong, out of fairness to earlier small licensees, would not give RCA a special license to use and resell rights under Armstrong's patents, RCA resorted to other techniques, including refusal to pay Armstrong royalties due him from RCA production of television sets with FM sound. Careful review of the evidence indicates that RCA did not care much one way or the other about FM, but was not going to let anything stand in the way of television!

Some of the 1944 testimony, concerning military uses of frequencies as high as 300 MHz, was classified. Participants in the hearings had access to the data, but they could not utilize it or communicate it to their backers or the press. Consultants had to be members of the RTPB. This became important when the recommendation was made to move FM from its 42 to 50 MHz allocation "upstairs" to a position closer to 100 or even 120 MHz. The recommendation was based largely on flawed classified information provided by former FCC engineer Kenneth Norton, who predicted that FM would experience serious interference on the 40 to 50 MHz band when the 11-year sunspot cycle reached its peak in 1947 and 1948. Although RTPB's

Panel 5 (FM) recommended an expanded band in the 50 MHz area, the FCC, after announcing most other allocations, decided on June 27, 1945, to move FM to the 88 to 106 MHz band. A few months later it added the 106 to 108 MHz band previously reserved for facsimile. This new allocation for 100 channels provided 60 more than on the old band and reserved 20 of them for educational uses. The FCC never explained how television, whose AM picture transmissions were especially susceptible to interference, would avoid the sunspot problem. On the other hand, Armstrong never explained how he could have a nationwide FM system with only 40 channels.

The move "upstairs" gave Armstrong more channels but at the unacceptable, to him, cost of starting over, since it made existing transmitters and receivers (perhaps 400,000) obsolete. Armstrong initiated several futile appeals to the courts, the legislative branch, and public opinion. He tried without success to make the FCC rescind its order and retain a couple of the old channels for relay purposes. His case sparked hearings in both the House and the Senate into FM and FCC allocation policies, but much recrimination failed to topple the FCC's decision. FM was trapped. The newer television service had won primary attention, and war-end demand for radio receivers was satisfied by the manufacture of AM sets. The manufacturing industry was afraid to confuse the buying public or divide the industry's priorities. Resolving the situation by ignoring FM took care of part of the problem, but the television manufacturing industry was split as well.

6.8.2 Allocations Hearings and Decision

The arguments over moving FM up to the 88 to 108 MHz band were but a sideshow to the main event between RCA, which wanted postwar television immediately, following "proved" standards, and CBS, which tried to delay full exploitation of television until it had completed research on color and high definition in the upper frequencies. (The situation was analogous to the Westinghouse decision at the end of World War I to use suddenly surplus manufacturing capacity for the production of broadcasting receivers.) If there were rival products, such as television *and* FM, or different television standards, the resulting public confusion might force manufacturers to divert facilities to less profitable lines of merchandise. Or, if one company controlled the patents and know-how, such as RCA with its television system, then other corporations might find themselves in the cold.

As a result, toward the end of World War II, the industry was divided. To RCA's great satisfaction and profit, almost the entire manufacturing industry favored RCA's position: the immediate establishment of postwar television using prewar standards, and the postponement of potential improvements in both standards and allocations to a vague future. CBS, lacking a strong patent position in black-and-white television, wanted to promote its system of color television and steal a march on RCA. It advocated further research on monochrome and color and an allocation system able to accommodate the foreseeable expansion of television—in particular, a large number of channels in the UHF band, with only temporary assignments on VHF. CBS asserted that delaying the innovation of higher-definition or color television would freeze the television system into the technical standards and allocation mold of 1941. The public had invested $2 million in receivers by 1944, but this was nothing compared to the hundreds of millions of dollars that it was expected to spend on television within two years of the war's end. CBS management and engineering witnesses called attention to the expensive military research on the UHF band during the war and the possibility of its leading to a practical high-band color television system within a year—if everybody worked on it.

To gain manufacturing allies in its fight against RCA, as well as to show genuine interest in UHF, CBS ordered a UHF transmitter from General Electric and cooperated in the development of UHF receivers with Zenith, but it received little support before the FCC. The CBS system, which promised far better quality of both black-and-white and color picture than we now have, would require complete redesign of receivers to permit them to operate on the UHF band with a bandwidth of 16 MHz. Eventually, CBS managed to fit its color system, but not the proposed high-definition monochrome system, within a 6-MHz standard channel. Supporters of "television now" attacked CBS for trying to marshal public and industry support, while WCBS-TV (then WCBW) repeatedly announced that its broadcasts were not inducements to buy televisions sets "at this time." Resentful of its proposal to abandon the VHF band and all previous planning, they accused CBS of trying to hamstring television because of its investment in AM broadcasting and its lack of a television set manufacturing subsidiary, and of trying to strengthen its own position while posing as a champion of science. Although many of these charges were valid, the opposition could not destroy the basic soundness of the CBS call for extensive serious planning for technical quality, the most logical allocations scheme, and the greatest amount of competition.

The lineup of opponents to CBS was formidable. As soon as the war ended, most electronics manufacturers would have excess plant capacity and some factories built with government money would be ready for purchase and conversion to television-receiver production based on prewar technical standards. The introduction of new standards would require tooling up, and the delay might cause producers of black-and-white television to miss out on profits from the expected postwar surge of buying. In addition to RCA, manufacturers, broadcasters, and individuals who feared postwar unemployment and were looking for new industries to take up the slack all opposed these CBS proposals. They were joined by such bodies as the just formed Television Broadcasters Association.

Perhaps the greatest handicap of CBS was that it was moving counter to the demand for consumer goods. Its argument that postwar demand for radio and phonograph equipment could keep them busy while they engineered a new television system failed to convince an industry, and a country, impatient for glittering new services. The industry felt that the available television system should be exploited to the fullest, regardless of its shortcomings.

These shortcomings, generally recognized, included the psychological barrier that establishing television on VHF would create to changing later to UHF, and the existing allowance of too few channels for a nationwide, competitive television system. RCA, ignoring the lessons of television's false start in 1940, DuMont, and others believed that it was better to get started immediately on VHF and trust that future problems could be solved.

The most important support for the RCA position came from the RTPB Television Panel. It recommended at the hearings that television could and should be established in black-and-white, on 6-MHz channels on VHF frequencies. It suggested that 30 contiguous channels on the VHF band would be sufficient. On reviewing the latter proposal, the RTPB's Allocations Panel badly mangled it by recommending 26 channels, divided into seven segments rather than one continuous band. All were to be in VHF, with nine below 108 MHz. The three uppermost channels were for *local* or *community* use, with low power and antenna, and would probably be needed only along the densely populated Atlantic seaboard. The RTPB Allocations Panel also suggested providing some 30 additional channels, each 20-MHz wide, for experimentation and future development.

Virtually all parties testifying at the FCC hearings agreed that at least 25 to 50 channels would be needed eventually and that their most logical location would be in the UHF. But, as a Philco executive put it, "There is no good reason why the public should not enjoy our present television while . . . research is going on." The pressure for immediate activation of 15 or so channels did not stop. The rebuttal to this pressure, by soon-to-resign FCC Chairman Fly, was disregarded: "I am rather regretful to see editorials talking about the necessity of freezing television at the prewar standards because there were 7,000 receivers in the market and in the hands of consumers. . . . If we are going to have that cry with 7,000 receivers we will never change [the system] basically . . . when the quantity of receivers may run into millions. . . ."

It would be hard to overemphasize the importance of the 1945 decisions that stemmed from these hearings. Much of their structure remains, and they are the source of many of today's problems. The January 15, 1945 report of the commission proposed assigning television only 12 VHF channels (six between 44 and 80 MHz, six between 180 and 216 MHz) as compared to the 25 or 30 proposed by the RTPB panels. Channels allocated to television in 1940 were permanently lost to military and other governmental uses. Spectrum space was so short that 11 of the 12 channels would have to be shared with government and nongovernment fixed and mobile services on a geographical mutual noninterference basis. The scheme did barely allow enough space for a maximum of seven stations in the largest cities but not enough for nationwide competitive service.

After further hearings and oral briefs early in 1945, including more classified testimony from military witnesses, the FCC issued its Final Reports on May 25 and June 27, 1945. Television received another channel near the high end of the VHF (174–180 MHz), and FM (see pp. 249–253) was definitely moved up to 88 to 108 MHz, freeing the old FM band (44–50 MHz) for television's channel 1 as proposed earlier.

The June 27 report had four extremely serious drawbacks:

1. It required television to share channels with fixed and mobile services, a dangerous practice for a service highly susceptible to interference.
2. In discarding the engineering criterion of a continuous band of channels, it increased the cost of sets by requiring expensive switches that would cover four bands over a range of 172 MHz (from the bottom of Channel 1, at 44 MHz, to the highest part of Channel 13 at 216 MHz) rather than continuous tuning over only 78 MHz (13 channels at 6 MHz each).
3. It rendered prewar FM investment obsolete and delayed the start of postwar FM on a frequency band considered by many less suitable than its previous band.
4. And most important, it authorized full-fledged exploitation of television on an inadequate number of channels.

The FCC decision to use the thirteen VHF channels was separate from its decision to reject CBS proposals for wide-band color television on the UHF band. Although it was unanimously agreed that thirteen channels were too few for nationwide, competitive service, no provision for correcting this situation was made other than labeling some UHF channels "experimental," although the FCC did speak of VHF as "temporary," with UHF the future "home" for television. In an ostensible effort to free television from its wartime fetters and speed its progress, the FCC actually bound the new service in a straightjacket (see p. 319).

Faced with the weight of opinion that RCA and its allies mustered, the FCC could not have done other than establish postwar television with prewar transmission and definition standards. RCA had worked *within* the industry to achieve its goals. As will be seen, RCA reaped the benefits from the tremendously rapid expansion of television service by selling sets and taking in huge patent royalties. Still working on its own color system, RCA fostered a "don't rock the boat" attitude in the industry with respect to color. The resulting FCC rejection of CBS's color and wide-band proposals encouraged expansion of black-and-white television service. The FCC, apparently eager to place its imprimatur on the winning side, approved.

6.8.3 The Petrillo Affair

In June 1940 James Caesar Petrillo, of the Chicago local, was elected national president of the American Federation of Musicians. Soon afterward he demanded that broadcasters playing recorded music pay fees through the union, in addition to those paid to ASCAP and other performing rights societies (see p. 214) and "stand-by" fees paid to musicians by the networks since 1937, whenever they used recorded music more than once. When Petrillo's negotiations with the networks broke down in June 1942, he announced a complete ban on recording both for home use and broadcasting as of August, depending on public demand for music to pressure the record companies and networks to pay graduated fees directly to the union.

Petrillo struck what many considered a low blow in 1943 when he banned the traditional NBC broadcasts from the Interlochen, Michigan, Music Camp because the student musicians were not members of AFM, although many of their teachers were. The union barred the teachers from working at Interlochen, although the camp's director gave up his union membership in protest. Petrillo made the Interlochen ban stick under threat of a national AFM strike banning the performance of all kinds of music.

In Summer 1943 Petrillo was asked to lift the recording ban on grounds of "national morale"—at least insofar as it affected music heard by the fighting forces. After Petrillo ignored these requests, the National War Labor Board ordered the AFM ban lifted in mid-1944, but the union stood fast. Even a plea from the President in October 1944 could not move Petrillo. The ban on recording ended only when Decca Records and WOR in September 1943 and then Columbia and RCA in November 1944 gave in to AFM demands.

In Spring 1944 Petrillo started a campaign to employ AFM members as *platter turners* (technicians who actually put records on turntables) in radio stations, and in February 1945 he ran out his next big gun, aimed at broadcasters alone. He ordered AFM musicians to refrain from playing for FM, which in the war years often rebroadcast AM programming, unless the parent AM stations hired duplicate stand-by orchestras of AFM members. No television work was permitted, pending further study. That battle would peak after the war, even though Petrillo successfully withstood outraged public opinion and even a new law, the Lea Act, which forbade "featherbedding" and union "coercion"—designed to curb his power in 1946 (see p. 333).

Petrillo's muscle-flexing was a hint of rising union strength in the ranks of broadcast and broadcast-related employees. As the industry grew far beyond its wartime size after 1945, unionization became increasingly important. Foreshadowing jurisdictional disputes to come was a battle between the AFM and the National Association of Broadcast Engineers and Technicians (NABET) over control of radio station disk turners. In Chicago, Petrillo's home town, the AFM won, but the technicians' unions won in other large markets while smaller towns were less unionized.

6.8.4 Office of Censorship

The first post-Pearl Harbor attempt to control what radio stations might say about the war effort came from the National Association of Broadcasters. Shortly after December 7, 1941, the NAB issued a list of 16 "do nots" to guide news reporters away from disseminating information of possible value to the enemy. Soon after, the government set up the Office of Censorship, under former newsman Byron Price, to oversee communications inside the United States. The office, operating under the premise that "what does not concern the war does not concern censorship," worked for voluntary cooperation of the various media. To secure industry cooperation and obtain the services of industry experts, it set up a broadcast division under the direction of a radio station executive. Most NAB rules soon were made official. In its first version on January 15, 1942, the "Code of Wartime Practices for American Broadcasters" noted that censorship was voluntary and that broadcast management was responsible for finding potentially dangerous material in news and other programming, and commercial copy. Broadcasters controlled most programs voluntarily by spot checking and submitted a few—news commentary by Drew Pearson and *The March of Time* on Blue, and *We, the People* on CBS—for formal prebroadcast censorship. This code, revised in May 1942 and again in December 1943, contained many "suggested" restrictions:

- Broadcast no information on specific military installations, units, or disposition of enemy prisoners in the United States.
- In the event of an enemy attack, make no reports of damage inflicted—and no indication of an attack until it is over.
- Do not identify by name persons injured or killed in battle until the military authorities have indicated they have notified next of kin.
- Supervise musical request programs and "any program which permits the public accessibility to an open microphone is dangerous." This usually meant banning man-on-the-street interviews for fear that an agent could convey a message to the enemy through an innocent-sounding song or combination of words.
- Do not accept public service announcements by telephone; they must be in writing from a known source.
- Broadcast only those foreign language programs that are accompanied by full English-language scripts for checking.
- Ban weather forecasts; knowledge of wind direction or barometric pressure would be vital to an enemy bombing attack.

The 127 foreign language stations, broadcasting in 30 different foreign languages, offered a special problem. Stations broadcasting in German or Italian were carefully investigated, and the Office of Censorship required them to hire a linguist to check program content and to file translations of their programs. These expensive requirements forced many stations to drop foreign language broadcasts, just as World War I had helped diminish the foreign language newspaper in America.

Media people feared the tendency of bureaucracy to get too large and costly. They recalled the World War I efforts of the government to censor through the Creel Committee on Public Information, which many believed to have cut too deeply into film and the press. But the voluntary controls administered by the Office of Censorship seem to have worked well and with little controversy. There was common recognition of what was needed, and common resolve to accomplish it with the least conflict.

6.8.5 The FCC Investigates . . .

Cooperation is not a word to describe wartime activities of the FCC. The strongly held views of Chairman James Lawrence Fly—the first chairman to have the ear of the President—did not agree with those of most broadcasters and, as it turned out, many congressmen. Most of the commission's activities had little to do with the war, the province of the War Production Board, the Office of War Information, and the Office of Censorship. The FCC monitored enemy broadcasts, kept watch for unauthorized transmissions, and continued investigating station and network ownership.

The proposed chain broadcasting regulations of May 1941 (see p. 210) entailed the FCC in much legal wrangling. In January 1942, the Federal District Court for the Southern District of New York ruled that the court had no jurisdiction over the NBC–CBS suit against promulgation of the proposed FCC rules. That same month, the Justice Department filed antitrust suits against CBS and RCA–NBC. That action, backed by the Mutual network, forced the major networks to appeal to the U.S. Supreme Court, which agreed in June 1942 to review the chain regulations. Its decision of May 10, 1943, was one of the legal landmarks in broadcasting history. In *NBC v. the United States*, the court, by a vote of 5-to-2, not only upheld the FCC's right to enforce the chain broadcasting regulations but also reinforced its rights under the Communications Act of 1934 to act in its best judgment under the "public interest, convenience, or necessity" rubric. The court held that regulation and selection of licensees was within the jurisdiction of the FCC as assigned by Congress, and that such regulations did not conflict, as the networks had claimed, with the First Amendment. This was the most important upholding to date of the FCC's powers. NBC reluctantly shed the Blue Network (see p. 231), and in October the government and Mutual withdrew the antitrust suits against NBC and CBS, having accomplished their purposes. The FCC regulations went into effect in mid-1943, leading to station sales in cities where one licensee had owned more than one station, and to the long, difficult, physical and financial untangling of the Red and the Blue networks.

FCC investigation of newspaper ownership of radio stations also dragged on during the war. Begun in Summer 1941, the hearings continued on and off until January 1944, when the commission "concluded, in the light of the record of this proceeding, and of the grave legal and policy questions involved, not to adopt any general rule with respect to newspaper ownership of radio stations." The commission submitted the results of its hearings to the interested congressional committees and decided to face the issue case by case instead of making rules. This did not end the matter; both the Justice Department and the FCC were working on newspaper–broadcasting station ownership divestiture for decades.

6.8.6 ... and Is Investigated

During the early 1940s the FCC was more the subject than the instigator of investigation. In 1940 RCA pushed a Senate investigation of the FCC after Chairman Fly forestalled RCA's plan to inaugurate commercial television with inadequate technical standards (see pp. 165–168). For years disgruntled parts of the industry and critical members of the House and Senate had sought congressional investigation of the FCC, especially for alleged inaction on monopolistic control of broadcasting. While its chain broadcasting investigation helped allay some of the concern that the FCC did not go far enough in promoting the public interest, many thought that the commission

---

A Landmark Supreme Court Decision: 1943

The Act [of 1934] itself establishes that the Commission's powers are not limited to the engineering and technical aspects of regulation of radio communication. Yet we are asked to regard the Commission as a kind of traffic officer, policing the wave lengths to prevent stations from interfering with each other. But the Act does not restrict the Commission merely to supervision of the traffic. It puts upon the Commission the burden of determining the composition of that traffic.

While Congress did not give the Commission unfettered discretion to regulate all phases of the radio industry, it did not frustrate the purposes for which the Communications Act of 1934 was brought into being by attempting an itemized catalogue of the specific manifestations of the general problems for the solution of which it was establishing a regulatory agency. That would have stereotyped the powers of the Commission to specific details in regulating a field of enterprise the dominant characteristic of which was the rapid pace of its unfolding.

The question here is simply whether the Commission, by announcing that it will refuse licenses to persons who engage in specified network practices (a basis for choice which we hold is comprehended within the statutory criterion of "public interest"), is thereby denying such persons the constitutional right of free speech. . . . The licensing system established by Congress in the . . . Act of 1934 was a proper exercise of its power over commerce. The standard it provided for the licensing of stations was the "public interest, convenience, or necessity." Denial of a station license on that ground, if valid under the Act, is not a denial of free speech.

Source: National Broadcasting Co., Inc. et al. v. United States et al. 319 U.S. 190 at 215–216, 219, and 226–227 (May 10, 1943); the opinion written by Mr. Justice Felix Frankfurter.

had gone too far, including in 1942 congressmen, constituent broadcasters, and newspaper publishers. Leadership of the anti-FCC group fell, however, on Georgia Congressman Eugene E. Cox (ironically, a former supporter of the commission) for reasons that were less savory than economic conservatism. The FCC had reported to the Department of Justice that Cox had illegally received payments from a Georgia station for representing that station's views before the FCC. Early in 1943 Cox pressured the House Speaker to appoint a five-person committee to investigate the FCC. Naturally, as proposer of the resolution, Cox became chairman of the committee!

The hearings, beginning in mid-1943, were not friendly. At the first session the FCC's general counsel was threatened with expulsion from the room for trying to speak to the committee. Cox and most of his fellow committeemen complained that the FCC had delved into programming and business aspects of broadcasting beyond its prerogatives, played political favorites in official actions, and entered wartime fields that were properly the Army and Navy's. They charged that Chairman Fly dominated the commission and helped his friends get station licenses. They said that the FCC was unpatriotic, in failing to implement a proposal to fingerprint radio operators; that it operated its monitoring service inadequately and drew manpower for it from military needs; and that it harbored potential subversives. They said that the FCC spent too much time and attention on broadcasting and neglected telephone and telegraph problems. The hearings dragged on for months, even with the resignation from the committee of chairman Cox, two general counsels (the second of whom, John J. Sirica, became the federal judge who presided over the Watergate break-in trial in the early 1970s), and most of the staff. With President Roosevelt's support of Fly and the personal nature of some of the charges, it was not surprising that the hearings had few results other than some FCC personnel changes, some specific findings that led to proposals to amend the 1934 Communications Act, and a mound of paper. Chairman Fly resigned early in 1944, Commissioner Payne was not reappointed, and Commissioner Craven declined renomination, although he returned to the FCC in the mid-1950s. In retrospect, the whole investigation may have been an exercise. But it made the commission even more cautious and responsive to congressional wishes and whims and taught Congress the publicity value of an FCC investigation, ensuring that commissioners would be familiar with Capitol hearing rooms in years to come.

6.9 Radio in a World at War

Of all the wars of this century, radio had its greatest impact in World War II. Wireless had limited use in World War I, before broadcasting developed. Television was making strong inroads into radio's audience by the Korean War of the 1950s and had become dominant by the Vietnam War. Radio was effective in three ways during the 1939–1945 war: as a tactical and strategic aid to military coordination of air, sea, and ground forces; as a source of domestic information and entertainment (see pp. 235–236); and as a medium for international propaganda (see p. 263).

6.9.1 Domestic Effects on Other Media

Radio helped tie the country together during the dark years of 1942 and 1943, when we "hung on" while our war machine geared for maximum effort, and the brighter 1944 and 1945 period, when we knew the enemy had to give in. Radio news reported the war at home and abroad, delivering more news to more citizens than any combination of print and film media. Radio's unique impact came from its mixture of programming-as-before combined with greatly increased news, news features, and commentary. Radio could entertain and inform the public faster and better than other means.

One reason for radio's success was the effect of the war on other media. Short supplies and poor quality of paper for newspapers and magazines helped push many advertisers to radio. Some newsprint went for comic books, which had their high point of readership in these years. Born in the mid-1930s, the comic book followed American fighting men around the world, often telling adventures of characters first heard on radio. The paperback book also bloomed during the war. If soldiers were not reading comics or listening to Armed Forces Radio, they were often reading paperback fiction, which took up less shipping space than books in hard covers.

Hollywood went to war as much as radio. The stereotypical brutal German Nazi and sadistic "Jap" or "Nip" plied their evil ways on the screen even before we entered the war. Serial film characters turned their attention from fictional criminals to the Axis, in an orgy of entertainment propaganda. Perhaps more important to the morale of fighting men, many Hollywood stars went on the USO circuits, setting an example for radio and stage personalities. Military personnel around the world viewed Hollywood films, distributed and exhibited under difficult conditions. As did radio creative personnel, many filmmakers lent their talents to the government for the duration; some, like Frank Capra, who directed the *Why We Fight* film series, worked in the service as professionals. Members of both industries, of course, joined the armed forces in other capacities and many saw combat.

The popular music business, at the height of the big band era when the war began, was hit hard in April 1942, when the War Production Board cut shellac supplies for records to 30% of 1941 consumption. The material was needed for wartime use, and its scarcity drastically reduced record output for several years. Not affected were most broadcast transcriptions, which already were recorded on vinyl, the plastic material from which all records soon would be made. The AFM recording ban discussed on p. 257 also reduced record industry output.

6.9.2 American Broadcasting Overseas

Overseas broadcasting by the United States took two forms: broadcasts intended for American troops abroad, and the fledgling propaganda efforts of the Voice of America. Troop broadcasting started out with a temporary, low-power unauthorized transmitter in Alaska, which tried to bring domestic radio fare to soldiers in one of the most physically demanding theaters of war. Army brass who discovered this operation recognized its potential value to morale. An attempt was made to meet this need through shortwave. However, because such facilities already were overtaxed, the Armed Forces Radio Service (AFRS) turned to medium-wave transmissions of two kinds: large, stations at major bases and smaller, low-power temporary units that could follow an army on short notice. The military either climatized and issued receivers or, where troops were stationed in one location for a while, obtained some by purchase or, in occupied territory, by "moonlight requisition."

Frequently AFRS ran into difficulties with technical matters, overly zealous censors, publicity-hungry senior officers, and the sensibilities of nations in which troops and AFRS might be stationed. AFRS stations primarily programmed domestic network radio fare: the programs minus the commercials, plus music recordings and a heavy dose of news. The Armed Forces Network (AFN) appeared in England in mid-1943 and soon operated more than 50 low-power stations on bases throughout the United Kingdom. After D-Day, shortwave relays delivered broadcast material to France. The 20-hour AFN broadcast day contained regular AFRS fare, orientation programs, and public service announcements. AFN and AFRS programs had a minor propaganda effect on civilians near the bases, who trusted the news "that the Americans tell themselves" more than the output of overt psychological or political warfare outlets.

Our strategic overseas effort was the Voice of America (VOA). The government began production of radio programs in January 1942 and first applied the name "Voice of America" to the programming in February. From its start, VOA broadcast in a variety of languages to several parts of the world—broadcasts were carried on privately owned shortwave stations in this country, which the government took over for the duration late in 1942, or on new government-owned transmitters. After its formation in mid-1942 (see p. 235), OWI became responsible for VOA and rapidly built up a worldwide production and broadcast operation. By the end of the war, VOA had major production centers in New York and San Francisco, with more than 1,000 programs a week coming from New York alone. Programming consisted mainly of music, with news, commentary, entertainment programs from domestic radio, and programs specially designed for VOA broadcasts, often using well-known radio characters.

6.9.3 Axis Radio Propaganda

Starting in the late 1930s, the Rockefeller Foundation funded a shortwave listening project at Princeton University to monitor and translate German, Italian, Japanese, and other foreign broadcasts. In March 1941 the U.S. government took over this work when it created the Foreign Broadcast Intelligence Service (FBIS), later the Foreign Broadcast Information Service, as a function of the FCC. The service regularly published summaries and digests of broadcasts, and recordings of some of the more important ones. In operation 24 hours a day, seven days a week, FBIS covered the world, receiving more than 1 1/2 million words a day in late 1942 and 2 1/2 million words a day by 1944. The FBIS continued after the war as part of the CIA and still issues respected summaries of Soviet, Chinese, and other foreign broadcasts.

The domestic audience for foreign broadcasting was quite small; perhaps 5% or 10% of the total population had and used shortwave listening equipment, typically as an "additional feature" on larger console and table model radios. It was estimated that only 150,000 Americans tuned directly to generally English-language broadcasts from Germany, with fewer hearing Italian or Japanese transmissions.

German international radio broadcasting came under the Ministry of Enlightenment and Propaganda headed by Dr. Joseph Goebbels, a "natural" propagandist and one of Hitler's closest advisers. German radio transmitted to the world at large and to countries that were specific military targets. Broadcasts of the first type stressed the correctness of the German position on world issues, the fine life inside Nazi Germany, and the heroic exploits of German military and naval forces. The second kind created a climate of fear and fomented internal strife in the target country by stressing German military strength and supporting the rights of dissident or minority groups, particularly those of German origin. One of Goebbels' most famous, or infamous, radio personalities was "Lord Haw Haw," the microphone name for British turncoat William Joyce, who broadcast to the British Isles for the Nazis starting in 1939. His nickname came from his affected upperclass-English style. Joyce failed to sway his audience, however, for the British laughed at him even as he advised them of locations for upcoming bombing raids. Later in the war, Berlin transmitted "Axis Sally," an Ohio woman named Mildred Gillars, who tried to destroy the morale of the Allied forces by playing big band music and messages of impending doom. The soldiers usually listened to the music and ignored the message. At the end of the war, the British captured Joyce and hanged him as a traitor. American authorities tried Gillars and imprisoned her until 1961.

The Italians seemed to follow Germany's example, but without success. In addition to Mussolini's, the most famous voice used by Italy for overseas broadcasts to the United States belonged to American expatriate poet Ezra Pound. Pound declaimed the wonders of Fascist Italy and the damnation of the democracies fighting it. The Americans captured Pound, but committed him to a mental hospital for a number of years as unfit to stand trial.

The primary mission of Japanese overseas broadcasts during World War II was to convince other Asians of the inevitability and benefit of the "Greater East Asia Co-Prosperity Sphere" being built with the force of Japanese arms. For the American fighting men in the Pacific, Japanese broadcasting primarily meant Tokyo Rose (Iva Ikuko Toguri and others), who played band records and offered them a broadcast soft shoulder, telling them that, while they were fighting, other men were wooing their wives and sweethearts at home. Although the music was popular—one story claims that we parachuted new recordings on Tokyo to replace the old, scratchy ones (but the new batch all broke on landing)—the propaganda was largely ignored. The Americans captured and fined Toguri and sent her to prison. She later worked in Chicago while hoping for a pardon, finally granted in 1977.

Allied nations also broadcast beyond their borders, especially the British. The BBC was the main Allied voice heard in Europe for four long years, after Germany had conquered most of the continent in 1940. It provided balanced news and, increasingly, coded messages to specific resistance groups to coordinate guerrilla action with Allied military forces. The BBC's newscasts probably had the highest credibility of any nondomestic broadcasting service in the world, although it lost much of this on D-Day as it confused the Germans with false statements about the invasion.

To the listener, American broadcasting during World War II changed only in respect to increased war-related content and the freezing of physical growth. However, as in World War I, the prospect of postwar change, particularly in television, was enormous. The demand for consumer goods, the possible postwar uses for electronic war matériel factories, the GIs' new skills in electronics and broadcasting, peacetime use of new leisure—all were crying for action. However, many key questions were put off until after the war even though, as will be seen in the following chapters, the answers turned out to be not readily available.

6.9.4 Period Overview

Although the war cramped radio, like the rest of the nation, with respect to personnel and material supplies, these were some of radio's best years in respect to economic success and public esteem. Radio's wartime news role was indispensable. The low number of stations, artificially restricted due to the construction freeze, shared in a feast of wartime advertising income while print media suffered from paper shortages. With potential competition from FM and television also delayed by the war, the AM network-dominated radio establishment reached its zenith.

Apart from that economic fact, the war years are important for the groundwork they contributed to postwar changes. A fourth national network, now ABC, resulted from the chain broadcasting rules and the 1943 Supreme Court case upholding the FCC. This court decision became a precedent for future FCC regulatory incursions into various aspects of the industry. While they achieved little public recognition and only limited discussion within much of the industry, the 1944 allocations hearings set the stage for television's postwar dominance (see pp. 283, 336–338) and FM radio's birth and temporary decline (see pp. 276–278). The issues, complicated in themselves, were made more so by wartime secrecy requirements. While the future was being set, the public took more notice of the less important Petrillo affair and the politically charged Cox hearings about the FCC.

The war years are best described as a profitable hiatus in the continuing development of American broadcasting. The war had global importance, and radio, apart from its important news function, took a back seat for the duration together with other civilian roles. But, as in the Depression, radio remained available to the public and served important information and entertainment functions.

Selected Further Reading

(Alphabetical within topics. For full citations, see Appendix D.)

For general accounts of wartime radio, see Barnouw (1968), Dryer (1942), Kirby & Harris (1948), and Lichty & Topping (1975). Radio journalism reached its apogee during this period—see Bliss (1991). For biographies of Edward R. Murrow, see Kendrick (1969), Persico (1988), Smith (1978), and Sperber (1986). Cloud & Olson (1996) relate the lives of "Murrow's Boys." See also the biography of Elmer Davis by Burlingame (1961), and autobiographies by Kaltenborn (1950) and Sevareid (1946). White (1947) includes a chapter on D-Day coverage, and NBC (1944) surveys that network's wartime effort. Bulman (1945), Culbert (1976) and Fang (1977) examine major commentators.

Studies of the wartime listening audience include Chappell & Hooper (1944), Lazarsfeld & Stanton (1941, 1944), Lowery and DeFleur (1995), and Merton (1946). Useful material on the Petrillo situation is found in Warner (1953) and White (1947).

Contemporary assessments of radio's wartime propaganda role include Childs & Whitton (1942), Huth (1942), Lean (1943), and Rolo

(1942). Fejes (1986) reviews 1930s U.S. broadcasting to South America. The BBC's many wartime activities are reviewed in Bergmeier & Lotz (1997), Briggs (1970), Delfiner (1974), Ettlinger (1943), and Kris & Speier (1944). Americans (like Tokyo Rose) and others who broadcast for the Axis are discussed in Cole (1964), Duus (1979), Edwards (1991), and Howe (1990).

Many recordings of actual broadcasts (particularly CBS news broadcasts) during World War II are available in the National Archives, and can be accessed in Ryan (1963).

"Television was already conducting itself provocatively, trying to get radio to pucker up for the kiss of death. Young men with crew cuts were dragging TV cameras into the studios and crowding the old radio actors out into the halls."———*Comedian Fred Allen in* TREADMILL TO OBLIVION

CHAPTER 7

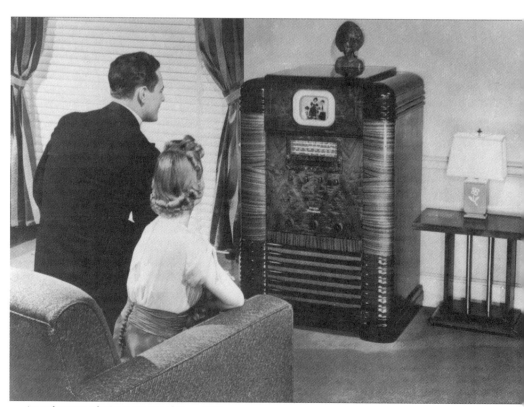

An early 1940s television set. *David Sarnoff Library.*

ERA OF GREAT CHANGE (1945–1952)

Red Barber (writer and later broadcaster) and WCBS-TV cover a baseball game, 1949. *Photofest.*

Chapter Outline

Amerian broadcasting made the transition from a small radio system dominated by four networks to a far larger AM–FM radio and television system in which networks concentrated on television and left radio stations to their own programming resources during the seven years from late 1945 to early 1952. A reader only familiar with today's broadcasting would hardly recognize the limited system of 1945, while the 1952 system contained all the elements to be found a quarter-century later, and most of those present today.

This same short period also marked a massive change in American life. By the Fall of 1945, World War II was over and the United States had become the most prominent country in the world. Confusion and expectation accompanied the end of wartime rationing and shortages and the implementing of plans for postwar consumption. Military personnel flooding home, though obviously welcome, clogged an overcrowded and changing employment market, and put an additional strain on inadequate amounts of housing. Millions of war-delayed marriages were celebrated and consummated, leading to the postwar baby boom and resulting demographic "baby boom" bulge down through the years. The G.I. Bill of Rights provided financing for hundreds of thousands of veterans to go to college. One industry after another endured union–management arguments and strikes. Postwar inflation was fierce. Every industry or service was in transition, particularly transportation and communication. The Hollywood motion picture industry almost succumbed to an important court case, a debilitating search for communist influences, and, finally, competition with an upstart: television.

The United States was also caught in international transition from 1945, when we dominated a world at relative peace, to 1952; when we were in a deepening cold war with the Soviet Union; facing both a newly communist China and a slowly expanding "third world" of newly independent nations attempting to maneuver between and manipulate both sides; and fighting a shooting war in Korea. The cold war almost exploded during the 1948–1949 Berlin Airlift, when the Western allies supplied West Berlin after the U.S.S.R. cut off ground access. The war in Korea, which started in June 1950, found American troops fighting a major war against communist Asian countries, although it didn't lead to a world war and atomic weapons were not used. All of this affected broadcasting.

Important changes in radio and television resulted from the FCC technical investigations and rulemaking proceedings discussed in 6.8 and 7.8. A lengthy and at times bitter debate on broadcasting's public service responsibility in the FCC, both houses of Congress, and the courts led to additional change. FM radio and television were being built on the profits of AM radio, which itself experienced a 59% growth in income and 156% growth in number of stations between 1944 and 1952 (see Appendix C, tables 1-B and 3-A). The relatively small "club" was rapidly becoming a major industry employing many people and having many problems. The radio audience in any one locality listened to familiar programming but sensed the imminence of television, which only one person in ten had seen by mid-1948. And its coming hit people with the same feelings of expectation and excitement that the original radio audiences had felt in the early 1920s.

7.1 Technical Innovations: High Fidelity and Television

Generally speaking, the public has taken little notice of technical controversies. But, in the 1945–1952 period, large corporations vying for a vast potential market in improved phonograph records drew considerable public attention. At the same time, magnetic tape recordings entered the home entertainment market, several years after the professional broadcasting industry had adopted simpler models. More sophisticated technology— notably the transistor, invented in 1948—was still in the laboratory, as industry wrangled over standards for recording and television.

7.1.1 Battle of the Speeds

For nearly 50 years, the 78-rpm record had been a mainstay of home entertainment and broadcast music. Many stations also used 15-inch or 16-inch 33 1/3-rpm electrical transcriptions for syndicated 15-minute programs but still had to depend on commercially available 78s for much of their musical programming. The 78 had many drawbacks: it was heavy and breakable; sound quality was mediocre; any musical selection that ran longer than four or five minutes took two, three, or more records; but most important, the constant need to change and turn records marred the appreciation of any extended piece of music. In an attempt to overcome this problem, RCA had test-marketed a 33 1/3-rpm standard-groove record for the home market in the early 1930s during the Depression; but, because it would play only on a new-style record player, the project folded within a few months.

In 1947–1948, however, engineers at CBS Laboratories, working under Peter C. Goldmark, devised a disc system with 33 1/3-rpm speed and *microgroove* recording, which had many more recording grooves per inch of diameter. These two factors made it possible to put 20 to 25 minutes on each side of a 12-inch disc. CBS introduced this long-playing (LP) record in

1948 to an enthusiastic public in the form of a new system: slower recording speed, finer grooves, vinyl record base, a better stylus, higher quality microphones and recording amplifiers—all resulting in a vast improvement in the fidelity of sound and convenience of playing records. At last, the average music lover could hear superb reproductions of the finest music at his or her convenience. The LP, together with FM availability and the interrupting of selections by commercials on AM stations, contributed to a drop in the amount of classical music programming on low-fidelity AM radio. AM stations preferred serving a mass audience to a smaller class audience; but the public now expected higher sound quality on *all* radio, and that would require a considerable investment by stations.

A few months later RCA introduced its EP or "extended play" disc, intended primarily for popular music. A lightweight 7-inch disc with a 1 1/2-inch hole in the middle—at first requiring another totally different reproduction system—revolved at 45 rpm and offered better sound quality than the 78-rpm record. Competition was tight for many months, with RCA even issuing symphonies and operas in the 45-rpm format, requiring a box of discs and killing the convenience of extended play. Eventually the public balked at having to invest in three separate systems in order to play available records. The RCA 45 became the standard format for popular single tunes, while classics and collections of popular music were recorded on the 33 1/3-rpm disc. RCA later unhappily adopted the 33 1/3-rpm LP for its fine catalogue of classical music. In short order, the 78 faded from the scene except for collectors, and record players capable of all three speeds came on the market. This standardization proved beneficial to all concerned and established a home music-reproduction pattern that lasted until cassette tape recording became popular in the 1960s.

7.1.2 The Coming of Tape and Hi-Fi

In the late 1940s, magnetic recording arrived on the domestic professional and consumer market. In 1947 Sears Roebuck sold a military-developed model with thin wire as the recording medium for $170—a very high price considering that the minimum wage was slowly rising from 25 cents an hour. It was intended mainly for business use, as its fidelity was too low for music and recording wire was very difficult to repair or edit. The machines were heavy and cumbersome but far more portable than earlier devices of comparable sound quality. The first tape recorders went on sale about the same time, using a 1/4-inch-wide paper base tape that allowed about 15 minutes of sound recording on a 7-inch reel.

If necessity is the mother of invention, then laziness may be the mother of necessity. The broadcast networks long had prohibited recordings because of their generally inferior quality, even refusing to bend the rules for on-the-scene news coverage during the war. Popular radio singer Bing Crosby wanted to record his program rather than follow the usual network practice of doing two live shows in one night to cover different time zones. NBC's ban on recordings kept him from pursuing other interests, including golf. Crosby had seen tape recorders in use in Europe when he was entertaining troops during the war, and his Crosby Research Foundation, which eventually amassed many patents on magnetic tape recording, developed recording techniques and equipment of high quality. He took his program, and high ratings, to ABC, which welcomed him and his ideas. New techniques and devices, including plastic-based rather than paper-based tape, soon followed, and by the early 1950s reel-to-reel tape recorders were standard equipment at most broadcasting stations. Time zone differences could be handled by a simple replaying of a tape, and, in recording studios, networks, and stations, the Magnecord or later the Ampex recorder became a programming standby.

Development of the LP record and magnetic recording led to a new consumer industry. The term *hi-fi* (short for *high fi*delity sound reproduction) was used in England before the war for certain custom designs, but now small firms such as Fisher or H. H. Scott began applying it to limited and even mass-production equipment. Hi-fi addicts became sophisticated as to the size and location of loudspeakers, the power and distortion of amplifiers, and the specifications of radio tuners. Many hi-fi sets—actually comprised of matched components—were designed to take advantage of the growing number of FM stations, many of which programmed classical music (see p. 302), the flood of LP records, and the promise of home tape recording. Where once only professionals purchased precision devices, now a groundswell of consumers bought high-priced components, mass-produced units that frequently promised more than they delivered, and even build-your-own kits from Heath and others.

7.1.3 ... and Television

The technical standards for television had been adopted in 1941 (see p. 168), but a number of important refinements appeared after the war. Chief among them was the new and sensitive orthicon camera tube announced by RCA in October 1945—and shortly afterwards, the image orthicon (IO) used for decades. This tube was a great improvement over the iconoscope and quickly became the standard. Since the IO could work with much less light, television became more sensitive to minor light variations than most motion picture photography. Actors no longer had to swelter under hundreds of foot-candles of light, station owners no longer had to pay for enormous quantities of power and light, and engineers welcomed the stability of the new tube.

Another development was the use of motion picture film in television programming. There were many problems involved in matching a mechanical-optical medium (film) providing 24 pictures a second with an electronic medium (television) operating at 30 pictures a second. A means of telecasting films soon was developed, using a film projector with a special shutter aimed at a television camera. A *film chain (or telecine)*, as this combination was known, became the key piece of equipment for new stations as it could run feature or even free industrial or commercial films more cheaply than live programming. A mirror device even permitted *multiplexing* more than one projector into a single camera.

But preserving televised images was harder to do. For years, once a program was telecast, it was lost; there was no good way of recording both picture and sound from the television screen. Finally, in the 1947–1948 season, a film camera was able to record pictures in synchronization off a specially bright television kinescope or picture tube—at a price: Film, or *kinescope*, recordings of television programs were less clear, less well defined, had less contrast than the original television picture, and were far poorer than an original film. Making *kines* was an art. The viewing public readily spotted even the best as a poor recording. Some programs were recorded in this way only for archival purposes, but the networks used kinescope recordings only to supply programs to affiliate stations not yet connected by wire or microwave relay for simultaneous transmission.

Kinescope recording was so unsatisfactory that several firms tried to develop an electronic system that would be more compatible with electronic television. Bing Crosby Enterprises conducted one of the first demonstrations of magnetic videotape recording in late 1951. Again, the singer was seeking a way to record his television musical variety program to avoid the inconvenience of doing it live. However, it took several years before videotape systems became commercially practical. By 1952 the tape still had to be moved at an almost fantastic 100 inches per second past the recording heads, but the picture was vastly better than kinescopes. Videotape would also be cheaper than kinescopes because the tape could be reused many times, could be played back immediately without processing, and, most important, was electronic—probably equal in quality to live television. Broadcasters would have to wait until the late 1950s, but the end product—if RCA and Ampex were correct—would be worth waiting for.

7.2 Growth of AM, FM, and Television

The 1946–1952 period is characterized by an almost explosive growth in number of AM stations as well as the arrival of large numbers of both FM radio and television outlets. Although the new services were growing rapidly, AM radio outdistanced them in new stations and additional communities served by at least one station.

7.2.1 Postwar Expansion of AM

The pressure to open new AM radio stations was intense. The natural growth of radio had been held back for more than 15 years, first because of the economic depression and then because of the wartime freeze in priorities. In addition, many returning military personnel wanted to apply wartime radio training and experience to broadcasting—many to start their own stations. Businessmen were aware of the financial potential of radio, the capital was available for starting new stations, and prospects for the tried-and-true AM industry looked more favorable than the new services of FM and television (see pp. 276–279), particularly since transmitting equipment and audiences were now available.

In addition, the FCC early in 1946 changed its technical standards for radio to allow more stations on the same or adjacent channels to be located in a given area. Since more stations on the same number of channels meant greater signal interference, the decision reduced the effective range of many stations and reversed the long-held policy of serving rural areas (overrepresented in Congress) through clear-channel stations. Under pressure from persons desiring licenses, the FCC decided that local radio listeners would be better off with reception of one or two local stations serving local needs than with reception of one or two distant signals. After the rules were changed, even though existing stations were to have been protected, AM stations increased from about 930 in 1945 to more than 2,350 seven years later.

More than two-thirds of this growth was in smaller stations in smaller markets. Often the new station was the first in a town that previously had relied on distant stations. From 1945 to 1949 alone, more than 560 communities received their first local AM radio station, some received more than one new AM station and an FM station as well. From 1945 to 1950, additional stations on formerly clear (one station only) channels increased by 10, while regional stations rose by 68 and local stations by 453! But, as noted, this growth was achieved at the cost of greater interference. Whereas less than 10% of AM stations during the war had operated in daytime only, nearly one-third had to be so limited by 1950, and many more had to lower power at night or use directional antennas to protect existing stations. All of this made AM radio more complicated and expensive, and in some communities led to inferior reception. Where before the war there might have been several clear or high-power stations in a major city, after the war new lower power stations in many of that city's suburbs fragmented both the listening audience and the advertiser's dollars (see p. 362).

Not all AM operators were successful. A few went under and many were only marginally profitable in the late 1940s, partly because of technical problems and partly because some officials and many broadcasters kept saying that AM was obsolete. They claimed that FM soon would replace AM and that television would then reduce or even eliminate radio as a major medium.

7.2.2 The FM Enigma

Expansion of postwar FM was clouded by Edwin H. Armstrong's losing fight to regain the prewar 40-MHz band for either FM direct broadcast or interstation relay, and by continuing difficulty in obtaining transmitters designed for the new 88 to 108-MHz band (see pp. 252–253). From 1945 to 1948, the 50 or so FM stations that had been on the air before the war could broadcast on both the old band and the new. At the end of 1948, low-band FM transmissions were canceled, and some 400,000 prewar FM receivers became useless. Armstrong sparked two congressional investigations but could not dislodge the FCC from its 1945 decision to move FM to the new band nor lengthen the time allowed for the changeover. Many listeners, stuck with expensive but useless receivers, were cautious about supporting the new medium further.

To allay some of this concern, the FCC consistently referred to FM as the preferred radio service, even suggesting that AM might eventually be phased out in its favor and that television would have limited importance for some time due to its costs. On the surface, it looked as though many people were taking the proffered advice. At the end of the war, more than 600 applications for new FM stations piled up and the commission allowed recipients a "conditional grant" to proceed with personnel, studio, and program planning prior to station construction. The initial screening allowed faster processing of the successful applicant's engineering submissions and got stations on the air in shorter time. Recognizing the demand for more channels, yet mindful that many potential licensees still in the military would be delayed in applying, the FCC held back some FM channels between 1946 and 1947, against strong industry opposition. By far the largest proportion of new FM licenses went to AM station operators; by 1949, for example, 85% of FM stations on the air were owned by AM licensees. Usually both stations were in the same town, with the FM outlet as insurance against possible AM demise or as protection against independent competition.

▪ **Postwar Patterns: Broadcasting Explodes**   The substantial and sudden growth of radio and television right after World War II marked a period of activity unique in broadcasting—all services were growing rapidly for the first time. That growth is apparent in this comparison showing stations actually on the air, authorized but not yet on the air, and pending applications for new stations—all for June 30 for each year. The FCC had dismissed without prejudice all wartime applications for AM and FM stations, explaining the "na" under "pending" for 1945 for both services.

	AM Radio			FM Radio			Television		
Year	On Air	Authorized (not on air)	Pending	On Air	Authorized (not on air)	Pending	On Air	Authorized (not on air)	Pending
1945	931	24	na	46	19	na	9	—	118
1946	961	254	680	55	401	250	6	24	40
1947	1,298	497	666	238	680	431	11	55	9
1948	1,693	331	575	587	433	90	29	80	294
1949	2,006	173	382	737	128	65	70	47	338
1950	2,144	159	277	691	61	17	105	4	351
1951	2,281	104	270	649	10	10	107	2	415
1952	2,355	65	323	629	19	9	108	—	716

Note: A freeze on new TV station authorizations was in effect from September 1948 until April 1952 (see p. 321).

Source: FCC *Annual Reports*. For summary data as of January 1, see Appendix C, tables 1-A and 1-B, which include information for educational stations, excluded here except for AM (about 25 on the air each year).

In its planning for FM, the FCC considered the lack of planning for AM assignments over the years. When AM stations applied for maximum power, the FCC had granted it as long as it did not cause major interference to an existing station, even though it might prevent smaller stations from getting started elsewhere and deny AM stations in the same market an equal technological chance to compete for advertising business. To avoid creating the same problem with FM, the FCC decided that all FM stations in a single area should be roughly equal in coverage, could compete for advertisers fairly, and would not cause interference elsewhere.

But the FM boom of the 1940s was short-lived. Total authorizations began to drop in 1949, and the stations-on-the-air count dropped the following year and kept dropping—as the number of AM and television stations continued to grow. FM's fortunes declined because:

1. FM equipment companies had to take time to reengineer to the new higher band at the same time that prewar equipment became obsolete.
2. The resulting confusion in the minds of broadcasters, potential advertisers (see pp. 294–295), and the public made buyers suspicious.
3. FM receiver sales were erratic and only a fraction of the number promised were manufactured (see p. 314).
4. Common AM-FM ownership for more than 80% of the FM outlets lessened aggressive pursuit of FM success, and the limited money, time, and personnel were frequently committed to television.
5. Duplicated programming on many AM-FM stations (see pp. 301–302) made the newer radio service pointless to most potential listeners.
6. Few FM networks offered special programming.
7. Advertisers showed little interest and support.

In addition to these problems, FM had to compete with both its sister media: established and growing AM and more exciting television. By 1952, FM's future looked bleak to all but a handful of independent station operators who programmed classical and other music for a small audience of hi-fi buffs. FM was a class service in what was supposed to be a mass medium. Two years later, frustrated by FM's decline and exhausted financially and mentally by constant patent royalty battles with RCA, Edwin Armstrong killed himself, ending his two-decade fight for "radio's second chance."

7.2.3 Establishment of Television

As the postwar period began, only six television stations were on the air, in New York, Washington, Schenectady, Chicago, Philadelphia, and Los Angeles, broadcasting a few hours a day. Due to some confusion on final allocations (see pp. 253–256 and 319–320) and the high cost of station construction, television's postwar start was far slower than had been the case for either AM or FM. The additional investment, in the absence of public support, made investors wary. Television equipment was more complicated to manufacture, and equipment makers wanted first to meet the highly profitable demand for AM station equipment and receivers.

When the television Freeze began in September 1948 (see p. 321), only 34 stations were telecasting from 21 cities to about one million sets. The Freeze would artificially limit television to larger markets. Even if there had been no government-imposed moratorium, high capital and operating costs probably would have slowed television's establishment in smaller markets. Even in one-station markets with an audience monopoly, high costs so reduced advertising income, determined essentially by audience size, that few stations operated in the black in their first years. Yet, the demand for transmitters increased each year of the Freeze, as stations that had received construction permits got on the air. The major manufacturers of television transmitters—RCA, GE, and DuMont—were running six months late when the Freeze began, and were hard pressed to meet the demand when it ended. Pioneering would pay off handsomely. The 107 stations that got on the air before or during the Freeze became the major money earners of the industry for more than a decade afterward.

Since in most cases pioneer television stations were owned by the licensees of AM outlets, they had some broadcast experience and the AM operation often was the source of developmental money. However, television was so sufficiently new and different that owners had to feel their way through problems of construction, equipment, programming, and daily operation. With few television-experienced personnel, a young war veteran might become a director in a matter of months, weeks, or even days—and had to learn everything on the job. This led to mistakes but also to a feeling of teamwork that lasted until the industry grew to the point of being impersonal. In one respect early television pioneering was markedly different from radio in the 1920s. Television had the advantage of being able to recruit radio's managers, and the pattern was clearly set: as soon as possible network interconnections of stations would cross the country (see pp. 286–287), bringing common programming to all.

7.2.4 The First Debate Over Pay-Television

An emotional issue was whether television should be supported by direct payments from the public instead of indirect advertising revenues. The idea was not new—there had been pay-radio and even pay-television proposals in the 1930s—but the great increase in television costs over those of radio revived it in the late 1940s. Zenith, the giant Chicago radio and later television manufacturer, under the direction of Commander Eugene F. McDonald, Jr., was the major proponent of pay-TV, but also working on

▪ Early Television Studios

Most pre-Freeze television stations varied greatly in layout, construction, and equipment. In the largest cities, giant radio studios designed for large studio audiences—including NBC's famous 8H, the home of the NBC Symphony Orchestra—were converted to television, and downtown motion picture and stage theaters were used as well. Most stations established a makeshift studio (few could afford two) in a building designed for some other purpose, with too low a ceiling for proper lighting, inadequate or nonexistent air conditioning, poor soundproofing, and a rabbit's warren of offices and corridors. Two studio cameras and their control units, at least one film chain for showing motion pictures, slides, or stills, and a network connection were all that was needed. Some studios were also oddly shaped or had supporting columns that interrupted space, camera movement, and lighting; some were housed in war-surplus Quonset huts. When a building was specially built, it was usually of inexpensive cinderblock construction. Although engineers liked the even illumination of fluorescent lighting, creative production people used motion picture lighting techniques because fluorescents could not be dimmed and were inappropriate for dramatic lighting. Too often, in the earliest studios, cameras moving over irregular wooden floors produced bumps and wiggles on the air. Microphones designed for radio had to be positioned so close to the actors that they often appeared in the picture. Monochromatic (black, white, purple) makeup had thankfully been discarded, but few studios bothered with anything but shades of gray for their settings. Soundproofing followed radio practice, and absorbent materials were draped everywhere the fire inspectors would permit, to soak up echoes and camera noise and other movement. Since all programs were live, actors and other talent had to watch not only script, director, and clock but camera as well. The tremendous heat from the lighting (an actor could lose seven to ten pounds during a performance) made air conditioning essential for the sake of both people and equipment; but because of power demands, cost, and noise from air conditioners, many studios were uncomfortable hothouses even in the dead of winter. Even CBS had to use converted space for its New York studio; and if a camera broke down, as frequently happened with handmade equipment, the show had to go on with only one camera.

Television stations operated by networks and large AM radio stations whose owners had been planning them for years still had too little space, even though the height in the studio may have appeared enormous to radio veterans; some studios had several cameras in each, and interconnected control facilities provided flexible operation. The needs for set construction and storage, repair space, and ready access for large and awkward equipment were usually overlooked by those without stage or feature film backgrounds, further reducing the number of "more than adequate" television studio installations. Television was new, experimental, in the red, and faced an uncertain future.

---

specific proposals and techniques were New York-based Skiatron and, on the West Coast, Telemeter, owned primarily by Paramount Pictures. Each firm had its own system, but all involved sending a scrambled picture via a normal broadcast channel and making the unscrambling technique available to customers on a pay-per-viewing basis. This channel would be useless, of course, to persons who did not pay.

Zenith's "Phonevision" system initially sent signals over telephone wires to unscramble the television signal, which came over the air in scrambled form. This system was the first to receive a major test, when, early in 1951, some 300 families in Chicago were equipped with the telephone lines enabling them to purchase programs in addition to seeing regular "free" television. Many thousands of families had applied, and the sample was expected to be a cross section of urban population program interests. For three months the pay channel, an experimental station licensed to Zenith, supplied feature films and other special entertainment at least three times a

An early television drama takes place under the hot television lights (note the protective hat on the cameraman) and with boom mikes and theatrical sets. These programs were the training ground for the first generation of television technicians and on-air personnel. Courtesy of Wisconsin Center for Film and Theater Research.

day. Zenith maintained that the test was a major success, even though film distributors refused to supply first-run films for the venture. Early in 1952, armed with the test results, which could be interpreted in various ways, Zenith petitioned the FCC to allow regular pay-TV programming in major American cities. In the meantime, Skiatron tested its "Subscriber-vision" in New York, using the facilities of WOR-TV and another sample of 300. Telemeter conducted tests in Los Angeles and wealthy Palm Springs.

Backing for pay-TV came from major professional sports teams concerned about television inroads on their gate receipts (see p. 337) and from cultural organizations, such as symphony orchestras, seeking a new source of revenue. Violently opposed were movie makers and theater owners, although they accepted theater-shown pay-TV events, and commercial television broadcasters. Another group argued for pay-TV via cable, which did not occupy a scarce broadcast channel and was less susceptible to illegal unscrambling by ingenious technicians and tinkerers. Indeed, to prove that cable was the only practical method, one party had a standing offer to "decode" any unscrambling device used with on-air pay-TV. All sides flooded the public with propaganda booklets and articles and appealed to the FCC for a clean-cut decision on pay-television, which the commission deferred until late 1968 (see pp. 416–417).

7.2.5 Effects of Growth on Ownership Patterns

The drastic adjustment in postwar broadcasting is perhaps best seen in relation to station ownership. Between 1923 and 1945 only a limited infusion of new owners and ideas occurred because the number of stations grew slowly and not many changed hands. From 1945 to 1952, however, the near tripling of AM stations and the arrival of FM and television produced a flood of new owners.

Prewar AM radio was controlled by companies or individuals concerned with station operation in major and medium-sized cities, where virtually all stations were on the air day and night and transmitting power increased steadily over the years. One of the largest ownership classes was newspapers, which owned some 30% of all stations by 1940. But by 1952 they dropped to just over 20%, as newspapers concentrated on the newer media and independent broadcasters, many of them war veterans, opened AM stations.

The new stations tended to be in smaller towns and suburbs, had less power (most were on regional or local channels), often were restricted by directional antennas or limited to daylight broadcast hours, and had to face competition from FM, television, and older AM stations. These variances led to far greater divergence of goals at industry conventions than before. A large proportion of the new stations competed without network affiliation, which, prior to 1947 or 1948, had been considered almost essential to rapid success. This was due to two factors: The networks did not want or need affiliates to overlap in geographical coverage, and the role of radio networks was declining (see pp. 283–286). The overall effect was to create greater diversity in AM operations.

Most FM stations were built by AM licensees. They not only possessed experience in broadcasting but often were first in line for the new services, wanting to protect their AM investment and possibly profit from new financial opportunities. AM licensees owned roughly four-fifths of FM stations, which usually only duplicated AM programming (see pp. 301–302) and occupied channels that an independent (non-AM) owner might otherwise have used. This is not to suggest a conspiracy, but it helps explain FM's impending problems of survival. Newspaper owners moved into FM as they had earlier built or purchased AM stations. Throughout the 1945–1952 period, with minor fluctuations, newspapers controlled about one-third of the FM stations on the air.

Most early television stations also were operated by AM licensees. Television required some outside revenue to survive several years of massive losses, and, with the exception of stations that were supported by receiver sales—DuMont, GE, and RCA, for example—this came from AM income. Newspapers were bigger owners in television than they had been in either radio medium. By the beginning of the Freeze in 1948, they controlled nearly one-third of the television stations. More important, since they held a large number of approved applications, by 1952 they owned more than 45% of television stations. Television costs tended to encourage multiple-station ownership, whereby an owner could apply economies of scale to management even if it had only one station in a given region, because television owners often were larger corporations with nationwide interests, whereas radio was generally considered small local business.

The coming of FM and television raised a phenomenon that had disappeared from AM broadcasting with enforcement of the duopoly rule: a single owner possessing more than one station in the same market. AM-FM, AM-TV, and AM-FM-TV combinations lessened the diversity potential of new media and new owners, for now a single owner could run three stations—and sometimes the newspaper, too—in the same market. Some smaller communities had only one media owner. Critics became increasingly concerned about this concentration of media control (see pp. 470–471).

7.3 Radio Networks Give Way to Television

At the end of the war in 1945, 95% of all radio stations were affiliated with one or more of the four national networks. Only seven years later, affiliation had dropped to just over half of all radio stations on the air. In the same period, television networks grew from vague proposals into powerful combinations having affiliation agreements with virtually all on-air television stations. Between these two developments, radio as a national advertising and programming medium gave way almost totally to television.

7.3.1 The Old Order Passes

Oddly enough, the radio networks ranked in number of affiliates in reverse order to their importance in broadcasting. CBS and NBC led in importance and impact, but ABC had about 50 more affiliates than either of them and Mutual had two and one-half times as many, although these usually were smaller rural stations lacking the audience pull of the major stations affiliated with NBC and CBS. Newest of the major networks was the American Broadcasting Company, as the Blue Network was known after 1945 (see p. 232).

CBS had named 37-year-old Dr. Frank Stanton as its president early in 1946, although William Paley retained ownership control. From this position Stanton became a spokesman for the broadcasting industry during the

■ **The CBS Team**   CBS radio in its most important days and CBS television for its first quarter-century was shaped primarily by two men: Starting in 1929 William S. Paley (left) served first as president and then as chairman; and Frank Stanton (right) served as president from 1946 to 1971. Both men are shown in the late 1960s. For the competing NBC executive team, see page 359.

Photos courtesy of CBS Inc.

next 25 years, much as David Sarnoff of RCA spoke for most of the electronics industry. Both NBC and CBS observed their 25th anniversaries in 1951 and 1952, with promotional hoopla about the great past days of radio and the wonderful coming days of television. Inter-network rivalry continued, with both ABC and CBS making major talent raids (see pp. 297–298) on bigger NBC. As early as 1947, ABC sought merger partners to bolster its financial position (see p. 288). A swap in call letters was arranged over several years to identify flagship stations more easily with their network; for example, CBS's WABC call letters went to the American Broadcasting Company's New York outlet (the WJZ call letters went to Baltimore), while CBS obtained the call letters WCBS from a station in the South.

Even with the FCC chain broadcasting rules (see p. 259), the national networks exercised great power over individual affiliates. In several cases, when local radio stations wanted to substitute a local program for a network program, network officials threatened to reconsider the station's affiliation contract. Even though the station licensee, by law, had the responsibility for what went over the air, until 1948 or so such threats had great effect, for network affiliation was the key to success.

Later, however, as more radio stations became independent and television networks expanded, the radio network declined in importance almost as fast as it had risen, leaving a residue of news, brief features, special events, and well into the 1960s such die-hard entertainment programs as Arthur Godfrey on CBS and Don McNeill's *Breakfast Club* on ABC. With audience interest focusing on television, advertisers and popular programs soon moved to the newer medium. By the 1951–1952 season, large chunks of time previously network-programmed were coming back to the affiliate radio stations for local programming.

The change in role was not unexpected. Early in 1949, NBC President Niles Trammell predicted that "within three years, the broadcast of sound or ear radio over giant networks will be wiped out." But apparently most network executives did not agree. For various reasons, chiefly its much higher costs, they felt that television would grow slowly enough to make a gradual radio-to-television transition during the 1950s. But the public's interest in and advertiser fascination with television, as well as the impatience of radio executives to make a mark in television, left network radio a dying operation by 1950.

Some attempted to introduce different types of radio networks. Several were limited, regional FM-only arrangements. But in late 1947, the exclusively FM Continental Radio Network added eastern and midwestern stations for its programs of music originating from several sources by using tapes, AT&T wires, or off-air relays, whichever was more effective. FM inventor Edwin Armstrong, whose own W2XMN in Alpine, New Jersey, was an important affiliate, secretly met nearly all the expenditures of the operation. Continental went out of business after Armstrong's death. For a time in the 1940s, both ABC and CBS proposed special networks for their FM affiliates, with high-fidelity duplication of AM network programs. This proposal was aimed at protecting the network organization should AM die off, but, in the end, a few FM stations simply affiliated with conventional low-fidelity AM-based networks.

More interesting, and generating considerably more publicity, was the establishment of the Liberty Broadcasting System. Begun as a single station in Texas by Gordon McLendon in 1948, LBS was based on skillful re-creation of baseball games by McLendon, who combined wire service reports of an ongoing game with sound effects records to make his listeners think they were hearing a play-by-play description. The legality of the method was questionable, because the ball clubs controlled the rights to game broadcasts. By 1949 McLendon's station was feeding the games to more than 80 others in the Southwest. Recreating both baseball and football games—and carrying many as direct play-by-play broadcasts—McLendon's operation had expanded to 200 stations by 1950 and was assuming network stature, with six hours of programming per day. McLendon announced plans for a nationwide network with 16 hours a day of varied programming, just when the established networks, except for Mutual, were letting their radio operations slide in favor of television. By June 1951, the Liberty network had 400 affiliated stations and boasted a strong news department with a growing reputation. Then the organization started to come apart. To obtain funds for continued expansion,

Liberty brought in a Texas oilman whose role and conservative views soon decimated the news staff. At about the same time, several ball clubs brought suit against Liberty. The costs of litigation, plus natural advertiser and broadcaster aversion to legal controversy, led to suspension of network operations in mid-1952. A couple of revival attempts failed, and Liberty's former affiliates either signed with one of the big four or turned independent.

Perhaps the radio networks assisted in their own demise when they provided the initial financial support for television stations and networks, a training ground for personnel, and models for television network organization, operations, and programming.

7.3.2 The New Television Networks

The expansion of television networks has to be examined in relation to (a) the technology and implications of coaxial cable and microwave relay, and (b) the actions of individual networks. The required technology for interconnection of television stations was understood by the early 1940s, but wartime priorities and the high cost of installation in relation to a very few stations and receiver owners delayed action. As with existing radio network interconnections, AT&T would provide the means of television networking and rental charges to stations and networks would pay for it—another direct outgrowth of the 1926 radio group-telephone company agreement (see p. 76). The first coaxial television cable (see Appendix B), between New York, Philadelphia, and Washington, D.C., was laid early in 1946. Television stations in the three cities were thus able to carry the Louis–Conn heavyweight championship boxing match, and the Schenectady station received the telecast by relay and rebroadcast it to its small audience. The wide publicity given to that event helped convince many persons that television networks were not far off. By November 1947, the cable was extended from New York to Boston, interconnecting the major population centers of the coastal Northeast. Turning west, AT&T engineers interconnected stations in the East with those in the Midwest by late 1948 so that major cities in the eastern half of the nation were receiving network programs simultaneously. Major interconnection links ran from Boston to Washington, from Philadelphia west to Chicago, from Milwaukee south to St. Louis, and from Detroit to Cincinnati. Further expansion of network lines took more time since population centers were farther apart.

In an almost direct parallel to the events of the early 1920s, the embryonic television networks clashed with AT&T over the rates to be charged for use of the coaxial cable. AT&T wished to establish a permanent tariff as soon as possible and discontinue experimental use of the line. When the broadcasters, judging the proposed rates far too high, refused to pay, AT&T cut off the service. Before a compromise was reached, a New York station used old Western Union twisted-pair telegraph lines to carry the video signal of the six-day bicycle races from Madison Square Garden to the studio—just as, more than 20 years earlier, the same licensee had used Western Union wires to carry the same races on radio during a similar battle.

Because the South and the West had fewer stations and viewers, in spite of a north–south interconnection installed on the West Coast in 1950, AT&T would take much longer to recoup its coaxial cable investment in these regions. Of course, the cable also could carry thousands of simultaneous telephone conversations, but telephoning also was greatest between major centers of population. Construction began on the main trunk east–west line in 1950. On most of this route point-to-point microwave radio relay towers with the same signal-carrying capacity as the coaxial cable were built about 30 miles apart, so that each tower would receive the signal, beef it up, and retransmit it to the next tower. All this was done at electronic speeds, with only a fraction of a second elapsing from initiation of a television signal on one end of the line to its reception on the other. The line was ready to test in late Summer 1951, just 36 years after completion of the first transcontinental telephone line. AT&T had laid plans for an inaugural program on all four networks late in September, but when President Truman was scheduled to address the peace conference officially ending the war with Japan in San Francisco on September 4, that occasion was used to open the coast-to-coast link. Ninety-four stations carried the address to about 95% of the country's television sets, with a potential audience of a million viewers. A few weeks later, regular national network telecasting began, sharing the one line. One of the first broadcasts was CBS's new *See It Now* series with Edward R. Murrow (see p. 312). A shot of Murrow in front of television monitors showing *live* scenes from both the Atlantic and the Pacific oceans proved that television had obliterated distance and opened a window on the world.

The development of television networks differed in several respects from the rise of the radio chains. First, the video webs grew directly and rapidly from radio organizations, complete with personnel, funding, and expertise, and they led the television industry from the start rather than following individual stations as radio had done. This also speeded the industry's development. Second, virtually all stations were affiliated with one or more (frequently two or three) networks at a time; the only independent stations in those early years were in New York and Los Angeles. Third, networking developed on a broad front, with no fewer than four competitors throughout this period. As with radio but to a greater degree, the networks initially lost money, with even owned-and-operated stations earning too little to cover the massive capital expenditures, but were operated with the expectation of future profits. Fourth, although radio networks could use conventional AT&T or even Western Union wire lines, television networks depended on installation of coaxial cable or microwave circuits for intercity connections. Fifth, television offered more program variety from the start than radio did in its earliest years (see pp. 302–311 and 128–135).

It was clear as early as 1941 that owners of profitable radio networks would undertake the formation of television networks. First into the ring after the war was NBC, which by February 1946 had an informal four-station network of flagship WNBT in New York and affiliates in Washington, Philadelphia, and Schenectady. Since new stations nearly all immediately assumed a primary or secondary affiliation with NBC, by Fall 1948, the first "network season," NBC had nearly 25 affiliates throughout the Northeast and into the Middle West, plus some noninterconnected affiliates on the West Coast. Before 1948 most stations programmed on their own, receiving only a few programs from the fledgling networks.

Because ABC was the newest radio network and a weak third in importance (see pp. 231–232), it decided to move rapidly into television to attain equality with NBC and CBS. It signed an affiliate in Philadelphia even before opening its first owned-and-operated station. Expansion into television was a heavy investment for a network controlled largely by one man, Edward Noble, who had a majority ownership stemming from his purchase of the Blue Network from NBC in 1943. As a result, ABC floated a series of stock sales in the late 1940s to fund network expansion. Even by 1947 there were rumors that ABC was seeking either a merger partner or a purchaser to gather sufficient capital to compete with better-financed CBS and NBC. Early in 1951, ABC admitted that it was negotiating with International Telephone & Telegraph, CBS, and General Tire & Rubber. The latter two companies planned to split up the network if successful in their bids. But Noble decided against division of the network and turned to a new prospective partner, United Paramount Theaters (UPT), headed by Leonard Goldenson.

UPT was the exhibition side of the original Paramount motion picture company, divorced from the production side as a result of a court mandate following an antitrust consent decree (see p. 337). UPT had money to invest in broadcasting and, after intensive bargaining, ABC and UPT announced in May 1951 that they would exchange stock and merge, with Noble as chairman of the board, and Goldenson as president. The two firms' boards approved the deal that summer and asked for FCC approval, required because transfer of control of stations was involved. The FCC held long hearings on UPT's antitrust problems in the motion picture field and their potential influence on its operation of a broadcasting network, and also weighed the basic question of such concentration of media control. Final approval of the merger in February 1953 gave ABC cash to continue television expansion, which almost had stopped in 1951 for want of capital. But this time ABC was still in a weak third position from which it took more than two decades to recover.

CBS was a relatively small company among American businesses, unable to command the financial leverage of RCA. It entered television strongly backing its own color system and holding back on network expansion until the color decision was made (see pp. 321–324). As a result, unlike both NBC and ABC, CBS had to purchase rather than build most of its O & O stations in major markets. Its choices were fairly limited and the stations it bought could not contribute much to network startup costs.

■ Network-Owned Television Stations: A Changing Cast

For decades, many of the most important television stations in the larger markets were owned-and-operated (O-&-O) by the networks themselves, and provided much of the profit for the networks. The number of such stations was limited by FCC rules to 5 VHF stations and 2 UHF until 1985, when the limits were raised. The following table shows network-constructed (C), -purchased (P) or -merged (M) O-&-O stations for the three major commercial networks from 1941 until 1985. The Fox network was started in 1986, when the multiple ownership rules (see pp. 282, 470–471, and 576–577) were relaxed, and WB and UPN started even later. Cities are listed by their 1968 market rank. For each station entry, the top line gives the 1985 call letters (or the call used when the network owned the station, omitting any "-TV" suffix) and the channel number, while the second line gives the date the station began operating under network control, with the code for whether it was constructed, purchased or acquired through merger. Termination dates are shown for stations no longer network owned. O-&-Os as of 1985 are boldfaced.

Market Rank/City	ABC	CBS	NBC
1. New York	**WABC (7)** **(1948, C)**	**WCBS (2)** **(1941, C)**	**WNBC (4)** **(1941, C)**
2. Los Angeles	**KABC (7)** **(1949, C)**	KTTV (11) (1948–1951, P) **KCBS (2)** **(1951, P)**	**KNBC (4)** **(1947, P)**
3. Chicago	**WLS (7)** **(1948, C)**	**WBBN (2)** **(1953, P)**	**WMAQ (5)** **(1948, C)**
4. Philadelphia	**WPVI (6)** **(1985, M)**	**WCAU (10)** **(1958, P)**	WRCV (3) (1955–1965, P)
5. San Francisco	**KGO (7)** **(1949, C)**	—	—
7. Detroit	WXYZ (7) (1948–1985, P)	—	—
8. Dallas-Ft. Worth	—	—	—
9. Washington	—	WTOP (9) (1950–1954, P)	**WRC (4)** **(1947, C)**
10. Houston	**KTRK (13)** **(1985, M)**	—	—
11. Cleveland	—	—	WKYC (3) (1948–1955, C) (1965, P)
12. Atlanta	—	—	—
13. Minneapolis–St. Paul	—	WCCO (4) (1952–1954, P)	—
16. Miami	—	**WCIX (6)** **(1988, P)**	**WTVJ (4)** **(1987, P)**
18. St. Louis	—	KMOX (4) (1957–1986, P)	—
19. Denver	—	—	**KCNC (4)** **(1986, M)**
23. Hartford–New Haven	—	WHCT (18) (1956–1958, P)	WNBC (30) (1956–1958, P)
30. Milwaukee	—	WXIX (19) (1954–1959, P)	—
35. Raleigh-Durham	**WTVD (11)** **(1985, M)**	—	—
38. Buffalo	—	—	WBUF (17) (1955–1958, P)
63. Fresno	**KFSN (30)** **(1985, M)**	—	—

ABC: ABC built the first five stations it owned. Technically, the licenses did change hands when ABC merged with United Paramount Theaters in the 1950s and again when Capital Cities bought ABC in 1985, adding three stations.

CBS: CBS station interests in markets 2, 9, and 13 were minority interests, not controlling shares, ranging in each case from 45% to 49%. Its short-lived operations in markets 21 and 24 were the only CBS ventures into UHF operation. Of those, the Milwaukee station has since been deleted entirely. The present CBS station in market 2 is wholly owned.

NBC: For the story behind NBC ownerships in markets 4 and 8, see text 8.3. The Cleveland station is the only one owned by the same network at two separate times. NBC's short-lived experiments with UHF are found in markets 21 and 28. Its New York station has used a variety of call letters (WNBT, WRCA-TV, WNBC-TV). GE bought NBC's parent, RCA, in 1986.

Call letters and channels—particularly of stations that started as experimental stations—changed during the years.

All data from two sources: Network Study Staff, Federal Communications Commission. *Network Broadcasting.* 85th Cong., 2d Sess., House Report 1297 (1958), page 575, table 48, and *Broadcasting Yearbook.*

A fourth television network was *without* radio connections. In 1944 Allen B. DuMont put WABD, named for himself, on the air in New York with announced plans for a postwar television network. After the war, DuMont started WTTG—named after his chief engineer, Thomas T. Goldsmith—in Washington, and pressed ahead with his network plans. His financial support came from a prosperous television manufacturing business. DuMont's plan was to expand along the Atlantic Coast and then pick up affiliates and other O & Os inland as receiver ownership increased and the AT&T coaxial cables expanded westward. This plan did not succeed. New television stations typically took on a primary affiliation with a major network, usually NBC or CBS, and at best made a secondary or tertiary connection with ABC and DuMont—with DuMont often left out. To earn income, the DuMont network offered to sublease its AT&T-supplied network lines in daytime hours for closed-circuit use at $11,000 an hour, but there were no takers. The affiliated stations grew in number, but few took many DuMont programs. As the Freeze on new stations (see p. 321) continued, it became obvious that DuMont's lack of network success had more than financial roots. There were too few channels in the major markets, only a handful with as many as four commercial stations on the air. As a result, he became an ardent proponent of providing an adequate number of competitive channels in most markets.

Within six years, television networks went from paper plans to operating coast-to-coast entities. Television networking was based on the radio model—except that the networks, rather than the advertising agencies, had to bankroll expensive program development (see p. 296)—and has changed little since. Virtually all on-air stations, other than those in the few cities with four or more commercial channels or in the hinterland beyond network service, were affiliated with one or more of the national networks.

7.4 Rebirth of Educational Broadcasting

The outlook for noncommercial educational broadcasting was brighter in 1945 than it had been for 15 years. First, there was a new radio service: noncommercial FM broadcasting. Second, pressures were building for similar channel reservations for educational television. Educational organizations that had nearly been squeezed out of the AM band since the mid-1920s would finally have opportunities and room to broadcast.

7.4.1 Expansion into FM

Placement of the educational allocation on the 88 to 92 MHz band in 1945 (see p. 253) made educators especially optimistic. The number of FM educational stations on the air grew steadily from six in 1946 to more than 90 in 1952—14% of all FM stations on the air. The NAEB helped lay plans for a national FM network of stations, with an interim tape-recording program exchange to serve the many university-owned stations in the Midwest and community and educational institutions elsewhere. The concept of the NAEB Tape Network started when Seymour N. Siegel, acting manager of New York City's noncommercial AM-FM station WNYC, saw his first handmade American magnetic tape recorder late in 1946. In 1951, the NAEB received a Kellogg Foundation grant to establish permanent headquarters at the University of Illinois and begin a tape duplication operation to facilitate a noninterconnected "bicycle network," in which one station's programs were shipped to other stations in succession. More than 40 stations soon were participating. Efforts to set up a national interconnected noncommercial FM network, however, lagged until the late 1960s. Some regional networks were established: in Wisconsin, by 1952, a state-supported eight-station network provided a full day's programming to most of the state.

Perhaps chastened by earlier experiences with educational AM radio, colleges, school districts, and municipalities applied for FM licenses very slowly. Apart from past disappointments and the problem of cost—especially for colleges and universities straining to serve millions of postwar students—potential educational FM station operators were wary of the continuing scarcity of FM receivers (see p. 314) and television's possible effect on radio. Late in 1948 the FCC, recognizing the burden of high cost and the limited or campus-only uses planned by some colleges, allowed educational FM licensees to broadcast with as few as 10 watts of power (enough for a 2 to 5-mile range) instead of the normal, more expensive lower limit of 250 watts. By requiring fewer technicians with high training, the low-power class added many new stations. Of the 92 educational FM stations on the air in 1952, more than one-third were 10-watt operations.

7.4.2 Hopes for Educational Television

More than anything else, the lobbying effort for educational reservations for television (see pp. 327–328) forced a not yet completely mended split among educational broadcasters. Some concentrated quietly on radio and other traditional media, while others focused on high-pressure lobbying and fundraising for educational television (ETV). The problems were immense; few schools or districts could afford television broadcasting, and commercial broadcasters, contending that they could meet educational needs, tried to defeat any reservation of channels for education. That claim had been voiced before, in the late 1920s and when Congress debated the Communications Act of 1934. It sparked educators to work together to convince their boards that ETV was worthwhile, and to maintain the right to seek their own station.

In October 1950, with the enthusiastic backing of FCC Commissioner Frieda Hennock, a successful lawyer who was the first woman commissioner, representatives of several organizations met to form the Joint Committee (later Council) on Educational Television (JCET). With foundation and other support, JCET mounted an intensive campaign for educational television channel reservations. This organization first was seen as an ad hoc group that would cease operations as soon as the FCC provided the reserved channels, but its need for permanence soon became clear. For one thing, JCET had to fight a two-front battle—getting the needed allocation on the one hand and finding and encouraging potential educational broadcasters on the other. CBS, having to *buy* into top markets because of its late entry into television station ownership, and the National Association of Broadcasters were the chief opponents of reserved channels for education. They contended that educators were not ready for television and that, at most, some UHF channels, not allocated to television, would suffice. Also bothersome were conservative educators who only recently had grasped the potential benefits of radio, let alone far more expensive and complicated television. In addition to lobbying, JCET provided a public information program to mobilize public opinion in ETV's favor until a prestigious cooperating organization, the National Citizens Committee for Educational Television, took over this function.

Reasoning that proof of the lack of aired educational material would influence FCC decision makers, NAEB sponsored content analyses of the programs of commercial stations in major cities. The first, covering a January 1951 week of New York television, found virtually no educational programming. Studies in other cities during the 1951 through 1954 period showed the same pattern (see table on page 304).

In Spring 1948 at least five universities were active in ETV. The University of Iowa had applied for a station, Iowa State University had received a construction permit, the University of Michigan was providing educational programs over a Detroit station, as was American University on a Washington, D.C., network outlet, and Kansas State University was continuing experimentation. To get coverage over a wide area at limited cost, educators took part in Westinghouse and Glenn L. Martin aircraft company experiments with "Stratovision" in the late 1940s (see pp. 325–326) and provided regular airborne transmissions in the 1960s (see p. 423).

In February 1950 Iowa State's WOI-TV at Ames, Iowa, became the first nonexperimental educationally owned television station. Taking some programs from the networks and selling advertising, the station was able to support a variety of educational programming without expense to the university. WOI-TV soon sent material to other schools for placement on commercial stations until they could have their own educational channels.

For the first time since they allowed AM licenses to slip from their fingers in the late 1920s and early 1930s, educational broadcasters had something to work and plan for—expansion into FM and television. The allocation of specific reserved channels, in the early 1940s for FM and in 1952 for television, saved educators from having to compete for outlets with potential commercial broadcasters. After three decades of commercial broadcasting, nonprofit licensees and potential licensees now had a chance to show what *they* could do.

7.4.2.1 *Industrial Video*

Although the days of routine use of television for surveillance and for "home movies" (camcorders) were to be decades in the future, there was a growing use of non-broadcast or "industrial" video that started right after World War II that expanded independently of broadcast television. First used by the military in airborne applications (the forerunner of "smart bombs"), this use soon moved to rail, aviation, bank, and electrical power monitoring. In some industries, television could monitor processes in environments that humans couldn't survive. With television, one night watchman sitting in a control room could replace several who formerly had to patrol in all kinds of weather. Lower quality television equipment also might be used for economical employee training, a practice that burgeoned after the development of inexpensive videotape recorders in the 1960s.

7.5 Radio Advertising Supports Television

The end of the war saw the end of the excess profits tax and 10-cent-dollar advertising (see pp. 232–234). But now consumer advertising for goods and services would expand as industry reconverted to civilian needs. Advertising time and space sales more than doubled from 1945 to 1952, from just under $3 billion to well over $7 billion. Newspapers continued to receive about 35% of the expenditure, with broadcasting in second place with 15%. The percentages changed little, but from 1945 to 1952 broadcast advertising volume increased from $425 million to more than $1,078 million. While television got little of that prior to 1950, by 1952–1953 television and radio divided the ever larger broadcast advertising pie about evenly. However, these overall figures tend to hide a number of important—and, for some broadcasters, serious—internal developments.

7.5.1 The Changing Economics of Radio

Major shifts were occurring in radio advertising. First, advertising agencies had less control of programs, especially after CBS moved in 1946 to take more control of network programs. Criticism about the role of agencies in radio may have been involved, but the rationale for the switch was that it gave the networks more of radio's potential profits, needed for their expansion into television. The agencies, on the other hand, while willing to risk money to develop new radio programs to sell to advertisers, refused to risk the amounts that would be necessary for television programming and reduced all their broadcast programming (see p. 296). Also, as audience and advertiser interest in television waxed, interest in network radio waned each year.

While radio advertising revenue was rising, the network share of it, including O & O stations, fell from $23 million to just over $11 million—a drop of more than 50% in seven years. The four networks' share went from 47% in 1945 to 26% in 1952. As early as 1948, more and more programming became sustaining and networks repeatedly cut their time charges, but to no avail. Advertisers changed to local spot radio and other media, including television. Once network radio started to slip, it went fast.

Locally, two conflicting trends spelled financial trouble for many postwar AM stations. As radio went from a national to a local advertising medium, its competitive stance changed. The local radio station proportion of radio income increased from one-third of radio's revenues in 1945 to well over one-half just seven years later. Although the increased revenue was welcome—and overall radio advertising was up too—the pot had to be split among more stations than before and competition with other media was fierce. Whereas up to and during the war radio competed mostly against magazines and a few major newspapers for a national or regional audience, after 1950 it competed directly with the well-entrenched chief local advertising medium: newspapers. There were twice as many daily newspapers as radio stations at first, but the postwar growth of AM and FM radio balanced these numbers by 1949, and today there are more than seven times as many stations as newspapers.

The very growth of radio was one of its worst problems, since more stations meant more licensees scrambling for available advertising dollars. New stations commonly operated in the red for a longer period, with perhaps one-third of *all* stations losing money in any given year. Stations allowed on the air only during daylight hours suffered in their search for advertisers, as did those with low power or especially restrictive directional antenna patterns. Early in 1947, the FCC issued *An Economic Study of Standard Broadcasting*, which suggested that the financial outlook for radio was dim because the increasing number of new stations would get ever smaller pieces of the advertising pie. The FCC report suggested that "old" radio markets would have the most difficulty, with new stations taking advertising from old ones; whereas in "new" radio towns the first station would have only the local paper as competition.

However, even though *network* radio was dying, at no time prior to 1953 did *overall* radio revenues fail to grow each year (see Appendix C, table 3-A). AM radio's share of all advertising income dropped from 15% in 1945 to 9% in 1952, but the total dollar value kept increasing.

While AM radio had problems in distributing income, at least it had the income to distribute. FM stations usually had little or no income at all. The reasons for FM's failure to attract money during its period of growth were several and serious, and, as will be seen in future chapters, none of them was easily overcome.

Foremost was that advertisers saw FM radio as duplicative. They were spending on AM, and frequently on television, and could not figure any gain by adding FM. To a large degree, they were right; most FM stations merely duplicated the programming of their sister AM stations, making the FM audience, such as it was, a free bonus. This mass giveaway of FM time was almost fatal to the few independent FM stations that tried to sell advertising. In addition, few FM stations had information to show to advertisers as to how many listeners in the market owned FM receivers. Advertiser analysis of FM receiver sales (see p. 314) suggested a small audience. Stations not duplicating AM programming had a reputation for "fine music" programming, which, although admirable to their faithful listeners, attracted far too few people to attract advertisers. Of those stations trying to sell time, few published rate cards, making it clerically hard for prospective purchasers.

Total FM revenues did not pass $1 million until 1948, and at no time during this period was the FM industry collectively even close to the black. A few big independent stations did fairly well in major markets—thanks to loyal audiences providing some direct support for the programming—but most were a drain on their owner's finances. Chiefly because of this drain, in the face of radical adjustments in AM radio, and the continuing demand of television expenses, hundreds of FM stations folded after 1950. Since FM obviously had peaked and now was in decline, broadcasters cut their losses and concentrated on AM and television.

7.5.2 Video Commercialism

Though soon to become the leading national advertising medium, television began in this country in a limited, local setting, and advertising revenues did not begin to cover programming and technical expense. Thanks to the precedent of more than two decades of radio advertising, advertising promised from the start to become television programming's prime support. The major question was: When would television reach enough big city audiences to make network television worthwhile, for advertisers feared its huge cost. As one research report put it late in 1949, "We seriously doubt that television will ever become a truly nationwide medium (as compared with present radio patterns and service) if it has to depend on the economics of advertising alone."

Television costs in the late 1940s generally ran 10 times higher than those for radio. Construction of a station without live production facilities, equipped only for reproducing movies or programs from another station, cost much more than the typical radio station. Construction of a fully equipped station with at least one studio, a film and slide chain, and network capability cost considerably more. Running such a station took many more trained technical and business personnel. A typical network prime time program cost between $6,000 and $8,000, and even the far less costly local programs ran much higher than radio's finest show. The visual demands of television—sets, lighting, costumes, makeup, the costs of buying and maintaining television cameras and other studio equipment as well as the personnel to operate them—all added up. Finally, the costs of laying coaxial cable or setting up microwave links, even in 1949 and 1950 when the network reached only from the eastern seaboard to the Midwest, led AT&T to raise its hourly charges to at least 10 times the comparable charge for radio network lines. These initial construction and continually rising operational costs kept the television broadcasting industry as a whole in the red until 1952, and many stations were money losers long afterwards.

Faced with time charges high enough to cover such costs, advertisers moved into television very cautiously, and some agencies stayed out completely, fearing that their standard commission would never cover the work and costs of getting into television. The agencies also abandoned the field of network program development, which they had dominated since the late 1920s. Companies that began to advertise in the 1946–1948 period aimed to secure a time slot on a given station, to obtain rights to talent or program ideas, to gain experience while the rates were comparatively low, or just to experiment with the new medium. When polled, most sponsors had little idea of the impact of their messages, especially since audiences were so limited. Advertisers without radio advertising experience were extra cautious.

Early commercials ran from the "standard" minute format to occasional *pitches* or advertising "programs" of 15 or 30 minutes. Early television commercial experiments sought an effective combination of visual and aural appeal at the least cost. The simplest advertisements were merely signs held before a television camera while an announcer off camera voiced the brief message. Slightly more involved ads combined slides and announcer talk. Even more complex was the silent film with live announcer—the first format to use movement in a commercial. The sound film, especially with animation and other visual sleights of hand, quickly became popular with sponsors, despite its costs. Many sponsors chose the lower costs but greater simplicity and greater risks (particularly if something went wrong during a demonstration) of live television. A television commercial could cost as little as $50 or as much as $10,000 to *produce*—before buying time on which to show it to an audience. Product identification became of utmost importance, and symbols or animated characters introduced on television spread the advertising message by word of mouth and other media.

Gillette, which continued to back sporting events on radio while moving into television, sponsored the Joe Louis–Billy Conn heavyweight fight of June 1946—the first interconnected "network" program. Bristol-Myers sponsored a series of travel films, becoming the first sponsor of any television series.

During these early years most advertisers sponsored entire programs and became identified with the program and its stars. For example, Texaco's identification with *Texaco Star Theater*—the Milton Berle show, a Tuesday night institution—sold a lot of gasoline (see pp. 305–306). Although the network often owned the program, full sponsorship allowed the advertiser considerable control. As rising costs made partial sponsorship or spot buying necessary, the advertiser's influence on the program faded.

Television advertising was placed with individual stations until 1949 when the eastern and midwestern branches of the networks were connected. Network advertising started when interconnected stations supplied a widespread audience for the same program at the same time. Network advertising accounted for at least half of the 1949–1952 television advertising (see Appendix C, table 3-B), as local advertising dropped from one-third to less than one-quarter and national and regional spot ads rose in importance. Thus the emphasis of television advertising was set nationally from the start. The first network rate card, issued by NBC in June 1949, offered advertisers 19 interconnected stations for $7,000 an hour; New York alone was $1,500. Adding other noninterconnected stations, which would insert the ad by film, raised the price to around $10,000 an hour for 34 affiliates. These rates appeared astronomical to advertising agency and advertiser personnel used to radio's prices, but in a few years they would seem amazingly cheap.

7.6 Programming: Both Heard and Seen

No startling new programming types appeared in the immediate postwar years. Strong inter-network rivalry in both radio and television marked the difficult transition of many programs from radio to television, and the decline of national radio and the rise of network television produced some programming changes and trends.

7.6.1 Decline of Network Radio

Before radio networks disappeared, they had two or three very good years—and before they succumbed had a lively knockdown fight over top stars and their shows. Television helped instigate the radio "talent raids" of 1948 and 1949. CBS started them when it realized that it was behind in the race for television affiliates.

Headed by Chairman William Paley, who had a bent for showmanship, CBS, realizing that radio stars might also become popular on television, came up with a novel interpretation of the tax laws. If a star formed a corporation with himself or herself as the major asset, employee, and stockholder, the network could then purchase control of the program from the corporation for a great deal of money and the star would pay a tax on capital gains rather than on straight income, which was more heavily taxed. The first major acquisition came in September 1948, when CBS "stole" *Amos 'n' Andy* from NBC in a $2 million deal with stars Freeman F. Gosden and Charles Correll. CBS then enticed Jack Benny and Edgar Bergen ("Charlie McCarthy") from NBC and Bing Crosby from ABC. The *Ozzie and Harriet* show and Red Skelton also went over to CBS before other stars started getting better deals from their own networks. Many of the CBS contracts were personally negotiated by Paley. The networks tried to counter one another's gains with lawyers and also with advertising and promotional battles in the press. Most of these changes took place in the 1948–1949 season (coincidentally, the first network TV season) but continued into the following year, when NBC came back with offers to CBS stars and managed to hire away Groucho Marx, Bob Hope, Kate Smith, and Ed Wynn and their shows. To prevent further migrations, the networks hurriedly placed under long-term contracts each program and star then working for them. Ironically, none of this had a lasting effect on network radio, all but defunct within five years, but strengthened CBS's financial and programming resources for television.

Radio's trend toward cheaper music and quiz shows, as opposed to drama, in prime time indicated increasing psychological pressure from television. *Stop the Music* (see below), a big money show based on music, was followed by *Break the Bank, Hit the Jackpot, Sing It Again* on the

---

■ **Network Radio Programming: Fred Allen and *Stop the Music***

Two developments in this period epitomize what was happening to radio network programming—and both affected radio comedian Fred Allen. For 15 seasons Allen's Sunday night hour (later a half-hour) on NBC had been one of the 10 most highly rated shows. His first problem was more a public relations man's dream than anything else. One of Allen's key joke targets had been the many NBC vice presidents: Allen noted that their job, on finding a molehill on their desk in the morning, was to make it a good-sized mountain before they left that afternoon. Things came to a head, however, when Allen ran overtime on the April 27, 1947 show and his comment about NBC having a vice president in charge of program ends—who saved minutes and seconds of program time until he had two weeks' worth, at which time he took a vacation—was cut off the air. The problem snowballed the following week when NBC cut off Bob Hope and Red Skelton when each tried to joke about Allen's hassle. Newspaper stories and ads indicated that ratings of all the affected programs were going up. It was a tempest in a small teapot, but the enmity between Allen and NBC brass did not help him later when he had ratings trouble.

In 1948, ABC began *Stop the Music*, a national music quiz program starring Bert Parks. It placed telephone calls at random across the country. When a person answered, Parks would call to the show's orchestra to "stop the music!," and the caller who could name the tune being played—the assumption was that he or she would have been listening to the program—won big prizes. ABC put this program opposite Allen's Sunday night slot with bad results for the comedian. His show dropped from the top 10 to number 38 while the new quiz show went to the number 2 slot within a few weeks. Genuinely concerned about the effect of the competing show on his audience, Allen posted a bond to guarantee a $5,000 prize to anyone listening to his program who missed an opportunity to answer a *Stop the Music* call correctly. There were several fake attempts to collect, but no genuine payoffs. But the result was that Allen went off the air in June 1949 as the quiz show mania took over much of radio's network audience.

networks and similar programs on local stations. While most network variety and straight music shows used live bands, the local stations, and soon ABC, began to use transcriptions, breaking the old taboo on recorded music over network radio. Music, which always had been strong in local radio, now penetrated daytime network programming. The late 1940s saw development of the *musical clock* format of music, weather, time checks—hence the format's name—news on the hour, and commercials. A local *disc jockey* ad-libbed chatty background material. Indeed, the concept of the disc jockey as opposed to the anonymous, regimented studio announcer began to grab hold in local radio, as declining network programming left stations to their own devices. No longer a mere announcer playing records, making commercial announcements, and introducing news and other program segments, the *jock* began to build his own on-air personality, tailoring music and other elements to reach informally out to the audience. Though the heyday of such a role was yet to come, the basic idea was set. On New York stations such programs as *Milkman's Matinee* and Martin Block's *Make-Believe Ballroom* were popular. On smaller stations, to the unhappiness of unions and the joy of station management, disc jockeys ran their own control boards and played their own turntables, without the help of an engineer—a combination or *combo* of duties that was to become the rule for radio.

Much of the music on networks replaced faltering daytime serials. While ratings of the long-running titles remained strong, attempts to begin new serials met with little success. Loyal audiences kept this type of program on the air, but fewer people listened than before and during the war. Competing with the soap operas was an increasing number of music, quiz, and human interest programs. One of them that ran for years on radio and later on television was *Queen for a Day*, which started on Mutual in 1945. Host Jack Bailey would pick women from the audience who had sad tales to tell, and the audience would applaud according to how miserable a particular life was. The woman garnering the loudest applause measured on a volume meter was crowned queen for that day, and got prizes and, to the extent feasible, whatever she had requested to make her life happier. This sort of participation by the studio audience was not new, but the human interest element of *Queen for a Day* was unusual.

Realizing that it would be hard to support radio programming as advertisers left for television, broadcasters toyed briefly with the idea of direct audience support—or pay-radio. Under this scheme, listeners would pay a nickel a day, $18 a year, to hear programming without advertising. There was strong opposition, and the plan was shelved when one of its proponents, William Benton, founder of the major advertising agency of Benton & Bowles, became U.S. Senator from Connecticut. The concept of pay-radio was revived briefly in 1947–1948 when several stations expressed interest in a home music service based on patents of the Muzak Corporation, but the idea died.

The only noticeable trend was the slow decline in total network programs and the increase in sustaining programs. A typical network affiliate

■ **Types of Radio Programs Broadcast in 1946**   Shown below are the program types broadcast by 85 sample radio stations representing all types of AM stations in all sizes of markets, for a week in November 1946. Compare this table to the slightly different data for 1932 (page 133), and 1925 (page 81) to see the continuing major role of music, the increase in drama on the air, and the great increase in news and public affairs programs. This table includes both networks and local programs.

Program Types and Subtypes	Percentage of Time	
Music		**41%**
Old familiar and western	7%	
Popular and dance	26	
Classical and semiclassical	8	
Drama		**16**
Daytime serials	6	
Mystery	3	
Comedy	2	
Other	5	
Other Entertainment		**14**
Women's (homemaking)	1	
Comedy and variety	7	
Quiz and audience participation	6	
Information		**23**
News and commentators	13	
Sports of all types and formats	4	
Talks	3	
Farm programs	2	
Forums and panels	1	
Other		**8**
Religion and religious music	6	
Unclassified miscellaneous	2	
Total		**102%** (error due to rounding)

For large stations, about one-third of the schedule was local and live, about one-quarter was recorded or transcribed, and the remainder was network material. Non-network stations devoted nearly two-thirds of their schedules to recorded material, chiefly music. Of the full sample of 85 stations, about one-third of the time on the air was sustaining, with little variation by station size. For all but the largest stations, most news came from the networks.

Source: After Kenneth Baker, Table 4 "An Analysis of Radio's Programming," in Paul F. Lazarsfeld and Frank N. Stanton, eds. *Communications Research 1948–1949* (New York: Harper, 1949), pages 51–72, mainly page 58.

now originated more programming than it took from the network—a reversal of the two-decades-long trend of network domination. The conviction that television would soon make all radio programming obsolete gave the radio business a general feeling of foreboding. Bright, young, and not so young, programming executives looked for opportunities to move over to the newer medium. A straw in the wind was the increase in *simulcast* programs in the 1950s, in which popular radio programs became television programs, with the audio portion carried on radio. Radio listeners reacted with annoyance to unexplained references or disconcerting studio laughter.

▪ Radio Drama at Its Height

Since all new entertainment media seem to draw from the content of older media (television from the movies, the movies from the stage, and so on), it is no surprise that early radio featured a great deal of aural drama in addition to other programming.

An entire new art form developed, with its writers (such as Norman Corwin and Arch Oboler), directors (60 years later, the anniversary of Orson Welles' 1938 "War of the Worlds" broadcast still was marked), and actors (many of whom later made their mark in the movies or on television). Although long rehearsals were a rare luxury, these programs melded words, voices, music, and sound effects (a new art form in itself!) into audience-gripping experiences.

While some programs (such as the Columbia Workshop) experimented with new forms of radio drama—including the use of blank verse—most dramatic radio programs used more conventional material. Some programs, such as the *Lux Radio Theatre*, used familiar plots and well-known stars from the stage or motion picture screen. Many of these programs later had life on television, but there still are some who would claim that the audio-only *Lights Out* or *Suspense* was more frightening than most recent big-screen horror films, that *X-Minus-One* was better science fiction than its television counterparts, or that an evening soap opera of the caliber of *Those We Love* has never been equaled.

Many programs had extraordinarily loyal audiences including soaps like *One Man's Family* and *Those We Love*, adventure programs like *I Love a Mystery*, and sitcoms like *Vic and Sade*, *Myrt 'n' Marge*, and *Easy Aces*.

Of special interest during World War II and after was an increase in radio "thriller" programs, aimed primarily at school-age boys (see Appendix C, tables 4-A, B, C). Popular programs were *Challenge of the Yukon* (with Sergeant Preston of the Royal Canadian Mounted Police and his dog King, around the turn of the last century), *Sky King* (a modern rancher using his airplane, the "Songbird," as well as a convenient pair of young relatives with whom the audience could identify), *Roy Rogers* (the singing cowboy star), *Straight Arrow* (a western with an Indian point of view), *Mark Trail* (as much nature education as adventure), and *Space Patrol* (young cadets learning the ropes in a future century). Traditionally, the thrillers were "stripped" or "across the board" at the same hour five days a week after school and had the serial element of suspense—hanging from one episode to the next. They were often the focus of radio and cereal package premium offers or items enclosed in cereal boxes. Some of these programs made the transition to television quite well (*Sky King, Roy Rogers, Superman, The Lone Ranger*), while others—including the very popular *Jack Armstrong, Tom Mix*, and *Captain Midnight*—either lasted on video briefly or did not make the move at all.

Several programs for parents and older children also soon transferred to television. Crime-detective drama included *Sam Spade, Dragnet* (low-key police realism in Los Angeles), and *Lineup* (police work in San Francisco). Comedy was also strong, especially *Our Miss Brooks* (Eve Arden as a long-suffering high-school teacher who loves a biology instructor from afar). While most of these shows were off radio by 1952 or 1953, a few went to television for lengthy runs. Then, they faded out for years, only to be revived for a new audience in the 1970s fascinated by nostalgia. Recordings were sought by collectors, and old radio programs played in the evening, usually on selected stations in larger markets, drawing sizable audiences, especially college students, from prime time television. As noted on p. 433, a few original dramatic presentations for radio appeared in the 1970s, but the late 1940s marked the height, and 1970s drama was mostly not-so-instant replay.

Many of these programs gave the impression of waiting for the time when they could abandon radio completely.

7.6.2 FM: Fine Music and Duplication

FM did not offer much that was new. Ever since the standard (AM) broadcasters had convinced the FCC in the 1944 and 1945 debate that FM would develop much faster if it could duplicate AM shows, the FCC had allowed unlimited AM–FM duplication. To protect AM advertisers from discrimination, the networks and many local AM stations took this one step further: co-owned FM stations could duplicate AM programming only if they carried *all* AM programs and advertisements. Since about 80% of the FM stations going on the air in the late 1940s were owned by AM stations in the same market, most FM stations carried AM programs. This sharply reduced the motivation of the public to buy FM receivers.

The independently owned-and-operated FM stations—fewer than 90 of the more than 700 on the air—opted for inexpensive musical programs, either background music hardly ever marred by talk or ads, or classical music and commentary. They also started issuing monthly program guides, which detailed the station's offerings for the coming month and often community events as well. In some cases these guides made more money through subscriptions and advertising than advertising carried on the FM station itself.

In many ways, FM was temporarily out of the running. Whether or not it was a "conspiracy," the AM industry effectively throttled FM development by making the new medium sound just like AM but without static and costing more for a receiver. Lacking sufficient unique appeal, FM—not surprisingly—did not attract audiences (see p. 314) and stations began to leave the air (p. 278).

7.6.3 Early Television Entertainment

Of all the periods in broadcasting history, two share the excitement of audience expectancy that the American public felt toward broadcasting. The first was in the early 1920s when radio was getting underway, the second was the period when television was beginning to reach across the country. While radio programs continued to attract large audiences, attention was now focused on the generally unexperienced television medium.

In 1945 the few television stations that had started in 1940 or 1941 returned to the air after wartime suspension with only a few hours of broadcasting a day, mostly on weekday evenings. Much early television programming was radio material with the addition of limited visual elements. Except for some theatrical or short subject films, most programming was live. From 1946 to 1952 television spread into daytime and weekend hours, started to use many different kinds of programming, mostly entertainment formats that had developed on radio, and became dominated by the networks.

As new stations increased competition in a few large markets, and as more television receivers were sold (see p. 315), stations began to offer programs in the afternoons. By the early 1950s, most stations were on the air in the morning and on weekends as well. The increased air time called for more programming material—again, usually local and live. Every station had its cooking expert; a late afternoon children's program host, usually a cowboy or a clown; a general interview host for daytime shows; and a small local news staff. Local programming filled daytime hours and weekend mornings, and networks filled evening hours.

Prior to Fall 1948 all television programming was local, with only an occasional special event being carried by more than one station at a time. Even network-owned stations operated as local independents. But, thanks to even local operators' experience with radio's formats and talent, program variety quickly approximated radio's, with music, variety, drama and comedy, quiz and other audience-participation shows, newscasts, and special events.

At the same time, video experimented with format, as radio had in the 1920s. Even early limited-length schedules had program hours to fill, and nearly anything could be tried as long as it did not cost too much; television was losing money in this period. Technicians, creative programmers, and performers had an exciting time trying, changing, and discarding formats. There were few restrictions or regulations. The twin aims were to fill air time and to see what would work best.

One format many television executives considered a natural was the motion picture, once the technical problem of converting 24 pictures a second to 30 was solved. But what they had in mind was the short; many doubted that the feature film would ever be available for home television. The pattern of television programming, except for sports and public events, fell into 10- and 20-minute segments rather than radio's 15-minute program pattern. Indeed, until the influx of ex-radio executives in the late 1940s, television scheduled programs in multiples of 20 minutes, long enough for two film reels of 1,000 feet on 35mm and a couple of commercials. Television programmers were uncertain as to how long audience attention could be held. With radio one could use imagination, but with television the audience had to pay total attention which, it was believed, programs of an hour or longer could not command. In addition, the motion picture industry, alarmed over the growth potential of television, refused to sell television any post-1948 and very few earlier movies. This visual media competition increased in the 1950s (see pp. 371 and 398–399).

Network programming dominated most evening hours on television from the start, and gradually expanded to daytime and weekends. Program managers quickly learned to fill local off-hours with the least expensive fare they could find—usually short films or off-network or independently produced and syndicated programs. They also ran old network output in fringe hours— a trend that was to increase in importance during the 1950s and 1960s as more old programs on film or videotape became available for reruns.

There was no question that advertiser-supported entertainment would be the basis of television programming just as it had been in radio. Because of its higher costs, getting the largest possible audience was even more important to video than radio, as the key to attracting advertiser money. The NAEB survey of a week on New York's seven stations in January 1951 (see box, page 304) showed that of 564 hours telecast, 25% was drama

■ **Changing Patterns of Television Programming: 1951–1954**   The most extensive analyses of early television programming were the series of programming studies conducted and published by the National Association of Educational Broadcasters. Here are the major findings of those content analyses.

Program Type	New York 1951	New York 1954	Los Angeles 1951	Chicago Summer 1951	New Haven 1952
Drama	25%	38%	26%	26%	24%
Comedy	3	9	3	3	4
Crime-detective	10	13	8	5	9
Western	6	4	6	6	—
Domestic/romance	5	4	5	1	9
Other drama	1	8	4	11	2
Music and Variety	18	15	16	12	19
Serious (classical)	1	1	—	}3	}4
Popular and light music	3	6	6		
Variety programs	14	8	10	9	15
Other Entertainment	12	8	8	15	11
Personalities	5	3	2	8	1
Quiz shows	7	5	6	7	10
Information	31	24	39	39	36
News	5	6	12	5	12
Weather	—	1	—	1	—
Public discussions and events	2	3	2	3	1
Other information	4	2	4	2	6
Sports	10	5	5	21	11
Homemaking	10	7	16	7	6
Other	14	14	11	8	9
Religion	1	2	1	—	1
Children's shows of all types	13	12	10	8	8
Total	100%	99%	100%	100%	99%
Number of stations:	7	7	8	4	1

Source: Los Angeles Television: May 23–29, 1951, by Dallas W. Smythe and Angus Campbell. (Urbana, Ill.: NAEB, 1951), pages 6, 79; The Purdue Opinion Panel, *Four Years of New York Television: 1951–1954* (Urbana, Ill.: NAEB, 1954), pages 69–75; Donald Horton, Hans O. Mauksch, and Kurt Lang, *Chicago Summer Television: July 30–August 5, 1951* (Urbana, Ill.: NAEB, 1951), pages 15, 25, 27, 55; and Dallas W. Smythe, *New Haven Television: May 15–21, 1952* (Urbana, Ill.: NAEB, 1953), page 106. © National Association of Educational Broadcasters. By permission.

(including 10% police/crime and 6% western), 14% was variety and vaudeville, 13% was entertainment for children, 10% each was sports, homemaking, and interviews/news, while only 4% was informational apart from news. The week covered offered little important programming and only one hour of serious music. Advertising was heavy, especially in the daytime and particularly on the DuMont and NBC stations. A year later the researchers found that crime shows had increased to 15% of the total for

■ **Radio to Television: The Goldbergs**   Running on CBS television from January 1949 to September 1953, *The Goldbergs* was based on a long-running radio series about the daily lives of a poor Jewish family in the Bronx. The program was built around the character of Molly, played by program creator Gertrude Berg.

Photo credit: Photofest.

■ **The Great TV Comedy Teams** Two mainstays of network television programming in the 1950s were the situation comedy—epitomized by Lucille Ball (left) in the original 1951–1961 *I Love Lucy*, with Vivian Vance and William Frawley (as Fred and Ethel Mertz), and then-husband Desi Arnaz (right)—and the comedy-variety program, such as (on facing page) *Your Show of Shows*, in which Sid Caesar and Imogene Coca and possibly the best-ever team of writers brightened the screen with sophisticated humor.

Photo credit: Photofest

New York, thus giving 25% of the programs over to what the NAEB termed portrayals of lawlessness (crime and western combined) while variety shows had declined. The NAEB later found basically similar conditions in Los Angeles and Chicago television: predominantly entertainment with emphasis on action-adventure drama. Advertising took up about 20% of the broadcast time in Los Angeles compared to about 15% in New York, including some program-length pitches.

The industry's own awards stressed entertainment too. The annual Emmy Awards, named after the image orthicon television camera tube, or

Photo courtesy of National Broadcasting Company Inc.

immy, were first made in 1949 for the previous season. For three years, they honored only entertainment programs over Los Angeles stations. Six awards were made in 1949 and 11 in 1950. In February 1952 the awards attained coast-to-coast coverage and applied to national content. Six awards that year went to entertainment programs and one to Senator Estes Kefauver (see p. 312).

With the single exception of sports broadcasts, variety programs were more abundant on network television evening prime time than any other type during this period. And, just as radio networks had prospered with

Amos 'n' Andy, so did television expand on the antics of Milton Berle. Labeled by extensive publicity as "Mr. Television," or "Uncle Miltie," Berle was the host and chief screwball of *Texaco Star Theater*, which began on June 8, 1948, and was amazingly popular—far more popular than the Fred Allen radio program with the same name for the same sponsor—for the next five years. Berle knew how to use the visual "sight gags" possible only on television and was happy to make a fool of himself. He delivered one-liners and topical jokes, used weird costumes and settings, and had top-flight guest stars who joined in the antics. For an audience becoming used to television, the combination was highly entertaining.

A calmer version of the variety show—actually, closer in spirit to vaudeville—was *Toast of the Town*, which began on June 20, 1948, with Broadway gossip columnist Ed Sullivan as host and lasted more than two decades as the *Ed Sullivan Show.* Sullivan was wooden and ill at ease in front of a crowd, but he had a talent for selecting stars, potential stars, and other acts for his program. The very first program featured the then little-known comedy team of Dean Martin and Jerry Lewis, making their television debut amidst a classical pianist, the Broadway composer–author team of Richard Rodgers and Oscar Hammerstein II, and a boxing referee. This mixture of high culture, popular interest, and three-ring circus became the hallmark of several television shows, all modeled to some extent on Sullivan's.

Many other long-lasting television stars started in these early years of network television. Garry Moore began a daytime variety show in 1950 and was on television in various capacities for decades. In Chicago, *Garroway at Large* began in 1949, a low-key program epitomizing the "Chicago School" of television and reflecting the low profile approach of Dave Garroway. Three years later, Garroway was the initial host on NBC's *Today* show. Suffering at first from its early hour of 7 A.M. (ET) and perhaps excessive gimmicks, this live two-hour combination of news, weather, features, interviews, and some performances, programmed with short lengths of viewer attention in mind, made *Today* a lasting fixture. *Today*, and its sister *Tonight* show, hosted over the years by Steve Allen, Jack Paar, Johnny Carson, and Jay Leno are good examples of unique television formats—both devised by NBC's brilliant network chief of the early 1950s, Sylvester "Pat" Weaver.

Another rapidly accepted staple of early television was the talent contest, a radio holdover made more interesting to both performer and listener by the addition of sight. In 1949 the long-running *Original Amateur Hour* (see p. 182) went on television, now under the direction of Ted Mack, as did radio personality Arthur Godfrey's *Talent Scouts.* Both programs were to last a decade or more on network television, spurring some local station copies.

A common musical format of early television was the 15-minute or half-hour *filler* show (though few called it that then) featuring a singer or orchestra playing popular music interspersed with ads. Local stations favored such programs because they were simple and inexpensive to produce, with few or no guest stars or other gimmicks. Some were built around well-known orchestras (e.g., Paul Whiteman, Wayne King) and singers (e.g., Vaughn Monroe, Kate Smith) but other programs created stars. One was a former Pennsylvania barber named Perry Como, whose relaxed informality—he looked out of place in a necktie—brought him a network program in 1950 after two years as a featured personality in a variety show. However, some well-known performers did not "make it" on the intimate medium of television. One was Frank Sinatra, a spectacular recording and radio artist, who did not do as well in television in the 1950–1952 seasons, or again in 1957–1958.

A musical program built more on an idea than on its stars—one of whom was Sinatra—was *Your Hit Parade*, which had run for 15 years on radio when it moved to television in 1950. The program played the top-selling tunes of the week selected by a "survey," plus a few extras. Extensive sets and dances helped maintain interest, especially when the same tunes were in the "top ten" for weeks. When the faster paced rock music came in, often instrumental and dependent for success on the styling of a particular artist or group, this type of program went into decline.

As on radio, little "serious" or classical music appeared on television. *Voice of Firestone*, beginning in 1950, was one of the few such programs regularly shown. Although it was attractive to its sponsor and audience, the network killed the program because the audience was too small to provide audience flow to adjacent programs. A cultural highlight of television's early years was Gian Carlo Menotti's opera, *Amahl and the Night Visitors*, which was commissioned by NBC and first shown on Christmas Eve 1951. An estimated five million viewers, at that time a sizable audience, viewed it in the first of many Christmastime showings.

Music and variety formats were important from the start but never dominated the medium as they did radio. Although they were "good television," they were expensive and not well suited to the visual element of television. The particular advantage of variety and musical programs in the early days of television was that they could be simulcast on radio with little or no loss in content.

The situation comedy rapidly became a mainstay of television programming. A number of such programs came directly from radio in 1948 and 1949, with others following later. Among the most popular programs were the *Life of Riley* with William Bendix, one of the earliest programs dealing with a blue-collar worker; *Our Miss Brooks*, a wisecracking teacher played by Eve Arden; *The Goldbergs*, written by and starring Gertrude Berg in a Jewish, New York setting; and *Amos 'n' Andy*, with black actors playing the leads instead of originators Gosden and Correll. The last left the air finally in 1966 because blacks resented the stereotypes and whites never related to it as they had to the radio version.

I Love Lucy appeared in 1951 and set a standard for television comedy for decades to come (see p. 306). On the surface, it was just another situation comedy, but the combination of the zany Lucille Ball, her Cuban husband

Desi Arnaz (until they were divorced in real life), and a fine supporting cast instantly gave it a high rating. Under varied titles and with changes of cast, the show stayed on the air until the 1970s. One show was particularly memorable—when nature and art combined to have Lucille Ball and "Lucy Ricardo" give birth during the same week. Many years later, the son joined the cast. Another long-lasting situation comedy reflected something of a real life marriage. *Ozzie and Harriet*, formerly a radio program (see p. 243) starred the real family of bandleader Ozzie Nelson.

Other comedy also caught on, particularly programs such as Jack Benny's, or (George) *Burns and* (Gracie) *Allen.* On television, these programs were a mixture of situation comedy and variety. One of the best was *Your Show of Shows*, a variety format with great writing and inspired sketches by Sid Caesar, Imogene Coca, and a supporting cast that included Carl Reiner. The unusual 90-minute format focused on Caesar's satiric commentary on everyday life, and became such a classic that a film put together from old kinescopes was successful in the 1970s. Bob Hope did stand-up humor and slapstick sketches on several programs before his own *Bob Hope Show* debuted in 1952. Except for some of the longer variety formats, the television comedy show dealt for a half-hour with a narrow range of predictable, but often funny, situations featuring actor-comedians, frequently unknowns, of varying quality.

Another early genre was the half-hour crime-detective show, long a radio staple. The best known was *Dragnet*, which began on television in 1951 with a low-key, starkly realistic portrayal of a Los Angeles police team at work. Its musical theme became instantly recognizable, and its approach, use of jargon, and true-to-life characters became a model for many police-based series. Most other early shows, some of which had transferred from radio, were low-budget and relied on violence, before it was of much concern, rather than on plot or characterization.

However, these first years of network television are perhaps best remembered for their path-breaking work in prestige anthology drama. In the 1948–1949 season *Studio One, Philco Playhouse*, and *Kraft Theater* all went on the air live for a half-hour or more each week. "Anthology" programs used a different cast and story each week, staying away from the stereotyping and restrictions of the weekly serial or situation series. Many present television stars, and a number of film and stage personalities, entered television in these programs. Slightly less prestigious were anthology series hosted by a movie star; Ronald Reagan for *Death Valley Days* or Loretta Young, who might play a role in several shows a year. *Studio One*, on CBS, programmed adaptations of novels, stories, or plays, while *Philco Playhouse* aired original drama. These and other drama programs provided a valuable outlet and training ground for stage or radio actors and new plays; the legitimate theater and television were much closer at this time than the motion picture industry and television, partly because most television production was in Broadway's backyard. By 1951, 16 anthology series, each presenting a different live drama each week, made up 12% of prime time programming. While such programs had great audience appeal at first, partly due to the higher income and education of early set owners, anthology audiences began to drop off as program costs doubled from 1949 to 1952 and a larger audience wanted diversion rather than serious drama.

Most early programming for children of school age also used the dramatic format. One popular format was the western (there were no "adult westerns" until the mid-1950s) including *Hopalong Cassidy, The Lone Ranger*, and *The Cisco Kid*. Originally network programs, they have returned over and over again in syndication. A few of these, produced by farseeing creators, were shot in color and had a revival in later years, when color telecasting came along. Another children's program type was the science-fiction thriller such as *Captain Video, Tom Corbett, Space Cadet*, or the first (1950) television version of *Superman*. This series, based on the hero of radio, comics, and films, was another example of the universality of a good archetype or gimmick.

A favorite of the youngest audiences was the children's equivalent of the variety show: circus, puppet, or animal. Some of them were *Super Circus* (1949), with music, circus acts, animals, and, of course, clowns; the immensely popular *Howdy Doody*, which began in New York in 1947; and the appealing *Kukla, Fran, and Ollie*, a Chicago product with the very human Fran Allison and two Burr Tillstrom puppets. Although attracting adults as well as children, *Kukla, Fran, and Ollie* did not have the audience size of *Howdy Doody*, which featured a western puppet character, host Buffalo Bob Smith, Clarabelle the clown, and a "peanut gallery" of children in the studio. It was a late afternoon "must" until 1960, and Buffalo Bob Smith was able to tour colleges successfully for another decade or more, reaching the same audience. In 1952 a program aimed at the youngest preschoolers, *Ding Dong School*, offered the conversation, low-key instruction, commercials, and entertainment of Miss Frances, a former professional teacher.

The remaining important format with respect to time on the air and audience size was sports programming. Boxing, basketball, and bowling were most common in 1948 and 1949 but dropped sharply within four years. The Wednesday and Friday night prizefight telecasts, together with baseball's World Series and special events in golf and racing, enlarged television's audience in neighborhood bars more than almost any other format. Throughout this period, wrestling and roller derby matches offered more spectacle than sport, and their stars became well-known personalities. These programs, often scripted, were not intended as pure sports contests; wrestling, in particular, was often played as melodrama.

Quiz and panel programs came over from radio as mainstays of both evening and daytime television programming. One of the first was the Goodson-Todman production firm's *What's My Line?*, which began in 1950 and was still showing in syndicated form decades later. Somehow, its panel of articulate celebrities trying to guess a contestant's occupation held audience interest. Others of this genre were *I've Got a Secret*; the *Quiz Kids*, featuring child prodigies and playing more on human interest than knowledge; *Beat the Clock; Strike It Rich* (the show with a "heart line" for announcement of donated special prizes for those with tear-jerking problems); *Truth or Consequences*; and *Queen for a Day* (see p. 299). Groucho Marx's *You Bet Your Life* was more a vehicle for Groucho's talk and gags than a true quiz show. Appealing to many who also liked quiz programs was *This Is Your Life*, where host Ralph Edwards surprised a famous personality by confronting him or her with persons from the past, who would tell the personality's life story and engage in tearful reunions.

7.6.4 Rise of Television Journalism

Radio news in the 1946–1952 period was dominated by radio, newspaper and wire service newsmen who had reported World War II. Edward R. Murrow, the best known, became a CBS network vice president and member of the board—positions he soon gave up for full-time news work on both radio and television. Network and local newscasts, a legacy of the immediate prewar and war years, continued although reduced in number of hours from the wartime peak. The audience still turned to radio for fast-breaking news. News veterans who broadcast into their second and even third decades were Drew Pearson; Edwin C. Hill; Fulton Lewis, Jr.; Gabriel Heatter; Lowell Thomas, whose nightly news program on NBC and later CBS lasted from 1930 to 1976; and Walter Winchell, who often spoke more gossip than solid news. One of the more famous and long-running news interview programs, *Meet the Press*, began during this period, as did *Capitol Cloakroom*, which presented interviews with senators and representatives.

Both NBC and CBS televised daily 15-minute newscasts in the networks' first season. The NBC *Camel News Caravan* had John Cameron Swayze narrating clips of newsreel film, while *Douglas Edwards with the News* did the same on CBS. Swayze was to last until 1956 and Edwards until 1962.

Supplementing regular newscasts was a series of special events. In 1951 television covered the welcome given General Douglas MacArthur after President Truman had relieved him of command in Korea, and the closing ceremonies of the San Francisco peace conference that officially ended the war with Japan. Perhaps the televising of the 1950 and 1951 Senate hearings into organized crime in the United States made the greatest audience impact. As the little-known Tennessee Senator Estes Kefauver chaired hearings for weeks in various parts of the country, viewers saw the world of organized crime unfold. The high point was the testimony of reputed gangster leader Frank Costello, who demanded that the cameras stay off his face—so they focused on his hands instead. The nervous movement of the hands, tied to what he was saying, clearly portrayed a man under extreme pressure. These hearings informed the country about organized crime and catapulted Kefauver into the limelight in time for the 1952 presidential race.

The first television public-affairs series on a network was *See It Now*, hosted by Edward R. Murrow and produced by Fred W. Friendly, the team that had created radio's *Hear It Now*. Beginning in 1951, this weekly half-hour program usually focused on a newsworthy and often controversial (see p. 378) person or news event.

7.6.5 Election Broadcasting

Another indication of the passing of an age was the 1948 election campaign. That radio still could make or break candidates was demonstrated in a Portland, Oregon, debate between Harold Stassen, former governor of Minnesota, and front-running Governor Thomas E. Dewey of New York, both Republican presidential candidates. The two men debated whether the Communist party should be outlawed. Stassen lost the debate with his poorly expressed liberal views and subsequently lost the primary to Dewey. Given the political realities of that year, at the height of the cold war with the Soviet Union, both Dewey and the polls figured he had the November election in the bag. But on radio, although Dewey was the "better" speaker, with a more traditional "radio voice" than his opponent, President Harry S Truman, he tended to speak over the heads of his audience. Truman had the difficult task of offsetting minority party incursions from Progressive Party nominee Henry Wallace on the Democratic left and States' Rights Party nominee J. Strom Thurmond on the right. Truman's radio talks were sometimes abruptly cut off for lack of funds to pay for the entire program, although the parties also heavily used spot announcements and short political programs. Truman won a famous political upset and by 1951 became the first President to allow audio recording of his news conferences—at first just for checking reporters' notes but a few months later for direct broadcasts.

The 1952 presidential campaign was the first to be televised nationally to a majority of the population, although some politicians had appeared on camera as early as 1928 and the 1948 campaign had been covered in cities with television. Both conventions, and preconvention primaries, were broadcast. However, the highlight of the election year—ironic in relation to the events that occurred 22 years later—was the September 23, 1952 nationally televised address of the GOP vice-presidential candidate, Senator Richard M. Nixon of California. Nixon had been accused of having access to a multi-thousand-dollar secret "slush fund" given to him by supporters. General Eisenhower, the Republican presidential nominee, was ready to dump Nixon, but the latter asked for a chance to clear himself. That night Nixon, speaking without notes, explained his financial condition in a half-hour, emotional address later called the "Checkers" speech, because of its reference to a pet dog his daughters had been given and were going to keep "no matter what." Listeners reacted to the speech with telegrams and calls urging the GOP leaders to keep Nixon on the ticket. The rest of the election was predictable, although neither major candidate came across well on television: Eisenhower because he bumbled and often misspoke or mispronounced words, and Illinois Governor Adlai Stevenson because he often spoke over the heads of his listeners. In Massachusetts, Congressman John F. Kennedy won a Senate seat against incumbent Henry Cabot Lodge after a series of televised debates. The television networks provided detailed election-night coverage for the first time. Nationally, the 1952 campaign proved the value of television spot advertisements for making voters aware of candidates rapidly and was the start of politicians' concern with television *image.*

In five years or so, television networks and stations had developed most of the program formats the medium would use for decades to come. The prior existence of radio had enhanced the growth of television, which used many of the same shows and performers—particularly in these transitional years when many shows were presented on both media at the same time.

7.7 The Increasing Demand for Broadcast Services

Audience attention immediately after the war focused not on television but on radio. Television was no closer in 1946 to most Americans than it had been in 1941 when only a few thousand people had receivers in a few cities. Readers of magazine and newspaper stories knew about television, but immediate ownership was beyond most people. Far more concern centered on radio—how to get those old sets repaired or replaced. After four years of war there was a tremendous demand for radio receivers—and everything else.

7.7.1 Meeting the Continuing Demand for Radio

As can be seen in Appendix C, table 6-A, the number of radio families increased by nearly 10 million in the 1945–1952 period. At the same time, the number of cars with radios more than doubled so that, by 1951–1952 a majority of cars had radio. These bare figures hide a number of interesting developments.

Virtually all manufacturing effort was put into the AM market in the postwar 1940s. More than 50 million AM receivers were made in 1946–1948 alone, to replace older sets and satisfy the major immediate postwar demand. The phenomenon of the multiset household bloomed: as radio prices came down, the number of sets per household increased. Bedrooms and kitchens now contained small $15 table model receivers with plastic cases and simplified internal circuitry, in addition to larger sets in living rooms.

For FM radio, the story was different. Two things combined to hold down receiver production: the 1945 allocation change for FM, which forced major reengineering by the manufacturers, and the great demand for AM sets. Naturally, with all major companies tooled up for the ready-made AM radio market, it got precedence. While more than 50 million inexpensive AM sets came off the lines, FM production was limited to only 2.9 million units in the 1946–1948 period—less than 6% of AM production. Furthermore, FM sets cost $50 or more, as they were more complicated and manufacturers had start-up costs to recover.

Much FM production was of large and expensive console radios and television sets. Because the new FM band was located just above VHF television channel 6, and because television's sound system was FM, about one-third of the television sets made in the late 1940s had FM radio reception capability built in. This proportion dropped to 20% by 1952 and disappeared a few years later. As FM's fortunes waned, FM trade groups and set makers tried to promote FM receiver purchases, but few urban areas had more than 10% FM set penetration by 1952. Caught between the lack of audience and too few stations to attract any, FM broadcasting found itself unable to break the vicious circle before the 1960s (see pp. 349–351).

7.7.2 Trends in Television Receivers

Unlike AM and FM radio, television had to build its postwar audience from scratch. Only a fraction of the 8,000 to 10,000 receivers in use before the war were still working when peace came. In 1946, some 6,500 were made and sold in New York, Los Angeles, Chicago, Philadelphia—communities that had stations on the air at that time. Television set manufacture started slowly because of AM demand, supply bottlenecks (picture tubes, for example), uncertainty over final spectrum allocations (see pp. 253–256), the possibility of black-and-white obsolescence due to color, and the chicken-or-egg relationship between high prices and consumer demand. Picture tubes, blown and shaped by hand at first, could not be made in quantity. Some early sets were sold in kit form to meet demand and reduce price. DuMont announced the first postwar television receivers for sale in May 1946, followed several weeks later by RCA. Philco came into the market in 1947 and many others by 1949, although the sales process was confused and unorganized.

A television set was a sizable investment. The typical 5-inch to 7-inch receiver cost from $375 to $500 in mid-1948—several weeks' pay for the average worker. In addition, the buyer paid an installation fee ranging from $45 to $300, depending on antenna requirements, and usually invested in a one-year service contract and a roof-top antenna, especially in cities more than 30 miles from the transmitter. Fully three-fourths of early receiver production went to East Coast cities; half to New York. The small screen sizes led to a brisk market in large magnifiers, costing from $10 to $60 each, set in front of the receiver to enlarge the picture. In 1949 and 1950, larger screen

■ TV Receivers from the Early 1950s   As noted in the text, the earliest (1947–1950) television receivers were expensive, often costing several hundred dollars. These newspaper ads of the early 1950s taken from metropolitan papers give an idea of what was available then for what price. Multiply by seven to approximate 2001 dollars. All sets then were black and white.

9-PC-41
Projection **$795**
model
Plus $3.61
Fed. Tax

Motorola

TABLE
MODEL
TELEVISION
WITH
BIG 16-INCH
PICTURE!

- Big-as-life pictures on 16-inch rectangular tube!
- Easy to operate, just two simple controls!
- Built-in antenna gives powerful performance!
- "Performance Tested" to insure you long, dependable service!
- Beautifully styled, modern, walnut-effect bakelite cabinet!
- Pictures clearer than ever, just as the TV camera "sees" them!

MODEL 17-T-3

$219.95
Plus
Tax and
Warranty

Big 12½-Inch Television!

new
"BROADVIEW"
SCREEN
gives 25% more
picture area

SIMPLIFIED
CONTROLS
even a child
can operate it!

Brighter,

clearer, steadier pictures

by *Motorola*

Here's a big screen permitting an entire roomful of people to see comfortably. Features the new BILT-IN-TENNA—no installation in "good signal" areas. Here's cabinet beauty to complement your lovely furniture. Hand rubbed to satin-smooth "piano finish." Mahogany or blond. See it, hear it, compare it today. CONVENIENT TERMS.

New Zenith TV Console

Model 2438R. 165 sq. in. "2-in-1" screen. 18th century cabinet, mahogany veneers and hardwoods. Only

$319.95
Plus Fed. Tax

*Model
Shown
Only* **$279.**95 $6.00 includes 1 year
parts warran-
ty and tax.

sizes were made, with the 10-inch set becoming the standard, although DuMont, long a leader in this area, offered a $500, 20-inch tube (not complete set) as early as 1947. Zenith introduced a circular picture (actually, almost all tubes then were circular but covered with a rectangular mask) and garnered a good portion of the market in 1949–1950 before rectangular tubes were marketed. Although the screen looked larger, the circular shape chopped off much of the sides of the rectangular picture being transmitted. As set sales increased and competition became stronger, the cost of receivers dropped so that a typical small-screen set cost only $200 by the early 1950s. Manufacture was slightly limited after 1951 by the Korean War military equipment demands (see p. 323).

Still, the television audience increased (see Appendix C, table 7-A) from almost zero to more than one-third of the nation's homes in the few years covered in this chapter. As the number of set owners grew, the market became more organized and inadequate manufacturers and sales organizations were squeezed out. The installation charge came down sharply or was eliminated. In 1952 not only was a television receiver a far better product, with a much larger screen, but it sold for perhaps half of its 1948 price. Most people saw their first television program in a public place, either a store window or a neighborhood bar—"We have TV" signs were a sure-fire come-on, especially just before a major sports event. With that initial exposure and increasing advertising by television stations and sales outlets, a few families made the plunge, and then more followed.

The receiver soon dominated the early television home. It usually went into the living room, relegating radio to another room, and became the center of attention for the family, and their non-television-owning friends. Some families without sets installed outside antennas in order to keep up with their neighbors. For the first week or two the family looked at virtually every program and marveled at the phenomenon. Slowly, the fascination declined, and individual family members began to watch specific programs. In a very short time, television replaced most radio, reading, and weekend movies—to the detriment of the other media.

Television's expansion was much faster than radio's: radio had taken a decade to reach a 33% penetration, but television managed it in only seven years. Initially, the large cities and the Northeast generally had more sets than elsewhere. Although people in rural areas without stations, particularly in the South and Midwest, went to great lengths to receive distant signals, these regions naturally had the slowest rate of television set sales.

7.7.3 Developments in Audience Research

In the late 1940s, the last years of AM radio hegemony over broadcasting, two excellent major surveys of public attitudes toward radio and its content appeared, both under the direction of Paul Lazarsfeld. *The People Look at*

Radio (1946) showed that the vast majority of persons surveyed in 1945 thought the radio did a good or excellent job, ranking higher than the churches, newspapers, schools, or local government. An expanded and updated survey published in 1948 as *Radio Listening in America* showed that, while television was just getting underway, the majority of listeners still liked radio, but it had slipped in favor of newspapers as the prime source of news now that the war was over. These volumes provide a useful picture of the radio audience just before television radically changed audience habits and views.

Prior to 1950, radio ratings were dominated by C. E. Hooper's "Hooper-ratings," based on coincidental telephone call surveys. With the coming of television, A. C. Nielsen's meter-produced ratings (see pp. 205–206 and 247–248) began to cut into Hooper's near-monopoly. Clients endlessly debated the merits of the two systems. Advertisers and broadcasters complained about having to pay for two different services doing the same job, and Hooper began losing clients to Nielsen. Early in 1950 Nielsen purchased Hooper's national rating service, leaving him free to measure individual local markets but giving Nielsen a virtual monopoly over national television ratings. Nielsen has provided meter-based national television ratings ever since, although other companies later participated (see pp. 384–385).

Until 1952 most research into television viewing habits was simple: who owned sets, how much they watched, and what products and services they bought. A New York advertising agency began periodically and systematically to poll a New Jersey town of 40,000 people (dubbed "Videotown") near New York City to see how television was changing the population's lives. The surveys showed having television was prestigious, as well as high satisfaction with television and increasing amounts of time spent watching it daily. Families tended to be together more of the day because of television, but it was soon realized that a family watching television did not necessarily communicate more; they just sat in silence and watched, sometimes with their non-television-owning visitors.

Television was recognized as different in many ways from radio. For one thing, since it required less imagination than radio, it focused attention more than radio. Television made personalities appear more human when seen as well as heard, gave the viewer a sense of sharing in events, and appealed to young children. These capabilities forewarned social scientists of its potential impact on families and American life.

Each of the networks issued research reports for agencies and affiliates, and these today make excellent snapshot views of television's progress. They show that the early television-owning American household was not typical but had a higher income (receivers were expensive) and above-average education. Early audience profiles also showed that television-owning families were larger and younger, spent more time every day with television than with all other media combined, and bought more products in general (and cars and appliances in particular). But most Americans, especially those removed from large cities or the Northeast, probably did *not* own a television set.

At least one concern of the 1970s cropped up in the first days of television: its effect on young children. Suddenly the home environment harbored a medium with sound and pictures less easily controlled than other media and attractive to very young children. Television critic Robert Lewis Shayon's *Television and Our Children* suggested that the answer to such problems lay in family control over their children's viewing habits and in organized community action to encourage better children's programming and less violence on the air. Such arguments grew louder in the decades to come (see pp. 385–386 and 457–459).

7.8 Regulating Expansion

The Federal Communications Commission found itself in the thick of the broadcasting transition of the 1945–1952 period. Probably the most important and certainly the most time-consuming controversy was television allocation—how to apportion sufficient channels to allow a choice of content in most regions without sanctioning interference from or to stations already on the air. At the same time, the commission issued its clearest statement yet on "public service responsibility" for broadcast licensees; the commission's staff fretted over the increasing number of radio stations trying to divide a relatively static advertising pie; a Chicago union leader was tying broadcasters into knots; and the industry was acquiescing in the blacklisting of entertainers accused of communist sympathies.

7.8.1 Mess in the Making: 1945 through 1948

As the war ended, there were enough television channels and enough skepticism about television's future in the smaller markets that an applicant could easily obtain a license. However, in larger markets, particularly in the crowded Northeast, there were not enough channels. The FCC engineering staff tried to apply sound engineering standards in assigning channels to the various cities and to avoid co-channel interference by allowing sufficient geographical distance between stations on the same channel. Their plan, based on the May and June 1945 decisions (see pp. 253–256), specified the communities for licenses, market-by-market, and the number of stations, or channels, at each location. This would ensure some coverage for rural areas and would ease the administrative burdens on both commission and applicant, since expensive engineering surveys would be unnecessary. The only alternative would have been a grab bag analogous to the unsatisfactory AM radio solution: Letting applicants fight for what they considered the best channel in the best location, no matter how many stations in other towns thereby could not be started. Since the number of channels, 13, had been determined, the only other major variable was the distance between stations operating on the same or adjacent channels. Power and antenna height were less important variables (see Appendix B, Waves, etc.). Although FCC engineers hoped to allow a margin for safety against interference by 200-mile co-channel spacing, such spacing would give New York City—always wanting more stations because it was the nation's largest market—only four of the seven available channels if the rest of the congested portion of the Eastern Seaboard was to get adequate service. (Since adjacent channels would give interference if used in the same market, only 7 of 13 could be used in any one city.) The FCC quickly found itself in a political box: New York *had* to have the maximum number of stations, yet, with Congress still dominated by rural interests, service also had to be provided to smaller communities.

The compromise solution, reached after several trials, gave New York its seven channels by eliminating two of the three "community" (low-power) channels and, among other compromises, by locating (in the FCC's own words) "television stations . . . somewhat closer together in the eastern part of the United States than was done in the original Commission proposal." No allocation plan gives something for nothing. In this case, the price of seven channels in New York was neglect of the safety factors previously deemed necessary to protect television against tropospheric interference. Instead of the 200-mile separations proposed originally, the plan adopted by the commission toward the end of 1945 (see pp. 253 ff.) called for separations of only 150 miles. This distance took care of anticipated interference but made no provision for the possibility, particularly at the height of the sunspot cycle, of radio waves traveling, as Armstrong and others had warned, through the lower atmosphere (troposphere) and causing very bad interference between stations on the same channel.

The FCC took steps in 1947 to solve two other problems with the 1945 television allocation plan. First, only one (community) channel was used solely by television; the other 12 channels were shared with the safety and special services. Although the assignments were based on mutual noninterference, this was obviously an impossible standard. Second, establishment of television in Canada and Mexico conflicted with U.S. television.

After considerable thought, the commission in May 1948 deleted channel 1 (44–50 MHz) and turned it over to the safety and special services. In exchange, the other television channels would be free of fixed and mobile services sharing. Although the television industry made a protest as a matter of form, it generally agreed that 12 *exclusive* channels were preferable to 13 channels if 12 of them were subject to sharing. The safety and special services also were pleased at this compromise until they later outgrew channel 1 and had to fight to share some lower UHF television channels in the most congested areas and take over—together with common carriers—the upper 15 UHF channels in 1970. The border station problem was solved by international agreements governing assignments of channels to cities within 250 miles of the border with Mexico in 1951 and Canada in 1952.

The chief problem remained. As television grew in popularity, the demand for new stations became insistent. The commission, apparently unable to foresee the consequences of its actions, repeatedly narrowed the mileage separations between stations on the same or adjacent channels. Although broadcasters were pleased to receive the new channels, safety factors had been thrown away.

By Fall 1948—less than three years after the television broadcasters and potential broadcasters started putting pressure on the FCC through the public and individual congressmen to get stations for *their* cities—it was obvious that a major error had been made. As more stations went on the air, and as the sunspot cycle reached its zenith, the shortcomings of the 1945 allocation table became unbearable. For example, mutual interference between stations in Detroit and Cleveland, a little more than 90 miles apart, was making reception impossible well into the heart of each city. The situation called for drastic action, of a sort not seen since the FRC acting as "traffic policeman of the airwaves" had cleaned up the AM band using the Radio Act of 1927.

In September 1948, with only 50 or so stations on the air but with an additional 50-plus construction permits outstanding, the effect of narrow separations, heightened by the sunspot phenomenon, led to a flood of complaints from broadcasters and the public that the FCC could not ignore. After hearings, on September 29 the commission "ordered applications for new TV stations placed in the pending file." They remained there, not for the six to nine months suggested by FCC Chairman Wayne Coy, but for nearly four years. The reasons for instituting the now-famous *television Freeze* were not the only reasons it took four years to lift. The Freeze provided time for RCA and CBS to continue their fight over color television, committees to resolve the use of UHF frequencies, pressures for an educational channel reservation system to mount, and interference problems to be settled.

7.8.2 The Television Freeze: 1948–1952

The "temporary" Freeze on new television stations lasted until April 14, 1952. Although the FCC acted on no new applications, it allowed stations holding construction permits to go on the air. The people who had television enjoyed expanded programming, but people in other areas looked forward to the end of the Freeze as ardently as the potential licensees.

Arrayed against those wishing access to a competitive television structure were the 108 "pre-Freeze" stations, including the outlets owned and operated by the networks. This group worked in various ways to maintain the Freeze and hold off potential competition, while promoting scarcity and inequality of television channels to ensure the least competition when the Freeze eventually lifted. Manufacturers, too, were glad to sell millions of sets, using well-understood prewar technical standards, to viewers of pre-Freeze stations.

The maneuverings of the haves and have nots focused on a lengthy series of commission hearings, which determined the eventual end of the Freeze and future shape of television. These hearings covered five substantive issues, related chiefly by their differential values to the two groups involved. The issues, not in any special order, were:

1. Color television standards
2. Reduction of tropospheric interference
3. Possible spectrum locations for additional channels
4. City-by-city assignment of channels and criteria for these assignments
5. Educational television channel reservations.

7.8.2.1 *Color Television Standards*

Hindsight tells us that color television standards might better have been considered separately from the main Freeze hearings. Regardless of the motives of participants in the imbroglio, the color phase delayed the end of the Freeze by more than a year. The color controversy was incorporated into the general hearings partly because it raised problems of spectrum allocation until 1949, when both CBS and RCA managed to make their respective systems work within the 6-MHz-channel bandwidth in use for black-and-white television.

Although CBS had lost round one of its fight for a wide-band color system during the 1944 hearings (see p. 253), the setback did not stop the firm for long. While CBS's main field of endeavor had been radio broadcasting, it recognized the potential of television and wanted a place of leadership in the new medium similar to RCA's. Despite the conclusion of most electronic manufacturers and engineers that commercial color television was years in the future, CBS sought to marshal public opinion behind the notion of "color now." In doing so, it may only have confused prospective set buyers. RCA, in order to protect its own extensive investment in color research, was forced into a public demonstration of its admittedly outmoded (1941) system. By showing its system, although RCA protested that a good electronic color system (as contrasted to the mechanical CBS system) was at least five years away, RCA admitted that there was something to the CBS claims after all.

During the hearings, CBS had to contend not only against the public's growing investment in the VHF black-and-white system but against RCA's improved all-electronic compatible color system. Because the CBS system was not compatible, black-and-white sets would be unable to pick up color telecasts in monochrome. Another drawback was the large, noisy, and hard to synchronize and maintain mechanical color wheel used to filter, transmit, and reconstitute the primary colors in sequence, but CBS said that could be overcome by further engineering work. In spite of repeated public statements that RCA would sell its color kinescope (picture playback) tubes to anybody, CBS never was able to purchase any in order to demonstrate that electronic rather than mechanical color reconstitution devices could be used at the receiver end.

RCA, in addition to publicizing the advantages of all-electronic compatible color, which it continued to perfect over the next several years, questioned CBS's motives in asking for immediate color standards. RCA representatives maintained that the industry, happily making black-and-white sets, should agree on new standards before the public heard about them. This was, of course, a complete reversal of RCA's position during the 1940 standards fight, when RCA tried to force through its own standards for commercial use in the face of violent opposition from the industry.

In hearings over its petition, the fringes of the industry supported CBS and the major established firms such as DuMont and Philco supported RCA. The FCC tended to depend on older elements of the industry in preference to CBS, with its limited experience in engineering and manufacturing. The same established companies also supplied most of the leadership for the Radio Technical Planning Board (RTPB) and Radio Manufacturers Association (RMA) committees, to which the FCC continued to listen.

However, after long and acrimonious hearings and demonstrations, the commission approved the CBS color system in October 1950, over the entries of RCA and Color Television, Inc. Neither RCA, which appealed the FCC decision up to the Supreme Court and an 8 to 0 decision in 1951 upholding the commission, nor the rest of the manufacturing industry would accept this decision. John Crosby, columnist for the *New York Herald Tribune*, summed up the color decision in his October 24, 1950, column:

> And God said, Let there be light: and there was light.
>
> And God saw the light, that it was good: and God divided the light from the darkness.
>
> And the FCC saw color and said, "Let there be color," and there was color. Or at least there was an edict decreeing color. And the public tried to divide the black and white from the color and discovered only confusion. Next to the FCC's, God's problem was comparatively simple.

Few CBS-standard color sets ever were made, although the company purchased some manufacturing facilities to make its challenge of RCA credible. While manufacturers were balking at the idea of constructing non-compatible, clumsy small-screen television sets and paying CBS a royalty for the privilege, RCA worked hastily to improve its own system. CBS recognized that its meager support would soon evaporate, since the new compatible RCA system would not disrupt existing television broadcasting, stop the profitable manufacture of black-and-white sets, cause public resentment over sets that would become obsolete overnight (even though CBS proposed that monochrome television on the VHF band be continued, for a while, at least) or cost the manufacturing industry additional royalties. Accordingly, the decision by the National Production Administration (NPA) in October 1951 that color television was "nonessential" to the stepped-up Korean War effort had the effect of getting CBS off the hook. The FCC also learned that it was unable to control the manufacturing industry and force the innovation of something the industry did not want.

Although in December 1953 the FCC rescinded its 1950 order approving the CBS system and approved RCA color—in the slightly improved and modified version recommended by the National Television System Committee (NTSC)—manufacturers showed almost as little inclination to go ahead with RCA as with CBS color. The industry had no reason to consider color until the vast market for monochrome sets became saturated, and the cost was too high ($1,000 and up per set) and there were too few color programs for the public to buy many of the complicated RCA sets.

The war between CBS and RCA really had ended with the NPA decision to halt production of CBS color-standard sets. After some bitter words between RCA's Sarnoff and CBS's Stanton, even CBS joined the NTSC effort to perfect a compatible color system. Although CBS had not been able to innovate its color system, in a sense it had won the war. Not only had the NPA order saved it from incurring serious loss, but it had gained time needed to compete with RCA in the television broadcasting field. RCA held the trophy of having its color system accepted but, as we shall see later, could not persuade the broadcasting and manufacturing industries to accept color fully for more than a decade. As a footnote to the CBS system, it should be noted that specialized medical closed-circuit television units used the slightly better color rendition of the CBS system for many years and that color pictures transmitted from the moon in the early 1970s came from CBS-type cameras—built by RCA! There were a number of self-satisfied smiles around CBS when the moon pictures came through.

7.8.2.2 *Interference Reduction*

Since the most obvious cure for tropospheric interference is increased mileage between stations on the same channel, this problem could be and was solved within a few months, although the specific solution was not promulgated until the Freeze ended in 1952. Technical developments, such as *offset carrier*, by making it easier to tune stations also would alleviate the problem without affecting home reception. Instead of the 150-mile or less separations it had approved in reports and decisions from 1945 through 1947, the commission toyed in 1949 with extremely rigid standards of 220-mile VHF co-channel separations. But in its 1952 *Sixth Report and Order*, the FCC imposed 190-mile co-channel separations over most of the country. In the Gulf states, where propagation characteristics were different, the new standard was 220 miles. In the crowded Northeast, the FCC had to compromise, with a 170-mile standard. No station had to leave the air, but several were moved about on the VHF band in order to eliminate the worst examples of interference, such as in the Detroit-Cleveland area (see p. 320).

The commission held firmly to these new standards after they were established. Having once been burned, it was unwilling to reduce safety margins again, even though many of its prediction formulas came under attack as being inconsistent with measured characteristics of signals. To provide a third channel for Pittsburgh, it created a complicated new rule allowing a shift in assigned channel to a community within 15 miles of a listed major community rather than supporting a co-channel situation short-spaced by little more than a half-mile. Most observers applauded the greater separations, particularly the 108 "pre-Freeze" stations, which would face less competition from new licensees. However, parties that wished to obtain VHF channels after the Freeze objected, claiming that a bit of interference was a small price to pay for healthy competition and multiple program sources, since increases in separation meant fewer local stations.

7.8.2.3 *Obtaining Additional Channels*

To provide for a competitive nationwide television system, the commission had to find more channels for television. Increasing co-channel mileage separations reduced the number of stations possible on the 12 remaining VHF channels and made the problem worse. However, even those in favor of greater access were not in favor of starting in the untried UHF band, with its concomitant problem of receiver conversion. Accordingly, the FCC made unsuccessful attempts for a number of years to obtain additional VHF channels from the military and the FM band. Although for a while in the mid-1950s FM, then in the doldrums, had to fight hard to retain the 88 to 108-MHz band (see p. 350), the FCC was unable to overcome the political support FM enjoyed as a legacy from Armstrong's efforts. The military flatly refused to turn over a great amount of its spectrum to television, even after several requests and studies. The Department of Defense argued that the "national security" required the reservation of these frequencies, even if they were not in full use.

The "outs" made some proposals that would have shoehorned in additional stations through less than maximum power, directional antennae, and reduced mileage separations. The FCC, with the growing administrative problem of allocation of the AM band as a warning, and also with a tender regard for the established service areas of the pre-Freeze stations, turned down these proposals.

Of necessity, the question became not *whether* to utilize the UHF band (470–890 MHz) set aside in 1945 for television experimentation and future broadcasting but, rather, *how much* of it to use. Proposals ranged from a half-dozen channels up to the maximum possible, 70. To counteract the advantages enjoyed by the established pre-Freeze stations, it was suggested that *all* television be moved to the UHF band. The commission rejected this proposal, because of the already huge investment in VHF transmitters and receivers and because the propagational characteristics of the UHF band were such that some persons in rural areas would lose reception if the bands were changed.

The commission decided to allocate the entire 70 UHF channels to television but then restricted the upper end (channels 70–83) to low-power translators and other devices that provide television service inexpensively to smaller communities, and eventually turned it over to other services (see p. 416). Of extreme importance, the commission made no move to transfer all television from the VHF to the UHF bands, in spite of vague proposals to that effect that it had made in the mid-1940s (see p. 255).

One interesting experiment, with some implications for later proposed use of space satellites for direct broadcasting, was *Stratovision*. This system, originally proposed by Westinghouse and the Martin aircraft company, consisted of a standard television transmitter built into a transport airplane, which circled at 30,000 feet while sending out television signals. Tests conducted in 1946 and afterward (see p. 292) showed that transmission of this kind could achieve reliable coverage over a circle of from 50 to 200 miles in diameter. Once, the aircraft was used to link up the eastern and midwestern isolated segments of AT&T's coaxial cable network so that the Midwest could enjoy the World Series. Stratovision saved money over the equivalent ground transmitters, but it interfered with assignments of frequencies to ground-based stations and did not accommodate differences in population density. Analogous to AM clear-channel stations and eliminating much of the need for both coaxial cables or microwave linking stations and the many small stations otherwise needed to cover the nation, Stratovision must have seemed attractive to the FCC. However, the same small station operators and members of Congress who earlier had managed to restrict clear-channel AM stations to 50,000 watts objected on the grounds that Stratovision might be monopolistic. The commission dropped the idea when it found that some 20 channels would be needed to supply the entire nation with four signals and that the necessary perturbations of the aircraft would disastrously affect the principles of "fair, efficient and equitable distribution of television facilities to the various communities." Westinghouse donated the equipment to a university, and the principle was ignored until Midwest Program on Airborne Television Instruction (MPATI) started flying in the 1960s using nonbroadcast channels (see p. 423), and proposals for direct-to-home space satellite broadcasting became more frequent in the 1970s (see p. 411).

7.8.2.4 *City-by-City Assignments*

Despite the pleas of potential broadcasters hoping for equality of access to a given community and of ABC and DuMont, the FCC finally assigned channels to communities by a system of priorities. These priorities ignored population density, the key to successful advertiser-supported station operation, and adopted a strict interpretation of Section 307(b) of the Communications Act, which calls for a fair geographic apportionment of channels to the several states and to the United States as a whole. Multiple services or programming choices for the public were only a secondary priority.

The published priorities were to provide:

1. At least one television service to all parts of the United States.
2. At least one outlet for local expression (station) to each community.
3. A choice of at least two services to all areas.
4. At least two program outlets or stations to each community.

Assignments of channels that remained unassigned would follow the same pattern. Educational reservations (see p. 327) would be assigned to major educational centers, and to larger cities in a proportion of one educational for every four commercial assignments. Above all, the boat would not be rocked if possible: no existing station would be moved from a VHF to a UHF channel, or even from a lower (channels 2–6) to a higher (channels 7–13) VHF channel. However, under the FCC plan, almost all cities would be intermixed with both UHF and VHF channels assigned in the same community.

Channels would be assigned through an *assignment table*—a technique devised by the commission in the mid-1940s for both television and FM. Although the FCC originally referred to a television "allocation table" when distributing channels city-by-city, it really meant "assignment table," the term used in the United States for many years but replaced in the early 1980s by "allotment." This chapter will use the term *assignment* for the earmarking of a channel for a given community or user, and the term *allocation* for the setting apart of a group of channels for a given service, such as television. (See Appendix B.) Without such a table, an applicant for a station in an eastern state would be in competition with all applicants east of the Mississippi. The FCC had successfully defended this technique in court and further strengthened it in the preliminary (1951) and final (1952) reports ending the Freeze, by holding that applicants for a channel not specified in the table would have to secure an amendment through lengthy and costly rulemaking proceedings—a major deterrent to making such changes. The only flexibility was to permit unlisted cities to apply for UHF "flexibility" channels and, as mentioned earlier, to allow an applicant in an unlisted town within 15 miles of a listed city to apply for assignment of a channel that met the mileage separation rules for the town in order to serve the city. Los Angeles joined New York in having seven VHF channels and several UHF channels assigned, largely because most of the VHF channels were already on the air. No other cities had as many VHF channels assigned.

The maneuvering among applicants for real or imaginary advantages of channel assignment or speed of obtaining a license could fill another book. City fought city, existing station fought applicant, and applicant fought applicant—but all parties grew weary and accepted most commission decisions, even DuMont, which had proposed its own nationwide assignment scheme based on different separation standards. The adopted assignment table, as amended in some cases, still determines availability of channels.

7.8.2.5 *ETV Reservations*

Educators hailed a suballocation within both the UHF and VHF bands to noncommercial educational television broadcasting, but it further restricted the number of channels assigned for commercial use in a given community. Reservation of educational channels in the assignment table was an advance over the practices on the AM band, where some 200 stations licensed to educational institutions in the 1920s had shrunk to a bare two dozen in the 1950s (see pp. 78, 122–123 and 175–177). However, it did not go as far as the FM separate educational allocation of 20 specifically inviolate channels contiguous to the commercial FM band, which any FM set could receive.

The ETV suballocation, or rather assignment, was championed by Commissioner Frieda Hennock who, with the aid of educational organizations (see pp. 291–292), persuaded the commission to adopt reservations for educational television. Educators gradually realized that this might be their only chance to obtain broadcast channels and soon became an effective lobby. First enunciated in 1951, the criteria for establishing a reservation were explained in the FCC's *Sixth Report and Order* of April 1952 (see pp. 328–330): When more than three VHF channels were assigned to a city, one would be for education. Forty-six educational centers also would receive a reservation, 23 of them the only VHF channel in the community. A UHF channel would be reserved where a given market, not an educational center, had *fewer* than three VHF assignments or where all VHF channels already were in use. Unlike FM, the reservations could be for any of the 82 television channels.

Opposition to these reservations was strong but unsuccessful. It came chiefly from DuMont and others who were fearful of establishing channel scarcity in major markets. Other objectors included the NAB, which suggested—much as in 1934 (see p. 176)—that "voluntary cooperation" between broadcasters and educators would be satisfactory to both, and Senator Edwin Johnson (D-Colorado), who had led a congressional fight for the approval of CBS color and a speedy end to the Freeze, and whose desires for competitive broadcasting led him to suggest that commercial licensees be required to give a certain amount of time each day to educators. The commission rejected the latter proposal on legal grounds, as well as proposals by educational institutions to make ETV stations partly commercial so that they would be self-sustaining.

In a final move, possibly inspired by President Truman's emphatic support of ETV, the FCC refused to place a definite time limit on using the educational reservations, although procedures for protesting them or changing them to commercial status were to have been established after a year. Slow-moving educational institutions still had an opportunity to obtain a television license four decades later. By 2001, more than 370 ETV— or, as they have since come to be called, *public television*—stations were on the air, nearly one-quarter of the television stations in the United States.

Their existence allows commercial stations to ignore to some extent the discriminating ETV audience and also helps restrict potential commercial broadcasters from some markets.

7.8.3 The *Sixth Report and Order*: Seeds of Future Problems

On April 14, 1952, more than 42 months after the start of the Freeze, the decisions described above were made public and final as the FCC issued its *Sixth Report and Order.* That it took six "Reports and Orders" to reach final decisions suggests the complexity of the issues. The FCC had to deliberate in the face of strong urging by manufacturers, smaller networks, new station applicants, and the public in unserved or underserved communities to lift the Freeze at the earliest possible moment. Having incorporated virtually all its television problems into one omnibus hearing docket, the FCC was not inclined to loosen the leash on new television stations until it had made decisions on *all* problems. Thus, we have the spectacle of selection of a color television system holding up consideration of UHF use, technical standards, allocation, and assignment. The group seriously interested in retaining the Freeze for its own sake, the pre-Freeze broadcasters, did not have to come into the open. As a matter of fact, their heterogeneity was such as to make unanimity impossible, since each of the 15 network owned-and-operated stations would favor the objectives of its parent network, to gain more affiliates and increase its nationwide salable "circulation." Much of the delay was due to people like Senator Johnson, who insisted that the color issue be decided before the allocation phase could come to a hearing. Such political pressure counterbalanced the efforts of manufacturers and organized labor to lift the Freeze and provide more television-related jobs, and the importunings of communities with limited or no television. When the FCC refused to lift the Freeze for such relatively unserved areas as Hawaii and Alaska, Senator Johnson grew nervous over the growing public pressure and assured his constituents that they would have television in time for the 1952 World Series. They did.

As with any FCC decision of this magnitude, the *Sixth Report and Order* included compromises that were later to plague the industry, the public, and the commission. Two of the most important were intermixture and the methods for serving smaller communities.

Under the *Sixth Report and Order*, cities would be intermixed with both VHF and UHF channels. Opponents of this scheme pointed out the grave disparity between the service the two bands could offer, and the economic disadvantage for a UHF station in a city with VHF stations assigned. If the VHF station had been operating during the Freeze, and the public had been saturated with VHF-only receivers, the problem would be compounded. DuMont's rejected plan provided at least some equality of outlets for the four networks in a majority of larger communities able to support television. Other organizations urged on the FCC their own assignment plans, some of which tried to avoid intermixture. Even the report of the President's Communications Policy Board, issued a year before the *Sixth Report and Order*, clearly foresaw drawbacks to intermixture:

> The proposed plan of the FCC contemplates the allocation of both VHF and UHF stations to the same community. There is little possibility that a UHF station can compete successfully with a VHF station. Within practical limits of power, a UHF station cannot serve as large an area as can a VHF station. For a considerable period after the UHF stations commence operation, particularly in cities where there are VHF stations, there will probably be few UHF receivers and consequently a limited audience.

And also, consequently, there was a limited amount of advertising agency interest in buying time on the station.

Because of theoretical propagation characteristics and equipment availability, the commission decided to support the fiction of equivalence of VHF and UHF. As a result, UHF stations in intermixed markets had ever increasing financial problems, forcing hundreds off the air (see pp. 387–391). In the mid-1960s the commission and Congress belatedly took remedial action, after more than a decade of agonizing and conducting hearings (see p. 415).

Although the FCC understood the political power of rural and small-town areas in Congress, the *Sixth Report and Order* did not serve those areas adequately. It was recognized that small towns rarely could not generate enough advertising revenue to support a full-fledged station, and that propagation characteristics of both VHF and UHF prevented many areas of the country from being served by a television equivalent to a clear-channel radio station. But the FCC did not do anything substantive to supply such service.

However, even before the Freeze was well underway, people in some underserved communities had taken matters into their own hands. The first community antenna, now cable, television (CATV) in the United States was developed in 1949. In numerous isolated mountainous regions, particularly in Pennsylvania and Oregon, cooperating citizens or businesses established for the purpose placed antennas on neighboring peaks and strung wires from the antennas to homes in the valleys. In other isolated communities, clever electronics experts rigged the receiving antenna to receive the distant station and fed the signal into a homemade *repeater* or *booster* transmitter of low power in the valley. Such boosters gave good service to the valley community but, since all transmitters can cause interference farther than they can give service, caused widespread interference to the "parent" station.

At first, the FCC ignored cable and tried to close down the boosters, but they were too hard to track down and too easy to establish again virtually overnight and had too much political support. Governor (former Senator) Edwin Johnson of Colorado appointed booster operators to his personal communications staff and successfully defied the FCC to act against them. The FCC attempted to provide alternatives—*satellite* stations with no original programming, and *translators* to move the received signal high into the little-used UHF channels—but failed (see p. 389). Although cable is now the primary service in most big cities as well as small towns, it originally provided service to communities with poor off-the-air reception into the late 1970s. Distant signal importation and specialized "pay-cable" services were for the future. All that has changed is the commission's regulatory stance, and the belief of many people in its future (see pp. 467–470).

Although the *Sixth Report and Order* was the result of much thought, work, and argument, its intended effect has not been realized. Because of its imperfections—and the imperfections of other policy statements by the commission and other government agencies—the number of on-air television signals available today in a given community is far below the expectations engendered by the allocation and assignment plans. Television's growth in the United States has been phenomenal, but it has not been smooth. Political and economic force has aborted many organizational patterns for the medium. The shortage of television broadcast stations or, perhaps, cable channels today restricts the viewing fare of the average citizen, sharply reduces the potential number of nationwide program sources (networks), creates conditions of monopoly or near-monopoly in many communities, raises costs beyond the reach of the local advertiser, and restricts opportunity for new talent. At the same time, there is a critical shortage of space in the radio spectrum for services other than television.

7.8.4 Public Service Responsibility

On March 7, 1946, the FCC issued what may have been its single most important programming policy document. Entitled *Public Service Responsibility of Broadcast Licensees*, but bearing a deep blue paper cover that gave it its popular title, the "Blue Book" contained five major parts. First, it gave examples of station promises for programming (providing local live public service programs, limiting advertising) versus their performance (inexpensive recorded music and a heavy proportion of ads). The second section provided the legal rationale for the FCC to act in the area of programming, chiefly in the process of choosing between competing applicants. Part three outlined what the FCC thought of as public service factors. These included the need for sustaining programs to:

1. Provide a balance to advertiser-supported material.
2. Offer programs whose nature would make them unsponsorable.
3. Serve minority tastes and interests.
4. Cater to the needs of nonprofit organizations.
5. Allow experimentation with new types of programs.

Charts and tables were used to show that networks usually aired sustaining programs at hours when few could listen, reserving the prime hours for advertiser-supported programming. The commission noted that when networks did provide public service material, most of their affiliated stations rejected it for a locally sponsored show. The third part of the "Blue Book" also outlined local station practices in programming and advertising that made it difficult to hear discussion of public issues on the air. Part four provided tabular statistical data to show how broadcast profits had increased from 1937 to 1944, which presumably would have allowed broadcasters to pay for some of the suggested improvements. The last part of the "Blue Book" was a summary that reiterated the importance of the station licensees in policing their own product. The FCC would favor renewal applications from stations that had met their public service responsibilities, defined as: sustaining programs, local live shows, discussion of public issues, and no excessive advertising. The "Blue Book" conclusions were described as neither regulations nor proposals for new rules but rather as a codification of FCC thinking to help licensees and regulators alike. Yet, this *was* the first major FCC statement on broadcast programming policy, although the commission previously had acted against specific stations on specific matters.

Initial reaction of the broadcasting industry to the "Blue Book" was calm but predictable; it claimed that the government was violating radio's freedom of speech since the Communications Act forbid the FCC to censor. A month later the issue heated up with the publication of *Radio's Second Chance* (1946) by Charles A. Siepmann, who was thought to be chief writer of the "Blue Book." Actually, although Siepmann—a former British broadcaster accustomed to the public service philosophy of the BBC—had been a consultant on the "Blue Book" project for a short while, FCC economist Dallas Smythe, Commissioner Clifford Durr and others had put most of the report together. In his book, Siepmann criticized American broadcasting and brought down on the FCC and himself the wrath of an industry fearing that the FCC was planning specific programming rules. Newspapers were divided, some defending the report and others fearing a government takeover of radio. The trade press—particularly the business weekly, *Broadcasting*—attacked it mercilessly, although no station was ever taken to hearing or off the air for not meeting "Blue Book" standards. Baltimore's WBAL, held up as a bad example in the "Blue Book," won its license renewal over a competing application from columnist Drew Pearson.

Still, the report had some solid results over time: The NAB strengthened its self-regulatory radio code, broadcasters had a clearer notion of what the FCC was looking for in comparative license renewal and application hearings, the FCC showed that it had the backbone for once to speak out if not act in a controversial area, and the "Blue Book" provided the commission with a useful precedent and the industry with a rallying point.

A specific area of public service received special attention in 1948 and 1949, when the FCC reversed itself over the right of stations to editorialize on the air. In 1941, while passing on a competing challenge to Boston radio station WAAB's license renewal, the FCC decided that "the broadcaster cannot be an advocate" or, in other words, that a licensee should not use the airwaves he controls to propagate his own opinions. Some broadcasters, and others claiming that it would limit the free speech rights of broadcasters, attacked this *Mayflower* decision, named after the competing applicant, the Mayflower Broadcasting Corporation. But, although a few stations ignored the rule, no licensee challenged the FCC in court. Most broadcasters did not editorialize anyway because they disliked antagonizing sponsors and segments of the audience by taking sides on any question. Some broadcasters even avoided any mention of labor unions because the topic was "controversial."

After hearings in which the NAB took a leading role, the FCC issued a report in 1949, *In the Matter of Editorializing by Broadcast Licensees*, which "clarified" the 1941 decision. It stated that "Only insofar as it is exercised in conformity with the paramount right of the public to hear a reasonably balanced presentation of all responsible viewpoints on particular issues can such editorialization be considered to be consistent with the licensee's duty to operate in the public interest." That decision generally was hailed as allowing broadcasters more of the rights enjoyed by print media under the First Amendment. The way was opened for editorializing, which started slowly in the 1950s. Even more important, the precedent was set for what was later called the Fairness Doctrine (see pp. 463–467).

An important case in this area opened in February 1948, when the Radio News Club of Southern California formally charged that G. A. Richards, president and controlling stockholder of stations KMPC in Los Angeles, WJR in Detroit, and WGAR in Cleveland, had ordered his news employees to slant the news—against President Roosevelt and his family in particular. Voluminous hearings began in 1950, but Richards' death in May 1951 rendered the matter moot in the opinion of the FCC Hearing Examiner. After Richards' heirs "rejected" the earlier practices, the commission closed the case without penalty, and the stations were soon sold.

7.8.5 The Petrillo Affair (continued)

To add to broadcasting's economic complications in the postwar years, the American Federation of Musicians (AFM) was still making demands (see p. 257). In October 1945 it ordered networks to hire duplicate orchestras or forgo use of network programs on FM. A month later it gave local stations the same order, helping speed the end of studio orchestras at all but the largest stations, as most turned to recorded music completely. Congress reacted to the AFM pressure by passing the Lea Act (after Congressman Clarence F. Lea, D-California, its sponsor) in April 1946, which made it unlawful to force a broadcast licensee to, among other things, hire unneeded personnel, pay salaries in lieu of those unneeded personnel, pay more than once for a single service, or pay for services that were not performed. After a series of court appeals, the Supreme Court of the United States upheld the act in June 1947. Further weakening the power of unions was the passage six months later of the Taft-Hartley Labor Relations Act. Faced with these restraints, AFM President Petrillo agreed in 1948 to a two-month trial of using one orchestra for AM-FM programming—and then caved in on the issue for good. In the meantime, radio stations had begun to rely more on recorded music and disc jockey programming, further weakening the ties between broadcasting and live music.

7.8.6 Self-Regulation and Blacklisting

The roles of trade and professional groups in broadcasting reflected the confusion of the period. There seemed to be a trade group for every kind of station—FM, television, would-be educational stations, new stations, old stations, and, of course, the National Association of Broadcasters (NAB). NAB, essentially a conservative association of members of the broadcast station establishment, working hand-in-glove with Sol Taishoff, the publisher-editor of *Broadcasting* magazine, had to re-evaluate its functions with the coming of television. In 1951, to eliminate the rival Television Broadcasters Association, it changed its name—for seven years anyway—to the more cumbersome National Association of Radio and Television Broadcasters (NARTB). (*Broadcasting* became *Broadcasting•Telecasting* at around the same time.) NAB's temporary shift in title helped pacify new television license holders who felt the organization was overly beholden to old-line AM radio operators. All groups spent as much time bickering with one another about roles and priorities as they did educating the public and politicians to their point(s) of view.

The NAB directed its major attention toward what it saw as government encroachment on programming decision making. As a result of the "Blue Book," oft-repeated threats of specific legislation, and public pressure to improve radio and television program standards, the NAB completely revised the 1939 radio code. "Standards of Practice," issued in 1948, was more stringent on limitations on advertising time. Although many stations adhered to them, they were still unenforceable. As more stations went on the air, especially in sparsely populated rural areas or urban regions with great competition, the struggle for economic survival often prevented adherence to the NAB code standards. "Standards of Practice" and the motion picture code served as models when the NARTB issued its first Television Code early in 1952, basically an unoriginal, proscriptive recitation of things the licensees should *not* do. The single means of enforcement was not much of a threat: NARTB's right to prevent the station's display of the Television Code Seal on the air and in advertising.

The period of the communist scare and blacklisting—in which the industry, through fear and cowardice, let others control it—was a grim era in

■ The Big Red Scare: 1950

If the Communist Party USA exacts a heavy financial toll of its members and dupes, it has been no less energetic in seeing to it that they get ahead in show business, while articulate anti-Communists are blacklisted and smeared with that venomous intensity which is characteristic of Red Fascists alone. . . . Those who are "right" are "boosted" from one job to another, from humble beginnings in Communist-dominated night clubs or on small programs which have been "colonized" to more important programs and finally to stardom. Literally scores of our most prominent producers, directors, writers, actors and musicians owe their present success largely to the Party "boost" system, a system which involves not only "reliable" producers and directors, but also ad agency executives, network and station executives, writers, fellow-actors and critics and reviewers. In turn, the Party member or "reliable" who has "arrived" gives the "boost" to others who, the Red grapevine whispers, are to be helped. . . . Contrary-wise, those who know radio and TV can recite dozens of examples of anti-Communists who, for mysterious reasons, are *persona non grata* on numerous programs, and who are slandered unmercifully in certain "progressive" circles.

The purpose of this compilation is threefold. One, to show how the Communists have been able to carry out their plan of infiltration of the radio and television industry. Two, to indicate the extent to which many prominent actors and artists have been inveigled to lend their names, according to . . . public records, to organizations espousing Communist causes. This, regardless of whether they actually believe in, sympathize with, or even recognize the cause advanced. Three, to discourage actors and artists from naively lending their names to Communist organizations or causes in the future.

Excerpts from *Red Channels: The Report of Communist Influence in Radio and Television* (New York: Counterattack, 1950), pp. 4–5, 9.

It is quite clear that whereas the editors and publishers of *Red Channels* and *Counterattack* do not consciously strive for the same objectives as the agents of Communism, their methods and techniques are very similar and so are their standards of morality and their respect for the essential "Blessings of Liberty" guaranteed by the Constitution and the Bill of Rights. As the vigorously anti-Communist *Saturday Review of Literature* has said, "*Red Channels* accepts Red Doctrine: to accuse is enough." It would be difficult to imagine any doctrine more profoundly un-American.

Playwright Robert E. Sherwood's reaction as he introduced an American Civil Liberties Union report on the subject, Merle Miller's *The Judges and the Judged* (New York: Doubleday, 1952), p. 9.

broadcasting and film and the arts generally. Blacklisting was the process of secretly refusing to employ someone, usually in this case a creative talent (actor, writer, producer, director) solely because of a frequently unsupported claim that he or she was a communist, had communist, "fellow traveler," or ultraliberal left-wing inclinations, or had been duped by communists. The vicious thing about blacklisting is suggested by its name. It was done by small groups of self-appointed investigators who made surreptitious reports to advertisers, agencies, stations, and networks indicating that someone either should not be hired because of his or her political beliefs or was "cleared" for employment. Potential employers who did not pay attention to these messages could expect to have their own patriotism impugned. Potential employees not cleared were seldom told why, and no executive ever admitted the existence of the blacklists. Blacklisting worked, from about 1948 until the early 1950s, because its organizers hit the broadcast system at its weakest point: the advertiser. Under threats of product boycotts, advertisers pressured agencies and broadcasters not to hire someone for fear of losing sales, or at least creating controversy, which all advertisers shun. With advertisers representing the broadcasting industry's source of income, no one in broadcasting would speak out against the practice or even admit it existed—only persons who had been blacklisted themselves, and they were no longer in broadcasting.

Perhaps the most successful and ironically, considering its secretive nature, the most visible blacklisting group was American Business Consultants, based in New York. Consisting of three former FBI agents, it issued a newsletter called *Counterattack* and often published special monographs. On June 22, 1950, it issued *Red Channels: The Report of Communist Influence in Radio and Television*, some 200 pages of detailed background information on 151 broadcast personalities, whom it suggested were at least sympathetic to communist thinking. *Red Channels*, carefully avoiding outright accusations, reprinted reports from the House Un-American Activities Committee and other official and unofficial groups, using the umbrella of official sources—mixed with some "guilt by association" and innuendo—to brand persons as undesirable. An accident of timing made *Red Channels* particularly effective: Three days after it was published, North Korea invaded South Korea and the United States entered the Korean War or "police action." Other than this one report, which was widely distributed, blacklisting remained institutionalized behind closed doors. Advertising and package agencies and networks soon assigned a "security checker" to make certain that anyone hired was "clean" with the blacklisters. Some stations and networks even required new employees to take a loyalty oath. Actors and writers who "confessed" their associations and informed on their colleagues before the House Un-American Activities Committee or prominent unofficial groups usually could be expunged from the blacklist. The insidious process continued until a celebrated case (see pp. 396–397) helped break the system.

7.9 The Impact of Television

That radio and television listeners and viewers were becoming more concerned about broadcasting's role in their daily lives was demonstrated by the rising clamor of complaints that helped lead to the 1948 revision of the NAB code, and in group action. In the late 1940s radio listener councils that sought programming of more value to the local community reached a peak. These councils were active in New England, the Midwest (often sparked by university activists), and California. They issued lists of good programs, conducted audience surveys, held informational meetings, produced special programs in cooperation with some stations, and generally encouraged greater educational use of radio. Although in Europe such groups often met for communal listening to special programs, that pattern did not develop here. Some councils organized around program production, frequently in association with a university, while others merely studied the industry and its problems and then pressured or at least advised local station managers to improve their programming. None of these groups covered a wide enough area or lasted long enough to have a lasting impact on the industry.

Many critics and professional broadcasters became increasingly concerned that radio was changing from a varied format, with something for everyone, to a stereotyped format of popular music and news with high advertising saturation. The increase in radio stations and expansion of television put such a financial strain on most radio broadcasters that they could not afford to accommodate many community requests for change.

7.9.1 Television's Domestic Effect

Of concern to all other mass communication media, as well as operators of any means of recreation or entertainment, was the impact of television. Two media that felt the immediate brunt were radically changed—radio and the movies. We have already discussed radio's loss of drama, variety, other entertainment—and advertisers—to television, and radio networks dried up to little more than news services with some sustaining entertainment programming (see pp. 297–301). As radio in the 1950s became more a local advertising medium, concentrating on recorded music, television became the evening-in-the-home entertainer and national advertising medium.

Hollywood, however, seemed in some ways totally unprepared. This was understandable, because the movie industry was fighting two important battles not directly connected with television. It lost the battle with the federal government over the right of large production studios to own chains of theaters. When the Paramount studio was forced in 1948, after a decade of antitrust litigation, to divest itself of its theater chain, panic set in. All major studios had to sell their theaters, keeping the production studios and distributing organizations, and with the sale went the benefits of vertical integration and a guaranteed market for the hundreds of feature films made each year. The motion picture industry also encountered blacklisting, although here it often surfaced in public, during emotional congressional and other hearings where actors and other movie people fell over one another in informing, with or without evidence, on old friends and enemies. Some of the accused took the Fifth Amendment, or refused to testify—at the cost of a jail term in a number of cases. The scars are still evident.

After 1950, television provided another punch to an industry no longer secure in its role or its profits. As early as 1949 motion picture attendance was off by 20% and employment was down by 25%, with lower-ranking workers, and not the top-heavy management, being laid off. As fewer films were made, more people were out of work. The former film audience was staying home, or going for a ride now that wartime transportation shortages had ended, and the movie audience soon dwindled from a family affair to an opportunity for teenagers to date. After 1950 the abandoned motion picture theater became a common sight. Hollywood unfairly blamed everything on television and tried to boycott the video medium. Stars under contract were not allowed to appear on television, old films were not released to networks or stations for television showing, and television workers were shunned in the movie colony. It was an ostrich act, which had to change radically when the American feature film industry faced even greater problems in later years.

Professional sports promoters also worried about the effects of television on game attendance. Televised sports events often had the direct result, according to team management's perceptions of the data, of reducing the gate receipts. Team owners were caught between the lure of substantial income from selling rights to a game to a network or station and the sight of empty seats and reduced parking and concession income as the fans stayed home to watch in comfort. Research sponsored by a number of professional teams showed that television had little effect on attendance over a season. Still, local game *blackouts* date from those early years, with many variations depending on the personal opinions of team owners. Only in 1973 did Congress impose restrictions on the blacking out of sold-out games in pro football (see p. 443).

Television affected other institutions as well. Advertisers began to shift vast sums of money into television that had once gone to radio or the print media. Likewise, television was radically changing the process and appearance of national elections and between-campaign politics (see pp. 312–313). There were rumors and reports of changes in family life styles, sleeping habits, children's entertainment and activity preferences (it was a lot more fun and easier to watch the *Lone Ranger* than to go outside and play cowboys and Indians), eyesight problems, and juvenile delinquency. However, many of these developments were merely hinted at during the late 1940s and early 1950s; television's impact on children would not be readily observed in the United States until later (see pp. 385–386 and 457–459).

7.9.2 Postwar Broadcasting Abroad

While television preoccupied most of this country right after World War II, radio remained the preeminent broadcast medium abroad. Even by late 1952, few countries outside the United States had television, and most of the transmitters and approximately 85% of the world's television sets were American—even though the country had only a little more than 5% of the world's population. The major foreign countries using television regularly were Canada, Cuba, Mexico, and Brazil in the Western Hemisphere and using U.S. technical standards, and France and Great Britain in Europe, each using different technical standards.

In the United Kingdom, the BBC resumed television transmissions in June 1946 by including in the opening program the same film cartoon that had been the last thing seen when BBC television left the air at the outbreak of the war in 1939. The French had conducted some experimentation and programming in Paris under German occupation during the war, and had continued transmissions after the war. But television in most other countries was limited to one or two transmitters and a few hundred or few thousand receivers—about where American television had been before the war.

With radio, a far more important and widespread medium, the main postwar job abroad was rebuilding and replacing transmitters, systems, and receivers. Since radio was easy to reconstruct and immediately useful once rebuilt, many countries put their mass communications effort in radio. German radio, under Allied occupation, was restructured along local and regional lines with no national radio organization whatever—in reaction to the Nazi centralized control of broadcasting and other media. In Japan the American occupation forces held strict control over radio at first, gradually easing it in the late 1940s to permit NHK to resume as the principal broadcasting organization. The United States allowed some Japanese international broadcasting early in 1952, expanded it when Japan's utility as a base during the Korean War became apparent, and then ended the occupation.

International broadcasting after 1945 became a weapon in the cold war with the Soviet Union and its allies, which intensified after 1947. For the first time, the United States was active in such communication in "peacetime." The Voice of America had started with the wartime operations of the Office of War Information (OWI) (see pp. 235–236) but had moved to the State Department. It operated in many languages and beamed news, music, and other programming to most areas of the world. In addition, the United States government set up three radio services *in* Europe. Radio Free Europe, which for years claimed to be privately supported when it was in fact supported clandestinely by the CIA, tailored its programming to the nations of Eastern Europe that the Soviets had occupied in 1945. Radio Liberty, also U.S. government-supported although declaring its private status, broadcast directly to the Soviet Union. Radio in the American Sector of Berlin (RIAS) was overtly run by the State Department, and was heard throughout East Germany. Much of the programming was music and "straight" news, with little direct propaganda, although the services varied (Radio Free Europe, for instance, at first held out hope of freedom to the European satellites of the Soviet Union and was largely programmed by refugees from the Communists) and *any* content, even if not directly controlled by the government, might be called propaganda. The Soviets spent huge sums building transmitters to send out noise to "jam" the incoming signals in urban areas. Penalties were imposed for listening to foreign broadcasts, although much "radio" broadcasting in the Soviet Union was wired or "rediffusion" much like CATV, and thus the audience could not select programs. Other nations broadcast to the world on the international shortwave bands as well, particularly the BBC, which had been doing so since the 1930s, and the Soviet Union.

After much preliminary work a major International Telecommunications Union meeting was held in Atlantic City in 1947 to revise the international frequency allocation table. Few changes in American broadcasting were necessary, but it was desirable to allocate the frequencies that had been opened up by wartime research. This conference, like other ITU meetings, showed that international cooperation *could* be achieved in the telecommunications field.

7.9.3 Period Overview

As the length of this chapter attests, summarizing the important events and trends of 1945–1952 is not easy. Overall, the period contained the transition from the AM radio-only broadcast industry, which had been around since the early 1920s, to a system incorporating AM and FM radio and VHF and UHF television, with such services as CATV and pay-TV in the wings. The industry was far bigger and more complex in 1952 than in 1945. The radio establishment helped pave the way for the new television network establishment; indeed the ownership of the new medium came essentially from the groups that had controlled prewar radio. The organization and operation of early television is the overriding theme of this period.

This short space of time also saw the fortunes of educational broadcasting rise as reserved frequencies became available first in FM and then in television. These decisions paved the way for the spectacular expansion of educational, later "public," broadcasting in the decades after 1950. But in the rush to television, some things were given short shrift. FM radio, the chief initial loser, entered a long period of decline after a short burst of postwar growth. Even television met problems as a result of the complicated FCC allocations proceedings during the Freeze. Although intended to correct earlier FCC mistakes, the 1952 *Sixth Report and Order* created UHF television stations as second-class citizens—a condition that soon would be abundantly clear.

Television expanded far more rapidly than radio simply because it built on the existing radio structure. Thus television used radio program formats with added video, networks were operated along radio lines, the role of advertisers was never in doubt, and radio set makers learned to make television sets. With its rapid growth and more complicated organization, the overall pattern of expanding television was the same as radio. Compared to radio's initial impact on American society (see pp. 99–100), television's effects on motion pictures, sports, and leisure patterns were felt in less than half the time. The new medium quickly dominated America's life style.

The 1945–1952 period brought such radical changes that today's broadcasting can almost be said to date from this era rather than from the pioneering of the 1920s. While FM radio and television suffered from growing pains, they benefited from the lessons of AM radio. The greatest growth of both new broadcast services, and the transformation of AM radio's functions, were to come in the Eisenhower years—between 1952 and 1960.

Selected Further Reading

(Alphabetized within topics. For full citations, see Appendix D.)

Contemporary studies of radio at its post-war peak include Bryson (1948), FCC (1947), Landry (1946), Midgley (1948), Siepmann (1950), Waller (1950), White (1947), and Wolfe (1949). More recent studies, taking a longer view, include Barnouw (1968), Bird (1999), Keith (2000), and Lichty & Topping (1975). Early commercial television techniques and operation are described in Dunlap (1942, 1947), Dupuy (1945), Eddy (1945), Hutchinson (1950), and Kempner (1948). Television networking is traced in Bergreen (1980), Campbell (1976), FCC (1958), Halberstam (1979), Hawver (1994), and Quinlan (1979) that deal with ABC, and both Metz (1975) and Slater (1988) that focus on CBS, and MacDonald (1990), while local station history is to be found in Murray & Godfrey (1997).

Radio program resources are noted in chapter four. Criticism of both radio and television is collected in Crosby (1952), and Gross (1970). Focusing specifically on television's programs and impact in the 1950s are Allen (1956), Boddy (1990), Heldenfels (1994), and Sturcken (1990).

Reference works on television programs for this and the remaining chapters include encyclopedias edited by Brown (1992), Newcomb (1997), and Slide (1991); pictorial histories such as Blum (1959), Chiu (1998), Goldstein & Goldstein (1983), Greenfield (1977), Marschall (1986), Settel & Laas (1969), and Shulman & Youman (1966); and such program directories as Brooks & Marsh (1999), Erickson (1989) on syndicated programs, Gianakos (1978–1987), Goldberg (1993) on revivals and sequels, McNeil (1996), Rose on program genres (1985), Shapiro on network schedules (1989–92), and Terrace (1979). Works dealing with types of programs include Adir (1988) on comedy, Davis (1995) on children's programs, Glut & Harmon (1975) on television heroes, Hawes (1986) and Skutch (1988a) on early live drama, MacDonald (1987) on the western, Melton, Lucas, & Stone (1997) on religion on radio and television, Rose (1986) on performing arts programs, and Stempel (1992) on television drama and comedy writers. O'Dell profiles 15 women television pioneers (1997). Books on specific television stars and programs over the years are now numberless, most of them written for fans.

Major radio audience surveys include Lazarsfeld & Field (1946), and Lazarsfeld & Kendall (1948), while Spigel (1992) assesses initial television impacts. Regulation is discussed in the FCC "Blue Book" (*Public Service Responsibilities of Broadcast Licensees*) (1946), Kahn (1984), Slotten (2000), and Warner (1948, 1953). Blacklisting is described in Cogley (1950), *Counterattack* (1956), and Vaughn (1972). Foreign radio and television systems are described best in the many studies published by Unesco (1947–51, 1950, 1951, 1953).

"On the evening of March 7, 1955, one out of every two Americans was watching Mary Martin play *Peter Pan* before the television cameras. Never before in history had a single person been seen and heard by so many others at the same time. The vast size of the audience was a phenomenon in itself as fantastic as any fairy tale. The age of television had arrived."———*Leo Bogart,* THE AGE OF TELEVISION, *page 1*

CHAPTER 8

Walter Cronkite and technicians squeezed into a convertable, 1952. *New York Public Library.*

> "... we are convinced that the UHF band will be fully utilized, and that UHF stations will eventually compete on a favorable basis with stations in the VHF."———*FCC SIXTH REPORT AND ORDER (1952), paragraph 197*
>
> "[potential UHF operators] had better study astronomy to figure up their balance sheets and buy lots of red ink."———*Commissioner Jones in dissent to the SIXTH REPORT AND ORDER*

THE AGE OF TELEVISION (1952–1960)

Bob Hope and Bing Crosby. *Photofest.*

Chapter Outline

Television came to the fore and radio faded into the musical wallpaper business during the 1952–1960 period. This chapter takes us from the end of the FCC Freeze on television station construction in 1952 to the quiz show and payola scandals in 1959 and 1960, which caused a shakeup in the FCC and new public awareness of the business of broadcasting. For television the period opened with growth and excitement but ended with questions and recriminations.

The 1950s were the Eisenhower years—a time of conflicting images. After two decades of Democratic administrations, General Dwight D. Eisenhower won the 1952 Republican presidential nomination from the more conservative Ohio Senator Robert A. Taft and then won the election from Adlai E. Stevenson (see p. 313). Since the Freeze had ended early in 1952 (see p. 328), plans for building hundreds of television stations were well advanced by the time "Ike" moved into the White House. Viewers absorbed the political turnover and subsequent shifts in international relations, particularly after the death of Stalin in March 1953. Wisconsin's Senator Joseph McCarthy, riding high in his witch hunt for communists everywhere, had a rendezvous with television that ended his power in American political life. The Supreme Court issued its famous school desegregation decision, which led to political and social crises aired in detail on the nation's television screens. In New York, the United Nations headquarters was completed with provision for television and radio coverage of important events.

The 1950s had many fads: the Davy Crockett craze, inspired by a television show; automobile tailfins; small kids writing the letter Z on everything, just like the hero of the Disney television series *The Mark of Zorro;* hula hoops; silly putty; rushing home from school for the five-minute episode of *Crusader Rabbit*; evangelists Billy Graham and Oral Roberts on television; the sack dress, which made a woman look like a chic sack of potatoes; rock 'n' roll music; telephone booth stuffing; swooning over pop singer Elvis Presley. The few fads that were not based on or inspired by television shows were at least reported widely by the medium.

People had more leisure time, and television quickly became the most popular way to spend it. Families had much larger incomes since the war had ended the Great Depression, while workers spent less time on the job. The work week very slowly shrank to less than 40 hours by 1960.

Additional leisure came with increasing purchases of washing machines, dishwashers, garbage disposals, dryers, and power mowers. As people spent many hours a day watching television, audiences dwindled for nearly every other kind of entertainment. The television audience grew faster than that for any other medium or means of recreation. By 1958 more homes had television than the 1939 number of radio homes; that is, though far more expensive, television achieved near-saturation in half the time it took radio.

Virtually all the developments in radio and television were predictable from occurrences of the revolutionary 1946–1952 period, since television built on and expanded the industry established by radio. AM continued to grow and change, despite fears that it was doomed by television; interest in FM radio faded away until it began a slight upturn at the end of the decade; and television's growth, problems, and promise filled the news of broadcasting. The 1952–1960 period was in nearly every way an age of television, more so than any time before or since.

8.1 Stereo and Videotape Technology

Two developments in broadcast technology in this period soon proved of immense value. The first was single-station stereophonic radio broadcasting, and the second was the perfecting of the videotape magnetic recording process for television.

8.1.1 Stereo and Multiplexing

The idea of stereo was not new. There had been lab experiments with stereophonic sound in the early 1900s, and in the 1920s stereo radio binaural broadcasts had been made from the stage of the Berlin Opera House, using six microphones in three pairs, half of each pair fed to a separate AM transmitter. In this country, some AM stations that played classical music experimented with two-station AM stereocasting, with one station broadcasting the right channel and the other the left—but listeners to only one station got but half a signal and offering the same program on two different wavelengths wasted spectrum space.

Nevertheless, in 1952 the *New York Times*-owned WQXR tried AM–FM two-station stereocasts, using AM for the right sound channel and FM for the left. In 1954 Boston's WCRB began four hours a week of such programming, boosting it to 40 hours a week by 1959. These early broadcasts were nearly always of live music, as there were few sources of stereophonically recorded music even on tape. After 1958 commercially recorded stereo records became available and recorded music could be readily broadcast in stereo. Even the networks got into the act when NBC broadcast the *Bell Telephone Hour* stereophonically in 1958 over its four O & O AM and FM stations. CBS followed suit, and television also was used when ABC stereocast the Lawrence Welk program on television and AM. Other experiments or demonstrations intermixing AM, FM, and television channels showed that FM stations offered such better sound reproduction quality that the two channels sounded very different. In addition, since the coverage area of these broadcasts obeyed the propagation laws of the frequency bands on which the two services operated, the AM half of the signal reached out much farther. The obvious notion of FM–FM two-station stereo was impracticable since few people had a single FM receiver, let alone two.

Faced with these technical limitations but responsive to audience interest in stereo broadcasts, broadcasters, particularly the hard-pressed FM operators, began to petition the FCC for commercial use of experimental single-station stereo broadcasting. Common technical standards would be needed so that all stations would broadcast the same sort of signal and all stereo receivers could pick up any stereo signal.

Meanwhile, some FM stations (see p. 350) had discovered a way of making money. While it made use of their transmitters, it was not broadcasting. In the late 1940s, stations in urban areas had developed *storecasting*—the sending of music directly into stores and offices over special receivers that, on transmission of a special tone, automatically cut out talk, leaving only the background music. Income came from rental of these receivers to business establishments. Although recognizing the stations' need for income, the FCC ruled against such use of the broadcast signal in the early 1950s, claiming that these customers had a stronger say in selection of music to be broadcast than regular listeners, a contravention of the 1934 Communications Act.

The commission ruled in 1955 that FM stations, instead of shutting off the special receivers with a simple tone in a process called *simplexing*, could storecast only by *multiplexing*—a more complicated process whereby the station transmitter sent out two different but simultaneous signals, one to the stores, one to the general public. Although broadcasters objected to the expense that this would entail, the FCC stuck to its guns. But storecasting and single-station FM stereo came into conflict, because both required some form of multiplexing. In the mid-1950s, broadcasters did not know how to transmit more than one FM subcarrier signal at a time. Yet, because storecasting was a ready moneymaker, and stereo offered FM a way out of its downward slide in audience appeal, broadcasters wanted to be able to provide both services at once.

Seventeen different stereo systems initially were proposed. Unfortunately, few of them allowed simultaneous storecasting. To try to sort out the conflicting systems, the industry resorted to an approach used earlier for television allocations and standards (see p. 250): It set up a committee of engineering experts from the industry to eliminate inferior systems by a series of comparative tests. In 1959 and 1960, this National Stereophonic Radio Committee (NSRC), working with FCC engineers, cut the number of competing systems to seven. Easily eliminated were those that did not allow storecasting and stereo at the same time, since by now some 250 stations were engaged in storecasting. While the tests dragged on, many stations kept using AM–FM two-station stereo.

Finally, in April 1961, the FCC set as the industry standard one that combined the Zenith and General Electric systems. Of the 15 other proposals, some had come from firms that merely wanted to promote stereo or FM, but most, of course, came from individuals or companies that wanted to exploit strong patent positions. As will be seen in the next chapter, this 1961 decision contributed to a new era of FM expansion through stereo while preserving storecasting and other Subsidiary Communications Authorizations (SCA) multiplexed services.

8.1.2 Videotape Recording

In the 1950s a magnetic tape recording process for television achieved broadcast quality. Since 1948, programming had been of three types: live, film, or kinescope recording (see p. 275), which was noticeably fuzzier and grainier than live or regular film. The search to replace the kinescope recording process had begun after the war, and a magnetic videotape system had been publicly demonstrated in 1951 and 1952. Late in 1953, shortly after FCC approval of color television standards (see pp. 321–323), RCA demonstrated a videotape recording (VTR) system for both color and monochrome television. The system, like earlier ones, showed promise but had serious technical problems.

The unveiling of a practical VTR took place in April 1956 at the NAB convention in Chicago. Ampex, a small California-based firm that had worked on audio tape recorders for Bing Crosby in the early 1950s, demonstrated a working black-and-white VTR system. Within days, Ampex took in $4.1 million in orders, even though these models, using a 2-inch tape moving at 15 ips, cost about $75,000 each. Now, finally, West Coast stations had a high-quality, practical means of delaying East Coast broadcasts without having to use film or kinescopes, or simply having New York repeat the show live. CBS apparently was the first broadcast organization to make this use of videotape recording, in November 1956.

In 1957 Ampex and RCA pooled their patents and knowledge so both could build compatible systems for color and black-and-white. Ampex, being first with a workable system, had sold more than 600 by early 1960, more than two-thirds of them to networks. After the introduction of the VTR, the networks rarely used the "kine." Because of the many network orders and high unit cost, fewer than 200 television stations had bought a VTR by 1960, and these naturally were the bigger stations in the larger markets.

The arrival of tape led to changes in television programming and production. It made editing much faster than with film because the tape did not have to be processed. It made special effects possible with the push of a button, and far cheaper than on film. It produced higher quality than either kinescope recordings or 16mm film. Hollywood makers of film for television, particularly series programs, had to find ways of paring down their costs to compete with videotape. Using an erase/rerecord (make/remake) system, one could easily remove a mistake in an original production. Audience participation shows, during which producers always worry about an obscenity or libel going over the air, could now be taped in advance. Although shot-by-shot editing was difficult and expensive until new electronic devices were invented in the late 1960s, VTR gave the programmer greater flexibility. Some critics claimed, however, that actors rarely gave performances with the same intensity as in the "live" days, since they knew that a "fluff" or mistake could be removed, however expensively, before it went on the air. Above all, program production was no longer tied to air dates and hours. Although it took years for the full benefits of VTR to be felt, its potential was obvious from the start.

8.2 The Spurt in Station Population

Until 1958 or so, broadcasting was characterized by growth of AM and television and decline of FM radio. For the first time, growth in itself was questioned: How many AM stations could be accommodated without unacceptable interference? Was UHF anywhere near as good as VHF for television? Should stations in the same medium—radio or television—in the same market have roughly equal power and range? Was there enough advertising income to cover all the new stations? These were the have versus have-not arguments of previous decades, but now increasing numbers of three different kinds of broadcasting stations complicated the fray.

8.2.1 AM Growth and FM Adjustment

In 1945 radio engineers agreed that the spectrum could take only about 900 AM stations without undue interference. But, as the result of FCC relaxation of engineering standards for prospective station licensees after World War II (see p. 276), the number of AM stations grew to 2,400 by 1952. Again, many engineers thought that was the limit. But more than 100 stations were added each year of the 1950s. As small stations went on the air in smaller towns, and more were shoehorned into the cities, the number of AM stations rose to 3,500 by 1960, and an average of 30 stations was operating on each frequency in the United States. This is misleading of course, as Class IV (local) channels had hundreds of stations squeezed on each, and a few of the Class I (clear) channels had only one or two stations on each.

    This growth of AM was achieved at some cost. First, an increasing proportion—one-third in 1952, nearly one-half in 1960—of AM stations was restricted to daytime operation so that these stations did not conflict with other, usually older, stations at night, when radio waves travel farther (see Appendix B). More stations also had to use directional antennas to reduce interference. At the same time, power used by AM stations continued to climb, so that the 100-watt station became the exception rather than the rule. Local stations had to increase power, within FCC set limits, simply to stay abreast of other stations on the same frequency that had acquired higher power. By 1960, 18% of the 3,456 AM stations were on clear channels with all, except for a handful of Class I stations, using lower power, directional antennas, or going off the air at night; 54% were regional outlets using 5,000 or 10,000 watts of power; and 27% were low-powered (250–1,000 watts) local stations. If nothing else, the addition of one thousand AM stations in the 1950s showed that, although network radio was dying (see p. 356), radio stations still were thought of as successful business opportunities. By 1960, virtually every American town of respectable size, and most suburbs of major cities, had their own AM radio station or stations.

On the other hand, more FM stations went off the air than went on. The 616 FM stations on the air in 1952 had shrunk to 530 five years later. Most were owned by AM stations, which duplicated their programming over the FM outlets and hung onto them in case FM should ever amount to anything. In several large cities, their owners kept FM stations on the air in hopes that they might someday be valuable. Few FM stations made money and most lost substantial sums. But the FM audience kept about the same size—mostly devotees of the few classical music stations in the largest cities.

Other groups needing radio spectrum space soon began to eye the FM allocation. In 1955, for example, the National Association of Manufacturers petitioned the FCC to share the FM band with land mobile and other services with pressing needs. Two years later there was a similar attempt at spectrum "raiding," and even television made a pitch for additional VHF channels at the expense of FM (see p. 389). In each instance, the majority of the industry stood fast, and the FCC decided to leave the FM band alone. Still, the threat to reduce its number of channels was implicit if FM's fortunes did not change for the better.

Then in April 1957 the trade weekly *Broadcasting* noted that, for the first time since the late 1940s, applications for new FM stations outnumbered stations going off the air. Some owners of groups of stations announced plans to set up separate programming for their FM stations and talk of an FM network was heard. Something was relighting FM's fire. By mid-1958 there were 548 stations on the air, the first increase in a decade, and two years later there were nearly 750 commercial FM operations—an all-time high. Applicants were competing for the same channels in cities where shortly before no one had cared.

Subsidiary Communications Authorizations (SCA) for services such as storecasting were proven moneymakers for FM outlets, but they could not alone explain what was happening. More important, especially in major cities, was the increasingly crowded AM spectrum. Since there was practically no room for a new AM station in any sizable city by the late 1950s, the only way to get a new radio signal on the air, especially at night, was to use FM. In addition, when television's first major growth spurt (see below) slowed down, investment money and labor became available for FM. The country was going through a cultural boom, and people discovered the independently programmed minority of FM stations that specialized in classical music. Production of FM receivers had picked up, with lower-cost imports from Germany and later from the Far East (see pp. 382–383). Finally, transistor AM–FM radios, introduced in the mid-1950s, had AFC (automatic frequency control) to prevent the annoying *drift* of tube-type receivers. All these factors helped break the vicious circle of no audience/no advertisers/no money for stations/no stations/no programs/no audience and finally produced the growth in FM that had been expected when it was approved for commercial operation in 1941. FM radio was still a secondary radio service, but the increasing number of stations on the air and growing audience suggested that it was here to stay.

8.2.2 Rapid Expansion of Television

When after four long years instead of the expected six months, the Freeze ended in April 1952 with the *Sixth Report and Order* (see pp. 328 ff.), the effect was much like unplugging a pipe. The television industry exploded, growing from the 108 pre-Freeze stations in 1952 to more than 530 in mid-1960. Distribution, which had been very irregular with six or seven stations in New York and Los Angeles but no service in many areas of the country, evened out as many medium-size towns got their own television station or stations. After a few years, there weren't many single-station markets. No longer could one station carry the best or most profitable programs of all four networks—ABC, CBS, NBC, and until 1955 DuMont—plus its own local programming and make a huge profit from pitting advertisers and networks against each other. With the coming of additional stations to a market, each with a network affiliation (invariably, the third and fourth wound up with ABC or DuMont), television competition in the modern sense began.

The end of the Freeze led to stations being established on the UHF band. Initially, hope was expressed—the engineers knew better—that the UHF allocations would provide universal television service, with a wide choice of programming. What many applicants forgot, however, was that UHF stations had much less coverage than their VHF competitors, partly due to poor receiver design.

Station operators and advertisers soon recognized that the typical VHF station on channels 2–6 would give reliable coverage to 65 to 70 miles, channels 7–13 traveled about five miles less, and UHF stations were lucky to reach much past 30 to 40 miles (lower-numbered channels giving better service). The FCC had tried to solve this problem by allowing channels 7 through 13 to use 316 kw of power as contrasted to the 100 kw allowed on channels 2 through 6; the UHF stations were allowed 1,000 kw (later 5,000 kw or 5 megawatts). Even with this adjustment, coverage differences remained—and canny advertisers placed most of their business with VHF stations. Compounding the problem, few UHF-capable receivers were produced in the early 1950s and still fewer after 1956. All pre-1952 sets, and about five-sixths of those manufactured between 1952 and 1963 could receive only VHF channels. If a UHF station was started in a town, owners of sets would have to buy new ones (and few did) or an *outboard* conversion device that cost $30 to $50 and attached to the antenna terminals. Because antenna placement was more critical for UHF, and because the converter rarely gave a picture as good as the picture from channels the set was engineered to provide, there was little stimulus for people to watch UHF stations if they had a choice. When there were enough VHF channels in a market, network affiliations and the better programs went to them, and most of the audience did not even know about the UHFs. There had to be at least a two-to-one ratio of UHF to VHF stations for a majority of the potential audience to invest in all-channel sets or converters. Thus the typical UHF station could not compete, since it had a smaller coverage area and, within that, a meager audience. The combination was to prove almost fatal to UHF and did result in more than 100 UHF stations going dark.

The FCC had decided to intermix VHF and UHF stations in the same market (see p. 329), supposedly to assure even competition. More than 100 stations started on UHF channels as soon as they could after the Freeze, each hoping to do as well as the pre-Freeze VHF stations. But shortly, after having spent hundreds of thousands or even millions of dollars, they found that few advertisers cared about UHF stations and their tiny audiences, and networks were uninterested in affiliating a UHF station, unless it was the only non-affiliated station in town. Within months, UHF operations were failing for lack of operating funds and audience interest.

Although VHF and UHF were regulated as one service, while they were not really equal, and FM as a separate service from AM, there was a strong parallel between UHF television and FM radio. Both services came after a sister service—VHF television and AM radio—had become entrenched. Both started strongly—FM in the late 1940s and UHF in the mid-1950s—only to fall quickly on bad times and decline in number of stations on the air. Both services lacked network affiliations and advertiser interest. Audiences were small because neither television nor radio owners cared to spend money for converters or new receivers. In both services, broadcasters with ownership interests in the older, competing service had little concern for the newer service. In both cases, the best urban markets initially were filled with the older services, leaving only smaller markets, with less economic and political clout, as building areas for the newcomers. There were increasing threats in the 1950s that FM and UHF spectrum allocations would be divided with other services, as they were not fully being utilized.

Ironically the FCC and various congressional committees stated that FM and UHF were to be favored services. There were constant comments in official reports and hearings about moving the older radio and television operations over to FM and UHF frequency assignments, which were technically better and would at least put all operators on an even footing. At times the commission appeared like the nervous doctor who cannot pinpoint the ailment but is sure that further ministrations will help. FM started an upturn after 1957 but UHF continued sliding slowly downhill throughout the 1950s. New rules and legislation of the 1960s would give both secondary services a shot in the arm.

Thus, during the 1950s, television's commercial growth took place in the VHF band. The 108 VHF stations in 1952 had grown to 344 in 1956 and 440 by 1960, but the number of commercial UHF stations was only 97 in 1956 and dropped to 75 by 1960 (see p. 387).

8.2.3 To Pay or Not to Pay: The Debate Intensifies

To a number of struggling UHF operators and some who had gone off the air, there appeared to be one salvation: pay-television. In the postwar years (see pp. 279–283), debates over the idea and some experimentation had started something of a battle between those in favor, led by Zenith, and those against, led by the broadcasting networks, motion picture producers, and theater owners.

Through the 1950s there were several pay-television systems. Zenith's "Phonevision" system, which had been tested in Chicago in 1951 (see p. 280), sent a scrambled audio and visual signal over the air and used a separate telephone wire to decode or unscramble it. The customer secured "decoding" information by mail, phone, or vending machine and set a five-number "code translator" attached to his home receiver to unscramble the transmitted signals. Zenith suggested that stations devote 15% of their time to pay operations and 85% to advertiser-supported programming. A second firm, Skiatron, planned to send its signals by wire, not over the air, and unscramble them by use of a printed electric circuit on a punch card, purchased at a neighborhood store, inserted into a box attached to the viewer's set. Though this system could be used over the air, Skiatron concentrated on establishing programming companies that would distribute programs only by wire. Telemeter also used a wire system, decoded by inserting the proper sum into a coin box on the home set. Various other companies, changing from year to year, used similar technology, although one proposed simply sending the unscrambled audio by telephone wire. Each firm claimed that pay-TV would provide new kinds of programming—cultural events, plays, sporting events then not seen on television, first-run films—and would do it without interruptions for advertising.

Arrayed against the pay-TV proponents were the broadcasting and most of the film industries. They claimed that pay operations would spell the end of "free," advertiser-supported, television. The pay operators would be able to siphon off whatever kinds of programming they wanted, because even a small sum per viewing home would amount to millions of dollars. In addition, pay-TV would inflate talent costs. It could pay higher fees than regular television did because it could pass all costs on to the viewers without worrying about pricing itself above rival advertising media. Finally, pay-TV would raise the cost of advertising since it would leave fewer viewers for commercially sponsored programs—at a higher cost-per-thousand to the advertisers.

Agitation for pay-TV grew following the Zenith demonstration and a later, six-month test by Telemeter, owned by Paramount Pictures, in the exclusive desert community of Palm Springs, just outside the Los Angeles market. That test was limited to 200 subscribers, and few results ever were announced. In September 1954 Skiatron, following Zenith's example of 1952, formally asked the FCC to approve regular pay-TV operations, inviting support by suggesting that only UHF stations could be pay stations—for the first three years, anyway. In Spring 1955, the FCC held hearings on the proposal, and government policy makers and the public were inundated with petitions, newspaper editorials, booklets, reports, and other propaganda on both sides. Many public opinion polls, other than those commissioned by broadcasters, favored giving pay-TV a chance. But opponents convinced some powerful figures in Congress that what seemed attractive to some would mean less "free" television to many. This produced several bills to outlaw pay-TV, but none reached a vote.

In Spring 1956, the FCC proposed a two-to-five year test to determine the viability of pay-TV. It would limit the test to programs other than those then aired over commercial television, to cities with at least three operating stations, and to UHF outlets. This proposal merely inflated the debate. In October 1957 the commission issued its First Report on pay-TV, with specifications for putting the test into practice. Any of the various pay-TV techniques could be used, only 20 markets could be affected at one time, and a given system could be tried in up to three cities.

In the meantime, an extensive test of pay-TV by wire was taking place over a Bartlesville, Oklahoma, cable system. Making use of two different channels, and offering programs from noon to midnight at $9.50 a month, this system depended heavily on first-run films shown repeatedly over a short period. The Bartlesville operation started with 800 subscribers, but after the novelty wore off the number dwindled and the form of payment was changed from a monthly fee to a per program charge. When the operation closed down in April 1958, it was losing $10,000 a month. Operators blamed the loss partly on the release of newer films to commercial television (see p. 375). Pay-TV enemies heralded this failure as proof that people given a choice between regular television and pay-TV would shun the latter. (Although there are similarities between this experiment and the pay-cable operations of today, there was no attempt in the 1950s to identify CATV with pay-TV, particularly as the few CATV systems could not carry many signals and had not yet entered the larger cities where pay operations would be most profitable.)

Just as the Bartlesville test was proving too expensive to continue, a House committee held hearings and in February 1958 issued a "sense of the Committee" resolution asking the FCC to delay application of its 1957 rules until Congress was able to consider and act. In the face of this pressure and a huge flow of mail, the FCC hastily issued a Second Report postponing pay-TV. But there was little movement in Congress, and the FCC's Third Report of February 1959 provided specifications for a more limited test of pay-TV. After more FCC and congressional hearings, only three applications were filed and only one of these resulted in an actual test in the United States (see pp. 416–418).

In Canada, one test was conducted in the late 1950s. Telemeter offered pay-TV programs to Etobicoke, a suburb of Toronto. The 1,000 subscribers paid a $5 installation charge and a per program fee for use of any of three channels, two of which carried only movies. Telemeter claimed to have 3,000 families on a waiting list and estimated that it might reach 5,000 homes by late 1960.

Indicating the validity of warnings by commercial broadcasters that pay-TV would funnel off popular programming, Skiatron contracted with the Giants and Dodgers baseball teams, then recently moved to California from New York, to telecast only on pay-TV. This scheme failed when the Los Angeles City Council refused to sanction a pay-TV system in the city.

And there pay-TV stood—about where it had in 1952 insofar as hard data on its potential was concerned. But the passing of time worked against the on-air pay-TV proponents. As commercial television expanded and offered more feature films, the financial and programming rationales for pay-TV faded. Backers of pay systems tired of fighting other industries, FCC bureaucracy, and congressional indecision. And the audience did not seem to care, judging from the nebulous success of the pay-TV tests.

8.2.4 The Expansion of Cable Television

Cable television did not create much controversy (see p. 330), as it grew fairly quickly in the mountain areas of Pennsylvania and the Far West. By 1952, some 70 systems served 14,000 subscribers. Typically, for an installation fee and then a monthly charge of about $5, a subscriber got one or more signals "imported" from afar. By 1960 more than 650,000 television set owners were reported to be subscribing to 640 fairly small and local cable systems. Television stations in this period usually welcomed cable because they provided more listeners for a station's programming.

At this time *cable* and *pay* television were very different. Cable subscribers paid a set fee for being hooked to the system and a monthly charge for reception of some or all the stations they could not receive directly off the air. Pay-TV viewers paid "per program" and usually could receive "free" programs as well. The line between these two types of service was to merge in the late 1960s when, ironically, over-the-air pay-TV had faded in potential importance while the innocent-appearing CATV systems had become one of the broadcasters' major problems (see p. 467).

8.3 The Domination of Network Television

The trends of the late 1940s continued to the point where the radio webs had shrunk to little more than AM news outlets by 1960 and television networks were almost entirely VHF affiliates. There were almost continuous investigations by Congress and the FCC (see pp. 391–392) into monopolistic tendencies of networks in general and NBC and CBS in particular.

In 1952, half the AM stations on the air were affiliated with one or more networks, but by 1960, although there were 1,000 new stations, only one-third of AM stations maintained affiliation. Clearly, the networks no longer dominated radio programming and economics in an era when all attention, including that of network personnel, was turned to television. In the early 1950s, network radio cut its rates in an attempt to retain advertisers, but most sponsors preferred television or spot advertising on individual radio stations. Many major stations gave up network affiliation to program on their own rather than be tied to a system that failed to attract listeners. The Westinghouse Broadcasting Corporation, a major group owner, pulled four stations out of NBC in August 1956 to go to full-time local programming. Other stations stayed with the networks only for their news services and those daytime programs that retained some following (see pp. 365–367).

What had been the largest network in affiliates, Mutual, fell on hard and scandalous times. From 1956 to 1959, ownership of the network changed six times, with one management convicted of stock manipulation and another accused of selling a guarantee of favorable mention on its news programs to Dominican Republic dictator Rafael Trujillo. As a consequence of all these factors, more than 130 stations dropped their Mutual affiliation.

The other radio networks drifted along in the wake of television. Ironically, some "new" radio network programs derived from television shows. The only real program innovation of lasting importance in the period was NBC's *Monitor*, which began in 1955 as a 40-hour over-the-weekend "magazine" program. The combination of talks, interviews, news, music, comedy, and sports was a hit with listeners and advertisers.

The only major attempt at FM-only networking, the Continental Network (see p. 285), was unable to expand beyond the East Coast, except for mailing recordings to other affiliates. This limited experiment ended early in 1954 with the suicide of FM inventor Edwin H. Armstrong, who had been quietly paying for telephone line interconnection of these FM stations. Several regional FM interconnection arrangements dried up at the same time. Even at their peak, they too had been limited to the Northeast.

More than anything else, the middle and late 1950s were marked by the domination of network television—and that meant NBC and CBS. But this period also saw the demise of one nationwide network and the bare survival of another.

The one to die was DuMont, the only television network not built on radio's profits. Although it was fragile from the start, the network did not stop operations entirely until late Summer 1955. DuMont's chief problem was always being number four at a time when most markets had fewer than four stations. CBS or NBC had first pick of affiliates, with ABC or DuMont clutching at the leftovers. Stations with more than one network affiliation (common in the 1950s) hardly ever chose to carry DuMont programming, and advertisers understandably shied away from placing ads few would see. Thus DuMont made only one-third to one-tenth of the revenue of the other networks. In January 1955 DuMont was feeding only 21 hours of programming a week to its affiliates—the three prime time hours each night—and by August, although it claimed to have 160 affiliates, it only sent them just over five hours a week. DuMont then sold its profitable Pittsburgh station and withdrew to manufacturing and research activities, later selling its stations in New York and Washington, D.C.

Barely surviving was ABC, which had had many financial crises and always seemed to arrive at a television idea just after CBS and NBC had been there and cleaned up. The end of DuMont cleared time on some stations for ABC programming, and the ABC-Paramount Theaters merger (see pp. 288, 290) provided money needed to pay debts and update facilities of their O & O stations. But ABC lacked a star vehicle on which to build audience popularity, something analogous to NBC's early use of Milton Berle. All networks wanted such a boost, and for once ABC was the winner. Early in 1954, ABC signed a contract with Walt Disney Productions to air some of the "appeal to the whole family" Disney films and a new Disney-developed family television program. That show, premiering in Fall 1954, was *Disneyland*, which was followed a year later by *The Mickey Mouse Club* afternoon children's program. The popularity of these programs improved ABC's image and appeal to advertisers even as they promoted Disney's new amusement park. This and the increase in number of three-station markets following the Freeze improved ABC's competitive position against CBS and NBC by the late 1950s.

All television networks went through important evolutionary changes in these years. Probably most important, the networks were increasingly producing and controlling their own programs. This trend away from sponsor or agency programming control was to come to a head with the quiz show scandals (see pp. 376–377 and 393–396). Second, after 1954 the networks relied less on half-hour or hour series and offered more *specials*, one-shot plays, and documentaries of longer duration (see p. 378). Third, the networks were making initial investment in color equipment and programming, although only NBC, on behalf of its parent RCA, was actively promoting color (see pp. 321–324). Like the special programming, the move to color was mainly for the sake of prestige. Hence, NBC consistently offered most color hours, followed by a reluctant CBS, with ABC not even trying until 1958. From a total of 68 hours transmitted in 1954, color programming rose to nearly 500 hours in 1956 and more than 650 hours two years later. Nearly all the color shows were specials and most were live or on film, as color videotape recording was not yet perfected. There were few color productions—650 hours a year is less than two hours a day—because color equipment and color broadcasting were costly, CBS and ABC were reluctant to support RCA's manufacturing adventures, and not many expensive color television receivers were being sold (see p. 384).

In the early years, most network productions had originated in New York or Chicago. By the 1955–1957 period, however, nearly all production activity had moved to the West Coast, as television drew more heavily on Hollywood's hungry film production talent pool (see p. 337). The shift left administrative and fiscal control in New York and creative work in Hollywood.

In these years the networks had their greatest influence over television development, for without an affiliation a local station was almost doomed to failure. NBC had the most affiliates, although its proportion dropped from more than 55% to about 42% of all stations between 1953 and 1960. CBS started the period with half as many affiliates as NBC but ended with nearly the same number. ABC was one-third to one-half the size of its two competitors (see Appendix C, table 2-D).

NBC's programming was dominated at first by network President Sylvester "Pat" Weaver, the driving force behind the radio network's *Monitor* (see previous discussion) and such television innovations as *Today*, *Tonight*, and the specials. But the real power at NBC was in its owner, RCA. Soon RCA Chairman David Sarnoff's son Robert, who had earned his programming spurs as producer of the award-winning documentary series *Victory at Sea*, took over the operation of NBC.

CBS continued under the leadership of Chairman William S. Paley and President Frank Stanton and a succession of television network presidents. Its programming tended to stick to the proven: for example, Arthur Godfrey, whose folksy humor and ability to pick talent had proven invaluable to CBS radio from 1941 until the network stopped airing entertainment programming in the 1960s, at one point had two prime time programs on CBS: *Arthur Godfrey and His Friends* and *Arthur Godfrey's Talent Scouts*.

▨ **Sarnoffs and Weaver: NBC's Executive Team**   David Sarnoff (left), operating head of RCA almost from its start in 1919, is seen talking with NBC/TV Network (1949–1953) and NBC president (1953–1955) Sylvester (Pat) Weaver (center)—creator of the concept of "spectaculars" and the *Today* and *Tonight* shows—and with his son Robert Sarnoff (then NBC chairman), who was to lead RCA after the senior Sarnoff's retirement in 1969. The younger Sarnoff was fired in 1975. Their CBS competitors are shown on page 284.

Photo credit: Indelible, Inc.

These programs overlapped for eight and a half seasons, and Godfrey hosted both of them (and a 90-minutes a morning radio program) every week. It was estimated that Godfrey alone accounted for the unmatched figure of more than 12% of the network's revenues in 1953.

After the DuMont demise, each network owned all they could: five VHF stations. Not wishing to enter unprofitable markets, each concentrated on the largest cities and shunned ownership of the two permitted UHF stations, although both CBS and NBC owned one or two for short periods. Ironically, ABC, the weakest of the networks, had the best O & O lineup: a station in five of the top seven markets (albeit on channel 7), with ABC as the original licensee. CBS and NBC, on the other hand, bought and sold several stations in the 1950s, jockeying for ownership of the most stations in the top five or six markets (see box on page 289).

This led to a strange deal between group owner Westinghouse and NBC. In 1955, NBC offered to buy KYW-TV, Westinghouse's Philadelphia station, in exchange for NBC's stations in Cleveland plus $3 million. Westinghouse probably would not have considered the deal except for NBC's threat to withdraw television network affiliations from other Westinghouse stations if Westinghouse did not accept. The swap took place in 1955. A year later, the Justice Department accused NBC of coercing Westinghouse with the threat of affiliation cancellations. After several years of FCC and court actions and appeals (and the intervention of other parties who hoped to gain from the situation), the FCC decided on *status quo ante*—to put everything back where it was before. In 1964 Westinghouse returned to Philadelphia, keeping the $3 million, and NBC went back to Cleveland. Observers who saw the initial deal as an example of raw network power concluded that concentration of network ownership of stations in the country's largest markets might be against the public interest.

8.4 The First ETV Stations

A small number of groups and individuals had lobbied to get channel reservations for educational television (see pp. 291–293 and 327–328) and had succeeded with the *Sixth Report and Order's* reservation of 242 channels. Lobbying effort then switched from national to state and local governing bodies and other sources to obtain money for such stations quickly, for the FCC had reserved the educational allocations for only one year, after which commercial applications might be accepted. Though later extended indefinitely, the deadline provided the impetus to get stations on the air. The Ford Foundation, working mostly through the Fund for Adult Education (FAE) and the Fund for the Advancement of Education (also FAE), provided seed money for the campaign. The National Citizen's Committee for Educational Television was formed to convince the public of the potential values of educational stations. Their job was

1. To sell the notion of educational television to universities and other groups that would serve as licensees.
2. To gain public interest and organized action in favor of such stations for alternative programming.
3. To convince community leaders that such stations would be outlets for local talent and local government and other agencies in action.
4. To save the ETV channel reservations from reallocation.

A milepost was reached when the first educational channel on a reserved frequency took to the air—the University of Houston's KUHT, in May 1953. (WOI-TV, at Ames, Iowa, was on a pre-Freeze nonreserved channel.) The second station was KTHE on channel 28 in Los Angeles. However, its sponsors, the University of Southern California and the Alan Hancock Foundation, had financial and other difficulties, and after several months it went dark—the first ETV outlet to close down. Los Angeles was without an ETV station until KCET, Community Television for Southern California, reactivated channel 28 in 1964. New stations required raising tax monies, foundation support, or aid from other sources. In many cases, commercial broadcasters donated help and equipment—sometimes in the nick of time. These altruistic-seeming donations also prevented or discouraged new competing commercial stations, since an ETV station in a market occupied a channel but rarely attracted a large audience. Also, ETV stations provided cultural and special-interest programs to small audiences and reduced the pressure on commercial stations to carry such programs. In mid-1955, there were 12 ETV stations on the air, by 1958 there were 35, and by 1961 there were 51, but half the states had none. As with commercial channels, most of the reserved frequencies were UHF—182 of the 274 reservations the FCC had made by 1960—but as with the commercial outlets, most of the early ETV stations were on the VHF band.

Once on the air, educational broadcasters had to fill their operating hours. Having no network to provide programming, and being unable to use ordinary television fare, most ETV stations operated for only a few hours a week. Some of these were devoted to in-school broadcasts, sometimes paid for by school districts, and others, to cultural and entertainment programs. Even by 1959, the typical ETV station was on the air for only 35 hours a week, half the time of the typical commercial station, and used mostly local productions. However, in May 1954 the National Educational Television and Radio Center had been established in Ann Arbor, Michigan (it later moved to New York City) and began to provide several hours of programs to the four stations then on the air. By 1958, 30 stations were getting a minimum of six hours a week from this cooperative, chiefly as kinescope recordings or film. By 1959, having lost interest in radio, it supplied members with eight hours of programming a week—a quarter of all ETV programs. Major producing stations were WGBH (Boston), WQED (Pittsburgh), WTTW (Chicago), and KQED (San Francisco). The programs were distributed by mail, in a bicycle network from one station to the next.

Most ETV stations were under the control of a single educational institution, usually a college or university, although some school boards were interested. A few were genuine community stations, managed by nonprofit associations, with representatives from educational and civic agencies. Alabama was the first to establish a state network of several educational outlets offering concerted programming. Other states followed suit as funding became available.

Educational stations generally offered two separate types of programming: programs with general cultural content—adult education, foreign films, public affairs, general educational material, concerts—and instructional television (ITV). ITV was designed for the classroom (broadcast or closed circuit), or for individual viewing as a series of instructional units from kindergarten through college, for which credit could be given. The first purely instructional effort by a commercial national network was NBC's *Continental Classroom*, which began in October 1958, airing from 6:30 to 7:00 A.M.(!) It began with a series of lectures on nuclear physics and dealt over many decades with a variety of other subjects. This program obviously was not aimed at everyone, although some of its loyal viewers were able to arrange local college credit for the work done via television.

8.5 Advertising: Local Radio and National Television

There is a myth among broadcasters and students of broadcasting that radio began to lose money in the 1950s as television was beginning to make it. While the importance of radio (particularly radio networks) in national advertising did decline, its income increased during this period. However, as the pie was sliced in more pieces, radio and television exchanged positions until in 1960 television was receiving twice the advertising dollars of radio—but radio kept making money.

What *did* decline was the economic clout of radio networks. In 1952, the webs still took in 25% of radio advertising revenues, but as more unaffiliated stations went on the air and advertiser interest in radio networks declined, that share plunged to 6% in 1960. In the same period local advertising revenues, already 52% of radio income in 1952, increased to 62% by 1960. NBC was hit harder and faster than CBS, partly because many NBC shows had lower ratings—a possible result of the 1948 CBS "talent raid" (see pp. 297–298).

Individual stations adjusted to the changing advertising pattern, which in turn was affected by audience size and interests. In the 1950s, evening prime time, which formerly drew the biggest radio audiences, gave way to morning and evening "drive time," when people in autos were on their way to and from work. In larger cities drive time was more easily sold and brought in greater revenue. Some local stations did their own programming and sold their own advertising so that they could retain all the income, rather than the small fraction passed on under network arrangements. Still, roughly one third of AM stations, particularly new ones, were losing money in 1960. Broadcasters found out again that the advertising pie could be successfully divided just so far.

This problem was especially acute for the independent FM station operators. As an industry, FM radio didn't make money and almost all stations were in the red, though total FM income jumped from $2.6 million in 1952 to $9.4 million in 1960.

Overall, radio as an advertising medium declined from 9% of all advertising dollars in 1952 to 6% in 1960. But, as advertising in general increased throughout the Eisenhower years, radio's total revenues increased from $624 million in 1952 to $692 million in 1960. So, most radio stations operated with an adequate profit margin, and the larger clear-channel stations made excellent profits.

Television's income increased spectacularly in these eight years, growing from $454 million in 1952 (about 6% of all advertising expenditures) to over $1,600 million (13% of all advertising) by 1960 (see Appendix C, table 3-B). But television pattern changes were opposite to radio's. Local advertising declined (from 23% of television revenue in 1952 to 17% in 1960) as did network advertising (from 57% to 50%) while spot advertising increased from one-fifth to one-third of all television income. The networks' own income increased, but their proportion of the pie dropped as many non-network-owned stations came on the air.

It has been suggested by both broadcasters and their critics that a television license was, in effect, "a license to print money." A VHF station with a network affiliation, as nearly all had, usually was in the black within a couple of years of going on the air even though it frequently cost $1 million or more to establish. Unfortunately, and not unexpectedly, this profitable picture did not extend to UHF stations. Although only about half the operating UHF stations were losing money in 1960, many others had failed for lack of income or operating capital. With their more limited range and often without network affiliation, UHF stations had too small an audience to interest national and regional advertisers. They attracted only local advertising, aside from some national spot business, and some independent UHFs had a reputation for low standards of advertising acceptance. Quarter- and half-hour programs that consisted of advertisements with a bit of entertainment thrown in to hold viewers were common. Many UHF stations did not subscribe to the NAB Television Code simply because they had to sell all the commercial time they could, regardless of how many spots were aired in an hour, or what type of products were advertised. Although UHF rates were lower than competing VHF station rates, UHF stations could not attract more business and thus make up for the lower rates per spot because advertisers wanted to reach the largest possible audiences in each market.

On the networks, and to some extent on local stations, an important sponsorship change was taking place. In 1952, one advertiser normally sponsored an entire program, just as in radio. Some major manufacturers of consumer goods controlled several programs. In 1951, for example, Procter & Gamble had become—and still is—the biggest television advertiser, as it had been in radio, with several daytime soap operas and evening programs. But as the television audience increased, as programs got more complex, and as talent and production personnel demanded larger salaries, programming costs went up sharply. Networks, being able to cover their increased expenses without having a cost-per-thousand greater than competing media, raised their advertising rates until, by the late 1950s, half-hour or hour network programs were beyond the reach of many advertisers.

Starting with longer programs, and then with shorter series episodes, networks began to develop new types of advertiser support. First appeared alternating or shared sponsorship, where two noncompeting firms would share the sponsorship of a single program by alternating weeks or some other segment. In this way they cut their costs while maintaining a regular identification with the program and exposure to potential buyers. When the number of participating sponsors rose above two, identification was reduced, but it didn't disappear. An early example was the Arthur Godfrey radio variety program, which was sold in 15-minute segments to participating advertisers. Television's *Today* operated the same way. Daytime and then prime time programs required shared sponsorship as costs continued to rise. By 1957–1958, about half the network shows were still fully sponsored by one firm, while 28% were under an alternation arrangement, and 20% used a participating format. By 1960 this was the standard for specials and hour-long series, while full or alternating sponsorship still was prevalent for half-hour shows. (*Participating* advertising was placed within a designated program, and *spot* advertising was placed anywhere in the station's schedule according to the class of time, based on audience size, purchased by the advertiser.) Both spot and participating advertisers paid a rate that covered the advertising time, a *pro rata* share of the program adjacent to the spot, and a profit for the program packager, usually a network. When advertising agencies relinquished television programming control to program packagers and networks, spots were sold without sponsorship, and the two-decades-long relationship between sponsor and program, amounting to sponsor control of programming, ended.

Television time rates and the cost of production became prime issues with advertisers. In the late 1950s, production of a one-minute commercial cost between $3,000 and $15,000, depending on the degree of production difficulty. In the years under discussion, talent costs went up 60% to 85%, a major part of an overall 20% cost increase. On top of the production cost and the cost of duplicating and distributing the filmed commercials themselves (which was, of course, spread over a number of airings) the advertiser had to buy network time. Full sponsors had to absorb costs that for a prime time hour rose from $33,000 in 1952 to more than $87,000 by 1960, and spot advertisers had to absorb their share of the program's costs. Even though they led to good sales results, these expenses drove many smaller firms out of television advertising and back into radio or print, while big national firms made heavy use of national and regional television. But numerous television advertisers grew from almost nothing to highly profitable size in a few years because of their sponsorship of a popular program—although their fortunes could dwindle almost as fast. Probably the best example was relatively unknown cosmetics maker Revlon, which grabbed a major portion of the cosmetics market through its sponsorship of highly popular quiz shows during that format's heyday of the late 1950s. Revlon held its improved product position despite the quiz show scandals (see pp. 376–377). On the other hand, when research demonstrated that many children watched the Lucille Ball program, a tobacco company sponsor dropped the program. Although it was the most popular show on the air, it did not reach enough *smokers* to pay off.

8.6 Programming Trends in the Fifties

While advertiser and audience interest was centered on television programming developments, radio—even network radio—did not dry up and blow away. The rise in revenues during most of this period (see pp. 362–363) suggested that radio stations had to be doing something right; neither the influx of new radio stations nor program competition from television was killing them. Television was firmly established by 1952 and was falling into recognizable program cycles much like those radio had experienced.

8.6.1 Revival of Local Radio and Coming of Top-40

Network radio ended in the late 1950s. As late as the early and mid-1950s network schedules resembled the great days of the two previous decades in that a variety of sponsored programs were available day and night. Interestingly, at no time before or after the 1953–1954 season have the radio networks presented so many programming hours per week. But by 1956, the total began to drop off sharply. The first signs were simulcasting of popular shows on radio and television, and eventual transition to television alone, and the continuing broadcast of sustaining programs for prestige and to create the semblance of a going operation.

In the evening hours, formerly prime time, only variety and musical programs and various types of talk shows increased in hours per week after 1952. The light music format, which had not been popular on network radio since the 1930s, returned in the late 1950s with 15- and 30-minute filler programs built around singers—similar to television offerings of the same period. The only markedly different radio format was NBC's *Monitor* (see p. 356).

This is not to say that all creative talent had left radio for television. A variety program, the *Big Show*, was one of the most ambitious ever attempted of its type. NBC produced an adult science-fiction program called *Dimension X* (later re-titled *X Minus One*). Two decades later, when NBC rebroadcast many of the original episodes, they played well, even in an era of space flight. A major evening program format in the late 1950s was news, and by 1956 there were more hours of news broadcast than any other type of network program. Today, of course, news is the main if not only reason for the existence of radio networks.

Soap operas continued to dominate daytime radio, although they were heard for one half and then for only one third of their previous hours per week. The soaps were one of the last bastions of advertiser support in network radio at a time when most network shows had become sustaining, partly because many soap operas were owned and produced by their sponsors. Another lasting network radio daytime program format was general talk variety programs such as Arthur Godfrey on CBS and Don McNeill's *Breakfast Club* on ABC.

But total radio network programming dropped drastically in the late 1950s. Local affiliates first dropped sustaining musical programming because they wanted to go their own ways, and then they dropped most remaining sponsored programs except news because they brought in insufficient

▪ The End of Radio's Daytime Serial: 1960

Friday, November 25, 1960, 2 P.M. Eastern Standard Time, marked the conclusion of one of the most distinctive eras in domestic mass communications; after nearly thirty consecutive years of broadcasting the radio soap operas had ended. "Goodbye, and may God bless you," Ma Perkins told her loyal audience as she finished her 7,065th and final broadcast. Young Dr. Malone also bid "a sad goodbye" to his audience. The Second Mrs. Burton did the same, introducing members of her cast for quick goodbyes. Local radio stations along the CBS network line continued with their transcribed spot announcements, time signals and station breaks as radio moved relentlessly forward, never pausing to mourn the departed nor, indeed, even heeding their loss. . . .

A major drop-off began in 1955 when only nineteen serials were renewed for the Fall season. Among those which did not return were such veterans as "Lorenzo Jones," "Stella Dallas" and "Just Plain Bill." The total dropped to sixteen in 1956, ten of which were on CBS and the remainder equally divided between NBC and ABC. They were discontinued altogether by ABC the following season. There were virtually no changes in 1958 but the 1959–60 season represented another serious diminution. NBC listed but one serial, "True Story," and CBS, dropping "Backstage Wife," "Our Gal Sunday" and "Nora Drake," was down to seven titles. NBC discontinued its only serial, along with its other entertainment programming, at the end of the season and "Helen Trent" was dropped from CBS.

The 1960–61 season began with a total of six serials, all on CBS and all on borrowed time. The programs were owned by sponsors who were no longer interested in using them. Rather than discontinue the serials entirely, CBS chose to lease the properties by paying royalties to Procter and Gamble and other owners. Other sponsors were then sought to fill the four commercial positions within the programs. No regular pattern was followed in this application of spot advertising and there was none of the earlier commercial identification with a particular serial. Only half-sold through most of 1960, they dropped to 25% sold toward the end of the year. "Best Seller" was introduced by the network in a final attempt to instill new vitality in the daytime serial by dramatizing novels but it was too late. Affiliated stations increased their efforts to force discontinuance of the serials altogether, determined to obtain release of the time for local sales and operations. In mid-August CBS announced that the last Friday in November would be the final broadcast date for the remaining serials. Each program thus had time to tie all of its loose ends together and to resolve its current complications. Significantly, none closed with such finality that the plot could not be resumed on a moment's notice.

Source: George A. Willey, "End of an Era: The Daytime Radio Serial," *Journal of Broadcasting* 5:97–115 (Spring 1961), at pp. 97, 102–103. By permission.

advertising revenue to warrant network costs. Many affiliates no longer automatically cleared time for network shows. The last radio soap operas and evening dramatic programs died in 1960. *Gunsmoke*, one of the latter, converted to an extraordinarily popular television program that lasted more than two decades. Present to the end was a version of the show that had given network radio its first impetus—*Amos 'n' Andy*. The blackface program had converted in the late 1950s from situation comedy to musical variety with short comedy bits between popular tunes, but it too was eventually dropped. In place of these vestiges of big-time radio, CBS announced a new programming plan, intended to preserve the physical network for prestige, emergency, and news: 10 minutes of news on the hour supplemented with five-minute feature shows during the day, and a loosely formated Arthur Godfrey show. Period.

In the 1950s the networks no longer controlled affiliates but merely supplied them with part of their program input. Radio networks were set in a mold by 1960–1961: news on the hour, the ability to air breaking news, and little else. But in a changing and frightening world, special news events were to remain radio's forte, as it could deliver flash or bulletin stories faster than any other medium. Other programs aired on radio (e.g., political conventions, sporting events) also were carried on television, albeit with different commentators. Radio networks became vestigial. Stations without network affiliations offered a minimum of "rip 'n' read," or "yank 'n' yell," newscasts, comprised of the wire services' five-minute summaries read by a disc jockey. However, in times of great stress or national disaster the networks often allowed independent stations free use of their coverage.

With radio networks no longer providing programs or income to local stations, by the late 1950s radio stations had to rely on their own resources for the first time since the 1920s. Most stations followed the networks with a music and news format, soon known as standard (later MOR, for *middle-of-the-road*), which usually meant trying to program a bit of something for everyone, with emphasis on vocal and orchestral popular music. Traditional radio sound lingered in such operations, which offered recorded music about half the time, sometimes adding local talk programs, and in general aiming for the widest and largest possible audience.

While a majority of radio stations used an MOR format in the 1950s, a new trend was developing. Freed from the restraints of network shows and schedules and seeking ways of attracting listeners in markets with increasingly competitive radio stations, some stations began to specialize in a particular kind of music. This was not new; there had been classical music stations, usually FM, and, in some rural areas, country-and-western (C & W) music stations. Now stations in markets with a substantial black population began to program "rhythm and blues." There were perhaps 20 such stations in 1952 and about 50 by the end of the decade. Stations that went to a background orchestral "good music," or *wallpaper*, format with little or no talk frequently engaged in store-casting (see p. 347), and were among the first to adopt automation for assembling and playing the day's programming.

The format that was almost to take radio by storm began slowly. Looking at sales of phonograph records, program directors at several stations decided to emphasize the tunes that were selling well. Station owner Todd Storz in Omaha and theater and station owner Gordon McLendon in Dallas are often given credit for originating what was to become known by the late 1950s as *Top-40* radio. Storz tried the idea as early as 1949, bringing it to full force by the 1953–1954 season. He operated in major markets while McLendon adopted the format in smaller and medium-sized markets because the formula was relatively inexpensive. Essentially, it was a tightly controlled, fast-paced format that usually involved playing each hour a certain number of what program directors, disc jockeys, and a growing number of "tip sheet" newsletters expected to become hits, three or four "top 10" tunes as measured by record sales, an old favorite (as time went on, "old" might mean anything that came out more than a few months before), and fast-paced orchestrals and vocals. The tunes were divided by spot commercials (frequently delivered by the disc jockey), weather forecasts, time announcements, and news on the hour. Strong station identification became more important than selling the network or a local or network program. The process of station identification became an art far beyond the mere repetition of station call letters and city required by the FCC. The jingle, used extensively for commercials in the past, was revived to give a station a specific image. Identity built on call letters, frequency location on the dial, or key talent, was constantly repeated until listeners knew it by heart. Directly tied to station identification were the station's on-air staff, who grew from mere announcers into *disc jockeys* (DJs) or, after station publicity people got involved, *personalities.* Their stock in trade was to create a specific approach to the music, intermixed with talk, jokes, and comment usually delivered at a rapid pace with little or no "dead" air space or silence.

Thus was born *formula* or *Top-40* or *rock* radio in the period between 1952 and 1954. It expanded from about 20 stations in 1955 to hundreds by 1960, although most imitators copied the outward format of the pioneers without really understanding the formula. It was a unique format that only radio could accomplish. It was aimed at teenagers, who were the fastest growing segment of the population, had growing disposable income, and had plenty of time to listen. Time and time again, an MOR-format station would take the plunge and achieve dramatic increases in listeners and income. When one rock station played the same music as another, with much the same sound, the personalities on the air contributed tremendously to a station's success. An unknown announcer named Alan Freed came out of Ohio to become one of the most important jocks on a New York radio station, and soon worked himself into a commanding position in the music world. Another, Dick Clark, became almost an industry unto himself first in radio and then television, in Philadelphia (see p. 372). Other personalities soon were affecting everyday life and manners of the youth of most major cities, and attracting negative comment from persons who disapproved of those manners and that music.

While radio always had been an important adjunct to sheet music and phonograph record sales, Top-40 radio personalities now developed virtual life-or-death power over popular music record makers and sellers. If a song was played, it usually meant instant success and profit, and even an excellent record was doomed to failure if it could not get an airing on one of the key Top-40 stations. Thus, the jocks (and sometimes the program managers) at the 50-kw rock 'n' roll stations in New York, Chicago, St. Louis, Los Angeles, and Philadelphia suddenly found themselves waited on hand and foot not only by their fans but by recording groups and record salesmen who depended on radio. Many disc jockeys responded to this adulation and flattery by accepting payments, gifts, and favors in return for playing specific records, always asserting however that they played only those records they had judged to be good. The *payola* business became a public

■ **The Rise of Formula Radio**   With formula or Top-40 radio, radio became more than a carrier of media content originating elsewhere; it became central to a type of entertainment.

Rock's radio and record orientation is critical in distinguishing the music as a folk idiom. Although rock was not the first folk music style to use records and radio, it was the first to express itself *primarily* through these mechanical, impersonal media. Before rock, popular records and radio shows were inspired by live situations—Broadway shows, nightclub performances, and other personal appearances of a group or individual. Radio tried to duplicate these situations; Pop disk jockeys like Al Jarvis and Martin Block described "make-believe ballrooms" which created the atmosphere of a large dance hall, and in which songs were experienced as if a particular musician were performing in person instead of on records. Similarly, folk music traditionally emerged from live situations—from groups sharing a common experience of work or play, or from an individual singing to his people. With rock, however, records became the primary, common bond among artists and listeners, and radio shows provided the primary, common situation in which the music was experienced. Without consciously describing a hootenanny or trying to elicit the atmosphere of one, the rock radio show generated the experience of a folk gathering. The unique feature of this experience was that it existed only in the mind and emotion of the individual listener; he did not pretend that the records he heard were anything but records, because the sounds he absorbed were realities in themselves.

The rock disk jockey played an instrumental role in this experiential folk reality. Because he spontaneously participated in the event—rather than structuring it and separating it from himself by assuming the role of a detached "master of ceremonies"—he encouraged the listeners to react in equally spontaneous and personal ways. Moreover, when the disk jockey audibly hammered the beat to one of his favorite songs, or sang a few of its lyrics, and when he breathlessly read the news, weather and sports, he gave the radio show a pace which—to listeners accustomed to an older radio style—caused everything to blend indiscriminately together. But this style also surrounded the show with a total atmosphere that was typical of rock. In the dense fabric of sounds which characterized the radio event, the records assumed the imprint of performances and the show assumed the immediacy—although not the illusion—of a live folk gathering.

With rock, the radio and record media assumed lives of their own. They became ends in themselves instead of means to other ends.

Source: Carl Belz, *The Story of Rock* (New York: Oxford University Press, 1972), pages 46–47. By permission.

scandal (see p. 394) at the end of the decade to match that of the television quiz shows, and a degree of cleaning up was instituted.

For most of the 1950s, the important thing was combining records and radio to create instant events in the minds of listeners—the task of the disc jockey. Reflecting the times, the DJ had to get popular stars and music on the air without making radio sound Negro-oriented, even though much of the impetus for what Alan Freed titled *rock 'n' roll* was the blacks' rhythm and blues. Program directors were concerned that too much "black" sound would alienate their basically white suburban listeners, and thus the early rock stars, except for Chuck Berry, were all white. The first star was Bill Haley and his Comets, who mixed country and western with the new rhythm. In 1956 the first rock superstar arrived—Elvis Presley, a former C & W singer whose career rose dramatically after he appeared on the Ed Sullivan television show. The cameras were limited to shooting him from the waist up, since his pelvic gyrations were deemed too hot for television—or at least for Sullivan. Viewers of the show heard little singing as the girls in the audience screamed with excitement, reminding many of the similar reaction to Frank Sinatra at his concerts a decade earlier. Before 1960 Presley had 18 records each selling more than one million copies. Fan magazines turned to radio again, as it was the rock stars' major medium. Formula format continued with modifications as the mainstay of radio for many years.

The country and western boom came on the heels of rock 'n' roll popularity. After 1957, C & W records were heard on many stations, and C & W specialty stations began to appear in the Northeast, heretofore out of reach for country stars and songs whose "natural" audience was in the South and Midwest. Another type of music allied to both C & W and rock was the folk music of the Kingston Trio and similar well-rehearsed groups whose songs were musically enjoyable and had much less "bite" than the socially significant folksongs of the 1930s and before. By the late 1950s rock was being recycled, stations playing "oldies but goodies" or "golden oldies" years after they were in the Top-40.

8.6.2 The Age of Television Entertainment

In the 1950s as quiz shows and westerns filled evening prime time, sponsors produced fewer and fewer programs. As late as 1957, sponsors or advertising agencies still produced about one-third of the network shows, especially daytime programs, while networks produced another third. The remainder came from the *packagers*, companies that combined talent, production facilities, and ideas for specific programs or series under contract to a network. Typically, a packager developed or bought the program idea and, if the network was interested, produced a *pilot* or sample program. If the network and a potential sponsor were still interested, the packaging company would then produce series episodes. For each program, the packager would assemble talent, technical facilities (sometimes rented from the network), and personnel, so that the network would purchase a finished film or tape package. By 1960 these companies produced about 60% of television network programming, networks about 20%, chiefly news and documentaries, and sponsors about 14%. The packagers made most of their profit from syndication to individual stations of programs no longer aired on the network. Frequently, however, the networks acquired a financial interest in the programs produced by the packagers—a system that developed further in the 1960s.

Another important trend was the change from live to recorded programs. In 1953, 80% of the network shows were done live before television cameras at the time of televising so that any mistakes went out over the air—actors forgetting their lines, "dead" bodies getting up and walking off a scene, a stagehand walking outside a window that was supposed to be 25 stories high. The remaining 20% of programs were on film. By 1960, the

VTR (see p. 348) had taken hold, and one-third of network programs were taped—a process even then so good that most viewers could not tell the difference between live and tape. Live network shows were only 36% of the total, and continued to drop sharply in the early 1960s, with the remaining third being filmed. The kinescope virtually disappeared from network use.

Stations had used syndicated, filmed programming for their off-network hours from the beginning. At first this had consisted of some original material and old theatrical films. By 1955 a good part of syndicated offerings was off-network material—programs that had finished their first runs on the networks. But in 1960, after a short-lived attempt in 1957–1958, the networks began showing feature films, which then were not available for station syndication. As a result, the stations expanded their network television schedules, typically from 48% to 61%, and reduced local live and syndicated film material, from 22% down to 11% for local live and from 14% to 13% for theatrical film available for station use.

That television was voracious in its use of material was demonstrated by its rapid turnover. From 1955 to 1959, the networks averaged 46 new programs each season. Only about 20 of these returned for a second year, and many failed to make it through their first season. Such short runs were costly for networks and packagers, because a program that had been in active production for less than a year was unattractive for syndication. Why some programs last and others do not never has been clearly understood, but in the mid-1950s observers suggested four reasons: sponsor satisfaction, personality continuity of the host or characters, a low-pressure format, and familiar situations. Another influence on program selection if not longevity was imitation, for as soon as a format became popular, other networks or producers aired their own versions, rapidly satiating public interest until the format began to decline for lack of material and viewers. The television *adult western* format (see pp. 374–375) is an excellent example.

Another trend was the gradual lengthening of programs. Whereas in the early years program directors had been concerned about holding interest for longer than 15 or 20 minutes, the half-hour show had become standard by the early 1950s. As the decade wore on, the hour-long program became prevalent, and 90- and even 120-minute special programs became almost common. Some program types, such as situation comedies, stayed with the half-hour format. The general trend was to lessen the lock-step progression of programs on all networks at the same hour. For instance, a very popular hour-long program might be scheduled so that its second half would overlap the start of a program on another network.

One of the most interesting developments of this period was the *spectacular.* Beginning in 1954, with the coming of limited colorcasting by NBC, these special programs made lavish use of settings and costumes, color, and major names to attract huge audiences from the humdrum of series formats, even though they often emphasized spectacle over content. As noted at the head of this chapter, one of the most important was *Peter Pan*, telecast by

NBC for two hours, live, in color, in early March 1955. Mary Martin's bravura performance was seen by nearly 70 million Americans, making it the largest audience for any single event in history up to that time. Early specials marking major anniversaries of the Ford Motor Company or the electric light were telecast on two or three networks at once. Specials were expensive, and programmers at first were unsure of their appeal to viewers used to programs on regular schedules. In the 1954–1955 season, there were only 41 hours of specials, but in 1959–1960 there were six times as many. NBC broadcast more of these programs than the other networks, thanks to the prodding of Pat Weaver; CBS was second, although similar in approach; and ABC seldom was in the running. Content, intended for large audiences, varied from lavish variety specials to documentaries and drama, which usually appeared in inverse proportions—more drama, less documentary, and so on.

An important program was NBC's *Tonight* variety show, which began on September 27, 1954, with Steve Allen as host. This still aired 90-minute agglomeration of talk, guests, music, sketches, and jokes started at 11:30 P.M. (ET) and took network programming into the wee hours of the morning. *Tonight*, with Jack Paar taking over as host in 1957, quickly attracted a following of night owls.

Straight musical programming consisted of former radio orchestral shows, including the semiclassical *Voice of Firestone* and the popular *Your Hit Parade* (see pp. 182 and 308), and light music shows. The latter, generally 15-minute filler programs featuring a single singer, faded from television after 1954 in favor of general variety shows. Rock music came to television in 1957 with *American Bandstand* on ABC, hosted by Dick Clark for two hours late every afternoon. This program, begun in Philadelphia in 1952, became a nationally televised teenage dance party with guest star visits. To save rehearsals and to give the audience the sound they were used to, the singers merely moved their lips in synchronization (*sync*) to a record. Youthful fans responded to the dancers and new dances as much as the music itself. Clark built on this program and his radio popularity to form an interlocking, highly profitable empire of music publishers, production, and other companies. Many local stations had similar programs, which were relatively easy to produce, but they never had the impact of rock radio.

Four major kinds of drama dominated network television in the 1950s: daytime soap operas, general and anthology drama, situation comedy, and, at the end of the decade, adult westerns. The familiar housewife-pointed serial drama grew slowly after 1953, until it reached 20 hours a week by 1960, partly from extending the programs from 15 to 30 minutes in the middle of the 1950s and partly from additional programs. Prestige anthology drama flourished. During the 1953–1956 period it was at its height, with some 20 programs per week on the three networks. After 1958 such programs were presented as specials, comprising between one-quarter and one-third of all special programming. In either category, the shows usually ran an hour or longer, although there were a few half-hour programs in the 1950s; were presented live or, toward the end of the decade, on tape; used changing characters and actors in different stories; and presented adaptations as well as original plays.

Playhouse 90, started by CBS in Fall 1956, probably typified the best of television anthology drama. This weekly, 90-minute, live, original drama series allowed optimal development of characterization and plot. Programs such as *Studio One, Kraft Theater*, and the *U.S. Steel Hour* had proven very successful as early as 1953. Rod Serling's "Patterns," on the *Kraft Theater* program, had so much response that it was repeated, live, a few weeks later. It was later made into a movie, as were his "Requiem for a Heavyweight" and Paddy Chayefsky's low-key but warmly satisfying "Marty." For the first time people on the street talked about television theater—plays written by Chayefsky, Serling, Reginald Rose, and others, and produced and directed by people like John Frankenheimer, Delbert Mann, and Franklin Schaffner. These creative people, many of whom later moved to the feature film industry, understood the television medium and concentrated on images that would move from the small screen into the minds and emotions of the television audience. Some programs used major stars in substantial dramatic roles, but others used "unknown" actors, including many from radio drama, with great success. One program, dealing with the death of Stalin, precipitated an international incident and rebounded on Soviet attitudes toward network newsmen stationed in Moscow.

Naturally, with the pressure of weekly deadlines, the quality was uneven—something that is often overlooked in reviewing the "golden age" of television drama. Many programs were thoroughly panned by critics. Although new series aired (e.g., CBS's suspenseful *Climax* and shorter programs like *Death Valley Days* and the *Jane Wyman Theater*), rising costs and declining ratings reduced the anthology format to an occasional special.

A continuing staple through the 1950s was the half-hour situation comedy. Paced by the long-running Lucille Ball program under the title of *I Love Lucy* and other labels, this type peaked in 1954 and 1955 and then dropped with the onslaught of the western adventure show. But this drop may be misleading, for the televised situation comedy is one of the most long-lasting formats ever devised for broadcasting. Though it fluctuates, it continues strong. Usually built on a "typical" but actually very atypical American family, it spawned subgenre such as the rural situation comedy, first successful with *The Real McCoys.*

Another situation comedy sub-genre saw humor outside of the family and maybe the law. Robert Cummings appeared as a leering photographer surrounded by beautiful models, and hopelessly pursued by his eminently sensible but very plain assistant. This program, which ran for five years, was familiar to moviegoers who had seen Cummings play similar parts in films. Comic Phil Silvers created one of television's unique characters,

Army Sergeant Ernie Bilko, in the last part of the 1950s. Sergeant Bilko ran rings around his camp commander and his colleagues but often got his comeuppance while trying to make money in slippery ways.

A television staple that dwindles but never disappears is the crime-adventure-detective genre. The most successful of the television crime fighters of the 1950s was lawyer *Perry Mason*, played by Raymond Burr, who brought the Erle Stanley Gardner character to life in 1958. In 1956 film director Alfred Hitchcock brought his suspense and macabre sense of humor to television. His half-hour thrillers with weird twists were famous almost more for the director's opening and closing monologues than for the dramas themselves. Crime à la Chicago's bootlegging days showed up on *The Untouchables*, with a machine-gun narration by gossip columnist Walter Winchell and a wonderful cast of old automobiles. Despite protests from Italian-Americans that all the villains appeared to be Italians, the program had high ratings for years. *Peter Gunn*, a series notable for its improvisational jazz theme and background, had a detective who, like most television heroes, usually won but often took a beating in the process. Running through the 1950s and, after a break, again in the late 1960s was the archetype *Dragnet*, created by and starring Jack Webb in a realistic account of police operations in Los Angeles. Another show with a California setting was *77 Sunset Strip*, which had a good theme, fast cars, Hollywood living, and a new idol for teenage girls, Edd "Kookie" Burns. It and other Warner Brothers productions, such as *Hawaiian Eye*, were so formula-written that, during a writers' strike, they exchanged old scripts and merely changed the characters' names. David Janssen, later star of other popular series, was *Richard Diamond, Private Eye*, whose telephone-answering service operator "Sam" (only her attractive legs were seen on the screen) was Mary Tyler Moore. Every television season most networks offered such programs.

In the late 1950s, the western became the most popular type of television series drama. There always had been westerns on television—even one produced live each day in a station backyard in Philadelphia—but like *The Lone Ranger* and other radio westerns, they were aimed at younger listeners. *Hopalong Cassidy*—originally a series of inexpensive movies—was tremendously popular among youngsters. *The Cisco Kid* and other westerns were major television syndication items. The *adult western*, with three-dimensional characters, arrived in Fall 1955, with *Gunsmoke*, a former radio show, serving as the archetype. The four continuing characters—a frontier U.S. marshal, his assistant, the female saloon owner, and the grizzled doctor—anchored two decades of episodes that concentrated on character and incident rather than on the old action-adventure, good versus bad, of children's programs. Although the cast changed, *Gunsmoke* became one of television's longest running programs. The growth in western-located programs was rapid: from six shows in 1955–1956 to 18 in 1957–1958 and 30 in 1959–1960, the year in which *Bonanza*, the second most successful western program, made its debut. This hour-long show was built around a ranch-owning patriarch played by Lorne Greene (formerly a top announcer for the Canadian Broadcasting Corporation) and his four, later three, sons. The episodes on the Ponderosa Ranch were to fill television screens for 14 seasons and then continue into endless years of syndication. Many other westerns did too, such as *Have Gun–Will Travel*, which set a high standard for acting, as its cultured gunman-hero, Richard Boone, roamed the West for hire. The overwhelming popularity of the western format was brief but some programs achieved ratings of more than 40, when a rating in the low 20s was considered good, for weeks at a time. The American West of the late 1800s had long been a major theme of the movies and printed fiction, and it fascinated television audiences steadily through the 1960s, although with diminishing popularity.

Most of Hollywood's feature films were not available to television in the 1952–1960 period. Films made prior to 1948 often were syndicated to local stations, but most film producers and distributors kept the classics and post-1948 production away from television. Their reasons were economic. Films made after August 1948 were bound by a contractual requirement that performers be paid additional income for television showings. In addition, film producers were afraid that, if they sold their product to their chief competing medium, old films showing on local stations would cut into the potential theater audience for new films or re-releases. The major producers held this front tenuously through the 1950s and then agreed to a common release date for most of their old productions, holding on only to classics and recent films still valuable for theatrical release. Thus in 1956–1957, thousands of Hollywood feature and short-subject films flooded into television, usually as "packages" of good and not-so-good films from a given studio. Why the sale in 1956 after years of holding off? Simply because Hollywood was hurting financially and needed the income badly enough to cause the studios to sell their own heritage and ignore the potential disadvantages. Interestingly, in light of later events, feature films appeared in *network* schedules in 1956 and 1957 only in limited numbers and did not return until the early 1960s. At the time, it still was economically more feasible for networks to prepare and present original material. The network also feared that theatrical films would not attract large audiences, because many people already had seen them.

A number of innovations were made in children's programs, reducing reliance on *Hopalong Cassidy*. In 1956 CBS began a morning show for preschoolers, *Captain Kangaroo*—a mixture of songs, education, fun, and a bit of light philosophy. Bob Keeshan, who was actually in his 30s, played the easygoing elderly sea captain in such a way as to charm parents and children alike. Once in the late 1950s, when CBS contemplated taking *Captain Kangaroo* off the air, brief mention of these plans in the trade press and newspaper television columns brought thousands of letters from outraged parents, many of them connected with the broadcasting industry. CBS executive Hubbell Robinson promised that the program would remain.

However, this outpouring of support attracted the previously missing advertisers to the point that many parents sighed for the days of fewer commercials and more program content. Most network programming for children consisted of action-adventure shows and cartoons presented in the late afternoon or on Saturday or Sunday morning. The ABC-Disney deal led to *Disneyland* for all ages and to the *Mickey Mouse Club*, which in 1956 practically owned the grade-school audience in the late afternoon. Soon the cast's wearing of caps with Mickey Mouse ears caused a nationwide fad, and the show's theme song became a camp hit among older children. The Disney organization again syndicated the original shows in the 1970s, long after many of the young performers had risen in show business or sunk to obscurity. The success of this revival led to a later—unsuccessful—version, featuring a cast that better reflected American cultural and ethnic diversity.

8.6.3 The Quiz Shows: Success and Scandal

Even more emphatically but more briefly than westerns, big money quiz shows grabbed the nation's fancy. The *$64,000 Question*, under the sponsorship of Revlon cosmetics, began on CBS on June 7, 1955, and within a month was the most popular program on the air, with a Nielsen rating of 41.1. It was based on a radio quiz program that had doubled the ante up to $64 as the contestant answered each succeeding question. The televised *$64,000 Question* was a triumph of psychological appeal for vast sums of money and of format, with quickly famous isolation booths, bank-guarded questions developed by university researchers, and participants who had expert knowledge in unlikely fields. So the nation saw a Marine captain who was a cooking expert, a grandmother fascinated with baseball statistics, a woman psychologist knowledgeable about boxing (Dr. Joyce Brothers, who had deliberately memorized boxing data to get on the show, and who later had her own broadcast advice program), a shoemaker who knew grand opera, and a 10-year-old math whiz. The show's producers received 15,000 to 20,000 applications a week, and cut that number to about 500 "possibles." Of those they selected only about 15 each week. Louis Cowan, whose organization developed the idea for the program, became a high CBS executive. The *$64,000 Question* became so popular that it was followed by the *$64,000 Challenge*, where winners from the first show were challenged by other contestants. At one point *Question* and *Challenge* were one and two in the ratings, and Revlon had to change its advertising because it had run out of product!

Next came *Twenty-One*, in which harder questions received more points, and it took 21 to win a match; *Dotto*, trying quickly to identify a face that gradually emerged as dots were slowly connected; and others in both evening and daytime hours. The prize money made weekly headlines. Several contestants won more than $100,000, and even the losers earned a new Cadillac as consolation.

■ **TV's Isolation Booth Era**   The format was fairly similar on all the big money quiz shows before the end came in a blaze of cheating and scandal—curtains, the sponsor's name in evidence, the ubiquitous isolation booths presumably precluding hankypanky by the competitors, and the velvet-chained stands for the contestants before the questions were asked. This shot is from *$64,000 Challenge*, the program for successful contestants from *$64,000 Question*.

Photo credit: Indelible, Inc.

But this success did not continue. By late 1957 and early 1958, ratings were falling off and some newer shows were unsuccessful. It was difficult to maintain a fever pitch of interest among viewers. But much more serious were the mutterings from various quarters that the shows had been rigged— an accusation that program producers and contestants vigorously denied. But the denials were false and the dam had to break: too many people knew what was going on. The first news of something seriously wrong came in August 1958 when *Dotto* was abruptly canceled from both CBS (morning) and NBC (evening). Several contestants had claimed that the program had been rigged, and one had written to the FCC. Within days, some 20 quiz shows left the air in television's first major programming scandal. Network officials claimed ignorance, program producers said that people did not understand commercial television's purposes and practices, and advertisers said nothing. In 1959 a New York grand jury investigated the matter, but its final report in July was not made public. Responsibility for investigation— which the public demanded, particularly after popular winner Charles Van Doren had admitted complicity in cheating on *Twenty-One*—then devolved on Congress and the FCC. The shock waves that went through the industry as a result of the quiz show and payola scandals made many wonder about the merits of the high pressure and stakes of broadcasting and especially of the demand for high ratings to please advertisers (see pp. 393–394).

8.6.4 Development of Television Journalism

News programming on most television stations and networks changed little during this period. The networks each offered a 15-minute early evening roundup, which by the late 1950s contained more network reporting and newsfilm shooting than the simple newsreel of the early 1950s. In 1956 NBC replaced John Cameron Swayze as news anchor with a team of reporters first assembled for reporting the 1956 elections (see pp. 379–380), Chet Huntley and David Brinkley, both experienced broadcast journalists. Douglas Edwards continued to hold down the CBS evening news, and John Daly anchored the ABC program. Local stations usually scheduled a half-hour of news, weather, and sports—often in the form of three 10-minute programs—prior to the network news and then offered a recap at the end of network programming at 11 P.M. (10 P.M. in the midwestern and mountain states). This format did not change until 1963, when the CBS and NBC programs were lengthened to a half-hour (see p. 443).

Supplementing the regular network news programs were many special events. There is space here for only a few highlights. The June 1953 coverage of Queen Elizabeth II's coronation in London was a technical tour-de-force. The time differential of five hours between London and New York, the transatlantic distance, and the desire of people in North America to see

▪ A Pioneering TV Documentary Team   Top CBS newscaster Edward R. Murrow (left) teamed up in the late 1940s with producer Fred Friendly (right) to do a series of radio and record documentaries. After a run of *Hear It Now* on radio, in 1951 the two created *See It Now* as the first continuing television documentary series—best remembered for the attack on Senator McCarthy discussed in the text. Friendly later headed CBS news.

Photo courtesy of Edwin Ginn Library, Tufts University.

what transpired as soon as possible were interesting problems. The time differential and the need to transport film actually helped, for what happened in London up to 1 P.M. would have arrived in the United States too early for viewing if satellites had then been available. Still photographs transmitted from London by wirephoto were telecast in New York within 10 minutes of being taken. But film coverage of the day's events, photographed mostly by the BBC, or taken from their television coverage, was carried by special airplane flights to the nearest North American cities with network connections and fed into the vigorously competing commercial networks and into Canada's CBC. By late afternoon and evening of Coronation Day, Americans were seeing the events within 12 hours of their occurrence.

The television networks also moved rapidly to cover President Eisenhower's illnesses in 1955 and 1956. The Suez fighting and Hungarian uprising of late 1956, coming toward the windup of an American political campaign, tested television news, which attempted to cover complicated events in three areas at once. In 1959, Soviet leader Nikita Khrushchev visited the United States for several days and was followed by a mob of reporters. Televised scenes of Khrushchev banging his shoe on a desk at the United Nations gave a unusual image of international politics. Television also covered the rise of Fidel Castro in Cuba, from early network specials on the rebels in the Sierra Maestra in 1957 and 1958 to lavish coverage of Castro's 1959 triumph and takeover. Most such news events were carried on regular newscasts.

8.6.5 Political Broadcasting

The exception was, of course, politics. The era saw three major political events: the Army-McCarthy Hearings in 1954, and the 1956 and 1960 election campaigns. Also, the presidency came closer to the people when President Truman in 1951 permitted excerpts from recordings of presidential news conferences to be aired, and President Eisenhower in 1953 allowed filming, and later videotaping, of news conferences for delayed, censored use. Before, reporters could only paraphrase, and later quote, the President's remarks from stenographic, and later recorded, transcripts.

Joseph McCarthy (R-Wisconsin) was riding high in 1953 when he began an investigation of communism in the U.S. Army. Due to a number of events too involved to relate here, this culminated in a series of televised hearings before McCarthy's investigative subcommittee from late April to early June 1954. For television, it was the most important long-term live reporting since the Kefauver crime hearings of 1951 (see p. 312). But shortly before the hearings started, on March 9, 1954, CBS newsman Edward R. Murrow had used one of his weekly half-hour *See It Now* broadcasts to expose the senator's vicious tactics—and did it by showing films of the senator's own speeches. Keeping in mind the political mood and the usual lack of aggressive investigative reporting or commentary on television, the broadcast took considerable courage, as well as some of Murrow's and program producer Fred Friendly's money. They advertised it in selected newspapers because the network was worried about any controversy and particularly controversy of this sort. The program together with a later one created a storm of reaction, with thousands of calls and letters, most of them favorable to Murrow's stand. A short time later McCarthy was given the chance to respond as he saw fit.

These broadcasts helped rouse interest in the Army-McCarthy hearings. For nearly eight weeks, the networks, particularly ABC, which had the least revenue to lose, scrapped morning programs to carry all or part of the hearings and, to their surprise, saw daytime ratings increase by 50%. Soon viewers became familiar with the pounding questioning by McCarthy and his chief aide, Roy Cohn, and the gentlemanly effective cross-examination by Army counsel Joseph Welsh who, over the weeks, revealed McCarthy as a bully who played with facts, people's reputations, and important issues for his own political gain. Much of the American public turned from McCarthy in disgust, and he soon faded from prominence, after being censured by the Senate. To a great degree, television had destroyed McCarthy's public esteem merely by showing what happened—even though television's regular news programs had helped build him up. One unfortunate lasting effect of the McCarthy hearings coverage was identification, in the public mind, of the Constitutional right of "taking the Fifth Amendment" with guilt.

The 1956 presidential race was something of a replay of the 1952 campaign, with the same candidates but a more important role for television. For one thing, there were now four times as many television stations and twice as many home receivers. Second, as President Eisenhower had been seriously ill, television was used as the primary means of getting his image and message to the people. This saved his strength and let him concentrate more on the Suez and Hungarian crises. There was a greater use of five-minute programs at the end of shortened popular entertainment programs, rather than the half-hour political broadcasts of 1952, which alienated many viewers whose favorite shows had been pre-empted. Television had become of primary importance in broadcast political campaigning, reporting, and advertising, as shown by television political revenues surpassing radio's for the first time.

The 1960 campaign featured two very different men and two quite different approaches to television. Senator John F. Kennedy used a relaxed, modern style, born of his need to overcome the handicap of being a member of a wealthy Catholic family not well known to the national public. Vice President Richard Nixon often ignored ideas of his television advisers, apparently feeling that his 1952 "Checkers" speech had proved his television skill.

The highlight of the campaign was four "Great Debates," the first televised face-to-face confrontation of candidates for presidential office. In Summer 1960, Congress had suspended, for that campaign and for the offices of President and Vice President only, Section 315 of the Communications

■ **The "Great Debates" of 1960**   The four debates between Vice President Richard M. Nixon and Senator John F. Kennedy in the fall of 1960 probably decided the election—for in the first debate Nixon came across as gray (in several ways) and evasive compared to the crisp Kennedy style. In part because incumbents dislike giving exposure to challengers, the next national television debates were not held until President Ford and Governor Carter met in 1976.

Photos courtesy of State Historical Society of Wisconsin and the *Milwaukee Journal*. (Lot 3424, Env. 24, 9/26/60)

Act, which required that candidates for a given political office be given equal opportunity to use broadcasting facilities. Relieved of the "equal time" obligation to fringe candidates, the three major networks offered, and the Nixon and Kennedy camps accepted, time for several debates. The first, televised live on September 26 on all three networks, may have cost Richard Nixon the election. He looked haggard, owing partly to a light suit against a light background and to a tired and furtive look he seemed to have on television—partly due to an unwillingness to take network technicians' advice on makeup—while Kennedy appeared confident and outgoing.

Interestingly enough, listeners on radio thought that the candidates were about even or that Nixon did better. But more persons saw the program than heard it, and Kennedy got exposure he could not have received in any other way. Nixon, who had been leading in public opinion polls, lost much of his carefully cultivated aura of experience and leadership. Nixon fared somewhat better in the three subsequent debates in October, with varied formats, but the damage had been done. Plans for a fifth debate fell through at the last minute, and both candidates relied instead on election eve *telethons* from their respective headquarters. Some historians believe that the debates provided the less well-known Kennedy with the narrow margin by which he won in November. On election night, the networks introduced the use of computers to predict winners. They blew it. Early in the evening, CBS predicted a Nixon landslide victory about the time NBC was saying that Kennedy would take the election by a wide margin. Only early the following morning did the true thin margin of the Kennedy victory become clear.

8.7 Viewing Trends and Research

As in every period discussed thus far, the broadcast audience increased in the 1950s. The proportion of homes with television sets rose from just over one-third in 1953 to nearly 90% by 1960—a truly phenomenal increase. The radio audience also grew, with even FM receivers selling well by the end of the decade. But as audiences increased so did concern about the effects of broadcasting, especially about the effects of television program content on young viewers.

8.7.1 Cheaper Receivers—and More of Them

AM radios in the 1950s were smaller than earlier sets and, in the latter part of the decade, truly portable. People still bought console radio-phonograph combinations, but the volume market in radio was in table, clock, portable (with batteries), and other smaller-size sets for every room of the house. Plastic cases and tube sets were the rule; transistor portable radios— lightweight and using inexpensive batteries—did not appear until the cost of transistors lowered in the last half of the decade. The typical home radio sold for $20 to $30, and the typical purchaser was a radio owner who wanted an extra set. The proportion of automobiles with radios increased in these eight years from 55 to 68%.

For most of the decade, the FM receiver market remained low and stagnant. Each year from 1953 through 1958, no more than 700,000 sets were sold; for four of these years, fewer than 300,000 were sold. At the same time, 10 to 15 million AM radios and 5 to 7 million much more expensive television sets were sold each year. The least expensive FM receiver sold for about $50, more than double the price of a typical AM set, and distribution of FM sales and service outlets was inadequate. Then, in late 1958 and 1959, for the first time in eight years, more than one million FM receivers were sold. In 1960, nearly two million were sold—about 10% of them imports from Germany and Japan, where war-devastated electronics industries had been rebuilt into advanced-technology, highly efficient operations. The average FM-AM set price came down to about $30, only $10 to $15 above the cost of an AM-only radio. The use of transistors and circuit innovations, known as AFC, that prevented frequency "drift" as sets warmed up made FM receivers far more attractive. Other reasons for the growth of FM broadcasting have been previously discussed (see pp. 350–351), but public awareness and advertising of sets helped a great deal.

Television continued to absorb the most attention and the most money. In 1952–1953, the typical set had a 12-inch, 14-inch, or 16-inch screen and cost about $250 plus installation—about a month's wage. When you could buy a 21-inch set, it cost more than $400. Virtually all sets were American-made and black-and-white; only 500,000 color sets were manufactured between 1953 and 1960, as contrasted to more than 52 million monochrome sets. While volume production continued to lower prices, it took the arrival of small portables in 1956 to bring the cost of a television set to less than $100. Nearly half (45%) of U.S. homes had television sets in 1953, although many markets in the Northeast had more than 80% set saturation, and some in the South had only a handful of sets. By 1960, however, regional variations had evened out considerably: the northern states were running about 90% and the southern states less, but the national average was 87%. But, even in 1960, less than 75% of homes in isolated rural areas had television, due to receiver cost and distance from transmitters.

The television market was influenced by two post-1952 developments. The first was the establishment of UHF stations, bringing about a need for UHF reception capability. Some receivers offered both VHF and UHF tuners built in, but the number of such sets declined annually from 1.4 million in 1954 to 400,000 in 1958—a small fraction of the 6 to 7 million sets sold yearly. Set manufacturers claimed that there was insufficient demand for the more complicated and $10 to $30 more expensive all-channel sets, while UHF operators and some potential viewers countercomplained that the manufacturers wanted to concentrate on the more lucrative VHF market. The only way to get UHF reception in a receiver built without UHF tuning was to purchase an externally mounted converter costing $30 to $50. Converters did not sell well; their quality was uneven, usually no better than "fair," and could cause interference to other sets on the same or different channels. The limited sale of UHF reception equipment increased the inequality between stations on the two television bands and placed further pressure on the FCC or Congress to relieve it (see pp. 387–391).

The other new element in television, color, took hold slowly for technical and economic reasons. Color adjustment on early sets was very difficult,
with blue faces and green lips particularly common; color programming
was scarce; and color sets cost at least $800 for a number of years. The first
1953–1954 model year color sets had 12-inch to 14-inch screens, and at
$1,000 it is not surprising that only 5,000 were sold. But as the sets im-
proved and as color programming on the networks increased, so did interest in color receivers, sparked by the enthusiastic reviews of color programs
by newspaper television columnists. Between 1956 and 1960, from 80,000
to 120,000 color sets were sold each year, and prices crept downward into
the $500 to $800 range. RCA built 90% of them. By late 1959, less than 1%
of American homes had color. As these households relegated the old black-
and-white set to stand-by or bedroom service, and as others bought newer
black-and-white receivers, television homes with more than one set rose to
10%. To stimulate set sales, color programming rose from 68 hours in 1954
to nearly 700 hours in 1959. Most was on NBC; in 1959 CBS offered only
6 1/2 hours of color and financially pressed ABC offered none and said that
it had no plans for color. Obviously, NBC's color programming was tied to
parent RCA's manufacturing role, and CBS saw no reason, after the torpe-
doing of its own color plans earlier in the decade (see p. 321), to put money
in RCA's pocket. Color was only an expensive toy for a small minority. The
pundits who claimed that color television would "make it big this year"
constantly had to backtrack.

8.7.2 Broadcast Viewing and Listening Trends

By the late 1950s, the A. C. Nielsen company clearly dominated the national television rating field despite competition from the American Research Bureau (ARB, later Arbitron), its closest rival, The Pulse, Trendex,
and others. The Nielsen meter, placed in a sample of 1,200 homes across the
nation, provided the audience data used by programmers to change network programs from season to season. In addition to regular ratings reports
sent to customers, Nielsen published related research showing that by 1960
the average television household had the set on for roughly six hours a day.
Most daytime viewing was done by *heavy viewers*, households that used
the set for 10 or more hours a day.

The methods of testing audience preferences and habits had been refined since the early 1930s. ARB depended on listener diaries, booklets in
which test families, changed for each *sweep*, kept track of their viewing and
some demographic factors. In the 1950s, Trendex tried to revive coincidental telephone calling for specific programs rather than for all shows on the
air, but advertiser and agency interest was insufficient to support its expense. Its main appeal was overnight readings on specific programs, so that
decision makers would not have to wait two weeks or more to act on a show

in trouble. In 1958 ARB borrowed Nielsen's meter idea but tied a small sample by telephone line to a central processing computer to derive overnight "Arbitron" ratings for New York. Again, expense limited this operation. All methods had drawbacks: the diaries suffered from errors and nonresponses; meters measured tuning rather than viewing.

An important development in the 1950s was the increasing demand by advertising agencies for demographic information. Knowing that a large number of people had looked at a given show was no longer enough. Advertisers wanted to know the ages and sexes of viewers, their income, and other factors believed crucial to product sales decisions. The Home Testing Institute made the first attempt to supply these figures with its "TVQ" or "Television Quotient" service, and other market research organizations, including the rating services, attempted to provide similar information, leading to higher costs for stations and networks. One can argue that this was a sign of what some social scientists later called the decline of the *mass* media concept. For now, instead of focusing on a maximum size undifferentiated audience, advertisers sought a specific audience for specific products or services. The result was a series of programs and supporting advertisements aimed carefully at a specific mini-audience and not at a mass one. This trend was to continue.

The ratings services fell into public disfavor as a result of the quiz show scandals, although it did not stop their use. For the loss of favorite programs the public blamed the ratings services rather than the decision makers who used the data the services provided, and now the quiz show situation added a moral dimension. Time and again in subsequent regulatory proceedings (see pp. 393–394), the argument was raised that the need for high ratings had caused the quiz show deceptions. Growing concern about the derivation, validity, reliability, and role of ratings led in the 1960s to major congressional and industry investigations of methods used.

Amidst the television hoopla, radio was overshadowed but not forgotten. The first in-depth look at radio in more than five years, widely reported in the trade press, was a 1953 Politz study. It showed that, while the *pattern* of radio listening had changed with the coming of television, the increase of radio listening in cars, in daytime, and away from the home had kept total radio listening high.

8.7.3 Children and Television: Phase One

From the start, families with children were among the first to buy television sets—at the urging of the children. Television became a natural babysitter, freeing parents and older children. Parents soon learned what researchers later found out: children as young as three years old were regular and heavy users of television. Parents worried that their children might be getting ideas from television that they were ill-equipped to handle—first apparent in the child's loud urging to buy some television-advertised product. A more serious concern was the constant action and violence seen on many cartoon shows, slapstick comedies such as *The Three Stooges*, and westerns aired when young children could see them. The number of fights, shootings, and killings broadcast in any week made viewers wonder what young children were learning. This concern had been expressed over radio and motion pictures in the 1930s and 1940s, and over comic books later, but people had worried then about radio's overtaxing the child's imagination. Now, they feared that *any* child, of any age, seeing mayhem on television day after day would become desensitized and accustomed to this behavior, even to the extent of adopting such values in his or her own life.

This concern led Senator Estes Kefauver (D-Tennessee) to hold hearings in 1952 into the causes of juvenile delinquency. The hearings touched often on the potential lessons to be found in daily television fare. The same committee looked into the problem again in 1954 and 1955, when witnesses cited examples of behavior models shown in adult action-adventure programs often watched by children. They associated the child's habit of imitation with the opportunity for young television viewers to follow violent examples. Some experts' testimony at the hearings suggested, however, that televised violence might be good for children as catharsis, which implies that *watching* violence takes away the need for *doing* violence. Most observers and researchers disagreed—and continued to disagree (see p. 457 and 556)—with one another.

The first two in-depth research studies on the interaction of children and television appeared in the late 1950s. The first, by Himmelweit, Oppenheim, and Vince (1958), was based on observations and interviews of several thousand children in England, while the second, by Schramm, Lyle, and Parker (1961), reported results of research in ten American cities during the 1958 through 1960 period. The chief finding of both studies was something parents long had known: that from its arrival in the home, television dominated other media and family activities. Its great novelty appeal lasted a few weeks and then, like another toy, it became part of the child's daily input. No physical effects showed up, although parents had worried about posture and eyesight in the early years of television, and about an increase in passivity—the *narcotizing dysfunction* of the mass media. The effect of television on school progress varied so much from child to child that generalizations were hard to make. The medium seemed to open children's eyes to the adult world faster, and in many youngsters sparked interest in new things, but others simply sat in front of the set, looking at whatever was on the tube. The determining factor seemed to be not the television set or its content but the child's background and emotional or psychological makeup before he or she ever saw television. Both studies showed that sixth-grade children, about 11 years old, watched television the most—about four hours a day.

8.8 Crises of Regulatory Confidence

Only the Cox-Lea investigations during World War II (see p. 261) had filled the regulatory picture with more investigations, soul-searching, and a feeling of smashed standards in broadcast content and operation than during the 1951–1960 period. Members of the FCC testified on Capitol Hill more than they minded their own shop. One possible explanation for these events of is that mistakes of the first decade of television had to be shaken out to make way for a fresh approach. That certainly happened!

8.8.1 The UHF Mess

Throughout this chapter we have mentioned the plight of UHF stations. When the FCC issued the *Sixth Report and Order* in April 1952, it did not create the competition it claimed to desire (see pp. 328 ff.). At best, the commission could create conditions and facilities for competition, hoping that new broadcasters would provide the actual competition and service to the public. However, the FCC established *unequal conditions*, which necessarily meant unequal competition. As the first UHF stations went on the air, they discovered that the stated FCC policy of equality of facilities in a given market did not exist in practice.

When UHF stations had to compete with VHF stations in the same market—a condition called *intermixture*—they were in trouble, particularly if the VHF station or stations had been operating for some time. In addition to the preponderance of VHF-only sets in such communities, the viewing habits of the audience, and the network affiliation contracts with pre-Freeze stations, a UHF operator had to neutralize or overcome the greater coverage area or range of VHF transmission. Both networks and advertisers relied on the concept of unduplicated population coverage or "circulation" in awarding affiliations and contracts. This basic inequality was aggravated by FCC moves to permit many VHF stations to increase antenna height and power, at a time when transmitter manufacturers were unable to construct high-powered UHF transmitters. Also, despite promises to the contrary by receiver manufacturers, only a small proportion of television receivers was able to pick up any UHF channels (see p. 383); all-channel set production peaked at 35% in the first half of 1953 and dropped below 9% by 1958, although field conversions raised the total proportion of UHF-capable receivers to more than one-fifth.

The FCC was too busy processing applications and issuing construction permits to worry about UHF operators for some years. Congress made it clear that the FCC's first priority was to meet the needs of television-hungry constituents. Surviving UHF operators lived on hope alone. Approximately 165 UHF stations went on the air between mid-1952 and mid-1959—and nearly 55% of them later went dark. The high point of 127 UHF stations came in March 1954; five years later there were fewer than 80.

The FCC's hope (or, in light of the commission's penchant for ignoring engineering advice, fantasy) that UHF and VHF were equal was not immediately obvious from the *Sixth Report and Order.* Of the 1,275 communities to which channels were assigned, 110 were to be VHF only, 910 UHF only, and only 255 (20%) intermixed. Also not immediately apparent from the *Sixth Report and Order* was the fact that of the top 162 markets, 8 were to be VHF only, 31 UHF only, and 123 (76%) intermixed. Considering the cost of establishing even the smallest station, it is no wonder that only 308 communities out of 1,275 had stations in operation in June 1958, and that virtually no UHF station was doing well against entrenched competition in the larger markets.

The loud complaints of UHF operators against the manufacturers, advertisers, networks, competition, and commission were to a large extent justified. Manufacturers were not interested in designing better all-channel sets or in promoting them, although their argument that there was little demand for UHF sets has pragmatic merit. Advertisers went where the people were, and VHF operators could hardly be expected to nurture their competition. The networks gave lip service to UHF but tended to give affiliations to VHF stations. Each established a plan (CBS's "Extended Market Plan" and NBC's "Program Service Plan") to provide network programs to some isolated UHF stations at practically no cost. This would give advertisers a few thousand more viewers and help the station sell spots before and after the network programs. After the FCC declared new multiple-ownership rules in Fall 1954, allowing a single entity to hold five VHF and two UHF stations at the same time, both NBC and CBS bought two UHF stations apiece. Two were in the Hartford area and the others were in Milwaukee (CBS) and Buffalo (NBC), but all had been sold by early 1959 (see box on page 289).

The predicament of UHF stations stemmed mainly from three problems:

1. The technical inequality of UHF stations with respect to coverage.
2. Intermixture, and the vast inertia of millions of VHF-only receivers.
3. Lack of confidence in the capabilities of and need for UHF television.

None of these would easily yield to wishful thinking, persuasion, or the marketplace.

It was recognized fairly early that solutions to these problems might lie in one or a combination of the following:

1. Unscrambling the egg (deintermixture) so that each community would be *either* VHF *or* UHF.
2. Converting to an all-UHF system, which would make all stations equal but would be very expensive for existing VHF stations and would reduce the number of signals that rural areas could pick up.

3. Converting to an all-VHF system, discarding the UHF band for television and picking up a probably limited number of channels from FM or government.
4. Promoting the manufacture and sale of all-channel sets by removing excise taxes or—in an analogy found in the Wireless Ship Act of 1910 (see pp. 42–43)—forbidding the transport of VHF-only receivers in interstate commerce.
5. Making unspecified but major changes in the relationships between networks and affiliates.
6. Somehow reducing coverage of VHF stations so that they would be comparable to UHF.

Another industry-staffed engineering group, the Television Allocation Study Organization (TASO), was established under FCC auspices to study technical ramifications of these and similar proposals—an act that delayed FCC decisions for another few years. Meanwhile, 75% of UHF stations showed losses.

Some of the proposals would not provide sufficient help and some were politically or technically infeasible. Neither FM broadcasting, which started to grow again in 1960, nor the military, who were asked several times up through 1958, was willing to give up VHF spectrum space. UHF operators, although many had little confidence and staying power, saw no advantage in abandoning their toehold. Broadcasters and the commission supported the idea of all-channel sets but recognized that any addition to consumer costs would be unpopular with Congress. Since range was affected more by antenna height than by power at these frequencies, reducing VHF power would seem to be ineffective, and allowing UHF stations to go to 5 million watts would not necessarily give a farther-reaching signal—if a transmitter could be made to deliver that power and UHF broadcasters could afford to buy it.

Because the UHF situation became caught up in the larger and politically more urgent issue of getting television to small communities, it received more and more congressional attention. At this time, before the Supreme Court "one man-one vote" decisions, rural areas and small communities had disproportionate political clout and representation in Congress. As a result, political rather than technological factors often ruled FCC decisions (and indecision) in respect to: CATV; then-illegal on-channel *boosters*, which retransmitted on the same channel as the orginal signal, causing considerable interference; translators, which picked up a signal and retransmitted it on a high-UHF channel in a small community; and satellites, essentially regularly assigned transmitters that originated no programming of their own, merely repeating the programs of a parent station (see p. 330).

The FCC, under pressure from Senator Charles Potter's (R-Michigan) Communications Subcommittee of the Senate Commerce Committee and

recognizing the political unlikelihood of a radical solution, started a series
of hearings in 1955. It grasped at every straw, including the possibility of
obtaining military spectrum space, "drop-in" of VHF channels without doing violence to the mileage-separation standards set forth in the *Sixth Report and Order*, and selective or total deintermixture.

The hearings gave UHF backers a platform, and they tried to make the
most of it. They proposed moving all television to the UHF band, limiting
color to UHF, and adding channels. They gave the compromise of deintermixture mild support but applauded removal of excise taxes on all-channel
receivers. Although VHF operators, aided perhaps overly much by the
NARTB, gave their views; and the networks, led by CBS, indicated their
lukewarm approval of UHF; the hearings bogged down in politics.

As with most political decisions, what emerged after FCC hearings in
1955, 1956, and 1958 was a compromise: selective (that is, in as few communities as possible) deintermixture in markets where it could be achieved
without disrupting many existing stations and their audiences. A few markets
were successfully deintermixed in the late 1950s, particularly in California's
San Joaquin Valley, but the UHF situation sat on almost dead center until
the mid-1960s. The Television Allocation Study Organization (TASO) final
report advocated that the UHF be abandoned and television stick with a de-
graded, due to drop-ins, VHF system. In February 1959, shortly after TASO
reported, the commission proposed alternatives for further study, coordination, and discussion:

1. A 50-channel VHF system, retaining the present 12 VHF channels.
2. A continuous 50-channel VHF system, abandoning channels 2 to 6
   but moving farther in the spectrum above channel 13.
3. A contiguous 25-channel VHF system retaining channels 7 to 13.
4. The existing 82-channel VHF-UHF system.
5. A 70-channel all-UHF system.

These untested proposals each had its proponents among the commissioners. Although deintermixture and slight degradations of the VHF spectrum were believed to be practical and acceptable, the FCC said that they
would not solve the problem.

The FCC requested and received $2 million to test UHF propagation
characteristics—especially in large cities—about which there were much
disagreement and little data. Using for the study the channel assigned to
New York's Municipal Broadcasting System station WNYC-TV (which
managed to have the test transmitter donated to it at the conclusion of the
experiment some years later), the commission prodded dormant UHF construction permit holders, and waited noisily for Congress to agree on the
best course. Senator Potter's investigation had merged into a study of network operations by Senator John Bricker (R-Ohio) and, after the Democrats
took over the Senate Commerce Committee in 1955, by Senator Warren

Magnuson (D-Washington). Magnuson, who was very interested in television policy, covered a tremendous amount of ground in the course of his Television Inquiry of 1956–1958 (see next section). Until members of Congress resolved their conflicting viewpoints, it was improbable that any commission decision in the UHF area would stick. More than a decade went by from the end of the Freeze to the first real legislative action—and UHF was still a troublesome issue more than a decade after that (see pp. 415–416).

8.8.2 The FCC Investigates the Networks—Again . . .

In Fall 1955, somewhat in response to Senator Bricker, the FCC decided that, because of the many changes in broadcasting, it was time to look again at the roles and practices of networks. Money and staff limitations and recognition of the reduced role of radio networks concentrated the investigation on television. Under the direction of University of Cincinnati Law School Dean Roscoe Barrow, extensive research was conducted in and about the networks (e.g., network-affiliate relations, option time, program sources, network ownership of stations, and advertising revenues). The first report, issued in October 1957, provided a detailed review of commercial television and the organization and economic status of the major networks, with a brief chapter on the radio industry. It also provided recommendations that shook the industry.

Most important, the Barrow report urged that the networks be put under direct FCC regulation. The long-standing FCC regulation of network-owned or affiliated stations was considered insufficient for the complicated role and importance of television networks, which dominated television far more than radio networks had dominated radio. In addition, the report recommended:

1. A ban on option time—specific times during the day when by contract the network had priority on station time.
2. Limits on network ownership of stations.
3. A ban on *must-buy* stations—a technique that required an advertiser to pick his lineup of stations so that a minimal nationwide network identity would be preserved at all times.
4. Publication of affiliation agreements.
5. A right of nonaffiliates to obtain network programs when the local affiliate rejects the network feed.
6. Penalties such as fines and forfeitures for breaking these or other rules.

While the industry immediately complained that such rules would destroy the structure of broadcasting—a familiar lament (see pp. 210–212)—the FCC took these initial recommendations under advisement.

In June 1960, the network study staff issued a second report, focusing on network program procurement. Described as "interim," it covered months of testimony from broadcasters, producers, critics, and others. It described current network practices in getting and using programming, including standards for program development and acceptance, and made some very tentative conclusions about public service programming. Further interim and detailed studies, without recommendations, were issued in 1963 and 1965.

This examination of networks was unlike the 1939–1941 investigation in several ways. For one thing, none of its recommendations promised changes as fundamental as the chain broadcasting rules upheld by the Supreme Court in 1943. Second, it was far more intensive and exhaustive than the 1941 Chain Broadcasting Report, yet it dealt with but a decade of television network operation. Finally, the 1957 report was the first in a series prepared by a regular, not ad hoc, part of the commission staff, showing that the networks could expect continuing scrutiny.

However, the two investigations also were alike. Both came up with specific recommendations to temper business practices that appeared to restrain competition. Both were undertaken following congressional pressure, for the 1957 network study grew out of several years of House and Senate hearings on networks and the FCC. In both cases the final rule changes instituted by the FCC stuck, despite strong industry opposition (see pp. 210–211 and 418–419).

8.8.3 . . . and Congress Investigates the FCC—Again

In March 1957 the House Committee on Interstate and Foreign Commerce formed a Subcommittee on Legislative Oversight to look into problems of certain regulatory agencies, which this committee was to "oversee" or supervise. The subcommittee was chaired at first by Congressman Morgan Moulder (D-Missouri) and later by full committee chairman Oren Harris (D-Arkansas). Almost from the start, the FCC became a prime target for the subcommittee chief counsel, New York University law professor Bernard Schwartz. Schwartz had little patience for diplomatic convention and made a habit of leaking to the press his latest findings on real and imagined shortcomings of the FCC. Those leaks led to Schwartz's firing in January 1958. He promptly wrote a book charging a political cover-up of regulatory commission shenanigans. In Spring 1958 the committee began hearings into the qualifications and activities of FCC commissioners, concentrating on their use of free industry-provided television sets and travel and on their ex parte (outside the normal forum for adjudication) contacts.

On March 3, 1958, FCC Commissioner Richard Mack resigned under fire, after it became known that he had accepted a sizable bribe to vote for an applicant for a Miami television channel. Mack was the first commissioner forced from office but not the last. Congress, concerned about chumminess between segments of the broadcasting industry and its regulators, focused on the Mack case. In April 1958 the subcommittee issued its report, calling for a code of ethics for administrative agency personnel, and the right of the President to remove commissioners for neglect of duty.

The subcommittee also investigated fairness in comparative application cases and the possible need for antitrust action against some broadcast owners. During the Summer and Fall of 1958, hearings continued into ex parte contacts, trafficking in licenses, mergers, and pay-offs—all considered against the public interest. The quiz show scandals and the payola problem (see next section) took up most of the subcommittee's time in 1959 and 1960. A 1959 Attorney General report to the President called for legislation to strengthen and clean up the operations of the FCC and the FTC, and also dealt with the ethics of commissioners and staff members. This aspect received more attention just a few months later.

Early in 1960, pressure built up to get rid of FCC Chairman John C. Doerfer. He had used very poor judgment, especially in light of the ongoing investigations, had taken pleasure trips on a broadcaster's yacht, and had submitted double and triple billing for official trips. When he took yet another trip on group station owner George B. Storer's yacht, President Eisenhower asked for his resignation. Doerfer was dissuaded from going on television with his side of the story, and he resigned. The black eye on the regulator, the FCC, naturally eased congressional pressure on the regulated, the broadcasters. Early in 1961 the Subcommittee on Legislative Oversight ended its activities before the hearings resorted to personality battles or vendettas like the Cox investigation of the early 1940s (see p. 261). This time, the FCC clearly had ethical problems that needed airing.

For more than a decade after 1950, there was almost always at least one congressional hearing or staff study of FCC activities underway in either the House or Senate or both. This period of investigation involved not only the commission's internal operations but also problems of the broadcasting industry. Although some broadcasting investigations may have been the result of prodding by a publicity-hungry congressman on a commerce, small business, or appropriations committee, the hearings of the late 1950s were more useful and less emotional than those of the early 1940s. The Senate Commerce Committee maintained a watchful eye on the FCC, and the commission knew it. Specific legislation and rule changes resulted, unlike the fizzle of earlier investigations.

8.8.4 The Quiz and Payola Investigations

Investigations of network quiz shows (see pp. 376–377) drew most of the public attention. In late 1959, the focus shifted from New York and its grand jury proceedings to Washington where both a congressional committee and the FCC held hearings. The highlight, or low point, of the congressional hearings came when the *Twenty-One* winner Charles Van Doren confessed his complicity in the rigging process, thus admitting that he had committed perjury before the New York grand jury. Van Doren's confession shocked the nation, more so because he was a relative of author-scholars Carl and Mark Van Doren and a faculty member of Columbia University. Former contestants, network officials, advertisers, agency representatives, and others also appeared before both the committee and the FCC and testified to the rigging story, giving a good picture of the pressures that brought about such unethical behavior. A rigged contest or quiz was a fraud on the public. Van Doren resigned his post at Columbia, and he and others fell into public disgrace although they weren't jailed. It was several years before he could publish again under his own name. The networks established stringent procedures for supervision of the few quiz shows still on the air and hoped that the worst was over. Although some quiz show producers found it harder to get on the air for a few years, in general the episode became forgotten—until Robert Redford's 1994 award-winning movie, *Quiz Show*, was distributed.

But just as the quiz show situation was settling down, payola, a form of corruption in radio, arose. Record manufacturers had recognized the importance of the disc jockey (see p. 368–369) in selling records. A few plays of a new tune on an important market's top rock station could spell the difference between wild success and failure. To persuade programmers and disc jockeys that a given record had Top-40, or Top-10, qualities required salesmanship in addition to sending the DJ a sample record.

But the persuasion soon moved past consideration of the record's merit to gifts of money, liquor, and even women and occasionally drugs. In short, bribery. Important disc jockeys enriched themselves while accepting "guidance" in evaluating new records—a payola process dating back to the era of big bands. But in the late 1950s, concern over this illicit business practice— a fraud because the public counted on the DJ's professional judgment and not his self-interest in selecting records—combined with older generations' distaste for and impatience with rock music to put the whole issue before Congress. A House investigating subcommittee heard testimony from many famous disc jockeys, including Alan Freed and Dick Clark. Freed's disclosure that he had freely partaken of payola stopped his career cold, while Clark's widespread and interlocking business interests, which obviously entailed conflict of interest if not outright payola, marred his reputation. These revelations led to legislation intended to curb commercial bribery in record selection, and to reaffirm the licensee's responsibility for whatever went on the air.

The House committee and the FCC also examined the practice of radio or television *plugola*, closely related to payola. This involved programmers or show hosts deliberately mentioning the name of a product or service. In due course the plugger would receive some of the product, or a case of whiskey, or cash. This was not sponsorship, because the station or network

▓ **Charles Van Doren on How the Quiz Shows Were Rigged**   After considerable soul-searching, the popular quiz show winner finally appeared before the House committee investigating the quiz programs and told the shocked audience how he had been co-opted:

[*Twenty-One* Producer Albert Freedman] told me that Herbert Stempel, the current champion, was an unbeatable contestant because he knew too much. He said that Stempel was unpopular, and was defeating opponents right and left to the detriment of the program. He asked me if, as a favor to him, I would agree to make an arrangement whereby I would tie Stempel and thus increase the entertainment value of the program. I asked him to let me go on the program honestly, without receiving help. He said that was impossible. He told me that I would not have a chance to defeat Stempel because he was too knowledgeable. He also told me that the show was merely entertainment and that giving help to quiz contestants was a common practice and merely a part of show business. . . . Freedman guaranteed me $1,000 if I would appear for one night. . . .

I met him next at his office, where he explained how the program would be controlled. He told me the questions I was to be asked, and then asked if I could answer them. Many of them I could. But he was dissatisfied with my answers. They were not "entertaining" enough. He instructed me how to answer the questions: to pause before certain of the answers, to skip certain parts and return to them, to hesitate and build up suspense, and so forth. On this first occasion and on several subsequent ones he gave me a script to memorize, and before the program he took back the script and rehearsed me in my part. This is the general method which he used throughout my fourteen weeks on "Twenty-One." He would ask me the questions beforehand. If I could not answer them he would either tell me the answers, or if there was sufficient time before the program, which was usual, he would allow me to look them up myself. . . . When I could answer the questions right off he would tell me that my answers were not given in an entertaining and interesting way, and he would then rehearse me in the manner in which I was to act and speak.

After the first program, on which I tied Stempel three times, Freedman told me that I would win the next evening and be the new champion. My guarantee was increased to $8,000. I again agreed to play, and I did defeat Stempel. . . . I asked [Freedman] several times to release me from the program. . . . He told me I had to be defeated in a dramatic manner. A series of ties had to be planned which would give the program the required excitement and suspense.

Source: House Committee on Interstate and Foreign Commerce, Special Subcommittee on Legislative Oversight. *Investigation of Television Quiz Shows.* Hearings, 86th Cong., 1st Sess., 1960. Volume II, pages 625–626.

received no revenue from it, but the on-air personality received a welcome boost in effective annual income. This practice infuriated station management, who saw it as undercutting its advertising rate card.

In December 1959, Attorney General William Rodgers reported to President Eisenhower on the need for legislation to eliminate false and deceptive programming and advertising. At about the same time, FCC Chairman Doerfer announced a plan for expanding network public service programming—a form of penance, although it was not labeled as such. It called for minimal public service programming on each network, rotating in prime time. The networks had previously relegated such programming to fringe hours but, desperate to regain viewers' respect, they agreed to

Doerfer's plan and announced several new documentary and public affairs programs for the following season. Thus, by 1959–1960, action by the FCC (hearings into quiz show and payola scandals), Congress (more hearings, and some legislation), and the Attorney General (a report with recommendations) all coalesced into Communications Act amendments that made rigged or otherwise deceptive programming punishable by law rather than merely admissible as possible evidence of unfitness of licensees at renewal time. The rigged programs left the air for good. Payola and plugola, however, while diminished, have continued to exist more or less underground. The various scandals, a failure of self-regulation, tarnished the image of broadcasting and paved the way for stronger governmental regulation.

8.8.5 Self-Regulation: Improving Television's Image

To undo some of the damage of the quiz show debacle, the National Association of Broadcasters set up a concerted public relations campaign. In October 1959, it created the Television Information Office (TIO), headquartered in New York and sponsored by television stations and networks, to give the public favorable information about all aspects of television. Its initial project was an Elmo Roper survey on public reactions to television following the quiz investigations, the first in a long series of similar, well-publicized reports. TIO also organized a library, provided study guides on specific television programs and series for elementary and secondary schools, and ran full-page ads in such prestige magazines as the *New Yorker* and *Saturday Review* to convince opinion leaders that television could be beneficial.

8.8.6 Blacklisting Continues

One industry wound continued to fester during the 1950s: the blacklisting of talent for their political beliefs (see pp. 334–336). In 1953 several members of the American Federation of Television and Radio Artists (AFTRA, the performers' and announcers' union) and individuals with American Legion and advertiser connections created Aware, Inc., which attacked alleged communist influences in broadcasting. Feeding on the anticommunist mood spearheaded by Senator Joseph McCarthy, this self-appointed group formalized the process of "clearing" performers whose backgrounds had been questioned—often by Aware itself. By competing for jobs with those it attacked, Aware members had at least one possible conflict of interest other than that of union members engaging in what might be considered a management activity. Aware's officers created a 12-step process through which an accused performer could publicly declare his rehabilitated thinking and again become employable. That Aware was operating in several guises became obvious when, after the New York AFTRA chapter held elections, Aware began investigations of the candidates it had opposed. Only after a long and emotional fight did a group of independents capture control of AFTRA in 1955, ending the relationship between a union and a minority of its members operating on ideological grounds.

In the meantime, a candidate for AFTRA office found himself in deepening trouble. John Henry Faulk, a very popular New York radio personality, lost his CBS radio job in Fall 1957 and suddenly found himself unemployable. His dismissal followed initiation of a lawsuit against Aware, which he accused of having caused an end to his radio sponsorship. CBS kept mum. But here the typical blacklisting case took an unusual turn. Faulk decided to fight and, with the financial aid of CBS's Ed Murrow and other friends, took the matter to court. Aided by celebrated lawyer Louis Nizer, Faulk won a series of important preliminary decisions, only to be faced with dwindling financial resources. By 1960 the case grew progressively more complicated with the addition of other defendants who had allegedly organized a boycott or otherwise affected Faulk's and others' employment. Finally, in Summer 1962, Faulk won and was awarded more than $3.5 million—a record in libel judgments (although, because of the death of the chief defendant, he collected only a small portion of it). The decision was upheld on appeal two years later, effectively putting an end to the blacklisting movement. Blacklisting not only lost credibility but was exposed as the product of a few self-appointed—and often self-serving—extralegal guardians of political morality. In addition, of course, relations between the United States and the Soviet Union as well as the political tenor of the country had changed substantially between 1953 and 1962. Although numerous books, plays, and movies have been written about blacklisting, including Faulk's own, dispassionate chronicles are rare; too many of the persons hurt as both victims and prosecutors are still alive . . . and have long memories. But there is little doubt that the blacklisting decade was a fearsome time in which to work in broadcasting and other media; one never knew when all jobs would suddenly close up or when one would be disavowed by one's friends, without warning or explanation.

8.9 The Age of Television

By the late 1950s researchers knew that television focused individual (and national) attention more than radio had, and that it was more concrete. But both media had a neutral point of view and a limited program choice, and both were virtually universal, with common symbols and syntax readily understood by the audience. Radio apparently stimulated the imagination more than television, but television was more glamorous and live television could provide a sense of "here and now" that was unmatched by any other medium. Like radio and sometimes more than radio, television seemed official and highly credible. But few viewers noticed these distinctions; they simply looked at and enjoyed television, and found new uses for radio's music and news.

The nation's colleges and universities paid little attention to television at first. It might be used as a tool (see pp. 291–293 and 360–361), but, except for a few social scientists, it was not studied formally as a medium (see p. 317). This was partly because professional training requires costly equipment and also because of the typical academic wait-and-see-if-it-is-more-than-a-fad approach to new things. It has been said that an academic discipline is identified by a professional association and a scholarly journal. The small University Association for Professional Radio Education (UAPRE) was organized in 1948, nearly died for lack of specific activities, and reorganized in 1956 as the Association for Professional Broadcasting Education (APBE). APBE, which changed its name in 1974 to the Broadcast Education Association (BEA), began publication of the quarterly scholarly *Journal of Broadcasting* in the Winter of 1956–1957. The organization's purpose was to combine broadcasters, through an association with the NAB, and educators in the common goal of solid career and liberal arts education in broadcasting. It now has approximately 260 colleges and universities, several dozen associate or corporate members, and approximately 1,200 professors and students as members.

8.9.1 Television and Other Media

By 1960 television was no longer a fascinating toy for the few; it was nearly universal. Thus, when households spent more time with television, other media sometimes suffered.

By and large the print media were not affected, though both newspapers and magazines sometimes catered to public interest in television at the same time that they downgraded the medium with which they were competing for advertising revenue. In the 1950s, television and print co-existed successfully, and such durable magazines as *TV Guide*, directly related to the growth of interest in television, *Sports Illustrated, Playboy*, and *American Heritage* all got their start. Many newspapers and general magazines published a television column, to join the few remaining radio columns. It can be argued that reviews or esthetic comment had little effect on audiences, since most reviews appeared after the public had seen the program. One critic said, in an aphorism long credited to comedian Jackie Gleason, that "television reviewing is like describing an accident to the victims." But such discussions occasionally influenced television policy makers. Reviews by *New York Times's* Jack Gould and *New York Herald Tribune's* John Crosby, and other critics of stature, were frequently quoted and discussed in professional television circles, in colleges and universities and, less frequently, by other readers and viewers.

The relationship between motion pictures and television was another story, since television was one of three main causes of the decline of the feature film (see p. 337). By 1953, 25% of the nation's theaters had closed, with only drive-ins continuing to expand in number. Unemployment in Hollywood was up, while those still working feared both the film blacklist and industrywide economic uncertainty. However, the filmmakers put out more color films (remember, most television was black-and-white) and experimented with widescreen techniques impossible to reproduce on the home screen. The first of these was the three-dimensional (3-D) film, for which the audience wore cardboard and plastic glasses that converted a blurry picture to striking realism. The fad lasted for about 18 months and two or three dozen 3-D films. In its place came Cinemascope and similar processes that used a new wide film stock and special projection lenses to provide a picture about half again as wide as the normal movie. In 1956, a few theaters (some later were specially built for the process in major cities) were converted for Cinerama, which used three cameras and three projectors for a 165° wide picture with stereo sound. This gave a larger-than-life, realistic, and spectacular three-dimensional effect but was expensive and required major modification to theaters and very careful adjustment. Less expensive wide-screen techniques such as Cinemascope, however, rapidly became common even though they required special lenses for showing and subsequent cropping of the picture when later shown on a television screen.

The other prong of the film industry's response to television was to withhold all older films from television showings. But the film companies could not keep a united front (see p. 375), and after early 1956 thousands of old Hollywood films started appearing on local stations, further depressing business at the neighborhood movie house. Having given in to television to this extent, Hollywood experienced a slow takeover by television in the late 1950s. By 1960–1961, when feature films were still scarce on the networks, a good proportion of the film industry's employment and production was in filming series for network television showing. Although feature film workers decried the "takeover" of the film industry by television, live television workers in New York, now out of their jobs, wondered whether Hollywood had not taken over television! Although many television series were inspired by hit movies, now some television programs (see p. 373) were made into films for release in theaters.

8.9.2 Television Around the World

The worldwide expansion of television had been delayed by World War II and its aftermath, but by the 1950s many countries were building television systems. A "buy at home" philosophy, and the opportunity to build a state-of-the-art system by starting from scratch, led to a variety of technical standards, particularly in Europe, since Latin America and Japan had adopted the 525-line system used in the United States. France had an 819-line system and Great Britain had a 405-line system, but Europe eventually settled on two slightly different 625-line systems, one for eastern Europe and one for western. By 1960 eight countries each had more than one million television receivers in use: the United States, Great Britain, France, West Germany, Italy, Canada, Russia, and Brazil. In several of these countries, receivers were in public places, as in the United States before the mid-1950s when there seemed to be more sets in bars and store windows than in homes. Because of these publicly located sets, the television audience in many of these countries was larger than the number of receivers might imply. In the United Kingdom, the high cost of the "telly" was overcome through monthly receiver rentals rather than purchases.

Countries in the Western Hemisphere generally followed the United States model of private ownership and commercial operation, except for Canada, which had a BBC-modeled Canadian Broadcasting Corporation (CBC) as well as many private stations. In other countries, television was directly or indirectly operated by the government, even though costs sometimes led to the acceptance of advertising. In Great Britain, the BBC had operated television since it started in 1936 except for a shutdown during the World War II period ending in 1946. But in 1954, after a long, involved parliamentary and behind-the-scenes debate, a commercially supported television system (ITV) was established as an alternative to the BBC. Supervised by the Independent Television Authority (ITA), which franchised regional program production companies ("programme contractors") to use ITA-owned transmitters, the new service was supported by advertising rather than receiver license fees as was the BBC—although license revenues were diverted to aid ITA in its formative years. Rather than program sponsorship, ITV used the *magazine* system of television advertising, with advertisers buying spots but having no control over their placement. The best programs were put "on the network" and aired by other contractors.

Japan and Canada developed similar competing systems in which one channel or network was operated by the government and another privately. Most major foreign cities had only one to three channels of television fare, compared to the three to seven in the larger American cities.

Considering the high cost of television programming and the short geographical distances in Europe, it is not surprising that members of the European Broadcasting Union decided to exchange programs. This exchange, called "Eurovision," also permitted efficient pooling of effort for coverage of important sporting and other events. In eastern Europe, the International Radio Television Organization (OIRT) started a similar venture, "Intervision." Although there were political and technical problems, the two systems occasionally exchanged nonpolitical programs.

In 1953 the U.S. Information Agency (USIA) was established to operate the Voice of America and print, film, and television propaganda activities of the United States government. Except for overseas operations directly under the control of an ambassador, it took over most State Department operational information functions and operated most overseas information and propaganda activities. Although the USIA distributed some material to be shown on foreign television systems, most American television programs went abroad through the efforts of commercial networks and program packagers. Foreign television systems provided an additional market for an American product, following the long-standing example of the feature film industry, as well as a new means of intercultural communication. Some commentators wondered what a constant fare of *I Love Lucy* would do to foreign opinions of the United States, and what effect it might have on the customs of foreign countries.

In Canada, television programming began from CBC stations in Toronto and Montreal in September 1952. A few months later, the government allowed expansion of the government-controlled CBC as well as privately operated television stations. By 1956, there were 9 CBC and 30 commercial television outlets. As mentioned before, Canada used U.S. technical standards, and operated only on the VHF channels. About half the Canadian population also could and did tune in to stations in the United States, since Canadian cities are mostly located in a narrow band just north of the border. The CBC stations were supported by the proceeds of a 15% excise tax on receiver sales. By 1960 private stations had increased to 38, while CBC stations remained at 9, including 3 that broadcast in French. Few Canadian cities had more than one channel until after 1961. Television viewing was divided almost evenly between U.S. and Canadian channels, and much of the fare on Canadian channels then was American.

Mexican television began in the early 1950s when commercially run channels went on the air from Mexico City under authority of licenses that were good for 25 years. In 1953, the two major station operators combined to form Telesistema Mexicano S.A., which in the 1950s was to control the content of virtually all television in the country. By 1960 there were 25 stations on the air, all on VHF channels. A few stations located near the U.S. border programmed in English, very profitably directing their broadcasts to the north. For domestic consumption, most program content was produced in Mexico but was like the American fare—with the substitution of bullfights for baseball. Having got into television quite early, Mexico quickly became one of the chief program suppliers for the rest of Latin America, and later expanded into the United States with affiliated stations in markets with large Spanish-speaking populations such as Los Angeles and New York.

8.9.3 Period Overview

This space of eight years can be thought of as the evolution that followed the 1945–1952 revolution. There were no fundamental changes in the industry; radio and television expanded within the patterns set in the immediate postwar years. AM radio and VHF television led this growth, with television networks becoming dominant in the broadcasting industry. FM radio had started out of its long decline by 1960, in part through subsidiary services and stereo; but UHF television was in serious trouble with small audiences and limited advertising income and usually no network affiliation. There was growth in educational television and FM, but the audiences were very small and funding was a paramount problem.

To many observers in later decades, these were the golden years of television programming—primarily because most network programming was live and often spontaneous, and high-quality anthology drama was plentiful, because television production was cheaper than the movies or Broadway and thus more hospitable to young playwrights. Some of this perceived quality was actually present, but part was due to the audience, who in the early 1950s had more income (due to cost of television receivers) and education than the general population. Yet the medium's problems were evident in growing concern about television violence, the quiz show scandals, and so on. Many persons in the industry, in government, and among the public felt that television had grown too fast to develop ethics commensurate with its huge role in society. Part of the problem was that the impact of television was becoming hidden by its very ubiquity.

No longer was the television set a novelty. No longer would programs seen the night before be the main topic of conversation at work or at play. Now television was merely something one sat in front of in the living room, and radio was something that provided music and news in the car, the bedroom, or the kitchen. There are many who believe that we are the poorer for that change—when the excitement died, broadcasting became ordinary and familiar. Ed Murrow, in a 1958 speech to his colleagues in the Radio-Television News Directors Association, summed it up with "This instrument can teach, it can illuminate; yes, and can even inspire. But it can do so only to the extent that humans are determined to use it to those ends. Otherwise it is merely wires and lights in a box."

Selected Further Reading

(Alphabetical within topics. For full citations, see Appendix D.)

The best contemporary descriptions of broadcasting in the 1950s are Columbia Broadcasting System (CBS, 1956) on network operations, Diamant (1971) on early television commercials, FCC (1958, 1963, 1965), Head (1956), Seehafer & Laemmar (1959) on advertising, U.S. Congress, Senate Commerce Committee (1956), and Wylie (1955). See works on 1950s television cited in chapter seven. Early educational television is described in Alford (1966), Blakely (1979), Caristi (1997), Hill (1965), Powell (1962), and Saettler (1968).

For television programs, see chapter seven. Bluem (1965) asseses early documentaries while Mickelson (1998) narrates the rise of CBS television news. Allen (1993) and Chester (1969) relate television's growing political role, while Kraus (1962) details the "Great Debates" of 1960. For the changing music on radio, see Eberly (1982), Fong-Torres (1998), Garay (1992) on Gordon McLendon, Passman (1971), Segrave (1994) on the payola scandal, and Wes Smith (1989)—plus any of the many books on Dick Clark and *American Bandstand*.

Studies of the television audience are to be found in Bogart (1956), Elliott (1956), and Steiner (1963). The seminal studies of television and children noted in the text are in Himmelweit, et al. (1958), and Schramm, et al (1961). For the relationship between the Cold War and audience research in this period, see Glander (2000), and Simpson (1994).

Studies of regulation in this period include Baughman (1985), Coons (1961), Emery (1971), Schwartz (1959), and Smead (1959). Anderson (1979), and Stone and Yohn (1992), relate the story of the quiz show scandals. The end of blacklisting is told by Faulk (1964), and Vaughn (1972). For developments in other countries, see further reading for chapters seven and nine.

CHAPTER 9

Advertisement for an early Sony portable TV set, 1963. *New York Public Library.*

"... there always will be, of necessity, a TV wasteland. The three TV networks must produce 10,950 hours of entertainment per year, in contrast to only 600 hours demanded of the entire moving picture industry of our country and the 125 hours per year demanded of the Broadway theater."———*Ed Sullivan testifying before the FCC, 1961*

ACCOMMODATION AND ADJUSTMENT (1961–1976)

Comedians Dean Martin & Jerry Lewis, popular well into the 1970s, in an early 1950s TV series. *Photofest.*

Chapter Outline

Television was not *all* wasteland, in spite of Newton Minow's observation. In a crisis or for special events, it was the medium to which everyone tuned. Perhaps the most dramatic occasion was in November 1963, when radio and television served as the ears and eyes of the American people, bearing witness to the shocking assassination of President John F. Kennedy. For four days almost all at home watched solemn and terrible events, listened to attempts to make them meaningful, and finally found some relief in the tributes from the nation's performing artists. It made no difference that most people got the first news by word-of-mouth, or whether they saw the shooting of the suspected assassin on their screens two days later—broadcasting brought the American people together.

Another FCC Commissioner, Lee Loevinger, has called the journalistic function of the media "essential." Just a year before President Kennedy's assassination, listeners and viewers had stayed close to radio and television for ten days as the United States and the Soviet Union stood on the brink of nuclear war over Russian placement of missiles in Cuba. News and special programs gave gripping accounts of the crisis, and President Kennedy delivered clear warning over the air of his intentions. After 1965 the steady buildup of American troops and commitment to South Vietnam was covered in the "living room war"—perhaps the most frustrating war this country has ever fought. The dramatic peak and possible turning point of American public opinion may have been the 1968 Tet offensive and the summary execution of a communist guerilla suspect on a Saigon street before NBC cameras. In 1968 there also were domestic assassinations and a violent demonstration outside the Democratic national political convention in Chicago. A year later, the nation and much of the world were watching when Neil Armstrong became the first man to walk on the moon. Toward the end of this period, the nation watched the fall of a President, as the Watergate scandal finally led to Nixon's resignation, the brief administration of the first nonelected President, Gerald R. Ford, and the second set of "great debates" during the campaign leading to President Jimmy Carter's administration.

The 15 years from the cold winter day when John Kennedy was inaugurated to the warm summer evening when Richard M. Nixon resigned were increasingly complicated and tension-filled. The country careened from domestic problem to foreign crisis and back again. In a world where many people wanted simple black-and-white answers, even the gray alternatives were getting harder to find.

Many Americans understandably retreated, when possible, to another world—a world of small pictures that provided hours of entertainment. Millions found *Perry Mason*, *The Beverly Hillbillies*, and *The Lucy Show* a welcome respite from the harsh truths of news programs. Daily serials and game shows on television, and music and talk on radio, helped pass the hours for housewives and youth. Radio, liberated by the transistor from the weight and expense and fragile tubes of earlier models, appeared everywhere. It was soon a standard accessory of the nation's urban youth—to carry a blaring radio on the street was the symbol of being "with it" and "tuned in." The general public listened to an academic theorist, Canadian Marshall McLuhan, who spoke fluently, if sometimes confusingly, of the degree to which broadcasting, and to a lesser extent other media and elements in society, had become an integral part of modern life.

But behind the scenes, generally unknown to the public, were the tensions of an industry beset with growth and change. More stations went on the air, dividing the audience and the advertising pie into ever smaller pieces with sometimes devastating results for the newcomer. The television industry feared mounting competition from cable television, and the FCC was caught in the old problem of how much to protect an existing industry in the face of a new one. Public concern about violence on the air and its effect on youth pushed Congress into sponsoring the biggest research effort ever connected with broadcasting (see pp. 457–459), and questions about fair treatment of controversial issues plagued broadcast management. Government concern, sometimes politically inspired, about concentration of ownership added to the industry's headaches.

9.1 Changing Technologies

In 1960–1961, most broadcasting equipment—home receivers and station and studio equipment—used electronic tubes similar in principle to those manufactured in the 1920s. The invention of the transistor by scientists in the Bell Labs in 1948 did not have an effect on broadcasting until the early 1960s, when their cost fell low enough to allow their widespread use. Transistors permitted more compact construction, cooler operation and thus longer life, and use of much less electric power. By the late 1960s transistors were giving way to even more compact successors, which were direct outgrowths of the nation's space research. First came printed circuits that reduced a series of tubes, resistors, capacitors, and other components to a sheet of plastic with many of the components literally painted or printed thereon and with sockets for transistors studded about. Then came truly microscopic integrated circuits, which were grown in a solution and then cut apart, and which incorporated the equivalent of transistors as an integral part of the tiny structure. The trend to smaller and more rugged—if some- what sensitive to heat, humidity, and static electricity—components made automatic assembly of virtually all electronic equipment possible and hence easier, quicker, and less expensive.

There had been rather unsuccessful automated radio programming ex- periments as early as the 1940s. But now, with more reliable electronics, timing units could be connected to long-running tape playback machines, allowing a station to be prerecorded and run automatically for hours. FM stations, short of cash to pay personnel—always the largest part of any broadcasting station's operating costs—often were the first to use automa- tion. Their music-and-little-talk formats of the 1950s and early 1960s lent themselves to this approach. Several companies specialized in offering both the equipment *and* the programming suitable for automated opera- tions. While this led to distant stations sounding almost alike, companies rarely sold a given programming service to more than one station in a mar- ket, thus maintaining the appearance of program format competition.

Coming at the same time as automation, and, indeed, forming part of most automation systems, was the tape cartridge. Reel-to-reel magnetic tape recordings had increasingly replaced disc records until about 1960. In that year a small plastic-enclosed *single hub* self-contained cartridge of tape, activated by a shove into the slot of a special tape player, was devel- oped. Foolproof; no need to set up the reels or find a starting place on the tape—just grab the cart and shove it in. This made the fast-paced formula or Top-40 station far easier to operate. Cartridges were used mainly for com- mercials and other segments from 15 seconds, or even less for station IDs, to about 10 minutes. As carts became available in half-hour and hour lengths, their use in radio broadcasting grew, with much programming orig- inally in other formats transferred to carts. From the studio the cartridge spread to the consumer in the form of playback machines, and radio recorders, in automobile and home.

By 1964, however, the cartridge had competition from the even smaller and lighter *two hub cassette*, developed by Philips (Norelco in the United States), the giant Netherlands electrical manufacturing company. While the cassette did not have the impact of the cart in broadcasting, other than pro- viding reporters with small and lightweight recorders, it made rapid gains in the consumer market. Philips wisely made it cheap and easy for any manufacturer to make cassettes, not restricting it to their own companies, which led to rapid adoption of the technology. Cassette-radio combinations became increasingly popular.

The next home audio development seemed likely to be four-channel or quadraphonic hi-fi systems. But disagreement over standards for the new service between advocates of the *matrix* and the *discrete* systems, and the high cost, virtually doubling the cost of a stereo system, led to very slow adop- tion. Although the first quadraphonic broadcasts had been aired in Boston and New York in 1968, using two cooperating FM stereo stations in each city, true *quadraplex* (four channels over one station) transmissions were not tried until the early 1970s. Because such transmissions required dropping any Subsidiary Communications Authorizations (SCA) the station was operating, few stations had an incentive to inaugurate four-channel broadcasting.

Problems of audio standards seemed simple when contrasted to video variations. By the late 1960s, two roads for video expansion seemed possible: cable television or home video recording systems. Some crystal ball gazers saw both in the cards: cable now, and home video systems later. Cable, having grown slowly since 1949 (see pp. 355–356), was already present on the broadcast scene. By the early 1970s some people predicted that CATV would oust over-the-air broadcasting. Possibilities included store purchases by cable, doctors' visits by closed-circuit television via cable, two-way interconnection with computers—the PC was years away—using a telephone as the home terminal, meter-reading and home protection devices activated through cable, and other *wideband communications* devices leading to the "wired nation." But in a couple of years cable seemed to have lost momentum, and the economic recession of the mid-1970s shelved most of these ideas (see pp. 417–418), although the number of homes served by cable continued to grow.

Economics and burgeoning technology also played a large part in delaying home video systems that could play whatever a person selected whenever he or she wanted. Programming was to be for the individual. The first home videotape recorders (VTR), essentially the same as the relatively inexpensive helical-scan machines used by industry and education, had little impact when they appeared in 1965, although they cost far less than quad-head broadcast-quality VTRs. Laboratories also were developing new systems based on videotape, film, and even lasers, and promising them first for industry and education and shortly afterward for the home market. In the late 1960s, CBS Laboratories promoted, but later sold, its Electronic Video Recording system (EVR). This heralded combination of film and television was supplanted by another possible pot of gold at the end of the rainbow, the video disc. Developed first by Philips, the video disc, on its own special machine, could provide both picture and sound for a half-hour or so on. Other companies were developing their own, incompatible technologies. The benefits of the disc over a cassette videotape system, several of which also were being developed, were analogous to those of the phonograph disc over the cylinder; countless copies could be stamped out at very low cost per unit. But this market too was held back by unsettled standards and the economic downturn of the mid-1970s.

Late in 1975, a premonition of the future appeared on a few store shelves. Sony "Betamax"[1] system videocassette recorders (VCRs) were

---

[1]The word "beta" refers to a Japanese brush stroke that completely covers the surface underneath it—just as the Betamax VCR uses the entire tape surface for a signal. See Lardner (1987).

reaching the market, initially in a console including a 19-inch color television monitor for $2,295. The price dropped (to about $1,300) when the first Betamax tape decks were placed on sale in February 1976. Even these first relatively limited machines (the tapes had only a one-hour capacity) allowed the television viewer to become a programmer—recording material off the air for playback at a later time, or *time-shifting*. Several months later, the Universal and Disney film studios sued to stop sales of the machines for fear their copyrights would be imperiled by home tapers of movies shown on television. Publicity about the suit and initial ads for the machine led to half the country's population telling pollsters they knew what a Betamax was barely a year after its introduction. The introduction of the VCR would create a significant watershed in the history of broadcasting in the space of remarkably few years (see pp. 490–493).

A major development in long-distance communication, threatening to destroy AT&T's long-held monopoly on network interconnections and making remote pickups possible from almost everywhere in the world, is the communications satellite. Predicted in detail as early as 1945, the technology for these devices was developed after 1957 when the Soviet Union launched the first artificial orbital satellite. It took only a few years to progress from placing a tape recorder aboard a satellite to broadcast a Christmas message from President Eisenhower (1958) and bouncing signals off a passive orbiting balloon named *Echo* (1960) to using active satellites that could receive messages and retransmit them on another frequency. Most early satellites were in orbits from a few hundred to a few thousand miles high, including AT&T's pioneering *Telstar*, launched in July 1962, which was capable of relaying television pictures across the Atlantic when in the proper orbital position. Later ones were placed in equatorial geosynchronous orbit 22,300 miles high. In this orbit, a satellite maintains its position relative to the earth, appearing to be stationary and thus providing an easy target for transmitting and receiving antennas on the ground.

These satellites, starting with *Early Bird* and going through various more sophisticated *Intelsats*, were generally launched by the National Aeronautics and Space Administration (NASA) for the Communications Satellite Corporation (COMSAT), a corporation created by Congress after considerable debate. COMSAT not only handled the U.S. side of international satellite circuits but managed the global network for the multinational International Telecommunications Satellite Organization, INTELSAT. Although AT&T owned *Telstar* and, originally, a large portion of COMSAT stock (which was divided roughly 50–50 between the general public and U.S. common carriers such as AT&T and Western Union), it sold most of its interest in COMSAT in the early 1970s. The FCC had approved a domestic satellite policy, which effectively limited the Bell System to providing local ground connections at transmitting and receiving stations. Although the Soviet Union in the 1960s and Canada in the early 1970s had established domestic communications satellite systems, the rush in the United States did not occur until Western Union's *Westar* was launched in 1974. Several companies leased channels on *Westar* and then retailed access to them at a considerable saving over AT&T land-line tariffs.

The networks began to investigate interconnection by communications satellites in what might be thought of as the first breach in the 1926 agreements between RCA and AT&T (see p. 76). The development of mobile ground stations—such as the one President Nixon took on his trip to China in 1972—together with satellites permitted full telecommunications facilities, including several television channels, almost anywhere.

One creative contribution of the communications satellite to television, however, awaited the late 1975 announcement by Home Box Office, a Time-Life pay-cable subsidiary, that it planned to use a *Satcom I transponder* to deliver its movies to participating cable system *head ends* nationwide. Systems that purchased a television receive-only (TVRO) antenna could now carry a pay-cable service, charge subscribers an additional fee, and share the proceeds with HBO. Early in 1976, a then little known entrepreneur named Ted Turner announced that he too was going to make the programming of his Atlanta UHF station available to cable systems, using a transponder on the same *Satcom I* satellite. Coining the term "superstation" to describe his concept, Turner figured that a diet of movies and sporting events (especially those of the professional teams he owned, the Atlanta Braves baseball and Hawks basketball teams) carried on his independent channel 17 would be a good supplement for the many television markets hitherto restricted to network fare. By the end of 1976, Turner's station was being carried by 20 cable systems in different parts of the country.

Together, the HBO and Turner moves dramatically expanded the role of cable television. Satellite transponders solved the age-old problem of expensive and time-consuming expansion of terrestrial networking by substituting instant nationwide distribution of a signal. Cable systems would have to buy a receiving antenna. However, once that step was taken, they would be able to provide Turner's and HBO's programs—and other signals promised for the late 1970s—as added incentives for cable subscribers.

9.2 Station Population Explosion

Broadcasting station growth continued, but the pattern was different. Despite FCC efforts to slow growth (see p. 413), the number of AM stations increased from about 3,600 early in 1961 to approximately 4,500 by 1976—even though engineers had considered the AM band crowded with only 950 stations in 1945. But radio's most prominent expansion—a surprise to long-time industry observers—was in FM. Commercial FM stations grew from about 800 in early 1961 to more than 2,100 by late 1976. Even more dramatic, educational FM stations increased from just 170 to more than 800. All told, there were nearly 3,700 FM stations on the air by late 1976—a dramatic turnaround for a one-time "loser" service. Television grew somewhat more slowly—from 560 commercial stations, mostly on VHF, in 1961 to more than 700 commercial stations, all but 200 of them VHF, by late 1976. Educational TV station growth was substantial—from just 52 outlets in 1961 to more than 250 (many of them merely repeater transmitters) 15 years later.

From such figures (see Appendix C, Table 1-B for details) come three interesting conclusions: (1) FM was now the fastest-growing broadcast service; (2) educational FM and television grew very rapidly, finally providing educational and cultural interests with the coverage they had wanted for so long; and (3) even by 1976, only 352 UHF stations actually were on the air, nearly half of them educational, versus more than 600 VHF stations, only 97 of them educational, even though the FCC had made far more UHF channels available. The quarter-century-old VHF-UHF problem (see pp. 387–391) had obviously not been resolved. At the same time, the sustained growth of other services led to problems of spectrum crowding.

9.2.1 Slowing AM and Expanding FM

It is hard to believe that for nearly half of the period 1961–1976 there was a freeze on new AM license awards. From May 1962 to July 1964, and again from July 1968 to February 1973, the FCC stopped most licensing of new AM stations while seeking rule changes to limit growth on that band. The problem had technical, economic, and political aspects, all interrelated. Most stations starting after 1961 were limited to daytime operation. Although most regions, particularly metropolitan ones, did not need another daytime station, adding nighttime stations would have caused massive interference elsewhere. By the mid-1970s, the largest markets were served by from 20 to 70 different AM or FM radio stations. In some places there were too many stations to divide the available advertising dollars effectively; 40% of radio stations were already marginal or losing money. Television had taken much of the audience, and salable program formats were few. But politically, it was difficult to persuade persons wanting to get into the radio industry and smaller communities that desired more outlets that AM growth had to stop. Finally, at the end of the second AM freeze in 1973, the FCC issued stringent rules for considering a request for a new AM station. Such a station would have to provide a first service—that is, for a community in which at least 25% of the coverage area or 25% of the population had no radio service at all. If an unused FM channel was available in the area to be served, no AM grant would be made.

Earlier, in Fall 1961, the commission had decided to resolve the question of clear channels, which had been dragging on since the allocation hearings of 1944. Complaints about the inherent unfairness of the clears, originally established by the Federal Radio Commission in 1928 (see pp. 144–145 and 171) to provide service to rural areas, and the desire to make room for low-power AM stations had finally overcome the arguments for their retention. The FCC decision was to "break down" 13 of the 25 1-A channels in the United States. Naturally, the high-powered stations on these channels fought this move through the final judicial decision of November 1963 that upheld the FCC. By the early 1970s, very few clear stations were still clear, or operating alone on that channel day and night. Some remained clear, or protected by the width of the continent, at night, but many new low-power or daytime-only stations had been squeezed in to provide local service.

As the number of FM stations grew, the commission found it had to improve its assignment structure. To avoid the first-come first-served shoe-horning typical of AM since broadcasting's start, both FM and television channels eventually were assigned to specific communities to permit orderly and efficient growth and to avoid concentration of facilities in the largest cities. In July 1962 this resulted in the establishment of three main classes of FM station plus provision for 10-watt noncommercial educational stations: Class A, low power (100 watts to 3,000 watts), and a restriction on antenna height to 300 feet above average terrain leading to a service radius of about 15 miles, and a distance between stations on the same channel of 65 miles; Class B (5 kw to 50 kw), 500-foot limit, 40-mile service radius, and 150-mile co-channel spacing; and Class C, high power (25 kw to 100 kw), 65-mile service radius, and 180-mile co-channel spacing. Using these standards, the commission assigned nearly 3,000 potential stations to about 1,800 communities. Classes A and B were to be used primarily in the crowded Northeast and in Southern California, while Class C would be allowed only in other parts of the country. Most existing stations were "grandfathered."

This reassignment ended several years of concern and a short freeze on issuance of new FM licenses. With the thaw, and with the stereo standards decision (see pp. 346–348), the number of FM stations began to increase rapidly. Most new stations were equipped for stereo broadcasting, and older ones slowly converted, so that about one-quarter of FM stations were broadcasting in stereo by 1965 and about two-fifths by 1971. Studio and transmitter changes were costly, and for a while there were too few stereo receivers to make the decision pay off. But with the increasing availability of stereo, and later four-channel, sound in tapes, records, and broadcasting, more stations took the plunge. By the mid-1970s, a large majority of FM outlets could broadcast in stereo.

As FM stations approached AM stations in service area and size of audience, FM channels assumed greater value to broadcasters. The commission, taking notice of their potential equality, considered separating AM and FM ownership in the same community. A 1963 rule led to partial nonduplication of programs between the two radio services (see p. 433) in all but the smallest markets. The FCC was constantly considering eventual breaking up of AM-FM ownership and programming combinations in the same market. FM stations were bringing steadily higher prices, with the first million-dollar sale taking place in 1968. Soon, the majority of FM licensing cases required comparative hearings, as would-be broadcasters competed for channel assignments. In addition, the unusual loyalty of FM audiences caused problems as stations changed hands and new managers tried to change format. A classical music FM station in Chicago (WFMT) was sold to the *Chicago Tribune's* WGN and ran into a well-organized public complaint campaign fearing it planned to adopt a different music format. WGN finally gave the station to an educational operator who would continue the classical music format. A New York classical music station (WNCN) changed hands and went to a pop format in 1974, raising an outcry from listeners. Political considerations of "concentration of power" gave strength to these protests. Despite, or because of, all this, FM stations in some markets achieved respectable audience ratings in competition with AM stations for the first time.

The multiplicity of broadcasting stations—approximately 9,000 by 1976—made heavy paperwork for both the commission and the stations. Smaller stations especially complained bitterly to Congress and the commission. Finally, in 1973, the FCC cautiously started a process initially called "re-regulation" to simplify and loosen some technical and record-keeping requirements.

9.2.2 Television: UHF, STV, and CATV

In the 1960s, many of the parallels between UHF television and FM radio disappeared. While FM grew and even prospered, UHF television grew so slowly that even a 1962 law requiring UHF and VHF reception capability on all new sets sold in the United States did not immediately help (see p. 454). Few new UHF stations went on the air, few UHF-equipped sets were made before the mid-1960s, and broadcasters, advertisers, and viewers showed little interest in UHF (see p. 387 ff). It was a circle that UHF was unable to break. However, in the decade after the 1964 effective date of the all-channel receiver law, UHF added 111 stations while VHF added only 47, largely because of a shortage of desirable VHF channels.

VHF scarcity was implicit in the 1952 *Sixth Report and Order* (see pp. 328 ff), and became evident with the 1965–1966 reassignment and reallocation of television frequencies. While the original plan offered a total of 551 commercial VHF assignments, only about 40 of these, mostly in very small western towns, were not on the air by late 1976. On the other hand, of

590 commercial UHF assignments, nearly 400 were still vacant. Much the same pattern existed for educational television (see p. 423), although a much higher proportion of UHF assignments was in use. In 1952, 242 educational channel reservations had been established, a number raised to 615—508 on UHF—in 1966. In 1966 the FCC stopped assigning channels 70 through 83. For various reasons, television stations on the top 14 channels had poorer coverage capability than stations lower in the spectrum, and most higher numbered channels were used only for low-power translators. This waste of spectrum space, combined with other options for its use—translators or the growing and aggressive land mobile, safety, and special radio services—led to the FCC's decision to remove these 84 MHz permanently from television broadcasting in May 1970.

This reallocation plus the earlier all-channel receiver legislation effectively ended FCC plans for deintermixture or any other 1950s proposals for rescuing UHF (see p. 388). The general hope now was that natural replacement of sets would increase the number of UHF homes and that the growing audience would attract advertising money and improve station finances.

Another matter temporarily laid to rest in this period was pay or subscription broadcast television (STV). The focus of long debate in the 1950s (see pp. 282 and 353) and a battle with Connecticut film theater owners that went all the way to the Supreme Court, over-the-air pay-TV was given a test from 1962 to 1968 over channel 18 in Hartford. Like so many other earlier tests, it was inconclusive.

The biggest operational attempt at pay-TV took place in California, using wires to provide three programs besides those received from free on-air television channels. Former NBC president Sylvester "Pat" Weaver led the Subscription Television company, whose 1964 venture had $25 million in capital, the backing of major corporations, and several important sports and entertainment contracts, including the Giants and Dodgers baseball teams. Pay-TV made a midsummer debut in the Santa Monica section of Los Angeles with about 4,000 subscribers paying to see new—but often not as new as hoped—films, educational and cultural features, and sports. Although STV briefly expanded to San Francisco, the costs of a public opinion fight against forces led by movie theater owners forced the Weaver group to curtail operations. In November, voters killed pay-TV by a nearly two-to-one margin on a ballot referendum initiated by the motion picture industry. The vote later was declared unconstitutional, but by then the company was out of money and out of business.

In Congress bills were introduced to outlaw pay-TV, and both sides sent out heavy propaganda. The battle took place in three arenas: the House Commerce Committee, which continued to hold hearings and ask the FCC to delay a decision; the FCC, which said it was ready to establish rules allowing STV operation under very controlled conditions; and the Hartford experiment, which was approved in 1968 for three more years, having already run for six. However, Zenith took that experiment off the air due to the impending FCC decision and the need to convert to color.

In December 1968 the FCC adopted rules allowing broadcast pay-TV but delayed implementing them until Congress had time to react. Movies to be shown for pay had to be less than two years old and sports events could not have appeared on free television in the previous two years; no continuing series could be aired. Pay-TV, over-the-air, could be established only in cities with more than four commercial stations and would have to operate a minimum of 28 hours a week. There could be no commercials, and at least 10 percent of offerings had to be other than sports or movies. Technical standards were announced in Fall 1969. A 1971 "antisiphoning" rule extended the ban on pay-TV use of sporting events to five years, and banned special sports events like the Olympic Games for ten years after their last free television showing. By 1974 three technical systems had been approved for operation, the first being Zenith's pioneering "Phonevision." Applications for stations in different markets had been approved by the FCC; but the first two over-the-air pay stations (one in Los Angeles, the other in a New Jersey suburb of New York City) did not get on the air until Spring 1977 (see p. 505).

Most of the then very limited pay-TV in the United States was a service of larger cable systems rather than broadcast. By mid-1976 more than 750,000 subscribers paid to receive programs on special channels of some 250 cable systems. The ability of these systems to charge for special programming made their operation far more attractive to investors.

Cable television had grown very slowly during the 1950s and early 1960s. By the mid-1960s, more than one million homes out of more than 60 million were on the cable, and more than 1,200 systems were operating (see Appendix C, Table 9-A, 9-B). Systems continued to increase in number and size, so that by late 1976 more than one in six of the nation's homes were hooked up to one of more than 3,700 cable systems, mostly in rural and suburban areas, particularly of the West. Cable's fortunes improved in 1965–1966 partly as a result of increased regulatory activity (see pp. 467–469). Some cable systems began to originate programming, most provided far better reception of color programs, and many larger towns began to see cable television. This last development reminded the FCC of past experiences with uncontrolled growth in big cities, and it put a freeze on signal importation into the nation's 100 top markets.

But cable was growing in other ways, although probably not as fast as industry publicity would have one believe. As equipment improved, systems expanded their capacity from three to five channels to ten or more, and the technology allowed 20 or more at a time, although only 12 percent of systems had this capability by 1976. As the investment required to build systems increased, the traditional "Mom and Pop" cable companies gave way to the better financed and managed Multiple System Operator (MSO). With this development the FCC became concerned over concentration of ownership, and in early 1970, it prohibited cable system ownership by telephone companies or television stations in the same market area, and of cable systems anywhere by national television networks. As more cable systems became program originators, the FCC tried various ways to prevent undue concentration of control.

This FCC action had, as a side effect, contention. Cable systems and some telephone companies, which charged cable high—perhaps exorbitant—rates to rent space on their poles, fought. Skirmishes between broadcasters and cable operators sometimes led to decreased service to the public. By the late 1960s, the National Cable Television Association (NCTA) was facing off against the National Association of Broadcasters in arguments over copyright, program carriage, signal importation, and other regulatory issues of economic and political importance to both sides. Congress took an increasing interest in cable. Broadcasters were not united, since cable provided larger audiences for many stations, especially the hard-pressed UHF outlets, and because many broadcasters owned cable operations in communities outside the range of their stations.

But the public was being told that cable was the greatest invention since the zipper with its new programming and new outlets for people with political, social, and economic interests not served by the broadcast system. New York and other large cities, already well served by on-air stations, acquired their first major cable systems. Unfortunately, the high cost of wiring in the city and insufficient new programming to interest potential subscribers left many cable operators—some of whom made money from tax loopholes rather than from any concern for the public interest—with a hand-to-mouth livelihood. The recession of the mid-1970s and the natural caution of many MSOs, particularly in light of the failure of the New York systems to make a substantial profit, seemed to dim cable's promise for the time being.

9.3 A Continuing Network Pattern . . . Ripe for Change

The basic pattern of network operation continued into the 1970s. The FCC finally banned option time agreements in mid-1963, an action first proposed in the 1941 Chain Broadcasting Report (see pp. 210–212 and 391–392), but by this time most industry observers felt it would have little effect, as FCC rule changes and competitive pressures had made network and affiliate relations more flexible. Early in 1965 the commission proposed limiting the financial control by networks to 50% of the programs they carried, with no part of syndication. The ostensible point was to enhance competition and possibly other points of view by allowing other production sources to enter the network television market. This rule aroused such strong opposition that the commission withdrew it but returned in May 1970 with another approach. This proposal would limit network programming in the top 50 markets between 7 P.M. and 11 P.M. (6 P.M. to 10 P.M. in the Central and Mountain Time Zones) to three hours—in effect, removing a half-hour the networks had programmed for their affiliates for years. The commission allowed syndicated "off-network" shows for the first year of the rule and then insisted on either station-produced shows or independently syndicated material, with the expressed hope that stations would use the time for local public affairs programming. The unfortunate result was a flood of inexpensive syndicated entertainment material— game shows, travelogues, some cheap variety and adventure programs— that was often worse than network programming. The Prime Time Access Rule (PTAR) was debated, modified slightly, nearly modified again, and debated some more. In 1972 the Justice Department filed antitrust suits against the networks in a possibly politically motivated attempt to further diversify program control. The suits were later dismissed and still later (1974) reinstated, leading many to predict a lengthy court battle ahead. However, as discussed on p. 509, although this lawsuit was settled out of court late in 1976, it was only one of the pressures on the network-station relationship of the time.

The long-lasting Yankee and Don Lee regional radio networks both folded in 1967. All national networks changed their top management, retiring pioneers in television and bringing in younger people, some with little or no broadcasting experience. Network broadcasting stopped being special and began to resemble other businesses. In 1967 a national labor dispute took most performers and live programs off the air. The American Federation of Television and Radio Artists (AFTRA), a performers union, called a strike over the wages paid announcers at network-owned FM stations. It quickly got out of hand, and CBS viewers tuning in the first night of the strike heard a bespectacled young man introduce the evening news with "This is Arnold Zenker substituting for Walter Cronkite." Except for a few like NBC's Chet Huntley who felt newsmen had no business on picket lines, news and entertainment figures respected the strike, and live shows were replaced with reruns or other canned programs. The dispute was settled just two hours before the scheduled beginning of the motion picture academy "Oscars" telecast, a major viewing event each year. Cronkite came back on that night deadpanning "This is Walter Cronkite, substituting for Arnold Zenker." Temporary news anchor Zenker, a lowly CBS executive, went to an on-air role in Boston and later in Baltimore on the strength of this sudden thrust into the spotlight.

ABC had particular problems that almost led to a controversial merger. By the 1964–1965 season, ABC had become competitive in ratings with both CBS and NBC. Long a distant third in popularity and advertising billings, ABC had gathered large audiences through the Disney program (see p. 376) and formula-ridden action-adventure shows. One year later, its new position of strength was in danger as the other two networks, led by NBC, began to program major amounts of time in color. ABC lacked sufficient capital to purchase color cameras, VTRs, and other equipment necessary for equal competition. While NBC prime time was nearly all color and CBS about half-color, ABC trailed into the season with 60% of prime time programming still in black-and-white. Its ratings and its reputation with advertising time buyers suffered.

ABC, casting about for new investment funds, and International Telephone and Telegraph (ITT), looking for new acquisitions, found each other late in 1965. Because ABC owned stations, such a merger would be subject to approval by the FCC and the Justice Department, whose antitrust division already was concerned with conglomerate ITT. The FCC held hearings on the proposed merger in September 1966 and approved the ITT takeover 4-3, even though the Justice Department had requested a delay. In January 1967, Justice requested that the FCC reopen the hearings. ABC stock dropped 14 points at the news. Faced with low ratings and consequent low income, ABC asked ITT for a $25 million loan. It did this partly to show how ITT would put money *into* the network rather than financially milking it, as some critics had anticipated. In March the FCC reheard the issues and on June 22, 1967, approved the merger a second time, by the same split vote. But a month later the Justice Department appealed the matter to the courts. Faced with further delay, ITT in January 1968 canceled the merger agreement. Those who felt that ABC would have been forced to temper its news coverage of ITT's many connections were delighted. ABC was left back in third place among the networks. That Summer, recluse billionaire Howard Hughes tried to buy controlling interest in ABC for $150 million, but ABC management was not interested.

As hopes for the ITT merger died, ABC took an innovative plunge into networking during this period–but in radio and not television. On January 1, 1968, it replaced the old ABC Radio Network with four separate networks: Personality (soon renamed Entertainment), Information, Contemporary, and American FM. Using the single ABC network line leased from AT&T, the four shared each broadcast hour in a set pattern, one network getting the first 15 minutes, the next network the second, and so forth. This kept costs down and, perhaps more important, allowed the FCC to waive the duopoly rule by using an obscure section of the 1941 Chain Broadcasting rules (which were not dropped until 1977). For the first time, networks were to be tailored to specialized station formats. *Each* network in a single market could have one affiliate. In a year ABC had twice as many radio affiliates as before, and soon more than 1,200 stations belonged to one of the four networks, making ABC by far the largest radio network operation, with about 30% of all radio stations. Mutual, formerly the largest radio network, suffered from the competition in the smaller markets that it had once controlled. It brought a law suit on the basis of alleged violation of the duopoly rule to enjoin ABC from the plan, but the suit was dismissed. That the Information network was, from the first, the largest of the four networks indicates the desire of stations for national news.

In 1972 Leonard Goldenson, the chief figure at ABC since the merger with Paramount Theaters in 1953, moved up to chairman of the parent company, and Elton Rule, manager of KABC-TV Los Angeles before his move to network headquarters in New York in the late 1960s, became president.

CBS had many changes in operating personnel. At the end of the quiz show scandals, CBS Television president Louis Cowan, who was closely identified with the genre, was eased out in favor of young executive James Aubrey. Aubrey ruled CBS with a steel hand early in the 1960s, earning the sobriquet "Smiling Cobra" for his cold-blooded decision making, and was highly successful at first in selecting network programs. His sudden dismissal in February 1965 in favor of another former station manager, John Schneider, mystified the television world. Aubrey offered no explanation, and neither did CBS President Frank Stanton or Board Chairman William Paley. In general, Aubrey did not fit the CBS image of quality so dear to Paley and Stanton. Some of his programming decisions apparently were based on cronyism rather than judgment, and by 1965 their ratings were wearing thin.

In 1973 Stanton, who by then was vice chairman of the CBS board, retired on schedule (to run the American Red Cross), and the broadcasting industry lost its most respected spokesman. Stanton would have liked, and expected, to move up to chairman, but Paley was not about to give up power in the corporation he had built. Stanton's finest moment had come in 1972, when CBS was attacked for its *Selling of the Pentagon* documentary (see p. 450) and Stanton had successfully stood up to the congressional committee chairman seeking to cite him and CBS for contempt of Congress. Many regarded his defense of the network on First Amendment grounds as a capstone to a distinguished career. CBS went "outside" for his replacement—first to a former ITT vice president, who died within a year of his appointment while Stanton was still available, and then to 37-year-old Arthur Taylor. Like ABC, CBS was beginning to rely on younger executives although Paley was unwilling to give up overall control. In a pattern common to other companies in which the strong founding executive remains active, Paley over the next decade went through several heirs–apparent, finding each wanting in some respect. Apparently Taylor and Paley did not hit it off personally, for while the network was doing well financially late in 1976, Taylor was suddenly relieved of his duties. Named in his place was a man with no broadcasting experience, John D. Backe, who had headed up CBS's publishing arm.

A highly successful company throughout this period, CBS began in the late 1960s to diversify its holdings. Although it could "beat" NBC in television ratings, it was a very small company compared to RCA. CBS Laboratories under Peter Goldmark developed important electronic devices, but CBS did not become a manufacturing concern. Instead, it purchased such diverse firms as Creative Playthings, Fender Guitars, and Holt, Rinehart and

Winston and other publishing firms. CBS's strong artistic style and sense of image, credited to Stanton, showed in everything from the design of their new headquarters, known as "Black Rock," to CBS stationery, to their television network programming.

At NBC, the retirement in 1969 and death in 1971 of longtime RCA head David Sarnoff cut an important string to the past. His son Robert took over active direction of RCA until he suddenly was fired late in 1975. Economic reverses of the 1960s and 1970s caused the parent company to drop out of space and computer activities to concentrate on electronics. In the early 1970s RCA briefly tried to sell NBC's radio O & O stations together with the radio network but could not find an acceptable buyer willing to take the package. In 1975 the NBC radio network replaced the long-running weekend *Monitor* with the first 7-day, 24-hour, live, all-news network service. The News and Information Service (NIS) would be available to any station, not just NBC affiliates, that cared to purchase it, and would run 50 minutes of each hour, leaving 10 minutes for NBC network or local news and features. An insufficient number of affiliates ended the venture early in 1977.

There was a serious attempt to form a fourth commercial television network in the mid-1960s. After the DuMont network collapsed in 1955, most observers believed that too few major markets had a fourth commercial television channel to permit a successful fourth network. Kaiser Broadcasting, a group owner and operator of UHF stations, kept announcing that it would start a UHF-based network if it could get its O & O stations in the black (which it had not managed by 1977 when it sold out to Field Enterprises). Then in July 1966 Ohio warehouse owner Daniel Overmyer, who had several UHF construction permits, announced plans to launch a fourth network with an eight-hour nighttime service, including two of news and two of a live show from Las Vegas. With former ABC-TV president Oliver Treyz to head the operation, the Overmyer Network (ON) signed up 85 affiliates by fall and then appeared to drift while it sought more affiliates. In March 1967 ON became the United Network when a West Coast syndicate gained control, and in May the United Network went on the air with a two-hour program from Las Vegas fed to 125 stations with 13 advertisers defraying most of the costs. This effort collapsed after 31 days when the network was unable to pay AT&T line interconnection charges. Various attempts to restart the network were made throughout the year, but none succeeded.

Several broadcast networks for special occasions—a harbinger of what was to come late in the decade with the new cable networks—were established. The most successful was the Sports Network, purchased by Howard Hughes in late 1968 after his abortive attempt to purchase ABC. The Hughes Sports Network operated on a special program basis, with various stations acting as affiliates depending on the events covered. UPI, AP, and Group W (Westinghouse) each offered audio news services to purchasers, and there were video (film) news services, but these were not full networks in the generally accepted sense. This is not to say that entrepreneurs did not think about establishing new conventional networks, but projected costs and the limited number of markets with more than three operating commercial television stations led to the shelving of these dreams.

9.4 Educational Broadcasting Goes Public

Until 1967, educational radio and television developed differently from earlier years in one important respect: the number of educational stations increased each year. Although only a couple of dozen noncommercial AM stations remained, educational FM stations rose in number from 186 in 1961 to 291 in 1966 and 804 a decade later, nearly a quarter of all FM stations, while ETV outlets doubled from 52 in 1961 to 114 in 1966 and again to 252 in 1976, more than one-quarter of all television stations. But the watchwords of these educational stations remained "local" and "inexpensive"; there was little national programming and very little money. The National Educational Television and Radio Center changed its name to National Educational Television (NET) in 1963 and eventually was providing up to 10 hours a week of programming on film or tape. But, as Sydney Head pointed out, "Despite remarkable progress, considering the odds, the course of educational television during the 1960s seemed dangerously parallel to that of educational radio—curving downward from a peak of high promise and fervent enthusiasm toward a plateau of mediocrity and neglect."[2] Some important help had come in 1962 with the first federal grants, requiring 25% local matching funds, to educational television. The National Association of Educational Broadcasters (NAEB) sponsored studies on the problems of educational broadcasting, usually arriving at the obvious conclusions that money and a national image were needed.

Funded primarily by the Ford Foundation, the Midwest Program on Airborne Television Instruction (MPATI) in 1961 revived Stratovision (see pp. 325–326). MPATI provided instructional television to schools in Indiana, most of Ohio and Illinois, and parts of Kentucky, Michigan, and Wisconsin from airborne transmitters on two UHF channels. Due to costs, scheduling problems, and the failure of some users to pay, MPATI finally sold its two airplanes and its transmitters in 1968, although it continued for a few years to produce and distribute programs on videotape.

A turnaround in the fortunes of ETV began in January 1967 with two important events. The first was the provision of several hours per week of interconnected live evening programming, with the Ford Foundation covering the interconnection costs. Later in the year NET, again with Ford

---

[2]Sydney W. Head, *Broadcasting in America*, 3rd ed. (Boston: Houghton Mifflin Company, 1976), page 182.

Foundation backing, presented the *Public Broadcasting Laboratory*, a two-hour news and feature program on Sunday evenings. The first program included a one-hour drama by blacks in whiteface, which bored and puzzled many viewers and which many southern ETV stations did not carry. Between 1951 and 1977, the Ford Foundation pumped $292 million into educational television stations, networks, and other operations.

The second, and most important, ETV event of 1967 was publication of the report of the Carnegie Commission on Educational Television, *Public Television: A Program for Action*. The commission had been established in 1965 by the Carnegie foundation. Its first decision was to distinguish among commercial television, entertainment for large or mass audiences; instructional television, generally in-class educational material; and public television, virtually everything else, with a large helping of public affairs, that was not supported by advertising. Among their final recommendations were (1) that a Corporation for Public Television be created to receive and disburse funds from government and other sources, (2) that it support at least two national and many more local production agencies, (3) that it seek ways to encourage interconnection of stations, and (4) that sufficient funds, not subject to the annual appropriation process, be provided through a 2% to 5% excise tax on television sets.

This report sold 50,000 copies in a few days, received wide attention, and led to rapid action. President Johnson mentioned public television—a term that caught on, over the objections of some commercial broadcasters—in his 1967 State of the Union address and shortly afterward proposed legislation along the lines of the Carnegie proposals. Eight months later, in November, the Public Broadcasting Act of 1967 became law. It created a Corporation for Public Broadcasting (CPB), as radio had been added at the congressional hearings. Unfortunately, the new corporation had to compete with the rising fiscal priorities of the Vietnam War, with a new Republican administration, which soon conveyed disinterest in a national system of public television, and with disagreement among educators as to whether the public television system should be centralized or station based and funded.

CPB could not legally operate stations or engage in program production. From March 27, 1968, to June 30, 1976, it received $376.2 million in income and gave out $310.7 million in grants, awards, and programs; its first federal appropriation had been $5 million in fiscal year 1969. CPB worked on four major areas of system development in its first months: grants to local stations with an immediate disbursement of $10,000 to all stations and the understanding that future grants would apply to individual needs and plans; interconnection of public television stations; underwriting national programs; and national publicity and research for public television.

A key problem present from the beginning was to plague public broadcasting well into the 1970s. Upon approving CPB, Congress had appropriated a few million dollars in seed money, much of it for facilities rather than for programs, without providing for long-term financing. The Carnegie report had made clear that isolation from the political process was crucial,

▪ **Carnegie Commission and the 1967 Act: The Creation of "Public" Television**   The first few paragraphs of the Carnegie Commission's 12 recommendations (the key ones are noted in the adjacent text) and part of the resultant 1967 act's "Congressional Declaration of Policy" make clear a substantial new role for public television.

The Carnegie Conclusions ... The Carnegie Commission on Educational Television has reached the conclusion that a well-financed and well-directed educational television system, substantially larger and far more pervasive and effective than that which now exists in the United States, must be brought into being if the full needs of the American public are to be served. This is the central conclusion of the Commission and all of its recommendations are designed accordingly.

The programs we conceive to be the essence of Public Television are in general not economic for commercial sponsorship, are not designed for the classroom, and are directed at audiences ranging from the tens of thousands to the occasional tens of millions. No such system now exists to serve us as model, and hence we have been obliged to develop a suitable new arrangement to bring this kind of television to the country. The Commission's proposal deals primarily with that new arrangement.

Although it provides for immediate assistance to existing stations, this is a proposal not for small adjustments or patchwork changes, but for a comprehensive system that will ultimately bring Public Television to all the people of the United States: a system that in its totality will become a new and fundamental institution in American culture.

This institution is different from any now in existence. It is not the educational television that we now know; it is not patterned after the commercial system or the British system or the Japanese system. In the course of our study, we examined all those and others: members of the staff visited Canada, England, Italy, Germany, and Sweden, and papers were commissioned on the Japanese and Russian systems. We found in many countries serious and skillful attempts to provide superior television programming, and in some countries highly successful attempts. But when such a system was successful it met the special needs of society in terms of that society's culture and tradition, and there was little or nothing we could expect to import. We propose an indigenous American system arising out of our own traditions and responsive to our own needs.

The 1967 Act ... Sec. 396.(a) The Congress hereby finds and declares—(1) that it is in the public interest to encourage the growth and development of noncommercial educational radio and television broadcasting, including the use of such media for instructional purposes; (2) the expansion and development of noncommercial educational radio and television broadcasting and of diversity of its programming depend on freedom, imagination, and initiative on both the local and national levels ... (5) that it is necessary and appropriate for the Federal Government to complement, assist, and support a national policy that will most effectively make noncommercial educational radio and television service available to all the citizens of the United States; (6) that a private corporation should be created to facilitate the development of [such] broadcasting and to afford maximum protection to such broadcasting from extraneous interference and control.

Source: Carnegie Commission on Educational Television, *Public Television: A Program for Action* (New York: Harper & Row, 1967), pages 3–4 and 47 U.S.C. 396(a).

and President Johnson had promised to furnish a long-range funding plan, which would permit CPB to plan ahead. He left office before this was done, and the Nixon administration, with its growing dislike for nationally oriented public television and unhappiness with what many Republicans perceived as excessive liberalism and independence in news and public affairs programming, dispensed annually a fraction of the recommended funds. This prevented long-range planning and hamstrung national development of public television. The problem was exacerbated as the Nixon administration proposed funding directly to local stations instead of the centralized programming agencies. The local stations were eager to augment their woefully inadequate funds and pick and choose among the national programs. Many local stations reflected their conservative populations and the business community, which provided most local voluntary financial support; and giving them the power to determine what programs they would "buy" from program suppliers would encourage programming that was politically safe.

Early in 1969, PBS (Public Broadcasting Service) was added to the alphabet soup, to oversee the interconnection process, mainly funded by the Ford Foundation, and other program distribution. It was not a program producer itself. It soon was controlled, however, by the managers of public television stations, many of whom had long resented the national program monopoly of NET and were just as unhappy over the centralized funding power of CPB, which they now needed for much of their support. From its start, PBS wrangled over control of funds for producing programs, which soon involved CPB, the stations, other program producers and supporters, and the Ford Foundation, until the OTP made it clear that federal funding under the Nixon administration would depend upon the system staying decentralized. Politically motivated bills tried to ban news and public affairs programs, using the reasoning that federal funds should not be used to suport a propaganda organ. Many congressmen objected to the high salaries of some on-air news people. Congress was nibbling around the edge, holding off funding until CPB would come around to the stations' and the administration's point of view. President Nixon vetoed a two-year funding bill, but a series of one-year authorizations for CPB passed. Congress was beginning to take an interest in public television (PTV), because substantial segments of the public had begun to watch.

PTV's adult audience increased to the point where some programs showed up in commercial rating service reports. Julia Child's *The French Chef*, produced by WGBH, Boston—one of the most prolific of the production centers for PTV, like KCET, Los Angeles; WNET, New York; and WTTW, Chicago—achieved great popularity. Perhaps most prominent were several British television programs, whose production and storytelling qualities far surpassed the run-of-the-mill commercial American situation comedies and adventure shows. The first of these was *The Forsyte Saga*, based on the Victorian-Edwardian novels of John Galsworthy. The 26 BBC-produced segments held audiences enthralled and increased listener donations. This was followed by *Masterpiece Theatre*, an all-inclusive title for other series and miniseries mostly produced by the BBC or the commercial IBA's program contractors, and hosted by English-American commentator and columnist Alistair Cooke. Some of these series dealt with historical subjects—*Elizabeth R* and *The Six Wives of Henry VIII*—but others dealt with less regal subjects. *Upstairs, Downstairs*, to some extent a weekly soap opera but also social history, depicted life in a London town house in the early 1900s as seen by the family and its servants. This series won several American Emmy awards. Public stations also made heavy use of classic and foreign films. NET public affairs programs such as William F. Buckley's *Firing Line*, the debate program *The Advocates*, *Black Journal*, *The Banks and the Poor*, and *The Great American Dream Machine* brought audience attention and more controversy, including displeasure from the Nixon administration and other conservatives. Essentially, public television was casting off its staid image and collecting larger and more varied audiences. Major companies frequently supplied funding for PTV series in exchange for a one-line credit: "*Masterpiece Theatre* is brought to you by a grant from Mobil Oil Corporation." These companies also often paid for newspaper advertising, which attracted larger audiences. Neither action was greeted with enthusiasm by commercial broadcasters.

In Fall 1969, PTV took a giant step forward in children's programming with the first airing of *Sesame Street*. Planned since the formation of the Children's Television Workshop (CTW) early in 1968, with Ford and Carnegie foundation and U.S. Office of Education funding, *Sesame Street* was quite different from such traditional PTV children's programs as *The Friendly Giant* or *Mister Rogers' Neighborhood* and commercial television's Saturday morning cartoons and adventure shows. It used modern commercial television techniques for education, having programs "sponsored" by different letters of the alphabet or numbers each day, having the show set on a city street, relying on very short animated cartoons with live and puppet segments, and breaking the show into short rapidly moving parts to keep the interest of preschool children. The show was an instant outstanding success, to the chagrin of the commercial networks that had turned down the idea before it had been offered to public television. *Sesame Street* was supported by a continuing research program, and changes were made in the format from time to time reflecting the results of that research. The CTW soon supplemented the preschool *Sesame Street* with *The Electric Company*, a half-hour program for older children that concentrated on words, spelling, and other concepts. CTW attempted an adult medical program in 1974, but it was soon withdrawn for major changes and, even after drastic surgery, ran only briefly.

By late 1976, concern over the future of public broadcasting centered on two important sets of questions: how the expanding system was to be adequately financed, and how the increased interorganizational squabbles (especially those between CPB and PBS) were to be resolved. These practical concerns, of course, did not get to what some felt was the heart of a philosophical question that hasn't yet been answered: is the proper role of public broadcasting being a successor to or incorporator of the older concept of "educational broadcasting" or, after the establishment of PBS, was it intended to be merely an alternative form of the same kinds of programming seen on commercial stations and networks?

9.5 Advertising Clutter and Consumerism

Perhaps more than in any other period of broadcasting's development, advertising itself was controversial. Advertiser demand for air time continued to increase, while costs and public concern about advertising effects also rose.

9.5.1 Trends: Clutter

The major trend toward local radio advertising continued during these 15 years, with the proportion rising to 70%. Total radio revenues more than doubled, but inflation in the mid-1970s and the larger number of stations on the air hid the effects of the revenue increase from the individual station. FM's advertising revenue position improved, but FM remained in the red. While overall FM revenues rose from less than $10 million to more than $308.6 million between 1962 and 1975, many more stations reported losses than profits. FM's problems were the same as in previous decades: compared to AM, there were too little data, audience, station services. But with increased specialization and improved ratings for some FM stations, some of this old refrain wore down. Station owner Gordon McLendon, often an innovator, tried broadcasting nothing but classified ads on FM station KADS in Los Angeles in 1966–1967—no programs, just ads. This experiment was not successful, and KADS reverted to a "normal" musical format.

In television, full sponsorship nearly disappeared as participating or shared advertising spread through both daytime and prime time hours. This change came fairly quickly; from the 1964–1965 season when only 48% of network ads were participating to 95% four seasons later. The long-standard one-minute commercial gave way to the 30-second spot. About 40% of spots were "30s" in 1964–1965; more than 80% four years later. Network advertising was so expensive that few advertisers could afford the steady weekly costs of full sponsorship, and research also showed that the 30-second spots sold goods and services almost as well at less—but not half—cost. Thus cost-spreading shorter ads became popular throughout prime time and daytime schedules. Unfortunately, their brevity resulted in a new pattern that audiences found irritating: the clustered or piggyback ad break. While the total time devoted to advertising did not increase, the number of commercial messages rose sharply as two 30s replaced one 60, or sometimes 20- and 10-second spots were strung together with 3-second quickies at station identification time. A prime time viewer often would see four or five ads in a row in the middle of a program, and the (in)famous midnight break on the late night network shows was cluttered with three to five minutes of national and local ads, promos (promotional announcements), and station breaks in a row. A survey showed 30 different products presented in the typical daytime hour. The public was not the only complainer; advertisers, concerned that their 30-second message in the middle of such clutter would never stick in the viewer's mind, spent more effort and money on the design of commercials. By the late 1960s the most clever were getting "Clio" awards in annual industry self-recognition. Listeners also accused the stations or networks of playing the audio of commercials louder than the program—often a bum rap; really a case of *more* audio, electronically compressed, than *louder* sound. Devices, such as the "blab-off," that enabled viewers to cut audio had a brisk sale.

But clearly television was doing something right. In the 1961–1976 period, its share of all advertising rose from 14% to 20% and total revenues increased more than 300%. Local advertising started to grow in importance again, rising from 15% to 25% of all television advertising. Non-network affiliated stations grew from 24 in 1961 to 97 in 1976 (see Appendix C, Table 2-D).

During the late 1960s the practice of advertising discounts became a concern within the industry. For a long time stations and networks had provided volume discounts for major advertisers to encourage large buys of time over long periods. The network discount practice came under investigation by the Federal Trade Commission, the courts, and Congress in the late 1960s, not so much for the discounts as for the allegedly unfair market advantage they gave major companies, creating difficulties for new products and smaller companies. In 1960, an FTC case taken to court prohibited Procter & Gamble from retaining the recently acquired Clorox company. The court had based its decision largely on Procter & Gamble's eligibility for massive discounts, due to the volume of its multiproduct advertising on the networks, and the unfair discrimination this position might exert on its competitors in the bleach field. This precedent made everyone more cautious and conglomerate mergers less attractive. The problem began to work itself out during the 1960s for several reasons. First, discounts for participating advertising were far smaller than for full sponsorship. Second, as television became a cause of antitrust actions against advertisers, discounts sometimes were eliminated. Finally, the increasing demand for television time did away with the networks' need to offer advertisers massive discounts.

All of the above, plus inflation, led to steadily rising prices for advertising time. The typical network prime time minute went from $30,000 in the early 1960s to over $100,000 by 1976. Special events, like the annual Super Bowl football game, brought upward of $225,000 for each minute, although network costs for rights to the game also were huge. Television was not a medium for advertising by most small businesses.

9.5.2 A Question of Fairness

For most of the 1960s, the most acute broadcast advertising question was whether cigarette advertising would be banned and, by extension, whether the government had the right to ban the advertising of any legal product.

The issue opened with the 1964 report of the Surgeon General, which declared, on the basis of scientific and statistical research, that cigarette smoking might be dangerous to the health of the smoker. In mid-1965, the FTC demanded that all cigarette advertising include a warning notice, a move blocked in Congress by tobacco-growing-state congressmen. Many critics saw the matter as one of fairness: since smoking cigarettes entailed controversy and public health, opposing views to cigarette commercials should be aired.

The first effective attempt to use this approach came late in 1966 when New York lawyer John Banzhaf requested WCBS-TV to provide time for antismoking spots. When the station refused, he appealed directly to the FCC. Most observers expected the complaint to disappear in the sea of bureaucracy but they were surprised. On June 2, 1967, the FCC decided that the Fairness Doctrine (see pp. 463–467) did apply in this case, and that the public should hear the antismoking point of view. Informally, FCC General Counsel Henry Geller said that one antismoking spot for every three smoking commercials would be a fair proportion. The Court of Appeals in Washington upheld the FCC decision. Governmental and voluntary health organizations made extremely creative spots and provided them to stations. Although the commission declared that the Surgeon General's report made this foray into commercial fairness unique, and thus not precedent-setting, advertisers, consumer advocates and environmentalists, and some lawyers were not so sure.

The increasingly active FTC and FCC proposed an outright ban on cigarette advertising on radio and television—the FTC wanted to include all media—and congressional hearings began to explore that idea. Broadcasters, alarmed because cigarette advertising accounted for about 10 percent of network advertising billings, offered many alternative plans, such as limiting ads to late evening and eliminating appeals to youth. Finally, under heavy pressure, the cigarette industry and the broadcasters split: the broadcasters suggested a four-year phaseout of cigarette advertising, and the cigarette people, concerned that FTC action might restrict them from other media, favored a quick and voluntary break with broadcast advertising. Indeed, if *all* tobacco companies were to drop television advertising at the same time, they could save a lot of money and no company would hold an advantage. They suggested termination in Fall 1970 if broadcasters would forgo contract provisions on canceled ads. The broadcasters—except for some who had voluntarily dropped tobacco advertising earlier—refused, and Congress then banned advertising by law.

After January 1, 1971—a date selected so that cigarettes could sponsor New Year's Day football bowl games one last time—no cigarette advertising would be allowed on radio or television. That last day was heavy with smoke, and during the late evening on January 1 tobacco company commercials filled the air as they used their expensive spots for the last time. From that date, $200 million in annual billings was lost to the broadcasters, who claimed the new law was unfair in that it did not affect the rival print media. They also pointed out that similar bans in other countries had done little to lower cigarette smoking—but that made little difference. In Fall 1973, Congress closed a loophole in the law by outlawing ads for "little cigars," which had been heavily advertised on the air during the previous year.

The cigarette matter was only the beginning of new FTC activity. Six months later, the FTC proposed an advertising claim substantiation program, whereby product makers would have to be able to support any and all claims made in print or broadcast advertisements. In broadcasting, this meant that erring sponsors would have to make "corrective" ads and telecast them for a specified time to counteract misleading ad claims. The heavy use of broadcasting by large multiproduct advertisers, even with diminished discounts, led to antitrust actions. Early in 1972, the FTC proposed that the four major cereal makers be broken up because of their market control, achieved chiefly through television ads concentrated in children's week-end programming.

This activity came to a head in February 1972 when the FTC proposed to the FCC that broadcasters should provide air time for *counteradvertising* to balance the views of commercial sponsors. The FTC felt that, if necessary, free time should be offered. The FCC demurred. A few test spots were produced, using the donated talents of actor Burt Lancaster to speak against Bayer's claims for aspirin superiority and to remind drivers of a massive recall of recent model Chevrolets, but very few stations used them. Proponents of counteradvertising said that it would enhance freedom of speech and that commercial advertisers, often notorious for false claims, should not have a monopoly on the publicly owned airwaves. As might be expected, broadcasters and advertisers united against this idea, because counteradvertising would (and here comes a familiar claim!) "ruin the industry." They believed that advertisers faced with counterads would leave broadcasting and go to print media, where no such threat waited. Proponents of counteradvertising noted that the antismoking spots of the late 1960s had not driven cigarette firms from the air; no one firm could afford to leave the field to others, and joint action would have violated antitrust laws. Broadcasters further claimed that arguments would fill the air and that free time was unfair to broadcasting since it was not required from other media. By 1976 it appeared unlikely that the counteradvertising concept would attain the force of law, although some stations accepted such advertising and law suits were started demanding such a right. The issue became one aspect of the battle for public access under the Fairness Doctrine (see p. 463 ff.), which included court suits against "misleading" ads.

9.6 Program Specialization and Cycles

Programming in both radio and television after 1960 was a matter of slow evolution of types, with program cycles of invention-imitation-decline being more important than revolutionary change. A common phenomenon in broadcasting was rapid copying of any program idea that showed it could gain an audience.

9.6.1 Radio Specialization

Until the late 1960s, the trend in AM radio was toward increased specialization of formats. A new all-news format spread to a few of the largest markets in the late 1960s. Their manpower requirements made all-news stations expensive, but they did very well in the ratings. Many more stations adopted all-talk formats that included, but did not depend on, news. Telephone call-in programs, discussions, interviews, news, and public affairs were the hallmarks of radio without music.

Some stations continued to specialize in music, although the Top-40 station, together with what had been rock music, slowly changed its sound, reflecting the evolution of popular music. It is difficult to summarize briefly the changes in music over 15 years. Music prior to 1964 had changed little from that of the late 1950s; Top-40 formula radio persisted. But the music of the Beatles drastically changed the sound of popular music after 1964; and after the Vietnam War became an issue in 1965–1966, college students' folk music turned into songs of protest. Singers were identified as much with their cause as with their music, and emphasis shifted from "sound," music and beat, to an appreciation of lyrics. Judy Collins and others made great music—sometimes with serious messages. The FCC warned management that it should clearly understand lyrics before airing a number, since some lyrics seemed to glorify drug usage; licensees would be held responsible for glorification of illegal actions. Another change of the mid-1960s was the increasing presence of black popular music artists on the air. In the 1950s, whites had performed rhythm and blues, which had originated as black music; now black soloists and groups turned their rhythm and blues into *soul music*. The center of this activity was Motown (*"Motor town"* = Detroit) Record Co., controlled by blacks, and having under contract a number of groups popular with both blacks and whites—notably Diana Ross and the Supremes. What became known as the *Detroit sound* of strong instrumental background to rhythmic music was reminiscent of the music of the 1950s.

Stations in the 1960s increasingly specialized in particular kinds of music. Some stations concentrated on programming music and other content by and for blacks, especially in the larger markets with sizable black populations, even though almost all licensees were white. Country and Western music spread from its southern home to the rest of the country, including the supposedly sophisticated Northeast. By the 1970s, every major market had at least one C & W operation. Other stations specialized in rock, the most popular; "middle-of-the-road" music; or "golden oldies." The latter based their appeal on replaying of music from the past—six months to a decade or two. These stations generally aimed at adults in the advertiser-desired ages between 18 and 35 who had listened to this music on radio as teenagers.

Some stations appealed to small specialized audiences—ethnic or religious groups, classical music fans, and listeners to a handful of listener-supported "underground" stations, such as those of the Pacifica Foundation, whose programming is too eclectic to categorize. As the fragmentation of audiences produced a fragmentation of advertising revenues, inexpensive and often automated formats became very desirable.

In May 1963 the FCC proposed that AM-FM operations in the same market and under the same ownership be required to program separately some of the time. This would reduce duplicated programming, which had characterized most FM stations since the late 1940s. The industry predictably claimed that any such action would harm FM by taking away popular programs. But the FCC was insistent and issued a rule in July 1964 specifying that, in markets of 100,000 or more, AM-FM stations must offer separate programming at least half the time. There was considerable legal wrangling, and whole classes of stations were given delays, but by 1967 most FM stations had come under the ruling, which was expanded to include smaller markets in the 1970s. The predictable result: FM began to specialize, and soon the air was filled with FM rock stations, FM Country and Western stations, as well as "progressive jazz" and the more traditional FM "beautiful music" and classical music stations. By the late 1960s the specialization had changed the decades-old idea that "FM is special," to the view that "FM is radio." An increasing number of receivers capable of receiving FM testified to the resulting audience appeal.

Nonmusical entertainment programming did not disappear. Catering to nostalgia buffs, returns of old radio drama and comedy programs appeared, first on stations appealing to college students in evening hours and then spreading to other stations for an hour or so a week at different hours of the day. In 1973, NBC began to broadcast repeats of *X-Minus-One*, a series of science fiction dramas from the early 1950s. Mutual offered several old shows, and a few specialty companies bought up broadcast rights to old series—*The Lone Ranger*, *The Shadow*, and some comedies—to syndicate them on tape to local stations. National Public Radio, the radio arm of CPB, funded several radio drama workshops, including one specializing in the use of stereo in radio drama. Beginning in 1974, CBS broadcast *Mystery Theater*, an hour-long original drama each night. Hosted by noted actor E. G. Marshall, the series provided the first network outlet for writing and acting talent in radio in more than two decades and was a success with listeners and advertisers alike. A child-oriented *Adventure Theater* followed two years later.

9.6.2 Economics of Television Programming

The most obvious differences between television programs of 1961 and the 1970s were the addition of color and the virtual elimination of live programming, although tape—using live television studio techniques—largely supplanted film. Color had languished after its 1954 introduction by RCA because of receiver and studio cost and lack of support from the rest of the industry with investments in monochrome. Only RCA's subsidiary NBC had programmed much color, while CBS had only occasional color shows and ABC had none. But by Fall 1965 all three networks had adopted color; NBC announced that its prime time schedule would be about 95% in color, CBS would produce half its programs in color, and ABC hoped to achieve 40%. Black-and-white television had reached nearly every home, and many sets purchased during the boom years were due for replacement. Color set quality had improved and prices had dropped. Advertisers and some far-seeing program packagers had been preparing commercials and programs in color.

Surveys had shown that color was associated with increased viewing and more attention to commercials, and for a time stations broadcasting more color had a ratings edge. But the cost of that edge was heavy. It was estimated that the networks spent $30 million to $40 million to purchase color equipment and add the required graphics, costumes, sets, and so on. Station costs also were high, since color cameras cost three times as much as monochrome cameras. To go "full color" was prohibitively expensive for most stations, but it cost them little to carry network programs and not too many thousands of dollars more to show color film. Hence, during that first color season, 97% of stations could carry network shows in color, 60% had color film and slide capacity, while only 15% could originate programs in color. The 1965–1967 period saw stations scrambling for color equipment—and for the money to pay for it. By January 1966, 70% of commercials were shot in color, and a year or so later monochrome commercial spots were rare, at least on a network. By December 1966, more color than black-and-white sets were being sold for the first time. Lower receiver prices led to more set production and importation and still lower prices. It was estimated that one-sixth of the nation's homes had color by 1967, and three-quarters by 1976 (see Appendix C, Table 7-A).

A major change in the source for television programming also occurred. Prior to the quiz show scandal (see p. 377), advertisers and their agencies produced about one-quarter to one-third of network programming, package agencies or companies produced about 45%, and the networks made up the difference—around 20% in typical years, much of it news. By the late 1960s and early 1970s, advertisers had almost disappeared as program producers, providing less than 3% of network shows, mostly daytime. Packagers now produced 80% of network programming and nearly all of prime time, although the networks often had a financial stake in the product. Programs produced by the networks themselves accounted for only 8% of a typical season's programming. This move from advertiser control was due only partly to the quiz show scandals. The most important factor was cost: up to a million dollars for a one-hour and perhaps two-thirds that sum for a half-hour program pilot by 1976. Regular program costs rose from $100,000 per hour in the early 1960s to about $300,000 for the same kind of show by late 1976. With packaging, networks could control their daily programming better than when advertising agencies controlled many productions. Advertisers were naturally more concerned with a single program than with an overall pattern, but the packagers had to cater to network needs and demands.

In the 1950s, most programs had been live or on film. But by the mid- to late-1960s the development of videotape recording (see pp. 348–349) did away with most live programs except news on the three networks and many local stations. Comedy and drama programs usually were shot on film so that syndication to smaller stations or overseas, which used different VTR standards, could help recoup costs. Tape often was used for music and variety programs, because its slightly sharper image and the pace permitted by "live" multicamera television practice gave it a more immediate look, and for talk programs and daytime serials, whose lower cost usually could be recouped in a single showing. In addition, of course, tape made use of existing, expensive television production facilities and could be shown without a delay for film processing.

Programs were running longer. The 15-minute show disappeared, the 30-minute format remained for situation comedies, while 60-, 90-, and even 120-minute dramatic or special programs became fairly common. Once in a while, a network would present a special program lasting the entire evening. There were more and more news and entertainment special programs and feature movies on network television (see p. 437) that ran an hour or two— or longer. To hold viewers over normal program switching periods, a few of these longer programs avoided ending an act or segment on the half-hour.

Then there was the problem of reruns. In the days of live television, there had been few program repeats, as shows either were produced year-round or had Summer replacements. Beginning in the 1960s, filmed and taped programs began to offer progressively fewer original episodes and more reruns each year, until, by the mid-1970s, some series had reruns for more than half the year. Unemployment in talent and craft unions in Hollywood spearheaded pressure to change this situation. By 1972 the problem had attracted White House interest, since President Nixon not only had no love for the networks but also had promised economic aid for the film workers in his home state of California. A White House agency, the Office of Telecommunications Policy, suggested that reruns cheated viewers and created much of the unemployment afflicting the movie industry. The networks replied that to reduce or eliminate reruns would cost so much that (1) they would have to program more inexpensive game and variety shows, (2) much program production would be forced out of the country to places with cheaper labor, and (3) reduced network profit ratios would mean fewer network news and public affairs programs, traditionally paid for by entertainment show profits. All of these would further reduce employment in the program production studios. The issue died with tacit recognition that reruns probably would stay, particularly since research showed that the audience for a rerun often was almost as large as for the original showing.

As the number of new programs in a given series in a year shrank from 39 to 26 or fewer, the use of *miniseries* with four to ten program episodes became attractive as *fill-ins* for canceled programs or as specials. This followed the British practice of making no more programs than could be made well, considering the long lead time for scripts and the fatiguing effect of a long-running series on performers and crew. The success of British miniseries on PBS (see pp. 426–427) paved the way for their use on commercial television, as did the rapidity with which networks would "kill" a series that did not initially do well in the ratings. A number of novels were serialized in this way starting in 1976, including Alex Haley's *Roots*, which achieved record ratings—as many as 80 million viewers—when it was aired for 12 hours over eight nights on ABC in January 1977.

Programming cycles became common by the early 1960s. Program types were invented, were imitated, and then declined. Some observers have suggested that after the early 1950s no new program types appeared—only adaptations of format, stars, and producers. New ideas were quickly exploited and imitated; a new show was built on a minor character in an earlier show, or merely followed a similar line. A prime reason for these *spin-offs* was cost. As a popular program lasted through several seasons, its creative or *above-the-line* costs, covering talent, direction, script, and music, increased far faster than the technical or *below-the-line* costs, partly because stars demanded a larger piece of a successful show. When the network could no longer make a profit on the cost per episode—although foreign sales and other factors had to be considered—it would cancel the show for a less expensive replacement as soon as ratings began to dip. Imitations of successful program types came in roughly three-year cycles, including periods for westerns, situation comedies, crime and detective, and action-adventure shows.

9.6.3 Television Entertainment Formats

The number of variety programs doubled after 1961 but then declined rapidly in the 1970s. Ed Sullivan finally left the CBS lineup in 1972, due to declining ratings and an aging audience, after a record run in his Sunday evening prime time slot. Other shows, built around singers—Dean Martin, Andy Williams—or comedians—Carol Burnett, Flip Wilson—came on, but had nearly disappeared by 1976. Quiz and audience participation programs also nearly disappeared in the network evening hours, although they remained popular during the daytime and on local stations.

In 1961 NBC started a trend with *Saturday Night at the Movies*, playing fairly recent theatrical films in prime time. The ratings were so high that the other networks joined in. In 1967 prime time movies played 12 hours a week on the networks and soon at least one network had one every night of the week. Films of all sorts—comedy, drama, musicals—were used; in the long run they were less expensive, better produced, and earned higher ratings than most comparable network series programs. Their popularity kept up until the 1975–1976 season.

For prime time showing, the networks needed more films appropriate for television than Hollywood could provide. They had exhausted recent feature films—production was drastically less than pre-1948 output—and most older films were too overshown or too unimportant for further syndication. Again, NBC led the way to a solution with *World Premiere* in 1966, presenting "made for television" movies—90- or 120-minute films shot on a television schedule of days rather than months. The speeded-up shooting schedule kept costs down, still put more entertainment values into a program than most series offered, and often led to better ratings than regular series. Once again, the other networks followed suit; in the 1971–1972 seasons, 100 such films were shown on all three networks. They were not cheap—about $400,000 for a 90-minute film in 1974—but when played twice, once as a rerun, they could recoup costs with good ratings and advertiser response. By the early 1970s, television films were doubling as series pilots or even as feature movies abroad. Earlier, when a pilot did not sell as a series, the half-hour or hour film had little sales appeal. But expanded to 90 or 120 minutes, such a pilot could be shown as a film, without a series sale, and its track record would contribute tremendously to its salability as a series.

Television comedy was consistently strong in prime time network programming. Situation comedies were particularly prone to the cyclical spin-off process. The long-running *Andy Griffith Show*—a comedy about a rustic sheriff—began in the 1961–1962 season and ran on network and in reruns through the decade, eventually spinning off *Gomer Pyle* (about a naive Marine Corps recruit from Andy's hometown), which in turn spun off *Mayberry R.F.D.* before CBS dropped rural programs in the early 1970s because they appealed to too old an audience to attract advertisers. In the same category was the immensely popular *Beverly Hillbillies* (about a hillbilly family, suddenly oil-rich, moving to Beverly Hills but keeping their country ways and clothes). This 1962 program spun off *Petticoat Junction* and Eva Gabor, Eddie Albert, and Arnold the pig in *Green Acres* (about rich city folks trying to make good in the country). Comedies of the mid-1960s featuring a monster, witch, or genie, included the long-running *Bewitched* (about a wife and her mother who were goodhearted witches), possibly the best of this lot; shows with talking cars or horses, and a "family" program based on the macabre cartoon characters of Charles Addams.

Some comedy shows stressed gimmick, some stressed plot, and many of the longest lasting featured a personality: Lucille Ball, Dick Van Dyke, and others. Van Dyke did not repeat the popular success of the award-winning *Dick Van Dyke Show* of the mid-1960s, but his co-star, Mary Tyler Moore, did. Her subsequent show—one of several successes packaged by her MTM Productions, under the leadership of her then-husband, Grant Tinker—was one of the few with a broadcasting milieu—a local television station's news department, *not* in Hollywood or New York.

The most important comedy program factory of the 1970s was Norman Lear and Bud Yorkin's Tandem Productions. They broke many barriers by adapting two successful British programs, which became *All in the Family* (about "lovable bigot Archie Bunker" and family) and *Sanford and Son* (about a black junk dealer). *Family* spun off *Maude* (about a middle-aged liberated woman), *The Jeffersons* (about Archie Bunker's black neighbors who move to a new, mainly white neighborhood), and others. The short run in 1975 of *Hot l Baltimore* (from the play about a sleazy hotel with a letter missing from its sign), which depicted homosexuals, prostitutes, and numerous older people in a comic light, and their syndicated *Mary Hartman, Mary Hartman* (an adult soap opera spoof that the networks would not touch, although many local stations did very well scheduling it against the late night news on other stations) showed that the barriers on subject matter were coming down. The change had been swift. As late as 1967, socially and politically oriented skits in the Smothers Brothers' comedy-variety show bothered the CBS continuity acceptance staff. Rising costs, slipped ratings, and alleged contract problems gave CBS the excuse to drop the program. The brothers sued CBS successfully but were not able to revive their show on a regular schedule until 1975 (on ABC). It was a dismal failure; their humor had been passed by as television and public taste changed.

A comedy program departing from the usual situation formula was *Rowan and Martin's Laugh-In*. Starting in January 1968 after some tryouts, it offered extremely rapid pacing, blackout comedy lines, a zany and inventive acting troupe of relative unknowns, and topical humor held together by comedians Dan Rowan and Dick Martin and stretching the ability to edit videotape to the limit. It was reminiscent of the innovative Ernie Kovacs show of 1955–1956 and subsequent specials before Kovacs's death in a 1962 auto crash. Several programs tried unsuccessfully to imitate *Laugh-In's* format, including one that succumbed after a single showing to affiliates' complaints about its bad taste. *Laugh-In* itself folded in mid-1973.

The hours devoted to western action-adventure programs diminished after 1961, with none scheduled for the 1976–1977 season. Only two had very long and successful lives: *Bonanza*, which lasted 14 seasons, and *Gunsmoke*, which lasted for 20. A flurry of war programs marked the early

1960s, nearly all of which replayed World War II. Some played it straight, like *Combat* or *12 o'Clock High*, and some tried an odd comedy form like *Hogan's Heroes*, which took place in a German prison camp; but most disappeared with the heating up of the real Vietnam War.

The tongue-in-cheek approach to action-adventure was best epitomized by *The Man from U.N.C.L.E.*, started in 1964, which showed intrepid agents of a mythical anticrime organization trying to outsmart a global underworld organization. It was a spoof on the popular "James Bond" spy films, and after a season or two it became more obviously comic. The bumbling spy reached new heights in the long-running *Get Smart* half-hour comedy, which first aired in 1965. Straight-faced television parodies of comic-strip character *Batman* and old radio character *The Green Hornet* on ABC created a short-lived student cult in 1966–1967. Fantastic but deadly serious was *Mission Impossible*, beginning in 1966 and going into syndication after 1972. It had a stock opening scene of the lead character retrieving from some out of the way place a cheap tape recorder that would "self-destruct in five seconds" after giving him instructions. Complicated mechanical and electronic gimmicks and plots were typical of this series, which ran for many years on the network and had healthy reruns and syndication with a 1988 sequel—and a high-budget feature film in 1996.

A limited science fiction movement peaked after 1966 with *Star Trek*, which depicted the "five-year voyage of the Starship *Enterprise*" and her diverse and stereotyped crew, including a pointed-eared alien executive officer. The voyage lasted only three years on network television, but the original programs still play in seemingly endless reruns. Its fans, known as "Trekkies," have created a cult, complete with annual conventions and the lobbying ability to force NASA to change the name of the first U.S. space shuttle to *Enterprise*. No other science fiction show—the childish *Lost in Space* or *The Invaders* or the British syndicated *Space: 1999*—had the attraction or lasting power of *Star Trek*, which later spawned feature films, a cartoon series, and, in 1987, the first of several sequels featuring a new generation of actors. A cult British series, *Dr. Who*, was never as popular in the United States.

Crime and detective programs were prevalent in the early 1960s and the mid-1970s. General formats of these two periods were frequently similar. *The Lineup*, a late 1950s show about veteran San Francisco police officers, was followed in the 1970s by *Streets of San Francisco*; the successful New York–based police detective *Kojak* of the 1970s reminded many of the superbly done *Naked City* of 1959–1963. Not all crime detective shows could be repeated, however. After nearly a decade, *Perry Mason* left the network lineup in 1966 (although it had highly profitable reruns), and star Raymond Burr's *Ironside*, about a wheelchair-bound police chief, was another long-term success. A revival of *Perry Mason* in 1973 was unsuccessful. However, until the 1970s television seemed unable to handle the uncompromisingly realistic look at police work of former Los Angeles Police Sergeant Joseph Wambaugh's *Police Story*. Most crime and detective programs continued their pot-boiling emphasis on action rather than on character and depth. For obvious production and audience distribution reasons, most shows of the genre were laid in New York City or California. The "good guys" were seen to lose occasionally, but familiar plot lines, themes, and characters remained, more so in the police and private detective programs than in lawyer-centered programs such as *The Defenders* (a 1960s program about a father-son team defending unpopular causes) and a mid-1970s special and miniseries, *The Law*.

Between *Ben Casey* and *Dr. Kildare*, which started in 1961, and *Medical Center* and *Marcus Welby, M.D.* a decade later, few medical programs had prime time popularity, but medical personnel and their adventures and love lives never left the networks, particularly the daytime soap operas, which often drew on medical locales or themes. By the early 1970s, medical dramatic programming was dealing more and more with controversial themes—abortion, euthanasia, costs of medical service, malpractice—in starker portrayals of hospital personnel, medical problems, and human character.

Regularly scheduled dramatic programs with little action but deep thinking did not last. George C. Scott as a concerned social worker in *East Side, West Side* was well reviewed by critics but insufficiently watched by the public, which wanted entertainment rather than conscience. Later shows about state legislators, *Slattery's People*, and even a U.S. senator, *The Senator*, met the same fate. Serious drama was limited in the late 1960s to the occasional special. The only regular anthology dramas of this period were on public television, and most were British imports.

The rise in public consciousness of racial and ethnic minorities in society was making television programming more complicated. Falling ratings and complaints from Italian-American groups about the preponderance of villains with Italian names forced the popular *Untouchables* off the network. Even though names were carefully changed during the last year of the show, the protest had achieved a life of its own. Mexican-Americans had the same effect on the "Frito Bandito" commercial cartoon character and, by the early 1960s, black concern about the lily-whiteness of television shows and commercials was bearing fruit. Though some network shows had starred blacks in the 1950s and 1960s, none lasted until Sheldon Leonard's *I Spy* in 1965 combined white Robert Culp and black Bill Cosby (then little known) as U.S. undercover agents. Their warm relationship and repartee as equals, together with an awakening racial consciousness, helped bring on more programs with black stars. The first series of the 1960s with one black star was *Julia*, a comedy about a divorced black nurse. Although a breakthrough, it received criticism for being too middle class. By the early 1970s, blacks were present in about one-third of all commercials and in many television shows. For a time, Flip Wilson's variety show won top ranking in the ratings. The color bar seemed broken.

In daytime hours, television consisted of reruns of situation comedies, soap operas, or quiz and other human-interest programs. All of these had low budgets and high profits, which often helped offset network losses from expensive, prime time television programs. Soap operas were thriving and expanding, with several becoming hour-long by 1976. Plot development remained lethargic, and differences between shows seemed slight except for *Dark Shadows*, telecast live with heavy gothic overtones, including a vampire. ABC briefly telecast *Peyton Place*, based on the best-selling novel, twice a week in prime time, but serials did not do well in the evening. In the early 1970s, although the serials maintained a certain decorum—no swearing, for example—they dealt increasingly with adultery, drugs, and other current controversies.

Game shows became a daytime staple, and for a time in the late 1960s they outrated the serials. Game programs had three basic formats: audience participation, panels—*Hollywood Squares*, for example, used entertainers or other "professionals" to participate in a quiz, often with scripted repartee—and human interest—or perhaps greed, as with *Let's Make a Deal*, in which studio audience members tried to get as much money or goods as possible. Local television stations adapted some of these and also used gimmicks like *Dialing for Dollars* as audience-building and advertising vehicles.

Talk programs now ran through the day on both network and local television. The magazine format of NBC's morning *Today* program (see p. 442), built around news and features, had many local station midday imitations aimed mainly at housewives. NBC was unsuccessful with another daytime talk program, the lavish *Home* of the early 1950s. Many men and women stars hosted talk or variety hours. Among the few who made national reputations were Dinah Shore and Mike Douglas. He began a low-key talk and variety program for Westinghouse's KYW, Philadelphia, in 1965 and had a syndicated solid hold on large daytime audiences a decade later. Merv Griffin had a similar show—in content and in ratings—in some markets.

The late evening hours became the domain of Johnny Carson after the former daytime quiz show MC took over Jack Paar's host job on the *Tonight* show in 1962. With band leader Skitch Henderson (and later "Doc" Severinsen), many guests, and announcer Ed McMahon, Carson presided over a late night, highly profitable institution on NBC that successfully and almost effortlessly fought off competing network programs with talk hosts such as Joey Bishop or Dick Cavett (ABC), or movies (ABC and CBS).

Sports programming was a staple of weekends. The last of the pre-scripted television wrestling programs left major stations early in 1964. By then television had revitalized professional football as the development of

▪ **Talk, Talk, Talk . . . Morning and Night**   Both *Today* and *Tonight* began in the 1950s, the brainstorms of then-NBC president Pat Weaver. The *Today* show (below) combined news and features for its early morning listeners—and in early programs the camera panned outside of the ground floor studio to show watching New Yorkers.

Photos courtesy of National Broadcasting Company, Inc.

videotape and videodisc "instant replay," starting in 1963, greatly added to audience interest. New Year's Day now belonged to football, much as Guy Lombardo and his orchestra was the expected harbinger of midnight on New Year's Eve. After 1967 the annual January Super Bowl earned enormous ratings and advertiser per-minute charges. The popularity and pitfalls of sports programs were illustrated in 1969 when NBC cut the last few seconds of a game to start a special children's program (*Heidi*) on time. In an unbelievable nine seconds, one team scored two touchdowns and won the game—but the enraged and frustrated television football fans saw none of it. The networks learned their lesson: stay with the sports coverage no matter how long the game might go. In 1975, as a result, a network stayed with a major game for 45 minutes into another children's special—and was roasted by enraged and frustrated parents.

ABC was more innovative in sports than the other networks. Its *Monday Night Football*, beginning in 1970, brought in audiences not reached by normal entertainment programming on the other networks. Its *Wide World of Sports*, on the other hand, attracted many viewers not normally interested in sports. Coverage of the 1964, 1968, 1972, and 1976 Olympics showed television technical ingenuity at its best, as ABC provided detailed and well-narrated coverage, usually by ex-athletes. In the 1972 Olympics, terrorists murdered Israeli athletes, and the sports-suddenly-turned-news

The *Tonight* show was hosted between 1962 and 1992 by Johnny Carson, shown here (right, below) with his announcer-foil Ed McMahon. Earlier hosts included Steve Allen (1952–1957) and the mercurial Jack Paar (1957–1962). Since Carson stepped down in 1992, Jay Leno has hosted the program.

team reported the story well. ABC's sports chief, Roone Arledge, was promoted to head of ABC News in 1977.

As the popularity of sports programs grew and all three commercial networks bid for the rights, television revenues became as important as gate or box office receipts to the various clubs and leagues. Sports fans had long objected to club contracts that required television blackouts for the area in which a contest was being played, even when the seating was sold out. This practice was stopped in 1973 when federal legislation banned football blackouts for games sold out three days in advance.

9.6.4 Growing Independence of Television News

For most of the 1960s, before and after evening network newscasts were lengthened from 15 minutes to a half-hour in September 1963, CBS's Walter Cronkite competed with the NBC team of Chet Huntley and David Brinkley for audience, while ABC ran a series of newsmen through its anchorman slot. It found long-term success in 1970 when Harry Reasoner left CBS and joined Howard K. Smith, another ex-CBS correspondent, to create a team. However, the Smith-Reasoner team broke up in 1975, with Smith becoming a commentator, the kind of position Eric Sevareid had at CBS until his 1977

■ **And now . . . the evening news with . . .** From 1963 to 1981, the CBS evening news was anchored by Walter Cronkite. A UP reporter until after World War II, Cronkite became one of the most trusted men in America. Although well known for his interest in the space program of the 1960s, his influence was most visible after he became a "dove" on the Vietnam War following a visit to Saigon during which CBS resident staffers showed him how the military manipulated the press. The left photo shows Cronkite in the 1960s. His chief competitor was the NBC team of Chet Huntley and David Brinkley from 1956 to 1971, then John Chancellor for several years. During and after the 1976 elections Chancellor (left) and Brinkley (right, in the right-hand photo) teamed together—and are shown here in the network booth above the floor of the Democratic convention that nominated Jimmy Carter for President.

Photo courtesy of National Broadcasting Company, Inc.

Photo credit: Indelible, Inc.

retirement—and Brinkley was at NBC until 1981. Reasoner became sole anchorman. In 1976 ABC hired Barbara Walters from the NBC *Today* show to be co-anchor in a million-dollar deal. At NBC, with Huntley's retirement in 1971, the anchor position reverted to John Chancellor, a veteran NBC news correspondent and the head of the Voice of America from 1965 to 1967. During and after the 1976 political campaigns, NBC teamed Chancellor with Brinkley.

Daytime network newscasts also grew during the late 1960s, partly because of news from Southeast Asia. Local stations frequently programmed more news than the networks, with short noontime programs, half-hour late evening shows, and up to an hour and a half adjoining the network news at the dinner hour. By 1976, the networks were proposing lengthening their evening newscasts to 45 or 60 minutes, against the strong opposition of their affiliates, who would lose revenue as a result. It didn't happen.

Spurred by the need to cover events in other continents—the Vietnam War, the Olympics—broadcasting networks turned to space communication satellites. Although each satellite use cost several thousand dollars, it permitted live coverage of some events and eliminated the complexities and red tape of air transport of film from overseas. Broadcast journalists also had, by the mid-1970s, a wide range of such electronic news-gathering (ENG) equipment as portable color cameras and videotape recorders, whose flexibility and ability to deliver live pictures led many television stations to replace their newsfilm equipment with a true television system.

A watershed of American history and of broadcast journalism occurred a few months after the networks lengthened their evening newscasts to a half-hour. Almost everyone old enough to remember can tell you exactly where he or she was on November 22, 1963, when the news came of President Kennedy's assassination in Dallas. The authors of this book both happened to be standing by UPI teletype machines, one in Madison, Wisconsin, and the other in Los Angeles. Although radio could respond immediately, the television networks had to take a few minutes to warm up cameras, insert a few hasty words into the normal programming, and switch over to four extraordinary days of news, commentary, and tribute. Although broadcasters, like the rest of the nation, were in shock, they somehow solved the logistic problems and produced the necessary pictures: preparations for the funeral, the first hours of the Johnson administration, varied tributes, the further shock of Jack Ruby shooting alleged assassin Lee Harvey Oswald, telecast live on NBC, and finally the almost unbearable emotion of the funeral and burial at Arlington National Cemetery. For all four days Americans remained glued to their sets. CBS research showed 93% of the nation's homes tuned in during the burial and the average home having a set in use for more than 13 consecutive hours. By the end of these four days, broadcasters could stand down from a job well done and commiserate with the rest of the country about the senseless assassination and the terrible feeling of loss—not just of a President, but of purpose and enthusiasm.

Unfortunately, the shooting in Dallas was but the first of a series of political assassinations and attempted assassinations. In April 1968 television covered riots that broke out in black ghettos after Rev. Martin Luther King, Jr.'s assassination in Memphis. Two months later, Senator Robert Kennedy was killed on the night of his California presidential primary victory. Live television did not catch the shooting itself—late at night in Los Angeles—but the networks stayed on the air to report the senator's condition and eventual death. For both Kennedy funerals, television was an integral part of impressive and symbol-laden ceremony. Through television, as it followed the train carrying the senator's body from New York to Washington, millions of Americans of all political persuasions joined vicariously with the hundreds of thousands who lined the tracks. Watching these events helped to achieve catharsis. The 1972 election process was similarly marred when a man shot and paralyzed Alabama Governor George Wallace at a rally. The horror of assassination loomed again in Fall 1975 when attempts were made in California on the life of President Gerald Ford and in 1981 when President Ronald Reagan was shot in Washington.

Some of the most exciting positive moments on television occurred during the "space race" of the 1960s with the Russians, after President Kennedy promised to put a man on the moon within the decade. Even the manned suborbital flights of 1961 were exciting although all that the viewer could see was the blast-off. With John Glenn's first orbital trip in February 1962, the nation hung on every minute of the several hours of coverage, although it was largely in the studio, with mockups and animation and interviews. In May 1963 Gordon Cooper used live television from space to show us what Earth looked like from orbit. Television covered the first space walk in 1965, showed the *Gemini* recovery live later that same year, and covered the disastrous flash fire in January 1967 that killed three *Apollo* astronauts about to make the first flight of their three-man spacecraft. On Christmas Eve, 1968, the mission commander of *Apollo 8* read passages from Genesis on live television while the spacecraft orbited the moon and we got our first closeup of the moon's surface. Seven months later, *Apollo 11* placed man on the surface of the moon itself. All the networks geared up with science reporters, ex-astronauts, explanatory animation, and models to explain the lengthy and complicated mission from liftoff to splashdown. On July 20, 1969, at 4:17 P.M. (EDT), the lunar module landed on the moon and even normally restrained CBS anchorman Walter Cronkite could not contain his joy and awe (see p. 448). At 10:56 P.M., Neil Armstrong became the first man to walk on the moon, and a small television camera covered the event live for Americans and millions of others who watched via satellite relay. For the next hours the world watched while the astronauts wandered over the surface, talked by telephone with the President, planted the American flag, and cavorted and worked. There also were live telecasts from the returning spacecraft, and of the splashdown and delivery of the astronauts to a germ-proof quarantine station.

Color television added great visual interest to later missions. The most suspenseful flight was that of *Apollo 13*, which aborted on the way to the moon because of a fuel cell explosion. Television kept the nation informed of emergency procedures that brought the crew safely home. Some viewers complained that space coverage was overdone, even during the *Apollo 11* and *Apollo 13* missions—they missed their favorite programs or resented the public relations exposure for the space program—but most viewers, judging from the ratings, were fascinated by every minute of it.

Television also provided momentum for the civil rights movement of the 1960s, in news reports, documentaries, and other programming. It also covered—and some would say caused or at least abetted—much of the urban racial and campus political and social unrest of the mid-1960s. In August 1965 television cameras covered the burning and looting by residents of large parts of the Los Angeles black community of Watts. A helicopter-borne KTLA camera provided amazing coverage, but television crews also went into the ghetto—many for the first time, residents complained—only to discover that they, too, were targets for frustration and rage. Riots in other cities, notably Washington, D.C., also occurred during this "long, hot summer." Some blamed the riots on unfulfilled expectations of blacks who had swallowed television's glamourized version of upper-middle-class white life. By the time of the riots in 1968 in Washington, Philadelphia, and other cities following Martin Luther King, Jr.'s assassination, broadcasters had learned what *not* to do. News teams, in addition to feeling like targets, had frequently encouraged violent, or more violent, action or confrontation simply by showing up at a protest with cameras and lights; and persons or groups who wanted to publicize their cause often alerted the news media to potential clashes.

After the racial conflict, the most important violence and protest that persisted in this period was over the war in Vietnam. Beginning with coverage of American "advisers" participating in small unit actions in the early 1960s, the nightly evening newscasts brought to millions of American homes the "living room war"—day-to-day life and death in battle. For more than seven years, families sat down to dinner in front of the television set and watched Americans and Asians shooting and being shot at in the longest war in our history. It was a war of small actions, and this is what television reporters and cameramen, anxious to make their marks as Murrow, Sevareid, and others had done in an earlier war, showed best. Critics contended that television's incomplete, piecemeal coverage had converted many Americans from a prowar or "hawk," or neutral, stand to an antiwar or "dove" stand during or after the early 1968 Vietcong and North Vietnamese Tet offensive. Coverage of peace marches on Washington and other such demonstrations by an expanding group of Americans led many to support this cause. Unrest on many campuses was strong, partly due to the war and partly due to Vietnam-related policies and politics. Starting at Berkeley, and spreading rapidly to Columbia, Wisconsin, and

■ CBS News Covers Man's First Landing on the Moon: July 1969

Sunday, July 20, 1969, about 4 p.m. (EDT). The three national television networks have scrapped normal program schedules to cover the initial moon landing by Astronauts Neil Armstrong and Edwin Aldrin on the *Apollo 11* mission. Here is how CBS's Walter Cronkite, assisted by former Astronaut Walter Shirra, reported the landing. (*Houston* is the Manned Spaceflight Center at Houston, Texas; *Capcom* is the capsule communicator at Cape Kennedy; *Eagle* is the landing craft; *Tranquility Base* was the name used by *Eagle* after the landing.)

Capcom: Eagle, you're looking great, coming up on nine minutes. We're now in the approach phase, everything looking good. Altitude 5200 feet.

Cronkite: 5200 feet. Less than a mile from the moon's surface.

Eagle: Manual altitude control is good.

Capcom: Roger. We copy. Altitude 4200 and you're go for landing. Over.

Eagle: Roger, understand. Go for landing. 3000 feet. Second alarm.

Cronkite: 3000 feet. Um-hmmm.

Eagle: Roger. 1201 alarm. We're go. Hang tight. We're go. 2000 feet. 2000 feet, into the AGS. 47 degrees.

Cronkite: These are space communications, simply for readout purposes.

Capcom: Eagle looking great. You're go.

Houston: Altitude 1600. 1400 feet. Still looking very good.

Cronkite: They've got a good look at their site now. This is their time. They're going to make a decision.

Eagle: 35 degrees. 35 degrees. 750, coming down at 23. 700 feet, 21 down. 33 degrees.

Schirra: Oh, the data is coming in beautifully.

Eagle: 600 feet, down at 19. 540 feet down at 30—down at 15...400 feet down at 9...8 forward...350 feet down at 4...300 feet, down 3½...47 forward...1½ down...70...got the shadow out there...50, down at 2½, 19 forward...altitude-velocity lights...3½ down...220 feet...13 forward ...11 forward, coming down nicely...200 feet, 4½ down...5½ down... 160, 6½ down...5½ down, 9 forward...5 percent...quantity light 75 feet. Things still looking good, down a half...6 forward...lights on...down 2½...forward...40 feet, down 2½, kicking up some dust...30 feet, 2½ down...faint shadow...4 forward...4 forward, drifting to the right a little...6...drifting right...

Cronkite: Boy, what a day.

Capcom: 30 seconds.

Eagle: Contact light. O.K. engine stopped...descent engine command override off...

Schirra: We're home!

Cronkite: Man on the moon!

Eagle: Houston, Tranquility Base here. The Eagle has landed!

Capcom: Roger, Tranquility. We copy you on the ground. You've got a bunch of guys about to turn blue. We're breathing again. Thanks a lot.

Tranquility: Thank you.

Cronkite: Oh, boy!

Capcom: You're looking good here.

Cronkite: Whew! Boy!

Schirra: I've been saying them all under my breath. That is really something. I'd love to be aboard.

Cronkite: I know. We've been wondering what Neil Armstrong and Aldrin would say when they set foot on the moon, which comes a little bit later now. Just to hear them do it. Absolutely with dry mouths.

Capcom: Roger, Eagle. And you're stay for T-1. Over. You're stay for T-1...

Tranquility: Roger. We're stay for T-1.

Capcom: Roger. And we see you getting the ox.

Cronkite: That's a great simulation that we see here.

Schirra: That little fly-speck is supposed to be the LM.

Cronkite: They must be in perfect condition...upright, and there's no complaint about their position.

Schirra: Just a little dust.

Cronkite: Boy! There they sit on the moon! Just exactly nominal wasn't it...on green with the flight plan, all the way down. Man finally is standing on the surface of the moon. My golly!

Capcom: Roger, we read you Columbia. He has landed. Tranquility Base. Eagle is at Tranquility. Over.

Source: 10:56:20 PM EDT 7/20/69 (New York: CBS Television News, 1970), pages 76–78. © 1970 CBS, Inc. By permission.

other campuses, the climax of this movement was the killing by Ohio National Guardsmen in early 1970 of four students during a protest at Kent State University.

Many reporters stationed in Vietnam felt that the United States was backing a string of dictatorships, that the war was morally wrong, and that it was being mishandled. Those who merely dropped in for a career-enhancing visit were taken in hand by Public Information Officers and consequently supported the war. But Walter Cronkite, after his second visit, delivered a strong negative commentary that reportedly caused President Lyndon Johnson to realize that the war had lost the support of middle America. ABC for several years offered a documentary overview of the week's events in Vietnam, but most network coverage was restricted to evening newscasts and occasional documentaries. Although reporters claimed that military control of their reporting, especially in countries like Thailand and Cambodia, made it difficult to get and transmit a true picture of what was happening, no previous war has been so accessible to reporters. The lazy reported the war from Saigon by relying on the military briefings known locally as the "Five o'Clock Follies"; the brave, ambitious, or foolhardy went out on combat patrols, where a number of them were killed or listed as missing. But there was little depth to the coverage. Obviously, television did play an important part in its first war, but it is an unanswered question whether the steady coverage of wartime violence deadened Americans to reality or whether the reporting showed the forest behind the trees and changed American thinking.

Television news and documentary units, especially those of CBS and NBC, were taking on increasingly tough subjects and saying something of value or importance about them. But controversy surrounding the television documentary was increasing. The 1960s began with the last of Edward R. Murrow's documentaries, *Harvest of Shame*, dealing with problems of migrant farm workers. When Murrow later was serving as head of U.S. Information Agency (USIA) for President Kennedy, he tried to suppress export of the program, but to no avail and much criticism. Programs such as *Biography of a Bookie Joint*, with films of gambling operations going on without police intervention, and *Battle of Newburgh* (about a town that cut off funds for many welfare recipients), led to public outcry and threats of legal action against the network responsible. Howard K. Smith's ABC documentary on *The Political Obituary of Richard Nixon*, just after Nixon lost the California gubernatorial election in 1962, raised sparks when Alger Hiss gave his views on his old tormenter. (Nixon, as a congressman, had been instrumental in sending former State Department official Hiss to jail for perjury for denying that he had been a communist agent.) Nixon supporters and other complainers and victims accused television of political bias and unfair reporting. CBS got into trouble with its "Pot Party at a University" segment of a Chicago local news show when it became known that the event had been set up for the cameras. Not only was the use of marijuana illegal but news "created" by the broadcaster was, at best, misleading to the public.

Perhaps the biggest complaint—and a congressional hearing—resulted from CBS's 1971 telecast of *Selling of the Pentagon*, a hard-hitting discussion of military public relations, which questioned spending large amounts of tax money in this way. The documentary angered conservative congressmen, though many admitted they had not seen the program, and they engineered a full-scale hearing on documentary practice, film splicing, editing of shows, and *out-takes* (unused film material). CBS refused to supply any materials not actually aired on the program, contending that such action would violate First Amendment freedoms and stifle all investigative reporting. An attempt to cite CBS and president Frank Stanton for contempt of Congress failed in what most broadcasters regarded as a victory. But several important points had been raised, and some documentary production methods were changed and controls of viewpoint tightened. What seemed acceptable and normal to a documentary maker might not appear so to a concerned viewer. Prior to 1964, the networks themselves had produced all news and news documentary programs. In 1963, ABC opened the door to other producers a bit by showing the David Wolper production of *Making of the President: 1960*. As television became the most commonly used and trusted source of information by the American public, its responsibilities increased.

The networks' news coverage received the strongest—generally politically inspired and planned—criticisms in the very late 1960s and early 1970s. In a televised speech to a Republican group in Iowa in Fall 1969, Vice President Spiro T. Agnew complained that three major networks had a stranglehold on the nation's news and thinking. He asked rhetorically who had selected the small group of network officials, editors, and anchormen who made news decisions. A week later he offered another complaint, and soon similar remarks from other politicians joined in a well-orchestrated campaign and safety valve for long-standing resentments. The broadcast industry responded with its usual defensiveness, emphasizing the dangers of governmental control of news. Agnew's comments ostensibly had been sparked by the network practice of commenting on a presidential speech immediately—what he called "instant analysis." That the networks usually had copies of presidential speeches to study hours in advance did not placate those who believed that the President should not be interpreted in this way. For a time in 1970–1971, CBS eliminated any post-speech analysis.

Many local stations joined in the clamor over network news control. They either had different political viewpoints—station owners frequently being more conservative than network news officials in New York and Washington—or wanted to avoid controversy that might interfere with sales of advertising time. The months-long confrontation, part of the Nixon administration's battle with more or less independent centers of information and power, was useful. Broadcasters had to consider their own actions and policies, explain them, tighten up sloppy practices, and improve their professionalism. Viewers had been directly exposed to critically important differences between government and media, and government and media both had re-evaluated their roles and assumptions. These struggles between media and government, including the release of the "Pentagon Papers" and the resulting legal clash between the *New York Times* and the government, and further disillusionment over Vietnam culminated in the biggest domestic news event in decades: Watergate.

Television did not play a strong role for the first year of the Watergate scandal of 1972–1974, which started with a "third rate burglary" and ended with the resignation of President Nixon. From discovery of the burglars in the Democratic Party offices in June 1972 through the election the following November, most investigative research was by the printed press, notably the *Washington Post*. Television stories and special programs became more common in 1973, but television's greatest value was its coverage of the Senate Watergate Committee hearings. Running from May through August 1973, and chaired by North Carolina's crusty Sam Ervin, these hearings were a fascinating live exposition of the political process in America, and were "must" television watching as a parade of witnesses told—or evaded telling—what they knew of the broad conspiracy to assure the re-election of Nixon and then to cover up the conspiracy itself. The members of the Senate committee soon became household names and faces, as the various witnesses supplied their pieces of the puzzle. For a time, the networks alternated coverage so that they and the viewers would have a choice between the hearings and regular entertainment programming. The more the viewers watched the hearings the more important the Watergate issues became in national affairs.

Newscasts and special news programs punctuated the course of the tottering administration. In October 1973 Vice President Agnew had to resign because of his acceptance of kickbacks when he was a Maryland official—to be replaced by Congressman Gerald Ford. Shortly afterward, when Nixon chose to fire the special prosecutor investigating Watergate, there was a "Saturday Night Massacre" that included several resignations and firings of top Justice Department officials and the firing of the special prosecutor. The story continued to build. Nixon professed innocence of the coverup, gave edited tape transcripts of his White House conversations to Congress—with the transcripts, in large binders, impressively piled behind him as he spoke on television. There were court battles over access to the tapes by Congress and by the new special prosecutor, arguments over a "missing" 18 1/2-minute portion of one tape, and further arguments over executive privilege and the right of Congress to subpoena the tapes. When the House Judiciary Committee in mid-1974 recommended impeachment, and the Supreme Court said that the President could not withhold the tapes, it was all over. On August 8, 1975, television and radio presented President

Nixon's resignation speech to a startled public as well as the swearing in of Vice President Gerald Ford the next day. The story finally ended with Ford's pardon of Nixon some weeks later.

9.6.5 Election Broadcasting

There were few changes in political campaign coverage in the 1964, 1968, and 1972 elections—but 1976 was different. The 1964 election fight between President Lyndon B. Johnson and Senator Barry Goldwater saw some of the strongest—some would say dirtiest—national political ads ever aired. A soon famous—though aired only once—Johnson spot intimated that Goldwater was likely to start an atomic war, and a Goldwater spot virtually accused Johnson of immorality. For election night, the networks and wire services joined together for the first time to coordinate reporting of election returns. The resulting Network Election Service (later, News Election Service) was to become permanent. The networks each took nine states, and the wire services split the rest. Although all "raw vote" tabulations were now common to all media, each network still used its own sample areas and computerized prediction techniques for forecasting or "declaring" winners—sometimes before polls closed in western states. This caused such an outcry that the networks had to delay "declarations" until the last polls had closed, although surveys commissioned by the networks indicated this action was not warranted.

The 1968 election was most notable for the debacle outside the Democratic convention in Chicago. Mayor Richard Daley tightly controlled the city and the location of cameras by the networks. It was not enough. When his police and the youthful antiwar and antiestablishment demonstrators clashed in front of the convention hotels several nights running, home viewers were treated to the dichotomy of calm inside the hall, as Vice President Hubert Humphrey became the nominee, and riots outside. Several reporters were arrested or roughed up inside the hall as well as outside, as the Daley forces sought to retain control in what was called a "police riot" in one official report. There were bitter postconvention assertions that television had biased viewers by covering the riots while neglecting the scheduled convention events. The networks replied that both were news events worthy of coverage. Daley supporters also claimed that the presence of the television cameras stimulated the rioting. The entire event was a prime hunting ground for researchers and contributed to Humphrey's subsequent loss at the polls. Convention coverage differed from previous years. ABC did away with its daytime and evening-long gavel-to-gavel coverage and concentrated its report into the late evening hours, and thus gained a ratings advantage by preserving its entertainment programs.

The 1968 campaign and the off-year elections of 1970 brought the talents of the professional image-makers fully into focus. Joe McGinniss' devastating *The Selling of the President 1968* exposed the media campaign behind Nixon, and many other candidates were accused of having been packaged and sold like consumer goods. Debate raged over the effects of television and other media usage, and experts analyzed the massive amounts of money that had been spent on mass media in attempts to persuade or even "buy" voters. By 1972, however, it was clear that television and image-building alone would not do the trick, and the image merchants lost some of their glamour and appeal. Expenditures on radio and television in the 1972 campaign, however, came to $60 million as compared to only $14 million spent on broadcasting in the 1960 race. Nixon, whose Committee to Reelect the President (CREEP) greatly outspent Democratic candidate Senator George McGovern, won by a landslide. As a result, a new federal law was passed that was designed to crimp the costs and style of campaigns after 1972.

The 1976 election campaign featured an old wrinkle—the "great debate" format pioneered in 1960 (see pp. 381–382). Late in 1975, in response to a petition from the Aspen Institute, the FCC revised its interpretation of Section 315. Its "Aspen ruling" held that debates and other coverage of candidates would be exempt from the equal opportunities provisions of the law if such political events were arranged by groups other than the candidates or the broadcasters, and if that broadcast coverage was "incidental" to the event taking place. Gerald Ford, in accepting the GOP nomination in August (after a tightly fought battle with former California Governor Ronald Reagan), challenged the Democrat's Governor Jimmy Carter to a series of debates—an unusual action for a sitting President, but taken because Ford was then far behind in the polls and was a bit unsure of himself, never having run in a presidential campaign before. There eventually were three debates between the presidential candidates, plus one between the vice presidential candidates, Senators Walter Mondale and Robert Dole. To comply with the FCC ruling, all were sponsored by the League of Women Voters, which had gotten practice with Democratic primaries during the Spring. As in the 1960 debates, when Nixon's appearance in the first debate cost him heavily, so did the debates affect the 1976 campaign. In the second debate, President Ford asserted quite clearly, and repeated when questioned, that Eastern Europe was not under Soviet domination. His campaign lost 10 days trying to explain that statement away, and the lost momentum likely cost him the election. Carter had appeared weak in the first debate (which had its audio cut off for 28 minutes due to a technical failure), but Ford's error in the second appeared to have greater impact in the end. Carter won the election. The 1976 elections were the first to be heavily covered using flexible electronic news-gathering (ENG) equipment, at both national and local levels.

9.7 Audience Ratings and Research

As much as the 1950s had been depicted as the Age of Television, it was not until the 1960s that we really began to determine how television was affecting us. Much research centered on the effects of television on children and youth, but there also was concern over its broader consequences.

Radio was in 96% and television in 90% of American homes at the beginning of this period, so growth in number of television homes slowed, although the number of television sets increased as people bought their second and third. Three-quarters of American homes had color sets by 1976. Transistors made radio and television sets smaller and lighter, and more and more sets were imported each year, first from Germany and then increasingly from the Far East. By the late 1960s, largely due to the labor economics of manufacturing abroad, virtually no radio receivers and very few black-and-white television receivers were manufactured in the United States, although U.S. firms had some foreign plants. In 1961, only 70% of cars had radios, but by the mid-1970s nearly 90% had, a substantial minority had added short-range transceivers in the Citizens Band, and even more had FM. Digital clock radios were popular in the 1970s, and very tiny transistor radios could be bought for as little as $5, with novelties—radios built into earphones or toilet paper holders—easily made.

Most homes of the early 1960s did not have the ability to receive UHF telecasts (see p. 383) and therefore UHF stations could not compete adequately with VHF stations in the same market. But in July 1961 the FCC proposed requiring all television sets be able to receive all channels. Congress approved the proposal in return for the commission's dropping all consideration of deintermixture (see p. 387 ff.), and President Kennedy signed the bill in July 1962, to take effect in mid-1964. Thanks to the steady market in portable and, after 1965, color television, the proportion of homes capable of receiving UHF broadcasts increased sharply from about 10% in 1961 to 90% in 1976. This act finally brought the UHF stations into the club, even though UHF tuners did not measure up to VHF tuners in quality in the same set until the manufacturers were pushed by the FCC in the late 1970s. The all-channel act was not the whole answer, but it helped immensely.

Noting the success of television's all-channel bill, those concerned with FM radio's lack of financial success tried but failed to get a bill passed that would require AM and FM capability in all radio, including automobile, receivers. The cost differential and manufacturer-dealer indifference held automobile FM radio sales down in the 1960s, preventing FM stations from cashing in on AM radio's big audiences in morning and evening drive time. By the early 1970s, FM saturation was about 60% compared to UHF's almost nonexistent capability when the 1962 all-channel television bill was being considered—thus reducing the need for all-channel radio legislation.

9.7.1 Viewing Trends and Ratings Problems

By 1961, 89% of the nation's families had a television set—47.2 million families. By late 1976, 97% owned television, but that small percentage increase covered a growth of more than 22 million families as the population rose. Thanks largely to the coming of color in the mid-1960s, retention of first-generation sets, and the relatively low cost of black-and-white portables, the proportion of multiset homes rose from 13% in 1961 to more than 45% by 1976. This is a far cry from the corner tavern announcing with great excitement in the late 1940s: "We have television!"

The basic pattern of television viewing remained as it had in the 1950s: Viewing was higher in Winter than in Summer and peaked between 8 P.M. and 10 P.M. Color-set owners viewed about seven hours a week more television than monochrome-set owners. Average daily household viewing slowly increased from about five hours in 1961 to about 6 1/4 hours in 1976. Roper (1977) collected data for the Television Information Office (TIO) that showed median individual viewing rose from 2:17 (two hours and 17 minutes) in 1961 to 2:53 in 1976. Families with children made heavier use of the set, and overall viewing decreased a bit as education and income increased; to 2:24 for the college educated and 2:40 for those in upper economic brackets. Women viewed the most and teenagers the least, while persons over 55 of either sex did the most viewing of all.

Viewership information, constantly updated, was generated by the two chief national ratings firms: the A.C. Nielsen Company, which had dominated national television ratings since 1949, and the American Research Bureau (ARB), later called Arbitron. After 1964 radio was measured only in local markets. At that point, radio was in 94% of American homes, sets were in use about 15 hours a week—down sharply from pretelevision days—and home receivers were giving way to portable and automobile sets, which were hard to measure. The radio pattern of listening remained the reverse of television—steady, except for a peak in the early morning, a brief spurt during afternoon drive time, especially in large cities, and a drop during television prime time.

The ratings themselves were in and out of trouble. Rumors of fraud and overdependence on ratings led to investigations in 1960–1961 by Congress, which commissioned an intensive investigation of ratings methods. The resulting report noted important shortcomings in ratings sampling and survey techniques, statistical standards, and use. In 1963–1964, the House Commerce Committee held further hearings, which included a 10-day grilling of top A.C. Nielsen personnel and uncovered shortcuts and skimping in research techniques that could cause significant differences in the results. Other firms also were examined, including a small company that faked much of its data in the back room, but the importance and problems of Nielsen took up much of the long hearings. From this investigation and its aftermath came several organizations intended to clean up the ratings and their image. The Broadcast Ratings Council included representatives of networks, broadcasting organizations, and advertisers to oversee ratings operations, making sure—for the benefit of advertisers as well as public relations—that gathering and reporting methods for ratings were valid and reliable and met standards for acceptable accuracy. The Committee on Nationwide Television Audience Measurements (CONTAM) was created by and for the networks to conduct a series of studies to find better ways to derive program ratings. In the 1970s, both organizations became involved with generating positive publicity and information on the ratings system on which networks, advertisers, and stations mutually survive. Statisticians agree that ratings firms now use generally sound methods, although the publicity they engender in station and network promotion efforts might be questioned, and some advertisers and ad agencies place far more reliance upon them than is warranted.

Just as the Lazarsfeld studies in the 1940s described the peak period of radio listening and Bogart's 1956 volume showed the rise of television, two books after 1960 demonstrated television's hold on the American public. The first was Gary Steiner's *The People Look at Television* (1963), based on a 1960 nationwide survey (with a substudy of New York viewers) underwritten by CBS. It showed that television generally had replaced other means of socialization, and that its popularity and use were high in nearly all sectors of the population except for those of high education and income. Although viewers nearly always claimed to want more cultural or educational programming when asked about program balance, they usually would pick more entertainment content when given a choice of material. Reactions to overall programming and advertising were highly positive; television was the one nonessential item in the typical home that was regarded as nearly essential.

A decade later this study was repeated, again with support from CBS, in Robert Bower's *Television and the Public* (1973). This update generally supported the earlier findings, although the public's fascination with television had worn off—it no longer was a constant topic of conversation and viewers were more critical of it. Television's impact as a news source was greater than in 1960, and parental concern and control over children's viewing were stronger than a decade earlier. Here the specific market surveyed was Minneapolis–St. Paul, and again viewers spoke of desiring more educational and cultural programming, while generally ignoring that choice when it was available. Researchers suggested that in both surveys viewers may have considered cultural programming a "proper response," regardless of their viewing preferences.

Issued about every two years, starting just after the quiz show scandals, were the Roper studies sponsored by the Television Information Office, an arm of the NAB, on what the public thought of television vis-à-vis other media. Early editions drew newspaper criticism for using a method whereby multiple responses showed television as far and away the most believed and most used news medium. Some of the questions used in these studies dated back to Lazarsfeld's work in the early 1940s, providing a longitudinal look at public reaction to broadcasting.

9.7.2 Television and Children: Phases Two and Three

The Kefauver hearings on television and juvenile delinquency in the mid-1950s (see p. 386) was the precursor of an even more intensive investigation in the early 1960s. The new probe came about because people were increasingly concerned over violence in the streets, juvenile delinquency, and the possibility that this behavior was related to violence in television programs. Some senators and staff members felt that broadcast self-regulation was not reducing violence on the air; others were well aware of the publicity value of hearings on this subject. In addition, some new research had suggested a direct cause-and-effect relationship between media violence and violent activities by viewers. In June 1961, Senator Thomas Dodd (D-Connecticut) opened what became nearly three years of intermittent hearings. In addition, the results of three committee staff monitoring reports of television content in 1954, 1961, and 1964 showed incidents of violence—a very difficult concept to define validly—on television to be increasing, especially at hours when children might be watching.

This second phase of concern over children and television ended late in 1964 with the publication of the hearings and a mimeographed interim report. That the final report never appeared and the interim report had limited distribution spoiled the potential effect of the hearings. The subcommittee suggested greater prime time network efforts in programming for children, revision of the FCC station application form to clarify the minimal public service and children's program requirements, addition of sanctions to give teeth to the NAB code, a mechanism for the public to voice its opinions of television, and the need for further research. The implied threat was congressional action if the industry did not police itself as it had promised in 1954.

These issues simmered until 1968. That year, in response to the assassinations of Senator Robert Kennedy and the Reverend Martin Luther King, Jr., President Lyndon Johnson created a Commission on the Causes and Effects of Violence with Milton Eisenhower as chairman. The commission's report contained a chapter on media violence and, more importantly, a lengthy staff report in book form on the issues and questions of media and violence. Other staff reports, accusing broadcasters of failing to clean up violence on the tube, led to Senate action some months later. Senator John Pastore (D-Rhode Island), powerful chairman of the Communications Subcommittee of the Senate Commerce Committee, wrote to the Surgeon General in March 1969 requesting creation of a research panel to evaluate the research literature and conduct original studies on the relation between television and violent behavior. Within six weeks, a research program

---

■ **Television Violence: The Surgeon General's Committee Reports (January 1972)** The following conclusions of the best-funded research program into the effects of television are a good example of the imprecision of much social science research. Newspaper accounts of the cautious qualifications contained in the committee reports varied widely. See pp. 556 ff for similar conclusions reached a decade later.

... there is a convergence of the fairly substantial experimental evidence for *short-run* causation of aggression among some children by viewing violence on the screen and the much less certain evidence from field studies that extensive violence viewing precedes some *long-run* manifestations of aggressive behavior. This convergence of the two types of evidence constitutes some preliminary indication of a causal relationship, but a good deal of research remains to be done before one can have confidence in these conclusions.

The field studies, correlating different behavior among adolescents, and the laboratory studies of the responses by younger children to violent films converge also on a number of further points.

First, there is evidence that any sequence by which viewing television violence causes aggressive behavior is most likely applicable only to some children who are predisposed in that direction. ...

Second, there are suggestions in both sets of studies that the way children respond to violent film material is affected by the context in which it is presented. Such elements as parental explanations, the favorable or unfavorable outcome of the violence, and whether it is seen as fantasy or reality may make a difference. Generalizations about all violent content are likely to be misleading.

Thus, the two sets of findings converge in three respects: a preliminary and tentative indication of a causal relation between viewing violence on television and aggressive behavior; an indication that any such causal relation operates only on some children (who are predisposed to be aggressive); and an indication that it operates only in some environmental contexts. Such tentative and limited conclusions are not very satisfying. They represent substantially more knowledge than we had two years ago, but they leave many questions unanswered.

Source: The Surgeon General's Scientific Advisory Committee on Television and Social Behavior, *Television and Growing Up: The Impact of Televised Violence.* (Washington: Government Printing Office, 1972), pages 17–19.

---

had been created and funded with $1.5 million from existing budgets—something of a record for this sort of government action.

Unfortunately, both politics and industry pressure worked against constructive results. The 12 researchers appointed to the panel included five from the networks, three from the academic research community, and "the naive four" with no background in the subject. The committee let contracts for 23 laboratory and field studies by a wide variety of researchers, as well as some literature review and synthesis. However, having been given a *de facto* veto power, the networks blackballed several well-known television-violence researchers as being no longer impartial since their opinions were well known—and allegedly antinetwork. The results were in by late 1971, and the report of the committee, issued in January 1972, appeared to have been written quickly and under pressure. Its inconclusive conclusion was that television violence can affect some of the viewers some of the time. This was not a new notion. Some of the studies themselves, however, published in full shortly after the report, pointed far more strongly to the conclusion that television violence does indeed help stimulate violent actions by some viewers in both short and long run. Controversy boiled in the trade and public press, and in hearings held by Pastore to sort out what the research expenditure and effort really meant. While there was criticism of the networks' role in the formation of the panel and writing of the report, broadcasters hailed it as clearing them of a never-admitted responsibility for causing violence. Critics said, "Ignore the report and look at the studies." Academicians worked over the data and strove to improve the questioned methodologies as well.

And there it probably would have died, like the earlier studies, except for one key difference. The 1970s was a period of vocal citizens' action groups (see p. 473), and one of the most vocal was Action for Children's Television. ACT had been formed by a group of Boston-area mothers concerned about violence on the air and excessive commercialism aimed at children, both on Saturday mornings and in other hours when children were likely to be viewing. ACT and other groups helped arouse public opinion to the extent that the industry and the commission, particularly after Richard Wiley became chairman in 1974, finally took action. The networks agreed to the suggestion from CBS president Arthur Taylor that, starting in Fall 1975, prime time network programming, except for news, before 9:00 P.M. (Eastern and Pacific time) would be for "family viewing" (see pp. 472–473) with limits on the depiction of violence. In addition, after 1972 most violent cartoons were removed from children's morning and weekend network programming. Critics agreed that the amount of violence was diminishing in the 1970s, but the disagreement over the definition of violence was illustrated in disputes over the findings by George Gerbner of the University of Pennsylvania, who regularly issued new editions of an "index" (later dubbed a "profile") that reported the incidence of violence on all network television programming. ACT, Pastore, and many researchers, critics, and other politicians kept this matter in the public eye—now that the incidence of real-life violence (coverage of the Vietnam War) no longer occupied as much of the evening news before "family viewing."

9.8 Regulatory Confusion

The regulatory scene became much more complicated in the 1960s and early 1970s for several reasons. First, conflicting views arose because there were more participants involved: new broadcasting stations, new groups familiar with and involved in the regulatory process, and new media—cable systems and potential operators of pay-TV and cable systems. Second, events had forced participants to look at problems in new ways. Earlier they had discussed the Fairness Doctrine, cable and broadcast television relationships, and ownership and control, but now these issues became much more salient and controversial and often intractable. Third, the proliferation of stations and services, such as FM and public television, together with such closely related media as audio and video recordings, produced greater competition within the industry. Fourth, and increasingly evident in the years to follow, was the beginning of a fundamental rethinking of the role of regulation. The very increase in means of program delivery seemed to some observers (especially some conservative economists and politicians) to negate the traditional conception of broadcasting as a "bottleneck" with a small and finite technological limit on number of outlets in a given locality. If technology's promise of a future of many channels and more choice came true, would traditional regulation be necessary any longer? This question was first faced with respect to cable television (see pp. 467–469).

9.8.1 Changing Cast of Regulators

On the regulatory scene, older groups changed and newer ones arrived. The FCC was shaken up to an extent not seen since the days of James Lawrence Fly in the 1940s. In 1961, after the conflict of interest scandals involving Commissioners Doerfer and Richard Mack, President Kennedy appointed thirty-four-year-old Newton Minow to the FCC chairmanship. Minow early served notice of his displeasure with much of what was broadcast when he spoke before the NAB of television as a "vast wasteland" (see this chapter's opening quotations) requiring more high quality television programming. The phrase caught on with the public. While the industry fretted over the newly critical FCC, Minow helped provide a Kennedy "New Frontier" activism to commission decisions. However, he was hamstrung by more conservative holdover appointees and, soon frustrated, he returned to private law practice in 1963. Minow was replaced by an even younger activist chairman, E. William Henry, until 1966. After Henry's departure, veteran Commissioner Rosel Hyde became chairman but could not readily control Commissioner Nicholas Johnson's highly public consumer activism (see below). President Nixon named conservative GOP leader Dean Burch as chairman in 1969. Serving until 1973, when he joined the White House staff, Burch was considered one of the FCC's better administrators, with the commission arriving at decisions in several controversial areas (particularly CATV) just before his departure. He also kept the FCC's factions communicating. Burch and Johnson both left in 1973, and General Counsel Richard Wiley was elevated to commissioner and in 1974 to the chairmanship. Wiley proved to be an even better administrator than Burch, establishing an atmosphere of hard work and more timely decision making.

During much of the 1960s, the team of Kenneth Cox and Nicholas Johnson issued reports and dissents attacking broadcasting organizations and practices, persuaded the commission to hold a couple of well-publicized citizens' gripe sessions outside of Washington, and supported greater citizen action to upgrade public service broadcast programming. Their approaches were different; Cox was generally low key, but the youthful

Johnson quickly took his campaign to the public. Johnson built a constituency with books like *How to Talk Back to Your Television Set* (1970), many articles and speeches, and detailed dissenting opinions to FCC decisions. He sometimes shot from the hip, but he awakened public interest and made people feel that they had a voice on the commission. At the opposite end of the political spectrum was Commissioner Lee Loevinger, one of the brightest men ever to serve on the FCC, a strong conservative whose well-honed legal mind generally matched the liberalism of Cox and the more radical opinions of Johnson. Both Johnson and Loevinger had been appointed to the FCC because they had ruffled too many feathers on earlier governmental jobs; Loevinger as head of the antitrust division of the Justice Department and Johnson as head of the Maritime Commission.

President Nixon soothed the broadcasting industry with his appointment of commercial broadcasters Robert Wells and James Quello but aroused the ire of consumer and minority groups. Yet Nixon also appointed the first black on the FCC, Benjamin Hooks. Hooks started quietly but by 1974 was making stronger statements on the place of minorities in broadcasting—and probably stepping on toes by insisting on enforcement of equal employment opportunity rules, even for PTV stations. Nixon also named the second woman to serve on the FCC, Charlotte Reid, who was much less important to the commission's deliberations than the first (see p. 291). For much of the period, the commission was ideologically divided.

By the late 1960s the FCC, designed in 1934, was beginning to suffer from overload, but in the 1970s it was nearly swamped. Regulating interstate telephone and telegraph as well as radio, it spent an increasing amount of time on complicated safety and special service rules, communication satellite policy, cable television, and processing paperwork for more than 9,000 broadcast and millions of other licenses. It had to act on everything: from the millions of letters insisting that a petition to require fairness on religious-body-owned stations was a "petition against God"—an attempt to remove all religion from the air—to the occasional complaint about obscene programming, particularly on educational stations—the Pacifica Foundation's WBAI, the University of Pennsylvania's WXPN—since few commercial broadcasters would so risk their licenses. As new technology and innovations made long-range policy questions more insistent, the FCC had even less time than in the 1930s to consider them.

Two kinds of studies had been undertaken to examine the FCC's policies and efficiency, particularly in the decision-making process. First were those concerned with organization—one conducted for the 1949 Hoover Commission on executive branch organization, one prepared under Judge Landis's direction for President Kennedy, and one prepared under Roy Ash's direction for President Nixon. Second were those concerned with telecommunication policy—the President's Communications Policy Board established by President Truman, and the President's Task Force on Communications Policy, reporting to President Johnson at the very end of his term.

In response to some of these analyses and the shortcomings of the FCC, and in order to accumulate more immediate power, President Nixon proposed to Congress early in 1970 that the Office of Telecommunications Management, a White House staff agency primarily concerned with government agency spectrum use and assignment, be converted to an Office of Telecommunications Policy (OTP). It would have a broader purview, including supervision of the more than 50-year-old Interdepartmental Radio Advisory Committee, and would be located within the Executive Office of the President to show its power to speak for the executive. The plan was activated in April, and Rand Corporation researcher Clay T. Whitehead was named to head the OTP. It quickly became clear that, while OTP would provide needed long-range policy planning and research, using facilities of the Office of Telecommunications in the Department of Commerce, its function was more actually political than technical.

OTP's first major coup was engineering a compromise between NAB and NCTA in Fall 1971 that led to the 1972 FCC cable rules (see pp. 467–469). Soon it was involved in seeking five-year license terms for broadcasters, a major broadcaster goal for most of this period; VHF channel drop-ins in large markets ostensibly to broaden competition; limiting program reruns, a result of administration concern for unemployment in the West Coast entertainment production unions; financing for public broadcasting; and limiting the Fairness Doctrine. After the demise of the Nixon administration in 1974, OTP almost dropped from sight and Whitehead resigned. Although it was kept alive by members of Congress who realized the potential value of long-range policy and research, after 1973 OTP had little of the power it once had, when the FCC, broadcasters, and many citizens had cause to become increasingly concerned about White House encroachment onto commission regulatory territory.

A third participant in the regulatory arena, in addition to the FCC and OTP, was the U.S. Court of Appeals for the District of Columbia, which the 1934 Communications Act had designated to hear most appeals from FCC decisions. Until the 1960s it usually had backed up FCC decisions on appeal, seldom taking it to task unless procedures had been badly mismanaged, and many broadcasters looked on it as the enforcement arm of the commission. Changing membership on the court, which has nine members—three of whom normally sit on a given case—and changing public pressures, however, changed the court's view of the FCC and the industry. This new view was brought home with a vengeance in March 1966 when a three-judge panel overturned an FCC decision that had refused to let a citizens' group participate in a license-renewal case. The Office of Communications of the United Church of Christ, headed by Everett Parker, had sought to speak for the 45% black population of Jackson, Mississippi, for the purpose of denying license renewal to WLBT. The panel of judges, in what became a landmark case, held that the public was entitled to participate (or have "standing") in such proceedings. Hitherto, such matters had been between broadcasters and the FCC, claiming to act on behalf of the public, and sometimes other broad-casters with an economic interest. By granting other citizen groups the right to be heard before the FCC, the court expanded public access to the decision-making process. In 1969, the court went further in the same case, ordering the FCC to lift WLBT's license and assign it to an interim operation—a *very* rare action—until a new "permanent" licensee could be selected. The decision spoke of the FCC's "curious neutrality in favor of an existing licensee." By 1970 some industry observers were referring to this increasingly independent and anti-FCC court as "broadcasting's preemptive court." Public interest groups rapidly understood that, if the FCC denied them standing or access, they could often obtain it on appeal. The preemptive role of the court seemed to expand by the mid-1970s.

Responsibility for long-range broadcast policy in Congress switched from the Senate (where longtime Communications Subcommittee head John Pastore retired late in 1976) to the House Communications Subcommittee under Torbert Macdonald (D-Massachusetts) and then Lionel Van Deerlin (D-California). With a professional and knowledgeable staff, the subcommittee held hearings into many aspects of communications, expressed concern about the limited role of cable versus broadcasting, and looked into the varied interrelationships of point-to-point communications and the broadcast-cable media. Late in 1976, Van Deerlin announced the subcommittee's most extensive project yet, aimed at a complete review and probable rewrite of the 1934 act (see pp. 562–566).

9.8.2 Fairness on the Air

The FCC's Fairness Doctrine (see pp. 332–333) caused controversy during the 1960s and 1970s. Politics, cigarette advertising, the Vietnam War, and other matters were reflected in the growing body of case law. Congress had perhaps inadvertently provided a seeming statutory base for the Fairness Doctrine in 1959, when it amended Section 315 (the political "equal opportunity" section of the Communications Act) to note that nothing exempted broadcasters from their responsibility " ... to afford reasonable opportunity for the discussion of conflicting views on issues of public importance." The Supreme Court's *Red Lion* decision in 1969 (see box on pages 464–465) firmly supported the idea that the concept of fairness, which was intended to benefit the average citizen and viewer and which previously had been included under the "public interest" standard, now had its own statutory authority. The FCC published specific regulations on the "personal attack" aspects of fairness in 1967 and 1968, and public notices that codified the case law and defined proper and improper adherence to the "controversial issues" aspects of the Fairness Doctrine—rigid rules for editorials—the station would have to seek out opposing views—and even more rigid rules for informing, providing texts, and providing rebuttal opportunities for persons who felt attacked. In

▪ Rise of the Fairness Doctrine: 1941–1974

January 16, 1941   Radio can serve as an instrument of democracy only when devoted to the communication information and the exchange of ideas fairly and objectively presented. A truly free radio cannot be used to advocate the causes of the licensee. It cannot be used to support the candidacies of his friends. It cannot be devoted to the support of principles he happens to regard most favorably. In brief, the broadcaster cannot be an advocate.

> FCC, *Mayflower* Decision, 8 FCC 333.

June 1, 1949   To recapitulate, the Commission believes that under the American system of broadcasting the individual licensees of radio stations have the responsibility for determining the specific program material to be broadcast over their stations. This choice, however, must be exercised in a manner consistent with the basic policy of the Congress that radio be maintained as a medium of free speech for the general public as a whole rather than as an outlet for the purely personal or private interests of the licensee. This requires that licensees devote a reasonable percentage of their broadcasting time to the discussion of public issues of interest in the community served by their stations and that such programs be designed so that the public has a reasonable opportunity to hear different opposing positions on the public issues of interest and importance in the community. The particular format best suited for the presentation of such programs in a manner consistent with the public interest must be determined by the licensee in the light of the facts of each individual station. Such presentation may include the identified expression of the licensee's personal viewpoint as part of the more general presentation of views or comments on the various issues, but the opportunity of licensees to present such views as they may have on matters of controversy may not be utilized to achieve a partisan or one-sided presentation of issues. Licensee editorialization is but one aspect of freedom of expression by means of radio. Only insofar as it is exercised in conformity with the paramount right of the public to hear a reasonably balanced presentation of all responsible viewpoints on particular issues can such editorialization be considered to be consistent with the licensee's duty to operate in the public interest. For the licensee is a trustee impressed with the duty of preserving for the public generally radio as a medium of free expression and fair presentation.

> FCC, "In the Matter of Editorializing by Broadcast Licensees," 13 FCC 1246, paragraph 21.

September 14, 1959   Nothing in the foregoing sentence [a modification of the "equal opportunities" for political candidates clause in Section 315 of the Communications Act of 1934] shall be construed as relieving broadcasters, in connection with the presentation of newscasts, news interviews, news documentaries and on-the-spot coverage of news events from the obligation imposed upon them under this Act to operate in the public interest and to afford reasonable opportunity for the discussion of conflicting views on issues of public importance.

> Public Law 86-274, 86th Congress (amending the 1934 Communications Act).

addition to broadcasters, those who opposed FCC intervention in programming on First Amendment grounds were unhappy about these steps.

A landmark case began with a 15-minute recorded program in which right-wing preacher Billy James Hargis attacked Fred Cook, author of a book critical of Senator Barry Goldwater, the Arizona conservative Republican candidate for President in 1964. Around 200 stations carried the program, and Cook, apparently with some support from the Democratic Party, claimed time to reply from all of them. Most offered him the free time required under FCC fairness rules. But WGCB—in the small town of Red Lion, Pennsylvania, 75 miles west of Philadelphia—sent him a rate card

June 9, 1969 It is the right of the viewers and listeners, not the right of the broadcasters, which is paramount . . . It is the purpose of the First Amendment to preserve an uninhibited marketplace of ideas in which truth will ultimately prevail, rather than to countenance monopolization of that market, whether it be by the Government itself or a private licensee . . . It is the right of the public to receive suitable access to social, political, esthetic, moral, and other ideas and experiences which is crucial here. . . .

In view of the scarcity of broadcast frequencies, the Government's role in allocating those frequencies, and the legitimate claims of those unable without governmental assistance to gain access to those frequencies for expression of their views, we hold the regulations [Public Attack Rules] and ruling [Fairness Doctrine] at issue here are both authorized by statute and constitutional.

Supreme Court decision in *Red Lion Broadcasting Co.* v. *FCC*, 395 U.S. 367.

May 29, 1973 If broadcasters were required to provide time, free when necessary, for the discussion of the various shades of opinion on the issue . . . the affluent could still determine in large part the issues to be discussed. Thus . . . a right of access . . . would have little meaning to those who could not afford to purchase time in the first instance.

If the Fairness Doctrine were applied to editorial advertising, there is also the substantial danger that the effective operation of that doctrine would be jeopardized. To minimize financial hardship and to comply fully with its public responsibilities a broadcaster might well be forced to make regular programming time available to those holding a view different from that expressed in an editorial advertisement. . . . The result would be a further erosion of the journalistic discretion of broadcasters in the coverage of public issues, and a transfer of control over the treatment of public issues from the licensees who are accountable for broadcast performance to private individuals who are not. The public interest would no longer be "paramount" but rather subordinate to private whim. . . . The congressional objective of balanced coverage of public issues would be seriously threatened.

Supreme Court decision in *Columbia Broadcasting System, Inc.* v. *Democratic National Committee*, 412 U.S 94.

June 25, 1974 The clear implication has been that any such a compulsion to publish that which "'reason' tells them should not be published" is unconstitutional. A responsible press is an undoubtedly desirable goal, but press responsibility is not mandated by the Constitution and like many other virtues it cannot be legislated.

Supreme Court decision in *Miami Herald Publishing Co.* v. *Tornillo*, 418 U.S. 241.

See also "Fall of the Fairness Doctrine" on pp. 568–569.

offering to *sell* reply time. Cook appealed to the FCC, which ordered the station to give the time. On WGCB's refusal, the issue entered the courts, with the station losing at all levels, and eventually reached the Supreme Court of the United States. There, it was combined with another case, in which the Circuit Court of Appeals in Chicago had upheld the attempt of the Radio Television News Directors Association to modify or loosen the editorializing and personal attack rules that they thought had restricted broadcast journalism. The two opposing decisions helped make these cases a fit subject for Supreme Court adjudication. The *Red Lion Broadcasting Co.* v. *FCC* decision in June 1969 was the most important broadcast-related court decision since the 1943 network case (see pp. 210–212). The court upheld the FCC's editorializing and personal attack rules and its right to enact a Fairness Doctrine, reaffirming the paramount importance of the listener or viewer under the 1934 Communications Act. In the early 1970s, two cases limited the Fairness Doctrine. The Business Executives Move for Peace in Vietnam (BEM) and the Democratic National Committee (DNC) tried separately to get broadcasters to sell them advertising time to comment on current issues of public importance. The broadcasters turned them down. In a 1973 decision, the Supreme Court upheld the commission's refusal to overturn broadcasters' judgment, suggesting that to allow such sales might undermine the licensees' decision making and responsibility for content aired over their stations.

The ostensible purpose of the Fairness Doctrine was to give the public access to more than one side of a controversial issue. Although a branch of the doctrine giving an individual who has been subject to a personal attack an opportunity to reply was codified into the FCC rules, most controversial issue cases were decided in accord with the principle that the public deserves to receive opposing views on controversial matters of public importance.

The FCC's decisions on controversial issue cases became increasingly involved and confusing to both broadcasters and the public. Many mistakenly thought that only the two most salient points of view on any given issue needed to be aired, or that carefully measured "equal time" was required, or that broadcasters should have no say in how different points of view were to be expressed. To help guide licensees, the FCC issued a primer in 1964, conducted a dialogue from 1971 through 1974 on all aspects of the doctrine, and issued a long public notice in 1974. Many still weren't sure what was required. Some critics complained that the doctrine was still too vague, that it involved government meddling in key areas of programming, and that its requirements might keep broadcasters from *any* discussion of controversial issues for fear of having to defend themselves before the FCC. Communications attorney Jerome Barron, among others, believed that the public interest would be served better by unlimited *access* to the airwaves by all who want it than by *fairness* left in the hands of the broadcaster. Bills to abolish the Fairness Doctrine were often introduced, reverting to an absolute view of the First Amendment stricture that "Congress shall pass no law" in this area. Yet many others, notably members of minority groups, rely on the doctrine for the opportunity to air their views. A decade later, in the late 1980s, all of this debate had escalated substantially (see pp. 567–569).

Although not part of the Fairness Doctrine as such, during the early and mid-1970s the FCC became active in supporting equal employment opportunity in the broadcasting industry, by requiring stations regularly to submit data on minority and female employment, and by considering such matters in comparative and license renewal hearings. The WLBT case (see pp. 462–463), in fact, involved claims of discrimination against blacks, both in employment and in program content, as did the FCC's 1975 action refusing to renew the licenses of eight stations of the Alabama educational television network. The latter case marked the first time a public television license had been lifted—though after litigation the chastened Alabama authority resumed control.

9.8.3 The Cable Conundrum

Although cable systems had provided limited television service—from one to three channels—to small communities since 1949 (see pp. 355–356), their competition with television stations was not immediately apparent. In the late 1950s, broadcasters began to object seriously to cable picking broadcast programs off the air and selling them to subscribers, with broadcast stations and program originators getting nothing for the use of their product. But there was little local or state regulation of cable until the early 1960s, and the FCC was contending that it could not federally regulate cable under the 1934 act because it was not a broadcasting service and was intrastate in nature.

In 1959, the FCC issued its first analysis of the relationship between CATV and broadcasting, focusing on three former UHF stations that claimed cable had helped force them off the air by not carrying their signals. Some leading cable operators pushed for federal regulation so as to avoid a confusion of local and state rules, while others wished to maintain the local orientation of their industry. In a 1962 case, the commission decided to take limited regulatory control over systems that used microwave relay to bring in distant signals (beyond off-air pickup range) to the *head end*, and imposed carriage and nonduplication rules to protect broadcast licensees from economically damaging conditions.

In 1965 the FCC expanded its microwave rules to cover both intra- and inter-state cable systems, and required that they carry any television station within 60 miles when requested to, and that they refrain from showing the same shows from a distant station for 15 days before or after the local television station airing. Less than a year later, another order limited CATV growth in the country's top 100 markets by requiring such systems to get specific approval for carrying distant signals. This was based on the belief that both cable and UHF would grow best in urban areas, because of the density of the population and lower costs of reaching that audience and that, if cable were unrestricted, financially weak local UHF stations might be forced off the air. The likelihood that cable would serve only *parts* of a given urban area, certainly not as great an area as a station, made it less in the public interest.

The Supreme Court upheld the FCC's authority to regulate cable if that authority was related in some way to the commission's statutory

■ **The Cable Regulatory Cycle**   Unlike the much longer trek of broadcasting from virtually no regulation in the 1920s to pervasive regulation just a few years later and deregulation in the 1980s, cable television passed from no regulation to severe restrictions—and back to virtually no regulation—in just under two decades. Later events on this chart are discussed on pp. 574–575 and 672–673.

Changing Cable Regulation

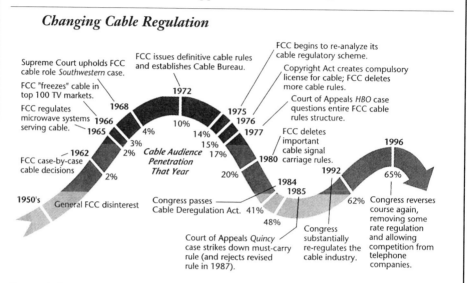

Over nearly four decades, the FCC's regulation of cable television has undergone substantial changes in direction. From virtually no regulation in cable's earliest years to substantial and detailed FCC regulation of the medium in 1972, cable was steadily more controlled. For the next two decades, cable was progressively deregulated, especially with the 1984 cable act that removed most remaining local franchise limitations. In 1992, Congress reversed course again and passed a strongly re-regulatory cable act, only to change course again four years later.

Source: Sydney W. Head, et al, *Broadcasting in America: A Survey of Electronic Media,* 8th ed. Houghton Mifflin Company, p. 354. Reprinted and updated with permission. Copyright © 1998.

regulatory power over broadcasting in *Southwestern Cable Co.* v. *United States* (1968). The next year, the FCC proposed that cable systems with more than 3,500 subscribers be required to originate some programming over one of the average of six to eight channels they carried. Court challenges delayed the effective implementation of this order, and it was eventually dropped.

The so-called definitive FCC rules on cable appeared in 1972. Cable systems were freed to expand in the top 100 markets, although with restrictions on the number and kind of signals they could carry. They had to offer channels to municipal governments and educational institutions and provide access for members of the public with something to say. New systems had to have at least 20 channels and existing ones had to have them by 1977–although these requirements were later postponed. Systems in smaller markets could import fewer signals, as the population was smaller and the harm to over-the-air local television stations might be greater. Older systems could continue to operate under the original, simpler regulations, but newer systems had to follow a maze of mandatory carriage and protection rules. Pay-TV over cable, which even by the late 1960s appeared more likely than pay-TV over the air, was officially permitted in the late 1960s. Specific rules on content, to prevent loss to over-the-air television of series programs and sporting events like the World Series, were included in the 1972 rules. Most of the restrictions were challenged, and the courts and the commission had dropped or modified many of them by 1977.

Yet, by 1977, the predicted cable revolution or "wired nation" was not happening. The downturn in the economy after the Vietnam War caused older systems to have increasing economic difficulties and discouraged expansion and construction of new systems. The largest cable MSO (multiple system operator), TelePrompTer, had serious reverses, and its president went to jail for bribing city officials to obtain a franchise. Expectations of the big cities becoming fertile markets for CATV were not borne out, and the "public access" channel did not take hold in New York, where it first was tried. Only a few "video freaks" and persons who wanted to see how far they could go with pornographic programming made full use of the channel, reaching a tiny audience.

Although the cable industry gained political friends by offering free service to 1974 candidates, the operators claimed that the three-level regulatory situation—federal, state, and city or other local franchising authority—in some states was stifling development and asked that legislatures "shed a tier" of regulation. The 1972 requirements for 20-channel capacity and originating various services made starting and operating cable so expensive that a fair return seemed doubtful, particularly since many of the best potential markets, underserved by broadcast television, had already been wired. Cable adherents claimed that the FCC was restricting cable to protect broadcasting, while broadcasters objected to the lack of reimbursement from CATV's "unfair" use of their programs. By 1976, faced with this confusion, and beginning to reassess its whole cable regulatory approach, the FCC decided to postpone implementation of many 1972 rules, including rebuilding.

Congress had been holding hearings on revisions of the 1909 Copyright Law for years, with little result, and a firm decision on cable's copyright liability had to wait until the law was changed, which it was late in 1976, to take effect a year later. Since, under FCC rules from the late 1960s, television broadcasters could not own cable systems within their primary coverage area, the battle lines were drawn, and the NCTA and NAB could find little to agree upon—even when forced to "agree" on copyright liability and licensing under pressure from the FCC and the OTP. In the meantime, as seen in Appendix C, Table 9-A and 9-B, cable continued to expand slowly, but the wired city or nation was a long way away.

9.8.4 Who Shall Own the Stations?

Monopoly control of broadcasting became an important issue again in the 1960s. The major concern was over the control of television stations, because they attracted by far the largest audience and showed up consistently as the major source of news. The slowly increasing power of group owners—firms, not networks, owning stations in several different markets—became apparent to Congress and the FCC by the early 1960s. Revived fears of newspaper dominance of broadcasting led to denial of one license renewal and new rules to keep television networks from controlling any CATV systems or local stations from controlling cable systems in the station's coverage area. The Justice Department intervened in several "concentration of control" cases. Whether or not a changing cast of commissioners was willing to go so far is uncertain, but the trend was toward "one station to a customer." Complicating these issues after 1970, members of minority groups became increasingly vocal about their lack of media ownership.

The commission's first major move, in 1965, was to propose that ownership of television stations in the top 50 markets be limited to three, only two of which could be VHF. Rather than operate by rule, the FCC proceeded case by case, but it waived the proposed rule in every case and finally killed the idea early in 1968. That year (1965), however, the FCC implemented a new comparative license procedure for use when two or more applicants desired the same broadcast channel. Key criteria were the applicant's capacity to attune to local concerns, to favor local control rather than group ownership, and to avoid connections with local newspapers or other broadcast stations. Unlike the 50-market ruling, this procedure was upheld on court review as was the requirement that licensees survey the public and community leaders in order to ascertain the community's needs.

A cold wind blew on broadcasters in 1969 when the FCC voted not to allow the *Herald Traveler* newspaper to retain the license for WHDH, channel 5 in Boston, apparently on grounds of cross-media ownership. Although technically the action stemmed back to the original 1957 grant for the station, which had been challenged because of *ex parte* contacts (which were later termed the "$100,000,000 lunch" by author Sterling Quinlan) and remanded by a court to the FCC for reconsideration, most broadcasters felt that their own licenses now were insecure, no matter how well the station had been programmed or for how long. In 1972, after appeals failed, the *Herald Traveler* gave up channel 5 to an independent, locally owned consortium and soon went out of the newspaper business. It was a convincing demonstration of the importance of television to the financial well-being of a newspaper-station combination. The new licensee of channel 5, operating as WCVB, demonstrated something else: programming many hours of locally produced programs a day can be profitable.

The unique WHDH decision not only shocked the industry, it also increased the number of petitions to deny renewal and caused many licensees to fear renewal time—once a simple formality. Their reaction led to FCC concern, triggered by congressional pressure, about the economic and psychological stability of the industry. As a result, it ill-advisedly issued a public notice early in 1970 on comparative broadcast proceedings, stating that the incumbent licensee would be relicensed every three years *unless* its programming and public service was shown to have been less than adequate. Unless such showing was made, competing applicants would not be considered. Most of the industry naturally liked this idea, but newly vitalized public interest groups and law firms protested. They claimed that the ruling was against the intent of the 1934 act, since it essentially gave indefinite licenses to incumbents. The Court of Appeals for the District of Columbia overturned the FCC proposal within a year, leaving some confusion, since the commission had repeatedly said that WHDH would *not* be a precedent. Parallel developments helped dispel the confusion to some degree.

In April 1968, the FCC initiated a rule-making docket on ownership— during the hearings on which it would consider most of the arguments and controversies. The commission adopted a one-to-a-customer rule in 1970, prohibiting common control of more than a single AM, FM, or television station in the same market. Since many major market operations were based on full or partial AM-FM-TV combinations, existing combinations could be retained until the stations were sold. AM-FM combinations could continue, but radio-television combinations had to be divested when sold.

In 1970 the commission undertook a long rule-making procedure on newspaper-broadcast station cross-ownership in the same market (see pp. 211–212). Early in 1975, a rule was issued essentially grandfathering existing cross-media combinations, but requiring divestiture in several small markets where the only paper and the only broadcast station were under common ownership (see pp. 575–577).

9.8.5 Self-Regulation and Citizen Action

The broadcasting industry after 1960 faced the worst heat in its history. While most viewers and listeners were satisfied with their program fare, many public service and special interest groups pressured the industry to improve with respect to advertising, especially commercials for children, amount of advertising time, and types of products advertised; program violence; ownership patterns; access for minority views and talent; portrayal of ethnic and religious groups; and minority and female employment. It was not an easy time to be a defender of broadcasting.

Much of television's public relations effort was shouldered by the Television Information Office (see p. 396), which continually issued reports, analyses, newspaper editorial reprints, slide presentations extolling American television, and its well-known survey series on what the public thought about television and other media (see pp. 456–457). TIO's parent, the National Association of Broadcasters, was affected by internal dissension caused by the wide range of broadcasting services, viewpoints, and goals. After a broadcaster-president died, the NAB tried to achieve political visibility by replacing him in 1961 with former Florida governor LeRoy Collins. Collins was a man of convictions, and his sympathetic view of those who would limit cigarette advertising and other issues brought him powerful enemies within NAB, and a relatively short tenure as president. He was succeeded by NAB staff member Vincent Wasilewski, whom the membership liked more, although while he was in office NAB lost many campaigns before the public and Congress. It fought against the ban on cigarette advertising and lost heavily, since even the tobacco companies knew it was time to quit and had retired gracefully—and profitably, since advertising costs went down and sales remained steady—leaving broadcasters holding the bag. NAB then focused on lengthening the broadcast license period to five years and presuming that a license would be renewed unless there were strong reasons against it. That campaign had not borne fruit by the end of this period. The NAB may have raised the First Amendment flag too often—every time somebody suggested the smallest change in American commercial broadcasting. As congressional committees tired of this line, the increasingly vocal minority and public interest groups became more effective.

NAB had to become defensive. The radio and television codes were frequently revised, but the revisions usually weakened them—except in instances where Congress had shown that tightening of standards was politically essential. The most serious problem was that the codes had no teeth. A station that violated their provisions only lost its right to show the code seal—surely a doubtful deterrent. Such long-banned products as personal hygiene products and hemorrhoid treatments found their way onto the nation's screens and loudspeakers as commercial standards came down in the wake of the cigarette advertising decision and the economic recession of the 1970s.

An example of the "Catch 22" problem in self-regulation arose in the 1975–1976 "Family Viewing Time" case. Although accounts differ (and those differences became very important), apparently FCC Chairman Wiley strongly encouraged the networks and the NAB to institute a policy of limiting violence in programs telecast before 9 P.M. (8 P.M. in the Central and Mountain zones). Then-CBS President Arthur Taylor championed this move, and the industry climbed on the bandwagon—except for the West

Coast package companies making about 80% of all television programs. Led by producer Norman Lear, they claimed that Wiley had violated the First Amendment by advocating such a provision in the NAB code, that the networks had violated the antitrust laws by agreeing to it, and that, even more important to the packagers, it cut into their potential revenues from syndication, as programs deemed violent and played on the networks only after 9 P.M. were similarly limited when played on local stations adhering to the NAB code. The program packagers took the issue to court. Late in 1976, a federal district judge in Los Angeles ruled that the "Family Viewing Time" self-regulatory rules were mainly due to excessive behind-the-scenes pressure from the FCC on the networks and the NAB. This important decision was appealed, but it put the whole self-regulatory process in doubt when it said that an industry's attempt to self-censor all its members was unfair, regardless of purpose. Each licensee had to make its own programming decisions.

Making NAB's job tremendously harder were the new activist groups concerned with broadcasting. They had gained impetus from FCC commissioner Nicholas Johnson, who, during his 1966–1973 term, had called for reforms and greater public input into broadcasting decisions. While listening groups had existed since the 1930s, few had made an impact on broadcasters or the general public. One of the most active of the new breed of public interest groups in the 1960s was one of the oldest—the Office of Communications of the United Church of Christ. It was the prime mover in the Jackson, Mississippi (WLBT), case (see p. 463), which helped open the regulatory process to public input. It continued to be active in other license cases, in studying the role of minority hiring in broadcasting, and in putting out useful publications on how to get the public involved in radio and television.

After several years of effective grassroots action, Action for Children's Television (ACT) (see p. 459) forced NAB code changes on commercialism and violence and an FCC hearing on the topic, and found funding for research studies. In the mid-1970s, ACT began to create local community groups with the same goals. The National Citizen's Committee for Broadcasting (NCCB), originally a public broadcasting support group in New York in the late 1960s, under ex-commissioner Johnson moved to Washington in 1974, started a bi-weekly magazine (*access*), and began to seek active input into broadcast decision making by connecting local groups with public service law firms, sources of financial support and necessary information. Other nonbroadcast-oriented groups—from the American Medical Association to the Parent-Teacher Association—became interested in, commented upon, and even, in the case of the PTA, threatened a boycott of advertisers' products because of violence.

Smaller groups concentrated on the employment and portrayal of women in television and radio; ethnic programming—trying to remove such negative images as *The Untouchables* (Italian-Americans), the television version of *Amos 'n' Andy* (blacks), the "Frito Bandito" commercials (Mexican-Americans); and blacks in broadcast ownership and programming. This last cause was aided in 1972 with the appointment of black Benjamin Hooks to the FCC (see p. 461). Many of these groups were very activist, applying for a license up for renewal or petitioning for its denial in order to get the broadcaster's attention, and then bargaining for whatever the group wanted, such as employment or more programming time. The beleaguered broadcasters thought of this as blackmail, but it was effective—although the FCC warned that the broadcaster could not delegate his authority to decide what should be aired. Broadcasting became a battleground of lobbyists, advocates, and pressure groups—all somewhat encouraged by the courts, a more open FCC, foundation-supported national organizations, and foundations themselves such as Markle and Ford.

Another factor, if only as a yardstick or precept, was the loosely organized groups of listener-supported radio stations—the Pacifica stations in Berkeley, Los Angeles, New York, and Houston; the "KRAB Nebula" stations; and some very independent independents in Seattle, San Jose, San Francisco, Dallas, St. Louis, Yellow Springs, and elsewhere. Several of these were established or otherwise nurtured by Lorenzo Milam, who put a substantial financial legacy and much time into many of these stations. His philosophy is best expressed in *Sex and Broadcasting*, a handbook on how to start a community radio station that poses seldom asked questions about the purpose of broadcasting.

Of particular interest were the first feeble attempts toward increased professionalism and self-policing by newsmen, both broadcast and print. In the late 1960s spurred by overt antagonism toward the press at the Democratic National Convention in Chicago in 1968 and by the Nixon administration's attacks on the media, several journalism reviews were established. These ranged from the prestigious *Columbia Journalism Review* to infrequently published magazines in a dozen other cities, and provided a much-needed public washing of dirty linen as well as seminars on journalistic ethics. Journalism had no single professional organization with the prestige and moral authority to establish and *enforce* a code of ethics in the way that law and medicine policed their memberships, although the Radio Television News Directors Association and the Society of Professional Journalists/Sigma Delta Chi tried. Accordingly, attempts were made, with foundation help, to establish a national "press council," the National News Council, to adjudicate claims of unfairness made against broadcasting and the printed press—although many major media refused to play. Some complaining groups, such as Accuracy in Media, and individual complainants were vulnerable to charges of bias themselves, but most wanted to improve the social responsibility of the media.

9.9 The Impact of Broadcasting (1960–1976)

Broadcasting, despite its growing diversity in programming, often brought the nation together. Most of these occasions were tragic, such as the assassinations of John F. Kennedy, Martin Luther King, Jr., and Robert F. Kennedy, and the resignation of Richard M. Nixon. But, more positively, in 1969 most of mankind watched Neil Armstrong step onto the moon.

9.9.1 Crises for Media Competing with Television

Television, it must be remembered, had captured the entertainment function of the mass media almost completely by 1960. Motion pictures had felt the pinch in the 1950s and, until the networks began heavy use of feature films in the early 1960s, the film industry was surviving on a few block-buster films, a few dependable stars, and by making television programs. Most television series were shot on film in Hollywood as well as many of the "made for television" feature films (see p. 437), which were emerging in the late 1960s. Although there was a new generation of moviegoers, and films for them, much of Hollywood's income in the early 1970s came from prime time network showings of recent movies. Still, unemployment in the creative trade unions in Hollywood was so high that the Nixon administration condemned the increasing use of reruns on television, which limited the need for original program material. In spite of this threat to the networks, Hollywood remained television-dominated, in both ownership and output. The independent producers—often successful directors or stars who could convince the banks that they were a good risk for a production loan—continued to turn out more important films than the major studios, although the surviving majors made enough notable blockbusters to cover the costs of less successful films.

Magazines felt the full brunt of television in the 1960s. The once popular *Colliers* died in 1957. By the mid-1960s, the *Saturday Evening Post* was in deep economic and editorial trouble, and after publishing bi-weekly for several years, the Curtis Publishing Company stopped publishing it in 1969. Many people said that television had stolen the audience for the mixture of fiction and fact that had made the *Post* a popular giant for over four decades. Then the two major picture magazines, which had started within a year of each other in the mid-1930s, ceased publication within a year of each other three decades later. *Look* went first, followed in 1971 by *Life*. The circulation was there nearly till the end, but advertisers had lost confidence in national general circulation magazines and thought that television would do them more good at less cost. Some national magazines tried to appeal more to advertisers by not renewing subscribers in poorer rural counties, much as CBS had killed its rural-oriented programs in 1971 (see pp. 437–438), but to no avail. Magazines became specialized, with the *Reader's Digest* being the only general circulation non-newsweekly magazine to survive into the mid-1970s. *TV Guide*, with its many regional editions and 1977 weekly circulation of approximately 20 million, was the nation's most popular magazine.

Newspapers faced increasing economic problems, only partly caused by radio and television taking away their late-breaking news role—the "extra" edition had virtually disappeared by the end of the 1950s—and television taking much of the entertainment function. In city after city, dailies died—New York's seven metropolitan dailies of 1961 had shrunk to three by 1968—generally to the benefit of advertisers who with one or two papers could cover the audience that once had been split among many. The soaring demands by labor unions, justifiably worried over technological unemployment, and the escalating costs of newsprint discouraged many publishers and investors. Business-oriented publishers raised their papers' daily price to readers and advertisers and then, as circulation and net profits dropped, killed them off or merged them. Some new suburban dailies and weeklies bucked this trend.

Increasing media competition and corollary costs contributed to a trend to media conglomerates in the 1961–1976 period, particularly in the book publishing industry, which had been generally removed from group ownership in the past. By the mid-1970s, several media empires had major holdings in print and broadcast media and often in film as well. It was argued that it took economies of scale to meet competition from other huge media empires, demands of large advertising agencies, inflation, and the costs of labor. The cost was loss of diversity in content, fewer outlets for advertising of new products or services unable to meet the price, and fewer jobs.

9.9.2 Television around the World

Two major developments were the coming of color and the use of communications satellites for news transmissions (see pp. 411–412, 444, 455). By the 1970s, most of the developed nations of the world had color television. Unfortunately, three systems were in competition for adoption: the American NTSC, the German PAL, and France's SECAM. The Western Hemisphere and Japan adopted the U.S. standard; Great Britain and most of Western Europe adopted the German system; and France, the USSR, and much of Eastern Europe, partly for political reasons, took the French system. Great Britain began color transmissions late in 1967. Canada had begun the year before, although an estimated 50,000 Canadian color sets had been tuned to colorcasts from south of the border before this. Japan and other Far Eastern countries quickly became the major sources for the world's television receivers. By the 1970s, more television sets were in use outside the United States than in it.

Transistors and then integrated circuits made radios smaller and more rugged, and their low cost and lack of need for power lines brought domestic broadcasting to many underdeveloped countries for the first time. Radio's low cost and ready access to rural areas made it a widespread ingredient in successful developmental communication in Africa, Latin America, and Asia. Developing nations that introduced television frequently supported it by advertising, and typically placed a single station in the capital city more for prestige and the pleasure of the ruling elite than for service to the public. American television programs and radio shows were popular, but toward the end of this period some countries established regulations limiting the showing of foreign import programs in order to protect their own artists, industry, and cultural independence. Even Canada passed strong laws to limit U.S. television advertising, programs, and other media influences that were considered harmful to the Canadian culture and media industry. Because of the language difference, Mexico was not as directly affected as Anglophone parts of Canada by U.S. stations. Indeed, Mexico had by the late 1960s become a major program source for the rest of Latin America and even for Spanish-language television stations in the United States.

9.9.3 Period Overview

As the title of this chapter suggests, this 15-year period saw more evolution than revolution for the media. FM radio and cable television grew to importance, while commercial television and AM radio grew more slowly. Public (formerly educational) broadcasting now was national policy and achieved national impact for the first time. Discussion continued on UHF and pay-TV.

Major issues in the 1960s and 1970s included financing of public broadcasting, the amount of advertising on both radio and television, the content of ads specifically aimed at children, violent program content, bias or suspected bias in broadcast journalism, responsibility for regulating broadcasting, political influence in the regulatory process, the increasing potential of cable television, all the issues surrounding the Fairness Doctrine, economic—and political and social class—concentration of ownership in broadcasting and other media, and a gnawing concern that broadcasting would serve the public's needs better if the public would express some interest. Few of these issues were clearly resolved by 1976, as the number of "players" in the broadcast issues arena and the economic stakes kept increasing.

The era began with an obvious major change at the FCC, as it went from years of complacency and even acquiescence to a period of strong regulatory activity. Relatively few issues were decided, however; diversity and confusion typically won out over clear-cut decisions and trends.

Selected Further Reading

(Alphabetical within topics. For full citations, see Appendix D.)

Contemporary views of broadcsting in this era are found in Cole (1970), Harris (1978), Head (1972, 1976), Mayer (1972), Skornia & Kitson (1968), Summers & Summers (1966, 1978), and White & Averson (1968). Early development of cable and other new technologies is found in Bagdikian (1971), Brown (1970), Kamen (1973), Lardner (1987), LeDuc (1973), Maddox (1972), and Smith (1972). Economic issues are the focus of Noll, Peck & McGowan (1973), and Owen, Beebe and Manning (1974). Diamant (1971), Hall (1984), and Price (1978) review top television commercials.

The dramatic changes in educational/public broadcasting are descibed in Blakely (1979), the Carnegie Commission report (1967), CPB annual reports (1970–1976), Day (1995), Engelman (1996), Gibson (1977), Koenig & Hill (1967), Macy (1974), Stone (1985), and Witherspoon & Kovitz (2000). Schramm et al. (1963) was the first national educational television audience study. "Underground" radio is the topic of Keith (1997), while Spigel & Curtin assess sixties television (1997).

For reference books on television programs, see chapter seven. Contemporary views of this era include Brown (1971), Cantor (1972), *The Eighth Art* (1962), Miller & Rhodes (1964), and the annual September "preview" issues of *TV Guide*. The made-for-television movie is chronicled in Marrill (1984), while the television output of two studios is found in Perry (1983, on Universal) and Woolery et al. (1985, on Warner Brothers). Children's television is covered in Fischer (1983) and Wollery (1983, 1985). Johnson (1971) and Sugar (1978) cover televised sports. Television journalism is covered in Barrett's reviews (1969–1982, originally annual then every two years), Bluem (1965) and Curtin (1995) on the documentary, Buzenberg & Buzenberg on the Dick Salent years at CBS (1999), Donovan & Scherer (1991), Einstein on documentary series and special reports (1987), Dunham (1997), Epstein (1973), Frank on NBC news (1991), Gates on CBS news (1978), Hammond on documentaries (1981), and Small (1970). Television's place in the Vietnam War is assessed in Braestrup (1977), Hallin (1986), and MacDonald (1985).

Politics and television during this period (and subsequent years) were featured in Chester (1969), Gilbert (1972), Lang & Lang (1983) and Lashner (1984)—both focused on Watergate, MacNeil (1968), McGinniss (1969), Mickelson (1989), Minow et al. (1973), Morreale (1993), Reinsch (1991), and West (1993).

Television audience studies include Beville (1988), Bower (1973), Cater & Strickland (1975), Glick & Levy (1962), Luke (1991), the National Institute of Mental Health (1982), Rowland (1983), Steiner (1963), and the Surgeon General's committee (1972). Regulatory issues are featured in Cole & Oettinger (1978), Emery (1971), Friendly on the *Red Lion* case (1976), Johnson (1970), Krasnow & Longley (1973), Levin (1971), and Jung (1996), Rowan (1984), and Simmons (1978)—all three on the Fairness Doctrine. Quinlan (1974) describes the WHDH decision. Compaine and Gomery (2000), Baer (1974), and Rucker (1968) all focus on questions of media ownership.

World broadcasting is described in Dizard (1966), Emery (1969), Green (1972), Head (1974), Paulu (1967, 1974), Segrave on U.S. television abroad (1998), Smith (1973), and Unesco (1964, 1975). The changing broadcasting scene in Great Britain is the subject of BBC *Handbooks* (through 1987), Briggs (1986, 1995), Harris on the "pirate" radio stations (1970), IBA *Handbooks* (annual), and Sendall (1982, 1983). Peers (1969, 1979) discusses Canadian radio and television.

> "The need for a fresh approach to broadcasting, now spurred by competitive challenges from cable and other video providers, is long overdue. This new approach concludes that broadcasters best serve the public by responding to market forces rather than governmental directives. It restores the broadcasting business to the unregulated status of American enterprise generally."————*FCC Chairman Mark Fowler, writing on his marketplace approach to broadcast regulation in the* TEXAS LAW REVIEW, *1982*

CHAPTER 10

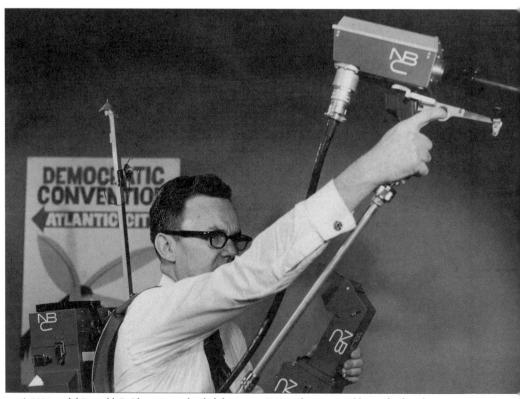

A 1964 model "portable" video camera that led the way to ENG in the 1970s and beyond. *Photofest.*

"No one doubted five years ago that . . . television would be altered quite drastically in this decade. Cable had already exceeded 30 percent penetration and HBO . . . was being spoken of as the likely fourth network. . . . Although no one can deny the impact of these technologies, the sweeping predictions about their inevitable progress were, as it turns out, overly optimistic. . . . Few of the early promises of the new media have been realized."———*Television critic Les Brown, summing up the mid-1980s in* CHANNELS FIELD GUIDE *1987*

CHALLENGE
AND COMPETITION
(1977–1988)

ABC's 1978 political convention control center. *Photofest.*

Chapter Outline

A few weeks after Jimmy Carter took office in 1977 as the 39th President of the United States, he appeared in an informal televised "fireside chat" much like those of President Roosevelt on radio four decades earlier, but wearing a sweater instead of a business suit. Carter tried to appear new and folksy at the same time—promising a continuation of past Democratic philosophy with few changes in government operation, and walking down Pennsylvania Avenue to the White House after he was sworn in. In contrast, 12 years later, as Ronald Reagan ended his two terms and George Bush, Sr., took office, the relationships of government and business (including the industry of broadcasting) that the United States had known for most of the twentieth century had undergone drastic changes as a result of rapid technological innovation and adoption of radical deregulation for ideological reasons.

After 1980, broadcasting's institutions were challenged more than ever before. Technological innovations and competitive pressures that began in the late 1970s forced broadcasters to adjust to an evolving—and soon mostly deregulated—marketplace of communication. For the first time, nonbroadcast electronic media began to dictate the direction of traditional over-the-air broadcasting. The dramatic changes that became increasingly evident in the 1980s had been gestating for years, as noted in chapter 9. As with most revolutions, however, these changes seemed to come—or we became aware of them—suddenly and often in combination, and they began to alter drastically the role of "broadcasting."

Perhaps these shifts were exacerbated by changes in the cast of characters. Manufacturing moved overseas. The young G.I.s who had returned from World War II to go into broadcasting were now contemplating retirement, and the first generation of broadcasters from the 1920s and 1930s had long since stepped down. Broadcasting was becoming a commodity, something to be bought or sold rather than a calling or a profession—and this attitude, reflected in the enrollment growth of business and law schools, fit right in with a growing trend toward economic conservatism in Washington.

The era covered in this chapter can be divided into two periods by the year 1980. The 1977–1980 period (the Carter years) marks a kind of calm before the storm. There was the excitement and uncertainty of widespread predictions about the possible demise of broadcasting as a result of the proposed introduction of as yet experimental new services such as broadband cable with unlimited capacity (the "wired city" concept) and direct broad-cast satellites. Still, even though there were some initial moves toward deregulation, broadcasting largely continued operating as it had before, ig-noring promised but not yet practical new competitors.

Indeed, some would argue that broadcasting stood at the peak of its performance on the eve of its 60th anniversary in 1980. Certainly, that year marked a gap in, if not an end to, the orderly growth that had started in the 1920s. Before 1980, much of television was still run by the station and network leaders who had helped to develop it and who still believed broadcasting had a concern with, and continuing responsibility to serve in, the public interest. The FCC continued to play a strong role in regulating broadcasting, despite increasing deregulation when Charles Ferris became chairman in early 1977. Only after 1980 did the long-promised new tech-nologies begin to make a real difference. The increasing penetration of ca-ble and videocassette recorders (VCRs) made these technologies a part of everyday life for their audiences, with both in more than half the country's households by 1987 (see pp. 551–552). At the same time, under Reagan-appointed commissioners, the FCC began to back—and then run—away from decades of public interest regulation, relying on the politically popu-lar (in a conservative administration) but unproven theory that marketplace competitive pressures would regulate broadcasting and other electronic media for the public good.

The changes that technology and deregulation brought about require a broader definition of such traditional terms as "broadcasting," "network," and "local station." "Broadcasting" has become a generic reference to any electronic means of delivering entertainment and information-news con-tent to consumers, while the term "network" no longer is restricted to a sys-tem in which local affiliates have to present the same content at the same time. In addition, delivery of programs to affiliates now is almost entirely by space communications satellite rather than terrestrial wires or mi-crowave relays. And "local station," by the 1980s, might include cable sys-tems and other distribution channels as well as individual stations. To members of the public, of course, the way a program reaches them is of little importance.

As this chapter will show, the expansion of delivery options and new economic pressures had substantial impact on the industry. However, programs—the content of broadcasting—were little changed (with rare ex-ceptions), although they were subject to ever-tighter budget limitations. Al-terations in broadcasting were not unique. They were occurring against a background of change elsewhere. For example, the once tightly regulated airline industry was thrown on its own competitive resources after 1978. This led to a mix of lower prices but often far poorer service from a lot of new, merged, and often short-lived airline companies, most trying to skim the cream of large market service, ignoring or overcharging many inter-vening cities and changing prices so rapidly that travel agencies' computers often had difficulty keeping track. The potential for deregulation of broadcasting and telecommunications services often was compared to the hypothetical and presumed benefits of a more competitive airline market, but the public was not as aware of all of the ramifications of this change.

The biggest telecommunications industry story started when the Justice Department moved against AT&T with an antitrust suit in 1974, a case that finally went to trial in 1981. Early in 1982, AT&T and the Justice Department settled out of court, subjecting AT&T and its operating companies to the continuing supervision of federal judge Harold Greene. The Bell System was broken up, with AT&T divested of its local, regulated operating companies and freed—in part—to engage in new, often unregulated ventures in the information and computer fields. The operating companies were reorganized at the beginning of 1984 into seven independently owned regional holding firms. The most radical changes insofar as consumers were concerned were in how they now obtained telephones (generally by purchase rather than lease), chose a long-distance carrier (where there had been little choice before 1980, now AT&T competed with lower-cost firms like MCI and Sprint), and paid their increasingly complicated phone bills. This restructuring of what had been one of the largest institutions on earth, and a paragon of technological efficiency, was thought by many to be another indicator of fundamental changes in the American economic system, which was becoming service oriented rather than manufacturing oriented, harder to enter against entrenched firms, and subject to many formal and informal controls because of multinationalism. Broadcasters and cable operators both kept a wary eye on this now partially unshackled colossus that might try to move back into the field it had left in 1926 (see pp. 74–76).

10.1 New Technologies

The pace of technological change in most fields accelerated after World War II. Cycles of innovation shortened because of the competitive pressure to market new ideas before someone else does. Sometimes shoddy "novelty" has been substituted for progress, leading to equipment designed to be thrown away by the consumer and replaced rather than repaired; sometimes bold new products have been embraced by the public. Yet the same competitive pressure can harm technological progress in the long run. In 1987, for example, under pressure to increase its short-term profits, CBS closed its research labs in Connecticut, where Peter Goldmark had developed CBS's early color television and LP record projects in the 1940s. RCA's David Sarnoff Research Center in Princeton, deemed unnecessary by its new owner, General Electric, was given to another research company for a tax write-off in the same year. Later still, the mission of Bell Telephone Laboratories became almost exclusively devoted to applied research, to the near-exclusion of basic research of the sort that had led to the transistor and

Information Theory. Changes in federal tax laws, often good indicators of real, as contrasted to rhetorical, public policy changes, removed much of the financial incentive for investing in research and development. While some inventions and innovations still came out of American laboratories, telecommunications manufacturing increasingly moved abroad, and the United States became a more service-oriented economy.

Broadcasting's once unique role was altered by the increasing availability of competing content delivery technologies. But, as will become evident, this technological change has improved the production and distribution processes rather than enhanced program content quality and variety. The dramatic changes of the 1980s, while based on years of earlier technical innovation, also were due to regulatory reconsideration. The increasing availability of new technologies contributed to arguments both for and against deregulation, as discussed on pp. 566–569.

10.1.1 Delivery: Getting Here from There

Put simply, many of the so-called new technologies are largely duplicate means of delivering similar programming from producer to consumer rather than a whole new system of communication, as was radio broadcasting in the 1920s. Until the early 1980s, with the exception of the relatively few homes wired for cable (see Appendix C, Tables 9-A and 9-B), radio and television retained their monopoly on electronic delivery of news and entertainment to households. But after 1980, other means of delivery, especially cable, VCRs, and (indirectly) satellites, became increasingly important.

Developed in the 1960s (see pp. 411–412), the geostationary- (geosynchronous-) orbit space communications satellite finally ended AT&T's lucrative monopoly of wire and, later, microwave broadcast network interconnection, which dated back to 1926 (see pp. 75, 77). In 1978, the Public Broadcasting Service began distributing programming to its 280 television affiliates by means of transponders (satellite devices that receive signals beamed up to them from earth and transmit back to earth on a different frequency over a defined area known as a "footprint") on the *Westar I* domestic communications satellite rather than using AT&T's land lines. The new system allowed better-quality transmission, more flexibility in sending programs between or within time zones or regions, and a greater choice of programs for stations—which could now choose among four channels of material instead of one—and it was cheaper. By 1980, with prices of television receive-only antennas (TVROs or "dishes") dropping, National Public Radio ended its terrestrial interconnection and moved to satellite. It is interesting that the last commercial television networks to switch to satellites were those that had been around the longest: NBC in 1985, followed soon by ABC and CBS. In addition, the 1980s saw the rise of many satellite-delivered cable networks (see pp. 514–517, Appendix C, Table 9-C).

Use of similar but more powerful satellites allowing direct service to the home was first proposed by Arthur C. Clarke in 1945, but given solid form in 1980 by the Communications Satellite Corporation (COMSAT). COMSAT's specially formed subsidiary, Satellite Television Corporation (STC), applied in December 1980 to the FCC for permission to design and launch the country's first direct broadcast satellite (DBS) service designed to reach rural areas and inner cities, both inadequately served by cable and over-the-air stations. (Of course, the satellite's coverage footprint would also cover wealthier areas.) STC's plan for DBS was but the first of many filed with the FCC in 1980–1982. The potential of DBS seemed bright, much to the consternation of traditional broadcasters, who feared instant obsolescence. They need not have worried. Though the FCC proceeded with spectrum allocations for possible DBS service, none of the many applicants survived, and only STC actually built satellites. The costs (estimated at $700 million through the first year of STC's operation) were too high for the limited potential audience. Further, none of the early DBS applicants resolved the central problem of programming—what to provide that was different from or better than what most consumers already had from over-the-air broadcasting, cable, and videocassettes.

One DBS operator did, briefly, show what could be done. United Satellite Communications, Inc. (USCI), with substantial financial backing from the Prudential Insurance Company, provided service to portions of the Midwest and Northeast in late 1984 using a Canadian ANIK satellite transponder. Expecting to serve several tens of thousands of homes, but actually reaching fewer than 11,000, USCI closed up early in 1985 owing some $47.6 million. By the late 1980s, a few companies, notably Hubbard Broadcasting of Minneapolis, were still expressing interest in a possible DBS service in the United States. But despite ever more efficient satellite technology, the daunting costs of design and launch and the inability to create programming sufficiently different from that already available made DBS in the United States seem unlikely for some years to come—although European and Japanese systems (often proposing high-definition television— see pp. 496–498) seemed more likely to succeed. A bootleg version of DBS was to be found in nearly a million American homes—often in localities with poor broadcast or cable service—that equipped themselves at high cost to pick up material from the low-powered communications satellites used by broadcast and cable networks. However, by the Fall of 1987, the commercial networks, under pressure from local affiliates, and most cable networks had "scrambled" their signals, in some cases willing (for a monthly fee approximating that of cable) to supply decoders to those with TVRO dishes at home.

While broadcasting looked to the skies for improved delivery systems, one terrestrial technology brought things back to earth. Developed in the 1970s, optical fiber or glass cables modulated by lasers began to spread across the country in the 1980s. Optical fiber has high signal reliability and a huge bandwidth capacity, thus lowering costs of delivery. Telephone companies first used it for high-density trunk circuits, and the first transatlantic fiber cable for voice and video communication went into service in mid-1988. Domestic communications satellite operators and telephone or other telecommunications systems saw optical fiber links as competition for many kinds of point-to-point communication, though for broadcast and cable services, satellite delivery was essential. Some wondered that when the costs of wiring homes with fiber optics declines, it may replace some present broadcast and cable services using the electromagnetic spectrum, raising the political and economic question of why we need to pay for two broadband (cable television and telephone-data) connections to our homes.

Other delivery technologies played minor roles in the electronic media delivery marketplace. Widely discussed, but having limited audience impact, were low-power television stations (LPTV) and "wireless cable" MMDS microwave broadcasting systems (see pp. 503–504). But in both cases, their programming was largely conventional broadcast fare, underlining our earlier point that the new delivery technologies were largely duplicate means of achieving the same end: getting news and entertainment from one producer to many homes—the essence of broadcasting.

10.1.2 New Technologies at Home

After 1980, an increasingly intense battle was fought for the loyalty and wallets of consumers seeking the latest in electronic communication gadgets. By the late 1980s, the most expensive (and potentially useful) of these gadgets was the home or personal computer (PC), which could acquire information, often in an interactive mode, through telephone lines using modems ("*mo*dulator-*dem*odulator"). PC games took up some leisure time people might otherwise have spent watching television. A second common gadget might be a cordless (radio) telephone or a telephone answering machine, both technically more reliable and useful to more people than the dwindling CB (Citizens Band) radio craze of a few years before, and a great deal cheaper than the cellular car phones installed by many business executives in the 1980s.

While electronic devices were filling the average home, the electronic innovations we are most interested in can be divided into four categories: audio recording, video recording, video text services, and improved video quality. Certainly the dominant trend in 1980s consumer electronics was to ever-better means of home recording and playback, for both audio and video. The recording industry's "battle of the speeds" in the late 1940s (see pp. 272–273) was but a precursor to a never-ending stream of rapidly introduced innovations in the 1980s, each seeking at least a niche of consumer acceptance. The struggle was complicated by the FCC's abandonment

▪ **Changing Transmission Modes**   Broadcast, cable and auxiliary services used an increasing variety of delivery systems in addition to over-the-air transmission by the 1980s. The major ones are compared here.

Medium	Description	Capacity/Use	Cost
Twisted-wire pair	Two insulated copper wires	Usually voice grade; typically one audio circuit; used for radio networks	Least expensive
Coaxial cable ("coax")	Insulated hollow copper cylinder with signal wire conductor	TV networks (until 1985) and cable systems; typically one video channel, but may carry more than two dozen	More expensive than twisted-wire
Optical fiber ("fiber optics")	Glass fiber strands carrying light beams within a protective cable	Multiple TV or radio channels or cable relay; very high capacity	Usually much more expensive than wire or coax
Microwave relay	Ultra-high frequency point-to-point radio carrier	Multiple TV or radio signals, linking cable systems, MMDS, and ENG relay; capacity similar to coax	Less costly than optical fiber
Satellite relay	Radio transponders on satellite receive from uplinks and transmit to downlinks	TV channel or multiple audio signals per transponder (usually 24 transponders per satellite); also SNG	Most expensive, but highly efficient for national or regional coverage

of its traditional role of selecting technical standards for broadcast services, leaving the success or failure of several technologies to an ill-defined marketplace (see pp. 569–571).

10.1.2.1 *Home Audio Recording*

Although the audiocassette continued to be improved to the point where it made major inroads into sales of LP records (and 45-rpm records and 8-track units had joined 78-rpm records as historical novelties), a major improvement in sound recording was a digital recording modulated by a laser, called the "compact disc" or CD, which had many advantages over traditional analog music recording. The CD, named for its just-under-5-inch size, was first introduced in 1983, offering fine sound reproduction at an initially stiff $800 for a player and at least $20 per disc. The discs were said to be indestructible and could be played endlessly without wear and resulting sound deterioration (though by the late 1980s there was concern about how long CDs would really last due to shortcuts taken by some CD makers). As with traditional record players, the CD player could not be used to record. But its superiority in quality of sound and absence of hiss or noise over analog-based disc, reel-to-reel or cassette tape made it a hit with audiophiles. Rising demand led to increased production, and costs dropped so that players could be had for $150 or so by 1987, and some CD discs were list priced under $12 and discounted below that. By 1986, a CD boom had developed, and what had been a niche market took on the trappings of a widespread consumer product, with home, portable, and automobile versions, stimulated by radio stations' increasing use of CDs on the air. By 1987, thousands of titles were available on CD (about half popular and half classical), cassettes were being relegated to a small section in music stores, and the traditional LP looked as if it also might be on the way out.

10.1.2.2 *Home Video Recording*

Leading the parade of home video products for most of the decade was the videocassette recorder (VCR), heralded as a true mass medium. Introduced in 1965 (see pp. 410–411), the VCR made hardly a dent in consumer interest until the early 1980s because of initially high average unit prices ($785 in 1978). Heating up competition and thus contributing to lower prices (down to $388 by 1986) was the fact that the Japanese producers of VCRs backed two conflicting standards—Sony's pioneering Beta format and Matsushita's competing VHS, introduced in 1977, which a decade later had won the war, at least in the United States. The differences were minor on the screen, but the cassettes were of different sizes and thus were incompatible. The public was attracted to buy as first VHS and then Beta increased the amount of recording time from an hour to as much as eight hours per ever-cheaper cassette. Increasingly complicated machines were capable of being programmed to record on a timer, without the need for someone present to push the buttons—although many never learned how, and "the blinking 12:00" became a symbol of technological inadequacy. VCRs with video cameras in the same box (known as *camcorders*) replaced most of the home movie business. As shown in Appendix C, Table 7-B, the penetration of VCRs rose sharply in the mid-1980s, reaching half of all television homes in 1987, the first broadcast-related service to achieve such a plateau since color television 15 years before.

 For the viewer, a VCR brought a large degree of viewing control into the home and away from the broadcaster or cable system owner. With such machines, viewers could practice time-shifting, recording of programs to watch when convenient rather than when scheduled by the network or station (see pp. 555–556). Further, home libraries of video material could be constructed. Now everyone could become his or her own television programmer, a fact that made life much more difficult for the ratings services (see pp. 553–556). This ability to duplicate freely broadcast and cablecast programming, especially motion pictures, led to adverse film industry reaction and eventually to unsuccessful legal actions to control VCR use (see p. 578). It led as well to businesses aimed specifically at VCR owners—rental (and sometimes sale) of cassette recordings of feature films and video programming was highly competitive but largely successful, due to low overhead and ability to meet a public desire. On the other hand, an attempt to cash in on the growing popularity of VCRs by ABC-TV's "TeleFirst" service from Chicago failed in just six months in 1984. ABC offered a subscription service of films telecast in early morning hours to preset VCRs. It signed up only 5,000 subscribers and lost some $15 million. The complications of setting VCRs for later recording, and the ready—and cheaper—local availability of rental tapes, doomed the venture. (Had it worked, many likely would have watched the previous night's recorded movie rather than prime time television, a factor ABC may not have thought through!)

The success of the half-inch VHS format in this country, and the desire of supporters of the Beta format to regain its market share, led to the development of new formats, such as Beta II and Super-VHS. While of higher pictorial quality, some of these machines are unable to play the tapes recorded on their less expensive relatives, and, of course, vice versa. While a plethora of different standards often limited playback to the home VCR for which the camcorder was bought, all of these units capture images in color and with sound. Some camcorders—either half-inch (VHS or Beta) or 8 mm—evolved to a quality level that has given them a role in nontheatrical or news production.

The application of the videodisc did not initially fare as well. First marketed by Magnavox in 1978 to sell copies of popular theatrical films to consumers, and given a big push by RCA after 1981, the videodisc was sold as a cheaper but playback-only alternative to the VCR. The videodisc industry also was plagued by several incompatible technologies, some based on lasers, others (like RCA's) based on mechanical (stylus-in-groove) techniques. Sharply lower VCR prices in the early 1980s, plus the videodisc's inability to record off the air, doomed the various videodisc systems, though many felt the disc's picture tended to be better than the VCR's, and it had significant uses in education and industry. RCA finally gave up on its product in 1984, after a loss of more than $500 million.

In the late 1980s, interest in the videodisc revived, thanks to the parallel, and far more successful, development of the audio compact disc (CD). Already available by 1987 was what seemed the best of all possible record worlds: machines that would play—but not record—audio CDs and laser videodiscs interchangeably. Paced by sales of music video discs, the

▪ The Consumer Digital Era   In the late 1980s, digital technology was increasingly common in radio and recordings and was beginning to make headway in television. By 1989, compact discs were in about 10% of American homes, while the digital audiotape recorder (DAT) was expected to be the next potential blockbuster mass acceptance product on the market. Videodiscs made an abortive market push in the early 1980s and, although it was thought that they would make a comeback in laser form, it was the DVD that took hold in the late 1990s. All relied on digital rather than analog recording and sound generation.

How a Laser CD or Videodisc Works
Information is etched into microscopic "pits" arranged in spiral tracks on the surface of the disc. Rather than being contained in the visible undulating grooves of the analog recording system used in vinyl LPs, data on a CD or laser videodisc are stored digitally as a sequence of 1s and 0s in the "pits" (indentations) and "lands" (places that weren't pits) of the disc surface. A focused laser beam "reads" the information in the reflected pits and lands. The signal is transferred to a prism, then directed into a photo detector for conversion into sound signals in CDs and video signals in videodiscs. A transparent plastic coating protects the information on the disc from physical damage and also carries the record label. The laser beam scans for information without physically wearing down the surface—thus laser-read discs, video or audio, theoretically should never wear out. (CD-ROMs for computers work in a closely related fashion.)

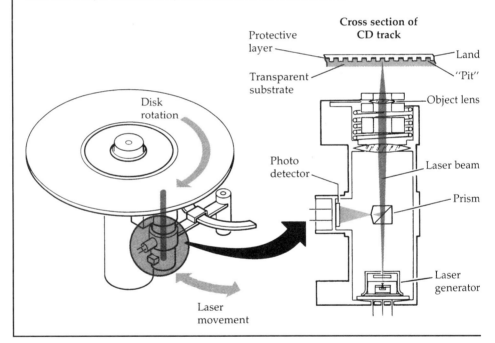

videodisc market showed signs of new life. Further, development of the CD-based read-only-memory (CD-ROM) computer memory technology paved the way for machines able to play any kind of CD disc: audio, video, or computer memory. Publishing ventures looked forward to placing enormous amounts of data—such as the complete Bible or U.S. Census—on a CD-ROM disk, with any section, page, or even word retrievable almost instantly with the proper computer commands. (The major cost is in preparing the content for recording, since existing automatic scanning devices for converting print to a computer storage medium are not perfect.) Industrial and training uses

How Digital Audiotape Works
A digital audiotape (DAT) machine uses a cassette of audiotape that is smaller than that used in an analog machine, but otherwise it is similar in operation. The tape records data in helical, or slanted, tracks, using two recording heads. Data on track one are oriented differently from those on track two, allowing a tight squeezing together of tracks without danger of interference. As with CDs (above), DAT machines "read" digital signals, 1s and 0s, which are then converted into analog sound for playback. Unlike CDs, DAT machines can be used to record and play back material.

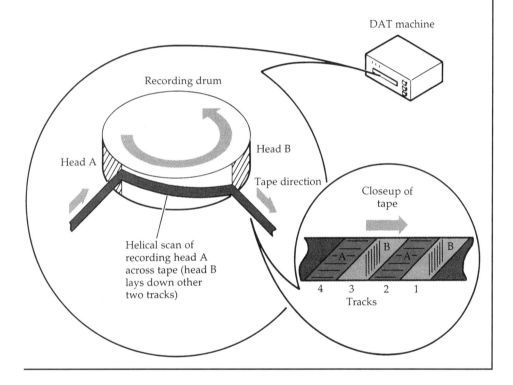

DAT machine

Recording drum

Head A

Head B

Tape direction

Closeup of tape

Helical scan of recording head A across tape (head B lays down other two tracks)

4   3   2   1
Tracks

of CDs, videodiscs, and CD-ROM were paving the way, said many observers, for major consumer product breakthroughs in the 1990s.

10.1.2.3 *Video Text Devices*

Despite much promotional hoopla and investment by several large media firms, two closely related new technologies, teletext and videotex, seemed unable to find a consumer market in America. Introduced first in Britain in the 1970s, then in Canada and France (using, as you might by now expect, differing technical standards), both of these are means to allow the viewer to select "pages" of printed information rather than the television picture being transmitted at the same time.

Teletext is a means of sending text and diagrams to a properly equipped television screen by use of one of the "vertical blanking interval" lines that together form the dark band dividing pictures horizontally on the television screen. The communication is one-way, with the transmitter sending one screen or "page" of information after another and able to store perhaps 200 at a time.

Videotex looks the same on the screen but reaches the home or office by cable and has an interactive ability (you can select any of possibly thousands of specific pages or screens by punching up numbers on a push-button

---

■ **Keeping Up with Technology**   With rapid improvements in studio and transmission technology and increased interest by foreign manufacturers in sales to American business, the annual equipment exhibition of the National Association of Broadcasters (NAB), the biggest of its kind in the United States (and, some say, in the world), has taken on increased importance. Until the early 1970s, this annual exhibition was held in Chicago or Washington, D.C., where hotel exhibition halls then were large enough to hold all the equipment demonstrations. As the industry grew, the NAB was forced to move to Las Vegas (where these photos were taken, at the 1988 exhibition) or Dallas, which have exhibition halls large enough to hold the hundreds of exhibitors, who occupy more space each year. By the end of the 1990s, it literally would be a five-*mile* walk to stroll once down each aisle. Electronic media engineers and managers count on this four-day exhibit and related convention technical sessions to get a sense of larger industry trends and to order new equipment. While the NAB's is by far the largest (more than 100,000 attendees!), other industry groups also have technical exhibitions.

Photos courtesy of the National Association of Broadcasters.

telephone or similar control). Both techniques could provide useful data—news headlines, airline schedules, weather reports, goings-on in town—to the subscriber. The French Telecom "Minitel" system, for example, supplied free terminals to homes requesting them that were intended to do away with printed telephone directories—and gain an audience base for other service providers. It remained in service through the 1990s.

The 1980s saw considerable policy debate in the United States about such systems and massive loss of money on them. Videotex attracted the most attention because it offered the ability to make thousands of pages of information, advertising, or entertainment available on a subscription basis at the push of a button. The Knight-Ridder newspaper chain introduced its "Viewtron" videotex experiment in Coral Gables, Florida, in October 1983 and spent nearly $30 million in programming and promoting the system in its first 14 months. In Southern California, the Times Mirror Company tried a similar system. By March 1986, both projects were wound up, with losses of $50–$60 million and $20 million, respectively. The public seemed confused by what was offered, disliked having to buy or rent decoding devices to receive the videotex signals, and was not very interested in the limited information made available. It seemed clear that videotex was best suited for business rather than home use. Newspapers were in the business of supplying content to consumers, so it is no wonder that they were early experimenters, just as they were when facsimile was proposed as a broadcast medium in the 1940s. By the late 1980s, the formerly AT&T owned regional Bell operating companies (RBOCs) were arguing in federal court that they should be allowed to provide such information services, a new wrinkle for a delivery-oriented, rather than content-oriented, industry. And, as again might be expected, newspaper chains (such as Knight-Ridder, which sold its television stations to provide capital for its own videotex plans) and other existing information providers were opposing any Bell market entry.

10.1.2.4 *Closed-Captioning*

A similar technology was of particular value and interest to a special and large minority of viewers. On March 16, 1980, NBC and ABC began to provide some of their programming with "closed captions," a teletext-like service providing subtitles for the hearing impaired. Broadcast on line 21 of the vertical blanking interval, the captions (termed "closed" because they require special equipment to see) are decoded and put on the screen by a device (sometimes built into the set) that for some years only Sears, Roebuck was willing to sell. ("Open" captioning for the deaf was used for a few years on PBS's late-night rebroadcasts of the *ABC Evening News,* and some religious and other programs insert a sign-language version in a corner of the picture.) Closed captioning grew slowly from 10 hours of ABC and NBC and 20 hours of PBS programming in 1980; CBS was promoting a form of teletext that included captioning among other services and did not join until 1984. By 1989, 200 hours a week—virtually all—of network prime time programs, all CPB-funded programming, and some daytime children's programs, sports, and even soap operas were being captioned. Many producers now insist on captioning. The U.S. Department of Education alone paid more than $6 million a year for captioning to nonprofit organizations (such as the National Captioning Institute and WGBH) and another $1 million to subsidize the manufacture of decoders. Captioning requires much time and skill, since only a few of the words spoken in the time available can be shown, making "instant captioning" of events rather rare.

10.1.2.5 *High-Definition Television*

Another potentially far-reaching technology was the initial development in the 1980s of several competing systems of "high-definition television" (HDTV). The idea of HDTV is not a new one—the definition of "high" has simply climbed higher over the years.

Considered in its modern context, however, HDTV dates from a 1,125-line, wide-screen, stereophonic system of television developed by the Japanese network NHK and first shown in the United States in 1981 (see table on next page). While HDTV offered a tremendous improvement in both picture and sound, it did so, as usual, at a price. When first demonstrated in 1981, the HDTV system required *six* normal 6 MHz television channels to send only one signal! By the late 1980s, band compression and other techniques had cut this to 8.1 MHz—still too much to be compatible with the American system of television allocation but workable for satellite or cable transmission, assuming receivers were available to consumers. For this reason, the Japanese proposed leaving their conventional television system alone and reserving HDTV for a direct broadcast satellite system. This "you can get the high quality of HDTV only if you buy new equipment" approach clearly differs from the quest in the United States for compatible systems (see pp. 321–323) but would open vast new potential markets for equipment manufacturers.

Partially out of fear of contributing to yet another Japanese consumer electronic product influx, and in a desire to control their own technical standards, by 1987 several European countries had begun cooperative development of their own high-definition television tied to their 50 Hz electrical system, thus making synchronization between transmitter and receiver easier to achieve. And in the United States, several "advanced" television systems (ATVs) suggesting a kind of middle ground—higher-definition pictures compatible with existing sets—were announced and initially demonstrated in 1987–1988. In mid-1988, the FCC bowed to political reality and decided that any broadcast HDTV system in the United States

---

▪ **HDTV: Improving the Picture**   By the late 1980s, the major technical issue in broadcast and cable television was the eventual adoption of one or more systems of high-definition television (HDTV). Companies—and countries—vied to have their product adopted as *the* system in order to reap the huge potential, manufacturing, and trade benefits of worldwide use by the late 1990s. Many systems and approaches were suggested—this table illustrates only a sampling of the major systems projected.

System	Country (firm)	Bandwidth Required*	NTSC Compatible?	Aspect Ratio (wide : high)	Number Scan Lines	Comments
For Comparison: The Current American Standard						
NTSC	United States	6 MHz	Yes	4 : 3	525	Present American TV system in use since 1941; with color since 1953
A. Single-Channel Systems						
ACTV I	United States (David Sarnoff Research Center)	6 MHz	Yes	5 : 3	525	Two-stage system: first would enhance existing NTSC (ACTV II is found below)
Super NTSC	United States (Faroudja Laboratories)	6 MHz	Yes	4 : 3	525/ 1,050	Improved system for current receivers
HD-NTSC	United States (Del Rey Group)	6 MHz	Yes"	5 : 3	525	Higher-definition version of current NTSC TV
MUSE-6	Japan (NHK)	6 MHz	Yes"	16 : 9 or 4 : 3	525	Improved current system (one of several "narrow" MUSE options)
B. Dual-Channel/Wideband Systems						
MUSE	Japan (NHK)	9.+ MHz	No	16 : 9	1,125	The pioneering system, demonstrated in United States in 1981. Four digital sound channels
Eureka	European Consortium	na	No	16 : 9	1,250	Designed around European 625-line, 50-field system; prototypes promised 1989–1990
Vista (Glenn)	United States (New York Institute of Technology)	6 + 3 MHz	Yes	16 : 9	1,125	Would use two separate channels: receivers and VCRs would be cheaper
ACTV II	United States (David Sarnoff Research Center)	6 + 3 MHz	No	5 : 3	1,125	Two-channel full HDTV
HDS-NA	United States (North American Philips)	6 + 3 MHz	Yes"	16 : 9	1,050	

*6 MHz is NTSC channel width—any system showing more would have to use an additional spectrum and would require a converter to allow viewing on an NTSC-standard set.
"There will be some picture degradation of an advanced signal when shown on current NTSC receivers, and the wider aspect ratio will be either lost or shown only by masking the top and bottom of screen.
na = not available

Sources: HDTV: Planning for Action (Washington, D.C.: National Association of Broadcasters, 1988), page 45; *Business Week* (January 30, 1989), page 59; Walter S. Baer, "New Communications Systems and Services," in Paula Newberg, ed., *Working Papers in Telecommunications Policy* (New York: Markle Foundation, December 1988), page 27.

---

would have to accommodate the need to continue to supply programming to the nearly 90 million homes with NTSC-standard sets—for a time. But it had taken the British more than two decades to make a similar switch-over from their pre-World War II 405-line system to a 625-line one, and that conversion was speeded by providing color telecasts only on the newer system. By the end of the 1980s it appeared that some means of supplying higher-definition pictures was inevitable—but what form it would take was not clear. Many members of Congress—and Pentagon officials—felt that it would be necessary to support U.S. industry in this endeavor to prevent yet another part of the domestic electronics industry from moving production overseas.

However, even though receivers were not available, as early as 1987 some farsighted producers were using HDTV as a production medium; very expensive prototype cameras and other equipment were snapped up for the production of commercials and theatrical "films," with conversion to NTSC or 35mm film making them available to those using existing standards.

This was not the only new production device. Field cameras and recorders no longer required weight lifters to carry and needed less light for a good picture than film; mobile satellite transmission equipment (used for news coverage in most larger markets by the end of the decade) could fit in a suitcase; highly sophisticated character generators for inserting graphics on the screen were developed; and computerized animation or "paint boxes" were affordable by larger stations. The latter two permitted an operator sitting at a PC keyboard to replace a studio full of carefully painted backgrounds and mechanical counters during election or sports coverage. At the National Association of Broadcasters' convention, almost every other equipment exhibit booth shows a use of computers. A couple of generations of broadcast videotape recorders had come and gone, with smaller, better-quality, lighter, and electronically controlled one-inch machines replacing the original two-inch, four-head broadcast VTRs for entertainment, and a whole family of half-, three-quarter, and one-inch portable equipment for electronic field production (EFP) and news-gathering (ENG) was now in use. Solid state CCD cameras were lighter and more rugged than those using pickup tubes, although they initially did not have studio quality. While one could no longer expect a studio camera to last more than a decade—as was the case with early generations of television equipment—the additional bells and whistles produced by manufacturers each year often were used to persuade budget managers that planned obsolescence was not altogether bad if one gained new capabilities—and if one's competition had just bought that same new piece of gear.

10.1.3 Technology Overview

At the simpler, cheaper, and smaller end of the spectrum of consumer devices were ever-smaller radio and audiotape cassette machines with tiny earphones, allowing radio listening, often with surprisingly high fidelity (some devices had five-band graphic equalizers), in private in the midst of public places. Often called "walkmen" (after a Sony trade name), these radios were miniature throwbacks to the earliest days of radio listening, when earphones were a limitation rather than a benefit, but they also threatened the shiny, large "boom box" stereo radio-cassette players, except where seeing—and hearing—one's media had a social role to play. As discussed on p. 570, the FCC's unwillingness to set technical standards for AM stereo radio has led that development to stagnate, even though its proponents' belief that stereo would enable AM once again to become more popular than FM ignores both the higher fidelity of FM broadcasting and the pivotal place of programming in listener preferences (see pp. 526–529).

Where broadcasters had been sharply concerned by the rising number of competing delivery systems early in the 1980s, by 1987 they were considerably calmer, possibly more nimble, and perhaps more resigned to added competition. It appeared that only cable television among delivery systems, and VCRs among consumer electronics devices for the home, had broken into the magic circle of electronic media reaching a majority of homes, and both relied heavily on broadcast programming. Many other delivery options were of little interest to audiences and advertisers alike (see pp. 524–525).

Still at the center of it all, as had been the case since the late 1940s, were the family television receivers. They were larger now (26 inches was a common screen size, and projection screens up to several feet in diameter were selling briskly by the late 1980s) and were mostly in color. They were also increasingly augmented by improved sound—including some programs in stereo—and related systems such as a "picture-in-picture" circuit that enabled a viewer to watch at least part of two programs at once. Television receivers were as common in the bedroom as in the living room, and sets could be found almost anywhere in the home. Handheld remotes allowed one to change channels, adjust sound volume, and control VCRs without leaving one's chair. No matter what delivery system was used, the home (and, increasingly, portable) receiver still was needed to interface the program supplier and the viewer.

10.2 Stations and Systems

From the very beginning of radio broadcasting in the 1920s, the local service nature of the medium had been central in the way stations were owned and operated, the type of programming they provided their listeners (at least some of the time), and the advertisers to whom they appealed. This was a national policy, declared most clearly in the language of the Communications Act of 1934. Early television followed suit, though national programming took hold far earlier in the history of that more expensive medium. Yet, certainly by the late 1970s if not before, the once-local nature of radio and television had fundamentally changed, with a variety of implications for both older and newer media. In the ever-tighter competitive search for programming, advertiser support, and audiences, broadcast stations had evolved from locally programmed media often reflective of their community of license to mere local outlets for one or more national networks (television stations and cable systems) or formats (radio). A major force driving this change was the high cost of local production of any kind of program compared with the ability of networks and syndicators to spread their production costs across many outlets.

To some extent, this shift was due to the increased number of stations on the air—nearly 13,000 by late 1988 (not counting LPTV and other minor services), compared with fewer than 1,000 at the end of World War II—all competing for audiences and advertisers. But the change was also the result of deregulation (see pp. 566–569) that saw the FCC pulling back from imposing any kind of local service requirements. Stations became more like any other businesses in the eyes of most broadcasters—who were rapidly entering managerial ranks from business schools and other industries rather than from lower operational positions in broadcasting—and in the eyes of their regulators, thus making a once unique service with special "protections" more vulnerable to competition from unexpected quarters.

A strong indicator of the shift in role of broadcasting was the rapid change in ownership, causing ever-higher station prices, that characterized the 1980s. This increase in mergers and takeovers was sparked by the FCC's relaxation of long-standing multiple ownership and "trafficking" rules (see pp. 575–577) combined with a perception that many broadcasting companies were worth far more than their stock prices indicated. The most important rule change was the lifting of the number of stations any one entity could own from the 7 AM-7 FM-7 television limit set in the 1950s to a new 12-12-12 rule in 1985 (see pp. 576–577). The first of the cross-media mega-deals in the 1980s was the Westinghouse Broadcasting takeover of TelePrompTer, then the largest cable MSO, for $646 million in 1981. Westinghouse sold off its cable acquisition just four years later (by then 115 systems serving 2.1 million subscribers) for a substantial profit by dividing its systems among several previously competitive cable MSOs. The widespread buying and selling of cable systems, usually noted only by the communities served (and those lending money for the purpose), obscured the slow movement of more and more systems into the control of the top 100 (or top 10) MSOs, another change from theoretical local control to control by national corporations.

Other major deals concerned network control (see pp. 510–513) and the purchase of stations for breathtaking prices. Australian press baron Rupert Murdoch purchased the highly successful Metromedia chain of seven television stations (reaching about a fifth of the nation's population, close to the limit established in the 12-12-12 rule) in 1985 for $2 billion—and he had to become an American citizen before the FCC would allow him to take over the station's licenses. (This action put him in some difficulty in his native country.) The buy was a key part of his plan to develop a fourth over-the-air network (see p. 512).

Desperate for a toehold in the second largest market in the country, Tribune Broadcasting (WGN in Chicago and WPIX in New York) paid out $510 million for the license of Los Angeles independent television station

KTLA in 1985—a record price for any single broadcast outlet. KTLA had been purchased for $245 million just two years before by Golden West Broadcasters, so the station had, in effect, increased in value by about $300,000 for each *day* Golden West owned it before the sale to Tribune. Critics of deregulation pointed to such transfers as proof that an important "scarcity" still existed when demand for stations could lead to such prices.

As with many industries, there seemed to be an almost frantic tendency for media organizations to merge with, buy out, or otherwise acquire other media firms in order to grow larger, often at the expense of potential competition (see p. 506 and Appendix C, Table 9-D). While most media companies are quite small when compared with America's manufacturing and service giants, recent large acquisitions have involved big money. Rupert Murdoch bought *TV Guide* for $3 billion. Warner Communications, already a major supplier of television programming (Warner Brothers studio), bought one of the most successful production houses, Lorimar Telepictures, in 1988, and then almost immediately announced a proposed merger with Time Inc. (a large MSO, owner of HBO and other cable networks, and magazine and book publisher) early in 1989. Warner and Time would have an annual revenue of approximately $10 billion and will be the largest worldwide television producer, the largest magazine publisher, the largest record company, the second largest cable operator, the largest pay-TV programmer, and the largest direct marketer of books in the United States.

10.2.1 FM Pulls Ahead

The radio business faced an increasingly difficult competitive situation after 1977 as a steadily larger number of stations fought for a more slowly expanding advertising market and listener pool. In most cities, radio stations had to make do with a smaller proportion of both. Some stations could not find formats to increase audiences quickly enough and either changed hands (some stand-alone AM stations were sold at a loss in the 1980s) or went off the air. But the decade after 1977 is mainly the story of an historical reversal, with the longtime second service, FM, finally coming out on top. Although the number of AM and FM stations were roughly the same, by the late 1980s FM radio stations collectively served about three-quarters of the nation's radio audience.

There were no surprise reasons for this change. For decades, it had been known by broadcasters and advertisers—and the public—that FM stations aired music with higher fidelity, were not subject to most natural and manmade static, could now be easily tuned, had a dependable and calculable service area, and could stay on the air 24 hours a day—unlike AM stations, which usually could meet only one or two of these standards. Further, by the late 1970s FM receivers in all sizes and price ranges were universally available. Almost all new automobiles now had AM-FM receivers, and many had audio cassette players. Now the public realized all of this, and its infatuation with stereo high-fidelity music caused it to gravitate toward FM. Although most FM channel assignments had been applied for by the mid-1980s, the FCC allocated an additional several hundred channels, causing the audience-advertiser pie to be split even more ways. Because of the FM signal's line-of-sight range, however, this step caused less interference on the FM band than adding more AM stations would have caused on its band.

The FCC's halfhearted support of AM stereo (see p. 570—actually, the commission avoided the decision on which system to adopt, leaving it to the marketplace, which had kept its hands off as well), its allowing of higher power for the smallest stations, and its arranging with Canada and Mexico for more U.S. AM stations to stay on the air for more hours helped AM, but not much. International plans to expand the standard broadcast band some 10 channels beyond its then 1605 kHz upper boundary would only provide more competition for the beleaguered existing AM broadcasters—but it would also supply a toehold in the business for hungry newcomers to the industry. The real reason for AM's decline, although each of the factors mentioned above is real, was programming (see pp. 526–527).

10.2.2 Is More Television Better?

Although some new television receivers have the ability to show more than one picture at a time, and the substantial majority of the public with VCRs can record one program while watching another, it is nevertheless true that one can pay attention to only one program at a time—and there is a finite amount of programming talent.

The need for more programming became evident in the late 1970s. The pressure came, in part, from a growing number of independent television stations, many on UHF. There were 78 such stations in 1980 and more than 250 by early 1989, strengthening their political clout to the point where the Independent Television Association (INTV) was able to schedule a dinner on the same night as the NAB's—and draw an equally impressive lineup of congressmen and regulators. The FCC had spent a lot of time and money in the 1970s on a variety of studies, reporting to Congress on how to improve UHF television transmission and reception, so that UHF, the proverbial second-class service, could compete more equally with VHF, though always subject to the basic spectrum propagation limitations imposed by nature.

The growing number of independent stations (from 120 in 1980 to nearly 300 in 1988) tended to be "lean and mean," willing to experiment with programming, technology, and other new ideas. Because the independent stations are able to move fast, it is probable that when higher picture definition becomes feasible they will jump faster than most network affiliates, if they can afford to. But the outlook is not all favorable. Most independent stations, except for a handful in the largest markets—such as WGN (Chicago), WPIX (New York), KTLA (Los Angeles), and WTBS (Atlanta), which are serving as superstations supplying programming to cable systems around the country—are constantly on the thin edge of bankruptcy. Programming costs are kept as low as possible—few have any news staff— and only nimble counterprogramming (for example, running entertainment programs while the network affiliates are airing news) brings in a large enough audience to attract advertisers. In markets where specialization pays off, independent stations tend to air older feature films, some sporting events, game shows, children's cartoons, and hour after hour of old network reruns. Even though independent stations brag about their status, there are few that would not jump at a network affiliation (even with as new an entity as struggling Fox—see p. 512) if one were offered.

Network affiliates (the number of which varied little in this period), on the other hand, often have fallen into a rut. Programming relies on the network and on tried-and-true syndicated programs. Even news, where the most competition occurs, tends to cloning of content and personnel. The number of affiliates of the three major commercial networks is unlikely to grow substantially, since no more than one station is affiliated in a given market. A fourth commercial network, such as Fox, would have to draw its affiliates from the ranks of independent stations, although as one network's programming goes down in popularity and another's goes up, there are occasional defections of strong stations from the weaker to the stronger network. This sort of change, of course, has a ripple effect through an entire market.

One attempt to broaden the variety of people able to own and operate television stations was the well-intentioned but apparently misguided attempt by the FCC to launch a low-power television (LPTV) system in the early 1980s. Based on results of some Canadian experiments, the FCC late in 1980 announced its intention to establish potentially thousands of spectrum allotments for tiny television stations. Most would be UHF outlets, using up to 100 watts of power (or in some cases VHF, with only 10 watts) for a coverage area with a radius of up to five or six miles. These new stations would be dropped into the existing allocation structure of full-power stations but with the new LPTV outlets forced to shield the larger stations from interference. The FCC claimed to be looking forward to a new age of neighborhood television stations and rural services where none existed thus far, and for outlets owned by members of minority groups and women, for a (relatively) low construction price of perhaps $200,000. Naturally, legislators representing the communities where the new stations would locate were in favor of the plan—and the goodwill the FCC got at first was perhaps its only reward.

Two problems arose immediately. For one thing, the FCC was so impressed with its brainchild that it allowed applications to be filed even before final forms and rules had been developed. Some individuals, groups, and firms (such as Sears, Roebuck and Co., which planned a network of more than 100 LPTV stations) filed literally hundreds of applications, and consulting engineers and lawyers cranked them out in assembly line fashion.

Belatedly calling for a freeze on new applications, the commission began to dig through the pile of paper, the processing of which had become more legally complicated than getting the new service on the air. The pressure from impatient LPTV applicants was one reason the FCC approached Congress requesting permission to select applicants by means of a lottery rather than by expensive and time-consuming comparative hearings. In 1982, Congress agreed, and, helped by new computers, the commission began to process applications, allowing the first stations to go on the air.

The other problem was more serious and long lasting—how to support such tiny stations. Advertisers were not usually interested in their miniscule audiences, and few stations could afford the fees to secure programming for pay-TV (already available on cable in most cases). While new networks of LPTV stations were a possibility, most knowledgeable broadcasters (and, eventually, many nonprofit or alternative media groups) decided that there was little to gain from LPTV. By the end of 1988, 455 LPTV stations were on the air (with call letters that included their channel number), mainly in rural and some suburban areas, and another 1,359 had been granted construction permits. But the dream of a viable new television service seemed as far away as ever, and the total LPTV audience was miniscule.

Another minor entry into the television outlet business was a service oddly named "wireless cable" to try to make its function more understandable to the public. More formally known as a multichannel multipoint distribution service (MMDS) or a multipoint distribution service (MDS), this is a microwave broadcast (rather than point-to-point) delivery system, originally created by the FCC in the 1960s for business-related common carrier use. With channels widened to carry video signals in the 1970s, and then with a total of eight channels allotted to each of the top 50 markets in 1983, MMDS took on the potential of competing with cable in some unwired urban areas. Being a "broadcast" service (although the FCC vacillated between regulating it as a common carrier or as a broadcast service), MMDS was far less expensive to build (just a transmitter and special antennas) than the wired connections between a cable system's headend and each home served. Subscribers still had to pay for their own receivers. But its operators suffered limited growth in the face of the cable industry's reluctance to sell them cable-controlled programming. By 1988, MMDS served only a small proportion of the national audience and faced a bleak future as the number of cities lacking cable service dwindled.

A variation of MMDS, keeping costs even lower, used leased time in the evenings on the instructional television fixed-service (ITFS) channels in the same band as MMDS that were owned and operated by educational or religious organizations for educational programming during the rest of the day. The payments from MMDS operators were very welcome to the educational licensees, and the MMDS operators benefited by not having to apply or pay fully for their own facilities. As the 1980s drew to a close, the future of this service was unclear.

An older television broadcast service saw a brief period of marginal success from 1977 to the early 1980s and then succumbed to newer competition. As noted on pp. 416–417, though the FCC had approved a new system of subscription television (STV) in 1968, the first two channels (in New York and Los Angeles) did not air until 1977 because of regulatory constraints. By 1983, about 27 pay stations were in operation, most offering scrambled pay signals at night and regular "in the clear" broadcasts during the day. Another 20 outlets were announced as being in various stages of planning. But the surface success was misleading, and the licensees knew it. Pay-cable, with multiple channels, was rapidly expanding and closing down opportunities for STV stations providing but a single channel of premium programming. By 1987, only two STV outlets remained in business, both of them LPTV stations. The former STV stations had nearly all converted to regular (independent) broadcast operations, some of them specializing in "home-shopping" programming, which became popular and profitable in the late 1980s.

10.2.3 Cable—The New Basic Distributor

One of the most important single changes in electronic media in this era was the expansion of cable television from a minority service to a majority distributor of video. As is evident in Appendix C, Table 9-B, the number of cable systems and subscribers increased substantially in this period. Cable penetration soared from just under 18% in 1977 to more than 52% in 1988. A variety of factors contributed to this rapid expansion after several decades of slow growth to the late 1970s.

Perhaps most important was the convergence of several kinds of demand. Television viewers were interested in getting clearer reception of local stations even in well-served markets and wanted some distant (usually independent) stations for their movies and sports. By the late 1970s, demand for pay-cable services by viewers interested in a new way to see films, and by cablecasters eager for a piece of additional income, helped to lead the way to cable expansion. After 1980, desire for the specialized new services (see p. 516), especially news and sports, attracted viewers who did not care about movies. Important too was the rapid deregulation of cable (see pp. 467–469) by the courts and the FCC after the mid-1970s. This had the effect of reducing uncertainty about what programming cablecasters could carry and settling the nagging question of copyright (see pp. 577–578).

As cable systems increased in importance nationally, they also became more controversial in many markets. The late 1970s were a time of frantic competition for long-term (usually 15-year) franchises in the last cities and suburban areas to be wired. The cost of applying for a major franchise, often several hundred thousand dollars, was a factor in industry consolidation, for smaller companies could not compete in the face of such financial pressures. Several scandals resulted from cable company payoffs to city officials, and plenty of perfectly legal but less than ethical means were used to obtain franchise agreements. Most popular was the technique of giving a small portion of the stock of an applicant to various officials and community leaders in return for their backing. Sometimes the fault lay with the city's excessive demands—in one case, a successful applicant had to promise to plant several thousand trees in the community. In what was logically an adversarial relationship, the main cable trade group, the National Cable Television Association (NCTA), constantly faced several associations of city officials, especially the National League of Cities, as each tried to get the upper hand in persuading Congress and the FCC. Until the late 1980s, cable did consistently well in these policy and legal face-offs, in part because of strong congressional support. Cable played on its "local" nature and often donated time to incumbent officials to curry favor.

As with broadcasting and other media, cable's expansion was fueled in part by a growing trend toward consolidation of ownership. Where the business had been characterized by "Mom and Pop" small-town community antennas into the 1960s, by the 1970s cable showed signs of both needing and attracting big money. Needing cash because of the capital-intensive nature of building new systems before any income was forthcoming, cable owners found that larger systems were more attractive to lenders. Cable became a more impersonal business as a result. By the late 1980s, Tele-Communications Inc. (TCI) was the largest multiple system operator (MSO), with about 20% of all cable subscribers. Its president, John Malone, constantly defended his firm's success while others held up TCI as an example of corporate greed and a portent of where cable was headed. Neither Mom nor Pop remained part of the cable picture (see Appendix C, Table 9-D).

For a brief time (1977–1984) many eyes were on Columbus, Ohio, as the Warner-Amex cable franchise there operated its "Qube" system featuring five interactive channels. Widely publicized across the country, the interactive channels allowed viewers to vote on simple questions in talk shows and the like. Many predictions were made about the potential for wide adoption of such technology for future polls and shopping. But Warner found that few subscribers used the feature after the novelty wore off, and Qube's interactive channels closed down in 1984 after a loss of some $30 million. Some pessimists felt the end of Qube might spell the real end of the wired city concept (in which homes would be connected by cable networks and computers rather than by broadcast channels) that had been discussed and debated for almost 20 years.

One final but always faithful indicator of cable's increasing importance among electronic media was the competitive reaction of other media. Jack Valenti, longtime Washington lobbyist for the motion picture industry, seemed to build his speeches in the 1980s around attacks on cable, describing it as a monopoly menace controlling a bottleneck delivery system into the nation's homes. The National Association of Broadcasters, too, was constantly bickering with the NCTA about such concerns as must-carry and cross-ownership rules (see pp. 575–577).

By late in the 1980s, it seemed that cable's success curve in both the marketplace and the policy arena was likely to turn downward. For one thing, most initial franchise construction was finished, leaving only system enlargement by reconstruction and, more likely, takeovers of small companies by larger ones. There was some concern that cable "overbuilds" (a hitherto rare situation in which a second company installs a parallel network in a given community, competing directly for subscribers) might result. For another, over half of the audience owned VCRs and often used them rather than watching either over-the-air or cable television.

10.3 Networks: A New Age

In the mid-1980s, American commercial broadcasting networks underwent more changes than they had since their establishment 40 to 60 years before. They changed ownership; they did not exactly welcome a great deal of competition; and even the definition of "network" changed. No longer was a network "two or more stations interconnected by some means or associated for the often simultaneous transmission of the same messages or programs." With VCRs and round-the-clock cable services such as CNN, the need for simultaneous transmission to the public disappeared, and the medium serving the public often was a cable system that carried the local affiliate broadcasting station. Interconnections now were by satellite links rather than wire or microwave circuits.

10.3.1 New Entrants

The worlds of broadcasting and cable networking were made more exciting, less predictable, and perhaps riskier by the activities of worldwide press baron Rupert Murdoch and broadcast and cable entrepreneur Ted Turner. Able to command the power of millions of dollars of their own and of other investors, both men moved to take important ownership positions in broadcasting and cable services. Turner came first with what became his "superstation," WTBS-TV in Atlanta, followed by the Cable News Network (see p. 540) and Turner Network Television (TNT!) in 1988.

Turner specialized in ideas that others had not thought of or had rejected. For example, his synergistic ownership of a small Atlanta UHF television station and the Atlanta Braves led to an attractive package for cable system operators when it was made available (for a small sum per month per subscriber) via satellite. In addition, Turner could charge advertisers national advertising prices for what originally was a small UHF station! Some of Turner's later investments—in companies owning feature films, such as MGM, for example—were to ensure plenty of "product" for WTBS to distribute. Turner, whose ability to plan and take risks led to his being captain of more than one America's Cup sailboat racing defender, at one time also tried to purchase CBS (see p. 511). His establishment of *CNN*, thought by many to be a financially foolish move, turned out to be a success. Although the bankers achieved stronger control over Turner's empire when he needed cash to start new ventures, his ability to come up with successful ideas has seldom been matched in broadcasting's history.

Rupert Murdoch, whose life story parallels those of other press magnates, such as the Canadian-born Lord Thomson of Fleet, started his career buying and operating newspapers in his native Australia. Soon he owned a major share of Australian commercial television broadcasting and expanded his activities to other continents, buying newspapers, magazines, and broadcasting stations. His interest in starting a fourth network—the first since the abortive Overmyer Network (see p. 422) 20 years before—predated his purchase of the Metromedia group of seven stations (see p. 500). In 1984, Murdoch had taken a half-interest in 20th Century-Fox, buying the rest in 1985. He announced his plans to combine the production capacity of the film studio with the former Metromedia stations, and future affiliated stations, to create the Fox television network. He planned to begin his new network slowly, with a late-evening program, and then expand into prime time, adding a day or so each year. In 1988, he added to his broadcasting-related properties with the $3 billion purchase of Triangle Publications, including the immensely popular (and profitable) weekly *TV Guide*—which might be a useful vehicle with which to publicize the Fox network.

In the United States, Murdoch had to become an American citizen (at some legal risk to his Australian broadcasting holdings) in order to buy television stations. In the 1986–1988 period, he owned television stations and major daily newspapers in the same cities—WNYW and the *New York Post*, and WFXT and the *Boston Herald*. Although such cross-ownership of media in the same market was against FCC rules, the commission traditionally granted waivers for a year or two until one or the other medium could be sold. Murdoch decided to fight the rule and showed himself to be a master of political public relations when he went on the offensive after a clause was inserted by Senator Ted Kennedy at the last minute into a Senate appropriations bill that forbade the FCC to drop the rule or grant indefinite waivers under the guise of "deregulation." It so happened that Murdoch's stations were the only ones waiting for such waivers, and he went a long way toward establishing himself as an underdog. Later, he tried to place some of his holdings in trust, but even that had to be modified to include a firm commitment to sell some. Meanwhile, as all-channel (VHF-UHF) receivers became universal, and as more UHF stations were established in larger cities, the Fox television network found many more independent stations hoping for a network affiliation than had been available to Overmyer (or Kaiser or DuMont before him; see pp. 290, 422). By keeping a close eye on expenses, Murdoch seemed more likely to succeed than his predecessors (see p. 512).

As discussed later (see p. 616), new radio networks appeared in the 1980s for the first time in decades as satellite delivery made specific kinds of music and talk formats less expensive.

10.3.2 Competitive Pressures

Broadcast networks flourished—as did the American economy, for the most part—in the late 1970s. The antitrust suits brought in 1972 (see pp. 419–420) were eventually settled—NBC's in 1976, with ABC and CBS falling into line in 1980. But while the overall pattern of network dominance of television continued, traditional over-the-air networks saw their audiences (in terms of percentages, if not absolute numbers fed by population growth) dwindle slightly every year after the mid-1980s as a result of competition from both VCRs and cable. An excellent snapshot of the television networks both at the peak of their power and on the brink of decline is found in the 1980 report of the third FCC network inquiry.

Following the Barrow report (see pp. 391–392), the FCC did not again assign a special staff to report on network television for two decades. An Office of Network Study reviewed network programming practices but had little impact on policy and faded from sight in the late 1960s. A few years later, however, affiliates' displeasure with the tiny amount of then-huge network profits being paid to them began to reach the ears of the commission as well as stockholders. Specifically, Westinghouse Broadcasting and Cable Inc., which owned stations affiliated with each of the three networks, filed a formal petition with the FCC in 1976 asking for an investigation of affiliate compensation and other network practices. Pressure from Congress contributed to the FCC's formation of a Network Study Special Staff in 1978.

Codirected by an attorney and an economist (an indication of how much the latter field had caught up with the former in helping to shape regulation of business), the inquiry developed or contracted for 18 staff reports issued in 1979–1980 examining both traditional broadcasting and the developing new services. Taken together, the studies, issued in only limited numbers, provide an excellent view of the industry as it existed at that time and how it was expected to develop. The final report took a very different approach from its 1941 and 1957 predecessors. It strongly criticized most existing commission rules limiting network behavior, saying that they usually did not work and, at any rate, that their economic cost was far higher than any social gain. The development of cable and other competing services sparked the network staff to urge on the commission a welcoming approach to newer services seeking to compete with the traditional networks rather than the generally restrictive approaches taken thus far.

But when the FCC moved to act on the study's recommendations, voices of the competition—those now "in" rather than those trying to gain a foothold—were heard loud and clear. A plan to drop the Prime Time Access

Rule led to heavy pressure from the program-producing industry based in Hollywood, which had been given new life by the rule when it was instituted in 1974. Similarly, a 1983 attempt to drop some complicated and somewhat arcane rules banning networks' financial interest in the entertainment programs they carried, or in their subsequent syndication, also brought Hollywood pressure groups out in strength. FCC chairman Mark Fowler was called in for an unprecedented dressing down (press releases spoke of a "briefing") by President Ronald Reagan, who may have thought back to his movie actor days when he made it clear that the FCC was to leave the network-limiting rules in place. Despite these careful studies showing the television networks to have less power than they once did, old rules set up to protect then-defenseless programmers from network controls would not be easily dropped, even after the ratings services and headlines showed everyone that the day of the all-powerful networks was done. In 1988, the FCC turned to another of the now-eight-year-old recommendations of its network study and announced plans to ease rules banning network ownership of cable systems.

10.3.3 Network Upheaval

> In a matter of months during 1986 the television industry was transformed beyond recognition. All three of the commercial networks—against which the progress of the other media inevitably is measured—came under new ownership or leadership. Each of the acquirers pledged to run these huge television machines in a more businesslike fashion than before, with fewer frills and executive perquisites, less staff, greater cost control and strict attention to the bottom line. So the networks have lost during the past year not only their near total domination of the television market but also their swagger, their corporate identities and perhaps also their hallowed traditions.—Les Brown, writing in *Channels Field Guide, 1987*, p. 9

The upheaval that longtime television critic Brown reports was sudden—it cracked open a closed network shop that had operated with unchanged ownership and surprisingly static management since 1953. The revolution began with the industry-stunning announcement in March 1985 that group owner Capital Cities Communications was taking control of the American Broadcasting Companies, operator of the ABC radio and television networks, in a $3.5 billion deal. ABC chairman Leonard Goldenson, who had taken over ABC in 1953 (see p. 288), had, on the eve of his retirement, decided to sell his shares. The FCC approved the sale in November (a marked contrast to the months of proceedings concerning ABC in 1953–1954). The company changed its name to Capital Cities/ABC. Cap Cities, as it was known, and its chairman, Thomas Murphy, had a well-deserved reputation for attention to the bottom line, and ABC was merely the first of the networks to resort to layoffs to prune overexpanded staffs and improve short-term profitability.

In contrast to the friendly takeover of ABC, Atlanta-based Ted Turner announced just a few months later a brash attempt at an unfriendly (his target was clearly not interested) bid for control of the much larger CBS. While given little chance of success by most Wall Street experts, the takeover attempt was in the headlines for weeks as both sides maneuvered. CBS chairman Thomas Wyman (he had replaced John Backe in 1980 and had become chairman when founder William Paley retired in 1983) headed the network's defense while overseeing its now widely diversified assets. Late in 1985, Turner withdrew his offer—having sold his own CBS stock back to the network for a tidy profit. In fighting off Turner, however, CBS had gone deeply into debt to buy back a fifth of its own shares. Thus weakened and needing cash, CBS had to sell off its St. Louis owned and operated station KMOX-TV and accept the friendly purchase of a large minority of its shares (just under 25%) by Loew's Inc. (chiefly hotels and movie theaters) chairman Laurence Tisch.

Late in 1986, after a boardroom tussle in which Tisch and Paley collaborated, Wyman was eased out and Tisch became the chief operating officer of the network. William Paley was brought back into the now largely ceremonial position of chairman. The Tisch era at CBS began with a new (for CBS) era of austerity, with extensive personnel layoffs, low resultant morale at CBS News (even an offer to buy the news division by several of its key employees), and the selling of many of the network's nonbroadcast interests. One of these sales, in early 1988, was of Columbia Records to Sony for $2 billion. The changes at CBS were reflected in its unaccustomedly poor audience ratings— the network ended the 1987–1988 season in third place for the first time in its history. A much smaller company than either of its competitors after all these sales, CBS in the late 1980s seemed ready to use its hoard of several billion dollars to expand its self-defined sphere of broadcasting (and possibly cable) operations. Late in 1988, CBS bought control of a VHF station in Miami, increasing its O & O holdings to five (see p. 289).

Change came as well to NBC. In January 1978, the network announced a substantial coup—it had hired away ABC program chief Fred Silverman to become its new president. Silverman was then an industry *wunderkind* who could do no wrong and who seemed to have a magic touch with programming. He had propelled longtime number three ABC to the top of the ratings heap. But this final shift (Silverman was the only executive to have had senior programming positions with all three networks) was one too many. NBC floundered through a series of expensive program disasters and stayed in the ratings basement. Finally, in June 1981, RCA's chairman Thornton Bradshaw replaced Silverman with the widely respected programming chief of MTM Productions, Grant Tinker. Tinker wrought wonders for NBC with his quiet, relaxed California style of management and sure sense of the right balance between high quality and popularity in programming. NBC moved to first place in network ratings in 1983 and stayed at or near the top for the rest of the decade.

But dramatic change was also coming for the senior network. Late in 1986, the broadcasting community was surprised to hear that NBC's parent, RCA, had been taken over by General Electric in a $6.28 billion deal—and that thus NBC would be under new ownership. The sale represented an ironic return to its origins by RCA—for, as detailed on pp. 57–58, General Electric had created RCA in 1919. A year later, Tinker retired as NBC's president to return to his first love, Hollywood program development, and the network was taken over by a GE official. One of Robert Wright's first decisions, in July 1987, was to sell off the NBC Radio Network (for $50 million to Westwood One), thus giving up on radio networking to concentrate on the more lucrative television service and then selling the NBC-owned and -operated radio stations piecemeal. The pioneering radio network was no longer in the radio business.*

As mentioned earlier (see pp. 290 and 422), the possibilities of a fourth commercial television network had been discussed and even attempted several times. But that inveterate acquirer of media properties, Rupert Murdoch, appeared in the late 1980s to be making the best try yet at establishing a fourth network in 1986 with the Fox (named after movie studio 20th Century-Fox, which he also owned) television network (see p. 508).

This is not to say that the Fox network found easy sailing: its first big show, a late-evening attempt to compete with the venerable *Tonight* show starring Johnny Carson, featured Joan Rivers (a frequent Carson vacation substitute). In only a matter of months, Rivers and Fox came to a parting of the ways, probably due to the program's low ratings—and Carson's resentment over her defection seemed likely to put a crimp in her future career. Fox then presented several prime time original (but inexpensive) series programs for two evenings a week. Ratings were poor, however, and by 1988, some affiliated stations were reverting to the independent mode of playing movies and off-network reruns rather than sticking with a ship only half afloat. But after Fox obtained the rights to popular specials such as the 1988 Emmy Awards, stations found the economics of affiliation with Fox more favorable. In June 1988, Fox's deleting all political content of a multihour rock concert in honor of black South African leader Nelson Mandela raised a great deal of protest, particularly from performers in the concert. (In the 1990s, Murdoch's Asian direct broadcast satellite venture was similarly attacked for its kowtowing to China.) Nevertheless, Fox's plans remained on schedule, with a third evening of prime time programming scheduled to start in mid-1989. Fox reported losses of $80 million in fiscal 1988—an indication of just how expensive starting up a fourth network could be.

Radio networking—or, in 1980s terms, national distribution of program formats—revived to some extent in the 1980s, thanks to both satellite

---

*RCA suffered further dismemberment when its consumer electronics division was sold to a French company. By this time, only one major American company—Zenith—still manufactured television receivers in the United States, and it gave up in the late 1990s.

▥ **The Networks' Eye in the Sky**   An artist shows how the early Westar VI satellite could cover the continental United States with "spot beams" aimed at Hawaii and Alaska (over the horizon in this view) from its geosynchronous orbit, 22,300 miles out in space above the equator. Communication satellites so located also allowed broadcast and cable networks in the 1980s to efficiently cover vast areas like the entire country, moving electronic media from reliance on terrestrial wire, cable, and microwave links to application of space age technology for their interconnection.

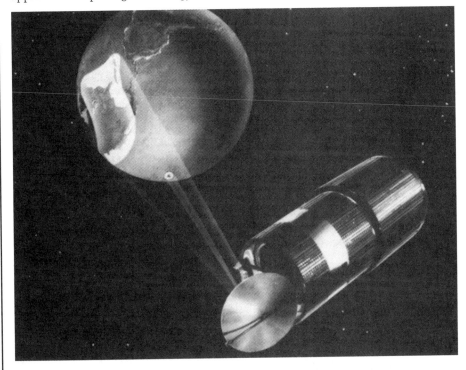

Courtesy NASA.

technology (see p. 486) and more competition among the increasing number of stations. Following television's example, a satellite transponder allowed a radio program service to reach hundreds of potential subscriber radio stations (many of them fully automated) without the need for expensive wired interconnections. By the late 1980s, despite some consolidation, there were more than 20 services, most delivered by satellite. Transtar Radio Network and Satellite Music Network, for example, together produced 15 different 24-hour music formats. National Public Radio and American Public Radio were early and successful users of satellite technology for program distribution.

At the same time, traditional radio networks—music and news services—changed hands. ABC had the most affiliated stations, as was the case for nearly two decades (see Appendix C, Table 2-B). Westwood One, a California-based syndicated program service, purchased the Mutual network from Amway in 1985 for $39 million and, as noted earlier, added the

NBC radio network to its growing holdings to broaden its role as a provider of middle-of-the-road features and music services. Westwood, then the second largest network operation, continued to operate as NBC, Mutual, and the original Westwood One program service.

10.3.4 Coming of Cable Networks

Although space communications satellites became increasingly important in both television and radio broadcasting program distribution in the 1980s, this was old hat to cable programmers. The pioneering efforts of HBO and Turner (see p. 411) started a bandwagon of new services (see the table below), all seeking to differentiate their content from rivals and all seeking to secure use of a transponder on one of the few satellites to which early cable system television receive-only antennas (TVROs) were aimed. Indeed, until TVRO costs declined after 1980, allowing a system operator to install multiple dishes aimed at different birds, it was important for cable program services to be on the same satellite as their competitors. Cable's demand for satellite transponders was equaled by the demand of other users (the

---

■ **Auxiliary Television Services 1977–1989**   While over-the-air pay broadcasting (STV, not to be confused with DBS) had a fairly short life span, multichannel multipoint distribution services (MMDSs) and low-power television (LPTV) appeared to offer a niche service option to full-power television stations by the end of the 1980s. For the success of competing cable, see Appendix C, Table 9-B.

Year	STV		MDS/MMDS		LPTV Stations on Air
	Stations	Subscribers (thousands)	Systems	Subscribers (thousands)	
1977		5	27	65	
1978	2	59	29	91	
1979	3	260	44	207	
1980	6	520	54	352	
1981	14	1,082	73	479	
1982	24	1,747	99	570	na
1983	29	1,823	na	570	na
1984	12	1,203	na	490	252
1985	6	622	na	440	316
1986	3	187	na	270	383*
1987	2	118	na	240	407
1988	2	100	na	200	346
1989	na	na	na	na	457

*1986 data as of February 25.

Sources: STV and MMDS data through 1982 from Paul Kagan associates, " Census of Pay TV Population," in *MDS Databook 1982*, page 13, as listed in Sterling (1984), pages 33 and 255 (see Appendix D for full citation), showing data as of June 30 (MDS) and December 31 of *previous* year for STV stations. STV and MDS data since 1982 from *Kagan Media Index* (May 17, 1988), page 8, citing data for last day of *previous* year. All LPTV data directly from FCC, showing outlets licensed (not all are on the air) as of December 31 of the *previous* year.

military and telecommunications carriers, for example), but it took several years to translate the demand into new satellite capacity in orbit.

Beginning with HBO's pioneering use of *Satcom I* in 1976, and lasting into the early 1980s, the driving force in cable networking—and hence in the overall growth of the cable industry—was the appeal of pay-cable services to the public. Pay pioneer HBO was always the largest in number of subscribers (Appendix C, Table 9-C). This Time Inc. service first faced competition after March 1978 when Showtime, another first-run movie oriented service begun two years earlier in California, started satellite distribution. Other services started in the next two years included The Movie Channel, which became the first to provide movies 24 hours a day; Cinemax, also owned by Time Inc. and counterprogrammed with HBO; The Playboy Channel, carrying soft-core adult material; and several short-lived rivals, including at least two that attempted to provide more high-brow arts and performance content.

All of these pay-cable networks worked in much the same way. The pay service bought pay-cable rights to theatrical films or other content and sometimes produced special events itself. It then persuaded the cable system operator to carry and promote its service. The cable system operator then set about collecting money from the subscribers. First, there was a flat monthly fee for "basic" service (originally just on-air stations, and later inexpensive national services, such as superstations in Atlanta, Chicago, Los Angeles, and New York, for which the operator paid a few cents per subscriber per month). With pay-cable, the operator also could charge an additional flat monthly fee (usually $7 to $10 by the mid-1980s) for everything carried by pay-cable services. (Usually, half of this fee was remitted to the pay-cable service.) Toward the end of the decade, many systems also offered pay-per-view (PPV), which brought in money for each showing ordered by the subscriber (see below). Each service offered a monthly menu of movies and specials, repeated on different days and at different times. Eventually, most cable operators had two or three tiers of service, each adding to the subscriber's cost.

By the mid-1980s, the pay-cable boom had flattened as the number of subscribers giving up service ("churn" in cable parlance) about equaled those signing up. Among the factors blamed were the increasing use of home VCRs (see pp. 410–411 and 490–493), the ever-rising prices charged subscribers (particularly after the 1984 Cable Communications Policy Act [see pp. 574–575] allowed cable operators to ignore restrictions in their franchises), and the limited amount of high-quality programming. The average cost per cable household per month had tripled to nearly $30, but the psychological limit still had not been reached. More than half of American households now subscribed to cable, and the cable MSOs looked around for additional ways to profit even while they engaged in wheeling-and-dealing consolidation. One way was a new version of an old idea—the notion of paying to see a specific program rather than subscribing to everything carried over a channel or tier. This would be analogous to buying a single issue of a magazine at the newsstand rather than subscribing for a year at a much lower price per issue. Over-the-air pay-TV proponents of the 1950s originally had planned to charge for specific programs (see pp. 353–355) but had been unsuccessful.

In the late 1970s, cable or MMDS operators in several major markets regularly transmitted scrambled pictures of special sports events. To receive an unscrambled picture, viewers could telephone the system and agree to pay a one-time charge to clear up the picture. The system's first regular national nonsports pay–per–view (PPV) services aired in November 1985 when Viewer's Choice, owned by Showtime/The Movie Channel, and Request Television began. PPV could be offered only on cable systems with computer-addressable decoder boxes, allowing instant descrambling of the PPV channel when viewers called to order a specific showing. The charges of $3 to $5 for each movie or event were very profitable for the cable operator, the PPV company, and the original supplier of the programming. PPV differed from HBO and other pay-cable channels by providing only a few first-run movies (often while they were still in theatrical release) or sporting events per month, heavily promoted and repeated at different times to catch all possible viewers. Much as the earliest television sets were to be found in public places like taverns, many members of the public first became aware of the possibilities of PPV by its availability in many hotel rooms.

Following the path of the pay services (but much less expensive to the supplier) came advertiser-supported basic cable networks, some of which charged systems to carry their service but were designed to be free of additional cost to viewers. However, speculation in the 1970s that there would be a flood of highly specialized cable services providing narrowcasts to targeted audiences, as a counter to the broadcast business, did not materialize. The costs of developing specific programming delivered by satellite to relatively small numbers of viewers were just too high. Some observers believed that the amount of talent needed to produce such programming also was near its limit. Thus, much of cable television increasingly began to resemble broadcasting in its content, even on services designed specifically for cable. Several cable networks tried to repeat the old radio approach of being all things to all viewers (such as the USA Network beginning in 1980, which relied heavily on broadcast reruns), while others took a specific programming niche (for example, Christian Broadcasting Network [CBN], one of the first and most widely successful conservative religious/family-oriented cable services; MTV, the first 24-hour music video service, beginning in 1981; C-SPAN, Cable Special Public Affairs Network, which, among other things, carried all proceedings from the House of Representatives and later the U.S. Senate on C-SPAN II, and The Weather Channel, starting in mid-1982). And, as discussed further on p. 540, Ted Turner's Cable News Network helped to change television journalism practice—and audience viewing habits—after 1980.

By the late 1980s, the impact of cable was being felt at the broadcast networks, each of which had lost audience and income from the competition, and in homes across the country, where the notion of "network" now included dozens of satellite- and cable-delivered services. One indicator of cable's increasing importance was growing concern over concentration among cable programmers and system operators. MSOs got larger, and independent system operators grew fewer (see Appendix C, Table 9-D). Another indication was the steady increase in space devoted to cable program listings in *TV Guide.*

10.4 Public Broadcasting (Still) Seeks Its Place

Public broadcasting both progressed and regressed in the years after 1977. This should come as no surprise. As noted on p. 426, interorganizational squabbles and questions of long-range funding pervaded the system in the mid-1970s—as they still did in the late 1980s. The problem was partially organizational politics, but underlying the malaise was a continued search for the right role—and an audience. Public television still lacked a cohesive sense of what its mission should be. Even public radio, always more focused, had troubles in the 1980s. As one wag put it, if public broadcasting officials were armed and asked to form a firing squad, they would stand in a circle!

One timely indicator of the problems was the report of a second Carnegie commission (Carnegie II). Those frustrated by many years of confusion centered their hopes on this effort, remembering the impact of the first commission a decade earlier (see p. 424). But times had changed. The second report, *A Public Trust,* issued in January 1979 after a year and a half of study, included a detailed accounting of what had been accomplished in public broadcasting's first decade and described the continuing problems of inadequate long-range funding and of insulation of programming from political pressures. Unfortunately, its call for substantially higher federal funding reached Congress in the midst of recession and belt-tightening. And its emphasis on a substantial restructuring of public broadcasting organizations—replacement of the Corporation for Public Broadcasting by a Public Telecommunications Trust—was largely ignored. Carnegie II was an interesting document, but it had nothing of the effect of the landmark first Carnegie report.

10.4.1 Politics As Usual

Carnegie II's relative lack of impact was due in part to entrenched factions in the various national organizations in public broadcasting. The battles of the 1970s involved hardened points of view, but the 1980s can be seen as one long and continuing struggle for both internal and external control of the Corporation for Public Broadcasting. This political infighting would be of mere parochial interest except that public broadcasting's establishment was thus ill prepared to face the Reagan administration's continued attempts in the 1980s to cut drastically (if not eliminate) federal funding of station facilities building, and operation of CPB. Although the policy of distributing CPB funds to local stations rather than centralizing production ensured that PBS programming was unlikely to be as offensive to the White House as that of a truly independent public broadcasting system would be, control of the corporation would ensure that this situation would continue.

The battle for control of the corporation centered on its 15-member board of directors, all appointed by the president. No matter who serves in the White House, CPB appointments are not a high priority, and thus the CPB board often was short of members. In addition, political appointees often have strong political views, which led to board battles over policies and personnel. For nearly a year in 1987, for example, the board considered a controversial content analysis of its own programming advocated by a right-wing Reagan appointee. When the board finally decided against the research, the member lost interest and resigned. The sharpest disagreements came while Reagan appointee Sonia Landau served as chair (1984–1987). Wife of a *New York Times* television columnist, Landau clearly had a political assignment—to bring CPB to heel by increasing its corporate underwriting and reducing federal funding. Policy and personality disagreements led in 1985 to the firing of CPB president Edward Pfister and the most severe public break between local stations and the Washington power structure in some years. The CPB board then fired Pfister's successor after only 10 months. His successor, Donald Ledwig, became CPB's sixth president in late 1987.

In the early 1980s, a financial crisis and scandal nearly ended National Public Radio. NPR had begun to seek means of self-support as funding from CPB seemed increasingly uncertain. Under Frank Mankiewicz, its president since 1977, NPR announced in 1982 an ambitious plan of further underwriting and sale of various services to allow total independence from the creaky federal funding process by 1988. The plans were too large and the base was too small—and by 1983 Mankiewicz was out and NPR was reeling from more than a $6 million deficit due to poor fiscal controls over expense accounts and expansive hiring practices. Congress investigated (some of the funds were federal), and things looked dark until CPB came through with a loan to allow operations to continue. For the first time, many individuals contributed to this national programming source in order to preserve their own listening choices. Nearly 100 employees were let go. The loan was paid back to CPB on schedule—but NPR lost some of its cherished independence from the political influences controlling CPB.

10.4.2 The Programming Dilemma

The audience knew little of the behind-the-scenes agony over finance and control, for it rarely directly affected what was on the air. Radio, particularly, continued to carve out a small but important audience interested primarily in news, public affairs, and the arts. Less than a third (about 280) of the more than 1,300 public radio stations (see Appendix C, Table 2-E) were "CPB qualified" and able to secure any of the dwindling pot of CPB funding. This meant also that only a small fraction of all public radio stations were carriers of NPR programming, with the remainder trying to attract local or specialized audiences, perhaps serving as a training ground for college or high school students of broadcasting or just indulging the preferences of whomever was in charge of programming.

But in almost every market of any size, at least one station carried National Public Radio. NPR's *Morning Edition* transported the low-key news and features approach of *All Things Considered* to a morning drive-time audience beginning in 1979, and *Weekend Edition* had its debut in 1985. Major congressional hearings, such as the Iran-Contra investigation, and inquiries into the fitness of nominees to the Supreme Court, were carried live by NPR as a matter of record. The fiscal crisis had eased sufficiently early in 1987 that *Performance Today* was begun (to mixed reviews) on a five-day-a-week basis.

In May 1980, Garrison Keillor's *A Prairie Home Companion* was first offered by Minnesota Public Radio. The weekly two hours of Keillor's creatively off-brand strain of humor quickly attracted a large (for public radio) and fanatically faithful late Saturday afternoon audience in most communities. The show typically was in three parts: an eclectic selection of musical performers (often folk or bluegrass), dramatic sketches, and a monologue about the doings in a mythical town called Lake Wobegon, Minnesota, with its strange yet familiar population of misfits, mixed with humorous "commercials" (for Powdermilk Biscuits, Bob's Pretty Good Grocery, the Ketchup Marketing Advisory Board, Bertha's Kitty Boutique, The Side Track Tap, Hoo-Hah! Hot Sauce, and the like). Keillor, a talented fiction writer for *The New Yorker* magazine, each week softly delivered a lengthy monologue about what was happening in Lake Wobegon and to its citizens (who reminded us of slightly larger-than-life reflections of people we knew). The program evoked a gamut of emotions in its audience, much as the *Vic and Sade* network radio program had in the 1930s and 1940s. The show was carried live from an old theater in the Twin Cities, although it occasionally went on the road and was simulcast on television a few times.

The popularity of *A Prairie Home Companion*—more people may have listened to it than to any other public radio program—helped Minnesota Public Radio create a new national organization, American Public Radio (APR), in 1981. Keillor finally became tired of the punishing creative requirements of *Companion* (it had been on the air in one form or another for 13 years), and production ceased in mid-1987. APR, meantime, had become an important program distributor and provided an option to NPR's material by carrying *MonitoRadio* (produced by the *Christian Science Monitor* newspaper, which was also edging into commercial radio and television) and other programs. Thanks to the availability of a satellite system, other programming was distributed nationally by stations with the funds to produce it, such as the jazz programming welcoming in the New Year from every time zone or Robert J. Lurtsema's unique blend of music and commentary on *Morning Pro Musica*, which originated in New England but had spread across the country.

Most public radio stations, even those controlled by school boards, were carrying less classroom instructional (often under 2% by the mid-1980s), a sad end to the high goals worked toward for decades by the National Association of Educational Broadcasters (which itself went out of existence by 1981).

Public television also became less overtly instructional and more of a general appeal medium. Indeed, except for a little during school hours, most "educational" programming also appealed to a general audience. Among those programs that might be classified in this way were *Sesame Street, Nova*, numerous nature programs, and other specials and miniseries. (Of course, such programming also existed on commercial television, but the commercial stations and networks would never label it "educational" for fear of audience turning off.)

The first regularly scheduled national evening newscast on public TV was the *Robert MacNeil Report*, starting in 1976 and expanded in 1983 as *The MacNeil/Lehrer NewsHour*, to become the country's only nightly hour-long newscast-interview-documentary (the format depended on the topic), although ABC's *Nightline* had similar content in a shorter time frame. Likewise, public television often seemed the only congenial home for controversial documentaries. *Frontline*, which often used the products of independent documentary filmmakers or video producers, was the only regularly scheduled documentary program in the mid-1980s. *Vietnam: A Television History* offered 13 hour-long episodes produced in 1983 by Boston's WGBH in association with British and French television companies to tell the entire story of the Vietnam wars from the 1940s to the 1970s. Because of the importance of television's on-the-spot coverage of that war, which affected (and was in turn affected by) public opinion (see pp. 447–449), the series was in part a study of the video medium itself and raised considerable controversy. It was not as controversial, however, as a multipart idiosyncratic view of black history titled *The Africans*, which raised the hackles of some Americans who objected to the left-wing approach of the program and demanded (and received) the opportunity to prepare a rebuttal.

PBS viewers still were attracted by old staples such as Sunday evening's *Masterpiece Theatre*, which continued to present British television dramas introduced by the urbane Alistair Cooke (and continued to make viewers wonder why American television could rarely do as well). A similar compilation of mostly British miniseries under the title of *Mystery!* did almost as well, extending the career of its host, one-time film horror star Vincent Price; Children's Television Workshop's *Sesame Street* was well into educating its third generation when it celebrated two decades on the air in 1989; *American Playhouse* presented U.S. productions from a consortium of public television stations beginning in 1982; and there were many documentaries dealing with nature and adventure. A number of the miniseries featured on these programs—such as *Jewel in the Crown*, about India during World War II and its achievement of independence—attracted audiences of extraordinary loyalty. Weekly current events programs like *Washington Week in Review* and *Wall Street Week* also had large and loyal audiences.

One indicator of the identity problem public television seemed to have was the blurring of lines dividing commercial entertainment from public television programming. A few public stations, seeking broader audiences at lowest cost, began to provide reruns of former commercial fare. The airing of movies, once intended to expose the audience to rare art films, started to concentrate on musicals and other popular fare—often to the annoyance of independent commercial broadcasters. In 1980, the critically acclaimed but low-rated *Paper Chase* series, which realistically portrayed law school students and practices (featuring veteran director-actor John Houseman as the senior professor) was rerun on public television after being canceled by CBS after only one season (1978–1979). (In 1983, the Showtime pay-cable service produced new episodes with much of the old cast, keeping the program alive for another year.) Similarly, *National Geographic Specials* and *Smithsonian*, among other series, often appeared on higher-paying commercial networks after their initial airing on PBS, carrying on a tradition ranging back to *The Finder* in the 1950s. Individuals also moved in both directions: Larry Grossman of PBS was president of NBC News for several years; movie critics Siskel and Ebert moved over to the better-paying commercial world; network newsmen Daniel Schorr and Roger Mudd moved from commercial to public television (which may have allowed more latitude, if less cash); and Bill Moyers went from PBS to CBS and back again in the 1980s as he sought an outlet for his documentaries and interviews that would allow him to say what he felt needed to be said.

10.4.3 Financing: A Gordian Knot

The financial crisis—almost a normal state of affairs for noncommercial radio and television stations—continued throughout the 1980s. Unfortunately, many felt that money itself was the chief problem, losing sight of the fact that disagreement on the basic mission (or at least on how best to accomplish that mission) contributed strongly to the continuing dearth of funds.

Lack of any action on the second Carnegie commission's recommendations (see pp. 517–518) laid the groundwork for the first major congressionally supported review of funding options. In a 1981 funding bill, Congress established the Temporary Commission on Alternative Funding for Public

Telecommunications (TCAF), made up of both public- and private-sector representatives, to study and experiment with options. TCAF operated through 1983 with support from the FCC and, under the authority of the 1981 act, conducted an 18-month experiment with overt advertising on 10 public television stations (public radio chose not to participate).

Following this experiment, TCAF recommended against advertising as an answer to public television's fiscal problems for fear that only major stations in large markets would receive sufficient revenue to justify added expense of sales staffs and higher union costs, and because acceptance of advertising and its implied search for larger audiences might well undermine the whole rationale of PBS as an alternative to commercial broadcasting. Although public television has always trumpeted its "commercial-free" status, most programs—since they often are prepared without knowledge of whether they will appear on public or commercial television—tend to be of the same length. As a result, PBS stations typically have four or five minutes at the end of each program to fill with promos and other material.

But it was clear to TCAF that the powerful commercial broadcasting industry would not sit still for continued spectrum reservations and other special benefits for a system supported by advertising in competition with regular commercial stations. So, after assessing several ideas, TCAF concluded that a less-threatening system of "enhanced underwriting" or more extensive announcements at the beginning and end of each program by corporations providing support for the program (and hardly distinguishable from short commercials in some cases) would be of greatest value. The FCC subsequently modified its rules and regulations to allow such an approach.

Still, enhanced underwriting, membership drives, and auctions were not enough, and public broadcasters trekked to Capitol Hill every year, seeking additional funding for the system. Budget pressures on Congress and the Reagan administration's lack of support in the 1980s led to "recisions" of money previously allocated. This situation made a hash of advance program financial commitments and other long-range planning—and effectively undid the whole rationale of three-year funding cycles. State contributions to public stations, once a major factor in overall funding levels, also declined under similar budgetary pressures.

On the local level, stations had little choice but to undertake on-the-air auctions and "membership" pledge week "begathons" to increase viewers' participation in financial support of "their" stations. While the $35–$50 basic membership category hardly paid for itself, since fund-raising is not cheap and a program guide had to be published and distributed, the stations felt that commitments of *any* amount would lead to larger audiences, a selling point for enhanced underwriting, and the opportunity to seek more contributions from members throughout the year. On the other hand, public stations that did on-the-air fund-raising knew that they often alienated much of their audience during the campaign, but saw no alternative in a time of reduced federal funding.

10.5 Advertising: Money and Motives

Outside of public broadcasting, advertising revenues remained the lubricant of the electronic media and one reason for the merger mania noted earlier (see pp. 500–501). While network television continued to be the country's prime national mass advertising medium during this period, changes in the old order clearly were in sight as early as the 1970s.

10.5.1 Broadcast Advertising: A Continuing Relationship

More than a few industry experts in the late 1970s were questioning how long a mass advertising-supported system of broadcasting could last amidst the growing number of delivery options and increasing specialization of content that then was just beginning to divide the audience. More than half a century of experience in reaching large, heterogeneous listening audiences seemed to be in jeopardy. Yet, 10 years later, broadcasting's major advertisers still were largely loyal to the national television networks, though they experimented widely with other options. The declining rate of growth in radio and television advertising revenues (see Appendix C, Tables 3-A, 3-C) was due to changes in listening and viewing and to a slower-growing audience divided among more and more different services, as discussed further on pp. 550–556.

For the first time, a substantial number of American homes had other ways to get electronic entertainment, chiefly videocassettes (often carrying promos for other films, if not actual advertising messages) and cable (a competitor for advertising itself). The growing number of independent stations also cut into the networks' revenues. In part, the ever-higher costs of television time and production lost it some advertisers. Newspapers still were the medium of choice for local retail and classified advertising, and other media, such as direct mail, grew in sophistication.

Still, through the 1980s, broadcasting remained an immensely successful advertising medium. The years after 1977 saw FM radio slowly develop into an important advertising medium for the first time in its varied history. AM's audience decline (see p. 552) translated in the mid-1980s into a parallel decline in its importance to advertisers. While the number of advertiser dollars put into any form of radio nearly tripled from 1970 to 1980 and almost doubled again during the first seven years of the 1980s, most of this was apparent rather than real, as a result of the monetary inflation of the period, and was matched by other media. (Between 1970 and 1985, television advertising revenues grew fivefold, as compared with radio's nearly fourfold increase and newspapers' better than threefold rise—though inflation accounted for more than half of these increases.) For both radio and television, local advertising revenues grew substantially faster than national "spot" advertising during this period, while network revenues climbed proportionately faster for radio than for television. During these 15 years, radio advertising constituted approximately 7% of all advertising, while television advertising's share grew from 18 to 22%.

Several threats to broadcast advertising arose in this period but disappeared without impinging on broadcasters' incomes. Early in the 1980s, bills were introduced in Congress to eliminate all advertising of wine and beer on television. ("Hard" liquor advertising always had been voluntarily refused by the industry as a public relations gesture.) Advertising of legal over-the-counter drugs also was questioned in mid-decade, with critics arguing that children seeing any pill-taking as acceptable might translate that image to the use of illicit drugs. Although the analogy of the law eliminating cigarette advertising in 1971 was raised, none of these limitations became law, in part because of effective lobbying by the wine, beer, drug, and broadcasting industries.

More fractious was the debate over advertising in children's programming. As a part of its radio deregulation decision (see pp. 566–567), the FCC removed its limits on the amount of advertising time allowed in programs aimed at children. Action for Children's Television and other groups petitioned the commission and courts for reinstatement of those guidelines. In 1988, Congress passed, but President Reagan vetoed, guidelines similar to those dropped by the commission. Concerns over so-called program length commercials (often cartoon shows with close tie-ins with commercial products) and selling by hosts of children's programs continued to trouble many critics. Indeed, it had troubled some broadcasters, as was evidenced in the advertising guidelines found in the now-abandoned (see p. 561) National Association of Broadcasters' code.

Often raised and always successfully beaten back were attempts by various states to tax advertising receipts, including, of course, radio and television (and cable) advertising revenues. In 1987, Florida's governor pushed through legislation to tax services, including advertising. Soon national advertisers were pulling their campaigns off Florida stations to avoid tax hassles—and moving trade association meetings from Florida to drive home the point. Pressure from those stations, other services affected, and Florida's tourism industry got the law rescinded in 1988.

10.5.2 New Media, Limited Appeal

As cable penetrated half of all homes in the country, glowing talk of the wired medium as a mass advertising vehicle was heard again. Cable's potential as an ad medium had been touted for years, but for several reasons the potential had never become practice. Cable's very success in providing more channels for its audience was at the core of the problem, for each new channel further divided the audience, making it harder to sell any one channel or program to a given advertiser. Individual cable networks often rose and fell on the results of their selling sufficient advertising time to cover costs. Cable systems' main revenue source had always been subscribers' fees, making the need for advertising secondary. While radio and television combined carried more than a quarter of all advertising in the country by the mid-1980s, cable television accounted for less than 1%. However, some analysts expected the networks' proportion of television advertising to continue to decline (from roughly half) while cable's might rise to nearly 5%, with most of the network loss flowing to local stations and syndicated programming rather than cable.

Not quite advertising in the accepted sense, but certainly a way of moving products, was the cable home-shopping craze of the mid-1980s. The notion of direct selling over the air was not new—it dated back at least a half century to early radio practice, and numerous products had been sold on a "per-inquiry" basis (with a commission going to the station). Also similar have been pitches for "greatest hits" records and tapes. In 1977, an AM station in Clearwater, Florida, offered home listeners a chance to call in directly and order products described on the air, and moved the concept to the local cable system in 1982. In July 1985, as the Home Shopping Network, it began national satellite distribution to cable systems across the country, offering system operators a small portion of the income received from their coverage area as an encouragement to carry the signal. A changing cast of hosts offered dozens of products during the course of a day at what were touted as deep discount prices, while cameras lovingly portrayed the item of the moment and constantly displayed a toll-free "800" number for viewers to use in placing their orders. In March 1986, a second HSN channel came on line to meet viewer demand. Other shopping services soon crowded on the air, some on cable and some on local UHF stations desperate for programming and revenue. Some of these stations eventually were purchased by one of the shopping networks. The process was the same in each case—products being shown constantly and huge batteries of telephone operators standing by to take orders and credit card numbers. Programming and advertising had merged to become one and the same.

Of the many other television delivery options offered in the 1980s, none except cable was large enough to garner much advertiser interest, although once in a while an advertiser would make videotapes of popular movies available at a drastic price reduction in order to be able to use the first few minutes of the tape for a commercial. Home VCRs actually were a threat to television advertisers because of the viewers' habit of "zipping" ahead through prerecorded ads, or else "zapping" (not recording) them in the first place. Surveys showed that a substantial proportion of those who recorded programs off the air generally skipped over the accompanying advertisements.

10.6 Programming

A television viewer at the end of the 1980s saw programming not much different from that aired a decade or two earlier. There was more use of computer graphics and somewhat more attention paid to sound quality, but most programming was still unpretentious entertainment. Some more attention was paid to "reality" (often defined as—or at least with—sex and violence), and there was a frantic search for successful formats to imitate. Poorly rated shows tended to leave the networks much faster by the late 1980s than a decade earlier—both because of better research and because of the risk involved in keeping an expensive show on the air. Radio formats tended to be aimed at those who liked either popular rock music or telephone-in talk, with hardly discernible differences between stations.

10.6.1 Radio's Survival

Radio programming changed remarkably little in the 1977–1988 period. Virtually no popular new format was developed. AM and FM stations continued to fragment the existing music and talk formats in search of specific audience niches as more stations crowded the airwaves. A "nostalgia" format appealed to more stations by the 1980s, but then there was more "golden oldie" rock music on which to base such an approach. Further, radio's audience was slowly aging and carrying its radio format preferences with it. More stations on the air simply meant that each station had a smaller piece of the pie—and seeking and holding that segment became both harder and more important.

   The most important radio shift was the decline of AM in the face of FM. As indicated on pp. 454 and 501, almost all new portable or automobile radios were AM-FM, and, with free choice, the audience tended to gravitate toward the better-sounding medium. In 1976, FM had about 40% of the audience and perhaps half that proportion of total radio income. A decade later, FM's audience and revenue shares both hovered at 70%. Crucial to the switch had been the FCC's nonduplication programming decisions of the mid-1960s (see p. 433), which forced FM stations to develop their own sound, which in turn attracted about half the national radio audience to FM stations by 1980. In the early 1980s, country, adult contemporary, Top 40 (usually called "contemporary hit radio" or CHR), album-oriented rock (AOR), and the old middle-of-the-road (MOR) format (combining talk, features, and some music) were the leaders, with country music being the single most common radio format. These same formats were strong at decade's end. With major markets often having 30 to 50 stations competing for listeners, focusing on specific demographic groups became more common. Some stations went for smaller audiences concentrated in demographic categories appealing to advertisers, such as men and women in the 18–45 age category or even women 18–35, rather than teens with less money to spend.

AM stations, to survive, looked to more specialized formats, including all-news, talk, and sports (all programs not helped by FM's better sound quality) and also specifically focused on ethnic minorities. All-talk stations, which featured telephone-in programs hosted by opinionated and controversial figures, attracted appreciable audiences. Several of these individuals, including Morton Downey, Jr., moved on to television. A few major market AM outlets struggled to survive with MOR formats not much different from radio three and four decades earlier. In small markets, of course, the limited number of outlets gave any radio station substantial flexibility in choosing its format. The traditional mix of news, personality, features, and some music had strong appeal, especially among older listeners. Likewise, especially in the South and Midwest, religious stations programming a mixture of conservative talk and features plus religious music and sermons (with monetary appeals) held a loyal audience.

10.6.2 Rising Risks in Television Programming

The arrival of VCRs and cable in a majority of homes by the late 1980s made those new media more important to the actors, writers, other creative people, and technicians who make television programs. The same was true with foreign rights to American programs as more countries found it popular and profitable to show American material. In 1981, and again in 1988, the start of the fall television season was delayed by strikes. The 1981 delay was caused by a July–September strike by the Screen Actor's Guild and the American Federation of Television and Radio Artists, who wanted more residual income from use of their programs on new media. This lack of a strong start contributed to a drop-off in network viewing levels for the entire season. The 22-week 1988 strike, which lasted until mid-August, saw the writers of television programs strike over similar issues plus a larger part of income from overseas sales. The new season was delayed into November, and fears were expressed again about pushing viewers tired of reruns to other services. While the "summer" (actually, September) Olympic Games and the presidential election campaign somewhat camouflaged the effect of the strike, the networks justifiably feared the potential for long-term negative effects. In the short term, of course, the strike concerned those striking and the companies struck (and the many ancillary industries, from restaurants to accountants, that depended largely on television production). Nevertheless, the strikes were an indicator of the growing recognition by others besides those in the executive suites of the changing economics of television programming.

The chief change was the ever-higher cost of making television shows. Program costs climbed, due in part to inflation and in part to improved production values (computer animation; location costs; a willingness to pay almost anything to hire actors who were "bankable," or so popular that they could command a large audience no matter what the program; and so on). A typical one-hour prime time drama that would have cost about $100,000 to produce in 1965 was up to about $300,000 a decade later, and to about $900,000 by the late 1980s, in spite of such cost-cutting practices as making programs in less-expensive Canada or using nonunion crews to the extent possible. As the cost of production rose, so did the risks attendant in making programs for television. Networks balked at paying more for their license to show a program (usually twice, before all rights reverted back to the program owner) so that, by the late 1970s, network payments covered only 90%—at best—of the per-episode cost of production. The production company was thus taking at least a temporary loss and the very real risk that the network would not renew the program for additional seasons, which would mean there would not be enough episodes (100 was the ideal number, but scheduling fewer first-run episodes made a difference in later years) to make the series attractive for eventual syndication.

By the late 1980s, successful syndication (domestic and often foreign) was required for a program merely to break even, let alone to make a profit. Until the 1970s, syndication nearly always provided profit over and above income from the network, which usually paid all actual production costs. There was little "first-run" (made for syndication) material. Passage of the Prime Time Access Rule (see pp. 418–419), the establishment of nearly 300 independent television stations by the late 1980s (see pp. 502–503), plus the increasing interest in recent (and even older) programming by basic cable networks changed that. In 1980–1981, 25 first-run syndicated shows aired at the start of the season. By 1986–1987, that number had jumped to 96. New companies developed to meet the demand, but there were problems as well. All production costs were up sharply, increasing the risk of program making and buying.

Syndication's image was of a steady diet of game shows and interview programs. Indeed, *Wheel of Fortune* (with the handsome Vanna White turning the letters) and *Jeopardy* were the top-rated syndicated shows of the late 1980s, followed closely by the Oprah Winfrey and Phil Donahue daytime interview shows, Merv Griffin having gone into big-time real estate. The cost of both formats was only a fraction of that of dramatic or variety programming. In 1988, *Wheel* cost about $8 million a year to make—but this daily program earned some $100 million!

To secure the rights for sufficient programming, many networks and producers went to measures that might not have been attempted in the past. International coproductions, involving money from one or more countries and creative talent from others, became common. WGBH (PBS) no longer had a monopoly of the many programs produced in England, with both good and bad programming going to the highest bidder (or the coproducer). An entrepreneur like Ted Turner might go so far as to purchase the films of an entire major Hollywood studio in order to be able to feed the always-demanding channels that he programmed. HBO frequently produced major programs with its own money, and consortia of stations or other cable program services did the same, although less often. Indeed, the expectations engendered by pro-cable publicity in the 1960s and 1970s, which held out hope that cable would become a source of tremendous amounts of higher-quality programming than the commercial broadcast networks, appeared to be ill founded.

10.6.3 Television Entertainment: Imitation and Evolution

In the late 1980s, prime time television remained a search for ratings success amidst slight variations of previously successful shows or stars. There was little that was new or different, for the risks in taking such a path were too great considering the costs of production, let alone the pressures of competing cable and VCR offerings. Of course, once in a while (as with *Hill Street Blues*) a new program so intrigued the audience (and other producers) that it was quickly imitated—but the process of innovation itself never really caught on. During other parts of the day, there was even less change. Soap operas and interview shows occupied most of the day, with morning programs such as the *Today* show and *Good Morning, America* starting off and NBC's *Johnny Carson* celebrity and variety show (and ABC's *Nightline*) serving as a nightcap after the local station's 11 o'clock news.

Although formulas remained the same, some genres changed more than others. Science fiction became less common, although fans of the long-running—it went through at least four actors in the title role—British import *Dr. Who* on PBS were a force to be reckoned with. In 1987 *Star Trek: The Next Generation* was aired (still without seat belts in the control room), and *ALF* began in 1986 on NBC. The latter could be considered either a throwback to earlier animal-centered comedy series featuring a "typical" television family or science fiction, since ALF was an "alien life form" from outer space with a smart-aleck mouth and a taste for cats (to eat). Paralleling the fate of feature films on the home screen, the western had almost disappeared from television, though the mini-series *Lonesome Dove* achieved very high ratings for CBS early in 1989.

10.6.3.1 *Network Jockeying*

In the mid-1970s, ABC briefly was the highest-rated network, thanks to the programming success of Fred Silverman (see p. 511). CBS moved back into its accustomed top spot in the 1979–1980 season. And then, in 1986, for the first time in television history, NBC nudged into top position and CBS slipped to third—a reversal of three decades' pattern. Later still, ABC slipped back down the mountain. No longer could a network plan a season's programs and then stick with them for several months to see if the audience would start to grow, as had happened often in the past. Now, if a program did not do well in the "overnight" weekly ratings, it was cut at once without compunction, since the advertisers could read the ratings just as easily as the networks. Each program not only had to build its own audience but had to deliver an audience to the programs that followed it later in the evening.

As before, all three networks would trot out special programs, typically made-for-television movies and mini-series, during the three ratings "sweep weeks" each year to try and bolster their image and ranking. To some extent, this occasional break with the regular pattern of weekly series added to the debate over whether to provide programming people merely watch or that which they watch and talk about. While conventional wisdom has it that few series (let alone most individual episodes) stay in viewers' minds, it was believed that specials—and the commercial spots they contain—often do. Networks were thus also able to capitalize on popular topics, stars, movies, or books without committing themselves to a full season's series (see also pp. 518–522).

In early 1983, for example, ABC offered 16 hours of *The Winds of War* (based on the popular Herman Wouk novel of World War II and featuring veteran movie actor Robert Mitchum in his first television role) and *The Thorn Birds* for nine hours (largely set in the Australian outback and exploring the pressures on an ambitious priest who falls in love). Both were highly successful audience-grabbers. Indeed, ABC came back with a *Winds* sequel (*War and Remembrance*) five years later that ran even longer (18 hours in November 1988 and 12 more early in 1989—said to be the most expensive program ever made for television up to that time, at a cost of over $100 million!). ABC found, however, that the program had marginal audience appeal, which made it likely that it would be the last miniseries this expensive. Also popular were "docudrama" specials, which retold history with a bit of license: biographies of John F. and Robert Kennedy and Lyndon Johnson; recreations of the life and work of Sam Houston and George Washington; refighting of various portions of the Civil War; famous recent murder cases; and visits back to the times of Napoleon, Peter the Great, and Columbus. A tendency to recycle became evident in the late 1980s, as "reunion" or "what do they look like now" specials featuring the original casts of frothy programs such as *Leave it to Beaver* and *Gilligan's Island* were presented to a nostalgic audience.

Some specials had substantial impact. Building on ABC's 1977 success with *Roots* (see p. 436), NBC offered a four-night dramatization of the life and death of the Jewish families during World War II in *Holocaust*, creating substantial controversy and widespread interest here and overseas (the series was eventually shown in West Germany, raising even more controversy in that country). Several programs dealing with the aftermath of a nuclear war (*Testament, The Day After*) generated strong reactions. More than half the country's adult population tuned in to *The Day After*, a several-hour view of a family in Lawrence, Kansas, after a nuclear exchange. Antiwar groups found that the program reinforced their message; "hawkish" groups claimed it was antidefense propaganda; all viewers found the images horrible and long lasting.

Another form of special reverted to former days of television music and variety, for a good cause. In July 1985, top music groups and individuals appeared free on a 17-hour marathon concert televised from London and Philadelphia to raise money for starving people in Africa. Dubbed *Live Aid*, some $75 million was raised in this series of musical acts seen by millions. The show used 14 satellites and was seen in 110 countries live (and in another 40 on tape). In later months, similar though less ambitious domestic versions sought to raise money for relief for economically distressed and weather-battered American farmers and other causes.

10.6.3.2 *New Dramatic Techniques*

Not all serious television programs were specials. *Hill Street Blues*, which began as a mid-season replacement in January 1981 on NBC, focused on the members of a police station in a depressed area in a large city. The characters were realistic, and so was the constant pressure of dealing with societal dregs and getting on with life. The viewer saw humor, pathos, and violence as he or she followed fully formed characters in a semi-serial fashion from week to week. Each episode took place in a single day, from the early morning roll call to late evening, with rapid cutting between multiple story lines and a cast of more than a dozen principals to keep track of. *Hill Street Blues* characters appeared as real (if somewhat larger than life) people, and it seemed appropriate to allow the line between the real (and ultimately fatal) health problems of the actor playing the precinct sergeant and the health of the fictional character to become fuzzy. The black humor of the fictional conditions of death of "Sergeant Esterhaus" became a posthumous tribute to the actor who portrayed him.

Another dramatic series that sometimes covered important topics but didn't take itself too seriously was *St. Elsewhere*. On NBC from 1982 to 1988, the program first took a realistic warts-and-all approach to life and death in a struggling urban teaching hospital, where more seemed to go wrong than right and where not all days were good ones. The title came from the mythical "St. Eligius Hospital" in Boston's slums, to which all sorts of people came for treatment—including the real Governor Dukakis (sprained ankle from jogging). As with *Hill Street Blues*, the comedy was often submerged in the trauma of trying to cope, interpersonal relationships could resemble a soap opera's, and the many intertwining plot lines and cast members were not easy to sort out.

Toward the end of its run, some of *St. Elsewhere's* programs dealt with unlikely events such as an out-of-body experience and a husband and wife ex-CIA team (Steve Allen and his wife, Jayne Meadows) who could disappear at will. A final program (which received a "jeer" from *TV Guide*) indicated that the entire series existed merely in the imagination of an autistic child who was a minor character. *St. Elsewhere* had a penchant for "in" jokes, in which actors would be addressed by the name of a character they played in some other program, and one episode contained a brief, unheralded scene in which almost the entire cast of the old Steve Allen show briefly gathered around a piano.

A similarly constructed program from the same production house (MTM), *Bay City Blues*, dealing with a minor league baseball club, ran out of story lines and audience early in its first year, but *L.A. Law*, which started in 1986, proved to be the same sort of success as *Hill Street Blues* and *St. Elsewhere*, appealing to a very large and loyal audience with its combination of good writing, action, tragicomic drama, and fine acting. Its multiple story lines told of the professional and private lives of associates and partners in a Los Angeles general practice law firm. A realistic (on the whole, greed outbalanced altruism) approach to the pressures of the job, combined with stereotyping of characters (the fatherly senior partner, the grasping managing partner, the philandering divorce lawyer, the sharp and ambitious women, black and Hispanic associates in the firm, and even the mentally retarded messenger) rapidly built the program to top ratings.

Many of these programs were created by Steven Bochco and produced under MTM (Mary Tyler Moore) Productions' auspices. The head of MTM when *Hill Street Blues* was first produced was Grant Tinker, ex-husband of Mary Tyler Moore, who went on to be president of NBC until shortly after it was sold to GE (see p. 511).

The differences between these programs and conventional ones were subtle. Whereas a *Barney Miller* or a *Night Court* brought a couple of intersecting and predictable plots to a location (few of these programs had more than a couple of sets) populated by permanent members of the cast, a *Hill Street Blues* or *L.A. Law* took the cast out into the streets or to other locations and let them interact with a large group of other actors and a large number of unpredictable parallel plots, few of which would be tidily resolved by the end of the program.

10.6.3.3 *The Unusual...*

The 1980s saw some of the last barricades against sensitive topics crumble. Homosexuality and even AIDS frequently were the subjects of story lines, as were drug abuse, the posttraumatic stress disorder affecting Vietnam veterans, child abuse, alcoholism, and other problems. The Vietnam War finally arrived on the same screen in programs such as *Tour of Duty* and *China Beach. Golden Girls*, starting in the Fall of 1985, showed with good humor one of the most overlooked minorities in America as it followed the lives of four clearly over-50 (or -60) single women living in Miami and still seeking men and/or happiness. The mixture of personalities and situations was a rare case of television not focusing exclusively on youth and beauty, and we laughed with, not at, the Golden Girls.

There seemed to be a new "problem" theme or two each year that appeared in some guise in almost every series. Some of this was due to the typical "copycat" approach to developing new program series, but some also was due to low-key efforts by the federal government to sensitize the creative forces of television to what Washington thought was the problem of the year. Sometimes the creative heads of studios, networks, and production houses were brought to the White House to receive a briefing—and then went back to their typewriters (or, more likely, word processors) to prepare and produce

---

▪ **The Vietnam War as Television Drama**   The 1972–1983 CBS hit *M*A*S*H*, set during the Korean War (1950–1953), helped make wartime comedy/drama popular. In 1988 network television ventured into the far more controversial waters of the Vietnam War with *China Beach* on ABC and *Tour of Duty* on CBS. *China Beach* stories centered on the women (nurses, entertainers, enlisted personnel, and their commanding officer) and the men they work and live with at a military rest and recreation center and base hospital in 1968, the peak year of American fighting in Vietnam. Unlike most of *M*A*S*H*, *China Beach* was serious drama in an hour-long format. But like the earlier program, *Beach* and *Tour* focused on the various personal impacts of a far-off and unpopular war.

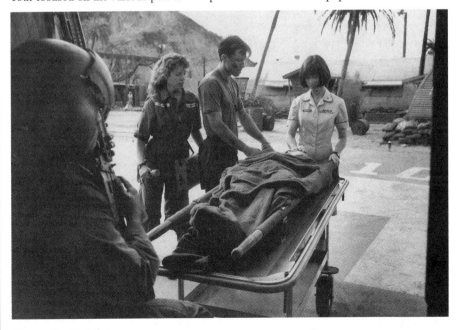

Photo credit: Photofest.

scripts giving their own slant on the matter. While the effect of this strategy usually was benign, some were concerned that it might lead to having television present only one approach to political, as well as medical or social pathological, matters, which in the future might allow an unscrupulous government and an unwary television industry to brainwash the public.

A stand-out "conventional" series was *M*A*S*H*, which had begun on CBS in 1972 and lasted for 11 years. Its combination of humor and empathy set against the activities of an army medical unit in Korea during the early 1950s' war built on an antiwar ethic growing out of the frustrating Vietnam War. The humane and antimilitary messages of Gene Reynolds and Larry Gelbart (producers and writers) and Alan Alda (the principal actor, who moved into directing) were positive and aroused resentment only among brass hats and stuffed shirts. While most regular comedies used a laugh track, it was noteworthy that *M*A*S*H*'s laugh track was never used in the operating room scenes. Alda's character of Hawkeye Pierce was the essential glue that kept things together, surrounded by the psychiatric-discharge-

■ **Cosby—Comedy Success**   Bill Cosby, as New York obstetrician Dr. Cliff Huxtable, applied gentle common sense in the raising of his son and daughters. He is shown here with two of his "children." Showing the trials and joys of parenthood—for which Cosby always had just the right response—*The Cosby Show* first aired in the Fall of 1984 and helped propel NBC to ratings leadership for the first time in history.

Photo credit: Photofest.

seeking Corporal Klinger in nylons, the naive yet shrewd Corporal "Radar" O'Reilly, and the professional and sexy chief nurse Major "Hot Lips" Houlihan. Over the years, the program survived many cast changes: new M.D sidekicks for Hawkeye; a new commanding officer in the form of commonsensical Colonel Sherman Potter (played by *Dragnet* veteran Harry Morgan) to replace the somewhat fey reservist Lieutenant Colonel Blake (played by McLean Stevenson); and the switch from one broadly buffoonish foil to a more urbane one. Some of the programs were unique: in one, the entire half-hour was shot in black-and-white as a television documentary might have looked in the 1950s, with the actors ad-libbing in character. In another, three generations of the Alda family were featured, and in one episode the camera showed only what an injured soldier would have seen. Some episodes were downright sad and insightful rather than funny. The two-and-a-half-hour final episode of *M*A*S*H*, telecast on February 28, 1983, was the most-watched television show in history, with a 60.3 rating and a 77 share of those watching television at that hour! Naturally, *M*A*S*H* continued in syndicated reruns.

Another ground-breaking situation comedy started in the Fall of 1984 when Bill Cosby returned to prime time as a New York doctor married to an attorney. The relationships between the couple and their five children remind one of *Father Knows Best*, but this family happened to be black. The *Cosby Show* quickly helped carry NBC to the top of the ratings heap as Bill Cosby's impeccable timing (honed by many years as a stand-up comic), recognizable family situations, and supporting cast maintained a broad appeal. Other "family" sitcoms tended to appeal to one demographic group or another—but Cosby was universal (see facing page).

10.6.3.4 . . . *and the More Usual*

More typical television drama built around people (as opposed to situations or action-adventure) thrived in these years. The crusty but credible Lou Grant character (played by Ed Asner) went from being a television news director on the old *Mary Tyler Moore Show* to an editor on the mythical *Los Angeles Tribune* newspaper on the *Lou Grant* program, which ran on CBS from 1977 to 1982. Its opening titles were notable in the first season for providing a half-minute music-and-film documentary montage on how newspapers are made—and end up as the absorbent lining for a bird cage! Both programs provided dramatic backgrounds for presenting the ethical problems of journalism. A decade later, the yuppie generation became the focus of ABC's *thirtysomething*, which combined humor and drama in an hour-long slice of life of young married professionals coping with new child, new job, or new home. Each week, the program offered more insight than situations in the accepted comedy sense, although those viewing over a generational gap might find trivial some of the problems faced by the cast. *The Days and Nights of Molly Dodd* appealed to many of the same critics and audience members, but not enough to find it a permanent network slot.

"Evening soap opera" was one term describing CBS's *Dallas*, which first aired in the spring of 1978 as a made-for-television film and began series telecasts that fall. It seemed that everyone was following the nefarious affairs (literal and figurative) of J. R. Ewing, Jr., played with a wonderful sense of evil by Larry Hagman. A huge audience was hooked by the last episode of the 1979–1980 season when J. R. was shot–and all Summer, fans of the show had to await the new episodes in the Fall to answer the question "Who shot J. R.?" Nearly 80% of all those watching television that night saw the November 21, 1980, program which answered the question. Beginning in 1981, CBS followed up with *Falcon Crest*, starring veteran actress Jane Wyman as the domineering matriarch of a California vineyard. *Crest* built its success on the same manipulative types of characters and stories as *Dallas*. Over on ABC, beginning in January 1981, John Forsythe played Blake Carrington on *Dynasty*, the story of still another greedy big-money (oil) family, this time set in the Denver area. Much of the program built around the rivalry of Carrington's gorgeous past (Joan Collins) and present (Linda Evans) wives, all set against the glamour of luxurious settings and costumes and devious plots. Other programs, such as *Knots Landing*, reached a similar audience. All of these programs also were popular abroad and were extremely profitable. Of course, daytime soap operas also retained their popularity (and their low production costs), moving further and further into story lines that featured explicit sex. A remarkably broad range of viewers, from college students to army trainees to retirees, were devoted to soap operas and had to get their "fix" each day.

Even without the deeper insights into the human condition provided by programs focusing on the individual rather than the situation, the action-adventure drama category, another longtime television staple format, continued to draw audiences in the 1980s. Some drama labeled action-adventure also focused on fantasy. *Charlie's Angels* professed to be about three female investigators working for a heard but never seen boss (played by John Forsythe when he was not on *Dynasty*). In fact, it was a vehicle for fast action and beautiful women during its ABC run (1976–1981) and was often criticized for its possibly sexist exploitation of "the girls" as they constantly hid their detective roles within an undercover disguise (which often hid little else). *Fantasy Island* also ran on ABC, from 1978 to 1984, building each 1-hour episode around the arrival of new guests at a mysterious resort island where a lifelong dream could come true. As the series went from season to season, the plots seemed ever more unlikely.

Any setting could be home to programs of different types. The world of law had *Paper Chase* (law school), *L.A. Law*, and *Night Court* (a funny and sometimes vulgar comedy). Medicine had programs ranging from comedy to the macabre. The military, big business, police forces, college, and almost any other professional setting could house a television program of some sort. About the only rare subject was the kind of daily work done by most Americans from nine to five. True, Flo was a waitress in *Mel's Diner*, "Ski" worked for a brief time in a steel mill, *Taxi*'s drivers seemed to do some work, and Jackie Gleason achieved fame as a bus driver. Yet the life of the "working stiff" was rarely portrayed on television.

One program that may be thought of as an exception was *Cheers*, which was set in a Boston neighborhood bar. This program, which ran on NBC from 1982 to 1989, grew steadily in popularity for several of these years. Plots were subordinated to character, and audiences felt that they knew a real Sam Malone (a jock—former baseball player—who owned the bar and had a large ego about his attractiveness to the opposite sex and not too many brains); Diane (a mousy blonde know-it-all who seemed his direct opposite and with whom he fought for the first years of the show); barflies Cliff (a postman who knew nothing) and Norm (an overweight, henpecked accountant); and sharp-voiced waitress Carla. When the actor playing "Coach," the bartender, died, the audience at home grieved with the cast on the screen. On programs such as *Cheers*, the "chemistry" or relationship between the male and female leads was extremely important. When the lead characters on *Moonlighting* consummated a hitherto uncertain relationship, ratings dropped.

Conventional situation comedy clearly remained a prime time staple throughout these years, as it had been for decades. And the overall format varied little—half an hour, usually with a laugh track and a regular cast. Some programs were superficially like others in terms of setting, but there was a big difference between the unconventional *Hill Street Blues* and the conventional *Barney Miller*. This is not to deprecate *Barney Miller*, which was a literate and low-key half-hour ABC sitcom from 1975 to 1982. Although it too followed big-city cops in the station house, it was a comedy (with some serious moments) that looked to the past for its production values rather than to the future.

Even more traditional were programs like *Love Boat*. In 1976, ABC ran several two-hour specials about life and love on a cruise ship. There was enough audience-pleasing fantasy and light romance in the two or three independent short stories in each "cruise" that ABC decided to commission Aaron Spelling to bring the idea back as a series in the Fall of 1977. The program ran into the mid-1980s, benefiting ABC and the Princess cruise ship line, which always sold out when it could announce that *Love Boat* filming would take place on a particular voyage. Actors portraying the ship's crew provided continuity, while guest stars (who got a free tropical cruise as well as pay) appeared in the vignettes, which were all based on some aspect of the love story formula.

Over the years, the networks have presented programs that purported to show (humorously) what goes on in the broadcasting industry. Feature and made-for-television films like *Network, Broadcast News, Special Bulletin* (another nuclear disaster drama), and *11 o'Clock News* took care of the serious end. Even radio programs from the 1940s like the *Jack Benny Show* used this approach, as did television programs like the *Mary Tyler Moore Show* and *Good Morning Beantown.* One of the zaniest of the genre was CBS's 1978–1982 *WKRP in Cincinnati.* This radio station's flashy sales director, zonked-out jazz DJ and hip black DJ, takes-himself-too-seriously news director, sexy front office secretary with brains, slightly confused general manager, and "normal" program director made up the cast.

10.6.3.5 *Among the Missing*

What was missing from television in the 1980s? Reviewing popular network programs of past decades, you find few or no variety programs in prime time after the late 1970s. Likewise, despite several attempts to revive the genre, the "adult western" remained a staple of the distant past, finding little audience interest in the 1980s. Music was mainly a matter of themes and background—even popular singers like Dolly Parton could not make a go of prime time television. On the other hand, old programming (even in black-and-white) had new life on cable and independent stations, and those wanting pop music could always listen to radio or watch MTV on cable.

10.6.4 More News at All Times

Television news became both more available and more watched by the late 1980s—but not always on the networks. Local stations had realized with a vengeance the desirability of having the reputation of being "first'" in news, and cable services like Cable News Network (CNN) and Cable Special Public Affairs Network (C-SPAN) cut into network news audiences. PBS, with its *MacNeil/Lehrer NewsHour*, became a player. Overall, television news now showed it could attract audiences and thus advertisers and revenues. In the early 1960s, network news programs were 15 minutes long (on weekdays only), and local stations typically provided no more than a half-hour divided into news, sports, and weather. By the late 1970s, network news was half an hour long (often with a 15-minute program on Sunday night), and most stations provided half an hour or possibly an hour of local news. Cable originated nothing. But 10 years later, the situation had radically changed. The networks supplied short news breaks throughout the day in addition to their flagship news programs in the early evening and the soft features and news of the *Today* show and its competition often took over the agenda-setting role previously held by daily newspapers. A large number of people (including many newsmakers, who previously had gotten into the habit of watching the networks' weekly news interview programs, such as the long-running *Meet the Press*) tuned in at 11:30 P.M. to watch ABC's *Nightline*; and local television stations might present news programs in the early morning, at noon, wrapped around the network news in the early evening for a total of as many as two hours, and at the end of the network entertainment schedule at night. "News junkies" who were still unsatiated could listen to all-news radio in many markets, view one of CNN's two channels, find numerous radio outlets that aired sports or financial news all day, and even buy a special radio receiver to obtain U.S. Weather Service forecasts directly without having to wait for them on The Weather Channel on cable.

To some extent, the increase in amount of news was based on expanding technological options. As noted on p. 498, by the 1980s most television stations had converted from use of news film (which, while less expensive at first, required developing and could not be reused) to videotape, usually gathered by mobile or even portable video units collectively labeled as electronic news-gathering equipment (ENG). Live telecasts could be made from remote sites so long as the signal could be microwaved back to the station. If it was not necessary to have the signal live, it could always be videotaped in the field and brought back to the station for editing. In a competitive market, one might see reporters and crews anywhere. However, microwaves were of use only where one had a clear line of sight to the receiving station, and the demand for channels seemed never to end. If a station wanted to cover a story in another city, it had to accept delays and pay through the nose for a connection through the telephone company or a satellite common carrier. Although some stations with helicopters for news and traffic coverage used them as relays for distant ENG microwave signals, this was uneconomical and often technically difficult—and dangerous. (Several helicopters owned or leased by both radio and television stations for reporting on traffic conditions have crashed, some with loss of life.)

In the mid-1980s, a new solution, satellite newsgathering (SNG), allowed major market station news crews to operate from trucks housing a satellite transmission antenna. Such vehicles, substantially larger than the vans in which conventional ENG crews could travel, often cost several hundred thousand dollars. SNG combined with ENG placed stations more in control of their own news coverage and lessened their traditional reliance on network news department outtakes to supplement local news. By the late 1980s, several SNG networks, notably CONUS (for "continental U.S.," set up by Minneapolis-based Stanley Hubbard), interconnected stations across the country on an ad hoc basis depending on the news story and its location. Since members of this association agreed to provide service to other members if their equipment was not tied up, a station sometimes found itself feeding a news event to affiliates of a rival network that would in turn feed it back to the originator's competition! All of this spelled more news options for local news directors, though.

These additional options were mixed blessings. Since the station with the highest-rated local news typically retained that lead throughout the evening's schedule, the news department came under much closer scrutiny by station management. The high costs of new hardware (such as computers for the weathercasters or SNG trucks) did not carry over to higher salaries for news personnel—except, of course, for anchors, who were able to charge as much as the traffic would bear but whose tenure often ran from rating book to rating book, since they acted and were treated as entertainers.

The cable industry finally jumped on the news bandwagon in the 1980s. Considerable expectations surrounded the start-up of Ted Turner's Cable News Network, which was announced in 1978 and began operation in June 1980. Turner offered to provide something that only all-news radio stations had supplied before—24 hours of news and features. Based in Atlanta, CNN was thought by some (especially those in broadcasting) to be a joke or gimmick that would not last. How could a video news service sustain itself without the backing of a network or some other existing news organization? And would Turner fiscally be able to afford a true news service? But starting with fewer than two million cable homes, CNN soon established itself as a lasting player. Because of its constant availability, its effective tie-in with European news agencies, and its reliance on young and hungry staff members whose apparent interest was in getting out the news and not in gaining a few minutes of air time to benefit their own careers, CNN grew in importance. At the beginning of 1982, CNN provided a second channel, CNN Headline News, with half-hour updates. The clear audience success of the service brought competition. ABC and Westinghouse set up their Satellite News Channel in 1982 and marketed it to cable systems. Both CNN and SNC lost money, which discouraged ABC and Westinghouse more than Turner, who was able to buy out the competition for $12.5 million in October 1983. CNN showed the networks that a lot of people clearly wanted access to national news at times other than the traditional six o'clock. The networks responded by giving *Nightline* (ABC) a regular time period and by trying an all-night all-news service (NBC's *Overnight*) for a short while. As one result, Linda Ellerbee, the outspoken and down-to-earth cohost of that and several other programs over the years, finally decided to try to produce her own shows—from which she could not be fired when network strategies changed.

When longtime ABC sports chief Roone Arledge was given the network's news portfolio in 1977 and instructed to get the third-ranking news operation up to competitive status with CBS and NBC, he experimented with several formats in the evening newscast. One unsuccessful approach had three or four anchors in as many cities. Finally, Arledge settled on Peter Jennings, who had anchored for ABC in the early 1970s but admittedly had done a miserable job then, in part because of lack of experience. After several years of foreign reporting, Jennings made a far more appealing and creditable anchor for ABC in the 1980s, frequently coming out on top in the weekly ratings wars.

Another bright ABC star was Ted Koppel, who was assigned to a nightly series of programs starting at 11:30 P.M. East Coast time dealing with "America Held Hostage" by Iran's imprisonment of American embassy officials in 1979. As the captivity of the American diplomats extended into 1980 (they were released the day Ronald Reagan was sworn in as President in 1981),

■ **Network Anchors . . . The Next Generation**   In the early 1980s, all three broadcast networks changed anchors from those who had long held the posts (see pp. 540–543). Dan Rather replaced Walter Cronkite on CBS early in 1981. Tom Brokaw moved from the early-morning *Today Show* to replace NBC's John Chancellor (who stayed on to deliver editorials once or twice a week), and Peter Jennings returned to ABC, (he had briefly been an anchor in the late 1960s). The ratings seesawed back and forth among the three networks through the decade.

Photo courtesy of Capital Cities/ABC News.

Photo courtesy of Tom Brokaw.

Photo by Anthony Edgeworth.

other topics were covered. The program's name was changed to *Nightline* and its length was regularized, dropping to half an hour (with the authority to extend beyond that if needed). Koppel, a superb interviewer, was one of the few in the news business who had the background, intelligence, and insight to hold his own against newsmakers with their own agendas and thus obtain useful and revealing information. ABC created short documentaries on a few hours' notice to set the stage for each program. *Nightline* provided a regular outlet in addition to the weekend interview programs (such as *Meet the Press*) for people with important things to say. While many of the subjects covered on *Nightline* (and on a long-form version of the program aired several times a year) were picked in advance, it always seemed able to provide a perspective on important events that had taken place the same day. The program became increasingly influential, and not only as a late-evening tonic for those stuffed with entertainment programming and CNN during the day. Koppel's staff was particularly good at obtaining people with opposing points of view to debate their positions face-to-face (or, since they might be at affiliated stations all over the country, face-to-monitor), and Koppel had the ability usually to keep them on the subject, although half an hour was hardly enough to cover a topic in depth.

CBS News went through years of internal agony in the 1980s as the network with the Murrow tradition and the Cronkite image fell on bad times, poor judgment, and worse luck. It began with the retirement in 1981 of longtime anchor Walter Cronkite (see p. 445), eased out by network management worried about losing up-and-coming Dan Rather to the competition as well as by the increasingly older demographics of the *CBS Evening News* audience. Ratings dipped when the sometimes overly intense Rather took over. More serious was a combination of changing CBS news directors and the growing pressure from headquarters to cut costs—particularly after Laurence Tisch assumed effective control (see p. 511). While Rather rebuilt the show according to his own agenda (Cronkite was not even allowed to participate in the 1984 election coverage, though he did play a role in 1988, when Rather felt more settled in his post), he made some mistakes. One was an apparently petulant several minutes of dead air when a sporting event ran overtime, and another was allowing himself to be manipulated by Vice President George Bush in an interview early in 1988. Layoffs and political infighting severely hurt CBS's image and performance, and a number of veterans moved on to other jobs. The level of internal conflict was reflected in several books (typically written by the losers) about executive turnover and the decline of news division independence and prestige during that period. At one point, some of the present and past members of the staff offered to buy CBS News from the parent company. Nevertheless, by the time Douglas Edwards (whose network anchoring assignment had started 40 years before) retired in 1988, CBS News was quite different from the organization it had been during its glory years.

NBC's new generation came on board with less fuss as longtime *Today* host Tom Brokaw replaced John Chancellor in 1982. David Brinkley left after more than 30 years at NBC to become a commentator on ABC News. NBC's prime time ratings success helped to propel the quiet-spoken Brokaw to the top of the evening news ratings heap. Networks increasingly were willing to accept (or recruit) those who had been successful elsewhere and even hire those who had not made their previous career in broadcast journalism. When Larry Grossman was eased out of the NBC News presidency in 1988, the network went to the newspaper industry for Grossman's successor.

In spite of all the new technology and changes in personnel, network news was still only 30 minutes long at the end of the 1980s—the same length it had been for a quarter of a century, and occupying the same period. The networks had tried several times to persuade their affiliates to accept longer evening network broadcasts, but the money being made on local news and syndicated shows continued to limit network news feeds to half an hour. Further, network documentary production was down sharply in the 1980s from levels of years before. The number of documentaries and news specials on the three major networks shrank to a total of 31 in 1987—versus 51 in 1977 and 100 in 1967. Many of the surviving documentaries were more entertainment or soft news features than hard-hitting investigative reporting. Few hard-nosed documentaries or similar programs remained— and they often attracted legal problems (see pp. 579–580). The small audiences and advertiser dislike of controversy in documentaries all but did in the genre, except for an occasional special dealing with the problem of the year and PBS's *Frontline.* The networks closed down their documentary units and concentrated on 90-second reports for the evening newscasts.

A "softer" format did successfully survive. CBS's *60 Minutes* thrived and stayed among the top-ten-rated programs for decades. Its formula of offering three or four stories a week and some important and many softer features brought imitations like ABC's *20/20.* When the costs of entertainment programming rose, several networks looked to their news divisions for relief—spawning such programs as CBS's *West 57th.* This development was exacerbated by the 1988 Hollywood writers' strike, since newswriters were not affected. Syndicated feature programs under such names as *Chronicle, PM Magazine,* and *Evening Magazine* occupied the profitable "prime time access" period between the network news and the start of entertainment programming at 8 P.M. (7 P.M. CST) for those stations that wished to counterprogram game shows such as *Jeopardy* and *Wheel of Fortune.* Even the often-parodied *Lifestyles of the Rich and Famous* fit into this category.

During this period, the Middle East replaced Vietnam as the hot spot most often shown on home television screens. No longer was this oil-rich region simply the scene of conflict between Jews and Arabs, for now Americans were intimately involved. On November 3, 1979, in the aftermath of the Ayatollah Khomeini's ouster of the Shah of Iran, a mob of "students" stormed the American embassy in Tehran, taking several dozen prisoners from among the staff. While the Carter administration made fruitless and apparently weak efforts to free the captives (including an abortive rescue

attempt by helicopter), the networks covered the Islamic Shiite revolution
in Iran and its overflow into once-peaceful Lebanon. Night after night,
scenes of the civil war in Beirut or interviews with often veiled spokespersons of one sect or another were shown on network newscasts—often making no more overall sense to American viewers than the recently abandoned
Asian war, which also lacked clear reasons, sides, and lines of fighting. The
taking of a number of individual hostages in Beirut in the 1980s and the
blowing up of both the American embassy and a barracks (killing more than
200 Marines) kept the story hot. Critics expressed concern about network
coverage of terrorists, since some terrorists seemed to engage in deadly acts
solely to facilitate access by their spokespersons to American television
screens.

To some extent, the story was "terrorism" rather than "the Middle East."
Such stories as the bombing of Pan Am Flight 103 over Scotland at the end
of 1988 and American attacks on Libyan aircraft and cities all could fit into
this framework. The hijacking of TWA Flight 847 in July 1985 and the two-
week drama that ensued illustrated the problems of trying to balance
hostage and family concerns with the public's demand for news, any news,
of progress in negotiations for the hostages' freedom. (This dilemma was
given a reprise when a made-for-television movie on the hijacking was
shown in 1988, shortly before one of the hijackers was brought to trial.)

Television faced severe problems of access to other stories. The military had learned its lesson in Vietnam: allowing reporters independent access to an armed conflict would open more doors to questions about the
wisdom of engaging in the conflict in the first place. The almost farcical
invasion of the Caribbean island of Grenada in 1984 was poorly covered at
first because the Pentagon would not allow reporters near the island for
several days. Criticized by all media, the Pentagon suggested guidelines
for future "pool" reporting. These were tested in the 1987–1988 crisis in
the Persian Gulf, when gunboats and aircraft tried to sink oil tankers of
neutral nations during the dragging Iran–Iraq war and a large force of U.S.
Navy ships was sent to the area. Twice in less than a year, American ships
were attacked, and one American ship shot down an Iranian airliner by
mistake, killing all aboard. The media found—not to their surprise—that
they were almost totally at the mercy of what the military would allow in
coverage. Some reporters operated independently, and the monitoring of
radio transmissions (honed to a fine extent during previous Israeli–Arab
conflicts) also proved useful. But without "credentials," it was impossible
for the news media to prevail against the curtain of military might
dropped over the region.

Many viewers and listeners were reminded of the assassination of President John F. Kennedy when, early in 1986, the space shuttle *Challenger*
blew up just over a minute after launch. Only CNN had been carrying the
launch live—we had become that used to routine and safe space travel—
but the networks soon joined in the coverage. Over and over we watched
the videotape of the exploding shuttle. For days, the media badgered the

families of the astronaut crew and besieged the National Aeronautics and Space Administration for more information. Nearly three years were to pass before NASA again sent a shuttle into orbit, in late September 1988. During congressional hearings on the disaster, television viewers had a fine moment when physicist Richard Feynman, live and without rehearsal, dunked a flexible o-ring—which he suspected of causing the failure—into ice water and cracking it to demonstrate the probable cause of the disaster. In the meantime, broadcasters as well as other industries and the military worried about their inability to place new or replacement communications satellites in orbit, since the United States had allowed its rocket booster capability to deteriorate, expecting to be able to use the shuttles whenever needed. Some satellites eventually were launched into orbit using vehicles produced by other countries. Even the USSR and China offered launch services—for a price.

Domestic news—disasters, scandals, government hearings—also received substantial coverage, made easier by the new news-gathering technologies. But ability to show pictures did not always mean that the full story was being told. When the Three Mile Island nuclear power plant near Harrisburg, Pennsylvania, vented radioactive waste into the air in mid-1979, the media (so said a later investigating commission) stressed more "what if" stories about a potential meltdown than factual "what is" material about the hour-by-hour events inside the plant—adding to the audience's concern with, and stress over, events. (Of course, the power company and government spokespersons provided as little information as they could—a foolish move in light of the success of an entertainment film, *The China Syndrome*, which had opened that month and had almost the same scenario as TMI.) When a Soviet nuclear plant at Chernobyl burned and let loose a huge amount of radioactivity over much of Europe in 1986, television reports seemed to fall into the same trap, partially—again—for lack of definitive official information.

10.6.4.1 *Sports*

Sports on television continued to fascinate many Americans. Two of the five largest audiences in U.S. television history were for Super Bowl football games—and the other games in this series were right behind. The jokes about "couch potato" fans of televised football (especially on weekend afternoons) seemed perennial. Some of the most profitable cable program services, such as ESPN, provided the viewer with nothing but sports. As a result, it was far easier to pry money and new equipment (such as stop-action videotape recorders) from managers for sports than for news.

Sports coverage during these years continued to be punctuated by the quadrennial Olympic Games, covered in this period mostly by ABC. The 1980 Winter Games were highlighted by an emotional win by the U.S.

hockey team against a more experienced Soviet team. The Summer Games never came off on U.S. television, as NBC was faced with a U.S. government boycott of the Moscow-based games due to the Soviet invasion of Afghanistan the year before. NBC had paid $85 million for the rights to televise the games and lost about $25 million even after insurers paid up. In 1984, with the Summer Games in Los Angeles, ABC provided 180 hours of coverage from 30 locations as much as 190 miles apart all over the Los Angeles area. The ceremonial opening and closing sessions, staged by impresario David Wolper and held in the old 1932 Olympic Stadium, harked back to the massed entertainment of old Busby Berkeley musical movies from the 1930s. Some 80 million viewers from all over the world watched. ABC covered the 1988 Winter Games in Calgary in a visual feast but found that the audience numbers were down as the U.S. athletes did not do well in the nationalistic or chauvinistic race for medals. The 1988 Summer Games in Seoul, South Korea, covered by NBC, which had paid a record $300 million for the rights, were held under some of the tightest security arrangements ever seen. While the 14-hour time difference between Seoul and the eastern United States was a factor, many observers felt that one reason for a severe drop-off in audience size and interest was the lack of audience familiarity (and, perhaps, level of experience) of NBC's on-air crew.

Television coverage of a professional sport often meant the difference between financial success and failure. Tennis and golf tournament winners moved into the big money because of increased television attention to their playoff games. Virtually all professional baseball and football teams, and players of other sports such as basketball and hockey, signed coverage contracts with one or more stations or networks, and the resulting television income was considerable. Even college teams got into bidding wars. In 1988, the Chicago Cubs, the last major league baseball team to restrict itself to the traditional afternoon contests at home, began to play under lights at Wrigley Field. This came about when the other organized baseball owners exerted pressure because their clubs were losing gate receipts by not playing televised night games in Chicago. By the late 1980s, cable was flexing its muscles and seemed likely to play a more important role in covering some sports events, including perhaps a share of the Olympics, before the 1990s would draw to a close.

10.6.5 Media/Politics; Politics/Media

Television played an expanding role in American politics in the decade covered here, in part because of the development of new services. Chief among them was the cable industry sponsored and supported C-SPAN (Cable Special and Public Affairs Network), developed initially to cover the U.S. House of Representatives after that body approved television access in 1979. C-SPAN took its feed from the House-controlled cameras and thus became a visual record of debates on the floor. C-SPAN also covered some hearings. In 1984 a political controversy arose when the House Speaker, Democrat Tip O'Neill, allowed the cameras to pan the floor of the House to show how few members were present for some late-afternoon GOP speech-making. The Speaker was slapped on the wrist, and the cameras were ordered to remain focused on the podium—but the coverage continued, although little used by commercial networks.

The Senate took much longer to decide that the benefits of coverage outweighed the disadvantages. In 1978, radio was allowed to carry the floor debate on the ratification of the Panama Canal treaty, and NPR carried the entire three days, while CBS and NBC aired only the first day. Otherwise, television coverage was limited to various Senate committee hearings, which over the years have created substantial video drama—the 1951 Kefauver crime hearings, the Army-McCarthy hearings of 1954, and the investigations of the teamsters in the late 1950s (see pp. 378–382). Both houses had long recognized that the public expected to see some congressional events on their screens, including ceremonial proceedings such as the annual presidential State of the Union address, and matters of major importance such as the House of Representatives' proceedings leading toward impeachment of President Nixon or the Iran-Contra hearings. When the House of Representatives decided to allow television coverage, the Senate agonized in a series of hearings and reports. By the 1980s, it was clear that the lower house was getting more publicity and news coverage thanks to the presence of the cameras—and that finally tipped the balance for the politicians in the Senate. After an experiment with limited coverage, the Senate finally opened its floor to full-time cameras under control of the presiding officer, causing C-SPAN to set up a second channel.

Television covered three presidential elections in this period: 1980, 1984, and 1988. In the first two, an incumbent president was running for office. In all three, television played the dominant role in carrying the candidates' images and messages to the voters.

President Jimmy Carter (serving from 1977 to 1981) made effective use of the medium, doing well in debates with President Gerald Ford, including one in which a technical bobble caused both candidates to stand silently behind their podiums for nearly 20 minutes. Carter won the election and started his term with the inaugural-day walk down Pennsylvania Avenue with which this chapter began. He held regular news conferences and appeared on talk shows. But despite his successes in such things as bringing Egypt and Israel to an agreement, Carter carried with him a public perception of ineptitude.

Former California governor Ronald Reagan, his opponent in 1980, was a master of the media, even gaining approval for "taking charge" with an "I paid for this microphone!" comment during a New Hampshire primary campaign debate that Reagan had, in fact, paid for. It had been expected by the Carter camp that there would be several one-on-one televised debates with Reagan. But Representative John Anderson's third-party quest for the job gave broadcasters equal-time problems, so only one debate took place. The October 28 face-off was in Cleveland, was produced, as before, by the League of Women Voters, and was carried by all three networks. The debate did not seem to play any pivotal role this time. On election night, Reagan was declared winner early—by NBC at 8:15 P.M. EST—rekindling the old debate about the impact of such early declarations on voters in states where polls were still open. West Coast voters had several hours left to vote, and some later research argued that thousands had remained home, with resultant impacts on many local and statewide races.

Reagan ironically made more limited use of television than did Carter, despite the new President's theatrical film background and reputation as "the great communicator." While he continued his weekly radio program throughout his two terms in office, Reagan seldom held traditional press conferences, forcing reporters to yell questions at him during "photo opportunities" in hopes of some give-and-take. Although part of this was blamed on the need for security—Reagan had been seriously wounded in an attempted assassination early in his first term—much of it was due to the universal desire of politicians to control news. Reagan came over well, folksy but seemingly in charge, in televised Oval Office speeches. His personal popularity insulated him from attack and even from sharp questioning by reporters such as ABC's Sam Donaldson, who assumed the mantle worn by CBS's Dan Rather in the Nixon administration. Other Republican candidates and policy issues tended to fade out of sight, as did Reagan's own penchant for making errors in public utterances (a tendency that seems to have afflicted many Presidents of recent years).

In late 1983, the FCC revisited its policies on televised political debates. It reversed several previous decisions and held that broadcasters could produce debates without fear of equal-time requests from excluded minor party candidates. No longer would the networks have to go through the charade of covering a debate as if they were mere bystanders rather than the reason the debate took place. Despite the rule change, the League of Women Voters retained its role in 1984 by sponsoring two debates featuring presidential candidates and a third featuring vice presidential candidates.

Ever since the 1950s, political campaign managers had been controlling more and more of what the public could see of a campaign, although it was impossible for them to control everything. For example, the 1984 campaign will be remembered for having the first woman on a major party's national ticket as New York Congresswoman Geraldine Ferraro ran for Vice President on the losing Democratic ticket with Senator Walter Mondale. Many felt that she more than held her own in the vice presidential debate with Republican George Bush, and the media focused on her—and on her husband's financial problems—more than it had on most vice presidential candidates in the past. An obscure 80-year-old Chicago manicurist named Clara Peller, who had played in a television commercial as a fast-food

■ **Covering the Conventions**   Television coverage of political conventions continued to dominate the quadrennial rituals in the 1980s (left picture is of the 1988 Republican National Convention). The formation of Cable News Network (CNN) in 1980 led to its playing an important role, often providing the "gavel-to-gavel" coverage that was once the hallmark of network television. Starting in 1988 the traditional networks limited their coverage to a few prime time hours into which convention planners had moved all important events. Even less coverage was provided during the conventions of the 1990s as primary elections took away the suspense of the party gatherings by preselecting candidates.

Photos courtesy of National Association of Broadcasters.

customer wondering "Where's the beef?," found her question underlining the Mondale theme that the Reagan administration lacked substance. On election night, due in part to pressure from Congress, the networks tried to avoid jumping the predictive gun that had raised so much controversy in 1980 and were somewhat more cautious in making early predictions.

The 1988 race seemed to start earlier than ever—as far back as 1986, when the first candidates declared for both parties in what was seen as a wide-open race without an incumbent for the first time since 1968. On the Republican side, long time television evangelist Pat Robertson declared for the GOP nomination, and for a time it appeared that those years of preaching might translate into votes. After a strong showing in early primaries, Robertson was undone, in part, by television tapes of some of his earlier religious claims. (Scandals involving other television evangelists such as Jimmy Swaggart and Jim Bakker also did not help Robertson's cause with the average voter.) Former Colorado Senator Gary Hart was the Democratic front-runner until reporters, acting on what was almost a dare of Hart's, discovered his apparent dalliance with a model. Jesse Jackson, building on his 1984 race, made a creditable showing in early primaries and electrified the drawn-out process with his televised oratory.

More than in earlier elections, the 1988 race was called a "media campaign" as press and television "horse race" stories made and broke candidates until the first primary votes were counted. The networks jumped to conclusions, and the politicians and public followed. There were televised network-sponsored debates among the initially long list of candidates (six or seven for each party) before most primaries. By the time the Democrats met in convention in Atlanta, it was clear that the electorate found the drawn-out process boring. Consequently, the networks continued their practice, started in the Summer of 1984, of not carrying the proceedings of each political convention "gavel to gavel." Indeed, even with the coverage abbreviated to two hours or so per evening (not including CNN and C-SPAN, which, by carrying the entire convention, gave the networks an excuse not to bother), the network coverage tended to consist as much of reporters roaming the halls to try to find a delegate or official with something to say than of presenting on the screen the carefully scripted convention itself. This was particularly true during the Republican convention, when Senator Dan Quayle's military record became a subject of controversy just prior to his nomination as George Bush's running mate. The handlers of both presidential candidates, Massachusetts Governor Michael Dukakis and Vice President Bush, groomed their men to deliver outstanding acceptance speeches—and both did. But audiences for the network's abbreviated coverage were lower than ever before—cable and independent stations saw huge ratings jumps, even for grade B movies. It appeared likely that the traditional four-day convention coverage was doomed to further streamlining, with television paying attention only to highlights—and any real news (or rumor) they could garner in spite of the best efforts of the political party managers to script the event.

The 1988 debates—two for presidential and one for vice presidential candidates—took place on schedule, one under auspices of the League of Women Voters, which refused publicly to do more because of the tight control of the political parties. Unlike the situation in 1960, few people changed their minds as a result of the debates—and many stations did not even bother carrying them. Still, Dukakis's weaker presentation and stiff personal style, especially in the second debate, helped cost him the election. Even more important to Bush's win, however, was his campaign's masterful establishment of a media agenda through orchestrated attacks on the media, short negative commercials, and his being sure to provide "sound bites" (a few seconds of slogan or pithy quote rather than a detailed presentation of the issues) to the news media (particularly television) in time to make the evening news on a daily basis.

10.7 Audience Changes and Constants

One important basis for assessing the impact of broadcasting and other technologies has been the comparative pace with which the potential audience purchased the product (such as a receiver or player) and the resultant "penetration" of service into American homes at any given time. Optimistic talk of new technologies in the 1970s usually stumbled over the crucial detail of just how many or how few Americans could (or would) use the new option. For example, despite the hoopla, only 13% of American homes had

CD players at the start of 1989, whereas 11% had home security alarm systems and 21% had home computers (many of them not used), according to the Electronic Industries Association.

Cable television, though first developed in the late 1940s, took until 1972 or 1973 to reach even 10% of the nation's homes (see Appendix C, Tables 9-A, 9-B) and reached half the homes only in 1988—40 years after first appearing. Radio took a decade to reach 50% penetration (see Appendix C, Table 6-A). But the videocassette recorder took only 12 years from the first sales of the Betamax in 1975 (see pp. 410–411) to reach the 50% of homes standard (see Appendix C, Table 7-B), helped along by falling prices and the VCR's relation to expanding cable and other services worthy of home recording. It also led to a new retail business—the rental of videocassettes of feature films at some store in almost every neighborhood. The growth of VCR usage contributed more to the decline in movie theater attendance than anything had since television itself burgeoned in the 1950s. In the more distant future, we may look back and see 1987 as a watershed year, when these two "new" electronic media—cable and VCRs—became more important to the average member of the audience than the radio and television stations that had provided so much for so many years.

Continued expansion of television receiver ownership naturally provided outlets for the new services as well as for broadcast television. By the start of 1989, 95% of American homes had color, and 60% had more than one receiver (see Appendix C, Table 7-B). More than 98% of homes had television and radio sets. Because of intense competition, television set prices actually fell during this period, particularly if the high rates of inflation in the late 1970s and early 1980s are taken into account. In 1988, a 19-inch color receiver for the living room might have been bought for as little as $250, and one of the many black-and-white sets purchased for other rooms of the house, or even for portable use, for as little as $69.

A small but growing minority of homes had top-of-the-line television receivers with stereo sound (about 15% early in 1989, with another 11% that could be adapted for stereo), pictures-within-pictures, built-in digital tuners for cable, displays indicating which channel was being viewed, or large display screens. These ranged in size from about 30 inches to several feet diagonally—and were in perhaps 2 to 5% of homes and a much larger proportion of taverns, following the pattern of usage set in television's earliest days. Some home projection television receivers could cost as much as $3,500. Most television sets were made in the highly competitive Far East—first in Japan and then (as Japanese costs rose) in Korea, Singapore, Hong Kong, Taiwan, and elsewhere, including China. By 1987, only Zenith among major manufacturers still made television receivers in the United States, and the number of American-made television sets exported was only half a million. Although American manufacturers made and sold another six million sets in the United States, these figures are small when compared with the 15.11 million sets made abroad and imported that year.

(In 1977, the equivalent figures were about 340 thousand, nearly 4 million, and 7.5 million—showing both a near-doubling in total number of television sets sold in the United States and a faster rate of growth in the proportion of imports.) Almost three-quarters of all VCRs, which barely existed in 1977, were built abroad in 1987.

Television usage—or, more precisely, the number of hours any television set was turned on in the average home, a figure that had regularly climbed several minutes per week for years—began to dip slightly in the late 1980s, down from a peak of 7 hours and 8 minutes of daily use recorded in 1983–1984. Homes with pay-cable service generally viewed more per week than did homes with only basic cable or those with only off-air broadcast service. Since these figures included all family viewing (see Appendix C, Table 8-A), they should not be confused with figures for the amount of time that given individuals or demographic groups watched.

Likewise, radio-listening patterns changed perceptibly in the late 1970s. After years of bringing up the rear, FM radio stations reached larger national audiences than AM stations in 1979, and soon the top-rated stations in most markets were all FM outlets—except for all-news AM stations, which reached more people but for only a few minutes a day. The reasons for the belated success of FM were varied, including the usually fewer advertisements, better sound quality (including stereo), and more musical format variety (see pp. 501–502). By the late 1980s, AM stations collectively shared only a quarter of the national radio audience (see pp. 526–527).

Both radio and television were forced to share ever more audience time with prerecorded materials: rented or purchased videocassettes and audiocassettes (now available everywhere and accessible at any time through tiny, lightweight portable players and earphones) or compact discs. Whatever the source of the sounds, more than a few critics—and long-suffering parents—argued that whatever kind of music teens listened to, especially with earphones, the audio levels were usually so high that serious hearing losses would likely result in later years.

10.7.1 New Methods, New Media

That the audience generally continued to be pleased with the service given them by television was evident in the biennial Roper Organization surveys done for the television industry (see pp. 455–457). Overall public opinion changed little from year to year after 1976, with 68 to 74% of the audience feeling that television was doing an excellent or good job and only 29 to 23% feeling that the job was fair or poor. Television ranked better, overall, than did newspapers. As the source of the typical person's news, television had consistently outranked newspapers and radio since about 1970. Although the television industry pays for this professionally conducted survey, the consistency of findings at least argues television's prominent place

in American life for more than three decades—nearly twice as long as network radio had held this position.

Suggesting some degree of dissatisfaction, however, were the findings
of a 1980 national survey that built on related studies tracing back two
decades (see pp. 455–457). Robert Bower's *The Changing Television Audience in America* (1985) concluded that there were both consistencies and
changes in audience reactions to television. While overall public reactions
to television had, Bower reported, "drifted from high enthusiasm to modest
appreciation" from 1960 to 1980, this was due in part to increased education ("higher education decreases admiration for television as an institution") and in part to a wearing off of the novelty of the medium after
35 years. But viewing was up about 27% from 1960 to 1980, pointing out
again that publicly expressed attitudes toward the medium are often poor
predictors of actual viewing behavior. Parents' favorable reaction toward
"the big babysitter," children's television, rose until 1970 but has declined
since, as more is learned—and expressed in competing media, such as
newspapers and magazines—about television's sometimes negative impact
on children's development (see pp. 556–558).

Yet another "effect" of the media might be measured in the increasingly
successful campaigns by politicians and special interest groups to discredit
the traditional watchdog role of the mass media. The messenger was attacked
rather than whatever it was that the media had uncovered, making some
wonder if the eleventh commandment ("thou shalt not get caught") was not
becoming more important in America than the other ten (see pp. 558–559).

Ratings firms were put under increasing pressure from advertising
agencies to update their techniques because of the expanding number of
channels delivering programs into the home, the growing sophistication of
advertisers, and improved methodologies developed by academic and commercial researchers. Until 1987, "the ratings" were not substantially different in approach or form from those of three decades before. The costs of this
audience research to the networks, stations, and advertising agencies that
paid for it continued to rise, however, since it was essential to the commercial broadcasting system. That was one of the factors that led to takeover of
the two largest ratings companies by larger, well-funded new parents. Arbitron had become a part of Control Data in 1967, while the A.C. Nielsen
Company was purchased by Dun & Bradstreet in 1984. A new player and
method entered the scene in late 1984 when the British company AGB introduced the "people meter" with an experiment in Boston. While AGB did
not last (it ended operation after just 11 months, unable to get the networks
and major advertising agencies to support its attempt to compete with
Nielsen), people meters did.

People meters are electronic devices that measure when a television receiver is on, to what channel it is tuned, and—unlike traditional meters—
who is actually watching (see p. 554). Developed independently by several firms during the 1980s (and actually used by regular ratings services in

■ **People Meters** The "people meter" machines used by Nielsen and Arbitron in the late 1980s did not look very special, but they heralded a vastly improved system of audience ratings. Here are the three devices that form the Arbitron system: (left) the large box contains the measurement devices and sits atop the home television set; (middle) the "joy stick" device, called a Scan Wand by Arbitron, is used to scan universal product codes after purchase and is then returned to its base unit so the code information can be tallied with television watching; and (right) the small hand-held unit allows the viewer to punch in a number assigned to each member of the household (up to eight), plus up to nine guests. A viewer "prompt" (a question mark in the upper left-hand side of the screen) appears every half hour if no new audience information has been entered by the hand-held unit. In the early morning hours, each ScanAmerica household's people meter is "read" by the national computer to help form overnight and national ratings and product purchase reports. However, in 1995 (see p. 665) Arbitron withdrew from the television ratings business.

Source: Arbitron, ScanAmerica Press Office.

Europe before its introduction here), the people meter promised more information of interest to advertisers, though at some risk to broadcasters, since some people—particularly children—failed to indicate their presence when queried by the people meter, thus reducing overall ratings. A.C. Nielsen had the strength and advertising agency support to start phasing out its Audimeter-diary methods and move to people meter techniques, finally replacing its traditional procedures in September 1987. In 1989, Nielsen reported initial development of a scanning device—rather than push buttons—to determine who was in the room.

The networks, already under pressure from cable and other services, were very unhappy with what they called a rush to the new system. They complained about the sample size (initially 2,000 homes, as compared with the national Nielsen meter sample of 1,700—but planned for an increase to 5,000) and composition (too many cable and pay-cable homes were included for the networks' taste) of the people meter national sample. Critics argued that the frequent button-pushing called for by the new system would quickly bore or tire audiences, thus skewing results. The new means of measurement showed that television viewing overall was off by about 10%, while many specific program ratings were sharply different from ratings obtained in the older way. Columns of trade magazines were filled with arguments and conflicting data as to why this occurred and whether it was an artifact of the technique. However, since the advertisers were pleased, conversion to people meters continued.

Arbitron also proposed a new technique, engaging in an extensive experiment in Denver called "ScanAmerica," which combined a Universal Product Code reader (able to interpret those thick and thin lines found on almost all packages nowadays) with a people meter so that sample households could easily report product purchases. Researchers presumably could now compare actual viewing behavior with resultant buying decisions—the kind of research connection that advertisers had wanted for years and that had been enjoyed only by some small marketers who took orders only by telephone and kept track of which commercial had aired immediately before the call.

The researching of local market television audiences was not directly affected by people meters in the late 1980s. The comparatively high cost of these electronic devices continued to restrict local market researchers to written diaries and (sometimes) telephone calls.

Measuring the audiences for newer and still-developing electronic media, especially cable and VCR use, posed another major methodology problem in the 1980s. Researchers wondered about the effect of increasing remote control usage on viewers' behavior (more channel switching and thus less "loyalty"—countered by tacit agreement among some networks to air commercials at exactly the same minute, to reduce the amount of channel surfing), whether cable and VCR use added to or took away from time spent with broadcast services (a bit of both, with more hours viewed overall, but nearly all of the added time went to the new services), how to measure viewing delayed by VCR time-shifting, and whether wholly new methods were needed to portray fairly and accurately the audience for newer multichannel, services. By the mid-1980s, Nielsen was issuing regular ratings reports for all major advertiser-supported and pay-cable networks. A lot of information on patterns of VCR use was also emerging—including the fact that a substantial proportion of material recorded was never viewed!

Audience research had gone a long way along the road from estimating set-tuning to estimating individual viewing. But it had to be acknowledged that the amount of attention paid to the set while "viewing," and the amount of commercial information comprehended and retained, were studied only in the laboratory. Still largely ignored by the commercial industry was any possible system of qualitative ratings that would regularly seek data on viewers' reactions to, if not the effects of, what they watched. Even such a seemingly simple bit of information as what kind of radio-listening went on in automobiles was on shaky methodological grounds. And to go from these figures to deciding that a given commercial reached a given member of an audience *and* caused him or her to buy a particular product or service clearly was not justified. The ratings (see Appendix B) were the only game in town for the advertisers, and they were improving—but they most decidedly were not yet perfected.

Advertising agencies constantly improved their own tools for assessing potential consumers, spending large sums on such techniques as "psychographics" (categorizing people in psychological rather than demographic terms) and "focus groups" (which were subject to intensive interviewing and debriefing). Assisting in defining these problems and finding means to overcome them was the industry supported and directed Electronic Media Ratings Council (EMRC), formerly the Broadcast Ratings Council (see pp. 455–456), whose research concerns extended in 1982 to cable and VCRs. As with its predecessor, the EMRC performed a combination auditing and accrediting function, helping to ensure that ratings surveys met at least minimal—and common—standards of reliability, although shying away from many questions of validity.

10.7.2 Kidvid (Phase Four)

The late 1970s saw what may have been the peak of serious government interest in improving television programming for young children. The effort came in parallel actions at two federal agencies. First, an FCC task force study issued late in 1979 found that broadcasters were not in compliance with the FCC's 1974 policy statement, which called for voluntary action to increase educational programming and for less advertising in children's television (see p. 459). The staff recommended mandatory program quotas for school-age and preschool children's programming. At the same time, a Federal Trade Commission staff study strongly recommended limiting or eliminating all advertising in programming aimed primarily at children, calling it "inherently unfair." Numerous members of Congress found these reports excellent public relations vehicles on which to stand, while others declared them to be antibusiness and moved to oust the FTC chairman.

But the election of Ronald Reagan, and the resultant change in personnel and deregulatory priorities at both commissions (see pp. 559–560), stopped these recommendations in their tracks. Late in 1983, after an FCC hearing on the policy issues involved, the commission issued a new statement that once again rejected any mandatory children's programming requirements and simply restated the commission's 1974 call for voluntary action. That weak action was insufficient for the activist views of Action for Children's Television (see p. 459), which took the FCC decision to court. The U.S. Court of Appeals upheld the FCC's decision, arguing that the agency had changed its thinking on children's programming, an action certainly within the commission's power. When the FCC later deregulated television advertising time guidelines, including those for children's programs, ACT appealed again, and this time the Court of Appeals agreed, noting that the FCC had not adequately justified its deregulatory action. In 1987, the FCC reluctantly was forced to reopen the question of the amount of advertising in children's shows.

Concern over the hypothesized impact on children of violent behavior portrayed on television was fed by several legal cases in the late 1970s. In 1977, 15-year-old Ronnie Zamora went to trial in Florida, accused of murdering the elderly lady next door when he was surprised during an attempted theft. His attorney tried a novel defense: he argued that Ronnie could not tell the difference between the real world and television due to his addiction to—the lawyer said "intoxication" with—such programs as *Kojak* and *Police Woman*. The jury was not convinced, and young Zamora received a life sentence. (Interestingly, this case was the first covered by television cameras after Florida allowed television news to record in its courtrooms.)

The murder-after-watching television argument, however, merely gave ammunition to those concerned about television's effects. That concern was further fed just a year later, when an NBC made-for-television movie, *Born Innocent*, simulated a brutal rape in a women's prison. Just days after the showing, a young girl was similarly attacked by several others. Her parents sued the network for having shown the program that "caused" the attack on their daughter. A California court, however, concluded that NBC had not tried to incite the rape, and thus the First Amendment protected the network from any findings of responsibility.

A more definitive statement of television's impact came in a two-volume 1982 National Institute of Mental Health report titled *Television and Behavior: Ten Years of Scientific Progress and Implications for the Eighties*, an assessment of research conducted during the decade after the famous Surgeon General's report (see pp. 457–459). Given the huge body of research in this field (some 3,000 studies issued after 1972—90% of all research publications on the influence of television on human behavior ever produced), the new report synthesized what was already known rather than reporting on original research or proposing more. The report took a broader view, reviewing violence studies (now found to conclude that televised violence did have a fairly direct effect on subsequent real-life behavior) but going beyond that to include broader social impacts. Noting that by 1982 half of all Americans had never known life without television, the report claimed that the medium had become an embedded part of daily life, with deep and only partially understood impacts on our perceptions of social groups and issues, health concerns, and the role of the family. Television was an informal educator of considerable importance.

Although most (not all) researchers agreed that the evidence supported the report's conclusions, it should be noted that the majority of the studies reviewed were content analyses of one kind or another, as opposed to the more conceptually and methodologically difficult studies of the impact of that content.

At least one important theoretical concept emerged in this period—the study of mass communication's role as the prime agenda-setter for society. Researchers in many universities noticed that concern with a given issue rose in opinion polls after coverage of that issue in print and broadcast media. A 1977 book by Donald Shaw and Maxwell McCombs raised agenda-setting to a more practical level by providing many examples. A stellar example (in both senses of the term) was the mid-1985 worldwide telecast of the Live Aid concert discussed on p. 531. While initial news reports helped place the famine on the public agenda, the concert prompted millions to help solve the problem.

10.7.3 Other Audience Effects and Criticism

The legal quibbling in the Zamora and *Born Innocent* cases did not deter further attacks on the medium from those who saw television as something that could subvert society. A growing number of people, particularly Protestant religious fundamentalists and the "Moral Majority" group organized by the Reverend Jerry Falwell, joined by political conservatives who objected to television news's coverage of things they would rather not have covered (such as U.S. involvement in Central America), felt that television itself was evil, and that its content should be regulated (few called for its abolition) on moral grounds. Many broadcasters were timid about responding to these attacks, but producer-writer Norman Lear (*All in the Family, Maude*) organized a counter group, People for the American Way, to combat head-to-head those who would restrict television's ability to reflect changing social mores and provide progressive political and economic views.

Yet the impact of television continued to attract the anger of those who felt harmed or limited by its power. Conservative television evangelists claimed to reach huge audiences in the 1980s and began to flex their political muscle in the elections of 1984 and 1988, attacking television even while using it (although their power waned by 1988 as first Jim and Tammy

Bakker and then Jimmy Swaggart were alleged to have committed improper acts). The right and the left both complained about the coverage of their organizations by the national networks. Former evangelist Pat Robertson on the right and ex-Colorado senator Gary Hart on the left both ran antimedia campaigns during the primaries of the 1988 election. Senator Jesse Helms started a weak attempt to take over CBS in the mid-1980s, calling on his right-wing followers to "become Dan Rather's boss," thus controlling the network's news output to their liking. As the primary provider of news for most Americans, television news was constantly battered—as is the historical fate of most messengers bearing bad news—from all sides, even though repeated reputable studies of television news content generally showed no clear pattern or evidence of bias. However, more and more, by one means or another, the independence of the mass media was under attack, and the public joined in with glee. This tendency was far more destructive than the traditional polarization between the tending-to-be-more-liberal editorial staffs and the tending-to-be-more-conservative managers and owners. Of course, the increasing tendency of all news media to provide entertainment rather than the information citizens in a democracy need in order to make valid decisions made some observers feel that the crime was suicide, not murder, whenever the news media lost public respect.

10.8 Rethinking Regulation

During the 1980s, the continuing political debate over the proper relationship between government regulators and the electronic media industry heated up. While much of the focus was on FCC chairman Mark Fowler's clearly stated ideological bias in favor of marketplace solutions to industry problems, a small but vocal minority kept alive a more traditional view of regulation's benefits. And the FCC was not the only arena—Congress played a very active role in deciding on electronic media policy matters.

The policy debate after 1977 was chiefly defined by two schools of thought in continuous collision. On the one hand, "traditional liberals" argued that the "public interest, convenience, and/or necessity" wording of the 1934 act meant that government should continue playing an important central role in charting the direction and operations of electronic media to make sure the industry served the public, and that the success of the current system in serving the public showed the wisdom of that course. On the other side, "marketplace conservatives" claimed that government regulation cost far more than the limited value derived from it (for either the industry or consumers) and thus that years of past regulatory precedents were now merely baggage to be discarded so that the public could benefit from the effects of highly motivated competition. Both sides relied on ideological argument more than on reliable data, but weren't willing to carry their argument to the extreme. Sometimes—as with the dismissal of the "spectrum scarcity" argument by conservatives—any attempt to analyze the matter objectively would run afoul of very slippery definitions of such basic terms as "market" and "competition."

Deregulation in broadcasting had begun in the mid-1970s under FCC chairman Richard Wiley (from 1972 to 1977) and accelerated under Charles Ferris (mid-1977 to early 1981). Serving both Republican and Democratic presidents, Wiley (a Republican) and Ferris (a Democrat) both believed that changes were necessary and proposed regulatory trade-offs for broadcasting. In return for retaining and even expanding such structural regulation as ownership limits and employment guidelines, the FCC would back away from consideration of more direct content controls, such as specific program or advertising guidelines. The latter type of proposals suffered constant attack on First Amendment grounds anyway and were by far the most controversial measures considered by the commission over the years. So regulators worked under an increasingly clear compromise premise in the late 1970s: government should help to set a broad structural arena within which broadcasters could operate freely.

Extreme deregulation, aimed at "getting the government off industry's back," came with Mark Fowler's chairmanship of the FCC from 1981 to early 1987. The compromise was abandoned, together with all but the most generalized support of the "public interest, convenience, and/or necessity" standard. The cast of regulatory players also changed in this period. Members and committees of Congress, with their own agendas and with membership changes from every election, exercised closer control over what they considered to be their creature, the FCC. Initially, Fowler had the backing of Congress for the FCC's deregulatory push. But after the mid-1980s, Fowler, and his successor, Dennis Patrick, found fewer supporters on Capitol Hill, in part because Congress felt the FCC was moving too far too fast and in part simply because Congress, with more substantial staff backing, wanted to play a more direct role in the policy sandbox.

The executive branch was not idle. Presidents ignored questions of telecommunications policy at their own political peril. Joining the fray early in 1978 was the National Telecommunications and Information Administration. NTIA was the lineal descendant of the once-powerful Nixon White House-based Office of Telecommunications Policy. Now a part of the Department of Commerce, NTIA had the functions of advising the executive branch on telecommunications issues, representing the President's telecommunications policies, and keeping peace among federal government users of the electromagnetic spectrum (through IRAC). As international meetings of the ITU and other organizations became more common and more central to domestic electronic media developments, the Department of State also took a more active role.

The industry continued to play in all the Washington arenas, although the entry of new players based, in part, on new technology tended to splinter points of view as the 1980s wore on. The National Association of Broadcasters continued to play the umbrella organization role, trying to represent the many different parts of the industry, from large networks to tiny market radio stations. (Indeed, the National Radio Broadcasters Association, an expansion of an FM radio trade group of the 1960s, merged into the NAB early in 1986, much as had the Television Broadcasters Association more than 30 years before.) But the points of view on regulatory issues grew more disparate, and the NAB found itself criticized loudly from all directions. Specialized groups spoke up increasingly for independent stations, large stations, daytime operators, and newer media, such as cable, all of which disagreed with NAB positions at one time or another.

The NAB's position as the industry spokesman and leader was not helped any when, in June 1979, the Justice Department filed an antitrust suit against the NAB's radio and television codes. Justice claimed that the code guidelines served to restrict the market for advertising (by limiting the amount of advertising per hour)—thus driving up costs for sponsors. After a March 1982 decision on one small part of the advertising code went against it, the NAB signed a consent decree with the government, effectively ending both the advertising and program guideline codes, which had been around since 1939 (radio) and 1952 (television). Although the demise of the codes was greeted with a sigh of relief from those who had been skirting and violating them, there was significant negative public relations fallout from the unseemly haste with which the NAB dropped the entire idea of program standards, particularly those dealing with children's programs.

The networks, which had always relied on their own "standards and practices" offices rather than the NAB code, and many stations continued to enforce programming and advertising codes of their own. By making it desirable for advertisers to meet one fairly high standard rather than different standards for each station, the networks and conscientious stations thus prevented the anticipated flood of substandard and even harmful programming and advertising.

On the other hand, although citizens' groups such as Action for Children's Television remained active, the desire of the networks to cut costs, and the FCC's abdication of responsibility for content in the name of "deregulation," led to a substantial reduction in staffing in the network standards and practices departments in the late 1980s. The Television Information Office, founded by the industry as a public relations arm in the aftermath of the quiz show scandals at the end of the 1950s (see pp. 376–377 and 393–394), was eliminated early in 1989.

The 1980s were not a settled time for broadcasters. Although many welcomed the fruits of deregulation, Congress made it clear that sooner or later there would be a price, perhaps in the form of rent (called a "spectrum use fee") for a channel. Broadcasters were frequently reminded that they could not have it both ways: if they were "special" because of their role in meeting the public interest, they probably should be subject to at least some generalized content-service guidelines. If, on the other hand, they were just like any other business, they should be subject to the fees that the federal government makes for use of public resources.

Broadcasting, although in the public eye, was an ever-smaller part of the larger telecommunications scene in the 1980s. Fundamental structural and service changes in the telephone industry, fed in part by the need to provide cheap and efficient computer communication networks (outside the scope of *Stay Tuned*), were causing far more fundamental changes to the common carrier telecommunications industries than were changes in broadcast regulation, although the latter were more likely to be noticed by the general public.

10.8.1 Congress Tries to Rewrite the 1934 Act

From 1977 until 1982, Congress was deeply involved in its most serious attempt thus far to review and replace completely the half-century-old Communications Act of 1934. Driven by changing technology and a belief that the spectrum scarcity argument accepted by the Supreme Court in the 1969 *Red Lion* decision should be overcome by such a rewrite, as well as a rapidly changing common carrier regulatory scene, members of first the House and later the Senate moved through several generations of hearings and bills in what was touted as a "basement-to-attic" review of American domestic communications policy.

The process began with an ill-conceived attempt by AT&T in 1976 to persuade Congress to amend the 1934 act essentially to reinstate its by-then crumbling telephone monopoly status.* Initially backed by many members of both houses, the bill never came to hearing, let alone a final vote. For, despite its title as the "Consumer's Communications Reform Act," the hands of special interests were all over its provisions, and it was soon seen as far too narrow and reactionary. (A later bill was numbered S. 611—the same digits as the Bell System's repair service telephone number.)

Congressman Lionel Van Deerlin (D-California), one of an increasing number of congressmen with a broadcasting background, took over the chairmanship of the House Communications Subcommittee concerned that the issues raised in the "Bell bill" needed resolution—but so did many other long-hanging controversies in broadcast and cable regulation. Perhaps it was time to reinvent the wheel. In May 1977, armed with special appropriation support, the Van Deerlin subcommittee staff issued an 800-page set of Options Papers outlining the current regulatory status of all services regulated by the FCC, along with the options Congress might consider in changing those relationships. Among the possible changes discussed were

---

*The Department of Justice had brought suit to break up AT&T in late 1974. Even by 1976, it was evident that the legal procedures would drag on for years. AT&T also was troubled by a series of FCC and court decisions that had introduced competition into long-distance service by specialized common carriers, such as MCI and Sprint, and into the customer premises equipment market (the *MCI* decision of 1969 allowed others to connect to "Ma Bell's" lines). Yet AT&T was still closely regulated and required to provide service on a near-universal basis, no matter how expensive that was to accomplish.

Rewrites and Deregulation This chart compares and contrasts the original requirements of the Communications Act of 1934, the proposals of early rewrite bills in 1978–1979, and the status a decade later—before the Telecommunications Act of 1996—of those same requirements.

1934 Act	1978–1979 Proposals	Deregulation by 1989
Regulation needed to: Promote the public interest, convenience, or necessity	"To the extent marketplace forces are deficient"	As in 1934 act
The Regulatory Agency FCC, with 7 members	Communications Regulatory Commission, with 5 members	FCC, with 5 members
Fees No provision	Spectrum fee on all licenses, to be used to pay for FCC, public broadcasting	Application fees for all services
License Terms 3 years maximum (renewable)	Indefinite for radio; 10 years for TV	7 years for radio, 5 years for TV
Renewals Okay if in public interest; comparative hearing if competing applications	Lottery proceeding for competing applications with minority preferences	Comparative process intact for radio-TV; lottery for new services with some minority preferences
Program Regulations None: gives FCC limited discretion	Eliminate program guidelines, limits on advertising, Fairness Doctrine, ascertainment	All proposals later adopted in modified form by FCC
Political Broadcasting Original Section 315	Would continue for TV, might be eliminated for radio. Would exempt some campaigns	Section 315, though modified, still in place
Public Broadcasting None: added in 1967	Eliminate CPB and set up a program endowment; allow editorializing	CPB still in place; stations can now editorialize
Ownership Limits None: FCC can adopt; FCC set 7-7-7 in 1954	One station per market; otherwise no limit on number of stations	Still one per market, but 12-12-12 nationwide
Cable Regulation None	Would eliminate then-existing FCC rules, require cable systems to get consent of broadcasters before carrying signal	Most FCC rules gone; cable enjoys retransmission consent under copyright act. 1984 cable act largely deregulatory

almost total deregulation of radio content requirements, different funding mechanisms for public broadcasting, and ways of having licensees pay for the right to use the spectrum. The papers were designed to stimulate and crystallize thinking, one staff member even assuring a group of academics that the committee would consider all ideas, even "crazy ones." Instead, they often stimulated fear and opposition.

A year later, Van Deerlin introduced H.R. 13015, hopefully titled the "Communications Act of 1978." Among other things, the huge bill, which was designed to supersede the 1934 act, called for replacement of the FCC with a five-member Communications Regulatory Commission, which would regulate "only to the extent marketplace forces are deficient" and would thus do away with the "public interest, convenience, and/or necessity" standard in the existing legislation. For electronic media, the bill envisioned the total deregulation of radio, no federal regulation of cable (leaving that to state and local authorities), lengthening the television station license period from three to five years and extending it to "indefinite" after a decade, no more multiple ownership of stations in the same market (though "grandfathering" of the many existing radio-television combinations would be allowed), and limiting of one person's or firm's ownership to no more than 10 radio and 10 television stations (instead of the existing 7-7-7 limit, or 21). To replace the Fairness Doctrine, the bill proposed a more general "equity principle" that called for balanced treatment of controversy but did not require coverage of issues in the first place. The "equal-time" political broadcasting requirements would be eliminated on radio for national and statewide races. It sounded too good to be true—and there was a kicker, which broadcasters instantly rallied against. All licensees (not just broadcasters) were to pay a spectrum license fee to operate, the funds going to defray the cost of regulation and to serve public, minority, and rural telecommunication needs. Extensive hearings in Washington's July heat received testimony from a divided industry and a divided FCC—several commissioners were firmly against the radical changes proposed. Van Deerlin was forced to agree that the rewrite needed rewriting.

In March 1979, Van Deerlin introduced H.R. 3333, which carried broadcast deregulation even further. It provided that there would be no enforcement of Fairness Doctrine and EEO requirements for radio. In addition, the bill proposed indefinite licenses for the aural broadcast services and elimination of comparative hearings and substitution of random selection—lotteries—for new stations. There would be no radio ownership rules, and public stations would be allowed to carry some commercials. But the new bill still contained the spectrum license fee as a trade-off. And *Broadcasting* editorialized that with the new rewrite, "Van Deerlin threatened to steal the all-purpose security blanket"—the 1934 act—which, despite its faults, the players clearly understood. Other critics attacked the lottery provision, suggesting that giving a license to the luckiest rather than the best qualified was a concept that should stay in the Las Vegas casinos. (Another proposal, not in the bill, that proposed that licenses be auctioned off, was met with approval only by those with lots of money.)

By then, as the subcommittee headed into further weeks of hearings, positions had hardened and there was clearly too much controversy and disagreement among and within the many industries involved. Van Deerlin thus reluctantly agreed that his staff would concentrate on common carrier matters, which seemed to need the most fixing, rather than a complete rewrite.

After the 1980 elections, the focus shifted to the Senate. Van Deerlin, surprisingly, had lost his bid for re-election (his opponent said the congressman was away in Washington doing his best to raise constituents' telephone bills!). Representative Timothy Wirth (D-Colorado) took over the House subcommittee chair. The Senate bills of the next two sessions focused mainly on common carrier matters, and though S. 611 and S. 622 did drop the call for a spectrum fee while proposing longer broadcast license periods, they still called for a lottery for new licenses and for some regulation of cable. These bills were stalled in committee and went nowhere. A final attempt in the House, delayed for more than a year while the subcommittee held extensive background briefings with experts to hone its knowledge, came to grief under lobbying pressure from AT&T.

While no new comprehensive act resulted, the rewrite process was not a total waste of time and energy. Members of Congress were now more knowledgeable about communications issues. While the initial rewrite had been radical in its departure from existing institutions and practices, subsequent versions looked more and more like the existing FCC and national telecommunications policy. Congress realized that without any clear industry agreement on the makeup of a replacement, the existing act, amended as needed, would have to continue to serve.

Congress focused as well on FCC membership and practices. Several commissioners who served in this period, among them chairman Ferris and commissioners Fogarty and Dawson, had moved up from congressional staff jobs. (Despite the fact that the President may nominate anyone as a commissioner, the chief executive often uses such posts as a way of gaining congressional favor.) That certainly helped Congress keep an eye on the commission! Further, several of the provisions in the defunct rewrite bills did see the light of day. A massive budget reconciliation bill in mid-1981 slipped in an extension of broadcast licenses from three years to five for television and seven for radio—something long sought by the industry. Cable was largely deregulated in 1984 (see pp. 468 and 574).

But the 1980s are perhaps best seen as a time of increasing tension between Congress and the FCC. Mark Fowler frequently took his strong ideological views to the Hill, where they did not always sit well with those skeptical of his reliance on marketplace regulation. He appeared to flout congressional interests—as when the commission proposed elimination of the Section 315 political broadcasting provisions dear to all candidates, particularly incumbents. He seemed unwilling to compromise with Congress until forced. The tension came to a peak in 1982 over President Reagan's appointment of Stephen Sharp, the commission's general counsel, as a commissioner. Fowler strongly urged the appointment, angering several in the Senate who thought the seat had been promised to someone else. Sharp got his seat—but the commission was reduced from seven to five commissioners (now serving five-year terms), and Sharp served for less than a year. In 1983, congressional displeasure with the FCC's generally independent policy direction led to a change in the commission's legal status from a permanent government agency to one that had to be, in effect, recreated every two years! The idea was to get the FCC's attention and force it to toe the congressional line more closely. Fowler's successor in 1987, former White House personnel

officer Dennis Patrick, seemed more conciliatory in manner but just as confrontational and ideological in intent. When the FCC unilaterally declared
in mid-1987 that it would no longer enforce the Fairness Doctrine (see
pp. 567–569), members of both houses angrily sought ways to "punish" the
commission and to insert their endorsement of the doctrine in a "veto-proof"
bill so that President Reagan or his successor would have to approve it, a scenario reminiscent of congressional ire at then-chairman Fly in the 1940s.

10.8.2 Broadcast Deregulation

A content analysis of material written about American broadcasting in the
decade 1978–1988 would show *deregulation* as one of the most discussed topics. The move to lift some requirements and restrictions from broadcasting
had been coming for a long time. It was obvious that many rules were honored
in the breach rather than the observance and that far too many waivers and exemptions were granted. If rules were not enforced, they were useless. Further,
for reasons already explored in this chapter, the place of broadcasting amidst
its rising competitors was clearly changing. No longer was radio or television
the only game in town. The introduction of new media, especially cable, that
were unfettered by the limitations of the electromagnetic spectrum, increasingly called into question some of the basic underpinnings of past regulation.
Scarcity of channels was politically—if not physically—removed from the
argument. In an administration that showed little sign of defending public
ownership of natural resources and parks, the idea that public ownership of
the airwaves justified regulation was laughable.

A step in the right direction, from the FCC's point of view, came in a
March 1981 Supreme Court decision that held that the commission need
not become involved in decisions over which radio music or talk formats
might best serve a given market. The court opinion resolved a controversy
that had rumbled through the 1970s, culminating in a 1979 lower court decision holding that the FCC did have to play a role when a station wanted
to switch away from a "unique" format desired by some members of the
public in a given market. The Supreme Court held that the First Amendment clearly left such decisions to station owners, not regulators.

More widely seen as the real watershed of deregulation, however, was
the elimination of four requirements dealing with radio proposed late in
1978 during the Ferris regime. The FCC had initially planned to limit the
deregulation to major markets in which many stations competed. By the
time the FCC held two days of oral hearings in September 1980, the plan
had been expanded to cover all commercial radio stations and had become
highly controversial. Critics felt the FCC was abandoning its proper role as
an overseer of the airwaves. Some were misinformed—hundreds of letters
expressed fears that religious, agricultural, or other service programming
might disappear if no longer "required" (it never had been).

The FCC's 1981 decision dropped "ascertainment," which required applicants to go through a complicated process to determine or ascertain just what the "city of license" (the community where the station was located by terms of its license) needed or wanted from its radio stations, especially in public service programming. Further, stations would no longer have to maintain detailed program logs and keep them open for public inspections. Those complaining about radio content would now have to keep their own records to back up complaints, making it extremely hard for them or the commission to determine if the stations had indeed been operating in the public interest. And the FCC did away with two "processing guidelines" that guided staff decisions on applications: no longer would stations have to promise even minimal public service programming or specify maximum amounts of advertising to be aired. Both would be left to the as-yet-unproven concept of "marketplace competition." The commission had come a long way from its abortive 1963 attempt to limit the amount of advertising content on the air! After the old rules were lifted (and similarly abandoned for commercial television and public broadcast stations in mid-1985), the FCC retained but two program areas of concern: political programming and obscenity.

Many other attempts at reregulation and deregulation followed, most of them dealing with control of industry ownership, entry, and structure (see pp. 571–577). Overshadowed were hundreds of technical changes consolidating duplicate requirements and the like. But it was not quite that easy. "*Re*regulation," not "*de*regulation," was still the buzzword for several years. Broadcasters, initially pleased at ascertainment's elimination, discovered that beginning in 1985 they would have to file a quarterly "problems and programs" list, specifying key community problems and the programs that were broadcast to deal in some way with those problems. Gone were the old but fairly specific guidelines that broadcasters could easily meet and know the FCC would not bother them. Now, managers had to make daily determinations on coverage of public affairs, knowing such a listing had to be prepared four times a year.

Getting the most attention in the mid-1980s, however, was a growing FCC campaign to end the Fairness Doctrine. FCC chairman Mark Fowler had hinted at such an action in his first package of proposed amendments to the 1934 act submitted to Congress late in 1981. Specifically, he argued that Congress should eliminate Section 315 and Section 312(a) requirements on political broadcasting. Congress, aware of the value of broadcasting to its own campaigns, demurred. The commission began to build a record, arguing the fact that the huge and growing number of broadcast stations, plus additional services, made the 1927 political broadcasting clause and 1949 Fairness Doctrine no longer necessary. (A further supporting factor was that an ever-growing proportion of the population now lived in or near large cities, weakening congressional interest in rural areas with few stations.) While most citizens' groups felt the Fairness Doctrine was the only entrance

■ **Fall of the Fairness Doctrine**   Compare these quotes with those on pages 464–465, which describe the "Rise of the Fairness Doctrine." These excerpts from FCC inquiries and decisions, several court decisions, and a failed legislative attempt to codify the doctrine show the changing thinking about the doctrine in the 1980s in the face of an increase in stations and competing services—and substantial shifts in regulatory ideology.

June 9, 1969 "If experience with the administration of these doctrines indicates that they have the net effect of reducing rather than enhancing the volume and quality of coverage, there will be time enough to reconsider the constitutional implications"—Supreme Court in *Red Lion Broadcasting Co. v. FCC*, 395 U.S. 367, at 393.

July 2, 1984 "The prevailing rationale for broadcast regulation based upon spectrum scarcity has come under increasing criticism in recent years.... We are not prepared to reconsider our long-standing approach *without some signal from Congress or the FCC that technological developments have advanced so far that some revision of the system of broadcast regulation may be required.*"— Supreme Court in *FCC v. League of Women Voters of California*, 468 U.S. 364, at 376–377, footnote 11, emphasis added.

August 7, 1985 "Based on the voluminous record compiled in this proceeding, our experience in administering the doctrine and our general expertise in broadcast regulation policy determinations, we believe that as a policy matter the fairness doctrine no longer serves the public interest.... Notwithstanding these conclusions we have decided not to eliminate the fairness doctrine at this time. The doctrine has been a longstanding administrative policy and a central tenet of broadcast regulation in which Congress has shown a strong ... interest."—FCC, *Report* on Gen. Docket No. 84282, "Inquiry into ... Fairness Doctrine Obligations of Broadcast Licensees," 102 FCC 2d 145, at 246–247.

September 19, 1986 "We do not believe that the language adopted in 1959 made the fairness doctrine a binding statutory obligation; rather it ratified the commission's longstanding position that the public interest standard authorizes the fairness doctrine. The language, by its plain import, neither creates nor implies any obligation, but seeks to make it clear that the statutory amendment does not affect the fairness doctrine obligation as the Commission had previously

ticket for their opinions to be heard over the air, a number of other groups—such as the Radio-Television News Directors Association (RTNDA)—felt that the doctrine actually reduced broadcast controversy because station owners preferred to eliminate all controversy rather than donate time for mandated rebuttals. At first, under some pressure from Congress and other critics, the FCC backed off any attempt at outright repeal, given the general belief that Congress had codified the doctrine into law with its 1959 amendments to Section 315 and that the Supreme Court had endorsed this with the 1969 *Red Lion* decision (see pp. 463–467). But in 1985, the commission sent a major policy report to Congress arguing for repeal. Facing little likelihood of action there, in August 1987 the FCC took the final step and unilaterally eliminated the Fairness Doctrine, using as a vehicle a fairness case remanded to it by the Court of Appeals for further action (see box above).

Despite the trend to deregulation, enforcement of existing rules and regulations continued. The most controversial decisions concerned RKO General, a group owner of radio and television stations and a subsidiary of General Tire. In mid-1980, the FCC denied renewal of three RKO television applied it. The words employed by Congress also demonstrate that the obligation recognized and preserved was an administrative construction, not a binding statutory objective."—U.S. Court of Appeals for the District of Columbia Circuit, *Telecommunications Research and Action Center* v. *FCC*, 801 F 2d 501, at 517.

April 2, 1987 "(7) For more than thirty years, the Fairness Doctrine and its corollaries, as developed by the Federal Communications Commission . . . have enhanced free speech by securing the paramount right of the broadcast audience to robust debate on issues of public importance; and . . . (8) the Fairness Doctrine (A) fairly reflects the statutory obligation of broadcasters under th[e] Act to operate in the public interest, (B) was given statutory approval by the Congress . . . in 1959, and (C) strikes a reasonable balance among the first amendment [sic] rights of the public, broadcast licensees, and speakers other than owners of broadcast facilities."—Last two "findings" of H.R. Bill 1934, 100th Cong., 1st Sess., proposing new Section 315(a) to the Communications Act, passed by Congress in June 3, 1987, but vetoed by President Reagan June 19.

August 6, 1987 "We find that the fairness doctrine chills speech and is not narrowly tailored to achieve a substantial government interest. We therefore conclude . . . that the fairness doctrine contravenes the First Amendment and thereby disserves the public interest. . . . Accordingly, we . . . conclude that the Constitution bars us from enforcing the fairness doctrine"—FCC, Memorandum Opinion and Order in Complaint of Syracuse Peace Council against Television Station WTVH, 2 FCC Rcd 5043, at 5057–5058, paragraph 98.

October 11, 2000 The U.S. Court of Appeals for the District of Columbia Circuit orders the FCC to "immediately repeal" the last vestages of the fairness doctrine: the political editorializing and personal attack rules.

station licenses, citing serious rule violations and misrepresentation to the commission. On appeal, one of the denials was upheld (for a Boston television station), while the others were thrown, together with 12 remaining licenses, into a massive legal process while the commission tried to determine RKO's fitness to be a broadcaster. Dozens of applicants vied for the licenses in question. In mid-1987, a tentative decision found RKO unfit and recommended lifting of all RKO licenses. Eventually, the FCC allowed RKO to sell off the remaining stations, but at a fraction of their normal worth. The case illustrated one of the worst examples of length and cost of regulatory proceedings and added to the industry and congressional pressure for substantial streamlining of FCC investigative and legal procedures.

10.8.3 Technical Standards

Until the 1980s, the FCC played a consistent and essential role in determining, testing, and enforcing technical standards for broadcast services. This role had developed in part because of the limited technological knowledge about radio when the 1927 and 1934 acts were drawn up. Technical standards for equipment and broadcast signal quality were needed to ensure uniform (or at least minimum) quality and as a support to interference-free allocation of the spectrum. This position often helped establish an industry, as, for example, in the shaping of modern television during the 1940s (see pp. 253–256 and 318–331). But during the Fowler regime at the FCC, this role of the commission as a national technical overseer was strongly questioned for the first time. In August 1981, the commission did away with the first-, second-, and third-class radiotelephone licenses, which had been issued for generations as indicators of varied levels of expertise for station engineering personnel, replacing them with a new "general" license. The commission then blandly announced that high technical quality was still required of all station licensees—but how they ensured that quality was going to be up to them in an era of shrinking government resources.

The next stage in the commission's departure from the setting of technical standards came about when it was faced with establishing standards for AM stereo broadcasting. Not a crucial decision in itself (except to AM station owners, who were hoping stereo would help counteract FM's growing success in attracting large audiences), it became a watershed in FCC technical thinking. At first, after several years of consideration, the FCC in April 1980 selected, by a vote of 5-to-2, one of five proposed standards then in competition for AM broadcasters desiring to transmit stereo signals. Radio engineers ridiculed the technical basis for the decision, and the commission withdrew it shortly thereafter. Two years later, by then a very different body in both membership and political thinking, the FCC voted 6-to-1 to allow AM stereocasts, but without selecting one of the five systems. The commission claimed that the marketplace would do the selecting, though there was some doubt even as to what the marketplace was in this case (radio manufacturers? broadcast stations? the general set-purchasing and listening public?). The FCC also argued that by not selecting a system, it was avoiding years of delay that would be caused by legal challenges. The result? By the late 1980s, AM stereo was only a minor factor in the AM business, with perhaps 10 percent of all stations using one system or another (by 1989, only two systems were left, and the Motorola system was winning a *de facto* victory, especially after General Motors selected that system for installation in its cars). Despite several revisits to the issue, the FCC stuck by its guns, claiming that government had no business making such a decision, both for lack of money and facilities to do so and because of the dominant deregulatory philosophy, which said that this was not a fit subject for regulatory action.

The AM stereo precedent was applied in March 1982 when the commission approved a low-power television service, with few restrictions on it save a strict requirement not to interfere with full-power television stations (a necessary rule in a political sense, since the viewers of the existing full-power stations would be sure to generate congressional action if interference developed). In June of the same year, in approving a system of DBS (see p. 487), the FCC set no technical rules, merely requiring no interference with other services and even said PBS "wasn't broadcasting." This decision had the further effect of eliminating any early possibility of using DBS to introduce a system of HDTV (see pp. 496–498) broadcasts directly to American homes. In March 1983, the FCC declined to pick specific standards for teletext, allowing television stations to transmit teletext signals so long as they did not cause interference with other signals. With television stereo, the commission in 1984 decided to "protect" an industry-agreed-on standard but did not, again, specifically require one approach. It was clear that in the future this FCC would generally approach any new service with the assumption that no standard would be selected other than a requirement that the new service not interfere with older services already in place, and even that practical rule was not sacrosanct.

While deregulating at home, the FCC, other government agencies (especially the Department of State and NTIA), and private telecommunications carriers and manufacturers were playing a far more active role in international standard-setting bodies such as the International Standards Organization and the International Consultative Committee for Radio, both based in Geneva, Switzerland, the latter a part of the International Telecommunication Union. With increasing trade in consumer and industry electronics, worldwide participation in developing agreements on standards became progressively more important in the 1970s. Different countries often rallied behind their standards because of the tremendous potential profits to be made, as had happened with color television (see p. 476). France, Britain, and Canada all backed conflicting standards for teletext early in the 1980s, while Japan and Europe (and, belatedly, the United States) were squaring off on standards for systems of high-definition television later in the decade (see pp. 496–498).

10.8.4 Entry and Equity

Fundamental policy questions of market entry and of equity of treatment across services faced the FCC throughout this period, often stimulated by new services made possible by new technologies. In a search for "a level playing field" for competition, the commission generally tried to avoid regulating new services at the same time it largely deregulated existing services. Cable television became caught in the middle of the switch in regulatory policy and came full circle in less than 20 years (see page 468). The first important question, however, dealt with a class of people, not media.

There was little disagreement by the 1970s that American minorities owned far fewer media outlets than would be suggested by their proportion of the nation's population. In response to petitions from several government and minority groups, and in an attempt to increase the number of stations in the hands of members of minority groups, in May 1978 the FCC agreed to two new methods of transferring licenses. If a station were sold to a minority-controlled licensee, the seller would receive a tax certificate that would cut or delay his or her capital gains tax. If an existing station was in trouble with the commission, that station could change hands (prior to the start of any formal FCC hearing on the problem) in a "distress sale to a minority group" for no more than 75% of the fair market price of the property. In April 1979, a Rhinelander, Wisconsin, television station was the first to transfer under the distress sale rule. In 1982, the policy was extended to members of minorities who had controlling roles but as little as 20 percent equity interest. By early 1989, 160 stations had passed into minority hands by means of tax certificates alone. In 1986, the commission began to reconsider the constitutionality of such minority preferences. It initiated a public inquiry and suspended granting of both tax certificates and distress sales pending a hearing. This angered Congress, which in proceedings for the FCC's 1987 appropriation successfully demanded that the inquiry be abandoned and both policies reinstated.

Facing continued demand for more broadcasting stations from all sides (except from existing stations and the NAB, which wondered if more were always better), the FCC during this decade examined many ways to squeeze more traditional broadcast operations into the existing spectrum space allotted for each service. For AM, the FCC considered, approved, and then reconsidered and rejected a change from the long-existing 10 KHz channel bandwidth to 9 KHz spacing, as is used in Europe and Asia. This change might have allowed 400 or more additional AM stations to squeeze onto the air. Pressure from existing AM stations fearful of the costs of the change, as well as of more competition, killed the idea in 1981. In another action, Western Hemisphere spectrum allocation changes, agreed to in meetings of the International Telecommunication Union beginning in 1979, called for extending the upper limit of the AM band from 1605 to 1705 KHz late in the decade, the first such expansion since 1952 (see box, p. 95). Although this band was used by broadcasting elsewhere, its use in the United States first required the moving of police transmissions to another band. The first of several hundred new stations in the United States and Canada was expected to be on the air by 1990. Likewise, the squeezing of more stations into the FM band was the result of FCC Docket 80–90 (the numbers indicated the 90th proceeding initiated during 1980), which may permit as many as 800 new FM stations. All of this expansion would be made possible primarily by improved—but unproven—technology and interference-reduction techniques.

More controversial have been attempts to expand the number of television stations on the air. For many years, the commission had attempted to solve the shortage of television channels by planning to "drop in" as many as several hundred allotments into the assignment table on a case-by-case basis. Naturally, existing broadcasters in those communities objected. The debate was vigorous, with some government agencies supporting the idea (to take pressure off those who wanted to enter the television broadcasting

business without the cost of buying an existing station) and others opposing it. Eventually the plan fizzled, with only four such VHF drop-in channels added in a 1980 decision.

While initially the cause of less debate and more promise, the FCC's
creation of a low-power television (LPTV) service described on pp. 503–
504 led to more headaches in the early 1980s as the application process
bogged down. Part of the problem was that this was the FCC's first serious
attempt to get a new service on the air with a minimum of regulatory paperwork. The commission's approach to totally new services now was generally quite simple—when in doubt about regulation, don't. Perhaps the
best example from the mid-1980s was the short life of direct broadcast
satellites (DBSs). First seriously proposed in a detailed six-volume filing
by COMSAT's subsidiary, Satellite Television Corporation, to the FCC in
December 1980, the notion of DBS briefly took the policy world by storm.
Here was a potential system that seemed to suffer few of the limits of
terrestrial broadcasting; would bring in a new player (thus presumably
adding to the diversity of program sources), and would specifically
be aimed at underserved rural, and later innercity urban, viewers. Once
the satellite was in orbit, most costs, except for programming, would be
paid by the consumer. The FCC moved with the regulatory speed of light,
and in a series of decisions over the next two years decided to move an existing microwave service out of the 12.2–12.7 GHz (gigahertz—one GHz =
1,000 MHz) spectrum space assigned by international agreement to DBS.
FCC rules were generous—applicants could decide whether they wanted
to be regulated as broadcasters or as common carriers. There were no ownership, financial, or technical regulations. Obviously, there would be no
requirement for local service. The only requirement laid on the many applicants (more than a dozen by 1982) was to show "due diligence" in planning and ordering satellites and launch capacity. But as "due diligence"
deadlines approached in 1982 and 1983, the DBS balloon quickly sprang a
leak. None of the prospective operators had resolved the old problem of
programming—what to provide potential viewers that they did not already
have. Further, when all the numbers were in, the costs of satellite design,
launch, and operation quickly surpassed any estimates of revenue. By
1983–1984, DBS was back to the blue sky category—for an indefinite time.
But no one could blame the FCC for regulatory delay in this case! Of
course, whether the public interest was best served by this concentration
of FCC resources and attention is open to argument. (See also pp. 487–488).

When other prospective technologies were proposed in the 1980s, the
commission again moved quickly and provided few regulatory impedi-
ments. Teletext services were authorized with few restrictions of any kind.
MMDS grew out of a common carrier service first set up in the early 1960s
(see p. 504).

Subscription television (STV), the existing over-the-air single-channel
pay system originally approved in 1968, also benefited from the FCC's

retreat from regulation. STV had languished in a morass of regulatory red tape so soggy that no stations went on the air until 1977 (see pp. 416–417). Beginning in 1979, the STV rules were slowly unraveled to allow more flexibility in station assignment and operation. Rules eliminated over the next several years included those allowing no more than one STV station to a market, a minimum of 28 hours of "conventional" (nonsubscription) programming per week, and a special application process. By 1983–1984, regulation was no longer impeded STV's future. The problem lay with STV's single-channel limitation and, once again, the need for programming.

More complicated and dragged out, and with the courts playing a major role, is the story of the FCC's deregulation of cable television, partly summarized in the box on page 468. This story had more positive results for the service in question. Under pressure from several groups, including recommendations from Congress and independent business groups, the FCC had begun to re-examine its cable policy as early as 1975, just three years after issuing so-called definitive regulations clearly restricting cable to ancillary status, behind broadcast television. In March 1977, an appeals court decision overturned many of the FCC's pay-cable rules as unduly restrictive or protective of broadcasting. After 1977, many relatively minor restrictions were lifted by an FCC steadily moving toward a lower regulatory profile. In the Summer of 1980, the FCC deleted two important and related rules that had limited the broadcast signals cable systems could carry. In 1984, after years of hearings but little action, Congress passed the Cable Communications Policy Act, which added a new title (Title VI) to the 1934 Communications Act. The cable act, the first federal legislation devoted to the medium, was a clear victory for the cable business. It generally limited regulation to a few local rules and lifted virtually all controls on cable programming and subscription rates, as well as limiting fees to be paid to cities and other franchising authorities—to their dismay and annoyance. The National League of Cities was the clear loser in this law, while the NCTA and the NAB struck an uneasy truce under the congressional gun. While some provisions called for various types of local "access" channels for school, government, and public use, many argued—correctly—that those requirements would be challenged on the basis of the First Amendment. The FCC and the courts also chipped away at the last vestiges of local control by allowing a second cable operator to come into a community to offer competition (called "overbuilding") and by making it very difficult for a municipality to refuse to renew a franchise when its term was up.

The longest-lasting FCC headache with cable concerned the must-carry rules, which soon became entwined with the "syndication exclusivity" (syndex) rules applied to television stations. First established in 1965, the must-carry rules required cable systems to carry all "significantly viewed" television stations within their system's coverage area. The rule, which dated from the period when cable was seen as supportive of broadcasting, was designed to ensure local stations equal access to viewers who might be cable subscribers. There was little controversy over this requirement, even from cable operators, until the late 1970s and early 1980s, when the number of cable networks mushroomed (see pp. 514–517). The increase in cable networks put pressure on older systems with limited channel capacity, which had to carry broadcast signals in place of much more profitable pay-cable or other cable networks. Further, with deregulation of other content requirements, and the 1984 legislation, the must-carry rules seemed to many to be out of sync with the changing view of cable. In the 1985 *Quincy Cable TV Inc. v. FCC* decision, the Court of Appeals for the District of Columbia Circuit held that the must-carry rules violated the intent of the First Amendment by limiting cable system program choice because of an ill-supported FCC fear of cable's impact on broadcasting. In 1986, after considerable wrangling among broadcast and cable industry trade groups, the FCC established a new must-carry rule. The new rule was to run for five years and was supposedly designed not to protect broadcasters but to maximize the viewer's variety of choice of channels. The new approach still did not survive court review—late in 1987, the revised rules were struck down again, on largely similar grounds, by the same court.

Broadcasters, especially newer independent stations and public broadcast outlets, were fearful about how long they would continue to be carried on nearby cable systems. During the same period, the broadcasters lost almost every court battle to prevent cable from carrying superstations and other outlets that also were running the syndicated programming that now cost those stations so much—and that originally had been sold with the assurance that no other station could air it in that community. The sniping grew intense, with both sides looking to the courts as well as the commission. One development that was particularly annoying to broadcasters, who had spent a great deal to make their channel numbers well known, was the arbitrary "move" of many stations to different channels on cable with unfamiliar numbers. Clearly, the pendulum had swung to the other side—and it was cable that seemed to be winning every fight against the older medium of on-the-air television in every forum.

10.8.5 Regulating Competition

With the FCC's structural rather than behavioral or content approach to regulation, questions of ownership, mergers and acquisitions, and concentration of control arose frequently in this period. To the commission, at least until the early 1980s, constraints on the media's "urge to merge" were a primary means of attempting to preserve some diversity in points of view in the local community. (The FCC never really tried to come to grips with determining if there really was any relationship between diversity in ownership and diversity in content.) But the economic pressures supporting increased concentration, especially the ever-higher costs of buying and programming for stations and systems, led to many changes in the FCC's ownership rules in the 1980s.

The FCC's rule banning all but existing newspaper-broadcasting cross-ownership, promulgated in 1975 (see pp. 470–471), came under court review late in that decade. The Court of Appeals for the District of Columbia Circuit overturned the FCC in the Spring of 1977, contending that if cross-ownership was bad, as the court felt the commission's record suggested, *all* cross-ownerships in the same market should be divested. Ironically, although this court tended to have a conservative bent, this was the same conclusion sought by President Franklin D. Roosevelt in the 1930s in an attempt to counter the power of newspaper owners who tended to oppose him. The industry faced a draconian situation: forced breakup of several dozen station-newspaper combinations across the country. On appeal in 1978, the Supreme Court ruled 5-to-4 that the FCC's original plan of forcing the divestiture of only a select few egregious cases was preferable. Most existing combinations could continue—at least until their sale, when a breakup would be mandatory.

Cable cross-ownership rules, set up in 1970, also were examined in the 1980s. The economic tension between telephone companies and cable systems was kept alive by the debate over an FCC rule, carried over into the 1984 cable act, that prevented telephone companies from operating cable systems in their franchise area. The telephone companies argued that cable would never get to some rural areas unless telephone companies, with their engineering skills and tradition of "universal service," supplied it. But many feared the concept of a single company controlling both telephone and cable lines into homes and remembered the bitter battles CATV systems had to wage in order to secure space on telephone poles for their wires. For somewhat similar potential conflict of interest reasons, the ban on co-owned and colocated television stations and cable systems stayed in force. By 1988, the FCC was investigating whether cable cross-ownership rules could be lifted, arguing that cable as a mature medium could operate and expand with less structural control.

Rules limiting regional concentration of broadcasting stations faded as a result of deregulation. Rules limiting any single licensee to no more than one VHF station in the top 50 markets (a rule never enforced while on the books), regional concentration rules, and even limitations on "trafficking" (sale of a license in less than three years, considered to be *prima facie* evidence that the owner was interested more in buying and selling than in serving the public) were all swept away by the Fowler FCC—and helped contribute to the merger and takeover activity of the mid-1980s discussed earlier in this chapter.

The number of stations any one entity should be allowed to own in the nation had been argued for half a century. For some three decades, the FCC rule on broadcasting was to allow no more than 7 in each service (AM, FM, and television—but only 5 of the television stations could be on VHF), for a

possible maximum of 21. Even though only one licensee actually did acquire the maximum, in 1985 the commission raised that limit, first for radio
and then for television, to 12 stations of each type. (The television limit,
however, had the additional restriction that no more than 25 percent of the
nation's population may be served by a given licensee, even if reached with
fewer than 12 stations.) The commission acted after failing to get Congress
to agree that no ownership limits whatsoever should be imposed on radio.
Furthermore, Congress would not support a commission proposal to drop
all ownership limits by 1990. On the other hand, none of the newer media
had ownership limits. LPTV, DBS, and other broadcast services established
in the 1980s had no artificial or noneconomic ownership ceilings. The
motion picture industry, among others, constantly pushed the FCC and
Congress to set up broadcast-comparable ownership limits on the number
of cable systems or subscribers any one MSO could control (see Appendix C, Table 9-D). But by 1988, there was still no rule limiting ownership of
either cable systems or cable networks.

One cable venture did run up against antitrust law, however. In 1980,
Getty Oil and four film studios (Columbia, MCA, Paramount, and 20th
Century-Fox) agreed to cooperate in a new venture called Premiere, which
would compete with HBO in the thriving pay-cable market. The film studios were unhappy with what they felt were low rates paid by HBO, and
thus each agreed to supply a nine-month exclusive license for its films to be
shown on Premiere. Announced in April, the venture was in trouble six
months later when the Department of Justice filed suit to halt it, arguing
that Premiere would be a restraint of trade. Premiere initially continued
planning, but a New Year's Eve injunction to stop its planned start-up two
days later killed the venture.

10.8.6 Regulating Rights

The post-1976 period was a tumultuous one in several areas of law affecting media's relationship to individual rights, as reflected in copyright, libel,
and obscenity legislation and litigation. Feelings that the media had become too big and intrusive clashed with beliefs of those who felt that First
Amendment freedoms were being threatened. Only a few highlights of a
contentious period of often confusing trends can be noted here, because the
courts became quite inconsistent and the number of law cases involving the
media expanded to the point where several publishing services now index
and abstract them.

Two-thirds of a century after its predecessor, a new copyright act finally
passed in 1976, to be effective at the beginning of 1978 (see p. 469). It
quickly came under pressure from constantly changing technology—and
some old controversies as well. The act took into account, said its authors,
both cable and broadcast interests. Cable would now have a "compulsory

license" right to carry any broadcast signal without having to ask permission or pay the station directly. In return, cable systems had to pay a copyright royalty, based on cable system revenue and the number of distant signals carried. Congress established the Copyright Royalty Tribunal to set the royalty rates, collect the fees, and decide how they should be allotted. Each year, the collection and payout decisions were subject to legal appeals and dragged-out proceedings. Broadcasters said that the fees paid were far too low given the value of the programming carried, while cable systems claimed that broadcasters were being given an expanded audience at no cost to them. Pay-outs typically took three to four years, given all the legal hassles—and most of the money wound up in the pockets of the motion picture production companies. A decade later, Congress did away with the cumbersome royalty tribunal process altogether.

Another hotly contested question of competing rights concerned the authority of home videocassette recorder owners to record material from broadcast and cable channels. Part of the issue was resolved in the 5-to-4 Supreme Court decision in January 1984 in the "Betamax" (*Universal Studios v. Sony*) case. After a highly unusual two sessions of oral argument, the court ruled that the recording of material off the air for private home usage was not a violation of the filmmakers' copyright. The court held that most recording was for time-shifting purposes, not for any money-making reason, and demonstrated thereby an awareness of the political furor that would have resulted had it decided the other way. (Delays in litigation make a difference: a year earlier, only half as many VCRs were owned by the public, and the Supreme Court's hands would not have been so tied.) The film industry, later joined by the music business, turned to another forum and urged Congress to amend the Copyright Act to require those selling VCRs and blank tapes to collect a small royalty fee to be turned over to various copyright holders. This proposal did not get very far, since much blank tape is used for camcorder making of home movies and recording of other noncopyright material.

A related concern by the mid-1980s was the right of satellite-delivered program services to protect their signals from unauthorized reception. Led by HBO in January 1986, cable networks began to scramble their satellite signals to prevent backyard television receive-only antenna owners from getting programs free. The commercial television networks, for various reasons—including the embarrassment of unplanned, unscripted, and incomplete "back channel" transmissions designed only for communication with affiliate stations being seen by the public—also started to scramble. Sales of the ever less expensive backyard dishes, which had been running in the tens of thousands per month before scrambling began, dropped sharply as the once free signals disappeared into a haze of electronic noise. Owners of backyard dishes descended on Congress demanding access to the satellite signals, and a few highly publicized incidents of breaking briefly into network signals with signs of protest highlighted the argument.

By 1989, however, nearly all satellite-delivered cable services had scrambled their signals, though many would provide service to individual homes equipped with decoder boxes for a monthly fee. Sales of backyard and rooftop dishes began to move upward again. Although this development was encouraging to those touting DBS, it was recognized that there was a vast difference between access to one or a few DBS program sources and access to more than a hundred satellite transponders—even if the equipment one had to buy for the latter was large, unsightly, complex, and made the neighbors complain of zoning law violations!

One of the first legal issues faced by radio broadcasters in the 1920s—payment for music used on the air—was still contentious six decades later. Every three to five years, as contracts from ASCAP and BMI came up for renewal, committees representing the radio and television stations would argue that royalty rates demanded by the music-licensing agencies were too high, or that television stations were hit unfairly when forced to buy blanket music licenses covering thousands of songs just to get the rights to use a few bits of sound track or theme music. A March 1985 Supreme Court decision held that such blanket licensing for television stations did not violate antitrust law. The negotiating process usually managed to convince broadcasters that they had fought successfully, but the basic tension between the music and broadcast industries remained.

Countless times in the late 1970s and into the 1980s, people famous or unknown sued a broadcast station, cable system, or network for harm, real or imagined. Most of these cases alleged libel—that the person's reputation had been harmed by broadcast of some falsehood. The networks and stations fought back vigorously, generally preferring to fight rather than apologize or voluntarily pay damages. As the law of defamation, and that of privacy, grew ever more complicated, the only sure thing that could be said was that a lot of lawyers were getting rich.

Two of the more widely discussed cases resulted from programs aired on CBS. Both dealt with aspects of the Vietnam War, and both were interviews conducted by Mike Wallace. In a *60 Minutes* profile, a highly decorated army officer, Anthony Herbert, was interviewed by Wallace about his attacks on the army's role in the war. Then the program questioned some aspects of his record. Herbert sued, claiming that the edited segment was defamatory and had injured his reputation. Though the case was eventually dismissed, along the way the Supreme Court issued a landmark—and to media journalists, dangerous—precedent. In its 1979 opinion in the case of *Herbert* v. *Lando* (Barry Lando was the segment's producer), the Supreme Court ruled 6-to-3 that Lieutenant Colonel Herbert's lawyers could probe the producers and reporters involved to determine their "state of mind" at the time the interview and editing took place. The court reasoned that since public figures had to prove "actual malice" (a legal term that really translates as having "knowledge that something was untrue, or with reckless disregard as to whether it was true or not") on the part of the media before winning a libel judgment, such questioning was a legitimate way to determine if such malice had been present.

The other case also never went to a jury for final verdict (a large fraction of cases are settled or dismissed beforehand, but not until each party has spent a great deal of money in lawyer's fees), but it received even closer attention. In January 1982, CBS broadcast *The Uncounted Enemy: A Vietnam Deception*, a documentary alleging a high command cover-up of enemy force figures in the late 1960s. A few months later, the former U.S. commander in Vietnam, General William Westmoreland, sued the network for what he and other "hawks" called character assassination, claiming that Mike Wallace's interview with him was edited in a way that distorted his true views and specific answers. The case went to trial in New York in October 1984, at the same time as a similar case involving an Israeli political figure and *Time* magazine, the juxtaposition garnering wide attention as once-powerful figures relived their key decisions. Just before the case would have gone for the jury's assessment—probably in favor of CBS—the general abruptly withdrew his suit and CBS issued a statement of correction and amplification of Westmoreland's role no different from that promised before the trial. Both sides claimed victory, although in the end Westmoreland had nothing to show for two years of effort (fortunately for him, his legal fees were paid by a conservative public interest law firm). Even so, CBS News's careful internal self-examination (the "Benjamin Report") of its editing process showed that operational improvements were necessary. The case appeared to show that the "actual malice" standard a public figure or public official had to demonstrate was a very steep cliff indeed. (Private figures, however, merely had to prove negligence—that the material defamed the identified victim, and the media couldn't prove that it was true—in most states.)

Obscenity has seldom been a serious problem for broadcasters, though some audience members decry what they perceive as widespread portrayal of sexual activity. One incident, however, led to a landmark decision. Comedian George Carlin's nightclub monologue on "seven dirty words you can't say on the air" was aired by a New York FM station on a serious program dealing with language at 2 P.M. one October afternoon in 1973, repeating no-no terms no fewer than 106 times in 12 minutes. A listener driving into the city with his teenage son heard the segment and complained to the station and the FCC. The FCC, some of whose members apparently were looking for a chance to condemn breaches of their standard of morality (one commissioner frequently took issue with the lyrics of rock music), immediately invoked an obscure section of law (dealing with "indecency," not "obscenity") and took the station to court. Ironically, this was the same licensee (the Pacifica Foundation, a listener-supported nonprofit organization that had several stations) about whose programming an earlier FCC had issued a ringing declaration that the airwaves were not to be restricted to the "wholly inoffensive, the bland." After a lower court decision in favor of the

station, the Supreme Court in June 1978 reversed on a 5-to-4 vote and upheld the FCC's fine levied against the station, arguing that broadcasting's
First Amendment rights were limited because of its availability in the home
and especially its ready accessibility to children. Thus, the court held, the
FCC had taken the right approach in telling stations to "channel" possibly
objectionable broadcasts to hours when children were less likely to be present in the audience (informally, after 10 P.M.). As was typically the case, the
commercial broadcasting industry did not rally to Pacifica's support. Also
as might be expected, the FCC refused to define "indecency," leaving stations the choice of risking sanctions—or making almost all such programming less offensive and blander. Some stations, of course, took the risk with
"topless radio" and telephone-in and interview programs that were quite
explicit when it came to sexual matters. Predictably, it took the FCC until
1987 to bring action against these "indecent" commercial programs. However, in April and again in December 1987, in cases against three stations,
the FCC issued public policies setting up a more general definition of indecent material and setting aside the midnight to 6 A.M. time period as a "safe
harbor," when parents could be assumed to control the set, a time period for
stations to have somewhat more latitude in what they broadcast to adults.
The decision seemed both to free broadcasters (in the six-hour period after
midnight—a so-called "safe haven" that was removed by Congress in 1988
in a law later overturned by the courts) and to tie them to a somewhat vague
standard (for the other 18 hours of the day), to the concern of First Amendment purists.

On the other hand, even the commission could not overlook the changes
in American mores, where four-letter words were used in situations hardly
dreamed of a decade or two before and where "jiggle" or "T&A" portrayals
of well-endowed women and men, and steamy encounters between them,
were a staple attraction in prime time—as well as daytime and late-night—
programming.

The 1984 cable act made illegal the cable transmission of obscene material (while preempting local regulation of content for any other reason, including indecency—a concern of many, given the content of some pay-
cable channels). Several states, notably Utah, tried more specific restrictive
laws—the very existence of the Playboy Channel was offensive to some
legislators—but were defeated on court appeal, since the 1984 federal cable
law preempted state action in this area as well as others.

10.8.7 Regulation Overview: Abandoning the Trust

By 1988, the electronic media could look back on more than a decade of
confusion, competition, and courtroom and congressional pressure—and
substantial progress in deregulation. Licenses now ran for longer periods
and it was harder for a challenger to petition to deny a station's license

renewal; the FCC played a much-diminished role in content; the Fairness Doctrine was dead, since congressional supporters didn't number enough be able to override a presidential veto; and citizens' action groups typically were demoralized and ineffective. The FCC had come to be perceived by the industry as cooperative and market oriented, not as a regulator or critic. On the other hand, many citizens felt that the commission had abdicated its responsibilities.

10.9 Impact

Long before the 1980s, broadcasting had become an integral part of every American's daily landscape. We awoke to radio news and weather and traffic reports. We switched on one of the network morning shows to have some light news and entertainment while getting dressed and eating breakfast. We drove to and from work with four- (or six- or eight-) speaker AM and FM stereo and tape decks in our cars. After watching the evening's prime time fare, or a rented videocassette, we might go to sleep after a late-evening television news wrap-up or stay up with a late-night show or cable movie rerun. We denied that the derogatory term "couch potato" applied to us and pointed to our careful selection of programs from *TV Guide* or the newspaper.

A radio receiver was nearly always within reach—even when traveling on mass transit, thanks to featherweight earphones of superb quality. While 2-inch portable television sets were only a novelty item in the 1980s, who was to say what they might become in later years? The 1980s might have been another period of consolidation, simply underlining this universal availability of receivers and programming with improved technology. We had more options from which to choose and somewhat more control over what we watched and heard—so long as it was chosen from what the station licensee or cable system operator made available to us.

10.9.1 Competing for the Consumer

Other media continued to respond to the changing challenges of broadcasting and its newer brethren. Newspapers increasingly took on the short and snappy story approach of television news, perhaps best epitomized by the rise of *USA Today*, the first attempt at a truly national American newspaper designed as such from the ground up. Published by the huge Gannett chain based in Washington, D.C., and printed in plants all over the country, *USA Today* first appeared in selected sample markets in 1981 and was soon sold across the country from ubiquitous sales boxes designed to look like television sets. *USA Today* made creative use of color (becoming perhaps the first newspaper best known for its weather page!), short stories from every state, and focused writing backed up with photos and clear diagrams and tables. Although deprecatingly called "McPaper" (a reference to the homogenized food to be found across the nation at the sign of the golden arches), *USA Today* met and exceeded all of its financial and circulation predictions. (A televised version launched in the Fall of 1988, however, received terrible reviews and soon failed, since the very appeal of the print *USA Today*—the reader's ability to turn to the section and page that interested him or her—was lost in the necessarily linear presentation of television.) Other papers followed suit. At the same time, newspapers also provided more soft and entertainment news as their hard news function diminished further in the face of competition from round-the-clock radio and television news availability, as well as, later, the Internet.

Although newspapers remained the medium of choice for some types of advertising—local department stores, for example—the handwriting was on the wall: the overall circulation of newspapers in this country had only remained steady while the population grew. Younger generations were finding newspapers more and more irrelevant, except for some advertisements and entertainment features such as sports, the comics, and even horoscopes. Yet another trend, similar to that found in most industries, was the ever-growing concentration of ownership in the newspaper business. Between 1963 and 1988, the number of daily newspapers in the United States dropped by 6 percent to 1,645—but the proportion of those owned by a group or chain more than doubled, from 31% to 74%. In some cases, editorial quality was improved, but since these companies tended to be publicly traded in the stock market, decisions were increasingly made for the sake of short-term profits. In order to support the ideal of editorial diversity, Congress passed the Newspaper Preservation Act (known to the more polite of its many detractors as the "failing newspaper act"), allowing supposedly independent papers to engage in joint operating agreements (JOAs) that would save both papers enormous sums in printing and advertising sales costs—and make it harder for new competition that was not part of the JOA to enter the market.

Magazines continued to proliferate and specialize. Consumers in the 1980s were hit with a flood of computer magazines of all types, one of which could claim that its hundreds of pages (mostly advertising) made it the largest magazine in history—until the next month saw that record broken. Color became universal in advertising and editorial material except for small-circulation "serious" periodicals. *Life*, which had folded in 1977 in the face of competition from television for its advertisers, was brought back as a glossy monthly with limited editorial content. *Life's* publisher, Time Inc., did not fare so well with a short-lived national cable television guide, dropping millions in an ill-planned venture marked by a lack of understanding of the multichannel medium (despite the fact that Time Inc. owned the HBO and Cinemax services, plus a huge cable MSO). A sign of the changing composition of the American public was the rise of *Modern Maturity*, a membership publication of the American Association of Retired Persons aimed at senior and retired citizens, to the top of the circulation charts, where it joined other magazines with more than 10 million sub-scribers: *National Geographic, Reader's Digest*, and *TV Guide. TV Guide* it-self continued to flourish and was sold with two other magazines for $3 bil-lion to media tycoon Rupert Murdoch in mid-1988.

Perhaps most affected by changes in the electronic media was the Hollywood movie community. Buffeted by television's onset in the 1950s, and in the dumps economically because of shrunken audiences by the 1960s, Hollywood regained some of its old production power in the 1970s—though producing more for television networks than for theaters. Box office blockbusters remained rare, and the sure-fire ones often were cofinanced and coproduced with European companies, reflecting the mo-tion picture industry's century of experience of finding profits in distribu-tion abroad. But a much more substantial revival of production developed after 1980, sparked by the expanding program needs of the two new serv-ices, cable and VCRs. The latter made effective use of both old films and of-ten substandard "exploitation" films of various kinds (terror and horror films were big among teen renters in the mid-1980s), which had heretofore had few outlets. Cable networks and the expanding channel capacity of in-dividual cable systems created an almost insatiable demand for product, which breathed new life into film and tape program production.

Independent and "runaway" (to other, cheaper locations) production, using portable equipment rather than big 35mm and 70mm studio cam-eras, abounded. Some started to experiment with HDTV for feature films, with the edited product to be dubbed to 35 mm film for release. Cable pay-per-view services developed in the mid-1980s often showed top new films just after their initial theatrical showings—and provided a substantial in-crease in movie industry revenues even as the number of theaters in sepa-rate locations shrank. The number of theater "screens" (a more accurate fig-ure than the number of "theaters," since many old movie palaces had been divided and almost all of the new shopping mall film centers had multiple screens) rose in the 1980s for the first time in decades, perhaps a result of the fact that the cost of seeing a film in a theater had soared.

Many creative figures in Hollywood unsuccessfully objected to the computerized *colorizing* of old black-and-white films for use by television (particularly Ted Turner's superstation, WTBS), even while many far-sighted observers suspected that HDTV would soon replace celluloid. Di-rectors and actors accused the newer medium of bastardizing the product of the old in pursuit of increased revenue and of ignoring the effects of col-orization on the original intent of the films' creators. But the larger ques-tions of art versus commerce took a back seat to the ever-growing need for more talent and for that talent's own economic concerns. These concerns were epitomized by a lengthy strike of television writers in 1988 against producers and production houses (which delayed the 1988–1989 television season), chiefly over the question of increases in residual payments to writ-ers for programs being rerun.

Hollywood expanded in more traditional ways as well. By the late 1980s, perhaps epitomized by Rupert Murdoch's takeover of 20th Century-Fox to make films (and shows for his Fox network), came a return to vertical integration (the big studios controlling chains of first-run theaters as guaranteed outlets for their product). This practice had been banned by the Justice Department in a series of consent decrees in the 1940s and 1950s (see p. 337), but by the late 1980s, theatrical film had sufficient competition from television, cable, and home video that the government no longer seemed concerned about such ownership concentration. The metamorphosis of several studios into rental facilities for independent producers also appeared to reduce their power. But regardless of the number of feature films and theaters, the new kings of Hollywood were the television program producers, some of whom also made movies, reflecting a tendency for actors, directors, and producers to work in both media.

10.9.2 Changing Electronic Media Worldwide

Just as newer electronic media modified broadcasting's role in the United States, so did they change radio and television elsewhere. In Britain, by the mid-1980s the long-revered BBC was under pressure more severe than any seen since the days of John Reith. Commercial radio had joined commercial television to offer British listeners a greater choice. The Conservative government, thanks to the fact that its leader, Margaret Thatcher, was enjoying the longest term as prime minister in the 20th century, was able to push the BBC into being more a carrier of other producers' material than the closed shop of high-quality and elitist goals it had been for decades. New networks ("channels") were devised with careful spectrum allocation planning, giving the commercially supported Independent Broadcasting Authority parity (and then some) with the BBC's two main channels. Cable appeared; local radio flourished; VCRs became popular in the United Kingdom before they did in the United States (given the few over-the-air channels in Britain). DBS was on the horizon—and the choice of programs included a growing proportion (previously restricted to 14%) of popular shows from the United States. Critics argued that one of the world's premier broadcasting organizations was being threatened with reversion to "just another broadcaster" status. Clearly the public service image of the BBC was being forced to change to a more entertainment-based one.

Deregulation of broadcasting slowly spread overseas from the U.S. model, without necessarily the same amount of intellectual ferment but with an equal chance for some of those involved to make a great deal of money. French broadcasting, for example, had a revolution. Long a government operation, French television became a privately operated entity in the early 1980s. On the horizon was a potential competitor of considerable clout as the French telephone authority installed thousands of "Minitel" videotex terminals in homes across the country in a bid to leapfrog over the existing limits of poor French telephone service and telephone books.

In Canada, by the end of the decade, an overwhelming proportion of the population received its television via cable. The CBC continued to serve the two primary language groups—English (a favorite service of many radio listeners on the U.S. side of the border) and French—across the nation, but it maintained a wary eye on the cultural and economic colossus to its south. Canadian cable systems, to the dismay and anger of U.S. stations located near the border, were authorized to delete U.S. commercials from American entertainment television. At the same time, Canadian manufacturers could not deduct from their taxes any payments for advertising on U.S. stations. Nevertheless, Canadian talent increasingly made its way to Hollywood— only to return in order to shoot "Hollywood" films in the much cheaper surroundings of our neighbor to the north.

Complicating life for many Americans was the growing 1980s deficit in the balance of trade. The formerly robust American dominance of trade in telecommunications began to reverse by the late 1970s, led by offshore (foreign-based, but often American-owned) manufacturing and imports of radio and television equipment. The consumer electronics market had become largely an import sector even by the late 1960s. Costs of labor and parts were lower in the Far East (initially Japan and more recently Korea, Taiwan, Hong Kong, and Singapore—and China). By the end of the 1980s, virtually no radios or VCRs and very few television sets were being made in America by U.S. firms—or had been for years. After 1981, however, even industrial telecommunications equipment markets became import rather than export centers. Protectionist pressures grew in organized labor and its congressional allies. Only one American export product remained strong, despite active protectionist moves by other countries: television programming.

Partially due to the interest in increasing sales abroad, American companies became more active in international meetings held to set technical standards and make spectrum allocation decisions. Because these meetings usually were held under the auspices of the International Telecommunication Union or one of its constituent bodies, planning for such meetings had to take place under State Department auspices (with help from the NTIA and the FCC) and required a great deal of debate before the U.S. delegation could decide on a national position. Emerging technologies, such as HDTV (see pp. 496–498), were particularly problematic. Neither European countries nor the United States were enchanted with the idea of giving over the future of television to a Japanese-developed technology that would threaten their own still-viable consumer electronics industries.

International meetings, attended by often sizable U.S. delegations made up of both government and private sector personnel, also worked for improved spectrum efficiency (crowding of more services into the same space) and debated questions of equal access by all nations to the important geostationary communications satellite orbit 22,300 miles out in space. The loss of launch capacity caused by suspension of U.S. space shuttle flights for nearly three years following the 1986 *Challenger* disaster and some mishaps in European space rocket launches added spice to the situation— particularly after the USSR and China offered to loft other nations' satellites for a reasonable price.

Sometimes these meetings were confrontational. American response to an increasingly politicized Unesco was very negative. Long a center of important research and action on communications, especially for developing nations, by the late 1970s this Paris-based U.N. specialized agency, under the direction of Secretary General M'Bow, had become increasingly obsessed with Third World social and political issues. This had caused discomfort for many Western countries that felt that the educational, scientific, and cultural emphasis for which Unesco had been designed was being buried in political controversy. Of most concern to American media was Unesco's support of a "New World Information Order" (NWIO), a scheme calling for greater Western support for Third World communication concerns. These included training (no problem there); access to the worldwide telecommunications networks, including satellites—which, it was pointedly emphasized, passed directly over the territory of many Third World nations (also acceptable); control over information that leaves a nation, to include licensing of reporters and other government oversight of media, such as a willingness to punish one's own reporters who offend another country (all of this repugnant to Americans used to operating under the First Amendment); and control by a country over what information comes into its territory (which most Americans would call "censorship"). The 1980 Unesco publication of an extensive report on the NWIO by a commission headed by Ireland's Sean MacBride brought American unhappiness with Unesco's direction to a new peak. Finally, after several more years of attempting to work change from within, the United States pulled out of Unesco membership (thus depriving the organization of about a quarter of its income) in an attempt to apply pressure to change Unesco's goals back to research and support of educational and cultural activities (it had been less involved in scientific matters). If nothing else, this debate helped to illustrate the growing central role of communications in the lives of most countries—and the growing interdependence of the United States with the rest of the world.

10.9.3 Period Overview

If the 1961–1976 period discussed in chapter 9 was one of evolution, the 1977–1989 period was clearly more revolutionary. Broadcasting no longer had a huge consumer market largely to itself as cable and VCRs developed as majority service providers. The networks, dominant in the late 1970s, faced a declining audience by the 1980s, as well as a host of cable network competitors. Programming looked and sounded much the same throughout this period—there simply was more of it produced for cable and VCR audiences, as well as a still-growing number of broadcast stations.

The relationships of government and the electronic media underwent a fundamental shift in the 1980s, a shift likely to outlast any short-term political changes. The FCC no longer was seen as a "national nanny," as Mark Fowler once called it. Indeed, television was no longer perceived as something special—it now was, to use another Fowler phrase, simply a "toaster with pictures" and thus should be regulated no more or less than most other businesses. There was general agreement in Congress and the FCC that past days of close regulation and guidelines were gone for good. Just as clearly, there also was disagreement about some important details of the trend toward less regulation, especially concerning ownership limitations, the Fairness Doctrine, and programming for or received by children. The pace of deregulation had slowed by the late 1980s, partly due to congressional unhappiness with the commission and partly due to a dwindling number of things left to deregulate, but indicating that a period of consolidation and consideration was at hand.

In the end, the public was receiving technically better quality material by the end of the 1980s, though largely more of the same so far as content was concerned. Yet surveys showed that the audience was generally pleased with—or, at least, did not want to discard—electronic media. As broadcasting approached its three-quarter-century mark, it appeared to maintain its central role in the lives of most Americans.

Selected Further Reading

(Alphabetical within topics. For full citations, see Appendix D.)

Cable's developing status is discussed in Baldwin and McVoy (1988), Banks (1996), Garay (1988), Mair (1988), Rowman (1983), and Webb (1983). The intertwined stories of Ted Turner and CNN are related in Bibb (1993), Goldberg and Goldberg (1995), and Whittemore (1990). Among the many assessments of "new" technology in this period are Antebi (1982), Braun and MacDonald (1982), Compaine (1984), Cook and Vaughan (1983), Ganley and Ganley (1987), Graham (1986), Greenberger (1985), Gross (1986), Hecht (1999) on the rise of fiber optics, Reid (1984), Singleton (1986), and Smith (1976). Braun (1994) relates the short, sad story of AM stereo.

Contemporary assessments of the broadcasting industry are found in Bedell (1981), Block (1990), FCC (1980), Goldenson (1991) and Quinlan (1979) on ABC, Tunstall and Walker (1981), and Williams (1989) also on ABC. Tensions in public broadcasting are illuminated in Carnegie (1979), CPB annual reports for this period, National Association of Public Television Stations (1984), and the Temporary Commission on Alternative Financing for Public Telecommunications (1982–1983). The commercial industry is further described in Arlen (1980), Heighton and Cunningham (1984), and Poltrack (1983).

Entertainment programming sources are listed in chapter seven, but for this period see network-level assessments in Christensen and Stauth (1984), Eliot (1983), Gitlin (1983), and Sklar (1980). The growing role of religious broadcasting is made evident in Frankl (1986), Hadden and Shupe (1988), and Horsfield (1984). Critical studies of sports television include Klatell and Marcus (1988), Powers (1984), and Rader (1984). Also see the titles for books on broadcast journalism listed in chapter nine, plus Benjamin (1988), Boyer (1988), Diamond and Bates (1992), Einstein (1987), Garay on television in Congress (1984), Henson on television weathercasting (1990), Madsen on *60 Minutes* (1984), and Nimmo and Combs (1985). Studies of network anchors include Fensch (1993), Goldberg and Goldberg (1990), Matusow (1983), and Powers (1977). Political television in this period is described in Bishop et al. (1978), Blume (1985), Kraus (1979), Robinson and Ranney (1985), Robinson and Sheehan (1983), and Swerdlow (1984).

Audience research is reviewed in Adler et al (1980), Beville (1988), Bower (1985), Comstock (1978), FCC (1979) and FTC (1978)—both on children's television, Frank and Greenberg (1985), Heeter and Greenberg on cable audiences (1988), Meyrowitz (1985). Studies of policy and increased deregulation are found in Bensman (1983 and 1985), Brenner and Price (1986), Cowan (1979), Ferris et al. (1983 to date), Kahn (1984), Krasnow et al. (1982), LeDuc (1987), Levin (1980), Pool (1983), and Powe (1987).

Radio and television around the world are discussed in Alisky (1981), Browne (1982), Codding and Rutkowski (1982), Head (1985), Katz and Wedell (1977), Lent (1978), Soley and Nichols (1987), Unesco (1980), Winship (1988), and the *World Radio-TV Handbook* (annual).

"Everything [in the communications industry] changes so fast. No one can keep up with innovation or transactional options."———*Howard Stringer, CEO of Sony America, quoted in Ken Auletta, "Annals of Communication: What I Did at Summer Camp," THE NEW YORKER, July 26, 1999.*

CHAPTER 11

Pentagon news briefing during the Gulf War, early 1991. *Department of Defense.*

> "... to provide for a pro-competitive, de-regulatory national policy frame-work designed to accelerate rapidly private sector deployment in advanced telecommunications and information technologies and services for all Americans by opening all telecommunications markets to competition ..."———*Purpose of Telecommunications Act of 1996, as expressed in the Senate Conference Report*

A NEW MARKETPLACE (1988–2001)

September 11, 2001: Photograph from live television of the fireball as a hijacked jet hits World Trade Center tower. *Associated Press, NBC.*

Chapter Outline

No history book can deal adequately with the ever-moving present. Thus, trying to choose an event or a date with which to start this chapter necessarily is arbitrary and presumptuous. The 1991 Gulf War or other conflicts, the deaths of Princess Diana or John F. Kennedy, Jr., President Clinton's impeachment, the Columbine High School shootings, or some natural disaster seemed very important at the time, but true history requires more hindsight and a focus on trends and principles. So, this chapter is designed to shed some light on more recent trends and events in order to place broadcasting's story in a modern context. Most changes of the 1980s were brought about by a changing cast of characters within an industry driven by growing competition. During the 20th century's final decade this competition had intensified in a merging and changing marketplace.

One consistent, basic, and important change widely evident in the 1990s, however, is that the concept of broadcasting as a public service now is barely given lip service. Starting about 1980, it became—and remains—widely accepted that manufacturers, broadcasters, advertisers, and programmers would fixate on the bottom line. Broadcasting stations and networks now are merely another asset to be managed. This philosophical change, reflected in most aspects of American life, clearly is to be reckoned with until the pendulum swings again. Deregulation, combined at times with just plain greed, makes clear that phrases such as "the public interest, convenience and necessity" no longer have the power that they had for the first six decades of American broadcasting.

As media players become fewer and larger, it becomes more difficult for individual listeners and viewers to have any influence. In Washington, the sole political goal seems to be getting re-elected (which often means serving the interests of media owners), and the means are avoidance of both controversy and new taxes. At the broadcast station level, the goal is short-term profit for stockholders, and there are many means to that end.

Another evolutionary change in the 1990s has been a recognition that program creation and delivery are increasingly two separate industries. Program creation often was seen as pushing the edge of the envelope on sexual and violent content; copycatting was the strategy of choice in program development; and news became more entertainment-oriented. Program delivery was characterized by ever more channels from a growing number of providers, including cable, satellite transmissions, and the

593

Internet. Indeed, once distinct fields as "television," "photography," and "computers" were losing their identity as they converged to a single multi-color, multimedia screen in front of which people were spending more time—and that screen increasingly was connected to the Internet.

11.1 Converging Technologies

During the 1990s, communication industry buzz words included "convergence," "digitalization," and "Internet," with the "dot.com" of "e-commerce" achieving mythic proportions (at least until a financial shake-out beginning in early 2000). Instead of remaining separate and clearly defined, electronic media programming, distribution, manufacturing, infor-mation, and telecommunications increasingly overlapped and merged. Every company wanted to be a player in this evolving entertainment/information mega-industry.

Computers by now were both the symbol and the essential and often in-visible tool of television, as well as many other aspects of American life. The sinews of mass communication—from editing of words and images to billing of customers—now depend on computers. Computers, too, had evolved—with processor speeds doubling every 18 months after 1965, and the RAM provided on a $1,200 machine in 2001 is at least ten thousand times that provided on its much more costly 1982 predecessor. Most im-portant, today's computers usually have access to the Internet.

In December 1996, the television manufacturing industry even decided to modify the proposed technical standards for high-definition digital tele-vision in order to accommodate the wishes of computer manufacturers, dropping the old interlaced scanning technical standard in favor of the pro-gressive scanning used for computer monitors. One could envision watch-ing television programs on one's computer screen, or *vice versa* in the years to come, in the same way one can use the same device to listen to a CD mu-sic recording or install a new program on one's computer using CD-ROM. Specialty "electronic boutiques" were to be found in shopping malls, or in catalogs on the Internet, catering to those who simply *had* to have the latest gadget or gimmick.

Were all of these devices necessary? No, but they certainly were de-sired. A video production house—or a university—without the latest equip-ment lost customers (or students). Yet, everyone understood that first, there was a lot of vaporware (a term originally referring to a computer software product announced and advertised, but not really ready for sale), and sec-ond, it was literally impossible to be equipped at a "state of the art" level, since next week's magazines, catalogs, or trade shows would offer some-thing newer. Some products survived on the basis of real quality and relia-bility, but most new hardware becomes obsolete or obsolescent almost as fast as new software.

Despite this rapid pace of change, some measures indicated that industry was *less* involved in research, rather than *more* as the times might have suggested. As discussed on pp. 485–486, many larger industrial research labs, such as those run by Bell Telephone Laboratories (now part of Lucent Technologies, an AT&T spinoff), GE, and CBS, were either closed or had modified their mission in the late 1980s to ignore the breaking of truly new ground in favor of applied product development. More ominously for American industry, a great deal of product development and most manufacturing moved overseas. The classic example is the VCR. It was invented in the United States, but with the exception of a few European models, all manufacturing is in the Far East. Japan, however, has found itself in the same situation as the United States with manufacturing costs too high to be competitive. Consequently, while many of the world's major electronics manufacturers, such as Sony and Panasonic (Matsushita) are headquartered in Japan, actual manufacturing takes place in Korea, Indonesia, or Malaysia and, increasingly, China.

Finally (although not strictly within the scope of *Stay Tuned*), the telephone industry changed even faster and further than broadcasting. There were many mergers and acquisitions that nullified much of the 1982 consent decree that broke up AT&T. In particular, AT&T itself invested deeply in the cable industry and by 2000 was the largest MSO. The seven Regional Bell Operating Companies (RBOCs) had shrunk to four by 2000 through mergers. Instead of wires, much of the action was in wireless cellular telephone service, first analog and then digital. Cellular telephone companies were seeking more spectrum space and doing other planning for a third generation ("3G") of cell phones that included global positioning system and Internet access, services already available in Europe and parts of Asia. Other voice and data transmission systems, including the Internet, cable, and various personal communication services (PCS) cut into conventional telephone revenues, but opened new opportunities. Like firms in every part of telecommunications, telephone operating companies merged. Plain old telephone service, or POTS, now was a tool of the past, its successors often merely adjuncts to the computer and using radio waves for transmission. However, some proposed PCS systems consisted of blue smoke and mirrors, and others—such as the worldwide Iridium system—misjudged the demand (and the pricing) for their service and quickly went under. In 2000, Iridium had to pull the plug on its $5 billion dollar fleet of 68 satellites and was planning to let them to burn up in the atmosphere—to the satisfaction of radio astronomers and others who had suffered technical interference from Iridium's transmissions—but new owners bought the system for a relative pittance ($25 million) and secured government contracts to give it a new lease on life.

On the low-tech end of the technical spectrum was the demise of the original use for radio—using Morse code for saving lives at sea. In 1995, the U.S. Coast Guard stopped listening for distress messages on the traditional

500 kHz emergency frequency in use for nearly a century. Four years later, the U.S. Navy stopped using Morse code, except for signal lamps for messages sent between ships observing radio silence. Replacing the simple and reliable SOS was a voiced call on higher frequencies of "mayday" (French for "help me")—or an automatic signal bounced from a satellite. These changes—which placed a great deal of reliance on easily interfered with satellite technology—left amateur radio operators as the only regular users of continuous wave (CW) and other Morse transmissions. In 2000, the FCC reduced the Amateur code test requirement to only five words per minute, in recognition of the turn by most amateurs to other technologies. But more than a few of America's three million hams must have smiled at the science-fiction adventure movie *Independence Day*, which showed Morse as the only way to communicate securely and reliably over long distances after enemy aliens disabled the world's communication satellites.

11.1.1 Delivery: DBS and Cable

To most viewers or listeners in the 1990s, the multiplying means of delivering television or radio signals to their receivers were seen as natural evolution. While local television stations continued to broadcast, roughly two thirds of American households received their television by means of cable during this period. Cable systems provided many more channels than formerly, including a number of cable programming services, although those systems offering more than 100 channels sometimes found that there was too little programming available to fill them. Talk of 500-channel systems using fiber optics or other wideband techniques was heard frequently during this period but, once again, ran afoul of the obvious fact that much programming would be duplicative. Who would want to pay for 500 channels of the same thing? To paraphrase an old Bob Dylan song, lots of channels and nothing much on.

In a few larger cities, multichannel multipoint distribution services (MMDS, or "wireless cable") provided programs on about 30 channels, using super high frequencies and small line-of-sight receiving dishes and converters. MMDS, directly competing with cable and with the same national programs, reached more than a million subscribers by the mid-1990s.

Direct Broadcast Satellite (DBS) service finally became a consumer reality after years of debate and false starts. First to those locations not served adequately by cable, and then in direct competition with cable, DBS systems offered most content provided by cable—except for local stations until late 1999 when new legislation allowed DBS systems to carry local signals. A single high-powered satellite could place a strong footprint over much of North America, as was earlier the case for parts of Europe, permitting the use of small 12- to 18-inch dishes for reception. Use of video compression technology allowed transmission of more channels, making DBS offerings more diverse than those of many terrestrial cable systems.

The first modern U.S. DBS system placed in service was DirecTV, launched by Hughes in June 1994. It was quickly popular, with people unable to receive cable (or unhappy with it) signing up at a faster rate than they had bought any other consumer electronic product or service in the past. While the industry hoped to reach a goal of at least 15 million U.S. subscribers by the turn of the century, it didn't quite make it, with firm figures reaching only about two-thirds of that level. Early in 1996, when AT&T bought 2.5% of DirecTV, the price they paid extrapolated the total value of the firm to $5.5 billion. Yet, of more than two dozen applications for DBS/DSS processed by the FCC after 1981, only four—U.S. Satellite Broadcasting Co. (USSB), Hughes DirecTV, Primestar, and EchoStar—survived mergers, bankruptcies, and FCC actions to become operational by the end of 1996. Since then, Hughes has purchased USSB (for $1.3 billion) and now serves more than half of the market . . . but is coveted by Rupert Murdoch.

But the global nature of satellite communication made it easy for multinational corporations (such as the media empire of the ubiquitous Rupert Murdoch, with DBS systems serving several continents) to make their own rules for this potentially lucrative business in an era of deregulation. Deals for the control of satellite transponder channels, between sometimes-unlikely partners, became commonplace. The several hundred million dollar cost of a satellite, its launch, and necessary insurance, restricted the hardware itself to the larger companies.

On the other hand, thanks to competition with other DBS providers and cable, consumer cost for a small receiving dish with a direct line of sight to the desired satellite dropped from more than a thousand dollars in 1994 to $199 by 1997, including large hardware discounts given to those who signed long-term agreements for the program service. Monthly fees, which had to cover operating costs, profits, and license fees charged by content copyright holders, generally were only slightly higher than cable's. Although some people still used the older large dishes that could be aimed at more than one satellite, scrambling of signals on most satellites (and the fee paid to have them unscrambled) and availability of the cheaper DBS served to restrict expansion of this market.

Despite DBS inroads, cable remained king. Where cable service was considered adequate, there was little reason other than price to switch to satellite. The proportion of the audience willing to bother with an antenna to receive a relatively small number of on-air channels steadily declined. An increasing number of subscribers watched premium channels and thus paid higher monthly bills (see pp. 619–624).

By the late 1990s, cable operators were promoting cable modems, with very high speed connections to the Internet, on systems that had been rebuilt from coaxial to fiber optic cable. Since surfing the Internet and broadcasting were competitors for people's leisure time, this development didn't help broadcasting—but it did make cable more profitable. Similarly, cable proposed using its facilities for voice telephone service, but cable's spotty record for consumer service led to a wary reception of both initiatives. Other utilities connected directly to homes, including local or regional telephone and electric power companies (whose own deregulation allowed them to spread into other fields), also were making strategic agreements with Internet service providers. Such formerly rare moves of one industry into areas long claimed by another were becoming more common—and uncertainty bred fear and a new label: convergence.

11.1.2 Home Entertainment

By 2001, the home television set might boast a screen up to 35 inches for direct-view, and perhaps five feet across for projection units. They were cheaper, flatter, and thinner, although flat screens to hang on the wall (a goal since electronic television was invented) were only starting to appear. Novelties such as battery operated sets, and experiments such as units that could be worn like eyeglasses, achieved little popularity. Nobody bothered to repair smaller sets, since they could be replaced for $100 or less. Features such as *picture-in-picture* were selling points, as was the ability to plug television audio into high-quality stereo loudspeakers. Some could be used with computers—or, more commonly, with computer games. Television audio was now increasingly supplied in stereo, and a closed-caption system for the hearing-impaired continued in widespread use. A device that would prevent the showing of scenes rated as violent by the networks, the *V-chip*, was available—but rarely used in homes, even those with small children, even though virtually all the major broadcast and cable networks were more-or-less voluntarily encoding ratings information in their signal or planned to do so. Many sets were truly *cable ready*, although cable systems using older technologies still required rental and use of their own set-top control boxes—as did some newer digital cable systems. Almost all electronic entertainment devices now had remote controls that could be pushed by the most sedentary "couch potato," while universal remote controls could operate a variety of audio and video electronic equipment.

Although the television set continued to be the focus of most electronic home entertainment, even in homes with special media rooms or home entertainment centers featuring theater sound and projection video, there were evolutionary changes elsewhere—many involving the computer. The Internet and the World Wide Web became accessible to millions of people who prefer to surf through the world's information offerings, or chat with like-minded people, pursue hobbies, or buy and sell products using their computer—now with larger screen, in full color, and often able to display television pictures. While some used this capability to satisfy a desire for pornography, others applied it to self-improvement, though many still wondered what all the excitement was about. Ironically, the failure of videotex/teletext on broadcast or cable television (see pp. 493–495) turned out to be transitory in terms of content, since all of the applications once proposed for these text services—and more—now are found on the Internet, indicating that the earlier concept was fine but that the means of delivery (and promotion) were inadequate.

Each player in the home entertainment game is aware that many prior technical limitations no longer apply, now that almost everything is digitized and can be manipulated by microchips. Economic factors may delay innovations, but can't stop them if public demand is there, or can be created. Once an old technology has been depreciated for tax purposes (and some of it actually is expensed on an annual basis), if a new model can be built, and someone will pay for it, it will be produced. The best example is the computer itself, new models of which become obsolete within days of their introduction. The belief that graphics should be central in modern communication has led to a bloating of the code used for programming— but ever-cheaper memory has allowed that to occur. Similarly, the amount of information that can easily be transmitted over an everyday telephone wire has jumped far beyond what was thought possible just a few years ago.

11.1.3 Audio and Video Recording

The audio LP record faded away in the late 1980s, although some audiophiles claimed that analog recordings, however scratchy, had a "live" quality that digital recordings couldn't match. The audiotape cassette, by the mid-1990s, also was on its way out after a long and successful run, except for those with large collections of music in this format or radio stations that still found them useful in automated systems. Replacing both was the compact disc, or CD. When portable CD players, some little larger than the Walkman, and units for automobiles became available, more music listeners switched over. Perhaps because they had become the new standard, although at first they could be successfully duplicated only by professionals, the cost of CDs did not drop nearly as fast or as far as earlier formats did when mass produced. Enough money was being made that proposed improvements in the CD system largely were ignored, although devices that could hold and play up to 300 CDs (making selection easy while taking up little space) were available by the start of the new century, and the research lab held units of even higher audio quality.

In the mid-1990s, the inability to make their own CDs was the only major limitation for consumers, and a major advantage for the record companies. That limitation paved the way for a major policy debate about allowing American sales of yet another new technology, the digital audiotape (DAT) recorder and player. Developed in Japan, and originally priced around $2,000 per unit, the DAT obviously was seen as a menace by record companies concerned that consumers or well-organized pirates with a DAT could make digital copies of CDs without losing any of their vaunted sound quality. (To record from a borrowed CD onto a conventional analog cassette tape, besides being a probable violation of the copyright law, introduced hiss and other noise that even the best cassette systems couldn't avoid.) Fearful of heavy sales losses if DAT machines became popular, the recording industry pressured Congress to ban the sale of DATs or, failing that, to require limiting their ability to record copyrighted material. Columbia Records, the largest record company in the world, spearheaded the move toward a "notch" system of recording that would ruin any attempted DAT dubbing. The National Institute of Standards and Technology (NIST), however, found the system delivered inferior sound and was easily circumvented. (Columbia Records may not have been too distressed; early in 1988, CBS sold its record company to Sony for a billion dollars—and Sony was an early backer of DAT.) But until Congress acted, no major Asian manufacturer risked tariff retaliation by exporting DAT equipment to the United States. Although some DATs are being sold, most of the public, perhaps mindful of the costs of switching to yet another format, has ignored it.

In the late 1990s, two further technological developments caused the recording industry to again fear for its future. The first, bypassing DAT technology, was the availability of blank CD disks that anyone could "burn" or record on. The second, later in the decade, was *MP3* computer software that enabled many of the antipiracy codes on musical recordings to be ignored and the recordings of choice downloaded from the Internet. The providers of such music to the public, such as Napster, claimed that they only allowed people who could demonstrate that they had legally purchased the recording to download it for their convenience, but this was questioned and nullified by the courts in 2000. According to a Harvard Law School Berkman Center report, by 1999 "MP3" had replaced "sex" as the Internet's most searched term. Although the Recording Industry Association of America (RIAA) fought back in court against "pirating" and "bootlegging," the use of MP3 already has led to such varied results as a billion-dollar business and restrictions imposed by several university computer centers because computer resources were being swamped by students downloading music. Although there are legal arguments (based on the "first sale doctrine" that allows people to resell records or books that they purchased in the first place) for allowing downloading, it is never safe to predict what the courts or Congress will decide to do—or ignore the possibility that the next generation of music software will prevent such activity unless someone has paid the original source for the copying—otherwise, why would artists bother to record?

U.S. video recording in the 1990s was all-VHS, except for professional users and a few with older camcorders that used different formats. During the 20th century's last dozen years, the price of VCRs and blank tape dropped, remote controls became more complex and complete, and a few innovations—such as the ability to automatically fast-forward through commercials—were developed. However, since many people still didn't know how to program their VCRs to record programs for playback at another time, objectors to the introduction of almost any complex new technology used the cautionary image of "millions of Americans with their VCRs endlessly blinking 12:00." One technique that made it easier to time shift was a device that worked with newspaper or *TV Guide* program listings, and with VCRs designed for the purpose, that allowed the VCR to be programmed merely by punching a number into a remote control.

The consumer video product ballyhooed most in the late 1990s was *DVD* (Digital Versatile—or Video—Disc). Its backers argued that DVD will replace CD-ROM, video discs, and other, more exotic, recording devices for interactive multimedia, because of its high capacity (possibly as much as 18 gigabytes, equivalent to a feature movie, on a single disc) and high speed access. Although interactive, the cost of recording on these new high-capacity devices may be higher than the average consumer would be willing to pay—but, as with the VCR, costs of such hardware can drop rapidly, with DVD players in 1999 costing half what they had cost two years before. A variant, Divx, used by Circuit City's video rental business to preclude illegal copying, offered nothing to the consumer and soon died. While the cost of manufacturing audio and computer CDs has dropped, it is still only a secondary video recording medium, restricted for the most part to industrial, educational, and rental movies, and unable to accommodate most movies on a single disk. A similar product, 12″ analog laser video discs, has the capacity for interactive video.

11.1.4 Digital Picture Manipulation

The improvement of digital storage devices now allows video and film-makers to create pictorial images in the computer—and modify them at will. Being able to *morph*, or change shapes from one image to another, allowed creators of video advertising and entertainment the chance to explore a dramatic new technique. Other previously impractical special effects could now be inserted in commercials and feature films—and even home "movies." The price of professional equipment has dropped almost as fast as the home computer, which, with all of its color, high-capacity storage, and bundled programs, costs about a quarter (in current dollars) as much as its 1982 counterpart. Semiprofessional video recorders in 2001 cost only a small fraction of the price of those sold in the mid-1980s. As a result, although stations, networks, and production houses spend many thousands of dollars to buy professional special effects generators and graphic "paint boxes," the industrial videographer or advanced amateur could buy one that does almost all of the same things for a few hundred dollars. One early unit was ironically called a Video Toaster, and was sold as a consumer device.

These new and inexpensive devices are creating a growing similarity between film and video—and even home computers. While Hollywood studios still have the facilities to attract the best talented personnel to produce feature motion pictures, even the most spectacular—such as the *Star Wars* films of George Lucas—use video for editing (on a computer, which also can be used to create characters and scenes that never really existed) and reap much of their revenue from the sale of videocassette copies. The "filmmaker" of the past often is now a "videographer," even though many still refer to the product as film. Home movies can be converted to video at a neighborhood copy center, photo or computer store, and the family camcorder has replaced the home movie camera. The contents of old still photograph albums can be converted to magnetic videotape, floppy disk or CD—or to any digitalized form that can be stored in the computer and manipulated, to be viewed or printed on demand.

One important psychological result of this ability to manipulate pictorial matter has been a weakening of the aphorism "pictures don't lie." While feature motion pictures such as *Zelig* and *Forrest Gump* at first amazed movie theater audiences with the insertion of modern actors into historical scenes, this soon became common, particularly in commercials— or the annual Academy Awards show. Once the idea was out, people started thinking about other ways to use such techniques. As a result, much less expensive software quickly was devised that could be used to change what used to be thought of as unchanging pictorial history. If you didn't want a former spouse in a photograph—get rid of him or her at the neighborhood photo shop, or with your home computer.

11.1.5 High-Definition/Digital Television

A similar path is being taken by digital television. While the first attempts at high-definition television (HDTV) used analog technology, including initial Japanese demonstrations in the 1980s (see pp. 496–498), it became obvious around 1990 that almost all electronic television transmission and recording would soon be digital, and that HDTV should be as well. This understanding wasn't sufficient to produce an agreed-on standard, although soon HDTV was merely a part of what was increasingly being called DTV (Digital Television). U.S. politicians and manufacturers liked the idea of creating a new consumer product, one that would help redress the balance of payments with Japan and lay the groundwork for a resurgent U.S. electronics manufacturing industry. As early as 1990, several firms developed computer simulations, and later, actual experimental equipment demonstrations were shown at the huge Consumer Electronics and National Association of Broadcasters (NAB) trade shows. The NAB, however, decided to emphasize a vaguely defined *multimedia*, and ended its special HDTV showings after a few years.

▓ **HDTV and NTSC**   Several photos of the inside of the cargo bay of a NASA space shuttle demonstrate the digital future of television. Those on the left are all-digital HDTV (note their clarity), those in the center show how HDTV looks when downconverted for viewing on an analog NTSC receiver, and the photos on the right exemplify the relatively poor picture definition of a regular NTSC analog picture. What you can't see, of course, is the far better digital sound that is also featured in the HDTV receiver.

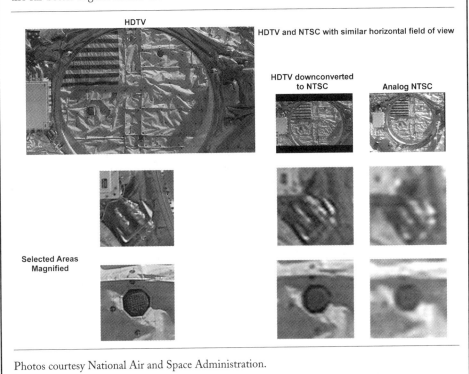

HDTV

HDTV and NTSC with similar horizontal field of view

HDTV downconverted
to NTSC

Analog NTSC

Selected Areas
Magnified

Photos courtesy National Air and Space Administration.

After nearly a decade of hearings, preliminary reports, and even a suspension of the antitrust laws to permit cooperative and comparative laboratory tests of HDTV and ATV (Advanced Television) systems by an Advisory Committee on Advanced Television Service under the direction of former FCC Chairman Richard Wiley, the FCC in 1996 approved a "Grand Alliance" package of technical standards that combined the best of several HDTV systems. The commission was virtually ordered to establish HDTV by Congress, which was looking for a way to rejuvenate the American electronics industry and respond to pleas from entrepreneurs for frequencies that could be used for personal communication devices and other profitable systems. The FCC set a schedule for introduction of the system, and projected the end of analog NTSC service by 2006. In November 1998, some stations in the top ten markets began to offer a few hours a week of digital television transmission—even though receivers still cost as much as many automobiles. By 2001, nearly two thirds of Americans were within the transmission range of at least one of the several hundred stations then offering HDTV—but almost none could afford to see the broadcasts in their digital glory. As late as November 1999 fewer than 20,000 sets a month were sold (which was a 45% increase over the previous month, probably due to the Christmas season). Even HDTV's supporters didn't anticipate a price much lower than $2,000 in the foreseeable future, while a good NTSC analog color set sold for less than $300.

It was clear even by 2000 that the transition to HDTV was going to take far longer than its supporters hoped. The reasons for this delay were (and remain) both technical and economic. Some adherents (such as Sinclair Broadcasting, in 1999) continued to recommend revised technical standards, there was considerable unexpected difficulty with interference in urban areas, and the need to operate HDTV stations on new channels created other problems.

There was even disagreement over what the "HD" of HDTV meant, in practice. The FCC's 1996 decision, which was quite detailed with respect to channel allotment, audio, and such details as aspect ratio (adopting a widescreen ratio of 16:9 rather than the familiar 4:3) allowed up to 18 different video formats, some providing 1,080 lines of vertical definition (as contrasted to the 525-line NTSC standard adopted in 1941), but some supplying only 480 lines—which, since they are digital, still provided a sharper picture than analog sets. To complicate things further, some broadcasters planned to use interlaced scanning (i), and others the progressive (p) scanning used for most computer monitors. The major broadcast networks, under political pressure to provide leadership, reflected this confusion. For example, ABC planned on using 720p during the evening and only 480p during the day; Fox planned to transmit both to its affiliates; while both CBS and NBC committed to the true HDTV of 1080i. The International Telecommunication Union questioned whether even 720p was really HDTV.

The shift from HDTV to DTV gave stations a remarkable choice: instead of transmitting the superb pictures of HDTV, they might use their new channel and digital compression to provide four (or more) simultaneous NTSC-standard programs—a potentially much more profitable course, and one that could help achieve the rhetorical goal of 500 channels in every home. After all, the typical news program, soap opera, or talk show does not need high definition. While multiple channels might ease the financial cost of stations' transition—such a practice might make true HDTV very rare.

The cost to stations of conversion to HDTV was bound to be high. For a period of years, they would have to provide NTSC signals on their existing channel, while offering a growing number of hours of DTV (or HDTV) transmission on a second channel (granted without cost as part of the FCC's 1996 decision). Additionally, production equipment was very costly. When color was adopted in the 1950s (see pp. 321–324), a station merely had to install a minor piece of transmission equipment to transmit network programs in color, later adding a color film chain camera to run motion pictures and slides, and new cameras only when competition made it necessary to supply local live pro-gramming in color. Much station equipment could remain the same. But HDTV requires stations to invest in new—and very expensive—transmitters, cameras, videotape recorders, and, in many cases, towers and antennas to cope with the fact that all stations will provide their HDTV signals on a new channel. Even the set for the local news will have to be upgraded, for HDTV makes all too clear what is real and what is a cheap imitation background.

The broadcast industry, already beleaguered by competition from other video distribution systems cutting into its profit margin, grew increasingly concerned about these new costs of doing business. Congress, responding to broadcaster appeals, passed a law in 1997 requiring the FCC to continue both systems (and, thus, allow broadcasters to continue to use both chan-nels) until 85% of the national audience owned HDTV receivers. Language in a 1998 budget law, also largely written at the industry's behest, restricted the FCC's intention to auction off the "old" channels for mobile personal communication devices and other services. Now, even if only 5% of house-holds in a given market continue to rely on analog signals, the effective date of returning the old channels for auction will be delayed. Hence, stations probably will be able to retain a multichannel transmission capability—and spread out their HDTV investment—over many years.

The FCC's original goal of phasing out NTSC seven years after the start of DTV already has been frustrated by the political inertia of many billions of dollars worth of receivers in nearly a hundred million homes. Why re-place your TV set until you have to? Is the "new" DTV/HDTV programming really worth the high cost of a new receiver? The only realistic likelihood of speeding up the process would be if those who wished to take over the old channels for other purposes mustered enough political clout to persuade Congress to pass a "speedup" law. After all, *any* FCC decision can be overturned by Congress. Although a new industry might result from HDTV, few members of Congress want to be in the position of supporting a deci-sion that would force voters to spend thousands of dollars each on some-thing they don't believe they need.

There are a number of historical precedents for this slow adoption of new technology. The first American color television receivers were sold in 1955 (at prices, adjusted for inflation, comparable to HDTV sets of today), yet it took more than 17 years before the majority of households had color. The United Kingdom went through a similar upheaval when it established 625-line television on UHF in 1964—and it took more than two decades for it to be politically feasible to cease broadcasting the old 405-line VHF sig-nal. (And it would have been easier in the U.K. in the 1960s, since many sets were leased rather than owned, and a "carrot"—color would be trans-mitted *only* on the new standard—was provided to balance the "stick" of closing down the 405-line service.) More recently, the Japanese NHK tele-vision network began an analog HDTV service with coverage of the 1988 Tokyo Olympics, and was providing an eight-hour-per-day schedule by

1991. Yet, even a decade later, only a few thousand receivers had been sold, at prices equivalent to tens of thousands of dollars.

Based on past history, the higher picture quality of DTV, its wide-screen format, stable color, and high-quality audio may not be sufficient to attract large audiences—even if prices drop quickly. There will be some willing set buyers—those who want to be "the first on the block," those to whom television provides art forms rather than information, sports fans, nature and movie buffs, and others. No doubt, programs—and commercials—will look better on HDTV, but will they be perceived as something "extra" in the way of programming? DTV isn't really like the first 1940s television receivers, which provided something truly new to the households that owned them, something that they couldn't have enjoyed before in another format.

11.1.6 Digital Radio Delayed

Digital audio broadcasting (DAB) ironically was slower than digital television in gaining FCC approval. Though discussed and researched in the 1980s, with the Eureka-147 technical system up and running in Europe by the mid-1990s, industry disagreements stood in the way of the FCC selecting an American DAB standard from nearly a dozen incompatible systems. This delay was due, in part, to a shared desire by industry and commission to incorporate digital radio in the same frequency bands already providing AM and FM service ("in band") so that a transition from analog to digital might be accomplished more smoothly.

Terrestrial stations fearful of satellite competitors delayed things further. In the late 1990s, the FCC authorized two satellite providers to supply digital audio radio service (DARS) direct to homes. Service began in 2001. While many Americans already enjoyed digital music service on cable or DBS channels, the new DARS operations presented a distinct threat to terrestrial broadcasters still squabbling over their own digital radio standards.

Although most telecommunications services have switched, or are switching, from analog to digital, the near-term future of digital radio broadcasting still cannot be predicted. However, using historical precedents for adoption of new technologies, it seems likely that at some point in the early 21st century the radio industry will be fully digitalized—after many arguments, false starts, and a transition period. Most radio control rooms and recording studios already are partly or fully digitalized. It also seems very unlikely that existing broadcasters will relinquish control over their industry willingly to newcomer entrepreneurs like those who started DARS.

11.1.7 The Internet as Broadcaster

The rapid adoption of the home computer since the IBM-PC was introduced in 1981, and the amazing growth in use of the Internet in the late 1990s, has created a revolution comparable to the introduction of the printing press 500 years ago. By 2001, roughly half of American homes had access to the Internet, at home, school or workplace, with no sign that the rate of growth was abating.

Some argue that the Internet is not a "mass medium," as it lacks the centralized structure of all previous print, film, and electronic media services. No single company or group of companies, much less any individual, can dictate what is available from the Internet at any one time. To some extent, the Internet and the World Wide Web reflect the cooperative anarchy of the Internet's founding. But, as a technology capable of being used to deliver entertainment, information, and persuasion (advertising) to millions at the same time, it certainly has many parallels to the rise of both radio and television.

Initial users of the Internet, just as with radio and television, tended to have curiosity, lacked fear of technology, and were largely well-to-do, white, and male. But just as older media soon transcended these characteristics, the Internet has become easier and less expensive to use, and the needed computers have become both cheaper and more capable. As a result, Internet users increasingly reflect a cross-section of America.

When the Internet's predecessor university and military scientific research high-speed computer network, Arpanet, was established in 1969, few thought it would lead to applications like distribution of music (see p. 600), the distribution of a new Stephen King story solely through the Internet early in 2000, and several proposed schemes for distributing motion pictures and graphic arts electronically. While the history of the Internet itself—with its rapid increases in speed, capacity, interconnectiveness, and applications, such as e-mail and e-commerce—is outside the scope of this volume, several events in Internet history affect broadcasting.

First, the conversion of the backbone National Science Foundation (NSF) scientific network from one available only to a few universities and military laboratories to an "open to all users" free-for-all operation, and its moving from NSF oversight to shared (although not centralized) private control between 1992 and 1995, made the idea of reaching the general public a possibility. Second, the early 1995 lifting of bans against Internet commercialization led directly to today's e-commerce. A *de facto* standard, the World Wide Web, made it easier to post specialized material on the Internet, particularly graphics, audio and links to other sites. The first browser software, Mosaic, became available in 1993, followed soon by Netscape Navigator, the first commercial browser, and Microsoft's Internet Explorer. When monthly flat-rate (rather than hourly) pricing was introduced by America On Line in 1996, all of the elements of today's Internet phenomenon were in place.

During its first decade, the Internet's "high-tech" and "e-commerce" firms created many billionaires—but financial conservatives wondered how companies with little or no income could gain so much in value, even while they admired the results in their own stock portfolios, at least until many "dot.coms" ran into a fiscal brick wall in the Spring of 2000.

Nevertheless, retail sales over the Internet—from books sold by new firms like Amazon.com and traditional mass booksellers like Barnes & Noble, to clothing and gifts sold by catalog merchants who moved some of their operations to the Web—expanded greatly, although profits were rare. In 1999, Christmas sales over the Internet were three times those of 1998. Such sales were up again in 2000, but by a smaller amount.

Broadcasters initially were perplexed by the Internet, and were concerned about its competition for their audience's time and attention. Indeed, some advertising revenue already was being diverted from the traditional media (including radio and television) to Internet sites that spread banner advertising throughout their offerings. Soon, the networks and most major-market radio and television stations also had a Web presence. These sites ranged from mere program listings or background material to full-time audio "stations" *streaming* their content directly to home computers. By the early 2000s, many listeners changed their habits, enthralled by the clearinghouse sites that allowed Internet users to select their own programming, music, or talk, from hundreds of sources, in their home town, across the nation, or abroad. Some musical artists, no longer sure that they would receive adequate payment for their creative talent through royalties paid by record companies on sales of conventional CDs, tried ingenious ways of using the Internet, from providing previews of new tunes to the sale of an entire album over the Internet—without any physical recording changing hands.

11.1.8 Recording Technology: Here Today, Gone Tomorrow

One problem of media recording technology is of particular importance to historians—including this book's authors—as well as media professionals and consumers. Nobody knows how long magnetic tapes and diskettes can retain their message, people and firms toss out irreplaceable records, while newspapers, books, and motion picture films crumble into dust every day. E-mail is transitory. When we run into a defective backup computer disk, or find that lovingly recorded audio cassettes no longer are playable, then news reports of 15-year-old videotape melting at the National Archives and early CD-ROM program disks showing decay after only a decade raise a justified fear for one's camcorder movies—and for the television programs one remembers from childhood.

The picture isn't entirely bleak, particularly with respect to motion pictures that have been maintained well—such as the reissue of the original 1977–1983 *Star Wars* trilogy in 1997—and audio disk recordings that have been stored under controlled conditions and rarely played. (One of the authors of this book recently was shocked to hear a broadcast late one night of a recorded radio program on which he had appeared a half century before.)

Occasionally, treasure troves are still being unearthed as, for example, the discovery in the Fall of 2000 of 47 boxes of long-lost scripts and other memorabilia from early television's *Your Show of Shows* and other productions in a locked and painted shut closet. (*Your Show of Shows* was an intellectual precursor of *That Was the Week That Was* and *Saturday Night Live*, and is credited with causing many people in the early 1950s to buy their first television sets.) These materials had been stashed away by Max Liebman, a producer from this legendary era, more than 40 years earlier—and forgotten after his death in 1981. The closet had once opened into the "writer's room" made famous in television (Carl Reiner's *The Dick Van Dyke Show*), movies (*My Favorite Year*), and on Broadway (*Laughter on the 23rd Floor,* by Neil Simon). Some of the writers who had used this room, in addition to Reiner and Simon, were Sid Caesar and Imogene Coca (the stars of the program), Woody Allen, Larry Gelbert (*M*A*S*H*), Mel Brooks, and others. Kinescopes (an early recording method) believed to have once been in the closet were now gone—but Sid Caesar is believed to have a complete set. Obviously, finding such raw material from broadcasting's past is a tricky combination of archeology and detecting.

While some sound recordings of many events and radio programs of the past century exist in the hands of collectors—a few outstanding examples were aired by NPR in "Lost and Found Sound" segments played during news programs in 1999—the vast bulk of past television programs are irretrievably lost. So, the problem of preserving and exhibiting the few surviving television programs is particularly acute. There are two parts to the problem: legal and technical. If intellectual rights to a work haven't been secured, it may be illegal to reproduce it, because of the extension of the period of copyright in the late 1970s (see pp. 577–579) and the so-called "Sonny Bono law" of 1995 that extended copyright protection to as long as 95 years. Further complications were caused by the complex ownership and talent contracts used in the entertainment business, and imperfect systems for indexing and locating, often making it impossible to locate original tapes or negatives. But even if a buyer has the originals, they may no longer be physically usable, although there are some kinds of archival film that are expected to permit new prints of feature films to be struck for decades to come and the later types of CD-ROM, because of their digital structure, may last for as long as their backers claim. Maybe.

But maybe not. In spite of the salvage efforts of corporations, institutions, and individuals, it seems probable that the number of video programs from the 20th century that will be viewable in the year 2050 may be even smaller than the amount of programming that has survived from the first 40 years of radio's existence.

11.1.9 Technology Overview

Related evolutionary developments that most affected the broadcasting industry after the late 1980s were the convergence of broadcast, computer, and other technologies, and the nearly universal adoption of digital electronic technology as a replacement for analog circuits. Once a signal—audio, video, computer data—is converted to digital form, it can be manipulated and transmitted at will. With the proper devices at both ends, almost any signal can be sent through almost any channel and recorded and stored in digital form, without distortion or loss. This makes using a computer terminal for the viewing of television programs practical. At the same time, a wide-screen color home television set might be used as a massive multimedia computer monitor, particularly for playing games. As a result, the dedication of various kinds of processors and monitors to particular uses is likely to diminish, with the *use* or content of the information being manipulated and monitored being much more important than how we label it or the delivery system employed. It may be significant that Bill Gates, of Microsoft, now owns several of the world's photographic archives.

In addition to the convergence and digitalization of electronic media (and, we should remember, works in any medium can be converted to an electronic signal), distance has become irrelevant. Almost any signal, from a broadcast network's to an e-mail message, may go around the globe for the same cost as across the street thanks to the use of geosynchronous space communication satellites. While new technologies (such as DTV) may take some time for public acceptance, the delay is almost always now because of financial (or, less commonly, regulatory holdups) not technological or scientific barriers.

11.2 Stations and Delivery Systems

While the number of broadcasting stations on the air continued to inch upward toward the turn of the century, the importance of each one shrank. A majority of the public received television via cable, on which a local television station was merely one program service (admittedly with a preferential right to be carried) among many. More stations were controlled by fewer owners—following consolidation patterns being set in almost every other industry, from automobiles and airlines to newspapers, magazines, books, and motion pictures. In radio, when the limits on multiple ownership were dropped by the FCC (see p. 669), and those who had started stations during the quarter-century after World War II started to retire, the number of radio stations that one licensee might own climbed from a maximum of 12 AM and 12 FM to several dozen in the mid-1990s, and in one case more than 1,200 by the year 2001. With one licensee now allowed to own several radio stations in the same market, overhead and personnel costs could be, and were, slashed.

Although station "localism" had been a goal of the Communications Act of 1934, during the last two decades of the 20th century localism largely disappeared as stations became outlets for national programming. Without governmental or public pressure to present more expensive local programs, fewer stations did so. Television stations made most of their profits from selling time on inexpensive network or syndicated programming—actually, selling the attention of their audiences to advertisers—and now usually considered profit, rather than the "public interest, convenience and necessity," as their only goal. Many radio stations wound up carrying the satellite transmissions of a disk jockey from some comfortable clime like California, losing most sense of location or culture, since they all sound much alike. Broadcast programming—and, in another sense, broadcasting's audiences—now were commodities.

11.2.1 Radio

As detailed in Appendix C, table 1-B, the number of U.S. radio stations grew from 10,068 in 1987 to more than 12,500 by the turn of the century, more than 2,000 of which were noncommercial FM outlets. By 2000, more than 60% of all radio outlets were FM. While FM stations were sold for higher prices than AM stations, few now believed that radio station ownership was the way to make lots of money. The distinction between AM and FM stations became one of format rather than technology. Virtually all new radio receivers tuned both AM and FM channels, and many received other services, such as government weather forecasts or the audio signal from VHF television. Because of its old bugaboos—static, especially during summer thunderstorms, and limited audio bandwidth, which led to lower sound quality—a large proportion of AM stations, particularly in larger communities where there was competition, were formatted as all-news or all-talk stations. Most FM outlets, on the other hand, aired various kinds of popular music—and often found it hard to convince audiences that their playlist was different from other stations'.

During the long-running 1990s bull market on Wall Street, the price of buying almost any broadcast station grew far beyond the actual value of land, facilities, and even the traditional measure of "good will." Family owned local facilities, such as KING, Seattle, or KTVK, Phoenix, were too attractive to remain controlled by individuals no matter how much some family members would have desired to stay in the broadcasting business. Brokers and buyers of stations (and cable systems) tended to look for the synergy of combined management, as well as whatever dollar figure represented long-term value—and then would bid whatever bonanza they thought it would take to acquire the property. Amid the commercial growth, the number of noncommercial educational stations also increased. Also, stations broadcasting more than 15 hours of religious content a week doubled from 1980 to 1995 and roughly half of the 1,500 religious stations were commercial.

Although it was easier to use trade press figures to calculate the price of monopoly cable systems (based on an amount representing the system's number of subscribers and what the buyer thought each subscriber would be worth), fuzzier formulas were devised for radio and television stations, each of which tended to have unique factors of audience, facilities, and location. Often, the purchase was merely to obtain a facility and not an existing audience—since a new owner would quickly substitute his or her own judgment for earlier decisions on programming formats. After the FCC allowed the same licensee to own more than one station in a market (a privilege extended to television in 1999), an owner could minimize costs and competition and maximize profit. Nobody worried about FCC rejection of a transfer, or the possibility that licenses would be revoked for other reasons. As sellers walked away from the table with enormous sums of money, new buyers came armed with plans for cutting personnel and other costs in order to meet interest payments on the money borrowed for the purchase.

Because of FCC deregulation, availability of satellite program services, and the continued trend toward automated operation, the number of radio station employees didn't rise as fast as did the number of stations. And many of these employees were kept on a tighter leash, with mandatory playlists being common. Continuing the process started in the 1950s of airing formats rather than programs, fully automated or satellite-provided content became the norm. Few disk jockeys, even in larger markets, were given the opportunity to achieve the fame—and income—of d.j.s of past eras, with the exception of a few superstars such as Howard Stern and Don Imus. Both Imus and Stern were syndicated to many radio stations, and even had their programs appear on television.

In 1999, harkening back to the original licensing principle of localism, the FCC raised the potential of a new class of non-commercial low-power FM (LPFM) stations. Paralleling the notion of low-power television (see pp. 503–504), and reviving the short-lived Class D 10–watt educational FM stations licensed in the middle of the century, the commission proposed various classes of LPFM—some propagating as much as 1,000 watts (service out to as far as 20 miles) and some micro-FM stations using 10 watts (covering two miles or so) or even less. The smaller stations would cover only geographically limited communities or neighborhoods, and would be very inexpensive to build. This proposal grew out of thousands of requests for means to serve small and localized audiences. It also was intended to regularize some small, illegal "pirate" operations in numerous localities, and reduce the drain on FCC funds being spent to eliminate them.

The LPFM proposal led to a firestorm of conflict. Those in favor of localism and diversification of voices on the air were strongly in favor. Community, cultural, and educational groups—and some retailers—thought of this as a chance to get into broadcasting, inexpensively. Existing FM broadcasters (including many noncommercial stations serving rural areas through repeaters), who saw interference and inefficient use of spectrum or audience-reducing competition, were just as strongly opposed. Debates were fierce, and no-holds-barred lobbying of Congress made it clear that this plan wouldn't be implemented quickly. Late in 2000, congressional action severely limited the number of possible LPFM outlets. This act created its own backlash in 2001 as activists did their own lobbying.

11.2.2 Television

Few television stations—there were 1,600 on the air by 2001—were willing to specialize as much as radio. As before, the typical 1990s television station still was a network affiliate that produced little of its own programming. Operations were more businesslike, and most executives were good company men and women—willing to move from job to job and city to city without objection. As the number of owners dwindled, this was a necessary strategy for a long(er) career. While this gave multiple station licensees more managerial flexibility, it made it less likely that employees would learn enough about a community to become a major player in it. One-time broadcaster professionalism was giving way to managerialism within a shrinking number of conglomerates. Corporate headquarters staffs increasingly made many decisions that previously had been made at the local level, including what equipment to buy, and when, what contributions to make to which local charities, what to charge for commercial time, and what kind of spin to put on problems that arose. While this was efficient in some ways, it could also slow the decision-making process, adversely affect morale, and make stations more and more alike.

Conventional industry belief continued to be that the station that had the highest rating for the local evening news would be likely to have the highest ratings for the rest of the evening prime time period. This wasn't always true—if a network were having a particularly bad year with its prime time programs, its affiliates would be likely to suffer as well.

The decrease in number of locally originated programs gave rise to a corps of freelance directors and producers who might be brought in if the station felt it had to cover some special event—a charity telethon, the visit of a dignitary, a special holiday celebration, a sports match of local interest—that further reduced the number of technicians and creative people on the station payroll. Cooperation among stations for such coverage was greater than before, since most managers considered it to be merely the paying of dues, without any real impact on the bottom line. As a result, one might see an unapologetic WCVB in Boston—a station that at one time was famous for its local live broadcasting—cutting away from the middle of the Boston 4th of July fireworks display for a commercial (to be fair, this coverage was jointly produced by WCVB and the A&E cable network). Following in the footsteps of the networks, larger stations might make arrangements with such partners as major local newspapers and even foreign broadcasters such as the BBC to conduct polls on the 2000 Presidential election campaign.

As discussed on pp. 602–606, the most significant event of the 1990s for most television stations was approval by the FCC of digital high-definition television. The logistics of such a move—for example, there aren't enough qualified riggers to build all the new towers that will be required within the few years allowed—are costly, as is the possibility that the public might decide not to buy expensive new receivers. This expense, coupled with the increasing competition for audiences and advertising by cable and the Internet, reduced station profitability.

The same ownership rule changes that affected radio stations also affected television, but later and to a somewhat lesser degree. To all intents and purposes, until the very end of the 1990s a given licensee could own no more than one station in a market (with the exception of some educational licensees), although under the 1996 Act a single owner could operate stations serving up to 35% of the nation's population.

11.2.3 Cable Systems

Although the cable television industry—now the dominant means of television distribution, to more than two thirds of all American homes— continues to try to position itself before the public and the Congress as an assortment of nearly 11,000 "mom and pop" small business operations, in reality the ever-larger number of cable subscribers is being served by fewer and fewer MSOs (see Appendix C, table 9-D). In the Spring of 1997, Tele-Communications Inc. (TCI), headed by John Malone, alone served nearly a quarter—more than 14.3 million—of the 60.9 million cable subscribers constituting 62.8% of U.S. television households. But mergers and sales in this industry occur almost every week. In the Spring of 1999, TCI became a part of AT&T. In 2001, the takeover of the entire Time Warner conglomerate by AOL further changed the face of the industry, although Wall Street and Washington regulators seemed less enthusiastic about this merger than the principals. More mergers were to come.

The choice of what programs are available is in the hands of very few entities. Both the number of major content providers—cable "networks"— and the number of MSOs is shrinking. In 1999, the top five cable multiple system operators in terms of size (Time Warner, ATT Broadband, MediaOne, Comcast, and Cox) combined served 36.8 million homes, roughly three fifths of the total, and the top 10 served 73%—a figure that has fluctuated slightly, because of competition from DBS, disillusionment with higher fees, and other reasons. But then, in 2000, AT&T bought MediaOne for $58 billion, bringing it up to the FCC's mandated—but soon overturned by the courts—cap of 30% of American homes, and Comcast, in mid-2001, in turn offered some $56 billion to buy AT&T Broadband. The top 50 cable multiple system operators now serve 95% of U.S. cable subscribers. Nearly three quarters of cable homes also subscribe to one or more pay cable units, with many of them specifically addressable by the cable operator. Although the price paid per subscriber when cable systems were sold continued to rise, it didn't slow the industry consolidation. A rapidly growing number (2.7 million in 2000) also use cable modems to access the Internet.

The number of channels available to the typical cable household also grew during the 1990s. Approximately 12% of homes (around a fifth of cable homes) had access to more than 70 channels in 1997 and, as systems were rebuilt, more became available. While only a handful of cable operators faced direct competition in their service area, all knew of that possibility—since their equipment, from head end to service drop, was aging, municipal franchises were running out, and their reputation for service and reasonable pricing had gone downhill.

However, the price of cable service continued to rise. Holding a monopoly in almost every franchise area, and with federal law superseding state or local ordinances, the cable operator was free to raise rates without justification by increased cost of programming or technological advances. When the Telecommunications Act of 1996 (see pp. 667–670) reduced municipal and state control of cable and led to price abuses, Congress stepped in again, placing a temporary freeze on most price increases at the basic tier (see pp. 619–624) of service that ended in 1999. Pay and pay-per-view prices, however, rise at the will of the operator. Many viewers were surprised to find that such popular channels as CNN or ESPN—originally found on the first tier (see below) of service—had been shifted to higher cost upper tiers.

Even more annoying to many subscribers—and to some cable networks or program services—was another clause inserted into federal law at the instigation of local television stations. It mandated that each cable system *must carry* all local stations. While the rules for what constituted a local station were complex, the effect on older and thus smaller cable systems was to reduce channels available for popular program services. In some instances a system had to consider stations in two markets (such as Washington and Baltimore) as "local," forcing duplication of the same program on two or more channels. If this happened, a local station that aired nothing more than another home shopping service could "bump" public services like C-SPAN I and II, CNN, or the Weather Channel off the cable system. This situation led to heated negotiations over which services would be retained, with C-SPAN having some political leverage since it carried proceedings of Congress live, but nobody was really happy. (The possibility of profitable channels like HBO or MTV or ESPN being dropped was never considered). Systems in markets with a large number of foreign language speakers found it economically necessary to include at least one channel in that language—typically Spanish, but possibly Japanese or some other tongue—further exacerbating the shortage of channels.

An extreme example of the effects of channel shortage occurred in New York City in 1996, when Fox tried to persuade the cable operator (Time

Warner) to carry its new all-news service. Time Warner claimed that there were no empty channels on its "saturated" (full) system. Fox argued that Time Warner was protecting CNN and other services in which it held a financial stake, and secured the political backing of the mayor, who was anxious to increase the number of communications companies headquartered in New York. Since the City franchise gave it a channel to use for public/ governmental programming, the mayor decided to turn this over to Fox. Now it was Time Warner's turn to cry foul. Eventually, after much publicity, legal fees and newsprint, the courts held that the mayor had overstepped his authority and Fox lost out. In another battle including the same New York cable systems, Time Warner cut off ABC programs for a few days early in 2000 while negotiating the question of payment. The FCC stepped in quickly and reinstated ABC—but not before many prospective viewers had missed an episode of *Who Wants to Be a Millionaire.* This wasn't merely a local fight, since two of the largest entertainment business companies were involved—Time Warner and Disney/ABC. At the time, the FCC was considering AOL's plan to take over Time Warner.

11.3 Networks and Program Services—Are More Better?

While the number of corporations that operated networks or other programming and distribution services showed little if any growth, the number of program sources that they provided continued to expand.

11.3.1 Radio Programming Services

With the stellar exception of National Public Radio (see pp. 627–629), the traditional radio networks essentially remained mere news outlets. Although satellite syndication services offered virtually all musical formats, stations that wished to broadcast news on a regular basis found that the older radio networks—and newer competitors such as Associated Press audio—were glad to sign them up. Such service was considerably cheaper than operating one's own news department and national connections were particularly useful for political or sports events.

A special case is Westwood One, which started out in 1974 as a radio program producer by syndicating a popular music program hosted by Casey Kasem. Over the years, Westwood One has gobbled up a number of individual stations, the Mutual network (1985), NBC radio (1987), and Shadow, a multi-city traffic (and news) source for local stations. In 1993, the company purchased Unistar and turned management over to Infinity Broadcasting, then the largest station owner. Today, it is a rare market that doesn't have at least one station receiving satellite-distributed music programming from Westwood One. A quarter of Westwood One is owned by CBS, demonstrating that the relationships in this part of the industry are more than merely "complex."

11.3.2 Television Networks

Because of the proliferation of video program services—including any set owner who can program a VCR—it is increasingly difficult to characterize the plethora of national networks and program syndication services that serve stations and cable systems. But as cable and satellite services supplied U.S. households with more programming choices, the number of viewers tuned to the three oldest major networks (ABC, CBS, NBC) steadily declined. Although fully 90% of households were tuned to one of the three during prime time in the early 1980s, their audience proportion had declined by half by the end of the 1990s—to only 40% of the television audience by 2001.

Why, then, were networks still attractive to advertisers? The real story was not that the *proportion* of the audience reached by ABC, CBS, and NBC (and, to a lesser extent, Fox, and to a much lesser extent, Warner Brothers (WB) and United Paramount Network (UPN)) was in decline—it was that the overall *number* of their viewers remained so large. Because the viewership for most cable-only channels often was very small, the networks remained the only way of efficiently reaching a *mass* audience. The population of the United States was growing steadily—it has more than doubled since 1940—and thus network time cost advertisers just about as much (on a cost-per-thousand basis) as it did in years past. This was in spite of cable, in spite of the VCRs now found in four fifths of television homes, in spite of multiple sets in the typical home, and in spite of viewer dissatisfaction with the concept of "network programming."

At the same time, the glamour and power of running a television network has ended. Few today can name the executives running ABC, CBS, and NBC—in contrast to the widespread public recognition of a Sarnoff (NBC-RCA), Goldenson (ABC), or Paley and Stanton (CBS) decades earlier. Program chiefs are as unknown to the public as the "suits" in the boardroom. In part, this decline in image and prestige can be traced to the fact that all three of the major networks have changed ownership (usually more than once since the mid-1980s), and have been acquired by larger firms. As described on p. 512 NBC merely came along for the ride when giant General Electric acquired RCA in December 1985. CBS, which suffered under the cost-cutting control of Laurence Tisch of Loew's Theaters, was purchased by Westinghouse in November 1995. ABC, which had earlier merged with Capital Cities, a hard-nosed station ownership group, was purchased by the Walt Disney company in 1996. In September 1999, less than three years after Westinghouse had acquired CBS, Viacom, originally a syndicator of CBS programming partly owned by CBS until divested under a 1970 FCC rule, took over CBS in a $37.7 billion dollar merger. Viacom chief Sumner Redstone had started in the movie theater business in New England, and later expanded into video rentals (6,000 Blockbuster stores), cable (Nickelodeon, MTV, VH-1), motion picture production (Paramount), book publishing (Simon & Schuster), and broadcast (UPN) programming. In 2000, Viacom bought Chris-Craft Industries' 50% interest in UPN, a move that threatened the FCC's one-network-per-owner tradition.

Each of these purchases cost the buyer many billions of dollars. Some buyers, such as Disney, hoped for the synergy of being able to use CapCities/ABC to promote other activities—such as Disney animated and live-action films or the Disneyland and Disney World amusement parks. But such synergy might have more negative effects. Since Disney now had the inside track in getting programs onto ABC, there was little incentive for other production companies to try, allowing possibly less well written and produced programs to be aired. GE and Westinghouse (which had been among the earliest pioneers in radio, and which together had founded RCA, see pp. 57–62) and Viacom merely sought another profit center. Most of these purchases led to further rounds of cost-cutting at the networks—in 2000 CBS moved the last few newscasters out of their headquarters at "Black Rock," and all networks had pared down their production staffs—and a further decrease in the morale of their news divisions.

The three newer commercial networks all are associated with motion picture studios. Fox, owned by Rupert Murdoch's News Corporation, became a force early in the 1990s, programming head-to-head with the first three by the end of the decade (it had only programmed a few hours on four nights of the week as recently as 1992). Allied to the 20th Century-Fox movie studio, it soon picked a niche for itself, appealing to viewers in their 20s and 30s. Some Fox programs, such as *The Simpsons, Married . . . with Children, Ally McBeal, Beverly Hills 90210*, and *X-Files*, were among the top-rated on the air. Fox, claiming that it deserved some leeway since it was so young, presented almost no news (although some affiliates did) and was successfully able to ignore politics during the 1992 and 1996 elections. It started a news division late in the 1990s, after the potential income from news "magazine" programs became evident. Reflecting owner Murdoch's political colors, the news division was headed by conservative political operative Roger Ayles—although Fox claimed that it wasn't politically biased. By 2000, Fox accounted for almost 10% of the total audience—not bad for an organization founded in 1985.

Neither WB (Warner Brothers) or UPN (United Paramount Network) were as successful in developing new programs and cultivating an audience. Few cities had enough stations to allow affiliation with the fifth or sixth (or even the fourth, Fox) network. Nevertheless, with the future likely to bring even more channels to the home, any entity with programming in its stockroom and the ability to produce more was likely to become a good investment.

Since the program chiefs at the various studios and networks now tended to report through more layers of executives at the network and the parent corporation, they became correspondingly faceless to the general public. A very few, such as Brandon Tartikoff (head of programming at

NBC 1980–1991), were highly respected in the industry—but largely unknown outside. Only when an unanticipated firing or a major upheaval occurred would the news media pay any attention. Although decisions made for personal reasons rarely are questioned by top management when they are profitable to the network, in 1997 the 33-year-old chairman of ABC Entertainment, Jamie Tarses (earlier in charge of prime time series at NBC, and whose association with the popular *Friends* series had given her clout), was effectively demoted partly because she had given a key spot on ABC's schedule to a program produced by her boyfriend. She also didn't order any pilots from Dream Works, where her ex-husband worked. She was forced out two years later—to join a long list of top network executives who were powerful for a few years but made no lasting impact.

Because networks made less money than their owned-&-operated stations, one program might make the difference between profit (and bonus) and loss (and dismissal). Partly to establish revenue streams, networks tried other options including merchandising associated with programs, cable networks (such as CNBC and MS-NBC, or a number of cable networks owned by Fox), selling program videotapes, and more overseas program distribution. Just as the motion picture industry nearly a century earlier, television was learning that if costs could be recouped domestically, then anything earned abroad was pure profit.

11.3.3 Cable Program Services

The number of new cable networks grew more slowly in the 1990s, because few cable systems were willing to make the investment necessary to accommodate more channels. There was, however, a brisk trade in merger and acquisition of existing cable program channels. Few new services made much impression on the public in the 1990s. Some, such as the History Channel and the Discovery Channel, successfully mounted major publicity campaigns to get viewers to persuade their local cable operator to carry the channel. But in general, the typical cable entertainment mix—classic off-network series, made-for-cable movies, some exclusive specials and series, occasional series that had just been dropped by a network, and programs pushing the envelope of titillation (such as Showtime's *Elvis Meets Nixon*)—changed little from system to system.

Most cable services are grouped into tiers. A tier is a level of service, often tied to a level of price. These vary in each cable system, typically including basic (local on-air stations and a few services such as home shopping and TBS); family (or second) tier, which might include Discovery, CNN, and C-SPAN; and premium—such as HBO and other first-run movie channels—for which an extra monthly charge is made. These categories are subject to change, as different content becomes available. Several lower-tier

---

■ **Cable's Plethora of Channels**   As of late 2000, the Cox Cable system in Fairfax County, Virginia (a suburb of Washington, DC) offered this selection over its 120 channels. Some services share channels (and are shown as part-time in this list). Such a system was cutting edge when it was first built in the mid-1980s by Media General, but is now approaching the average. As Cox rebuilds the system to a greater capacity and digital technology, dozens of additional channels are being added.

Local "Must Carry" Commercial Stations (8)
WRC-TV, Channel 4 (NBC owned-and operated local station)
WTTG-TV, Chnnel 5 (Fox owned-and-operated local station)
WJLA-TV, Channel 7, (ABC affiliate local station)
WUSA-TV, Channel 9 (CBS affiliate local station)
WTMW (TV), Channel 14 (local independent station)
WPXW-TV, Channel 15 (local PAX Family Television affiliate)
WDCA-TV, Channel 20 (local UPN affiliate station)
WBDC-TV, Channel 50 (local Warner Brothers Network affiliate station)

Local "Must Carry" Public Stations (5)
Maryland Public Television, Channel 22
WETA-TV, Channel 26, Washington, DC
WHUT-TV, Channel 32, Howard University
WNVC-TV, Channel 56, Northern Virginia Community College
WNVT-TV, Northern Virginia

Local Cable System Access and Origination (5)
Fairfax Access Network (community bulletin board, public access radio)
Fairfax International (non-profit public access)
Fox Cable Access Corporation (local public access)
News Channel 8 (local cable news channel)
Town of Herndon Access Channel

Local Cable System Government, School, College, and Library Channels (8)
Fairfax City Government Channel
Fairfax County Government Channel
Fairfax County Public Library

Falls Church City Television
Falls Church Public Schools Teacher Channel
George Mason University courses
Northern Virginia Community College courses
Red Apple: Fairfax County Public Schools

Basic Cable Network Services: (66)
  News and Public Affairs (11)
    Court TV
    CNBC (Consumer News Business Channel)
    CNN (Cable News Network)
    CNN Financial News
    CNN Headline News
    C-SPAN (Cable-Satellite Public Affairs Network)
    C-SPAN2
    C-SPAN Extra (daytime hours)
    Fox News Network
    MSNBC
    Weather Channel
  Documentaries (10)
    Animal Planet (animal-related)
    Discovery Channel
    Discovery Health
    Food Network
    History Channel
    Home and Garden Television
    The Learning Channel
    NASA
    Outdoor Life (part-time)
    Travel Channel
  Home Shopping Channels (5)
    Cable Marketplace (video classifieds)
    QVC
    Tour of Homes (real estate)
    Home Shopping Network
    Product Information Network

---

channels, including The Family Channel, Turner Network Television (TNT), and the USA Network, are occasionally producing made-for-television movies and other programming, including continuations of programs originally on the broadcast networks, such as *Babylon 5* on TNT and new productions of classics such as *Don Quixote*.

By the late 1990s, many cable networks produced a substantial amount of this original programming. For example, The Family Channel produced a television movie, *Mother Teresa, In the Name of God's Poor*, TNT

Foreign Language (3)
Arab Network (Arabic)
Telemundo (Spanish)
Univision (Spanish)
Music (3)
Country Music Television
MTV (Music Television)
Video Hits 1
Religion (2)
EWTN (international Catholic network)
Trinity Broadcasting (religion, inspirational)
For Women (2)
Lifetime
Oxygen
Sports (2)
ESPN
ESPN-2
Superstations (2)
WGN, Chicago
WTBS, Atlanta
Movies and Other (26)
American Movie Classics
Arts and Entertainment
Bravo Network (arts and movies)
Cartoon Network
Comedy Central
Cox Demand: schedule information for pay-per-view
Disney Channel
Entertainment Television
Fox Family Channel
FX ("bold, edgy" movies, series)
HTS ("Mid-Atlantic's regional network")
International Channel

Jazz Channel (part-time)
The National Network (wrestling, movies, sports)
Nickelodeon (for children)
Ovation (part-time)
Romance Classics
Sci-Fi Channel (science fiction and fact)
TNT (Turner Network Television)
Toon Disney (part-time)
Turner Classic Movies
TV Guide Channel: cable system program listings
TV Land (TV programs from 1960s-1980s)
Urban Contemporary (news, sports, music, comedy)
USA Network
The View (Cox information, services)

Pay Channels (12)
Cinemax
Cinemax-More
ESPN News
Fox Sports World
The Golf Channel
HBO
HBO Family
HBO Plus
HBO Signature
The Movie Channel
Showtime
Showtime 2

Pay-Per-View Channels (9)

Total Available Channels: 120

produced *Buffalo Soldiers*, and USA Network produced *Ms. Scrooge*. This was pretty standard fare, produced on a strict budget, but starring well-known actors in some cases—Geraldine Chaplin, Danny Glover, and Cicely Tyson in the three mentioned. Bravo and A&E (Arts and Entertainment) produced some original programming, such as a low-budget but highly popular daily *Biography* documentary program on A&E—and rebroadcast high-quality off-network programming, especially British mysteries, many of which originally had been first broadcast in the United States on PBS.

Feature motion pictures constituted the largest share of money-making cable programming. While lower-tier channels such as American Movie Classics, Flix, and Encore made many (mostly older) movies available, much more profitable were the so-called movie channels, including HBO (Home Box Office), Showtime, The Movie Channel, and Cinemax. These premium services usually were in the highest cost tier of cable service and often were lumped together under the term pay cable. A smaller and even more expensive tier was "*pay-per-view*," which required payment for each film or sporting event, such as a heavyweight boxing match. Although Showtime, The Movie Channel, and Cinemax generally restricted themselves to the repeated showing of (sometimes the same) motion pictures, HBO received praise for some of its lavishly produced rock concerts, documentaries, and dramas— including the highly praised *Sopranos* about a Mafia family. While the hard core of the Disney Channel audience were parents and their children, it frequently provided high-quality programming for other viewers.

Cable services such as the Family Channel (originally owned by the PTL religious organization, but now owned by Disney), Lifetime, USA Network, TNT, and Turner Broadcasting System (Superstation WTBS in Atlanta) generally programmed old network series. TBS/TNT aired many feature films— including a lot of westerns—from the huge Turner film library. Lifetime (jointly owned by Disney and Hearst and reaching many homes because it typically was on a lower tier) claimed to be concentrating on programs for women, to contrast with the stereotypical use of sports channels by men, but a look at its content—at one time including reruns of the superbly written, directed, and acted but violent *Homicide: Life on the Street* (dropped by NBC in 1999)—makes one wonder if it really is focused as advertised.

Another category might be labeled "specialty" or "genre" programming, and is aimed at fans or members of a particular group. Spanish-language programming on Univision and other services, other foreign language services, and Black Entertainment Television (BET) fall into this category. Concentrating on a specific kind of content are the Science Fiction channel, Comedy Central, the Cartoon Network, and The Playboy Channel (a premium channel that was restricted on most cable systems to the hours after ten at night). E! The Entertainment Channel acts to some extent as a *People* gossip magazine for those interested in entertainment, but also airs the raunchy Howard Stern disk jockey show. Some informational channels, such as Court TV (which had a loyal audience to its live coverage of some of the most interesting trials of the decade, but by the turn of the century apparently was just waiting to be sold, devoting more and more time to police-oriented off-network series, including *Homicide*), American Health, The Learning Channel, Discovery Channel, History Channel, Golf Channel, and Home and Garden channels might be placed in another category.

Although not as salient as before, partly because of scandals, and the aging of some well-known evangelists, there are several religiously oriented cable channels with loyal audiences, particularly popular in the South. Also aimed at a niche—in this case, sports fans—were highly popular services such as ESPN and the Sports Channel. During the professional football, baseball, and basketball seasons—which, thanks to media coverage and indoor sports arenas, had begun to overlap—these channels were in tremendous demand, although there were enough sporting events aired on the broadcast networks to keep many fans happy. Congress had mandated decades before that the baseball World Series not move to pay-per-view or some other cable channel that a large number of their constituents could not receive. Political pressure effectively forced some football games into the same category, including the Super Bowl and many traditional college matches.

With the exception of the premium-cost Disney Channel, Nickelodeon, and some programs on The Learning Channel and Discovery, there was little increase in the amount of programming intended for children. Indeed, there was little specialty cable programming for the 22% of the U.S. population that is younger than 15 years of age—or, for that matter, the segment (now 27% of the population) that is 50 or older.

Informational channels are a particularly important category of cable services. These include Turner's Cable Network News (CNN) and CNN Headline News, various financial services, the Weather Channel, and C-SPAN I and II. In some areas there are local and regional all-news channels such as New York's Channel One, New Jersey's Channel 12, and the New England Cable News Network. Newer to the genre are CNBC and MS-NBC, a looking to the future of computers-as-entertainment/information combination of NBC and Microsoft. C-SPAN, under the direction of Brian Lamb from its start, has a particularly important role to play as the carrier of live coverage of both the House and the Senate. It has always been funded by the cable industry, and has more than met the high hopes the industry had for its public relations value. Other C-SPAN programming comprises congressional hearings, speeches, and news conferences, Prime Minister's Questions from the British House of Commons (which viewers who appreciate debate and invective might classify as entertainment), and a *Booknotes* program emceed by Lamb that spawned a best-selling book of its own.

Although the industry may think of home shopping channels as informational, many who are addicted to this form of shopping think of it also as entertaining. Those, such as Barry Diller, who served as program chief at different times at all three major networks, looking toward the future of the cable industry think such programs are the future of the industry—because, unlike any medium limited to advertising, home shopping channels have immediate, hard dollar feedback as to what sells and how best to sell it.

There has been little recent change in the financial structure of the cable program industry. Pay-per-view uses a box office approach and the premium channels get so many cents a month for each subscriber from the cable systems. However, other channels get some income from cable systems for carriage and some from advertising. Although advertisers tend to look for larger audiences than cable can supply, some cable channels sell national advertising and some—such as the Weather Channel, with its many addressable weather forecast areas—can supply a package that would appeal to local stores and services. Most such local advertising, however, is sold by the cable system directly. In a few cases, such as home shopping services, the program provider will pay the cable system for carriage. Because many cable systems and cable program providers have ownership relationships, it is difficult to draw hard and fast rules.

11.4 Public Broadcasting: Hanging On

Outwardly, public radio and television appeared successful and healthy. The number of stations continued to grow slowly—to more than 2,000 FM (about a quarter of which were affiliated with NPR) and nearly 375 television outlets by the start of 2001. Some programs had audiences large enough to show up in the ratings books, and public affairs programming was important enough to arouse considerable political controversy and antagonism.

But this health was, in many instances, more apparent than real. Federal funding for the Corporation for Public Broadcasting (CPB), cut heavily by the Reagan and first Bush administrations in the 1980s, was not restored during the two Clinton administrations in the 1990s. As a result stations had to seek funding for programming, equipment, and facilities from other sources—and, in the process, became more competitive.

11.4.1 Letting Go

The licensees for some noncommercial educational stations gave up, and sold their stations to bring in money for other purposes. WNYC, licensed to the City of New York for nearly three fourths of a century (it first went on the air in 1924), was sold for budget-balancing purposes in 1996. WNYC-TV went to commercial interests for several million dollars, but WNYC(AM), an NPR affiliate and program source, was sold to the nonprofit Friends of WNYC for a manageable price, thus defusing much of the conflict that otherwise would have occurred. While those within the listening area of the station provided most of these funds (to be paid over several years), the national reputation of the station led to some contributions from non–New Yorkers. WNYC(AM) continued to supply national programs such as *On the Media* and local interview and telephone programs, while WNYC-FM continued mostly to air music.

Not so fortunate, however, were the listeners to stations such as WCAM (City of Camden, New Jersey, which was sold to a commercial firm in the 1970s), WDCU(FM) (University of the District of Columbia, sold to C-SPAN in 1997), or WFBE(FM) (Board of Education, Flint, MI, sold to Liggett Broadcasting for $6.8 million in 1997). Some large noncommercial stations— notably WBUR, Boston—extended their coverage by taking over smaller and hitherto independent ones.

Starting in the 1970s and accelerating in the 1980s, a number of universities decided to turn their stations over to the institution's public relations department, which then hired professional broadcasters in order to enhance the institution's image. This had the effect, however, of taking away a major laboratory resource from broadcasting students in those schools. Among the many stations making this move were KUSC (University of Southern California, Los Angeles, originator of the nationally syndicated *Marketplace* program), KLON (University of California, Long Beach, famous for its jazz programming, and now licensed to a local nonprofit organization), WRTI (Temple University, Philadelphia), and WBUR (Boston University). WBUR, a major source of NPR news programming, in the 1990s started programming several small FM stations and then acquired a larger AM station on Cape Cod, which effectively expanded its listenership in that area.

The Pacifica Foundation stations continued their tradition of internal strife. These venerable non-NPR affiliated stations, in markets such as San Francisco, Los Angeles, and New York, attracted audiences that sometimes were fanatical in their support. In 1999, the national board of the Foundation decided to exercise more control over its KPFA in Berkeley—and ran into a hornet's nest of staff and audience resentment and protest. Localism and program experimentation were fetishes at the station, and cutting back to archived programs was thought to be a slap in the face of the audience—and a possible warning that the station was to be sold. The fight has been bitter and at the expense of both staff and audience. Regardless of the legal ownership and eventual outcome of the Pacifica dispute, such changes in public radio caused nostalgia among those who remembered a less-structured, more venturesome side to noncommercial radio. Now that it was hard to tell the difference between a commercial network executive and one from a major NPR/PBS station, and truly independent licensees such as Lorenzo Milam (see pp. 471–475) were no longer on the air, many listeners felt that stations such as Pacifica's "belonged" to their communities. If enough of the proposed low-power FM stations were authorized, well and good—but few listeners wanted existing full-power public stations in their communities to disappear.

11.4.2 The Eternal Funding Problem

Those stations that were part of one of the national public broadcasting networks—National Public Radio (NPR) or Public Broadcasting (television) Service (PBS)—tried to raise local money to replace that previously provided by CPB. This effort led to longer and more frequent "begathons"—a week or more of pleas for contributions, often several times a year, with programs cut short (or skipped altogether) to accommodate the pleas. Memberships brought program guides, discount cards for local merchants, offers of tours of the station—and many requests for additional funds. In markets with several public stations, one might choose which to support by one's preference for the premium gifts offered—umbrellas, coffee cups, video or audio recordings.

During "pledge" weeks or months, some of the most popular programming of past years—*The Three Tenors, Peter, Paul and Mary*, British dramas, etc.—was presented. Personalities with whom the public identified made the "pitch" and local volunteers answered the phones. Some stations devoted many days of their schedule to auctions of merchandise and services provided by companies desiring free publicity. These fundraising efforts had two goals: to attract members, who now typically paid $60 for a minimum membership that had been priced at only $25 or $30 in the mid-1980s, and to be able to show corporations, foundations, and individuals who might be persuaded to underwrite programs or otherwise provide large sums of money that members of the audience were loyal and dedicated enough to contribute. Although only a small minority of public radio stations were "CPB qualified" (see pp. 517–523) and part of NPR, they were the larger and more popular operations. However, more than a thousand other public stations had to raise money in the same way.

A few public radio stations, in reaction, contacted the list of those who had contributed previously, and offered a deal: if you contribute now, we won't have a full-fledged fund-raiser, and can stick to our programming. When combined with the on-air promotion of matching gifts, this could cut down substantially on the amount of on-air time given over to the begathons. WBUR (Boston), one of the first to try this approach, was able to meet its goals in 1997 with only three hours of on-air fundraising. Several others, including Washington's WETA, had "on-line" days with just a few announcements encouraging listeners to go to a Web site to contribute, leaving the station's programs largely intact.

Another approach to raising money, considered suspect by those who believed that the noncommercial principle of public broadcasting was important, was the "enhanced underwriting" approved by the FCC in the 1980s. This extended the on–air description of those who supported, or underwrote, a program—and the product or service they represented. Originally, such an announcement only would say "Supported by the XYZ Corporation." But later, the announcement would go as far as "Supported by the XYZ Corporation, manufacturer of fine cooking gadgets for the home, available at your neighborhood supermarket"—followed by a lengthy description of the product or service. With the door propped open, enhanced underwriting announcements got longer and longer and essentially became indistinguishable from commercials. While the FCC's limited experiment in out-and-out commercialism had been rejected in the early 1980s, it seemed that it was acceptable under another label. Commercial stations continued to grumble about unfair competition. A combination of underwriting announcements, provision for on-air fund-raising and enhanced underwriting announcements, and promotions for other programs reduced program length for some PBS half-hour programs to the 22 minutes familiar to viewers of commercial television.

Those stations that originate programming have other sources of income. First, like any nonperishable product, the program might be sold or leased to others—such as PBS or NPR or some other group, including foreign broadcasters. Second, there is a steady market for scripts and for video and audio cassettes of programs (which can be sold at relatively high prices and which receive on-air promotion at the end of the program), which cost the producers nothing. Third, it is possible to package several programs of a series and sell them (or, in some cases, give them away as premiums during on-air fund-raising campaigns). Fourth, many programs—including those for children—can offer merchandising tie-ins, often sold in stores. Usually, rights to produce these items—such as *Barney* dolls—were sold by the programmers to other firms specializing in such items. In the mid-1990s, when the CPB budget was being debated, various members of Congress wondered why public broadcasting got so little of the merchandising money. As a result, some contracts were rewritten to public broadcasting's benefit. Fifth, advertising in program guides, and commissions from sales of CDs and audiocassettes made available through the NPR Recorded Music Service. If there were other ways to make money—books, toys, music, or even seminars such as Louis Rukeyser's seminars on making money in the stock market—somebody in public broadcasting was, or soon would be, exploring the option.

One fund-raising technique that might not be obvious to the average listener is in the sale or exchange of subscriber mailing lists. "List brokers" find that public broadcasting station subscriber lists can be readily sold—and that the stations, in turn, are always looking for good lists for their direct mail subscription solicitations. In 1999, however, when it became known that a few stations had exchanged lists with political party committees (primarily but not exclusively Democratic) Republican members of Congress were outraged. Heads rolled, and prohibition of such practices was proposed in the House of Representatives, which had the leverage of federal funding approval to hold over the stations' heads.

11.4.3 Public Radio Programs

Programming on public radio changed very slowly. Some stations still carried some in-school broadcasts, children's programs were a local staple, and classical music or jazz found a commercial-free home. But more than 350 stations got much of their major programming from NPR.

Affording some competition for NPR was Public Radio International (PRI, previously called American Public Radio, an outgrowth of Minnesota Public Radio). The public rarely realized that their local NPR station might get some of its programming from PRI, in spite of on-air identification. One of the most popular public radio programs was the telephone-in *Car Talk* (featuring "Click 'n' Clack, the Tappet Brothers"—Tom and Ray Magliozzi, one of whom actually ran a garage). *Car Talk* dispensed information, opinion, and *ad lib* humor on everything from how to keep a teenager from wrecking the family car to troubleshooting engine problems. It had a particularly active "shameless commerce division" from which one might order a wide variety of promotional merchandise.

Garrison Keillor's *A Prairie Home Companion* (see p. 519) retook its old name after a couple of seasons in the late 1980s calling itself *The American Radio Theater*. This live musical variety program, performed in front of a large audience in a theater in St. Paul, Minnesota, or on the road, stuck to its highly successful formula. Fans of the show listened not just for the music, but also for the sly humor of the pretend commercials and the often-poignant News from Lake Wobegon ("where all the women are strong, the men are good looking and the children are above average").

National Public Radio's most important programming, however, remained news and public affairs. Throughout the day, one minute after the hour, a headline news service provided an up-to-date account of domestic and foreign news often overlooked by the commercial news services that were concentrating more and more on crime and disaster. Several hours a day were devoted to *Morning Edition*, *Talk of the Nation* (a telephone-in program), and the long-running afternoon *All Things Considered* (affiliates could broadcast up to two hours of *ATC*, although many of the features and minidocumentaries would be repeated, often more than once). *All Things Considered* (copied from the excellent but less ambitious Canadian Broadcasting Corporation's *As It Happens*), nailed down the 5 P.M. slot on most NPR stations soon after its debut in 1971. (It now starts at the beginning of drive time, 4 P.M., and there is a *Weekend Edition*.) Although Bill Siemering, its originator, went into station management, the ever-changing cast and crew became familiar visitors to millions of homes. Several of *ATC*'s on-air staff—such as John Hockenberry, Cokie Roberts, and Linda Wertheimer— moved full or part time to the commercial networks, with Roberts and Wertheimer among the more influential Washington reporters.

Talk of the Nation is actually two programs. During the first four weekdays, each of its two hours typically is devoted to a special current topic, with guest experts eventually giving way to callers. On *Science Friday*, however, the topic is always science-related, and covers a wide variety of topics that laymen find interesting. Another NPR program, *Fresh Air*, with Terry Gross, attracts a substantial audience to her superb interviews with figures in the arts, music, and current events.

Many stations created new programs, in the hope of persuading other stations to share the cost—or even to make a profit. Most, of course, go nowhere. But some locally produced programming is aired over the full NPR network (such as *Car Talk* from WBUR), or syndicated to a smaller lineup of stations (such as *Marketplace* from KUSC). However, the hoped-for

■ While the excessively sweet nature of the dinosaur star drove some adults up the wall, *Barney and Friends* became a public television staple in the 1990s. Popularity of program-based products raised questions in Congress as to why PBS did not share in more of the income from such sales.

Photofest.

benefits to be gained from making their programs attractive to other stations could be a two-edged sword: when *The Connection*, with Christopher Lydon, started to be syndicated from WBUR, making the program less focused on the Boston area, neither Bostonians nor other listeners were pleased. In 2001, Lydon's desire for *Connection* ownership came into conflict with management's desire to keep syndication receipts for the station, resulting in the departure of the entire program staff. This was a particularly clear example of the age-old conflict between creatively and financially-oriented people, with the listening public caught in the middle.

11.4.4 Public Television Programming

Television programming on PBS only received minor adjustments in the 1990s. *P.O.V.* (*Point of View*) sought out and aired original short films, an almost inexhaustible source of content. *Masterpiece Theatre* (renamed *Exxon-Mobil Masterpiece Theatre*, to give more credit to the corporate underwriter) continues to devote most of its broadcasts to high-quality British drama. *New York Times* essayist Russell Baker stepped into the shoes of founding host Alastair Cooke, a BBC overseas correspondent who had been an American citizen since World War II. Similarly, when Vincent Price's health failed, noted British actress Diana Rigg took over as host of *Mystery*, another program consisting mostly of British miniseries.

While it is hard to find recent PBS programs that provoke the kind of American viewer attention given *Upstairs, Downstairs* and other programs of the 1970s and 1980s, overall quality remained high. Helen Mirren starred in several award-winning *Prime Suspect* mystery miniseries as an edgy Scotland Yard detective who had to devote as much energy to political infighting as she did to finding killers. Robbie Coltraine starred in *Cracker*, playing an overweight gambling (and boozing and womanizing) addict who also was a brilliant forensic psychiatrist—not to be confused with a 1997 American version, with a different cast, that suffered badly in comparison to the original. Three well-received plays by author/politician Michael Dobbs—*House of Cards, To Play the King*, and *The Final Cut*—featured Ian Richardson as Prime Minister, perhaps the most urbane, murderous example extant of the corruptive influence of power.

Although nudity appeared on PBS long before it was on commercial broadcasting in the United States, the language and themes of some episodes of *Cracker* apparently were too rough for politically sensitive PBS, and were seen instead on the Bravo cable channel. When PBS aired a miniseries called *Tales of the City*, it garnered acclaim, large (for PBS) audiences—and a tremendous amount of criticism for airing strong sexual themes and language. When *More Tales of the City* was produced, PBS wasn't willing to touch it and it ran on cable. Some astute observers wonder if PBS's concerns about losing present audience members weren't overshadowing the possibility of acquiring new viewers.

While not all of the miniseries on these two flagship programs were British—some were American, including some commissioned by PBS, and some were Australian, Canadian, or from other countries that made versions in English—they continued to make it possible for PBS to continue to supply good programs without the financial outlay that would be required to commission U.S. production of every one of their programs. Since most expenses were already covered by showings in the United Kingdom, these imports were priced at an affordable level, and the quality was high, even for sitcoms like *As Time Goes By*, starring Academy Award winner Judi Dench—since the American buyers could pick and choose the best. Some programs on the *Nova* science-oriented series were produced by the BBC and some by WGBH in the United States. Typically, a British sitcom or drama had a beginning, middle, and end as a series and the writing was consistent, since only as many episodes would be produced as could be done well—which was rare in American television, with its insatiable appetite for content, and whose producers always hope that their program will be picked up for another year, and that it would amass enough episodes to profitably enter syndication.

Although it often appeared that PBS was becoming indistinguishable from the commercial networks, there were two important structural differences. First, Congress acted as though the small sums appropriated to CPB gave Congress the right to dictate content. Second, although much program funding came through CPB, individual stations were the actual producers. In 2001, Pat Mitchell, the new head of PBS, decided to eliminate funding for the *Mystery* series both because of lingering legislative dislike of all things foreign and because many felt that too much money was going to WGBH, Boston, the producer of many of PBS' most popular series. Apparently, Mitchell hoped that original programming produced by other stations might attract larger and younger audiences. Because of the economic facts of life–it was always less costly to import programs from abroad than to try to produce them oneself, and the commercial networks might always be more nimble than PBS in finding ways to attract younger audiences—this was a major gamble.

Public television always had to expect that popular programs might be lured away by commercial television. Perhaps the first was a children's program, *The Finder*, which moved to CBS as *Let's Take a Trip* in the 1950s. This happened many times, with traffic in the opposite direction quite rare. The commercial networks had the money to seduce most talent away from the low-paying public sector. When some audience potential was shown—as, for example, with the sport of tennis—it was only a matter of time before it moved to a commercial network. Frequently, programs that originally appeared on PBS, such as the miniseries that constituted *Mystery*, were rerun on the A&E cable channel, not PBS.

It was on the public affairs front that public television not only competed with, but often surpassed the commercial networks, with documentary, history, and public affairs series run under the *Frontline, American Experience*, and *Nova* titles. These programs featured important and interesting topics, were well produced, and enjoyed appreciative audiences. *Frontline* was the only regular documentary series on television after the middle-1980s. Pageantry and nature were sure-fire content for other programs seen on PBS, together with concerts ranging from the late John Denver to the Boston Pops and—especially during fund-raising periods—tenors, both Italian and Irish.

Two half-hour programs on Friday nights showed how a simple public affairs format, produced intelligently every week, could both build an audience and achieve recognition across the country, particularly in Washington and on Wall Street. The first was *Washington Week in Review*, which consisted of three or four "talking heads"—usually newspaper reporters—discussing the most important news developments of the week from a Washington perspective. Unlike the commercial news interview programs, such as the long-running *Meet the Press*, this program was not designed to provide a pulpit for a person in the news. Rather, a diverse group of experienced reporters gave their best assessment of a particular event or development and answered the questions of their peers. The program's goal was to inform—unlike *The McLaughlin Group*, which also appeared on PBS but, because of the combative nature of its host, tended to provide more heat than light.

Wall Street Week, however, became America's most-watched financial information program, in an era when interest in the stock market grew to its highest point since the 1929 crash—even after the "dot.com" stock market meltdown in 2000. The format was simple: host Louis Rukeyser, a journalist who grew up in a family of knowledgeable Wall Streeters, opened with a monologue—replete with plays on words—about the events of the week, and then he and a panel that changed every week answered viewer questions and devoted most of the program to interviewing a financial expert in some field. The program, which originated in 1972, explained complex matters in understandable language, and brought back guests after six months or a year to be graded on the quality of their forecasts. It was produced live at Maryland Public Television, which often had to cross its collective fingers when weather and travel conditions between Wall Street and Owings Mills, Maryland, became tricky. It was "must" viewing by brokers, since they were bound to hear from their clients the next day about what *Wall Street Week* said this week.

Although few public stations could afford to produce their own regular news programs—and woe betide them if the audience grew to expect a program that couldn't be justified on economic terms, thus stranding its audience—almost all PBS stations carried the well-respected network *NewsHour* program. Originally co-anchored by Robert MacNeil, a Canadian who had a successful news career on American network television, and Jim Lehrer, an experienced Texan newscaster, the program soon was known as *The MacNeil/Lehrer Report*. When MacNeil retired to devote more time to writing books, it adopted its present name, *The NewsHour with Jim Leher*. In terms of ratings, it couldn't hold a candle to the declining early evening news programs of the commercial networks—but its audience consisted of the movers and shakers in the nation's political and financial worlds, as well as other broadcast journalists.

While these public affairs programs are generally thought of as belonging to PBS, they actually are produced by one of PBS's member stations, such as WGBH (Boston), WNET (New York), and WTTW (Chicago), and other stations in Washington, Los Angeles, Seattle, Pittsburgh, St. Louis,

San Francisco, Buffalo (Mark Russell's monthly satirical political one-man revue), Maryland Public Television and others. Some programs are produced in association with private companies affiliated with their stars, because Congress has mandated that no executives or performers paid in part through CPB funding may make more than a member of Congress—a sum that seems large to members of the public, but tiny to those looking at the salaries paid commercial show business or sports figures. However, there is no limit to the amount that may be paid to a production company, and that company can pay its talent what it wishes.

While some PBS stations broadcast in-school educational programming during the day, almost every public television station served children with low key, nonthreatening programming—including cartoons and the ever-popular *Sesame Street,* which was also was seen in versions designed for and produced in many foreign countries. Other PBS stations also syndicated children's programs, such as *Bill Nye, The Science Guy* from Seattle.

The success of home refurbishing programs such as *This Old House* stimulated a commercial version (with the original PBS star) and led to the successful network sitcom *Home Improvement.* WGBH, which produced *This Old House,* had similar success with a low-key (and low budget) *Antiques Roadshow.*

11.5 More Advertising

Audience members who thought that the 1990s brought more advertising—both in terms of number of messages and total amount of time devoted to commercials—were correct on both counts.

11.5.1 Commercial Content and Techniques

While there were few major changes in broadcast advertising after 1987, the minor changes made things look and sound different. The ability to "morph" and otherwise manipulate pictures (see pp. 601–602) allowed creative ideas full rein, and the home television screen became filled with talking frogs, climbing penguins, sports utility vehicles in impossible places, and all sorts of other real and fanciful creatures and situations.

Against this background of fantasy, some advertisers and entertainment programmers strove for realism—which led to a number of newspeople succumbing to the easy money and appearing in commercials, fictional programs, or feature films. Most networks quickly adopted rules against this practice, with ABC being the most rigid and CBS being willing to occasionally allow a real news person to appear on a fictional program like *Murphy Brown.*

Some advertising humor amused audiences—but it had to do so without annoying too many viewers or cause people to forget just what it was that was being advertised. Some older pitches, still remembered by generations of viewers, were the lonely Maytag repair man, created by Stan Freberg and originally starring Jesse White (who was replaced only after many years in the role); Madge the Manicurist, who sold Palmolive dishwashing liquid from 1965 to 1992; Fred, the Dunkin' Donuts baker from 1981 until the end of the 1990s; and Mr. Whipple, who admonished viewers to "not squeeze the Charmin" tissue for more than a quarter of a century after 1964.

Broadcast advertising continued to rely on 20- and 30-second commercials, with some shorter and very few running a minute in length. After the demise of the NAB code in the mid-1980s, however, each hour had more time devoted to commercials and promotions (which both were useful to the program department and reserved the time slot for commercial sponsors should they become available) since neither the industry nor government felt like imposing restrictions as they had in the past. While most stations aired as many commercials as they could, those competing with others in their market might voluntarily restrain themselves to enhance their reputation. One special case is the Super Bowl football game, with its huge audiences and resulting near-unbelievable price for each commercial—which acted as a showcase for the industry to show off their most creative ads.

The tendency of business to form conglomerates has led to occasional interactions between commercials of unrelated branches of the same company. Since spots are vastly more common than program sponsorship, and more of them can be inserted in each hour, both because of reduced length and more minutes per hour devoted to advertising, it often is hard to find the programming among the commercials. *Clutter* annoys both advertisers and audiences. Some even think back nostalgically to when a "commercial break" was one ad, for one product, set off at each end by a couple of seconds of black. The pressure for advertising on television has squeezed out another old standby—product protection. For the first several decades of broadcasting, stations and networks would commit to not airing a spot for a competing product for a set period of time—often 15 minutes. Today, cheek-by-jowl competing ads—particularly for automobiles—air all the time. These and other practices continued to increase advertising on television (see Appendix C, table 3-C).

11.5.2 Forbidden Advertising

The advertising of hard liquor had always been a "no-no" in American broadcasting, even after the end of Prohibition in 1933. Distillers and distributors feared the imposition of other restrictions on advertising of their products by the federal government, and broadcasters didn't wish to risk losing the ability to carry beer and wine advertising, which accounted for roughly 10% of industry advertising revenue. Numerous broadcasters, particularly in the so-called Bible belt middle of the nation, knew that much of their audience was opposed to liquor. Occasionally someone attempted to advertise hard liquor on radio or television, but either the station or the advertiser was always convinced by their peers that such advertising was unwise. However, in 1997 some distillers, in an atmosphere of deregulation (see pp. 562–569 and 670–672), decided that they were unlikely to have further restrictions put on their print and broadcast advertising if they aired commercials late in the evening. Actually, they reasoned, this would be a win-win: either they were allowed to advertise hard liquor or, should the Congress decided to prevent all broadcast alcohol—including beer and wine—advertising, then the hard liquor companies would still be better off than before, since the rival beverages would not have an unfair advantage in terms of media access. The broadcast media would be the only ones to suffer. Yet, by 2001, very few hard liquor ads had actually aired, which may have helped the National Association of Broadcasters repel periodic assaults on broadcast wine and beer ads.

This was but one skirmish in the question of First Amendment rights of commercial speech. Another that seemed to reappear with almost clock-like regularity was concern over the advertising of medicine and drugs. Critics argued that such advertising at least indirectly promoted use of all drugs, even illegal ones. One could count on expressions of congressional concern, particularly near election time. Industry groups would call for further research, and then there would be a slow fade-out, with no action taken. Other worrisome content included condom advertising (on some radio stations as early as the 1970s), which, however, didn't raise as many hackles as the partial nudity, sexual innuendo, and strong language used by advertisers whose products or services encouraged such content—for example, 900-number telephone sex services.

11.6 Commercial Programming

To many in the business, "programming" really means program scheduling. The limited number of high-quality programs available—from original dramas to home movies, and from sports to public affairs—was hard to expand, and thus the highest priced programming executives measured their successes and failures strictly on the basis of how many people were viewing and listening (ratings) or what proportion of those listening or viewing were watching their particular offering (share). Most new broadcast content in the 1990s actually was traditional (sports and special events), from other media (such as feature films or books), recycled previously broadcast material, exciting and low cost true-life car chases and "reality" programs like *COPS* and *Survivor*, and news magazine shows. The reasons for this lack of originality are many: schedulers can get swamped, original material can be unpopular, it costs a great deal, and the risk is great—one can never be sure if a new genre or program will be popular.

As always, a great deal of programming was recycled. Not only has broadcasting been around long enough to develop generations or cycles of genre programming such as police, medical emergency and the like, but the tapes and films (and even, in a couple of instances, the kinescopes) of some older series were taken out, dusted off, and aired. Programs that had been aired in the U.K. often were refurbished for American audiences, or vice versa. A program that had appeared on one network one year might appear on another—or on a cable channel—the next, particularly nature shows. The ideas for previously successful programs were reused—for example, it would be hard to count the numerous series featuring the characters of Sherlock Holmes or Robin Hood.

11.6.1 Pushing the Envelope

A new generation of producers and writers often tended to go beyond the tacit boundaries of good taste, usually with the approval of network executives and advertisers who usually cared only about the size of the viewing audience, but sometimes merely to impress their peers.

Partial nudity appeared on prime time, accompanied by thousands of words produced by newspaper columnists and even news anchors. This wasn't uncommon overseas—one British observer pointed out to an American group that "we enjoy rather more sex and rather less violence"—but until the first episode of the well-written *NYPD Blue*, which showed a major character's entire nude backside, it was rare in U.S. commercial network programming. Sometimes, it is hard to provide justification or motivation for such material—which is one of the factors that led to the development of television content ratings systems (see pp. 670–672). For example, one 1997–1998 program, *Oz*, placed in a men's prison (where male nudity, including branding on one character's buttocks in the first episode, might be expected), managed to include some female nudity. A character asked his girlfriend to parade outside his prison window in the buff. Far fetched? Exploitive? Perhaps ... but the program's writer/producer, Tom Fontana (who also was responsible for outstanding programs such as *St. Elsewhere* and *Homicide: Life on the Street*), claims that this actually happened in a prison, and that he didn't invent the story.

The amount of violence portrayed on television stimulated the most criticism. Recognizing this, and the possibility of governmental action, the cable industry sponsored a three-year academic research study into how much violence was evident in entertainment programming. Three volumes of results appeared in the mid-1990s, largely confirming the critics. While the "worst" program or network might vary, the addiction of television— and its audience—to crime and extreme adventure never diminished.

Language also pushed the envelope. Although the FCC's guidelines for hours when children might be in the audience (see p. 671) were uncertain, some words that hitherto might have been considered indecent started to turn up on drama programs, talk shows, and even cartoons such as *South Park* and *The Simpsons.* This change has permeated society, the media—and this volume.

11.6.2 Radio Formats

With the exception of public broadcasting, radio stations remained "formatted" rather than "programmed," as had been the case since the 1950s (see pp. 365–370). By the 1990s, differences in AM and FM radio, although based on their sound quality and propagation characteristics, were purely programmatic. Typical FM stations played varieties of rock music, while AM stations became noted for talk and news. In larger markets with more stations, niche formats—all-news, sports, ethnic programs—could be made profitable. A minority of stations would concentrate on some musical specialty for all or part of the day, such as country, jazz, or soul, or even a few hours of Frank Sinatra or Broadway show tunes, and then plug into a syndicated satellite program service when drive time was over. Station management did what it could to reduce costs by sharing them with other stations their group operated in the same market (see p. 610), and by using satellite-delivered syndicated programming services rather than more costly, and often uneven, local production. This could lead to the loss of some familiar local sounds—for example, three generations of the John Gambling family ended their 75-year (!) run over WOR, New York, in the Fall of 2000. Most content decision makers at the local level were copycats, who looked for what was being neglected in their communities and then ordered formats from syndicators who claimed to have a winning formula.

Nevertheless, while still making money, radio rarely made waves—except to shock people, as with "shock jock" Howard Stern's smut and innuendo-filled programs or the confrontational Don Imus, both based in New York. Stern's antics cost the licensee of Infinity, which provided the syndicated program, millions of dollars in FCC fines. But neither man would have been on the air if he weren't hugely popular.

Radio still could serve the public interest. News headlines, traffic, and weather during morning and evening drive time (ever longer as traffic congestion increased in urban areas) remain useful and profitable. When a weather or other disaster occurred, radio often could be on the scene faster than television, and the habit of listening to radio for information about loved ones in the path of danger remained. Some stations relied on volunteers, articulate people—often with a clear-cut point of view—to run telephone-in or talk programs for little or no money. Political leaders—including the President every Saturday—often had regular radio programs.

Highly successful conservatively oriented national talk show hosts, such as Rush Limbaugh—who took credit (or blame) for determining the Republican outcome of the 1992 and 1994 elections, lost much of their clout later in the decade. (By 2000, some of their role was taken on by the less partisan—i.e., equally nasty to both candidates—late-night television talk show hosts like Jay Leno and David Letterman.) While still popular, they no longer could claim to be the voice of the people talking back to big government. It may be that too many had similar right-wing political/ economic views, or it may be that the public merely wanted something else—health news, for example, or stock market advice—but the talk show's season in the sun appeared to be over.

11.6.3 Television Entertainment

It is, of course, too early to assess which television programs of the last decade of the 20th century will be remembered into the 21st. Indeed, the various end-of-the-century attempts of *TV Guide* and others to list the "top 100" shows of the 20th century rarely showed much agreement. But those that stood out from the pack—and, in any given year, the network prime time pack is about 60 programs deep—tended to fall into a limited number of genres. Some virtually disappeared—music, variety—and westerns, which had been seen virtually every night on every network in the 1950s

▪ Inflation hit the radio *$64 Question* of the 1940s and even the television *$64,000 Question* of the late 1950s when host Regis Philbin helped to propel *Who Wants to Be a Millionaire?* to instant success in 1999, marking the return of big-money quiz formats to prime time television for the first time in more than 40 years.

Photofest.

(see pp. 370–375), were virtually gone by the 1980s and haven't yet returned. "Private eyes" are similarly scare. Others hung on by their fingertips.

But program cycles of invention, imitation and decline still existed, even though they can take a long time to come full circle. Forty years after the scandals of the 1950s (see pp. 376–378), the quiz show format returned. Dating back to 1930s radio, the formerly powerful quiz show had been reduced to programs like *Win Ben Stein's Money* until a limited series based on a British original, *Who Wants to Be a Millionaire*, won the summer 1999 ratings jackpot for ABC—and was immediately added to the fall schedule for no fewer than three nights a week. There was an interesting difference, and not just the amount of money involved, between *Twenty-One* and the *$64,000 Question* in the 1950s and *Who Wants to Be a Millionaire* at the end of the century. Questions in the 1950s were quite difficult, but for the more recent program they were very easy—and contestants were given "lifeline" calls and hints. Once again, the public was being seduced by voyeurism rather than an opportunity to test themselves against the contestants. The success of *Who Wants to Be a Millionaire* led, predictably to *Who Wants to Marry a Multimillionaire*—which also appeared to be on the road to success until the first couple separated right after the honeymoon. One new quiz show, with elements of *Survivor*, was the 2001 British import *Weakest Link*—which nastily ejected one contestant after every round of questions.

The networks continued their affair with tearjerker miniseries—usually with the name of a potboiling romance, adventure, or horror genre author above the title—but few serious dramas. There were many interviews with musical stars on the late evening shows, but almost no musical or variety programs. Disaster films were common, but there were only a limited number of long-form dramas exploring the human condition on other than a superficial level—most of which, in the mid-1990s, for example, seemed to be adaptations of Jane Austin novels. In a nutshell, there were few programs to talk about the next morning.

Science fiction programs trading on the popularity of *Star Trek* (whose franchise continued running through *ST: The Next Generation*, *ST: Deep Space Nine*, and *ST: Voyager*), and the movie trilogy *Star Wars*, were common in the 1990s. There were even science fiction aspects to sitcoms such as *Red Dwarf* or *Third Rock from the Sun*, starring John Lithgow in the implausible story of alien voyagers with inappropriate human bodies in a college town, which followed in the extra-terrestrial footsteps of *My Favorite Martian* (1963–1966) and *ALF* (1986–1990). Obviously, the aliens had been watching U.S. television before they landed.

Police and medical drama was very common throughout the late 1980s and 1990s. Some were of very high quality, with excellent writing, direction, acting, and camerawork. Others were merely entertaining, and some were very forgettable. *NYPD Blue*, produced starting in 1993 by Steven Bochco, was a darker version of his ground breaking *Hill Street Blues*, which had aired between 1981 and 1987. Without the humor of its predecessor, it nevertheless deeply explored many aspects of the life of members of a New York police precinct—although it sometimes descended into soap opera.

Not really a police drama, since it focused on a family of organized crime members, the *Sopranos* gained critical acclaim and a large audience on HBO for its acting and writing. While some of those who didn't subscribe to HBO may have wondered what all the fuss was about, others started to think seriously about subscribing.

■ NBC's *NYPD Blue* broke new ground in its use of language (and some nudity) in late prime time as it portrayed the lives and loves of a New York City police precinct. Dennis Franz (right) played a skeptical and hard-boiled detective who became the series' chief draw. While owing much to *Hill Street Blues, NYPD Blue* didn't have its humor or lack of cast turnover.

Photofest.

Homicide: Life on the Street got even more deeply into the lives and cases of an ensemble cast representing members of the Baltimore Police Department homicide squad. Only one actor in the original cast was known to most television viewers—and he was not the star. Indeed, he left after a couple of years (his character had "misbehaved" at a police convention), as did numerous others. But the program went on without a hitch. A police department featuring a command structure with an outstanding level of vicious incompetence at the top and an awesome but compassionate black Italian lieutenant at the bottom, and such continuing story lines as recovery of one detective from a stroke and difficulties several detectives had trying to procure additional income from a bar they purchased across from the station, were interspersed with realistic police work. The program ended its lengthy network run in 1999 because of low (but loyal) ratings. It already had taken up residence on cable channels, such as Court TV. In 2000, a successful made-for-TV-movie brought everyone (including two ghostly characters who had "died" earlier) back to investigate the shooting of the lieutenant and wrap up loose ends.

Law & Order also changed its cast frequently in the years after its start in 1990, but didn't seem to have much difficulty keeping its audience. Fictionalizing contemporary real felony cases, the first half-hour usually featured police tracking down and arresting a suspect and the second half-hour featured members of the New York district attorney's staff attempting to secure a conviction. They didn't always win, but the program was successful enough that a spinoff (featuring a refugee from the cancelled *Homicide*) joined it in 1999, and a third joined the "franchise" in 2001.

Most other police dramas were derivative, and many were violent and—like their predecessors—often ignored the law, while allowing the actors playing the "bad guy" an opportunity to emote. Programs like *Martial Law* (featuring a real overweight Asian judo expert), *Walker, Texas Ranger* (starring another martial arts expert), and *Nash Bridges* kept the genre going.

A far cry from the superficial *Perry Mason* courtroom/detective drama (which ran for more than 16 years starting in 1957), *L.A. Law* started in 1986 and continued into the 1990s. The story of members of a Los Angeles law firm, its internal politics, and some of its cases, the series had a generous amount of black humor, including the death of the managing partner in the opening episode (one partner immediately demanded the deceased's office) and the death of another partner when the elevator door opened to an empty elevator shaft. This formula could be repeated endlessly, with different approaches—it could be stark (*Law & Order* or *Murder One*), humorous (*Ally McBeal* or the older *Night Court*), or both (*The Practice*).

An unusually well-crafted program, *West Wing*, first aired in 1999. It was a very fast-paced portrayal of a dedicated group of White House staff members, with Martin Sheen playing liberal President Bartlett with considerable gusto. This hour-long drama, with lighter moments, was

West Wing depicted President Josiah (Jed) Bartlett (Martin Sheen, center) and his senior staff including C.J. Craig, the quick-witted press secretary (Allison Janey, left), in an NBC series offering good writing and often pointed comment on current news developments or social concerns.

Photofest.

unafraid to reflect real-life major problems of government, foreign affairs, and society. Not all of the solutions "worked," but almost none of the characters were one-dimensional and viewers inadvertently learned a lot about government. (A number of former White House staffers served as consultants.) During the 2000 election campaign, quite a few automobiles in California sported "Jed Bartlett for President" bumper stickers.

Other adventure programs focused on the dangers of real life, even though the odds against some of the more improbable mishaps were high. Among the latter were *Emergency!* and *Rescue 911* with William Shatner introducing a mix of live action and recreated real-life stories of police, fire, emergency medical, and rescue personnel at work. Some viewers watched the show to see if any of the victims would *not* be saved. It happened very rarely! (There also was, among other examples of this genre, a syndicated *Rescue 8* in the 1950s, *Code 3* in the early 1990s, and *Rescue 77* later in that decade.) Even less expensive to produce—since there never was any need to recreate parts of an episode with paid actors—were programs like *COPS*. Here, a camera operator rode along with police officers and captured pictures and sound of cases—high-speed traffic chases were particularly popular—for limited editing and Fox network airing. Sometimes only a brief voice-over at the end would save the program from being only a chase without a resolution. Cheaper programs aired on-the-spot snippets of the "worst traffic accidents" variety. It remains to be seen whether a 1999 Supreme Court decision restricting television "ride alongs" with police will crimp the ability to tape such material.

It was only a matter of time before these "reality" programs moved to another plane, since they were both cheap to produce and popular. *Survivor* originated in Europe, but achieved an unheard-of level of popularity

When *Survivor* first aired on CBS in the Summer of 2000 (based on an earlier British program), the "reality" program attracted a huge and growing audience eager to see which person survived the longest by not getting "voted off" the island by fellow castaways. A few months later, a second series set in the Australian outback, did nearly as well and a third was planned for an African location while other producers and networks joined the bandwagon with variations.

Photofest.

■ NBC's *ER* (Emergency Room) continued television's fascination with medical mayhem, with (R to L) George Clooney, Eriq La Salle, Sherry Stringfield, and Anthony Edwards depicting the emergency room medical team of a downtown Chicago hospital. The program's popularity became so important to NBC that it agreed to record per-episode payments to the stars, driving *weekly* costs for the series well above $10 million.

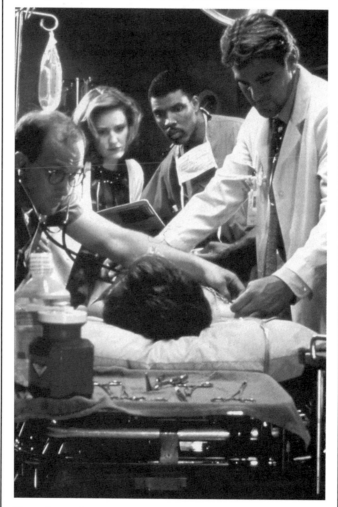

Photo © 1995 Warner/MPTV.NET.

in the United States in the Summer of 2000. The idea was simple: "maroon" a diverse (and, the producers hoped, attractive to viewers) group of people in an isolated spot (a south Pacific island for the first series) for 39 days, constantly tape them, devise tests for them to meet, eliminate them one-by-one (mostly by vote of the surviving participants), and then award the "survivor" a million dollars—while building suspense with weekly edited programs of their progress. The first series attracted as many as 40 million people to the final two-hour program (followed by a town-hall interview program with all 16 castaways), and an estimated 110 million watched at least one episode—causing *Survivor* to become the most viewed program in commercial television history. CBS rapidly made plans for additional series—the next in the Australian outback—and other networks looked for their own version of the program with mixed success. *Big Brother* did reasonably well in Europe, but not in the United States. PBS aired *1900 House*, a series that showed a British family trying to live in a restored London house as their grandparents had lived at the turn of the last century—a challenge that created considerable viewer interest. Those who thought more deeply about the difference between these programs noted that *1900 House* put a premium on cooperation, and *Survivor* put a premium on backstabbing and greed.

Medical programs, successors to *Ben Casey*, *Dr. Kildare*, and *St. Elsewhere*, tended to be more soap opera than the top-rung police dramas of the 1990s. Particularly popular were *ER* (Emergency Room), a very highly rated series in 1995–1996 and for a number of years thereafter. In 1998, *ER* also became the most expensive prime time hour-long production—at $13 million per episode, as much as ten times the norm—as its actors demanded and received huge salaries knowing full well that NBC badly needed this program's continued ratings. *ER* had a remarkable ensemble cast, including George Clooney, whose movie acting career took off as a result. One of the most heartwarming episodes featured 1950s pop singer Rosemary Clooney, his aunt in real life. *Chicago Hope* at first starred Mandy Patinkin, whose acting career was often eclipsed by his singing career. Like Clooney, he eventually left the show for other career opportunities, but it continued to limp on without him. In 1999, *Third Watch*, which combined elements of the police, rescue, and medical genres, went on the air—bringing the concept of derivation to new heights, although it often was well done.

Making no pretense at presenting high culture were syndicated programs such as *Baywatch* (much like a police series/soap opera in well-filled bathing suits—very popular around the world), *Xena: Warrior Princess*, and *Hercules: the Legendary Journeys*. The latter two made no pretense at being other than entertaining fiction. Attractive "hunks" of both sexes in limited clothing, grade school plots, and lots of swordplay (and a little wizardry) made an entertaining and mindless thud-and-blunder product. Their success led producers to other mythological or remote historical settings (the short-lived *Roar* was set in fifth-century Celtic Europe).

As discussed on p. 630, several British series and miniseries such as *Cracker* and *Prime Suspect* became popular among those who admired fine dramatic writing and acting. An instant cult grew up around *Absolutely Fabulous*, a half-hour sitcom featuring a dysfunctional female household that was deeply into the trendy fashion/art/theatre scene in London.

■ One of the biggest success stories in the 1990s was NBC's *Seinfeld*, which was a top-rated program for several seasons, built around New York comic Jerry Seinfeld and his coterie of sometimes offbeat friends.

© Don Zaitz, 1993/Castle Rock, NBC/MPTV.NET.

In the United States, sitcoms were among the bright spots in programming, although the recorded laugh tracks and formulaic writing proved tiresome to some viewers. Appealing particularly to younger audiences were *Seinfeld*, the top-rated program for two seasons—with the final episode, in 1998, earning news coverage across the nation. Although *Seinfeld* had an established comic (Jerry Seinfeld) as star, the high level of writing, direction, and ensemble acting was sufficiently credited for the show's success that other members of the cast—after eight years of trying—were able to pressure NBC into giving them very large pay raises. However, when the show left the air, few cast members landed on their feet.

Programs like *Seinfeld* were much of the reason why NBC consistently pulled ahead of the other major networks in the ratings in the 1990s. (ABC was second, and former "Tiffany network" CBS a distant third—even losing place to Fox occasionally.) Indeed, the Thursday night lineup on NBC (*Friends, Seinfeld,* and *ER*) has been credited for NBC's first-place position.

Frasier, a spinoff of the hugely popular 1980s' *Cheers*, appealed to a wider audience, with its tales of a psychiatrist, his querulous father, prissy brother, Cockney housemaid, and very insightful dog. The sitcom genre itself evolved, and frequently featured more complex and multifaceted episodes. For example, *Murphy Brown* starred Candice Bergen as a broadcast journalist of a considerably more complex nature than Mary Tyler Moore's "Mary Richards" of two decades before. At one point, in a somewhat confusing 1992 election campaign, Vice President Dan Quayle attacked Murphy—a fictional character!—for having a child out of wedlock, in itself a theme (like "Murphy's" bout with breast cancer) hitherto classified as "drama" not "comedy." *Roseanne*, one of the few sitcoms featuring a blue-collar family, albeit a loud and demonstrative one, reached #1 in the ratings chart, and was on ABC for several years starting in 1988. Television's top-rated program episode of the 20th century was the February 1983 final two-hour installment of *M*A*S*H*, the Korean War medical comedy, which earned CBS an audience share of 60.3 at a time when few programs had a share above 20. How unusual this was is evidenced by the fact that the #1 network in 1999 probably enjoyed an audience smaller than the third place network a decade earlier, because of the splintering of the audience among networks, cable, rental videos, and other means of distribution.

Other sitcoms often had bizarre premises, such as *Third Rock from the Sun*, mentioned earlier. Even more original (apart from *Third Rock's* basic gimmick) was *Northern Exposure*—a traditional sitcom that first aired in 1990, with memorable characters placed in a town of Cicely, Alaska, a setting that occasionally allowed otherworldly or, at best, highly coincidental, themes. Even "conventional" sitcoms might have an unexpected twist: the last episode of *Newhart* in 1990 ended with Bob Newhart waking up in bed with his "wife" from *The Bob Newhart Show*, which was last telecast in 1978—thus turning the entire eight year run of the second show into a dream!

The serial drama, of course, often meandered into other genres, such as police/adventure or comedy. But there were usually some programs worth noting like *thirtysomething* (which explored the world of Yuppies—Young Urban Professionals, a sociological term) that aired between 1987 and 1991, giving rise to a number of programs that tried to achieve the same audience pull, with both older and younger groups of characters. Serials such as *Melrose Place, Beverly Hills 90210, Felicity,* and *Dawson's Creek* were aimed at younger viewers, while more traditional programs like *Murder, She Wrote* and *Diagnosis Murder* were deliberately aimed at older ones.

Children, however, were given short shrift by commercial television. Although the profitable Saturday morning cartoons continued, it wasn't until Congress twisted the broadcast networks' arms with the Children's Television Act of 1990 (see p. 670) and other statutes that additional television programs for children were produced, although not as many as had been common in the 1950s and 1960s.

Despite decades of experience—and a growing number of roles for African-American and other ethnic minorities—the networks could be amazingly short-sighted, and even blind. The 1999–2000 season began with 26 new prime time series—but only one of them (*City of Angels* on CBS) featured a black in a leading role. The NAACP and other groups protested, and several producers furiously wrote in more parts for members of minority groups. For example, *West Wing* added a special personal assistant to the president who was a young black man—who later started going out with the president's daughter, an arrangement that the networks, always wary of offending members of the audience, never would have even thought of showing even a decade earlier.

A number of serial dramas, some with comedic overtones, crossed over the line to a darker look at the world and the supernatural: *Twin Peaks*, laid in a rural area, was quite weird; and *X-Files*, about FBI agents who operate within a paranoid world of UFOs, aliens, and other strange concepts. *Buffy the Vampire Slayer* was aimed directly at young audiences, as was its spinoff, *Angel*. The line between reality and fiction grew ever thinner, as programs such as these—and some so-called documentaries—accepted the supernatural and bizarre as their premise.

A number of programs presented religious themes, such as *Touched by an Angel* on CBS (which explicitly used God as the cornerstone of the program), *Nothing Sacred* on ABC (which won a Peabody award), and *Seventh Heaven* (an Aaron Spelling program about a minister's family, and at one time the most popular show on the WB network). *Touched by an Angel* was the second most highly rated drama on television during the 1999–2000 season.

Using cartoon characters—with voices supplied by well-known actors to a great extent—were *The Simpsons, Beavis and Butthead*, and *South*

▪ *The Simpsons* cartoon family became a popular staple of the Fox Network in the 1990s. While teenage Bart Simpson took center stage at first with his defiance of authority, over the years the program has developed some 50 characters, some of them minor, each with clearly identifiable traits (and often the voices of well-known stars), and all contributing to the series' social commentary. It is the longest running network prime time cartoon series.

Photofest.

Park. These were a far cry from Disney cartoons or family fare like *The Jetsons* or *The Flintstones. The Simpsons* were in classic sitcom form, with a family getting into difficulties—often reflecting some of the angst and discouragement of their real-life counterparts in the audience—and often crossing the line into humorous bad taste. *Beavis and Butthead* were two teenagers who were almost always in bad taste, and *South Park* truly pushed the envelope!

Inexpensive, but popular, were programs that typically used home movies or tapes, such as *America's Funniest Home Videos*, produced by Vin DiBona. Once such a program achieved success, imitators followed to the point where many of the videos seemed overly convoluted and almost certainly made with the television program in mind.

Daytime programming continued to be a mix of soap operas and audience talk shows. Both Mike Douglas and Merv Griffin had left the air, and Oprah Winfrey's *Oprah!* dominated the scene. When she started touting books on the air, their sales shot up. Other hosts such as Montel Williams and Maury Povich reached fewer viewers. When this genre multiplied, the producers and hosts had to search ever harder for people to interview and themes to explore. Jerry Springer, a former politician, unleashed his biases and went for the jugular. Jennie Jones' program had an episode in which a man admitted to his sexual attraction to another man—who shot and killed him a few days later. While that episode was never released, Jones may have spent more time in lawyer's offices and courtrooms than the studio. This caper resulted in a $25 million judgment against the production's owners.

Soap operas tried new character and plot gimmicks to the extent that it was hard to think of ways that would surprise the audience. Language also became far more free. For more than a decade, probably the only thing that actually would shock (and gratify) the loyal audiences to these shows— many of whom were college students—would be if always-nominated, never a winner Susan Lucci would win a Daytime Emmy Award from the Television Academy (she finally did, in 1999).

The Emmy Awards themselves were among the few major nonsports events produced for airing on a network. Once a "family" gathering, where people in the industry congratulated each other, since the 1970s they had been produced for the nation—and public recognition of the importance of the art being honored. The Emmys (television), the Tonys (Broadway stage), the Oscars (motion pictures), and the Grammys (recordings) each received its own night—and, on the network carrying the program that year, a great deal of additional publicity. The Oscars, in particular, had enormous television audiences, frequently were entertaining (comedian Billy Crystal was particularly good as host), always ran long, and were rehashed on talk programs all the next week.

Few television writers, producers, or directors stood out from their peers in the 1990s. Steven Bochco, David Lynch, Tom Fontana, and, later,

▪ Jay Leno, host of the *Tonight Show*, greets guest Billy Crystal. Leno took over the late-night NBC program when long-time host Johnny Carson retired in 1992 after three decades in the job.

Photofest.

David E. Kelley, did so in the United States. Some used their success with popular shows to convince the networks to air programs that they found more satisfying. An example of this was the warm, well-written, and well-acted low-key comedy-drama *Brooklyn Bridge*, featuring a Jewish family in post–World War II Brooklyn—a series that probably never would have been produced if its creator/producer Gary David Goldberg had not also created the profitable and long-running *Family Ties*. The extreme example was Dennis Potter, whose British television miniseries *Pennies from Heaven* and *The Singing Detective* were among the most imaginative programs ever broadcast. Knowing that he was about to die (in 1996), he wrote (and two different British networks produced) *Karaoke* and *Cold Lazarus*. Where the chief character (played by Albert Finney) ended and the real Dennis Potter began is something that viewers of these many-layered plays might never untangle—but would never forget.

11.6.4 The Sports Money Machine

From the earliest days of broadcasting there was a seemingly insatiable audience appetite for sport. While reports of up-to-date scores might be considered news, and would be presented in news programs, most coverage of sports is really only another form of entertainment. The only fly in the ointment during this period was the astonishing rise in fees paid by networks to carry professional football and other sports—and some evidence of declining audiences. Where CBS had paid "only" $28 million to telecast the National Football League's games in 1964–1965, three decades later, Fox paid $1.5 *billion* for a three-year contract. A later seven-year deal (1998–2005) for the same league cost Fox $4.4 billion—but obviously Fox felt that the expenditure was worthwhile. These prices were partly in recognition of the fact that the broadcast audience for sport continued to be far larger than the number of people willing to buy tickets and attend the games in person.

It is arguable that professional football exists today because of television, and many millions of fans gain almost all of their knowledge of their favorite sports from the tube. The Olympics provide exposure to "new" sports for the casual viewer to enjoy. Many stations carry play-by-play of the home teams, international contests in sports such as golf and soccer bring out the sometime fan, and coverage of marathons elicits "there but for the grace of God, go I" sighs. Few newscasts would be complete without time devoted to scores and personalities, and radio programs like *Only a Game* appeal to those who claim to detest sports. Today, although there is an occasional all-sports radio station (WFAN, New York, is the latest incarnation of pioneer WEAF), ESPN and its imitators and clones on cable (ESPN 2 and ESPN News have joined ESPN Classic) are among the most profitable cable channels. Two decades after its 1979 founding, ESPN was the fifth largest network (broadcast or cable), as measured by gross revenues.

Many sports remained closely bound to national cultures. U.S. baseball was growing in popularity in Japan and in Latin America, even though the so-called World Series only had American teams participating. Cricket remained a game engendering fierce loyalties in Great Britain and in many former colonies—whose teams sometimes beat the mother country. Professional and college basketball remained largely an American fascination, while hockey appealed to audiences in Canada and in its neighbor to the south. However, "football" means something different in the world outside the United States. It is what Americans call soccer, and is the most watched and most played sport in the world. Even when the soccer World Cup finals were held in the United States, and in 1999 when the U.S. women's team beat women from the People's Republic of China in a hard-fought game in double overtime, soccer has never achieved the popularity in the United States that it had in the rest of the world. All of these sports, and the various international competitions in them, such as the World Cup, are carried around the world on television.

The Olympic Games remain particularly newsworthy, even though they now are on a two-year schedule, with alternating summer and winter games. Olympic Games coverage is largely restricted to the network that has paid the most to the games' organizers. As with professional sports, fees paid to cover the Olympics have burgeoned during the 1980s and 1990s, now constituting the largest portion of host city and Olympic Committee income. In 1994, the winter games helped CBS earn a 48 share of the audience—the only Olympics broadcasts to reach the fabled top ten. But Internet reports of Olympic events in 2000 in far-off Sidney, Australia cut seriously into the U.S. audience for the tape-delayed broadcasts.

As with some news programs, there no longer is a firm line between some sports and scripted entertainment. Professional wrestling, for example, is one of the most highly rated shows on basic cable—and has been telecast profitably for decades. Professional wrestlers are now important enough to be tapped to throw out the first pitch at baseball games, and even enter politics, such as Minnesota Governor Jesse Ventura. Highly scripted, much of the appeal of wrestling matches is spectacle and mayhem.

There were, however, disquieting indicators that the public could have *too much* sports programming. The professional football Super Bowl, which in the 1980s were four of the top ten rated programs of all time, didn't reach that level once in the 1990s. ABC's long-running *Monday Night Football* ratings also slipped, and major league baseball no longer was the topic of as much morning-after water cooler conversation. And the high cost of the most popular sports events was leading networks to seek—or, in some instances, create—new events that would have lower cost and for which high audience interest could be created.

11.6.5 News and Public Affairs

Entertainment values increased substantially in most news programs in the 1990s, even while cost-cutting accelerated.

11.6.5.1 *Network News Implodes*

There were few changes in network newscasting that were immediately obvious to the viewer. The major network anchors—Dan Rather at CBS, Peter Jennings at ABC, Tom Brokaw at NBC—continued in their posts, while they and their audiences aged. Second-tier anchors were mostly to be found on the news magazines (see pp. 657–659), although Ted Koppel's *Nightline* occupied a special and influential position, usually at 11:30 P.M. The line between news and entertainment often was blurred in many ways. For example, CNN reporters were encouraged by Time Warner (which owned CNN) to appear in the 1997 motion picture *Contact* (a movie that also drew the ire of the White House for its inclusion of misleadingly edited actual video footage of President Clinton). Viewers soon learned that ABC's entertainment reportage often focused on Disney films and Broadway shows, and Fox's on 20th Century-Fox's movies (and *TV Guide* on Fox television)—examples of the synergy and bias expected from media conglomerates (see pp. 617–618). Fox news also was noticeably more politically conservative.

What the audience couldn't immediately see was the lower quality of network news because of the financial effects of the drop in viewership of the flagship evening newscasts from a combined share of nearly three fourths of the viewing audience in the early 1970s to less than half the viewing audience by the middle of the 1990s. In 1971, the combined rating for the three national network evening newscasts was 37.2, a number that dropped to 23.9 in 1995. Shares of the total television news audience dropped during the same period from 73% to 48%—and continued down.

It can be argued that the problem was circular: the drop in viewership was due to a drop in journalistic quality, which in turn was caused by cost-cutting. The drop in journalistic quality probably is an amalgam of the morale problems caused by network downsizing, the tendency to air vicarious entertainment instead of the kind of news that it takes a professional (rather than an Internet information provider) to supply, and network treatment of the news as a profit center (which started when Don Hewitt's *60 Minutes* started to make money and give network executives the idea that all news broadcasting should make a profit). What may have been lost is the use of journalism as a means of meeting their public interest responsibilities. The downsizing also caused those network correspondents still on the payroll to be spread thinly, with fewer and fewer stationed abroad. To cover foreign events, the networks relied on foreign counterparts, freelancers, and—for stories that could justify the expenditure to the accountants—flying in correspondents and satellite transmitters. (In the industry, it was called "parachuting," and was more economical than having resident correspondents.)

Even those economies were not enough, and just at the end of 1999 three networks—ABC, CBS, and Fox, which wanted to get into the game—agreed to pool video coverage into a Network News Service, a cost-cutting effort whose conceptual forerunner was the 1964 Network (now "News") Election Service intended to reduce the cost of obtaining voting results. NBC originally decided to go it alone, with its broadcast network and CNBC and MS-NBC cable news services.

There was a clear softening of news at both the local and national levels. Locally, few stations could resist the "if it bleeds, it leads" approach to selecting lead stories, and some deliberately sought out stories of crime and disaster. Although such an emphasis led to the strange situation where most U.S. citizens believed that the streets of their communities were more dangerous than police or FBI statistics showed, such coverage also led to high audience ratings. One group owner, Sunbeam, became known for how its Miami station concentrated on crime—which was bad enough in reality, but not as bad as Sunbeam's television news would have one believe. Although city tourist authorities complained, their protests had little effect on what was covered. When Sunbeam bought a station in Boston, a toned-down version of the same news judgment was employed. The worst effect of this was that competing stations modified their own news coverage in order to avoid being scooped on crime, accident, and similar stories.

Another change in the news was emphasis on "evergreen" features involving attractive children or animals, parades or fireworks, as well as local developments that the station had adopted as a contribution to "civic journalism." Since a news program runs a scheduled length of time and since commercials, sports, and weather rarely would be cut, it meant that news of long-range political, social, and economic developments got short shrift. Nationally, the same change in emphasis was evident in most network flagship evening newscasts. They started providing more special features and consumer and health information than either breaking news or in-depth news of politics and other trends and ideas. To be fair, other media such as newspapers and news magazines also were moving from news to features and "infotainment."

While it got harder to justify expensive in-depth coverage of most stories—except, of course, stories like coverage of wars in which U.S. military forces took a major part, sudden deaths of personalities like Princess Diana and John F. Kennedy Jr., the bombing of the Oklahoma City Federal

■ Longtime sports broadcaster and defendant O.J. Simpson (second from right) sits alongside his attorneys, from left, Johnnie Cochran Jr., Robert Blasier, and Peter Neufeld during closing arguments in what was probably the most widely watched murder trial (Los Angeles, September 1995). Simpson was found not guilty, but later lost a civil trial dealing with the same murders. The verdicts in both trials exacerbated racial tensions in America.

AP/Wide World Photos.

Building and the subsequent trial of the chief suspect in Denver, the bombing at the Atlanta Olympic Games in 1996 (whose extensive coverage was partly due to the number of reporters in town for the Games), the fate of Elian Gonzalez, and the O.J. Simpson murder case—once one network latched on to a story, others felt that they had to follow. Every network and station covered the 1990s O. J. Simpson case from the slow-motion chase on Los Angeles freeways to the criminal trial and its not–guilty verdict and on to the civil trial and its contrary verdict. At least one station (KTLA, Los Angeles) covered every minute of the trial. Possibly the media panic over having to juggle coverage of the verdict in the Simpson civil trial, of voyeuristic titillation to the majority of the public, at the same hour as President Clinton was making his 1997 State of the Union address to Congress and the entire nation, is a sign of the way journalism is going.

A few other major international news stories broke through. Chief among them was the fall of communism in Eastern Europe—beginning in late 1989, and continuing through the end of the Soviet Union itself two years later. Viewers all over the world watched in amazement as the Berlin Wall came down, or as the flag of the U.S.S.R. flying over the Kremlin was replaced by the flag of the Russian Republic. (Two years later, the world again watched in awe and apprehension as a plot to take over the fledgling Russian government was turned back—with riveting pictures of tanks in the street, a burning legislative building, and reporters everywhere to tell us what we were seeing.) The very existence of radio and television, showing what life was like in the West, probably hastened the end of the communist regimes—and other modern technologies, such as fax machines, direct dialing, audio- and videotapes, and computers played their parts as well. Less well covered, to the dismay of those concerned, were stories of the famines in sub-Saharan Africa, conflicts in the Balkans and elsewhere, and similar important but untelegenic developments.

The most dramatic coverage was of the first true "living room war," fought in the Persian Gulf in 1990–1991, which showed how much better broadcast journalism technology had become in the 15 years since the end of the Vietnam War. One of CNN's anchors, Bernard Shaw, was in Baghdad during the brief conflict, which started when Iraq invaded and occupied U.S. ally Kuwait, and his pictures and descriptions of cannon, rockets, bombs, and missiles going off outside his hotel window—live—enthralled his audience. He was allowed to broadcast, using a suitcase-size satellite transmitter (although it permitted the U.S. military to see how successful their attacks had been) because Saddam Hussein, the ruler of Iraq, needed a direct link for his propaganda messages to the United States. Both sides approved Shaw's presence, although some of the general public objected to an American newsman broadcasting messages from the enemy.

When the American and allied forces took to the desert to push Iraq out of Kuwait early in 1991, a large pool of reporters and camera operators almost fell over one another trying to get the most dramatic pictures of

Operation "Desert Storm" or simply human-interest interviews with soldiers from their own city or state. Some of them showed Iraq's Scud missiles fired at Saudi Arabia and Israel (which, although not a combatant, feared germ or gas attacks) being countered by Patriot antimissile missiles. It reminded many of the movie *Star Wars*.

Upon their return, however, many reporters told of censorship difficulties with the military commanders—and many months later, stories emerged about the poor performance of the American Patriot missile, to the unhappiness of the military and manufacturers who had been singing its praises. Another story that received inadequate coverage—almost none for several years—was about the medical problems suffered by some U.S. troops who had served in the Gulf. But the top generals involved found that television had made them household names and faces. The field commander, Gen. Norman Schwarzkopf—whose father, head of the New Jersey State Police in the 1930s, used to "narrate by proxy" the *Gangbusters* radio program—was treated with the same acclaim as General Douglas MacArthur during early phases of the Korean War. General Colin Powell, Chairman of the Joint Chiefs of Staff, could have ridden his fame to a Presidential nomination had he only said the word—and he did become Secretary of State a decade later.

U.S. troops were involved in several other parts of the world during the 1990s, and it soon became evident that the increasingly suspicious military was using access-limiting tactics to prevent the media from fully covering conflicts in which the United States was involved. Many senior commanders still resented some aspects of coverage of Vietnam, which they believed led to the U.S. pullout, and had practiced control procedures in short-lived hot spots like Granada and Panama. Others cringed at the sight of Marines crawling up a beach when entering violence-torn Somalia—with news camera operators and their bright lights crawling backward, in front of them, making the Marines easy targets had the Somalians wished to contest the landing. The grim fighting in Kosovo in 1999 was an opportunity to give the impression of open reportage, while restricting the media in many ways. It wasn't just on-the-spot coverage that was restricted: a CNN/*Time* magazine documentary that claimed to have uncovered military use of poison gas in Cambodia in the 1970s was so heavily attacked by ex-military officers that the program was discredited, and Peter Arnett, one of CNN's most noted correspondents, was severely disciplined while producer April Oliver and a colleague were fired. Other government agencies—notably the FBI during the siege of the Branch Davidian compound near Waco, Texas in 1993—imposed their own restrictions.

While the space program, after the *Challenger* disaster in 1986, now rarely got more than a minimal amount of coverage, the landing of a "cute" robot vehicle on Mars in 1997 surprised many news professionals with the amount of public interest—which might have been whetted by the bright and long-lasting appearance of the Hale-Bopp comet a few months before.

The loss of two Mars landers in 1999 caused hardly a ripple—after all, the last manned flight to the Moon had occurred in 1972, and Mars was a long distance away.

Surprising many newspeople and viewers alike was the huge emotional reaction to the accidental death in 1997 of Great Britain's Princess Diana and—two years later—the death of John F. Kennedy Jr. in an aircraft accident. Massive news coverage continued for weeks. The bombing of the federal building in Oklahoma City in 1995 was made particularly poignant by the large number of small children who were killed. While the 1998 impeachment trial of President Bill Clinton was covered thoroughly, many felt that the coverage was focused more on the titillation of his relationship with Monica Lewinsky than with any constitutional questions, unlike the Watergate case that forced Richard Nixon to resign the Presidency a quarter century earlier.

An ethical problem that could affect the credibility of broadcast journalism stemmed from both a decline in professionalism and caps on network expenditures. For example, CNN talkmaster Larry King, whose program was as much entertainment as news, earned very large amounts of money in addition to his salary by being willing to speak to a wide variety of groups. Almost any newscaster could earn money without running afoul of journalistic or economic ethical standards by writing books or for the other print media. Sometimes this could tie in with programming, as with the best-selling history books that both Tom Brokaw and Peter Jennings produced at the end of the decade. All those whose faces were seen often on the air, including such second-tier news personalities as Cokie Roberts (of NPR and ABC) and Jeff Greenfield (originally of ABC and later with CNN), could command fees in the many thousands of dollars for giving talks to professional, social, and business organizations.

One of the few radio news program services, Monitor Radio, went out of business in June of 1997. An alternative to network and AP news, this respected service went the way of other *Christian Science Monitor* broadcasting activities when financial difficulties arose. Both public and commercial radio stations found this service useful, because of its thoughtful coverage and commentaries on both foreign and domestic news. Because of its affiliation with Christian Science, the usual news fare of disasters, disease, and crime largely were absent. Stations hunted for a replacement news source, with some signing on with the BBC World Service, which could provide news during most of the day via satellite.

11.6.5.2 *Magazine Shows Explode*

The networks increasingly placed their program focus on so-called magazine shows. Typically, they ran an hour, and concentrated on from one to three stories. The first of this genre was CBS's *60 Minutes*, which went on the air in 1968, became the first news-related program series to make the "top ten" in the ratings, and stayed in that exalted position for many years. Other early programs—some of which dealt with hard news and some of which covered stories that were of decidedly limited importance, except for those viewers for whom gossip constitutes news—included *Dateline NBC*, which in the 1990s went head-to-head with *60 Minutes* at 7 P.M. eastern time on Sunday evenings, and which had other editions on other nights— at one time five nights a week; *60 Minutes II*, intended to extend the franchise to another evening; *20/20*, with Hugh Downs and Barbara Walters on ABC (as many as four editions on various nights); *48 Hours* on CBS, which originally focused on collapsing two days of a continuing story into an hour; *PrimeTime Live*, on ABC; and *Early Edition.*

Newsmagazine programs had many advantages to the television networks since they were very cost effective, with a typical budget of perhaps $600,000 as compared to at least twice that an hour for most entertainment programming. Additional competition has resulted in somewhat lower audiences for any given program, but as a genre they are still very attractive to networks and advertisers. Although content duplications are more common than when only *60 Minutes* and *20/20* were on the air, there still seem to be many original—although often inconsequential—stories available, surprising for a genre that (while it may recycle some stories) tries to keep going all year around. One possible drawback to newsmagazines is that disgruntled subjects of stories are more likely to sue for defamation or privacy invasion. Another is that the hosts or stars of these programs are spread very thin, and thus their content has become the responsibility of a legion of little-known producers.

News magazine programs expanded from two hours each on CBS and ABC in 1990 to five hours on NBC, three on ABC, and two on CBS in 1998. By 1999, the number of programs of this genre seemed to overwhelm both network schedules (13 of 22 prime time hours on the three largest networks) and significant content. Some magazine programs concentrated on sob stories, health oddities, crime, and other topics that were chosen for their interest rather than their importance. Some tried to engender fear rather than knowledge. Some latched on to a formula that devoted the hour to a particular murder case or other event or scandal. Although some correspondents and anchors were very experienced—several *60 Minutes* correspondents and executive producer Don Hewitt were in their 70s—others were far less so, and even money-makers were subject to cost-cutting.

Somewhat different from the rest was *CBS Sunday Morning*, whose low-key, beautifully shot, humane coverage of the arts, ideas, and sometimes events that normally don't get covered, attracted a faithful audience. For 15 years, CBS newsman Charles Kuralt—best known for his "On the Road" segments on the *CBS Evening News*—presented this material with meticulous attention to the words he wrote and the subjects he covered.

Kuralt, whose rumpled, balding appearance was a living reproach to the typical blow-dried anchor until his lamented death in 1997, was one of the last who wrote all of his own copy (he had started out as a writer for newsmen like Ed Murrow). When Kuralt stepped down, he was replaced by Charles Osgood—who also had a way with words, most often heard in his five-minute programs (sometimes with poetry written about the day's events) weekday mornings on CBS radio.

The growth in number of magazine shows could not maintain the audience interest the way that the original *60 Minutes* or *20/20* had in past years. Some of the news magazine clones ignored the originals' attention to significant topics and detail, focused on scandal, gossip, and exploitation, and then wondered why their audiences weren't as large. Fox, for example, offered a magazine show that, as one wag put it, always had at least one package per program on oversexed prostitutes and/or teenagers. Even more of a loss was the serious single-topic documentary format formerly exemplified by *CBS Reports* and only seen in the late 1990s on PBS' *Frontline* and occasional specials. As might be expected, magazine programs tended to have a short life. *West 57th*, which took its name from the address of CBS news, *Eye to Eye with Connie Chung* (CBS), *Now* (NBC), and *Day One* (ABC) all died quickly.

A special case was *Nightline*, with Ted Koppel. This program—typically airing at 11:30 in the evening on east and west coasts, after the local late news on most affiliates—started in November 1979 (see pp. 540, 542) and never stopped being "must" viewing. Koppel, who had remarkable skills as an interviewer and as someone who knew what was going on in the world, made *Nightline* one of the major programs—another was the long-running Sunday *Meet the Press*—on which the politically ambitious liked to appear. Koppel had no reservations about asking tough questions, was well-prepared, and was not bound by a scripted scenario. For several years the length of the program fluctuated, depending on the topic being discussed and how interesting Koppel and his producers thought the topic and the guests of the evening were. However, ABC found that it was possible to sell the time following *Nightline* for a pretty penny—most recently, the political satirical program *Politically Incorrect*, with Bill Maher, has occupied that slot—and restricted it to a half hour. The program typically includes a minidocumentary about the topic of the evening, followed by questioning that can be either too long (if the guests are dull) or too short (if the guests are interesting).

11.6.5.3 *Politics and Broadcasting*

The 1992 election, with incumbent Republican George Bush losing to Arkansas Governor William Clinton was out of the ordinary for broadcasting. Many stations and some networks decided to *not* carry each party convention in its entirety. A third party, dedicated to the election of and funded by wealthy industrialist H. Ross Perot, provided most of what excitement there was, particularly when Perot stepped out of the race, and a short time later returned to it. Political commercials often were vicious, and speeches and debates predictable. Clinton won, to the surprise of those who thought that a Republican dynasty that started with President Ronald Reagan in 1980 would continue. Perot garnered a respectable 19% of the vote.

After the 1994 congressional election, much had changed. This election gave both the House and the Senate to the Republicans in a landslide, for what looked like many years to come. While nobody could be certain, most observers gave part of the credit for this overwhelming Republican vote to radio talk shows. Most talk show hosts were antigovernment, claimed to be libertarian, and appealed to the many disaffected members of the listening public. Candidates sought to appear on these programs, and what the self-appointed "talkmeister"—such as Larry King, who was seen as neutral, and had a huge radio and television audience, and the far more conservative Rush Limbaugh—said was treated with great respect by many candidates. In 1994 right-wing talk shows apparently had great power, even credited with defeating House Speaker Thomas Foley (D-WA). But by the 1996 election, the public seemed to have concluded that talk shows were of much less value in making up their minds. While many shows were as virulent as before, their audiences shrank, except for the hard core of regular and often vocal listeners.

But, for the 1996 elections, even though few of his major initiatives had been successful, President Clinton had adopted the middle ground on many issues, and played the media masterfully, which was one of the reasons why Senator Bob Dole lost. Few broadcasters paid much attention to the political conventions of 1996. While C-SPAN and other cable services carried the programs from gavel to gavel as broadcasters once had, the commercial networks carried only a sampling of the most important speeches, debates, and events for an hour or two here and there each evening. The carefully scripted plans of the political parties for coverage were wasted. The same political boredom affected election night broadcasts, which were much the same since the pioneering days of the 1920s. Traditionally, election night meant that all major news departments were carrying the same sort of material, and thus competition between them for being first and audience was constant. In 1996, in markets with many political races to decide, there was some of the old excitement, but one had the feeling across the nation that station management—and audience—would be just as happy airing entertainment program reruns. After all, cable didn't have a tradition of election night coverage, and thus was unhindered in its quest for audiences and advertisers.

Early in 1998, the investigation of President Clinton's investment in a real estate development (known as"Whitewater") by special prosecutor Kenneth Starr took a new turn, one that filled the airwaves for more than a year.

Starr decided to focus on Clinton's sexual dalliance with a young former intern, Monica Lewinsky. It was a highly public, partisan, and lengthy process, that led to Clinton's impeachment—the first impeachment of a sitting president in nearly a century and a half—in the House, but acquittal in the later Senate trial. Although Republicans maintained that Clinton's peccadillos were the equivalent of President Nixon's abuse of power during the 1972–1974 Watergate case, the public—even after months of "all Monica, all the time" newscasts—wasn't nearly so extreme. Some may have turned cynical, but not everyone adopted the "they're *all* crooks!" approach. Yet, the move of news from information to "infotainment" was almost complete, and much of the public today would be hard pressed to distinguish between gossip and news, and between scandal-mongering and editorial opinion.

While the general public continued to grumble about the growing cost of campaigning, which had caused some members of Congress to retire prematurely, and the sources of the money to run a campaign—a nonpartisan list would include corporations, labor unions, and foreign economic or political interests—they weren't grumbling loudly enough to persuade Congress to enact a campaign finance reform law, since such a law would make life more difficult for incumbents, and for broadcasters who probably would be required to provide some free time for candidates. Broadcasters looked forward to campaign spending every four years, and giving away time (i.e., audiences), their only commodity, was a frightening prospect—particularly since the First Amendment protected competing print media from having to give away their inventory.

The national political conventions were treated by the networks in 2000 in much the same cavalier way that they covered the 1996 conventions. For the 2000 election night coverage, all of the networks continued to use pooled News Election Service reports of the results of "exit polls" and vote tablulations. And fell on their faces. ABC, CBS, NBC, and Fox (as well as every other media organization trying to interpret the vote) all managed to "declare" that Florida had gone for Vice President Al Gore, then that it had gone for Gov. George W. Bush, and then that it was too close to call—each network tracking its competition within a few minutes of each other on each zig and zag. It turned out that Florida indeed was too close to call—with only a few hundred disputed votes separating the candidates and the electorial college votes from Florida necessary to win the closest election in a century. From election night until a month later, when the results of the presidential race were finally known, all broadcast and print news media gleefully reported anything that they could about the vote count in Florida—from the fall of a chad (the little piece that falls out of a punch card) to the spin of a high priced lawyer. Public interest in the counting of ballots for the 2000 election far exceeded public interest in the substance of the campaign, possibly because of the limited charisma of the two main candidates and possibly because of having been conditioned to expect that horse races are exciting and worth viewing.

11.7 Audience Fragmentation

Television and radio were both considered necessities—by rich and poor, by exclusive clubs, welfare departments, and prison wardens. While there are a few families that do not have or use receivers, this was generally a matter of choice—particularly among some of the most wealthy and highly educated—and not a matter of price or availability. Both broadcast media are in almost every home, in almost every room. They are used many hours a day. To many, they are essential.

The more choices available in a given media market, the more fragmented audiences become. While the television broadcast networks—and a very few cable channels such as HBO or ESPN—could still deliver a mass audience, most audiences were small, easily described or defined, self-selected, and loyal. This doesn't mean that they tuned to one station all the time. Most people watched a few television stations and specialized cable channels out of all those available. If they were sports fans, they would turn to ESPN or the Sports Channel, news junkies would spend a lot of time with CNN and their favorite local station newscasts, and so on. They might also use a program guide to select network prime time programs. Radio listeners usually selected only a handful of radio stations to tune to—perhaps one for news, one for local traffic and weather, one for sports, one for music that required some thought when the listener was fresh, another "easier" station for when she or he was tired—out of all those that might be available (more than 100 in some markets). Some people, of course, "surfed" the dial, and anyone could decide to select another programming source at any time, but most members of the audience were creatures of habit.

Of course, they can only select from what is available. For example, less coverage of political conventions and campaigns (see pp. 659–661), may help explain why fewer than half of qualified voters actually voted in 1996. (On the other hand, some broadcasters argue that this reverses cause and effect—public lack of interest in politics results in less coverage on radio and television.) While the public may become overloaded by political coverage and tune out, on the other hand fear of crime in the streets apparently is more the result of excessive media coverage (see p. 653) than it is of real danger.

11.7.1 The Art of Choosing

Audience selection among network programs became easier with devices that allowed VCRs to be programmed in advance using a number assigned to each program. These numbers were published in the ever-larger weekly newspaper program guides, and in *TV Guide* itself. This magazine—with one of the largest magazine circulations in the nation—had "dumbed down" its editorial content after Walter Annenberg sold its nearly five dozen separate editions to Rupert Murdoch for $3 billion, but still provided program listings for the thousands of programs and movies available in a particular market, saving a great deal of time that otherwise would be spent surfing during an evening of television watching.

VCRs, now found in more than 80% of American homes, gave rise to a new business that took off in the 1980s: the rental and sale of videocassettes. Video stores can be found in most malls or shopping centers. There are more than 90 million video rentals a week, nearly one per television household. Federal law has now banned keeping of records on an individual's movie choices—on grounds of preserving privacy—an action greeted with a sigh of relief by those who rented pornographic films. Carrying an inventory that ranged from a few titles on a shelf in a village general store to thousands in a major city emporium, this business flourished for several decades. In 1997, however, Blockbuster—the largest video store chain, an arm of Viacom, which is now the owner of CBS—gave several explanations to stockholders why the number of rentals was going down. One was that a growing number of viewers had many-channel cable service or satellite (DBS) receivers—and once they had access to more than 100 channels, they didn't need to rent. Another was that many viewers were buying, not renting, and building up a library of favorites. Yet other reasons dealt with the smaller number of new films being released, the uncertainty caused by the approval of digital television—and the weather (when it is good, people are outdoors, rather than watching television). All of these reasons have some validity. The public also was interested in video games, whether a Nintendo hooked into their television set or installed on their home computer or downloaded from a satellite or from the Internet.

As early as 1997, the public started to show concern about the governmentally mandated obsolescence of their television receiver and VCR (see pp. 600–601). By 1999, those stations that were already transmitting DTV (at least one station in markets servicing more than three-fourths of the U.S. population) were proclaiming their foresight, and the networks were producing some programs—such as NBC's *Tonight* show with Jay Leno—for the new standard, but the mass public still wasn't buying. Regardless of whether DTV would actually be in their market by early in the 21st century, if someone needed a television set because the old set had broken down, or because the idea of having a set in another room in the house seemed good, they went out and bought a new NTSC set. Prices were low, there were remote controls for everyone—although males still continued to try to monopolize their use—and DTV was a long way away, wasn't it?

11.7.2 Patterns of Viewing and Listening

The 1990s were an era of "more"—more channels and more watching, although *what* was watched was changing. In 1990, 65% of homes owned more than one television receiver, whereas by 2000 that number had climbed to 76%. The number of cable subscribers grew even faster, from 56 to 76% of American homes in the same decade. VCR ownership grew from 65 to 85%, while the use of remote controls expanded from 77% to virtually everyone by the turn of the century. Use of television, as measured by the number of hours the set was operating, rose to 7 hours and 24 minutes by 1999, up from 6 hours and 55 minutes a decade earlier.

But the "more" is particularly evident in the growing number of viewing options. In 1990, the typical home could receive 33 channels, but could choose from among 62 at the end of the decade—nearly twice as many. The typical audience share of the varied video services has changed substantially. According to Nielsen data, in the late 1980s about two thirds of viewing was of network affiliates, independent stations took about 20%, basic cable 13%, pay cable about 7%, the remaining 4% watched public television. But a decade later the numbers were very different—the network affiliates only attracted 54% of viewing, independent stations had declined by almost half to 11%, while basic cable had ballooned up to 41%. The other choices showed little change. (Because of overlap, these proportions do not add up to 100%.)

Another option, not yet well recorded, is the Internet. In early 1999, Nielsen began regular Internet audience measurement, so there is the beginning of an historical record. At that time, the Internet audience—a perhaps misleading label—was growing by 1.8 million people a month. The typical Internet household was on line about 7.5 hours per month, just under a half hour per surfing session.

Radio usage remained fairly steady throughout the 1990s, and the Internet has only incidentally impacted radio listening because many people attend to both activities at the same time. However, as more radio stations take to the air, and as more stations stream their audio through the Internet, the audience for each becomes a smaller overlapping sliver of an already heavily divided pie.

11.7.3 Effects, Real and Otherwise

In the late 1990s, the cable television industry funded a three-year investigation of television violence. Conducted by academic researchers at several universities, the resulting three reports demonstrated that violent programs remained very much a staple of American programming. The broadcast networks, however, largely ignored these findings partly because, with the television ratings scheme and related V-chip in place, they may have felt that they had met their responsibility.

However, news coverage of violence in schools, particularly the extensive coverage of the Columbine High School shootings in Littleton, Colorado in 1999, made such content—both news reports and police/adventure dramatic programs—a convenient target, one that couldn't be swept under the rug. Legislators, police, and others, including many parents, felt that there *had* to be a connection between fictional violence on television and real violence in the schools. Such a simple cause-and-effect relationship—copycat crime—has rarely been demonstrated, but there is clearly a lot of smoke, and many believe that where there's smoke, there's fire. Just as important, television sets the agenda, and the more violence shown on television—even though only a small handful of the thousands of schools in the nation are involved—the more people think violence is pervasive. This is similar to the public belief that the streets are much more unsafe than is reflected in the statistics gathered by law enforcement officials.

11.7.4 Rumbles over Ratings

The business of finding out how many (and which kinds of) people were watching and listening grew both more complicated and less crowded in the 1990s. The key problem for both stations (which paid for the ratings) and advertisers (who used them) was the lack of choice among ratings companies as the business settled into monopoly. There also were substantial technical problems to overcome, such as how to measure audiences of new channels and new media.

After years of playing a weak second to A. C. Nielsen, Arbitron tried to improve its competitive position with its "ScanAmerica" system, which combined program ratings and product-use data and thus would be of great use to advertisers and advertising agencies. But the high cost of the system and lack of sufficient industry support forced Arbitron to abandon this effort in 1992, and two years later Arbitron withdrew completely from providing local market television ratings.

By then the sole provider of both national and local TV ratings, Nielsen generated a great deal of broadcaster discontent. Nielsen continued to use paper diaries for local ratings because they cost less, even though they weren't as accurate as machine data. On the national level, Nielsen had initiated "people meter" ratings, measuring individual rather than household viewing, in 1987, using a sample of 5,000 households. But the television networks, unhappy that people meter data showed a steady erosion of their audience, always seemed to be on the verge of dropping Nielsen service—except that there was no alternative. In 1997, Nielsen again became a separate company after several years as part of Dun & Bradstreet and later Cognizant. Eighteen months later, Nielsen was sold to the Dutch publisher VNU NV for $2.7 billion, and pledged to continue operating as it had during its first half century.

Arbitron, having left national ratings to Nielsen, focused on local radio ratings, a market that Nielsen had abandoned in 1964 and Birch-Scarborough left in 1991. Continuing to rely on two-week written diaries, Arbitron regularly surveyed some 260 radio markets—the 95 largest all of the time, and the remainder in the Spring and Fall. National radio program service ratings were derived by RADAR (Radio's All-Dimension Audience Research), which was performed by Statistical Research Inc. using telephone survey methods for a week at a time twice a year.

Measurements of newer media were slow to develop, since there were substantial methodological problems counting such scattered audiences. Nielsen had first provided cable ratings in 1979, and upgraded that service with more market-level information in 1992, allowing a comparison of cable with broadcast station tuning. Nielsen also measured use of VCRs, including the time-shifting function, four times a year. Several firms, of which Media-Matrix was dominant, provided estimates of Internet use—total amount of time spent on the Web, which sites got the most "hits," and so on.

11.8 Legislation, Deregulation, and Policy

During the 1990s, regulatory concepts dating back to shortly after the Civil War were quietly overturned. The "public interest, convenience and necessity" seemed less and less to be the basis for governmental decision making. Selecting a licensee on the basis of what might most benefit the public became suspect, and wealth (spectrum auctions) and luck (lotteries) substituted. The "deregulation" of the 1980s became *no* regulation in the 1990s. The very idea of regulation was considered archaic and impractical. During the 1990s, if someone thought of a possible way to make money, the necessary spectrum would be found by the FCC—perhaps at a price—and sometimes needless of interference and economic damage that might be done to other services. Communications efficiency, built into the Communications Act of 1934, gave way to desire—for example, when vulnerable radio circuits were used to replace more reliable wire circuits in order to save a few dollars and a bit of time and effort.

Government's various roles—as facilitator, user, and regulator—remained, but sometimes were used inappropriately, as when Congress assigned the Pentagon such varied tasks as leading roles in research for high-definition television and breast cancer research. When the biggest user of electronics, the government, wanted something, it would get made—and then the manufacturer would seek civilian uses. Generally, they were successful, as witnessed by such successful adaptations as the Boeing 707 jetliner and the ever-more-useful GPI (geographical position indicator), which measures how long a signal takes to reach any four of many orbiting satellites, and uses those figures to plot exact (if a U.S. military user) or approximate locations (if a civilian hiker or boater, since the military is justifiably wary of having unfriendly parties use GPI as an aid for targeting missiles), thus enabling cell phone (or automobile) companies to suggest restaurants or gas stations in one's immediate neighborhood.

Regulation was almost abandoned in many arenas, with the motto being "that regulation is best that regulates least." By 2001, the FCC no longer showed any real advocacy for regulation in the public interest. Ideas like "the free marketplace" and the resulting "untrammeled competition" were the current philosophy all over Washington, even if the government's other roles, as provider of facilities and research and as industry's biggest customer, came in conflict with a strict interpretation of this philosophy.

11.8.1 A New Telecommunications Law

The single most important change in policy in the 1990s was the passage of a substantial package of amendments to the Communications Act of 1934 that became collectively known as the Telecommunications Act of 1996. That some change was needed had been recognized for years, at least as far back as Rep. Van Deerlin's 1978–1979 attempt to totally replace the 1934 Act (see pp. 562–566). But deciding exactly what changes should be made, and how to implement them, delayed final action of the Telecommunications Act for some time. The 1994 Republican takeover of both houses of Congress indirectly led to more delay, as both White House and Capitol Hill relearned the delicate arts of compromise and leadership.

The 100-page legislative package that had been developed over several years finally was signed into law in February 1996. Most provisions dealt with common carrier (telephone and data), with only a few sections specifically concerned with broadcasting or cable. But these were sufficient to cause dramatic change. The broadcast license period was extended to eight years for both radio and television, up from the five years for television and seven for radio adopted in 1981. This reduced paperwork for both industry and government and served to reduce broadcaster anxiety.

Another related change served the same end, but may be more far-reaching. For decades, broadcasters had lobbied Congress for "renewal expectancy"—a term signifying that a licensee could count on renewal unless found guilty of a serious transgression. While it seldom happened in practice, station owners always seemed to fear that a competing application at renewal time would cost them their license—or, at least, would throw the renewal into a comparative FCC hearing to decide which applicant (the existing licensee or the challenger) would provide the better public service. A few notorious and expensive cases in the past kept the issue high on the broadcasters' agenda. The 1996 act contained a provision that required the FCC to take formal action to turn down an existing licensee before it could even consider a competing application—a very unlikely event. This provision gave broadcasters virtually all they wanted and greatly limited the FCC's—or any challenger's—freedom of action. The effective result of the new law was to mandate renewal of any license if: the station had served the public interest, had not been found guilty of "serious violations" of the Act, and had committed "no other violations" of the Act or FCC regulations

---

■ **Telecommunications Act of 1996 and the Electronic Media**   These key provisions selected from the electronic media part of this landmark legislation (which was largely devoted to the common carrier telecommunications industry) demonstrate the political strength of those in Congress who wished to implement a new political and economic ideology. Where shown, the section number refers to the amended Communications Act of 1934.

Purpose of the act:
To promote competition and reduce regulation in order to secure lower prices and higher quality services for American telecommunications consumers and encourage the rapid deployment of new telecommunications technologies

Program ratings:
Require, in the case of an apparatus designed to receive television signals that are shipped in interstate commerce or manufactured in the United States and that have a picture screen 13 inches or greater in size . . . , that such apparatus be equipped with a feature designed to enable viewers to block display of all programs with a common rating [such as those adjudged by the ratings process to have high amounts of violence or sexual content]. *. . (303 (x))*

License period:
Each license granted for the operation of a broadcasting station shall be for a term of not to exceed 8 years. (307 (c))

License renewals:
. . . the commission shall not consider whether the public interest, convenience, and necessity might be served by the grant of a license to a person other than the renewal applicant . . . [unless the renewal applicant has failed to meet each of the following three standards:]
   (A) the station has served the public interest, convenience, and necessity;
   (B) there have been no serious violations by the licensee of this Act or the rules and regulations of the Commission; and
   (C) there have been no other violations by the licensee of this Act or the rules and regulations of the Commission which, taken together, would constitute a pattern of abuse. (309 (k) (1, 4))

Ownership of radio stations:
. . . eliminate . . . any provisions limiting the number of AM or FM broadcast stations which may be owned or controlled by one entity nationally [and] *eliminate . . . the restrictions on the number of television stations that a person or entity may directory or indirectly own, operate, or control, or have a cognizable interest in, nationwide and . . . by increasing the national audience reach limitation for television stations to 35 percent . . .*

Cross-media ownership:
. . . permit a person or entity to own or control a network of broadcast stations and a cable system . . .

"which, taken together, would constitute a pattern of abuse." It would be a tall order to find a station in violation of these provisions, considering current regulatory and enforcement criteria, and thus renewal may be expected in virtually all cases.

As a result, there has been destruction of the ability of listeners, groups, and communities to effectively challenge existing licenses. Ever since the courts held in the 1960s that the public had legal "standing" in license granting or renewals (see pp. 460–463), the very existence of this possibility served as a partial bar to unreasonable licensee actions or FCC decisions. But under the 1996 Act, the public has lost this leverage.

A third change probably already has had more impact than Congress intended. It required the FCC to remove all restriction on how many radio stations an owner could control across the country and also opened up opportunities for owning a number of stations in the same market. Long-standing (and enforced) FCC *duopoly* and *multiple ownership* rules that had prevented ownership of more than one station of a type (AM, FM, or television) in any one market were largely swept away for radio in 1996 and television in 1999. This enabled station owners to minimize costs and competition, and thus maximize profits. While no one owner could control more than half of the stations in any market, in the largest cities (those with 45 or more radio stations) one owner cold have up to eight stations (no more than five in the same service, AM or FM). In a market with as few as 14 stations, a single owner could now own up to five, no more than three in the same service.

An almost immediate result was a sharp trend toward radio industry consolidation. In the first year after passage of the 1996 Act, multiple-station ownership grew amazingly—with upward of 200 stations licensed to a single licensee. By 2001, the largest group (Clear Channel Communications and AMFM) ballooned to more than 1,200 stations, with several others controlling several hundred stations each. Market-by-market, buying and selling went on as companies tried to position themselves in the potentially profitable situation of having a strong multi-outlet position. Individual radio station prices shot up amid all this merger and acquisition activity. The Justice Department finally slowed things down by issuing an informal ruling to the effect that, in spite of the 1996 Act, no one owner could control more than half the radio advertising revenue in a single market—or the antitrust laws would be brought into play.

In mid-1999, the FCC announced that one entity could control two television stations in the same market if there were at least eight other stations operating there. The "if" reduced the effect of this change to approximately the 50 largest cities. A single owner could control overlapping stations—as might happen, for example, in the crowded Eastern seaboard, involving cities such as Baltimore and Washington, D.C.

Continuing the relentless march toward deregulation, in early October 2000 the FCC suspended the political editorializing and personal attack rules for the 2000 election campaign—and was almost immediately trumped by the U.S. Court of Appeals for the District of Columbia, which ordered the commission to "immediately repeal" the rules on procedural grounds. While this case may go through further appeals, the National Association of Broadcasters (NAB) and the Radio-Television News Directors Association (RTNDA) (which has been fighting against the Fairness Doctrine since 1980, see pp. 566–569) both claimed it a notable victory toward removing the last vestiges of the Fairness Doctrine, most of which had been repealed by the FCC in 1987. RTNDA's position has always been based on the First Amendment—against external restraints on journalistic judgment. NAB's position may have been based more on financial considerations. What little objective research exists on the benefits/demerits of the Fairness Doctrine for the general public has had little attention paid to it, as contrasted to the oratory that has been employed by the proponents of this deregulation. The small group of public interest advocates who still favored the Doctrine on the basis that the airwaves belonged to the people could only hunker down and wait for the regulatory pendulum to swing again in the future.

Although the FCC continued to search for new efficiencies (such as placing all license actions and identifications in a computerized database, assigning unique numbers to each licensee) and explored ways of increasing its license fee income, not all of these efforts were successful. The amount of money the FCC could raise by lotteries or by auctioning spectrum for personal communications devices was greatly misperceived. Some of the winners in the first ($10.2 billion) auction of this spectrum had to ask for a bailout, bankruptcy, or both. This failure to move ahead not only cost the FCC fee income, but it prevented any use of the frequencies in question until the matter was settled in extensive further FCC and court proceedings.

11.8.2 Legislating Decency/Protecting Children

As a product of their never-ending struggle to be re-elected, many members of Congress focused on the possible (i.e., not really proven) cause-and-effect adverse impact of broadcasting (and other media) on children. Since this clearly is a useful political issue, hearings have been held fairly regularly since the 1950s (see pp. 385–387) about the impact of televised sex and violence, or about the lack of sufficient educational programming or moral emphasis. In the Children's Television Act of 1990, Congress mandated that television stations air at least a minimal amount of "pro-social" programming each week. The FCC was required to monitor and limit the amount of advertising carried in such programs to 12 minutes per hour on weekdays and 10.5 minutes on weekends. Although the now-defunct NAB Code once required such limitations, this was the first time that Congress had passed a law mandating a specific kind of program or limiting the amount of advertising on the air.

In subsequent rulemaking, the FCC defined this Act to control programs intended primarily for an audience of those who were 12 years old or younger. Under pressure both from children's advocates and the White House, the FCC in 1996 followed up with a requirement that the "minimal amount" be three hours of such "pro-social" programming a week. The new rules required that the shows be aired at reasonable times (neither too early nor too late for children) and made the word "educational" clearer in intent.

Protecting children from violence, sex, obscenity, and other antisocial messages on television or radio has proven harder to accomplish, thanks to the First Amendment. The Telecommunications Act of 1996 took a different route by requiring manufacturers to include a "V-chip" ("V" for violence) in all new television receivers. This computer chip would allow parents to automatically block out programs they didn't want children to view, using a rating system that networks and stations employed to identify such programs. While the Act did not mandate a particular content rating system, it gave the FCC the right to establish a committee to decide on a system if the industry couldn't agree on one. After fulminating about potential court appeals based on the First Amendment, broadcasters decided that discretion was the better part of valor and agreed to establish a system based in part on that used by the motion picture industry, and even began to encode the rating information on their channels. However, after all of the debate, the public—even parents of small children—seemed little interested in buying (and programming) V-chip receivers.

The seemingly unending concern with indecency and obscenity on the air (see pp. 580–581) didn't slacken in the 1990s. The FCC attempted to define a "safe harbor" for the airing of indecent but otherwise protected speech. Congress became concerned that, since children could be in the audience at any time, they could be exposed to obscene and indecent material. In 1990, obeying a mandate from Congress, the FCC completely banned this sort of content—only to be reversed a year later by the courts on the grounds that this law was too broad to survive under the First Amendment. Congress, in 1992, then mandated that such programs be allowed only between midnight and 6:00 A.M. That limitation was soon modified, and the current safe harbor between 10:00 P.M. and 6:00 A.M. was established. Congress entered the scene again in 1996, with a broad statute (the Communications Decency Act, part of the larger 1996 Telecommunications Act)

■ Television Code Categories

(1) Solely for children:

TV-Y	Appropriate for all children (specifically designed for Children 2–6)
TV-Y7	Designed for children aged 7 and older; who can distinguish between reality and make-believe.
TV-Y7-FV	Same, but with fantasy violence that may be stronger than in other programs

(2) For all audience members:

TV-G	General audience; little or no violence, strong language, sexual situations.
TV-PG	Parental guidance suggested as may have some violence sexual situations, language or suggestive dialogue
TV-14	Parents strongly cautioned: same limitations as above
TV-M	Mature audiences only. May be unsuitable for those under age 17.

(3) Additional content warnings (Added in late 1997)

V	Violence
S	Sexual content
L	Strong language
D	Suggestive dialogue
FV	Fantasy violence

forbidding both obscene (not protected by the First Amendment) and indecent (protected, although punishable under earlier statutes if broadcast) speech. An amendment, named after Nebraska Senator James Exon, spread a broad blanket of prohibition across the electronic media, telecommunications generally, and the Internet—and was appealed within hours of being signed into law. Within a year, the Supreme Court had decided by a vote of 7 to 2 that it was far too broad and vague to be constitutional, in spite of its laudable goal of protecting young children.

Related to this, but receiving much more public attention, was Howard Stern. The New York–based "shock jock" DJ became the center of controversy in the early 1990s. His employer, Infinity Broadcasting, racked up huge FCC fines for Stern's suggestive and indecent sexual innuendos. By 1993 the fines totalled $1.7 million, in part because Stern was carried on stations across the country and each airing was considered a separate violation. With a number of station sales and purchases held up by the FCC because of the fines, Infinity finally paid them in two installments. Although complaints about Stern showed little sign of abating throughout the decade, his popularity on both radio and television assured at least near-term continuation of his program.

11.8.3 Cable's Regulatory Roller Coaster

Attempting to limit obscene or indecent material on cable has proved even more complicated and contentious than it has with traditional broadcasting. Several states attempted to mandate control of indecent cable program content in the 1980s, but were overturned on appeal when the courts held that, as a subscription medium, cable is not as intrusive as broadcasting. In the Cable Act of 1992, Congress gave cable system operators the *option* of banning indecent programming on public or governmental access channels, or at least moving such programming to a single channel. Courts upheld this provision, as it left the choice in the hands of system managers. As part of the 1996 Telecommunications Act, Congress *required* that cable systems completely block or scramble both the audio and the video portions of any cable service primarily dedicated to showing explicit sexual content, unless it were limited to the "safe harbor" hours of 10 P.M. till 6 A.M. This requirement survived court review in 1996–1997, in part because it still provided system operators with a choice—they could schedule this programming for hours when children were unlikely to be in the audience.

Cable had other bouts with legislation. After deregulation of cable in the 1984 Act (see pp. 574–575), cable's subscription rates soared at a far faster rate than general inflation. At the same time, the industry's reputation for service dropped sharply, and complaints flooded into the FCC and the Congress. Despite the public relations activities of the cable industry, the perception of cable being greedy led to a congressional revisit of the issues in 1992, followed by reinstatement of some regulation of the industry. Local franchise authorities again were given some rights to control basic cable rates, and the FCC was told to establish rules setting up reasonable rates for other tiers. The FCC responded with decisions that rolled back basic cable rates a bit between 1993 and 1995 (pay cable and pay-per-view were not affected by this law), although few consumers noticed much difference, and many complained about the complexity of the new rules.

The 1992 Act also reinstated another cable industry concern, must-carry (see p. 575). *Must-carry* requires cable systems to carry all television stations within their coverage area. Originally mandated by the FCC in the 1970s on the behest of television broadcasters, these rules had been twice overturned by court review in the mid-1980s as unconstitutional. But the television industry, fearful that any stations not carried on cable would wither away, lobbied for the return of these rules—and Congress finally acted accordingly. The 1992 Act also mandated that cable programmers sell their programs and services to competing modes of delivery (e.g., DBS, MMDS) at nondiscriminatory prices. This helped reinforce the FCC's post-1979 ideology that the best regulation would be effective competition.

In 1996, the Congress again reversed course. Persuaded that other media competitive with cable were developing, the Telecommunications Act relaxed or rescinded much of the rate regulation structure that had developed since 1992 and further deregulated basic tier rates in 1999. If rates again climb so high that Congress becomes aware of public unhappiness, this matter will no doubt again be revisited. Another unresolved question was that of cable's carriage of digital television signals—which would require major investment in new facilities. As this is being written, there was no firm requirement about must-carry, or about the idea that cable should carry broadcast HDTV signals—thus making the new service virtually unavailable to two thirds of the national audience (see pp. 602–606).

11.8.4 Torts and Ethics

Although the laws of libel and slander, concerns about invasion of privacy, and questions of broadcasting's access to court proceedings had long been subjects of discussion in newsrooms, a number of news operations tangled with the law in unusual ways. For example, ABC's *PrimeTime Live* program telecast a segment in 1992 that attacked the Food Lion grocery chain on several grounds, including false labeling and unsanitary handling of meat. To get the story, ABC producers (acting as reporters and camera operators) had lied about their current employment on application forms, and had been given jobs at Food Lion. Using hidden cameras and similar techniques, the story was reported. Food Lion cried "foul," and, instead of bringing suit for defamation (in which it would have had to prove "actual malice" on the part of ABC), it sued on grounds of trespass, obtaining employment using false credentials, not doing the task for which they were employed by Food Lion, and similar torts (injuries). A North Carolina jury agreed strongly with Food Lion and, in 1996, ABC was assessed more then $5 million. Although this sent a strong message to television newsrooms—as did an earlier case in which NBC used pyrotechnic devices to make sure that an "unsafe" gasoline tank exploded—on appeal the damages ABC was to pay were reduced, first to $315,000, and then to a token $1 from each of the two producers.

Another widely publicized case also concerned food. When the popular daytime talk show host Oprah Winfrey claimed on the air that she would never eat another hamburger after hearing criticisms of beef safety, the Texas Beef Group sued under a state "agricultural products libel" law, claiming that the broadcast had cost their industry millions in lost sales. Relocating her program temporarily from Chicago to Amarillo, Texas, for the trial, Winfrey added to the publicity. After a six week long trial, the jury found in favor of Winfrey, although winning it had cost her between a half million and a million dollars.

Numerous other instances of problems with both the law and ethics—e.g., the NBC gas tank fakery mentioned above, and an eventually discredited CNN/*Time* program about American military forces using poison gas on American defectors in Cambodia (see p. 656)—apparently is just one part of a blurring of the line between entertainment and information, "infotainment." Since news is now expected to be a cash cow for both stations and networks, personal ambition and competitive pressures make it increasingly difficult for reporters, editors, producers, and anchors to avoid shortcuts, "do the right thing," forgo sensationalism, and meet their responsibilities to the audience.

11.8.5 Players and Arenas

Congress continued to micromanage telecommunications, including broadcasting. The FCC, shorn of much of its authority and now down to five members, struggled to keep abreast of the many changes in technology, ownership, and the political climate. In the 1990s, tenure on the commission tended to be short, and membership often was successfully proposed to the White House by powerful members of Congress. While individuals like Chairman Kinnard in the late 1990s attempted to demonstrate independence and authority, this posturing rarely was successful or lasting. Because the FCC was supposed to oversee electronic media industries of vital concern to the public, a member of Congress could garner much desired publicity by attacking the FCC on any subject, from low-powered FM (see pp. 612–613) to the move of the FCC's headquarters from its convenient location in the middle of the lawyer's enclave in Washington to an isolated spot in southwest District of Columbia. With Michael Powell assuming the chairmanship when the George W. Bush administration started in 2001, and with a Republican majority on the commission, it looked like more emphasis on market forces rather than public interest regulation in the future in the FCC as well as Congress.

11.9 **Into the 21st Century**

The new laws discussed above have helped displace the old standard of "the public interest, convenience, and necessity." The Telecommunications Act of 1996 adopted the marketplace concept as the best way of promoting the public interest—even though there is very little research as to whether this approach really works. One side effect of such a philosophy has been to weaken the standing of members of the general public in challenging licenses. Most legislators and members of the FCC genuinely believe that unlimited competition is the best way of achieving the public interest. Unfortunately, in order to ensure that competition exists, there is a strong tendency to redefine "the market" to include every electronic entertainment medium (including computers) as a member. (The equally likely possibility that unlimited competition is one of the first steps on the road to monopoly is similarly unproven.)

Another casualty in many communities is the loss of localism. Local programs cost more to produce than network or syndicated shows—and broadcasting is a business. Elimination of many of the restrictions on number of stations an entity may own means that both the stations and the audiences they serve are nothing more than commodities, as are the programs they produce and watch.

Yet, there is little outcry from the public. Instead, one can see that nearly everyone is plugged in—to radio, cassette or CD player, television set, computer, VCR, telephone—much of their lives. And these lives are being lived at a faster pace, thanks to the Internet and other electronic media.

The Internet is not "broadcasting," but it clearly is rapidly growing in importance. As an almost anarchistic web, it is neither controlled by large conglomerates nor by government. This isn't to guarantee that this situation will continue—and the growth in only a handful of years of advertising, e-commerce, and exchange of information between Web sites is a sign that change is fast upon us—but it is quite clear that the public has taken the Internet's effectively unlimited information (and entertainment) resources to heart.

While the electronic media promised to obliterate distance, it wasn't until space communications satellites were introduced that distance truly became irrelevant. Now, news can be gathered from anywhere without delay, and programs can be distributed over a third of the globe as easily as across town. DBS has become common around the world, even though terrestrial transmissions remained the norm, particularly in the United States.

11.9.1 Changes around the World

In other parts of the globe, similar changes occurred—with due regard for national regulatory systems. For example, Rupert Murdoch's "Star" DBS system (founded in 1991, with Murdoch taking over two years later), with a footprint serving most of Asia, is very careful to avoid content that might offend the largest potential market in the world, the People's Republic of China. Murdoch and his News Corporation avow no responsibility except to the bottom line. The ability of smaller nations to restrict potentially damaging or subversive content was less clear, although at one time Germany attempted to restrict many Internet sites they thought indecent—only to have a worldwide outcry against the practice. CompuServe, one of the major American Internet service providers (ISP), had immediately complied, but its subscribers put pressure upon the company to rescind that action.

Some nations have moved away from international shortwave broadcasting in favor of satellite transmissions to local stations in other countries; for example, BBC programs from the United Kingdom are currently aired over many stations in the United States. On June 30, 2001 BBC ceased broadcasting via shortwave to most of North America. Moreover, in Spring 2001, Swiss radio announced that they were planning to drop international shortwave and most direct satellite transmissions in favor of increased Internet usage for audio and connections to European cable systems for video.

The International Telecommunication Union (ITU) underwent its first major reorganization in a half century in 1994, when it scrapped its old structure and elevated the goal of assisting developing nations in meeting their communication needs to the same level as its traditional task of setting technical standards and determining spectrum policy in order to coordinate and regulate radio and wire transmissions that crossed national boundaries. Previously, many decisions were made between pairs of nations—and often at the working rather than the policy level. Now there are other goals, but overall telecommunications allocation decisions remain in ITU hands, continuing its status as a stellar example of international political and technical cooperation for more than a century.

However, even with the mechanisms provided by the ITU, a number of worldwide technical standards never were adopted, because too much money and political reputation would be put at risk. The standards for digital television (see pp. 602–606) are a case in point. Some developing countries still yearn after the goals of the 1980 UNESCO Report (Sean MacBride, *Many Voices, One World*), which would have justified censoring communications across borders in some cases, or restricting imports of VCRs or satellite reception equipment, or access to the Internet, in others—all in the name of preserving national or religious identity. However, the economic need of most nations to be part of the World Trade Organization, whose members agreed to open their national telecommunications systems to competition and potential outside ownership, has limited barriers at the border in most instances.

In some nations, the ideological push for competition led to the abandonment of long-standing policies. For example, in the United Kingdom, great care had been taken for nearly four decades to ensure that virtually every home would be able to receive BBC-1, BBC-2, and ITV (commercial) television signals. But there were too few frequencies available to provide the same level of access to any new networks—and the Conservative governments of Margaret Thatcher (1980–1991) and John Major (1991–1997) had many entrepreneurs demanding a chance to make money with television. So, a law was passed in 1990 giving them the chance to become the highest bidder for the available channels. Thus, Channel Four, started in the early 1990s, and a fifth channel established in 1997 could not be received by anything like the full British population. The establishment of satellite services such as Murdoch's BSkyB may have further reduced the potential profitability of new channels—but that wouldn't stop those who still believed that it was impossible to lose money on television. In the meantime, the BBC went through several directors-general and a great deal of staff unrest in both its domestic and World Service branches as cost-cutting and lowering of program quality to compete with ITV became the order of the day. A new (commercial) Radio Authority licensed several hundred local—often *very* local—stations.

Canada had a different experience. Since the national government wished to cut costs, the Canadian Broadcasting Corporation found itself with much less money—and more expense, since the cost of new technologies and the need for service in both English and French was high. Premier Jean Chretien's government cut the network's subsidies by 30%, and further cut its international shortwave services. At the same time, a growing number of private radio and television stations picked up some of the domestic programming slack. Canada remained torn between its desire to remain free of the cultural colossus of the south—the United States, with hundreds of stations that could be seen or heard by Canadian viewers and listeners, most of whom lived within less than 100 miles from the border—and its financial difficulties. Although quite a few U.S. television shows are filmed or taped in Canada because of substantially lower costs, this only has a local effect. Throughout the 1990s there were skirmishes about the carriage of programming from the United States on Canadian cable systems—which served almost the entire population—and even about the tax deductibility of Canadian payments for advertisements in magazines published in the United States but distributed across the border. Curbs on imports of popular music helped promote a thriving Canadian music business—which has a strong presence in the United States as well. There is something ironic in this, since a great many Canadian musicians, actors, writers, and producers have had highly successful careers in Hollywood.

▪ Epilogue: September 11, 2001

By 2001, most Americans thought that traditional network news was an increasingly irrelevant "dinosaur." They also figured that mass displays of patriotism, common when the U.S. entered World War II, would never appear again. They were wrong on both counts.

On Tuesday, September 11, 2001, terrorists hijacked four commercial airliners loaded with passengers and fuel, and deliberately crashed two of them into the twin 110-story towers of the World Trade Center in New York City, and a third into the Pentagon. The fourth smashed into a field after passengers tried to regain control from the hijackers. Thousands lost their lives, including hundreds of emergency personnel crushed when the WTC towers collapsed.

Nobody knew at first whether the first crash was an accident or a deliberate act. The impact of the second jet into the other WTC tower removed any question. All networks immediately began full-time live coverage, combining news (such as grounding of all air travel) and considerable specu-lation and rumor, much of which later proved false.

Fortunately, New York had greatly improved its emergency responses after a 1993 bombing in the same World Trade Center. Media technology—including minicams, satellite trucks, and cell phones—had greatly improved broadcasting and cable's ability to respond as well. "Crawls" generated at the bottom of network pictures reflected content convergence with banner-ridden Internet Web pages. Satellites allowed commentary from anywhere in the world. Minicams—and even consumer video cameras—gave astounding multiple views of events. Although transmitters for New York television stations had been destroyed, most of the nation and New Yorkers with cable never noticed.

For the first time since the 1963 assassination of President John F. Kennedy (see p. 444), Americans absorbed four full days of continuous television and radio network coverage of a sin-gle event. By week's end, networks had offered more than 90 hours of non-stop coverage, com-pared to about 70 hours in 1963. The top anchors—Peter Jennings (ABC), Dan Rather (CBS) and Tom Brokaw (NBC)—seemed to go without sleep for days. The older networks were joined by CNN ("breaking news" choice for many viewers) and Fox news. Commercials disappeared, as did entertainment programming except on a few cable channels. Stations and channels without their own news operations aired reports from "hard" news sources. Broadcast news did its tradi-tional job exceptionally well, linking the world to news of the grim destruction and its long-lasting aftermath.

Instead of the classical music that provided emotional succor in 1963, there were inspiring inter-views with some of the volunteers—emergency crews, construction workers, medical personnel—who dug into the world's largest mountain of rubble, often with bare hands and shovels, seeking the all-too-few survivors. Their actions, and many interfaith church services, contributed to a grow-ing patriotic fervor as the fact sank in that America had become a battleground. Congress almost unanimously gave President Bush power to wage war against the then-unknown terrorists. National Guard units were called up and flags sprouted on homes and highway overpasses.

Only after five days did entertainment programs (and commercials) begin to trickle back on the air, and professional sports restart (although hampered by air travel slowdowns caused by security measures), but it was hard to return to a "business as usual" mentality even after stock markets opened on Monday. The world had changed, argued many of those who called local radio stations to talk about their feelings. But nobody knew whether the early cooperation, contributions, and volunteerism would continue when faced with the more mundane aspects of life.

Sixty years earlier, when President Franklin D. Roosevelt asked Congress to declare war against Japan following the sneak attack on the U.S. fleet at Pearl Harbor (see pp. 223–226), he began: "Yesterday, December 7, 1941, a day that shall live in infamy . . ." After the terrorist attacks, an NPR commentator, recognizing the wall-to-wall coverage by the national networks, said "September 11, 2001, a day that shall live in imagery . . ."

Selected Further Reading

(Alphabetical within topics. For Full citations, see Appendix D.)

The fast-changing electronic media scene at the turn of the millennium is described in Auletta (1991 and 1997), Baker and Dessart (1998), Compaine and Gomery (2000) on ownership trends, Grant (1991–1996), Hilliard and Keith (1999) on low-power TV, Keating (1999), MacFarland (1997), Parsons and Frieden (1998), Steinbock (1995), and Walker and Furguson (1998). Digital television is the focus of Brinkley (1997), de Bruin and Smits (1999), Dupagne and Seel (1998), and Van Tassel (1996).

The growing importance of public broadcasting is made evident in Collins (1993) and Looker (1995)—both focusing on NPR—Jarvik (1999) on *Masterpiece Theatre*, Land (1999) and Lazar (1999)—both of which profile Pacifica radio—and McCourt (1999). Public television's development is reviewed in Stewart (1999). Eastman and Furguson (1997) is a useful analysis of program decision making in the late 1990s. See titles relating to broadcast journalism in the selected further readings of chapters 9 and 10; also Foote (1998), Gunther on ABC news (1994), Hilliard and Keith (1999) on hate radio, Hunt (1999) and Thaler (1997) on the O. J. Simpson frenzy, Keith (1995) on Native American broadcasting, Murray's (1999) encyclopedia of television news, and Spragens (1995) on television magazine news programs.

A current survey of commercial audience research is Webster, Phalen, and Lichty (2000). Among discussions of policy are Krattenmaker and Powe (1995), Lipschultz (1996) on the FCC and indecent programs, and Price on the V-chip (1998).

Changing international electronic media are described by Allen (1995), Avery (1993), Boyd (1999), Browne (1999), European Audiovisual Observatory (1995–date), Noam (1992), Smith (1998), Tracey (1998), and Woods (1992 and 1999).

"We are getting deeper and deeper into our subject. A few moments ago we were wading. Now we are swimming. Let us hope that we shall not drown. There is only one way to understand a subject, and that, to mix the metaphors a little more, is to take the bull by the horns."———*Raymond Yates and Louis Pacent, THE COMPLETE RADIO BOOK (1922)*

CHAPTER 12

Television antennas sprouting, late 1940s or early 1950s. *National Archives.*

LESSONS FROM THE PAST FOR THE FUTURE

TV reception from satellite dishes, 2001—and later. *Ruth Mandel.*

Chapter Outline

W hile the past may appear complex, it nevertheless is possible to discern patterns and trends that illustrate—and even explain— the evolution of broadcasting over the eight decades since its start. But the future is *always* cloudy, particularly when trying to predict the fast-changing development of the electronic media. This doesn't stop us— and others—from trying!

12.0 Evolution

It is unlikely that the guesses of *any* of the players in this game, including broadcasters, entrepreneurs, inventors, content providers, cable and DBS operators, regulators, legislators, managers, financiers, talent, manufactur- ers, engineers, critics, and others will be fully correct. So, we certainly aren't pretending to be omniscient—*no* prediction is a "sure thing"—but in this chapter we offer both our opinions and a number of questions intended to highlight both past trends and likely future directions.

12.0.1 Questions and Trends

As pointed out in the first chapter of *Stay Tuned*, many of today's institutions are the descendents of events, trends and ideas of years past. For example, although the 21st century opens with something "new," the promise of a dig- ital broadcasting system (one that would require replacement of existing receivers), we went through an analogy of this development when color television was adopted in the 1950s. So, are the claims valid that today's multi-billion dollar gamble (using the consumer's money) will revitalize the American electronics manufacturing industry and give the audience more new content on more channels than they possibly could hear or view? Will the continuing covergence of print, broadcast, and the Internet change the face of all mass media—and even the concept of mass communication? Stay tuned.

The general public doesn't fully understand (or care about) the economic, technological, and political forces that change the mass media. Most people haven't thought of the implications of recent developments, such as global- ization of the mass media or whether the Internet will be a friend or foe of older media. Most people seek content choices and low prices. But many in the various industries that make up the electronic media are thinking ahead, and are using the lessons from the past for their own benefit.

For example, the FCC approved digital television standards in the 1990s. But the FCC has its own agenda, and the new rules allow a broadcaster to provide *either* one channel of high-definition television *or* four (or more) channels of NTSC television. Since there is a lot of old (hence, inexpensive) programming available for NTSC, and since it is likely that a station will have a larger total audience for four channels peddling familiar fare than for one channel purveying new (even though possibly of higher quality) content, which choice do you think most broadcasters will make? After all, even though some electronic media (such as cable) rely on direct payment by the audience, the fiscal backbone of American broadcasting is still advertising and audience size is the key to advertising income. Will the public, after buying their new DTV set wonder what ever happened to the HDTV that attracted them in the first place? Will the FCC and Congress really be willing to render obsolete all those NTSC television sets in American voters' homes? Will those who plan to produce HDTV programming other than sports, nature shows, and pageantry find a mass audience, or will they use costly other means of distribution (e.g., DVD)? Stay tuned.

Regardless of how DTV/HDTV content is distributed, when (if?) NTSC transmissions are eliminated, more than 100 million American households will have needed to buy a new—and expensive—DTV receiver, as well as a new VCR/larger computer hard drive/other device capable of recording and playing HDTV (and the family's "home movies"). Is this financially likely? Will attending to these gadgets, including the ubiquitous home computer, occupy more of people's lives? Stay tuned.

And will the continuing convergence of print, broadcast and Internet services fundamentally change what we read, see and hear? The proliferation of choice made possible by these new media and techniques will have many intended and unintended consequences. For example, can the agenda-setting function of major network newscasts continue, now that their combined audience share has shrunk below 50%? Will the public interest concept continue to decline in importance, being replaced by adoption of a commodity approach (i.e., *everything* can be bought and sold)? Stay tuned.

The innovations that constitute modern electronic media have been adopted ever more rapidly. Although it took the telephone 80 years to reach 34 million homes, electric wiring 62 years, the automobile 49 years, the electric refrigerator 37 years—it only took radio 25 years, television 10 years, and the Internet less than a half dozen years to reach the same number. There are other series of "how long did it take" figures using different bases (50 million users, a fourth of American households (which takes account of the enormous growth in population in the past century), etc.), but the basic lesson is the same—it is taking less and less time for a desirable invention— such as cellular telephones—to spread across the nation. (It should be remembered, though, that these new gadgets are hardly of equal importance.

In fact, in 1999, CNN considered radio only the 40th most important story of the 20th century.)

12.0.2 Seeking Patterns

Though *broad*casting first became important in the early 1920s, by the end of the 1990s there was an increasing industry focus on specialized *narrow*casting. The number of U.S. radio and television stations has increased 25-fold in the last three quarters of the 20th century. Instead of three or four national networks, and a handful of independent stations, the average American household now can choose among 50 or 100 video channels, as many as 100 radio signals, thousands of titles from the neighborhood video outlet or CDs from the nearby music store—and the entire Internet.

It is obvious that no single channel can ever again enjoy the audience levels common as late as the 1980s, except for occasional specials such as the Super Bowl or the first series of *Survivor*. This has serious implications for the profitability of individual broadcast (or cable) services, the marketing and advertising of goods and services, and the unity of knowledge and attention of the population.

All of these developments have led to a *lack* of continuity in our culture, a *lack* of understanding by politicians and the public of the potential roles and potential of electronic media, a *lack* of programmers who demonstrate good taste, a *lack* of stations that still feel that they have a public service obligation, and a *lack* of corporations with goals other than profit and growth. The public is in the middle of this fermenting caldron, with little impartial information on which to base the decisions it still is able to make.

Even as the number of choices for content and delivery systems expands, the number of those who actually control the electronic media continues to shrink. Instead of a maximum of 21 stations, a single licensee now can own thousands. In 2001, the FCC allowed a major network to control a smaller one, and was considering elimination of the wall between newspapers and stations in the same community. Such media *kieretsu* (a Japanese term for an interlocked web of agreements, activities and joint ventures) as Microsoft, Disney/ABC, AOL/Time Warner, GE/NBC, ATT/TCI, News Corp., and CBS/Viacom are strategically placed to benefit from, and probably dominate, new media developments. Today, they engage in various combinations of broadcast television (networks and stations), cable, film and video production, Internet technology and content, satellite transmissions, home video/games/interactive programs, sports teams and venues, print media (newspapers, magazines, books), telephone and personal wireless communication, music and recordings, and theme parks. Some are involved in manufacturing and retailing. The long-range impact of such growing concentrations of ownership across so many media and services probably will exceed what we now can imagine.

In many ways, programmers, manufacturers, and the conglomerates and *kieretsu* that control them appear to be on the same side, with the consumer/audience on the other. At least since the late 1970s, government also seems to be on the side of the *kieretsu*, raising the question of what effect this will have on the the 21st century. Stay tuned.

Whether broadcasting (or other electronic media) is thought of as a business or an industry, an art, an application of technology, an embryonic profession, a force shaping our culture, an establishment or institution, a social phenomenon—and it is all of these and more—its roots, whether growing for a century (in terms of technological development) or only for 80 years (in terms of broadcasting itself), offer many useful patterns, principles and trends—and precedents.

Our purpose in this final chapter is twofold: (1) to identify patterns, themes, and concepts from the past that help explain *why* things happened as they did and (2) where possible, to suggest implications and lessons for the future. As acknowledged earlier, we are aware of the potential pitfalls of prediction and extrapolation, particularly in a field as rapidly changing as this, since history is not truly cyclical. Thus we intend to err on the side of caution. To the extent possible, this chapter parallels the internal structure of its predecessors in examining the difficulties and opportunities caused by technological innovation; the linking of local outlets (stations) into national services (networks); the evolution of educational (later, public) broadcasting; advertising and other financial support and economic competition; program cycles and strategies; the changing size and behavior of the audience; government policy and regulation/self-regulation; and the primary reason for the study of broadcasting in the first place: the many social roles and impacts of American radio and television on the people.

12.1 Innovating Technologies

12.1.1 Invention and Innovation

Not all aspects of technological development or innovation are strictly technical. Consider the differences between "invention" and the less easily achieved "innovation"; the interwoven concepts of "not invented here," national security, and economic nationalism; the battles over a finite amount of usable spectrum space; the industrial or government research team as contrasted to the individual inventor; the search for common standards for any new device; the varied roles of government; the economic and marketing system into which an innovation is introduced; and the different goals of manufacturers and users.

There are large differences between conceiving or inventing something, which requires creativity and imagination; its development, using engineering or scientific skills and luck; and its successful introduction or innovation, which requires financial, promotional, legal, and marketing skills—and more luck. The number of inventors in this field who died destitute—one even died of starvation—testifies to the need for a sound business head at the innovation stage. Edwin Armstrong, an inventor of outstanding talent, had been a successful innovator until he tangled with RCA over FM. Marconi and Alexander Graham Bell had good business managers, but Fessenden, de Forest, Stubblefield, Farnsworth, and many others did not. They never enjoyed sufficient good fortune or entrepreneurial skill to innovate successfully.

12.1.2 External Forces

The "not invented here" syndrome (i.e., it wasn't created in our shop, so we will have nothing to do with it) often has led to the disregard of inventions from competing laboratories or other countries, and the consequent wasted motion of duplicated effort. While less important in the United States since domestic electronics manufacturers abdicated in favor of their Asian competition, it still crops up in the form of agitation for "American" standards for high-definition television. Closely allied to NIH is the desire of each country to control its own telecommunications (and energy) systems, for both national security and economic reasons. An example is when the U.S. Navy objected to sale of the Alexanderson alternator to British Marconi after World War I. However, the need to coordinate radio frequencies on a worldwide basis has limited the effect of this factor.

The combination of these forces has led many nations to try to develop similar telecommunications devices and to establish tariff barriers or subsidies to protect domestic interests. However, strictly profit-motivated economics probably would lead to failure of a "go it alone" policy because manufacturing tends to move to countries where costs are lower. For example, no television sets have been manufactured in the United States for years—and high costs have moved set production from Japan to Malaysia, Korea, Indonesia, China, and Mexico.

Governments of many Third World countries have supported political initiatives—such as the Unesco-sponsored New World Information and Communications Order in the early 1980s—that would give each nation equal access to the world telecommunications networks regardless of investment or other contributions. Also affecting both the introduction and use of new technology is the current support by industrially developed nations of international free trade and associated economic groupings of nations such as the European Economic Community. The World Trade Organization and the World Bank are probably more important than the desires of any one nation.

Further, the very nature of shortwave broadcasting and increasing use of DBS and the Internet makes cultural and political isolation more difficult. The fall of communism in eastern Europe in 1989–1991 is perhaps the best recent demonstration of the effects of peoples communicating directly with peoples.

Some technological developments seem to have a life of their own. Small, incremental improvements keep older technologies—from automobile engines to radio receivers—in use, no matter how obsolescent they may be. Gordon Moore, Intel's CEO, made a prediction decades ago that the amount of processing power that could be put on a computer chip would double every 18 to 24 months and that the cost would drop at the same time—and, to date, this has happened. For decades after the first geostationary commercial space communication satellite was launched in 1974, it was thought that there would need to be only a handful of them, but by 2001 there were some 200 in orbit, plus many times that number of military satellites belonging to many nations. Only the need to avoid interference, and international cooperation, has made it possible to provide efficient service.

12.1.3 Technological Trade-offs

Another principle involves the need of radio communication services for frequency spectrum space. This has led to many trade-offs between technical efficiency, fiscal economy, and political realities. At first, radio equipment could be imprecise, inefficient, and relatively inexpensive, because spectrum space was plentiful. As demand rose and spectrum space grew scarce, communication services required more sophisticated and expensive equipment. But in the case of broadcasting, investment by the general public in receivers designed for older frequency bands or standards delayed technological advances. It has long been thought that no member of Congress seeking re-election could allow the FCC to render obsolete all those expensive receivers in constituents' living rooms. As a result, at the start of the 21st century, television is still "frozen" into mostly 1941 technical standards—and congressional support of the FCC's decision to adopt DTV may well change because of this political factor. Other services, from amateur to maritime, have found, however, that they must constantly be aware of the FCC's current penchant for awarding frequencies on the basis of their highest and best use—which tends to reflect the political strength and savvy of those with other uses for those channels.

In most previous instances, a new standard allowed an older one to continue in use, as in the case of FM stereo serving older receivers monaurally. Only if the new standard was marketed effectively and the new devices were cheap enough, could the public be persuaded to relegate the older form to another room, to relatives who might find it useful, or to the discard pile. In radio's earlier years, discarded receivers were an inexpensive source of spare parts for young experimenters, but the complexities of solid-state circuitry now make this use problematic.

The replacement of black-and-white television sets in the living room by color took two decades, but it did eventually happen—although black-and-white portable sets are still sold. The British needed even longer to shift all television from the VHF to the UHF band, even with the "carrot" of allowing color only on the UHF, an important lesson as we contemplate the innovation of HDTV. Over the years, a number of new standards for musical recordings have come and gone, even with public inertia and unwillingness to discard older recordings (such as 78-, 33 1/3-, and 45-rpm disks, eight-track cartridges, and audiocassette tapes). The market life span of each standard may be growing shorter; the compact disc (CD) was still new to the public when DAT (digital audiotape) reached a level of development that caused its backers to suggest that DAT would soon replace CDs. Newer technologies—possibly computer based—may leapfrog both. Or, as has happened in the past, the older standard continues to serve a specialized niche for quite a while—after all, not everyone wants to buy a complete replacement musical library every decade or so; Betamax videotapes were available for many years after VHS won that war. But manufacturers have become aware that there is a small but profitably significant public that can be depended on to buy almost any consumer electronics product so long as it is "new" and "better." This initial market may be enough to create a "buzz" that gives a new device or standard the publicity to attract a wider-based sales demand.

The complexity, throwaway quality of many products (often difficult to repair even by the few repairers left), and pricing is often reflected in the financially impractical (but marketing wise) attempts to sell "state-of-the-art" equipment, both consumer and professional. There still are trade-offs; for example, more sensitive cameras created savings in lighting instruments and the electricity to run them. Any major showing of new hardware—the EIA Consumer Electronics Show, the National Association of Broadcasters convention or the Society of Motion Picture and Television Engineers exhibition—is an opportunity to see how quickly manufacturers issue new models with bells and whistles to attract buyers, even though more managers and fewer engineers now make decisions on equipment purchases at the NAB. When coupled with the shorter life expectancy of such equipment—studio cameras once could be counted on for a decade's service but now must be replaced much more frequently—it is no wonder that accountants in the electronic media industries find it accurate (as well as advantageous for tax reasons) to quickly "write off" equipment.

Some trade-offs are not, strictly speaking, technical. The desire of manufacturing corporations for quick profits probably has had more effect than all of the world's electronics inventors and engineers put together.

12.1.4 Individual *vs.* Industrial Inventing

In most technical fields in the past half century, invention has increasingly come from industrial or government laboratory teams rather than individual inventors. Even in the early 1900s, such radio inventors as Fleming and

Alexanderson worked for large corporations, but others—e.g., Marconi, Fessenden, Farnsworth, de Forest, and Armstrong—worked alone or with a few subordinate helpers, and had to scratch for funding. The increasing complexity of telecommunication technology and the enormous cost of continuing research now favor team effort supported by large companies. On the other hand, market-driven planned obsolescence often places a premium on styling and gimmicks rather than solid technical advances. While there still is a place for the small company with an excellent product—if financing can be found—it is no accident that the transistor came from Bell Telephone Laboratories and color television in its present configuration from RCA. The videotape recorder, first produced by then very small Ampex, nevertheless required more than a decade of financial support by a variety of foundations and corporations for its development. Only a handful of companies can now afford to design, develop, and manufacture any full line of electronic equipment, and even fewer are willing to take the risk. Economic pressure on all companies for short-term profits seems to be steering them toward applied rather than pure research. Even this applied research rarely is directed to items that would not be immediately profitable, such as high-quality UHF tuners for television sets, until attention is focused by the public or by government. With the removal of most consumer electronics production to the Far East and Mexico and deletion of tax advantages, research and development by American firms in this field has dropped substantially in recent decades—with full consequences we don't yet know.

12.1.5 Patents and Standards

Two interconnected principles guide the adoption of inventions. First is a search for a common standard or specifications for a new device; second is the drive by each major company to have a commanding patent control position for products built to that standard. Sometimes this patent strategy is modified, as when N.V. Philips of the Netherlands allowed all manufacturers to use its audiocassette patents in an attempt to build up that industry. But the more common pattern is reflected in the drawn-out battles over patents for the telephone (Bell versus several others), the vacuum tube (Fleming versus de Forest), the regenerative circuit (de Forest versus Armstrong), FM radio (Armstrong versus RCA), television camera tubes (RCA versus Farnsworth), audio recording speeds (RCA versus CBS), video recording formats and speeds (Sony versus many others), and so on.

These battles sometimes shaped entire industries. Examples are the attempt to innovate mechanical scanning television before electronic scanning was perfected, the development of mutually incompatible color television systems in the late 1940s and early 1950s, and the more recent plethora of competing recording modes. While in the past the FCC made official determinations of standards, it now often defers to an ill-defined market—which often tends to make the buying public, wary of multiple standards, shy away from the product entirely (as with AM stereo). On the other hand, in the 1980s the market made VHS a *de facto* videocassette recording standard in the United States, beating out Beta. We don't yet know the future of HDTV, digital audio broadcasting, or higher-quality VCR or videodisc formats. Because legal, laboratory, and public relations battles are so expensive and lengthy, usually only the largest corporations are able to play.

For general acceptance and total overthrow of one type of communication device by another, the marketplace is rarely sufficient, and generally either the industry or the government must impose a new standard or specifications by fiat. The risks are large, but so are the rewards: once the FCC, the public, or some international or industry body puts a stamp of approval on a technical standard, it is extremely difficult for a new and competitive technological approach to enter the market. Only when the government intervenes on the side of innovation, or a company decides not to exploit a patent position, or the rest of the industry gangs up on a leader, or a new idea (such as television itself, VCRs and the Internet) catches the public's fancy, does the field open up. Even then, good inventions and innovations may get buried under the weight of a 900-pound gorilla—as happened with Microsoft's domination of personal computer operating systems.

12.1.6 The Roles of Government

In addition to its more obvious roles as both regulator and user of communication services, the government also is a facilitator. Congress appropriated the money that enabled Morse to build the first electrical telegraph line in the 1840s and, more than a century later, through the military and NASA, financed the development of space communications satellites. It is doubtful if either technology would have been innovated without government assistance. More recently, it established the Internet and became deeply involved with HDTV. The government also administers the patent system. The Navy-administered patents pool during World War I showed how industrial cooperation might be established in peacetime and World War II research opened up vast reaches of the electromagnetic spectrum. The Navy also stimulated the formation of RCA. During both world wars, the government created the conditions for a tremendous burst of activity in industrial laboratories designing and building war-related devices.

Sometimes, however, the government acts *against* technological innovation by yielding to the greatest pressure, frequently from groups already in place in that industry, as during the periods when the FCC benefited AM and later VHF television station owners by using regulatory activity or inactivity to delay innovation of FM radio, UHF, and cable. More recently,

▪ **Here a Dish, There a Dish**   Beginning in the 1980s, the electronic media landscape across America changed rapidly. Various satellite receiving antennas cropped up at cable head ends and television stations as domestic communication satellites became the preferred means of networking local outlets. Taken at a headend near Washington, DC, several types of antenna are shown in the left-hand photo, though the 10 meter TVRO in the foreground is the most common type (although 3 and 5 meter "dishes" often are used). The transmission tower in the background mounts microwave dishes on its side, for renting space on the tower is another way to generate station income. At the same time, small consumer TVROs of 12 or 18 inches in diameter (page 693) appeared on the roofs or sidewalls of homes and apartments as subscribers sought better program packages and prices than those offered by local cable systems.

Christopher H. Sterling.

congressional and FCC willingness to assist entrepreneurs who wish to market wireless telephone has led to shortages of spectrum space for other uses (even the military has had to relinquish some) and cellular phone and PCS towers are sprouting like weeds in urban and suburban areas.

Also, even if the government does approve a particular standard, that doesn't stop corporations from deciding not to play the game—as was the case with the FCC's approval of an inadequate standard for television in 1940, and may be a reason for delay in adoption of DTV. Even though 60% of American viewers could view DTV over more than 100 stations by 2001 (if they bought DTV receivers), almost no informed observers believe that the original deadline (2006) for dropping NTSC broadcast service will be met, whatever Congress says.

12.1.7 Inertia of Older Technology

The innovation of equipment and techniques in the broadcast studio and at the transmitter was more conservative than in most telecommunications fields, principally because most broadcasters were satisfied with the status quo and had little financial incentive to improve. Hence, transmitters grew larger and more efficient but not essentially different. Studio control equipment became more flexible and more complex as both a reflection and a precursor of programming flexibility and complexity in both radio and television. Adoption of solid state equipment took place only when broadcast station management realized the cost savings inherent in such devices. The advent of color programming in the late 1960s required the purchase of new and expensive equipment but did not lead to many new program ideas, and we'll soon see whether HDTV follows the same path. At the start of the 21st century, the substitution of digital for analog equipment seems to be following a similar route, bringing the viewer a marginally improved picture and with nearly invisible improvements in reliability and noise reduction. Even though we now expect to see SNG "reporting live via satellite" on television news programs, the use of costly space communications satellites for other program production really is very limited, although they have found an important niche in program distribution.

So, the story of technical innovation in the broadcast studio is replete with new "toys" for production people, but little change in content. One important exception, for which everyone had a use, was magnetic recording. In radio, recordings progressed from inferior techniques banned from the networks to a virtually omnipresent mode of programming. Tape permitted nearly random access to segments not possible with discs. In television, while film could be edited, until the advent of videotape all non-film programming was live. With VTR, the programmer could edit, store, and rearrange at will—although losing some of the spontaneity of live production. When wedded to lightweight, portable color television cameras, the new generation of VTRs made possible electronic news-gathering (ENG) by one-person crews. The VCR now permits the consumer to accomplish some of the same functions at home, as well as the ability to *timeshift* programs.

The broadcast receiver industry also has been cautious about adopting new technologies, but for political as well as economic reasons. Billions of dollars' worth of receivers in millions of voters' homes causes tremendous political inertia, since most people aren't about to replace perfectly good equipment without a good reason, and a government agency telling them to do so is not a "good reason." At the same time, manufacturers also are rarely willing to sponsor research or tool up for production unless they see a competitive advantage in the fairly short term—it is much more efficient to copy the work of others. The expansion of color television came only after black-and-white television had reached nationwide saturation. High-definition television (HDTV) now is delayed in part by a saturated low-definition receiver market. Digital television (DTV) is starting to move only because of governmental insistence. The unwillingness of American business to take risks also may be reflected in the fact that the logical union of direct broadcast satellites (DBS) and HDTV, already taking place in Europe and Japan, is merely being talked about in the United States.

So far, with the exception of broadcast facsimile in the 1940s, no broadcast medium has been completely abandoned when a new medium or standard has been introduced and adopted. A black-and-white television set built in 1941 can still be used, despite the later introduction of color and UHF. An 8-track audiocassette tape machine or 78-rpm record player will still play music—from the right recordings. Many new devices use as a selling point that they are "downward compatible" with existing ones, although this flexibility is unlikely to survive manufacturing strategies that produce devices that cannot be repaired or adjusted, carefully meter out small and cosmetic improvements, and design built-in obsolescence.

In another arena, Congress' political goals sometimes ignore technical realities, such as the vulnerability of space satellite communications to solar flare interference, or when short-term profits for business constituents are more attractive than improving or even maintaining a current system or medium. This already has happened in the point-to-point field, where the military frequently abandons large embedded systems, such as use of the traditional radiotelegraph distress frequency of 500 kHz. It can be argued that the Clinton administration's push for HDTV and better display monitors was more a political rather than a technical decision. Although there were technical studies as early as the 1940s that suggested the best frequency band to use for each kind of service—for example, using lower frequencies for signals that needed to reach around the world (see Appendix B)—the general strategy has been for each new service to try to get the lowest possible vacant frequencies, because equipment already has been designed to use them. Today, this often means moving "upstairs" from earlier versions of the same service: FM radio broadcasting had to move to the 88–108 MHz frequency band, much higher than AM radio; second generation cell phones use channels that are hundreds of MHz higher than first generation ones, and so on. However, since the government now is interested in securing revenue from auctioning frequencies, a rational allocation of ever-scarcer frequencies seems even less likely.

Getting ahead of the pack doesn't always pay off. FM radio didn't benefit after World War II when its backers tried to label AM radio—an entire existing industry and its technology, entrenched in the home—as obsolete. The Iridium satellite-based public telephone system failed utterly. Achieving success for future innovation will take either powerful financial backing and acceptance of its standards by most of the industry for their own economic reasons, or strong political pressure to allow a direct approach to the public, as in pay-TV by cable. AM stereo, for example, had neither. While individuals have invented and small companies have built "better mousetraps," the investment in manufacturing design and assembly lines is almost prohibitive except for the largest firms, here and abroad. If a small company's product is truly competing in the market, it generally means that one of the large players has bought the product (or the company) from its originators. The public may benefit from innovation and from economies of scale and production—solid state receivers are cheaper and require less electricity than vacuum tubes, permitting the development of high-quality, battery-operated, portable equipment at a reasonable cost—but generally, technological innovations *per se* make little difference in the content and effects of broadcasting. As a rule, the public tends to hold on to obsolescent devices while they are still usable (and not embarrassingly old if seen by visitors), so it typically requires decades for the new to replace the old, even with the design of appliances with built-in obsolescence intended to speed the replacement cycle, and a resulting shortage of technicians willing to repair inexpensive equipment.

12.1.8 A Few Predictions

Since the future is unknown, any predictions we can make are necessarily vague. It seems likely that changes in technology will continue to be evolutionary, since real revolutions—as when transistors made compact battery-operated equipment available to all, or as when computers and the Internet were integrated into daily life—are rare. So there probably will be more bells and whistles, similar to such recent developments as remote control tuners with memory and HDTV program production, even though such programs may be distributed using the NTSC standard. The general public's infatuation with home entertainment centers will create some demand for better television audio (in stereo) and video. Manipulation of signals by internal computer chips may permit receivers to fool eyes and ears into believing they are experiencing higher quality without using an inordinate amount of the electromagnetic spectrum. Specialized uses of the television channel—such as closed captioning for the deaf, interactive video games for children, or interfacing with home computers—will burgeon as DTV is adopted. Convergence will be the buzz word in the industry, but the general public will still think of their living room screen as "television," much in the way that a SUV is a "car."

But, although the Internet and two-way cable already make it technically possible to vote, work or buy groceries from one's home, it is likely to be some time before we close our doors and maintain our connection to the world electronically. The Internet may have many different but substantial impacts on broadcasting. By the start of the new century, most stations probably had some kind of Web presence, often permitting the *streaming* of their signal, so that people all over the world may experience what is now the rather poor quality picture and somewhat better sound of what at one time was a local station. This technology, only a few years old, is bound to improve, and the external antenna and specialized receiver may go the way of the dodo.

One way to predict at least the rate of change in the future is to step back in time, and think about the changes in broadcast technology that took place over the past decade or two. There were many. Spectrum-greedy techniques (such as DBS) became political rather than technological problems. Wireless means of connecting equipment have superseded wires in many applications—but without a concomitant increase in reliability, however convenient they are. Broadcasters benefited from time base correctors that permitted use of cheap VTRs on broadcast channels, while at the other end of the economic spectrum, production houses installed terribly expensive computer-controlled nonlinear tape editing devices such as those produced by Avid and other firms. New types of cameras, such as the CCD, required no alignment, lasted for years, needed little light, and are so small that the lens is larger than the rest of the camera.

Digital already is replacing analog transmission systems, leading to a "cleaner," noise-free picture and sound. Stereophonic music is now aired on most FM radio stations, and many television stations already transmit in stereo. The long-held dream of television receivers thin enough to hang on a wall has only recently been realized, remote controls and other conveniences are everywhere, the television and computer industries realize that agreement on monitor standards is necessary, and large-screen projection television sets are now common in homes able to set up "home entertainment centers" or "media rooms." Home VCRs permit everyone to be his or her own programmer, through ever-more-easy-to-make off-air recordings or rentals from the local store. All networks now use space communications satellites for distribution.

In the new century, it is (fortunately) unlikely that all entertainment media will be replaced by such frightening specters as direct electrical stimulation of the pleasure center of the brain, which would easily provide the ultimate "high." But with better quality audio and video, the line between reality and fantasy will be ever more blurred—and what effects will that have? Decisions still are unmade as to how content is to be distributed in the 21st century. Will we benefit more from cable television (which ties television sets to a fixed wire) and DBS (which tethers them to a dish antenna)—or would high-quality miniature portable television sets or programming through the Internet be more attractive? Who will control the "last mile" of broadband service to the home? Will *everything* be wireless (with all of the problems of uncoordinated spectrum usage that is entailed), or will fiber optics become the transmission medium of choice? Stay tuned. The home VCR took less than a decade to reach the number of homes that cable took 40 years to reach—but can this rapid market saturation of new devices to be exceeded in the future? Stay tuned. For the first time, we may have more channels available through cable than we have worthwhile (defined as you will) programming to fill them. Each of these technologies—and many others not mentioned or even dreamed of—will affect the electronic media and the audiences of the 21st century.

12.2 A Local Station Service . . .

From the start, the FCC's practice of granting licenses to *local* radio and television stations (mandated by Congress many years ago) has worked at cross-purposes with the *national* economic character of network advertising and their ability to cover the nation instantly.

12.2.1 National/Local Dichotomy

Responding to the American federal political principle of sovereign states and local electorates, the FCC licenses stations to provide service to a specific legal, political, and technologically determined community. It has made almost every broadcast transmitter a separate "station," applying regulation to this level rather than to the national networks whose programming attracts most advertisers. A similar fiction considers every cable system as a separate unit, without regard to the multiple system operator (MSO), which almost certainly controls it. For many years, the FCC strictly limited the number of stations a licensee may own in order to ensure local expression, furnish advertising facilities for local businesses, and assuage congressional fear that a handful of companies might dominate the media. The expectation was that the local station was a force in its geographic or social community. In times of crisis or disaster or local political activity, only local broadcasting stations could rapidly provide necessary information. Other media, such as cable, might be technically capable but rarely have the will, equipment, or personnel for local reporting and programming. Local outlets also provide training grounds for new talent since to jump right from college onto a national stage—even if only on a little-watched cable channel—is not a good way to learn one's craft.

But the localism philosophy clearly is in full retreat, as is a legislative tendency to favor rural areas to counteract the "one person, one vote" Supreme Court decisions starting in 1962. For better or worse, the tendency toward greater ownership concentration is likely to continue for some time, as legal limits on number of stations a licensee may own are reduced or eliminated. DBS is likely to lead to even greater national—and international—concentration than now provided by the networks or group owners. Even a truly local medium, such as *low-power FM* (LPFM), in trying to establish itself against the economic desire of advertisers and existing stations to reach the maximum number of people, may have to develop its own networks, if it survives. But the political pendulum swings, and in the distant future this trend toward concentration may be thought of as a temporary policy aberration. Or it may not. Stay tuned.

Let's take another example. Although economies of scale led radio broadcasting from wholly locally owned and programmed stations to a system of content control by national networks in the late 1920s, after World War II the pendulum swung back. With network executives preoccupied by television, the demise of network radio, and thousands of new AM and FM stations, local radio program control seemed to reappear. But this was only an illusion, since formulaic music content (e.g., Top 40), imitation of successful formulas, syndication (often by satellite), and a limited number of national music program sources soon predominated. Although there is some news and talk, particularly in markets large enough to accommodate such minority programming profitably, even it is often syndicated, and radio today—with 10 times the number of outlets as at the end of World War II—*is* what David Sarnoff labeled it eight decades ago: a "music box."

12.2.2 Programming: A Push for Profit

It is no surprise that radio formats, let alone specific programs or talent, can often change overnight if the licensee believes it desirable. Licensees are continually scanning the local market, looking for a potentially profitable niche. Today, that often-narrow window of opportunity is all-important, and stations may discard decades of good will and history by changing call letters as well as format, and calling the result a "new station."

Television is slightly different. Most stations air the same network programs at similar times in most areas, limiting the actual content diversity available. The 20% or so of stations that are independent (non-network affiliated) usually rely on syndicated fare (often old network programs) for much of their schedule, since profits can be made from low costs as well as high income.

The result, for both radio and television, is a host of local transmitters offering a limited number of similar programs. Confirming this pattern is the FCC practice of permitting absentee and group ownership of stations, which means that station management and ownership is not the same as local community control. Those who control perhaps hundreds of stations no longer owe special loyalty or service to any single community, and the station (and its audience) becomes just another indistinguishable commodity to buy and sell. This isn't to say that many stations, usually smaller ones in smaller markets, don't have conscientious operators who are as much a part of their community as was the traditional small-town newspaper publisher. But such smaller operations are threatened, causing 600 of them to complain to the FCC in 2001 that the growth in number of network O-&-Os has given the networks (and other large group owners) too much power.

A similar national pattern has evolved with cable television. Although cable operators have from dozens to hundreds of channels to fill, there seem to be either never enough or far too many. "Too many" only applies to systems with 100 channels or more, which often duplicate a great deal of content and give over many channels to home shopping. But even as late as 2001, many cable systems still only provided as few as 50—or even 20—channels, forcing often-difficult choices of what to carry. With stockholders breathing down management's neck, it isn't hard to make the choice between a channel that brings in additional income (e.g., home shopping) or a free public service (e.g., C-SPAN). Here again, primary program fare on cable systems is anything but "local." It consists of rebroadcasts of network affiliates (including PBS), both old and new feature films (e.g., HBO, Cinemax, Bravo, AMC), sports (e.g., ESPN), superstations (e.g., WTBS, WGN) from elsewhere in the country with "independent" programming, and a growing number of national cable-only services providing news (e.g., Cable Network News (CNN) and MS-NBC), or aimed at those interested in gardening, health, weather, religion, children, health, science-fiction, golf, history, and a myriad of other topics.

As with radio and television in recent decades, the number of locally originated cable programs is tiny. During the 1985–1987 period, when the FCC's *must-carry* rules were not in effect, cable system operators often made local independent stations pay for carriage. Some local network affiliates were dropped when a big-city affiliate of the same network was added. These practices led to new FCC must-carry rules hated by cable operators and loved by broadcasters, particularly marginal local television stations. The cable industry has ratcheted up its fight against must-carry, particularly with respect to DTV transmissions that might duplicate NTSC broadcasts. This is a complex matter, with strong arguments on both sides. Today, stations can negotiate such matters as channel placement with cable operators, and even threaten to levy a charge for carrying the channel. In 2000, during such negotiations, the Time Warner cable system in New York City briefly stopped carrying the ABC affiliate during a time of very popular programming—leading to a public relations disaster and FCC censure. Despite this adverse public reaction, the soon merged Time Warner and AOL heated up the conflict with Disney/ABC even more. Each tried to use its own political, economic and public relations clout to secure carriage of programs it owns.

In a sense, videocassette recorders (VCRs) might be considered as the ultimate in local programming control. Anyone can become his or her own programmer, choosing from a variety of rented, purchased, and home-recorded content—almost all of it national, not local, in origin. The streaming of broadcast content on the Internet similarly allows the recipient to control what music he or she listens to, although the economics of this "ancillary broadcasting" remain unclear.

12.2.3 Haves and Have-Nots

The tension between the haves and have-nots among broadcasting stations has been a continuing theme over the decades. Those already on the air have little economic reason to encourage competition. AM radio and, later, VHF television station licensees became the broadcasting "establishment." AM radio resisted both FM and television, but when the financial potential of television became evident, farsighted AM licensees often started television stations. The roughly 100 VHF stations on the air before the Freeze (1948–1952) epitomized this dominance, forcing UHF stations licensed after 1953 to struggle—and more than 100 to fail.

Both AM and VHF shared several attributes: they generally had been successfully established long before the directly competing FM and UHF services were introduced; they received the most revenue; and they controlled the industry's trade associations. Advertiser acceptance, network status, and larger audiences belonged to the older and generally more powerful AM and VHF services as late as 1980, when cable began to level the playing field and eliminate UHF television's technical handicap. FM, with its better sound quality and more organized programming, grew after 1965 to become the most audience-appealing (by 1980) and profitable segment (in the 1990s) of the radio broadcasting industry, in spite of AM's feeble attempts to use stereo to compete.

Any potentially competitive service (in the past including FM radio, UHF television, on-air pay-TV, or cable television, and today including DBS, satellite-delivered broadcasting and HDTV) or government regulation threatening the livelihood of existing stations is strongly attacked at the FCC, in the courts, and in Congress. Logically, older services try to keep newer competitors from full development by political action (politicians are very sensitive to the wishes of any medium that helps elect them) and economic pressures, or by themselves becoming involved in the newer medium—which helps contain the potential competition by occupying one of its channels.

In recent years new classes of have-nots have appeared wanting to get in. These include minority groups that either lack funding to purchase a station or, because of the startling growth in number of stations (nearly 12-fold since World War II)—lack channels on which to build a new station. Local community-supported stations and cable systems often are looked down on by more traditional and larger profit-oriented broadcasting stations. A move to establish very low power television stations (LPTV), with very small coverage areas, predictably has rarely been successful. A parallel move (often spearheaded by community activist "pirates") for low-power FM (LPFM) was cut off by the "haves" even earlier—being strongly opposed by existing broadcasters (both commercial and non-commercial) warning of interference and worrying about further splintering of audiences.

Although it is popularly believed that a broadcasting (particularly television) license is tantamount to a license to print money, a surprising number of stations have gone bankrupt, and others jump for any income source, such as home-shopping services. To launch a *new* service successfully against an entrenched and uncooperative industry is even more difficult than gaining a foothold in an existing service.

The truism that "them that has, gets" holds particularly true in the electronic media. Many stations pioneered by those willing to take risks achieved financial success which supported the political power often used to perpetuate their status. Later owners of these stations—often large conglomerates willing to enter any profitable industry—benefited from their predecessors' struggles. In such circumstances, both the haves and the have-nots feel ill-used. The clear implication is that any new service can succeed only by overcoming the opposition of the powerful existing industry. Economic resources, talent, and programs are hard to get as the new service struggles for public recognition and acceptance. Without such acceptance, manufacturers of consumer electronics are unwilling to do anything and advertisers ignore the new medium.

12.2.4 Obsolescence—the Ultimate Prediction

Some experienced media observers argue that transmitter-based local stations already are obsolete and will soon disappear. They suggest that broadband (probably fiber-optic) wired connections—a frightening specter to both broadcaster and cable operator (except those now owned by telecommunication companies like AT&T)—being installed by telephone companies will be the likely future. Large cable system operators have decided to go the same route, with broadband fiber optic links allowing them to offer Internet and telephone connections as well as video and audio. DBS operators since 1999 have both the right and the responsibility to carry local signals to subscribers in that area. "Broadcasting" might eventually degenerate into a content service sharing broadband transmission paths with the Internet to feed programs and movies automatically into home video recorders. Such possible changes will not happen quickly, since investment in the status quo by both the public and broadcasters is too great for the existing system to be junked overnight. And it may be that—if one doesn't want local content— the corner video store or the Internet will become the most popular content distribution mode in the early 21st century instead of local stations. But *if* some new and exotic electronic media service fills a public need or wish better than broadcasting, change probably will come—slowly and marked by some accommodation between the new service and the existing industry. However, if it does not fill a public need or desire, no matter how much ballyhoo is engendered, the new medium is unlikely to succeed, as broadcast facsimile and other services learned in the past. Stay tuned.

12.3 ... with National Program Suppliers

The most important thing about the three older commercial networks (ABC, CBS, and NBC) is their long-term dominance of broadcast programming, economics, and public image.

12.3.1 Network Dominance

Perhaps surprisingly, the big three have remained on top in terms of revenue, even though cable, VCRs, DBS, independent stations, Fox, WB, UPN, PBS, and the Internet have made serious inroads into major network audience levels, particularly during prime time. In the 1970s, the three large commercial networks reached more than 90% of television households in prime time; three decades later, that proportion had dwindled to less than two thirds of households and was dropping. No one network consistently dominated during the past half–century. ABC, for example, made the circuit between have and have-not at least twice, and in 2001 appeared to be in its third cycle. Because the need to have network outlets in many communities in order to be truly national runs afoul of technical shortages of channels, as well as limited talent to create popular programs, it has been difficult to establish new networks except at the very beginning of a medium's development. Fox, benefiting from Murdoch's huge investment, acquired an audience for some programs, but remains smaller than ABC, CBS, and NBC—and WP and UPN are much smaller than that.

Since their formation for radio in the late 1920s, networks have controlled audience loyalty, in spite of their varied roles as carriers of others' programming, increasing use of Hollywood product, great caution in accepting let alone adopting change, and some usurpation of their program distribution role by cable, satellites, MMDS, and VCRs. Their chief strategy, economy of scale—more affiliates, in larger markets, with which to reach larger audiences and thus command greater advertiser income at no increase in production cost—has led to bland programming designed to appeal to the largest possible audiences and to please cautious advertisers. As long as national advertisers pay, networks are content.

Each network tries to be all things to all viewers or listeners, with due regard for attracting the 18–45 year old women consumers most desired by advertisers. Each is extremely wary of innovative programs, preferring to jump on the bandwagon only after someone else has pioneered a successful venture. In this way, program cycles (invention, imitation and spin-offs, decline and—years later—resurrection), develop and are copied. Broader strategies—such as careful scheduling of an entire evening of similar programs to attract and retain a similar audience, or the heavily promoted miniseries—go through similar cycles.

12.3.2 East Coast/West Coast

In their respective heydays, radio (1930s–1940s) and especially television (1950s–1990s) networks repeated the film industry pattern of centralized financial control in New York with production facilities in Hollywood. This split has led to many of the same money-versus-creativity conflicts that affected major Hollywood film studios. Networks have more control over their product, since they control the national distribution system, even though many entertainment programs are produced by independent packaging agencies or production houses, partly because of an FCC edict in force from the early 1970s into the 1990s. While New York and Chicago also were major production centers for national programming in radio and early television, since the early 1950s the Los Angeles area has been the center for almost all production except news, public affairs, and some serials, although actual filming or taping may be done wherever costs are lowest—such as in Canada, some of whose cities look much like those in the U.S. Another similarity with feature motion pictures is found in the fact that, like film, the real profits are to be found in overseas distribution of product and programs. If the costs of a program have been covered domestically (usually on the second or third rerun), then whatever is paid by foreign television systems is almost entirely profit to the program owner.

The two oldest networks, NBC and CBS, traditionally have been the strongest. After dominating radio, they quickly did the same in television and continued to do so for a quarter-century. ABC, founded in 1945, was the weakest financially and, until it briefly jumped into first place in the mid-1970s, was the weakest in programs as well. But by the middle 1980s, NBC was far ahead, and ABC once again was bringing up the rear. A few years later, one-time ratings leader CBS was in last place, even falling behind Fox in some time periods. From year to year, it is a horse race, with seasonal wins often decided by fractions of a rating point or a single program.

For various reasons described in previous chapters, the DuMont network did not survive past 1955, an attempt to establish a fourth network failed in 1967, and Rupert Murdoch's Fox Television Network (started in 1987) found that its magic path to profitability lay in inexpensively produced programs aimed at teenagers and young adults. The Warner Brothers Network (WB) and United Paramount Network (UPN), founded in 1995, have a long way to go, since few markets have enough channels for them. The 1999 acquisition of CBS by Viacom, which already owned UPN, probably will affect this situation. Public television networks are discussed below. Commercial radio networks were almost moribund after television became a national medium, existing only for the news and an occasional special program. NPR is discussed on pp. 710–714.

The organization of a company often made a difference. For example, CBS usually could move faster than NBC in matters such as the "talent raids" in the late 1940s because broadcasting was the keystone of its business, whereas NBC was only a small part of huge RCA. (Now that NBC is part of even larger General Electric, this situation may have gotten worse.) On the other hand, a talented program chief could make a big difference: Fred Silverman brought ABC from behind to parity in the 1970s (only to fail dismally when he later took over NBC's programming); but innovative programs modeled on his experience with the MTM production house helped Grant Tinker when he moved NBC into the number one spot in the mid-1980s. A few other network programmers, such as Brandon Tartikoff of NBC (1980–1991), or in production studios, such as Grant Tinker, Aaron Spelling, Steven Bochco, and David E. Kelley, may occasionally have copied from themselves, but were noted both for original and creative writing and the ability to juggle more than one program at a time.

12.3.3 Owning Networks

Until 1985–1986, network ownership remained remarkably stable, despite a few changes around the margins, such as Mutual changing hands more than once, NBC radio being forced to divest itself of the Blue Network (which became ABC) in 1943, and ABC's merger with Paramount in 1953 (see pp. 288, 290). But then, encouraged by FCC deregulation, liberalized limits on station ownership, Wall Street's realization of broadcasting's profit potential, the death or retirement of many longtime network executives, and the frenzied national climate of merger and acquisition, all three networks changed hands in less than two years—and then later changed again. Although network rivalry remained, leadership and corporate goals had shifted.

Capital Cities, a very successful and hardnosed group station owner, bought and merged with ABC in 1985. ABC became the "Mickey Mouse" network in 1996 when Disney purchased Cap Cities/ABC. RCA (and, hence, its subsidiary, NBC) was purchased by General Electric in 1986, bringing the story of RCA full circle (see p. 57). The NBC radio network was sold, and NBC television is now but a small and insecure part of behemoth GE. CBS technically remained independent for a time but, partly because of William Paley's inability to find a successor to whom he was willing to entrust his legacy. (CBS had been known as "Bill Paley's candy store.") But in 1986, it fell under the financial and operational control of Laurence Tisch, the chairman of Loews Inc., a major corporation with entertainment and hotel interests. CBS has since been sold twice, first to Westinghouse (which spun off its manufacturing business and adopted the CBS name) and then again, in 1999, to Viacom, a former CBS syndicator now controlled by movie theater (and UPN, MTV, Blockbuster Video, and other firms) owner Sumner Redstone. Layoffs, sell-offs, and other belt-tightening measures showed that the new owners considered networks to be businesses like any others—requiring that the "bottom line" be served.

Ownership of television broadcasting networks is important partly because there are so few of them. There are a host of regulatory, technological, and economic reasons for the limited number. Few markets have four or more commercial channels assigned, putting the fourth-place network (usually Fox) in a position of playing endless "catch-up." Any fourth (let alone fifth or sixth) network has a much smaller potential national audience than the three major chains, since these channels frequently are on UHF with less range and coverage than their VHF competitors. Although the networks often are blamed for encouraging scarcity of competition, national policy has long reflected the need to keep potential interference low in order to avoid irritating viewers of existing stations. Since the original networks had the foresight to build or buy stations in the largest markets (see pp. 286–290), this reasonable policy has been a source of economic benefit to them. While networks as such rarely made much profit until the 1970s, the handful of network-owned-and-operated stations in large cities always were extremely profitable.

12.3.4 Operating Networks

Because the Communications Act of 1934 does not provide for direct FCC network regulation, they have been regulated through their affiliated stations. Well into the 1970s, a network could control its affiliates' programming through a one-sided contract giving the network a first option on much of the station's time. Officially, contracts were renewed annually, but in fact they recognized what could be a lifetime relationship. Although in the early 1940s the FCC had limited mandatory radio option time and two decades later eliminated television option time (and promulgated the Prime

Time Access Rule in the 1970s)—networks remained the stronger partner in the network-station marriage.

In the beginning, few stations ever switched networks. If a market had too few channels, a less desirable network might have to accept secondary status. However, when ABC became a strong competitor, several stations did switch from one of the then-weaker other networks. This precedent of "disloyalty" led to less permanent affiliations, as did the fact that a group owner might have stations affiliated with two or three networks and thus be familiar with their strengths and weaknesses. Although many object to the concentration of national programming in so few hands, it may also be argued that the networks are the *only* institutions—other than a tiny handful of newspapers, the Associated Press news wire service, and CNN—that have the fiscal strength to support national and international news-gathering operations. And even these few news services often have cost-saving exchange or cooperative arrangements with other media organizations.

Until the early 1950s radio and later, television networks, acted almost as common carriers, distributing programs produced or controlled by advertising agencies and often having only a limited say in program content or scheduling. Although this was a comfortable relationship during radio network days, the networks had to take over the programming function when rising television costs made developing and producing programs too risky for individual advertisers or even large advertising agencies. The pace of this trend quickened as escalating costs led to a drop in sole sponsorship, and the development of alternate or multiple sponsorship led to an even greater loss of advertiser control. Eventually, the networks found it cheaper to farm out most program production to packagers and production houses, notably West Coast movie studios suffering from a decline in feature film attendance that was partly caused by television. A 1970 FCC rule made this division of function official, restricting the networks' right to produce most of their prime-time programs—and limiting their ability to benefit from after-network-run syndication income. In 2000, in its deregulation frenzy, the FCC repealed its rule prohibiting networks from owning programming they air in prime time. As a result, 13 of 18 new programs scheduled to appear on the top four networks were owned by the network, and producers like 20th Century-Fox and Warner Brothers were responsible for 37 shows on the six commercial networks. The exception throughout this period was network news and public affairs programs. For prestige (and supervision of content for fear of libel suits), the networks themselves had always controlled news. By World War II, network radio news had become a major means of informing the public. Television news, starting as little more than a newsreel introduced by a talking head, quickly became the most used and believed national news medium and still is, although audiences have dwindled.

12.3.5 Cable Networks

By the early 1980s, a new type of national program distribution affected the viewing of many Americans. Cable, no longer content to be a mere carrier of on-the-air stations that could not be received in remote areas, started selling a second tier of cable-only program services. Among the first (June 1980) and most important was Cable News Network (CNN), television's first all-news network. Started by Ted Turner, whose independent Atlanta "superstation" WTBS already was a major source of cable sports and movie programming, CNN soon evolved into two channels that "news junkies" and those who need to know will turn to, even though it lacks any local news. During national or international crises, CNN often replaces the television networks as the place to view—but during quiet times, its audience drops off, some turning to competitors such as MSNBC, a joint project

Satellites Extend the Reach   Echostar VI, launched in 2000, is one of several direct-to-home or DBS satellites serving the U.S. market. Such domestic communication satellites are known for their large square panels of solar batteries that stretch for yards, as well as smaller receiving and sending antenna dishes. The core electronics that allow multiple video or audio signals to be stored and retransmitted are in the center.

Echostar satellite artwork courtesy of Lockheed Martin Missiles & Space.

of Microsoft and NBC. Turner later became part of Time Warner (now AOL/Time Warner). He no longer runs CNN and has been eased out of AOL/Time Warner. Radio developed its own specialized networks, some temporary (to carry a certain sporting event), and some permanent, such as NPR and the Bloomberg financial news network.

Entertainment cable services, epitomized by Home Box Office, which supplies uncut and uninterrupted feature films in exchange for a monthly subscription fee, soon followed. Roughly half of those with cable subscribed to this second (or third) tier of pay-cable programming. All transmit by satellite to cable system head ends and, until suppliers started to scramble their satellite signals, unintentionally to viewers who had installed satellite receiving dish antennas in their yards in order to tune in for free. A fourth tier developed in the 1980s—pay-per-view (PPV) movie (or sporting event, such as a championship boxing match) services making it easy to indulge in impulse viewing. Larger cable systems often provided several such channels, as well as an even larger number of home shopping channels.

A particularly significant development has been the growth of multiple system operators (MSOs) at least one of which (AT&T) is right up against—or beyond—the original cap on proportion of the population (30%) it is allowed to serve. The top 20 MSOs serve all but a tiny fraction of U.S. homes, and the proportions are even more extreme in countries such as Canada. The growth of cable, and of DBS, has led each distribution method—cable, DBS, and on-air broadcast—to feel beleaguered and friendless. The larger one of these organizations becomes, the more likely it is that further acquisitions (here and abroad) will be questioned by agencies such as the FCC, the FTC, and the Justice Department—which has already won court cases breaking AT&T into several parts (some of which already have merged back together), and may break software giant Microsoft into two, each of which will be among the world's largest corporations. The AOL/Time Warner merger was held up by governmental anti-trust questions. European common market regulatory authorities have also gotten involved.

12.3.6 Public Broadcasting Networks

Although often overlooked by commercial broadcasters, there *is* another major network: PBS (Public Broadcasting Service). In most markets, the FCC in the early 1950s reserved approximately a fourth of all channels for noncommercial educational television. Almost all of these channels are now occupied by stations, and most are affiliated with PBS, which supplies programs in a manner roughly similar to the way the other networks operate. For many years decisions on *which* programs would be produced—by stations or independent producers, not PBS or CPB—or purchased were made by the stations through a complicated bidding-commitment procedure made necessary by the fact that federal funding is supplied to stations and not to PBS or CPB. Recently PBS was given more power to fund program production which, in 2001, PBS President Pat Mitchell used to diversify sources of programs and reduce dependence on British programs in the hope their replacements would appeal to a younger audience. It is unclear whether such a course of action will be feasible. In public radio, as in commercial radio, the networks are of limited importance, with only about one-sixth of noncommercial FM stations being affiliated with NPR (National Public Radio). Nevertheless, some NPR news and public affairs programs, and even entertainment programs from NPR or Public Radio International (PRI, originally American Public Radio, a group of stations organized by Minnesota Public Radio, which does not have the overhead or some of the governmental restrictions of NPR)—have large, loyal audiences.

12.3.7 Current Status and What May be Next

Although the networks are the obvious target for critics of any of broadcasting's real or imagined shortcomings, and networks themselves are prone to complain at the slightest interference in their activities, they (and their owned-and-operated stations) have done extremely well financially, which is one reason why they are now being bought and sold. But not everything has gone their way. They lost one tenth of their income—perhaps $200 million in early-1970s dollars—when cigarette advertising was banned; citizens' group pressures reduced the income from children's programs; the Prime Time Access Rule forced them to return some prime time inventory to their affiliates; and new program delivery competition from cable, VCRs, PBS and later the Internet made substantial inroads on their prime time audiences; election campaign reforms reduced election time revenues; and costs of acquiring sports events such as the Olympic Games and covering major news events kept rising. For many years, they were greatly restricted in their ownership of programs, including a ban on syndicating them in the United States.

These conditions led to serious dwindling of the networks' share of the total audience. The public still watched ever-more television—but it now was seeing programs over cable, DBS or VCRs. Indeed, the networks themselves—after decades of terrestrial linking through telephone lines and coaxial cable—turned the bulk of the job over to communication satellites in the mid–1980s. In decades to come, while the network names may continue, the Internet might be used to distribute television programs. Yet, because of population growth, the profits of their O & O stations, and their relationships with creative talent, the traditional networks continue to profit, and the symbiotic relationship between network and affiliated station has proven to have more merits than demerits for all concerned—although relationships have become increasingly acrimonious. Since the program purchase-scheduling-delivery functions remain essential to the electronic mass media today as in the 1920s, the networks probably will continue in the business of efficiently sharing expensive middle-of-the-road programs across the nation—although a minority think that specialized cable services or even the Internet will eliminate the need for common denominator programming. Stay tuned.

One relatively unexamined factor is the possibility of synergy—the whole being greater than the sum of its parts—resulting from the increasing concentration of ownership. The top 25 group owners controlled nearly 40% of some 1,200 commercial television stations in 1999, up from only 25% in 1996. Multiple system owners in the cable industry are even more concentrated (see Appendix C, table 9-D). It isn't improbable that these entities will think about going into the program production business themselves, which would put even more pressure on the traditional networks. Whether such vertical integration would pass muster with the FTC or the Justice Department's antitrust division will depend on the politics of the time.

12.4 The Public Broadcasting Alternative

The development of educational—later public—radio and television took place despite limited public knowledge or support, indifference, and even hostility of commercial broadcasters, regulatory caution based on political concerns, and the overriding and interrelated questions of what precisely is the mission of such a system and its financial support—and consequent probable control of content.

12.4.1 What's It For?

Central during decades of public broadcasting is the continuing lack of agreement on what it is expected to do for its audience. From the start, radio broadcasting was held up as a great potential educational force, as was television in its turn. Such a platitude has currency, particularly as definitions of education have broadened—from the classroom to a variety of cultural activities and interests. But when the narrow educational role became less appealing, public broadcasting faced a host of questions. Should it be an alternative to commercial radio and television? A chance for education in the home or expansion of adult education programs at the college level? An adjunct to in-class instruction? A general cultural service? A locally oriented service or a national one? Controlled by the community, the educational establishment, or by counterculture organizations? Should it emphasize opportunities for minority interests? Should it be another national network in competition with existing commercial nets? All of these questions remain active, and the confusion over the mission of American public service broadcasting has been reflected in the names applied to it: instructional, educational, and public—or cultural, community, and alternative.

This vagueness of national purpose and consequent dearth of financial capitalization have intimidated and frustrated generations of leadership in public broadcasting, and provided feed for critics. From the beginning, educators have too often failed to grasp opportunities, frequently set their sights too low, and have been subservient to those in government and elsewhere who might have been good allies but turned out to be less helpful as masters.

In Great Britain and many other countries, the publicly controlled broadcasting system was established as an instrument of national policy long before commercial broadcasting—which became dominant, but not overwhelmingly so—was allowed. In the United States, commercial broadcasting began first and remains primary while educational broadcasting has had to subsist on crumbs. This was self-defeating because there never was enough money to produce programming and promotion that could build general public support.

12.4.2 Growth

Approximately 200 noncommercial AM radio stations in the 1920s shrank to a couple of dozen by the late 1930s. Apparently once the glamour of the new medium wore off, fiscal caution and the apprehension of classroom teachers who feared for their jobs were sufficient (especially in the Depression) to choke off funds needed to upgrade facilities to FRC standards and continue operating. During the 1930s and 1940s, a few educational broadcasters kept alive the dream of regaining access to broadcast channels in every community. Commercial broadcasters were using most of the AM channels previously and briefly occupied by the educators and, in spite of commercial broadcasters' assurance to Congress that adequate time for educational programming would be provided, fulfillment of the dream had to wait until educators won reservations on FM channels in 1940 and on television in 1952. These set-aside channels, which were the latter-day fruition of an unsuccessful attempt to secure them in the Communications Act of 1934, provided the stimulus that eventually led to more than 300 noncommercial television stations and more than 1,400 noncommercial FM radio stations. The number of noncommercial FM and television stations (including those operated by religious groups) has approximated a fourth of all FM and television outlets for decades, and their audiences have grown to the point where programs often show up well in the ratings and are listened to or viewed at least occasionally by the majority of Americans.

Still confused about its purposes, educational broadcasting slowly grew out of the demonstration stage although equipment manufacturers may have benefited more than students or the general public. But the continuing lack of agreement on common goals led to a corresponding lack of public concern. As a result, political and economic pressure was never adequately mobilized to support ETV/PTV and the resulting lack of money was a symptom more than a cause of its malaise. For, despite all the rhetoric, ETV has seldom attempted to be more than a limited alternative to commercial entertainment. Its programs tend to appeal to a well-educated minority or, as its critics would say, an elite. Only with occasional movies or high-quality drama, much of the latter from Britain, some music (typically featuring popular semi-classical artists, such as tenors from Italy and Ireland), comedy, and satire, and some children's and "how to" programs, have public television stations been able to garner substantial audiences.

Both listeners and contributors have continued to come largely from a narrow spectrum of society. One can argue that these are the decision makers and movers, but this group already is well served by other media. Public broadcasting, as created by congressional action in 1967, is just barely a medium for the general public, although more and more programming is aimed lower in order to address political and fiscal pressures.

12.4.3 Seeking Funds

Largely because of its fuzzy sense of mission, public broadcasting remains hampered by restricted funding, lack of a consistent long-range funding plan, and political influence on decision making. Members of Congress and other politicians object to tax monies going to independent programming supporting various political and social views they may not favor themselves. Accordingly, for decades noncommercial educational radio stations were legally prevented from editorializing or endorsing political candidates, and local pressure frequently was even more severe. It is significant that many years passed before an educational broadcaster challenged the constitutionality of this situation.

A few municipalities, school districts, and universities had provided minimal support for educational broadcasting each year until the late 1950s, when such outside agencies as the Ford Foundation offered help. In 1967 the Carnegie foundation's report proposed a new name, "public television," and a new vision and generated enough pressure on Congress for the government to establish the Corporation for Public Broadcasting, with some tax support for equipment and programming.

Educational broadcasters, willing to do almost anything for money, have discovered that "he who pays the piper calls the tune." They also have found that a promise to fund is not proof of money forthcoming. More than three decades after the first Carnegie Commission report, and two after the second, a true long-range funding plan isolated from short-term political pressures is still only a dream. Proposals for "dedicated" funding from excise taxes on receiver or station sales remain unlikely in the face of industry pressure and political ideology. Internal dissension is rampant. Public television often is called elitist, yet its role of providing programming not generally supplied by commercial television is recognized—and some of it is very good. Cautious governing boards of local public television stations are at loggerheads with the alphabet soup of national organizations. Government remains ambivalent—and no recent president seems to have wanted another effective network to parry and has ensured this condition by directing the dribble of federal funding to local rather than national organizations.

Finally, public television's limited success in attracting underwriting funds from commercial firms has alienated many commercial stations—which now view it as competition to be fought rather than as a public service to be supported. After federal funding was reduced in the 1980s, public television stations were allowed to give "underwriting" and later "enhanced underwriting" credits, virtually indistinguishable from commercials, to firms that contributed to a program's production costs—and as a result were strongly attacked both by commercial stations and by those who appreciated receiving programming *without* commercial interruptions.

12.4.4 A Few Predictions

The long-term future of public broadcasting is unclear. With the support of tax and foundation money, there is little danger that it will blow away. But without that support, and with fewer and fewer apparent differences between public and commercial television programming, even the minority

■ **Decades on Sesame Street**   By the beginning of the new century, *Sesame Street* had contributed to children's development for more than three decades over PBS, a remarkable record.

Photofest.

that now supports public broadcasting may turn away, removing the last stimulus for governmental fiscal support. Not only are there a number of cable networks—A&E, Bravo—that carry many of the same programs as PBS, but there also are several—the Discovery Channel, C-SPAN—that carry in their entirety important hearings, political conventions, and the like. Finally, such public affairs programming annoys the many who would rather be viewing the originally scheduled entertainment programs, on PBS or the commercial networks.

The immediate future appears to hold few programs with the wide public appeal of *Sesame Street* or some *Masterpiece Theatre* offerings, more bickering over a limited financial pie, a growing struggle with cable television operators who have little interest in carrying PBS stations, and continued infighting among competing organizations. When those in public broadcasting can confidently sell a substantial portion of the general public on clearly defined goals and aims, receive support with fewer strings attached, and stop the nearly constant internal and political bickering, then this service may become more than a stepchild to commercial radio and television. But at the start of the 21st century there are no guarantees that any of this will happen. Stay tuned.

12.5 Dollars and Sense

Despite initial attempts to find other means of financing broadcasting, a strong debate over the propriety of broadcast advertising in the mid-1930s, and concern over many aspects of it since, advertising has been the chief support of American broadcasting since the late 1920s. In turn, radio and then television have become major advertising media. Advertising's dominant role has affected program content and production, widened the differences between the haves and have-nots, and helped establish different roles for today's radio and television.

12.5.1 Programs as Bait

Because most broadcasting is advertising supported, programs are only a means to an end: attracting consumer audiences to sell to advertisers. (When an advertiser buys "time" or "space," these are merely the historic units of measure for adverting sales purposes.) Programs become bait to gather audiences, which networks, stations, and, to a lesser extent, cable systems then sell to advertisers. Thus the majority of programs tend to be mass entertainment, with information (news and public affairs) receiving just enough time to ensure a good public image, or cheapened to popular gossip- and scandal-mongering content. Mass appeal programs generally are bland and politically neutral, aiming to offend as few while entertaining as many as possible. Program content appeals to a low common denominator so that the largest number can enjoy it—and attend to the increasing number of supporting commercials. To the advertiser, so long as the "cost per thousand" remains the same and the audience's demographic mix is desirable, it does not matter if the message appears in the form of a 30-second spot or an "informational" underwriting identification on supposedly "noncommercial" PBS.

12.5.2 Origins

In the United States, following the initial sale of commercial time in 1922, the rush to adopt this method of financing soon carried all before it. Other possible approaches for securing operating income had been suggested: annual license fees on receivers (as levied in Great Britain and elsewhere); general tax revenues (which support a few municipal and university stations today); special taxes; annual subscriptions (currently received by many PTV and some public radio stations); donations (received by public or religious broadcasters); operation of stations as auxiliary enterprises by receiver manufacturers and retailers; or combinations of these. All of these were and remain far less common than commercial sponsorship, both here and abroad. A few stations have been supported out of the pockets of an individual or firm for altruistic, political, religious, or public relations reasons, or to save on federal taxes, since one can reduce one's taxes by losing money supporting an unprofitable business. But by 1928 radio had become a mass advertising medium, and through the 1940s the larger advertising agencies controlled radio network programming.

On the other hand, the high (and rising) costs of producing television programs turned off advertising agencies, so the networks had to take over this function themselves when television burgeoned in the late 1940s. Until the late 1950s, when the quiz show scandals forced networks to supervise programming more strictly to protect their affiliated stations from FCC sanctions, advertisers still could easily veto the content of most sponsored programs. At the same time, the cost of sponsoring an entire program had risen beyond the capacity of most corporate sponsors.

12.5.3 Advertising

As a result, broadcasting slowly adopted a modified "magazine concept," which allowed advertisers to buy national or local spots within programs and allowed advertiser support without complete advertiser control. This system has shaped most of today's American electronic media—even the Internet. Most national television advertising goes to the networks and larger stations (and, to a lesser extent, cable networks) partly because of the convenience to the advertiser of using only one large outlet instead of many smaller ones. Local advertisers, unable to afford the prices charged national ones, must use smaller and less efficient independent stations or fringe time on larger ones. Independent stations, often on less desirable UHF channels, must handle the same large and fixed operating costs on the smaller amounts of money generated by local ads, and hence often are willing to "break" their published rates or arrange barter deals in order to have enough income flow to pay their bills. Most radio stations must scramble even harder.

Competition between radio and television for advertising is restricted by the interaction of advertisers' desires for efficiency, the demise of radio networks that forced radio to become a local advertising medium, and technological factors that limit the number of networks and make most smaller stations inherently and permanently inferior as advertising media. Once a new medium or approach—FM, UHF television, cable, pay-TV, home video recording—has won a long, expensive struggle to get public, government, or industry support or approval—such as, for example, the 1962 all-channel receiver bill that helped UHF—the battle has just begun. Now it must start the *marketing* fight against those stations or other institutions that hold an economic advantage.

12.5.4 Direct Payment

Cable television has discovered that large potential profit is to be gained from a form of subscription (payment by the month for unlimited use of "basic" advertiser-supported programming), added to shared income from pay-TV, and from direct "pay-per-view" programming—the last two without advertiser support. If basic subscription fees paid out-of-pocket costs, much of the rest was pure profit, and some early operators and multiple system operators (MSOs) stayed in the business because they could invest the large and regular cash flow and because of the enormous capital gains that could be made when they sold the system. This was largely a function of the tax laws, which allowed deductions for financing as well as operating expenses and levied low-rate capital gains taxes on profits from the sale. Then the new owner would go through the same process.

However, this changed in the late 1970s, when the first "cable only" programming, such as current feature films on HBO, was distributed by satellite to local systems. Suddenly there was an opportunity for the system operator to profit every month by sharing in an extra monthly fee charged the subscriber. Since much of the wiring was already in place, pay-cable was a money-maker for cable operators from its inception.

By 1987, the magic "half of American homes subscribe to cable" figure had been reached. Of those, about half also took one or more "tiers" of pay-cable. As the proportion of those using cable (basic and pay) grew, the average income per subscriber per month climbed rapidly, from $5 or less to $30, $40, or more for many cable systems. The larger audiences attracted an increasing amount of local and national spot advertising to the cable system for additional revenue. However, it took a long time for many large cities to get cable, for economic, political, or technological reasons—costs of wiring a large city are high, as are public expectations of quality, since urban audiences already are well served by on-the-air broadcasting. Television manufacturers touted "cable ready" tuning, and *TV Guide* successfully fought potential competition by covering cable as well as broadcast television in its pages. The public still watched television—but now it was seeing most network or non-network shows on cable or by pickup from a rooftop satellite receiving dish.

12.5.5 Specialization

While most national advertisers still find television to be the medium of choice (matching newspapers' share), the "pie" of their expenditures now has to be cut in ever-smaller wedges. Viewers with up to 100 advertising-supported cable channels to choose from are harder for advertisers to reach than viewers with only three or four on-air network affiliates. The growth of advertising-free (pay) cable, PBS, and rented cassettes among those competing for the viewer's attention makes the advertising agency's job more difficult. The old concept that a television station license was a license to print money is obsolete, even though the high price tags on stations and cable networks indicate that they still are considered extremely valuable properties. The money is still there, but it has to be earned rather than "picked up off the ground."

12.5.6 Other Income Sources

All companies are constantly on the lookout for additional ways of making money. The proportions of advertising and subscription (by the month) income will vary, depending on competition and public acceptance. For example, advertising has been the mainstay for commercial television, but has been far less effective on the Internet or in motion picture theaters. Public broadcasting has found some funding in the promotion of tours and seminars, as commercial radio has benefited from rock concert promotions. The cable industry relies on monthly subscriptions for the most part, as do many print media. The sale of books, tee-shirts, records, and similar merchandise (although sometimes disguised as "premiums," or gifts provided in recognition of donations) is common, some network programs have merchandising tie-ins ready by the time the first episode is aired, and the sale of products over television may, some day, result in income for stations other than those labeled as "home shopping" outlets as is the case in the U.K.

12.5.7 A Few Predictions

While many think "convergence" refers only to technologies, it also applies to industries. Although the go-go years of conglomerates controlling a host of unrelated industries seem to have passed, the combination of ambition—some would say greed—and governmental and public acceptance of the ideology of deregulation and unrestricted growth is leading to fewer and fewer entities controlling ever-larger portions of any given medium or industry—and a consequent shrinkage in the number of independent entities. This has proven true in banking, airlines, automobile manufacture, petroleum, drug stores, and a myriad of other industries. In communication fields as different as personal computer operating systems and newspapers, it has become extraordinarily difficult to establish new firms or preserve smaller and older ones. The product of huge mergers of a few years ago (like Time Warner and Turner) is suddenly absorbed by another communications entity (AOL) that is looking to expand in a related area. Many business leaders believe that the only alternatives are growth or death. The Congress's removal of most restrictions on broadcast station ownership soon led to hundreds of stations being controlled by one company. One company—Gannett—controls hundreds of newspapers and only a handful of cities now have competing papers. One firm owns more than 1,200 radio stations. Cable, supposedly an industry with thousands of "mom & pop" companies, actually is heading toward oligopoly–the top 25 companies serve more than 90% of American homes; the top 5 serve approximately two-thirds.

A cartoon shows three fish of varying size. The smallest one, about to be gobbled up by the middle one says: "The world is unjust." The middle one, about to gobble the smallest one, but about to be eaten in turn by the largest fish, says: "The world can be just." The largest one has no doubts: "The world is just." What effects will this concentration of control have on the American public? It can be argued that, in A. J. Liebling's words, "Freedom of the press is guaranteed only to those who own one."*And it also can be argued that the ultimate result of unregulated competition in a given industry is likely to be monopoly—with consequent monopoly pricing and reduction in service. Broadcasting isn't at that point yet, but it will require much public vigilance to avoid a situation where our sources of news, as well as entertainment, are restricted to a handful of *kieretsu*. Stay tuned.

12.6 Programming: An Expanding Menu

Programs resulting from increased competition are neither as bad as some critics say (typically, they decry tendencies toward consensus, timidity, and the lowest common denominator approach) nor as good as some idealogues touting the virtues of competition and diversity would have us believe. Some of the awards hanging on the "I love me" walls of stations

---

*Liebling, A.J. *The Press.* New York: Ballantine, 1961. p. 30. (Originally published in *The New Yorker*, May 14, 1960.)

are well-deserved, although others may be a substitute for a feeling of real accomplishment in the public interest. This ambivalence is reflected *TV Guide's* 2000 list of "100 most memorable moments in TV history": the two highest ranked "moments" were astronaut Neil Armstrong's first walk on the moon in 1969—and Lucille Ball's "Lucy in the Candy Factory" episode of 1952.

12.6.1 Unoriginality . . .

Most programs are "more of the same," produced as inexpensively as practicable. Even such highly profitable programs as *60 Minutes* keep a close eye on costs, and their many imitators and clones may be on even tighter budgets. Something touted as "new" is usually a variation on what has been done before or merely a gimmick or something to titillate the audience rather than a carefully crafted artistic advance. Since audiences are sold to advertisers, programs continue to serve as the lure used to attract viewers. Hence, programs mostly—in addition to a little congressional and public pressure—reflect demands from advertisers that, in turn, reflect varied audience preferences and the profit interests of owners and managers. From these has come program standardization and a cyclical, largely imitative, development of program types and themes.

The needs of networks as well as the constraints imposed by early recording media led to standardized program lengths, generally in 15-minute increments. Radio of the early 1920s and after 1960 has been more free-form. Program formats usually are defined by the need to insert a certain number of commercials at exact times, often determined by computer or previously distributed schedule. If the particular "availability" has not been sold, the network may insert an unpaid program promotion or public service announcement so that the schedule is maintained—and the public is further conditioned to expect program interruptions. Even PBS programs originally produced abroad without the straitjacket of commercial scheduling generally adhere to this pattern, with regular climaxes written into scripts to motivate audience viewing during and beyond the commercial interruption.

Successful early programs led to standardization of program types. Musical, variety, drama, comedy, sports, and game formats all were common by the late 1930s, and most programs since then are but modification and adaptation, and still are aimed at women from 18 to 45, who determine most consumer purchases.

For many reasons, there has been little real program experimentation. First, with few exceptions, radio has had a shortage of real talent and new ideas. Vaudeville performers were shocked to see routines that might have pleased stage audiences for a lifetime gobbled up by radio's national listenership in days or weeks. Television's appetite for content, especially with 18- to 24-hour programming days, is prodigious, forcing mass production of proven formats. Second, few advertisers wish to risk supporting nonconventional programs, since the stakes are so high. They generally must appeal to the largest possible audience without antagonizing parts of it. Third, costs and thus risks are always rising. Radio programs seemed cheap to produce; even television of the late 1940s rarely cost more than a few thousand dollars a week for a network show. But by the 1990s an hour of dramatic prime time programming might cost a million dollars before it could be sent to the home screen. A consequence of high cost is reduction in number of shows created for a season from 39 (in network radio's day) to less than half that number today. Indeed, one of the major reasons for producing new episodes at all is the hope that there will be enough episodes (nominally 100) to make the show attractive for syndication—and residuals. This tendency of networks, advertising agencies, and production studios to play it safe with accepted methods and formats explains why most programmers follow conventional ideas and copy past successes. Even the most highly creative are urged to copy their own previous successes.

Setting the Entertainment Pattern   George Burns and his wife Gracie Allen made up one of radio's pioneering comedy teams in the 1930s just as Milton Berle was the first hot television property in the late 1940s. Both radio and television relied on the widespread appeal of comedy to attract large audiences and grateful advertisers.

Culver Pictures.

12.6.2 . . . and Originality

But, every so often, frequently in unsponsored sustaining time, on public television, or in another country or medium, one program or idea that is a bit different from others of its genre becomes popular; less often, a producer will support a program that is substantially different; and once in a while, the gamble pays off. Most recently this happened with voyeur shows, such as *Survivor* or *1900 House*. A few years ago self-contained miniseries were in vogue, possibly reflecting apparent reductions in audience attention spans. (This latter effect also is evidenced by fast-moving programs such as *Sesame Street* and the practice that rarely allows a network television news story to be more than 90 seconds long.) Music videos crossed the line between promotion and entertainment. In the late 1990s, the newsmagazine and "reality-based" programs from *COPS* to *America's Funniest Home Videos* became popular—particularly among network executives who appreciated their low cost. Norman Lear showed that current controversies could be the subject of situation comedies such as the 1971–1983 *All in the Family*. Close copies were soon produced in a process of imitation that continued until audience ratings for that type of program began to decline. By then, another program format or genre would be on the upswing of *its* cycle. Generally, it takes from one to four seasons for a program type to run its course, and some types have returned to popularity every "TV generation" of 10–15 years. By this token, we may be overdue for returns of the western drama and the comedy-variety form—but the cycle isn't that predictable. In 2000, for example, the big-money quiz show returned—although it took longer because of the scandals of the late 1950s. (Indeed, Appendix C tables 4 and 5 show a remarkable similarity between recent network television program types and radio programming of the 1930s and 1940s.)

The cautious networks rarely are interested in program ideas from outside that do not fit into a mold developed in their own headquarters. The competitive scheduling of network programs has become an art with the trappings of a science. The programming chiefs rely not only on rating services but also on the track records of major packagers such as MTM (*The Mary Tyler Moore Show, Rhoda, Hill Street Blues, St. Elsewhere*), Lorimar (*Dallas, Falcon Crest, Knots Landing, Perfect Strangers, ALF*), Warner Brothers/ Lorimar (*Growing Pains, China Beach, Night Court*), Desilu (*The Lucille Ball Show*), Tandem (*All in the Family, Sanford and Son, The Jeffersons*), and producers such as Steven Bochco (*Hill Street Blues, L.A. Law*), David Kelley (*The Practice, Ally McBeal*), and Aaron Spelling (*Charlie's Angels, Dynasty, Hotel, Fantasy Island*), and a few others. Spin-offs (or rip-offs) from successful series are preferred by networks to new program ideas from new sources. It is unlikely that this pattern will change until channels are provided to support more than four or five on-air networks or unless new means of distributing programs are further developed. Those demonstrated in the past include temporary sports networks, first-run syndication of serials (such as

Baywatch, or *Xena, Warrior Princess*), miniseries, and occasional dramatic programs distributed over ad hoc networks consisting of both independent and network-affiliated stations. Cable networks tend to seek out inexpensive off-network programs to distribute, leavened with independent productions and sporting events, although HBO, A&E, and a handful of other cable channels regularly (but not often) produce special programming of their own.

It is possible to "milk" or extend the life of a program or format by making cast changes, going from a serial format to a story-contained-in-one-episode approach, or emphasizing some aspect of the program (such as sex and violence) until it is virtually a parody of itself. But some of the best program series—including *M*A*S*H, Hill Street Blues, Seinfeld,* and the *Mary Tyler Moore Show*—decided to retire voluntarily while still popular, often wrapping up many of the loose ends in their story lines in the final show. Of course, these programs had produced enough episodes to be profitable in later syndication, and some of the talent would receive large residual payments for the rest of their lives.

12.6.3 Tactics

It has been said that there are only a dozen or so major literary plots, and television and radio drama have reused them so often that they have become nearly as conventionalized—with stock characters, pacing, and plot—as the lengths or genres of the programs themselves. Most avid television watchers can predict the outcome of a program or subliminally know when the plot is building in suspense and interest toward a commercial interruption. The staples of genre, plot and attractive performers, are always in the wings, ready to reappear. This familiarity becomes a comfort to persons who use television for companionship. Even those who turn to television for more than relaxation and entertainment are unwilling to do so *all* the time.

Hence, the very sameness of broadcasting seems to be one of its greatest strengths. Rather than responding to presumed or possible audience *needs*, electronic media tend to cater to the public's *desires*, which are reduced to the limited choice of programming aired. Since much of the audience finds change uncomfortable and stability welcome, broadcasters and advertisers use these attitudes to establish continuing audience preferences and habits. About the only change is in the amount of information that today's audience seems to be able to absorb. The 20-second spots of today, with improvements in message construction and production, seem to be as effective as their 1-minute forbears of three or more decades ago.

Locally produced programs are rare, in spite of the efforts of organizations like the National Association of Television Program Executives and the overseas examples of cooperative program exchanges. Local formats for both radio and television rarely could compete with networks except by copying them. A half dozen of today's radio formats have no network counterparts

▪ **Network Hegemony**   For television's first four decades, the larger networks dominated broadcast news. Each evening millions would tune to CBS (see Walter Cronkite on p. 445) or NBC. Chet Huntley [left] from New York and David Brinkley [right] from Washington co-anchored the NBC evening news from the late 1950s into the 1970s. They are shown at the 1956 Democratic convention. Later network anchors are shown on p. 541. Network and local station newscasts helped to spell the end of the evening newspaper—just as CNN and the Internet would drastically diminish the traditional network news role by the late 1990s.

Photo courtesy National Broadcasting Company.

since radio networks no longer provide large amounts of programming—but *do* have a similarity from market to market that cannot be blamed solely on the success of program consultants. In television, the term "local origination" generally is a misnomer. It really means nationally syndicated programs (particularly game shows like *Jeopardy* or *Wheel of Fortune* or, sometimes, "soft" or feature "magazine" news programs and a whole judiciary system of syndicated "judge" programs) or feature films shown with local commercials.

12.6.4 The Importance of News

The chief exception to this are news programs. Not only do some broadcasters still believe that the FCC and Congress look with favor on programming news and public affairs as being "in the public interest," a sizable minority of the public feels a need to be well informed on local matters—a need not satisfied by the networks or CNN. The proportion of Americans who read newspapers is steadily dropping, leaving the electronic media as the only game in town. Therefore, local broadcast news also supplies a major share of local spot revenues—more so now that most of the networks are sharing the costs of stock footage of breaking news events and are the primary supporters of the Voter News Service on election night. Indeed, evidence suggests that a strong early evening local news program will lead its audience to that station's evening prime time programming as well. In other words, money spent on the 6 o'clock local news program will pay off by helping "win" audience ratings for the entire evening. But even here the approach is standardized—with radio's "rip 'n' read" superficiality torn from the AP wires, and television newscasts virtually indistinguishable from one another except for their highly paid blow-dried anchors and gimmicks suggested by consultants, such as "happy talk" interaction among on-air presenters.

Replacement of a news anchor by a network occasions considerable nervousness (and coverage by other media)—and as this book goes to press, that hasn't happened for two decades—since Dan Rather moved into Walter Cronkite's chair at CBS in 1981. The last few holdovers from World War II radio network commentary days have died—Bob Trout staying in harness until his death in November 2000 at the age of 91—and the expression of opinion scares those in the executive suites, so today caution and objectivity are rigorously maintained. Although more women are seen on television newscasts, with Barbara Walters's salary reaching the same stratospheric level of many male network anchors, and women have occupied a large proportion of producer and other behind-the-scenes positions for many years, it wasn't until the late 1980s that a woman was to be seen doing NFL play-by-play.

If presented at all, editorials are bland; limits on time and cost restrict what might be aired on evening newscasts; and negative reactions to infrequent controversial documentaries has made it harder to get them on the air. Success beyond the conventional newscast *is* possible, although rare. An example is CBS's *60 Minutes*'s long stay in the list of top 10 programs in terms of ratings, and ABC's unexpected success with *Nightline* starting in 1980—both of which show that news can attract audiences and advertiser support, which, of course, has made news operations subject to the same economic demands as entertainment programming—and even greater fear that the Internet will continue to syphon viewers from network news.

These economic demands and fears have led to much less coverage of national politics (see Appendix C, table 5-G) and far more to exciting but superficial novelty, sex, and violence titillation and scandal. The journalist's public watchdog function has been submerged under a sea of caution and concern for the bottom line.

The meaning of the word "Infotainment" has gone from a condemnation to an objective description. Although the coverage of the recount of the Florida vote in the 2000 presidential election was extensive—perhaps

■ **Televising Sports Then and Now** An NBC television crew broadcasts baseball on TV for the first time during a game between Columbia University and Princeton at New York's Baker Field in 1939. Two mobile vans sent the television signal to the transmitter at the Empire State Building for broadcast to the handful of homes equipped with television sets. Six decades later Seattle Mariners' Ken Griffey Jr. is seen through a center field TV camera while standing on first base. Money paid by networks to carry professional sports had transformed the economics of the sports business.

AP Photo.

AP Photo/Eric Gay.

excessive—during the campaign itself many Americans got their political ideas from jokes during the nightly monologues of Jay Leno and David Letterman.

There is some justice to the complaint that the networks spend huge amounts of money for sophisticated hardware and personnel to report news, political events, sporting events such as the Olympics, political assassinations, and other disasters, but spend very little time or money on interpretations or implications of the news—the in-depth of information a democracy needs in order to reach valid decisions. Foreign correspondents no longer are stationed where the news is being made; they merely "parachute in" with a portable satellite transceiver, even in such battlegrounds as Kosovo. Indeed, the once-important documentary has been debased and confused in the public mind by the networks' entertainment divisions, which show fictional presentations of (sometimes) real events in "docudramas." What few public affairs documentaries are aired are to be found on PBS and cable channels such as Discovery, the History Channel, and the Learning Channel. One interesting experiment in 2000 was a joint venture of ABC's *Nightline* and PBS's *Frontline*: a two-hour special (on *Frontline*) on the Clinton administration, which may reflect the frustration of traditional news people at the commercial networks's unwillingness to schedule serious public affairs programming. Superficial biographies and "gee, whiz" tabloid accounts of improbable events, magazine shows, and "reality" are filling the time once used for providing the in-depth knowledge the public needs to make its decisions. After more than six decades we still lack an answer to the question of the proper balance between two legitimate interests: that of industry in profit and that of the public in news and public affairs.

12.6.5 A Few Predictions

Some—often those wanting a piece of the pie—claim that an increase in number of channels (and thus available programs) will automatically lead to "class" rather than "mass" programs. This idea has been accepted by some groups who believe that their program wants would be better served if there were more outlets. However, just as a mass audience can mean profits for advertiser-supported broadcasting, sheer size also is attractive to electronic media supported by direct subscription or purchase. So, virtually every programmer would prefer a large rather than a class audience, no matter how defined. The name of the overall industry is *broad*- not *narrow*-casting. Will cable, the Internet, pay-TV, videodiscs, videocassettes, DBS, and the like really give us a golden age of program diversity and high quality? Not likely. The evidence we have indicates that it is nearly always more profitable to copycat existing entertainment to attract the most potential buyers at the least per-unit cost. So, although our best sense of the likely future is "more of the same"—stay tuned.

All News, All the Time   Created in 1980, CNN became the first stop for news junkies by the 1990s. Its coverage of the short but intense Gulf War in 1990–1991 marked its coming of age as a respected news source, depended upon even by the Pentagon itself. CNN audiences always increase during major news stories, but drop off on humdrum news days.

Photofest.

12.7 And What of the Audience?

As reflected in the desires and needs of listeners and viewers, the public interest is paramount—according to public pronouncements of politicians, the Supreme Court, most broadcasters speaking at public hearings and meetings, and almost everyone else. Yet, because of broadcasting's commercial support, pleasing advertisers usually comes first. Further, "the public" really is many publics, as advertisers recognized decades ago. The average person today does not remember a time before television, but has completed more formal education than his or her ancestors, is growing older, and some may have more leisure time—or are more willing to spend most of the time they have after work in front of the tube.

The audience, although passive, is essential. Although earlier predictions that there would be more leisure time in which to pay attention to the media have fallen afoul of a national desire to garner dollars to buy "things" even at the cost of longer work weeks for most adult household members, the media audience is still huge and supports the advertisers who support programs.

With respect to the adoption of new technology, the public generally demands programming service *before* investing in receivers, VCRs, and other expensive home entertainment devices. During the 1950s and 1960s, whenever there was special scheduled programming—*Peter Pan*, the Olympics, the Academy Awards, even public affairs such as national political conventions—people rushed out to buy their first sets. Later, people bought color sets to see special programs (and even ads) transmitted in color. Although free-enterprise purists argue that competing devices or standards be allowed to fight it out in the marketplace, neither the public nor manufacturers are willing to take much risk by investing in devices that might not be adopted. So, everyone usually waits until the government or a united industry determines technical standards and specifications. However, since the FCC now tends to defer to the market, questions on standards and formats are waiting, in the final analysis, for the public to commit itself, usually basing this commitment on which standard is most actively promoted or has the most political support.

12.7.1 Activists and Passivity

Research shows that most viewers are content to let the experience wash over them with little overt reaction. Even switching between a growing number of channels seems to be more a result of boredom, overfamiliarity with a given program or format, and increasingly limited attention spans than a conscious decision to change. "Water cooler" discussion of a program the next day with relatives, friends, or co-workers is ever more rare. Broadcasters and advertisers have relied on head-counting research—the ratings and associated *demographics*—to determine the success of the programming they supply and make it the primary criterion for retaining or dropping a program. The claim that the majority of the public is satisfied with current broadcast fare has some validity, even though the public has no choice beyond the menu which networks, stations, and cable systems provide. Yet, in a country of more than 280 million people, even a small minority may contain millions of potential audience members!

There are a few exceptions to general passivity in the form of small and temporary activist citizens' groups like Action for Children's Television (ACT). Voluntary feedback—phone calls or letters—is rare but sometimes is effective enough to bring back a canceled program, or cause a network or station to drop one, since one person willing to communicate with programmers may represent hundreds or thousands of others who may be disaffected but not willing to exert themselves. A handful of audience groups work to persuade the FCC and Congress that action of some kind is needed, usually with respect to programs containing sex and violence, although now that the FCC no longer requires stations to retain program logs and, with changes made by the 1996 Act, it is almost impossible to challenge a license renewal. Other legal approaches are unlikely to succeed. On the other hand, if enough members of Congress can be recruited, any cause may succeed.

Growing sophistication of advertisers and the increasing number of stations and cable systems has led to a redefinition of "mass communication," particularly as applied to radio. The many highly specialized stations of today have loyal but relatively small audiences for very specific types of programming. Some advertisers, realizing that a "class" or "niche" audience with interest in their product or service might be more desirable than a much larger but indifferent "mass" audience, have geared their time-buying accordingly. Increasingly sophisticated advertisers rely on demographics (data on audience composition for a given program) and *psychographics* (data on audience likes and dislikes), which allow them to groom and aim their messages at a particular target. Sociological categories such as Yuppies ("Young Urban Professionals") and Dinks ("double income, no kids") weren't precise enough for time buyers. The shrinking number of research and measurement services have developed techniques, such as people meters, to better determine audience characteristics, even of the still mass-oriented networks, so that advertisers may match their efforts to potential customers.

12.7.2 Worry about Effects

Researchers, critics, and other observers rarely agree on the effects broadcasting has on its audiences although virtually everyone agrees that there *are* effects. Since the mid-1950s, concern about the effect of televised violence on children has elicited a series of congressional hearings, millions of dollars' worth of research, two important government and several private reports, reflecting several schools of thought on the issue. Yet the research had to be stimulated from outside, by nonindustry groups, since broadcasters were unwilling or unable to determine broadcasting's impact. People spend more time with radio and television than with almost any other activity, but the theoretical constructs and objective data to determine the effects of such attention are only slowly becoming available. Broadcast time salesmen cite a great deal of research, much of it self-serving, to convince advertisers that radio or television would be the most persuasive medium for selling goods and services, but very little definitive research on passivity, violence stimulus, stereotype formation, or other hypothetical or real effects has been done. Radio and television can provide a learning experience, but just what is learned, by whom, and with what effect is not well understood even after decades of speculation and a great amount of research.

Fearful of change, the industry recognizes that if the public becomes truly aroused by the problems that programs emphasizing violence and sex may cause for children, it is bound to lead to government restrictions or possible public relations–conscious advertiser boycotts. Mandates for often-invalid subject matter screens for Internet terminals in schools and libraries show the direction of legislative thinking. But the few cases of an imitative violent act in real life following a violent act on the television screen rarely show a direct cause-and-effect relationship on close analysis. In cases that seem to show a relationship, it usually can be shown that the person had exhibited abnormal tendencies previously and that Wilbur Schramm's conclusion that "some kinds of stimuli have some kinds of effect on some kinds of people sometimes" still holds.

12.7.3 Critics and Criticism

Yet this does not satisfy those who believe that the mass media are to blame for many—perhaps most—of the world's evils. To forestall more onerous regulations, for many years broadcasters advocated self-regulation, which culminated in 1975 with the short-lived "family viewing" time restriction on airing violent programs in the early evening. Although some broadcasters blamed this development for a drop in prime time ratings and use their raunchiest or most violent episodes during ratings sweeps periods, and there is a general disregard of the millions of children who watch television after nine o'clock and of the many violent scenes on the evening news, self-regulation was not the last word. When an antitrust legal challenge to the NAB's self-regulatory code on advertising was successful in 1982–1983, the NAB quickly abolished *all* program standards, leaving it up to the networks' and stations' own self-interest to parry public objections. On the other hand, in the mid-1980s the FCC disowned its 1964 *Pacifica* decision that the airwaves are not wholly for the inoffensive and bland when it came to "indecency," responding to a handful of complaints and relegating serious (as well as possibly prurient) content to a "safe harbor" in the middle of the night, when children might be expected to be in bed.

"Media-bashing" tends to be a favorite pastime of critics and politicians alike, and there is a tendency to blame the media (film, radio, comic books, television, and records, in that general order, over the years) for anything that goes wrong with our children or our society. But to the general public, getting higher-quality receivers at reasonable prices and being able to get a distant signal over the air or through cable with an entertaining program were far more important than any hypothetical dangers from content. Static mattered more than sociology, and big-name sports and entertainment was more important than high culture. This self-generating cycle supported the economic rationale for limiting programming experimentation. Most people wanted to be entertained; even at the height of World War II, during an early 1970s landing on the moon, or in the middle of the 1991 Gulf War, complaints flowed into stations about news cutting into favorite shows. News and documentaries had low ratings, and when combined with the unpopularity of the war in Vietnam, the unpleasantness of the Iran-Contra affair, or lack of drama in political conventions, it is no wonder that the networks often shunned such special public affairs programming. On the other hand, since tabloid-fodder like the O. J. Simpson case and the Clinton-Lewinsky scandal of the late 1990s appealed to the prurient-minded, they received a tremendous amount of air time—and fewer complaints.

At the same time as the public exhibits general satisfaction, there is more research and increasing congressional, conservative religious group, and other social critic interest in using television (and cable) as a whipping boy and placing restrictions on it. While a handful of activists try to improve the system, most citizens, virtually addicted to media that did not exist a generation or two ago, relax and watch and listen. Although the negative effects of broadcasting have rarely bothered most people, the public is aware that there are many things that are pathological about today's society and world—and is looking for scapegoats. Consequently, it considers broadcasting—a messenger telling us about the world's problems—as an obvious and vulnerable target due to its presence in the home. On the one hand, broadcasting is condemned as *causing* social ills; on the other hand,

■ **Staying Tuned**   While youth were often the first to pick up the wireless habit, their elders could also be persuaded to tune in . . . just as today's older generation came belatedly to the Internet's many services. The development of radios with loudspeakers, and using household electricity rather than batteries (or crystal sets), paved the way for radio to become a medium used by all members of the household. In some ways, this was a revolution as important as the invention of radio itself.

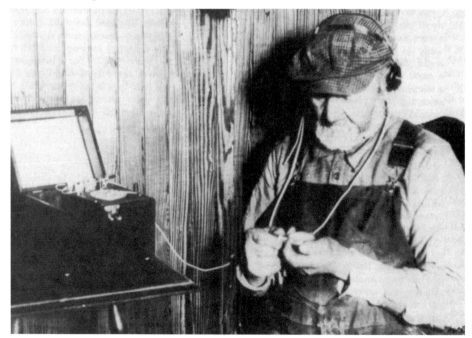

Photos courtesy Smithsonian Institution. (76-14662 and 76-14658)

radio and television also are attacked for not doing something to *cure* them. A surprising proportion of people say that, despite the First Amendment, they are willing to accept some kind of governmental control—over programs and Internet content directed to adults as well—if it will eliminate material deemed potentially harmful to children.

12.7.4 A Few Predictions

The coming of expensive and physically larger digital television, including HDTV, probably will return television viewing to the living or media room, and may reduce the use of second (or third) sets in bedrooms and kitchens. The public will not turn away from television as its primary entertainment medium, although news may be attended to on the Internet rather than the networks in the future. Radio will continue to become wallpaper, and few will listen to whatever local service remains, although new services offering "jukeboxes in the sky" or radio via satellites aimed at the driving

public were being introduced in 2001. It is very unlikely that definitive research into adverse effects of the media will be accomplished—but that will
not stop activists from attacking the media or legislators from regulating
them. Congress's adoption of the principle of deregulation apparently
applies more to the business aspects of the media, and not their content.
It will be easier to program one's own entertainment through the use of
VCRs—and eventually, computers—for time-shifting and the playback of
rented movies, which also are available on DVD. Audience research will
become ever more sophisticated, with personal portable people meters
capable of measuring attendance to all sources of information, persuasion
and entertainment—including the Internet.

12.8 A Changing Policy World

Running through America's electronic media history is a search for the
meaning of the elusive "public interest, convenience, and/or necessity."
Promulgated in the Radio Act of 1927 and continued under the Communications Act of 1934 (and even in the far-reaching 1996 amendments), this is
the criterion against which all regulation of broadcasting is measured, yet it
never has been satisfactorily defined either by Congress, which thought it
up, the FCC, which has to administer under its terms, or the courts, which
have to deal with the result. This may have some advantages in that it permits interpretations that reflect current reality rather than an idealized and
rigid fiction. Surprisingly, recent proposals to do away with the public
interest standard in the interests of allowing the broadcaster more freedom
actually tend to be far more rigid.

12.8.1 Reluctant Regulator

Part of the problem is the FCC's traditional reluctance to regulate. This is not
just a recent development, although emphasis after 1980 on deregulation
and marketplace ideology indicates that this reluctance has reached such an
extreme that one wonders if members of the FCC believe in any of the principles spelled out in the Communications Act. Rarely if ever possessed of
clear jurisdiction, sufficient information on which to base decisions, or the
power to enforce them, this politically sensitive body traditionally has
ignored or postponed problems—and no wonder. For years, the Court of
Appeals for the District of Columbia Circuit has overturned many FCC
decisions, further reducing the incentive to make them. Although many
participants in the regulatory arena practice delaying tactics in order to maintain the status quo for their own advantage, at the commission delay seems
virtually a goal in itself. Even so, the trend, from the first enactment of radio
laws in 1910 and 1912 until the end of the 1970s, was toward greater government supervision. At that time, growing case law precedent, congressional

interest in anything that affects the interests of its constituents, and the accretion of cases and policies into formal doctrines established a situation in which many broadcasters felt themselves narrowly circumscribed.

Other than during the chaos of the mid–1920s, the broadcasting industry has always maintained that the less regulation, the better. The chaos of unrestricted competition, in a field inherently limited by the strictures of the electromagnetic spectrum, was ended when Congress passed the Radio Act of 1927—with the enthusiastic approval of both the listening public *and* broadcasters. So long as the federal role was limited to such technical matters as clearing the airwaves of interference, most broadcasters had little objection to the new agency. But in the self-perpetuating nature of most bureaucracies, the FRC and, later, the FCC moved into programming areas to serve better that ill-defined "public interest." From then on, a low-grade war was waged between private enterprise and government bureaucracy, punctuated by moments of high drama as dirty laundry (such as the late 1950s' quiz show, payola, and plugola scandals or the behavior of incompetent or dishonest commissioners) was washed in public while pious promises were made about doing better in the future.

In its first six decades, the commission varied between "leaning tower of Jell-O" accommodation with, or even subservience to, the industry and mutual antagonism, which built to one peak with the 1946 "Blue Book" and to another during the several years of FCC activism that started with Chairman Minow's "vast wasteland" speech in 1961. Although no major revisions in law or regulation resulted from these activities, the climate changed after Minow was appointed, and broadcasters no longer possessed the informal control over the commission they had long held. In recent years, broadcasters and most members of the now-five-member commission have been on the same side of the ideological fence—but, unfortunately for broadcasters, their most important adversary has become the cable and the DBS industries, toward which both Congress and the FCC seemed to be leaning.

12.8.2 The Faceless Staff

In evaluating government's role in broadcasting, it is good to remember that the several agencies involved—Congress, the FCC, the OTP and its NTIA successor, and the courts—are not monolithic. They are composed of a changing cast of people with varied goals. Commissioner Johnson's interest in eliminating cross-media ownership in the 1960s had a very different philosophical base from President Nixon's 1970s attack on the ownership of television stations by the *Washington Post*, which opposed him. Most FCC members were appointed because of their earlier activities and views, with some getting the position because of old political debts, some because of service as a staff member of either the FCC or Congress, and some because a president wanted someone who thought as he did. Most recently, the nod often has gone to individuals who have the backing of influential members of Congress—and who fit into an unwritten quota system for women and members of minority groups. With a seven (now five) year term of office, the Communications Act expected the members of the FCC to be independent—but most members have not proven strong enough to stand up to the chairs of powerful congressional committees.

Behind the scenes, however, were "the staff"—the generally unknown congressional committee aides, FCC senior civil servants, and politically oriented technocrats of the NTIA—who had their own goals and a great deal more continuity than their elected or appointed superiors—and who often were not averse to educating, arguing with, or (more rarely) subverting their masters. Most of these people worked conscientiously in the public interest, but their length of tenure often froze their points of view, including a tendency to protect the status quo.

Although current controversies occupy our attention, they are seldom truly current. Most regulatory problems have been around for a long time; some take decades to reach a decision. Precedent often becomes so encrusted that various sides in a dispute often have difficulty finding new approaches to long-standing issues. Nevertheless, identification of some of the themes underlying today's problems may help explain them.

12.8.3 Concentrating Ownership

One such theme is concern over concentration of ownership of broadcasting stations and cable systems, a concern typically pushed on the FCC by left-wing populist members of Congress. Restrictions were instituted on multiple ownership of stations in a given market, on cross-ownership between media, and on particular combinations such as television station-cable ownership within a station's coverage area starting in the 1930s and continuing through the 1950s. The courts generally supported this FCC and Justice Department activity, starting with the Supreme Court's 1943 upholding of the commission's chain broadcasting (network) rules. Existing combinations have been allowed to continue, and some no-holds-barred attempts have been launched to persuade the FCC to grant waivers, notably by Rupert Murdoch, who wanted to own both newspapers and television stations in New York and Boston in 1988. After changes were made early in 1999 that allowed such cross-ownership, it was anticipated that the prohibition against newspapers owning stations in the same market soon would disappear. Under the old rules, changes in corporate ownership led to such extremes as pioneer NBC having to divest itself of its owned-and-operated radio stations in order to retain television stations in the same markets after purchase of its parent, RCA, by GE in 1985. Since members of Congress concerned about economic concentration were scarce in the late 1990s, what antitrust actions were undertaken by the Justice Department (such as the *Microsoft* case) seemed to be out of bureaucratic habit rather than conviction.

The commission's partial relaxation of the multiple ownership rules in 1985 predictably led to a large increase in station sales, abetted by relaxation at the same time of rules against "trafficking" in station licenses. In 1996, almost all restrictions were removed for radio, permitting a single licensee to own hundreds of stations, including several in the same market. Three years later, the FCC announced that it was planning to relax same-market ownership rules for television—one of the stimuli for the Viacom-CBS merger. This was a triumph of the ideology of deregulation, which had started in the late 1970s, originally touted as removing only outmoded and technical clauses from the rules. By allowing stations to be bought and sold for short-term gains ("trafficking"), the FCC removed one of the last regulations that was based on the concept that the broadcast media were "special" and subject to the public interest standard.

12.8.4 Seeking Fairness

Perhaps the FCC's most important and longest-running policy donnybrook was the Fairness Doctrine, which started simply enough when the FCC decided in the 1941 *Mayflower* case that the broadcaster should not be an advocate. The FCC then changed its mind in 1949, holding that a broadcaster *could* be an advocate if he or she provided an opportunity for opposing views to be heard. As the doctrine evolved case by case over the years, it split into two parts: the right of the public to hear opposing views on controversial matters of public importance (incorporated in Section 315 of the Communications Act in 1959), and the right to respond for those personally attacked during such a presentation (incorporated in the FCC rules in 1967). In its 1969 *Red Lion* decision, the Supreme Court upheld both.

The Fairness Doctrine, which was primarily intended to benefit the public by encouraging the airing of varied opinions on matters of public concern, became a rallying point for activist citizens' groups after 1964. When it was used in 1967 to require that stations broadcasting cigarette commercials (a law prohibiting this practice didn't take effect until 1971) provide free *anti*smoking spots, many in the industry and elsewhere felt that expanding the Doctrine to cover a commercial product was a dangerous precedent, in part because the requirement did not affect nonelectronic media. Different groups seized on the decision to demand time to respond to other commercials on consumerism or environmental issues. With the aid of the courts, the FCC later managed to put the lid back on this Pandora's box.

This did not stop citizens' groups from pressuring for increased access. They tried to use the Fairness Doctrine and other regulations to achieve something different from fairness: *access* to the airwaves for persons who had something to say—in the way they (and not the broadcaster) wanted it said. Argued best by attorney Jerome Barron, this concept led to little-used public access channels for CATV in the FCC's 1972 rules, to parts of the 1984 cable act, and to continuing pressure on broadcasters in the form of petitions to deny license renewal (until they, too, were eliminated in the 1996 Telecommunications Act).

Congress and the commission, both now believing that the Fairness Doctrine had been pushed too far, instigated hearings, revision proposals, and court tests of the doctrine's procedures—and even of its basic desirability. In a nutshell, the Doctrine had become a hot potato—particularly since post-Watergate election reform laws and many 1970s libel law case law changes further muddied the waters—and, with support from broadcasters, the FCC became loath to apply the Fairness Doctrine. In 1985 the commission let it be known that it was looking for a way to dump the doctrine as unconstitutional. While this would please conservatives in and out of government, as well as broadcast journalists and others who felt that the doctrine interfered with their First Amendment rights, the Democratic majority in Congress felt so strongly that the doctrine should be retained that when the FCC did drop it in 1987, Congress tried to restore it—only to have the bill vetoed by President Reagan. And there things stood during most of the Bush and Clinton administrations. However, broadcasters—led by the Radio-Television News Directors Association, which consistently maintained that the Doctrine actually worked to lessen public debate, since licensees were loath to risk having to carry time-gobbling opposing points of view—never gave up on their opposition to the Fairness Doctrine. In the Fall of 2000, as the Clinton administration wound down, a federal judge effectively killed the last two elements of the Fairness Doctrine, ending nearly 60 years of debate.

12.8.5 Lobbying

Supposedly held accountable by the Communications Act, broadcasters came to distrust continual FCC's investigations and rule changes, and "harassment" by citizens' groups, some of which had financial support from tax-exempt foundations or even government agencies. Until this trend was reversed in the early 1980s under the Reagan administration, government increasingly seemed to guide and limit the licensee's authority over station operations. The FCC, itself under pressure, at first tried to walk in the middle of the road, refereeing confrontations between broadcasters and listener groups to the dissatisfaction of both. The commission's typical tactic of delay proved ineffectual as citizens' groups found their way to the usually more receptive courts, a not-surprising development in an ever more litigious society. When in the late 1960s the WLBT decision (see pp. 460–463) gave some types of citizens' groups standing before the FCC, it expanded the list of participants in the regulatory arena, although this right was limited in the 1990s. These newcomers, like other players, soon found it advisable to negotiate their concerns directly with broadcasters rather than take the long road through the commission and the courts.

In many cases after the mid-1960s on, broadcasters often found that their own causes were not doing well. Much of this was due to an inability to lobby Congress as effectively as the rival motion picture and cable industries, partly because of corporate unwillingness to give up specific advantages for the common good—in 2000, for example, NBC (and shortly thereafter Fox) withdrew from the NAB because of NAB's position in support of ownership limits on local stations. CBS also dropped its membership the next year. During this period, cable had steadily improved its ability to lobby both Congress (which was particularly pleased by "free time" each week) and the FCC. The FTC, the antitrust division of the Justice Department, and other agencies developed popular antibroadcast ideas for increasing regulation of broadcast advertising and building intramarket media competition until the laissez-faire atmosphere of the 1980s buried these efforts. Congress made increasing demands on broadcasters for the carriage of political campaigning at bargain prices. Anti–job discrimination laws— one of the few areas under active FCC regulation during the Reagan era— and a requirement that broadcasters survey community leaders and the public to ascertain the community's needs as part of the license renewal process added to the mound of paperwork required of each broadcaster. On the other hand, Congress in 1981 finally lengthened license terms (to five years for television and seven for radio) and in 1996 raised both to eight years and made it almost impossible to challenge an existing license.

Although these increasingly complex regulations led broadcasters to think that the commission was firmly in the citizens' group ("enemy") camp during the 1960s and 1970s, such was not the case. Some regulations were mandated by Congress, some were the product of normal bureaucratic expansion, and others were the consequence of court decisions or were in response to real abuse of the public interest. The increasing number of multimillion-dollar libel suits reflected the case law of defamation, not a policy of the commission. The FCC's policy of delay fitted in well with the goals of those broadcasters who were economically powerful at a given time. Commission action or inaction—as contrasted to commission rhetoric— generally favored broadcasters over outsiders, AM over FM, VHF over UHF, and television broadcasters over cable until the newly found political strength of the cable industry caused a flip-flop. Only when the need for new services or technologies became absolutely clear did the commission approve stereo and nonduplication rules to help FM, support the all-channel receiving set law to help UHF television, and loosen restrictions on pay-TV and cable. The courts—in decisions on cable television, or on the copyright law—showed careful attention to political winds but settled into this same pattern. Even then, the new regulations seldom were even-handed.

Usually regulators protected the existing service; sometimes, as with cable in the mid-1970s, they favored the new service; but always they claimed to be serving the public interest.

12.8.6 Other Agencies

Broadcasters are subject to laws and policies that are not within the purview of the FCC. For example, although a federal shield law protecting the confidentiality of reporters' sources has never gotten anywhere, many states have such laws—and also permit cameras and microphones in courtrooms. Locating radio transmission towers involves the FAA and a number of state agencies, with the FCC's approval based on the decisions of others. Gavel-to-gavel coverage of the House of Representatives' proceedings over C-SPAN, a public affairs cable service (that ironically initially was not available in the District of Columbia) was an initiative of the House, not the FCC, following the Nixon impeachment hearings. (The more conservative Senate followed suit in 1986.) Even after the Freedom of Information Act was passed in 1966, journalistic access to government information—particularly in the courts and in those parts of the executive branch that use the excuse of "national security"—became more difficult each decade. Copyright, minimum wage, and a host of other laws apply to broadcasters without FCC intervention.

A 19th century humorist named Peter Finley Dunne reminded us that the Supreme Court, however myopic it may be, carefully follows the election returns. So does the Congress—and most other governmental bodies follow Congress's lead. Re-election is the primary goal of most legislators, so if a vocal constituency advocates content filters for the Internet, they probably will be installed regardless of the First Amendment. If Senators and Representatives are convinced that their more vocal constituents need protection, a flurry of laws to that end are proposed, regardless of minority points of view. At the start of the 21st century, most members of Congress believe that their *active* constituency consists of business executives, and the laws that are passed reflect this. If others believe that the public interest would better be served with a different policy, it is up to them to organize. Sometimes—as in analyzing the argument over whether the copyright laws should be extended to promote private interests rather than the diffusion of knowledge—one has to examine the politics of the economy rather than the principles of the Constitution. A wise man once suggested that it is better not to view the messy making of sausage, newspapers and laws. If we are afraid of the mess, then we probably have the government we deserve.

12.8.7 Self-Regulation

Self-regulation in broadcasting is one barometer of public concern over radio and television's role in society. Like most such industry self-regulatory efforts, the NAB codes (1929–1982) were intended to influence public opinion. They had little policing effect, no matter how much effort was devoted to their wording. With some exceptions—the informal ban on hard liquor advertising and the briefly in force provision for "family viewing" time are two—the codes were platitudes, often ignored if the industry was in economic difficulty. Most important, not all stations were code members, many did not feel bound by them, and the only enforcement penalty was withdrawal of permission to use the code's symbol or seal—which hardly anyone noticed anyway. Consequently, when a 1982 federal court decision struck down television code limitations on the amount of commercial time allowed per hour, the NAB readily eliminated any pretense of maintaining industry-wide programming and commercial time standards. Apparently today only the carefully honed ability of networks to avoid controversial material and congressional and political interest in the protection of young children from sexually explicit or other "indecent" programming prevent even more "anything-goes" programming.

12.8.8 Planning Ahead

Finally, it should be noted that there never has been a consistent long-range communications policy in the United States, except as inadequately sketched out in the 1934 and 1996 acts, the latter being largely implementation of a market basket of ideological position statements. The pressures of budget and day-to-day duties have restricted both congressional and the FCC's long-range vision—indeed, some members of the FCC and Congress would like to abolish the regulatory body altogether. Congress is too concerned with politically inspired hearings and re-election fund-raising and lacks the continuity for such planning; and broadcasters are running day-to-day businesses. In 1951 and again in 1968, presidential commissions examined U.S. telecommunications policy, but most of their quite-different recommendations were ignored. When the OTP was formed in 1970, it seemed to be a step toward continuing policy research at a high government level, but it quickly became mired in politics and short-range goals.

It is this lack of long-range, policy-oriented thinking that has led to government *reaction* to recurring problems rather than *anticipation* of their recurrence, even with an increase in telecommunications policy research and establishment of the NTIA in the 1970s. In the 1980s and 1990s, doctrinaire conservative economists dominated policy that previously had taken account of technical constraints and broad political economy theory. Much of the agenda of the Reagan (1981–1989) and earlier Bush (1989–1993) administrations was determined by ideological economic principles, and both administrations preferred to develop new policies within conservative think-tanks rather than in the give-and-take of traditional policy-making procedures. This movement was strong enough that the Clinton administration (1993–2001) never felt it had the power to swing the pendulum in the other direction, even before the 1994 Republican takeover of Congress.

12.8.9 A Few Predictions

After nearly three fourths of a century of broadcast regulation, the controlling phrase "public interest, convenience, and/or necessity" is likely to remain undefined beyond what the current political situation says it means, with resultant regulatory confusion and lack of goals. Not only does the 1934 Communications Act respond slowly to change, it often is administered— or funded—by people who seem to have little loyalty to its principles. This uncertainty guarantees that philosophical and operational regulatory problems will remain with us in the future.

The swings from regulation to reregulation to deregulation and back again ensure that the current situation will not remain stagnant. It might be said that the debate is between those who believe "that government is best which governs *least*" and those who believe "that government is best which governs *best*." At one time, both sides cited the public interest standard as backing their positions. Today, this standard is in eclipse and there appears to be little appeal in Washington of the idea that broadcasting is unique and important in our society and that it should be carefully nurtured—or restrained, if necessary.

In other words, since the early 1980s broadcasting has lost its once "special" status and has been lumped in with other electronic media as just more contenders for use of the electromagnetic spectrum. And this seems likely to continue until something changes the political system. The idea that the public interest standard (may the best—as far as the public interest is concerned—applicant win the channel) should be abandoned in licensing in favor of auctions (may the wealthiest applicant win) or even lotteries (may the luckiest applicant win) seems likely to hold sway for some time.

The continual application of ad hoc solutions to seemingly permanent problems has taken a toll. Because both industry and government understandably are looking out for themselves, the public interest suffers as a result. Concerted action by knowledgeable and impartial citizens could change this pattern but would require preparation, popular support, and funding. Past experience suggests that it would be desirable to have solid, impartial research and policy initiatives supported by funds generated outside of either bureaucratic or industry control—and an outlet to present these views to the public. The potential of such a "third force" in the electronic media is great, but its likelihood seems disappointingly small.

12.9 And if There Were *No* Broadcasting?

But what if radio and television broadcasting had never developed? How would life in this country differ? The answers to such questions suggest the dramatic impact of more than eight decades of American broadcasting.

▪ **The Sarnoff "Radio Music Box" Memo**   This is the frequently-reprinted 1920 version of a memorandum looking toward using radio telephony for broadcasting rather than point-to-point communication. written by David Sarnoff to his then-supervisor at the Marconi company, E. J. Nally, in 1916. The earlier version has been lost since the early 1920s. See pp. 46–47. (Courtesy of Louise Benjamin)

"...a plan of development which would make radio a 'household utility' in the same sense as the piano or phonograph. The idea is to bring music into the house by wireless. ....The problem of transmitting music has already been solved in principle and therefore all the receivers attuned to the transmitting wavelength should be capable of receiving such music. The receiver can be designed in the form of a simple 'Radio Music Box' and arranged for several different wavelengths, which should be changable with the throwing of a single switch or pressing of a single button. ....The box can be placed on table in the parlor or living room, the switch set accordingly and the transmitted music received. There should be no difficulty in receiving music perfectly when transmitted within a radius of 25 to 50 miles. ....The same principle can be extended to numerous other fields as, for example, receiving of lectures at home which can be made perfectly audible; also events of national importance can be simultaneously announced and received."

Whether 1XE went on the air before 8XK is unimportant—but how broadcasting has affected the people of the nation is vital knowledge.

Clearly, life without broadcasting would in some ways be a throwback to the days before 1920—but even without broadcasting the world would not have stood still, and we cannot look back nearly a century and say, "That's how it would be today, without broadcasting." We can only resort to a guessing game, a form of reverse futuristics, similar in some ways to taking the data in this book and extrapolating ahead to the last quarter of the 21st century and whatever the electronic media have evolved into.

12.9.1 Daily Life

Even the smallest unit of social life, the family, would offer a substantially different milieu in which to grow up. Without broadcasting's wider socializing effect, the family would have a far more important social role than it has today. Family members probably would fill their ever-longer hours of leisure with activities less passive than watching television—and might even do more things together. Our entertainment media would be very different: the film industry would be thriving, and newsreel theaters might be popular. Vaudeville would have remained both a major entertainment medium and a way for aspiring legitimate theater and motion picture performers to hone their acts and their abilities—which would have more than satisfied "father of radio" Lee de Forest, who reportedly argued against establishing networks in favor of a circuit of vaudeville performers moving on from station to station! Recreational reading of magazines and books of all types would be greater. Even with 21st-century transportation and the telephone, local communities would be more important. Home, school, church, and immediate neighborhood might play larger roles in the absence of pictures of the "greener grass" elsewhere. Our personal and collective identities would be with our community, city, state, or region rather than with the nation or world, which probably would have major consequences for the distribution and sale of retail goods, personal travel (would you wish to take a flight or an ocean voyage without modern electronic communication and navigation systems?), and international politics. Libraries would be more important, and education would concentrate more on improving literacy.

Without broadcast journalism's ability to tell us almost instantly what is happening anywhere at any time, we are left with newspapers or magazines (and motion picture newsreels) that take hours or days to publish admittedly more complete news, even when the event warrants speed. We would find it much harder to identify with happenings far away when the news doesn't reach us for such a long time. Lacking the cohesive effect of electronic media, regions of the country, let alone of the world, would be far more different from one another than are today. Fads and information on living and social styles would travel more slowly and penetrate less deeply when passed on only by print, film, and word of mouth. Even our language would be different, as there would be no broadcast media to help override regional dialects and usage. English might not be so dominant. Our knowledge of other areas would be limited to memories of personal travel or to images from the printed page, still photographs, and movies. Results of international diplomatic—and sports—meetings would take at least a day to reach us, and the sport would lose much of its thrill when reduced to print rather than conveyed live or on videotape by satellite. Familiar sports, as played by *local* teams rather than distant national leagues, would be preferred over accounts of exotic events (such as many of the Olympic games), that have to be seen to be understood. Indeed, without enormous payments for the rights to television coverage, sports organizations would be very unlike those of today.

12.9.2 Social Movements

In addition to a slowing down of new fashions and ideas, there would be substantial political and economic impacts from the absence of broadcasting. No longer could a political idea or a national leader mobilize or galvanize an entire populace—particularly persons who cannot or will not bother to read—in a day or two. The civil rights movements for minorities and women would have progressed much more slowly without constant broadcast news coverage, and incorporation of these themes into dramatic television offerings. If we had been engaged in wars in Vietnam or the Gulf without television, our views of them would probably have changed more slowly—if at all. The Soviet Union might have lasted longer. Without the necessity to cater to television's visual appeal, other presidents might have been elected (or Watergate more easily covered up). This alternative world would be unimaginably different.

12.9.3 Other Media/Other Regions

In the economic sphere, many products and services would suffer without broadcast advertising, since advertisers would be forced to use print or perhaps film for national advertising. On the other hand, like today, direct mail and point-of-purchase displays and billboards would receive the most advertising dollars. Naturally, the consumer electronics industry—and the related trade deficit with Asia—would be *much* smaller. Such general circulation magazines as *Life, Look,* and the *Saturday Evening Post*, all of which went out of business in the decades after television was introduced, still might be thriving as mass audience advertising vehicles, with circulations in the tens of millions. With these large circulations, advertisers probably would want to have more say about content in order to avoid offending potential consumers. Careers of show business personalities would rise and decline much more slowly. The recording industry would boom, although musical stars would develop more slowly than today's overnight sensations. Many performing arts groups would have larger live audiences than they now do.

Overseas, suspicions of a country's neighbors might be higher than today, with its worldwide boundary-crossing television and radio—or, since radio also is used for propaganda, the effect might be a wash. Economically, groupings of nations like the European Community would be much less likely. Language differences would be more important and harder to overcome. Human nature being the same the world over, the motion picture might be the only "universal" medium, as it was in the first decades after it was introduced.

But, of course, since radio and television (and the Internet) *were* successfully innovated, we need to look backward a bit in order to forecast the future intelligently. The coming of radio in the 1920s took the nation by storm and had substantial effects on print, film, and phonograph records—as well as on the family, economics, and politics. But, unlike the complete displacement of the horse and buggy by the automobile, some older media, particularly records, thrived on their own improving technology and lived in symbiosis with radio. Radio has taken over the role of the newspaper extra, but it is not suited to disseminate the comic strip or the political cartoon or to serve as a medium of record. When television arrived in the late 1940s and early 1950s, this dislocation was repeated. Radio, after less than 25 years, was virtually eclipsed as a national (but not as a local) medium. Television joyously took over radio's content, just as movies took over the content of the Broadway theater. The movie industry itself was shattered for decades, expanding output in the 1980s only because of demand from cable, VCRs—and a new young audience for "blockbuster" films. But, radio did not *eliminate* recordings or movies, and television did not *eliminate* radio—so it is probable that the Internet will incorporate some of the content of older media, and not replace them.

12.9.4 Summing Up

For nearly half a century, television has been the dominant mass medium in the United States, with other media scrambling for significant and profitable niches. It has carried an increasing proportion of national advertising and has given a majority of citizens most of their news. The motion picture industry primarily is its handmaiden, while the newsreel and the national weekly picture magazine have disappeared entirely. Minor league sports have all but disappeared in the face of major league television coverage; although many new teams and leagues have been established solely because of expected television income.

But broadcasting and other electronic media are more than mere economic institutions. They have given us moments of laughter and high and low drama—including wars, and the death, resignation and impeachment of Presidents—and have extended our eyes and ears to the entire world and even to the Moon . . . and Mars. They have brought us closer together. Except for the dwindling few born before 1920, we have all known radio all of our lives. Those born since 1950 have grown up with television—their "local" community is defined by it in many cases—and they will spend more time with television than with almost any other activity. They make up the first television generations. Those born since 1970 missed the exciting growth of the early years, and by not remembering anything different and accepting television as it is, they unfortunately may be unaware of much possibility for improvement. Those born since 1980 are the computer generation, one fully used to two very different screens and the ability to get information (and entertainment) from the Internet on demand, and who consider scores of television channels their birthright.

The violence and sex, beauty and laughter, emotion and reason provided by society's ambiguous mirror, which both reflects and projects, have affected and will affect them. They, in turn, will change American society, including, in full circle, the electronic media. While the impact of broadcasting may not always have been beneficial, it has been deep. To understand what has been heard and seen over radio and television during the past four fifths of a century is to understand American life better. As for the future—

Stay tuned . . .

APPENDIX A
A SHORT CHRONOLOGY OF AMERICAN BROADCASTING

This *very* selective chronology of highlights is divided into periods paralleling the chapters in the text and is restricted to what we feel are the most important events of each year. In periods of consolidation or evolution, such as the 1990s, there are relatively fewer "events." The material has been gathered and condensed from (see bibliography for full citations) Barnouw (1966, 1968, 1970, 1990), *Broadcasting* (1970, 1976), Dunlap (1951), Head (1976), Kempner (1948), and several unpublished sources of which the most useful was L. W. Lichty's "A Chronology of American Television to 1966" (unpublished).

The Prehistory of Broadcasting (to 1919)

1725 Gray (England) discovers the principle of conduction by observing electricity carried several hundred feet through a hemp thread.

1753 An anonymous published letter (England) suggests wired communication with a wire connection for each letter of the alphabet.

1794 Chappé (France) devises optical/mechanical telegraph system using signals on towers between major French cities.

1832 Morse (United States) develops basic sense of what will become his electrical telegraph system and code.

1840 Morse receives telegraph patent applied for in 1837.

1843 Bain (Scotland) devises basic principles of transmitting pictures (later known as *facsimile*), much of it applicable later to television.

1844 First telegraph circuit, between Washington and Baltimore, is officially opened with message "What Hath God Wrought?"

1858 First underwater telegraph cable is laid across the Atlantic but works for only a few months.

1861 Coast-to-coast telegraph lines put 18-month-old Pony Express out of business.

1862 Caselli (France) transmits a crude image by wire between two towns.

1864 Clerk Maxwell (Scotland) theorizes existence of electromagnetic waves.

1865 International Telegraph (later Telecommunication) Union is founded.

1866 Atlantic cable is successful on third major attempt. • Loomis (United States) conducts wireless telegraph experiments in Virginia and sends signals about 15 miles.

1872 Loomis acquires world's first patent on a wireless system but fails to commercialize it for lack of funds.

1873 May (England) discovers that selenium can produce electricity in direct relation to amount of light received.

1876 Bell (United States) applies for patent on telephone device, then demonstrates same at Philadelphia Centennial Exposition.

1877 Edison (United States) succeeds in first audible reproduction of recorded sound—basis of phonograph and subsequent recording methods. • Carey (United States) proposes bank of selenium cells, each with wire conductor to similarly arranged bank of lights on reception end, for crude means of picture transmission.

1880 Leblanc (France) suggests the principle of scanning to allow faster transmission of pictures using only one wire.

1884 Nipkow (Germany) patents the scanning disc with spiral of holes with which to scan and later reproduce pictures.

1885 American Telephone and Telegraph (AT&T) is formed from several earlier phone companies.

1887 Hertz (Germany) proves Clerk Maxwell theories in series of laboratory experiments.

1888 First photocell is developed, later of great importance to television.

1892 Stubblefield demonstrates his wireless telephone system.

1894 Jenkins (United States) begins theorizing about television system using mosaic system. • Lodge (England) introduces and improves Branly (France) coherer as a wireless detector. It becomes the standard for two decades.

1895 Marconi (Italy) sends wireless telegraph messages approximately a mile on his father's estate during initial experiments.

1896 Marconi arrives in England, demonstrates his improved system, and leads in formation of what will become in 1900 the "British Marconi" firm.

1897 Braun (Germany) develops cathode-ray oscilloscope as crude electronic display tube.

1899 Marconi sends wireless signal across English Channel. British and American navies experiment with several wireless systems. • American Marconi, British-controlled subsidiary of main firm, is founded. • Wireless calls for aid bring about first rescues of crew and passengers from vessels in distress in European coastal waters.

1901 Marconi and aides send Morse code letter *S* across the Atlantic Ocean, demonstrating potential for long-range communication applications of wireless.

1903   Berlin is site of first international radio conference, which proposes greater cooperation in ship-to-shore communication.

1904   United Fruit Company begins to build its network of radio stations in Central America and Caribbean countries to coordinate banana shipping. • Fleming (England) patents two-element vacuum tube, or valve.

1906   Fessenden (United States) transmits voice and music program from transmitter at Brant Rock, Massachusetts. • De Forest (United States) develops three-element tube, called triode or Audion. • Pickard and Dunwoody (United States), among others, develop crystal detector—first inexpensive and easily duplicated detecting device. • Berlin is site of second international radio conference, which adopts "SOS" emergency call and demands all companies and ships equipped with apparatus from various manufacturers to communicate with one another in emergencies.

1907   Rosing (Russia) receives a faint television signal by using Braun tube and adding photocells.

1908   Campbell Swinton (England) suggests a completely electronic system of television.

1909   Herrold begins broadcasts from San Jose, California, and schedules them regularly shortly thereafter.

1910   First United States radio law, Wireless Ship Act of 1910, calls for radio and operator on all oceangoing passenger vessels.

1912   *Titanic* disaster dramatically shows value of wireless as 700 of 2,200 persons are saved after midatlantic iceberg collision. • Second United States Wireless Ship Act requires two radio operators on all vessels at sea. A month later, Radio Act of 1912 provides first regulations for land radio stations and amateur operators. • De Forest discovers amplification potential of triode, which leads to AT&T purchase of telephone rights to three-element tube.

1915   Coast-to-coast telephone service established. • American Radio Relay League set up as association of amateur operators. • General Electric and British Marconi tentatively agree that GE will sell Alexanderson alternators exclusively to Marconi.

1916   De Forest broadcasts presidential election returns in Wilson-Hughes race. • Sarnoff files "radio music box" memo with officials of American Marconi, who are interested only in international and ship radio for private messages.

1917   United States enters World War I. The navy takes over radio transmitters—especially the Alexanderson alternators, the only reliable long-distance wireless transmitters—for the duration, or closes down facilities; establishes system until 1920 of indemnifying companies for patent infringement—essentially a patents pool—so that best equipment can be made for wartime use.

The Beginnings of Broadcasting (1919–1926)

1919   Navy continues control of radio facilities after war as battle rages over government's role in future of wireless; Congress holds hearings (May–June). • British Marconi resumes negotiations with GE for alternator, still demanding monopoly rights, but after Navy intervention, GE forms RCA to safeguard American radio interests. RCA acquires rights to alternator (October) and assets of American Marconi, and enters into first patent cross-license agreement with GE (November).

1920   President Wilson orders Navy to relinquish control of amateur and all other nongovernment radio facilities (March). • AT&T joins RCA-GE cross-licensing agreement in step leading to postwar civilian-controlled patents pool (July). • To outflank position of RCA, Westinghouse purchases two key receiver patents from Armstrong (October). • To encourage sales of radio receivers, Westinghouse establishes KDKA in East Pittsburgh, based on experimental station 8XK run by their engineer Frank Conrad. Initial KDKA broadcast is of Harding-Cox presidential election returns (November).

1921   Westinghouse attempt to compete in international radio collapses as RCA has tied up most foreign contacts. Westinghouse joins RCA patents pool, splitting receiver manufacturing rights with GE 60-40. United Fruit also joins pool (June). • Thirty broadcasting stations go on the air, including six owned by Westinghouse and others operated by GE and RCA. Only two frequencies (channels) are in use for broadcasting.

1922   Hoover hosts first radio conference in Washington, which calls for government regulation of radio technology, limited advertising, and classes of stations based on kind of service (February). • With hundreds of new stations, Hoover adds new frequency for stations of higher power and high quality programming. First use of four-letter station calls (August). • AT&T enters broadcasting, seeing it as extension of toll telephone operation. First paid-for commercial announcement on WEAF (August).

1923   Jenkins transmits unmoving facsimile silhouettes from Washington to Philadelphia by wireless (March). • Zworykin (United States) patents iconoscope camera tube, key to an electronic television system. • Second radio conference reiterates suggestions of the first and calls for temporary licensing guidelines until Congress will act (March). • Planning meeting in Chicago leads to formation of National Association of Broadcasters, to fight ASCAP demand for payment from radio stations for all music used on the air and to seek government technical regulation. • Hoover announces three classes of stations and assigns greatly increased frequency spectrum, about two thirds of current AM band, to two of them (June). • RCA enters broadcasting by taking over programming of Westinghouse's New York outlet and building a station in Washington and another in New York. The New York stations, WJY and WJZ, become major competition for AT&T's WEAF. • First multiple station hookup combines WEAF (New York), WGY

(Schenectady), KDKA (Pittsburgh), and KYW (Chicago) (June). First lasting hookup between WEAF and Massachusetts station comes a month later. • Federal Trade Commission report, aimed mainly at RCA, criticizes monopoly in radio equipment and patents (December).

1924 First coast-to-coast radio program demonstrates use of telephoneline circuits and lays groundwork for planned national AT&T network, using WEAF as originating station (February). • Third and largest radio conference in Washington calls for broadcasting use of entire 550–1,500 kHz band and urges research into monopoly and station interconnection (October). • Competition between Telephone Group (WEAF and allied companies and stations) and Radio Group (RCA, GE, Westinghouse, and others and their stations) affects decisions on programming, station interconnection, patents, and equipment manufacture.

1925 Baird (England) gives public demonstration of mechanical (Nipkow disc) system of television by transmitting silhouettes (April). • Jenkins (United States) sends first filmed (moving) images by wireless using mechanical television system (June). • Fourth and last radio conference in Washington agrees that limit on number of stations may be required, radio is not a public utility, and limited advertising is acceptable (November).

1926 *Zenith* case shows limits of 1912 act when federal court holds Secretary of Commerce cannot prevent firm from changing station frequency, thus wiping out Hoover's voluntary regulatory scheme. U.S. Attorney General releases opinion that Secretary of Commerce can only process license applications and not regulate them. With all controls ended, licensing of 200 new stations adds to interference chaos on the air (Fall).

The Coming of Commercialism (1926–1933)

1926 Internal strife within industry is resolved as Telephone and Radio groups sign three-part agreement including provision that AT&T will exit business of broadcasting station operations (July). • RCA forms National Broadcasting Company (NBC) (September). NBC purchases WEAF from AT&T for $1 million and begins regular broadcasting on NBC-Red, based on old AT&T chain of stations (November).

1927 NBC-Blue network, based on New York's WJZ, begins operations with 1927 Rose Bowl broadcast (January). • President Coolidge signs Radio Act of 1927, which creates Federal Radio Commission (FRC) (February). • New FRC orders stations back to frequencies assigned by Hoover and sets broadcast band at 550–1,500 kHz (April). • Columbia Broadcasting System (CBS) goes on the air with 16 stations for a long and shaky start-up period (September). • Ives (United States) transmits both still and moving pictures, as well as synchronized sound by wire. • Farnsworth (United States) transmits first electronic television pictures. • Millions listened to radio coverage of Lindbergh solo transatlantic flight (May).

1928   Baird transmits television picture across the Atlantic and later demonstrates mechanical color television. • Zworykin develops and patents a much-improved iconoscope tube. • The FRC allocates several 10 kHz channels in the standard (AM) band for television. • Congress passes Davis Amendment to Radio Act, which calls for equality of radio service in five regions in the country (March). • Radio generally is becoming accepted as advertising medium, though it carries only 2 percent of all advertising this year. • FRC announces plan to allocate clear, regional, and local AM channels (August). • Paley buys control of CBS; is named president in early 1929. • NBC begins fulltime (but not 24-hour) coast-to-coast operation.

1929   In the *Great Lakes* case, the FRC analyzes what the public interest means for a broadcasting station. • National Association of Broadcasters issues a code of radio advertising and programming ethics (April). • Crossley's Cooperative Analysis of Broadcasting offers first system of network program ratings. • FRC becomes permanent body after several short-term extensions (December).

1930   Formation of conflicting National Advisory Council on Radio in Education and National Committee on Education by Radio. • Lowell Thomas begins national daily newscast, on NBC-Blue (and broadcasts regularly until May 1976). • RCA takes over GE and Westinghouse research efforts in television as part of the reorganization of roles of each firm following antitrust action.

1931   Court upholds FRC denial of license renewal to Brinkley's KFKB because of past programming and personal attacks on the air (February). Appeals court dismisses appeal of FRC denial of Schaeffer license because of profanity uttered by candidate for public office; saying licensee is responsible (March). FRC rescinds license of Baker's KTNT in Iowa for personal attacks and other program matters (June) and of Shuler's Los Angeles station for personal attacks (November). The latter decision is later upheld as not being improper government censorship. These four cases help solidify the FRC's right to examine programming for public interest. • Metropolitan Opera Broadcasts begin with Milton Cross as announcer (until his death in 1974).

1932   Radio reports the Lindbergh kidnaping, one of first tragedies covered on the air (March). • University of Iowa begins scheduled educational broadcasting with mechanical television (the station staying on the air to 1939). RCA initiates 120-line electronic television field testing. • GE and Westinghouse end long legal wrangle with agreement to sell all RCA stock; RCA, now fully independent, competes with former owners (November).

1933   First of President Roosevelt's famous "Fireside Chats" (March). • As newspaper-radio tensions rise, Associated Press limits sale of news to local stations. CBS gathers network news on its own (April). • Biltmore Agreement between networks and news agencies eliminates independent radio reporting by networks (December). • RCA initiates use of Zworykin's iconoscope-kinescope combination and raises picture definition to 240 lines.

• Armstrong receives the four key patents to new FM radio system (December).

Radio's Golden Age (1934–1941)

1934 Three independent organizations are established to gather and sell news for radio in fight against Biltmore Agreement (March). • Station WLW begins experimentation with 500,000 watts (until mid-1939) (May). • Roosevelt signs Communications Act of 1934 replacing FRC with Federal Communications Commission (June). • A new network, first called Quality and then Mutual, is started by owner and joint operator stations WOR, WGN, WLW, and WXYZ (September).

1935 RCA and Armstrong end cooperation over FM radio. Armstrong announces his FM system, and RCA achieves 343-line interlaced television scanning and announces million-dollar television research program (May). Armstrong demonstrates his FM system (November). • United Press and International News Service agree to sell news to radio stations and networks, marking effective end of Biltmore Agreement (May).

1936 Congress repeals Davis Amendment requiring equal radio service in five zones, thereby allowing for more stations and greater power in areas of high population (June). • FCC holds engineering conference and hearings on future of FM and television (June). • BBC (England) initiates regular television broadcasts comparing Baird mechanical with EMI-Marconi electronic systems (November). • New York to Philadelphia coaxial cable is tested (December).

1937 American Federation of Radio Artists (originally "Artistes"), a union for announcers and performers (later known as AFTRA), is formed (July). • In wake of chaotic Hauptmann (Lindbergh kidnaping) trial, American Bar Association adopts Canon 35, banning radio, recordings, and photography in courtrooms (September). • FCC allocates 19 channels for experimental television (October), and Philco demonstrates 441-line television pictures.

1938 FCC makes first educational allocation in broadcasting, 25 channels in 40-MHz band (January). • First FM station, Armstrong's W2XMN in New Jersey, goes on the air (April). • Wheeler-Lea Act gives Federal Trade Commission right to curb false and misleading advertising (April). • Radio's reporting of month-long Munich crisis is first major use of shortwave for live coverage of international event (September). • Orson Welles's production of *War of the Worlds*, the most famous single radio broadcast, scares many listeners (October).

1939 Associated Press begins to supply news without charge for sustaining programs on NBC (February) and later begins to sell news (June), thus finally ending the Press-Radio war. • FCC issues a memorandum on 14 types of objectionable programming (March). • Unable to buy his patents, RCA signs television patent license agreement with Farnsworth. NBC starts regular television programming with opening of New York World's Fair (April). • New NAB code goes into effect: disallows liquor advertising or paid controversial ads, and limits all advertising to 10 percent of each hour (July). • Facing rising pressure from ASCAP for higher royalties, NAB establishes its own music licensing organization, Broadcast Music, Incorporated (BMI) (September). • BBC suspends television operations for the duration of World War II (September).

1940 FCC gives go-ahead for limited commercial television as of September, using 441-line standard (February), but rescinds order after RCA pushes receiver sales against FCC desires and understandings (March). • Radio correspondents provide regular reports from Europe at war, especially eye-witness accounts from Murrow in London, Shirer in Berlin and France. • CBS demonstrates its color television system—a mixture of electronic and mechanical methods (August). • Justice Department prepares antitrust action against ASCAP, BMI, and radio networks for music monopoly (December); settled by consent degree in February 1941.

1941 Commercial FM radio operations are authorized (January). • FCC issues *Mayflower* decision, which is understood to eliminate licensee editorializing (January). • Nearly all stations change frequencies, many only slightly, as the North American Regional Broadcasting Agreement (NARBA) goes into effect between the United States, Canada, Mexico, and Cuba (March). • FCC issues *Chain Broadcasting Report* with eight important recommendations; most upsetting to the industry is requirement that NBC give up either Red or Blue network (May). • FCC approves commercial television with 525-line standard and FM sound—effective July 1. CBS and NBC stations operate stations by the first day. • FCC begins two and one-half year investigation of press ownership of radio stations (August).

Radio Goes to War (1941–1945)

1941 Largest radio audience to date, estimated at 90 million, hears Roosevelt declare war. Amateur stations are closed down, and weather forecasts are limited for the duration (December).

1942 Wartime code bans man-on-the-street and ad-lib interviews, and most quiz shows (January). FCC bans construction of new broadcasting stations in areas with primary (local) service (February) and freezes all station construction except for operations underway, to conserve war material. Receiver production is ended, and shellac, used in records, is sharply limited for civilian use (April). • President Roosevelt creates Office of War Information (OWI) and names newsman Elmer Davis to head it (June). • American Federation of Musicians, under new president Petrillo, announces no musicians will play for recording sessions—beginning of a long strike (August).

1943 Supreme Court upholds FCC's chain broadcasting regulations, forcing NBC to shed one network, forbidding exclusivity, and curtailing option time (May). • Congressman Cox begins lengthy House investigation of the FCC (June). • E. J. Noble purchases the Blue network from RCA for $8,000,000, and the FCC approves the transfer (October).

1944 FCC ends newspaper-broadcasting ownership investigation without drawing up new rules (January). • Networks allow FM stations to carry AM programs without extra charge to sponsors (January). • FCC holds major allocations hearings on spectrum above 30 MHz, concerned especially with future of FM and television (September–November). • Networks sign with Petrillo's AFM, on his terms, after an appeal from President Roosevelt fails to end strike. Two-and-a-half-year-old recording ban is ended (November).

1945 Blue Network becomes American Broadcasting Company (April). • FCC delivers television allocation of 13 VHF channels (May) and FM service is moved up to 88–108 MHz band (June). • The war ends, and the FCC begins to process backed-up station applications; receiver production is resumed; OWI is abolished (August); amateur bands are released to civilians (November).

Era of Great Change (1945–1952)

1946 FCC's "Blue Book" makes strongest statement yet on licensee's responsibility in public service programming (March). • BBC reestablishes television broadcasting with 405-line prewar standards (June). • RCA publicly demonstrates all-electronic system of color television (November).

1947 Strong anticommunist attacks on broadcasting include *Counterattack* newsletter and early blacklisting. • Zenith announces Phone-vision system of pay-TV by wire, setting off two decades of experimentation and intense debate (July). • Over a period of several months, interconnection of television stations by both microwave and coaxial cable develops, connecting stations in both the East and Midwest (late 1947 through Spring 1948).

1948 AFM lifts ban (begun in late 1945) on musicians playing for television or on AM-FM simulcast programs (March). • Broadcast and nonbroadcast sharing of television channels is eliminated, but channel 1 deleted for other uses (May). • Scientists at Bell Telephone Labs demonstrate transistor (June). • NBC and CBS announce plans for major television network expansion by 1950. First ABC television station goes on air in New York (August). Midwestern AT&T coaxial cable network opens, linking existing stations from St. Louis to Buffalo (September). • After hearings on allocations (June–September), FCC orders Freeze on stations license applications for television, while it attempts to solve problems of interference and sufficient spectrum space (September).

1949 Eastern and midwestern television networks are connected, linking 32 stations in 14 cities. First televising of presidential inaugural (January). • FCC releases report which allows stations to take editorial positions if they treat opposing views fairly—later seen as birth of Fairness Doctrine (June). • FCC disallows (after October 1) certain giveaway shows with jackpots as violations of the U.S. Criminal Code prohibition on lotteries. • FCC begins television hearings, initially concentrating on choice of color system (September).

1950 FCC allows Zenith to test Phonevision for 90 days in Chicago (February). • Editors of *Counterattack* issue *Red Channels*, which causes more blacklisting in radio and television (June). • Korean War leads to restrictions on civilian construction, including radio and television sets, although reduced production continues. • FCC approves CBS mechanical-electronic color system (October).

1951 Televised sessions of hearings on crime by Senate committee catapult Tennessee's Senator Kefauver into prominence (January). • ABC and United Paramount Theaters merge, with UPT's Leonard Goldenson becoming top man at network (April). • First coast-to-coast live television broadcast features President Truman's address to Japanese peace treaty conference in San Francisco, uses AT&T microwave facilities that cost $40,000,000 to build (September). • Manufacture of color television equipment is stopped for duration of Korean War (October).

1952 NBC begins the *Today* show (January). FCC issues *Sixth Report and Order* on television allocation, ending Freeze and opening UHF band to television broadcasting (April). • First major amendments to Communications Act of 1934 become law; allow FCC to issue cease and desist orders as well as revoke licenses; require lower time charges for political ads (July). • First commercial UHF station takes to the air in Oregon (September). • Bing Crosby Enterprises demonstrates magnetic videotape recording machines to replace kinescopes (films) previously used to record television programs (December).

The Age of Television (1952–1960)

1953 After two-year legal wrangle, required because station licenses were involved, FCC approves merger of UPT and ABC (January). • RCA and then NTSC ask FCC to adopt RCA compatible system of electronic color; and even CBS announces it will telecast with the system in the fall (June–July); FCC approves (December). • Armstrong demonstrates multiplexing system for FM—the basis of later storecasting and stereo operations (October). • FCC extends license period of television stations from one to three years, and limits ownership of stations for single owner to five television (later extended to seven with addition of two UHF), seven AM, and seven FM stations (November).

1954 ABC and Disney studios sign a long-term contract, which generates the famous *Disneyland* and greatly strengthens ABC's competitive position (April). • Weeks of televised Army-McCarthy hearings mark the beginning of the downfall of Senator Joseph McCarthy.

1955 President Eisenhower opens news conference to first television newsfilm coverage, with films shown later after both White House approval and editing (January). • House and Senate Commerce committees issue reports critical of network monopolies, calling for major changes in regulation (February). • FCC authorizes Subsidiary Communications Authorizations (SCAs) for FM stations to transmit music into stores and other business places, providing badly needed source of FM station income (March). • NBC announces *Monitor* weekend radio network program, which lasts into 1975. • DuMont television network switches over to film presentations with live coverage only for special events and sports. Network disappears altogether in September. • First major congressional investigation of television effects on juvenile delinquency ends, calling for FCC program censorship, stronger NAB code, and other changes (August). • Commercial television starts in England (September).

1956 Major film companies sell rights to "post-'48" films for television showing (January). • Ampex demonstrates successful black-and-white videotape recorder (April).

1957 Major test of pay-TV begins in Bartlesville, Oklahoma (September). • FCC study of television network development and practices recommends more than 30 rules changes (October).

1958 FCC Commissioner Mack resigns for accepting bribes to vote for station applicant in the Miami channel 10 case (March). • FCC decides that regulation of cable television is beyond its authority because that service is not broadcasting (April). • United Press and International News Service merge to form UPI. (June). • Rumors of television quiz show rigging turn out to be true—programs are taken off the air, and investigation begins in New York (summer).

1959 In amending Section 315 of 1934 Act, exempting newscasts from equal opportunity for political candidate roles, Congress appears to give statutory backing to Fairness Doctrine. • Mutual network undergoes several changes of control to reduce financial pressures. • At congressional hearings, former quiz show contestants admit complicity in rigging process (October–November). To improve its image, industry forms Television Information Office, surveys audience reaction to the quiz and other scandals; networks promise more prime-time news programming.

1960 Attorney General Rogers says FCC and FTC have power to regulate payola and plugola problems, as well as quiz show rigging (January). • FCC Chairman Doerfer resigns under fire for failing to maintain arms-length distance from broadcasters he is regulating (March). • Daytime serials and most other radio network entertainment programming ends, leaving news and special events coverage. • In first basic programming statement since 1946 "Blue Book," FCC outlines the responsibilities of licensees in public interest programming. • Congress suspends Section 315 for the 1960 election of national officials, paving way for four televised "Great Debates" between Nixon and Kennedy. Those debates, especially first one, probably change course of election. • Program of airborne television transmission for educational use in the Midwest (MPATI) begins after 15 years of plans and experiments (December).

Accommodation and Adjustment (1961–1977)

1961   Newton Minow is named FCC chairman by President Kennedy (January). He sets tone for commission by depicting television as a "vast wasteland" at NAB meeting (May). • First presidential news conference covered live by radio and television (January). • Edward R. Murrow leaves CBS to head USIA (January). • FCC approves standards for FM stereo broadcasting (April), and stations begin using new means of transmission (June). • First man-in-space television special coverage is for suborbital flight of Alan Shepard (May). • FCC ends a 16-year controversy by breaking down 13 of 25 Class I-A (clear channel) frequencies to allow more local AM stations (September).

1962   John Henry Faulk wins libel judgment of $3.5 million, helping to end blacklisting era (June). • Government begins financial grants to help support construction and facilities of educational television stations. • Telstar, first means of relaying television signals by space satellite, is launched into orbit for AT&T by NASA (July). • Comsat, the Communications Satellite Corporation, is formed after long congressional hearings (September). • Legislation is passed calling for all new television sets by early 1964 to have UHF reception capability (September).

1963   CBS and NBC begin half-hour evening newscasts, up from 15-minute length (September). • Television covers four days following assassination of President Kennedy (November).

1964   Release of Surgeon General's report on dangers of smoking increases pressures for cigarette advertising limitation (January). • Supreme Court, in *New York Times* v. *Sullivan* case, makes conviction for libel unlikely in reporting of public officials' duties and character (March). • Networks and wire services set up election reporting service to pool results in upcoming fall election (June). Previous election campaign had brought complaints over television ads. • Subscription Television begins to provide pay-TV to homes in California cities (July), but referendum—later held to have been unconstitutional—rejects STV, and forces system to close down (November).

1965 First commercial synchronous communications satellite, Early Bird, goes into orbit and allows constant Europe-to-United States television (April).

1966 FCC takes over regulation of cable systems, calling for carriage of all local signals, same-day nonduplication, limited distant signal importation (February). • Television coverage of Vietnam War expands as fighting increases and United States becomes increasingly embroiled. • Court of Appeals for the District of Columbia says in WLBT case that audiences of stations have a right to be heard in FCC legal proceedings (March). ABC applies to FCC for permission to merge with ITT (April), FCC twice approves on split votes, but Justice Department pressure kills merger at end of 1967. • Overmyer Network is announced as a fourth commercial chain of television stations, claiming 85 stations to take a two-hour nightly feed from Las Vegas (October).

1967 Thanks to Ford Foundation grant, NET offers first coast-to-coast network interconnected educational telecasts (January). That same month, Carnegie Commission report offers many recommendations, helping to start era of *public* television and radio. • Overmyer (now named United) Network goes on the air (May) but soon stops operations due to lack of funds (June). • FCC, in first commercial application of Fairness Doctrine, announces that anti-smoking spots are needed to balance cigarette ads (June). • ABC announces (August) and gets FCC approval for (September) plan for four radio networks operating on a single telephone interconnection line, each network to cater to a different type of radio program format. • Corporation for Public Broadcasting is created by Public Broadcasting Act of 1967, based on Carnegie Commission recommendations (November).

1968 ABC splits radio operation into four separate networks (January). • Heavy coverage of aftermath of Martin Luther King, Jr., assassination shows major riots in some cities, helps to prevent others (April). Two months later television covers shooting and funeral of Senator Robert Kennedy (June). • Supreme Court, in *Southwestern Cable Co.* case, upholds FCC regulatory authority over all cable television systems (June). • Television networks receive many complaints over coverage of violence in Chicago streets during Democratic convention (August). • President's Commission on Communication Policy issues report, sees cable supplementing broadcasting services (December).

1969 FCC resolves long-controversial status of channel 5 in Boston by lifting license from *Herald-Traveler* newspaper and awarding it to local group with no other media holdings (January). • Senator Pastore requests Surgeon General to investigate effects of television violence on viewers, especially children (March). • Public Broadcasting Service is formed to operate public television station interconnection (April). • In *Red Lion* decision, Supreme Court upholds FCC's Fairness Doctrine noting that needs and rights of viewers to diversity of views are more important than rights of broadcasters (June). • Apollo 11 mission puts man on the moon, and television takes the story around the world, with live television from surface of moon (July). • FCC requires program origination by cable systems with more than 3,500 subscribers, but rule not effectively enforced (October). • *Sesame Street*, product of Children's Television Workshop, begins daily telecasts on public television stations and quickly wins critical and children's acclaim. • In speech at Des Moines, Iowa, Vice President Agnew attacks television news and its perceived bias. This marks beginning of Nixon administration's antimedia campaign (November).

1970   FCC adopts rule to disallow AM-FM-TV or radio-television station ownership combinations in the same market in the future, while grandfathering (allowing to stand) existing combinations (March). • FCC limits network prime-time television programming to three hours a night—the Prime Time Access Rule, or PTAR—and effectively eliminates network control of syndicated programming (May). • Television UHF channels 70–83 inclusive reallocated to nonbroadcast (mostly land mobile) uses (May). • President Nixon names Clay Whitehead as first director of new Office of Telecommunications Policy (June).

1971   Ban on radio-television advertising of cigarettes begins after Congress passes restrictive legislation (January). • *Selling of the Pentagon* documentary on CBS creates wrangle between Congress and networks, and near contempt citation for CBS' Stanton, over television documentary and general news methods (January). • FCC releases rules for license applicants to follow, defining community ascertainment process (March)—seen by some as expanding "public access" movement in broadcasting, now five years old.

1972   Surgeon General's committee report on children and television viewing suggests there may be a causal relationship between video violence and some children's subsequent actions (January). • FCC issues definitive rules for cable television, allowing but restricting scope of cable in top 100 markets (February). • Justice Department files antitrust suit against three television networks, charging excessive control of programming and advertising (April). • Administration-sponsored reorganization of public broadcasting begins, stressing local stations rather than national service—partly as a result of President Nixon's dislike of independent public affairs programming on PBS.

1973   FCC begins "re-regulation," or lessening of some administrative requirements, mainly for local radio stations. • Supreme Court rules, in BEM and DNC cases, that broadcasters are not required to sell time for editorial advertisements—a setback for advocates of greater media access (May). • Senate (Ervin) Watergate Committee hearings are carried on television for several weeks and help focus national attention on the scandal (spring and summer).

1974   Westar, first U.S. domestic communications satellite, is launched. • Television covers impeachment hearings against Nixon in first video coverage of House (July). Television covers the last days of Nixon administration, including first presidential resignation speech (August).

1975   FCC adopts rule restricting future newspaper ownership of local market radio stations (January). Expansion of Citizens Band radio begins to create administrative headache for FCC and interference in other services, including broadcasting. Electronic newsgathering—ENG, or use of videotape and live portable television cameras rather than film—expands rapidly among local stations. • Beginning of substantial pay-cable television operations, including Home Box Office (HBO). • NBC radio network drops *Monitor* and other programs and begins first national full-time radio news service (June). • FCC interprets Section 315 to add more exemptions (September). • RCA Chairman Robert Sarnoff, son of David Sarnoff, is forced to resign by board of directors because of RCA's financial performance (November).

1976   After nearly two decades of discussion, Congress passes a new copyright law to replace the 1909 act. Among many other things, it requires cable operators carrying distant signals to pay fees to broadcasters (October). • For the first time since 1960, presidential candidates "debate" one another (October). • In a sudden move, CBS fires Arthur Taylor as president, naming John Backe as successor and likely eventual replacement for network founder William Paley, who announces his own plans to step down early in 1977 (October). • Federal judge in Los Angeles finds "Family Viewing Time" standard of networks and the National Association of Broadcasters TV Code to be illegal, partially because of findings of undue FCC pressure on the industry to adopt this self-regulation move. Decision places effect and impact of entire NAB radio and television code structure in doubt (November). • House Communications Subcommittee announces plans for total revision of the Communications Act of 1934 (December).

Challenge and Competition (1977–1988)

1977   Alex Haley's *Roots* is serialized in ABC miniseries with huge audience and great impact (January). • NBC ends experiment with an all-news radio network service as too few stations affiliate (May). • Congress begins an unsuccessful five-year effort to rewrite the Communications Act (May). • The first two STV (over-the-air pay-TV) stations air. • OTP is disbanded, with most functions going to the Department of Commerce (October). • "Qube" interactive cable experiment begins (it will end in 1984) in Columbus, Ohio (December).

1978   New copyright law, the first complete revision since 1909, goes into effect (January). • Showtime begins satellite distribution and becomes HBO's chief rival (March). • FCC approves distress sale and tax certificate policies to increase minority station ownership (May). • First of "rewrites" of 1934 act introduced in House (June). • Second Supreme Court *Pacifica* decision upholds FCC concern over indecent and obscene programming (June). • Magnavox markets first videodiscs.

1979 "Carnegie II" report urges vast infusion of federal funds into public broadcasting (January). • House of Representatives sessions are regularly shown by C-SPAN (March). • First station is transferred to a minority group under "distress sale" policy of FCC (April). • FTC staff recommends elimination of advertising on children's television while an FCC task force calls for enforcement of program quotas for young children's fare (November). • FM surpasses AM in size of total national radio audience.

1980 NBC and ABC begin to offer closed captions for the deaf on some programs (March). • Cable News Network (CNN) begins 24-hour news service (June). • FCC drops most of its remaining cable television rules (July). • Third FCC broadcast network inquiry completed (December). • COMSAT announces extensive DBS plans, beginning two-year push for authorization (December). • "Premiere" pay-cable network stopped by Justice Department's antitrust action (December).

1981 Complicated news day as Ronald Reagan is sworn in as President and U.S. embassy hostages return from Iran (January). • HDTV is first demonstrated in the United States. • FCC begins a "freeze" on new LPTV applications (April). • Mark Fowler becomes chairman of FCC and implements strong deregulation policy (May). • Radio licenses extended to seven years, television to five in congressional budget bill (August).

1982 Radio deregulation drops several rules for commercial stations (March). • FCC formally approves new low-power television service rules (March). • NAB drops its self-regulatory codes in a consent decree with the Justice Department (March). • Ten-year review of television violence studies released by the National Institute of Mental Health finds clear connection between what is viewed and subsequent actions.

1983 Final episode of *M*A*S*H* is most-watched program in television history (February). • FCC is changed from permanent agency to one requiring reauthorization every two years. • NPR experiences financial crisis due to overexpansion and loose management. • FCC creates MMDS or "wireless cable" service (May). • Compact discs first introduced to consumer market.

1984 Supreme Court issues "Betamax" decision allowing home taping of off-air signals (January). • As part of its settlement of a government antitrust suit, AT&T divests its local operating companies (January). • Congress passes Cable Communications Policy Act. • Radio deregulation is expanded to cover television and public broadcasting (July). • United Satellite Communications, Inc. begins brief DBS operation using a Canadian satellite but closes up early in 1985. • RCA pulls out of videodisc market after a half-billion-dollar loss. • National candidates debate election issues on television (September–October).

1985 Seventeen-hour-long "Live Aid" concert is broadcast by satellite from Philadelphia and London to 100 countries in famine fund-raiser (July). • Home Shopping Network begins national service–first of a host of competing services (July). • Capital Cities announces it will buy ABC network for $3.5 billion to create Capital Cities/ABC—first network to change hands since 1953 (November). • First pay-per-view cable services air (November). • GE announces plans to take over RCA and its NBC networks (December). • NBC is first of commercial television networks to begin using satellite rather than land-line distribution. • FCC increases number of stations one entity can own from 21 (7 AM-7 FM-7 TV) to 36 (12-12-12).

1986 HBO is first cable service to scramble its signals to limit piracy (January). • Knight-Ridder and Times Mirror close down their videotex marketing efforts begun in 1983–1984—with a combined $80 million loss (March). • NBC wins seasonal ratings race for first time in television history (April). • Coverage by radio and television of Senate proceedings begins (June). • Laurence Tisch takes effective control of CBS (September). • Fox Broadcasting Company airs first show on way to becoming a fourth network (October). • NBC changes hands as RCA is bought (for $6.4 billion) by General Electric (June–December).

1987 Space shuttle *Challenger* explosion is covered by television (January). • NBC Radio Network is sold to Westwood One (July). • FCC drops Fairness Doctrine (August). • People meters are first used to provide Nielsen ratings (September). • Cable and VCR penetration both pass the 50 percent mark. • FCC's attempt to retain must-carry rules for cable systems is overturned in court (December).

1988 CBS sells Columbia Records, world's largest record company, to Sony. • Twenty-two-week writer's strike, ending in August, delays fall television season. • Rupert Murdoch buys *TV Guide* (August). • FCC decides that any future broadcast HDTV system must be compatible with existing receivers and will have to fit within present broadcast spectrum allocation (September). • Ending more than 65 years of history, WNBC (AM), the former AT&T station WEAF, is sold and becomes an all-sports outlet. • National candidates debate election issues on television (September–October). • There are more than 12,000 radio and television stations on the air.

A New Marketplace (1989–2001)

1989 Fall of communism in Eastern Europe reported and probably hastened by widespread television coverage. • Time Inc. and Warner Communications merge to become world's largest entertainment company. • Half

of American homes now receive television service by means of cable.
• Sony buys film and television studio Columbia Pictures Entertainment
for $3.4 billion (November).

1990 Potential system of digital HDTV is first announced and demonstrated using computer modeling (June). • Sale of first consumer DAT
recorders. • Congress passes Children's Television Act mandating a few
hours a week of programs directed toward younger viewers as well as limits on advertising in such programs (first legal limit on broadcast advertising time).

1991 Gulf War widely covered with live broadcasts, though highly
restricted by military (January-February). • Television and international
radio cover short-lived coup in Soviet Union as leadership stays in touch
with events by tuning to BBC and Radio Liberty broadcasts (August). • Digital
HDTV lab testing begun in U.S. (April). • Matsushita (Panasonic) buys
MCA for $6.9 billion.

1992 First over-the-air digital HDTV experimental transmissions (March).
• Third party candidate Ross Perot spices up presidential election coverage, but political conventions no longer fully covered with live TV (July-
August). • FCC allows ownership of up to 18 AM and 18 FM stations
nation-wide, and up to two of each in major markets. • Digital compact
cassettes (DCC) first marketed. • Radio Broadcast Data Service (RDS) first
introduced in U.S. • Arbitron closes down its network television ratings
service (September). • Cable Act, passed over President Bush's veto, rein-
states many regulations including "must carry" rules (October).

1993 NBC admits rigging a crash test of a truck for a news program and
pays damages to General Motors. • Major HDTV system players merge into
so-called "Grand Alliance" to develop a single system (May). • FCC lifts
the financial interest and syndication rules, freeing networks to become
more active in entertainment programming. • FCC adopts specific stereo
AM technical standard after years of debate (November).

1994 Arbitron exits local television ratings leaving entire television market to Nielsen. • Hughes launches DirecTV, first American DBS system.
• ITU substantially reorganized for first time in nearly a half century.
• Aided by winning NFL television rights, Fox network gains a number of
big-market affiliates from the older three networks. • Viacom buys Paramount Communications for $10 billion and later purchases Blockbuster
video rental chain for $8 billion. • FCC increases national ownership limit
on radio to 20 AM and 20 FM stations. • Inception of direct broadcast
satellite services in the U.S.

1995 Coast Guard ceases listening for 500 kHz Morse Code distress signals.
• World Wide Web begins operation on the Internet. • Congress terminates
FCC minority tax certificate program (March). • Inception of Universal
Paramount Network (UPN) and Warner Brothers Network (WN). • FCC

repeals prime-time access rule (PTAR). • Disney buys Capital Cities/ABC for $19 billion (August). • Infinity Broadcasting pays $1.7 million in FCC fines because of indecent broadcasts by Howard Stern (September). • National obsession with O. J. Simpson murder case and trial, with "not-guilty" verdict becoming most watched moment in television history (October). • Seagram buys MCA from Matsushita and renames it "Universal Studios". • Westinghouse buys CBS network for $5.7 billion and takes on the network's name (November). • Time Warner buys Turner Communications, including CNN, for $7.6 billion. • DVD technical standard selected.

1996 Telecommunications Act of 1996 mandates V-Chips in television receivers and deregulates radio ownership, permitting one licensee to control hundreds of stations including up to eight in the largest cities, and extends broadcast licensees to eight years (February). • Communications Decency Act portion of 1996 Act challenged, and later overturned by courts as unconstitutional. • CBS (Westinghouse) buys Infinity Broadcasting for $4.7 billion, combining nation's two largest radio station operators (June). • AOL introduces flat Internet pricing increasing use of World Wide Web which, in turn, apparently cuts into television audiences. • FCC approves "Grand Alliance" HDTV technical standards (December).

1997 Under strong political pressure, broadcast industry reluctantly adopts a complex program content rating system tied to V-Chips to help viewers concerned about effects of sex, violence, etc. on their children to select programs (January). • FCC adopts final rules for digital television and sets 2006 as deadline for end of NTSC analog services (April). • Confusing HDTV's future, ABC and Sinclair announce they plan to use digital technology for multiple channels, not high-definition service (August). • Death of Britain's Princess Diana creates world-wide mourning covered by television (August-September). • First DVD players sold in U.S. • Westinghouse sheds almost all business activities except CBS.

1998 FCC reallocates television channels 60-69 to eventual non-broadcast use (January). • Impeachment trial of President Clinton covered by television from floor of U.S. Senate (February). • AT&T announces plans to take over the largest multiple cable system operator, TCI (June). • Inception of American HDTV transmissions in largest markets (November). • FCC reorganizes and increases the number of its operating bureaus, adding units for wireless and international telecommunication. • Most of FCC's EEO rules are found unconstitutional. • Hughes Corp, operator of DirectTV satellite service, takes over two smaller competitors—US Satellite Broadcasting and then Primestar (December).

1999 Congress allows DBS systems to carry local broadcast signals. • FCC ceases cable rate regulation in accord with 1996 Act (March). • With announced takeover of Media One, AT&T becomes largest U.S. operator of cable television systems (May). • Viacom, already controlling UPN, announces plans to take over CBS (September). • *Who Wants to Be a Millionaire?* returns big-money quiz shows to prime time after four decades.

• Unhappy with NAB stand favoring limit on television station ownership, Fox and later CBS and NBC drop their memberships in the trade association, weakening its traditional "umbrella" role for the industry. • "Magazine" news programs expand to fill large parts of network prime-time schedules.

2000   AOL moves to acquire TimeWarner for $135 billion in largest take-over in history (January). • Iridium international mobile satellite system closes down with $5 billion loss; reopens with new owners and lower prices (March). • FCC authorizes low power FM outlets (LPFM), over industry (including NPR) opposition; authorization both challenged in courts and quickly quashed by Congress chiefly on grounds that LPFM would cause interference to existing FM stations. • Celebrity and spectacle fill airwaves again with death of John F. Kennedy, Jr. (July). • Tape-delayed Olympic games in Australia fail to attract expected audiences (August). • Brief elimination of ABC network signal by Time-Warner cable systems (including New York City) during ratings sweep week focuses public and FCC attention on access to cable systems. • "Reality" TV programs, many originating in Europe, spread through network prime-time schedule, including top-rated *Survivor* and *Big Brother*. • Clear Channel Communications buys AMFM Inc. for $16.6 billion, creating nation's largest owner of radio stations (initially about 900). • Political news coverage diminishes until cliff-hanger of Presidential election night brings back the audience (November). • Television provides blanket coverage of month-long Florida recount and legal battle over election results, ending with Supreme Court decision (December).

2001   President George W. Bush names Michael Powell new chair of FCC and latter promises a strongly deregulatory regime (February). • Arguing high station costs and the lack of HDTV receivers in the hands of listeners, television industry asks FCC to delay deadline for conversion to HDTV operation (May). • *Who Wants to be a Millionare?* ratings drop after program is overexposed with multiple broadcasts each week—network trims schedule to but twice a week (June). • The BBC and Radio Switzerland announce that short-wave broadcasts to North America will end, but programs will continue over cable networks and local stations in some countries and over the Internet worldwide. • Comcast bids $56.5 billion for AT&T Broadband which, if successful, would make Comcast the nation's largest MSO (July). • Thousands of radio stations providing their programs and related services by audio streaming over the World Wide Web. • Fox Family Channel sold by Murdoch to Disney-ABC, giving Murdoch funds to attempt acquisition of Direc TV for $5.3 billion and adding to his DBS empire (July). • CNN introduces "younger appeal" look to its Headline News (attractive faces, busy graphics) and is criticized widely for cheapening both appearance and content (August). • Four days of continuous television, cable and radio coverage supply information to the nation and reflect its horror, as terrorists hijack four airliners and destroy the World Trade Center in New York, and damage the Pentagon, killing thousands (September).

APPENDIX B
GLOSSARY

This glossary has an essay form in preference to the typical circular set of definitions. Most terms deal with technology, although some deal with business and economics or broadcast programming. The technical basis for broadcasting is a subject for a book in itself, but it is also important as a factor in the development of electrical-electronic communication, together with politics, economics, the arts, and the social structure. Indeed, technology is less flexible than but fully intertwined with these other factors. Sometimes we can find a way around apparent technical or physical barriers—for example, by sacrificing quantity for speed, or by accepting less-than-perfect reproductions—but we can never ignore them.

Most words not found in this glossary can be readily found in a dictionary or are explained in context in the text. When a term has more than one meaning, the one most pertinent to broadcasting or other electronic media is used. We have tried to limit the brief explanations that follow to specialized terms and their interrelationships. Internal cross-references are supplied except where they would be unduly duplicative or easily found as, for example, within the entries for *Broadcasting* and *Broadcast Media.* Terms that are mentioned in an entry but which are discussed in fuller scope elsewhere in this glossary are printed in **boldface**, but internal cross-references are listed as (*see* Such-and-so). The most efficient way to absorb this technical terminology rapidly may be to read the entire glossary as if it were a mini-textbook.

ABC American Broadcasting Company, originally Blue Network, Inc., later American Broadcasting—Paramount Theaters and Capitol Cities—ABC, purchased by Disney in 1995. *See* Network.

Actors Equity *See* Unions.

Aerial *See* Antenna.

af (audio frequency) *See* Receiver.

Affiliation, Affiliates *See* Network *and* Ownership.

AFM (American Federation of Musicians) *See* Unions.

AFTRA (American Federation of Television and Radio Artists) *See* Unions.

AGVA (American Guild of Variety Artists) *See* Unions.

Allocation, Assignment, Allotment, Licensing Because all radio transmissions can cause *interference* in the form of manmade *static* or degradation of signal over a greater distance than they can give service, and since different frequencies (*see* Waves) have different characteristics, the FCC must apportion certain bands of frequencies or channels to a given service, such as television broadcasting or ship-to-shore or amateur radio—*allocation*; divide an allocated frequency band to reserve designated frequencies or sub-bands for use by certain users or in specified geographical areas—*assignment*; and authorize a given user to operate a radio transmitter on a discrete frequency at a particular location or locations under specified conditions—*licensing.* In recent years, the FCC and NTIA (see below) often have used the word *allotment* rather than *assignment* for the second stage (and sometimes the first stage) of this process, and NTIA has added to the confusion by using the word *assignment* for what the FCC would call *licensing.* (For a period in the 1950s and 1960s, the FCC itself confused "allocation" and "assignment" in some public documents.) Because federal government agencies use about half the radio spectrum, allocation, which is circumscribed worldwide by international agreements and treaties (*see* ITU), and assignment for these stations is administered by the *Interdepartment Radio Advisory Committee* (*IRAC*), now a part of the *National Telecommunications and Information Administration* of the U.S. Department of Commerce. The FCC standards for granting a broadcast station license involve citizenship, character, financing, and technical competence or facilities. Before a license is issued, a *construction permit* (*CP*) gives the potential licensee authority to build the station Licenses are granted for distinct periods—three years until the 1980s, then five years (television) or seven (radio), now (since 1996) eight years for both broadcasting services. Licenses may be—but rarely are—revoked for cause. Sometimes, when the FCC has many applications for the same channel, it holds *comparative hearings.* In recent years, licenses in some services have been granted on the basis of *auctions*, where the prospective licensees offer money to the government, or *lotteries*, in which the luckiest applicant wins the right to use a particular frequency.

When unexpected demand or unexpected technical difficulties arise with a given service or allocation to it, the FCC institutes a *freeze* on new licenses until the problem is resolved. In choosing between competing applicants—particularly between different services applying for the same band of frequencies, as in the recurrent conflict between television broadcasting and land mobile for the UHF television band—the FCC must make its decision in light of the touchstone criterion set forth in the Communications Act: the *public interest, convenience, and/or necessity.*

Alternating Currents (AC)   *See* Vacuum Tube.

Alternators   *See* Transmitter.

Amateur (also known as a *ham*)   An individual interested in radio technique solely with a personal aim and without pecuniary interest, characterized by self-training and technical investigations. To become an amateur operator, a person must pass tests of technical knowledge and (until 1999) ability to communicate in **Morse code**, as contrasted to the simpler requirements for *Citizens Band* (CB) operators. In exchange, amateurs may, depending on their class of skill, use much higher power than CBers may, a variety of frequencies, some permitting very long-range communication, and techniques forbidden to CBers. Many amateurs build or modify their own equipment. Amateurs frequently provide outstanding public service in times of disaster; their spectacular breakthroughs in technological and operational development contributed particularly to early broadcasting; and the military and naval forces, especially during World War I, eagerly recruited their services as trained radio operators. The frequencies allocated to amateurs throughout the spectrum permit them to communicate with other amateurs around the world. Amateurs communicate "person-to-person"–although they may start a conversation by calling "CQ," a general call to anyone who may be listening. They do *not* "broadcast" intentionally to the general public, but anyone with the proper receiving equipment may listen.

AM Channels   The FCC's channel allocation and station classifications for AM radio remained basically unchanged for more than a half-century until adjustments were made in the 1980s and 1990s. In 1988 the standard broadcast (AM) band was extended to 1705 kHz, adding 10 new channels for a total of 117 10-kHz wide channels. After debate, in 1997, the FCC selected nearly 100 existing stations to move from lower but crowded frequencies into the new band extension, rather than licensing new operators. They were given as many as five years to make this shift, and they were allowed to broadcst on both the new and the old frequencies during that period.

In the mid-1990s, the commission also simplified its classfication of AM stations into four types which, between them, utilized the traditional three types of channels (clear, regional, local):

A   unlimited time stations on clear channels, using power from 10,000 watts to 50,000 watts (1% of all AM stations)
B   unlimited time stations on clear or regional channels, using power from 250 watts to 50, 000 watts (35% of all AM stations)
C   small stations operating on local channels using power from 250 to 1,000 watts (21% of all AM stations)
D   daytime-only stations, or those operating with less than 250 watts of power at night, on either clear or regional channels. Class D outlets must operate so as not to interfere with any Class A or B station (42% of all AM stations).

Prior to the 1990s, with the standard broadcast (AM) band starting at 535 kHz and ending at 1605 kHz, 107 channels were divided into three categories with five classes of stations operating on them. A *clear channel* is one on which only one *dominant station* operates at night for several thousand miles, although a number of low to medium power *secondary stations* may share it with the dominant station during the day. The United States, Canada, Mexico, and other North American countries are signatories to the North American Regional Broadcasting Agreement (*NARBA*), negotiated in 1937 and revised in 1950. Each country has channels on which one of its stations is dominant. The treaty also provides that each dominant station use at least 50,000 watts of power; in the United States, 50 kw is also the upper limit because of a "Sense of the Senate" resolution in the late 1930s. (*See also* Waves *and* Bandwidth.)

The following are the ways in which standard broadcast (AM) channels were long classified in the United States:

60   **Clear channels**—one dominant station in most instances.

    24   Class 1A—one U.S. dominant station on each, with only 1–7 other, lower power stations sharing the channel by day and none by night.

    17   —dominant station in Canada, Mexico, Cuba, etc., may be used by some U.S. lower power stations by day.

    19   Class 1B—two or, in some cases, more stations sharing each channel at night, with from 1 to 40 or more Class II U.S. stations and others in other countries sharing the channel during the day.

41   **Regional channels** (Class III)—each generally used by from 20 to 70 or more stations spaced several hundred miles apart, using 5 to 50 kw of power.

  6   **Local channels** (Class IV)—each generally used by 150 to 175 stations using low power (250 watts at night, 1 kw during the day), often spaced only a few tens of miles apart so that their tower lights sometimes can be seen farther than the signal reaches

107   Channels from 540 through 1,600 kHz. Since each channel is 10 kHz wide, the total standard broadcast band was from 535 through 1,605 kHz. Additional channels were added between 1,605 and 1,705 kHz after a 1988 international agreement extended the band to 1705 kHz, which made available 10 additional regional channels. However, in 1997, the FCC decided instead to move some existing stations to the new channels in order to reduce interference. Although the above classifications are still in use, the FCC also classifies stations from A (the most privileges) to D (the least), depending on the maximum power and hours of operation permitted (see above).

Amperes   *See* Circuit.

Amplification   *See* Receiver *and* Vacuum Tube.

Amplitude Modulation (AM)   *See* Modulation

Antenna, Aerial   A metallic device used for the sending and receiving of electromagnetic waves; often in the form of a tower or series of towers but frequently a horizontal length of wire, often a *parabolic reflector* or *dish*, and sometimes a short vertical *whip*. Most broadcasting stations use vertical antennas; shipboard stations string antennas between the vessel's masts. For efficiency, an antenna must bear a relationship to the wavelength (*see* Waves) of the frequency for which it is designed, usually one half or one quarter wavelength. If it does not bear such a relationship, the antenna will not *resonate* properly to the transmitted or received wave. Hence, since wavelength increases as frequency diminishes, we find that standard (AM) broadcast stations use their entire tower as an antenna, whereas FM broadcast stations, on a much higher frequency, have only a small antenna on top of the tower. The international radiotelegraph distress frequency, 500 kHz, is very short to use as a wavelength for long-range use over water, but it was chosen many years ago because antennas for that frequency could fit physically between the masts of the typical oceangoing ship. A VHF television or FM receiving antenna is roughly five feet wide, whereas a UHF television antenna—of higher frequency and thus shorter wavelength—is less than two feet wide. At even higher frequencies, precisely aimed *dishes* from 2 to 100 feet in diameter are used to focus the extremely short waves precisely onto the antenna element located at their focal point. It is also possible to "aim" huge antenna arrays on the shortwave (high-frequency) band and even to construct a directional system with towers to reinforce and cancel one another so that a standard broadcast (AM) station causes minimal interference in one or more directions. *Directional antenna* (*DA*) installations are particularly useful for AM today, since the FCC has put a large number of stations on almost every channel. Transmitting antennas can be oriented to supply *horizontal, vertical*, or *circular polarization*, the first two of which require similarly oriented receiving antennas for efficient reception. These techniques generally permit a reduction in interference so that stations on the same frequency can be located closer together.

AOL   America OnLine, the largest Internet Service Provider (ISP). In 1999, bought Time Warner. *See* Ownership.

AP (Associated Press)   *See* News.

ASCAP (American Society of Composers, Authors and Publishers)   *See* Copyright.

Aspect Ratio   *See* Television Signals.

Assignment   *See* Allocation.

ATM   Asychronous (information) Transfer Mode (or Automatic Teller Machine, used in banking).

AT&T   American Telephone & Telegraph Company. *See* Bell System.

ATV   Advanced Television. *See* HDTV.

Auctions   *See* Allocation, Assignment, Allotment, Licensing.

Audience   *See* Communication.

Audio   Of or pertaining to audible sound, or its broadcasting, or recording and reproduction.

Audio Streaming *See* Internet.

Audion *See* Vacuum Tube.

Automation The totality of mechanical and electronic techniques and equipment used to achieve control of a process, equipment, or system. Many automated radio stations use automatic playing of music tapes and recorded commercials to cut down on use of engineers and other personnel. In its favor, automation cuts down the boring, repetitive, and complex tasks that often lead to on-air errors, particularly at station-break time ("panic periods"). More and more broadcast equipment, including transmitters, is operated by unattended automation. Most automated devices today are computer controlled.

Bandwidth The bandwidth, the amount of electromagnetic *spectrum* space efficiently occupied by a **channel**, depends on the amount of information that one wants to transmit. For example, a dot in Morse code takes an appreciable fraction of a second to form but requires only one "bit" of information: the telegraph key is momentarily depressed, and a brief spurt of electricity is sent down the line or to the transmitter. In a radiotelegraph system, such a signal requires only about 50 *Hz* of bandwidth. (A *Hertz*, or Hz, is equivalent to one cycle per second of alternating current; a kiloHertz [kHz] to one thousand cycles per second, a megaHertz [MHz] to one million cycles per second. The terms kilocycle [kc] or megacycle [mc] were used until the 1960s, when it was internationally agreed to honor Heinrich Hertz, one of the earliest wireless experimenters.) Voice requires more: although your hi-fi system may state on its nameplate that it handles audio frequencies from "20 to 20,000 Hz," the human voice rarely requires more than 5,000 Hz (or 5 kiloHertz or 5 kHz) of bandwidth. In fact, the typical telephone system transmits only some 2,500 Hz, accounting for the tinny sound of a telephone conversation, which has lost its highest and lowest voice frequencies. This is all that is needed for maximum intelligibility, although radio stations using telephone lines for networking or picking up programs from remote locations have special equipment at both ends to extend the response of the telephone system to 5 kHz or, in the case of high-fidelity FM, as much as 15 kHz. A single picture on a television set, requiring only a tiny fraction of a second to form, contains a great deal of information—but requires 4.5 MHz (*see* Television Signals). High-definition television (HDTV) requires even more bandwidth, one of the reasons for its slow rate of adoption in many countries.

If the necessary bandwidth is not available, it is possible to transmit the information by sampling—the human eye and ear can "remember" through such processes as persistence of vision, which makes it possible to perceive motion in a series of still pictures on a film—or by presenting the information in sequential rather than simultaneous form, as in television *scanning.* For example, some early experimenters with the telegraph used a separate wire circuit for each of the 26 letters of the alphabet, a logical although inefficient and expensive configuration. One of Morse's and his associates' contributions was the use of a code for sending the letters of the message one after the other as electrical pulses through one wire. (*See also* Television's Early Technological Development.)

Base   *See* Land Mobile.

Bell System   The former name for the American Telephone & Telegraph Company and its operating companies, Long Lines Department, and manufacturing arm (Western Electric). In 1984, the Bell System (familiarly known as *Ma Bell*) was broken up as the result of an antitrust agreement with the Justice Department. While AT&T is still in the long-distance and computer fields, there are now four remaining independent "Baby Bells" or regional Bell operating companies (*RBOC*) out of seven; competition in long-distance carriage; manufacturing; new technologies such as integrated service digital networks (ISDNs), and so on, at all but the level of the local operating companies—which themselves want to get into cable television. AT&T itself has migrated into the cable television industry, and by 1999 was the largest MSO. Bell Atlantic, in addition to being the operating company in New England, New York, and the Middle Atlantic states, merged with GTE, which itself controlled roughly 10% of the nation's telephones, and now goes by the name of Verizon. The RBOCs have been slowly obtaining permission to get into the long distance business, and some long distance carriers have been considering getting into the local telephone business. All have been concerned at the rapid growth of cable television, which also can supply voice and data (via the Internet) communication connections to the home.

Beta   *See* Recordings.

Binaural   *See* Modulation.

Blanking Interval   *See* Television Signals.

BMI (Broadcast Music, Inc.)   *See* Copyright.

Boosters   *See* Satellite.

Broadband   A channel or channels able to carry a great deal of information. *See* Allocation, Assignment, Allotment, Licensing, and Bandwidth.

Broadcasting   A radiocommunication service of transmissions intended to be received directly by the general public. This service may include transmissions of sounds—**radio broadcasting**—or transmissions by **television, facsimile**, or other means. Broadcasting—to everyone—should be distinguished from two-way or point-to-point communication, which was called *narrowcasting* in the early 1920s. *Narrowcasting* now refers to the programmer's focus on a specific audience rather than on the public as a whole or on a technical bandwidth limitation. (*See* Mass Communication.)

Broadcast Journalism   *See* News.

Broadcast Media   In the United States, standard broadcast (AM) stations; frequency modulation (FM) stations, both commercial and noncommercial educational; television stations, both commercial and noncommercial educational; international (shortwave) stations; and experimental facsimile and other classes of service.

Cable (also *CATV* or *Community Antenna Television*)   Although the word "cable" was used after the mid-1850s to refer to underwater telegraph lines, particularly between continents, and still has that connotation, since the 1950s it has been used as a shortened form of "cable television," a system for distributing television (and sometimes radio) to homes in an area by means of wire rather than radiocommunication. Although systems from the late 1940s into the 1960s typically provided very few channels and were sometimes a cooperative or nonprofit public service, modern systems can provide from 35 to 120 or more channels and operate as profit-making businesses. In addition to providing interference-free reception of local stations, modern systems bring in signals from distant cities and sometimes provide *local origination*, government, educational, and *public access* channels and *pay-cable* service (*see* Pay-TV). The "*wired city*" is a proposal that telecommunication services in the United States, including television and access to computers, will and should eventually be distributed by a *wideband* (great information-carrying capacity) cable directly to individual homes. Telephone companies and CATV operators both are eyeing this possibility of a new line of business.

A CATV system typically consists of a *head end*—the location where signals from local stations or microwave (*see* Waves) or **satellite** signals are picked up and amplified for retransmission through the system—several miles of *trunk lines* either on poles or underground, and individual *service drops* or wired connections to individual subscribers, together with the various amplifiers and other devices that are needed to push the signal through the system. A *two-way cable system* permits some signal transmission from the subscriber's home back to the head end—for remote reading of utility meters, information as to whether a *pay-cable* or **pay-TV** signal is being used, and so forth. In the 1970s some experimentation and planning went on for *interactive cable systems* allowing a complete two-way voice and picture communication process. Most CATV systems charge subscribers a monthly fee for each *tier* (such as basic or pay) of service. A trend is toward multiple system operators (*MSOs*), who own or operate cable systems in several communities. Most regulation of cable is through municipal *franchising*, although some states and the federal government (FCC) have promulgated some regulations and standards. In the 1980s, the FCC preempted much local regulation but did not install its own. In Europe, CATV would be called *rediffusion*, a term applied to wired radio (particularly in the United Kingdom and the Soviet Union) as well as wired television. A *master antenna system* (*MATV*) typically serves only a single institution or apartment house and rarely offers the auxiliary services mentioned above. An *SMATV* system is an MATV that receives its programming directly from a satellite dish.

Call Letters   Combinations of letters and sometimes numbers used to identify radio stations over the air. Blocks of initial letters are assigned to a particular country, a practice started as a result of the London International Radiotelegraph Conference of 1912. The United States has been assigned all of the blocks with the initial letters W, K and N, and much of A, although both A and N calls tend to be used mostly by the armed forces. Several N (for Navy) stations were used for early radio experimentation. In broadcasting, W is generally used east of the Mississippi and K west, with a few exceptions—usually older stations such as KYW, Philadelphia, and KDKA, Pittsburgh. An X following a number generally means an experimental station (9XM, 8XK, W2XR) with numbers in these early calls, and in amateur licenses, representing geographical districts. Some calls (FM in the early 1940s, LPTV today) used two digits to indicate the assigned channel. Although some pioneer stations still have three-letter call signs, most are four-letter, with many FM and television stations using those suffixes to create five- and six-letter calls (WNYC-TV). Stations may select their own call signs, within FCC guidelines and rules, leading to ingenious acronyms (WIOD, Miami = Wonderful Isle of Dreams; WGN, Chicago = World's Greatest Newspaper, the original licensee the *Chicago Tribune*) or associative meanings (KOP = Detroit Police Department; WILK = Wilkes-Barre, Pennsylvania).

Camcorder   *See* Recordings.

Carrier Wave   *See* Modulation *and* Transmitter.

Cartridge   *See* Recordings.

Cassette   *See* Recordings.

Cathode   *See* Vacuum Tube.

CATV (community antenna television)   *See* Cable.

C-Band   *See* Satellite.

CBS (Columbia Broadcasting System)   *See* Network.

CCD (controlled capacitance discharge)   *See* Television Camera Tubes.

CD (compact disc)   *See* Recordings.

CD-ROM   A "compact disc—read only memory" recording used primarily for computer information.

Cellular Telephone   *See* Land Mobile.

Chain Broadcasting   *See* Network.

Channel   A channel is an arbitrarily defined group of radio frequencies occupying a segment of the spectrum wide enough to permit operation of a station of a given service. For example, a channel for a standard (AM) broadcasting station is 10 kHz wide, but one for a television broadcasting station is 600 times wider (6 MHz) in order to handle the additional information of a picture.

Character Generator   A device (often called a *Chyron*, for a popular brand name) for inserting titles and other words and material into a television picture.

Chicago School   A laid-back approach to television variety and drama, as typified by much network programming from Chicago in the 1950s and 1960s.

Chip   *See* Vacuum Tube.

Circuit   A pathway which ends at the same place it began. In *electrical circuits*, electricity flows from the source, through a switch or other control device and a *load*, and back to the source. The source may be a *generator*, a rotating machine that produces electricity when spinning; a *battery*, a chemical source of electricity; or, as in the case of radio, a *transmitter*. The load may be a lamp, a motor, a heater, or something similar that does a certain amount of work–produces light, motion, heat, and so on. If there is no load, there is also no *resistance*—an electrical property measured in *ohms* related to the amount of energy (*watts*) the load requires to do work; and, if a conducting path, a wire, connects one side of the source to the other without a load, we have a *short-circuit*, a condition demanding an infinite amount of electricity, which quickly results in a burned-out wire or generator—or fuse, if such a protection was inserted in the circuit. There are two basic electrical circuits: *series*, which is like a chain, through each link of which all the *current* flows; and *parallel*, which requires both sides of the source to be linked to each load, as, for example, all outlets in a house must have two wires connected to them. With a parallel circuit, one part of the load may be disconnected without having any effect on the others; with a series circuit, the removal of any part of the circuit "breaks the chain." Current is measured in *amperes*, calculated by dividing the *voltage* in the circuit (the amount of "pressure," measured in *volts*) by the resistance.

In a simple electrical telegraph circuit, the elements consist of batteries (the source), a key (a switch which can be manipulated on and off very rapidly), the wire connecting the sending and receiving stations, a relay at the receiving **station**, and a *return wire* to the other terminal of the battery. (Actually, since the *ground* will conduct electricity, in most cases the earth itself is used for the return part of the circuit, with both the return wire from the relay at the receiving station and one terminal from the battery at the sending station connected to it.) The *relay*, or *sounder* in early telegraph language, consists of a fine coil of wire wound around a piece of soft iron, the thinness of the wire providing some resistance in the circuit. Electricity passing through the coil converts the iron core into an *electromagnet*, which is set up to attract or repulse another piece of iron or steel that hits it with an audible "click" and then is pulled away by a spring as soon as the current is off. These clicks form the dots and dashes of **Morse code**.

A radio circuit is comparable: the source of electricity is a **transmitter**, which is "keyed" or "modulated" much as the electrical telegraph circuit is keyed manually. However, instead of needing a wire conductor to connect sending and receiving stations, radio **waves** can be sent through the atmosphere from an antenna connected to the transmitter and through the ground for a return. A circuit, in radio terms, generally if a little loosely applies to a two-way pathway using a particular frequency or **channel**. It may also refer to the arrangements of components within a transmitter, receiver, or other electronic device—the design of the unit, in electronic terms. This latter usage is derived from the fact that *electrons*, tiny units of energy, must travel in a circuit from source back to source to do any work.

Citizens Band (CB)   A two-way usually mobile radio service that any member of the public (not just truckers) may use. Simple to operate, CB consists of low-power fixed and mobile stations intended for personal or business communication, radio signaling, control of remote devices, and almost anything else not prohibited. It differs from broadcasting in that it is a short-range, point-to-point service, and it differs from amateur radio in that amateurs have technical skills and use radio more as a hobby than for personal or business communication. CBers may not engage in technical experimentation. Some channels have been formally or informally assigned to special uses: channel 9 for emergencies, channel 19 for truckers. Citizens Band radio was established by the FCC in 1958 but grew slowly until the mid-1970s, when suddenly millions of units were sold, perhaps sparked by the desire of motorists to avoid traffic police ("smokey") enforcing speed limits during a gasoline shortage, and the service assumed the status of a fad complete with its own songs and movies and references on comedy television shows. In 1977 the number of CB channels was increased from 23 to 40 because of demand for more space. (*See also* Amateur.)

Clear Channel   *See* Channel.

Closed Caption   *See* Modulation.

Closed-circuit   Not broadcast; availability intentionally restricted as to location through use of wired circuits or radio frequency band used.

Clutter   Term applied to the ever-larger number of commercials, station and network promotions, and station identifications aired during every television (or radio) commercial break. Clutter was not a major problem until shorter (:30 seconds or less) commercials became common, although the total number of commercial minutes per hour also has been climbing. Some consider the growing use of small network or cable service logos in the corner of the screen to be a form of visual clutter.

Coaxial Cable   A cable consisting of two concentric metallic conductors—a thin wire or pipe in the middle and, separated by a carefully and evenly sized insulator, an outer conductor of woven metal mesh or a larger pipe. Most coaxial cable is flexible with an outer plastic sheath for insulation and mechanical protection; the kind that has rigid piping generally is restricted to short runs carrying high current, such as from a powerful transmitter to an antenna. Coaxial cable can carry a tremendous **bandwidth** and has made long-distance—beyond the range of off-the-air pickup—television transmission or program distribution practical. Much of the intercity television (and telephone) network (and, indeed, most video signals carried by wire within a studio or in a **cable** system) requires coaxial cables, since ordinary wires do not carry a television signal satisfactorily. The rest of the intercity network uses wideband *microwave* (*see* Waves) point-to-point transmission and reception systems. Although modern practice has produced cables utilizing several coaxial conductors independently covered by the same outer sheath, permitting very wide bandwidths to be carried, the new *fiber optic cable*, an extremely fine thread of fiberglass modulated with light waves by a **laser** and capable of carrying a tremendous amount of information, is being increasingly used in their stead.

Coherent   *See* Laser.

Coherer   *See* Receiver.

Coincidental   *See* Ratings.

Color, Colorburst, Color Wheel   *See* Television Signals.

Colorization   *See* Colorizing.

Colorizing   Using a computer to add colors to a black-and-white feature film. Turner Broadcasting (Turner Classic Movies, superstation WTBS, etc.), now part of AOL/TimeWarner, is particularly noted for this practice, which many purist movie fans disapprove.

Common Carrier   A transportation or communication activity—airlines, truck lines, and telephone companies—which undertakes to accept for transmission at published nondiscriminatory rates all correspondence—freight, passengers, messages—tendered by members of the public. A common carrier is often a *public utility*, an organization operating under a franchise from a government and charged with certain activities necessary for the public welfare, that accepts regulation of rates in exchange for monopoly or near-monopoly status. By law, broadcasting is not considered a common carrier and is not regulated as such for rates or program content. On the other hand, while cable might better fit under the "common carrier" label, it actually fits into both classifications (or neither one) because of special legislation, FCC rules, and court decisions.

Communication   The transmission and reception of information through any medium between and among humans and/or machines and/or animals (*see also* Mass Communication, Mass Media). *Information,* according to the theory developed by Shannon, Weaver, and others, is anything (particularly, but not exclusively, knowledge and intelligence) that someone desires to have transmitted, together with any intelligence transmitted—intentionally or not. *Intelligence* is an old word for "news," information of military value, as well as information understandable to or capable of being deduced by the recipient or *audience*, the eventual recipient(s) of a message. A *message* is intentionally coded (into speech or some other form) and transmitted as information. Most messages have *meaning*, which means that there is a sharing of concepts between a communicator and the audience. A *symbol* or *sign* or code has meaning to the extent that its connotations and denotations are mutually understood by communicator and audience. (*See also* Signal.)

Community Antenna Television   *See* Cable.

Comparative Hearings   *See* Allocation.

Compatible   A new technological advance is said to be compatible if it will *not* render existing receivers or other equipment obsolete and can, for instance, play the same recordings.

Conduction   *See* Radiation.

Conductivity   *See* Waves.

Conelrad   *See* Emergency Broadcast System.

Conglomerate   *See* Ownership.

Construction Permit (CP)   *See* Allocation.

Continuous Wave (CW)   *See* Modulation.

Convergence   The obliteration of distinctions between media, at the production level (e.g., using HDTV and computer editing to create feature motion pictures to be shown in theaters) or in the home (e.g., the use of a computer monitor to watch television programs or vice versa).

Copyright, Performing Rights Societies   Literally, the power to control the right to copy a literary work (such as books or plays), music, paintings. The U.S. copyright system was established in Article I, Section 8 of the Constitution (*see* Invention, Innovation, Patents). Although one copyrights a piece by labeling it, prior to publication or distribution, with a © or the word "copyright," the name of the copyright owner, and the year, it is wise to *register* the copyright with the U.S. Register of Copyrights in order to have dated proof of notice of copyright. *Infringement* of copyright—copying without permission—is a federal offense. A 1976 copyright law (effective January 1, 1978) put obligations on CATV for the first time, and grants copyright for the author's life plus 50 years. *Performing rights societies* such as *ASCAP* (American Society of Composers, Authors and Publishers) and *BMI* (Broadcast Music, Incorporated) administer the copyrights held on most music for the benefit of the copyright holder(s); some European music is controlled by *SESAC*, Incorporated. Started in 1914 when composer Victor Herbert objected to the playing of his music in a restaurant (benefiting the restaurant but not Herbert), ASCAP licenses performance of all music owned by persons for whom it acts as agent. (Recording, dramatic, and other rights are licensed case by case.) Each station pays a small percentage of its gross revenues for the right to play all ASCAP music. Each year, ASCAP distributes these monies to its members according to a complex formula and following a sample survey of actual renditions of each piece of music. In 1939–1940, ASCAP raised its rates to the point where broadcasters rebelled and organized a rival organization, BMI. Today, most stations have contracts with both organizations—although the relationship is never placid and often has been complicated by court supervision.

Counterprogramming   *See* Programming.

Cross-media Ownership   *See* Ownership.

Crystal Control   *See* Transmitter.

Crystal Set   *See* Receiver *and* Vacuum Tube.

Current   *See* Circuit.

DAT (digital audiotape)   *See* Recordings.

DBS (direct broadcast satellite)   *See* Satellite.

Decoherer   *See* Receiver.

Demographics   Measurement of the division of audiences into groups by age, gender, educational attainment, income, etc., for purposes of aiming advertising at desired targets.

Deregulation   Policy of FCC (and other government agencies) after the mid-1970s to remove existing regulations and rely on market forces such as competition for control of potential excesses.

Desktop publishing   Using computers, and usually special software, rather than older printing technologies such as moveable type and photo offset techniques, to prepare (and sometimes produce, in small quantities) printed materials.

Detection   *See* Vacuum Tube.

Diaries   *See* Ratings.

Digital/Analog   Digital signals are a series of discrete "on" or "off" conditions, based on rapid sampling rather than a continuously varying one as in an analog signal. Digital inherently is able to ignore static and other interference and is capable of very high quality reproduction (as in audio *CD* or *DAT* recordings), but it requires a far greater bandwidth than does an analog signal. Almost all computers use digital signals, and the newest (and most expensive) models of all types of other devices are now designed for digital processing.

Diode   *See* Vacuum Tube.

Diplexing   *See* Modulation.

Direct Current (DC)   *See* Vacuum Tube.

Direct Wave   *See* Waves.

Directional Antenna (DA)   *See* Antenna.

Discrete   *See* Laser *and* Modulation.

Dish   *See* Antenna.

Dominant Station   *See* Channel.

Dot Sequential   *See* Television Signals.

Downlink   *See* Satellite.

DTV   Digital Television. Fostered by Congress, and approved by the FCC in the 1990s, it can be used to broadcast *HDTV* or as many as four NTSC-quality broadcasts on the same channel. Separate DTV channels were set aside for existing broadcasters, who were expected to return to the FCC the channels used for analog transmissions after a substantial proportion of the population had bought the expensive receivers needed for DTV.

DVD ((Usually) Digital Video Disc)   *See* Recording.

Duopoly   *See* Ownership.

DX-ing   A hobby, quite popular in the first decades of radio, of attempting to receive stations far beyond normal reception range. Most stations in a given city cooperated by going off the air one night a week, the "*silent night*," so that listeners could pick up stations elsewhere in the country. Silent nights had stopped by the late 1920s as more stations went on the air, competition increased, and broadcasting became more familiar, but DX-ing continues today among amateur and some broadcasting listeners, particularly of FM and television near the height of the 11-year sunspot cycle when freak reception is more common.

E-commerce   *See* Internet.

Edison Effect   *See* Vacuum Tube.

Editorials   *See* News.

Educational Television   *See* ETV.

Electrical Circuit   *See* Circuit.

Electrical Transcription   *See* Recordings.

Electromagnet   *See* Circuit.

Electromagnetic Energy   A class of phenomena such as radio waves, heat (infrared) waves, light waves, X-rays, gamma rays, and cosmic rays. These waves are propagated at the speed of light—approximately 186,300 miles per second, or 300,000,000 meters per second—and differ chiefly in the degree to which waves of various frequencies or lengths are reflected from or pass through different physical media. The electromagnetic spectrum is composed of all types of waves, from electrical and radio waves alternating a few times per second through visible light waves with frequencies measured in billions of Hertz (cycles per second) and even beyond. (*See* Waves.)

Electrons   *See* Circuit.

Emergency Broadcast System   The EBS system was designed to alert the public in case of imminent tornado, flood, hurricane or other disaster. It is activated many times a year. It originated as "Conelrad" (CONtrol of ELectromagnetic RADiation) early in the Cold War. That system required all participating (AM only) stations to switch to 640 and 1240 kHz with low power in order to both alert the public about a possible atomic attack and prevent the use of known-location transmitters as "homing" devices for aircraft. As television became more popular, and as the Cold War thawed, the system evolved into EBS (still the most familiar name), which receives alerts (typically through AP wires and key stations) and transmits warnings to the general public as well as to special receivers turned on by the combination of tones and brief shutdowns of transmitters. Although emergency management authorities would like to be able to turn on radios remotely, this feature is not generally available.

ENG (electronic news-gathering), **EFP** (electronic field production), **SNG** (satellite news-gathering).   *ENG* uses portable, battery-operated electronic equipment—microphones, television cameras, VTRs—for acquiring television **news**, in contrast to the use of portable film cameras for this purpose. In the process, tapes are taken back to the station or sent by means of a mobile or portable transmitter, as a **remote**. Editing may be done in the field or at the station, and the coverage may be aired "live" if the signal can be sent back to the station by microwave or by helicopter or other relay. *EFP* is the use of similar equipment for the field production of more complex programs or commercials. *SNG* is the use of a space *satellite*, rather than microwave, transmitter truck, with the signal received at the station. With SNG, the station or network can receive news program content from almost any place on earth. ENG became dominant in many markets in the 1970s after development of portable color equipment (including *time base correctors* permitting the use of less expensive videotape recorders over the air), in spite of its high initial cost, partly because it permitted immediate replay of pictorial material without film processing delays.

ETV, ITV, PTV (*educational, instructional*, and *public* television)   Originally *educational* broadcasting was the generic term for classroom instructional, adult education, and cultural programming, particularly when aired over noncommercial educational stations. *Public* broadcasting, popularized by a 1967 Carnegie Commission report, generally refers to broadcasting on noncommercial stations. *Instructional* television generally has been restricted to in-class or other **closed-circuit** or videotaped uses. The same descriptive words can be applied, with suitable modification, to radio.

Ex Parte   Contact with a regulatory body (such as the FCC) or court by only one party to a dispute.

Facsimile   A system of **telecommunication** for the transmission of fixed images (*television* transmits moving or transient images) with a view to their reception in a permanent (paper) or semipermanent form. Includes the *wirephoto* process used by wire services to send pictures—by wire or radio—to newspapers early in the 20th century. Experiments with broadcast facsimile were conducted the 1940s, and industrial interest in the technique was exploited as early as the 1970s. Systems using blank lines in a television picture to transmit "pages" of information to the home video screen, such as Britain's CEEFAX, are **teletext**, not facsimile. In the 1980s, inexpensive and reliable equipment made "FAX" transmissions over regular dial telephone circuits very popular among businesses of all sizes. (*See also* Television's Early Technical Development.)

Family Viewing   *See* Programming.

FAX   *See* Facsimile.

Feedback   Feedback is any situation whereby a portion of the output of any process or system influences the input into the system in the future. *Negative feedback* is used to control or "dampen" the process; *positive feedback* reinforces the ongoing process and is usually detrimental. In **mass communication**, any means of responding to a particular message (letters to the editor, sales, audience ratings) is an example of feedback.

Fiber Optic   *See* Coaxial Cable.

Fields   *See* Television Signals.

Field Sequential   *See* Television Signals.

Filament   *See* Vacuum Tube.

Film Chain   *See* Television Camera Tubes.

Fixed   *See* Land Mobile.

Fleming Valve   *See* Vacuum Tube.

Formats (Program)   *See* Programming.

Formats (Videotape)   *See* Recordings.

Frames   *See* Television Signals.

Franchising   *See* Cable.

Freeze   *See* Allocation.

Frequency   *See* Waves.

Frequency Modulation (FM)   *See* Modulation.

FTP File Transfer Protocol   *See* Internet.

Full-motion Video   A term that came into use when computers and Internet connections had the necessary bandwidth to reproduce realistic motion over the Internet. Previously, video over computer connections was a sequence of individually scanned pictures—and looked like it.

Galvanometer   *See* Receiver.

Generations   *See* Recordings.

Generator   *See* Circuit.

Geostationary Orbit (GSO)   *See* Satellite.

Grandfathering   Allowing existing situations to continue regardless of new rules.

Grid   *See* Vacuum Tube.

Ground   *See* Circuit.

Groundwave   *See* Waves.

Guard Bands   *See* Television Signals.

Ham   *See* Amateur.

HBO (Home Box Office)   A major pay-cable service. *See* Cable.

HDTV (high-definition television)   Any of several means of improving television to the quality level of 16 mm or even 35 mm film. While far advanced in Japan (*MUSE*) and Europe for *DBS*, HDTV may become a production standard in the United States (for television programs and feature "films") rather than a direct-to-home delivery system in the near future. For a number of reasons—primarily the political urgency of ensuring that existing NTSC-standard sets (*see* Television Signals) are not rendered obsolete—the United States is experimenting with **ATV** (advanced television), which is *compatible* rather than incompatible with existing sets, even though it may not be capable of true high definition. Although initially an analog technology, HDTV became a digital service during the 1990s. The FCC has approved a variety of potential standards, although none have attracted the viewers' fancy by the start of the new millennium. *See also* DTV.

Head End   *See* Cable.

Helical Scan   *See* Recordings.

Hertz (Hz)   *See* Bandwidth.

Heterodyne   *See* Receiver.

High Band   *See* Recordings.

Holography   *See* Laser.

HTML (HyperText Markup Language)   *See* Internet.

HTTP (HyperText Transfer Protocol)   *See* Internet.

IATSE (International Alliance of Theatrical Stage Employees)   *See* Unions.

IBEW (International Brotherhood of Electrical Workers)   *See* Unions.

Iconoscope   *See* Television Camera Tubes.

Image Dissectors   *See* Television Camera Tubes.

Image Orthicon   *See* Television Camera Tubes.

Incoherent   *See* Laser.

Induction   *See* Radiation.

Information   *See* Communication.

Information Theory   *See* Morse Code.

Infotainment   A word coined from the two words "information" and "entertainment," reflecting the debasement of information content.

Infringement   *See* Copyright.

Innovation   *See* Invention.

Instructional Television   *See* ETV.

Integrated Solid State Circuits   *See* Vacuum Tube.

Intelligence   *See* Communication.

Interactive Cable Systems   *See* Cable.

Interference   *See* Allocation.

Interlaced   *See* Television Signals.

Intermediate Frequency (IF)   *See* Receiver.

International Telecommunication Union (ITU)   A specialized United Nations agency, founded in 1865 as the International Telegraph Union, now particularly concerned with radio frequency *allocation* matters as well as international technical and operational standards for all forms of telecommunication.

Internet   The Internet is a worldwide distributed network for the interconnection of computers. Before the sale of personal computers "took off" in the early 1980s, most businesses, governments, and other institutions using computers relied on direct connections, typically through leased telephone lines. (While space communication satellites can be used, the lag caused by the vast distance between a synchronous satellite and earth led to transmission complications.) The Internet grew from *Arpanet*, a network initiated in 1969 by the Department of Defense for the exchange of large quantities of scientific and engineering data by its contractors, including the national laboratories and a number of major universities.

The development of programs for *e-mail* (transmission of electronic messages between or among computers), FTP (File Transfer Protocol), and the *modem* (a "modulator–demodulator" device that takes electronic signals from a computer and inserts them in a telephone line), led to wider use of transmitted messages and shared data. Before the Internet became widely available, individuals might dial and connect to one or more *BBS* ("bulletin boards") for textual information or exchanges on a specific topic. The first major switched system or flexible e-mail connections between individuals was *Bitnet*, operated informally by colleges and universities. After the Internet became available to private users in the early 1990s, and Internet Service Providers (*ISPs*) started selling access, most BBS were replaced by e-mail "listservs," "chat rooms," or "Usenet newsgroups" and, later, Web sites.

Some used the Internet for inexpensive telephoning—since costs remain the same for the user whether the other party is in the next room or across the world. The Internet quickly became a seamless web of interconnections, initially (late 1980s) used for corporate messaging and later (mid-1990s) for individual communication.

At the same time, the amount of information that a modem could transmit or receive had grown from 300 bytes to more than 56,000 bytes (a measure of information roughly equal to one digit or letter) per second. Special lines, provided by telephone companies (DSL) or cable systems (using "cable modems") allow speeds ranging from 10 to 100 times as fast, and even much higher speed *broadband* connections are being planned. These higher speeds, as well as the improvement and ever-lower cost of *scanners* (for converting pictures to bytes) and other equipment led to the transmission of pictures (first line drawings and monochromatic still pictures, then color, then moving pictures) and sounds as well as words and data—and also to the use of the Internet for commercial advertising. While commercial messages were a rarity on the Internet as late as 1995, by 2000 advertising appeared on a huge proportion of *home pages* (i.e., the first page you see when you log on to a site) accessible through the *World Wide Web.*

Nobody knows how many *servers* (computers configured to make *Web sites* available for those searching for them—or for the information they contain—on the Internet) or *routers* (devices that cooperate to deliver messages, chopped into small later-reassembled *packets*, across the Internet, between servers and their clients) there are operating at any moment, and nobody could possibly draw a comprehensive map of the Internet. There are literally billions of Web pages available, from those of individuals who put out pictures or text of interest only to distant relatives, to news media that can keep up to the minute without breaking into existing programming or editions, organizations and corporations that can make information available far more effectively than with printed materials, and governments able to communicate with constituents quickly and cheaply. Through the use of *browsers* (software for bringing up and displaying Web pages) such as Netscape Navigator or Microsoft Internet Explorer, it is possible to locate material—text, graphics, audio, video—using simple and logical language or by clicking on a simple *hyperlink* rather than the often-lengthy specific address of the source one is looking for. Furthermore, a number of firms provide index services, *search engines*, and otherwise make it easy to find a Web page. The popularity of browsing (or *surfing*) has made the World Wide Web's "WWW" prefix synonymous with the Internet to many people. A *URL* (Uniform Resource Locator) gives every site a unique address.

E-commerce, using the Internet to sell services, merchandise (e.g., booksellers such as Amazon.com and Barnes & Noble), or information (most large newspapers and databases such as Lexis/Nexus), has given rise to a number of "dot.com" firms, so-called because of their location in the ".com" (commerce) domain of the Internet. (Other top-level domains are .edu (education), .org (organizations), .gov (government), and several approved in late 2000 by a formerly governmental but now private organization known as ICANN.) The development of supposedly secure encryption that permits the safe and confidential sending of credit card numbers, banking and medical information, and other sensitive data through the Internet greatly aided the rise of e-commerce.

Although acronyms such as *HTML* (HyperText Markup Language, used to form Web pages) or *HTTP* (HyperText Transfer Protocol, the system of communication rules used by the Web) aren't understood by everyone, they are employed by roughly half the U.S. population and the same number of computer users overseas every day. The Internet has become a mass medium in its own right. Complex scientific and engineering data are now moving to a much smaller, but tremendously faster, government-sponsored Internet 2 network.

The traditional media also have embraced the Internet. By 2000, more than 3,700 radio stations in the United States were engaged in *Internet radio*, and were *streaming* their signals over the Web—obliterating the restrictions nature or the FCC had imposed on their traditional transmitters and antennas and making possible a worldwide audience. Video was making early moves along the same lines, although ordinary telephone modems were too slow for *full-motion video*. However, a form of pseudo-video has become popular with *Webcams*—a video camera pointed at some supposedly interesting scene (from an individual going about everyday business to the hatching of falcon eggs) updates its image on a Web site every few seconds or minutes. Television stations also used the Internet to post additional information about news or programs, as well as audio and other—sometimes interactive—information. The major music recording companies had to resort to the courts in 2000–2001 to close down *Napster*, a service that used *MP3* audio coding software to permit the *downloading* of recorded music (to be listened to over increasingly high quality computer loudspeakers, or on CDs "burned" or created at home) from the 'net—without any royalties being paid to the copyright holder. As modems grew faster and DVD video recording easier, the motion picture industry started worrying that they, too, would find the Internet a major competitor. Popular author Stephen King "published" a novel on the Internet in 2000, a chapter at a time, promising to continue if enough people paid a small fee (through the Internet) for each chapter. Not enough did. While definitions of words like *Webcasting* are subject to change almost without notice, the concept that motion pictures, graphics, sounds and text could be converted to or originated as bits of information and transmitted electronically, seems to have taken hold. While some argue that the Internet can become the next generation of television (aided by the standards for DTV, which are more compatible with computer monitors than with conventional television), others go beyond that goal and maintain that the ongoing convergence in the visual media will result in a computer/Internet takeover of all media.

Internet Radio   *See* Internet.

Invention, Innovation, Patents   *Invention* is the act or process of developing something new—a device, a process, a thing—through study and experimentation. *Innovation* is the introduction of an invention into use or into the marketplace. The U.S. Constitution (Article I, Section 8) empowers the federal government to issue *patents*, which guarantee to the inventor exclusive rights for 17 years to manufacture, or to *license* the manufacture of the invention, in exchange for monetary *royalties*. In exchange, the invention goes into the public domain after that period, or it may be renewed once. The intent of a patent system is to encourage both invention and use of that invention widely, rather than keep it as a *trade secret* for an indefinite period. (*See also* Copyright.)

Ionosphere   *See* Waves.

IRAC (Interdepartment Radio Advisory Committee)   Now part of **NTIA**. *See* Allocation.

ISP (Internet Service Provider)   *See* Internet.

ITFS (instructional television fixed service)   Channels set aside in the 12 GHz band for televised school instruction; channels are often leased to MDS operators at night.

Kinescope Recorder (Kine)   *See* Recordings *and* Television Camera Tubes.

Ku-Band   *See* Satellite.

Land Mobile   A family of radiocommunication services, generally the **safety and special services**—police, forestry—but sometimes the **common carrier** services such as mobile telephone. Includes **cellular** telephones that enable one to keep in touch over a wide geographical area, with no loss of quality, because of continuous computer-directed assignment of the call to the closest transmitter-receiver site from which the call can be connected to the wire network. Mobile units in cars and airplanes may be associated with *fixed* or *base* stations that communicate with a number of mobile units. Since the late 1940s, the growth of land mobile has clashed with the growth or preservation of television broadcast frequency bands, since both services need vast amounts of spectrum space with similar characteristics. Showing an insatiable demand for land mobile channel bandwidth are a variety of PCS (personal communication service) systems—from cellular telephones (now in their second generation in the U.S. and third generation in Europe and Asia) to the original (failed) Iridium system that launched scores of low-orbit satellites, but couldn't persuade the public to sign up.

Laser   An acronym for *l*ight *a*mplification by *s*timulated *e*mission of radiation. Any one of a number of devices that can convert incident electromagnetic radiation of mixed frequency (*incoherent*) energy to one or more very specific or *discrete* frequencies of highly amplified and *coherent* visible radiation. Can be used for carrying great amounts of information or, because of the coherent nature of the radiation and its sharply aimed focus, for cutting materials; also for *holography*, a technique for recording and reproducing three-dimensional "pictures."

License   *See* Invention *and* Allocation.

Licensee   *See* Ownership.

Licensing   *See* Allocation.

Line-of-Sight   *See* Waves.

Lines   *See* Television Signals.

LMDS   Local Multipoint Distribution Service.

Local Oscillator   *See* Receiver.

Local Origination   *See* Cable.

Long Playing (LP)   *See* Recordings.

Longwave   *See* Waves.

Lotteries   *See* Allocation, Assignment, Allotment, Licensing.

LPFM (Low-power FM broadcasting)   In the late 1940s, a term sometimes applied to Class D (10 watt) noncommercial educational FM stations. After the FCC mandated that such stations either use higher power (100–1000 watts) or accept interference from other stations, many Class D stations left the air. Community groups, schools, churches, and others became active in arguing for licensing of more such stations in the 1970s and 1980s, arguing that the public deserved a voice in communities served mostly by increasingly alien group–owned stations. Frustrated by FCC inaction (the result of pressure from commercial and some noncommercial FM stations and people who thought that *repeaters* were more important), some groups established illegal stations. If they caused interference, the FCC closed them down. In 1998, the FCC approved new class of LPFM stations, but instituted strict rules to prevent interference to existing stations—and refused to license any previously illegal station. Congress all but eliminated LPFM in 2000, but agitation for such a service wouldn't go away.

LPTV (low-power television)   A television service authorized in 1981 designed to service extremely small areas. Supposedly intended for minority groups and others with a programming affinity. Since there effectively are no multiple ownership restrictions, some large corporations applied for hundreds of channels in various localities. Several thousand are on the air.

Mass Communication   Simultaneous (or nearly so) process of essentially one-way communication from a single source addressed to a mass audience. The message usually is reproduced in quantity through mechanical or electronic devices. A *mass audience* is more than two undifferentiated persons voluntarily engaged in the same communications behavior or activity, but not necessarily interacting in other ways. **Feedback**, often economic, may alter the content of mass communication but does not alter the one-way nature of a given mass communication event. (*See* Communication.)

Mass Media   The means or channels of mass communication: primarily newspapers, magazines, radio (sound) broadcasting, television broadcasting, motion pictures, and, secondarily, the theater, recordings, and books. Heterogeneity of content within the medium, but not necessarily any specific item or example, and voluntary attention by the audience are common characteristics of the mass media.

Master   *See* Recordings.

Master Antenna Television (MATV)   *See* Cable.

Matrix   *See* Modulation.

MDS or **MMDS** (multipoint distribution service or multichannel multipoint distribution service)   A microwave service, sometimes using channels leased from *ITFS,* typically used to provide *HBO* and other pay-cable services in cities where cable is not yet fully installed. The MDS operator generally leases special *downconverter* tuning devices that pick up the microwave signal and convert it to the television frequencies expected by the television set. Often called "wireless cable" to emphasize the program service being provided.

Meaning   *See* Communication.

Mechanical Scanning   *See* Television's Early Technological Development.

Message   *See* Communication.

Microgroove   *See* Recordings.

Microradio   Another term for LPFM.

Microwave   *See* Waves.

MIDI   (Musical Instrument Digital Interface) Computerized control system that allows a keyboard to "talk" to studio synthesizers for creating music electronically.

Modem   *Mo*dulator-*Dem*odulator. *See* Internet.

Modulated Continuous Wave (MCW)   *See* Modulation.

Modulation   A radio signal generally consists of a *carrier wave* and one or two *sidebands.* (Sophisticated systems such as *single sideband* do not strictly follow this pattern, but they are not used for broadcasting, except for television's *vestigial sideband* [*see* Television Signals].) The carrier wave **signal** generally is on the center frequency of the **channel** on which the **transmitter** is operating and, unless used in an "off-on" manner to transmit **Morse code**, carries no intelligence itself. The *information* or intelligence or *message* is carried in the form of *modulated* sidebands. Sometimes the modulation is a variation in the strength or *amplitude* of the sideband; sometimes it is a swing of *frequency* within the channel; sometimes it has other forms, such as *pulses.* The first two (amplitude modulation, or AM, and frequency modulation, or FM) are used for broadcasting. AM takes up less spectrum space but is more prone to interference on most bands. Television uses FM for sound and AM for picture. Some radiotelegraph systems use the modulation of a tone, interrupted to produce dots and dashes, on a *continuous wave* (*CW*) or *modulated CW* transmitter. Within each channel there may be space to put additional information; a telegraph signal, using very little **bandwidth**, can generally be added to a telephone channel, with the telegraph sound being filtered out at the telephone. In addition, the bandwidth of a channel can often be divided and made more useful by *diplexing* or *multiplexing*—inserting two or more signals on the same channel in such a way that each may be retrieved independently at the receiving end. Since 1955, the FCC has allowed FM broadcast stations to obtain a *Subsidiary Communications Authorization* (*SCA*) that will permit it to use one or more *subcarriers* within the total channel bandwidth of 200 kHz but outside the modulated frequency swing of the main program channel.

These subcarriers generally are used for *stereophonic* (*stereo*) music transmissions. In a *binaural* system, the human condition of two ears feeding one brain is extended backward from ears to two loudspeakers, two amplifiers, two signals from the receiver, and two microphones. Stereo permits listeners with proper equipment to hear the music stereophonically and other listeners to hear it *monaurally*. In recent years *quadrasonic* systems, which give the illusion of four sound sources surrounding the listener, have been developed, some using the *discrete* system—four separate isolated channels fed to four speakers—and others the *matrix* system—reduction and encoding of four channels into two, and decoding back into four at the receiver or player, a less expensive but slightly less efficient process. Other FM stations use their subcarriers for *storecasting* or *transitcasting* or for even more specialized services such as **facsimile** or special programming to the blind or, using teletypewriters, the deaf. (*See* Waves.) *Transitcasting* is an SCA service supplied to trains, buses, and similar conveyances by FM stations. Since the driver or crew usually controls the receiver, the riding public becomes a captive audience to the broadcast station and its music, and sometimes commercial messages. After some public outcry and the decline in public transit use after the early 1960s, transitcasting became rare. A similar service is *storecasting*, in which a music service—sometimes labeled *Muzak* after the franchised trademark used by the largest of such firms—is delivered over a subcarrier or over leased wire lines to stores, doctors' offices, and other business places. If broadcast, special receivers able to pick up the subcarrier are supplied for a monthly fee.

Television multiplexing is less common, although an audio program cue and intercom for station personnel in the studio or field, called *IFB* (*interruptible foldback*), stereo sound, or a *Secondary Audio Program* service (*SAP*) such as a simultaneous language translation can be found.

Particularly common are means of providing printed captions for the deaf on a **closed caption** basis, in which a special receiver or decoder must be purchased to pick up the *character-generated* captions on a line of the **VBI** or *vertical blanking interval* between pictures. *Open captioning* may be seen by everyone, without the need for a special receiver, but it is deemed by programmers to be disruptive to those with normal hearing and is not common. The open use of sign language, usually shown in an insert in the picture, is chiefly found in telecasts of religious services.

Monaurally   *See* Modulation.

Morphing   From the word "metamorphosis," or change of physical form. Refers to the practice of using a computer to create major changes in appearance, particularly in feature films. Typically, the images flow into one another.

Morse Code   Code that permits transmission of the alphabet as a series of short and long pulses of electricity or signal: "dots and dashes." It was invented by Samuel F. B. Morse and his associates (especially Alfred Vail) in the 1830s for use with the electrical **telegraph**. Because it made use of the fact that some letters are more common in English than others, it was an unconscious use of some of the principles of *information theory* (*see* Communication) to achieve greater efficiency—the letter *e,* for example, is very common and is coded as a quickly and easily transmitted dot, whereas the infrequently used letter *z* requires two dashes and two dots.

MOS   *See* Television Camera Tubes.

Mosaic   *See* Modulation.

Motion Pictures   A visual record of a story or event, stored in the form of images, and usually the associated sound, on film, for later projection at such speed as to give an audience an illusion of motion; also, the projection of same. In a television studio, films generally are projected in a film chain (*see* Television Camera Tubes).

MPEG   (Motion Picture Experts Group) A video camera format for encoding (and later editing and transmitting) graphics such as motion pictures via the Internet. *See* Recording.

MP3   A format for transmitting sounds (including musical recordings) via the Internet. *See* Recording.

MSO (multiple system operator)   *See* Cable.

MTV   A cable programming service specializing in short *music videos.*

Multimedia   An overall term for the convergence of audio, video and computer media in the home or for business presentations.

Multiple Ownership   *See* Ownership.

Multiplexed   *See* Modulation *and* Television Camera Tubes.

Must-Carry Rules   *See* Cable.

Mutual Broadcasting System (MBS)   *See* Network.

NAB (National Association of Broadcasters)

Television Code   *See* Programming.

NABET (National Association of Broadcast Employees and Technicians) *See* Unions.

Napster   The most popular of several services briefly (until legal action closed it down in 2000) used for downloading musical recordings from the Internet without paying royalties to the copyright holder.

NARBA (North American Regional Broadcasting Agreement)   *See* AM Channels.

Narrowcasting   *See* Broadcasting.

Network   Two or more stations, often broadcasting stations, interconnected by some means, or associated for the often simultaneous transmission of the same messages or programs. When one station picks up the signal off the air from another, it is a *relay.* Broadcasting networks were referred to as *chain broadcasting* in the 1920s and 1930s, and colloquially are known as *webs* or *nets.* Since the late 1970s, various pay-cable program services, such as *HBO* (Home Box Office), *Showtime,* and *CNN* (Cable News Network), and *"super-stations,"* such as WTBS in Atlanta, WPIX in New York, and others that provide programming by satellite to cable system operators, as well as collections of stations such as PAX, have been referred to as "networks," further confusing the issue. In 2001, there were seven national broadcast television networks in the United States—American Broadcasting Company (*ABC*), now owned by Disney; Columbia Broadcasting System (*CBS*), now owned by Viacom; National Broadcasting Company (*NBC*), which is owned by General Electric; the *Fox* broadcasting network (owned by Rupert Murdoch); Warner Brothers Network (*WB*); Universal Pictures Network (*UPN*); and the Public Broadcasting Service (*PBS*), funded in part by the *Corporation for Public Broadcasting.* National radio networks include ABC (which supplies four separate services), CBS, NBC (is owned and operated by Westwood One), and National Public Radio (*NPR*). *American Public Radio* also provides programming to public radio stations. (The *Mutual Broadcasting System* closed down in 2000.) Most television stations and just over half the country's radio stations are affiliated with networks. In the United States, a network generally consists of the program-producing and central administering organization, a number of *owned-and-operated* (*O & O*) stations (*see* Ownership), and a greater number of independently owned but *affiliated* stations. The network generally produces, or buys from independent producers or *packagers,* programs that are beyond the resources of a single station and "sells" them to national advertisers for program production costs and the aggregate sum of the time charges of all affiliates airing the program. Stations may refuse to carry network programs, since the station licensee is legally responsible for everything aired over the station. The affiliates receive only 25 to 35% of their normal time charges but gain in other ways. They can sell *spots*—commercial advertisements—immediately before and after the program, during *station break* or *station ID* (identification) periods, for high prices because of advertiser desire to reach the large audiences attracted by the expensive network programs. The networks also supply affiliates with some *sustaining*—not *sponsored* by commercial advertisers—programs without cost, as well as with prestigious news programming. Until the mid–1980s, networks usually paid for interconnecting the stations by microwave or **coaxial cable** facilities supplied by AT&T, but since about 1985 they lease relay facilities on space communications **satellites** for that purpose.

News   The timely report of an event of interest to a number of people, often obtained through the *wire services* or *news agencies*—organizations that gather news and transmit it, usually by *teletypewriter,* to media clients for dissemination to the public by various means. The main wire services used in the United States are the Associated Press (*AP*), the struggling United Press International (*UPI*), and *Reuters,* an English firm. Frequently considered part of *broadcast journalism* are *public affairs* programs, which consist of news and feature material dealing with government and public issues that help citizens make reasoned decisions on such matters, and *editorials*, which are clearly identified, on-the-air expressions of opinion by a station licensee or his representative on a topic of public interest and concern. (*See* ENG *and* Remote.)

NII   National Information Infrastructure. Term adopted during the Clinton–Gore administration (1993–2001) to refer to aspects of telecommunications policy.

Nipkow Disc   *See* Television's Early Technological Development.

Noise   *See* Signal.

NTIA   National Telecommunications and Information Administration of the U.S. Department of Commerce.

NTSC (National Television System Committee)   *See* Television Signals.

O & O (owned and operated)   *See* Network.

Off-network   *See* Programming.

Ohm   *See* Circuit.

On-line and Off-line Editing   Different forms of computerized video editing systems.

Optical Fiber   *See* Fiber Optic.

Orthicon   *See* Television Camera Tubes.

Outside Broadcast (OB)   *See* Remote.

Ownership   Although physical facilities and "goodwill" may be owned, the Communications Act of 1934 (and the Radio Act of 1927 before it) reserves title to the entire electromagnetic spectrum to the people of the United States, with the government administering it. Hence, although someone may own a transmitter, the public owns the channel on which it is operating. The broadcaster merely has a permit to use it in the public interest for a few years; in practice, licenses are renewable and have rarely been revoked during or at the end of their term. The FCC has frequently investigated the issue of concentration of control and has issued reports, orders, and rules frowning on *cross-media ownership*, overlapping ownership of a newspaper and a broadcasting station in the same market; prohibiting *duopoly*, one licensee from controlling more than one station of the same service in a single market; and limits *multiple ownership*, the total number of stations an individual or company may own nationally in each broadcasting service. This number, for many years, was 7 standard (AM), 7 FM, and 7 television, with no more than five of the television stations on the VHF part of the spectrum. In 1985, these numbers were increased to 12-12-12, and then in 1992 individual licensees were allowed to own up to 18 AM and 18 FM stations in the Unites States, and up to two of each in major markets. As a result of the Telecommunications Act of 1996, all multiple-ownership restrictions were dropped for radio, and modified substantially for television. However, the commission no longer routinely approves AM-FM-TV combinations in the same market, although those already licensed to a single individual or company may continue until a change of ownership occurs. Many multiple or group owners have stations in different towns; in recent years *conglomerate* companies—firms that own or control numerous companies in different fields—have entered the field of broadcasting. The number of stations owned by a given entity has burgeoned from a maximum of 21 (Park Broadcasting in 1984) to more than 1,200 (Clear Channel/AMFM). In some major markets, with as many as 20 or 30 radio outlets, almost all are owned by no more than three or four licensees. **Network** *affiliation* is *not* the same as ownership; many group owners have one station affiliated with one network, a second station with another network, and so on. The *licensee*, or station "owner," is responsible for everything broadcast over the station since, at least in theory, he or she is a trustee for the public.

Package, Packager   *See* Network *and* Programming.

PAL (Phase Alternation by Line)   *See* Television Signals.

Parabolic Reflector   *See* Antenna.

Parallel   *See* Circuit.

Patents   *See* Invention.

Pay-TV, Pay-Cable   A television distribution system in which members of the audience pay a special charge for particular programs. Originally planned as an over-the-air service, and the subject of a number of demonstrations and experiments from 1951 on, most pay-TV is now in the form of separate *pay-cable* channels (such as HBO, Showtime, and The Movie Channel) for which additional monthly charges are levied. Sometimes, pay-TV charges are on the basis of pay-per-view (PPV), the cost to the viewer varying depending on the individual program, using a variety of hardware to prevent nonpaying viewers from descrambling or obtaining the pay program(s). *Scrambling* is a process that mixes up picture or sound elements during transmission but permits normal reception on a set with the proper (leased) equipment attached. Home Box Office was the first (1976) to establish a system to provide pay-cable programs to the head ends of cable systems using space communications satellites or, in some instances, microwave. Most "free" or pay national programming services, including PPV, distribute in the same way. The last on-air pay-TV stations tended to be independently programmed.

People Meters   *See* Ratings.

Performing Rights Societies   *See* Copyright.

Phosphor   *See* Television Signals.

Picture Elements or **Pixels**   *See* Television Signals.

Plate   *See* Vacuum Tube.

Plumbicon   *See* Television Camera Tubes.

Polarization (horizontal, vertical, or circular)   *See* Antenna.

PPV (pay-per-view)   *See* Pay-TV.

Precision Offset Carrier   *See* Transmitter.

Prime Time Access Rule (PTAR)   *See* Programming.

Production House   An organization, sometimes associated with a motion picture studio, that specializes in *packaging* and producing television programs or commercials. Examples are MTM and Lorimar.

Programming   Among terms needing definition are the short–lived *family viewing* (FV) *time*, the period from 7 P.M. to 9 P.M. Eastern and Pacific time which, starting in 1975, was to contain only content suitable for the entire family. This standard was written into the *NAB Television Code* after pressure from Congress and others concerned about the possible effect of violence and sex content on children. FCC chairman Wiley's "encouragement" was a factor in a federal judge's decision in 1982 that individual stations should control their own programming; concerted or mandatory (NAB code) advertising restrictions were illegal. The NAB promptly dropped the entire code idea: program content as well as advertising; radio as well as television. *PTAR*, or the *Prime Time Access Rule*, was a 1974 FCC action that required affiliated stations to program at least one hour during prime time, 7 P.M. to 11 P.M. Eastern and Pacific time, from non-network sources, to encourage a diversity of programming and programming sources. A *format* is a type of program (or *genre*) such as a soap opera; the term may also refer to the specific organization of content of a particular show. A program *stripped* or *across the board* is scheduled at the same time each weekday. When a different program is shown at the same time each weekday, the strategy is called *checkerboarding*. *Counterprogramming* is the scheduling of material usually not aired by competitors at that hour, e.g., entertainment when most stations are airing local news. *Station* or *affiliate time* is the prime time period (usually from 7 P.M. to 8 P.M. Eastern and Pacific time) not programmed by the network. Many non-network programs are *syndicated*—either *off-network*, having been shown on a network in the past, or original—and sold to individual local stations. A *spin-off* is a program developed around a character or a situation in a successful program. A program *package* is the program idea, writers, stars, director, and so forth assembled by a *packager* for production or sale to a network or for syndication.

Propagation   *See* Waves.

Public Access   *See* Cable.

Public Affairs   *See* News.

Public Broadcasting Service (PBS)   *See* Network.

Public Interest, Convenience and/or Necessity   *See* Allocation.

Public Television   *See* ETV.

Public Utility   *See* Common Carrier.

Pulse Modulation (PM)   *See* Modulation.

Quad Head (Quadruplex)   *See* Recordings.

Quadrasonic   *See* Modulation.

Radiation, Conduction, Induction   Electricity can travel from one point to another in a variety of ways. *Conduction* requires a conductor, usually a piece of wire, to carry the current. However, something not specially prepared as the conductor can also serve, as, for example, the earth, salt water, or some other common **circuit** ground. *Induction* uses the principle that an object may be electrified, magnetized, or given an induced voltage by exposure to a magnetic field. During the late 1800s several experimenters, particularly Nathan B. Stubblefield, arranged two loops of wire a distance apart and sent an electrical signal through one of them. The resulting magnetic field was picked up by the other loop, some distance away—up to three miles in some cases. Although the method was generally used for **Morse code**, speech could be transmitted in this way. Most of the energy in an induction field is, however, contained in the vicinity of the transmitting loop. At higher frequencies, it is possible to *radiate*—diffuse from a center, as when a balloon is blown up—the signal for great distances. Generally radio communication requires frequencies above those used for telegraph or voice, although any radio frequency may undergo **modulation** with the audio frequencies of speech and allow the code or the speech to ride piggyback on the radio frequency wave. *See* Waves.

Radio, Radiocommunication   A general term applied to the use of electromagnetic, or Hertzian, waves to communicate. An earlier term was *wireless*.

Radio Broadcasting   Strictly speaking, multiple-address radio telephony (*see* Broadcasting).

Radiotelegraphy   *See* Telegraphy.

Radiotelephony   *See* Telephony.

Radio-Television News Directors Association   *See* Unions.

Ratings   Estimates of audience size and composition used to measure the popularity of programs. Ratings are compiled by a *rating service* such as A. C. Nielsen or Arbitron or, in earlier years, the Cooperative Analysis of Broadcasting, C. E. Hooper, and others. Methods include telephone calls that are *coincidental* with the program, *diaries*, and various kinds of recorders, including *people meters*, which require each viewing member of the household periodically to push a button that is recorded at the ratings company, but do quickly secure information about individual (rather than household) viewing. The results are expressed either as *ratings*, the proportion of all television homes that are tuned to a given program, or *share*, the proportion of homes using television at that time that are tuned to the particular program and frequently include additional demographic data of value to advertisers. Advertising agencies also use many other kinds of research data, such as *psychographics.*

Receiver   A device for the reception of electromagnetic waves carrying modulated radiocommunication signals, generally including (or attached to) an antenna; tuning components; a detector; and enough amplification stages to permit use of a loudspeaker. Among the earliest devices for detecting radio waves were the *galvanometer*, a sensitive electrical meter that would show, by deflection of the meter's pointer, when a signal was present, and the *coherer*, a glass tube containing metallic filings that would clump together or cohere when an electric current passed through. A *tapper* or *decoherer* would disperse the filings between each dot or dash. Later, the *crystal set* (*see* Vacuum Tube) was employed, since electric current could flow only in one direction through it and it did not need decohering. The diode vacuum tube supplanted the galena or other crystal for this purpose. Greater and greater *selectivity*—the ability to choose between competing signals—and *sensitivity*—the ability to receive weak signals—were obtained with the *regenerative, superregenerative, heterodyne,* and *superheterodyne* receiver circuits. Receiving sets using the last named circuits worked most efficiently at a single frequency, the *intermediate frequency* or *IF*, no matter what the frequency of the station being received. In essence, this type of receiver used a *local oscillator* to generate a "local" radio frequency signal within the set, which would be a certain number of kiloHertz—the value of the IF—above or below the frequency of the station to which the receiver was tuned. In tuning to the frequency of the desired station, one would automatically change the local oscillator or transmitter since the same knob controlled both tuning condensers. The two frequencies would "beat" against one another, leaving the resultant intermediate frequency, the difference between the two signals, which would always be the same. The generally relatively low IF—a common frequency used in AM radios today is 455 kHz—permits simple and rugged design of components and, beyond the tuning stage, use of only one frequency. The equipment can be designed for that one frequency rather than to correspond with the broad range of frequencies used by the various transmitting stations within range. As a result, almost all radio receivers today combine tuning or radio frequency (*rf*) stages, a detector stage, and a number of intermediate frequency and audio frequency (*af*) stages of *amplification*—boosting the signal without otherwise changing its characteristics. The word "receiver" is now commonly used for high-fidelity tuner-amplifier combinations that are attached to external loudspeakers, with the word "radio" used for cheaper self-contained units. A television receiver is similar to a radio receiver in function: the desired channel is tuned in much as in the radio receiver and the resulting signal is eventually fed to the picture tube (kine-scope) and loudspeaker for reproduction of the picture and sound.

Receiving Station   *See* Station.

Record Communication   A term to distinguish nontransient communica-tion. For example, the telegraph is a record communication; the telephone is not. Film is a record communication; "live" television is not.

Recordings   Reproduction of musical or other performances stored in the form of magnetic patterns in tape, or grooves in plastic discs. Motion pic-ture film also is a form of recording as are a number of other forms—even writing falls in the category—that are used in broadcasting. The earliest sound recordings were made on wax cylinders. Later, discs, usually 10 or 12 inches in diameter, rotating at 78.26 rpm, were used. The *electrical tran-scription* (*ET*), used for radio broadcast programming for many years, con-sisted of a 15-inch or 16-inch disc revolving at 33⅓ rpm, which gave 15 minutes of playing time per side using standard width grooves. In the late 1940s, Peter Goldmark and a CBS Laboratories team developed the *LP* (*long-playing*) record for home use. It was 10 or 12 inches in diameter and revolved at 33⅓ rpm but used an extremely fine *microgroove* that en-abled one side to hold more than 20 minutes of music. This analog format was popular into the 1990s, particularly for classical music. While popular music also was supplied on LPs, disc jockeys often had to select one hot "cut" out of many on the "album." At the same time the LP became popu-lar, RCA introduced a 7-inch, 45-rpm microgroove disc with an oversize center hole, but after a long marketing struggle it was restricted to popular music, one tune to a side. The higher quality of microgroove led to the rapid phasing out of the 78-rpm disc. More recently, the highest-quality audio re-productions have come from **CD**s or *compact discs*, which are computer controlled, using **digital** rather than **analog** signals that virtually eliminate hiss or *noise*. Another use for this system, called *CD-ROM* (compact disk-read only memory), is used interactively with computers for the storage and retrieval of vast amounts of data. *Reel-to-reel* magnetic tape recording de-rived from magnetic wire recording machines and from steel tape continu-ous loop recording machines used for such things as telephone weather forecast announcements in the early 1940s. While still used professionally, reel-to-reel sound recordings have been replaced in homes with easier to handle, self-contained devices that give good sound reproduction. The most common such device, until the **CD** became popular, was the twin hub *cassette*, in which the tape is permanently threaded on supply and takeup reels and the entire unit is placed over shafts driven from the motor. For some years, there also was the single hub 8-track *cartridge*, which, although a bit bulkier and more complex, plays multichannel music with higher fi-delity and is even easier to insert in the playback device than the cassette. A form of *cart*(ridge) machine is used for short audio recordings, usually commercials, in radio broadcasting. A digitalized system, *DAT* (*d*igital *a*udio*t*ape), which can make perfect copies (or *dubs*) of CDs or other DATs, is technically available but has been held up in this country because of the apprehension of record companies and other copyright holders.

Television or video recordings originally were made by the *kinescope* (television picture tube) *recorder*, in which a motion picture camera photographed the images on a special television picture tube of great brightness. The quality of the resulting *kine* was not high, partly because the U.S. television system scans 30 complete pictures per second but a sound movie camera photographs only 24 frames per second. There also were contrast and other problems. Color kinescope recordings were made as color television became common. While sometimes reruns were aired via kine, the primary use of this technique was archival, although it sometimes was used (in conjunction with a "hot" or one-minute film processor) to project sporting events in theaters, the earliest form of "pay-TV." One advantage of kinescope recording was that, before electronic standards converters were developed, it could ignore the differences between different television standards such as NTSC, PAL and SECAM, and distribute in a "universal" film format. Even today, the technique has a growing number of adherents, since it is now possible to shoot, edit and do full post-production in an all-digital electronic form, and then use laser scanners to create a *HD* version on 35 mm or 70 mm film almost identical to that which would have resulted from using film throughout.

In the late 1950s, magnetic *videotape recording* (*VTR*) was developed, revolutionizing the industry. The first bulky *quad head* or *quadruplex* videotape recorders used a revolving assembly of four record-playback heads over which 2-inch tape was transported at 15 (usually) or 7½ inches per second (ips), with the heads briefly overlapping as they turned at high speed, providing a picture almost indistinguishable from "live." Although now considered obsolete, the quad format, employing open reels rather than cartridges or cassettes, is still used for much archival and historic tape storage, since it was the *de facto* standard from 1956 until the late 1970s. (RCA and Ampex did have a 2″ cassette system, with internal reels, used primarily for commercials.) Later, *high band VTR*, which used a high-frequency—10 MHz—carrier, yielded a very high signal-to-noise ratio, and its excellent interference-free picture enabled more *generations* (successive duplicates) to be made from the original recording, or *master.* Color recording and electronic editing to the exact frame desired are now possible on even the relatively inexpensive *helical scan* VTRs used for industrial and educational purposes. In these VTRs the tape is wrapped in a spiral (helix) around a large-diameter, fixed drum within which a record-playback head revolves. Helical scan VTRs, first in a 2″ format, and then in 1″ or 1/2″ formats, and 3/4″ *U-Matic* cassette VCRs are much less expensive, recording for longer lengths of time than the now-obsolete quad head machines or early 1″ professional helical scan models, but at the expense of image quality. By the early 1980s, professional videotape recording had adopted a 1″ helical-scan standard (Type C) that permitted substantial savings in cost and weight and was used widely until the late 1990s.

In the 1980s, the home VCR (*videocassette recorder*), in a variety of formats, such as *VHS* and *Beta* (and more recently, *Super-8* and *S-VHS*) became a very popular consumer item (see Appendix C). Although VHS and Beta engaged in a bitter marketing struggle, Sony threw in the towel and abandoned the possibly better quality Beta in 1988, which was the end of the 1/2-inch-composite-analog-consumer-distribution-format competition. VCRs usually are used for *time-shifting* (recording for later playback) or for the playing of videocassettes of motion pictures rented or purchased from retail outlets—which has become a major industry in its own right. When combined with a small camera, these recorders are called *camcorders* and have replaced the home movie camera and projector. First used for stop-action recording during sporting events, various kinds of *videodiscs*—thin, flexible plastic discs used to record and play back video and audio material by magnetic, laser, or other complicated processes—are now being used in the home in the same way as musical recordings, particularly in the *DVD* (digital video disk) format available from video rental stores. Since there is no worldwide agreement on technical standards, even with videodisc's many potential

▪ Some Audio Recording Formats

	Medium	Speed	Usual Size (diameter)	Frequency Response (Hz)	Usual Playing Time (minutes, one side)	Notes
Standard	Mechanical	78.26 rpm	10", 12"	100–6,000	7 (12")	Standard groove
Transcription (ET)	Mechanical	33⅓ rpm	16"	70–8,000	15	Standard groove broadcasting programs
Wire recorder	Magnetic		2"	100–6,000	60	.01" thick wire
Long-playing (LP)	Mechanical	33⅓ rpm	10", 12"	20–18,000	25 (12")	Microgroove
45-rpm (RCA)	Mechanical	45 rpm	7"	100–8,000	5	Microgroove for popular music; later 60–16,000 Hz
Reel-to-reel	Magnetic	1⅞ to 15 ips	7"	20–15,000	60 (3¾ ips) 15 (15 ips)	¼" wide magnetic tape; consumer can record
Cassette (micro size)	Magnetic	1⅞ and ¹⁵⁄₁₆ ips	2½" × 4" 1¼" × 2"	20–14,000	30–60	Original frequency response was low; consumer can record
Compact disc (CD)	Laser optical		120 mm	15–20,000	70	Digital; playback only
Digital audiotape (DAT)	Magnetic	8.15 mm/sec	2" × 3"	15–22,000	120	Digital cassette; record or playback

Note: This is not an exhaustive list. It is arranged chronologically. Some formats—like magnetic wire recorders and eight-track cassettes—have come and gone; others, such as 16-rpm records, never really had much use. Others were used for specialized purposes: 10" reels for professional audiotaping, reel-to-reel speeds as high as 60 ips, early field recordings on motion picture film, audio cartridges (carts) for broadcast commercials, and so on. Playback time for magnetic tape depends on the thickness of the tape and how much can be put on a reel or into a cassette. Some reel-to-reel and cassette formats permit multiple tracks of recording. Improvements were made to each format during its existence that enhanced audio fidelity, particularly to the audiocassette and the 45-rpm record, which now exists in a 12" format for high-fidelity professional use as well as in the format familiar to consumers.

⬛ Some Video Recording Formats

	Medium	Reel, Cart, Cassette, or Disc	Usual Width	Usual Playing Time (minutes)	Notes
Kinescope	Optical (film)	Reel	16 mm or 35 mm	60	Poor quality; now obsolete
Quadruplex	Magnetic	Reel	2″	30–60	Broadcast use
Helical scan	Magnetic	Reel	2″	30–60–120	Industrial, broadcast use
Helical scan (types A, B, C)	Magnetic	Reel	1″	10–180	Mostly boradcast, some industrial use
Cartridge	Magnetic	Cart	2″	5–20 ⎫	Carts and cassettes
Cassettes	Magnetic	Cassette	2″	5–20 ⎬	used by stations for commercials
U-Matic (color under)	Magnetic	Cassette	.75″	20–60	Limited broadcast use
Beta	Magnetic	Cassette	.50″	270	Primarily home use
VHS	Magnetic	Cassette	.50″	360	Primarily home use
Betacam VHS-C	Magnetic	Cassette	.50″	20	Used for ENG and as camcorders
ED Beta	Magnetic	Cassette	.50″	360 ⎫	Higher quality, but
S-VHS	Magnetic	Cassette	.50″	270 ⎬	not compatible with earlier with designs;
Video 8	Magnetic	Cassette	8 mm	120 ⎭	nonbroadcast
Videodisc	Optical or mechanical	Disc	7″ diameter	120+	Usually playback only
D-1, D-2, etc.	Magnetic	Reel	1″	60	Digital, broadcast use
DVD	Optical	Disc	7″ diameter	120+	Usually for rented (laser) feature films

Note: Literally dozens of formats have been used for video recording. Most are mutually incompatible. Above are those most commonly found in television broadcasting stations, listed chronologically. When magnetic videotape recording (VTR) became possible in the late 1950s, kinescope recordings became obsolete—but they may be the only source for programs aired before 1960. The many motion picture film formats used by television news departments are not included here. Although some broadcasting stations use home videocassette recorders (VCRs) for their news operations, these machines do not meet the FCC's technical broadcasting standards.

advantages—inexpensive materials, simple duplication processes—it has not yet replaced videotape *cartridge* and *videocassette* systems for short and even long messages in home machines, but is coming up fast.

Although the use of *time base correctors* now permits relatively inexpensive VTRs (typically Betacams) to be used for over-the-air broadcast, particularly in **ENG** and **EFP** applications, it seems probable that the industry will continue using 1″ digital professional machine as its standard, although new professional *formats* appear almost as frequently as home VCR formats. The workhorse *U-Matic* format, typically for non-broadcast use, is being phased out, and its replacement is still uncertain. One difficulty with the lack of agreement on *compatible* VTR and VCR formats is that it frequently is virtually impossible to *dub* (or copy) from one to another unless the signal is separated into its *luminance* (monochromatic brightness) and *chrominance* (color) components, known as Y and C. Even then, dubbing often is quite difficult because of nonstandardized plugs, cables, and electronic parameters. Editing, however, has become a matter of pushing a few buttons rather than physically slicing tape with a razor blade.

Rectifier   *See* Vacuum Tube.

Rediffusion   *See* Cable.

Reel-to-Reel   *See* Recordings.

Regenerative   *See* Receiver.

Register   *See* Copyright.

Relay   *See* Network.

Relay, Sounder   *See* Circuit.

Remote   A broadcast or part of a broadcast that originates from outside the studio. In the United Kingdom, a remote is called an *outside broadcast* (*OB*). In the early days of radio, such a broadcast was called a *Nemo*, presumably reflecting telephone company usage—"*not emanating main office*"—although possibly associated with the "Little Nemo" comic strip about fanciful dreams off in the middle of nowhere. (*See* ENG *and* News.)

Repeaters   Unattended transmitters used to repeat the signal of a parent station. Used in television (also "satellites") for locations without sufficient population to make a full-fledged station financially viable or, in FM radio or television, to fill in areas the parent station's transmitter and antenna cannot cover because of mountainous terrain, etc. In the west, repeaters may be the only practical way to serve isolated small communities and homesteads with broadcast content.

Residuals   Payments made to actors and other artists for the airing of programs in syndication or otherwise beyond the original number of contracted showings.

Resolution   *See* Television Signals.

Resonating Frequency   *See* Waves.

Retransmission consent   Under FCC rules, a cable system needs to secure retransmission consent for transmission of programs aired on local television stations. This rule, and "must-carry" (a requirement that cable systems carry all local stations), are major negotiation points between the cable and the television broadcast industries, with the viewing public caught in the middle.

Return Wire   *See* Circuit.

Reuters   *See* News.

rf (radio frequency)   *See* Receiver.

Rotary Arc   *See* Transmitter.

Royalties   *See* Invention.

RTNDA   *See* Radio-Television News Directors Association.

Safety and Special Services   The FCC traditionally divided the radio stations under its supervision into **broadcasting, common carrier**, and safety and special services—a term that includes every other kind of user, from amateur to police. Other titles (such as "Mobile") may be used for FCC bureaus.

SAG (Screen Actors Guild)   *See* Unions.

Satellite A body in orbit around another, larger body. Often used in a political sense ("the former Soviet Union's satellites of Poland, East Germany ..."), the word has two meanings that concern broadcasting. First, artificial *space communications satellites* are launched by rocket into an orbit approximately 22,300 miles above the equator. This height and orbit enable them to remain stationary (*synchronous*) with respect to one spot on the earth's surface and high enough to "see" roughly one third of that surface. Hence, line-of-sight radio frequencies can be used to cover entire continents or oceans. Typically, each channel requires a separate *transponder* (a receiver picking up the signal from earth, which responds by changing its frequency and retransmitting the signal to many terrestrial television receive-only (*TVRO*) dishes located at television stations and cable system head ends). The signal from earth to satellite is called an *uplink*; the return signal—particularly when used for *SNG* (satellite news-gathering) is called a *downlink.* Most satellite relays operate on SHF microwave frequencies, such as the *Ku-* and *C-bands* (nomenclature originally applied to radar). These satellites can *relay* virtually any kind of electronic signal—telephone, television—point to point from one large earth station to another. They also are successfully used with small receive-only dish **antennas** at pay-cable (*see* Pay-TV) installations, network affiliates, and remote villages and towns and by more than a million private citizens in areas where over-the-air and cable signals are hard to get. *DBS*, or direct satellite-to-home broadcasting, appears to be some years away because of the need to increase power in the satellite and provide special antennas on rooftops, but is being introduced abroad. In reaction to the many dishes in private hands, networks and pay-cable companies have taken to *scrambling* their signals so their programs cannot be viewed without a special decoder. Second, a satellite is a television station that does not originate its own programming but retransmits the programs of a parent station. Satellite television stations operate on a channel regularly assigned to their community and not on the parent station's channel, as do *boosters*, or on one of the upper UHF television channels with very low power, as do *translators*, which "translate" the parent station's signal up to the high UHF.

Scanning *See* Television's Early Technological Development *and* Television Signals.

Scrambling *See* Pay-TV.

Screen Directors Guild *See* Unions.

SECAM (Séquential Couleur à Mémoire) *See* Television Signals.

Secondary Station *See* Channel.

Selectivity *See* Receiver.

Selenium *See* Television's Early Technological Development.

Semaphore A device for sending coded signals visually by means of flags, lights, or mechanically moving arms. Developed to a high degree of efficiency in the century before introduction of the electrical telegraph, semaphore today survives to a limited extent in the navy, where signal lamps using Morse code have taken over from the sailor who holds two small flags and moves them to a different position for each letter, and in railroading, which uses a simple code based on the position, ranging from vertical to horizontal, of short paddles mounted on towers.

Sensitivity   *See* Receiver.

Series   *See* Circuit.

SESAC (originally Society of European Stage Authors and Composers) *See* Copyright.

Service Drops   *See* Cable.

Share   *See* Ratings.

Short-circuit   *See* Circuit.

Shortwave   *See* Waves.

Sidebands   *See* Modulation.

Sign   *See* Communication.

Signal   Sometimes referring to any transmission (including one without intentionally encoded information or desire for **communication**), the term generally refers either to a message or to the actual electromagnetic wave propagated from a **transmitter**. The mere presence of a carrier wave signal indicates the important fact that a transmitter exists, but, technically, information is carried in the **modulation** of the signal, not in the signal itself. *Noise* in a channel is that which can interfere with reception of a message. Generally, noise is either electrical/mechanical (such as *static*) or semantic (imperfect agreement on the connotations and denotations of symbols or signs). The *signal-to-noise ratio* (S/N) is often used to describe the relative amount of interference in a given channel.

"Silent Night"   *See* DX-ing.

Single Sideband (SSB)   *See* Modulation.

Skip   *See* Waves.

Skywave   *See* Waves.

SMATV (Satellite Master Antenna Television)   *See* Cable.

SNG   Satellite news-gathering.

Solid State, Transistor, Chip   *See* Transmitter *and* Vacuum Tube.

Space Communications Satellite   *See* Satellite.

Spark Gap   *See* Transmitter.

Spectrum   *See* Waves *and* Bandwidth.

Spin-off   *See* Programming.

Sponsored   *See* Network.

Spots   *See* Network.

Static   *See* Allocation *and* Signal.

Station   The place or position from which a service is provided or operations are directed; in other words, a *transmitting station* in a given radio-communication service. A *receiving station* is the place—the home, the car—where a receiver is located. In recent years, the general public has mistakenly taken to calling their cable systems "stations."

Station Break, Station ID   *See* Network.

Stereophonic   *See* Modulation.

Stereoscopic   *See* Television Signals.

Storecasting   *See* Modulation.

Subcarriers   *See* Modulation.

Subsidiary Communications Authorization (SCA)   *See* Modulation.

Superheterodyne   *See* Receiver.

Superpower   In the United States, any standard (AM) broadcast station that uses more than 50 kw of power. Only one station, WLW (Cincinnati), was operating with such power (500 kw), from 1935 to 1939, after which the U.S. Senate frowned on superpower. However, the proposal remains active, and high-powered stations operate in other countries, notably Cuba and Mexico. In the 1920s, the term referred to lesser amounts of power.

Superregenerative   *See* Receiver.

Superstation   One of a half-dozen independent (non-network-affiliated) broadcasting stations (the first was Ted Turner's WTBS in Atlanta) whose programs are uplinked to a satellite and then made available to cable system operators for a small sum per subscriber per month. Generally, these stations (WGN in Chicago, WPIX and WWOR in New York, and KPIX in San Francisco, for example) feature movies, old reruns, and sporting events.

Sustaining   *See* Network.

Symbol   *See* Communication.

Synchronizing   *See* Television Signals.

Synchronous   *See* Satellite.

Syndicated   *See* Programming.

Talent   A generic term referring to a person or persons appearing on radio or television as actor, announcer, singer, performer, on-air news reporter, and so forth. This meaning is the one most commonly used in broadcasting; it probably is derived as a sarcastic extension of the dictionary definition, which refers to persons with gifts, aptitudes, or abilities of a superior quality.

Tapper   *See* Receiver.

Telecine   A *film chain*; a facility at a station or network used for the projection of motion picture film over a television system. Consists of a projector or projectors, an optical multiplexer and a television camera.

Telecommunications   Any transmission, emission, or reception of signs, signals, writing, images, and sounds or intelligence of any nature by wire, radio, visual, or other electromagnetic systems of communication An implication from the first part of the word (*tele-* = far, distant) is that the communication takes place over a substantial distance.

Telegraphy   A telecommunication system for the transmission of written matter by a signal code, through a wire channel unless the term *radiotelegraphy* is used to signify use of a **radiocommunication** channel.

Telephony   A telecommunication system for the transmission of speech or other sounds, through a wire channel unless the term *radiotelephony* is used to signify use of a **radiocommunication** channel.

Teletext, Videotex   Now obsolescent techniques for sending numerous "pages" to the home, generally using a television set as the display device. Teletext used a *vertical blanking interval* (*VBI*) line, was one-way, and sent up to 200 pages in sequence, over and over again. Videotex usually was transmitted over a wider cable channel and was interactive to the extent that the viewer could select which of thousands of pages of news, weather, sports scores, airline schedules, menus, and so forth, were desired. Such systems (such as CEEFAX) were in use in the United Kingdom by both BBC and ITA (using different systems), and France from the 1970s into the 1990s, but were never successfully innovated in the United States. Although touted as a potential major component of the "wired city" concept of the 1960s, these technologies have largely been superceded by the more-flexible Internet.

Teletype   *See* News

Television   A telecommunication system for the transmission of transient images of fixed or moving objects; also the broadcast service of the same name, which includes both the picture and the accompanying sound.

Television Camera Tubes   Although the original television pickup devices, which converted light energy into electrical energy, were mechanical (*see* Television's Early Technological Development), all-electronic camera tubes were devised and introduced in the late 1930s. These were generally of a storage-discharge type, storing the light falling on the tube face and then discharging it into the system by scanning the storage element with an electron beam. The all-electronic camera tubes included the *Iconoscope* of Vladimir Zworykin (RCA) and the *Image Dissector* of Philo Farnsworth. These were combined into the *orthicon* and *image orthicon* tubes by RCA engineers in the early 1940s. The image orthicon (*IO* or *orth*) tube, in use for more than a quarter-century, was replaced for high-quality broadcast uses by the *Plumbicon*, which used a lead oxide—Pb is the symbol for lead—for a key part, and for industrial and other nonbroadcast uses by the lower resolution quality (*see* Television Signals) and less sensitive—needing more light for a good picture—*vidicon* tube The vidicon is used in *film chains*—motion picture and slide projectors are *multiplexed* through an optical device that focuses two or more sources of program material at a small vidicon television camera—in television studios because light levels from film or slide *projectors* are high and can be controlled. A *kinescope* is either a television picture tube used at the receiver end of the system or a kind of television **recording**. The solid state *CCD* or *controlled capacitance discharge* device is becoming popular for **ENG, EFP**, and **camcorder** use. It is rugged and very lightweight, although it needs some picture quality improvement before it replaces tubes in studio cameras. While the better CCD devices are getting close to comparability with three- or four-tube cameras, even newer solid state *imaging devices* such as *MOS* are in the wings.

Television's Early Technological Development   Television's first practical technological development was recorded when English telegraph engineer Joseph May discovered in 1873 that the element *selenium* was capable of producing small amounts of electricity in direct response to the amount of light falling on it. His supervisor, Willoughby Smith, notified the prestigious Society of Telegraph Engineers in England, and today both men are given credit for the discovery.

Within a couple of years, various inventors designed methods for putting this discovery to work in a television system. Although the actual devices were imperfect, the principles were straightforward. G. R. Carey of Boston in 1877 proposed a crude imitation of the human eye: a bank of selenium cells and lamps that could be used for breaking up pictures and sending the elements over wire. Three years later English scientists Ayrton and Perry tried out such a mosaic device. Fournier and Rignoux first transmitted actual images in France in 1906. Following the telephone's invention by Alexander Graham Bell, who had also experimented with the use of light waves rather than wire to transmit voice, inventors in several countries proposed or demonstrated a rash of television—or still-picture, nonmoving, **facsimile**—devices.

Some of these, like today's animated advertising signs, used a wire to connect each selenium cell—the pickup device, analogous to one facet of the eye—with a small electric lamp—the reproduction device, in a *mosaic.* The more lamps, the more detail could be put into the picture. In some versions the lamps simply were "on" or "off," while in others their intensity varied in direct response to the different intensities of light projected on each cell. This approach, experimented with for many years, required an impractical amount of wiring and a mechanically awkward arrangement of cells and lamps. To reproduce a picture equal in detail to a 23-inch television screen of today would require more than 350,000 lamps, each not more than one-fortieth of an inch in diameter!

French scientist Maurice Leblanc developed a technique in 1880 to avoid this quandary, using the principle of *scanning,* in which each picture element was viewed successively rather than all at once as in the mosaic devices. Each picture was divided into lines and each line into minute segments. His approach was analogous to the solution of a similar **bandwidth** problem in telegraphy.

By 1884 basic principles of scanning had been incorporated in some *mechanical* devices L. B. Atkinson's apparatus employed a drum fitted with tangential mirrors, each successive mirror being oriented through a small angle so that, as the drum rotated, the picture would be scanned in a series of lines that would be projected on a single selenium cell. The resulting electrical output of the cell could be transmitted over a wire circuit, as at this time there were no wireless transmission devices. As with all television systems, rotating drums at both ends of the circuit had to be *synchronized* in order to transmit the image successfully. No full description of Atkinson's device was published, and many writers give credit for the mirror drum to a European, Lazare Weiller, who proposed a similar system in 1889. The scanning disc and other devices quickly overshadowed the *mirror drum*, although experimenters used it for many years—E. F. W. Alexanderson of General Electric as late as 1927.

The scanning disc, basis for almost all mechanical scanning systems for several decades, was invented in 1883 and patented in early 1884 in Germany by Paul Nipkow. Lacking the money to extend the patent on his "electrical telescope," he allowed it to lapse and worked for the next 32 years as an engineer for a German railway signal company. Although he lived until 1940 and is generally recognized as the inventor of a system that could reproduce moving objects, Nipkow never built a working model of a complete transmission-reception system, since he lacked means of synchronizing the discs, adequate light sources, amplifiers, photocells, and all the sensitive and increasingly complicated tools of later experimenters.

The *Nipkow disc* looked like a phonograph record, perforated with a single spiral of small holes, each hole a fraction of an inch closer to the center of the disc and a fraction of an inch farther along the rim of the disc than the preceding one. When the disc was placed directly between a narrow-beam light source (although sunlight and gas lamps were used, the electric lamp was the most common) and an object and then rotated, the light would shine through only one hole at a time. In one complete turn, the narrow beam would illuminate every part of the object, moving across it in what appeared, because of the speed of rotation and the persistence of vision, as slightly curved lines or streaks. In practice, the light merely illuminated the object, and a selenium cell—after 1888, a more sensitive device called a *photocell*—"looked" at the scene through each hole as the disc revolved. At the receiving end, a neon lamp varied rapidly in brightness in response to the current produced by the photocell, and the viewer observed it through a Nipkow disc rotating in synchronization with the disc at the other end of the circuit. A mask, of the same size at both ends of the circuit, blocked out part of the disc and focused both the cell and the viewer's eye at the same relative place. Persistence of vision caused the combination of varying-intensity neon lamp and rapidly spinning disc to reproduce a crude picture of the original object in the viewer's brain. The picture, at first, was only an inch or two wide, being limited chiefly by the size of the holes, the diameter of the disc, and the speed of rotation—each of which led to mechanical problems. (*See also* Bandwidth, Television Signals, *and* Television Camera Tubes.)

Television Signals   The *resolution* or sharpness of a television picture is measured in terms of *picture elements*, or *pixels.* In gross terms, the resolution of a picture is the product of the number of horizontal *lines* scanned for each picture times the number of complete pictures, sometimes called *frames*, analogous to frames of a motion picture film, per second. However, not only are some cameras, recorders, and receivers incapable of providing maximum resolution, but the 525 lines used in an *NTSC* (National Television System Committee) system are *interlaced*—much as one interlaces his or her fingers by placing those on one hand between those on the other. First the odd-numbered lines are transmitted and then the even-numbered so that in one second we actually see 60 pictures or *fields* of 262½ lines each. Because of the persistence of vision in human beings, transmission of 60 half-fields produces a moving picture with better resolution, particularly when something on the screen is moving rapidly, than a 30-frame noninterlaced system. The use of 60 pictures per second originally permitted locking or *synchronizing* the picture in the studio to the picture at home through the 60 Hz power line frequency. (In much of the world, 50 Hz power is used, resulting in 50-field, 25-frame television in those countries.) A strong synchronizing signal, produced by a synchronizing or *sync* generator at the studio or transmitter, does most of the work in keeping the picture at home in step with the one in the studio. In *scanning* a scene, the beam of electrons in a television camera tube sweeps across the target, onto which the scene is focused by a lens, from left to right and then, during the *blanking interval*, returns to the left without generating a signal, drops down two lines because of interlacing, and sweeps across again. The *aspect ratio*, or the ratio of horizontal to vertical size, of a television picture is 4:3. Although *three-dimensional* (*3-D*) or *stereoscopic* television was experimented with as early as 1926, it is not now in use. (*See* HDTV.)

Now common, *color* was also the subject of experiments in the 1920s. In early times the image was focused through a spinning *color wheel* that fed each primary color in turn to one pickup tube. A modern studio color television system uses a system of filters to feed primary colors—red, green, blue, or sometimes their complements—to each of three camera tubes. Less expensive industrial systems use one-tube cameras. Very little additional bandwidth is required for the *colorburst* signal component of a television signal, since it is merely an instruction to the receiving set to produce various strengths of color signal at a given instant. Standards differ for television around the world; some countries use our NTSC (525 lines, 30 frames);

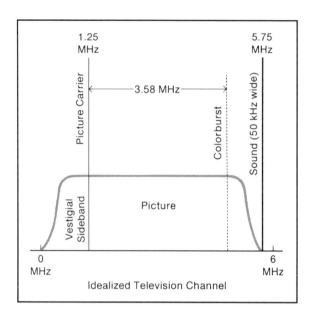

Idealized Television Channel

eastern Europe uses one form of 625/25 and western Europe a slightly different one. The British have closed out the 405/25 system they had used since the 1930s in favor of 625/25, and the French also have dropped their 819/25 system. Other standards were used prior to World War II. Three-color systems—*NTSC, PAL*, originally a German system, and the French *SECAM*, also used in Russia—are in use. Fortunately, it is now possible (but complex and often expensive) to convert programming made on one standard to another. The *field sequential* system was the original color system, since the lower speeds (60 fields rather than 15,750 lines per minute) were easier to use with mechanical color wheels. The *dot sequential* system is presently in use, since color picture tubes are now made with hundreds of little triangles consisting of red, green, and blue chemical *phosphor* dots that glow when hit by the focused electrons from the *guns* in the tube. However, the camera actually used by the astronauts during moon landings in the early 1970s was field sequential.

The channel for a 525/30 system is 6 MHz wide, but the actual picture needs only approximately 4 MHz. The rest of the channel is taken up with the sound portion of the transmission, *guard bands* to reduce interference from stations on adjoining frequencies, and a *vestigial sideband*—when present television transmission standards were adopted in 1941, NTSC engineers attempted to save frequency space by using only one sideband and a carrier, but the state of the art forced them to "waste" 1.25 MHz by providing a second sideband of reduced size and no appreciable value.

Time-shifting   *See* Recordings.

Trade Secret   *See* Invention.

Transceivers   *See* Transmitter.

Transducer   A device for converting one form of energy to another (as a microphone transduces sound energy into electrical energy).

Transistor   *See* Vacuum Tube.

Transitcasting   *See* Modulation.

Translators   *See* Satellite.

Transmitter   A device for radiating signals that might be received at a distant location. (The term is also used for the portion of a telephone that is spoken into.) It is fed or controlled by a microphone or other speech input equipment, or a telegraph key, or some other source of signal, and feeds to an antenna a composite signal that usually consists of a *carrier wave*, *modulated* by (has superimposed on it) the intelligence that one desires to transmit or send.

The earliest radiotelegraph transmitters employed the *spark-gap* principle whereby a high current or voltage jumps across a gap in a wire or other conductor. This spark will radiate over a wide band of frequencies, much as a bolt of lightning does. But when tuned to some extent and fed into an antenna of a certain wavelength, the spark cannot be detected over nearly as wide a band as lightning, thus conserving spectrum space. In the earliest transmitters, the spark was controlled by a telegraph key to produce dots and dashes. The *rotary arc* transmitters, developed later, were motors designed to produce an almost continuous arc, which could be fed to the antenna by a key. Because arcs offered a gentler approach to radiotelegraph than the spark gap, they—particularly the Poulsen arc—continued in use into the 1930s, generally aboard ships needing medium-range transmissions. The Alexanderson and other *alternators* (alternating current generators) were often pickup-truck-sized rotary electrical generators driven by motors at speeds, and hence frequencies, so high that they could send energy a long distance by **radiation** from an antenna without using wires. The Alexanderson alternator spun so fast that the output was of a frequency of alternations more than one thousand times that of the 60 Hz power supplied to houses today. Designed for transoceanic communication from fixed installations on shore, it was very reliable, efficient, and expensive. The current from the alternator could be fed to an antenna much more efficiently than could the broader signal from an arc transmitter, and attempts to secure exclusive use of the Alexanderson machine played an important role in establishing radio in this country.

Just before World War I the first practical high-powered *vacuum-tube transmitters* were tried, and a few years later they were placed in commercial service. **Vacuum tubes** permitted virtually silent operation, voice transmissions, and smaller, even mobile or portable, size. Although many low-power transmitters and *transceivers*—*transmitter* and *receiver* combined in a single unit, such as a walkie-talkie or a Citizens Band set—have used *solid state* technology for years, high-power broadcast transmitters with solid state devices rather than vacuum tubes were not available until the mid-1970s.

Early broadcast transmitters did not have many features we take for granted, such as limiters to prevent overloading or overmodulating the transmitter. Until 1925 or so transmitters were *tuned*, much as a radio receiver is tuned, and often drifted off frequency and caused interference to other stations. Eventually, *crystal control* was perfected—a technique based on the capacity of a quartz crystal of a given thickness to force a current flowing through it to vibrate at a certain, determined frequency. When mounted in an enclosure that kept the crystal at an even temperature and prevented heat expansion or contraction, the unit held the station at a specified frequency. Transmitters with crystal control for broadcast and other uses caused less interference. One of the FRC's first orders of 1927 required crystal control and other standards for broadcast transmitters. A technique known as *precision offset carrier* permits television stations on the same channel to be located a few miles closer to each other without interference. (*See also* Modulation, Waves.)

Transmitting Station   *See* Station.

Transponder   *See* Satellite.

Triode   *See* Vacuum Tube.

Tropospheric Forward Scatter   *See* Waves.

Trunk Lines   *See* Cable.

TVRO (television receive-only satellite earth station)   *See* Satellite.

Two-way Cable System   *See* Cable.

Unions   Labor unions are plentiful in broadcasting and even more plentiful in the motion picture industry, which provides so many television programs. Among the most prominent are *AFTRA*, the American Federation of Television and Radio Artists (formerly AFRA), which serves announcers, actors, and other talent; *AFM*, the American Federation of Musicians, which has jurisdiction over virtually all musicians and a small number of turntable operators in Chicago radio stations; *IATSE*, the International Alliance of Theatrical Stage Employees and Moving Picture Machine Operators of the United States and Canada, whose members range from stagehands on Broadway and motion picture projectionists to television technical crews (camera operators and so forth), particularly in New York; *IBEW*, the International Brotherhood of Electrical Workers, which also represents many technicians; and *NABET*, the National Association of Broadcast Employees and Technicians. Originally *NABET* stood for National Association of Broadcast Engineers and Technicians; the change from "engineers" to "employees" marked the trend in many unions to represent a broad range of job categories in a given station. A number of actors and singers belong to either *Actors Equity* or *AGVA*, the American Guild of Variety Artists. The *Screen Actors Guild* (*SAG*), the *Writers Guild of America* (West and East), and the *Screen Directors Guild* also have jurisdictions in broadcasting, but only the larger stations, networks, and program packagers, particularly those based in Hollywood, have direct connections with them. Although the networks may deal with dozens of different unions, most stations contract with only one or two or even none, with the technical and clerical staffs often represented by the same union. A few union contracts may affect the entire industry, but most are negotiated for the individual market. A professional association, such as the *Radio Television News Directors Association (RTNDA)*, is not, strictly speaking, a union organized for collective bargaining purposes.

UPI (United Press International) *See* News.

UPN (United Paramount Network) *See* Network.

Uplink *See* Satellite.

URL (Uniform Resource Locator) *See* Internet.

Vacuum Tube Before the *transistor* and *integrated solid state circuits* and devices came into almost universal use in the 1960s and 1970s, respectively, the vacuum tube performed the essential functions of electronic *detection* and *amplification.* Today, only the picture tube in a television set is still a vacuum tube. Modern solid state devices—the *transistor* and later developments such as integrated circuit *chips*—are essentially grown in laboratories and then cut apart, rather than manufactured, but fill the same functions as the vacuum tube.

Yet, without some kind of one-way *valve*—still the name for the vacuum tube in Great Britain and elsewhere—to permit only the positive half of each cycle of radio-frequency alternating current waves to pass, it would be impossible to *demodulate* or permit the audio-frequency signal superimposed on the radio-frequency waves to be detected. (A *rectifier*, used to convert *alternating current [AC]* to *direct current [DC]* for power supplies and other uses, works the same way, whether vacuum tube or solid state.) The *crystal set*, used as a **receiver** from the earliest days of radio until the 1930s, was a primitive *solid state* device that used as a *detector* a piece of galena or some other crystalline ore that would allow current to pass in only one direction.

The other major function of the vacuum tube, one that permitted today's selectivity and sensitivity, is **amplification**, the strengthening of a signal or current without otherwise changing its characteristics—much as power steering in an automobile amplifies the turning motions of the driver.

The principles of vacuum-tube theory are simple: opposites attract and likes repel, just as with a pair of bar magnets; electrons are negative by definition; and the amount of repelling or attracting is roughly proportional to the voltage applied to that part of the tube. Thomas Alva Edison first noticed the actions of electrons within a glass tube evacuated of air. The *Edison effect* is the blackening of the glass wall of a tube caused by the electrons boiling off the glowing wire of the *filament* within an electric light bulb and striking the glass hard enough to blacken it. Ambrose Fleming inserted a second element, known generally as the *plate*—although technically it was an *anode* and the filament a *cathode*—in the glass bulb and discovered that when a positive charge was placed on the plate, a current would flow between the filament and the plate but that no current would flow when a negative charge was applied. The device converted the weak AC radio currents picked up by an antenna attached to the plate to a pulsating DC and delivered the audio component that had been used to modulate the radio waves as sounds—dots and dashes or speech—in a pair of earphones. His device was known as the *diode* (two electrodes) or *Fleming valve.*

Lee de Forest, in the first decade of the twentieth century, discovered how to amplify weak electronic signals. If a grid or mesh of fine wire was placed in the tube between the filament and the plate, a weak negative voltage on that grid would repel the electrons coming from the filament A condition of no voltage on the grid would permit the maximum current to flow between the filament and the plate. Varying voltage on the grid would permit varying current flow in the main circuit. Accordingly, a weak current flow from an antenna or microphone or other source fed into the grid in such a way as to vary from zero to slightly negative would cause the extremely strong current flow in the main circuit to vary in precisely the same way—or, in other words, the weak input current was "amplified." De Forest called his tube an *Audion*, but the generic name is *triode*—a three-element or three-electrode vacuum tube.

Although there have been improvements—a separate *cathode* wrapped around the filament that acts as an oven, permitting a more even flow of electrons; increased complexity: two or three separate circuits within the same tube, generally operating with the same filament source of electrons; smaller sizes; and more rugged construction: sometimes metal or ceramic instead of glass—all vacuum tubes use the same basic principles.

Vacuum Tube Transmitters   *See* Transmitter.

Valve   *See* Vacuum Tube.

V-chip   A computer chip added to a television set that can be programmed by parents to block violence or other undesirable content as identified by signals of program ratings by stations and networks. Required in all new U.S. sets as of the late 1990s.

Vertical Blanking Interval (VBI)   *See* Modulation and Television Signals.

Vestigial Sideband   *See* Television Signals.

VHS (Video Home System)   *See* Recordings.

Video   Of, or pertaining to, the visual or picture portion of television.

Videocassettes and Videocassette Recorders (VCRs)   *See* Recordings.

Video Dialtone   Networks for the distribution of video over telephone lines. This technology hasn't yet been successfully innovated, except for special circuits in New York and other cities with large concentrations of media and advertising firms.

Videodiscs   *See* Recordings.

Video on Demand   A form of pay-cable, permitting the viewer to select the starting time of movies.

Video Streaming   *See* Internet.

Videotape Recording (VTR)   *See* Recordings.

Videotex   *See* Teletext.

Vidicon   *See* Television Camera Tubes.

Volts   *See* Circuit.

WARC (World Administrative Radio Conference)   *See* International Tele-communication Union.

Watts   *See* Circuit.

Waves, Propagation, Frequency, Wavelength   All *electromagnetic waves* or *electromagnetic energies* travel at 300,000 kilometers (roughly 186,300 miles) per second in free space, and a fraction slower in wire or other materials. What distinguishes these waves or parts of the *electromagnetic spectrum*—radio, infrared, visible light, ultraviolet, X-rays—from one another is their length, the actual distance from crest to crest or trough to trough. If one uses the analogy of water waves traveling at a constant speed breaking on a seacoast, it becomes obvious that as the wavelength grows, the number of waves per unit of time will drop proportionately, and vice versa. Hence, *longwave* = low frequency; *shortwave* = high frequency; *microwave* = upper ultrahigh frequency or beyond. (See chart, page 821.) Further, since wavelength, measured in meters, times frequency, measured in thousands of cycles per second, equals 300,000—the speed of light or electromagnetic radiation in kilometers per second—we find that the wavelength of frequencies used in the standard (AM) broadcast band ranges from more than 555 meters (approximately six football fields) long at 540 kHz down to only 187 meters at 1,600 kHz. As discussed under **antenna**, this has implications for equipment; a half-wave antenna in the middle of the very high-frequency (VHF) band used for FM radio is only five feet long. Because of the small size of tuning components at VHF or UHF frequencies (much as a combination of thickness and length of a musical tuning fork determines its pitch, so does a combination of two electrical values, capacitance and inductance, determine the *resonating frequency* of a piece of radio apparatus), the equipment is prone to drift off frequency as it heats up and metal expands. This is why early FM sets needed to be retuned after a period of use. Later sets avoided this problem with a combination of compensating circuits known as *automatic frequency control* (*AFC*) and the nonheating characteristics of most transistors.

Different wavelengths have different characteristics. Some—visible light—can be perceived directly by our senses but do not penetrate solid objects in the way that X-rays can. Some need a pathway, such as the wire used for 60 Hz electrical power, while others—radio and light—can travel or radiate in free space or atmosphere. Some will *attenuate*—that is, lose strength—very rapidly with distance, while others, if aimed or focused or guided carefully, will lose very little strength. Within that part of the electromagnetic spectrum used for radiocommunication, standard nomenclatures and characteristics apply (see box on page 821).

Radio waves occupy the electromagnetic spectrum below 100,000 MHz (megahertz, formerly designated mc, or megacycles per second). Above that part of the electromagnetic spectrum are infrared waves or rays, visible light (roughly 10^9 Hz), ultraviolet rays, X-rays, gamma rays, and cosmic rays.

The standard (AM) radio band runs between 535 and 1,705 kHz (kiloHertz). FM radio broadcasting runs between 88 and 108 MHz; noncommercial educational FM is between 88 and 92 MHz. VHF television is in three segments: 54–72, 76–88, and 174–216 MHz (channels 2–4, 5–6, and 7–13). UHF television (and some other services near the upper end) occupies the band between 470 and 806 MHz (channels 14–69). AM radio uses a bandwidth of 10 kHz, FM radio a bandwidth of 200 kHz, and television a bandwidth of 6 MHz.

Radio waves have three major means of *propagation*, and the efficiency of each varies with the frequency of the wave. *Groundwave*, for example, which hugs and travels along the earth's surface, is good for long-distance communication—up to worldwide in some cases—particularly when the ground *conductivity* near the transmitter is high, as is the extreme case with salt water, on frequencies from ELF into the medium-wave standard (AM) broadcast band. From about the middle of the standard broadcast band through the shortwave band, to about 30 MHz or even a little beyond, the most effective long-range mode is *skywave.* These wavelengths are such that signals bounce off the ionized layers that surround the earth, the *ionosphere*, at between 50 and 250 miles of altitude, much as a flashlight beam will bounce off a mirror. The bounce or *skip* may be calculated—the angle of incidence is equal to the angle of reflection, and the height is known—and the desired target area pinpointed by directional antenna arrays—a technique used for international shortwave but not for domestic broadcasting. Skywave useful range varies with time of day, season, and sunspot cycle. At high frequencies and above, groundwave is limited to only a few miles under normal conditions. Above the frequencies at which skywave is reliable, radio propagation is limited to about 125 percent of the distance to the optical horizon or *line-of-sight.* This *direct wave* propagation is the reason for the limited range of FM and television stations, whose antennas are rarely tall enough to send good signals more than 100 miles. A fourth transmission mode, *tropospheric forward scatter*, can be used for extensive distances in very expensive and huge military point-to-point systems at VHF

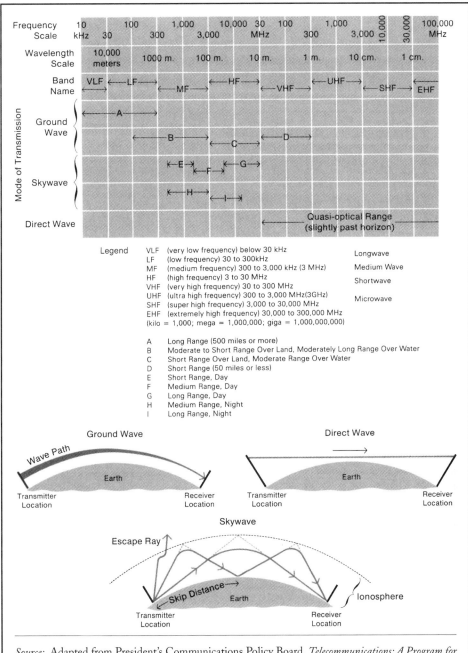

Source: Adapted from President's Communications Policy Board, *Telecommunications: A Program for Progress* (Washington: Government Printing Office, 1951), page 22.

frequencies and beyond. It scatters and bounces through the troposphere, which extends downward to the earth's surface. Space communication **satellites** use frequencies in this *quasi-optical* range because, although far away in distance, they have an unobstructed line of sight to the earth station antenna—over one-third of the globe. Since on almost any band, the lower the frequency, the higher the practical range—partly due to greater ease of designing equipment for frequencies that are familiar and easier to work with—television channels 2–6 often may be received for a greater distance than channels 7–13, and much farther away than frequently more powerful UHF television stations. This inequality in technical facilities for the same category or service of stations on the same band leads to economic, and consequently political, problems, particularly with respect to the standard (AM) band, where stations at the low end can expect more reliable groundwave coverage over a radius of around 100 miles than those at the high end. (*See also* Bandwidth, Channel, *and* Modulation.)

WB Warner Brothers Network   *See* Network.

Web or **Web Site**   *See* Internet.

"Webs"   *See* Network.

Webcasting   A term referring to the use of the Internet for broadcast-like transmissions to whomever may wish to log on.

Whip   *See* Antenna.

"Wired City"   *See* Cable.

Wireless   *See* Radio.

Wireless Cable   *See* MDS.

Wirephoto   *See* Facsimile.

Wire Services   *See* News.

World Wide Web   *See* Internet.

Writers Guild of America   *See* Unions.

APPENDIX C
HISTORICAL STATISTICS
ON ELECTRONIC MEDIA

The following tables provide an overall view of many aspects of broadcast and cable history. Some of these data originally were first assembled by L. W. Lichty and C. H. Sterling in 1967–68; a few were published in different form in Lichty and Topping (1975); and more extended information on many categories appears in Sterling (1984). Specific sources are shown for all tables, with a brief form used if the item is listed in the bibliography (Appendix D), or a full citation if not.

   Three points concerning all the tables: First, we have not noted all the exceptions or special cases that may occur but have pinpointed the more important. Second, where no information is shown, we have used the following system:

blank space	Indicates no such information (i.e., no television stations in 1921).
—	Zero or none.
na	Data unavailable, though theoretically the item or service did exist or may have existed.

Third, and an unfortunate measure of the times, we have found it increasingly difficult to obtain information to update many tables. Where data was plentiful and often free when we first wrote *Stay Tuned*, increasingly information is considered proprietary and is available only at often very high cost, or is no longer collected at all. Most of the FCC's broadcast and cable data gathering, for example, ceased in the early 1980s as a part of the larger trend to deregulation. You will find little information concerning computers or the Internet here, as data covering both is both inconsistent and poorly collected. Maybe next time—stay tuned.

Useful Tools for Historical Comparison: 1920–2000

This initial table offers basic data on the U.S. population, the total number of households in the country, and the consumer price index for every five years from 1920 through 2000. The population and household data is useful when considering the ownership of radio and television receivers, for example, or the penetration of other services. The Consumer Price Index figures (1982–84 = 100) allow one to determine a rough estimation of the impact of inflation on the actual dollar figures shown in later tables or referred to in the text. For example, to determine what financial data shown for 1950 means in terms of 2000 dollar values, divide the 1950 CPI index figure (24.1) into that for 2000 (172.2) to get 7.1 and then multiply any 1950 dollar figure by 7.1. To more easily determine the constant dollar value for any year to any other year, see the Bureau of Labor Statistics "instant calculator" available at *http://stats.bls.gov/cpihome.htm.*

Year	U.S. Population (millions)	U.S. Households (millions)	Consumer Price Index (1982–84 = 100)
1920	106.5	24.5	20.0
1925	115.8	27.5	17.5
1930	123.2	30.0	16.7
1935	127.4	31.9	13.7
1940	132.1	35.2	14.0
1945	139.9	37.5	18.0
1950	151.7	43.6	24.1
1955	165.3	47.9	26.8
1960	180.7	52.8	29.6
1965	194.3	57.3	31.5
1970	204.9	62.9	38.8
1975	216.0	71.1	53.8
1980	227.7	80.8	82.4
1985	238.5	86.8	107.6
1990	250.0	93.3	130.7
1995	263.1	99.0	152.4
2000	281.4	103.9(1999)	172.2

Sources: Population and households from U.S. Census Bureau; Consumer Price Index from U.S. Bureau of Labor Statistics, "Consumer Price Index, All Consumers, 1982–84 = 100" available at *ftp://ftp.bls.gov/pub/special.requests/cpi/cpiai.txt*

Table 1   Number of Stations: 1921–2000

Table 1 shows the number of stations actually on the air (regardless of license status) as of January 1 each year unless otherwise noted. Commercial and educational FM and VHF television were authorized in 1941, with UHF and noncommercial educational television appearing first in 1953. These figures should be used with some caution, as methods of counting varied with original source (Department of Commerce, FRC, FCC, or one of the commercial data firms). Basic station data here match that used in network affiliate tables 2-A and 2-B.

▪ 1-A   AM Radio Stations through 1940

1921 5		1931 612
1922 30		1932 604
1923 556		1933 599
1924 530		1934 583
1925 571		1935 585
1926 528		1936 616
1927 681		1937 646
1928 677		1938 689
1929 606		1939 722
1930 618		1940 765

▪ 1-B   Broadcasting Stations since 1941

		FM Radio		Television		
Year	AM Radio	Commercial	Educational	Commercial	Educational	Total
1941	831	18	2	2 (July 1)		853
1942	887	36	7	4		934
1943	910	41	8	8		967
1944	910	44	8	8		970
1945	919	46	8	8		981
1946	948	48	9	6		1,011
1947	1,062	140	10	12		1,224
1948	1,621	458	15	16		2,110
1949	1,912	700	27	51		2,690
1950	2,086	733	48	98		2,965
1951	2,232	676	73	107		3,088
1952	2,331	637	85	108		3,161
1953	2,391	580	98	126		3,195
1954	2,521	560	112	354	2	3,549
1955	2,669	552	122	411	11	3,765
1956	2,824	540	123	441	18	3,946
1957	3,008	530	125	471	23	4,157
1958	3,196	537	141	495	28	4,396
1959	3,326	578	151	510	35	4,600
1960	3,456	688	162	515	44	4,865
1961	3,547	815	175	527	52	5,116
1962	3,618	960	194	541	62	5,375
1963	3,760	1,081	209	557	68	5,675
1964	3,854	1,146	237	564	85	5,886
1965	4,044	1,270	255	569	99	6,237
1966	4,065	1,446	268	585	114	6,478
1967	4,121	1,643	296	610	127	6,797
1968	4,190	1,753	326	635	150	7,054
1969	4,265	1,938	362	662	175	7,402

(*continued*)

Year	AM Radio	FM Radio		Television		Total
		Commercial	Educational	Commercial	Educational	
1970	4,292	2,184	413	677	185	7,751
1971	4,343	2,196	472	682	199	7,892
1972	4,374	2,304	511	693	213	8,095
1973	4,395	2,411	573	697	230	8,306
1974	4,407	2,502	652	697	241	8,499
1975	4,432	2,636	717	706	247	8,738
1976	4,463	2,767	804	710	252	8,996
1977	4,497	2,873	870	728	256	9,224
1978	4,513	3,001	926	716	266	9,419
1979	4,549	3,107	982	724	274	9,636
1980	4,558	3,155	1,038	734	277	9,762
1981	4,589	3,282	1,092	756	282	10,001
1982	4,634	3,349	1,118	777	288	10,166
1983	4,685	3,421	1,090	813	293	10,304
1984	4,733	3,527	1,122	862	287	10,571
1985	4,754	3,716	1,172	904	290	10,836
1986	4,718	3,875	1,231	941	300	11,065
1987	4,863	3,944	1,261	999	296	11,363
1988	4,902	4,041	1,301	1,017	325	11,586
1989	4,948	4,174	1,383	1,062	338	11,905
1990	4,978	4,357	1,435	1,112	353	12,235
1991	4,987	4,392	1,440	1,117	353	12,289
1992	4,985	4,570	1,507	1,132	357	12,551
1993	4,961	4,785	1,588	1,147	362	12,843
1994	4,944	4,971	1,662	1,155	363	13,095
1995	4,913	5,109	1,733	1,160	363	13,278
1996	4,909	5,296	1,815	1,180	363	13,565
1997	4,857	5,419	1,864	1,190	365	13,695
1998	4,762	5,542	1,923	1,198	366	13,791
1999	4,793	5,662	2,017	1,221	368	14,061
2000	4,783	5,766	2,066	1,243	373	14,231

Sources: Most data on Tables 1-A and 1-B are derived from FCC records, many of which are reported only in secondary sources. Data for earlier years (1921–1959) taken from *Broadcasting Yearbook 1977*. For many years, *Broadcasting Yearbook* and *Television Factbook* published different figures. We have chosen to follow *Television Factbook* for the 1960–1975 period, with supplementary data, including 1976–1977, from *Broadcasting* magazine and/or *Broadcasting Yearbook*. Data from 1978 through 1983 are as reported in Sterling (1984), pp. 5–7 and 18–19, citing FCC data as provided in *Television Digest* and/or *Broadcasting*. Data for 1984–1989 are as reported by FCC for stations licensed on the last day of the *prior* year (so, December 31, 1987 data is shown here as representing January 1, 1988), with 1985 and 1988 figures as printed in *Broadcasting*, and 1986 data showing stations licensed as of February 25. Other sources or exceptions: (1) AM radio column includes educational stations, which dwindled in number from as many as 200 in the mid-1920s to approximately 25 in 1941 and since; (2) data for 1921–1926 include "total authorized" stations, those for 1927–1947 include "authorized" and/or "licensed," not necessarily stations actually on the air as reported for later years (1923 data for March 1, 1924 data for October 1, 1925 data for June 20, and 1926–1932 data for June 30); (3) educational FM figures through 1973 from Corporation for Public Broadcasting, *Status Report on Public Broadcasting* (Washington: CPB, 1974), p. 8, with remainder from the FCC; and (4) educational television stations, 1941–1947 gathered by Lichty and Sterling from FCC. 1990–99 as reported on FCC website, citing data for 31 December of the *previous* year (e.g., December 31, 1993 is shown here as 1994 data). Exceptions: 1990 data is as of 30 September and 2000 is as of 13 Dec; 1999 FCC figures from *Broadcasting & Cable* (13 Dec 99), p. 115. These are operating stations, not total authorizations.

Table 2   Network Affiliates: 1927–2000

Figures in the first three tables show the growth of national commercial radio networks over eight decades, with most figures as of January 1 of each year. In table 2-A, NBC figures include both Red and Blue networks (see table 2-C for details of NBC's two networks) until 1943, when Blue became independently owned (and was renamed ABC in 1945). Table 2-B details radio networks since 1965, which have increasingly included FM stations as affiliates. Total percentage of network stations is approximate, as many stations were affiliated with more than one network at a time. In 1968, ABC broke into four specialized networks, presaging the radio network specialization of the 1980s. All percentage columns are based on all commercial stations (AM only in table 2-A, AM and FM in table 2-B), not just network affiliates. Mutual ceased separate operation in 2000.

In table 2-D (television networks) because the DuMont network left the air in October 1955, and as most of its affiliates held a primary affiliation with another network, its figures are presented in the footnote. Through the 1950s, the separate network affiliation listings may not add to the number of network stations shown: multiple affiliations were more common in the days of fewer television outlets per market. Unfortunately, the respective networks were unwilling or unable to provide affiliate information after 1988 despite repeated attempts.

Table 2-E provides an approximate picture of public broadcasting network member (affiliate) stations. As apparently neither NPR nor PBS retain (or could provide) a record of their own affiliates, the table shows the number of "CPB-Qualified" radio stations (see text, p. 519) which is essentially what most NPR member stations are, their percentage of all noncommercial radio, the number of NPR affiliates as reported by Arbitron, and the total number of public TV stations (generally synonymous with PBS affiliates, though a few public television stations broadcast only to schools).

2-A Commercial Radio Networks: 1927–1964

Year	NBC Number	NBC Percentage	CBS Number	CBS Percentage	Mutual Number	Mutual Percentage	ABC Number	ABC Percentage	Total AM Stations	Network Stations Number	Network Stations Percentage
1927	28	4.1%	16	2.3%					681	44	6%
1928	52	7.6	17	2.5					677	69	10
1929	58	9.6	49	8.1					606	107	18
1930	71	11.5	60	9.7					618	131	21
1931	75	12.3	76	12.4					612	159	25
1932	86	14.2	84	13.9					604	170	28
1933	88	14.7	91	15.2					599	179	30
1934	88	15.1	92	15.8	4	.7%			583	184	32
1935	88	15.0	97	16.6	3	.5			585	188	32
1936	89	14.4	98	15.9	39	6.3			616	226	37
1937	111	17.2	105	16.3	80	12.4			646	296	46
1938	142	20.6	110	16.0	107	15.5			689	359	52
1939	167	23.1	113	15.7	116	16.1			722	396	55
1940	182	23.8	112	14.6	160	20.9			765	454	59
1941	225	27.1	118	14.2	166	20.0			831	509	61
1942	136	15.3	115	13.0	191	21.5	116	13.1%	887	558	63
1943	142	15.6	116	12.7	219	24.1	143	15.7	910	620	68
1944	143	15.7	133	14.6	245	26.9	173	19.0	910	694	76
1945	150	16.3	145	15.8	384	41.8	195	21.2	919	874	95
1946	155	16.4	147	15.5	384	40.5	195	20.6	948	881	93
1947	161	15.2	157	14.8	488	46.0	222	20.9	1,062	1,028	97
1948	167	10.3	162	10.0	519	32.0	256	15.8	1,621	1,104	68
1949	170	8.9	167	8.7	526	27.5	269	14.1	1,912	1,132	59

1950	172	8.2	173	8.3	543	26.0	282	13.5	2,086	1,170	56
1951	180	8.1	183	8.2	552	24.7	295	13.2	2,232	1,210	54
1952	191	8.2	194	8.3	560	24.0	302	13.0	2,331	1,247	53
1953	207	8.7	203	8.5	560	23.4	348	14.6	2,391	1,318	55
1954	212	8.4	205	8.1	560	22.2	360	14.3	2,521	1,337	53
1955	208	7.8	207	7.8	563	21.1	357	13.4	2,669	1,335	50
1956	205	7.3	204	7.2	558	19.8	342	12.1	2,824	1,309	46
1957	199	6.6	201	6.7	525	17.5	334	11.1	3,008	1,259	42
1958	203	6.4	200	6.3	431	13.5	299	9.4	3,196	1,133	36
1959	209	6.3	198	6.0	441	13.3	286	8.6	3,326	1,134	34
1960	202	5.8	198	5.7	443	12.8	310	9.0	3,456	1,153	33
1961	201	5.7	195	5.5	428	12.1	339	9.6	3,547	1,163	33
1962	200	5.4	206	5.6	510	13.8	342	9.3	3,618	1,258	34
1963	200	5.4	207	5.6	510	13.9	366	10.0	3,760	1,283	35
1964	202	5.2	227	5.8	500	12.8	353	9.1	3,854	1,282	33

2-B Commercial Radio Networks: 1965–1988

Year	NBC Number	NBC Percentage	CBS Number	CBS Percentage	Mutual Number	Mutual Percentage	ABC Number	ABC Percentage	Total Commercial AM & FM Stations	Network Stations Number	Network Stations Percentage
1965	209	3.9%	237	4.5%	501	9.4%	355	6.7%	5,314	1,302	24.5%
1966	215	3.9	239	4.3	520	9.4	361	6.6	5,511	1,265	23.0
1967	216	3.7	240	4.2	na	na	337	5.8	5,764	na	na
1968	217	3.7	243	4.1	515	8.7	500	8.4	5,943	1,457	24.5
1969	222	3.6	245	3.9	492	7.9	1,013	16.3	6,203	1,972	31.8
1970	220	3.4	247	3.8	523	8.1	1,175	18.1	6,476	2,165	33.4
1971	230	3.5	249	3.8	538	8.2	1,074	16.4	6,539	2,091	30.9
1972	231	3.5	242	3.6	545	8.2	1,169	17.5	6,678	2,187	32.7
1973	233	3.4	243	3.6	568	8.3	1,246	18.3	6,806	2,290	33.6
1974	230	3.3	248	3.6	632	9.1	1,293	18.7	6,910	2,403	34.8
1975	232	3.1	247	3.5	657	9.3	1,322	18.7	7,068	2,458	34.8
1976	223	3.1	257	3.6	684	9.5	1,353	18.7	7,230	2,517	34.8
1977	236	3.2	266	3.6	755	10.2	1,546	21.0	7,370	2,803	38.0
1978	245	3.3	270	3.6	800	10.6	1,554	20.7	7,514	2,869	38.2
1979	268	3.5	278	3.6	950	12.4	1,561	20.4	7,656	3,057	39.9
1980	281	3.6	321	4.2	934	11.9	1,574	20.4	7,713	3,110	40.3
1981	315	4.0	400	5.1	902	11.5	1,591	20.2	7,871	3,208	40.8
1982	370	4.6	425	5.3	876	11.0	1,631	20.4	7,983	3,302	41.4
1983	363	4.5	na	na	860	10.6	1,750	21.6	8,106	na	na
1984	318	3.8	na	na	841	10.2	1,745	21.1	8,260	na	na
1985	355	4.2	na	na	847	10.0	1,726	20.4	8,470	na	na
1986	478	5.6	na	na	na	na	1,893	22.0	8,593	na	na
1987	389	4.4	na	na	na	na	2,133	24.2	8,807	na	na
1988	475	5.3	na	na	731	8.2	2,251	25.2	8,943	na	na

Sources: For total number of stations: FCC. For number of their affiliates: the radio networks. NBC data after 1982 are for various dates, usually September, October, or November, and are from both the radio network and "The Source." Mutual data are from *Broadcasting Yearbook.*

2-C   NBC Red and Blue Radio Networks: 1927–1941

Year	Red (WEAF)	Blue (WJZ)	Alternates
1927	22	6	na
1928	17	11	24
1929	22	14	22
1930	22	17	32
1931	23	18	34
1932	28	22	36
1933	28	24	36
1934	28	20	40
1935	27	20	41
1936	26	18	45
1937	30	33	48
1938	36	44	62
1939	48	55	64
1940	53	60	69
1941	74	92	59

Source: NBC.

2-D Commercial Television Network Affiliates: 1947–1988

Year	NBC Number	NBC Percentage	CBS Number	CBS Percentage	ABC Number	ABC Percentage	Total Stations	Network Stations Number	Network Stations Percentage
1947	2	16.7%	1	8.3%	1	8.3%	12	4	33%
1948	9	56.3	3	18.8	6	37.5	16	17	100
1949	25	49.0	15	29.4	11	21.6	51	50	98
1950	56	57.1	27	27.6	13	13.3	98	96	98
1951	63	58.9	30	28.0	14	13.1	107	107	100
1952	64	59.3	31	28.7	15	13.9	108	108	100
1953	71	56.3	33	26.2	24	19.0	126	125	99
1954	164	46.3	113	31.9	40	11.3	354	317	90
1955	189	46.0	139	33.8	46	11.2	411	374	91
1956	200	45.4	168	38.1	53	12.0	441	421	95
1957	205	43.5	180	38.2	60	12.7	471	445	94
1958	209	42.2	191	38.8	69	13.9	495	469	95
1959	213	41.8	193	37.8	79	15.5	510	485	95
1960	214	41.6	195	37.9	87	16.9	515	496	96
1961	201	38.1	198	37.6	104	19.7	527	503	95
1962	201	37.2	194	35.9	113	20.9	541	508	94
1963	203	36.4	194	34.8	117	21.0	557	514	92
1964	212	37.6	191	33.9	123	21.8	564	526	93
1965	198	34.8	190	33.4	128	22.5	569	516	91
1966	202	34.5	193	33.0	137	23.4	585	532	91
1967	205	33.6	191	31.3	141	23.1	610	537	88
1968	207	32.6	192	30.2	148	23.3	635	547	86
1969	211	31.9	190	28.7	156	23.6	662	557	84
1970	215	31.8	193	28.5	160	23.6	677	568	84
1971	218	32.0	207	30.4	168	24.6	682	593	87
1972	218	31.5	209	30.2	172	24.8	693	599	86

1973	218	31.3	210	30.1	176	25.3	697	604	87
1974	218	31.3	212	30.4	181	26.0	697	611	88
1975	219	30.8	213	30.0	185	26.0	711	617	87
1976	218	30.7	213	30.0	182	25.6	710	613	86
1977	212	29.1	210	28.8	190	26.1	728	612	84
1978	213	29.3	208	28.6	195	26.8	716	616	86
1979	213	29.3	208	28.6	202	27.5	724	623	86
1980	213	28.6	200	26.8	202	27.1	734	615	84
1981	213	28.3	200	26.6	207	27.5	756	620	82
1982	215	27.8	200	25.8	206	26.6	777	621	80
1983	na	na	202	24.8	207	25.4	813	na	na
1984	206	23.8	202	23.3	210	24.3	862	618	72
1985	205	22.7	205	22.7	211	23.3	904	621	69
1986	207	22.0	204	21.7	214	22.7	941	625	66
1987	207	20.7	184	18.4	215	21.5	999	606	61
1988	208	20.4	na*	na*	222	21.8	1,017	na	na

* CBS reported its affiliates merely as "over 200."

Note: Figures above do not include the Du Mont network, as most of its affiliations were secondary or tertiary after prime affiliation with one of the other networks above. Du Mont figures (from *Broadcasting Yearbook*) were: 1949 (45), 1950 (52), 1951 (62), 1952 (62), 1953 (133), 1954 (195), 1955 (158). Du Mont suspended network operations late in 1955. In early 1967, the United (Overmyer) Network broadcast an evening program to 106 stations. The Fox network, discussed in 10.3, began with 111 affiliates in 1986 and had 122 by March 1989. All percentages are based on total number of commercial stations.

Sources: For total number of stations: FCC. For number of their affiliates: the television networks. Data for 1978–1982 from Sterling (1984), page 24, citing the networks; 1983–1988 from the networks to the authors.

⬛ 2-E   Public Broadcasting Network Member Stations: 1970–2000

	Public Radio Stations			
Year	"CPB-Qualified" Stations	As % of all Noncommercial Radio Stations	NPR Member Stations	Public Television Stations (PBS Members)
1970	73	18%	na	185
1971	96	20	na	199
1972	109	21	na	213
1973	132	23	na	230
1974	147	23	24	241
1975	159	22	na	247
1976	169	21	113	252
1977	176	20	187	256
1978	na	na	197	266
1979	na	na	208	274
1980	217	21	237	277
1981	na	na	259	282
1982	na	na	274	288
1983	na	na	275	293
1984	na	na	273	287
1985	288	25	327	290
1986	295	na	307	300
1987	na	na	316	296
1988	308	24	337	325
1989	313	23	348	338
1990	318	22	395	353
1991	373	26	398	353
1992	391	26	427	357
1993	400	25	472	362
1994	403	24	492	363
1995	407	23	535	363
1996	408	22	536	363
1997	694	37	564	365
1998	na	na	593	366
1999	na	na	602	368
2000	na	na	571	373

Source: Corporation for Public Broadcasting for baseline number of "CPB-Qualified" public radio stations. Percent of all stations based on total noncommercial radio stations data in Table 1-B. NPR member stations from Arbitron annual spring public radio nationwide measure, as reported to authors by TRAC Media Services of Tucson. For total number of public television stations, see table 1-B.

Table 3 Broadcast/Cable Revenue: 1927–2000

Figures show amount of advertising revenue accruing to national networks (including program, talent, time, commercial, and agency commission costs), national and regional spot (including commissions), and local advertising (including discounts and agency commissions). Discounts are excluded for networks and spots. Last column is radio (3-A) and television (3-B and 3-C) percentage of all U.S. advertising expenditure. Dollar figures are in millions; add 000,000. As radio proportional data changes little from year to year after 1960—save for the decline of national spot and the gain of local advertising—it is presented only every five years. Cable advertising revenue is reflected in table 3-C for the past two decades. Table 3-D offers information on the sources of public broadcasting revenue for every five years. To convert data to present-day dollar values, see "useful tools" on p. 826.

3-A   Radio Advertising; 1927–2000

Year	Network Dollars (millions)	Network Percentage	National Spot Dollars (millions)	National Spot Percentage	Local Dollars (millions)	Local Percentage	Total Dollars (millions)	Percentage of All Advertising
1927	$ 3.8	79.0%	$ .9	19.0%			$ 4.8	na
1928	10.3	73.0	3.9	28.0			14.1	na
1929	19.2	72.0	7.6	28.0			26.8	na
1930	27.7	68.0	12.8	32.0			40.5	2%
1931	37.5	67.0	18.5	33.0			56.0	3
1932	39.1	63.0	22.8	37.0			61.9	5
1933	31.5	55.0	25.5	45.0			57.0	5
1934	42.6	59.0	30.0	41.0			72.8	6
1935	62.6	55.6	$ 14.9	13.2%	$ 35.1	31.2%	112.6	7
1936	75.6	61.8	22.7	18.6	24.0	19.6	122.3	7
1937	88.5	53.8	28.0	17.0	48.1	29.2	164.6	8
1938	89.2	53.4	34.0	20.3	43.9	26.3	167.1	9
1939	98.6	53.6	35.0	19.0	50.2	27.3	183.8	9
1940	113.3	52.6	42.1	19.5	60.2	27.9	215.6	10
1941	125.4	50.7	52.3	21.2	69.5	28.1	247.2	11
1942	128.7	49.5	58.8	22.6	72.5	27.9	260.0	12
1943	156.5	49.9	70.9	22.6	86.2	27.5	313.6	13
1944	191.8	48.7	87.4	22.2	114.3	29.0	393.5	14
1945	197.9	46.7	91.8	21.7	134.2	31.7	423.9	15
1946	199.6	43.9	98.2	21.6	156.6	34.5	454.4	14
1947	201.2	39.7	106.4	21.0	198.8	39.3	506.4	12
1948	210.6	37.5	121.6	21.7	229.9	40.9	561.6	12
1949	203.0	35.5	123.4	21.6	245.0	42.9	571.4	11

1950	196.3	32.4	135.8	22.4	273.3	45.1	605.4	11
1951	179.5	29.6	138.3	22.8	288.5	47.6	606.3	10
1952	161.5	25.9	141.5	22.7	321.1	51.5	624.1	9
1953	141.2	23.1	145.6	23.8	324.4	53.1	611.2	8
1954	114.4	20.5	134.9	24.1	309.4	55.4	558.7	7
1955	84.4	15.5	134.1	24.6	326.4	59.9	544.9	6
1956	60.5	10.7	161.0	28.4	345.5	60.9	567.0	6
1957	63.5	10.3	186.9	30.2	367.5	59.5	617.9	6
1958	57.8	9.3	189.7	30.6	371.7	60.0	619.2	6
1959	44.1	6.7	206.4	31.4	405.8	61.8	656.3	6
1960	43.0	6.2	222.0	32.0	428.0	61.8	692.0	6
1965	60.0	6.5	275.0	30.0	582.0	63.5	917.0	6
1970	56.0	4.3	371.0	28.4	881.0	67.4	1,308.0	7
1975	83.0	4.2	436.0	22.0	1,461.0	73.8	1,980.0	7
1980	183.0	4.9	779.0	21.0	2,740.0	74.0	3,702.0	7
1985	328.0	5.0	1,319.0	20.0	4,915.0	75.0	6,563.0	7
1990	482.0	5.5	1,635.0	18.7	6,609.0	75.7	8,726.0	7
1995	480.0	4.2	1,959.0	17.3	8,899.0	78.1	11,338.0	7
2000	705.0	3.8	3,390.0	18.4	14,325.0	78.0	18,420.0	8

Note: Readers should be aware that ".0" has been added to parts of this table for typographical consistency—on percentages from 1927 through 1934, and on dollar figures from 1961 through 2000.

Sources: Research Department, McCann-Erickson (data reprinted in several sources, including *Television Factbook*) for data since 1935. Earlier information refers to estimated gross radio billings (and is thus not directly comparable to the post-1935 data) and comes from *Broadcasting Yearbook* 1951, page 12, table V. These represent advertising volume at the one-time rate, ignoring discounts.

3-B Television Advertising: 1949–1979

Year	Network Dollars (millions)	Network Percentage	National/Regional Spot Dollars (millions)	National/Regional Spot Percentage	Local Dollars (millions)	Local Percentage	Total Dollars (millions)	Percentage of All Advertising
1949	$ 29.4	50.9%	$ 9.2	15.9%	$ 19.2	33.2%	$ 57.8	1%
1950	85.0	49.8	30.8	18.0	55.0	32.2	170.8	3
1951	180.8	54.4	69.9	21.0	81.6	24.6	332.3	5
1952	256.4	56.5	93.8	20.7	103.7	22.8	453.9	6
1953	319.9	52.8	145.5	24.0	140.7	23.2	606.1	8
1954	422.2	52.2	206.8	25.6	180.2	22.3	809.2	10
1955	550.2	53.1	260.4	25.2	224.7	21.7	1,035.3	11
1956	643.1	52.5	329.0	26.9	252.6	20.6	1,224.7	12
1957	690.1	53.7	351.6	27.4	243.6	19.0	1,285.3	12
1958	742.0	53.5	397.0	28.6	248.4	17.9	1,387.4	13
1959	776.0	50.7	486.4	31.8	266.8	17.4	1,529.2	13
1960	820.0	50.4	526.7	32.4	280.5	17.2	1,627.3	13
1961	887.3	52.5	548.0	32.4	256.0	15.1	1,691.0	14
1962	976.0	51.4	629.0	33.2	292.0	15.4	1,897.0	15
1963	1,025.0	50.4	698.0	34.4	309.0	15.2	2,032.0	16
1964	1,132.0	49.5	806.0	35.2	351.0	15.3	2,289.0	16
1965	1,237.0	49.2	892.0	35.5	386.0	15.3	2,515.0	17
1966	1,393.0	49.3	988.0	35.0	442.0	15.7	2,823.0	17
1967	1,455.0	50.0	988.0	34.0	466.0	16.0	2,909.0	17
1968	1,523.0	47.1	1,131.0	35.0	577.0	17.9	3,231.0	18
1969	1,678.0	46.8	1,253.0	35.0	654.0	18.2	3,585.0	19

Year							
1970	1,658.0	46.1	1,234.0	34.3	704.0	19.6	3,596.0	18
1971	1,593.0	45.1	1,145.0	32.4	796.0	22.5	3,534.0	17
1972	1,804.0	44.1	1,318.0	32.2	969.0	23.7	4,091.0	18
1973	1,968.0	44.1	1,377.0	30.9	1,115.0	25.0	4,460.0	18
1974	2,145.0	44.2	1,497.0	30.8	1,212.0	25.0	4,854.0	18
1975	2,306.0	43.8	1,623.0	30.8	1,334.0	25.3	5,263.0	19
1976	2,857.0	42.6	2,154.0	32.0	1,710.0	25.4	6,721.0	20
1977	3,460.0	45.4	2,204.0	29.0	1,948.0	25.6	7,612.0	20
1978	3,975.0	44.4	2,607.0	29.1	2,373.0	25.5	8,955.0	20
1979	4,599.0	45.3	2,873.0	28.3	2,682.0	26.4	10,154.0	20

Note: Readers should be aware that ".0" has been added to parts of this table for typographical consistency, particularly for dollar figures for the years from 1961 through 1979.

Sources: Research Department, McCann-Erickson (data reprinted in several sources, including *Television Factbook*). McCann-Erickson has provided rounded and corrected data for several earlier years. McCann-Erickson data for 1976–1979 as reported to the authors from that company.

3-C Television/Cable Advertising: 1980–2000

Year	Broadcast Television						Cable Television		Total Dollars (millions)	Percentage of All Advertising
	Network		National/Regional Spot		Local					
	Dollars (millions)	%	Dollars (millions)	%	Dollars (millions)	%	Dollars (millions)	%		
1980	$ 5,130.0	45.0	$ 3,269.0	28.6	$ 2,967.0	26.0	$ 72.0	—	$11,438.0	20%
1981	5,540.0	43.2	3,746.0	29.2	3,368.0	26.3	160.0	1.2	12,814.0	21
1982	6,144.0	41.2	4,364.0	29.7	3,765.0	26.1	290.0	2.0	14,713.0	22
1983	6,955.0	41.2	4,827.0	28.6	4,345.0	25.7	452.0	2.7	16,879.0	22
1984	8,318.0	41.5	5,488.0	27.4	5,084.0	25.4	733.0	3.7	20,043.0	23
1985	8,060.0	39.7	6,004.0	29.6	5,714.0	28.2	989.0	4.8	20,298.0	21
1986	8,342.0	37.9	6,570.0	29.8	6,514.0	29.6	1,173.0	5.3	22,026.0	22
1987	8,500.0	37.1	6,845.0	29.8	6,835.0	29.8	1,321.0	5.8	22,941.0	21
1988	9,172.0	35.1	7,147.0	27.4	7,270.0	27.8	1,641.0	6.3	26,131.0	22
1989	9,110.0	33.2	7,354.0	26.8	7,612.0	27.7	2,095.0	7.6	27,459.0	22
1990	9,863.0	33.9	7,788.0	26.8	7,856.0	27.0	2,457.0	8.5	29,073.0	22
1991	9,533.0	33.8	7,110.0	25.2	7,565.0	26.8	2,728.0	9.7	28,189.0	22
1992	10,249.0	33.7	7,551.0	24.8	8,079.0	26.5	3,201.0	10.5	30,450.0	23
1993	10,209.0	32.2	7,800.0	24.6	8,435.0	26.6	3,678.0	11.6	31,698.0	23
1994	10,942.0	30.9	8,993.0	25.4	9,464.0	26.7	4,302.0	12.1	35,435.0	23
1995	11,600.0	30.7	9,119.0	24.1	9,985.0	26.4	5,108.0	13.5	37,828.0	23
1996	13,081.0	30.8	9,803.0	23.1	10,994.0	25.9	6,438.0	15.2	42,484.0	24
1997	13,020.0	29.5	9,999.0	22.7	11,436.0	25.9	7,237.0	16.4	44,130.0	24
1998	13,736.0	28.8	10,659.0	22.3	12,169.0	25.5	8,547.0	17.9	47,720.0	24
1999	14,698.0	30.6	10,925.0	22.7	12,595.0	26.2	9,807.0	20.4	48,025.0	23
2000	16,020.0	30.4	11,800.0	22.4	13,665.0	25.9	11,150.0	21.2	52,635.0	23

Source: McCann-Erickson.

Note: Network includes Fox as of 1990. Total includes syndicated program advertising which is not listed separately here (and grew from $901 million in 1988 up to $2.8 billion by 1999).

■ **3-D   Public Broadcasting Revenue: 1970–1999**

Table shows total public broadcasting system revenue (Corporation for Public Broadcasting, National Public Radio, Public Broadcasting Service and stations) and proportion of that revenue from various tax and non-tax sources.

		Source of Income by Percentage from:					
Year	Total Income (millions)	Federal Govt	State and Local Govt	Memberships and Auctions	Business/ Industry	Foundation	Other
1970	$ 154	15%	na	na	na	na	na
1975	370	25	44%	11%	7%	8%	5%
1980	705	27	39	15	10	3	6
1985	1,096	16	33	23	16	4	9
1990	1,581	17	30	23	17	5	9
1995	1,917	18	29	23	15	6	9
1999	2,150	14	25	27	15	6	13

Source: Corporation for Public Broadcasting data as presented in *Statistical Abstract of the United States* various years. 1999 data from CPB website.

Table 4   Radio Programming: 1927–1999

Tables 4-A through 4-D, based on data in Summers (1958), show trends in programming on the national commercial radio networks from their inception through the mid-1950s, when television had drastically diminished the role of network radio. Data for 1927 refer only to NBC's Red network, while data after that year include NBC-Blue and CBS and data after 1934 include Mutual. NBC-Blue became independent in 1943 and was renamed ABC in 1945.

The figures shown are the number of quarter-hours of that program type on the air for all networks for a single week–typically, the third week in January. Thus the data are indicative of that "season's" programming but are no more than that, especially as the "season" concept did not become important for the networks until well into the 1930s.

The tables cover (A) evening programs, or those on the air after 6 P.M., any day of the week, (B) weekday daytime programs on the air Monday through Friday before 6 P.M., (C) a total program summary combining the data in A and B plus weekend daytime figures, and (D) a percentage summary for selected years showing trends in program types. For convenience, the programs in the first three tables are divided into four major categories: variety, music, drama, and talk. Each is further subdivided into specific program types. Note the following in the set of tables:

Other than *children's variety*, programs directed at children are included in totals with adult programs.

Recorded music and *magazine variety*, to name the two most obvious types of program, do not appear in network schedules until the 1950s.

4-A   Evening Network Radio Programs: 1927–1956
(number of quarter-hours on commercial networks)

	1927	1928	1929	1930	1931	1932	1933	1934	1935	1936	1937	1938	1939
Variety													
Vaudeville and Comedy	—	4	6	12	9	5	28	32	30	28	38	36	38
Semi-Variety	—	—	—	8	18	37	8	23	18	16	16	6	6
Amateur and Talent	—	—	—	—	—	—	—	—	2	9	4	4	4
Hillbilly, Country & Western	—	—	2	2	—	2	7	9	10	20	10	8	12
General and Talk Variety	4	10	12	10	16	12	14	14	23	22	24	30	32
Children's Variety	—	—	—	—	—	—	—	—	—	3	—	—	—
Magazine Variety	—	—	—	—	—	—	—	—	—	—	—	—	—
Music													
Musical Variety	30	34	55	90	75	87	57	64	99	70	56	52	48
Light Music	8	28	34	46	37	60	44	27	29	34	25	20	12
Concert Music	39	76	68	62	62	33	44	48	47	49	36	48	28
Recorded Music	—	—	—	—	—	—	—	—	—	—	—	—	—
Drama													
General	—	—	—	—	—	—	—	2	2	6	8	6	14
Light	—	8	16	22	20	13	15	13	18	17	11	17	28
Women's Serial	—	—	—	—	—	16	15	15	13	5	—	—	—
Comedy, Comedy Situation	—	—	—	11	18	17	16	8	10	22	34	16	18
Thriller	—	—	2	6	9	19	38	34	35	22	25	23	33
Documentary, Information	—	4	—	2	—	3	4	4	4	7	8	12	8
Talk													
Human Interest	—	—	—	—	—	—	—	6	7	5	16	16	13
Quiz	—	—	—	—	—	—	—	—	—	—	6	8	18
News	1	4	2	4	13	12	19	27	28	31	34	23	33
Public Affairs, Forums	—	2	2	5	5	8	7	—	12	5	8	8	12
Talk	4	4	2	4	14	12	13	14	15	26	14	18	23
Sports Play-by-Play	—	—	—	—	—	—	—	—	—	—	—	2	2
Religion	2	2	2	4	14	4	2	5	5	5	5	5	7
Total Quarter-Hours	88	176	203	288	310	340	331	345	407	402	378	358	389

Under *drama*, "general" refers to anthology and prestige dramatic programs, while "light" is a catchall for series not covered in other categories.

Under *talk*, "human interest" means a program type concentrating on personalities and occupations and activities, though the nominal format of such programs was often audience-participation, panel, or quiz show in style.

Under *music*, all the programs shown were live except those labeled "recorded."

Note: Tables 4-A through 4-D are © by L. W. Lichty and are used with permission. Table 4-E details radio station formats since 1964 and is drawn from many different surveys, as listed in its footnote.

▪ 4-A   (*continued*)

1940	1941	1942	1943	1944	1945	1946	1947	1948	1949	1950	1951	1952	1953	1954	1955	1956
32	18	32	34	38	32	30	38	34	30	24	22	26	18	6	8	12
16	6	9	2	5	2	—	4	2	2	4	4	4	2	2	10	10
4	4	4	2	2	2	—	—	4	8	7	7	9	6	2	2	2
12	8	8	6	8	10	4	6	4	10	4	4	4	12	12	11	5
16	28	24	21	29	22	22	18	4	4	8	4	4	2	8	25	7
—	—	—	—	—	—	—	—	—	—	—	—	—	—	—	—	—
—	—	—	—	—	—	—	—	—	—	—	—	—	—	—	—	30
59	58	69	60	63	70	63	40	44	52	51	33	29	56	52	76	51
24	4	11	7	5	13	9	3	4	2	7	6	15	23	26	28	37
28	34	37	22	29	29	24	18	22	23	21	26	32	30	38	27	24
4	—	—	—	—	—	—	—	—	—	—	—	10	12	10	4	15
14	14	16	12	16	8	18	16	18	20	14	20	16	16	12	6	—
24	20	17	14	11	8	17	19	12	22	12	9	25	15	22	7	5
—	—	—	—	—	—	—	—	—	—	—	—	—	—	—	—	—
21	17	27	20	23	32	40	44	41	35	53	39	33	36	41	16	13
40	30	41	35	56	48	57	79	78	68	91	95	91	79	71	62	37
4	4	9	12	16	16	6	6	10	4	2	12	9	10	11	6	18
10	19	12	10	16	9	11	12	12	8	10	12	6	—	6	2	9
30	37	28	30	30	32	38	27	36	48	34	32	16	36	25	19	12
56	45	62	65	88	73	77	49	65	50	77	82	83	96	103	82	85
13	18	14	12	11	10	14	17	9	13	13	12	10	12	17	17	23
38	23	26	8	5	9	21	23	14	22	19	19	18	25	32	21	27
3	3	2	—	—	2	3	3	3	3	5	6	6	3	3	26	—
5	9	7	11	9	5	5	5	5	3	7	—	—	—	2	10	10
453	399	455	383	460	432	459	427	421	427	463	444	446	489	501	465	432

■ 4-B   Daytime Network Radio Programs: 1927–1956
(number of quarter-hours on commercial networks)

	1927	1928	1929	1930	1931	1932	1933	1934	1935	1936	1937	1938	1939
Variety													
Vaudeville and Comedy	—	—	—	—	—	—	2	—	5	4	—	—	—
Semi-Variety	—	—	—	—	—	—	—	—	—	—	—	—	—
Amateur and Talent	—	—	—	—	—	—	—	—	—	—	—	—	—
Hillbilly, Country & Western	—	—	—	—	—	—	—	—	—	—	—	—	—
General and Talk Variety	—	—	—	—	—	—	—	20	27	20	30	40	40
Children's Variety	—	—	—	11	8	15	25	—	12	10	7	4	3
Magazine Variety	—	—	—	—	—	—	—	—	—	—	—	—	—
Music													
Musical Variety	—	—	—	2	—	9	5	—	6	—	8	—	—
Light Music	—	10	27	18	30	62	54	92	49	87	45	42	65
Concert Music	—	—	4	8	4	6	9	20	16	13	18	16	16
Recorded Music	—	—	—	—	—	—	—	—	—	—	—	—	—
Drama													
General	—	—	—	4	4	4	8	8	4	4	4	4	—
Light	—	—	—	—	—	2	4	—	—	—	5	—	3
Women's Serial	—	—	—	—	—	—	20	43	48	88	154	240	225
Comedy, Situation Comedy	—	—	—	—	—	6	5	9	15	—	5	7	—
Thriller	—	—	—	—	—	5	14	13	18	25	27	41	30
Documentary, Information	—	—	1	—	10	10	10	10	12	10	12	10	20
Talk													
Human Interest	—	—	—	—	—	—	—	5	5	16	12	17	6
Quiz	—	—	—	—	—	—	—	—	—	—	—	—	—
News	—	—	—	—	—	—	6	—	—	10	29	18	—
Public Affairs, Forums	—	—	—	—	—	—	—	—	—	—	—	1	—
Talk	3	31	89	51	96	134	79	91	80	70	83	88	75
Sports Play-by-Play	—	—	—	—	—	—	—	—	—	—	—	—	—
Religion	—	—	—	—	—	—	—	—	—	—	—	5	5
Total Quarter-Hours	3	41	121	94	152	253	241	311	297	357	439	533	488

■ 4-C   Network Radio Programs: Summary 1927–1956
(number of quarter-hours on commercial networks)

	1927	1928	1929	1930	1931	1932	1933	1934	1935	1936	1937	1938	1939
Evening													
Variety	4	14	20	32	43	56	57	78	83	98	92	84	92
Music	77	138	157	198	174	180	145	139	175	153	117	120	88
Drama	—	12	18	41	47	68	88	76	82	79	86	74	101
Talk	7	12	8	17	46	36	41	52	67	72	83	80	108
Daytime													
Variety	—	—	—	11	8	15	27	20	44	30	37	44	43
Music	—	10	31	28	34	77	68	112	71	100	71	58	81
Drama	—	—	1	4	14	27	61	83	97	127	207	302	278
Talk	3	31	89	51	96	134	85	96	85	96	124	129	86
Weekend Daytime													
Variety	—	—	—	—	—	4	6	10	8	8	10	12	24
Music	—	2	10	14	27	56	55	66	58	62	65	55	56
Drama	—	—	2	2	2	15	12	19	16	7	16	11	18
Talk	16	22	15	21	25	26	24	22	23	35	38	36	35
Total by Type													
Variety	4	14	20	43	51	75	90	108	135	136	139	140	159
Music	77	150	198	240	235	313	268	317	304	315	253	233	225
Drama	—	12	21	47	63	110	161	178	195	213	309	387	397
Talk	26	65	112	89	167	196	150	170	175	203	245	245	229
Total Quarter-Hours	107	241	351	419	516	694	669	773	809	867	946	1,005	1,010

■ 4-B (*continued*)

1940	1941	1942	1943	1944	1945	1946	1947	1948	1949	1950	1951	1952	1953	1954	1955	1956
—	—	—	—	—	—	10	—	—	—	—	—	—	10	5	—	—
—	—	—	—	—	—	—	—	—	—	—	—	—	—	—	—	—
—	—	—	—	—	—	—	—	—	—	—	10	10	10	—	—	—
—	—	2	—	2	10	—	35	30	30	35	35	15	24	19	—	—
42	40	32	62	70	30	55	40	30	55	80	95	65	110	101	121	126
4	5	—	—	—	—	—	—	—	—	—	10	5	14	5	—	—
—	—	—	—	—	—	—	—	—	—	—	—	—	—	—	—	95
—	—	4	5	9	—	10	10	10	20	30	25	10	15	20	41	48
46	38	35	4	13	30	29	24	6	21	16	15	25	53	43	23	23
10	11	14	2	4	—	—	—	—	2	2	—	—	—	5	5	5
—	—	—	—	—	—	—	40	15	20	10	30	25	36	28	35	
—	—	—	—	—	—	—	—	—	—	—	—	—	—	—	—	—
—	—	—	—	15	14	14	9	13	15	20	20	10	15	28	33	23
305	300	275	200	220	195	200	165	180	165	160	135	175	140	135	130	95
5	5	5	—	5	5	10	10	10	10	—	—	—	—	5	—	5
20	26	35	25	30	40	50	45	45	40	42	35	35	15	12	12	8
19	10	10	10	10	10	10	10	10	—	—	—	—	—	—	—	—
4	—	—	—	10	30	45	58	70	85	70	50	50	44	53	35	28
—	5	5	—	15	15	15	41	50	50	31	50	60	45	35	35	13
10	20	41	49	50	50	51	50	50	35	35	40	30	51	73	63	55
—	—	—	—	—	—	—	—	—	—	—	—	—	—	—	—	—
68	68	76	33	37	42	44	37	36	54	45	55	40	48	15	18	25
—	—	—	—	—	—	—	—	—	—	—	—	—	—	—	—	—
5	—	—	—	—	—	5	—	—	5	5	5	5	5	5	—	—
538	528	534	390	490	471	548	534	580	602	591	590	565	624	595	544	584

■ 4-C (*continued*)

1940	1941	1942	1943	1944	1945	1946	1947	1948	1949	1950	1951	1952	1953	1954	1955	1956
80	64	77	65	82	68	56	66	48	54	47	41	47	40	30	56	66
115	96	117	89	97	112	96	61	70	77	79	65	86	121	126	135	127
103	85	110	93	122	112	138	164	159	149	172	175	174	156	157	97	73
155	154	151	136	159	140	169	136	144	147	165	163	139	172	188	177	166
46	45	34	62	72	40	65	75	60	85	115	150	95	168	130	121	221
56	49	53	11	26	30	39	34	56	58	68	50	65	93	104	97	111
349	341	325	235	280	264	284	239	258	230	222	190	220	170	180	175	131
87	93	122	82	112	137	160	186	206	229	186	200	185	193	181	151	121
16	12	15	14	30	18	20	12	10	12	14	22	24	23	58	66	90
63	64	66	51	60	43	69	63	53	47	47	50	52	108	83	78	80
16	17	18	14	36	30	34	39	39	35	39	38	36	36	27	22	16
53	58	65	50	62	60	70	69	58	77	79	90	77	107	99	92	92
142	121	126	141	184	126	141	153	118	151	176	213	166	231	218	243	377
234	209	236	151	183	185	204	158	179	182	194	165	203	322	313	310	318
468	443	453	342	438	406	456	442	456	414	433	403	430	362	364	294	220
295	305	338	268	333	337	399	391	408	453	430	453	401	472	468	420	379
1,139	1,078	1,153	902	1,138	1,054	1,200	1,144	1,161	1,200	1,233	1,234	1,200	1,387	1,363	1,267	1,294

4-D Network Radio Programs: Percentages 1929–1956 (summary, every three years)

Percentage of All Quarter-Hours:

Year	Variety	Musical	Drama	Interview, Human Interest, Quiz	News, Sports, Forums, Talks	Other* Programs	Total Quarter-Hours Broadcast per Week
1929	5%	56%	6%	—	28%	5%	351
1932	11	46	15	—	26	2	694
1935	18	39	25	2%	11	5	809
1938	15	24	38	4	16	3	1,005
1941	10	20	42	6	18	4	1,078
1944	16	16	38	7	19	4	1,138
1947	14	15	33	14	21	3	1,144
1950	13	15	36	13	19	4	1,233
1953	15	25	28	8	20	10	1,387
1956	31	23	16	5	19	6	1,294

*Includes Farm, Religious, Miscellaneous, and Unclassified.
Sources: Data in this table are derived from tables 4-A through 4-C.

■ 4-E Radio Station Formats: 1968–1999

Year/mkts	No. of Stations	Middle-of-the-Road	Top 40	Beautiful and Background	Country	Black Soul	News Talk	Religion	Oldies	Other
										Percentage of Stations Programing
1968 top-50 mkts	1,076	40%	15%	13%	11%	7%	—	—	—	14%
1973 all markets	4,193	22	26	8	21	14	3%	—	—	3
1978 all markets	2,653	17	32	13	17	5	3	5	—	6
1982 all markets	2,904	19	23	9	19	8	3	7	—	9
1988 all markets	2,939	26	19	6	15	7	5	7	—	13
1999 all markets	10,444	—	7	—	22	4	14	11	11%	31*

Notes: Categories vary over the years, so these must be considered as, at best, approximations of what stations were programming. Data through 1988 based on samples of AM and FM stations in top 50 markets for 1968 and all market sizes in other years. 1999 data includes most commercial stations on the air. "Oldies" category not included in years before 1999.

* "Other" for 1999 includes such formats as (with ranks within the top 30 formats): Hispanic (6), sports (15), ethnic (23), "pre-teen" (26), and classical (29).

Sources: Sterling (1984) for data through 1982, citing Lichty & Topping (1975) for 1968 and 1973 information. 1982 and 1988 data from James Duncan. 1999 from M Street Inc. as reported on Radio Advertising Bureau, *Radio Marketing Guide and Fact Book for Advertisers: 2000–2001 Edition,* p. 46, as provided on RAB website.

Table 5   Television Programming: 1949–2000

Tables 5-A through 5-E show trends in programs on the national commercial television networks from their inception in 1948 to either 2000 (prime time) or 1973 (daytime). Except for table 5-A, these tables show the number of quarter-hours of each program type on the air for a single week, typically the third week in January—parallel to radio data tables 4-A through 4-D. The data are thus indicative of that television season; that is, 1954 data refer in a general sense to the whole 1953—1954 television season.

The tables show (A) evening programs on the air after 6 P.M. (listed by hours rather than quarter-hours, and with somewhat different program categories than the other tables); (B) weekday daytime programs on the air Monday through Friday before 6 P.M.; (C) a total programming summary of number of quarter-hours and percentages, allowing a direct comparison of prime-time and daytime information plus that for weekend programming (also including cost and other measures of program change), and (D and E) detailed major network format types in both prime-time and daytime hours summarized from data provided by A.C. Nielsen. Tables 5-D and 5-E differ from tables 5-A through 5-C not only in source but because (1) they include only programs carrying advertising (the vast majority) and (2) they cover only 10 A.M. to 4:30 P.M. as "daytime." Table 5-F reports the available data on public television station programming—see notes to that table for program definitions pertaining only to public television. Finally, Table 5-G provides information on the television audience for national presidential campaigns.

The program types for tables 5-A through 5-E are more refined than those for radio, making direct comparisons a bit difficult. For example, "thriller" in the radio tables includes content classified as crime-detective, action-adventure, westerns, and suspense programs in television. Note also:

Table 5-A shows the weekly hours of programming on ABC, CBS, NBC (and, for later seasons, Fox, UPN and WB) from 6 to 11 P.M., Eastern time. The program categories shown in the table are defined as follows:

Variety: includes comedy, music, country, and talk variety formats, and in a very few cases miscellaneous or varied formats.

General drama: into the 1960s was primarily anthology; since then many are lawyer- and doctor-centered programs.

Movies: includes made-for-TV movies as well as those initially produced for theatrical release.

Action/adventure: also includes science-fiction/space.

Crime/detective: virtually all police or private-eye programs.

Western: while there were occasional 'cowboy' dramas during the past quarter-century, none since 1991 has lasted for a complete season.

SitC (Situation Comedy): (sometimes earlier Comedy Drama) also includes a small number of animated family comedies such as *The Flintstones* and *The Simpsons*.

Quiz: includes panel, audience participation, and human interest.

News: includes network evening news, documentary, documentary magazine, forum, and other information formats. The table covers not just 'primetime' programs but *all* network evening programs from 6 to 11 P.M. Eastern and Pacific time (5 to 10 P.M. Central and Mountain time), so that it includes the network evening news programs *World News Tonight, CBS Evening News*, and *NBC Nightly News*–their titles for the last half of this table, but broadcast under various titles earlier.

Talks: includes all sports programs (including football, since this sample is based on the fall schedule beginning with 1992–93 (as noted below), and religion. This category grew from 1989, since it also includes "reality" formats such as comedy "reality" programs like *Funniest Households Videos* and action or crime/action 'reality' such as *COPS, Rescue 911,* and *Unsolved Mysteries*—and most recently, programs such as *Survivor.*

Each TV season label is abbreviated (so September 1948 to August 1949 is shown in this table as 1949 and so on). Even by 1950 the then four networks (DuMont is included) presented nearly 90 evening hours each week. After 1955, when DuMont failed, there were generally about 80 hours. Then in 1971, FCC rules limited each network to three hours each night, so with evening news–which expanded from 15 to 30 minutes after 1964–the total is slightly less. After Fox is added, starting in 1990, the total is again about 90. WB and UPN, added in 1999, bring the total, including the evening news, to about 115, rounded up to whole hours.

The compilation in tables 5-A through 5-E was initiated by Professor Harrison B. Summers at Ohio State University in the 1950s, and was then revised and continued by Lawrence Lichty, now of Northwestern University, after 1960. Material for the 1948–49 through the 1976–77 seasons was based on a sample week of programming (third week in January); for 1977–78 through 1991–92 season the list is based on the last week of January and first week of February "regular" programs (i.e., at least five episodes a season, thus not including specials, one-time-only, or mini-series, during the regular season from September to April). From 1992–93 to 2001 data are drawn from the BJK&E Media Group–now TN Media Inc–based on programs for fall season.

Over the years L. W. Lichty has had assistance from a number of colleagues including C. H. Sterling, Kenneth Swerdlow, and Susan Leakey Watler up to 1977; M. T. Cozzola, 1978–87, Noah Arceneaux 1988–1991, and Steve Sternberg and Stacey Lynn of True North for data since 1993. Tables 5-A through 5-E are copyright © 2000 by Lawrence W. Lichty.

5-A Evening Network Television Programs: 1949–2001

Year	Variety	General/Drama	Movies	Action Adventure	Crime Detective	Western	Situation Comedy	Quiz	News	Talk/Sports
1949	22	6	9	—	1	—	1	3	12	28
1950	21	11	2	4	3	1	4	5	7	32
1951	42	16	3	6	4	2	4	5	6	33
1952	30	14	—	7	7	2	6	5	7	19
1953	20	11	—	5	6	2	9	5	11	14
1954	19	15	—	7	5	2	13	6	9	15
1955	25	20	—	2	3	2	15	6	9	7
1956	28	18	3	5	2	4	10	7	7	4
1957	26	19	3	7	2	4	9	6	7	3
1958	20	13	—	6	5	10	10	6	8	3
1959	17	9	11	5	8	16	7	2	8	3
1960	18	8	—	8	12	18	8	2	6	2
1961	9	7	11	8	10	14	13	1	14	2
1962	11	9	2	8	12	12	13	2	13	1
1963	17	14	4	9	5	9	12	1	12	1
1964	19	15	4	8	5	9	10	2	13	2
1965	20	9	6	11	2	6	16	1	13	—
1966	16	5	8	14	3	9	18	—	11	—
1967	12	2	12	19	3	10	13	1	13	—
1968	15	1	13	18	6	9	10	2	12	—
1969	17	3	14	8	10	10	11	2	13	—
1970	18	9	18	5	6	6	14	2	12	—
1971	17	9	16	2	12	6	13	1	12	—
1972	9	5	18	3	12	4	10	—	11	—
1973	13	6	25	5	11	3	11	—	12	—
1974	5	6	23	4	16	3	7	—	11	—

Year										
1975	6	7	19	4	20	2	9	—	11	—
1976	5	9	14	3	25	—	13	1	12	—
1977	8	8	12	9	19	—	14	—	13	—
1978	10	9	14	7	12	1	15	1	12	—
1979	8	15	14	9	10	2	14	1	13	—
1980	6	14	14	7	11	—	13	—	14	1
1981	5	14	13	8	10	1	13	—	14	3
1982	5	12	17	6	8	—	13	—	14	2
1983	1	14	16	11	8	—	14	—	13	3
1984	1	12	17	10	11	—	11	—	14	5
1985	1	11	15	11	14	—	11	—	13	2
1986	—	10	16	11	14	—	12	—	13	1
1987	—	12	15	10	12	—	13	—	15	—
1988	1	13	13	3	20	1	13	—	14	2
1989	1	16	12	5	12	2	14	—	15	3
1990	1	13	14	4	13	2	18	—	18	6
1991	4	14	16	4	9	2	18	—	17	9
1992	2	13	16	2	7	—	23	—	16	
1993	na	na	na	na	na	na	na	na	na	na
1994	3	12	14	4	8	—	24	—	20	7
1995	1	15	14	6	10	—	21	—	20	6
1996	1	19	14	5	6	—	25	—	18	4
1997	1	15	12	7	10	—	24	—	19	4
1998	1	16	10	7	10	—	22	—	21	4
1999	4	23	12	7	14	—	27	—	21	6
2000	1	30	13	9	10	—	22	—	22	6
2001	2	24	18	13	7	—	20	4	20	6

▪ 5-B   Daytime Network Television Programs: 1949–1973 (number of quarter-hours on commercial networks)

	1949	1950	1951	1952	1953	1954	1955	1956	1957	1958
Variety										
Special, Variety	—	—	—	—	—	—	—	—	—	—
Comedy	—	—	—	35	—	—	—	—	—	—
Ameteur, Talent	—	—	—	—	—	—	—	—	—	—
Country and Western	—	—	—	—	—	—	—	—	—	—
General, Talk	10	10	13	129	79	86	166	166	114	76
Music										
Musical Variety	5	—	20	20	40	50	30	10	10	55
Light Music	10	5	5	5	—	—	—	—	—	—
Drama										
General	—	—	—	—	—	—	—	20	20	30
Motion Pictures	—	—	—	—	—	—	—	40	30	—
Women's Serials	—	—	5	30	20	45	84	40	55	65
Action-Adventure	20	—	—	—	—	—	—	—	—	10
Crime-Detective	—	—	—	—	—	—	—	—	—	—
Suspense	—	—	—	—	—	—	—	—	—	—
Westerns	—	—	15	—	—	10	—	—	—	—
Comedy, Situation Comedy	—	—	—	—	—	—	—	—	30	10
Animated Cartoons	—	—	—	—	—	—	—	—	—	—
Quiz and Panel										
Audience Participation	20	30	24	28	42	44	40	40	50	80
Human Interest	15	5	8	1	25	25	20	30	35	45
Panel Shows	—	—	10	—	—	—	—	—	5	—
News and Information										
Newscasts	—	—	—	10	5	5	—	—	5	5
Forums, Interviews	—	—	—	—	—	—	—	—	—	—
Documentary, Information	—	—	—	—	—	20	—	—	—	—
Other Types										
Religion	—	5	—	—	—	—	—	—	—	—
Talk	15	90	28	11	—	—	27	—	—	—
Children's Shows	10	40	30	15	21	35	32	70	40	25
Sports	—	—	—	—	—	—	—	—	—	—
Miscellany	—	—	—	—	—	—	—	—	—	—
Total Quarter-Hours	105	185	158	284	232	320	399	416	394	401

▦ 5-B (*continued*)

1959	1960	1961	1962	1963	1964	1965	1966	1967	1968	1969	1970	1971	1972	1973
—	—	—	—	—	—	—	—	—	—	—	—	—	—	—
—	—	—	—	—	—	—	—	—	—	—	—	—	—	—
—	—	—	—	—	—	—	—	—	—	—	—	—	—	—
—	—	—	—	—	—	—	—	—	—	—	—	—	—	—
70	60	40	50	70	45	40	40	40	40	40	50	50	50	60
50	30	30	20	20	10	10	10	20	—	—	—	—	—	—
—	—	—	—	—	—	—	—	—	—	—	—	—	—	—
20	50	50	50	40	20	—	20	20	20	—	—	—	—	—
—	—	—	—	—	—	—	—	—	—	—	—	—	—	—
70	80	100	70	60	70	120	150	110	108	138	158	180	160	160
—	20	20	—	—	—	—	—	—	—	—	—	—	—	—
—	50	—	—	—	—	—	—	—	—	—	—	—	—	—
—	—	—	—	—	—	—	—	—	—	—	—	—	—	—
—	50	10	10	—	20	20	—	—	—	—	—	—	—	—
10	40	50	20	40	50	60	60	50	50	50	60	60	70	20
—	10	—	—	—	—	—	—	—	—	—	—	—	—	—
140	80	100	140	110	120	100	100	128	128	114	68	70	90	130
40	40	50	30	20	20	10	10	20	20	8	—	—	—	—
—	—	—	10	20	20	10	10	10	18	10	28	20	10	10
5	5	9	22	16	24	24	24	22	18	18	26	24	25	25
—	—	—	—	—	—	—	—	—	—	—	—	—	—	—
—	—	—	—	—	—	—	—	—	—	—	—	—	—	—
—	—	—	—	—	—	—	—	—	—	—	—	—	—	—
50	20	20	30	40	10	10	10	10	12	12	10	10	10	10
25	15	15	40	20	20	20	20	20	20	20	20	20	20	20
—	—	—	—	—	—	—	—	—	—	—	—	—	—	—
—	—	—	—	—	—	—	—	—	—	—	—	—	—	—
480	550	494	492	456	429	424	454	450	434	410	420	434	435	435

▪ 5-C Network Television Programs: Summary 1949–1973 (number of quarter-hours on commercial networks)

	1949	1952	1955	1958	1961	1964	1967	1970	1973
All Programming: Quarter-Hours									
Variety	66	249	278	161	95	134	116	195	150
Music	45	64	52	99	50	42	40	28	16
Drama	87	196	266	309	468	400	478	518	483
Quiz	68	93	108	167	170	180	174	102	142
News/Information	45	56	60	62	77	94	88	83	94
Other	166	145	157	75	97	88	74	84	86
Total	477	803	921	873	957	938	970	1,010	971
All Programming: Percentage									
Variety	14%	31%	30%	18%	10%	14%	12%	19%	15%
Music	9	8	6	11	5	4	4	3	2
Drama	18	24	29	35	49	43	48	51	50
Quiz	14	12	12	19	18	19	18	10	15
News/Information	9	7	7	7	8	10	9	8	10
Other	35	18	17	9	10	9	8	8	9
Total	99%	100%	101%	99%	100%	99%	99%	99%	101%

Average Production Cost: Prime-Time Programs

90 min. Drama	na	na	na	na	na	$181,000	$200,000	$300,000	$342,500
60 min. Variety	$5,900	$35,900	$67,700	$84,000	$110,000	115,700	182,170	193,210	204,286
60 min. Drama	10,800	21,100	34,100	65,450	86,640	120,810	176,520	203,610	213,636
30 min. Variety	3,800	16,700	24,600	44,100	63,000	65,000	na	100,000	na
30 min. Drama	3,500	13,200	26,100	36,200	42,270	59,030	88,690	103,960	104,194
30 min. Quiz	1,730	9,640	11,400	29,330	28,200	45,500	71,000	35,000	na
Movies	na	na	na	na	180,000	200,000	380,000	750,000	750,000
Movies for TV	na	na	na	na	na	na	na	400,000	418,333

Live-VTR or Film (Percentage of quarter-hours in prime time)

Live-VTR	34%	78%	65%	42%	17%	25%	19%	22%	12%
Film	na	25	40	69	81	54	67	51	58

Source: Lichty and Topping (1975), Table 36. Information in the last two sections (average production cost and live-VTR or film) is *only* for prime-time programs broadcast 7–11 P.M. Average production cost is actually the lease (rental) payment for all showings (usually two) for "Movies" while referring to production costs for all other categories. The percentage figures for live-VTR and film are based on prime-time quarter-hours—and may not add to 100% due to rounding.

▪ 5-D Network Television Prime-Time Program Types: 1973–1995 (number of quarter-hours per week)

Year	Variety	Drama/ Adventure	Film	Mystery	Situation Comedy	Other	Total
1973	20	40	64	68	48	12	252
1974	8	68	58	76	30	12	252
1975	16	68	40	84	44	12	264
1976	28	52	46	66	50	22	264
1977	16	60	48	48	64	28	264
1978	12	72	48	48	58	26	264
1979	—	48	56	56	68	36	264
1980	18	60	56	28	70	32	264
1981	16	76	40	48	60	24	264
1982	12	76	40	48	64	24	264
1983	8	104	48	28	52	24	264
1984	6	84	48	84	48	22	284
1985	4	90	40	82	48	20	284
1986	—	78	48	58	56	24	264
1987	4	72	36	80	72	20	284
1988	8	60	48	64	70	36	286
1989	10	80	48	52	84	26	300
1990	10	96	48	42	88	28	312
1991	16	68	56	40	100	32	312
1992	10	88	48	44	86	44	320
1993	14	76	56	36	92	50	324
1994	2	112	56	20	80	54	324
1995	4	106	56	20	96	42	324

Sources: All data derived from A.C. Nielsen. 1973–1982 from Sterling (1984), page 198. Figures are quarter-hour averages calculated by the authors from Nielsen data for the fall of each indicated television season. Totals may not add due to rounding. "Film" means feature films. Figures beginning in 1988 include the Fox Network "Other" includes news magazine programs; the majority of the category after by the mid-1990s. Beginning with data for 1996, however, Nielsen reported number of *programs* rather than number of *hours*, making it impossible to further update this table.

▥ 5-E   Network Television Daytime Program Types: 1973–1987 (number of quarter-hours per week)

Year	Daytime Drama	Situation Comedy	Quiz/Audience Participation	News/Other	Total
1973	148	20	158	13	340
1974	138	10	188	3	340
1975	158	10	168	3	340
1976	180	30	130	20	360
1977	180	50	120	10	360
1978	200	30	100	20	350
1979	210	20	120	10	360
1980	220	40	60	20	340
1981	220	30	80	10	340
1982	230	20	80	—	330
1983	210	30	90	10	340
1984	230	20	80	20	350
1985	220	10	110	—	340
1986	200	10	90	10	310
1987	220	20	100	—	340

Sources: All data derived from A.C. Nielsen. 1973–1982 from Sterling (1984), page 198; 1983–1984 from *Television Audience 1984* (Northbrook, Ill.: A.C. Nielsen Co., 1984), page 40; 1985–1987 from *Television Audience 1987* (Northbrook, Ill.: A.C. Nielsen Co., 1987), page 43. Figures are quarter-hour averages calculated by the authors from Nielsen data for the fall of each indicated television season. Totals may not add due to rounding. Some data for 1977–1982 are estimated from Nielsen data by the authors. After 1987, Nielsen stopped reporting number of hours and simply listed the number of programs making it impossible to further update this table.

■ 5-F Public Television Programming: 1964–1996

Percentages of Typical Weekly Programs (All Hours) on PTV Stations

Year	General Programs						Instructional		(Foreign or International Co-Production)
	News/Public Affairs	Information/Skills	Cultural	Children/Youth	Sesame Street	Other	Youth	Adult	
1964	13%	na	12%	10%		19%	41%	5%	na
1966	13	na	17	10		18	34	9	na
1968	14	na	17	10		10	42	8	na
1970	18	na	18	20		8	32	5	na
1972	19	na	12	21		20	25	4	na
1974	13	16%	18	11	21	4	17		(6)
1976	12	20	21	10	18	4	17		(8)
1978	11	24	22	9	16	5	15		(9)
1980	12	23	22	9	16	6	14	1	(13)
1982	12	25	23	8	15	5	13	1	(10)
1984	14	26	20	8	15	6	12	1	(13)
1986	16	30	21	7	11	2	15		(15)
1988	16	32	18	6	12	1	16		(14)
1990	18	32	19	6	11	1	14		(12)
1992	17	29	18	15	11	1	9	3	(11)
1994	19	27	16	20	9	1	6	3	(10)
1996	19	29	17	20	8	1	5	3	(10)

Definitions for this table (for 1974 and since; they vary slightly for earlier data) include:

News and Public Affairs: includes news and discussion programs; beginning in 1986, this also includes business or consumer programs.

Information and Skills: Includes history/biography, science, skills and how-to, and general information programs

Cultural: includes art and reviews, music/dance performances, drama, feature films, comedy/satire, and variety programs

General Children and Youth: includes *Mr. Roger's Neighborhood* and related programs.

Sesame Street: that program or *Electric Company*, both directed toward children and from the Children's Television Workshop.

Other: includes most sports, station promotion, auctions and other.

Instructional: specifically aimed at classroom use "or otherwise in the general context of formal education"

Foreign or international co-production: shown in parentheses as a percentage of all public television programs; do not add to or subtract from program type percentages.

Source: Data through 1972 from Sterling (1984) citing Corporation for Public Broadcasting, biennial survey of public television stations. Data since from CPB, same source, as reprinted in *Statistical Abstract of the United States*, annual.

▒ 5-G   Television Coverage of Presidential Elections: 1952–1996

Election Year (Winner-Loser)	Hours (All Nets)	Party Conventions		First Debate	Second Debate	Election Night	Viewing Alternatives*
		Democrats	Republicans				
1952 Eisenhower-Stevenson	119	na	na	No debates		na	na
1956 Eisenhower-Stevenson	60	na	na	No debates		na	na
1960 Kennedy-Nixon	55	29	28	60	59	66	na
1964 Johnson-Goldwater	60	29	22	No debates		56	na
1968 Nixon-Humphrey	73	29	26	No debates		59	na
1972 Nixon-McGovern	57	18	23	No debates		45	na
1976 Carter-Ford	60	25	32	54	52	52	na
1980 Reagan-Carter-Anderson	47	27	22	59	None	46	na
1984 Reagan-Mondale	25	23	19	45	46	36	17
1988 Bush-Dukakis	na	20	18	37	36	26	25
1992 Clinton-Bush-Perot	na	22	21	38	46	40	38
1996 Clinton-Dole	na	17	17	32	26	26	45

(Table header: **Total Rating, All Networks**)

Notes: A "rating" is the proportion of all television households that is watching a particular program or event. "Hours" in first column is total hours telecast from conventions by all networks (including DuMont in 1952, and CNN and PBS in 1992, 1996. Remaining columns are the total rating across all networks for events listed.
*"Alternative Viewing" in last column is total rating of all other viewing choices, broadcast or cable, *other* than election night reports.
Source: A.C. Nielsen Co. *Network Television Audiences to Primaries, Conventions, Elections* (1976), and *2000 Report on Television* (2000).

Table 6   Radio Receivers and Audio Market: 1922–1998

Though radio production was frozen during World War II (1942–45), the number of radio households grew as extra sets were distributed to those with none. As cars were junked during that period, however, car radios in use obviously declined. While household radios continued to increase in numbers with population growth after 1960, the percentage of households with radio and typical cost changed little as new audio products were introduced. For baseline data on number of households, see "useful tools" on p. 826.

▓ 6-A   Ownership of Radio Receivers: 1922–1959

Year	Radio Households (thousands)	Percentage of All Households	Average Receiver Cost	Cars with Radio (thousands)	Percentage of all Cars
1922	60	0.2%	$50	na	na
1923	400	1.5		na	na
1924	1,250	4.7		na	na
1925	2,750	10.1	83	na	na
1926	4,500	16.0		na	na
1927	6,750	23.6		na	na
1928	8,000	27.5		na	na
1929	10,250	34.6		na	na
1930	13,750	45.8	78	30	.1%
1931	16,700	55.2		100	.4
1932	18,450	60.6		250	1.2
1933	19,250	62.5		500	2.4
1934	20,400	65.2		1,250	5.8
1935	21,456	67.3	55	2,000	8.9
1936	22,869	68.4		3,500	14.5
1937	24,500	74.0		5,000	19.7
1938	26,667	79.2		6,000	23.8
1939	27,500	79.9		6,500	24.9
1940	28,500	81.1	38	7,500	27.4
1941	29,300	81.5		8,750	29.6
1942	30,600	84.0		9,000	32.3
1943	30,800	83.6		8,000	30.9
1944	32,500	87.6		7,000	27.5
1945	33,100	88.0	40	6,000	23.4
1946	33,998	89.9		7,000	24.9
1947	35,900	93.1		9,000	29.3
1948	37,623	94.2		11,000	33.1
1949	39,300	94.8		14,000	38.6
1950	40,700	94.7	26	18,000	49.6
1951	41,900	95.5		21,000	52.3
1952	42,800	95.6		23,500	55.3
1953	44,800	98.2		25,000	57.3
1954	45,100	96.7		26,100	56.4
1955	45,900	96.4	20	29,000	60.0
1956	46,800	96.3		30,100	57.9
1957	47,600	96.2		35,000	64.6
1958	48,500	96.3		36,500	65.5
1959	49,450	96.7		37,200	65.7

Sources: For radio households: National Association of Broadcasters (to 1950) and Radio Advertising Bureau (1950 to 1959). For cars with radio: Electronic Industries Association (to 1954) and Radio Advertising Bureau (1955 to 1959). Average receiver cost from Lichty and Topping (1975), page 521, table 41. Otto Schairer, in *Patent Policies of Radio Corporation of America* (New York: RCA Institutes Press, 1939, page 57), reports an average retail price for radio receivers of $120 in 1929 and $43.60 in 1937.

■ **6-B   Household Audio Market since 1960**

	FM Receivers as Percentage of			Households Owning		
Year	All Radios Sold	All Households	Automobile Radios Sold	Cars with Radio	Component Audio	Compact Disc
1960	8%	na	na	68%	na	
1965	15	na	6%	79	na	
1970	48	74%	14	93	na	
1975	65	93	38	95	na	
1980	78	95	78	95	na	
1985	na	na	na	95	39%	2%
1990	na	95	na	95	50	19
1995	na	95	na	95	53	48
1998	na	95	na	95	55	52

Sources: All data through 1980 as reported in Sterling (1984), pages 225–226, citing Electronics Industries Association estimates for all but household penetration of FM, which is from Pulse Inc. for data through 1975 and from Radio Advertising Bureau for data since 1975. Data since 1980 from Electronic Industries Association and Radio Advertising Bureau.

Table 7   Television Receivers and Video Market: 1946–2000

As with radio, the television market became "mature" with the full spread of color, UHF-tuning capability and, by the 1990s, widespread availability of remote controls. The households VCR became available after 1975 (see Table 7-B). More recently, other video products have appeared (and some, such as the laserdisc, have come and gone), including large-screen projection receivers and videocams. For baseline data on number of households, see "useful tools" on p. 826.

▪ 7-A   Ownership of Television Receivers: 1946–2000

Year	Television Households (thousands)	Percentage of All Households	Percentage of Television Households				Average Receiver Cost	
			Multiple Sets	UHF	Remote Controls	Color	B & W	Color
1946	8	.02%	—					
1947	14	.04	—				$279	
1948	172	.4	1%					
1949	940	2.3	1					
1950	3,875	9.0	1				190	
1951	10,320	23.5	2			na		
1952	15,300	34.2	2	na		na		
1953	20,400	44.7	3	na		na		
1954	26,000	55.7	3	na		na		
1955	30,700	64.5	3	na		.02%	138	$500
1956	34,900	71.8	5	na		.05		
1957	38,900	78.6	6	9.2%		.2		
1958	41,925	83.2	8	8.1		.4		
1959	43,950	85.9	10	8.0		.6		
1960	45,750	87.1	13	7.0		.7	132	392
1961	47,200	88.8	13	7.1		.9	125	381
1962	48,855	90.0	14	7.3		1.2	128	352
1963	50,300	91.3	16	9.6		1.9	118	346
1964	51,600	92.3	19	15.8*		3.1	109	348
1965	52,700	92.6	22	27.5		5.3	106	356
1966	53,850	93.0	25	38.0		9.7	98	371
1967	55,130	93.6	28	47.5		16.3	92	362
1968	56,670	94.6	29	57.0		24.2	74	336
1969	58,250	95.0	33	66.0		32.0	78	328
1970	59,700	95.2	34	73.0		39.2	75	317
1971	61,600	95.5	36	80.0		45.1	81	324
1972	63,500	95.8	38	81.0		52.8	79	319
1973	65,600	96.0	41	86.0		60.1	77	308
1974	66,800	96.1	42	89.0		67.3	79	316
1975	68,500	96.3	43	91.0		70.8	84	341
1976	70,500	96.4	45	92.0		73.3	89	349
1977	71,200	97.4	47	92.0		76.0	89	350
1978	72,900	97.6	48	na		81.0	85	350
1979	74,500	97.7	48	na		83.0	86	350
1980	76,300	97.9	50	95.0	na	85.0	89	367
1981	79,900	98.1	51	96.0	16	85.0	89	370
1982	81,500	98.1	53	na	20	88.0	88	364
1983	83,300	98.1	55	na	24	89.0	81	350
1984	83,800	98.1	55	na	30	90.0	83	334
1985	84,900	98.1	57	na	38	91.0	82	331
1986	85,900	98.1	57	na	47	92.0	81	328
1987	87,400	98.1	59	na	57	92.0	83	333
1988**	88,600	98.1	60	na	66	94.0	75	336
1989	90,400	98.2	63	na	70	96.0	na	na
1990	92,100	98.2	65	na	77	97.8	na	na
1991	93,100	98.2	65	na	80	98.1	na	na
1992	92,100	98.3	65	na	83	98.6	na	na

(*continued*)

▪ 7-A   (*continued*)

Year	Television Households (thousands)	Percentage of All Households	Percentage of Television Households				Average Receiver Cost	
			Multiple Sets	UHF	Remote Controls	Color	B & W	Color
1993	93,100	98.3	67	na	86	98.3	na	na
1994	94,200	98.3	70	na	90	99.0	na	na
1995	95,400	98.3	71	na	91	99.0	na	na
1996	95,900	98.3	72	na	93	99.3	na	na
1997	97,000	98.4	74	na	94	99.5	na	na
1998	98,000	98.3	74	na	95	99.5	na	na
1999	99,400	98.2	74	na	96	99.7	na	na
2000	100,800	98.2	76	na	na	99.8	na	na

* The all-channel receiver requirement passed by Congress in 1962 took effect in 1964.
** Estimates
Sources: NBC Corporate Planning data as reprinted annually in *Television Factbook,* except for UHF penetration data, which are from NBC Research based, in turn, on studies by the Advertising Research Foundation (to 1968) and U.S. Census reports. Average set prices taken from *Television Digest* (17:27:9) for 1960–1976, inclusive, using Electronic Industries Association data. Estimates for earlier years from Lichty and Topping (1975), page 522, table 42, and authors. Column on multiple sets is a compromise by the authors due to extensive disagreement on this statistic between various original sources (which is why figures are rounded to nearest whole number). Through 1963, the figures are those of NBC Research as published in *Television Factbook*—data closely paralleled by other sources. After 1963, the figures are a compromise most closely following data supplied by A. C. Nielsen Co. 1976 television household and color penetration data derived from estimates in Blair's 1977 *Statistical Trends in Broadcasting.* 1977 data supplied by *Television Factbook* staff. Color and UHF data generally from Nielsen fall survey of the previous year. Set prices for 1978–1988 from *Television Digest* (28:13:11 and 27:22:9), with black-and-white television prices reported to authors by *Television Digest* based on information from EIA *Consumer Electronics.* Television households 1978–1988 from *Broadcasting Yearbook 1988,* page G-16. Data for multiple-set and color households 1978–1986 from annual issues of *Television Audience* (Northbrook, III.: A. C. Nielsen Co.). 1988–2000 data from A. C Nielsen as cited by Television Bureau of Advertising website. Remote control information from Statistical Research Inc., "SMART TV Ownership Survey, Spring 1999" as presented in *TV Dimensions 2000* (New York: Media Dynamics, 2000).

■ 7-B   Household Video Market since 1975

Year	Sales to Dealers (in thousands of units)				VCR Households (thousands)	Percentage of TV Households with VCRs
	VCRs	Videodisc Players*	Video Cameras	Projection TVs		
1975	30	—	—	—	—	—
1976	55	—	—	—	—	—
1977	160	—	—	—	—	—
1978	402	—	—	—	200	0.3%
1979	475	—	61	29	400	0.5
1980	805	—	114	57	840	1.1
1981	1,361	157	190	139	1,440	1.8
1982	2,035	223	296	117	2,530	3.1
1983	4,091	307	414	144	4,580	5.5
1984	7,616	200	489	195	8,880	10.6
1985	11,853	200	517	266	17,660	20.8
1986	13,174	200	1,169	304	30,920	36.0
1987	13,306	220	1,604	293	42,560	48.7
1988	14,500	250	2,000	300	51,390	58.0
1989	9,760	120	2,286	265	58,000	64.6
1990	10,119	168	2,962	351	63,180	68.6
1991	10,718	206	2,864	380	67,000	71.9
1992	12,329	224	2,815	404	69,000	75.0
1993	12,448	287	3,088	465	72,000	77.0
1994	13,087	272	3,209	636	74,000	79.0
1995	13,562	257	3,650	820	77,270	81.0
1996	15,641	155	3,634	887	79,580	82.2
1997	16,673	349*	3,650	917	81,670	84.2
1998	18,113	1,079*	3,829	1,070	82,910	84.6
1999	21,652	3,700*	4,596	na	84,140	84.6
2000	na	na	na	na	85,810	85.1

Note: DVD sales figures replace videodisc player sales after 1996.

Sources: All unit sales figures from Electronic Industries Association, *Consumer Electronics Annual Review,* various issues. VCRs for 1975–1977 are estimates based on import figures from *Television Digest* (February 1, 1988), page 15. Video cameras for 1985–1988 and VCRs for 1988 from *EIA Consumer Electronics US Sales* (June 1988), page 7. VCR households and percentage of television households with VCRs: *Trends in TV* (March 1988), Television Bureau of Advertising, page 5.

1989–2000 data in first four columns of sales data from Electronic Industry Association/Alliance, *U.S. Consumer Electronics Industry 1998* and earlier issues. Last two columns from Television Bureau of Advertising, citing A.C. Nielsen data.

Table 8   Using Electronic Media: 1931–1999

Audience use of electronic media means *radio* through the 1940s, then *radio and television* into the 1980s. After 1980 the development of *cable networks* began to substantially increase the number of viewing options for most Americans. Table 8-A records typical daily household use of radio and television. Table 8-B demonstrates how the number of television channels receivable in the typical household substantially increased by the late 1980s and into the 1990s. And Table 8-C demonstrates how cable viewing options cut into traditional broadcast television audiences. For baseline data on number of households, see "useful tools" on p. 826.

▪ 8-A   Hours of Radio and Television Use: 1931–1999 (selected years)

Year	Daily Hours:Minutes per Household	
	Radio	Television
1931	4:04	—
1935	4:48	—
1943	4:48	—
1946	4:13	na
1950	4:06	4:35
1955	2:12	4:51
1960	1:53	5:06
1965	2:27	5:29
1971	2:52	6:02
1976	3:25	6:18
1981	3:19	6:45
1986	na	7:08
1990	na	6:53
1995	na	7:17
1999	3:06	7:26

Sources: Sterling (1984), pages 219–220, for data through 1981, citing diverse sources that are not strictly comparable but are still useful for trends. Specifically: **1931:** Lumley (1934), page 196, reporting on a survey of some 14,000 listeners in 10 cities; **1935:** CBS, *Radio in 1937* (New York: CBS, 1937), page 30, reporting on research in communities of 2,500 persons and over; **1943:** C. H. Sandage, *Radio Advertising for Retailers* (Cambridge, Mass.: Harvard University Press, 1945), page 140, citing Nielsen Radio Index research for January of total listening in cities over 100,000; **1946** and **1965:** Lichty and Topping (1975), page 523, citing A. C. Nielsen; **1950, 1955, 1960:** A. C. Nielsen; **1971** radio figure from *CBS Radio Network: Affiliate Research/Promotion Reference Guide* (New York: CBS, 1972), citing RADAR studies; television figure from A. C. Nielsen; **1976** radio figure from *Encyclomedia: Radio 1978* (New York: Decisions Publications, 1978), page 6; television from *Broadcasting* (April 3, 1978), page 48, citing Nielsen. **1981** radio from Radio Advertising Bureau, citing RADAR; television from Nielsen. **1986** from Television Bureau of Advertising, citing Nielsen. **1999** radio data is from Fall 1999 Arbitron *American Radio Trends* and refers to average weekday time (weekend is 5:15); Television data are from A. C. Nielsen.

▪ 8-B   Television Channels Receivable: 1964–1999

Channels Received Per Household	Percentage of all Television Households in:								
	1964	**1968**	**1972**	**1976**	**1980**	**1985**	**1990**	**1995**	**1999**
1 to 4	41%	18%	17%	12%	9%	—	—	—	—
5 to 6	33	22	22	23	20	—	—	—	—
7 to 9	22	40	41	38	28	—	—	—	—
10 or more	4	17	20	27	43	—	—	—	—
up to 14	—	—	—	—	—	50%	30%	na	11%
15 to 19	—	—	—	—	—	15	7	na	7
20–29	—	—	—	—	—	16	7	na	6
30–39*	—	—	—	—	—	19	56	na	5
40–49	—	—	—	—	—	—	—	na	7
50–59	—	—	—	—	—	—	—	na	12
60 or more	—	—	—	—	—	—	—	na	52
Average Channels per Household:									
Receivable	na	na	na	7.7	na	18.8	33.2	41.1	62.0
Viewed	na	na	na	na	na	na	na	10.4	13.1

* Actually, "30+" for 1985, 1990
Source: A.C. Nielsen Co., in annual issues of *Television Audience.*

Broadcast and Cable Viewing Share: 1980–1999
(*Audience shares are shown in italic font*; number of networks in roman font)

| | Broadcast Station Shares | | | Cable Program Service Numbers and Shares | | | | | |
| | | | | Basic | | Premium | | Pay Per View | Total Services |
Year	Affiliates	Independents	Public	Services	Share	Services	Share	Services	(Incl. other)
1980				19		8		—	18
1981				29		9		—	38
1982				30		11		1	42
1983				31		11		1	43
1984				37		10		1	48
1985				41		9		4	56
1986				54		8		4	68
1987				61		9		5	76
1988	*58%*	*20%*	*3%*	64	*17%*	8	*7%*	5	78
1989	*55*	*20*	*3*	64	*21*	5	*6*	4	76
1990	*53*	*21*	*3*	65	*24*	5	*6*	5	79
1991	*54*	*20*	*3*	67	*24*	7	*6*	4	82
1992	*53*	*21*	*4*	71	*25*	8	*5*	4	87
1993	*52*	*21*	*4*	80	*26*	9	*5*	7	101
1994	*52*	*21*	*4*	94	*26*	20	*5*	8	128
1995	*46*	*21*	*3*	104	*33*	21	*6*	8	139
1996	*43*	*20*	*3*	126	*36*	18	*7*	7	162
1997	*49*	*12*	*3*	131	*40*	14	*7*	6	164
1998	*46*	*11*	*3*	139	*41*	18	*6*	10	174
1999	na	na	na	147	*45*	43	na	9	214

Note: "Services" refers to the number of cable program services. Pay cable viewing share combines premium and pay-per-view shares.
Source: Nielsen Media Research as provided by Cable Advertising Bureau, *Cable TV Facts*, as made available on NCTA website.

Table 9   Growth of Cable Television: 1952–2000

Data for various dates (usually in the fall or January 1) in each year, show estimates of the number of cable systems, total number of cable subscribers, percentage of television households with cable, and the average number of subscribers per system. The latter figure is misleading, since even in 1977 only 22% of all reporting systems had 3,500 or more subscribers and only 10 systems had 50,000 or more. Beginning in 1975, Table 9-B shows the growth of pay and (in 1985) pay-per-view cable. Table 9-C illustrates the growth of selected national cable services. For baseline data on number of households, see "useful tools" on p. 826.

▪ 9-A   Cable Television Systems: 1952–1969

Year	Number of Systems	Number of Subscribers (thousands)	Percentage of Households with Cable Service	Average Number of Subscribers per System
1952	70	14	0.1%	200
1953	150	30	0.2	200
1954	300	65	0.3	217
1955	400	150	0.5	375
1956	450	300	0.9	667
1957	500	350	0.9	700
1958	525	450	1.1	857
1959	560	550	1.3	982
1960	640	650	1.4	1,016
1961	700	725	1.5	1,036
1962	800	850	1.7	1,063
1963	1,000	950	1.9	950
1964	1,200	1,085	2.1	904
1965	1,325	1,275	2.4	962
1966	1,570	1,575	2.9	1,003
1967	1,770	2,100	3.8	1,186
1968	2,000	2,800	4.4	1,400
1969	2,260	3,600	6.1	1,593

Source: Original estimates from *Television Factbook* and *Television Digest*.

◾ 9-B   Cable Television Systems since 1970

Year	Number of Systems	Number of Subscribers (thousands)	Percentage of Households with Cable Service	Average Number of Subscribers per System	Cable Households with Pay-TV	Pay-Per-View Have Access	Use
1970	2,490	4,500	7.6%	1,807	na	na	na
1971	2,639	5,300	8.8	2,008	na	na	na
1972	2,841	6,000	9.6	2,112	na	na	na
1973	2,991	7,300	11.1	2,441	na	na	na
1974	3,158	8,700	13.0	2,755	na	na	na
1975	3,506	9,800	14.3	2,795	23.6%	na	na
1976	3,651	10,800	15.5	2,958	22.3	na	na
1977	3,800	11,900	17.3	3,132	25.3	na	na
1978	3,875	12,500	17.1	3,355	35.0	na	na
1979	4,150	13,600	18.3	3,398	41.3	na	na
1980	4,225	15,200	19.9	3,787	50.6	na	na
1981	4,375	17,830	22.3	4,183	67.2	na	na
1982	4,825	24,290	29.8	4,352	75.6	na	na
1983	5,600	28,320	34.0	5,057	84.2	na	na
1984	6,200	32,930	39.3	5,311	84.1	na	na
1985	6,600	36,340	42.8	5,506	81.6	15%	3%
1986	7,500	39,160	45.6	5,221	78.1	16	4
1987	7,771	41,690	47.7	5,365	78.6	18	4
1988	8,413	43,790	49.4	5,205	81.2	21	5
1989	9,050	52,565	57.1	5,808	79.3	26	8
1990	9,575	54,871	59.0	5,731	77.1	30	10
1991	10,704	55,786	60.6	5,212	74.7	36	12
1992	11,035	57,212	61.5	5,185	77.5	42	13
1993	11,108	58,834	62.5	5,297	75.2	48	16
1994	11,214	60,495	63.4	5,395	72.2	52	17
1995	11,218	62,956	65.7	5,612	74.2	50	17
1996	11,119	64,654	66.7	5,815	75.1	54	21
1997	10,950	65,929	67.3	6,021	73.9	55	22
1998	10,845	67,011	67.4	6,179	72.2	55	23
1999	10,466	68,538	68.0	6,549	73.1	58	25

Source: Households with pay-TV from NCTA, citing Paul Kagan Associates. Pay-Per-View Access and use data from Statistical Research, Inc. "SMART TV Ownership Survey, Spring 1999," as reprinted in *TV Dimensions 2000* (New York: Media Dimensions, 2000), p. 151.

9-C   Selected Cable Network Services, 1980–2000

Type of Service	Start-up Date	Jul 1980	Oct 1984	Aug 1988	Jan 1992	Mar 1996	Jul 2000
A. Largest Basic Services							
A&E Television Network	4/81	—	12.0	34.2	51.0	65.0	65.0
American Movie Classics*	10/84	—	—	12.0	36.0	60.0	69.6x
Black Entertainment	1/80	3.7	8.0	20.0	31.0	44.2	44.2
C-SPAN	3/79	5.8	19.3	39.2	55.0	66.1	77.0
Cartoon Network	10/92	—	—	—	—	24.7	56.6x
Comedy Central	4/91	—	—	—	22.0	37.0	56.9x
CNBC	4/89	—	—	—	45.0	56.0	71.0
CNN	6/80	—	28.5	46.9	58.9	67.8	77.0
CNN Headline News	1/82	—	12.6	32.7	47.3	60.2	72.5
Discovery Channel	6/85	—	—	33.8	56.0	67.0	77.4
Disney Channel*	4/83	—	0.3	3.8	6.0	16.1	45.1x
ESPN	9/79	4.0	34.0	47.8	59.1	67.9	77.0
ESPN2	10/93	—	—	—	—	30.8	63.0x
(Fox) Family Channel	4/77	—	—	—	54.1	64.0	64.0
History Channel	1/95	—	—	—	—	15.0	55.2x
Learning Channel	10/79	0.3	5.0	12.8	15.6	45.0	72.0
Lifetime Television	2/84	—	20.1	39.8	53.4	64.0	75.0
MSNBC	7/96	—	—	—	—	na	20.0
MTV	8/81	—	22.6	42.7	54.9	65.9	72.2
Nickelodeon/Nick at Nite**	7/79	2.5	20.1	41.2	55.5	64.0	76.0
QVC (Fashion)	10/91	—	—	—	8.3	54.6	72.2
Sci-fi Channel	9/92	—	—	—	—	29.1	53.9x
TNN (Nashville)	3/83	—	17.9	41.1	53.9	64.8	75.0
TNT	10/88	—	—	—	54.9	66.6	76.8
USA Network	9/80	—	28.0	45.2	58.0	67.2	77.2
VH1	1/85	—	—	27.9	43.2	54.0	68.3
Weather Channel	5/82	—	12.0	36.0	50.4	61.7	74.0
B. Superstations							
WTBS (Atlanta)	12/76	8.9	31.0	45.7	57.7	67.6	78.0
WGN (Chicago)	11/78	3.9	14.2	24.7	34.9	na	46.2x
WOR (New York)	4/79	2.8	4.9	12.3	13.5	12.5	—
C. Pay Cable Services							
Bravo****	12/80	—	0.7	1.1	7.0	22.0	37.1x
Cinemax	8/80	—	2.5	5.1	6.3	8.9***	17.5x
HBO	11/72	8.1	12.5	15.9	17.6	20.8***	29.0x
Showtime	7/76	1.2	4.5	6.3	10.0	14.8	16.5x

Note: All figures are rounded to nearest 100,000. Excluded are text-only services, and cable program services not operating in 2000.

*Indicates began as pay cable network and became basic.

**Nick at Nite began 7/85.

***As of 31 Dec 1995. "x" indicates network subscribers for 1998–99 season as reported by A. C. Nielsen.

****Bravo is a basic service on many cable systems.

Sources: 1980 from Sterling (1984), pp. 207–208, citing *Cablevision* (January 12, 1981), p. 28; 1984 from *Channels Field Guide 1985*, pp. 53ff; 1988 from *Broadcasting* (22 August 1988)m pp. 32–33; 1992 from NCTA's *Cable Developments* (March 1992); 1996 from same source (data for Jan-Mar 1996); 2000 from NCTA's *Cable Developments* on line at *http://www.ncta.com/glance.html* A. C. Nielsen data (items with "x") from *2000 Report on Television.*

▨ 9-D   Concentration of Cable System Ownership: 1970–1999

As of Month/Year	Percentage of Total Cable Households Served by Multiple System Operators:		
	Top 5	Top 10	Top 50
2/1970	19.9%	31.3%	63.5%
6/1971	24.3	35.4	67.2
9/1972	32.1	43.7	70.5
1973	29.0	42.0	68.7
10/1974	32.3	45.2	74.5
10/1975	30.7	42.8	72.3
1976	na	na	na
3/1977	26.7	37.6	66.7
1978	na	na	73.9
1979	na	na	na
1980	na	na	na
4/1981	33.1	48.0	na
1982	na	na	na
4/1983	31.5	45.7	63.8
10/1984	34.8	51.5	88.9
10/1985	35.3	50.6	88.7
10/1986	32.8	47.9	88.0
10/1987	30.4	42.2	87.7
10/1988	32.3	46.8	90.0
10/1989	36.9	52.0	91.0
10/1990	38.2	53.3	91.4
10/1991	37.6	52.6	88.5
9/1992	40.0	52.2	85.0
9/1993	42.6	54.5	85.9
9/1994	42.7	54.8	86.7
9/1995	53.0	66.2	91.2
9/1996	56.7	70.0	92.5
9/1997	59.8	73.0	93.2
9/1998	55.8	69.7	91.6
9/1999	59.6	79.0	91.9

Source: Television Digest, Warren Communications News.

Table 10   Growth of Satellite Distribution: 1975–2000

While the specific number of television receive-only (TVRO) antennas is hard to come by, by the mid-1980s virtually all cable systems and television stations had access to at least one. According to the NAB, 85% of radio stations in 1985 and 90% by 1987 used TVROs. Most broadcast stations had more than one to allow reception from the increasing number of different satellites used to distribute video or audio signals. The first DBS satellite was launched in 1994. Beginning then, household satellite systems began a quick transition from large 3 to 10 feet in diameter dishes to far smaller antennas (often a mere foot across).

| | Domestic Satellites | | DBS | | Household Satellite Systems | |
| | | | | | Unit sales to dealers (thousands) | Percentage of Households with |
Year	U.S. Satellites	Transponders Carried	Suppliers	Subscribers (millions)		
1975	3	48	—	—	na	na
1977	6	120	—	—	na	na
1979	8	156	—	—	na	na
1981	8	156	—	—	na	na
1983	19	420	—	—	na	na
1985	29	504	—	—	na	na
1987	26	524	—	—	250	na
1989	na	na	—	—	300	na
1991	na	na	—	—	281	na
1993	na	na	na	na	349	na
1995	na	na	1	4.5	2,235	3%
1996	na	na	2	6.5	2,200	5
1997	na	na	3	8.4	2,200	7
1998	na	na	3	10.6	2,830	8
1999	na	na	3	12.3	na	10
2000	na	na	2	15.3	na	na

Sources: For data through 1983, see Sterling (1984), p. 34, which draws data from NAB and NCTA. DBS information from Satellite Broadcasting and Communications Assn. Website. Household Satellite system data from Electronic Industry Alliance. Households with satellite reception capability from Statistical Research, "SMART TV Ownership Study, Spring 1999," as reprinted in *TV Dimensions 2000* (New York: Media Dimensions, 2000), p. 106.

Table 11   Electronic Media Employment and Regulation: 1925–2000

Two final measures of the growth of electronic media are the expanding number of employees in radio, television and eventually cable television organizations, and the parallel growth of government regulation (here represented chiefly by the FCC annual budget and number of employees) for selected years.

■ 11   Electronic Media Employment and Regulation, 1925–2000

Year	Broadcast Industry Employees	Cable Industry Employees	Regulation (FCC) Budget		Percent Real Change	Number of FCC Personnel
			Actual $	Constant $ (1982–84 = 100) *(Dollar figures in millions)*		
1925	na		$0.2	$1.6	na	
1930	6,000		.8	4.5	385%	131
1935	14,600		1.1	8.2	181	442
1940	25,700		1.8	13.1	62	625
1945	37,800		6.2	34.5	163	1,513
1950	66,000 *(Radio 52,000; TV 14,000)*	na	6.7	29.2	(13)	1,285
1955	77,600 *(Radio 45,300; TV 32,300)*	na	6.9	25.7	(14)	1,094
1960	93,600 *(Radio 53,000; TV 40,600)*	na	10.6	35.6	38	1,396
1965	109,900 *(Radio 60,200; TV 47,700)*	na	16.9	53.7	51	1,502
1970	129,400 *(Radio 71,000; TV 58,400)*	na	24.6	63.8	19	1,553
1975	144,100 *(Radio 81,800; TV 62,300)*	24,300	46.9	87.2	37	2,073
1980	176,300 *(Radio 98,000; TV 78,300)*	33,654	76.0	92.3	6	2,094
1985	na *(Radio na; TV na)*	72,306	95.4	88.7	(4)	1,825
1990	na *(Radio na; TV na)*	102,656	107.5	82.3	(7)	1,705
1995	235,700 *(Radio 113,000; TV 122,700)*	116,056	184.9	121.3	48	2,022
2000	na	na	210.0	122.0	(—)	1,933

Sources: Data from Dept of Commerce (for 1925–30), Federal Radio Commission (for 1930), and FCC (since 1935). Data for 1930 combines Dept. of Commerce Radio Division ($295, 400), and FRC ($460,000), though personnel data includes only the FRC. Broadcast employment data from 1985–2000 from NTIA, citing U.S. Bureau of Labor Statistics. Cable employment data from FCC, as cited by NCTA.

Not included in figures above are data for Office of Telecommunications Policy (1970, 1975); and National Telecommunications and Information Administration (since 1980) which is as follows:

Year	Annual Budget (Millions)	Personnel
1970	$ 2.1	45
1975	8.4	60
1980	17.6	269
1985	42.6	294
1990	41.0	281
1995	113.3	336
2000	73.4	280

Source: James McConnaughey, NTIA. The 1995 budget jump was in part for special programs that were short-term.

APPENDIX D
A SELECTED
BIBLIOGRAPHY

This listing, which stresses American broadcasting although it provides a few titles from the United Kingdom and Canada, is selective—a complete bibliography, even one restricted to books, would fill a volume itself. What follows is designed to support the "Further Reading" annotations following each chapter and give readers multiple points of entry into the world of broadcasting history. Some publications not designed to be historical when published are included for the light they shed on a particular period or phase of broadcasting. Some titles, included only because of a shortage of material on a given topic, are of marginal quality.

In addition to the books listed below, a number of journals and magazines are noteworthy for publishing material on broadcasting history. Among them are the *Journal of Broadcasting & Electronic Media*, *Journalism History*, *Journal of Radio Studies*, *Historical Journal of Film*, *Radio & Television*, *Journalism and Mass Communication Quarterly*, *Communication Booknotes Quarterly*, and the *Smithsonian* magazine. A number of films on broadcasting history topics have been run under the *American Experience* PBS program label in recent years, including a superficial version of Tom Lewis' *Empire of the Air* (filmed by Ken Burns), and several more exacting documentaries on figures in the electronic media (e.g., Alexander Graham Bell, Rod Serling, Vladimir Zworykin, and Philo Farnsworth), generally funded by the Sloan Foundation.

Those who are particularly interested in specific radio or television programs will find excellent lists and descriptions in Brooks & Marsh, Buxton & Owen, Dunning, McNeil and similar volumes in the following bibliography. Brooks & Marsh also has a list of Emmy winners.

Postpublication reprint editions and bibliographies of special value are noted. (The New York Times Company closed down Arno Press in the early 1980s, but many of the books so annotated below, gathered into collections by the authors of this volume and others, are still available from Ayer Company Publishers, 6 Lower Mill Road, North Stratford, NH 03590 1-888-267-7323; www.scry.com/ayer/). Periodical entries include years of publication, frequency of appearance, and a brief line of description. For all books, the year shown is that of original publication unless a later edition is specified. American editions of books published originally in Britain are usually listed under the American publisher. Generally omitted are script collections, histories of individual stations, special material on old radios, and broadcasting in specific other countries (except the U.K.). As a rule, the latest edition of a title is cited.

While some of this material is in print or has been reprinted for the library market, most of it is not currently available outside of major libraries. We have intentionally omitted most materials, including dissertations, that cannot be found in most libraries—no matter how good they may be. Likewise, we list few periodical articles due to space limitations. The listing is current as of the middle of 2001.

Following the bibliography is a selected list of Web sites, museums, libraries, and archives for those searching for more information.

Abramson, Albert H. *Electronic Motion Pictures: A History of the Television Camera.* Berkeley: University of California Press, 1955 (reprinted by Arno Press, 1974).

———. *The History of Television, 1880–1941.* Jefferson, NC: McFarland, 1987.

———. *Zworykin: Pioneer of Television.* Urbana: University of Illinois Press, 1995.

Adir, Karin. *The Great Clowns of American Television.* Jefferson, NC: McFarland, 1988.

Adler, Richard P., (Ed.). *All in the Family: A Critical Appraisal.* New York: Praeger, 1979.

Adler, Richard P., et al. *The Effects of Television Advertising on Children.* Lexington, Mass: Lexington Books, 1980.

Aitken, Hugh G. J. *Syntony and Spark: The Origins of Radio.* New York: Wiley/Interscience, 1976.

———. *The Continuous Wave: Technology and American Radio, 1900–1932.* Princeton, NJ: Princeton University Press, 1985.

Albig, William. *Modern Public Opinion.* New York: McGraw-Hill, 1956.

Alford, W. Wayne. *History of the NAEB: 1955–1965.* Washington: NAEB, 1966. (For the earlier period, see Hill, Harold.)

Alisky, Marvin. *Latin American Media: Guidance and Censorship.* Ames: Iowa State University Press, 1981.

Allen, Craig. *Eisenhower and the Mass Media: Peace, Prosperity, and Prime-Time TV.* Chapel Hill: University of North Carolina Press, 1993.

Allen, Fred. *Treadmill to Oblivion.* Boston: Little, Brown, 1954.

Allen, Frederick Lewis. *Only Yesterday.* New York: Harper, 1931.

———. *Since Yesterday.* New York: Harper, 1940.

Allen, Robert C., (Ed.). *To Be Continued . . . Soap Operas Around the World.* New York: Routledge, 1995.

Allen, Steve. *The Funny Men.* New York: Simon and Schuster, 1956.

Aly, Bower, & Gerald D. Shively. *A Debate Handbook on Radio Control and Operation.* Norman: University of Oklahoma, 1933.

Anderson, Kent. *Television Fraud: The History and Implications of the Quiz Show Scandals.* Westport, CT: Greenwood, 1979.

Andrews, Bart. *Lucy & Ricky & Fred & Ethel: The Story of "I Love Lucy."* New York: Dutton, 1976.

Annals of the American Academy of Political and Social Science. Philadelphia: The Academy, bimonthly, 1890–present (in the 1980s, Sage Publications became the publisher for the Academy). The following issues (reprinted in a volume by Arno Press, 1971) deal exclusively with broadcasting: Stewart, Irwin, (Ed.), "Radio," Supplement to No. 142 (March 1929); Hettinger, Herman S., (Ed.), "Radio: The Fifth Estate," No. 177 (January 1935); Hettinger, Herman S., (Ed.), "New Horizons in Radio," No. 213 (January 1941).

Antebi, Elizabeth. *The Electronic Epoch.* New York: Van Nostrand Reinhold, 1982.

Appleyard, Rollo. *Pioneers of Electrical Communications.* London: Macmillan, 1930 (reprinted by Books for Libraries).

Archer, Gleason L. *History of Radio to 1926.* New York: American Historical Society, Inc., 1938 (reprinted by Arno Press, 1971).

———. *Big Business and Radio.* New York: American Historical Company, Inc., 1939 (reprinted by Arno Press, 1971).

Arlen, Michael J. *Living-Room War.* New York: Viking, 1969.

———. *Thirty Seconds.* New York: Farrar, Straus & Giroux, 1980.

Arnheim, Rudolf. *Radio.* London: Faber and Faber, 1936 (reprinted by Arno Press, 1971).

Arnold, Frank A. *Broadcast Advertising: The Fourth Dimension—Television Edition.* New York: Wiley, 1933.

Atkinson, Carroll. *American Universities and Colleges That Have Held Broadcast License.* Boston: Meador, 1941.

———. *Radio Network Contributions to Education.* Boston: Meador, 1942a.

———. *Broadcasting to the Classroom by Universities and Colleges.* Boston: Meador, 1942b.

———. *Radio in State and Territorial Educational Departments.* Boston: Meador, 1942c.

———. *Radio Programs Intended for Classroom Use.* Boston: Meador, 1942d.

Auletta, Ken. *Three Blind Mice: How the TV Networks Lost Their Way.* New York: Random House, 1991.

———. *The Highwaymen: Warriors of the Information Superhighway.* New York: Random House, 1997.

Avery, Robert K., (Ed.). *Public Service Broadcasting in a Multichannel Environment.* White Plains, NY: Longman, 1993.

Baer, Walter S. *Cable Television: A Handbook for Decision Making.* New York: Crane, Russak, 1974.

Baer, Walter S., et al. *Concentration of Mass Media Ownership: Assessing the State of Current Knowledge.* Santa Monica, CA: Rand Corp., 1974.

Bagdikian, Ben H. *The Information Machines: Their Impact on Men and the Media.* New York: Harper, 1971.

Baker, John C. *Farm Broadcasting: The First Sixty Years.* Ames: Iowa State University Press, 1981.

Baker, William F., & George Dessart. *Down the Tube: An Inside Account of the Failure of American Television.* New York: Basic Books, 1998.

Baker, W. J. *A History of the Marconi Company.* New York: St. Martin's Press, 1972.

Baldwin, Thomas, & D. Stevens McVoy. *Cable Communications.* 2nd ed. Englewood Cliffs, NJ: Prentice-Hall, 1988.

Balfour, Michael. *Propaganda in War 1939–1945: Organizations, Policies, and Publics in Britain and Germany.* London: Routledge & Kegan Paul, 1979.

Banks, Jack. *Monopoly Television: MTV's Quest to Control the Music.* Boulder, CO: Westview, 1996.

Bannerman, R. LeRoy. *Norman Corwin and Radio: The Golden Years.* University of Alabama Press, 1986.

Banning, William Peck. *Commercial Broadcasting Pioneer: The WEAF Experiment, 1922–1926.* Cambridge, MA: Harvard University Press, 1946.

Barfield, Ray. *Listening to Radio: 1920–1950.* Westport, CT: Praeger, 1996.

Barnouw, Erik. *A Tower in Babel: A History of Broadcasting in the United States to 1933.* New York: Oxford University Press, 1966.

———. *The Golden Web: A History of Broadcasting in the United States, 1933–1953.* New York: Oxford University Press, 1968.

———. *The Image Empire: A History of Broadcasting in the United States from 1953.* New York: Oxford University Press, 1970.

———. *The Sponsor: Notes on a Modern Potentate.* New York: Oxford University Press 1978.

———. *Tube of Plenty: The Evolution of American Television.* 3rd ed. New York: Oxford University Press, 1990.

———. *Media Marathon.* Durham, NC: Duke University Press, 1996.

Barrett, Marvin, (Ed.). *The Alfred I. DuPont-Columbia University Survey of Broadcast Journalism.* New York: Grosset & Dunlap (1969–1971), Crowell

(1972–1980), Everest (1982). (Note: main title varies; published annually to 1972 and biennially to 1982.)

Barron, Jerome A. *Freedom of the Press for Whom? The Right of Access to Mass Media.* Bloomington: Indiana University Press, 1973.

Barry, Gerald, et al., (Eds.). *Communication and Language: Networks of Thought and Action.* New York: Doubleday, 1965.

Batson, Lawrence D. *Radio Markets of the World, 1930.* Washington, DC: Department of Commerce Trade Promotion Series No. 109, 1930 (reprinted by Arno Press, 1971).

Baudino, Joseph E., & John M. Kittross, "Broadcasting's Oldest Stations: An Examination of Four Claimants," *Journal of Broadcasting* 21:1:61–83 (Winter 1977).

Baughman, James L. *Television's Guardians: The FCC and the Politics of Programming 1958–1967.* Knoxville: University of Tennessee Press, 1985.

———. *The Republic of Mass Culture: Journalism, Filmmaking, and Broadcasting in America since 1941.* Baltimore: Johns Hopkins University Press, 1992.

BBC. *War Report: A Record of Dispatches Broadcast by the BBC's War Correspondents with the Allied Expeditionary Force 6 June 1944–5 May 1945.* London: Oxford University Press, 1946.

BBC Handbook. London: BBC Publications, 1928–1987, annual. (Title varies: "Handbook" 1928–1929, "Yearbook" 1930–1934, "Annual" 1935–1937, "Handbook" 1938–1954, "Yearbook" 1943–1952, not published in 1953–1954, "Handbook" 1955–1980, and "Annual Report and Handbook" 1981–1987.) Publication ceased in 1987.

Bedell, Sally. *Up the Tube: Prime-Time TV in the Silverman Years.* New York: Viking, 1981.

Beniger, James R. *The Control Revolution: Technological and Economic Origins of the Information Society.* Cambridge, MA: Harvard University Press, 1986.

Benjamin, Burton. *Fair Play: CBS, General Westmoreland and How a Television Documentary Went Wrong.* New York: Harper & Row, 1988.

Benjamin, Louise M. "In Search of the Sarnoff 'Music Box' Memo: Separating Myth from Reality," *Journal of Broadcasting & Electronic Media,* 37:3: 325–335 (Summer 1993).

———. "In Search of the Sarnoff 'Music Box' Memo: Nally's Reply." Paper presented to the History Divison of the Broadcast Education Association, Las Vegas, April 2001.

———. *Freedom of the Air and the Public Interest: First Amendment Rights in Broadcasting to 1935.* Carbondale: Southern Illinois University Press, 2001.

Bennett, Jeremy. *British Broadcasting and the Danish Resistance Movement, 1940–1945.* Cambridge: Cambridge University Press, 1966.

Bensman, Marvin R. *Broadcast Regulation: Selected Cases and Decisions.* Lanham, MD: University Press of America, 1983, 1986.

———. *The Beginning of Broadcast Regulation in the Twentieth Century.* Jefferson, NC: McFarland, 2000.

Berg, Jerome S. *On the Short Waves, 1923–1945.* Jefferson, NC: McFarland, 1999.

Bergmeier, Horst J. P., & Rainer E. Lotz. *Hitler's Airwaves: The Inside Story of Nazi Radio Broadcasting and Propaganda Swing.* New Haven, CT: Yale University Press, 1997.

Bergreen, Laurence. *Look Now, Pay Later: The Rise of Network Broadcasting.* New York: Doubleday, 1980.

Beville, Hugh Malcolm, Jr. *Social Stratification of the Radio Audience.* Princeton, NJ: Princeton University Office of Radio Research, 1939.

———. *Audience Ratings: Radio, Television, Cable.* 2nd ed. Hillsdale, NJ: Lawrence Erlbaum Associates, 1988.

Bibb, Porter. *It Ain't as Easy as it Looks: Ted Turner's Amazing Story.* New York: Crown, 1993.

Bilby, Kenneth. *The General: David Sarnoff and the Rise of the Communications Industry.* New York: Harper & Row, 1986.

Billboard (1894—present; monthly, then weekly). Trade periodical, mainly of the music industry, with a good deal of information on radio music.

Bird, William L., Jr. *"Better Living" Advertising, Media, and the New Vocabulary of Business Leadership, 1935–1955.* Evanston, IL: Northwestern University Press, 1999.

Bishop, George F., et al. *The Presidential Debates: Media, Electoral and Policy Perspectives.* New York: Praeger, 1978.

Blake, George G. *History of Radio Telegraphy and Telephony.* London: Chapman and Hall, 1928 (reprinted by Arno Press, 1974).

Blakely, Robert J. *To Serve the Public Interest: Educational Broadcasting in the United States.* Syracuse, NY: Syracuse University Press, 1979.

Blanchard, Margaret A. *Exporting the First Amendment: The Press-Government Crusade of 1945–1952.* New York: Longman, 1986.

———. (Ed.). *History of the Mass Media in the United States.* Chicago: Fitzroy Dearborn, 1998.

Bliss, Edward, Jr., (Ed.). *In Search of Light: The Broadcasts of Edward R. Murrow, 1938–1961.* New York: Knopf, 1967.

———. *Now the News: The Story of Broadcast Journalism.* New York: Columbia University Press, 1991.

Block, Alex Ben. *Outfoxed: Marvin Davis, Barry Diller, Rupert Murdoch, Joan Rivers, and the Inside Story of America's Fourth Television Network.* New York: St. Martin's Press, 1990.

Blondheim, Menahem. *News Over the Wires: The Telegraph and the Flow of Public Information in America, 1844–1897.* Cambridge, MA: Harvard University Press, 1994.

Bluem, A. William. *Documentary in American Television: Form, Function, Method.* New York: Hastings House, 1965.

Blum, Daniel. *A Pictorial History of Television.* Philadelphia: Chilton, 1959.

Blume, Keith. *The Presidential Election Show: Campaign '84 and Beyond on the Nightly News.* South Hadley, MA: Bergin & Garvey, 1985.

Blythe, Cheryl, and Susan Sackett. *Say Goodnight, Gracie! The Story of Burns and Allen.* New York: E. P. Dutton, 1986.

Boddy, William. *Fifties Television: The Industry and its Critics.* Urbana: University of Illinois Press, 1990.

Boettinger, H. M. *The Telephone Book: Bell, Watson, Vail and American Life: 1876–1983.* New York: Stearn Publishers, 1983.

Bogart, Leo. *The Age of Television.* New York: Ungar, 1956, 1958, 1972. (1972 edition is a facsimile reprint of the 1958 edition, with extensive added notes.)

Boorstin, Daniel J. *The Americans: The Democratic Experience.* New York: Random House, 1973.

Bower, Robert T. *Television and the Public.* New York: Holt, Rinehart and Winston, 1973.

———. *The Changing Television Audience in America.* New York: Columbia University Press, 1985.

Boyd, Douglas A. *Broadcasting in the Arab World.* 3rd ed. Ames: Iowa State University Press, 1999.

Boyer, Peter J. *Who Killed CBS? The Undoing of America's Number One News Network.* New York: Random House, 1988.

Braestrup, Peter. *Big Story: How the American Press and Television Reported and Interpreted the Crisis of Tet 1968 in Vietnam and Washington.* Boulder, CO: Westview, 1977 (2 vols.). (Several shorter versions of this title were published.)

Braun, Ernest, & Stuart Macdonald. *Revolution in Miniature: The History and Impact of Semi-conductor Electronics.* 2nd ed. Cambridge: Cambridge University Press, 1982.

Braun, Mark J. *AM Stereo and the FCC: Case Study of a Marketplace Shibboleth.* Norwood, NJ: Ablex, 1994.

Brenner, Daniel L., & Monroe E. Price. *Cable Television and Other Non-Broadcast Video.* New York: Clark Boardman, 1986. Regular updates.

Briggs, Asa A. *The Birth of Broadcasting: The History of Broadcasting in the United Kingdom* [vol. I, to 1926]. London: Oxford University Press, 1961.

————. *The Golden Age of Wireless: The History of Broadcasting in the United Kingdom* [vol. II, 1926–1939]. London: Oxford University Press, 1965.

————. *The War of Words: The History of Broadcasting in the United Kingdom* [vol. III, 1939–1945]. London: Oxford University Press, 1970.

————. *Sound and Vision: The History of Broadcasting in the United Kingdom* [vol. IV, 1945–1955]. London: Oxford University Press, 1979.

————. *Competition: The History of Broadcasting in the United Kingdom* [vol. V, 1955–1974]. London: Oxford University Press, 1995.

————. *The BBC: The First Fifty Years.* London: Oxford University Press, 1986.

Bright, Charles. *Submarine Telegraphs: Their History, Construction and Working.* London: Crosby, Lockwood and Son, 1898 (reprinted by Arno Press, 1974).

Brindze, Ruth. *Not to Be Broadcast: The Truth about the Radio.* New York: Vanguard, 1937 (reprinted by Da Capo, 1974).

Brinkley, Joel. *Defining Vision: The Battle for the Future of Television.* New York: Harcourt Brace, 1997.

Broadcasting (1931–1941, biweekly; 1941-present, weekly). Title has varied: *Broadcasting & Cable* in 1990s. The most important trade journal of the broadcasting industry, with news, special analyses, statistics, and reviews of all aspects of radio and television, especially advertising, programs, the networks, and regulatory trends. The following special issues are of special value in broadcasting history: "Two Exciting Decades" (October 16, 1950), pp. 67–168; "Radio at 40 Enters Its Critical Years" (May 14, 1962), pp. 75–140; "Broadcasting at 50: Can It Adapt?" (November 2, 1970), pp. 65–154; "The First Amendment and the Fifth Estate" (January 5, 1976), pp. 44–100; "The First 50 Years of NBC" (June 21, 1976), pp. 29–92; "CBS: The First Five Decades" (September 19, 1977), pp. 45–116; "The 50th Anniversary Issue: On the Road to 2001," (October 12, 1981), pp. 115–311; "Sixty Years of NBC," (June 9, 1986), pp. 49–119, and "Cable: The First Forty Years," (November 21, 1988), pp. 35–49.

Broadcasting Yearbook (1935–present). Title has varied. Standard directory of broadcasting stations and other elements of the industry, with useful tables of data.

Brock, Gerald W. *The Telecommunications Industry: The Dynamics of Market Structure.* Cambridge, MA: Harvard University Press, 1981.

Brooks, John. *Telephone: The First Hundred Years.* New York: Harper & Row, 1976.

Brooks, Tim, & Earle Marsh. *The Complete Directory to Prime Time Network TV Shows, 1946–Present.* 7th ed. New York: Ballantine, 1999.

Brown, Les. *Televi$ion: The Business Behind the Box.* New York: Harcourt Brace Jovanovich, 1971.

————. *Les Brown's Encyclopedia of Television.* 3rd ed. Detroit: Gale Research, 1992.

Brown, Robert J. *Manipulating the Ether: The Power of Broadcast Radio in Thirties America.* Jefferson, NC: McFarland, 1998.

Brown, Ronald. *Telecommunications: The Booming Technology.* New York: Doubleday, 1970.

Browne, Donald R. *International Radiobroadcasting: The Limits of the Limitless Medium.* New York: Praeger, 1982.

————. *Electronic Media and Industrialized Nations.* Ames: Iowa State University Press, 1999.

Bruce, Robert V. *Bell: Alexander Graham Bell and the Conquest of Solitude.* Boston: Little, Brown, 1973.

Bryson, Lyman. *Time for Reason about Radio.* New York: George Stewart, 1948.

Buehler, E. C. *American vs. British System of Radio Control.* New York: H. W. Wilson "Reference Shelf" Series, VIII:10, 1933.

Bulman, David. *Molders of Opinion.* Milwaukee WI: Bruce, 1945.

Burlingame, Roger. *Don't Let Them Scare You: The Life and Times of Elmer Davis.* Philadelphia: Lippincott, 1961.

Burns, R. W. *British Television: The Formative Years.* London: IEE/Science Museum, 1986.

————. *Television: An International History of the Formative Years.* London: Institution of Electrical Engineers, 1998.

Burns, Russell. *John Logie Baird: Television Pioneer.* London: Institution of Electrical Engineers, 2000.

Burrows, A. R. *The Story of Broadcasting.* London: Cassell, 1924.

Buxton, Frank, & Bill Owen. *The Big Broadcast: 1920–1950.* New York: Viking, 1972.

Buzenberg, Susan, & Bill Buzenberg, (Eds.). *Salant, CBS, and the Battle for the Soul of Broadcast Journalism.* Boulder, CO: Westview, 1999.

Byron, Christopher M. *The Fanciest Dive: What Happened When the Media Empire of Time/Life Leaped Without Looking into the Age of High-Tech.* New York: W. W. Norton, 1986.

Campbell, Robert. *The Golden Years of Broadcasting: A Celebration of the First 50 Years of Radio and TV on NBC.* New York: Charles Scribner's Sons, 1976.

Cantor, Muriel G. *The Hollywood TV Producer: His Work and His Audience.* New York: Basic Books, 1972.

Cantor, Muriel, & Suzanne Pingree. *The Soap Opera.* Beverly Hills, CA: Sage, 1983.

Cantril, Hadley, with the assistance of Hazel Gaudet and Herta Herzog. *The Invasion from Mars: A Study in the Psychology of Panic.* Princeton, NJ: Princeton University Press, 1940 (reprinted by Harper, 1965).

Cantril, Hadley, & Gordon W. Allport. *The Psychology of Radio.* New York: Harper, 1935 (reprinted by Arno Press, 1971).

Caristi, Dominic. "First in Education: WOI-TV, Ames Iowa," pp. 195–209 in Michael D. Murray & Donald G. Godfrey, (Eds.), *Television in America: Local Station History from Across the Nation.* Ames: Iowa State University Press, 1997.

Carnegie Commission on Educational Television. *Public Television: A Program for Action.* New York: Harper & Row, 1967.

Carnegie Commission on the Future of Public Broadcasting. *A Public Trust.* New York: Bantam Books, 1979.

Carpenter, Humphrey. *The Envy of the World: Fifty Years of the BBC Third Programme and Radio 3, 1946–1996.* London: Phoenix, 1997.

Carpenter, Ronald H. *Father Charles E. Coughlin: Surrogate Spokesman for the Disaffected.* Westport, CT: Greenwood, 1998.

Carter, Samuel, III. *Cyrus Field: Man of Two Worlds.* New York: Putnam, 1968.

Cassata, Mary, & Thomas Skill. *Life on Daytime Television: Tuning-in American Serial Drama.* Norwood, NJ: Ablex, 1983.

Castleman, Harry, & Walter J. Podrazik. *Watching TV: Four Decades of American Television.* New York: McGraw-Hill, 1982.

Cater, Douglass, & Stephen Strickland. *TV Violence and the Child: The Evolution and Fate of the Surgeon General's Report.* New York: Russell Sage Foundation, 1975.

Chappell, Matthew N., & C. E. Hooper. *Radio Audience Measurement.* New York: Stephen Daye, 1944.

Chase, Francis, Jr. *Sound and Fury: An Informal History of Broadcasting.* New York: Harper, 1942.

Cheney, Margaret, & Robert Uth with Jim Glenn. *Tesla: Master of Lightning.* New York: Barnes & Noble Books, 1999.

Chester, Edward W. *Radio, Television, and American Politics.* New York: Sheed and Ward, 1969.

Childs, Harwood L., & John B. Whitton, (Eds.). *Propaganda by Short Wave.* Princeton, NJ: Princeton University Press, 1942 (reprinted by Arno Press, 1972).

Chiu, Tony, (Ed.). *CBS: The First 50 Years.* Los Angeles: General Publishing, 1998.

Christensen, Mark, and Cameron Stauth. *The Sweeps: Behind the Scenes in Network TV.* New York: Morrow, 1984.

Christman, Trent. *Brass Button Broadcasters.* Paducah, KY: Turner, 1992.

Clarke, Arthur C. *Voice Across the Sea.* (Rev. ed.). New York: Harper & Row, 1975.

Cloud, Stanley, & Lynne Olson. *The Murrow Boys: Pioneers on the Front Lines of Broadcast Journalism.* Boston: Houghton Mifflin, 1996.

Coates, Vary T., & Bernard Finn. *A Retrospective Technology Assessment: Submarine Telegraphy—The Transatlantic Cable of 1866.* San Francisco: San Francisco Press, 1979.

Codding, George A., & Anthony M. Rutkowski. *The International Telecommunication Union in a Changing World.* Dedham, MA: Artech House, 1982.

Codel, Martin, (Ed.). *Radio and Its Future.* New York: Harper, 1930 (reprinted by Arno Press, 1971).

Coe, Lewis. *The Telegraph: A History of Morse's Invention and its Predecessors in the United States.* Jefferson, NC: McFarland, 1993.

————. *The Telephone and Its Several Inventors.* Jefferson, NC: McFarland, 1995.

————. *Wireless Radio: A Brief History.* Jefferson, NC: McFarland, 1996.

Cogley, John. *Report on Blacklisting II: Radio-Television.* New York: Fund for the Republic, 1956 (reprinted by Arno Press, 1971).

Cole, Barry G., (Ed.). *Television: A Selection of Readings from TV Guide Magazine.* New York: Free Press, 1970.

————. *Television Today: A Close-Up View: Readings From "TV Guide."* New York: Oxford, 1981.

Cole, Barry G., & Mal Oettinger. *Reluctant Regulators: The FCC and the Broadcast Audience.* Reading, MA: Addison-Wesley, 1978.

Cole, J. A. *Lord Haw-Haw and William Joyce.* New York: Farrar, Straus & Giroux, 1964.

Collins, Mary. *National Public Radio: The Cast of Characters.* Washington: Seven Locks Press, 1993.

Collins, Robert. *A Voice from Afar: The History of Telecommunications in Canada.* Toronto: McGraw-Hill Ryerson, 1977.

Columbia Broadcasting System. *Crisis.* New York: CBS, 1938.

————. *Radio and Television Bibliography.* New York: CBS, 1942.

————. *Network Practices.* New York: CBS, 1956.

————. *10:56:20 pm EDT, 7/20/69: The Historic Conquest of the Moon as Reported to the American People by CBS News over the CBS Television Network.* New York: CBS, 1970.

Communication Booknotes Quarterly (1969–present, quarterly; under this title since 1998, previously *Broadcasting Bibliophiles Booknotes, Mass Media Booknotes, Communication Booknotes*). Short reviews of current literature in the field.

Compaine, Benjamin M., (Ed.). *Understanding New Media: Trends and Issues in Electronic Distribution of Information.* Cambridge, MA: Ballinger, 1984.

Compaine, Benjamin M., & Douglas Gomery. *Who Owns the Media: Competition and Concentration in the Mass Media Industry.* 3rd ed. Mahwah, NJ: Lawrence Erlbaum Associates, 2000.

Comstock, George, et al. *Television and Human Behavior.* Santa Monica, CA: Rand Corp., 1975 (three volumes, all annotated bibliography).

————. *Television and Human Behavior.* New York: Columbia University Press, 1978.

Connah, Douglas. *How to Build the Radio Audience.* New York: Harper, 1938.

Cook, Rick, & Frank Vaughan. *All About Home Satellite Television.* Blue Ridge Summit, PA: TAB, 1983.

Coons, John E., (Ed.). *Freedom & Responsibility in Broadcasting.* Evanston, IL: Northwestern University Press, 1961.

Cooper, Isabella M. *Bibliography on Educational Broadcasting.* Chicago: University of Chicago Press, 1942 (reprinted by Arno Press, 1971). Coverage of 1,800 items is far broader than title suggests, including all of broadcasting in well-organized and annotated indexed guide.

Cooper, Kent. *Barriers Down: The Story of the News Agency Epoch.* New York: Farrar & Rinehart, 1942 (reprinted by Kennikat, 1969).

Corporation for Public Broadcasting. *Annual Report.* Washington: CPB, 1969–present.

————. *Public Television Program Content.* Washington: CPB, 1974–present (biennial).

————. *Status Report on Public Broadcasting.* Washington: CPB, 1973, 1977, 1980 (title varies).

————. *Summary Statistics of CPB-Qualified Public Radio Stations.* Washington: CPB, 1970–present (irregular; title varies).

————. *Summary Statistics of Public Television Licensees.* Washington: CPB, 1970–present (irregular; title varies).

Counterattack, editors of. *Red Channels: The Report of Communist Influence in Radio and Television.* New York: American Business Consultants, 1950.

Corr, O. Casey. *KING: The Bullitts of Seattle and Their Communications Empire*. Seattle: University of Washington Press, 1996.

Corwin, Norman. *Thirteen by Corwin*. New York: Henry Holt, 1942.

———. *More by Corwin*. New York: Henry Holt, 1944.

———. *On a Note of Triumph*. New York: Simon & Schuster, 1945.

———. *Untitled*. New York: Henry Holt, 1947.

Covert, Catherine L., & John D. Stevens, (Eds.). *Mass Media Between the Wars: Perceptions of Cultural Tension*. Syracuse, NY: Syracuse University Press, 1984.

Cowan, Geoffrey. *See No Evil: The Backstage Battle over Sex and Violence on Television*. New York: Simon and Schuster, 1979.

Cox, Jim. *The Great Radio Soap Operas*. Jefferson, NC: McFarland, 1999.

Crosby, John. *Out of the Blue: A Book about Radio and Television*. New York: Simon and Schuster, 1952.

Crowley, David, and Paul Heyer. *Communication in History*. 2nd ed. White Plains, NY: Longman, 1991.

Csida, Joseph, & June Bundy Csida. *American Entertainment: A Unique History of Popular Show Business*. New York: Watson-Guptill, 1978.

Culbert, David Holbrook. *News for Everyman: Radio and Foreign Affairs in Thirties America*. Westport, CT: Greenwood, 1976.

Curtin, Michael. *Redeeming the Wasteland: Television Documentary and Cold War Politics*. New Brunswick, NJ: Rutgers University Press, 1995.

Czitrom, Daniel J. *Media and the American Mind from Morse to McLuhan*. Chapel Hill: University of North Carolina Press, 1982.

Dalton, W. M. *The Story of Radio*. London: Adam Hilger, 1975 (3 vols.).

Danielian, N. R. *AT&T: The Story of Industrial Conquest*. New York: Vanguard, 1939 (reprinted by Arno Press, 1974).

Davis, Henry B. *Electrical and Electronic Technologies: A Chronology of Events and Inventors*. Metuchen, NJ: Scarecrow, 1981–1985 (3 vols.).

Davis, Jeffery. *Children's Television, 1947–1990*. Jefferson, NC: McFarland, 1995.

Davis, Stephen B. *The Law of Radio Communications*. New York: McGraw-Hill, 1927.

Day, James. *The Vanishing Vision: The Inside Story of Public Television*. Berkeley: University of California Press, 1995.

De Bruin, Ronald, & Jan Smits. *Digital Video Broadcasting: Technology, Standards, and Regulations*. Norwood, MA: Artech House, 1999.

de Forest, Lee. *Father of Radio: The Autobiography of Lee de Forest.* Chicago: Wilcox and Follett, 1950.

Delfiner, Henry. *Vienna Broadcasts to Slovakia: 1938–1939—A Case Study in Subversion.* New York: Columbia University Press, 1974.

DeLong, Thomas A. *The Mighty Music Box: The Golden Age of Musical Radio.* Los Angeles: Amber Crest, 1980.

———. *Quiz Craze: America's Infatuation with Game Shows.* New York: Praeger, 1991.

Desmond, Robert W. *World News Reporting.* Iowa City: University of Iowa Press, 1978–1984 (4 vols.).

DeSoto, Clinton B. *Two Hundred Meters and Down: The Story of Amateur Radio.* West Hartford, CT: American Radio Relay League, 1936.

Diamant, Lincoln. *Television's Classic Commercials: The Golden Years, 1948–1958.* New York: Hastings House, 1971.

Diamond, Edwin, & Stephen Bates. *The Spot: The Rise of Political Advertising on Television.* 3rd ed. Cambridge, MA: MIT Press, 1992.

Dibner, Bern. *The Atlantic Cable.* New York: Blaisdell, 1964.

Dill, Clarence C. *Radio Law: Practice, Procedure.* Washington, DC: National Law Book Company, 1938.

Dinsdale, A. A. *First Principles of Television.* New York: Wiley, 1932 (reprinted by Arno Press, 1971).

Dizard, Wilson P. *Television: A World View.* Syracuse, NY: Syracuse University Press, 1966.

Donovan, Robert J., & Ray Scherer. *Unsilent Revolution: Television News and American Public Life.* New York: Cambridge University Press, 1991.

Douglas, Susan J. *Inventing American Broadcasting 1899–1922.* Baltimore: Johns Hopkins University Press, 1987.

———. *Listening In: Radio and the American Imagination.* New York: Times Books, 1999.

Dreyer, Carl. *Sarnoff: An American Success.* New York: Quadrangle, 1977.

Dryer, Sherman H. *Radio in Wartime.* New York: Greenberg, 1942.

Dummer, G. W. A. *Electronic Inventions and Discoveries: Electronics from its Earliest Beginnings to the Present Day.* 4th ed. Bristol, England: Institute of Physics, 1997.

Dunham, Corydon B. *Fighting for the First Amendment: Stanton of CBS vs. Congress and the Nixon White House.* Westport, CT: Praeger, 1997.

Dunlap, Orrin E., Jr. *Radio in Advertising.* New York: Harper, 1931.

———. *The Outlook for Television.* New York: Harper, 1932 (reprinted by Arno Press, 1971).

————. *Marconi: The Man and His Wireless.* New York: Macmillan, 1937 (reprinted by Arno Press, 1971).

————. *The Future of Television.* New York: Harper, 1942, 1947.

————. *Radio's 100 Men of Science: Biographical Narratives of Pathfinders in Electronics and Television.* New York: Harper, 1944 (reprinted by Books for Libraries, 1970).

————. *Communications in Space: From Marconi to Man on the Moon.* 3rd ed. New York: Harper & Row, 1970.

Dunning, John. *On the Air: The Encyclopedia of Old-Time Radio.* New York: Oxford University Press, 1998.

Dupagne, Michel, & Peter B. Seel. *High-Definition Television: A Global Perspective.* Ames: Iowa State University Press, 1998.

Dupuy, Judy. *Television Show Business.* Schenectady, NY: General Electric, 1945.

Duus, Masayo. *Tokyo Rose: Orphan of the Pacific.* Tokyo: Kodansha, 1979.

Dygert, Warren B. *Radio as an Advertising Medium.* New York: McGraw-Hill, 1939.

Eastman, Susan Tyler, & Ferguson, Douglas A. *Broadcast/Cable Programming: Strategies and Practices.* 5th ed. Belmont, CA: Wadsworth, 1997.

Eberly, Philip K. *Music in the Air: America's Changing Tastes in Popular Music, 1920–1980.* New York: Hastings House, 1982.

Eckhardt, George H. *Electronic Television.* Chicago: Goodheart-Willcox, 1936 (reprinted by Arno Press, 1974).

Eddy, William C. *Television: The Eyes of Tomorrow.* New York: Prentice-Hall, 1945.

Edelman, Murray. *The Licensing of Radio Services in the United States, 1927–1947: A Study in Administrative Formulation of Policy.* Illinois Studies in the Social Sciences, (Vol. 31). Urbana: University of Illinois Press, 1950 (reprinted by Arno Press, 1979).

Edmonson, Madeleine, & David Rounds. *From Mary Noble to Mary Hartman: The Complete Soap Opera Book.* New York: Jove/HBJ, 1977 [a paperback reprint and updating of *The Soaps* (New York: Stein & Day, 1973)].

Education on the Air. Annual proceedings of conference on educational broadcasting. Columbus: Ohio State University, 1930–1953, 1959.

Educational Broadcasting Review (1967–1973; bimonthly). In earlier years was published as *NAEB Journal* and *AERT Journal;* for later years, see *Public Telecommunications Review.*

Edwards, John Carver. *Berlin Calling: American Broadcasters in Service to the Third Reich.* Westport, CT: Praeger, 1991.

The Eighth Art: Twenty-Three Views of Television Today. New York: Holt, Rinehart and Winston, 1962.

Einstein, Daniel. *Special Edition: A Guide to Network Television Documentary Series and Special News Reports, 1955–1979.* Metuchen, NJ: Scarecrow Press, 1987.

Eisner, Joel, & David Krinsky. *Television Comedy Series: An Episode Guide to 153 TV Sitcoms in Syndication.* Jefferson, NC: McFarland, 1984.

Electronic Media. (1981–present, weekly). Very useful re: programming.

Eliot, Marc. *Televisions: One Season in American Television.* New York: St. Martin's Press, 1983.

Elliott, Philip. *The Making of a Television Series: A Case Study in the Sociology of Culture.* London: Constable, 1972.

Elliott, William Y., (Ed.). *Television's Impact on American Culture.* East Lansing: Michigan State University Press, 1956.

Ely, Melvin Patrick. *The Adventures of Amos 'n' Andy: A Social History of an American Phenomenon.* New York: Free Press, 1991.

Emery, Walter B. *National and International Systems of Broadcasting: Their History, Operation and Control.* East Lansing: Michigan State University Press, 1969.

————. *Broadcasting and Government: Responsibilities and Regulations.* 2nd ed. East Lansing: Michigan State University Press, 1971.

Engelman, Ralph. *Public Radio and Television in America: A Political History.* Thousand Oaks, CA: Sage, 1996.

Eoyang, Thomas T. *An Economic Study of the Radio Industry in the United States of America.* New York: Columbia University Press, 1936 (reprinted by Arno Press, 1974).

Epstein, Edward Jay. *News from Nowhere: Television and the News.* New York: Random House, 1973.

Erickson, Hal. *Syndicated Television: The First Forty Years, 1947–1987.* Jefferson, NC: McFarland, 1989.

Ettlinger, Harold. *The Axis on the Air.* Indianapolis, IN: Bobbs-Merrill, 1943.

European Audiovisual Observatory. *Statistical Yearbook: Film, Television, Video and New Media in Europe.* Strassbourg, France: EAO, 1994–present, annual.

Everson, George. *The Story of Television: The Life of Philo T. Farnsworth.* New York: Norton, 1949 (reprinted by Arno Press, 1974).

Ewen, Stuart. *Captains of Consciousness: Advertising and the Social Roots of the Consumer Culture.* New York: McGraw-Hill, 1976.

Ewen, Stuart, & Elizabeth Ewen. *Channels of Desire: Mass Images and the Shaping of American Consciousness.* New York: McGraw-Hill, 1982.

Fabe, Maxene. *TV Game Shows.* New York: Doubleday, 1979.

Fahie, J. J. *A History of Electric Telegraphy to the Year 1837.* London: Spon, 1884 (reprinted by Arno Press, 1974).

———. *A History of Wireless Telegraphy.* 2nd ed. Edinburgh: Blackwood, 1901 (reprinted by Arno Press, 1971).

Fang, Irving E. *Those Radio Commentators!* Ames: Iowa State University Press, 1977.

———. *A History of Mass Communication: Six Information Revolutions.* Newton, MA: Focal Press, 1997.

Farnsworth, Elma G. *Distant Vision: Romance and Discovery on An Invisible Frontier–Philo T. Farnsworth, Inventor of Television.* Salt Lake City, UT: PemberlyKent, 1990.

Fates, Gil. *What's My Line? The Inside Story of TV's Most Famous Panel Show.* Englewood Cliffs, NJ: Prentice-Hall, 1978.

Faulk, John Henry. *Fear on Trial.* New York: Simon and Schuster, 1964.

Federal Communications Commission. *Annual Report.* Washington, DC: GPO, 1935–present (1935–1956 reports reprinted by Arno Press, 1971).

———. *Reports* (1935–1986). Washington: GPO (official texts of decisions, reports, and orders). Replaced in 1987 by *Federal Communications Commission Record* (biweekly).

———. Engineering Department. *Report on Social and Economic Data Pursuant to the Informal Hearing on Broadcasting.* Washington, DC: GPO, 1938 (reprinted by Arno Press, 1974).

———. *Investigation of the Telephone Industry in the United States.* U.S. House of Representatives Document 340, 76th Cong., 1st Sess., 1939 (reprinted by Arno Press, 1974).

———. *Report on Chain Broadcasting.* Washington, DC: GPO, 1941 (reprinted by Arno Press, 1974).

———. *Public Service Responsibility of Broadcast Licensees.* Washington: GPO, 1946 (most of the text was reprinted in Kahn, Frank J., below, and fully reprinted by Arno Press, 1974). (The "Blue Book").

———. *An Economic Study of Standard Broadcasting.* Washington, DC: FCC Mimeo, 1947 (reprinted by Arno Press, 1974).

———. The Children's Television Task Force. *Television Programming for Children.* Washington: FCC, 1979 (5 vols.).

———. Network Inquiry Special Staff. *New Television Networks: Entry, Jurisdiction, Ownership.* Washington: GPO, 1980 (2 vols.).

———. Office of Network Study. *Network Broadcasting.* U.S. House of Representatives Report 1297, 85th Cong., 2nd Sess., 1958.

———. Office of Network Study. *Television Network Program Procurement.* U.S. House of Representatives Report 281, 88th Cong., 1st Sess., 1963.

———. Office of Network Study. *Television Network Program Procurement, Part II.* Washington: GPO, 1965.

Federal Communications Law Journal (1937–present, thrice yearly). Legal and scholarly articles, mainly on broadcast regulation. (Note: Was *Federal Communications Bar Journal* until 1977.)

Federal Radio Commission. *Annual Report.* Washington, DC: GPO, 1927–1933 (reprinted by Arno Press, 1971).

———. *Commercial Radio Advertising,* U.S. Senate Document 137, 72nd Cong., 1st Sess., 1932 (reprinted by Arno Press, 1974).

Federal Trade Commission. *Report on the Radio Industry.* Washington, DC: GPO, 1924 (reprinted by Arno Press, 1974).

_____.*Staff Report on Television Advertising to Children.* Washington: FTC, 1978.

Fejes, Fred. *Imperialism, Media, and the Good Neighbor: New Deal Foreign Policy and United States Shortwave Broadcasting to Latin America.* Norwood, NJ: Ablex, 1986.

Felix, Edgar. *Using Radio in Sales Promotion.* New York: McGraw-Hill, 1927.

———. *Television: Its Methods and Uses.* New York: McGraw-Hill, 1931.

Fensch, Thomas, (Ed.). *Television News Anchors: An Anthology of Profiles of the Major Figures and Issues in United States Network Reporting.* Jefferson, NC: McFarland, 1993.

Ferris, Charles, et al. *Cable Television Law: A Video Communications Practice Guide.* Albany, NY: Matthew Bender, 1983—present, title has varied (updated twice a year, 4 vols.).

Fessenden, Helen. *Fessenden: Builder of Tomorrows.* New York: Coward-McCann, 1940 (reprinted by Arno Press with a new index, 1974).

Fifty Years of A.R.R.L. Newington, CT: American Radio Relay League, 1965.

The First 50 Years of Broadcasting. Washington, DC: Broadcasting Publications, 1982.

Fink, Donald G. *Television Standards and Practice: Selected Papers of the Papers of the National Television System Committee and Its Panels.* New York: McGraw-Hill, 1943.

Fischer, Stuart. *Kids' TV: The First 25 Years.* New York: Facts on File, 1983.

Fisher, David E., & Marshall John Fisher. *Tube: The Invention of Television.* Washington: Counterpoint, 1996.

Flannery, Gerald, (Ed.). *Commissioners of the FCC: 1927–1994.* Lanham, MD: University Press of America, 1995.

Fleming, John A. *The Principles of Electric Wave Telegraphy.* London: Longmans, Green, 1906, 1910, 1916, and 1919. (First two editions are most detailed in their historical treatment.)

Fong-Torres, Ben. *The Hits Just Keep on Coming: The History of Top 40 Radio.* San Francisco: Miller-Freeman, 1998.

Foote, Joe S., (Ed.). *Live from the Trenches: The Changing Role of the Television News Correspondent.* Carbondale: Southern Illinois University Press, 1998.

Foust, James C. *Big Voices of the Air: The Battle over Clear Channel Radio.* Ames: Iowa State University Press, 2000.

Fowler, Gene, & Bill Crawford. *Border Radio.* Austin: Texas Monthly Press, 1987.

Fox, Stephen. *The Mirror Makers: A History of American Advertising and Its Creators.* New York: Morrow, 1984.

Frank, Reuven. *Out of Thin Air: The Brief Wonderful Life of Network News.* New York: Simon & Schuster, 1991.

Frank, Ronald E., & Marshall G. Greenberg. *The Public's Use of Television.* Beverly Hills, CA: Sage, 1980.

Frank, Ronald, & Marshall G. Greenberg. *Audiences for Public Television.* Beverly Hills, CA: Sage, 1982.

Frankl, Razelle. *Televangelism: The Marketing of Popular Religion.* Carbondale: Southern Illinois University Press, 1986.

Franklin, Marc A., et al. *Cases and Materials on Mass Media Law.* 6th ed. NY: Foundation Press, 2000.

Friendly, Fred. *Due to Circumstances Beyond Our Control. . . .* New York: Random House, 1976.

Frost, S. E., Jr. *Education's Own Stations.* Chicago: University of Chicago Press, 1937a (reprinted by Arno Press, 1971).

———. *Is American Radio Democratic?* Chicago: University of Chicago Press, 1937b.

Ganley, Gladys D., & Oswald H. Ganley. *Global Political Fallout: The VCR's First Decade.* Norwood, NJ: Ablex, 1987.

Garay, Ronald. *Congressional Television: A Legislative History.* Westport, CT: Greenwood, 1984.

———. *Cable Television: A Reference Guide to Information.* Westport, CT: Greenwood, 1988.

———. *Gordon McLendon: The Maverick of Radio.* Westport, CT: Greenwood Press, 1992.

Garner, Joe. *We Interrupt This Broadcast.* Naperville, IL: Sourcebooks, 1998. (Includes 2 audio CD recordings.)

Gates, Gary Paul. *Air Time: The Inside Story of CBS News.* New York: Harper, 1978.

Gerani, Gary, with Paul H. Schulman. *Fantastic Television*. New York: Harmony, 1977.

Gerrold, David. *The World of Star Trek*. New York: Ballantine, 1973.

Gianakos, Larry James. *Television Drama Series Programming: A Comprehensive Chronicle*. Metuchen, NJ: Scarecrow, 1978–1987 (5 vols., covering 1947–1984).

Gibson, George H. *Public Broadcasting: The Role of the Federal Government, 1912–1976*. New York: Praeger, 1977.

Gilbert, Robert E. *Television and Presidential Politics*. North Quincy, MA: Christopher Publishing, 1972.

Gitlin, Todd. *Inside Prime Time*. New York: Pantheon, 1983.

Glander, Timothy. *Origins of Mass Communications Research During the American Cold War: Educational Effects and Contemporary Implications*. Mahwah, NJ: Lawrence Erlbaum Associates, 2000.

Glick, Ira O., & Sidney J. Levy. *Living with Television*. Chicago: Aldine, 1962.

Glut, Donald F, & Jim Harmon. *The Great Television Heroes*. New York: Doubleday, 1975.

Godfrey, Donald G. "CFCF: The Forgotten First," *Canadian Journal of Communication*, 8:4:56–71 (September 1982).

———. *Reruns on File: A Guide to Electronic Media Archives*. Hillsdale, NJ: Lawrence Erlbaum Associates, 1992.

———. *The Father of Television: Philo T. Farnsworth*. Salt Lake City: University of Utah Press, 2001.

———. & Frederic A. Leigh, (Eds.). *Historical Dictionary of American Radio*. Westport, CT: Greenwood, 1998.

Godfried, Nathan. *WCFL, Chicago's Voice of Labor, 1926–78*. Urbana: University of Illinois Press, 1997.

Goldberg, Lee. *Television Series Revivals, Sequels or Remakes of Cancelled Shows*. Jefferson, NC: McFarland, 1993.

Goldberg, Robert, & Gerald Jay Goldberg. *Anchors: Brokaw, Jennings, Rather and the Evening News*. New York: Birch Lane, 1990.

———. *Citizen Turner: The Wild Rise of an American Tycoon*. New York: Harcourt Brace, 1995.

Goldmark, Peter C. *Maverick Inventor: My Turbulent Years at CBS*. New York: Saturday Review Press, 1973.

Goldenson, Leonard H. *Beating the Odds: The Untold Story Behind the Rise of ABC [. . .]*. New York: Scribner's, 1991.

Goldsmith, Alfred N., & Austin C. Lescarboura. *This Thing Called Broadcasting*. New York: Holt, 1930.

Goldstein, Fred, & Stan Goldstein. *Prime-Time Television: A Pictorial History from Milton Berle to "Falcon Crest."* New York: Crown, 1977.

Graham, Margaret B. W. *RCA and the VideoDisc: The Business of Research.* New York: Cambridge, 1986.

Gramling, Oliver. *AP: The Story of News.* New York: Farrar & Rinehart, 1940 (reprinted by Greenwood, 1969).

Grandin, Thomas. *The Political Use of the Radio.* Geneva, Switzerland: Geneva Research Centre (*Studies* X:3), 1939 (reprinted by Arno Press, 1971).

Grant, August, (Ed.). *Communication Technology Update.* Newton, MA: Focal Press, 1991–2000, annual.

Green, Timothy. *The Universal Eye: The World of Television.* New York: Stein and Day, 1972.

Greenberger, Martin, (Ed.). *Electronic Publishing Plus: Media for a Technological Future.* White Plains, NY: Knowledge Industry Publications, 1985.

Greenfield, Jeff. *Television: The First Fifty Years.* New York: Abrams, 1977.

Gross, Ben. *I Looked and I Listened: Informal Recollections of Radio and TV.* 2nd ed. New Rochelle, NY: Arlington House, 1970.

Gross, Lynne Schafer. *The New Television Technologies.* 2nd ed. Dubuque, Iowa: Wm. C. Brown, 1986.

Guide to Independent Television. London: Independent Television (later Broadcasting) Authority, 1963–1988, annual. (Note: title changed from year to year; *Television and Radio* was common in 1980s.)

Gunther, Marc. *The House That Roone Built: The Inside Story of ABC News.* Boston: Little, Brown, 1994.

Hadden, Jeffrey K., & Anson Shupe. *Televangelism: Power and Politics on God's Frontier.* New York: Henry Holt, 1988.

Halberstam, David. *The Powers That Be.* New York: Knopf, 1979.

Hale, Julian. *Radio Power: Propaganda and International Broadcasting.* Philadelphia: Temple University Press, 1975.

Hall, Jim. *Mighty Minutes: An Illustrated History of Television's Best Commercials.* New York: Harmony, 1984.

Hallin, Daniel C. The *"Uncensored War:" The Media and Vietnam.* New York: Oxford, 1986.

Halper, Donna L. *Invisible Stars: A Social History of Women in American Broadcasting.* Armonk, NY: M. E. Sharpe, 2001.

Hammond, Charles M., Jr. *The Image Decade: Television Documentary, 1965–1975.* New York: Hastings House, 1981.

Hancock, H. E. *Wireless at Sea: The First Fifty Years.* Chelmsford, England: Marconi International Marine Communication Co., 1950 (reprinted by Arno Press, 1974).

Harlow, Alvin F. *Old Wires and New Waves: The History of the Telegraph, Telephone, and Wireless.* New York: Appleton-Century, 1936 (reprinted by Arno Press, 1971).

Harmon, Jim. *The Great Radio Heroes.* Garden City, NY: Doubleday, 1967; Jefferson, NC: McFarland, 2001 (rev. ed.).

———. *The Great Radio Comedians.* Garden City, NY: Doubleday, 1970.

Harris, Jay S. *TV Guide: The First 25 Years.* New York: Simon and Schuster, 1978.

Harris, Paul. *When Pirates Ruled the Waves.* Aberdeen, Scotland: Impulse Press, 1970.

Hawes, William. *American Television Drama: The Experimental Years.* University: University of Alabama Press, 1986.

Hawks, Ellison. *Pioneers of Wireless.* London: Methuen, 1927 (reprinted by Arno Press, 1974).

Hawver, Walt. *Capital Cities/ABC: The Early Years, 1954–1986.* Radnor, PA: Chilton. 1994.

Head, Sydney W. *World Broadcasting Systems: A Comparative Analysis.* Belmont, CA: Wadsworth, 1985.

Head, Sydney W., (Ed.). *Broadcasting in Africa: A Continental Survey of Radio and Television.* Philadelphia: Temple University Press, 1974.

Head, Sydney W., & Christopher H. Sterling, et al. *Broadcasting in America: A Survey of Electronic Media.* Boston: Houghton Mifflin, 1956, 1972, 1976, 1982, 1987, 1990, 1994, 1998. (Head was sole author until 1982; subtitle has varied.)

Hecht, Jeff. *City of Light: The Story of Fiber Optics.* New York: Oxford University Press, 1999.

Heeter, Carrie, & Bradley S. Greenberg. *Cableviewing.* Norwood, NJ: Ablex, 1988.

Heighton, Elizabeth, & Don R. Cunningham. *Advertising in the Broadcast Media.* Belmont, CA: Wadsworth, 1976, 1984 (2nd ed.).

Heldenfels, R. D. *Television's Greatest Year: 1954.* New York: Continuum, 1994.

Henck, Fred W., & Bernard Strassburg. *A Slippery Slope: The Long Road to the Breakup of AT&T.* Westport, CT: Greenwood, 1988.

Henson, Robert. *Television Weathercasting: A History.* Jefferson, NC: McFarland, 1990.

Herring, James M., & Gerald C. Gross. *Telecommunications: Economics and Regulation.* New York: McGraw-Hill, 1936 (reprinted by Arno Press, 1974).

Hettinger, Herman S. *A Decade of Radio Advertising.* Chicago: University of Chicago Press, 1933 (reprinted by Arno Press, 1971).

Hettinger, Herman S., & Walter J. Neff. *Practical Radio Advertising*. New York: Prentice-Hall, 1938.

Hickman, Tom. *What Did you Do in the War, Auntie? The BBC at War, 1939–45*. London: BBC, 1995.

Hijiya, James A. *Lee de Forest and the Fatherhood of Radio*. Bethlehem, PA: Lehigh University Press, 1992.

Hill, Harold. *NAEB History, 1925–1954*. 2nd ed. Washington, DC: NAEB, 1965. (For continuation, see Alford, W. Wayne.)

Hilliard, Robert L., & Michael C. Keith. *The Broadcast Century: A Biography of American Broadcasting*. 2nd ed. Boston: Focal Press, 1997; 2001 (3rd ed.).

———. *Waves of Rancor: Tuning in the Radical Right*. Armonk, NY: M. E. Sharpe, 1999.

———. *The Hidden Screen: Low-Power Television in America*. Armonk, NY: M. E. Sharpe, 1999.

Himmelweit, Hilde T., A. N. Oppenheim, & Pamela Vince. *Television and the Child*. New York: Oxford University Press, 1958.

Historical Journal of Film, Radio & Television. (1980–present, quarterly). International journal with primary focus on visual media.

Hogben, Lancelot. *From Cave Painting to Comic Strip: A Kaleidoscope of Human Communication*. New York: Chanticleer Press, 1949.

Horsfield, Peter G. *Religious Television: The American Experience*. New York: Longman, 1984.

Hosley, David H. *As Good as Any: Foreign Correspondence on American Radio, 1930–1940*. Westport, CT: Greenwood, 1984.

Howe, Russell Warren. *The Hunt for "Tokyo Rose."* Lanham, MD: Madison Books, 1990.

Howeth, L. S. *History of Communications-Electronics in the United States Navy*. Washington: GPO, 1963.

Hubbell, Richard W. *4000 Years of Television: The Story of Seeing at a Distance*. New York: Putnam, 1942.

Hudson, Robert V. *Mass Media: A Chronological Encyclopedia of Television, Radio, Motion Pictures, Magazines, Newspapers, and Books in the United States*. New York: Garland, 1987.

Hunt, Darnell M. *O. J. Simpson Facts and Fictions: News Rituals in the Construction of Reality*. New York: Cambridge University Press, 1999.

Husing, Ted. *Ten Years Before the Mike*. New York: Farrar & Rinehart, 1935.

Hutchinson, Thomas H. *Here Is Television: Your Window to the World*. New York: Hastings House, 1946, 1948, 1950.

Huth, Arno. *Radio Today: The Present State of Broadcasting*. Geneva, Switzerland: Geneva Research Centre (*Studies* XII:6), 1942 (reprinted by Arno Press, 1971).

Independent Thinking: An Overview of the Independent Television Industry. Washington: Frazier Gross & Kadlec Inc., 1986.

Inge, M. Thomas, (Ed.). *Handbook of American Popular Culture.* Westport, CT: Greenwood, 1979–1981 (3 vols., each with extensive bibliographies).

Instant World: A Report on Telecommunications in Canada. Ottawa: Information Canada, 1971.

Jaker, Bill, Frank Sulek, & Peter Kanze. *The Airwaves of New York: Illustrated Histories of 156 AM Stations in the Metropolitan Area.* Jefferson, NC: McFarland, 1998.

Jarvik, Lawrence A. *Masterpiece Theatre and the Politics of Quality.* Lanham, Md: Scarecrow Press, 1999.

Jensen, Peter R. *Early Radio: In Marconi's Footsteps, 1894–1920.* Kenthurst, Australia: Kangaroo Press, 1994.

Johnson, Katherine E., (Ed.). *TV Guide 25 Year Index.* Radnor, Pa.: Triangle, 1979.

Johnson, Nicholas. *How to Talk Back to Your Television Set.* Boston: Little, Brown, 1970.

Johnson, William O. *Super Spectator and the Electric Lilliputians.* Boston: Little, Brown, 1971.

Jolly, W. P. *Marconi.* New York: Stein & Day, 1972.

Jome, Hiram L. *Economics of the Radio Industry.* Chicago: A. W. Shaw, 1925 (reprinted by Arno Press, 1971).

Journal of Broadcasting (1956–present, quarterly; added *and Electronic Media* to title effective with vol. 29 in 1985). Major source of scholarly research and reference on radio and television; many historical research articles and bibliographies, 15 reprinted in Lichty and Topping (see below). "A Bibliography of Historical Articles Published in the *Journal of Broadcasting* 1956–1982" (by J. M. Kittross) was published in *Historical Journal of Film Radio and Television*, 4:1:90–96 (1984). A 25-year index was issued in spring 1982; more recent indices on CD-ROM.

Journal of Law and Economics (1958–present, now twice yearly). Has published important articles on FCC, IRAC, media economics.

Journal of Radio Studies (1992–1998, annual; 1998–present, twice a year).

Journalism History (1973–present, quarterly).

Journalism Quarterly (1924–present, quarterly). Title has varied. General mass communications research. Cumulative indexes occasionally published.

Jung, Donald J. *The Federal Communications Commission, the Broadcast Industry, and the Fairness Doctrine, 1981–1987.* Lanham, MD: University Press of America, 1996.

Kahn, Frank J., (Ed.). *Documents of American Broadcasting.* (4th ed.). New York: Appleton-Century-Crofts, 1984. (Earlier editions also are useful.)

Kaltenborn, H. V. *I Broadcast the Crisis.* New York: Random House, 1938.

————. *Fifty Fabulous Years: 1900–1950.* New York: Putnam, 1950.

Kamen, Ira. *Questions and Answers about Pay-TV.* Indianapolis: Howard W. Sams, 1973.

Katz, Elihu, & George Wedell. *Broadcasting in the Third World: Promise and Performance.* Cambridge, MA: Harvard University Press, 1977.

Keating, Stephen. *Cutthroat: High Stakes and Killer Moves on the Electronic Frontier.* Boulder, CO: Johnson Books, 1999.

Keith, Michael C. *Signals in the Air: Native Broadcasting in America.* Westport, CT: Praeger, 1995.

————. *Voices in the Purple Haze: Underground Radio and the Sixties.* Westport, CT: Praeger, 1997.

————. *Talking Radio: An Oral History of American Radio in the Television Age.* Armonk, NY: M. E. Sharpe, 2000.

Kempner, Stanley. *Television Encyclopedia.* New York: Fairchild, 1948. Chronology, pp. 3–42.

Kendrick, Alexander. *Prime Time: The Life of Edward R. Murrow.* Boston: Little, Brown, 1969.

Kiernan, Thomas. *Citizen Murdoch.* New York: Dodd, Mead, 1986.

King, W. James. *The Development of Electrical Technology in the 19th Century: The Telegraph and the Telephone.* Washington: U.S. National Museum (Bulletin 228), 1962 (reprinted by Arno Press, 1977).

Kirby, Edward M., & Jack W. Harris. *Star-Spangled Radio.* Chicago: Ziff-Davis, 1948.

Kisseloff, Jeff. *The Box: An Oral History of Television, 1920–1961.* New York: Viking, 1995.

Kittross, John M., (Ed.). *Documents in American Telecommunications Policy.* New York: Arno Press, 1977 (2 vols.).

Kittross, John Michael. *Television Frequency Allocation Policy in the United States.* New York: Arno Press, 1979 (reprinting a 1960 University of Illinois dissertation; contains "Afterthoughts and Second Guesses.").

————, (Ed.). *Administration of American Telecommunications Policy.* New York: Arno Press, 1980 (2 vols.).

Klatell, David A., & Norman Marcus. *Sports for Sale: Television, Money, and the Fans.* New York: Oxford University Press, 1988.

Knightley, Phillip. *The First Casualty—From the Crimea to Vietnam: The War Correspondent as Hero, Propagandist, and Myth Maker.* New York: Harcourt Brace Jovanovich, 1975.

Koch, Howard. *The Panic Broadcast: Portrait of an Event.* Boston: Little Brown, 1970.

Koenig, Allen E., & Ruane B. Hill, (Eds.). *The Farther Vision: Educational Television Today.* Madison: University of Wisconsin Press, 1967.

Krasnow, Erwin G., & Lawrence D. Longley. *The Politics of Broadcast Regulation.* New York: St. Martin's Press, 1973, 1978, 1982. (With Herbert Terry for 3rd ed.)

Krattenmaker, Thomas G., & Lucas Powe. *Regulating Broadcast Programming.* Cambridge: MIT Press, 1994.

Kraus, Sidney, (Ed.). *The Great Debates: Background, Perspectives, Effects.* Bloomington: Indiana University Press, 1962.

————. *The Great Debates: Carter vs. Ford 1976.* Bloomington: Indiana University Press, 1979.

Kris, Ernst, & Hans Speier. *German Radio Propaganda: Reports on Home Broadcasts During the War.* London: Oxford University Press, 1944.

Lacy, Dan. *From Grunts to Gigabytes: Communications and Society.* Urbana: University of Illinois Press, 1996.

LaGuardia, Robert. *Soap World.* New York: Arbor House, 1983.

Land, Jeff. *Active Radio: Pacifica's Brash Experiment.* St. Paul: University of Minnesota Press, 1999.

Landry, Robert J. *This Fascinating Radio Business.* Indianapolis, IN: Bobbs-Merrill, 1946.

Lang, Gladys Engel, & Kurt Lang. *The Battle for Public Opinion: The President, the Press, and the Polls During Watergate.* New York: Columbia University Press, 1983.

————. *Politics and Television Re-Viewed.* Beverly Hills, Calif.: Sage Publications, 1984.

Lardner, James. *Fast Forward: Hollywood, the Japanese, and the VCR Wars.* New York: W. W. Norton, 1987.

Lashner, Marilyn A. *The Chilling Effect in TV News: Intimidation by the Nixon White House.* New York: Praeger, 1984.

Law and Contemporary Problems (1933–present, quarterly). Journal of the School of Law, Duke University. See, especially, "Radio and Television" (22:4, 1957, and 23:1, 1958) and "Communications," (34:3–4, 1969).

Lazar, Matthew. *Pacifica Radio: The Rise of an Alternative Network.* Philadelphia: Temple University Press, 1999.

Lazarsfeld, Paul F. *Radio and the Printed Page.* New York: Duell, Sloan & Pearce, 1940 (reprinted by Arno Press, 1971).

Lazarsfeld, Paul F, & Harry N. Field. *The People Look at Radio.* Chapel Hill: University of North Carolina Press, 1946 (reprinted by Arno Press, 1975).

Lazarsfeld, Paul F, & Patricia L. Kendall. *Radio Listening in America: The People Look at Radio—Again.* New York: Prentice-Hall, 1948.

Lazarsfeld, Paul F, & Frank N. Stanton, (Eds.). *Radio Research 1941.* New York: Duell, Sloan & Pearce, 1941.

————. *Radio Research 1942–1943.* New York: Duell, Sloan & Pearce, 1944.

————. *Communications Research 1948–1949.* New York: Harper, 1949.

Lean, Tangye. *Voices in the Darkness: The European Radio War.* London: Secker and Warburg, 1943.

Leapman, Michael. *Barefaced Cheek.* London: Hodder & Stoughton, 1983. (A biography of Rupert Murdoch.)

Lebow, Irwin. *Information Highways and Byways: From the Telegraph to the 21st Century.* New York: IEEE Press, 1995.

Le Duc, Don R. *Cable Television and the FCC: A Crisis in Media Control.* Philadelphia: Temple University Press, 1973.

————. *Beyond Broadcasting: Patterns in Policy and Law.* New York: Longman, 1987.

Lee, Alfred M. *The Daily Newspaper in America.* New York: Macmillan, 1937.

Leinwoll, Stanley. *From Spark to Satellite: A History of Radio Communication.* New York: Charles Scribner's Sons, 1979.

Lent, John A., (Ed.). *Broadcasting in Asia and the Pacific: A Continental Survey of Radio and Television.* Philadelphia: Temple University Press, 1978.

Lessing, Lawrence. *Man of High Fidelity: Erwin Howard Armstrong.* Philadelphia: Lippincott, 1956 (revised edition, Bantam Books, 1969).

Levin, Harvey J. *Broadcast Regulation and Joint Ownership of Media.* New York: New York University Press, 1960.

————. *The Invisible Resource: Use and Regulation of the Radio Spectrum.* Baltimore: Johns Hopkins Press, 1971.

————. *Fact and Fancy in Television Regulation: An Economic Study of Policy Alternatives.* New York: Russell Sage Foundation, 1980.

Levin, Murray B. *Talk Radio and the American Dream.* Lexington, MA: Lexington Books, 1987.

Lewis, C. A. *Broadcasting from Within.* London: George Newnes, 1924.

Lewis, Tom. *Empire of the Air: The Men Who Made Radio.* New York: Harper Collins, 1991.

Lichty, Lawrence W., & Malachi C. Topping, (Eds.). *American Broadcasting: A Source Book on the History of Radio and Television.* New York: Hastings House, 1975.

Lingel, Robert. *Educational Broadcasting: A Bibliography.* Chicago: University of Chicago Press, 1932.

Lipschultz, Jeremy H. *Broadcast Indecency: FCC Regulation and the First Amendment.* Newton, MA: Focal Press, 1996.

Lodge, Oliver J. *Signalling through Space without Wires: The Work of Hertz and His Successors.* (3rd ed.) New York: Van Nostrand, 1900 (reprinted by Arno Press, 1974).

Lohr, Lenox. *Television Broadcasting: Production, Economics, Technique.* New York: McGraw-Hill, 1940.

Looker, Thomas. *The Sound and the Story: NPR and the Art of Radio.* Boston: Houghton Mifflin, 1995.

Lowery, Shearon, & Melvin L. DeFleur. *Milestones in Mass Communication Research.* 3rd ed. New York: Longman, 1995.

Luke, Carmen. *Constructing the Child Viewer: A History of the American Discourse on Television and Children, 1950–1980.* Westport, CT: Praeger, 1991.

Lumley, Frederick. *Measurement in Radio.* Columbus: Ohio State University Press, 1934 (reprinted by Arno Press, 1971).

Mabee, Carleton. *The American Leonardo: A Life of Samuel F. B. Morse.* New York: Knopf, 1943 (reprinted by Octagon Books, 1969).

MacDonald, J. Fred. *Don't Touch That Dial! Radio Programming in American Life from 1920–1960.* Chicago: Nelson-Hall, 1979.

———. *Blacks and White TV: Afro-Americans in Television since 1948.* Chicago: Nelson-Hall, 1983.

———. *Television and the Red Menace: The Video Road to Vietnam.* New York: Praeger, 1985.

———. *Who Shot the Sheriff? The Rise and Fall of the Television Western.* New York: Praeger, 1987.

———. *One Nation Under Television: The Rise and Decline of Network TV.* New York: Pantheon, 1990.

MacFarland, David T. *Future Radio Programming Strategies: Cultivating Listenership in the Digital Age.* Mahwah, NJ: Lawrence Erlbaum Associates, 1997.

Maclaurin, W. Rupert. *Invention and Innovation in the Radio Industry.* New York: Macmillan, 1949 (reprinted by Arno Press, 1971).

MacNeil, Robert. *The People Machine: The Influence of Television on American Politics.* New York: Harper & Row, 1968.

Macy, John, Jr. *To Irrigate a Wasteland: The Struggle to Shape a Public Television System in the United States.* Berkeley: University of California Press, 1974.

Maddox, Brenda. *Beyond Babel: New Directions in Communications.* New York: Simon & Schuster, 1972.

Madsen, Axel. *60 Minutes: The Power & The Politics of America's Popular TV News Show.* New York: Dodd, Mead, 1984.

Maine, Basil. *The B.B.C. and Its Audience.* London: Thomas Nelson, 1939.

Mair, George. *Inside HBO: The Billion Dollar War Between HBO, Hollywood and the Home Video Revolution.* New York: Dodd, Mead, 1988.

Marconi, Degna. *My Father, Marconi.* New York: McGraw-Hill, 1962.

Marcus, Norman. *Broadcast and Cable Management.* Englewood Cliffs, NJ: Prentice-Hall, 1986.

Marcus, Sheldon. *Father Coughlin: The Tumultuous Life of the Priest of the Little Flower.* Boston: Little, Brown, 1973.

Marill, Alvin H. *Movies Made for Television: The Telefeature and the Mini-Series, 1964–1984.* New York: New York Zoetrope, 1984.

Marland, E. A. *Early Electrical Communication.* London: Abelard-Schuman, 1964.

Marling, Karal Ann. *As Seen on TV: The Visual Culture of Everyday Life in the 1950s.* Cambridge, MA: Harvard University Press, 1994.

Marschall, Rick. *History of Television.* New York: Gallery Books, 1986.

Martin, James. *The Future of Telecommunications.* 2nd ed. Englewood Cliffs, NJ: Prentice-Hall, 1976.

Matusow, Barbara. *The Evening Stars: The Making of the Network News Anchor.* Boston: Houghton Mifflin, 1983.

Mayer, Martin. *About Television.* New York: Harper & Row, 1972.

Mayes, Thorn L. *Wireless Communication in the United States: The Early Development of American Radio Operating Companies.* East Greenwich, RI: New England Wireless and Steam Museum, 1989.

McArthur, Tom, & Peter Waddell. *The Secret Life of John Logie Baird.* London: Century Hutchinson, 1986.

McChesney, Robert W. *Telecommunications, Mass Media, and Democracy: The Battle for the Control of U.S. Broadcasting, 1928–1935.* New York: Oxford University Press, 1993.

————. *Rich Media, Poor Democracy: Communication Politics in Dubious Times.* Urbana: University of Illinois Press, 1999.

McCourt, Tom. *Conflicting Communications Interests in America: The Case of National Public Radio.* Westport, CT: Praeger, 1999.

McGinniss, Joe. *The Selling of the President 1968.* New York: Trident Press, 1969.

McIntyre, Ian. *The Expense of Glory: A Life of John Reith.* London: HarperCollins, 1993.

McMahon, A. Michal. *The Making of a Profession: A Century of Electrical Engineering in America.* New York: IEEE Press, 1984.

McNamee, Graham, in collaboration with Robert Gordon Anderson. *You're On the Air.* New York: Harper, 1926.

McNeil, Alex. *Total Television: A Comprehensive Guide to Programming from 1948 to the Present.* (4th ed.) New York: Penguin, 1996.

McNeil, Bill, & Morris Wolfe. *Signing On: The Birth of Radio in Canada.* Toronto: Doubleday Canada, 1982.

McNicol, Donald. *Radio's Conquest of Space.* New York: Murray Hill Books, 1946 (reprinted by Arno Press, 1974).

Meehan, Diana M. *Ladies of the Evening: Women Characters of Prime-Time Television.* Metuchen, NJ: Scarecrow, 1983.

Melton, J. Gordon, Philip Charles Lucas, & Jon R. Stone. *Prime-Time Religion: An Encyclopedia of Religious Broadcasting.* Phoenix, AZ: Oryx, 1997.

Merton, Robert K. *Mass Persuasion: The Social Psychology of a War Bond Drive.* New York: Harper 1946 (reprinted by Greenwood, 1971).

Metz, Robert. *CBS: Reflections in a Bloodshot Eye.* Chicago: Playboy Press, 1975.

Meyrowitz, Joshua. *No Sense of Place: The Impact of Electronic Media on Social Behavior.* New York: Oxford University Press, 1985.

Michael, Paul, & James R. Parish. *The Emmy Awards: A Pictorial History.* New York: Crown, 1970.

Michelis, Anthony. *From Semaphore to Satellite.* Geneva, Switzerland: International Telecommunication Union, 1965.

Mickelson, Sig. *From Whistle Stop to Sound Bite: Four Decades of Politics and Television.* New York: Praeger, 1989.

————. *The Decade That Shaped Television News: CBS in the 1950s.* Westport, CT: Praeger, 1998.

Midgley, Ned. *The Advertising and Business Side of Radio.* New York: Prentice-Hall, 1948.

Milam, Lorenzo. *Sex and Broadcasting: A Handbook on Starting a Radio Station for the Community.* 3rd ed. Los Gatos, CA: Dildo Press, 1975 (reprinted by MHO and MHO Works, 1988).

Miller, Merle, & Evan Rhodes. *Only You, Dick Daring! Or, How to Write One Television Script and Make $50,000,000. A True-Life Adventure.* New York: William Sloane Associates, 1964.

Minow, Newton N., et al. *Presidential Television.* New York: Basic Books, 1973.

Mitz, Rick. *The Great TV Sitcom Book.* New York: Richard Marek, 1980.

Morreale, Joanne. *The Presidential Campaign Film: A Critical History.* Westport, CT: Praeger, 1993.

Morris, Joe Alex. *Deadline Every Minute: The Story of the United Press.* Garden City, NY: Doubleday, 1957.

Moseley, Sydney A. *John Baird: The Romance and Tragedy of the Pioneer of Television.* London: Odhams, 1952.

Mott, Frank Luther. *The News in America.* Cambridge, MA: Harvard University Press, 1952.

———. *American Journalism: A History 1690–1960.* 3rd ed. New York: Macmillan, 1962.

Murray, Michael, & Donald G. Godfrey, (Eds.). *Television in America: Local Station History from Across the Nation.* Ames: Iowa State University Press, 1997.

Murray, Michael D., (Ed.). *Encyclopedia of Television News.* Phoenix: Oryx, 1999.

Murrow, Edward R. *This Is London.* New York: Simon and Schuster, 1941.

Murrow, Edward R., & Fred W. Friendly, (Eds.). *See It Now.* New York: Simon and Schuster, 1955.

Nachman, Gerald. *Raised on Radio.* New York: Pantheon, 1998.

National Association of Broadcasters. *Broadcasting in the United States.* Washington: NAB, 1933.

———. *Broadcasting and the Bill of Rights.* Washington: NAB, 1947.

National Association of Public Television Stations. *Public Television and Radio and State Governments.* Washington: NAPTS, 1984 (2 vols.).

National Broadcasting Company. *The Fourth Chime.* New York: NBC, 1944.

National Institute of Mental Health. *Television and Behavior: Ten Years of Scientific Progress and Implications for the Eighties.* Washington: GPO, 1982 (2 vols.).

Newcomb, Horace. *Television: The Critical View.* 4th ed. New York: Oxford University Press, 1987.

Newcomb, Horace, (Ed.). *Encyclopedia of Television.* Chicago: Fitzroy-Dearborn, 1977 (3 vols.).

NHK (Nippon Hoso Kyokai). *The History of Broadcasting in Japan* and *50 Years of Japanese Broadcasting.* Tokyo: NHK, 1967 and 1977.

Nimmo, Dan, & James E. Combs. *Nightly Horrors: Crisis Coverage in Television Network News.* Knoxville: University of Tennessee Press, 1985.

Noam, Eli, (Ed.). *Television in Europe.* New York: Oxford University Press, 1992.

Noll, Roger G., Merton J. Peck, & John McGowan. *Economic Aspects of Television Regulation.* Washington: Brookings Institution, 1973.

Norman, Bruce. *Here's Looking at You: The Story of British Television 1908–1939.* London: BBC, 1984.

Nye, Russel B. *The Unembarrassed Muse: The Popular Arts in America.* New York: Dial Press, 1970.

O'Dell, Cary. *Women Pioneers in Television: Biographies of Fifteen Industry Leaders.* Jefferson, NC: McFarland, 1997.

O'Hara, J.C., & W. Pricha. *Hertz and the Maxwellians: A Study and Documentation of the Discovery of Electromagnetic Wave Radiation, 1873–1894.* London: Peter Peregrinus, 1987.

Owen, Bruce M. *Economics and Freedom of Expression: Media Structure and the First Amendment.* Cambridge, MA: Ballinger, 1975.

Owen, Bruce M., Jack H. Beebe, & Willard Manning, Jr. *Television Economics.* Lexington, MA: Lexington Books, 1974.

Owen, Bruce M. *The Internet Challenge to Television.* Cambridge, MA: Harvard University Press, 1999.

Paglin, Max D., (Ed.). *A Legislative History of the Communications Act of 1934.* New York: Oxford University Press, 1989.

Paglin, Max D, (Ed.), & Joel Rosenbloom & James R. Hobson, (Co-eds.). *The Communications Act: A Legislative History of the Major Amendments, 1934–1996.* Silver Spring, MD: Pike & Fischer, 1999.

Paley, William S. *As It Happened: A Memoir.* New York: Doubleday, 1979.

Paper, Lewis. *Empire: William S. Paley and the Making of CBS.* New York: St. Martin's Press, 1987.

Parsons, Patrick R., & Robert M. Frieden. *The Cable and Satellite Television Industries.* Needham Heights, MA: Allyn & Bacon, 1998.

Passman, Arnold. *The Deejays.* New York: Macmillan, 1971.

Paulu, Burton. *Radio and Television Broadcasting on the European Continent.* Minneapolis: University of Minnesota Press, 1967.

———. *Radio and Television Broadcasting in Eastern Europe.* Minneapolis: University of Minnesota Press, 1974.

———. *Television and Radio in the United Kingdom.* Minneapolis: University of Minnesota Press, 1981. (See also the same author's two earlier studies on the same topic from the same publisher: *British Broadcasting* [1956], and *British Broadcasting in Transition* [1961].)

Pawley, Edward. *BBC Engineering: 1922–1972.* London: BBC, 1972.

Peers, Frank W. *The Politics of Canadian Broadcasting: 1920–1951.* Toronto: University of Toronto Press, 1969.

———. *The Public Eye; Television and the Politics of Canadian Broadcasting: 1952–1968.* Toronto: University of Toronto Press, 1979.

Perry, Armstrong. *Radio in Education: The Ohio School of Air and Other Experiments.* New York: Payne Fund, 1929 (reprinted by Arno Press, 1971).

Perry, Jeb H. *Universal Television: The Studio and Its Programs: 1950–1980.* Metuchen, NJ: Scarecrow, 1983.

Persico, Joseph E. *Edward R. Murrow: An American Original.* New York: McGraw-Hill, 1988.

Peterson, Theodore. *Magazines in the Twentieth Century.* 2nd ed. Urbana: University of Illinois Press, 1964.

Phillips, Vivian J. *Early Radio Wave Detectors.* New York: Peter Peregrinus, 1980.

Picard, Robert G. *The Cable Networks Handbook.* Riverside, CA: Carpelan, 1993.

Pitts, Michael R. *Radio Soundtracks: A Reference Guide.* Metuchen, NJ: Scarecrow Press, 1986.

Poindexter, Ray. *Golden Throats and Silver Tongues: The Radio Announcers.* Conway, AR: River Road Press, 1978.

Pollay, Richard W., (Ed.). *Information Sources in Advertising History.* Westport, CT: Greenwood, 1979.

Poltrack, David F. *Television Marketing: Network, Local, Cable.* New York: McGraw-Hill, 1983.

Pool, Ithiel de Sola, (Ed.). *The Social Impact of the Telephone.* Cambridge, MA: MIT Press, 1977.

———. *Technologies of Freedom.* Cambridge, Mass.: Harvard University Press, 1983.

Pope, Daniel. *The Making of Modern Advertising.* New York: Basic Books, 1983.

Porterfield, John, & Kay Reynolds, (Eds.). *We Present Television.* New York: W. W. Norton, 1940.

Powe, Lucas A., Jr. *American Broadcasting and the First Amendment.* Berkeley: University of California Press, 1987.

Powell, John Walker. *Channels of Learning: The Story of Educational Television.* Washington: Public Affairs Press, 1962.

Powers, Ron. *The Newscasters.* New York: St. Martin's Press, 1977.

———. *Supertube: The Rise of Television Sports.* New York: Coward, McCann, 1984.

Presbrey, Frank. *The History and Development of Advertising.* New York: Doubleday, Doran, 1929.

President's Communications Policy Board. *Telecommunications: A Program for Progress.* Washington: GPO, 1951.

President's Task Force on Communications Policy. *Final Report.* Washington: GPO, 1968.

Price, Jonathan. *The Best Thing on TV: Commercials.* New York: Penguin, 1978.

Price, Monroe E., (Ed.). *The V-Chip Debate: Content Filtering from Television to the Internet.* Mahwah, NJ: Lawrence Erlbaum Associates, 1998.

Prime, Samuel I. *The Life of Samuel F. B. Morse.* New York: Appleton, 1875 (reprinted by Arno Press, 1974).

Public Opinion Quarterly (1937–present, quarterly). Scholarly research on public opinion, polls, and media audiences.

Public Telecommunications Review (1973–1980, bimonthly). Topical research and comment on public radio-TV. See also *Educational Broadcasting Review.*

Quinlan, Sterling. *The Hundred Million Dollar Lunch.* Chicago: O'Hara, 1974.

———. *Inside ABC: American Broadcasting Company's Rise to Power.* New York: Hastings House, 1979.

Rader, Benjamin G. *In Its Own Image: How Television Has Transformed Sports.* New York: Free Press, 1984.

Radio Annual (1937–1964, annual). Trade directory with statistics, information on stations and networks, and review of previous year.

Radio Broadcast. (1922–1930, monthly). Popular discussion of the industry combined with technical advice for home receiver makers.

The Radio Industry: The Story of Its Development. Chicago: A. W. Shaw, 1928 (reprinted by Arno Press, 1974).

Radio Regulation. Washington: Pike and Fischer, 1948–present (loose-leaf reporting service of FCC and court decisions).

Reed, Robert M., & Maxine K. Reed. *The Encyclopedia of Television, Cable, and Video.* New York: Van Nostrand Reinhold, 1992.

Reid, James D. *The Telegraph in America: Its Founders, Promoters and Noted Men.* New York: Derby, 1879 (reprinted by Arno Press, 1974).

Reid, T. R. *The Chip.* New York: Simon and Schuster, 1984.

Reinsch, J. Leonard. *Getting Elected: From Radio and Roosevelt to Television and Reagan.* New York: Hippocrene, 1991.

Rhoads, B. Eric, (Ed.). *Blast from the Past: A Pictorial History of Radio's First 75 Years.* West Palm Beach, FL: Steamline Press, 1996.

Rhodes, Frederick Leland. *Beginnings of Telephony.* New York: Harper, 1929 (reprinted by Arno Press, 1974).

Ritchie, Michael. *Please Stand By: A Prehistory of Television.* Woodstock, NY: Overlook, 1994.

Rivkin, Steven R. *Cable Television: A Guide to Federal Regulations.* Santa Monica, CA: Rand Corp., 1973.

Robertson, Jim. *Televisionaries.* Charlotte Harbor, FL: Tabby House, 1993.

Robinson, Michael J., and Austin Ranney, (Eds.). *The Mass Media in Campaign '84.* Washington: American Enterprise Institute, 1985.

Robinson, Michael, & Margaret Sheehan. *Over the Wire and on TV: CBS and UPI in Campaign '80.* New York: Russell Sage Foundation, 1983.

Robinson, Thomas Porter. *Radio Networks and the Federal Government.* New York: Columbia University Press, 1943 (reprinted by Arno Press, 1979).

Rogers, Everett. *Communication Technology: The New Media in Society.* New York: Free Press, 1986.

Rolo, Charles J. *Radio Goes to War: The "Fourth Front."* New York: Putnam, 1942.

Roper Organization, Inc. *Changing Public Attitudes toward Television and Other Mass Media.* New York: Television Information Office, 1959–1989. Title varies; issued approximately every 18 months for a total of 16 published reports. (When the TIO closed down in 1989, publication of this series was passed to the National Association of Broadcasters.)

Rose, Brian G., (Ed.). *TV Genres: A Handbook and Reference Guide.* Westport, CT: Greenwood, 1985.

———. *Television and the Performing Arts: A Handbook and Reference Guide to American Cultural Programming.* Westport, CT: Greenwood, 1986.

Rose, Cornelia B., Jr. *National Policy for Radio Broadcasting.* New York: Harper, 1940 (reprinted by Arno Press, 1971).

Rose, Oscar. *Radio Broadcasting and Television: A Bibliography.* New York: H. W. Wilson, 1947.

Rosen, Philip T. *The Modern Stentors: Radio Broadcasters and the Federal Government, 1920–1934.* Westport, CT: Greenwood, 1980.

Rosewater, Victor. *History of Cooperative News-Gathering in the United States.* New York: Appleton, 1930 (reprinted by Greenwood, 1970).

Rothafel, Samuel L., & Raymond Francis Yates. *Broadcasting: Its New Day.* New York: Century, 1925 (reprinted by Arno Press, 1971).

Rowan, Ford. *Broadcast Fairness: Doctrine, Practice, Prospects.* New York: Longman, 1984.

Rowland, Willard. *The Politics of TV Violence: Policy Issues of Communication Research.* Beverly Hills, CA: Sage, 1983.

Rowman, James W. *Cablemania: The Cable Television Sourcebook.* Englewood Cliffs, NJ: Prentice-Hall, 1983.

Rucker, Bryce W. *The First Freedom.* Carbondale: Southern Illinois University Press, 1968.

Ryan, Milo. *History in Sound: A Descriptive Listing of the KIRO-CBS Collection of Broadcasts of the World War II Years and after [. . .].* Seattle: University of Washington Press, 1963.

Saettler, Paul. *A History of Instructional Technology.* New York: McGraw-Hill, 1968.

Sander, Gordon F. *Serling: The Rise and Twilight of Television's Last Angry Man.* New York: Dutton/Penguin, 1992.

Sarnoff, David. *Network Broadcasting.* New York: RCA, 1939.

———. *Looking Ahead: The Papers of David Sarnoff.* New York: McGraw-Hill, 1968.

Scannell, Paddy, & David Cardiff. *A Social History of British Broadcasting: Volume 1, 1922–1939, Serving the Nation.* Oxford: Blackwell, 1991.

Schechter, A. A., with Edward Anthony. *I Live on Air.* New York: Stokes, 1941.

Schemering, Christopher. *The Soap Opera Encyclopedia.* New York: Ballantine, 1985.

Schmeckebier, Laurence F. *The Federal Radio Commission: Its History, Activities and Organization.* Washington, DC: Brookings Institution, 1932.

Schramm, Wilbur, Jack Lyle, & Edwin B. Parker. *Television in the Lives of Our Children.* Stanford, CA: Stanford University Press, 1961.

Schramm, Wilbur, et al. *The People Look at Educational Television.* Stanford, CA: Stanford University Press, 1963.

Schramm, Wilbur (ed. by Steven H. Chaffee and Everett M. Rogers). *The Beginnings of Communication Study in America: A Personal Memoir.* Thousand Oaks, CA: Sage, 1997.

Schroeder, Richard. *Texas Signs On: The Early Days of Radio and Television.* College Station: Texas A&M University Press, 1998.

Schubert, Paul. *The Electric Word: The Rise of Radio.* New York: Macmillan, 1928 (reprinted by Arno Press, 1971).

Schwartz, Bernard. *The Professor and the Commissions.* New York: Knopf, 1959.

Schwarzlose, Richard A. *The Nation's Newsbrokers.* Evanston, IL: Northwestern University Press, 1989, 1990 (2 vols.).

Seehafer, Eugene, & J. W. Laemmar. *Successful Radio and Television Advertising.* New York: McGraw-Hill, 1951, 1959.

Segrave, Kerry. *Payola in the Music Industry: A History, 1880–1991.* Jefferson, NC: McFarland, 1994.

———. *American Television Abroad: Hollywood's Attempt to Dominate World Television.* Jefferson, NC: McFarland, 1998.

Seiden, Martin H. *Cable Television USA: An Analysis of Government Policy.* New York: Praeger, 1972.

Sendall, Bernard. *Independent Television in Britain: Origin and Foundation, 1946–62.* London: Macmillan, 1982.

———. *Independent Television in Britain: Expansion and Change, 1958–68.* London: Macmillan, 1983.

Sennett, Ted. *Your Show of Shows.* New York: Collier, 1977.

Settel, Irving. *A Pictorial History of Radio.* 2nd ed. New York: Grosset & Dunlap, 1967.

Settel, Irving, & William Laas. *A Pictorial History of Television*. New York: Grosset & Dunlap, 1969.

Sevareid, Eric. *Not So Wild A Dream*. New York: Knopf, 1946 (reprinted by Atheneum, 1976).

Shapiro, Mitchell E. *Television Network Prime-Time Programming, 1948–1988*. Jefferson, NC: McFarland, 1989.

————. *Television Network Daytime and Late-Night Programming, 1959–1989*. Jefferson, NC: McFarland, 1990.

————. *Television Network Weekend Programming, 1959–1990*. Jefferson, NC: McFarland, 1992.

Shayon, Robert Lewis. *Television and Our Children*. New York: Longmans, Green, 1951.

Sheldon, H. Horton, & Edgar Norman Grisewood. *Television: Present Methods of Picture Transmission*. New York: Van Nostrand, 1929.

Shiers, George, (Ed.). *Technical Development of Television*. New York: Arno Press, 1977.

Shiers, George. *Early Television: An Annotated Bibliography to 1940*. New York: Garland, 1997.

Shirer, William L. *Berlin Diary: The Journal of a Foreign Correspondent 1934–1941*. New York: Knopf, 1941.

————. *"This is Berlin:" Radio Broadcasts from Nazi Germany*. Woodstock, NY: Overlook Press, 1999.

Shulman, Arthur, & Roger Youman. *How Sweet It Was: Television—A Pictorial Commentary*. New York: Shorecrest, 1966.

Shurick E. P. J. *The First Quarter-Century of American Broadcasting*. Kansas City: Midland, 1946.

Siepmann, Charles A. *Radio's Second Chance*. Boston: Little, Brown, 1946.

————. *Radio, Television, and Society*. New York: Oxford University Press, 1950.

Sies, Luther F. *Encyclopedia of American Radio, 1920–1960*. Jefferson, NC: McFarland, 2000.

Simmons, Steven J. *The Fairness Doctrine and the Media*. Berkeley: University of California Press, 1978.

Simpson, Christopher. *Science of Coercion: Communication Research & Psychological Warfare, 1945–1960*. New York: Oxford University Press, 1994.

Singleton, Loy A. *Telecommunications in the Information Age*. 2nd ed. Cambridge, MA: Ballinger, 1986.

Sivowitch, Elliot. "A Technological Survey of Broadcasting's 'Pre-History,' 1876–1920," *Journal of Broadcasting* 14:1–20 (Winter 1970–1971). Also in Lichty and Topping.

Sklar, Robert. *Prime-Time America: Life Behind the Television Screen.* New York: Oxford University Press, 1980.

Skornia, Harry J., & Jack William Kitson. *Problems and Controversies in Television and Radio.* Palo Alto, CA: Pacific Books, 1968.

Skutch, Ira. *The Days of Live: Television's Golden Age as Seen by 11 Directors Guild of America Members.* Lanham, MD: Scarecrow Press, 1998a.

———. *Five Directors: The Golden Years of Radio.* Lanham, MD: Scarecrow Press, 1998b.

Slate, Sam J., & Joe Cook. *It Sounds Impossible.* New York: Macmillan, 1963.

Slater, Robert. *This. . . Is CBS: A Chronicle of 60 Years.* Englewood Cliffs, NJ: Prentice-Hall, 1988.

Slide, Anthony. *Great Radio Personalities in Historic Photographs.* New York: Dover, 1982.

———. *The Television Industry: A Historical Dictionary.* Westport, CT: Greenwood, 1991.

Slotten, Hugh R. *Radio and Television Regulation: Broadcasting Technology in the United States, 1920–1960.* Baltimore: Johns Hopkins University Press, 2000.

Small, William. *To Kill a Messenger: Television News and the Real World.* New York: Hastings House, 1970.

Smart, James R., (Comp.) *Radio Broadcasts in the Library of Congress: 1924–1941.* Washington: Library of Congress, 1982.

Smead, Elmer E. *Freedom of Speech by Radio and Television.* Washington: Public Affairs Press, 1959.

Smith, Anthony. *The Shadow in the Cave: The Broadcaster, the Audience, and the State.* Urbana: University of Illinois Press, 1973.

———. *The Geopolitics of Information.* New York: Oxford University Press, 1980.

———. *Television: An International History.* 2nd ed. Oxford: Oxford University Press, 1998.

Smith, Delbert D. *Communication via Satellite: A Vision in Retrospect.* Boston: Sijthoff, 1976.

Smith, George David. *The Anatomy of a Business Strategy: Bell, Western Electric, and the Origins of the American Telephone Industry.* Baltimore: Johns Hopkins University Press, 1985.

Smith, Myron J., Jr. *U.S. Television Network News: A Guide to Sources in English.* Jefferson, NC: McFarland, 1984.

Smith, R. Franklin. *Edward R. Murrow: The War Years.* Kalamazoo, MI: New Issues Press (Western Michigan University), 1978.

Smith, Ralph Lee. *The Wired Nation: Cable TV—The Electronic Communications Highway.* New York: Harper & Row, 1972.

Smith, Sally Bedell. *In All His Glory: The Life of William S. Paley—The Legendary Tycoon and His Brilliant Circle.* New York: Simon & Schuster, 1990.

Smith, Wes. *The Pied Pipers of Rock 'n' Roll: Radio Deejays of the 50s and 60s.* Marietta, GA: Longstreet Press, 1989.

SMPTE Journal (1916-present, monthly). Some excellent coverage of video.

Smulyan, Susan. *Selling Radio: The Commercialization of American Broadcasting, 1920–1934.* Washington: Smithsonian Institution Press, 1994.

Smythe, Dallas W. *Structure and Policy of Electrical Communications.* Urbana: University of Illinois Press, 1957 (reprinted by Arno Press, 1977).

Sobel, Robert. *RCA.* New York: Stein & Day, 1986.

Socolow, A. Walter. *The Law of Radio Broadcasting.* New York: Baker, Voorhis, 1939 (2 vols.).

Soley, Lawrence C., & John S. Nichols. *Clandestine Radio Broadcasting: A Study of Revolutionary and Counterrevolutionary Electronic Communication.* New York: Praeger, 1987.

Spalding, John W., "1928: Radio Becomes a Mass Advertising Medium," *Journal of Broadcasting* 8:31–44 (Winter 1963–1964). Also in Lichty and Topping.

Sperber, A. M. *Murrow: His Life and Times.* New York: Freundlich Books, 1986.

Spigel, Lynn. *Make Room for TV: Television and the Family Ideal in Postwar America.* Chicago: University of Chicago Press, 1992.

_____. & Michael Curtin, (Eds.). *The Revolution Wasn't Televised: Sixties Television and Social Conflict.* New York: Routledge, 1997.

Sponsor (1946–1968, weekly, later monthly). Broadcast advertising trade magazine. See special issues on "40 Year Album of Pioneer Radio Stations" (May 1962); "CBS: Documenting 38 Years of Exciting History" (September 13, 1965); and "NBC: A Documentary" (May 16, 1966).

Spragens, William C. *Electronic Magazines: Soft News Programs on Network Television.* Westport, CT: Praeger, 1995.

Standage, Tom. *The Victorian Internet: The Remarkable Story of the Telegraph and the Nineteenth Century's On-line Pioneers.* New York: Walker, 1998.

Starch, Daniel. *Principles of Advertising.* Chicago: A.W. Shaw 1923.

Stedman, Raymond. *The Serials: Suspense and Drama by Installment.* 2nd ed. Norman: University of Oklahoma Press, 1977.

Steinbock, Dan. *Triumph & Erosion in the American Media and Entertainment Industries.* Westport, CT: Quorum, 1995.

Steiner, Gary. *The People Look at Television: A Study of Audience Attitudes.* New York: Knopf, 1963.

Stempel, Tom. *Storytellers to the Nation: A History of American Television Writing.* New York: Continuum, 1992.

Sterling, Christopher H. *Electronic Media: A Guide to Trends in Broadcasting and Newer Technologies, 1920–1983.* New York: Praeger, 1984.

_____. & Timothy R. Haight, eds. *The Mass Media: Aspen Guide to Communication Industry Trends.* New York: Praeger Special Studies, 1978.

_____. & George Shiers. *History of Telecommunications Technology: An Annotated Bibliography.* Lanham, MD: Scarecrow Press, 2000.

_____. (Ed.). *Encyclopedia of Radio.* Chicago: Fitzroy Dearborn, 2002 (2 vols.).

Stewart, David. *The PBS Companion: A History of Public Television.* New York: TV Books, 1999.

Stokes, John W. *70 Years of Radio Tubes and Valves.* Vestal, NY: Vestal Press, 1982.

Stone, David M. *Nixon and the Politics of Public Television.* New York: Garland, 1985.

Stone, Joseph, & Tim Yohn. *Prime Time and Misdemeanors: Investigating the 1950s TV Quiz Scandal—a D.A.'s Account.* New Brunswick, NJ: Rutgers University Press, 1992.

Storey, Graham. *Reuters: The Story of a Century of News-Gathering.* New York: Crown, 1951 (reprinted by Greenwood, 1970).

Studies in Broadcasting. Cambridge, MA: Harvard Radiobroadcasting Project, 1940–1948 (6 vols.; reprinted by Arno Press, 1971).

Sturcken, Frank. *Live Television: The Golden Age of 1946–1958 in New York.* Jefferson, NC: McFarland, 1990.

Sturmey, S. G. *The Economic Development of Radio.* London: Duckworth, 1958.

Sugar, Bert Randolph. *"The Thrill of Victory": The Inside Story of ABC Sports.* New York: Hawthorne, 1978.

Summers, Harrison B., (Ed.). *Radio Censorship.* New York: H. W. Wilson, 1939 (reprinted by Arno Press, 1971).

———. *A Thirty-Year History of Programs Carried on National Radio Networks in the United States, 1926–1956.* Columbus: Ohio State University, Department of Speech, 1958 (reprinted by Arno Press, 1971).

Summers, Robert E., & Harrison B. Summers. *Broadcasting and the Public.* Belmont, Calif: Wadsworth, 1966, 1978. (With John Pennybacker for 2nd ed.)

Surgeon General's Scientific Advisory Committee on Television and Social Behavior. *Television and Growing Up: The Impact of Televised Violence.* Washington: GPO, 1972.

Swartz, Jon D., & Robert C. Reinehr. *Handbook of Old-Time Radio: A Comprehensive Guide to Golden Age Radio Listening and Collecting.* Metuchen, NJ: Scarecrow Press, 1993.

Swerdlow, Joel L. *Beyond Debate: A Paper on Televised Presidential Debates.* New York: Twentieth Century Fund, 1984.

Swift, John. *Adventure in Vision: The First 25 Years of Television.* London: John Lehmann, 1950.

Tebbel, John. *The Media in America.* New York: Crowell, 1975.

Television (1944–1968, monthly). Feature articles on the television industry.

Television Digest (1945–present, weekly). Detailed and informed newsletter of broadcasting and electronics industries.

Television Factbook (1945–present, biennial to late 1950s, then annual). Major reference directory of entire television industry—with useful data and statistics.

Television Quarterly (1962–present, quarterly, though issued irregularly in mid-1970s). Official journal of the National Academy of Television Arts and Sciences.

Television/Radio Age (1953–1989, biweekly), covers programming and advertising. See NBC 60th Anniversary Issue, May 1986.

Temin, Peter, with Louis Galambos. *The Fall of the Bell System.* New York: Cambridge University Press, 1987.

Temporary Commission on Alternative Financing for Public Telecommunications (TCAF). *Report to the Congress.* Washington: TCAF/FCC, 1982–1983.

Terrace, Vincent. *The Complete Encyclopedia of Television Programs, 1947–1979.* 2nd ed. Cranbury, NJ: A. S. Barnes, 1979 (2 vols.).

————. *Radio Programs, 1920–1984: A Catalog of over 1800 Shows.* Jefferson, NC: McFarland, 1998.

Thaler, Paul. *The Spectacle: Media and the Making of the O. J. Simpson Story.* Westport, CT: Praeger, 1997.

Thompson, Robert L. *Wiring a Continent: The History of the Telegraph Industry in the United States (1832–1866).* Princeton, NJ: Princeton University Press, 1947 (reprinted by Arno Press, 1972).

Toll, Robert C. *The Entertainment Machine: American Show Business in the Twentieth Century.* New York: Oxford University Press, 1982.

Tracey, Michael. *The Decline and Fall of Public Service Broadcasting.* Oxford: Oxford University Press, 1998.

Tunstall, Jeremy, & David Walker. *Media Made in California: Hollywood, Politics and the News.* New York: Oxford University Press, 1981.

Turow, Joseph. *Entertainment, Education, and the Hard Sell: Three Decades of Network Children's Television.* New York: Praeger, 1981.

TV Guide. (1953–present, weekly). See especially the Fall Preview Issue each September.

Tyler, Tracy F. *An Appraisal of Radio Broadcasting in the Land-Grant Colleges and State Universities.* Washington: National Committee on Education by Radio, 1933.

Tyne, Gerald. *Saga of the Vacuum Tube.* Indianapolis, IN: Howard W. Sams, 1977.

Udelson, Joseph H. *The Great Television Race: A History of the American Television Industry, 1925–1941.* University: University of Alabama Press, 1982.

United Nations Educational, Scientific, and Cultural Organization (Unesco). *Many Voices, One World: Communications and Society Today and Tomorrow.* Paris: Unesco, 1980 (the "MacBride Commission" report).

———. *News Agencies: Their Structure and Operation.* Paris: Unesco, 1953.

———. *Press, Film, Radio: Reports on the Facilities of Mass Communication.* Paris: Unesco, 1947–1951 (7 vols.; reprinted in 3 by Arno Press, 1972).

———. *Television: A World Survey,* and *Supplement.* Paris: Unesco, 1953, 1955 (2 vols.; reprinted in one by Arno Press, 1972).

———. *World Communications: A 200 Country Survey of Press, Radio, Television, Film.* Paris: Unesco, 1950, 1951, 1956, 1964, and 1975. (Subtitle varies.)

United States, Congress, House of Representatives. *Radio Laws of the United States.* Washington: GPO, 1972 (revised from time to time with varied titles).

United States, Congress, House of Representatives, Committee on Interstate and Foreign Commerce. *Regulation of Broadcasting.* 85th Cong., 2nd Sess., 1958. (Prepared by Robert S. McMahon.)

———. *Investigation of Television Quiz Shows.* Hearings. 86th Cong., 1st Sess., 1960 (2 vols.).

———. *Responsibilities of Broadcast Licensees.* Hearings. 86th Cong., 2nd Sess., 1960 (2 vols.).

United States, Congress, Senate, Committee on Interstate and Foreign Commerce. *Television Inquiry.* Hearings in Six Parts, with several interim and special reports. 84th and 85th Congs., 1956–1958.

United States, Department of Commerce. "Recommendations of the [Second] National Radio Committee," *Radio Service Bulletin* (April 2, 1923), pp. 9–13 (reprinted, with next four items, in Kittross, 1977, above).

———. *Recommendations for Regulation of Radio Adopted by the Third National Radio Conference.* Washington: GPO, 1924.

———. *Proceedings of the Fourth National Radio Conference and Recommendations for Regulation of Radio.* Washington: GPO, 1926.

———. *Annual Report of the Commissioner of Navigation to the Secretary of Commerce.* Washington: GPO, 1921–1926.

———. *Annual Report of the Chief of the Radio Division to the Secretary of Commerce.* Washington: GPO, 1927–1932.

Van Tassel, Joan M. *Advanced Television Systems: Brave New TV.* Newton, MA: Focal Press, 1996.

Variety (1905–present, weekly). Major trade weekly of show business.

Vaughn, Robert. *Only Victims: A Study of Show Business Blacklisting.* New York: Putnam, 1972.

Vipond, Mary. *Listening In: The First Decade of Canadian Broadcasting, 1922–1932.* Montreal: McGill/Queen's University Press, 1992.

Vogel, Harold L. *Entertainment Industry Economics: A Guide for Financial Analysis.* New York: Cambridge University Press, 1986, 2001.

Waldrop, Frank C., & Joseph Borkin. *Television: A Struggle for Power.* New York: Morrow, 1938 (reprinted by Arno Press, 1971).

Walker, James R., & Douglas A. Ferguson. *The Broadcast Television Industry.* Boston: Allyn & Bacon, 1998.

Waller, Judith C. *Radio, the Fifth Estate.* 2nd ed. Boston: Houghton Mifflin, 1950.

Warner, Charles. *Broadcast and Cable Selling.* Belmont, CA: Wadsworth, 1986.

Warner, Harry P. *Radio and Television Law* and *Radio and Television Rights.* Albany, NY: Matthew Bender, 1948, 1953 (2 vols.).

Warren, Donald. *Radio Priest: Charles Coughlin, the Father of Hate Radio.* New York: Free Press, 1996.

Watson, Mary Ann. *The Expanding Vista: American Television in the Kennedy Years.* New York: Oxford University Press, 1990.

Weaver, Pat, with Thomas M. Coffey. *The Best Seat in the House: The Golden Years of Radio and Television.* New York: Knopf, 1994.

Webb, G. Kent. *The Economics of Cable Television.* Lexington, MA: Lexington Books, 1983.

Webster, James G., Patricia F. Phalen & Lawrence W. Lichty. *Ratings Analysis: The Theory and Practice of Audience Research.* 2nd ed. Mahwah, NJ: Lawrence Erlbaum Associates, 2000.

Wedlake, G. E. C. *SOS: The Story of Radio Communication.* Newton Abbot, England: David & Charles, 1973.

Weinberg, Meyer. *TV and America: The Morality of Hard Cash.* New York: Ballantine, 1962.

Wertheim, Arthur Frank. *Radio Comedy.* New York: Oxford University Press, 1979.

West, Darrell M. *Air Wars: Television Advertising in Election Campaigns, 1952–1992.* Washington: Congressional Quarterly, 1993.

White, David Manning, & Richard Averson, (Eds.). *Sight, Sound, and Society: Motion Pictures and Television in America.* Boston: Beacon, 1968.

White, Llewellyn. *The American Radio.* Chicago: University of Chicago Press, 1947 (reprinted by Arno Press, 1971).

White, Paul W. *News on the Air.* New York: Harcourt, Brace, 1947.

Whitfield, Stephen E., & Gene Roddenberry. *The Making of Star Trek.* New York: Ballantine, 1968.

Whittemore, Hank. *CNN: The Inside Story.* Boston: Little, Brown, 1990.

Wilk, Max. *The Golden Age of Television: Notes from the Survivors.* New York: Delacorte, 1976.

Williams, Christian. *Lead, Follow or Get Out of the Way: The Story of Ted Turner.* New York: Times Books, 1981.

Williams, Frederick. *The New Communications.* 2nd ed. Belmont, CA: Wadsworth, 1989.

Williams, Huntington. *Beyond Control: ABC and the Fate of the Networks.* New York: Atheneum, 1989.

Wilson, Geoffrey. *The Old Telegraphs.* London: Phillimore, 1976.

Winsbury, Rex, and Shehina Fazal. *Vision and Hindsight.* London: John Libbey, 1994.

Winship, Michael. *Television.* New York: Random House, 1988.

Winston, Brian. *Media Technology and Society: A History from the Telegraph to the Internet.* London: Routledge, 1998.

Witherspoon, John, & Roselle Kovitz, with an update by Robert K. Avery and Alan G. Stavitsky. *A History of Public Broadcasting.* Washington: Current, 2000 (2nd ed.).

Wolfe, Charles H., (Ed.). *Modern Radio Advertising.* New York: Funk and Wagnalls, 1949.

Wood, Donald N., & Donald G. Wylie. *Educational Telecommunications.* Belmont, CA: Wadsworth, 1977.

Woods, James. *History of International Broadcasting.* London: IEE, 1992 and 1999 (2 vols.).

Woolery, George W. *Children's Television: The First Thirty-Five Years, 1946–1981.* Metuchen, NJ: Scarecrow, 1983, 1985 (2 vols.).

Woolley, Lynn, et al. *Warner Bros. Television: Every Show of the Fifties and Sixties Episode-by-Episode.* Jefferson, NC: McFarland, 1985.

World Radio-TV Handbook. New York: Billboard Publications (annual).

Wylie, Max. *Clear Channels: Television and the American People.* New York: Funk and Wagnalls, 1955.

Yates, Raymond Francis, & Louis Gerard Pacent. *The Complete Radio Book.* New York: Century, 1922.

Year-Book of Wireless Telegraphy and Telephony. London: Wireless Press, 1913–1925 (annual).

Young, Peter. *Person to Person: The International Impact of the Telephone.* Cambridge, England: Granta Editions, 1991.

Finding Out More About the Development of Broadcasting

Although the books and journals listed in the bibliography above are the most common background resources for broadcasting scholars, they are not the only sources of information. Following are just a few of the more important Web sites, museums, archives, and specialized libraries for those interested in broadcasting history.

1. A Selection of Web Sites

This lists but a small fraction of the growing number of relevant and useful Web sites, most of which emphasize technological history. Additionally, there are many sites for specific radio and television programs and stars not noted here. Links on these sites will send you to many more. This list was assembled late in 2000.

Television Technology Web Sites

Early British Television History: the Background to Baird's Phonovision. <http://www.dfm.dircon.co.uk/tvhist1.htm>
  Concentrates on the work of John Logie Baird and his mechanical television system—including crude period recordings one can view through the site.

The Farnsworth Chronicles by Paul Schatzkin. <http://songs.com/philo/index.html>

Strongly biased toward the view that he has been underappreciated, this is a useful site on the life and work of Philo T. Farnsworth, containing a narrative biography, many graphics, and a chronology.

History of Color Television by Edwin H. Reitan Jr. <http://novia.net/~ereitan/>

Detail on the competition between the CBS (partially mechanical) and RCA (all-electronic) color systems and the fierce industry debate over color TV technical standards in the 1940s and early 1950s, the FCC's decisions adopting the CBS system (1950) and then the RCA system used today (1953), as well as the real inception of color broadcasting in 1954.

A History of Television by Jean-Jacques Peters of the European Broadcasting Union. <http://www.dvb.org/dvb_articles/dvb_tv-history.htm>

Sections on most technical aspects of the medium's development, handsomely illustrated with photos and clear color diagrams, with focus on Europe. Useful comparison with American sites.

The History of Television by *Broadcast Engineering* magazine. <http://www.technicalpress.com/Articles/History/History_TV.htm>

A technically oriented narrative with a host of photos (some in color) so that the site takes a while to download. This is part of a larger site including other aspects of television.

The Museum of Television (Toronto). <http://www.mztv.com/gallery.html>

This Canadian museum offers a virtual tour of three galleries (on mechanical television, TV at the 1939 World's Fair, and the Philco "Predicta" line of receivers) as well as TV inventors/inventions.

Page One: a History of British Television. <http://freespace.virgin.net/peter.culley/history.htm>

Exploration of the history and operation of both public service-oriented BBC and commercial companies, including some program history.

U.S. Television Chronology, 1875–1970 by Jeff Miller. <http://members.aol.com/jeff560/chronotv.html>

Includes specific sign-on dates of many U.S. television stations. Updating is constant and current.

HDTV—An Historical Perspective by Corey Carbonara. <http://web-star.com/hdtv/perspective.html>

Primarily text, divided into extensive chapters carrying the story back to the 1930s.

National Cable Television Center. <http://www.cablecenter.org>

Denver-based industry-sponsored museum and archive of CATV history.

TV Program History Web Sites

Most of the following sites, focusing on program genres (often with links to specific program Web sites) are created and maintained by amateurs rather than professionals. All show signs of consistent and current updating.

There are many sites devoted to specific programs not listed here. Also check sites of (or about) the major networks.

The DuMont Television Network by Clarke Ingram. <http://members. aol.com/cingram/televison/dumont.htm>

Steadily growing site on the role of the short-lived (1948–1955) DuMont national TV network and some of its programs (including *Captain Video*), as well as network founder and television inventor Allen B. DuMont.

Fifties Television by WebBoomers Inc. <http://www.webboomers.com/ lifestyles/nostalgia/50sTV/50sTV.htm>

Links to roughly two dozen top network programs of this era (including four sites for *I Love Lucy*).

Shadows of the Past: TV Westerns. <http://www.sptddog.com/sotp/ tvwesterns.html>

Arranges programs by decade, beginning with the 1950s, and then by program title. Many links to specific programs and stars.

TV in the '50s by Candace Rich. <http://www.fiftiesweb.com/tv50.htm>

Provides links to many television programs of the era, listed by type (drama, news, kids shows, comedy, variety, quiz, westerns) and then by specific program title.

Radio Technology Web Sites

In addition to these technology-oriented sites there are others for different inventors (Marconi, Tesla).

Edwin Howard Armstrong by Mike Datzdorn. <http://www.erols.com/ oldradio/>

Based on the extensive Harry Houck collection, this includes a host of historical documents in reproduction.

Antique Radio Page by D. J. Adamson. <http://members.aol.com/djadamson/ arp.html>

One of many designed for those who collect old radios, this includes books, articles, links, classified ads, and more.

Antique Wireless Association Electronic Communication Museum. <http://www.antiquewireless.org>

Details on the collection and its accessibility. (See "Museums" below.)

The Broadcast Archive by Barry Mishkind. <http://www.oldradio.com/>

Includes equipment and programming sections and links, plus detailed information about the FCC, old stations, and links to other archives and organizations. An amazing potpourri.

The RMS Titanic Radio Page. <http://www.netinfo.com.au/anars/>

Quite detailed page with information on the radio equipment used at the time (1912), the operators, and the actual messages sent and received from the doomed ocean liner.

Surfing the Aether. <http://www.northwinds.net/bchris/index.htm>
Extensive site with chronology arranged by decade and incorporating many links to people and developments.

United States Early Radio History by Thomas H. White. <http://www.ipass.net/~whitetho/index.html>
A wonderfully useful site that offers full copy of a variety of pre-1920 articles and documents plus the author's own valuable research on early radio station list publications, call-letter policies, and the like.

World of Wireless. <http://home.luna.nl/~arjan-muil/radio/history.html>
A Netherlands site (in both English and Dutch) that takes the story through World War II. Includes details of the owners' collection.

History of Recording Technology by Steve Schoenherr. <http://ac.acusd.edu/History/recording/notes.html>
Includes phonographs, tape recorders, and even musical jukeboxes. Offers a 16-part chronology with pictures and links.

Soundsite. <http://www.soundsite.com/index.html>
Reviews all aspects of current home entertainment audio and video technology, including data from manufacturers and brief chronology.

Radio Program Web Sites
Virtually any network radio entertainment program is the subject of a site or sites. Listed here are some general Web sites that are linked to a host of others.

Jack's List of Old Time Radio Pages. <http://www.pe.net/~rnovak/jack.htm>
Just that—a long list of links to all kinds of old time radio (OTR) sites, many of which allow you to hear whole program episodes. Also includes information on general radio history resources of all kinds. Regularly updated.

Radio Days. <http://www.otr.com/index.shtml>
Information on many old network radio programs (including some complete logs), OTR chat room, FAQs, and more.

Old Time Radio. <http://www.old-time.com/>
Includes many logs of program series, links to other sites, and information on collecting programs.

Olde Time Radio. <http://www.oldetimeradio.com/>
Allows one to listen to episodes of about a dozen old radio dramatic programs.

2. Museums

These U.S. museums and collections are open to the general public. Establishment of new institutions and relocation of older ones happens frequently, as those who compare this edition of *Stay Tuned* with the second edition will notice. There also are some private collections that sometimes are available to serious scholars, and specialized portions of other museums such as the Henry Ford Museum at Dearborn Village, MI. This list is only a beginning, so be sure to look for a collection or exhibition near you.

American Advertising Museum, 5035 S.E. 24th Ave., Portland, OR 97202. 503-AAM-0000 (503-226-0000). <www.admuseum.org/museum/ about.htm>

Excellent exhibit and extensive collection on both print and broadcast advertising, with screening of classic television ads. Call ahead, open weekdays only by reservation.

Antique Wireless Association Electronic Communication Museum, Village Green, Routes 5 & 20, Bloomfield, NY 14468. 716-657-6260. <www. antique wireless.org>

A very good collection of equipment, emphasizing the pre-broadcast days of wireless. AWA also is developing a useful research library and archive. Open only on weekends without advance reservations. Publishes quarterly *The Old Timer's Bulletin* with solidly researched articles and columns on early technology.

Bellingham Antique Radio Museum, 1315 Railroad Ave., Bellingham, WA 98225. <www.antique-radio.org/homeframe.html>

Offers extensive collection of old radio receivers. Web site provides considerable reference information. Wednesday-Saturday.

Information Age, National Museum of American History, Smithsonian Institution, 14th St. & Constitution Ave., NW, Washington, DC 20560. 202-357-2700. <Americanhistory.si.edu>

Permanent exhibit from the telegraph through modern computers, with extensive and rare material on radio and television broadcasting. Also see nearby exhibit on electricity and Thomas Edison.

Museum of Broadcast Communications, Chicago Cultural Center, Michigan Ave. & Washington St., Chicago, IL 60602-3407. 312-629-6000.

Includes very good museum, plus an extensive archive and listening/ viewing posts for radio and television programs.

Museum of Radio and Technology, 1640 Florence Ave., Huntington, WV 25701. 304-525-8890. <oak.cats.ohiou.edu/~postr/MRT/>

Located in a former school, this includes a large display of radios and related technology.

Museum of Television and Radio (formerly Museum of Broadcasting). Two locations: 25 West 52nd St., New York, NY 10019. 212-621-6600 and 465 North Beverly Dr., Beverly Hills, CA 90210. 310-786-1000. <www.mtr.org>

This well-established collection of radio and television programs now has two purpose-built locations with gift shops (also on-line). Issues valuable catalogs from exhibitions.

New England Museum of Steam and Wireless, 1300 Frenchtown Rd., East Greenwich, RI 02818. 401-885-0545. <http:/users.ids.net/~newsm/>
A good collection in both fields. Some useful publications.

Newseum, 1101 Wilson Blvd., Arlington, VA 22209. 888-Newseum (888-639-7386) or 703-284-3544. <www.newseum.org/newseum/aboutthenewseum/index.htm>
Located near the nation's capital, this foundation-supported facility offers a large and popular museum dealing with all aspects of journalism, plus an extensive research archive. It plans to move to a downtown Washington, DC location.

Pavek Museum of Broadcasting, 3515 Raleigh Ave., St. Louis Park, Minnesota 55416. 952-926-8198. Fax: 952-929-6105.
Extensive collection of radio receivers, television sets, and related broadcast equipment.

3. Libraries and Archives

This is a small selection. See also Donald G. Godfrey (comp.), *Reruns on File: A Guide to Electronic Media Archives* (Hillsdale, NJ: Lawrence Erlbaum Associates, 1992), for an annotated state-by-state guide. For the nation's capital, see Bonnie G. Rowan & Cynthia J. Wood, *Scholar's Guide to Washington, D.C., Media Collections* (Baltimore: Johns Hopkins University Press, 1994). Private collections of programs are *not* listed below.

American Archive of Broadcasting, Special Collections Reading Room, Thousand Oaks Library, 401 E. Janss Road, Thousand Oaks, CA 91362. 805-449-2660, ext. 228. Fax: 805-449-2675. <www.tol.lib.ca.us/1specoll.html>
Huge collection of printed and archival material, including many collections concerning specific radio stars. On-line catalog.

George H. Clark "Radioana" Collection and **Allen B. DuMont Collection,** Archives Center, National Museum of American History, Smithsonian Institution, Room C340, 14th St. & Constitution Ave., NW, Washington, DC 20560. 202-357-3270. For Radioana: <www.si.edu/lemelson/dig/radioana/index.html#timeline.
"Radioana" is one of the finest collections of paper materials of all kinds on the development of wireless and radio. Clark was an acquisitive RCA historian, who assembled an invaluable collection from radio's early years. There is a published and on-line register of contents which offers a useful chronology, information on important wireless companies, and a notion of how the collection developed. The DuMont Collection focuses on the rise of television. Contact the Center before planning a visit.

Library of American Broadcasting (formerly Broadcast Pioneers Library), Hornbake Library, University of Maryland, College Park, MD 20742-7011. 301-405-9160. Fax: 301-314-2634. <www.lib.umd.edu/UMCP/ LAB/>

This collection began as an effort of The Broadcast Pioneers Foundation in 1964, and was housed until 1994 in the National Association of Broadcasters building. Since then, it has been located in ever-larger facilities at Maryland. The collection includes books, pamphlets, periodicals, personal collections, oral histories, photos, audio/visual recordings, scripts and extensive vertical files. It is co-located with the National Public Broadcasting Archives.

Mass Communications History Collections, State Historical Society of Wisconsin, 816 State St., Madison, WI 53706. 608-624-6400.<ww.shsw. wisc.edu/archives/readroom/masscol.html>

One of the largest collections of individual and institutional archives in journalism, advertising, broadcasting and general mass communication, it was started in 1955 with the papers of H. V. Kaltenborn. It includes most of the NBC archives into the 1950s.

Motion Picture, Broadcasting and Recorded Sound Division, Library of Congress, James Madison Building, 101 Independence Ave., SE, Washington, DC 20540-4690.

Motion Picture and Television Reading Room, LM 336, <lcweb.loc.gov/ rr/mopic/>

Performing Arts Reading Room (includes radio and audio holdings), LM113, <lcweb.loc.giv/rr/record/rechome.html>

There are substantial holdings in both radio and television broadcasting in this collection, best accessed from the two reading rooms in the same building.

Motion Picture, Sound and Video Unit, Special Media Archives Services Division, National Archives and Records Administration, Archives II, 8601 Adelphi Road, College Park, MD 20740-6001. 301-713-6800, <www.nara.gov/ research/bymedia/mo_int.html#online>

Many catalog aids, some on-line, are available for this huge collection of thousands of news, documentary, and government radio, television and film programs.

National Public Broadcasting Archives, Hornbake Library, University of Maryland, College Park, MD 20742-7011. 301-405-9160, <www.lib. umd.edu/ UMCP/NPBA/index.html>

Established in 1990, includes records of the CPB, NPR, PBS, and related organizations as well as the papers of prominent individuals in public radio and television. This collection is co-located with the Library of American Broadcasting.

Radio Archive of the University of Memphis, Microforms Dept., McWhirter Library, University of Memphis, Memphis, TN 38152. 901-678-3174, <www.people.memphis.edu/~mbensman/welcome.html>

Created by Dr. Marvin Bensman, this is one of the better collections of radio programs on tape. See preceding paragraph for the URL of its on-line catalog.

UCLA Film and Television Archive Research and Study Center (formerly ATAS (Association of Television Arts and Sciences)-UCLA Television Archive), 46 Powell Library, University of California at Los Angeles, Los Angeles, CA 90024. 310.206.5388.<www.cinema.ucla.edu/ research.html>

One of the larger collections of film and videotape television programs.

Vanderbilt Television News Archive, Vanderbilt University, 110 21st Ave. South, Suite 704, Nashville, TN 37203. 615-322-2927. Fax: 615-343-8250, <tvnews.vanderbilt.edu/about.html>

Keeps and indexes videotapes of all broadcast television network newscasts and special events coverage since 1968.

AUTHOR INDEX

SUBJECT INDEX

This Subject Index is intended to help, without overwhelming, the reader. Accordingly, we have in non-rigorous fashion supplied a word or two about job titles, etc. for individuals, but we have not duplicated the Glossary from Appendix B. We urge you to use Appendix B for technical, business and programming terms. Because standard reference works provide dates of birth and death of many show business and political figures, only a few such dates are provided. The word (cable) in parentheses is intended to identify cable program services or channels. Most authors are to be found in the Author Index that precedes this Subject Index. Finally, the page numbers supplied do not provide context—particularly, as might be expected, in the conclusions reached in Chapter 12—so we advise that you read a page or two both before and after any cited page.